VAN TIL'S
APOLOGETIC

VAN TIL'S APOLOGETIC

READINGS AND ANALYSIS

Greg L. Bahnsen

P&R
PUBLISHING
P.O. BOX 817 • PHILLIPSBURG • NEW JERSEY 08865-0817

For a complete listing of Greg L. Bahnsen's books, articles, and tapes, contact Covenant Media Foundation, 4425 Jefferson Avenue, Suite 108, Texarkana, AR 71854-1529. Phone: 1-800-553-3938.

Printed in the United States of America

Composition by Colophon Typesetting

Library of Congress Cataloging-in-Publication Data

Bahnsen, Greg L.
    Van Til's apologetic : readings and analysis / Greg L. Bahnsen.
       p.   cm.
    Includes biblographical references and indexes.
    ISBN-10: 0-87552-098-7
    ISBN-13: 978-0-87552-098-8
    1. Apologetics. 2. Van Til, Cornelius, 1895–1987—Contributions in apologetics. 3. Apologetics—History—20th century. 4. Reformed Church—Apologetic works.   I. Title.
BT1102.B214   1998
239'.092—dc21   98–23866

To David

truly a "beloved" son
whose birth brightened graduate school days—
may the words of his namesake guide his every thought:
"In Thy light shall we see light" (Ps. 36:9).

Contents

Analytical Outline

In the outline below, numbered entries list the chapter sections, and indented entries are the reading selections from the writings of Van Til.

Foreword

Some years before his death (in 1987), Dr. Van Til asked several colleagues and friends to watch over the legacy left by his writings. In partial response to that request, this informal Van Til Committee decided to sponsor two projects: a Van Til reader of major size and an extensive bibliography of his writings. Over the years changes have occurred in the composition of the committee, but its purpose and these goals have remained the same.

The concern for a comprehensive bibliographic tool has been realized, entirely outside the oversight of our committee, by Eric Sigward in his producing *The Works of Cornelius Van Til, 1895–1987,* CD-ROM (New York: Labels Army Co., 1997). Many are indebted to Mr. Sigward for this valuable result of his tireless and self-sacrificing efforts, including the almost limitless search possibilities it affords.

The idea for this reader came from the late Greg Bahnsen himself. When he approached our committee a number of years ago, we were delighted not only with his concept of the shape the reader should take but with Dr. Bahnsen's interest in writing it. We believed him eminently, even uniquely, qualified among Dr. Van Til's former students for the task. Dr. Bahnsen's busy schedule and difficult health delayed the book's appearance, but we are grateful that he was able to complete the manuscript shortly before his untimely death in December 1995.

Our thanks to Presbyterian and Reformed Publishing for its commitment to this project and to Dr. James W. Scott for his editorial assistance.

Van Til, we believe, was a remarkable gift to the church. His thought continues to have unprecedented value for strengthening the church in its commitment to the whole counsel of God and for advancing its mission in the world. Our confident expectation is that this volume will prove effective both as an introduction to that thought and for promoting a deepening understanding of it.

For the Van Til Committee
Richard B. Gaffin, Jr.
K. Scott Oliphint

Preface

Generations of maturing Christian pastors and scholars have benefited from the biblical fervor and intellectual rigor of Cornelius Van Til's teaching and writing, particularly in the field of apologetics (defense of the faith). It is my hope that the present volume will help further generations to share in the philosophical profundity and transforming power of Van Til's thought.

A few things initially stand in the way of their doing so. The *first* is that Van Til authored a massive amount of material (some 30 books and syllabi, and over 220 articles, pamphlets, and reviews).[1] Nevertheless, no particular publication expounds the essentials of his presuppositional method in one place systematically, pointedly, and with topical clarity. Even his key book, *The Defense of the Faith*,[2] is at many

---

1. The writings of Van Til, both published and unpublished, have been collected in the CD-ROM entitled *The Works of Cornelius Van Til*, ed. Eric Sigward (New York: Labels Army Co., 1997).
2. Included in *The Defense of the Faith* (Philadelphia: Presbyterian and Reformed, 1955) are sections from the syllabi *Apologetics* (1947, 1953), *A Christian Theory of Knowledge* (1954), and *An Introduction to Systematic Theology* (1952), as well as the articles published in the book entitled *Common Grace* (1947), "Nature and Scripture" from *The Infallible Word* (edited by N. B. Stonehouse and Paul Woolley [Philadelphia: Presbyterian and Reformed, 1946]), a pamphlet *Particularism and Common Grace* (1952), a two-part article replying to J. O. Buswell from *The Bible*

points a compilation of segments of previous syllabi and articles, arranged in a crisscross pattern of topics, rather than a systematic and balanced unfolding of his apologetical approach in a discursive, practical, and readily outlined fashion. Some of the issues covered in it only weakly support the central purpose of the book (e.g., chapter 14, "Common Grace and Existentialism"), while other especially helpful and pertinent discussions are not included (e.g., the analysis of the method of argument with unbelievers in chapter 15 of *A Survey of Christian Epistemology*[3]).

Although he did not accomplish all that he would have liked,[4] Van

---

Today (1949), and a series of articles on Reformed apologetics in *Torch and Trumpet* (1951–52).

An abridged and revised second edition of *The Defense of the Faith* was published in 1963, and then a third edition (with only minor revisions) in 1967. References within the present book will be to the first edition, because it represents the fullest presentation of Van Til's position. The first edition of 1955 (in hardback) is now difficult to find, however, and so some readers may wish to use the following formula for converting the page references (to the original edition) that are given in the present book into the equivalent page numbers in the third edition:

for pages 24–37, subtract 16
for pages 40–167, subtract 17
for pages 171–98, subtract 20
for pages 240–67, subtract 59
for pages 303–53, subtract 94
for pages 358–97, subtract 98

The material on all other pages in the first edition is omitted in the third edition.

3. Published as vol. 2 of the series In Defense of the Faith (Philadelphia: Presbyterian and Reformed, 1969). According to Van Til's preface, the first edition of this syllabus was written in 1932 under the title *The Metaphysics of Apologetics*. (The work may represent an expansion of Van Til's 1925 Th.M. thesis at Princeton Seminary under C. W. Hodge, Jr. The Van Til Archives at Westminster Theological Seminary in Philadelphia contain a manuscript that appears to be from 1929; perhaps it is an early draft of what Van Til identified as the 1932 syllabus.)

4. Van Til was particularly distressed at the end of his life that he had never produced an exegetical study showing the extensive and necessary biblical support for the presuppositional method: "Apparently I have given occasion for people to think that I am *speculative* or *philosophical* first and *biblical* afterwards. . . . In short, I would like to be more exegetical than I have been. Dr. G. C. Berkouwer was right in pointing to my weakness on this point" (*Toward a Reformed Apologetics* [Philadelphia: privately printed, 1972], 24, 27). This criticism is mentioned in connection with James Daane in *Defense of the Faith*, 214.

It was to meet this expressed need and reinforce Van Til's outlook that the present author produced the syllabus *A Biblical Introduction to Apologetics* (1976). This syllabus is now published in Greg L. Bahnsen, *Always Ready: Directions for Defending the Faith* (Texarkana, Ark: Covenant Media Foundation, 1996).

It should be noted, though, that obvious and crucial biblical allusions are scattered throughout many of Van Til's writings (e.g., *Defense of the Faith*, 45, 109, 135,

Til was a prolific writer of syllabi, surveys, articles, and books. The best self-contained summary of his view is "My Credo," especially the concluding outline ("The Total Picture").[5] It is so compact, however, that one must already be familiar with Van Til's other works to interpret and apply it well. Thus, readers usually need to master a number of Van Til's writings in order to gain a general understanding of his system of thought.

The *second* obstacle that readers encounter is Van Til's style of writing. Frequently he used generalizations and passing allusions that presumed a thorough acquaintance with the history and development of Western philosophy, which most readers do not possess. He had a penchant for discussing issues and philosophers with abstract and (sometimes) vaguely worded principles. His surveys and summaries of positions or periods of thought could meander before reaching trenchant insights. His style could have been strengthened by more analytical, discursive, progressive, and precise development of his assessments and conclusions.[6] The organizing principles and particular expository manner of his longer publications are often of a diverse nature (i.e., hard to follow) or geared to historical surveys and analyses of individuals (which beginning students rarely find suitable). For

237, 241, 304, 307, 319, etc.; *A Christian Theory of Knowledge* [Philadelphia: Presbyterian and Reformed, 1969], 42). The biblical underpinnings of his position are noted explicitly in some syllabi (e.g., *An Introduction to Systematic Theology* [1952], which was revised and expanded many times, and finally published as vol. 5 of the series In Defense of the Faith [Philadelphia: Presbyterian and Reformed, 1974], 93, 96) and pamphlets (e.g., the opening pages of *The Intellectual Challenge of the Gospel* [London: Tyndale Press, 1950; reprint, Phillipsburg, N.J.: Lewis J. Grotenhuis, 1953], and at various places in *Paul at Athens* [Philadelphia: Presbyterian and Reformed, 1954]). They are also conspicuously displayed in his addresses and sermons (e.g., "Common Grace and Witness-Bearing," *Torch and Trumpet*, December 1954–January 1955 [reprint, Phillipsburg: Lewis J. Grotenhuis, 1956], republished in *Common Grace and the Gospel* [Philadelphia: Presbyterian and Reformed, 1972, chap. 5]; and *The God of Hope* [Phillipsburg: Presbyterian and Reformed, 1978]).

5. In *Jerusalem and Athens: Critical Discussions on the Theology and Apologetics of Cornelius Van Til*, ed. E. R. Geehan (Philadelphia: Presbyterian and Reformed, 1971), 1–21. This is a *Festschrift* commemorating Van Til's forty years of service as a professor and his seventy-fifth birthday.

6. John Frame notes: "But teaching the process of analysis was not Van Til's gift. Therefore even today there are many—both friends and enemies of Van Til's ideas—who have extremely confused notions of what he actually taught. . . . [T]he force of his bold, exciting summaries, illustrations, and exhortation is weakened by inadequate definition, analysis, and argument" ("Cornelius Van Til," in *Handbook of Evangelical Theologians*, ed. Walter A. Elwell [Grand Rapids: Baker, 1993], 161).

instance, it is disappointing to find a book entitled *A Christian Theory of Knowledge*[7] not working through the standard questions pertaining to the nature of knowledge. The book opens with themes of apologetical relevance, then turns to a lengthy and uneven historical survey, and later focuses upon selected individual writers (some of whom were already given such treatment in *The Defense of the Faith*). Likewise, *The Reformed Pastor and Modern Thought*[8] begins with a discussion of Calvinistic apologetic method, and then shifts to a historical survey—of philosophers and theologians—with short synopses at some points and extensive discussions at others.

A *third* hindrance is the actual content of what Van Til has to say. We find it strange to have our natural ways of thinking so thoroughly challenged and reformed. Because of the thorough changes they would require of us, revolutionary insights are often greeted with intellectual inertia—or downright hostility. R. J. Rushdoony was surely on target when he said of Van Til: "His critique is directed to the presuppositions of thought with a radical thoroughness. This fact accounts for the nature of Van Til's influence: he either reshapes the thinking of those who come within his orbit or incurs their consistent opposition."[9]

And then, *finally*, there is the ever-present difficulty that people have with thinking abstractly and using the special concepts and vocabulary of philosophy, particularly when Van Til's own terminology arises from the arcane parlance of a bygone generation of idealistic philosophers (e.g., "principle of individuation," "limiting concept," "concrete universal"). This factor is occasionally complicated even further by the novelty of some of Van Til's own ideas (e.g., common grace as "earlier grace"[10]) and his unusual use of terms (e.g., "analogi-

---

7. This book was based on an earlier syllabus of the same title (1954). Some of its contents appeared in *The Defense of the Faith*.
8. Philadelphia: Presbyterian and Reformed, 1971. In part, this includes portions of earlier addresses by Van Til from 1961 and 1966.
9. Foreword to Van Til, *The Case for Calvinism* (Philadelphia: Presbyterian and Reformed, 1963), viii (omitted in the 1975 printing).
10. See *Common Grace* (Philadelphia: Presbyterian and Reformed, 1947), now published (with identical pagination) in the expanded work *Common Grace and the Gospel*, 30, 72, 74, 75, 82–83, 85, 91. The original, longer version of this essay was published in *Proceedings of the Calvinistic Philosophy Club* (1941), and then edited and published as a three-part article, "Common Grace," in the *Westminster Theological Journal*, vols. 8 (1945): 39–60, 166–200 and 9 (1946): 47–84. Pt. 2 of *Common Grace and the Gospel* adds other relevant papers on the controversy over common grace (from 1951, 1953, 1954, 1966, and 1968), as well as a previously unpublished essay.

cal").[11] Sometimes a blessing can be a curse. Van Til was astute in using lively metaphors and illustrations, but sometimes his vivid rhetoric was troublesome to others.[12]

A need exists, therefore, for a volume that, in a supportive fashion, condenses, arranges, and clarifies the wide range of Van Til's writings that touch on apologetics. There is a welcome place for analyses of Van Til's creative and thoughtful contributions to other fields (e.g., theology, ethics, psychology, and history of thought), but the present work focuses specifically on his approach to apologetics.[13] My aim is to expound the presuppositional method of defending the Christian faith by highlighting and explaining the distinctives of Van Til's thought, providing carefully chosen selections from his body of writings, and taking opportunity to correct certain criticisms that have been voiced. This book, then, is something of an anthology with running commentary.

My hope is to make presuppositionalism readily understandable to readers who want an introductory exposure to Van Til in his own words and who are not specially trained in philosophy, but who are

11. Van Til recognized the trouble he might have caused himself, but also held (correctly, I believe) that opponents who paid attention to his publications should have been able to avoid misreading him so badly. He once wrote: "My main purpose is to seek to remove some misunderstandings that have developed with respect to my views. These misunderstandings may be my own fault, no doubt, in considerable measure. My terminology may sometimes be ambiguous. But I cannot believe that such misconstruction of my view as is now being advertised is fairly found in anything that I have written or said" ("A Letter on Common Grace," in *Common Grace and the Gospel*, 149 [reprinting *Letter on Common Grace* [Phillipsburg, N.J.: Lewis J. Grotenhuis, 1953]).

12. Perhaps the most famous case was Van Til's colorful application of the point that the Christian's approach to science must not, by means of a defective view of common grace, incorporate into itself the destructive force of autonomous thinking, which denies the revelatory character of all facts in nature and the necessity of God's providence to make scientific procedure intelligible. He said that then "we might as well blow up the science building [at Calvin College] with an atom bomb." In customary humility (and to the amusement of his followers) he later wrote about the hyperbole, "I have apologized for that statement" ("A Letter on Common Grace," in *Common Grace and the Gospel*, 195).

13. For a worthwhile exploration and interaction with the teaching of Van Til on a broader plane than is found here, I recommend John M. Frame, *Cornelius Van Til: An Analysis of His Thought* (Phillipsburg, N.J.: Presbyterian and Reformed, 1995). Beyond philosophical and apologetical issues, Frame explores and offers helpful evaluation of Van Til's broader teaching and insights in systematic theology and contemporary theology. With respect more specifically to Van Til's apologetics, Frame has great appreciation for Van Til, but is somewhat more critical than I am. His criticisms related to apologetics have to some degree appeared in previous publications, which I have attempted to address briefly throughout the present text.

willing to read and reflect upon basic issues pertaining to knowledge and Christianity at more than an elementary level. Because this is intended as an introductory exposure, not an advanced text for specialists, it will not delve into deeper or technical philosophical issues pertaining to Van Til's thinking and method, nor will it extensively examine possible ambiguities or difficulties that could benefit from clarification or correction.[14]

This book is an organized digest of what Van Til taught throughout his various publications about the underlying approach to apologetics. After an introductory sketch of the basic themes that drive Van Til's apologetic and a survey of his life, the book lays out his conception of apologetics and offers a simple description and illustration of his presuppositional method. We then explore and explain in more detail the relevant epistemological and psychological issues that bear on Van Til's way of defending the faith, culminating in a discussion of the transcendental argumentation that he endorsed—set in contrast to the more traditional way of using theistic proofs and empirical evidences. A few of Van Til's opponents are examined before his outlook is summarized in the conclusion.

It will be beneficial for the reader to stay in touch with, and remain aware of, the flow of thought in the book, especially since certain discussions are somewhat lengthy and the analysis is interspersed with blocks of readings. The progression of thought can be scanned by looking at the development of chapter sections (and the topics of the Van Til readings), which are listed in the analytical outline at the front of the book. I would suggest that the reader can most effectively learn and understand the thrust of Van Til's approach to defending the faith if he keeps referring back to this outline in order to grasp the significance of what he is reading at any particular point within the overall scheme.

Each section begins with a brief discussion of the announced topic. Selected readings from Van Til then follow the introductory discussions; the titles for the excerpts are my own. The readings are accompanied by explanatory commentary or footnotes, transitions, and occasional responses to critics.

---

14. For an example of an attempt at philosophical strengthening of Van Til's distinctive position, aroused by sympathetic criticism, see my doctoral dissertation "A Conditional Resolution of the Apparent Paradox of Self-Deception" (Ph.D. diss., University of Southern California, 1978). This is briefly summarized and applied to Van Til in "The Crucial Concept of Self-Deception in Presuppositional Apologetics," *Westminster Theological Journal* 57 (1995): 1–31.

Throughout this book, the quotations and extended readings taken from Van Til's publications (including his quotation of others) will be distinguished from my own comments by the use of a distinctive typeface, an example of which is provided by this sentence. Footnotes within Van Til's text usually provide my own running commentary; "CVT:" introduces his own footnotes. Full bibliographical information on any work written by Van Til is given whenever it first appears in each chapter, as well as in the bibliography at the back of the book.

For ease of reading or greater clarity of thought, I have sometimes taken the editorial liberty of breaking up longer paragraphs in Van Til's material. Also, in readings that combine a number of passages from a particular source, the order of the selected portions has sometimes been changed.[15] On rare occasion, Van Til's wording was slightly changed (or amplified) in a subsequent edition or republication of his work; in such cases I have followed the wording that seems best. A number of proofreading corrections have also been made.

There are many thanks to extend to others who helped me in one way or another in producing this book. I am grateful for the philosophically astute seminary instruction I received from John Frame, which set my feet in the right path for my doctoral studies. Heartfelt thanks go to Richard Gaffin for initiating, encouraging, and patiently waiting for the completion of this project through a number of medical and personal upheavals in my life.

I cannot find adequate expression for my gratitude to Randy and Marinell Booth for the cheerful, willing, and persevering hours of labor that they contributed to the preparation of the manuscript; it could not have been finished without them, and I will always remember their kindness to me. Likewise, my mother, Virginia Bahnsen, always seemed to be standing by, ready to type, check, or help in any way needed. If nominations for sainthood were appropriate in Protestant circles, I would surely promote the names of my hardworking and generous manuscript readers: Lonn Oswalt, Joseph Bell, and my assistant, Michael Butler.

The members of the Board at the Southern California Center for Christian Studies (P.O. Box 328, Placentia, CA 92871) are thanked for granting me the time and opportunity to engage in this writing project—and more generally for all of the administrative and personal

---

15. In these cases, the footnote reference for the reading selection in question will list the pages for the selected passages in the order in which they are presented here.

support they give to the teaching ministry here. I would also like to express deep gratitude to the session and congregation of Grace Presbyterian Chapel in Orange County, California, for their special financial gift, which kept me off the road (at speaking engagements) and provided a month for finishing the manuscript.

And, finally, although he is now in a better place, I would publicly acknowledge my debt to Cornelius Van Til for the hours of rewarding personal discussion, fellowship, and instruction he shared with me years ago—as well as the gracious confidence he expressed by inviting me, while a student at Westminster Seminary, to assist him in his scholarly labors and lecture in his stead when he was ill. I learned much from his words, as well as from his walk.

Chapter 1

An Introduction to Van Til's Apologetic

1.1 A Question of Ultimate Commitment

"Contentious disputes arise," wrote John Calvin, "from the fact that many think less honorably than they ought of the greatness of divine wisdom, and are carried away by profane audacity."[1] Calvin was commenting upon 1 Peter 3:15, a verse that has long been taken as the biblical charter for Christian apologetics. His words were not directed, however, at the "profane audacity" of the *unbeliever* who challenges the existence of God or the veracity of His word, but rather at those Christian *apologists* who fall short of recognizing and submitting to the superiority of God's wisdom as revealed in the pages of Scripture. Assuming for themselves the self-sufficiency and intellectual pride of autonomy,[2] they launch into battle with antagonistic unbelievers (who are themselves marked by the same self-sufficiency and intellectual

---

1. *Calvin's Commentaries*, ed. D. W. Torrance and T. F. Torrance, vol. 12, *The Epistles of Paul the Apostle to the Hebrews and the First and Second Epistles of St. Peter*, trans. William B. Johnston (1551; Grand Rapids: Eerdmans, 1963), at 1 Peter 3:15 (p. 290).
2. "Autonomy" refers to being a law unto oneself, so that one's thinking is independent of any outside authority, including God's. Autonomous reasoning takes itself philosophically as the final point of reference and interpretation, the ultimate court of intellectual appeal; it presumes to be self-governing, self-determinative, and self-directing.

1

pride) with an "audacity" that is "profane"—not befitting those who live under the lordship of Jesus Christ. The sorry result, as Calvin knew, is nothing but the kind of contentious disputes that should be shunned by servants of the Lord (2 Tim. 2:23–26).

In the words of 1 Peter 3:15, the personal prerequisite for offering a reasoned defense of the Christian faith is to have "set apart Christ as Lord in your hearts." Christ must be the ultimate authority over our philosophy, our reasoning, and our argumentation—not just at the end, but at the beginning, of the apologetical endeavor. If we are to "cast down reasonings and every high thing exalted against the knowledge of God," said Paul, then we must "bring *every* thought captive to the obedience of Christ" (2 Cor. 10:5).[3] An ultimate commitment to Christ covers the entire range of human activity, including every aspect of intellectual endeavor. To reason in a way that does not recognize this is to transgress the first and great commandment: "You shall love the Lord your God with . . . *all your mind*" (Matt. 22:37). In light of this, our apologetical method, not merely our apologetical conclusions, should be controlled by the word of Jesus Christ.

Very simply, if the apologist is to rid himself of profane audacity, his faith in the greatness of divine wisdom must be championed by means of a procedure that itself honors the same wisdom. After all, in Christ "*all* the treasures of wisdom and knowledge are deposited" (Col. 2:3). No exception is made for the knowledge by which the Christian defends the knowledge of Christ. This means that the apologist must *presuppose*[4] the truth of God's word from start to finish in his apologetic witness. It is only to be expected that, in matters of ultimate commitment, the intended *conclusion* of one's line of argumentation will also be the presuppositional standard that governs

---

3. A more appropriate motto for Van Til's apologetic could hardly be found than the title of Richard Pratt's practical manual for defending the faith in Van Til's presuppositional style: *Every Thought Captive* (Phillipsburg, N.J.: Presbyterian and Reformed, 1979). This is a very helpful, elementary book for the "uninitiated" (as Pratt puts it).

4. A "presupposition" is an elementary assumption in one's reasoning or in the process by which opinions are formed. In this book, a "presupposition" is not just any assumption in an argument, but a personal commitment that is held at the most basic level of one's network of beliefs. Presuppositions form a wide-ranging, foundational *perspective* (or starting point) in terms of which everything else is interpreted and evaluated. As such, presuppositions have the greatest authority in one's thinking, being treated as one's least negotiable beliefs and being granted the highest immunity to revision.

one's manner of argumentation for that conclusion—or else the intended conclusion is not his *ultimate* commitment after all.

The Christian's final standard, the inspired word of God, teaches us that "the fear of the Lord is the beginning of knowledge" (Prov. 1:7). If the apologist treats the starting point of knowledge as something other than reverence for God, then unconditional submission to the unsurpassed greatness of God's wisdom at the end of his argumentation does not really make sense.[5] There would always be something greater than God's wisdom—namely, the supposed wisdom of one's intellectual starting point. The word of God would necessarily (logically, if not personally) remain subordinate to that autonomous, final standard.[6] The situation is pictured well by C. S. Lewis: "The ancient man approached God (or even the gods) as the accused person approaches his judge. For the modern man the roles are reversed. He is the judge: God is in the dock. . . . The trial may even end in God's acquittal. But the important thing is that Man is on the Bench and God in the Dock."[7]

1.2 An Epistemologically Self-Conscious Apologetic

It has been the genius of Cornelius Van Til's approach to defending the Christian faith to see how entirely inappropriate is the intellectual attitude of putting God in the dock. The spirit of the apostle Paul arouses him: "Rather, who are you, O man, to reply against God?" (Rom. 9:20), and, "Let God be deemed true, though every man is a liar" (Rom. 3:4). Created men, especially as sinful rebels, are in no moral or intellectual position to challenge their sovereign Creator and Lord.

---

5. Ludwig Wittgenstein confessed that a devastating incongruity lay at the heart of his *Tractatus Logico-Philosophicus.* If he was correct in his eventual conclusion, then the premises used to reach that conclusion were actually meaningless: "Anyone who understands me eventually recognizes [my propositions] as nonsensical, when he has used them—as steps—to climb up beyond them. (He must, so to speak, throw away the ladder after he has climbed up it.)" (1921; reprint, London: Routledge & Kegan Paul, 1961, § 6.54, p. 151). In similar fashion, evangelicals sometimes utilize an autonomous apologetical method. Instead of assuming the authority of Christ, they use that method like a ladder to climb up to acceptance of Christ's claims, only then to "throw the ladder away," since Christ is now seen as having an ultimate authority that conflicts with that method.
6. R. J. Rushdoony has nicely encapsulated this fundamental concern in the title of his book summarizing Van Til's thinking, *By What Standard?* (Philadelphia: Presbyterian and Reformed, 1958).
7. *God in the Dock: Essays on Theology and Ethics,* ed. Walter Hooper (Grand Rapids: Eerdmans, 1970), 244.

A thoughtless approach to Christian epistemology[8] which forgets this runs the danger of transgressing God's clear prohibition: "You shall not put the Lord your God to the test" (Deut. 6:16).[9] Remember the example of Job, who dared to question God and demand answers from Him: "The Lord said to Job: Will the one who contends with the Almighty correct Him? Let him who argues with God answer Him! . . . Would you condemn Me to justify yourself?" (Job 40:1–2, 8). God is not in the dock; we are. His word and character are not questionable; ours are. And, as Van Til was acutely aware, this is not true simply in some narrowly "religious" or moral sense; it applies equally to man's intellectual reasoning (which is an expression of his religious posture).

Our Christian epistemology (or theory of knowledge) should thus be elaborated and worked out in a way that is consistent with its own fundamental principles (or presuppositions), lest it be incoherent and ineffective. Our "method" of knowing is determined by our "message" *as a whole*—thus being influenced by, even as it influences, our convictions about reality (God's existence and nature, and man's nature, relation to God, place in the universe, purpose, etc.). We ought not to espouse one thing theologically, and then practice something else in our general scholarship. One way to say this is to say that Christian scholars and apologists must be thoroughly "self-conscious" about the character of their epistemological position, letting its standards regiment and regulate every detail of their system of beliefs and its application. They always need to form opinions and develop reasoning in light of their fundamental Christian commitments. It has been Van Til's aim to bring this ideal of "epistemological self-consciousness" to bear upon the theory and practice of defending the Christian faith.

1.3 Arguing from the Impossibility of the Contrary

It has been the further genius of Van Til's approach to recognize that an epistemologically self-conscious method of defending the faith is not simply philosophically necessary (given the presuppositional issue) and morally appropriate (given the Creator-creature relation). It also constitutes the strongest intellectual challenge that can be directed to the thinking of the unbeliever. God's revelation is more than

---

8. Epistemology is the study of the nature and limits of human knowledge; it addresses questions about truth, belief, justification, etc.
9. Notice how Jesus himself, in an apologetical and moral contest with Satan, rested his case on a simple quotation of this stricture from the word of God (Matt. 4:7).

the best foundation for Christian reasoning; it is the only philosophically sound foundation for any reasoning whatsoever. Therefore, although the world in its own wisdom sees the word of Christ as foolishness, "the foolishness of God is wiser than men" (1 Cor. 1:18, 25).
Christians need not sit in an isolated philosophical tower, reduced to
simply despising the philosophical systems of non-Christians. No, by
taking every thought captive to Christ, we are enabled to cast down
reasoning that is exalted against the knowledge of God (cf. 2 Cor.
10:5). We must challenge the unbeliever to give a cogent and credible account of how he knows anything whatsoever, given his espoused
presuppositions about reality, truth, and man (his "worldview").

Van Til's presuppositional defense of the faith mounts a philosophical offense against the position and reasoning of the non-
Christian. Following the inspired lead of the apostle Paul, it rhetorically asks: "Where is the wise? Where is the scribe? Where is the
disputer of this world? Has not God made foolish the wisdom of the
world?" (1 Cor. 1:20). This theme is predominant in Van Til's practice of presuppositional apologetics. The task of the apologist is not
simply to show that there is no hope of eternal salvation outside of
Christ, but also that the unbeliever has no present intellectual hope
outside of Christ. It is foolish for him to build his house on the ruinous sands of human opinion, instead of the verbal rock of Christ
(Matt. 7:24–27). He needs to see that those who suppress the truth
of God in unrighteousness inescapably "become vain in their reasoning. . . . Professing themselves to be wise, they become fools"
(Rom. 1:21–22). Their opposition to the faith amounts to no more
than a "knowledge falsely so called" (1 Tim. 6:20–21), by which they
actually "oppose themselves" in ignorance (2 Tim. 2:23, 25).

The unbeliever attempts to enlist logic, science, and morality in his
debate against the truth of Christianity. Van Til's apologetic answers
these attempts by arguing that only the truth of Christianity can rescue the meaningfulness and cogency of logic, science, and morality.
The presuppositional challenge to the unbeliever is guided by the
premise that only the Christian worldview provides the philosophical
preconditions necessary for man's reasoning and knowledge in any
field whatever. This is what is meant by a "transcendental"[10] defense

10. The term "transcendental" should not be confused with the similar sounding
    word "transcendent" (an adjective for whatever goes beyond human experience).
    Transcendental reasoning is concerned to discover what general conditions must
    be fulfilled for any particular instance of knowledge to be possible; it has been

of Christianity. Upon analysis, all truth drives one to Christ. From beginning to end, man's reasoning about anything whatsoever (even reasoning about reasoning itself) is unintelligible or incoherent unless the truth of the Christian Scriptures is presupposed. Any position contrary to the Christian one, therefore, must be seen as philosophically impossible. It cannot justify its beliefs or offer a worldview whose various elements comport with each other.

In short, presuppositional apologetics argues for the truth of Christianity "from the impossibility of the contrary." Someone who is so foolish as to operate in his intellectual life as though there were no God (Ps. 14:1) thereby "despises wisdom and instruction" and "hates knowledge" (Prov. 1:7, 29). He needs to be answered according to his folly—demonstrating where his philosophical principles lead—"lest he be wise in his own eyes" (Prov. 26:5).

The basic points made in the last three sections of this discussion can now be recapitulated. Christian apologetics is a defense of religious faith, thus pertaining to the question of one's ultimate commitment in life. Apologetics entails intellectual reasoning in justification of one's beliefs, thus touching on the epistemological question of the final standard of knowledge. These observations make clear that the defense of the faith is unavoidably a presuppositional matter. Both the unbeliever and the believer operate in terms of certain espoused presuppositions or worldviews, aiming to develop their thinking in a way that is consistent with their respective ultimate commitments. The Christian apologist needs to argue with the non-Christian in an epistemologically self-conscious manner, which cannot happen if his reasoning and argumentation assume things that are actually contrary to his intended conclusion.

Therefore, the authority of Christ and His word, rather than intellectual autonomy, must govern the starting point and method of his apologetics, as well as its conclusion. He challenges the philosophical adequacy of the unbeliever's worldview, showing how it does

---

central to the philosophies of secular thinkers such as Aristotle and Kant, and it has become a matter of inquiry in contemporary, analytically minded philosophy. Van Til asks what view of man, mind, truth, language, and the world is necessarily presupposed by our conception of knowledge and our methods of pursuing it. For him, the transcendental answer is supplied at the very first step of man's reasoning—not by autonomous philosophical speculation, but by transcendent revelation from God. This makes Van Til's transcendental criticism of unbelieving thought different from what Herman Dooyeweerd calls "transcendental critique."

not provide the preconditions for the intelligibility of knowledge and morality. His case for Christianity, then, argues from the impossibility of the contrary. From beginning to end, both in his own philosophical method and in what he aims to bring about in the unbeliever's thinking, the Christian apologist reasons in such a way "that in all things Christ might have the preeminence" (Col. 1:18).

1.4 Cornelius Van Til

The outlook on apologetics that is sketched above was developed, refined, and applied by Cornelius Van Til for over half a century. His consistent adherence to the authority and supreme wisdom of God, infallibly revealed in the Scriptures, led him to promote a presuppositional method of apologetics that not only can forcefully communicate the intellectual challenge of the gospel—both to philosophy professors and to milkmen—but also can do so with humble boldness, rather than the "profane audacity" censured by Calvin. Being steeped in biblical instruction and having mastered the intellectual giants of Western thought, Van Til developed a conception and method of defending the faith which has, in light of the history of previous contributions, amounted to nothing less than "the reformation of Christian apologetics."[11]

Van Til may not have seemed to be a likely candidate for such an accomplishment, but God is in the habit of utilizing unlikely candidates to mount great victories for His kingdom—think of David and Goliath! Van Til "wanted to be a farmer. . . . Instead he became one of the foremost Christian apologists of our time," to use the words of David E. Kucharsky in *Christianity Today*.[12] Cornelius Van Til (later nicknamed Kees [pronounced "Case"]) was born on May 3, 1895, in a farmhouse in Grootegast, Holland, as the sixth of eight children to a devout dairyman-farmer who worshiped with the Reformed *Afscheiding* party (which had rejected the doctrine of the presumptive regeneration of baptized children). He was Dutch through and through, from wearing wooden shoes ("klompen") to being raised on the Heidelberg Catechism.

11. Greg L. Bahnsen, "Socrates or Christ: The Reformation of Christian Apologetics," in *Foundations of Christian Scholarship: Essays in the Van Til Perspective*, ed. Gary North (Vallecito, Calif.: Ross House Books, 1976), 191–239.
12. "At the Beginning, God: An Interview with Cornelius Van Til," *Christianity Today* 22 (December 30, 1977): 414.

At the age of ten, in the spring of 1905, his family sailed from Rotterdam to America to join Kees's older brother, Reinder (eleven years older than he), who had found the land amazingly inexpensive. The family settled in Highland, Indiana. Cornelius enjoyed the soil and animals, but he also advanced quickly in school. "Big Klompa" (as his teacher nicknamed him) learned English within a year. With his evident intellectual strengths, he was not to be a cucumber farmer after all. At age nineteen, he came under the conviction that he should become a minister. In 1914 Europe went to war, and Van Til went to Calvin Preparatory School and College, the educational center of the Christian Reformed Church. He worked his way through as a part-time janitor and loved the study of philosophy, at which his mind was adept. By the time he enrolled in Calvin Theological Seminary in 1921, he was already familiar with the works of Abraham Kuyper and Herman Bavinck and had added a knowledge of Hebrew, Greek, and Latin to his Dutch and English! He studied systematic theology under Louis Berkhof and Christian philosophy under W. H. Jellema.

American Christianity in the 1920s was reacting to the shock waves of theological liberalism, inspired by German higher criticism of the Bible and a Darwinian view of man. At that time, the man who stood head and shoulders above his peers in setting forth a Christianity worthy of scholarly defense was J. Gresham Machen of Princeton Theological Seminary. His forceful answer to one plank in the skeptical view of the New Testament, *The Origin of Paul's Religion,* was published during Van Til's first year in seminary. American philosophy in the 1920s was interacting with various responses to Kant's critical philosophy (absolute idealism, personalism, neorealism, and critical realism) and coming under the sway of naturalistic ideologies (pragmatism and positivism). Among the schools of noted academic stature was Princeton University, whose philosophy department was headed by the Scottish personalist, Archibald Allan Bowman (1883–1936).

For his middler year of seminary (1922), Van Til made the difficult decision to transfer to Princeton, where he could study simultaneously at the seminary and the university. During this time, he roomed with John J. de Waard (who was to become a lifelong friend),[13] managed the student dining club, and lived on the same floor in Alexander Hall with "Das" Machen, who was busy publishing numerous apologetical

---

13. De Waard was a fellow Dutchman who later entered the Orthodox Presbyterian Church with Van Til. In 1959 Van Til preached de Waard's funeral sermon, which is published in the *Presbyterian Guardian* 28 (1959): 214–15, 222.

studies (including his monumental *Christianity and Liberalism* [1923]). Van Til's seminary adviser, C. W. Hodge, Jr., was a grandson of Charles Hodge and the successor to B. B. Warfield. Van Til profited from the solid biblical instruction of men like Hodge, Robert Dick Wilson, William Park Armstrong, and Oswald T. Allis, but the professor closest to his heart was Geerhardus Vos, the respected Dutch scholar who championed the method of biblical theology to the Reformed community in America. Vos exercised a significant influence upon Van Til's decision to give himself to the academic and ecclesiastical struggles through which Machen would go. (When Vos passed away in 1949, Van Til preached his funeral sermon.)

Van Til wrote the prize-winning student papers for both 1923 (on evil and theodicy) and 1924 (on the will and its theological relations). The seminary granted him a Th.M. in systematic theology in 1925, after which he married his longtime sweetheart, Rena Klooster. At the university, Van Til's prowess in metaphysical analysis and his mastery of Hegelian philosophy gained high praise from A. A. Bowman, who offered him a graduate fellowship.[14] In 1927 the university granted him a Ph.D. in philosophy for a dissertation on "God and the Absolute."[15]

Men in the seminary had been keeping an eye on Van Til's work. His first published piece, written at the time he was awarded his mas-

---

14. Over a decade later, Van Til reviewed two books by A. A. Bowman: *Studies in the Philosophy of Religion* and *A Sacramental Universe*. The reviews appeared in the *Westminster Theological Journal* 2 (1939–40): 55–62, 175–84; they were reprinted in *Christianity and Idealism* (Philadelphia: Presbyterian and Reformed, 1955), 91–110. For further reading on Van Til's response to personalism, see *A Survey of Christian Epistemology*, In Defense of the Faith, vol. 2 (Philadelphia: Presbyterian and Reformed, 1969), chaps. 12–13, and his reviews of Albert C. Knudson's *The Doctrine of God* (in *Christianity Today* [a Presbyterian publication in the 1930s] 1, no. 8 [December 1930]: 10–13), of Edgar Sheffield Brightman's *Is God a Person?* (in *Christianity Today* 3, no. 11 [March 1933]: 7) and *Personality and Religion* (in *Presbyterian Guardian* 2 [1936]: 100), and of Ralph Tyler Flewelling's *The Survival of Western Culture* (in *Westminster Theological Journal* 6 [1944]: 221–27), as well as his address "Boston Personalism" (in *The God of Hope* [Phillipsburg, N.J.: Presbyterian and Reformed, 1978], 287–334).
15. Van Til published an article with this same title in the *Evangelical Quarterly* 2 (1930): 358–88. He was particularly an expert in the thought of Bernard Bosanquet (1848–1923), a British philosopher who discussed the problem of predication and emphasized the "concrete universal" (i.e., a generalization or unity not so vague or abstract as to suppress the specific qualities and differences within actual experience), and whom Van Til deemed the most advanced and sophisticated idealist of his generation (*Survey of Christian Epistemology*, 189).
    For more on Van Til's appraisal of idealism, see *Survey of Christian Epistemol-*

ters degree in theology, had been a review of Alfred North White-head's *Religion in the Making*.[16] It clearly exhibited the salient lines of Van Til's presuppositional approach: (a) locating his opponent's crucial presuppositions, (b) criticizing the autonomous attitude that arises from a failure to honor the Creator-creature distinction, (c) exposing the internal and destructive philosophical tensions that attend autonomy, and then (d) setting forth the only viable alternative, biblical Christianity. Van Til's next publication (in 1929) was a review of two works by Bavinck.[17] In it, another famous feature of Van Til's thinking came to expression as he insisted that the propagation and defense of the faith required believers to abandon the impossible notion of a "neutral territory" of truth between believers and unbelievers. By the time of the review's publication, Van Til was back at Princeton as a visiting lecturer.

When J. Gresham Machen declined the chair of apologetics at Princeton Seminary, deciding to remain in the New Testament department, the Board of the seminary was encouraged by William Brenton Greene (1854–1928), the retired professor of apologetics, to invite Van Til to lecture in the department for the 1928–29 academic year. After receiving his doctorate and making his first visit back to the Netherlands in 1927, Van Til had accepted the pastorate of the Christian Reformed Church (about seventy families) in Spring Lake, Michigan, a rural community of about one thousand people, thirty miles from Grand Rapids. Although installed for only a year, he took a leave of absence from the congregation and taught apologetics at Princeton. He impressed everyone so favorably there (even though he was the youngest instructor) that at the end of only one year the Board elected him to assume the Stuart Chair of apologetics and ethics. However, within weeks the General Assembly of the Presbyterian Church in the U.S.A. reorganized Princeton Seminary in such a way that control of the once conservative bastion of Reformed orthodoxy was turned over to men who desired to see many different viewpoints represented at Princeton and who favored a "broad church."

---

ogy, chap. 11, and his collection of articles and reviews, *Christianity and Idealism*; cf. his "Absolute Idealism," in *The Encyclopedia of Christianity*, ed. Jay Green (Wilmington, Del.: The National Foundation for Christian Education, 1964), 1:33–34.

16. *Princeton Theological Review* 25 (1927): 336–38. For a later discussion, see Van Til, review of *The Philosophy of Alfred North Whitehead*, ed. Paul Arthur Schilpp, in *Westminster Theological Journal* 4 (1942): 163–71.

17. *Princeton Theological Review* 27 (1929): 135–36.

Machen resigned and immediately started work to establish West-minster Theological Seminary in Philadelphia. Van Til likewise re-signed and returned to Michigan. During that summer, Van Til's only child, Earl, was born. About the same time, Machen handpicked Van Til to teach apologetics in the new seminary, even traveling with Ned B. Stonehouse to Michigan in August to plead with him to accept the position—after a previous visit from O. T. Allis had not persuaded him.[18] After declining at first, Van Til took up teaching duties at West-minster Seminary in the fall of 1929, where he continued in that min-istry until retiring more than forty years later. When Machen was un-justly forced out of the Presbyterian Church in the U.S.A. in 1936, Van Til supported him in the founding of the Presbyterian Church of America (which was soon renamed the Orthodox Presbyterian Church). Along with R. B. Kuiper, he transferred his ministerial cre-dentials from the Christian Reformed Church to the new denomi-nation, where he came to have a decided influence for years to come, both as a scholar and as a powerful pulpit preacher.

From the outset of his teaching career, Van Til sought to develop a distinctively consistent Christian philosophical outlook. He wanted to see everything in terms of a biblical world-and-life view. This was evident already in 1931, when he published articles on "A Christian Theistic Theory of Knowledge" and "A Christian Theistic Theory of Reality."[19] The first major syllabus produced by Van Til at Westmin-ster Seminary, *The Metaphysics of Apologetics*,[20] appeared in 1932. In it he traced various epistemological positions down through history, not-ing the bearing of metaphysical convictions[21] upon them, and ex-plained the necessity of a transcendental, presuppositional method of argumentation. He insisted that Christians must reason with un-believers, seeking to reduce the non-Christian worldview (in whatever

18. This is but one of many indications that Machen and Van Til saw their respective contributions to apologetics as complementing each other, not conflicting. For a fuller discussion of the relationship between Machen's historical defense of the faith and Van Til's presuppositional method, see Greg L. Bahnsen, "Machen, Van Til, and the Apologetical Tradition of the O.P.C.," in *Pressing Toward the Mark: Es-says Commemorating Fifty Years of the Orthodox Presbyterian Church*, ed. Charles G. Den-nison (Philadelphia: Committee for the Historian of the Orthodox Presbyterian Church, 1986), 259–94.
19. *The Banner* 66 (1931): 984, 995; 1032. Van Til begins *The Defense of the Faith* in the same way—with an exposition of the Christian outlook in metaphysics, episte-mology, and ethics.
20. This syllabus was subsequently retitled *A Survey of Christian Epistemology*.
21. Metaphysics is the study of the nature, conditions, extent, origin, structure, and

form it takes) to absurdity—by exposing it to be epistemologically and morally self-contradictory. Van Til's insight, a brilliant and apologetically powerful one, was that *antitheism actually presupposes theism.* To reason at all, the unbeliever must operate on assumptions that actually contradict his espoused presuppositions—assumptions that comport only with the Christian worldview. The unbeliever's efforts to be rational and to find an intelligible interpretation of his experience are, then, indications that he bears a knowledge of God the Creator within his heart, though struggling to suppress it (as the Bible itself speaks of sinful man's condition).

By the end of the decade, Van Til had produced major classroom syllabi covering the topics of apologetics, evidences, prolegomena to systematic theology, psychology of religion, ethics, and the (then new) "theology of crisis" of Karl Barth and Emil Brunner. In these syllabi, he was particularly adamant that in defending the faith, believers must not artificially separate philosophical apologetics (theism) from empirical evidences (Christianity in particular)—even as systematic theology (positive statement of the truth). These early syllabi were expanded, revised, and reissued many times over nearly half a century.[22]

Van Til's presuppositional approach to the defense of the faith has provided a powerful impetus for reform in Christian thinking, one which cuts in two directions. *Outwardly*, it directs a transcendental challenge to all philosophies that fall short of a biblical theory of knowledge, demonstrating that their worldviews do not provide the philosophical preconditions needed for the intelligible use of logic, science, or ethics. In this way, Van Til took the offensive against unbelieving philosophy, offering an internal critique of Plato,[23] Kant,[24]

---

relationships of whatever exists (especially that which may be beyond sense experience).

22. Many of these syllabi carried the disclaimer: "This syllabus is for class purposes only, and is not to be regarded as a published book." However, such a statement is surely "difficult of interpretation," since Van Til eventually stopped using the syllabi as a transcription of his lectures for students in class (cf. "for class purposes"), and he himself used important segments of them in his "published books." I interpret Van Til to have meant that the syllabi were like "drafts" along the way to a finished publication someday, thus acknowledging his own desire to possibly recast, explain, illustrate, or revise further if the opportunity afforded itself.

23. E.g., "Plato," *Proceedings of the Calvinistic Philosophy Club,* 1939, 31–44; *Survey of Christian Epistemology,* chap. 3.

24. "Kant or Christ?" *Calvin Forum* 7 (1942): 133–35; *Survey of Christian Epistemology,* chap. 9; *The Reformed Pastor and Modern Thought* (Philadelphia: Presbyterian and Reformed, 1971), chap. 3.

Dewey,[25] idealism, personalism, process philosophy,[26] etc., and striving to stay abreast of the contemporary philosophical scene.[27]

Inwardly, Van Til's presuppositional approach calls for self-examination by Christian scholars and apologists to see if their own theories of knowledge have been self-consciously developed in subordination to the word of God which they wish to vindicate or apply. Not surprisingly, then, Van Til's career as a Christian scholar led him into confrontation with a variety of defections from sound theology and a variety of defects in Christian philosophy, whether found in (1) the schools of modern theology, from Barth and Brunner[28] to Heidegger, Teilhard, Buber, Ferré, Tillich, Kroner,[29] the "God is dead" movement,[30] the Confession of 1967,[31] and the new hermeneutic of Fuchs and Ebeling,[32] or (2) the American Pres-

25. Review of *The Philosophy of John Dewey*, ed. Paul Arthur Schilpp, in *Westminster Theological Journal* 3 (1940): 62–73; *A Survey of Christian Epistemology*, chap. 9.
26. For references on Van Til's treatment of idealism, personalism, and process thought, see footnotes 14, 15, and 16.
27. E.g., "Recent American Philosophy," *Philosophia Reformata* 2 (1937): 1–24; review of *Twentieth Century Philosophy*, edited by Dagobert Runes, in *Westminster Theological Journal* 6 (1943): 72–80. The relevance of Van Til's presuppositionalism to modern epistemological issues is explored in Greg L. Bahnsen, "Pragmatism, Prejudice and Presuppositionalism," in *Foundations of Christian Scholarship*, ed. North, 241–92.
28. Already in 1935, Van Til had produced a syllabus entitled *Theology of Crisis*, and in 1937 he began publishing articles on neoorthodoxy, beginning with "Karl Barth on Scripture," "Karl Barth on Creation," and "Karl Barth and Historic Christianity," in *Presbyterian Guardian* 3 (1937): 137–38, 204–5; 4 (1937): 108–9. Many other articles were to follow throughout Van Til's career (e.g., "Has Karl Barth Become Orthodox?" *Westminster Theological Journal* 16 [1954]: 135–81), but he is especially remembered for the thorough assaults made upon neoorthodoxy in two major publications: *The New Modernism: An Appraisal of the Theology of Barth and Brunner* (Philadelphia: Presbyterian and Reformed, 1946; 2d ed., 1947; 3d ed., with five previously published essays on Barth, 1972); and *Christianity and Barthianism* (Philadelphia: Presbyterian and Reformed, 1962; 2d ed., with four additional essays, 1974).
29. *The Later Heidegger and Theology* (Philadelphia: Westminster Theological Seminary, 1964), reprinted from *Westminster Theological Journal* 26 (1964): 121–61; "Pierre Teilhard de Chardin," *Westminster Theological Journal* 28 (1966): 109–44; *Christ and the Jews* (Philadelphia: Presbyterian and Reformed, 1968; cf. previous syllabus, 1965); "From Cornelius Van Til" (a response to Nels F. S. Ferré, "Where Do We Go from Here in Theology?"), *Religion in Life* 25 (1955): 22–28; review of *Systematic Theology*, vol. 2, by Paul Tillich, in *Westminster Theological Journal* 20 (1957): 93–99; "Religious Philosophy: A Discussion of Richard Kroner's Book *Culture and Faith*," *Calvin Forum* 18 (1953): 126–28; *Reformed Pastor and Modern Thought*, chap. 4.
30. *Is God Dead?* (Philadelphia: Presbyterian and Reformed, 1966).
31. *The Confession of 1967: Its Theological Background and Ecumenical Significance* (Philadelphia: Presbyterian and Reformed, 1967).
32. *The New Hermeneutic* (Philadelphia: Presbyterian and Reformed, 1974). For fur-

byterian tradition, including past stalwarts such as Charles Hodge,[33] B. B. Warfield,[34] and W. B. Greene,[35] and more recent figures such as J. Oliver Buswell,[36] Gordon Clark,[37] Floyd Hamilton,[38] and Edward J. Carnell,[39] or (3) the teachings (e.g., on common grace[40]) of Dutch Reformed authors in the Netherlands and the United States—such as Kuyper,[41] Bavinck,[42] Berkouwer,[43] Dooyeweerd,[44]

---

ther discussions of modern theological trends by Van Til, see *The Great Debate Today* (Philadelphia: Presbyterian and Reformed, 1970) and *The New Synthesis Theology of the Netherlands* (Philadelphia: Presbyterian and Reformed, 1975).

33. *An Introduction to Systematic Theology*, In Defense of the Faith, vol. 5 (Philadelphia: Presbyterian and Reformed, 1974), chap. 4; *The Defense of the Faith* (Philadelphia: Presbyterian and Reformed, 1955), chap. 5.

34. Introduction to *The Inspiration and Authority of the Bible*, by B. B. Warfield (Philadelphia: Presbyterian and Reformed, 1948); *Defense of the Faith*, chap. 13; *A Christian Theory of Knowledge* (Philadelphia: Presbyterian and Reformed, 1969), chap. 8.

35. *Defense of the Faith*, chap. 13.

36. Ibid., chap. 10; *Christian Theory of Knowledge*, chap. 10; *Survey of Christian Epistemology*, appendix; *Introduction to Systematic Theology*, chap. 14.

37. *Introduction to Systematic Theology*, chaps. 13–14.

38. *Defense of the Faith*, chap. 13; *Christian Theory of Knowledge*, chap. 9.

39. Review of *An Introduction to Christian Apologetics*, by Edward John Carnell, in *Westminster Theological Journal* 11 (1948): 45–53; *The Case for Calvinism* (Philadelphia: Presbyterian and Reformed, 1963), chaps. 3–4.

40. Van Til finished his undergraduate course of study at Princeton Seminary in the same year, 1924, as the Christian Reformed Church affirmed its "Three Points" concerning common grace. Of the many things written by Van Til on this subject, note especially his second book, *Common Grace* (Philadelphia: Presbyterian and Reformed, 1947) and the helpful collection of relevant essays, *Common Grace and the Gospel* (Philadelphia: Presbyterian and Reformed, 1972).

41. "Reflections on Dr. A. Kuyper," *The Banner* 72 (December 16, 1937): 1187; *Defense of the Faith*, chaps. 8, 11, 13; *Christian Theory of Knowledge*, chap. 8.

42. "Bavinck the Theologian," *Westminster Theological Journal* 24 (1961): 48–64; *Defense of the Faith*, chaps. 8, 13; *Introduction to Systematic Theology*, chap. 5, where Van Til offers the assessment: "Herman Bavinck has given to us the greatest and most comprehensive statement of Reformed systematic theology in modern times" (p. 43).

43. *The Sovereignty of Grace: An Appraisal of G. C. Berkouwer's View of Dordt* (Philadelphia: Presbyterian and Reformed, 1969); *The Triumph of Grace: The Heidelberg Catechism* (Philadelphia: Westminster Theological Seminary, 1958), chap. 6; *The New Synthesis Theology of the Netherlands*, chap. 2.A; and reviews of books by Berkouwer, especially on Barth, in *Westminster Theological Journal* 11 (1948): 77–80; 12 (1949): 74–76; 18 (1955): 58–59.

44. Review of *A New Critique of Theoretical Thought*, vol. 1, by Herman Dooyeweerd, in *Westminster Theological Journal* 17 (1955): 180–83; response to Dooyeweerd in *Jerusalem and Athens: Critical Discussions on the Theology and Apologetics of Cornelius Van Til*, ed. E. R. Geehan (Philadelphia: Presbyterian and Reformed, 1971), 89–127; *Herman Dooyeweerd and Reformed Apologetics* (Philadelphia: Westminster Theological Seminary, 1974); "Biblical Dimensionalism," in *Christianity in Conflict* (Philadelphia: Westminster Theological Seminary, 1962–64), vol. 2, pt. 3, chaps. 8–9.

Vollenhoven,[45] William Masselink,[46] and James Daane.[47]

Van Til's prolific work as a teacher and writer goes beyond his constructive and critical contributions in apologetics and Christian philosophy. His presuppositional outlook not only cuts outwardly and inwardly; it has likewise cut a wide swath through a large number of related areas. Van Til produced valuable studies in the area of Christian theology (e.g., on equal ultimacy in the Trinity, absolute predestination, God's incomprehensibility, nature and revelation, theological paradox, and a nonintellectualistic view of man)[48] and ethics (e.g., on the necessity of the proper goal, motive, and standard).[49] Van Til's works also addressed intellectual history,[50] key figures in church history (e.g., Augustine and Calvin),[51] Christian culture,[52] and the necessity of Christian education.[53]

45. Reviews in *Calvin Forum* 1 (1936): 142–43 and *Westminster Theological Journal* 14 (1951): 86–87; "Professor Vollenhoven's Significance for Reformed Apologetics," in *Wetenschappelijke Bijdragen*, ed. S. U. Zuidema (Franeker: T. Wever, 1951), 68–71.
46. "Letter on Common Grace" (1953; now published in *Common Grace and the Gospel*); *The Banner* 95, no. 32 (1960); 96, no. 2 (1961); *Introduction to Systematic Theology*, app. 1; *Defense of the Faith*, passim.
47. *The Theology of James Daane* (Philadelphia: Presbyterian and Reformed, 1959); *Defense of the Faith*, passim.
48. *Introduction to Systematic Theology*, passim; *Defense of the Faith*, chaps. 1–2; *The Protestant Doctrine of Scripture*, In Defense of the Faith, vol. 1 (Philadelphia: Presbyterian and Reformed, 1967); "Nature and Scripture," in *The Infallible Word*, ed. N. B. Stonehouse and Paul Woolley (1946; reprint, Philadelphia: Presbyterian and Reformed, 1967), 255–93; "The Significance of Dort for Today," in *Crisis in the Reformed Churches*, ed. Peter Y. De Jong (Grand Rapids: Reformed Fellowship, 1968), 181–96 (expanded in *Sovereignty of Grace*). Cf. John M. Frame, "The Problem of Theological Paradox," in *Foundations of Christian Scholarship*, ed. North, 295–330.
49. *Christian Theistic Ethics* (Philadelphia: Westminster Theological Seminary, 1940, 1947; Phillipsburg, N.J.: Lewis J. Grotenhuis, 1952), In Defense of the Faith, vol. 3 (Philadelphia: Presbyterian and Reformed, 1974).
50. E.g., *Christianity in Conflict; Who Do You Say That I Am?* (Philadelphia: Presbyterian and Reformed, 1975).
51. *Survey of Christian Epistemology*, chap. 4; *Christian Theory of Knowledge*, chap. 4; "Calvin and Modern Subjectivism" and "Calvin as a Controversialist," *Torch and Trumpet* 9, no. 3 (1959): 5–9, and no. 4 (1959): 14–16.
52. E.g., "Calvinism and Art," *Presbyterian Guardian* 17 (1948): 272–74; "The Full-Orbed Life," in *Fundamentals in Christian Education*, ed. Cornelius Jaarsma (Grand Rapids: Eerdmans, 1953), 157–70; reprinted in *Essays on Christian Education* (Philadelphia: Presbyterian and Reformed, 1971), a collection of relevant articles from 1930 to 1969.
53. *Essays on Christian Education;* "What Shall We Feed Our Children?" *Presbyterian Guardian* 3 (1936): 23–24; "The Education of Man—A Divinely Ordained Need," in *Fundamentals in Christian Education*, ed. Jaarsma, 39–59.

So, then, the distinctive presuppositional method and outlook that Van Til promoted through his published writings have generated an intellectual revolution. Its impact has been felt outwardly (in the transcendental challenge to all unbelieving scholarship), inwardly (in the demand that Christian scholarship be developed in a way that is faithful to its ultimate commitments), and widely (in its relevance to numerous areas of life and study). By God's providence, Van Til himself, as an individual, personally exerted a wide influence within the Christian world.

In 1938 Van Til was appointed honorary professor at the University of Debrecen in Hungary, the oldest Reformed institution in Europe. (Hitler's invasion of Czechoslovakia stranded Van Til in Amsterdam, preventing him from reaching Budapest to deliver his acceptance speech.) Throughout his time at Westminster Seminary, numerous students from the Orient (especially Korea, Taiwan, and Japan) came to consolidate their understanding of the Reformed faith under his tutelage.

Many well-known Christian scholars and teachers in America studied under Van Til, including the popular apologists Edward J. Carnell and Francis Schaeffer.[54] During his career, Van Til also dealt in

54. Both of these men advanced their own versions of "presuppositional" apologetics, versions which miss the transcendental challenge of Van Til's outlook. Carnell treated the Christian worldview as a hypothesis (one among many) to be tested according to "synoptic" standards (e.g., coherence, historical veracity, and personal satisfaction) which are (mistakenly) taken as intelligible apart from—and thus more philosophically basic or authoritative than—the Christian worldview (*Introduction to Christian Apologetics* [Grand Rapids: Eerdmans, 1948], chap. 5, also pp. 41, 59, 61, 70, 72–73, 97, 99, 102, 106–7, 117, 119, 154, 164, 173–75, 178–79, 214ff., 268–69; *A Philosophy of the Christian Religion* [Grand Rapids: Eerdmans, 1952], 30, 31, 40, 106, 183, 185, 187, 270–73, 307, 321, 446, 449, 474, 495, 512ff.; *Christian Commitment* [New York: Macmillan, 1957], 76, 78, 101–3, 127, 133, 138, 142, 152, 198, 286, 287). Carnell wrote: "In the contest of hypothesis-making . . . the winner [is] he who can produce the best set of assumptions to account for the totality of reality. . . . Bring on your revelations! Let them make peace with the law of contradiction and the facts of history, and they will deserve a rational man's assent" (*Introduction to Christian Apologetics*, 94, 178). In Thomistic fashion, he insisted: "First we must know in order that we might believe" (*Philosophy of the Christian Religion*, 515; cf. p. 260).

Similarly, Francis Schaeffer treated a "presupposition" as merely a hypothesis to be tested over against competing presuppositions by the standard of observational experience (apparently taking this experience as presuppositionally neutral and rationally intelligible apart from the Christian worldview): "What I urge people to do is to consider the two great presuppositions . . . and to consider which of these fits the facts of what is. . . . It is a question of which of these two sets of presuppositions really and empirically meets the facts as we look about us in the

a critical fashion with the apologists J. Oliver Buswell (an inductivist) and Gordon Clark (a deductivist),[55] both of whom were at one time ministers in the Orthodox Presbyterian Church. In the mid-1930s, Buswell left that communion, subsequently taking issue with Van Til's consistent Calvinism and philosophical presuppositionalism.[56] In the mid-1940s, Clark became embroiled in ecclesiastical controversy over his views of God's incomprehensibility, the primacy of the intellect, and other matters, eventually leaving the denomination and severely criticizing Van Til's theory of knowledge.[57]

In the 1950s, Van Til debated certain Dutch authors over philosophical issues pertaining to common grace[58] and God's sover-

---

world" (*He Is There and He Is Not Silent* [Wheaton, Ill.: Tyndale House, 1972], 65, 66; cf. p. 81). Schaeffer claimed that religious proof follows "the same rules" as scientific proof (*The God Who Is There* [Chicago: Inter-Varsity Press, 1968], 109–11).

55. An "inductive" approach to knowledge begins with the observed particulars and draws generalizations and inferences with probability, whereas a "deductive" approach begins with general (universal) concepts or principles and fits the particular instances to them, drawing inferences with certainty.

56. See, e.g., his articles in *The Bible Today* 42 (1948–49). Van Til's response to Buswell's criticism is referenced in footnote 36 above. Buswell did not recognize that Christian presuppositions (e.g., God's sovereign control over the world to produce uniformity in nature) are philosophically necessary in order to render factual evidences and inductive reasoning intelligible. Since he insisted on developing an epistemology apart from Scripture (in order to test and accept Scripture as a hypothesis), Buswell's epistemology could be as readily reduced to skepticism as the philosophy of the unbeliever with its world of chance (e.g., Hume).

57. See chap. 8.5 below. Clark's own epistemology at first demanded that the Bible be treated as a hypothesis that must pass the test of logical coherence in order to be accepted. See "Special Divine Revelation as Rational," in *Revelation and the Bible*, ed. Carl F. H. Henry (Grand Rapids: Eerdmans, 1959), 37; *A Christian View of Men and Things* (Grand Rapids: Eerdmans, 1952), 24–25, 31, 92, 147, 273, 318, 324. He claimed: "The attempt to show the Bible's logical consistency is, I believe, the best method of defending inspiration" ("How May I Know the Bible Is Inspired?" in *Can I Trust My Bible?* [Chicago: Moody Press, 1963], 23).

But Clark later went so far as to deny altogether that knowledge is derived through sense observation—a position that has been easily reduced to skepticism, since one must use one's senses to gain knowledge even from the Bible. See "The Wheaton Lectures," in *The Philosophy of Gordon H. Clark*, ed. Ronald H. Nash (Philadelphia: Presbyterian and Reformed, 1968), 23–122; cf. Ronald Nash, "Gordon Clark's Theory of Knowledge," 125–75. Though sometimes called a presuppositionalist, the later Clark actually treated Christianity as an unprovable, fideistic first axiom, which is merely chosen or posited (*Three Types of Religious Philosophy* [Nutley, N.J.: Craig Press, 1973], 7–8, 104–7, 110). In both his rationalistic and his fideistic phases, Clark fell short of treating the Bible as the highest (self-attesting) authority and as the basis for a transcendental challenge to unbelief.

58. E.g., responding to William Masselink, *General Revelation and Common Grace* (Grand Rapids: Eerdmans, 1953).

eignty.[59] He was invited to become the president of Calvin Theological Seminary in Grand Rapids, but after being pulled back and forth in his mind, he determined to remain in his teaching post at Westminster.

In 1955 he published what would become his most commonly read book for explaining his apologetical system, *The Defense of the Faith*, a reworking and compilation of many previous syllabi and articles that positively presented the presuppositional method and replied to various critics of it. The presuppositional perspective was spread further, not only by the translation of his works by students in many countries, but also through Van Til's personal trips—to the Orient (Tokyo, Taipei, Taiwan, Hong Kong, and Seoul) in 1959, and to the Mexican state of Yucatán in 1962.

Those who came to know Van Til personally will testify that he was not only a man of principle and conviction, but also a man of warmth and compassion. His personal warmth and care were clearly manifest in the humor he would use in his lectures, the fact that his home was always open to students and visitors wishing to talk with him (sharing ginger ale and cookies on the porch), his street preaching in New York City, his tender letters of gospel hope to presidents and other public figures, and his continuing walks and evangelistic talks with the nuns who lived behind his home. Those who heard him pray knew of his deep passion for piety.

Testimony to the principled conviction by which he lived was found in Van Til's reluctant, but necessary, call for greater faithfulness even in a fellow scholar (and Dutchman) who was perceived as being closest to his position. In 1959 Herman Dooyeweerd was in America and lectured at Westminster Seminary. Although Van Til had been encouraged by Dooyeweerd's ideas thirty years earlier (when he met him in Amsterdam), he was distressed to see him now unwilling to base his philosophy on an exegesis of the text of Scripture (something Dooyeweerd eventually criticized as arising from Van Til's "typical rationalistic scholastic tendency"[60]). Fidelity to the Reformed faith and

---

59. E.g., responding to James Daane, *A Theology of Grace* (Grand Rapids: Eerdmans, 1954).

60. Dooyeweerd, "Cornelius Van Til and the Transcendental Critique of Theoretical Thought," in *Jerusalem and Athens*, ed. Geehan, 74–89. As late as 1962, Van Til was still attempting to read Dooyeweerd optimistically ("in the best possible light"). In vol. 1, pt. 3, of his massive syllabus on the history of apologetics, *Christianity in Conflict*, Van Til wrote, "Dooyeweerd is not asking for an independent philosophy such as would be based on human autonomy. His whole effort is to show that a Christian phi-

the self-attesting authority of Christ in Scripture meant that Van Til was unable to endorse his fellow Dutchman's approach.[61] This parting of the ways was exacerbated in the decade of the 1960s by certain disciples of Dooyeweerd in North America (e.g., the Association for the Advancement of Christian Scholarship), leading to tension between the two schools of thought (even between Van Til and his colleague in the apologetics department at Westminster[62]).

On the other hand, during and after this period, a number of younger students and teachers who had been nourished by Van Til's presuppositional approach began publishing, teaching, and making their own contribution to Christian scholarship (e.g., R. J. Rushdoony and John Frame). In the 1970s, Van Til was presented with two volumes of essays, honoring his achievement as a theologian and apologist: in 1971, *Jerusalem and Athens* (ed. E. R. Geehan), and in 1976, *Foundations of Christian Scholarship* (ed. Gary North).[63] In 1972 Van Til

---

losophy, as well as a Christian theology, must take its basic religious presuppositions from Scripture" (p. 168). This optimism faded as time went on. In the Van Til *Festschrift* (1971), Dooyeweerd accused Van Til of an extreme "rationalism" that claimed "that philosophical ideas are to be *derived* from the supra-natural truths of divine revelation" (p. 81). Van Til replied (in part): "You see then, Dr. Dooyeweerd, that I hold two points about Christian apologetics which apparently you do not hold. In the first place I believe that Christian apologetics, and in particular Reformed apologetics, is not really *transcendental* in its method unless it says *at the outset* of its dialogue with non-believers that the Christian position must be accepted on the authority of the self-identifying Christ of Scripture as the presupposition of human predication in any field" (p. 98).

Van Til's cordiality and humility were evident as he closed this long critical interchange: "But I must stop. I hope that by what I have said in this article, Dr. Dooyeweerd, I am enabling you to have a somewhat more satisfactory insight into my view; as I have, I think, by reading your letter and by rereading a good deal of your writing elsewhere, attained to a more satisfactory insight into your view. I hope this interchange of ideas between us may help others, after us, to listen more humbly to the words of the self-attesting Christ of Scripture in order that they may better bring the word of truth to all men everywhere— all to the praise of our triune God. Soon we shall meet at Jesus' feet" (pp. 126–27).

61. Van Til usually points out that, although there is value in Dooyeweerd's critique of secular systems of thought (especially their pretended autonomy), there is also a dangerous failure in Dooyeweerd's constructive effort, which is to develop a Christian philosophy apart from—and as an intellectual framework for approaching—the Bible's own explicit, verbal teaching.

62. Cf. Robert D. Knudsen, "Progressive and Regressive Tendencies in Christian Apologetics," and Van Til's response, both in *Jerusalem and Athens*, ed. Geehan, 275–305.

63. For further material on Van Til's life, see the biography by William White, Jr., *Van Til: Defender of the Faith* (New York: Thomas Nelson, 1979). Some readers will be disappointed that the book lacks systematic historical detail and analysis, while others will find its personal and impressionistic nature highly readable. The most comprehensive and helpful bibliography of Van Til's publications is the annotated

was named emeritus professor at Westminster Theological Seminary, and in 1976 the seminary named a new lecture hall in his honor.

Rena, his beloved wife of fifty years, passed away in January 1978. A young family came to live with him in his old home in the Philadelphia suburb of Ambler. The last time I saw him (in June 1985), he was pushing one of their children in a stroller and singing gospel hymns. On April 17, 1987, Cornelius Van Til, one of the towering Christian intellectuals of the twentieth century—who could confound scholars and sing to children—joined "all the saints who from their labors rest," and now hymns God's praise in heaven's choir.

A PERSONAL TESTIMONY: TOTAL SURRENDER[64]

As Christians we are not, of ourselves, better or wiser than were the Pharisees. Christ has, by his word and by his Spirit, identified himself with us and thereby, at the same time, told us who and what we are. As a Christian I believe first of all in the testimony that Jesus gives of himself and his work. He says he was sent into the world to save his people from their sins. Jesus asks me to do what he asked the Pharisees to do, namely, read the Scriptures in light of this testimony about himself. He has sent his Spirit to dwell in my heart so that I might believe and therefore understand all things to be what he says they are. I have by his Spirit learned to understand something of what Jesus means when he said *I am the way, the truth and the life*. I have learned something of what it means to make my thought captive to the obedience of Christ, being converted anew every day to the realization that I understand no fact aright unless I see it in its proper relation to Christ as Creator-Redeemer of me and my world. I seek his kingdom and its righteousness above all things else. I now know by the testimony of his Spirit with my spirit that my labor is not in vain in the Lord. "I know whom I have believed and am convinced that he is able to guard what I have entrusted to him until that day" (II Tim. 1:12, NASB). All of my life, my life in my family, my life in my church, my life in society, and my life in my vocation as a minister of the gospel and a teacher of Christian apologetics is unified under the banner *Pro Rege!*[65] I am not a

---

work by Eric D. Bristley, *A Guide to the Writings of Cornelius Van Til 1895–1987* (Chicago: Olive Tree Communications, 1995), also available in *The Works of Cornelius Van Til, 1895–1987*, ed. Eric Sigward, CD-ROM (New York: Labels Army Co., 1997).

64. An excerpt from "My Credo," in *Jerusalem and Athens*, ed. Geehan, 4–5.

65. Abraham Kuyper's famous slogan, *Pro Rege*—"For the King"—functions as a brief maxim for a thoroughly Christian world-and-life view, where all of our thinking and activity in every area of life is pursued in submission to the Lord Jesus Christ speaking in His word. This theme, coupled with the subsequent allusion (which

hero, but in Christ I am not afraid of what man may do to me. The gates of hell cannot prevail against the ongoing march of victory of the Christ to whom all power in heaven and on earth is given.

Van Til did not consistently develop) to historical optimism regarding God's kingdom in history, characterizes the distinctive "Reconstructionist" extension and application of Van Til's thought. Speaking of the "legacy" of Van Til, John Frame writes: "Van Til's ideas are being taught by various individuals and groups today. The 'theonomists' or Christian reconstructionists . . . are thorough-going Van Tillians in their epistemology" ("Cornelius Van Til," in *Handbook of Evangelical Theologians*, ed. Walter A. Elwell [Grand Rapids: Baker, 1993], 167).

As to ethics, Van Til wrote: "We wish to bring out that the real difference between Christian and non-Christian ethics goes much deeper than is often supposed. . . . *There is no alternative but that of theonomy and autonomy*. It was vain to attempt to flee from God and flee to a universe in order to seek eternal law there" (*Christian Theistic Ethics*, 134). "It is this point particularly that makes it necessary for the Christian to maintain without apology and without concession that it *is Scripture, and Scripture alone*, in the light of which all moral questions must be answered" (*Defense of the Faith*, 71). This entails the need for taking our sociopolitical ethics from Scripture, not from a supposed interpretation of "natural law" (cf. Gary North, *Westminster's Confession* [Tyler, Tex.: Institute for Christian Economics, 1991]). "The Old and New Testaments as a unit maintain that God, as man's creator and judge, must naturally set the ideal for man's life. . . . The Biblical *summum bonum* requires the absolute destruction of sin and evil in the individual and in society. . . . We have the further obligation to destroy the consequences of sin in this world as far as we can" (*Defense of the Faith*, 81, 82). In connection with the "internal self-consistency" of God's righteous character as the source of "any justice in a world of sinners," Van Til asserted that the believer "will seek the maintenance of God's laws for men everywhere and at all times, in ways that are themselves in accord with those laws" (*Introduction to Systematic Theology*, 245).

Regarding Augustine, Van Til wrote: "By his magnificent philosophy of history, seen in its totality as the fruit of reflection of God's revelation through Christ in all things, Augustine did point toward a reformation in philosophy and science as well as in theology . . . in the interest of tracing, better than would otherwise be possible, something of the progressive victory of Christ *in the world*" (*Christianity in Conflict*, vol. 1, pt. 3, 169 [emphasis added]). Van Til taught that, prior to the victory that is certain beyond history's end, we must in the present have the "courage to start with the program of the eradication of evil from God's universe. . . . We are making progress toward our goal" (*Defense of the Faith*, 82). Later he wrote: "Still further I know that Christ saved and saves his church, his people, that they may be a blessing to the world. . . . And it is the *world* that will be saved. Satan and all the powers of hell cannot prevail against the kingdom of heaven that Christ established and is establishing" (*Case for Calvinism*, 133). "According to the teaching of Scripture, in all that happens in the world of 'men and things' Christ is establishing his kingdom as he destroys the kingdom of Satan. . . . By means of this thought-communication God gave man the task of subduing the world. Quite properly this task has been called man's 'cultural mandate' " (*Protestant Doctrine of Scripture*, 103).

Nevertheless, Van Til nowhere developed or expressed a particular millennial eschatology (although he did favorably endorse an extensive, exegetical, and explicitly postmillennial tape series expounding the book of Revelation in the "Supplement Catalog" [April 1980] for the Mt. Olive Tape Library). It is probably distorting and reading too much into Van Til's use of the metaphor of "common grace as earlier grace" to make him into a "self-conscious amillennialist" with a progressively pessimistic view of history (contrary to Gary North, *Dominion and*

PRESENTING CHRIST WITHOUT COMPROMISE[66]

Throughout, my aim has been to show that it is the historic Reformed Faith alone that can in any adequate way present the claims of Christ to men for their salvation. The Reformed Faith alone does anything like full justice to the cultural and missionary mandates of Christ. The Reformed Faith alone has anything like an adequately stated view of God, of man, and of Christ as the mediator between God and man. It is because the Reformed Faith alone has an essentially sound, because biblical, theology that it alone has anything like a sound, that is biblical, method of challenging the world of unbelief to repentance and faith. . . .

In seeking to follow the example of Paul, Reformed Apologetics needs, above all else, to make clear from the beginning that it is challenging the wisdom of the natural man on the authority of the self-attesting Christ speaking in Scripture. Doing this the Reformed apologist must place himself on the position of his "opponent," the natural man, in order to show him that on the presupposition of human autonomy human predication[67] cannot even get under way. The fact that it has gotten under way is because the universe is what the Christian, on the authority of Christ, knows it to be. Even to negate

---

Common Grace [Tyler, Tex.: Institute for Christian Economics, 1987], 80–87; even North notes that Van Til did not give these issues much systematic thought (p. 87 n.). However, in his massive survey and analysis of the history of thought and culture, Van Til certainly had the spirit of reconstruction: "There is then not a square inch of space where, nor a minute of time when, the believer in Christ can withdraw from the responsibility of being a soldier of the cross. . . . Satan must be driven from the field and Christ must rule" (*Christianity in Conflict,* 1:ii).

66. Excerpts from the pamphlet *Toward a Reformed Apologetics* (Philadelphia: privately printed, 1972), 1, 20, 28.
67. "Predication" is the mental or verbal act of attributing or denying a property or characteristic (a "predicate") to a subject—as when someone affirms, "The sky is blue," or "George Washington fought at Valley Forge," or "Driving seventy-five miles per hour is no longer permitted by law."

Predication requires one intelligibly to differentiate and select individual things (particulars), to make sense out of general or abstract concepts (universals, classes, definable sets), and to distinguish them (so as *not* to make them identical) while in some sense *identifying* or relating them to each other. In the ordinary affairs of life, people readily engage in predication without difficulty—until they are called upon to give an analysis or philosophical account of just what it is that they are doing, what it assumes about reality, and how anyone could know.

Van Til would lay down this dialectical challenge: "How do we know that the many do not simply exist as unrelated particulars [so they are disjointed and different experiences so individual as to share nothing objectively in common, whether a nature, law-like tendency, or even a basis for applying the same word to them]? . . . On the other hand, how is it possible that we should obtain a unity that does not destroy the particulars [strip the particulars of their particularity]?" (*Defense of the Faith,* 42).

Christ, those who hate Him must be borne up by Him. A three year old child may slap its father in his face only because the father holds it up on his knee. . . .

Finally, it is my hope for the future, as it has always been my hope in the past, that I may present Christ without compromise to men who are dead in trespasses and sins, that they might have life and that they might worship and serve the Creator more than the creature. Rather than wedding Christianity to the philosophies of Aristotle or Kant, we must openly challenge the apostate philosophic constructions of men by which they seek to suppress the truth about God, themselves, and the world.

To be sure, it is the *grace* of God which we proclaim to men, and we must proclaim the gospel *suaviter in modo*,[68] but nevertheless, we have not been true to Christ if we do not say with Paul: "Where is the wise? where is the scribe? where is the disputer of this world? hath not God made foolish the wisdom of this world? For after that in the wisdom of God the world by wisdom knew not God, it pleased God by the foolishness of preaching to save them that believe" (I Cor. 1:20, 21).

We are children of the King. To us, not to the world, do all things belong. It is only if we demand of men complete submission to the living Christ of the Scriptures in every area of their lives, that we have presented to men the claims of the Lord Christ without compromise.

A CONSISTENTLY REFORMED APOLOGETIC [69]

To this point no notice has been taken of the fact that not all Reformed theologians follow the method briefly suggested so far. What has been called the Reformed method in the preceding discussion is implied in the basic contention of Reformed theology, namely, the self-sufficiency and self-explanatory character of the triune God. But that such is the case has not always been recognized.

The Reformed theologians of the Reformation period did not work out a Reformed apologetical methodology. This is not to be marveled at. They laid the groundwork for it. Some later Reformed theologians continued to use the Romanist-evangelical method of defending Christianity. At least they did so up to the point where the specifically Reformed teachings on the sovereignty of God in soteriology came up for discussion. Thus the apologetics of the Reformed theologians at Princeton Theological Seminary (prior to its reorgani-

---

68. That is, "gentle in manner."
69. Excerpts from *Christian Theory of Knowledge*, 19–21, 23–24.

zation in 1929 when the Reformed Faith was rejected in principle) used a method of argument similar to that employed in Bishop Butler's *Analogy*.[70]

Now Butler's work is perhaps the most outstanding historical example of evangelical non-Reformed methodology. It starts with assuming that man, though he has not taken God into account, has by his own principles been able to interpret the course and constitution of nature aright. Butler's argument is to the effect that, if men would only follow the same method they have employed for the interpretation of nature when they are confronted with the claims of Christianity, they will be driven to accept the latter as true. Men have seen evidence of substitution in nature and they have recognized it as such. So then, why should they not also accept the idea of the substitutionary atonement by Christ, the Son of God, as presented in Scripture? Men have admitted that the exceptional, the inexplicable, takes place in nature. There is a principle of discontinuity as well as a principle of continuity that men recognize in the world. Why then should they object to the possibility of the supernatural and of miracle? They can allow for these without in the least giving up their own basic principle of interpretation.[71]

It was against a position similar to this that Dr. Abraham Kuyper protested in his famous work *Principles of Sacred Theology*.[72] His argument is to the effect that apologetics of this nature gives over one bulwark after another to the enemy. Kuyper's contention is that the Christian must take his place directly upon the presupposition of the truth of the Christian religion as it is presented in Scripture.

Even so, both Kuyper and Bavinck did not work out their own principles fully; their primary interest was theological rather than apologetical. When they did engage in apologetical argument they sometimes employed the method which they themselves had criticized in others.

What has been called the Reformed method in the preceding discussion was, however, employed by both the men of Princeton and of Amsterdam to which reference has been made. At one point or another all the Reformed theologians of modern times argue that unless the "reason of man" and the facts of the universe be taken as they are taken in terms of the infallible revelation of God given to man in the Bible, human experience runs into the ground.

It is to this basic approach of Kuyper and Bavinck, of Charles Hodge and B. B.

---

70. CVT: *The Works of Joseph Butler, D. C. L.*, ed. by The Rt. Hon. W. E. Gladstone, Vol. I (New York: Macmillan and Co., 1896).

71. CVT: Cf. B. B. Warfield, "Apologetics," *The New Schaff-Herzog Encyclopaedia of Religious Knowledge*, ed. by Samuel M. Jackson (Grand Rapids: Baker Book House, 1951).

72. CVT: Abraham Kuyper, *Principles of Sacred Theology*, tr. by J. H. DeVries (Grand Rapids: Wm. B. Eerdmans, 1954). This is an abridgement of Kuyper's three volume work *Encyclopaedie der Heilige Godgeleerdheid* (Kampen: J. H. Kok, 1908–09).

Warfield and Geerhardus Vos (ignoring or setting aside the remnants of the traditional method that is found in their works) that appeal is made in this work.

It is of critical importance in the current scene that a consistently Reformed apologetic be set forth. . . .

In the first place, every Christian must tell the non-Christian that he must be *saved* from his false views of God and himself. The greatest love can be shown for the lost only by those who have themselves sensed most deeply the lost condition from which they have been saved. The best physician is he who tells the patient who needs surgery that he must be rushed to the hospital, not he who tells him to take a strong sedative.

It is this that the present writer has learned from those from whom he has been bold enough to differ at points. It is only in a subordinate way that he differs from the great theologians of the preceding generation. The greater part of what is presented here is due to the fact that the writer stands on the shoulders of the great Reformed thinkers mentioned above. He is merely gathering together the thoughts found over a widely diversified body of their writings in order to present briefly that which basically they have taught. The present book is no more than an effort to stimulate thinking along the lines of consistent Christian approach to modern thought.

The message of Christianity must ring out clearly in the modern tumult. If Christianity is to be heard above the din and noise of modern irrationalism and existentialism, it must think in terms of its own basic categories. If it has to import some of its materials from the enemy, it cannot expect effectively to conquer the enemy. It is the Christian Faith that alone has the truth; this should be its claim. It should be made with all modesty; those who have accepted it once were blind. They have been saved by grace. Little would it behoove them to regard themselves as the source of wisdom. But disclaiming themselves as the source of wisdom, they cannot make apology for God and for Christ the Son of God. If men would be saved, if they would save their culture as well as themselves, they must meet the requirements of God. There is no other way to truth. "Hath not God made foolish the wisdom of this world? For after that the world by its wisdom knew not God, it pleased God through the foolishness of preaching to save those that believe" (I Cor. 1:20, 21).

THE ALL-ENCOMPASSING CHALLENGE[73]

If then Christianity as interpreted in the Reformed creeds, as championed by Kuyper, Bavinck, Hodge, Warfield and Machen, is to be presented to men

---

73. An excerpt from *Defense of the Faith*, 279–80.

today, ministers must learn to understand the riches of their own position. Christianity is the *sine qua non* of the intelligibility of anything. Why am I so much interested in the foundations of science? It is (a) because with Kuyper I believe that God requires of us that we claim every realm of being for him, and (b) because with Kuyper I believe that unless we press the crown rights of our King in every realm we shall not long retain them in any realm.

Chapter 2

The Task of Apologetics

2.1 The Nature and Necessity of Apologetics

In ancient Greece an *apologia* was the defense offered in a court of law in answer to an accusation. Socrates was accused of atheism and of corrupting the youth of Athens; eventually he was sentenced to die. The dialogue by Plato in which we read the courtroom reply that Socrates offered is entitled *The Apology*—not indicating that Socrates "apologized" and said he was sorry, but rather that he defended his actions and integrity.

Christians in the ancient world knew what it was to have accusations and ridicule directed at them for their religious convictions and practices. The report of Jesus' resurrection was taken as an idle tale (Luke 24:11), a lie (Matt. 28:13–15), and an impossibility (Acts 26:8). For preaching it, believers were arrested by the Jews (Acts 4:20–23) and mocked by the Greek philosophers (Acts 17:32). On the day of Pentecost the disciples were accused of being drunk (Acts 2:13). Stephen was accused of opposing previous revelation (Acts 6:11–14). Paul was accused of introducing new gods (Acts 17:18–20). The church was accused of political insurrection (Acts 17:6–7). Experts openly contradicted what the Christians taught (Acts 13:45) and prejudicially vilified their persons (Acts 14:2). So, on the one hand, the Christian message was a stumbling block to Jews and utter foolishness to Greeks (1 Cor. 1:23). On the other hand, the early Christians had to guard against the wrong kind of positive acceptance of what they proclaimed. The apostles were confused for gods by advocates of pagan religion (Acts 14:11–13), given unwelcome commendation by soothsayers (Acts 16:16–18), and had their message absorbed by heretical legalists (Acts 15:1, 5). Twentieth-century believers can sympathize with their brothers in the ancient world. Our Christian faith continues to see the same variety of attempts to oppose and undermine it.

What kind of response should be made to such accusations and challenges? It is clear from the New Testament record that the believers in the early church were not content to be relativists, subjectivists, or eclectics. In the accounts of opposition that are mentioned above, Christians are not found replying that nobody can know anything for sure (especially about supernatural matters), in which case there is no absolute truth. Religious disagreements are not seen as irresolvable differences of personal upbringing, culture, or perspective. We do not read anything like "The Bible is true for me, but may not be true for you." Nor can we find any willingness to make common cause with false religiosity as long as Christianity is accepted as one among many legitimate points of view. Instead, what we find in answer to accusation, ridicule, and alternative religions is *apologetics*—the defense of the truth of Christian claims:

> [Peter proclaimed,] Let all the house of Israel therefore know for certain that God has made him both Lord and Christ, this Jesus whom you crucified. (Acts 2:36)

> But Saul increased the more in strength and confounded the Jews that dwelt at Damascus, proving that this is the Christ. (Acts 9:22)

> So [Paul] reasoned in the synagogue with the Jews . . . and in the marketplace every day with them that met him, including certain also of the Epicurean and Stoic philosophers. (Acts 17:17–18)

> I deem myself happy, King Agrippa, that I am to make my defense [*apologia*] before you this day. (Acts 26:2)

> Both in my bonds and in the defense [*apologia*] and confirmation of the gospel you are all partakers with me of grace. . . .
> I am set for the defense of the gospel. (Phil. 1:7, 16)

Those who were followers of Christ in the early church stood firm on His own categorical claim: "I am the way, and the truth, and the life; no one comes to the Father but by me" (John 14:6). Accordingly, they proclaimed Christ in such a way that the gospel about Him would be understood as objectively and exclusively true. Those who abided in His word would "know the truth" that sets men free (John 8:31–32).

First-century Christians were willing and able to defend that claim. After all, the truth is not clearly taught unless whatever contradicts it or whatever error stands over against it is refuted. Jude exhorted his fellow believers "to contend earnestly for the faith which was once for all delivered unto the saints" (Jude 3). Peter made it a moral imperative to be prepared to give a reasoned answer in defense of the Christian message: "Set apart Christ as Lord in your hearts, being ready always to give an answer to every man who asks you a reason concerning the hope that is in you, yet with gentleness and respect" (1 Peter 3:15). In light of the preceding passages, this verse is not an isolated encouragement to defend the faith intellectually; it should be seen in the wider context of the total New Testament witness, which emphasizes the vindication of Christian truth-claims. According to 1 Peter 3:15, the obligation to defend the Christian faith rests upon all believers—all the sheep of Christ's flock. It is all the more an obligation resting upon those charged with defending the flock (Acts 20:28–30) and setting before it an example as shepherds (1 Peter 5:1–3). Thus, one of the New Testament requirements for those who would be ordained as elders or teachers in the church is that they be "able both to exhort in sound doctrine and to confute the gainsayers" (Titus 1:9). We cannot avoid the conclusion, therefore, that apologetics has the strong warrant of New Testament example and command.

According to Cornelius Van Til, apologetics aims to defend the Christian faith by answering the variety of challenges leveled against it by unbelievers, thereby vindicating the Christian philosophy of life (worldview) over against all non-Christian philosophies of life (worldviews). There are many ways in which Christian truth-claims come under attack. Their meaningfulness is challenged. The possibility of miracles, revelation, and incarnation is questioned. Doubt is cast upon the deity of Christ or the existence of God. The historical or scientific accuracy of the Bible is attacked. Scriptural teaching is rejected for not being logically coherent. Conscious life following physical death, everlasting damnation, and a future resurrection are not readily accepted. The way of salvation is found disgusting or unnecessary. The nature of God and the way of salvation are falsified by heretical schools of thought. Competing religious systems are set over against Christianity. The ethics of Scripture is criticized. The psychological or political adequacy of Christianity is looked down upon. These and many, many other lines of attack are directed against biblical Christianity. It is the job of apologetics to refute them and demonstrate the truth of the Christian proclamation and worldview—to "cast down reasonings and every high thing that is exalted against the knowledge of God" (2 Cor. 10:5).

One of the distinctive insights that Van Til has given to presuppositional apologetics is that every line of reasoning that is exalted against the knowledge of God, and every kind of objection or challenge to the faith that is raised by unbelievers, arises from an attitude of the heart and within the intellectual context of a world-and-life view. Everybody thinks and reasons in terms of a broad and fundamental understanding of the nature of reality, of how we know what we know, and of how we should live our lives. This philosophy or outlook is "presupposed" by everything the unbeliever (or believer) says; it is the implicit background that gives meaning to the claims and inferences drawn by people. For this reason, every apologetical encounter is ultimately a conflict of worldviews or fundamental perspectives (whether this is explicitly mentioned or not).

The Christian must not only recognize this for the purpose of developing and responding to arguments with an unbeliever, but also be aware that the particular claims which the apologist defends are understood within the context of the entire system of doctrine revealed by God in the Scriptures. It is this entire underlying worldview that is being defended, even when we answer a more narrow, particular attack. We cannot talk about everything at once, of course, but the specific matters about which we argue with the unbeliever are always understood and defined within the broader framework of God's full revelation. Thus, we do not attempt to defend the resuscitation of a particular human corpse, and then attempt to add an argument that this revived individual is also a divine person (etc.); rather, we set forth and defend the resurrection of the incarnate Son of God. Likewise, the Christian apologist does not argue for just any kind of abstract, general theism ("a god of some sort or other"), but rather for the specific conception of God revealed within the Christian Scriptures. Thus, when all is said and done, apologetics becomes the vindication of the Christian worldview as a whole, not simply a piecemeal defense of isolated, abstractly defined, religious points.

Therefore, apologetics involves intellectual reasoning and argumentation regarding the Christian worldview. This is more than personal testimony and autobiography. It is a matter of intellectual analysis and confrontation. The loathing of such things in many quarters of the modern Christian community is unhealthy. Reasoning is not an unspiritual activity to be shunned, nor does "argument" automatically denote personal contentiousness.

There is a use of the mind and scholarly procedures which is indeed proud and ungodly—"walking in the vanity of their mind, being darkened in their understanding, alienated from the life of God, because of the ignorance that is in them, because of the hardening of their heart" (Eph. 4:17–18). Nevertheless, Paul just as clearly affirms that "you did not so learn Christ" (v. 20). Christians have been renewed in the spirit of their mind (v. 23; cf. Col. 3:10) and granted repentance "unto the knowledge of the truth" (2 Tim. 2:25). "We have the mind of Christ" (1 Cor. 2:16), in light of which we seek to develop a philosophy that is not patterned after worldly thinking and human traditions, but rather after Christ, "in whom all the treasures of wisdom and knowledge are deposited" (Col. 2:3, 8). Reasoning in this manner is an expression of true spirituality and godliness, an obedient response to God's requirement that in "whatsoever you do, do all to the glory of God" (1 Cor. 10:31), and that we "love the Lord your God with all your heart, and with all your soul, and with all your mind" (Matt. 22:37). God does not want our minds eradicated, but transformed (Rom. 12:2). When we begin to use our intellects in the service of our Creator and Savior, we naturally wish to make our best effort and produce work of the highest quality possible. It is obvious in the pages of the New Testament that this was the case with the disciples, whether they were fishermen, tax collectors, or studious teachers of the law. They put their minds to work, searching the Scriptures for better understanding, and reasoning with people to persuade them of its truth.

Yet they knew the difference between intellectual argument—the presentation of premises or reasons in support of an inference or con-

clusion, and the offering of evidence to substantiate claims—and interpersonal hostility or contentiousness. Thus, Peter, aware of the different ways an argument can be conducted, specifically reminded his
readers to offer their reasoned defense "with gentleness and respect"
(1 Peter 3:15). Paul wrote: "The Lord's servant must not quarrel, but
be gentle toward all, apt to teach, forbearing, in meekness correcting
those who oppose themselves" (2 Tim. 2:24–25). The proponents of
conflicting viewpoints can trade arguments and engage in intellectual
dispute in a manner that exhibits or leads to being puffed up—something that Paul censures in a multitude of ways throughout 1 Corinthians (especially as it stems from a lust for persuasive words of worldly
wisdom, 2:4–5). However, there is nothing in the nature of the case
which requires argumentation to be conducted in a proud and unlov-
ing fashion. Apologetics can be pursued with a humble boldness, one
which displays true concern for the error of the unbeliever's thinking and the destructiveness of his ways. This does not mean giving
even an inch on any issue of truth over which we disagree with the
unbeliever. But it does mean, as Dr. Van Til would always say, that we
keep buying the next cup of coffee for our opponent.

The appropriateness and necessity of apological argument with
unbelievers needs to be asserted, not only against anti-intellectualism
and false piety, but equally against the sophisticated opinion of someone like Abraham Kuyper that apologetics is intellectually futile.
Kuyper well understood that all men conduct their thinking and reasoning in terms of an ultimate, controlling principle—a most basic
presupposition, perspective, and mental attitude. For the unbeliever,
this is a natural principle (that takes man's thinking to be intelligible
without recourse to God), while for the believer it is a supernatural
principle (based on God's involvement in human history and experience, notably in regeneration, providing the framework necessary
for making sense of anything). These two ultimate commitments—
call them naturalism and Christian supernaturalism—are logically
incompatible and seek to cancel each other. They must in principle
create "two kinds of science," where each perspective (in principle)
contradicts whatever the other perspective says and denies to it the
noble name of "science."[1] Thus, the unbeliever is bent on distorting,
reinterpreting, or rejecting any evidence or argumentation that is set

---

1. *Principles of Sacred Theology*, trans. J. Hendrik De Vries (1898; Grand Rapids: Eerdmans, 1968), 150–56.

forth in support of, and which is controlled by, the believer's ultimate commitment. To be consistent, the unbeliever cannot even allow for the possibility that the Christian proclamation is true. Kuyper saw all this, but from it he drew a fallacious conclusion, namely, that Christian apologetics is useless, that there is no pressing need to reason with the darkened understanding of the unbeliever: "It will be impossible to settle the difference of insight. No polemics between these two kinds of science . . . can ever serve any purpose. This is the reason why . . . Apologetics has always failed to reach results."[2]

That conclusion does not follow, however, when other, equally biblical insights are taken into account. For instance, the unbeliever's intention may be to follow his naturalistic principle consistently, and he may claim to be doing so; but to do so in practice is not actually possible. He cannot escape the persuasive power of God's revelation around and within him; indeed, by the common grace of the Holy Spirit, he is restrained from successfully obliterating that testimony. He conducts his life and reasoning in terms of God's revelation (since there is no other way for man to learn and make sense of the truth about himself or the world), all the while verbally denying it and convincing himself that it is not so. In light of these things, not only is the apologist able to mount a compelling argument against the cogency of the unbeliever's espoused philosophy and the adequacy of his interpretation of the facts, but the unbeliever can also be expected to understand and feel the force of the apologist's reasoning. Van Til maintained: "Thus, intellectual argument will not, as such, convince and convert the non-Christian. It takes the regenerating power of the Holy Spirit to do that. But as in the case of preaching, so in the case of apologetical reasoning, the Holy Spirit may use a *mediate* approach to the minds and hearts of men. The natural man is quite able intellectually to follow the argument that the Christian offers for the truth of his position. He can therefore see that the wisdom of this world has been made foolishness by God. Christianity can be shown to be, not 'just as good as' or even 'better than' the non-Christian position, but the *only* position that does not make nonsense of human experience."[3]

Apologetical argument—intellectual reasoning that goes beyond mere testimony—must not, therefore, be disparaged or ignored, as if it were a futile exercise due to subjectivity in anyone's ultimate per-

2. Ibid., 160.
3. *A Christian Theory of Knowledge* (Philadelphia: Presbyterian and Reformed, 1969), 19.

spective or presuppositions. Van Til says that Christianity must be presented to men as the objective truth, and provably so. It is not only a moral lapse, but also an unjustifiable intellectual error, to reject the message of God's revealed word.

APOLOGETICS DEFENDS CHRISTIANITY TAKEN AS A WHOLE[4]

Apologetics is the vindication of the Christian philosophy of life against the various forms of the non-Christian philosophy of life.

It is frequently said that apologetics deals with theism, while evidences deals with Christianity. For that reason, it is said, apologetics deals with philosophy while evidences deals with facts.

Now there is, to be sure, a certain amount of truth in this way of putting the matter. Apologetics does deal with theism more than it deals with Christianity, and evidences does deal with Christianity more than it deals with theism. For that reason, too, apologetics deals mostly with philosophy and evidences deals mostly with facts. But the whole matter is a question of emphasis.

That the whole question can be no more than one of emphasis and never one of separation is due to the fact that Christian theism is a unit. Christianity and theism are implied in one another. If we ask, e.g., why Christ came into the world, the answer is that he came to save his people from their sins. But what is sin? It is "Any want of conformity unto, or transgression of, the law of God." And who or what is God?

True, we have here given the orthodox doctrine of the work of Christ, and the orthodox definition of sin. But we could just as well give any other definition of the work of Christ and we should find that it always involves a certain concept of God. If we say that Christ came to set us a fine example of morality and no more, then we have redefined sin to mean some weakness inherent in human nature and therewith we have redefined God to be something less than that absolute and holy being which orthodox theology conceives him to be. Christianity can never be separated from some theory about the existence and the nature of God. The result is that Christian theism must be thought of as a unit.

We may, therefore, perhaps conceive of the vindication of Christian theism as a whole [in comparison] to modern warfare. There is bayonet fight-

---

4. An excerpt from *Apologetics* (Nutley, N.J.: Presbyterian and Reformed, 1976), 1–2. A syllabus with this title was first issued in 1929, and was revised in 1947 and 1953. Two portions of the excerpt also appear in *The Defense of the Faith* (Philadelphia: Presbyterian and Reformed, 1955), 23–24 (where footnotes indicate dependence on a 1942 edition of the syllabus).

ing, there is rifle shooting, there are machine guns, but there are also heavy cannon and atom bombs. All the men engaged in these different kinds of fighting are mutually dependent upon one another. The rifle men could do very little if they did not fight under the protection of the heavy guns behind them. The heavy guns depend for the progress they make upon the smaller guns. So too with Christian theism.

It is impossible and useless to seek to vindicate Christianity as a historical religion by a discussion of facts only. Suppose we assert that Christ arose from the grave. We assert further that his resurrection proves his divinity. This is the nerve of the "historical argument" for Christianity. Yet a pragmatic philosopher will refuse to follow this line of reasoning. Granted he allows that Christ actually arose from the grave, he will say that this proves nothing more than that something very unusual took place in the case of that man Jesus. The philosophy of the pragmatist is to the effect that everything in this universe is unrelated and that such a fact as the resurrection of Jesus, granted it were a fact, would have no significance for us who live two thousand years after him. It is apparent from this that if we would really defend Christianity as an historical religion we must at the same time defend the theism upon which Christianity is based. This involves us in philosophical discussion.[5] To interpret a fact of history involves a philosophy of history. But a philosophy of history is at the same time a philosophy of reality as a whole.

Thus we are driven to philosophical discussion all the time and everywhere. Yet in defending the theistic foundation of Christianity we, in the nature of the case, deal almost exclusively with philosophical argument. In apologetics we shoot the big guns under the protection of which the definite advances in the historical field must be made. In short, there is an historical and there is a philosophical aspect to the defense of Christian theism. *Evidences deals largely with the historical while apologetics deals largely with the philosophical aspect. Each has its own work to do but they should constantly be in touch with one another.*

---

5. In *The Defense of the Faith,* Van Til added: "But to engage in philosophical discussion does not mean that we begin without Scripture. We do not first defend theism philosophically by an appeal to reason and experience in order, after that, to turn to Scripture for our knowledge and defense of Christianity. We get our theism as well as our Christianity from the Bible. . . . It is therefore the system of truth as contained in Scripture which we must present to the world" (p. 24). He later explains: "By the 'Christian philosophy of life' I mean the truths of Scripture as set forth by the classical Reformed theologians" (p. 37).

Two crucial things about Van Til's presuppositionalism must be observed here: (1) Any adequate apologetical argument must function (even if only implicitly) within a broader philosophical framework, and rests ultimately upon it. (2) The Christian gains his philosophical presuppositions, not abstractly or by speculation, but concretely and directly from the Scriptures at the very outset.

If we are to defend Christian theism as a unit it must be shown that its parts are really related to one another. We have already indicated the relation between the doctrine of Christ's work, the doctrine of sin, and the doctrine of God. The whole curriculum of an orthodox seminary is built upon the conception of Christian theism as a unit. The Bible is at the center not only of every course, but at the center of the curriculum as a whole. The Bible is thought of as authoritative on everything of which it speaks. Moreover, it speaks of everything. We do not mean that it speaks of football games, of atoms, etc. directly, but we do mean that it speaks of everything either directly or by implication. It tells us not only of the Christ and his work, but it also tells us who God is and where the universe about us has come from. It tells us about theism as well as about Christianity. It gives us a philosophy of history as well as history. Moreover, the information on these subjects is woven into an inextricable whole. It is only if you reject the Bible as the word of God that you can separate the so-called religious and moral instruction of the Bible from what it says, e.g., about the physical universe.[6]

This view of Scripture, therefore, involves the idea that there is nothing in this universe on which human beings can have full and true information unless they take the Bible into account. We do not mean, of course, that one must go to the Bible rather than to the laboratory if one wishes to study the anatomy of the snake. But if one goes only to the laboratory and not also to the Bible one will not have a full or even true interpretation of the snake.

BOTH APOLOGETICS AND EVIDENCES VINDICATE CHRISTIAN THEISM[7]

If we take apologetics in its broad sense we mean by it the vindication of Christian theism against any form of non-theistic and non-Christian thought. This

---

6. This is a crucial point for Van Til: the truths of the Bible stand or fall as an entire system. The apologist does not separate the "earthly" (observational) teachings and claims of the Bible from its "heavenly" (theological) teachings and claims, as though the former were in principle subject to verification, while the latter require a step of faith. Apologists who defend the historical "facts" reported in the Bible in order to lay a foundation for claiming that the Bible is likewise reliable in its theological "interpretation" of those facts engage in notoriously fallacious reasoning—as well as getting stranded behind "Lessing's ditch" (between the accidental details of history and the universal truth of religion). Furthermore, apologists who are clear about the plenary, verbal inspiration of the Bible will not be satisfied with the position of "limited inerrancy," as though Scripture might err regarding details of history or science, but is fully reliable when it teaches us about salvation. "If I told you earthly things and you do not believe, how shall you believe if I tell you heavenly things?" (John 3:12).

7. An excerpt from *Christian-Theistic Evidences*, In Defense of Biblical Christianity, vol.

vindication of Christianity has two aspects. In the first place, Christian theism must be defended against non-theistic philosophy. We have sought to do this in the course in apologetics. In the second place, Christian theism must be defended against non-theistic science. It is this that we must seek to do in the course in Christian evidences. Evidences, then, is a subdivision of apologetics in the broader sense of the word, and is coordinate with apologetics in the more limited sense of the word.[8]

Christian-theistic evidences is, then, the defense of Christian theism against any attack that may be made upon it by "science." Yet it is Christian theism as a unit that we seek to defend. We do not seek to defend theism in apologetics and Christianity in evidences,[9] but we seek to defend Christian theism in both courses. Then, too, in the method of defense we do not limit ourselves to argument about facts in the course in evidences nor to philosophical argument in the course in apologetics. It is really quite impossible to make a sharp distinction between theism and Christianity and between the method of defense for each of them.

Nevertheless, in evidences it is primarily the factual question with which we deal. Christianity is an historical religion. It is based upon such facts as the death and resurrection of Christ. The question of miracle is at the heart of it. Kill miracle and you kill Christianity. But one cannot even define miracle except in relation to natural law.

Thus, we face the question of God's providence. And providence, in turn, presupposes creation. We may say, then, that we seek to defend the fact of miracle, the fact of providence, the fact of creation, and therefore, the fact of God, in relation to modern non-Christian science.

But if the matter is put this way we may as well say that we are seeking to

---

6 (Phillipsburg, N.J.: Presbyterian and Reformed, 1978), i–ii. The syllabus upon which this book was based was issued in 1935 and revised in 1947 and 1966.

8. Notice, then, that for Van Til "apologetics" is *broadly* understood as any vindication of Christianity. In another sense—a *narrow* one, where "evidences" is its complement—"apologetics" is often understood as the defense of the faith against philosophically expressed criticism. Also, notice here (as Van Til goes on to point out) that apologetics and evidences are not distinguished by the kind of defense set forth (it will be philosophical and factual in both cases), but rather by the kind (or source) of challenge directed against the faith—whether it is philosophically or scientifically expressed.

9. Van Til here opposes the common notion that abstract or generic "theism" (the view that some kind of unspecified "god" exists) is first proved by philosophical arguments, which are then supplemented by scientific and historical arguments for the more specific version of theism known as Christianity. The only position that apologetics properly defends is the narrowly defined viewpoint of Christian theism. And this viewpoint is defended as a unit, without vainly attempting to segregate its "philosophical" and "factual" components.

defend Christian theism as a fact. And this is really the same thing as to say that we believe the facts of the universe are unaccounted for except upon the Christian-theistic basis. In other words, facts and interpretation of facts cannot be separated. It is impossible even to discuss any particular fact except in relation to some principle of interpretation. The real question about facts is, therefore, what kind of universal[10] can give the best account of the facts. Or rather, the real question is which universal can state or give meaning to any fact.

Are there, then, several universals that may possibly give meaning or statement to facts? We believe there are not. We hold that there is only one such universal, namely, the God of Christianity. Consequently, we hold that without the presupposition of the God of Christianity we cannot even interpret one fact correctly. Facts without God would be brute facts. They would have no intelligible relation to one another. As such they could not be known by man.

APOLOGETICS PROVIDES A BASIC METHOD
FOR ANSWERING EVERY CHALLENGE[11]

We hope to show how the Christian view of life may most effectively be proclaimed and defended. In this connection, we have in mind the responsibilities of the young pastor who must guide his people, especially his young people, into an ever deeper grasp of the Christian faith. But the Christian faith is frequently ridiculed. It is said to deal with what is purely imaginary. It is said to be logically contradictory. Appealing substitutes, which are often disguised in the words of Scripture, are offered for it.

How will the young pastor guide his flock, his high school and college people, in the midst of this confusion? . . . He needs a criterion by which he himself may be able to distinguish truth from error. He needs, in particular, to be able to discern whether the books he reads, and those his people read, hold to historic Christianity or not. He must understand the reasons why men reject historic Christianity. He must know how to evaluate these reasons.

---

10. In this context, Van Til uses the term "universal" for any truth of a general or abstract nature—whether it be a broad concept, law, principle, or categorical statement. Such general truths are used to understand, organize, and interpret particular truths encountered in concrete experience. As Van Til goes on to say, if one does not begin with some such general truths (universals) with which to understand the particular observations in one's experience, those factual particulars would be unrelated and uninterpretable—i.e., "brute." In a chance universe, all particular facts would be random, have no classifiable identity, bear no predetermined order or relation, and thus be unintelligible to man's mind.
11. An excerpt from *The Reformed Pastor and Modern Thought* (Philadelphia: Presbyterian and Reformed, 1971), 1–2.

Is historic Christianity really out of accord with the facts of science? If it is, must he hold to his convictions in the realm of religion *in spite* of the facts of science? Are Christianity and science to be thought of as operating in independent spheres?

Again, is historic Christianity out of accord with the demands of logic? Is it really or only apparently contradictory? Does it matter whether it is contradictory? Does Christianity maintain that that which is impossible according to logic has none the less happened in fact?

The young pastor may well be baffled by all this. He cannot hope to know as much about the facts of science as the non-Christian experts in science do. He may get some help from fellow Christians whose life task it is to study science. He may get some help also from his former seminary professors. But while they are "experts" in their specialized fields of research, they may not be able to show him *how* he may settle each and every issue.[12]

APOLOGETICS SHOULD BE PURSUED IN A LEARNED FASHION[13]

The unity and organized character of our personality demand that we have unified knowledge as the basis of our action. If we do not pay attention to the whole of biblical truth as a system, we become doctrinally one-sided, and doctrinal one-sidedness is bound to issue in spiritual one-sidedness. As human beings we are naturally inclined to be one-sided. One tends to be intellectualistic, another tends to be emotional, and still another tends to be activistic. One tends to be only prophet, another only priest, and a third only king. We should be all these at once and in harmony. A study of systematic theology will help us to keep and develop our spiritual balance. It enables us to avoid paying attention only to that which, by virtue of our temperament, appeals to us.

Moreover, what is beneficial for the individual believer is also beneficial for the minister, and in consequence for the church as a whole. It is sometimes contended that ministers need not be trained in systematic theology if only they know their Bibles. But "Bible-trained" instead of systematically trained

12. At this point, Van Til begins an extended discussion of the proper method for defending the faith—"a method of apologetics that meets the requirements of the hour. It alone challenges the natural man in the very citadel of his being. It alone is able to show how he who will not accept God's interpretation of life has no coherence in his experience" (pp. 30–31). If one is to develop such a powerful defense, it is necessary that "one's theology and one's apologetics go together" (p. 31).

13. An excerpt from *An Introduction to Systematic Theology*, In Defense of the Faith, vol. 5 (Philadelphia: Presbyterian and Reformed, 1974), 5–7.

preachers frequently preach error. They may mean ever so well and be ever so true to the gospel on certain points; nevertheless, they often preach error. There are many "orthodox" preachers today whose study of Scripture has been so limited to what it says about soteriology that they could not protect the fold of God against heresies on the person of Christ. Ofttimes they themselves even entertain definitely heretical notions on the person of Christ, though perfectly unaware of the fact. . . .

It is but natural to expect that, if the church is strong because its ministry understands and preaches the whole counsel of God, the church will be able to protect itself best against false teaching of every sort. Non-indoctrinated Christians will easily fall prey to the peddlers of Russellism [i.e., Jehovah's Witnesses], spiritualism and all of the other fifty-seven varieties of heresies with which our country abounds. One-text Christians simply have no weapons of defense against these people. They may be able to quote many Scripture texts which speak, for instance, of eternal punishment, but the Russellite will be able to quote texts which, by the sound of them and taken individually, seem to teach annihilation. The net result is, at best, a loss of spiritual power because of loss of conviction. Many times, such one-text Christians themselves fall prey to the seducer's voice.

We have already indicated that the best apologetic defense will invariably be made by him who knows the system of truth of Scripture best. The fight between Christianity and non-Christianity is, in modern times, no piece-meal affair. It is the life and death struggle between two mutually opposed life and world views.[14] The non-Christian attack often comes to us on matters of historical, or other, detail. It comes to us in the form of objections to certain teachings of Scripture, say, with respect to creation, etc. It may seem to be simply a matter of asking what the facts have been. Back of this detailed attack, however, is the constant assumption of the non-Christian metaphysics of the correlativity of God and man. He who has not been trained in systematic theology will often be at a loss as to how to meet these attacks. He may be quite proficient in warding off the attack as far as details are concerned, but he will forever have to be afraid of new attacks as long as he has never removed the foundation from the enemy's position.[15]

---

14. This is a distinctive insight of presuppositional apologetics, without which its approach cannot be properly understood and used. At base, every apologetical encounter—regardless of the specifics being discussed—involves an implicit conflict between two irreconcilable worldviews (fundamental convictions about reality, knowledge, and human conduct). Van Til encourages us to make these differences more explicit, so that it will be evident what is controlling the outcome of the dispute for each party.

15. Because all detailed arguments against the faith arise within the context of an an-

It should not be forgotten in this connection that the minister's duty is increasingly that of an apologist for Christianity. The general level of education is higher than it has ever been. Many young people hear of evolution in the high schools and in the colleges where their fathers never heard of it except as a far distant something. If the minister would be able to help his young people, he must be a good apologete, and he cannot be a good apologete unless he is a good systematic theologian.

In conclusion, we should observe that just as a thorough knowledge of the system of truth in Scripture is the best defense against heresy, so it is also the best help for the propagation of the truth. This is but the other side of the former point. . . .

The church will have to return to its erstwhile emphasis upon its teaching function if it is to fulfill its God-given task of bringing the gospel to all men. Its present recourse to jerky evangelism as almost the only method of propaganda is itself an admission of paupery. It is remarkable that what the church, generally speaking, still does in the way of teaching is shot through with modernism. The propaganda of orthodoxy seems to be limited almost exclusively to evangelization in the narrow sense of the term. When this propaganda turns to teaching as a means, it all too frequently employs uncritically the conceptions of "reason" and "fact" as these are understood by those who make no profession of Christianity.[16] The result is that there is no teaching of Christianity as a challenge to unbelief. Revivalists ought to make themselves unnecessary as quickly as possible. Orthodoxy must take over the teaching function of the church anew, and do it with a better knowledge of the requirements of that work than ever before.

It goes without saying that if all these benefits are to come to us as ministers and as a church, we must undertake our work in a spirit of deep dependence upon God and in a spirit of prayer that he may use us as his instruments for his glory.

---

tagonistic worldview, an effective defense must deal with the underlying philosophical questions. With an ability to do this, the apologist is prepared to answer challenges, the details of which have not been heard before (cf. "always ready" in 1 Peter 3:15).

16. If believers do not study or reflect upon philosophical issues pertaining to reason, factuality, knowledge, etc., then they have very little with which to guard themselves against uncritically working with philosophical concepts and principles that are basically worldly and contrary to Christ. The best way to avoid resting upon humanistic philosophy (cf. Col. 2:8) is to study it, recognize it for what it is, and be able to destroy its foundations. Medical doctors do not promote healthy bodies by refusing to study and master the various kinds of disease.

APOLOGETICAL REASONING WITH THE
UNBELIEVER IS NOT USELESS[17]

I am unable to follow him [Kuyper] when from the fact of the mutually destructive character of the two principles he concludes to the uselessness of
reasoning with the natural man.

The Arminian holds that on the Reformed conception of man there is no sense
to preaching. There would, the Arminian argues, be no approach to an identity
of meanings between the preacher and the man "dead in trespasses and sins" to
whom he preaches. The dead man cannot even count and weigh and measure.[18]
There is an absolute severance of all connection between him and the living.

For this absolute deadness of the natural man, the Arminian substitutes the
notion of degrees of deadness, in order thus to establish degrees of contact
with the truth. There can be no absolutely evil deed because then the will itself
would be destroyed. It is ambiguous or meaningless, says the Arminian, to
talk about the natural man as knowing God and yet not truly knowing God.
Knowing is knowing. A man either knows or he does not know. He may know
less or more, but if he does not "truly" know, he knows not at all. The Calvinist, he argues, is an absolutist who destroys the light of day.

In reply to this the Calvinist insists that there are no degrees of deadness.
The natural man does not know God. But to be thus without knowledge, without living, loving, true knowledge of God, he must be one who knows God
in the sense of having the sense of deity (Romans 1).[19] For the spiritual deadness of the natural man is what it is as suppression of the knowledge of God
given man by virtue of creation in God's image.

Hence Warfield was quite right in maintaining that Christianity is objectively defensible. And the natural man has the ability to understand intellec-

---

17. An excerpt from *Defense of the Faith*, 363–64.
18. By this, Van Til means that, in terms of the Calvinist's transcendental challenge,
    the unbeliever's espoused worldview or philosophy cannot make counting and
    measuring intelligible. (Counting involves an abstract concept of law, universals,
    or order—which contradicts the unbeliever's view of the universe as a random
    or chance realm of material particulars.) By rejecting God's word, the unbeliever
    would not in principle be able to count and measure things. As it is, unbelievers
    do engage in counting and measuring, but they cannot give a philosophical ac-
    counting of that fact.
19. Van Til here indicates that "knowing God" is not the same thing in every case
    where God is known. There is a knowledge of God in faith and blessing (which
    the unbeliever wholly lacks), as well as a knowledge of God in unbelief and curse
    (which the unbeliever cannot avoid). The latter is truly knowledge, and in terms
    of it the unbeliever can gain limited knowledge about the world and arrive at in-
    telligible interpretations of experience. The unbeliever denies this latter kind of
    knowledge because he does not have the former kind of knowledge.

tually, though not spiritually, the challenge presented to him. And no challenge is presented to him unless it is shown him that on his *principle* he would destroy all truth and meaning. Then, if the Holy Spirit enlightens him spiritually, he will be born again "unto knowledge"[20] and adopt with love the principle he was previously anxious to destroy.

2.2 The Relationship of Apologetics to Theology, Evangelism, and Philosophy

Artificial conceptions of the work of apologetics often lead to the conclusion that it is something other than theology, or Christian philosophy, or evangelism. Of course, the false distinctions that people sometimes promote here likewise entail artificial conceptions of theology, philosophy, and evangelism, too. It would be helpful to see just what apologetics has in common with theology, philosophy, and evangelism—as well as what makes it different. The key will be to recognize differences of *degree* between these activities and not escalate them into categorical differences of *kind*. Apologetics, theology, philosophy, and evangelism each involve the use of our minds for gaining and propagating knowledge. Although they work with different kinds of questions, audiences, or settings, they are nevertheless expressions of the Christian's underlying approach to intellectual method in general (or epistemology)—one's view of reasoning, and particularly its relationship to faith. It would be philosophically incoherent and damaging to hold that apologetics, theology, philosophy, and evangelism embody entirely discrepant epistemologies. According to Scripture, in Christ "*all* the treasures of wisdom and knowledge are deposited" (Col. 2:3; cf. Prov. 1:7).

Theology applies the word of God. So does evangelism. So does Christian philosophy. So does apologetics (just notice how often Scripture has been alluded to above). It ought to be clear, then, that these different tasks at least share a common commitment to the authority of God as revealed in His word. When believers attempt to find answers to the questions of philosophy, they should attempt to do so in a manner that is true to, and aims to draw conclusions in harmony with, their Christian commitment—or else they are acting (and using their reasoning ability) like unbelievers, rather than believers. The

---

20. That is, he will be transformed from the knowledge of God in unbelief and curse to the knowledge of God in faith and blessing; the latter is characterized by glad profession of what was once angrily suppressed.

way we use our mind (Col. 1:9–10, 21–23) is just as much subject to
the moral authority of God as the way we use our body—and we cannot serve two masters (Matt. 6:24). When believers attempt to evan-
gelize unbelievers and bring them to a knowledge of God's truth, they
should themselves be submissive and responsive to that truth, as well
as portraying it correctly—or else they will lack persuasiveness (Rom.
2:2, 21–24; 1 Peter 2:12) and will mislead those who are already in the
dark (Matt. 15:14; 23:15). When believers are asked theological questions about God's person and acts, or about man's relationship to
Him, their answers must reflect what God Himself has said—or else
they are only serving themselves (Rom. 16:17–18) and showing that
they know nothing (1 Tim. 6:3–4).

As it turns out, the apologist defends what the theologian has
learned, with the tools and insights refined by the philosopher, for
the evangelistic purpose of seeing the unbeliever's heart and mind
changed.

On the other hand, the work of the theologian, philosopher, or
evangelist cannot be carried out without to some degree defending
the truth of Christianity—in apologetics. All of these tasks are both
positive and defensive in nature. They are all interdependent. To be
sure, there are shades of difference between apologetics, theology,
philosophy, and evangelism—differences in the primary audience, or
type of questions addressed, or immediate aim. But all of these tasks
come under the common umbrella of applying God's word to the
hearts of men. This is what we were made for: to receive God's word
and apply it to our lives.

Adam was expected to do that in the garden. Because sin has entered
the picture, the application of God's revelation to our lives must now
take on a redemptive character. Now the word must be applied in a setting where faith and obedience to what God has revealed is either considered immature or openly repudiated. Nevertheless, in everything we
do as Christians—from understanding the world in terms of God's revelation (especially the system of doctrine revealed in the Bible) to persuading men to acknowledge that system of doctrine revealed in the
Bible to persuading men to acknowledge that system as true and bow
to the Savior—we are engaged in responding to God's word and applying it to ourselves and others. We are always "bringing every thought
captive to the obedience of Christ" (2 Cor. 10:5).

Apologetics is a way of doing theology, a way of doing evangelism,
a way of doing philosophy. If the work of these other areas is in vary-

ing ways an application of God's word, so must be the work of the apologist.

The observation that apologetics is, in particular, a distinctive way of doing philosophy (characterized by submission to God's revelation as one's highest authority) raises some questions about the use of philosophical vocabulary. Is it appropriate for the Christian apologist to utilize terminology that originated among secular and unbelieving philosophers? There is a sense, according to Van Til, in which apologetics (or theology for that matter) and philosophy are simply different "ways of speaking" about the same fundamental topics (what is real, how we know, and how we should conduct ourselves). Naturally, to drive home the word of God to the hearts of those who wish to think and speak philosophically, it would be necessary to talk their language. If you were to go as a missionary to an unevangelized Turkish tribe, you would learn to speak as a Turk or risk being unable to communicate effectively. Likewise, Van Til said that speaking to the "tribe" of philosophers required him to speak their language.[21]

On the other hand, Van Til was alert to the fact (somewhat before his time[22]) that philosophical terms are understood and function within their theoretical context. "The meaning of words derives from the total system of which they form a part."[23] Man's verbal behavior always assumes certain conventions and expectations within a community of speakers, and those conventions and expectations assume certain relationships, rules, and conceptions. The "later" Wittgenstein pointed

21. Of all the published criticisms that Van Til received over his career, perhaps the most shallow—nearly a textbook case of guilt by association—was the claim that his use of the vocabulary of idealism (for instance) showed him to be an idealist in philosophical commitment and outlook (e.g., Jesse DeBoer and James Daane: cf. *Defense of the Faith*, 5, 6, 228). Because Van Til spoke of God as the "concrete universal" (which, by the way, he argued, idealism itself could not find), J. Oliver Buswell charged that he was "deeply mired in Hegelian idealistic pantheism"! Van Til replied: "Judging merely by the sound of this term you charge me with holding Hegelianism. I specify clearly that my God is precisely that which the Hegelian says God is not, and yet you insist that I am a Hegelian" (pp. 241, 151).

22. In the early part of Van Til's career, unbelieving philosophers like the logical atomists and the logical positivists attempted to produce an ideal language that would be completely neutral, objective, and public—completely apart from any theory (wide or narrow) in which terms were used. The meaning of a specific expression, such as "e," it was thought, could be fixed and specified without reference to other expressions of the language in which "e" was found, apart from observation and referential terms. To put it mildly, such views are discredited today.

23. *The Intellectual Challenge of the Gospel* (London: Tyndale Press, 1950; reprint, Phillipsburg, N.J.: Lewis J. Grotenhuis, 1953), 9.

out that "the speaking of language is part of an activity, or of a form of life."[24] It is especially true of terms that are central to explanations within a form of life (or theoretical perspective) that they carry ideological baggage with them. Ancient Epicureans spoke of "atoms," as do modern physicists, but they clearly understand atoms in significantly different ways (e.g., only one of these schools would say that "splitting the atom" makes sense). This explains why philosophical arguments sometimes amount to arguments over how to define special terms, as when Socrates argued over the meaning of "justice," etc. Therefore, Van Til cautioned Christians that, although they must use the language of the philosophers, they must be careful not to understand crucial terms according to the unbeliever's underlying conceptions. Think again of our missionary to the Turks. He will utilize the Turkish language, but prudently—always explaining that the connotations or implications of an expression (e.g., "Creator," "power," "right," "sacrifice") must be seen in the light of biblical revelation, not the pagan cultural background. The same caution must be exercised when the Christian uses philosophy as a way of speaking to accomplish apologetical purposes.[25]

Let us return to the point that apologetics and theology, philosophy, and evangelism are interdependent. If apologetics is independent of the others, then the way is opened for the Christian scholar to operate autonomously—as though he were intellectually self-sufficient apart from God, who should be the basic authority over how to reason, and who has the right to be the final judge of what to believe or disbelieve. This tendency is evident in those who separate apologetics from theology (e.g., Warfield), those who separate philosophy

24. *Philosophical Investigations*, trans. G. E. M. Anscombe (Oxford: B. Blackwell, 1953), I, par. 23.
25. Van Til rhetorically asks: "Is it a sign . . . of paganism if one [merely] employs the word?" Elsewhere he asserts: "My critics assume that identity of words must imply identity of meanings." He explains: "Note the contrast said to exist between Christianity and idealism. Both use the term 'self-realization' but the connotation of this term is different in the two cases." Of a philosopher with whom he disagrees, he says: "Obviously we cannot reject what he says because he uses the term [in question]. We shall have to inquire into the *meaning* of the term." Using philosophical terms is not an indication of making common cause with unbelieving theories. "I use this philosophical language in order the better to be able to contrast the Biblical idea of the Trinity with philosophical theories that are based upon human experience as ultimate." So Van Til is eager to indicate: "The reader may note that the meaning I attribute to the phrase 'concrete universal' is sharply contrasted with the meaning attributed to the same phrase by idealist philosophers" (*Defense of the Faith*, 269, 54, 80, 270, 240, 43).

from theology (e.g., Dooyeweerd), and those who separate apologetics from evangelism or witnessing (e.g., Schaeffer, Kuyper). In every case, apologetics ends up proceeding to establish its conclusions apart from presupposing the word of God as the necessary condition of all intelligibility, and as though there were something more philosophically certain or authoritative than God's revelation.

In its own way, each of these dichotomizing positions shares the view of faith and reason advocated by Thomas Aquinas, rather than the view of Augustine. Simply put, Augustine argued that man's understanding and reasoning function only upon the foundation of faith in God. Reason has no self-sufficient ability to interpret experience and no true authority to judge the veracity of Christian faith. Augustine said, "I believe in order to understand." Understanding (reason) presupposes faith (the truth of the Christian message). Augustine repudiated any autonomous philosophy or use of human intellect. It could be said that Aquinas reversed this, saying that faith in God had to be founded upon the independent results of man's reasoning and understanding. The Thomistic approach assumes that fallen man is capable of reasoning in a proper way (prior to repenting of sin and submitting to the Savior) and that knowledge and intelligible interpretation of experience are philosophically possible apart from God's revelation (i.e., possible in terms of a basic perspective different from the Christian worldview). Man's own intellect, when used at its best, is thus granted the ability and the right to pass judgment on the credibility of God's word (its worthiness of faith). Reason—set up as a judge, not simply used as a tool—takes a privileged position alongside faith.

Warfield (and the old Princeton tradition[26]) held that apologetics must lay the foundation upon which systematic theology can work.[27] For Warfield, the inspiration of the Scriptures was not the foundational doctrine upon which the Christian scholar should proceed, but the last and crowning conviction to which he comes—based upon the demonstration of Scripture's general trustworthiness by man's right reason:

26. The method of apologetics that was advocated by professors at Princeton Seminary prior to its reorganization in 1929 (so as to broaden the school's perspective and weaken its distinctively Reformed witness) is often labeled the "old Princeton" approach. It was given definitive published expression by Charles Hodge and B. B. Warfield, but also taught in Van Til's day in William Brenton Greene's apologetics courses.

27. B. B. Warfield, "The Idea of Systematic Theology," in *Studies in Theology* (New York: Oxford University Press, 1932), 57, 74.

"Surely he must first have Scriptures, authenticated to him as such, before he can take his standpoint in them. . . . [Faith has] grounds in right reason."[28] We thus see two things about the philosophical (epistemological) perspective which Warfield encouraged the apologist to take: it should be (1) outside of a commitment to Scripture and (2) in agreement with the right reason of the unbeliever—in a word, autonomous. This kind of apologetic (where Christ is not the final authority) would prepare for and be the authoritative foundation of systematic theology (where Christ is the final authority).

Here we find two fatal flaws. First, Christ is made one's final authority only after He has been authorized by one's own reasoning (which is, therefore, the real "final" authority). In principle, each and every teaching or action of Christ could then be required on its own to pass the scrutiny of human reason, lest that particular provide the reason for refusing to have general (implicit) trust in Christ. Second, the autonomous non-Christian is mistakenly assumed to be capable of right reason, contrary to the clear testimony of the Bible that he abuses his mind and has an ax to grind against God. The unbeliever "becomes vain in his reasoning" (Rom. 1:21), "cannot receive the things of God's Spirit" as anything but foolish (1 Cor. 2:14), and "hates knowledge" (Prov. 1:7, 29). If Warfield had been consistent with this understanding (thankfully, he was not), he would have ended up with both bad theology, where man is the final authority, as well as bad apologetics, where the unbeliever's fundamental approach is unobjectionable.

The case of Dooyeweerd is somewhat parallel to that of Warfield. Warfield gave apologetics the responsibility for laying the foundation of systematic theology. Dooyeweerd taught more broadly that philosophy must establish the presuppositions of the sciences in general, including the science of theology.[29] Theology is for Dooyeweerd a "theoretical" discipline alongside other sciences, such as history, psychology, economics, biology, math, etc.—all of which are distinguished as theoretical sciences by the fact that they draw rational distinctions within one's experience and study one of the differentiated aspects (modalities) of experience in an objectified, logical way (un-

28. "Introduction to Francis R. Beattie's *Apologetics*" (1903), in *Selected Shorter Writings of Benjamin B. Warfield,* vol. 2, ed. John E. Meeter (Nutley, N.J.: Presbyterian and Reformed, 1973), 98.

29. Herman Dooyeweerd, *In the Twilight of Western Thought* (Nutley, N.J.: Craig Press, 1960), chaps. 5–7, each on "Philosophy and Theology."

like the naive or pre-theoretical experience of things in their undifferentiated wholeness).[30] According to Dooyeweerd, it is the task of philosophy to provide a coherent and total view of temporal experience in terms of which the mutual relations, inner structure, and nature of the special sciences are explained. The individual sciences (including theology) cannot provide this total view within which all the sciences are schematized, ordered, and regulated; only philosophy can do that.[31] Therefore, Dooyeweerd maintains that philosophy "delimits" theological science, that theological science "is in need of a philosophical foundation," and that "theology in its scientific sense is bound to philosophical fundamentals."[32]

Now then, even though he insists that philosophy is not dependent upon exegesis and theology, Dooyeweerd wants to deny that philosophy can be religiously neutral or autonomous. It is always done in the "radical grip of a central basic-motive." Philosophy may regulate theology, but philosophy itself is controlled by a personal, religious heart-attitude. Dooyeweerd would have the Christian philosopher do his work under the subjectively controlling grip of the "word of God"—not the text of Scripture (which would bring us back to a theoretical study subject to philosophically controlled presuppositions), but the "spiritual power" of its pre-theoretical theme of creation-fall-redemption as addressed to "the heart."[33] Thus, Dooyeweerd contends that philosophy should be "controlled by" the word (its spiritual power) but not "derived from" the Bible (its textual meaning). "The Bible does not provide us with philosophical ideas," and to say otherwise (to take philosophical content from Scripture) is scholastic "rationalism."[34]

30. For instance, think of the difference between the "pre-theoretical" (naive) *experience* of enjoying a good steak and the "theoretical" (scientific) *study* of the chemical components of meat, the body's digestive system, the economic forces that determine the price of steak, etc.
31. "Therefore, the Thomistic distinction between philosophy and dogmatic theology, as such, constituted progress when compared with the Augustinian view which identified this theology with Christian philosophy" (Dooyeweerd, *In the Twilight of Western Thought*, 130).
32. Ibid., 130–31, 148, 152, 157.
33. "This spiritual basic motive is elevated above all theological controversies and is not in need of theological exegesis, since its radical meaning is exclusively explained by the Holy Spirit operating in our opened hearts, in the communion of this Spirit" (ibid., 146).
34. "Cornelius Van Til and the Transcendental Critique of Theoretical Thought," in *Jerusalem and Athens*, ed. E. R. Geehan (Philadelphia: Presbyterian and Reformed, 1971), 81–84.

This is a troublesome conception of Christian philosophy. In it, once again, the verbal teaching of God's revealed word is subordinated to some controlling authority outside of itself—and that actually runs contrary to the Bible's own verbal teaching (Col. 1:18; 2 Cor. 10:5). The philosopher is placed in the privileged position of laying down for the exegete how the Bible may and may not be used, how its teachings must be broadly conceived, and what the Bible can and cannot say. Reason becomes a vestibule for faith (believing truths of theology). Philosophy is thereby rendered rationally autonomous, even if the philosopher's "heart is gripped" by the power of God's word. This granting of rational autonomy to philosophy is especially evident from Dooyeweerd's understanding of "transcendental criticism" as an inquiry into the conditions that make theoretical thought possible—an inquiry that does *not* assume a "transcendent" position (dogmatic theology), but can be successfully pursued by every philosophical position in general. The Christian's theological outlook is not to be brought into the "transcendental critique" from the very outset, but only later in the dialogue with unbelieving philosophies.[35] The deadly assumption here is that some philosophical reasoning is possible or intelligible for the unbeliever without presupposing the Christian worldview. That makes philosophical reasoning autonomous after all, and the apologetical case is lost from the very start.

Acknowledging subjective commitment (a gripped heart) does not remove this rational autonomy. Practically speaking, it is not clear how the philosopher is supposed to be "gripped" by a powerful theme whose truth is not in any way rationally interpreted and believed on the basis of the biblical text. This separation of power from meaning in God's word tends toward mysticism, subjectivism, and arbitrariness—all of which are deadly for the work of defending the faith. Moreover, the very distinction between theoretical and pre-theoretical thought is difficult to draw clearly and cogently since each candidate for explaining it ends up either making one of them impossible (e.g., only God sees all

---

35. *A New Critique of Theoretical Thought*, trans. David H. Freeman and William S. Young (Philadelphia: Presbyterian and Reformed, 1953), 1:37; *In the Twilight of Western Thought*, 58. By contrast, in Van Til's transcendental challenge to all unbelieving philosophies, the confrontation with transcendent theological truth "must be brought in at the first step" ("Response by C. Van Til" to Dooyeweerd, in *Jerusalem and Athens*, ed. Geehan, 108). This prevents the discussion from being an "abstract" and impersonal question of detached philosophy; the Christian philosopher from the outset presents the concrete, personal details of God's revelation as the position which stands over against unbelieving opposition.

truth in relation to all other truth, thus in a concrete, undifferenti-ated fashion) or placing them on a continuum (e.g., between more and less abstract reasoning or scholarly analysis). Dooyeweerd's scheme unduly confines the relevance of scholarly exegesis of Scrip-ture to the science of theology, rather than making it pertinent to the content and methods of all the other sciences.[36]

One may also take exception to Dooyeweerd's view of the philo-sophical task. The philosopher does not differ from the common man, except in the degree of self-conscious reflection upon, and hard work given to, philosophical questions (i.e., those which are system-atically basic to all other thinking, but not settled by any specialized science). The philosopher critically examines fundamental princi-ples and conceptual confusions, seeking explanatory and evaluative standards that are explicable, coherent, and justifiable. He then con-structively attempts to unify the results of the special sciences and every aspect of human experience into an overall world-and-life view. This provides an adequate description of what has been the aim of those scholars down through history who have been called philoso-phers. But there is nothing in this conception that would prevent the philosopher from doing his work in the context of a commitment to the verbal revelation of God in Scripture—indeed, attempting to an-swer philosophical questions in humble obedience to it (Ps. 119:24, 66, 98–100, 104–5, 128, 130, 160). Those who do not strive to do this are not religiously neutral, after all (Rom. 1:18–21; Col. 2:8), but will try to answer philosophical questions by suppressing God's revelation and treating their reasoning as a self-sufficient, final authority that can make sense of human experience and knowledge apart from Jesus Christ (which is a religious posture in itself).

Thus, Dooyeweerd's strict separation of philosophy from theology appears to be neither biblical nor necessary. Both disciplines answer similar questions (about reality, knowledge, and conduct), even if in somewhat different terms and settings. However, some would argue that the way in which philosophy attempts to answer those questions is different from the way in which theology does so. But such a view incorporates two objectionable assumptions. First, it assumes (perhaps from the long tradition of men doing philosophy with an autonomous attitude) that philosophy is in its very nature something that does not

36. Cf. John Frame, *The Amsterdam Philosophy: A Preliminary Critique* (Phillipsburg, N.J.: Harmony Press, n.d.); Robert A. Morey, *The Dooyeweerdian Concept of the Word of God* (Philadelphia: Presbyterian and Reformed, 1974).

stand under the authority of the Lord Jesus Christ. Those who work in submission to the Lord, accordingly, are automatically disqualified from doing "philosophy"—despite the fact that the critics of this mentality have their own lords and ultimate commitments. Second, it assumes that man's reasoning and interpretation of experience can be made intelligible outside of the worldview provided by divine revelation—thus begging from the outset the very question pursued by the Christian philosopher. It is precisely this assumption that the apologist challenges the unbeliever to make good.

When we turn to the relationship between apologetics and evangelism (or "witnessing," as Kuyper termed it), we must again disagree with those who suppose that the unbeliever can intelligibly study and interpret experience while at the same time denying the truth of the Christian worldview. Francis Schaeffer does this by isolating apologetics from evangelism, making apologetics a preliminary or preparatory vestibule for faith—what he calls "pre-evangelism."[37] Schaeffer does not contend that the non-Christian's worldview is philosophically unintelligible, but simply that it is incomplete. It is all right as far as it goes (it has "half the orange"), but it leaves out the supernatural (the "other half of the orange").[38] In light of this dichotomy between an area of natural understanding (which does not need Christian presuppositions) and an area of supernatural understanding (which calls for the Christian worldview), we can understand how apologetics becomes a first step, with evangelism following as a second. Schaeffer says:

> The truth that we let in first is not a dogmatic statement of the truth of the Scriptures but the truth of the external world and the truth of what man himself is. This is what shows him his need. The Scriptures then show him the nature of his lostness and the answer to it. This, I am convinced, is the true order for our apologetics in the second half of the twentieth century.[39]

This understanding of our procedure assumes that the unbeliever's philosophy can readily interpret both the external world and himself in an intelligible fashion on the basis of its autonomous presuppositions and rejection of biblical authority—understanding them well enough to see his spiritual "need." After this preparatory work of rea-

37. *The God Who Is There* (Chicago: Inter-Varsity Press, 1968), 137, 143.
38. *Death in the City* (Chicago: Inter-Varsity Press, 1969), 130–31.
39. *The God Who Is There*, 129.

son has been done, the evangelist can appeal to the unbeliever to repudiate his autonomy and accept the dogmatic truth of the Scriptures, which "answers" his spiritual need. Thus, Schaeffer's outlook suggests that apologetics and evangelism operate intellectually with different standards, goals, and methods—a twofold approach that is true to the traditional Thomistic method.

This is not at all true, however, to the New Testament witness. When we examine the speeches in Acts or the discourses in the epistles, it is extremely difficult to offer any objective line of demarcation between theology, apologetics, and evangelism. The apostles simply did not work in terms of a strict separation between these things. Where, for instance, in the Areopagus address of Acts 17 does Paul leave apologetics and begin evangelizing? For that matter, precisely where was he doing theology, and where apologetics? Such questions are futile, for they rest on muddled conceptions. The reason we cannot draw strict lines between the theology, apologetics, and evangelism of the Areopagus address is that in all three of these tasks Paul equally presupposed the authority of the word of God and was working in them all to apply it (whether positively stating the truth, defending the truth, or appealing to people to be changed by the truth).[40] The same thing is true of Paul's *apologia* recorded in Acts 26. We find testimony (his background and conversion, vv. 4–5, 16). We find theological commitment to the foundational authority of Scripture (vv. 6–7, 22, 27) and the lordship of Christ (vv. 13–15, 19). We find philosophical consideration given to the issue of what is possible and credible, distinguishing truth from madness (vv. 8, 25). We find apologetical claims to historical evidence (v. 26). We find evangelistic appeal for a changed heart and mind through faith and repentance (vv. 18, 20). Here again it would be unnatural to dissect Paul's discourse into rigid categories of theology, philosophy, apologetics, and evangelism. All of these concerns run together.

We should say, therefore, that apologetics is not separate from, or preparatory to, systematic theology or evangelistic proclamation. It partakes of both, developing the truth about God and offering witness to it. Like them both, it does not strive to act independently of God's word and authority. Apologetics works to develop a method of

---

40. Cf. Greg L. Bahnsen, "The Encounter of Jerusalem with Athens," *Ashland Theological Bulletin* 13 (1980): 4–40, now published in *Always Ready: Directions for Defending the Faith* (Texarkana, Ark.: Covenant Media Foundation, 1996).

gospel presentation that is consistent with the full teaching of Scripture and anticipates the personal needs of the unbeliever. To answer the objections of the unbeliever, the apologist needs to understand issues about truth, knowledge, interpretation of experience, philosophical worldview, etc., better than the unbeliever himself; the apologist must know the unbeliever and his world better than he himself does. When apologetical theory sets forth principles for responding to the unbeliever's attacks, then, these principles will touch on philosophical questions such as those in epistemology (the theory of knowledge)—in which case apologetics obviously entails philosophical considerations, just as much as it entails theological and evangelistic ones. Moreover, the specific kind of epistemological position taken by the apologist must be derived from the word of God, even as his theological and evangelistic positions and practices are, lest the manner in which he defends the faith prove inconsistent with (or philosophically undermine) the message he is defending.

It could be said that Van Til has labored to rid our thinking about apologetics, theology, philosophy, and evangelism of misleading dichotomies between them—polarizations that serve to overlook the ethically qualified character of man's every intellectual ability and effort. There are to be no other gods before the face of the Lord (according to the first commandment, Ex. 20:3), no other authorities over our thinking that detract from submission to the revealed word of God. The Lord's claim upon us, even upon our thinking and reasoning, is absolute and unchallengeable—just because He is the Lord (Rom. 3:4; 9:20; 11:33–34). Therefore, "take heed lest there shall be anyone who robs you by means of his philosophy, even vain deceit, which is after the tradition of men, after the rudimentary principles of the world, and not after Christ" (Col. 2:8). In that light, we must not artificially separate positive statement (theology) from its defense (apologetics), or separate the appeal for mental change (evangelism) from the intellectual reason for such change (apologetics), or separate general reflection upon conceptual foundations (philosophy) from the particular content of Christian concepts (theology, apologetics). Van Til rejects each of these dichotomies in order that our thinking and scholarship will not be divided into two phases, the first being autonomous and religiously neutral, and the second being submissive to Christ and biblically faithful. For Van Til, like Augustine, reason is not the platform (precondition) for faith, but vice versa.

APOLOGETICS AND THEOLOGY ARE INTERDEPENDENT[41]

About the matter of theological encyclopedia there has been a great deal of debate among Reformed theologians. There is only one point in this debate that we are here concerned to mention. That is the question of the relation of systematic theology to apologetics. On this point Dr. Benjamin Breckinridge Warfield, and with him the "Princeton school" of theology, differ from Dr. Abraham Kuyper and Dr. Herman Bavinck and the "Dutch school" of theology.

The point of difference concerns chiefly the nature of apologetics. Warfield says that apologetics as a theological discipline has to establish the presuppositions of systematic theology such as the existence of God, the religious nature of man, and the truth of the historical revelation of God given us in the Scriptures. In contrast to this, Kuyper says that apologetics must seek only to defend that which is given it in systematics.[42] Warfield argues that if we were to follow Kuyper's method we would first be explicating the Christian system and afterwards we would be asking ourselves whether perchance we had been dealing with facts or with fancies. Kuyper argues that if we allow apologetics to establish the presuppositions of theology we have virtually attributed to the natural man the ability to understand the truth of Christianity and have thus denied the doctrine of total depravity.

We cannot and need not discuss this debate in detail. Kuyper's basic contention that we must always keep in mind the distinction between the regenerate and the unregenerate mind need not imply that apologetics must come after systematics and must be negative only. Apologetics can very well come first and presuppose in general the system of truth brought out in systematics. It is true that the best apologetics can be given only when the system of truth is well known. But it is also true that the system of truth is not well known except it be seen in its opposition to error. The two disciplines are therefore mutually dependent upon one another.

On the other hand,[43] we hold that the basic contention of Kuyper with respect to Warfield's position is correct. Warfield often argues as though apologetics must use a method of approach to the natural man that the other dis-

---

41. An excerpt from *Introduction to Systematic Theology*, 2–3.

42. Van Til footnotes Warfield's *Studies in Theology* and Kuyper's *Encyclopedia of Sacred Theology.*

43. It should be noticed that Van Til does not side completely with Kuyper against Warfield—or completely with Warfield against Kuyper. He uses each to correct the errors in the other. Here he has disagreed with Kuyper's negative conception of apologetics, which subordinates it to systematics, but now turns to disagree with Warfield's subordination of systematics to the results of a neutral apologetic.

ciplines need not and cannot use.[44] He reasons as though apologetics can establish the truth of Christianity as a whole by a method other than that of the other disciplines because it alone does not presuppose God. The other disciplines must wait, as it were, till apologetics has done its work, and receive from it the facts of God's existence, etc. This distinction between the method of apologetics and the method of the other disciplines we believe to be mistaken. *All the disciplines must presuppose God, but at the same time presupposition is the best proof*. Apologetics takes particular pains to show that such is the case. This is its chief task. But in so doing it is no more neutral in its method than are the other disciplines. One of its main purposes is to show that neutrality is impossible and that no one, as a matter of fact, is neutral. We conclude then that apologetics stands at the outer edge of the circle of systematic truth given us by systematics in order to defend it.[45]

THEOLOGY AND PHILOSOPHY
CANNOT BE SHARPLY SEPARATED[46]

Before defending Christian theology we must speak of Christianity and its relation to philosophy and to science. Philosophy, as usually defined, deals with a theory of reality, with a theory of knowledge, and with a theory of ethics. That is to say philosophies usually undertake to present a life and world view. They deal not only with that which man can directly experience by means of his senses but also, and ofttimes especially, with the presuppositions of experience. In short, they deal with that which Christian theology speaks of as God. On the other hand Christian theology deals not only with God; it deals also with the "world." It would be quite impossible then to state and vindicate a truly Christian theology without also stating and defending—be it in broad outline only—a Christian philosophy.

The Roman Catholic apologists have worked out elaborate arguments to prove that theology and philosophy cover clearly differentiated domains of reality and follow clearly differentiated methods of investigation. Philosophy is said to deal with the domain of the natural reason, and Christianity is said to deal with the domain of faith. Theology, says Jacques Maritain, presupposes certain "fundamental truths of the natural order as an introduction to

44. Van Til footnotes Warfield's article "Apologetics" in the older collection of Warfield essays, *Studies in Theology*.
45. That is, apologetics and systematics stand within the same circle—having the same outlook and method—even though they function and are positioned within that general circle differently.
46. An excerpt from *Apologetics*, 23–24.

the faith" *(An Introduction to Philosophy*, p. 130). On the other hand, "the premises of philosophy are self-supported and are not derived from those of theology" (*idem*, p. 126). At a later point we shall consider this Roman Catholic doctrine of the relation of philosophy to theology more fully. For the moment it may suffice to stress the fact that the history of philosophy tells us of men who have sought to give us a totality view of reality as a whole. It is in relation to them that Christianity must be presented. Christian apologetics must, accordingly, in practice be a vindication of the Christian world and life view as a whole.

Calvinistic philosophers, such as D. H. Th. Vollenhoven (*Het Calvinisme en de Reformatie der Wysbegeerte*), H. Dooyeweerd (*De Wysbegeerte der Wetsidee*) and H. G. Stoker (*Kristendom en Wetenschap*) have also stressed the sharp difference of domain between philosophy and theology. However, they are vigorously opposed to the distinction between reason and faith as made by Roman Catholics. They speak of the frankly religious *a priori* principles that philosophy must take from the Scripture.[47] Their aim in making a sharp distinction between the domain of philosophy and that of theology is therefore primarily that of showing the variegated richness of the Christian life and world view as a whole. With this aim we are in full agreement. But Christian apologetics must concentrate on the central concepts of the Christian life and world view as a whole. It will stress rather the unity than the discreteness of a truly Christian theology and a truly Christian philosophy. It will make use of the main concepts of a true Christian theology and a true Christian philosophy, combining them for its own purposes.

DIFFERENT WAYS OF SPEAKING: THEOLOGY, PHILOSOPHY, APOLOGETICS, WITNESSING[48]

(A) We may further observe that in these two divisions of epistemology and metaphysics we deal from a philosophical point of view with that which theology deals with from a theological point of view. The six divisions of sys-

47. As we saw in our previous discussion, Dooyeweerd later made it clear that, while he could not agree with the pretended autonomy or neutrality of the Romanist view of reason, he nevertheless did not hold that philosophy's (undeniable) precommitments should be taken from the text of Scripture itself.
48. The sources for these comments by Van Til are:

   (A) *A Survey of Christian Epistemology*, In Defense of the Faith, vol. 2 (Philadelphia: Presbyterian and Reformed, 1969), xiv–xv.
   (B) *Introduction to Systematic Theology*, 1, 14, 15.
   (C) *Defense of the Faith*, 235.
   (D) "Nature and Scripture," in *The Infallible Word*, ed. N. B. Stonehouse and

tematic theology—theology, anthropology, Christology, soteriology, ecclesi-
ology, and eschatology—are all included in our theory of reality or metaphysics. Philosophy deals with no concepts that theology does not deal with.
It is but a matter of terminology.

(B) Systematic theology seeks to offer an ordered presentation of what the
Bible teaches about God. . . . It does not follow from this that it is about God
alone that we wish to obtain knowledge. It only means that it is *primarily* of
God that we speak. We wish to know all that God wishes us to know about
anything. The Bible has much to say about the universe. But it is the business
of science and philosophy to deal with this revelation. Indirectly even science
and philosophy should be theological. . . . Our theology should be God-
centered because our life should be God-centered. . . .

    What needs to be done, therefore, is to point out that the difference be-
tween theology and other sciences does not lie in the fact that God is any less
necessary for the one than for the other, but that the difference lies only in
the *degree of directness* with which God is brought into the knowledge situation. . . . It is true that we are more directly concerned with the Bible when
we deal with theology than when we deal with the other sciences, but it is not
true that in the other sciences we are not at all concerned with the Bible. Even
in the study of zoology or botany the Bible is involved. The Bible sheds its indispensable light on everything we as Christians study. There is a philosophy
of fact in the Bible that we use for the interpretation of every fact of our lives.

(C) I am interested in defending the metaphysics that comes from Scripture.
This involves: (a) the doctrine of the self-contained God or ontological Trinity, (b) the plan or counsel of this God pertaining to created reality, (c) the
fact of temporal creation as the origin of all the facts of the universe, (d) the
fact of God's providential control over all created reality including the supernatural, and (e) the miraculous work of the redemption of the world through
Christ.

    This metaphysic is so simple and so simply Biblical that non-Christian
philosophers would say that it is nothing but theology. . . . So I point out that
the Bible does contain a theory of Reality.

        Paul Woolley (Philadelphia: Presbyterian and Reformed, 1946), 282–83.
    (E) *Jerusalem and Athens,* ed. Geehan, 348, 125–26.
    (F) *Survey of Christian Epistemology,* 194–95.
    (G) *Defense of the Faith,* 40, 41. Here a footnote by Van Til has been brought up
         into the main text. The latter part of this reading is also found on p. 13 of
         Apologetics (apparently the 1942 edition only).
    (H) *Survey of Christian Epistemology,* v.

(D) And if theology succeeds in bringing forth ever more clearly the depth of the riches of the Biblical revelation of God in Scripture, the Christian philosopher or scientist will be glad to make use of this clearer and fuller interpretation in order that his own interpretation of nature may be all the fuller and clearer too, and thus more truly revelational of God. No subordination of philosophy or science to theology is intended here. The theologian is simply a specialist in the field of Biblical interpretation taken in the more restricted sense. The philosopher is directly subject to the Bible and must in the last analysis rest upon his own interpretation of the Word. But he may accept the help of those who are more constantly and more exclusively engaged in Biblical study than he himself can be.

(E) Here I have been trying to say over and over again that I'm only interested in stating and defending what Scripture teaches and from reading your [R. J. Rushdoony's] first pages you make me out to be a philosopher. Well, I guess I am one of sorts, but you put everything into a better perspective by pointing out that even in my philosophizing on the One-Many problem[49] I am trying to bring out that only the biblical answer to this problem is the true answer. Or, better, you point out that there is no intelligible speech about the unity and diversity of things unless the question itself is placed in a Christian framework. . . .

    [In response to Herman Dooyeweerd[50]]: In the University at Princeton I

49. The "one and many problem" is the underlying issue or challenge which has characterized many philosophical conundrums down through the history of philosophy. See the discussion below. Van Til referred repeatedly to this problem as one that showed the futility and failure of non-Christian reasoning. "Man's problem is to find unity in the midst of the plurality of things. He sometimes calls this the One-and-Many problem" *(Defense of the Faith, 41)*. Van Til maintained that the orthodox, biblical doctrine of the Trinity provides a guideline for resolving these difficulties by maintaining the equal ultimacy of unity (the one) and plurality (the many) in God—who has created the world to reflect the same equal ultimacy between one and many (cf. *Common Grace and the Gospel* [Philadelphia: Presbyterian and Reformed, 1972], 8).

50. In his contribution to Van Til's *Festschrift, Jerusalem and Athens,* Dooyeweerd took sharp issue with Van Til's claim that "the knowledge of God about himself, about man, and about the world was mediated to man from the beginning through ordinary language, including conceptual terms." Dooyeweerd sharply criticized as simplistic and unbiblical the view that obeying God's voice "means making every human *thought* subject to divine thought expressed in scriptural *concepts.*" He insisted "that verbal language would necessarily signify conceptual thought-contents is a rationalist prejudice that runs counter to the real states of affairs" (pp. 83–84). Dooyeweerd was loath to fall into Van Til's "metaphysical interpretation" of God and His attributes, rejecting statements by Van Til such as "God's being is exhaustively rational" (pp. 86–88).

had familiarized myself with the terminology and thinking of the history of philosophy, ancient and modern. What was I to do in order to set the biblical and more especially the Reformed points of view of reality, of knowledge, and of ethics as a challenge over against the man-centered view of men like Plato, Aristotle, Descartes, Locke, Leibniz, Kant, etc.? Should I devise a new terminology in order by means of it to express biblical truth, and thus make clear the differences between it and the thinking of man-centered philosophies? I could not if I had wanted to do such a thing. . . . I put Christian meanings into their words. I would tell them that my view of reality and knowledge—call it metaphysics and epistemology, if you wish—is taken from Scripture. To do otherwise would be for me to engage in vain speculation with the result that I would have an otiose deity dangling before my mind as my own projection into the void. Moreover, this is the terminology current in the English-speaking world in which I labor.

(F) Whatever may be said in favor of [Kuyper's] making a sharp distinction between the work of a Christian philosopher and an apologist, it is in practice impossible for any Christian to limit his task to that assigned to him by Kuyper. In the first place, the borderline between that which is *in theologicis* and that which is *in philosophicis* is so thin that it cannot always be discerned with exactitude. It can be no more than a matter of emphasis. In the second place, one cannot be exclusively defensive. . . . The diathetical, the thetical and the antithetical can at most be matters of emphasis. But all this does not touch the main point. The main point is that Kuyper has himself appointed to the Christian consciousness the task of reasoning with the non-Christian consciousness. In addition to that he has often been very much engaged in apologetics in his own reasoning. That is, he has constantly tried to set the whole of the Christian theistic conception of life in contrast with the non-theistic conception of life and has pointed out the advantages of the Christian position. But he has spoken of all this as *witnessing* to the world rather than reasoning with the world. . . . The *yes* of Hodge and Warfield in answer to the question whether it is possible to reason with the non-regenerate consciousness, and the *no* of Kuyper, have neither of them been unqualified.

(G) After we answer, in preliminary fashion, the question as to *what* we believe as Reformed Christians, we face the problem how to get people interested in our faith. Men in general do not use or even know our theological terms. But, to the extent that they are educated, they have had some training in secular philosophy. They have a non-Christian familiarity with the categories of God, man and the universe. If we are to speak to them and win them, it is necessary for us to learn their language.

There is no possibility of avoiding this. We can make no contact with men unless we speak to them in their language. I do not understand why my critics object when I use such terms as "concrete universal" or employ such terms as "the universal," "the particular," "the one and many." Especially do I not understand this on the part of those who are "experts in philosophy" and whose business it is to teach philosophy from the Christian point of view. The charge of "intellectual anabaptism" might well be lodged against me if, as a teacher of Christian apologetics, I failed to translate Christian truth in the language of the day. Is not the important thing that Christian meanings be contrasted with non-Christian meanings? The Apostles did not shun the usage of language borrowed from non-Christian sources. When they used the term *logos* must they be thought of as followers of Philo's non-Christian thought simply because he also used that term? . . .

We need do no more than take a few of the main concepts of the system of theology and state them in philosophical terms. So we need to use the language of the philosophers. But most philosophers have not been Christians. At any rate philosophical language has to a great extent been formed under non-Christian influence. Is it not likely then that we shall, if we use the language of philosophers, also import into the Christian scheme of things the problems of philosophy as these have been formulated by non-Christian people? . . . The answer is that we shall be obliged, to a large extent, to use the language of the philosophers or we shall have no point of contact with them. But we shall have to be on our guard to put Christian content into this language that we borrow.

(H) A preliminary survey of epistemological terminology brings out that this terminology itself has grown out of a milieu which has colored its connotation. It will not do to speak of the inductive and deductive methods as though theists and non-theists meant the same things when they use these terms.[51]

51. An assertion that "the meaning" of two utterances is "the same" (or "not the same") is easily misconstrued. When I say that the meaning of "atom" for the Epicureans is not the same as the meaning for modern physics, I am not claiming that they have absolutely nothing in common—as though modern physicists could actually be referring, say, to pigs! They may both be speaking of a small building block of material objects, but other senses of its "meaning"—what the term picks out, how it functions, what evidence is given for sentences using it, what logical implications or operations are called for, etc.—are not the same. The theories within which the term is used are different in philosophically important ways. Thus, they do not "mean" the same thing.

The term induction means one thing for a theist who presupposes God and another thing for a non-theist who does not presuppose God. For a theist induction is the implication into God-centered "facts" by a God-centered mind; for a non-theist it means the implication into self-centered facts by a self-centered mind. The same difference prevails in the case of such terms as analysis and synthesis, correspondence and coherence, objectivity and subjectivity, a priori and a posteriori, implication and linear inference and transcendental versus syllogistic reasoning. A non-theist uses all these terms univocally, while a theist may use any or all of them analogically.[52]

CHRISTIAN COMMITMENT INVOLVES A DISTINCTIVE METHOD OF KNOWING[53]

For the study of systematic theology the question of method is of basic importance. "If a man adopts a false method, he is like one who takes a wrong road which will never lead him to his destination."[54] Moreover, the question of method is the all-important point for modern science and philosophy. If orthodox theology desires to appear relevant to the modern situation it must adopt a self-conscious position on its own and on modern methodology in general. It is, to be sure, the task of apologetics rather than that of systematics to defend the orthodox over against [non-Christian] methodology. But if apologetics is to do its work properly it is important that systematics work out fully its own methodology. . . .

However, to find the proper method for the study of systematic theology we shall need to discuss, briefly, the question of methodology in general. It is only after it has been shown that Christian theism as a whole, in all its departments, has a methodology quite distinct from other general interpretations of reality, that the proper method to be followed in systematic theology will appear.

The question of method is not a neutral something. Our presupposition of God as the absolute, self-conscious Being, who is the source of all finite being and knowledge, makes it imperative that we distinguish the Christian theistic method from all non-Christian methods. . . .

52. As explained later, Van Til means here that unbelievers think autonomously (as though the Creator-creature distinction were irrelevant—i.e., "univocally"), whereas believers reason in terms of the light and guidance provided by God's revelation (reinterpreting experience by thinking God's thoughts after Him—i.e., "analogously").
53. Excerpts from *Introduction to Systematic Theology*, 8, 9, 18, 19, 21.
54. Van Til refers to Charles Hodge, *Systematic Theology* (New York: Charles Scribner's Sons, 1872), 1:3.

From this discussion of idealist logic, it appears how intimately one's theory of being and one's theory of method are interrelated. . . .[55]

There are two mutually exclusive methodologies. The one of the natural man assumes the ultimacy of the human mind. On this basis man, making himself the ultimate reference point, virtually reduces all reality to one level and denies the counsel of God as determinative of the possible and the impossible. Instead of the plan of God, it assumes an abstract notion of possibility or probability, of being and rationality. . . .

On the other hand there is the Christian position. When consistently expressed it posits God's self-existence and plan, as well as self-contained self-knowledge, as the presupposition of all created existence and knowledge. In that case, all facts show forth and thus prove the existence of God and his plan. In that case, too, all human knowledge should be self-consciously subordinated to that plan. . . .

The nearest that we can approach to bringing out the relation between the methods of the various sciences and theology, and then once more between the various theological disciplines among themselves, is to think of several concentric circles. God is at the center of these concentric circles. The large outside circle contains the facts of all the sciences, save theology. The second and smaller circle contains all the theological disciplines. The third and still smaller circle deals with theology proper. . . .[56]

It is therefore of the utmost importance to point out that there is a distinction between the Christian and the non-Christian conception of the place of human reason.

There have been, generally speaking, two tendencies among orthodox theologians on this question of the function of reason in theology. In the first place, there have been those who have been so afraid of "reason" that they have assigned to it no place at all. On the other hand, there have been those who have been very anxious to prove that theology has a perfect right to con-

---

55. That is, one's convictions about metaphysics (the nature of reality) will influence one's position on epistemology (the proper method for knowing things), even as one's epistemology will influence one's metaphysical beliefs. A person's metaphysic and epistemology will be coordinated with each other, constituting a specific world-and-life view set over against other world-and-life views (each with its own interdependent views of reality and the method of knowing).

56. By this illustration Van Til makes the personal knowledge of God (the innermost circle) the implicit source and required center for biblical exegesis (the second circle), as well as for history, physics, math, and every other use of human reason to acquire knowledge. Thus, all the particular intellectual disciplines share with each other a broader, common conception of method, in terms of which God must be presupposed.

sider itself a science. Both tendencies failed to distinguish between a Christian and a non-Christian use of reason.

In order to avoid these difficulties in some measure, we must attempt again to show that our conception of the place and function of human reason is directly involved in our conception of God. We must avoid the idea that human reason exists as a known and definable entity apart from God so that we may begin from it as from an ultimate starting point.

To make clear our position on the place of human reason in theology, it is necessary first to show that the place we accord to reason in connection with theology is basically the same as that which we accord to it in connection with the other sciences. As the theological method is but a specialized form of the Christian theistic method in general, so the place of reason in theology is determined by our conception of Christian theistic epistemology in general.[57]

REASON AND FAITH ARE BOTH UNITED IN COVENANTAL SUBMISSION TO SCRIPTURE[58]

Here it will at once be asked how a system of philosophy or science can be consonant with the doctrines of religion if these doctrines are given by authority and are all-inclusive in their implications. A solution of the problem as to the relation between theology and philosophy or science might be found, it will be argued, if theology is based on authority and philosophy or science is based on reason. By the employment of reason, science and philosophy may make certain assertions about reality, and by means of revelation theology may make additional assertions about reality. Thus the relation would simply be one of supplementation. Reason would think of itself as a rowboat which can go out into water but which dares not attempt to cross the ocean. Faith in authority would simply take over where reason finds the water too deep. If there would be any control of authority over reason at all, this control would be merely negative. It would be the control of a teacher who merely tells the pupil that he has not found the correct answer to his problem. The child can find the right answer of itself if only it tries again. (This is the Roman Catholic position on the relation of philosophy or science to theology. See e.g., Mahoney, *Cartesianism*, and Jacques Maritain, *Introduction to Philosophy*.)

57. To illustrate his call to recognize the difference between Christian and non-Christian methods (epistemologies), Van Til goes on in chaps. 4 and 5 to criticize Charles Hodge because "he does not clearly distinguish between two views that are diametrically opposed to one another in epistemology, and yet both assert the primacy of the intellect" (p. 31), and to criticize Herman Bavinck because of his "failure to distinguish Christian from non-Christian certainty" (p. 46).
58. Excerpts from *Apologetics*, 25–27, 29, 37.

Again, a solution of the problem of the relation between theology and philosophy or science may be found, it will be argued, if theology limits its assertions to the realm or dimension of the supernatural and if philosophy or science limits its assertions to the realm or dimension of the natural. Good fences make good neighbors. A true science will want to limit itself in its pronouncements to the description of the facts that it meets. It is of the essence of a true science that it makes no pronouncements about origins and purposes. So too a true philosophy will seek logical relationships between the facts of experience. But the absolutes of religion cannot be reached by means of these logical relationships. Reason therefore does not pretend to speak of God as he exists in himself. Thus both science and philosophy limit themselves to the phenomenal realm and gladly leave the realm of the noumenal to authority and faith. (This is a popular method of approach among orthodox as well as liberal Protestants.)[59]

However, it will be argued further, if one rejects both of these possible solutions and insists that the doctrines of religion deal with the phenomenal as well as with the noumenal while yet they are given by authority, one is bound to seek the destruction both of philosophy and of science. Such a concept of the relation of theology to philosophy and science, it will be contended, is monopolistic and totalitarian.

In reply it must first be admitted that a truly Protestant interpretation of Christianity cannot accept either of the two proffered solutions of the relation of theology to philosophy and science. A truly Protestant view of the assertions of philosophy and science can be self-consciously true only if they are made in the light of the Scripture. Scripture gives definite information of a most fundamental character about all the facts and principles with which philosophy and science deal. For philosophy or science to reject or even to ignore this information is to falsify the picture it gives of the field with which it deals.

This does not imply that philosophy and science must be exclusively dependent upon theology for their basic principles. It implies only that philosophy and science must, as well as theology, turn to Scripture for whatever light it has to offer on general principles and particular facts. In order to do

---

59. Van Til here refers to the famous attempt of Immanuel Kant (1724–1804) to save science while leaving room for faith. Kant's project involved sharply separating the sensible realm of "phenomena" (things as they appear—that is, objects interpreted through mental categories imposed by man's mind) from the unknowable and noncognitive realm of "noumena" (things as they are in themselves—that is, the uninterpreted external source of experience). Phenomenal objects of experience can be understood in a natural fashion, but supernatural matters (noumena) are beyond reason and understanding.

so they may ask the assistance of theology. It is the business of theology to engage in detailed exegesis of Scripture. The philosopher will naturally make use of the fruits of this exegesis. It is also the business of theology to present the truth of Scripture in systematic form. The philosopher and the scientist will naturally also make use of the fruit of this effort. Even so the Christian philosopher and the Christian scientist will be first of all directly dependent upon Scripture itself.

Our conclusion then must be that the defense and vindication of a truly Protestant theology require also a defense and vindication of at least some of the basic principles of a truly Protestant philosophy and science. . . .

Basic to the whole activity of philosophy and science is the idea of the covenant. The idea of the covenant is commonly spoken of in relation to theology alone. It there expresses the idea that in all things man is face to face with God. God is there said to be man's and the world's creator. God is there said to be the one who controls and directs the destiny of all things. But this is tantamount to applying the covenant idea to the philosophic and scientific fields as well as to that of theology. It is difficult to see how the covenant idea can be maintained in theology unless it be also maintained in philosophy and science. To see the face of God everywhere and to do all things, whether we eat or drink or do anything else, to the glory of God, that is the heart of the covenant idea. And that idea is, in the nature of the case, all inclusive.

There are two and only two classes of men. There are those who worship and serve the creature and there are those who worship and serve the Creator. There are covenant breakers and there are covenant keepers. In all of men's activities, in their philosophical and scientific enterprises as well as in their worship, men are either covenant keepers or covenant breakers. There are, to be sure, many gradations of self-consciousness with which men fall into either of these two classes. Not all those who are at heart covenant keepers are such self-consciously. So also not all those who are at heart covenant breakers are such self-consciously. It is a part of the task of Christian apologetics to make men self-consciously either covenant keepers or covenant breakers. . . .

Philosophy and science deal more especially with man in his relation to the cosmos, and theology deals more especially with man in his relation to God. But this is only a matter of degree. And the two forms of revelation[60] cover the dimensions or areas of both. . . . The two forms of revelation must therefore be seen as presupposing and supplementing one another. They are aspects of one general philosophy of history. . . .

All this is simply to say that one must be a believing Christian to study na-

---

60. The reference is to God's revelation in nature and His revelation in Scripture.

ture in the proper frame of mind and with the proper procedure. It is only the Christian consciousness[61] that is ready and willing to regard all nature, including man's own interpretative reactions, as revelational of God. . . . When man had not sinned, he was naturally anxious constantly to seek contact with the supernatural positive revelation of God. But it is a quite different matter when we think of the redeemed sinner. He is restored to the right relationship. But he is restored in principle only. There is a drag upon him. His "old man" wants him to interpret nature apart from the supernatural revelation in which he operates. The only safeguard he has against this historical drag is to test his interpretations constantly by the principles of the written Word. And if theology succeeds in bringing forth ever more clearly the depth of the riches of the biblical revelation of God in Scripture, the Christian philosopher or scientist will be glad to make use of this clearer and fuller interpretation in order that his own interpretation of nature may be all the fuller and clearer too, and thus more truly revelational of God. No subordination of philosophy or science to theology is intended here. The theologian is simply a specialist in the field of biblical interpretation taken in the more restricted sense. The philosopher is directly subject to the Bible and must in the last analysis rest upon his own interpretation of the Word. But he may accept the help of those who are more constantly and more exclusively engaged in biblical study than he himself can be.

IN THE INTELLECTUAL BATTLE, APOLOGETICS COORDINATES AND FOREWARNS[62]

Apologetics is the vindication of the Christian philosophy of life against the various forms of the non-Christian philosophy. . . .

By theological encyclopedia is meant the arrangement in the curriculum of the various theological disciplines. These disciplines are all centered about the Bible because the Bible is thought of as described above.[63] There are first of all the Biblical departments dealing with the Old and New Testaments respectively. In these departments the original languages, exegesis, and Biblical theology are taught. In all this there is a defense as well as a positive statement of the truth. The matter of defense of the truth of Christian theism

61. Van Til distinguishes between the unfallen, the fallen, the redeemed, and the perfected (glorified) consciousness of men—that is, the various inward spiritual conditions (and relationships to God) found in history, as they bear upon and affect the mental attitude and activity of men.
62. Excerpts from *Apologetics*, 1, 3–4.
63. Van Til has already described the Bible as totally authoritative and as the center, not only of every seminary course, but also of the curriculum as a whole.

cannot be left to the apologetic department alone. The specific truths of Christianity must be defended as soon as they are stated. Not one of them has been allowed to stand without attack, and the experts in each field can best defend them. Then comes systematic theology which takes all the truths brought to light from Scripture by the biblical studies and forms them into one organic whole. . . . When we have the system of truth before us we wish to see how it is to be brought to men, and how it has been brought to men. Since it is the word of God, of God's interpretation to men, it must be brought in God's name and with God's authority. In practical theology the matter of preaching the Word is taken up. Here too defense must be coupled with positive statement. Then church history takes up the story as to how this preaching of the Word has fared throughout the centuries. Have those to whom the preaching and teaching of the Word was entrusted brought it faithfully in accordance with the genius of that Word as the Word of God? Have men readily received it when it was preached faithfully? What has been the fruit if it has perhaps been poorly preached and half-heartedly received? Such questions as these will be asked in church history. And again, defense and positive statement go hand in hand.

This really completes the story of Christian encyclopedia. There has been in the disciplines enumerated a detailed and comprehensive statement of the truth. There has been in addition to that a defense of every truth at every point. Is there no place for apologetics? It would seem so. Yet perhaps there may be the work of a messenger boy. Perhaps the messenger boy can bring the maps and plans of one general to another general. Perhaps the man who is engaged in biblical exegesis is in need of the maps of the whole front as they have been worked out by the man engaged in systematic theology. Perhaps there will be a more unified and better organized defense of Christian theism as a whole if the apologist performs this humble service of a messenger boy. Then too the apologist may be something in the nature of a scout to detect in advance and by night the location and, if possible, something of the movements of the enemy. We use these martial figures of speech because we believe that in the nature of the case the place of apologetics cannot be very closely defined. We have at the outset defined apologetics as the vindication of Christian theism. This is well enough, but we have seen that each discipline must make its own defense. The other disciplines cover the whole field and they offer defense along the whole front. Then too they use the only weapons available to the apologist: namely, philosophical and factual argument. It remains that in apologetics we have no well-delimited field of operation and no exclusive claim to any particular weapon.

The net result then seems to be that in apologetics we have the whole field to cover. And it was this that was included in the analogy of a *messenger boy* and *scout*. This does not imply that the messenger boy or the scout must leave all the work of defense to the others so that he would have nothing to do but carry news from one to the other. No indeed, the scout carries a rifle when he goes scouting in the historical field. Then too he may have to and does have to use the large stationary guns that command a larger distance.

We have just now employed the figure of a fortress or citadel. We may think of the apologist as constantly walking up and down on or near the outer defense of the fortress. This will give the other occupants time to build and also enjoy the building. The others too must defend, but not so constantly and unintermittently. The apologist too must rest and must enjoy the peace of the fort but his main work is to defend and vindicate.

In this connection we must guard against a misuse that might be made of the figure of the fortress. It might be argued that this seems to put Christianity on the defensive. Is it not true that Christianity was meant to conquer the whole world for Christ? Yes it is. We have already said that we think of Christian theism, when we think of Christianity.[64] That covers the whole earth. If we can successfully defend the fortress of Christian theism we have the whole world to ourselves. There is then no standing room left for the enemy.[65] We wage offensive as well as defensive warfare. The two cannot be separated. But we need not leave the fort in order to wage offensive warfare.[66]

2.3 The Aim of Apologetics

What can the Christian hope to accomplish when he replies to the objections or challenges of the unbeliever or tries to make a case for Christian commitment? When anyone asks him for a "reason" for the hope that is within him (1 Peter 3:15), just how "reasonable" should he purport the faith is and show it to be? We need to pause and consider what goal apologists ought to set for themselves, if they would live up to the task that Scripture gives them in defending the faith.

64. That is, Van Til does not wish to separate philosophical theism in general from the historical particularity of the specific Christian message. The Christian system as a unity (a cohesive worldview) must be defended as such.
65. This is a distinctive thrust in Van Til's apologetic. Nothing in the whole world can be made intelligible by the non-Christian's reasoning or fundamental philosophy. If he wishes to reason about or understand anything, he has no philosophical place to stand except within the Christian framework of thought.
66. That is, as Christian thinking encounters and challenges the unbelieving world of thought ("wages offensive warfare")—say, in philosophy or evangelism—it need not abandon the same fundamental theory of knowledge that is utilized in theology and biblical study ("need not leave the fort").

God's word, which strongly and boldly claims that the Christian message is true, knowable, and provable, stands in sharp contrast to the experientialism and "evidentialism" that are prevalent in evangelical circles today.[67] To see this, notice should be taken of how the Bible presents "the intellectual challenge of the gospel," to use a title of Van Til's. He was quite explicit that one thing that stands out about his understanding of defending the faith is that in it "man has no excuse whatsoever for not accepting the revelation of God whether in nature, including man and his surroundings, or in Scripture. God's revelation is always clear."[68]

In the first place, Scripture never bypasses the mind and reasoning of those who are confronted with its message, making its appeal (somehow) straight to the emotions or simply calling for a noble commitment of the will. Conversion surely does involve emotional feeling and volitional dedication, but never merely so. Thus, Christianity that is patterned after the Bible is not fairly represented by what is called a "leap of faith." The gospel supplicates the intellect of its hearers, being not only able to satisfy the demands of their mind regarding its assertions, but claiming to be the only way of saving rationality in general. Conversion entails a critical use of a person's intellectual ability, one which demands new beliefs called "faith" (Rom. 10:9), a change of mind called "repentance" (Acts 3:19), and intelligent verbal activity called "confession" (Rom. 10:10). It is characterized by renewal in "the spirit of your mind" (Eph. 4:23) "unto the knowledge of the truth" (2 Tim. 2:25; cf. Col. 3:10), so that one may now love the Lord "with all your mind" (Matt. 22:37). Evangelistic

67. The particular approach to apologetics that is in view here is commonly called "evidentialism." It is popularly (and mistakenly) contrasted with another approach, which is designated "presuppositionalism." What is entirely misleading about this way of speaking is the suggestion that some apologists make their appeal to "evidence," arguing with presuppositionless neutrality, while others simply expose determinative "presuppositions" and are disinterested therefore in evidence or argumentation. Nothing could be further from the truth on both scores.

68. *Defense of the Faith*, 256. Objections that can legitimately be made against some assertion, or the lack of requisite evidence or warrant for that assertion, are sometimes said to "obscure" the truth of what is claimed; we say that "it is not clear" that the assertion is believable or how it is to be understood. Similarly, philosophers speak of the special clarity of the beliefs that they consider most certainly true (e.g., rationalists call self-evident truths "clear and distinct," while empiricists give special status to ideas or "reports" that are modeled on the allegedly indubitable experience of direct observation). This may help explain why, for Van Til, the "clarity" of revelation is not simply an abstract aspect of its meaning, but pertains to its truthfulness, warrant, or believability.

discussion with unbelievers cannot honestly evade this intellectual dimension of conversion and Christian commitment. It certainly did not do so in the New Testament. Believers there are found engaging in "refutation" (Titus 1:9), "proving" (Acts 9:22), "arguing persuasively" (Acts 19:8), and "reasoning" with unbelievers (Acts 17:2, 17; 18:4; 19:9).

In the second place, one will look in vain to find anything in the Bible like an appeal to the "probability" of its truth-claims. That may be the general spirit that pervades much of modern apologetics, but it is starkly absent from the biblical witness. With respect to a particular fact of history, Peter proclaimed on the day of Pentecost that all the house of Israel may "know with certainty" that God raised Jesus from the dead (Acts 2:36). Paul "confounded" the Jews not simply by giving some reason to think so, but by fully "proving that this is the Messiah" (Acts 9:22). The apostolic apologetic was bold and decisive, never conceding that non-Christians have any reason whatsoever for not coming to faith (even if their studied opinion is that Christianity is absurd). Those who do not believe the word of the cross have not simply made an intellectual mistake—for which there is, after all, some apparent reason—but have been utterly foolish (1 Cor. 1:18–20). That does not leave much room for acting like, or holding that, it is somewhat understandable that unbelievers think and reason as they do. With respect to the revelation of God in nature, Paul categorically declares that those who do not believe it are "without excuse" (Rom. 1:20—etymologically, "without an apologetic"!). After all, they do not merely have some vague and uncertain evidence for the living and true God, but actually "know" the truth about Him (vv. 19, 21). It would be an unwarranted misreading of Scripture to understand the kind of "certainty" that it claims for the truth and believability of the Christian message to be a "practical" or "moral" certainty of dedicated conviction—and not at the same time an intellectual or rational certainty.[69] Unbelievers are declared to be "futile in their rea-

69. E. J. Carnell spoke for a large group of evangelical apologists when, without due reflection, he declared: "Let us establish securely the fact that proof for the Christian faith, as proof for any world-view that is worth talking about, cannot rise above rational probability. . . . The more the evidences increase, the more the strength of probability increases." Nevertheless, he went on to say that the believer embraces the hypothesis of Christianity (characterized by mere probability as to its rationality) with "perfect moral or subjective assurance." However, when Scripture promotes and claims certainty for its own message, it is not merely speaking of the "perfect subjective assurance" that one can have in just about any silly no-

sonings" (Rom. 1:21)—arrogantly professing "wisdom," while in fact being downright "fools" (v. 22). The objections that even "thinking" unbelievers raise against the truth of Christianity are not given respect in the New Testament, but represent "ignorance" (Eph. 4:18) and "false knowledge" (1 Tim. 6:20).

The biblical witness to (1) the necessity of a rational defense of the Christian's truth-claims and to (2) the full certainty with which they can be demonstrated stands over against the attitude of "fideism." It is important to understand correctly what "fideism" means as a com-

---

tion (e.g., Santa Claus). Carnell must incorporate some kind of "leap of faith" when he, like others, concludes that "we have complete moral certainty from a system which is but rationally probable" (*An Introduction to Christian Apologetics* [Grand Rapids: Eerdmans, 1948], 113, 116, 118).

Now then, the critical philosopher must be allowed to ponder: just how "securely" does Carnell "establish" the dictum that worldviews cannot rise above rational probability and that they are supported only inductively (i.e., their probability increases with an increase of evidence)? He offers no proof of such claims at all, but simply lays them down as prescriptions. He seems to have naively believed that the inductive study of evidence takes place outside the context of some particular worldview, with its own philosophical baggage (cf. Greg L. Bahnsen, "Inductivism, Inerrancy, and Presuppositionalism," *Journal of the Evangelical Theological Society* 20 [1977]: 296–300).

As indicated, Carnell was not alone. R. C. Sproul popularizes a similar point in *Objections Answered* (Glendale, Calif.: Regal Books, 1978). The fact that the Bible claims something, he argues, is not enough in itself to authenticate that claim; Scripture must first be authenticated through historical reasoning about the "basic" trustworthiness of its manuscripts, leading us (rationally? psychologically?) "to believe confidently" that Jesus is divine (pp. 31–32). There is a "leap of faith" here (or some "circular reasoning," despite Sproul's disclaimer)—as though Scripture cannot be self-authenticating, but claims made by Jesus (found only in Scripture!) can be. Regardless, Sproul creates other difficulties for himself. His historical "chain" of reasoning already has two weak "links" (maintaining only the "basic" reliability of the documents, and circularly accepting Christ's interpretation of Himself, His resurrection, etc., on His own say-so), but he adds more. He must admit that substantial portions of the Bible are not even subject to the authenticating "historical research" that he demands, and with regard to those biblical statements which are subject to it, he admits that "not every biblical discrepancy has been resolved" (p. 26). Thus, Sproul's apologetical chain of reasoning is weak indeed.

Sproul concedes, then, that one's commitment to the infallibility of Scripture (a universal claim about the inability of the Bible to err) rests on the much narrower grounds of its mere "general reliability" (pp. 33–34). As an apologist, all Sproul can say is that "the direction of the evidence is very encouraging" (p. 26), while as a dedicated believer in Christ he wants to claim much more. He wants to speak of "the rock-solid intellectual integrity and truth of Christianity," banishing all skepticism and claiming (with Luther) that biblical claims "are surer and more certain than sense and life itself" (p. 18). We enthusiastically applaud this latter attitude, but observe that it is inconsistent with the former.

monly used term in religious philosophy.[70] One dictionary describes it as "a pejorative term for subjectivist theories which are based upon religious experience and which undervalue reason in theology."[71] Others are just as clear: fideism holds that "religious truths are inaccessible to human reason," thus amounting to a "reduction of religion to an irrational faith."[72] Fideism is the "view which assumes knowledge originates in a fundamental act of faith, independent of rational presuppositions."[73] According to this view, "Christian assertions are matters of blind belief and cannot be known or demonstrated to be true."[74] Fideism, we are told, is "based upon a leap of faith and a negation of rational constructions."[75] The fideist's faith is "exclusively determined by the emotions."[76] The *Encyclopedia of Philosophy* tells us that fideism is "a kind of irrationalism" wherein "truth in religion is ultimately based on faith rather than on reasoning or evidence"; religious tenets "cannot be established by proofs."[77]

70. Some critics of Van Til continue to misconstrue the nature of fideism, and then charge him with holding to it, even though their view has been refuted (see Bahnsen, "Inductivism, Inerrancy, and Presuppositionalism"). In the November 4, 1977, issue of *Christianity Today* (vol. 22), for example, R. C. Sproul described Westminster Seminary as teaching fideism, not because Van Til held that Christianity had no rational defense of any kind (and indeed shunned such a defense), but rather because it was "defended on grounds other than natural reason" (i.e., patterned after the natural man's claim to intellectual autonomy) ("You Can't Tell a School by Its Name," 220).

   The charge of fideism reappeared in 1984, in a book coauthored by Sproul, John Gerstner, and Arthur Lindsley. They take fideism to be, not an attitude that is set over against the offer of rational proof for a religious conviction, but, more narrowly, any approach set over against their own kind of rational argument (namely, one claiming to be religiously impartial, empirical, and inductive). They assert: "If the presuppositionalist offers any reason, he ceases to be a presuppositionalist," and "a faith in Scripture . . . that does not rest on reasons is fideism" (*Classical Apologetics* [Grand Rapids: Zondervan, 1984], 308–9).

71. Alan Richardson, "Fideism," in *A Dictionary of Christian Theology*, ed. Alan Richardson (Philadelphia: Westminster Press, 1969), 129.

72. *Philosophical Dictionary*, ed. Walter Brugger and Kenneth Baker (Spokane, Wash.: Gonzaga University Press, 1972), 140.

73. "Fideism," in *The New International Dictionary of the Christian Church*, ed. J. D. Douglas, Earle E. Cairns, and James E. Ruark (Grand Rapids: Zondervan, 1974), 374.

74. Van A. Harvey, *A Handbook of Theological Terms* (New York: Macmillan, 1964), 99.

75. R. C. Sproul, "Fideism," in *The Encyclopedia of Christianity*, vol. 4, ed. Philip E. Hughes and George R. Jaffray (Marshallton, Del.: National Foundation for Christian Education, 1972), 194.

76. Paul Poupard, "Fideism," in *Sacramentum Mundi*, ed. Karl Rahner et al. (New York: Herder and Herder, 1968), 2:336.

77. Richard H. Popkin, "Fideism," in *The Encyclopedia of Philosophy*, ed. Paul Edwards (New York: Macmillan, 1967), 3:201.

Van Til's presuppositional apologetic is, as anyone can see from the above, the *diametric opposite* of fideism. He taught: "We as Christians alone have a position that is philosophically defensible"; he spoke of being "certain . . . that Christianity is objectively valid and that it is the only rational position for man to hold."[78] Indeed, he clearly maintained that according to Christianity—and only Christianity—all of reality is "inherently rational";[79] "Christianity believes in an ultimate rationality," being the "very reverse of agnostic"—while unbelief is "an ultimate irrationality."[80] When the Christian defends his faith, then, he must not rest upon emotional appeals or a mere call to volitional commitment; he must exhibit the gospel as the rigorous intellectual challenge that it is. The unbeliever's position "ought to be refuted by a reasoned argument, instead of by ridicule and assumption."[81] Van Til saw Christianity as "alone able to save from scepticism . . . [and] modern irrationalism."[82] So rationally defensible is the Christian faith that Van Til could boldly assert: "Christianity is the only reasonable position to hold. It is not merely as reasonable as other positions, or a bit more reasonable than other positions; it alone is the natural and reasonable position for man to take."[83]

Anyone who knows Van Til's teaching and writings knows that he never tired of making known this high demand for the task of apologetics: "We cannot allow that if rational argument is carried forth on true premises, it should come to any other conclusion. . . . [The argument] is objectively valid, whatever the attitude of those to whom it comes may be. . . . [We must] press the objective validity of the Christian claim at every point."[84] Because the intellectual case for Christianity made by the apologist is "objectively valid," Van Til insisted that it "ought to be proof and witness for both unbeliever and believer."[85] He affirmed that "Warfield was quite right in maintaining that Christianity is objectively defensible."[86] In his introduction to B. B. Warfield's masterful work, *The Inspiration and Authority of the Bible*, Van Til said: "It might seem that there can be no *argument* between them [believer and unbeliever] . . . that the orthodox view of authority is to be spread only by testimony and by prayer, not by argument.

---

78. *Common Grace* (Philadelphia: Presbyterian and Reformed, 1947), 8, 82.
79. "Nature and Scripture," 277; also *Defense of the Faith*, 255.
80. *Introduction to Systematic Theology*, 13, 24.
81. *Survey of Christian Epistemology*, 23.
82. Ibid., 35.
83. *Defense of the Faith*, 256.
84. *Common Grace*, 61, 49, 95.
85. *Reformed Pastor and Modern Thought*, 98.
86. *Defense of the Faith*, 364.

But this would militate directly against the very foundation of all Christian revelation."[87]

Therefore, it is strange that some critics of Van Til have attempted to paint him as a proponent of fideism. For instance, John W. Montgomery charges that in Van Til's presuppositional apologetic we "give the unbeliever the impression that our gospel is as aprioristically, fideistically irrational as the presuppositional claims of its competitors." Montgomery fosters instead an appeal to historical argument ("evidences"), which hopes to show that the Christian truth-claim, particularly about Christ's resurrection, is "very probable," given the available data.[88] Clark Pinnock, writing in support of the same kind of "probabilism" and against Van Til's presuppositional apologetic, charges him with an "irrational fideism" that sees "truth in religion [as] ultimately based on faith rather than on reasoning or evidence"— one that "demands the non-Christian make a total and ungrounded commitment."[89] Although it may be little more than a shortcut to genuine analysis and interaction, or may merely indicate a superficial acquaintance with epistemological issues, some evangelical apologists have tried to dismiss Van Til by labeling his presuppositionalism with the prejudicial epithet of "fideism."[90] Such inaccuracy is difficult to account for. All we can do is point out the inaccurate scholarship of such critics in reading Van Til or in understanding philosophy. After all, Van Til, the alleged fideist, wrote words that were too strong even for his critics to utter: "Faith is not blind faith. . . . Christianity can be shown to be, not 'just as good as' or even 'better than' the non-Christian position, but the *only* position that does not make nonsense of human experience."[91]

---

87. Introduction to B. B. Warfield, *The Inspiration and Authority of the Bible* (Philadelphia: Presbyterian and Reformed, 1948), 38.
88. John Warwick Montgomery, "Once upon an A Priori . . .," in *Jerusalem and Athens,* ed. Geehan, 391.
89. Clark H. Pinnock, "The Philosophy of Christian Evidences," in *Jerusalem and Athens,* ed. Geehan, 422–23; cf. *Biblical Revelation—The Foundation of Christian Theology* (Chicago: Moody Press, 1971), 38–42.
90. For instance, Sproul et al., *Classical Apologetics,* 184–87, 307–9. Also, Norman Geisler, *Christian Apologetics* (Grand Rapids: Baker, 1976), 56–58. Geisler sees the "fideistic hitch" being that Van Til insists on assuming that the biblical worldview is true while arguing for its truth. But presuppositionalism contends that the biblical worldview must be assumed, not only in arguing for the truth of the Bible, but in order for any reasoning or argumentation to be intelligible. This is no fideistic "hitch," but the transcendental argument itself! Strangely enough, Geisler recognizes that Van Til could be interpreted in this transcendental fashion (p. 56, n. 25), but then chooses to portray him in a contrary way.
91. *Christian Theory of Knowledge,* 33, 19.

Van Til's presuppositionalism explicitly aims to provide rational and objective proof of the inescapable and certain truth of Christianity. The critical allegation of fideism against his apologetic is thus ridiculous. Indeed, his critics (Montgomery, Pinnock, Sproul, Geisler, etc.) themselves make no effort to present a proof of Christianity that rises above the level of rational probability.[92] Fideism maintains that the believer cannot (and perhaps should not) offer rational grounds for the full certainty of Christianity's truth-claims. Thus, Van Til is at the opposite pole from fideism, while his critics, ironically, stand closer to it, for they agree with it (to this extent) that full rational proof of Christianity cannot be given. Van Til aims for rational certainty, while his critics settle for far less, namely, probability. For the "evidentialist" critic of presuppositionalism, there is always a subjective "leap of faith" (without corresponding rational grounds) that must be added to the apologetical argument. Christianity may be presented as rationally sound, but only "probably" so; there is always some legitimate and "reasonable" ground for the unbeliever to balk at Christian commitment. That kind of position is a halfway house between fideism and the full strength of the biblical witness and challenge. That is why the *New Catholic Encyclopedia* speaks explicitly of something called "semifideism"—a view "which holds that man reaches truth by reason, but with probability only and not with certitude."[93] Indeed, in his early syllabus *Christian-Theistic Evidences*, Van Til himself spoke of those who take what is commonly

92. In most cases, the only kind of full "certainty" which these apologists offer the Christian—quite unlike the biblical witness—is subjective, moral, or practical (not rational, as with Van Til's program). Theistic proofs and historical/scientific evidences, according to them, can only show that the Bible is "very likely" true (and then, only in those areas which supposedly have the "independent" support of man's reasoning and research).

   For some of these authors, though, even this quasi-fideism is ultimately surrendered to complete experiential fideism. Montgomery, while wanting to challenge unbelievers with supposedly neutral "objective facticity," eventually admits the subjectivistic core of his own apologetic. The proof of Christianity turns out to be the experience of "satisfaction" it provides when one tries it. There are, however, "a welter of conflicting religious options, and one can become psychologically jaded through indiscriminate trials of religious belief." Thus, our apologetic can only aim to provide grounds for testing the Christian option first: "Christ deserves to be given first opportunity to make His claims known to the human heart" (*The Shape of the Past* [Ann Arbor: Edward Bros., 1962], 140; cf. *Where Is History Going?* [Grand Rapids: Zondervan, 1969], 38–39). For a fuller examination of Montgomery's approach to defending the faith, see my unpublished paper, "A Critique of the Evidentialist Apologetical Method of John Warwick Montgomery."
93. S. A. Matczak, "Fideism," *New Catholic Encyclopedia* (New York: McGraw-Hill, 1967), 5:908.

called today the "evidentialist" approach to apologetics as a "second and less consistent class of fideists." Evidentialist critics of Van Til who have inaccurately labeled his presuppositional apologetic "fideistic" are, when all is said and done, actually closer to the fideistic attitude themselves than he ever was, for they hold to semifideism.

FIDEISM (BOTH EXPERIENTIAL AND EVIDENTIAL) REPUDIATED [94]

All this does not mean that there were no believers in Christianity who observed the sceptical tendency of Butler's and Paley's arguments. On the contrary, there were many of these. We may perhaps place them into two categories. There were, in the first place, those who deemed Hume's criticism of Butler's argument as conclusive not only against Butler, but as conclusive against any intellectual argument for Christianity. [95]

Thinking that Butler's type of argument is the only type of argument conceivable, they gave up all hope when they saw their hero defeated by Hume. They saw no way of harmonizing the facts of the Christian religion with the "constitution and course of nature." They gave up the idea of a philosophical apologetics entirely. This fideistic attitude comes to expression frequently in the statement of the experiential proof of the truth of Christianity. People will say that they know that they are saved and that Christianity is true no matter what the philosophical or scientific evidence for or against it may be. And this is done not only by those who have had no opportunity to investigate the evidence for Christianity, but also by those who have.

But, in thus seeking to withdraw from all intellectual argument, such fideists have virtually admitted the validity of the argument against Christianity. They will have to believe in their hearts what they have virtually allowed to be intellectually indefensible.

A second and less consistent class of fideists, though denying the validity

94. An excerpt from *Christian-Theistic Evidences*, 34–35.
95. David Hume (1711–76) was a Scottish skeptic who demonstrated that a strictly empirical epistemology would rationally undermine any attempt to unite separate experiences—and thus undermine any reasoning by analogy from one experience to another experience (thus, say, causal reasoning from the past to the future). The "evidentialist" apologetic of Bishop Butler and William Paley claimed to rest on an empirical foundation, in which case Hume destroyed it as well—and even more, discredited the attempt to reason by analogy from natural experience to what might be expected of supernatural activity (cf. the title of Butler's famous work, *The Analogy of Religion, Natural and Revealed, to the Constitution and Course of Nature*, 1736). Van Til discusses this in chap. 2 of the syllabus from which this selection is taken.

of any philosophical argument for Christianity, turns to arguments taken from archaeology, biological science, etc., hoping in this way to show that the spade corroborates the Bible. This class of fideists approaches very closely to those who profess to follow the method of Butler. They seek a scientific or factual defense for Christianity. In fact, we may say that there is only a difference of degree between the three groups spoken of: (a) the direct followers of Butler, (b) the more consistent fideists, and (c) the less consistent fideists. There is in all of them an emphasis upon the appeal to "brute facts," whether those facts be external or internal. They differ only in respect to the relative faith they have in their ability to unite the "facts" in which they believe into a rational whole that will be able to withstand attack on the part of modern science and philosophy. The followers of Butler think that there is a defense of the Christian experience before the bar of philosophy as well as before the bar of science. The consistent fideists hold that no defense of any sort is possible. The inconsistent fideists contend that Christianity may be scientifically, but cannot be philosophically, defended.

THE GOAL OF OBJECTIVE, ABSOLUTELY CERTAIN PROOF [96]

Our argument as over against this would be that the existence of the God of Christian theism and the conception of his counsel as controlling all things in the universe is the only presupposition which can account for the uniformity of nature which the scientist needs.[97] But the best and only possible proof for the existence of such a God is that his existence is required for the uniformity of nature and for the coherence of all things in the world. . . . Thus there is absolutely certain[98] proof for the existence of God and the truth of Christian theism. Even non-Christians presuppose its truth while they verbally reject it. . . .

---

96. Excerpts from *Defense of the Faith*, 120, 121–22, 256. The last segment of this reading partially reproduces, as Van Til himself indicates, what he wrote in *Common Grace*, 49, 62.

97. Van Til maintains here that the only way to escape Hume's skepticism and to philosophically justify the "connections" (identity, causality, etc.) between separate experiences (see n. 95 above) is to presuppose Christianity as one's worldview. Given the existence of the God revealed in the Bible, there is indeed a "uniformity" in nature—by His sovereign control and trustworthiness. Thus, the personalism of Christian theism is the intellectual precondition for even the impersonal procedures of science itself.

98. The concept of certainty has fallen on hard times in the twentieth century, and references to "certainty" or "certain proof" are bound to be construed (or misconstrued) in different ways. The way in which Van Til uses the term is expressed by Harry Frankfurt in *The Encyclopedia of Philosophy:* "The claim that a basis for doubt is inconceivable is justified whenever a denial of the claim would violate

The second objection may be voiced in the following words: "While a Christian can prove that his Christian position is fully as reasonable as the opponent's view, there is no such thing as an absolutely compelling proof[99] that God exists, or that the Bible is the word of God, just as little as anyone can prove its opposite." In this way of putting the matter there is a confusion between what is objectively valid and what is subjectively acceptable to the natural man.[100] It is true that no method of argument for Christianity will be acceptable to the natural man. Moreover, it is true that the more consistently Christian our methodology, the less acceptable it will be to the natural man. We find something similar in the field of theology. It is precisely the Reformed faith which, among other things, teaches the total depravity of the natural man, which is most loathsome to that natural man. But this does not prove that the Reformed faith is not true. A patient may like a doctor who tells him that his disease can be cured by means of external applications and dislike the doctor who tells him that he needs a major internal operation. Yet the latter doctor may be right in his diagnosis.

It is the weakness of the Roman Catholic and the Arminian methods that they virtually identify objective validity with subjective acceptability to the natural man. Distinguishing carefully between these two, the Reformed apologist maintains that there is an absolutely valid argument[101] for the existence

---

the conditions or presuppositions of rational inquiry" ("Doubt," 2:414). Notice the next sentence in the selection from Van Til.

For a discussion of recent epistemological writings on the idea of certainty and how Van Til's outlook relates to them, see Greg L. Bahnsen, "Pragmatism, Prejudice, and Presuppositionalism," in *Foundations of Christian Scholarship: Essays in the Van Til Perspective*, ed. Gary North (Vallecito, Calif.: Ross House Books, 1976), 241–92. The related and unwarranted notion that truths which are necessarily so must reduce simply to matters of logic and semantics is criticized— and the bearing of its refutation upon apologetics is discussed—in my unpublished essay "Revisionary Immunity."

99. George I. Mavrodes shows how trivial this kind of hard-line pronouncement can turn out to be, given the fact that there is no single argument for any proposition (not just religious ones, like "God exists") which is guaranteed to be cogent and convincing to absolutely every single person (*Belief in God: A Study in Epistemology of Religion* [New York: Random House, 1970], 26–47; this same point is reflected in John M. Frame, *Apologetics to the Glory of God* [Phillipsburg, N.J.: Presbyterian and Reformed, 1994], 62, 64).

100. Although this is often overlooked in casual conversation, it is well to remember that there is a conceptual difference between "certainty" (a property of propositions) and "confidence" (a property of persons). Likewise, there is technically a difference between the "soundness" of an argument and its "persuasiveness." Only the latter is relative to people.

101. It should be clear from the context here that Van Til meant to claim more than that the argument is "valid" (i.e., that its conclusion necessarily follows from the premises). In the first place, the strong kind of argument that he is advocating

of God and for the truth of Christian theism. He cannot do less without virtually admitting that God's revelation to man is not clear. It is fatal for the Reformed apologist to admit that man has done justice to the objective evidence
if he comes to any other conclusion than that of the truth of Christian theism.

As for the question whether the natural man will accept the truth of such
an argument, we answer that he will if God pleases by his Spirit to take the
scales from his eyes and the mask from his face. It is upon the power of the
Holy Spirit that the Reformed preacher relies when he tells men that they are
lost in sin and in need of a Savior. The Reformed preacher does not tone down
his message in order that it may find acceptance with the natural man. He
does not say that his message is less certainly true because of its non-
acceptance by the natural man. The natural man is, by virtue of his creation
in the image of God, always accessible to the truth; accessible to the pene-
tration of the truth by the Spirit of God. Apologetics, like systematics, is valuable to the precise extent that it presses the truth upon the attention of the
natural man. The natural man must be blasted out of his hideouts, his caves,
his last lurking places. Neither Roman Catholic nor Arminian methodologies
have the flame-throwers with which to reach him. In the all-out war between
the Christian and the natural man as he appears in modern garb it is only the
atomic energy of a truly Reformed methodology that will explode the last *Fes-
tung* to which the Roman Catholic and the Arminian always permit him to
retreat and to dwell in safety.[102] . . .

I stress the *objective clarity* of God's revelation of himself wherever it appears. Both Thomas Aquinas and Butler[103] contend that men have done justice by the evidence if they conclude that God *probably* exists. (I have discussed the views of Aquinas in *The Infallible Word* and those of Butler in the

---

would also be "sound" (i.e., its premises would be true). Moreover, the truth of
its premises (or the soundness of secondary, tertiary, etc., arguments used for
those premises) is acknowledged or knowable without prior acknowledgment
or statement of the conclusion in the formulation(s). The kind of strong argument intended by Van Til represents a genuine "cognitive advance" (to use
Mavrodes's expression) because things which the unbeliever will acknowledge
turn out, without him realizing it, upon analysis to require or imply the truth of
the Christian worldview. Does this mean that the argumentation will be "convincing" in the sense of compelling the unbeliever openly to confess its soundness (or the truth of its conclusion)? Not at all, as Van Til goes on to say.

102. CVT: The use of such martial terminology is not inconsistent with the Christian principle of
love. He who loves men most will tell them the truth about themselves in their own interest.

103. In his writings, Van Til characteristically takes the Roman Catholic scholar
Thomas Aquinas (1225–74) as the key representative of "natural theology" and
the Anglican bishop Joseph Butler (1692–1752) as the exemplar of "evidentialist" apologetics.

Syllabus on Evidences.) I consider this a compromise of simple and fundamental Biblical truth. It is an insult to the living God to say that his revelation of himself so lacks in clarity that man, himself through and through a revelation of God, does justice by it when he says that God *probably* exists. "The argument for the existence of God and for the truth of Christianity is objectively valid. We should not tone down the validity of this argument to the probability level. The argument may be poorly stated, and may never be adequately stated.[104] But in itself the argument is absolutely sound. Christian-

---

104. Van Til spoke in this fashion to bring out the utter objectivity of the truth and cogency of the argument for Christian theism (cf. Plato holding that a triangle may never be adequately or perfectly drawn in this world on any particular occasion, and yet there exists perfect triangularity known to us all). Van Til did not say that there is some kind of argument that is beyond human ability to be stated, but simply recognized that particular attempts to state it might all prove inadequate in one way or another. Anybody who has taught logic or intellectual skills realizes that students sometimes present arguments which, although they are "getting at" or "struggling to express" a good point, have a form that calls for refinement and greater precision. Indeed, given different audiences with varied backgrounds and ways of thinking, just about any formulation of an argument can be "improved" by adaptation to the hearer. This is what Van Til meant by saying that the apologetical argument "may be poorly stated and may never be adequately stated." Still, "in itself" the argument's truth and cogency are objective, not subjective or merely probable.

John Frame expresses disagreement with Van Til's assertion that there is "absolutely certain" proof of Christian theism (*Apologetics to the Glory of God*, 77–82, 86; cf. p. 90). Of course, Frame is aware that Scripture speaks of a certainty about God's existence and the gospel that is more than personal assurance—considering its truth to be absolutely certain. Nevertheless, he holds that our arguments for the truth about God or the gospel are only probable (not absolutely certain) because there is "room for error" in the formulation of them. So even though he is dissatisfied with Van Til's distinction between an apologetical argument (say, as an ideal) and its particular statement or formulation, Frame must reintroduce a comparable distinction of his own—now between the "evidence" or "data" or "testimony" for God or the gospel (which is certain) and the formulation of the argument that attempts to "convey" this evidence (which, depending upon the degree of obscuring or distortion, is more or less adequate). Is this really an improved way of putting matters? It would not seem so.

First, Frame insists that "the justification for believing" is not merely probable (p. 86), even though the "degree of belief warranted" is (p. 81, n. 28). But one cannot really have it both ways. Second, there is a detrimental ambiguity lurking in Frame's use of the word "evidence"—meaning (1) the facts, or data, or objective situation that is experienced, and/or (2) the experience of those facts, which is expressed (or expressible) in taking the experience as support for a conclusion. The second sense virtually dissolves Frame's distinction between "evidence" and "argument," while the first sense makes his distinction subject to the same objections that he has with Van Til's way of putting matters. If "evidence" is not construed as something given expression in the context of supporting a conclusion, then what Frame is referring to as "justification of believ-

ity is the only reasonable position to hold. It is not merely as reasonable as other positions, or a bit more reasonable than other positions; it alone is the natural and reasonable position for man to take. By stating the argument as clearly as we can, we may be the agents of the Holy Spirit in pressing the claims of God upon men. If we drop to the level of the merely probable truthfulness of Christian theism, we, to that extent, lower the claims of God upon men" (*Common Grace*, p. 62). Accordingly I do not reject "the theistic proofs" but merely insist on formulating them in such a way as not to compromise the doctrines of Scripture. "That is to say, if the theistic proof is constructed as it ought to be constructed, it is objectively valid, whatever the attitude of those to whom it comes may be" (*Idem*, p. 49).

THE GOSPEL AS AN INTELLECTUAL CHALLENGE[105]

While the Apostle Paul was at Corinth the Lord spoke to him in the night by a vision: "Be not afraid, he was told, but speak, and hold not thy peace: for I am with thee, and no man shall set on thee to hurt thee: . . . for I have much people in this city."[106] Had Paul been afraid to bring the simple gospel of the death and resurrection of Jesus Christ to the city of Corinth with its Jews and with its Greeks? If so, he was afraid no longer after the vision had been given to him. "Where is the wise? where is the scribe? where is the disputer of this world? hath not God made foolish the wisdom of this world? For after that in the wisdom of God the world by wisdom knew not God, it pleased God by the foolishness of preaching to save them that believe."[107]

If the Corinthians would but look at the facts as they are, and particularly as they have shown themselves to be in the course of history, they would be compelled to acknowledge the bankruptcy of the wisdom of man. What an-

---

ing" by appeal to such evidence is as much an ideal construct as Van Til's "unstated argument." And if Frame rejects Van Til's notion of a certain "argument" because there is "room for error" in its statement, then by the same standard he must surrender the certainty of what he calls "evidence" for God and the gospel—since there is (equally) "room for error" in the statement or pointing out of that evidence (e.g., misconstrual of what is being naturally revealed, or adducing scriptural testimony where there is error regarding the original text, its translation, or its interpretation). Thus, Frame has not given us good reason to disagree with Van Til's claim that there is "absolutely certain" proof of Christian theism. Neither has he "rehabilitated" the notion that "probability" applies to all apologetical arguments.

105. Excerpts from *Intellectual Challenge of the Gospel*, 3–7, 40. The Scripture citations in the footnotes below are given by Van Til.
106. Acts 18:9–10.
107. 1 Cor. 1:20–21.

swer had Socrates, Plato and Aristotle been able to give to the deepest problems of life? Shall we say that they gave no answer? No, indeed; for they could not escape giving an answer. But the answers they had given were wrong. Their wisdom had been made foolishness with God. In the light of the narrative which Paul brought, the wisdom of the Greeks was not merely inadequate; it was sinful. Man had originally been made perfect. He had then in Adam broken the covenant that God had made with him.[108] He was now a covenant-breaker and, as such, subject to the wrath of God.

Having such a view of the nature of man Paul did not merely plead for a "complete system," for recognition of the "spiritual dimension" as well as the material. He did not want merely to add the idea of the personal confrontation with Jesus Christ to that of the impersonal study of the laws of nature.[109] In short, he did not ask for the privilege of erecting an altar to the living God, Creator of heaven and earth, next to the altars to gods that have been born of human minds. He pleaded for, and in the name of his Lord required of men, a complete reversal of their point of view in every dimension of life. The entire house of the interpretation of life had to be broken down. Many of the building blocks that they had gathered could no doubt be used, but only if the totally new architectural plan[110] that Paul proposed were followed.

But how could Paul expect that covenant-breakers should become covenant-keepers? How could those who had worshipped and served the creature more than the Creator be expected to turn from their evil way? Would they turn as soon as it was shown to them intellectually that the wisdom of this world has been made foolishness with God? Indeed not. Their minds being darkened, they would appear to others to see while yet they did not see. "But the natural man receiveth not the things of the Spirit of God: for they are foolishness unto him: neither can he know them, because they are spiritually discerned."[111] Or could they be expected to desire and will to

---

108. Rom. 5:12.
109. It has been a repeated mistake of apologists to approach unbelievers as though their interpretation of certain areas of reality (e.g., "nature") were quite intelligible in terms of their professed philosophy (regarding reality, knowledge, and ethics) and acceptable as far as it goes, simply needing to be supplemented with some propositions about the "supernatural." According to Van Til, the apologist's focus should not be restricted to this "added" dimension, but rather should encompass the entire range of human knowledge.
110. In terms of the analogy, the new architectural plan represents the newly adopted worldview of Christianity (with its own revealed theory of reality, theory of knowledge, and theory of ethics). Within this context, the "discoveries" or accomplishments of the unbeliever can be seen to be meaningful—to "make sense"—and to be profitably applied.
111. 1 Cor. 2:14.

believe that which might seem intellectually paradoxical to them? No, St. Paul did not expect that, "because the carnal mind is enmity against God; for it is not subject to the law of God, neither indeed can be."[112]

Yet the Apostle did not despair. He did not lower the requirements of the gospel in order to get men to accept it. Being truly all things to all men, sacrificing himself without limit for the sake of Jew and Gentile alike, he yet continued to insist always on the complete rejection of the "wisdom" of man and on the substitution for it of the "foolishness" of God.[113] For this he had good reason.

He knew all the evidence was for the truth of his message.[114] Can anyone really doubt that God, the God whom Paul preached, does exist? The eternal power and Godhead of Paul's gospel are clearly visible to all men everywhere.[115] God speaks His requirements through all the facts with which man deals. He speaks to men in the works of creation and providence; He speaks also to men through their conscience.[116] He spoke at the beginning of history in direct supernatural fashion to Adam. All men are therefore without excuse. There is no fault in the objective revelation of God to men. It is perspicuous; no one can escape being confronted with it. There is no area of impersonal relationships where the face of God the Creator and Judge does not confront man. It is not as though the evidence shows that *a* god exists or that God *probably* exists. If such were the case then there would be some excuse for man if he did not bow before his Maker. Paul makes bold to claim that all men know deep down in their hearts that they are creatures of God and have sinned against God their Creator and their Judge.

Nor is it as though the evidence for "theism" were clear but the evidence for "Christianity" were obscure. Paul boldly asserts that men are bound to believe the facts of Christianity to be true as soon as they hear of them. When he declares the fact of the resurrection of Christ, he asserts that

---

112. Rom. 8:7.
113. Christian conversion calls for a completely new intellectual outlook or orientation regarding everything that exists, not simply a change of opinion on a few particular points regarding God. The presuppositions that were previously taken for granted and professed as one's philosophy, being based on worldly and human thinking in rebellion against God, must be discarded in their entirety in favor of the "philosophy according to Christ" (Col. 2:8; cf. 2 Cor. 10:5).
114. If there is no evidence that is intelligible apart from the Christian worldview, then there is no evidence that counts against the truth of Christianity. And if no evidence counts against the truth of the Christian faith, it is not merely "probably" true or "probably" provable, but is known with absolute certainty. There is no reason (no evidence) that stands against it.
115. Rom. 1:19.
116. Rom. 2:14–15.

through it all men have been given assurance of the day of final judgment by the Son of man.[117]

Through Paul's gospel, then, "objective truth" stands before men as a challenge. Men cannot react neutrally towards it; they must accept it or suppress it because they do not want to believe it. Paul knows that those who cling to the "wisdom" of the world do so against their better judgment and with an evil conscience. Every fact of "theism" and every fact of "Christianity" points with accusing finger at the sinner, saying: "You are a covenant-breaker; repent and be saved!"

The truth Paul brings requires response, the response of repentance; and repentance is the work of the whole man. Paul's truth is "existential." He who rejects it virtually commits suicide both intellectually and morally.[118]

Yet Paul also knows that sin is of such a nature as to make men prefer intellectual and moral suicide to the truth of God in Christ. Repentance means the recognition of bankruptcy. It involves the suppliant's attitude— begging for mercy, for pardon, for life. It means fleeing from the city of destruction and pressing on to the celestial city even when Mr. Worldly Wise Man and all his friends are going in the other direction. It means bearing the offence of the cross. Will any of the wise of the world accept his gospel and repent?

Yes, they will. Paul is quite sure of that. He knows that God has much people in the city. He knows that he himself had been a persecutor. He remembers vividly how the Lord had appeared unto him. "Am I not an apostle? am I not free? have I not seen Jesus Christ our Lord? are not ye my work in the Lord?"[119] Now that Jesus has come into the world to save His people, His Spirit will set them free. That Spirit will take the things of Christ and give them to His people. God's work is one. God the Father so loved the world that He gave His Son that they who believe might be saved. God the Son came into the world to do the will of the Father. God the Spirit will give men hearts of flesh instead of hearts of stone. The believers in Corinth were the work of the Apostle. "Forasmuch as ye are manifestly declared to be the epistle of Christ

---

117. Acts 17:31.
118. This is Van Til's key point, and it merits reflection. The Christian message is not simply what is needed for the salvation of man's soul (i.e., from moral suicide), but just as much what is needed for salvation from the dilemmas that make nonsense out of his reasoning (i.e., from intellectual suicide). Many mistakenly assume that philosophy can get along all right apart from any reference to religious matters, but in fact philosophy needs Christ as its Savior. It is spiritual and eternal suicide to reject Christ and the gospel, but also intellectual suicide. Thus Augustine could say, "I believe in order to understand."
119. 1 Cor. 9:1.

ministered by us, written not with ink, but with the Spirit of the living God; not in tables of stone, but in fleshy tables of the heart."[120]

The natural man who of himself cannot discern the things of the Spirit is by that Spirit renewed in knowledge after the image of Him that created him.[121] "This renovation is said to be [*eis epignosin*], not *in* knowledge, much less *by* knowledge, but *unto* knowledge, so that he knows. Knowledge is the effect of the renovation spoken of."[122] Moreover "the knowledge here intended is not mere cognition. It is full, accurate, living, or practical knowledge; such knowledge as is eternal life, so that this word here includes what in Eph. 4:24 is expressed by righteousness and holiness."[123]

With this assurance that the Spirit of God, who had enveloped him in heavenly light and turned him from being a persecutor to being an Apostle, can and will enable men to turn from the wisdom of the world in order to accept his gospel, Paul goes forth boldly among men everywhere. Speaking for Him who spoke to Lazarus in his tomb, Paul does not hesitate to speak to those who are dead in trespasses and sins.[124] He expects that the Spirit will in sovereign mercy enable men to repent. It is God, the Spirit, who makes men do that which in their folly they would otherwise not have done. "Are not ye my work in the Lord?" If you who were enamoured of the wisdom of the world have now owned it to be foolishness, you must go forth with the same challenge that I presented unto you. "Therefore, my beloved brethren, be ye steadfast, unmoveable, always abounding in the work of the Lord, forasmuch as ye know that your labour is not in vain in the Lord."[125]

Shall we as Christians, facing the wisdom of the world in modern form, dare to do what Paul tells those who are his work in the Lord to do? Shall we dare to be steadfast and unmovable, never doubting the objective truth of the message that we bring, never doubting that the wisdom of the world has again been made foolishness with God? Shall we have full confidence that our labour will not be in vain in the Lord? . . .

It is thus that God has made foolish the wisdom of this world in the modern day no less than He did in the day of Paul. Instead of accepting the favours of modern man, as Romanism and Arminianism do,[126] we should challenge

120. 2 Cor. 3:3.
121. Col. 3:10.
122. CVT: Charles Hodge, *Systematic Theology*, New York, 1872, Vol. II, p. 99.
123. CVT: *Idem*, p. 100.
124. Eph. 2:1.
125. 1 Cor. 15:58.
126. Van Til's central objection to the apologetical approach taken in natural theology (Romanism) and evidentialism (Arminianism) is that it compromises with the natural man's claim to intellectual autonomy. It appreciates and hopes for

the wisdom of this world. It must be shown to be utterly destructive of predication[127] in any field. It has frequently been shown to be such. It is beyond the possibility of the mind of man to bind together the ideas of pure determinism and of pure indeterminism and by means of that combination to give meaning to life. Either modern man will have to admit that he knows everything or else he will have to admit that he knows nothing. The only alternative to this is that he claims both absurdities at the same time.

Let us again remind ourselves that what has been said does not mean that Christians are in themselves wiser than are other men. What they have they have by grace. They must be "all things to all men." But it is not kindness to tell patients that need strong medicine that nothing serious is wrong with them. Christians are bound to tell men the truth about themselves; that is the only way of bringing them to recognize the mercy, the compassion, of Christ. For if men are told the truth about themselves, and if they are warned against the false remedies that establish men in their wickedness, then, by the power of the Spirit of God, they will flee to the Christ through whom alone they must be saved.

---

any kind of favorable mention or acknowledgment or superficial agreement from the autonomous mind-set. And in order to win it over, it offers to make common cause with its presuppositions in a vain project of showing that those autonomous perspectives actually support nonautonomous conclusions. The favor of the natural man is thus gained at the cost of reinforcing the unbeliever's claim to ultimate authority and failing to intellectually challenge the alleged self-sufficiency of his reasoning.

127. On "predication," see chap. 1, n. 67.

Chapter 3

A Simple Summary and Illustration

An introductory overview of the presuppositional approach to apologetics would be beneficial before we consider deeper philosophical and psychological aspects of apologetical argumentation. One of the compelling features of presuppositionalism is its accessibility and suitability to believers at all levels of academic sophistication. It can profitably be explained to school children, be utilized by college students in any field, and satisfy graduate students and professors in philosophy. This summary will assume very little.

We have already covered the features that are characteristic of presuppositional apologetics in a very general fashion. In chapter 1, our opening exposure to the distinctive contribution of Cornelius Van Til emphasized three things. First, apologetical argument is religious in nature, involving one's ultimate commitment in life; thus, the apologist must both argue for the supreme authority of Christ and argue in a way that exhibits that commitment (1.1). Second, a person's method of reasoning not only determines, but is itself determined by, what he fundamentally believes about reality (God, man, and the world); the apologist's theory of knowledge should be self-consciously worked out as part of his total system of Christian belief (1.2). Third, unbelievers themselves need to be pressed by the apologist to become

self-conscious about the implications of their own underlying philosophies (whether implicitly assumed or explicitly professed); by demonstrating that these outlooks render reasoning meaningless or unintelligible, the apologist indicates that the unbeliever has no
intellectual ground on which to stand in attacking the faith and, even
more, proves the Christian worldview to be true from the rational impossibility of the contrary (1.3).

Van Til refers to the same three general concepts when he sums
up part 1 ("The Structure of My Thought") of the principal book intended to set forth his approach, *The Defense of the Faith:* "Herewith we
are led back to the question of Scripture as identifying itself as the Word of
God and of the system of truth set forth in Scripture as that in terms of which
alone human experience in all of its aspects has meaning."[1] The three components singled out for mention are the Bible's self-attesting status,
Christianity constituting an entire system of truth, and the defense of
that self-attesting system by displaying it as the precondition for the
intelligibility of human experience. Let me explain.

(1) What are we to make of this book called "the Bible"? Van Til
taught that Scripture must "identify itself." There are opinions and
standards of assessment outside the Bible that might be used to indicate how to categorize this book, what qualities (virtues or defects, literary or historical or philosophical) it could or does have, and how
to interpret its function and place in human experience. But the
standard that the Christian applies is the testimony of the Bible about
itself; its character and purpose are believed on its own attestation (or
witness)—being "self-attesting." Therefore, Scripture has final authority in the reasoning of the believer. (2) What Scripture gives us,
moreover, is not simply random bits of religious insight—the theological and ethical "conclusions" that we should affirm. It sets forth
"the system of truth," an entire worldview that simultaneously reveals
how we know what we know (epistemology), what the nature of reality is (metaphysics), and how we ought to live our lives (ethics). The
parties to apologetical discussion must realize that their respective
methods of reasoning and evaluating are consonant with their conflicting messages as a whole; that is, they function as they do because
of the "system" of which they are a part. (3) How then can the Christian system of thought (with its final, self-attesting standard) effectively
and intellectually challenge the non-Christian's system of thought

---

1. *The Defense of the Faith* (Philadelphia: Presbyterian and Reformed, 1955), 198.

(with its own final, self-attesting standard)? Van Til proposed that the Christian worldview "alone" provides an outlook wherein "human experience in all of its aspects has meaning." The alternative views reduce to absurdity because they render reason, science, ethics, etc., nonsensical or incoherent.

We will use this same three-point outline in the following summary of Van Til's presuppositional apologetic.

3.1 Apologetics as a Conflict Between Final Authorities

Most of us are accustomed to thinking of philosophy or academic debate in terms of intellectual detachment from the living of daily life. (Disputes over the nature of "substance" or about the analytic/synthetic distinction do not, after all, seem terribly relevant to grocery shopping, getting the kids dressed, or fixing the plumbing). Questions about the way we reason and think may be important, but they are ethically indifferent or "neutral" matters for scholarly investigation and debate. The moral quality of our lives is not an issue here, for ethics is thought to pertain to our conduct (daily affairs), along with the motives for our concrete behavior and inner attitudes (especially toward other persons). This general outlook is so widespread that it hardly rises to the level of conscious consideration and choice; we just take it for granted. Reasoning is one thing, and ethics is another. That is why Van Til's insights have such a revolutionary effect on most people. He insists (as does Scripture) that the way in which we use our minds—the way in which we reason, how we evaluate claims to the truth, the standards we adopt for knowing, etc.—is itself an ethical matter. This part of human behavior called "reasoning" is as much subject to moral obligations and assessments as anything else we do in the world. The "greatest" commandment teaches us to love the Lord our God with all our *minds*, too (Matt. 22:37)—to take every thought captive to the obedience of Christ (2 Cor. 10:5).

Thus, apologetical dialogue between the believer and the unbeliever exhibits not only two conflicting points of view (as to whether God exists, Jesus rose from the dead, etc.), but also two different moral stances. The believer and the unbeliever recognize two different final standards for living—including that aspect of living known as thinking, reasoning, and arguing. They are divided by their ultimate commitments, either to Christ or to some other authority (usually themselves). Van Til pointed out that sin comes to expression in the unbeliever's intellectual conduct and standards: "When man has become a sinner, his intuitive powers are as sinful as his reasoning powers. . . . Every man by his *sinful nature* seeks violently to suppress the voice of God."[2] "Thus the scientist in the laboratory and the philosopher in his study are both dealing with their materials either as a covenant-keeper or as a covenant-breaker. All of man's acts, all of man's questionings, all of man's affirmations, indeed all of his denials in any dimension of his interests, are covenantally conditioned."[3]

Christians must not fall into a false intellectualism here. "Intellectualism in the church has often made an easy compromise with the Socratic dictum that knowledge is virtue. Men often speak as though the only thing that the sinner needs is true information. This . . . is not the case. Man needs true interpretation, but he also needs to be made a new creature. . . . Sin is not only misinformation; it is also a power of perversion in the soul."[4] The non-Christian's opposition to the truth about God or the gospel does not arise from legitimate intellectual problems with the faith, but from a rebellious and rationalizing heart. "The sinner's problem from his point of view is to cast doubt upon this evidence, to make it appear as though the evidence were not clear. . . . It is the effort of every man to put the blame for his failure to serve God upon the elusive character of the evidence for God's existence."[5]

The two opponents in an apologetical encounter are thus intellectually living by two different ethical standards, but they are also arguing according to conflicting final standards for knowledge itself. They disagree on the ultimate authority that should be used to warrant or justify what a person believes as true. Suppose that a certain statue at Piccadilly Circus in London were described in a tour book as a depiction of Eros with his bow drawn, but that, because you have actually been there to see the statue, you assert that the tour book is in error. If your friend replies that those who write tour books are more likely to have the facts straight than you, your friend has attributed more authority to the tour book than to you on this matter. What he would claim to "know" about the statue of Eros is determined by the authority he has chosen to follow. Now, in the far more im-

2. *Common Grace* (Philadelphia: Presbyterian and Reformed, 1947), 62.
3. *The Protestant Doctrine of Scripture*, In Defense of the Faith, vol. 1 (Philadelphia: Presbyterian and Reformed, 1967), 4.
4. *An Introduction to Systematic Theology*, In Defense of the Faith, vol. 5 (Philadelphia: Presbyterian and Reformed, 1974), 130.
5. Ibid., 163–64.

portant dispute between the Christian and the unbeliever, they too
have conflicting final authorities for knowledge. As Van Til put it, they
disagree on the "reference point" to be used in assessing truth-claims
and interpreting experience. (In our illustration, one person gained
his perspective from the "point of reference" given in the tour book,
while the other's ultimate point of reference was his memory of an
eyewitness experience.) Believers and unbelievers have different presuppositions that give them their orientation to the world, to reasoning, and to living. "Either one thinks in terms of the authority of Scripture, making reason and all its activities subject to this authority, or else one
acts and thinks on one's own ultimate authority."[6] Or, as Van Til wrote elsewhere: believers should "agree that human experience and human logic
must be interpreted in terms of God and Christ rather than that God and Christ
must be interpreted in terms of human experience and logic."[7]

A person cannot have it both ways regarding his final standard or
ultimate reference point. He presupposes and reasons either according to the authority of God or according to some other authority.[8] Attempting to be neutral about God's ultimate authority in determining
what we know is a result of a bad attitude toward God's ultimate authority. It is a way of saying that one does not really need the work of
Christ to save him in his reasoning. "It is the self-authenticating Christ
who . . . shows us that in all our efforts as ultimate self-interpreters we are actually opposing the salvation that he offers. Every bit of supposedly impersonal
and neutral investigation, even in the field of science, is the product of an attitude of spiritual hostility to the Christ through whom alone there is truth in
any dimension."[9]

This is a critical point for apologetics. Van Til's approach recognizes
and points out that religious conversion entails a change in a person's
point of reference or ultimate standard for knowing and interpret-

6. Ibid., 192.
7. *Common Grace*, 104.
8. The complaint will be heard that, if we are arguing over whether God exists and
has final authority, we may not take that authority for granted while we are arguing about it. But the complaint is reversible, is it not? The Christian can reply: "If
we are arguing over whether God exists and has final authority, we may not take
for granted that He is not the final authority; the attempt to authorize (substantiate) His authority by some other standard would amount to the ruling that whatever authority He has cannot be final." A person's presuppositions are (as such)
presupposed even when someone is discussing or arguing about them. For example, philosophers who argue for the truth or validity of the laws of logic do not
put aside logic while arguing for it.
9. *The Case for Calvinism* (Philadelphia: Presbyterian and Reformed, 1963), 145.

ing anything at all. Hence, apologetics is at base an intellectual conflict over ultimate authorities for knowing and living. "When the sinner has by God's grace in Christ received this new light and this new power of sight then he sees all things in their proper relationships. Formerly he stood on his head while now he stands on his feet. Formerly he referred all things to himself as the final point of reference. Now he refers all things to God his Creator, and to Christ his redeemer as the final point of reference. His conversion was a Copernican revolution. It was not accomplished by steps or stages. It was an about-face. Before his conversion he looked away from the God and the Christ of Scripture. *After* his conversion he can't see a fact in the world that he does not wish to deal with to the glory of God. The words of Paul, 'Whether ye eat, or drink, or do *anything* else, do all to the glory of God,' are now his motto. Deeply conscious of his continued sinfulness he is, none the less, now, in the core of his being, a lover instead of a hater of God."[10]

It is now fairly easy to answer the age-old question of the relationship between faith and reason. Van Til affirmed the importance of reasoning and using our intellect as a tool, but he also understood that this tool would be utilized according to the direction, standard, or "reference point" of some ultimate authority (for ethics as well as for knowing). The unbeliever uses his reason (reasoning) in the service of his own personal authority, desires, and rebellion against God. The believer has been brought to a change of final authorities: "When God has reasoned with us and changed our minds till our every thought is brought into captivity to the obedience of Christ, we must use our minds, our intellect, our reason, our consciousness, in order to receive and re-interpret the revelation God has given of himself in Scripture. That is the proper place of reason in theology. There is no conflict between this reason and faith, since faith is the impelling power which urges reason to interpret aright."[11]

Of course the unbeliever finds this utterly unacceptable. But by what standard is it judged unacceptable? The unbeliever as much as the believer follows some ultimate standard, although he may be reluctant to admit it. For the unbeliever, the tool of reason (reasoning) would be transformed into the final judge for knowing anything (as though there could be some abstract thing[12] that might be venerated

---

10. *The Reformed Pastor and Modern Thought* (Philadelphia: Presbyterian and Reformed, 1971), 35–36.
11. *Introduction to Systematic Theology*, 30.
12. Cf. the logical fallacy of reification (or hypostatization): treating as a concrete or specific entity a series of events ("the winds of change") or an abstraction ("the federal government," "Mother Nature").

as "Reason"), thus replacing the final authority or standard of God's revelation.[13] Van Til was keenly aware that "we cannot speak of human reason in general, or of the human consciousness in general. . . . 'Reason' in the case of the non-Christian is employed by such as assume themselves to be self-sufficient, while 'reason' in the case of the Christian is employed by those who through regeneration have learned to think of themselves as creatures of God and of their task in life as keeping covenant with God."[14] This is the focal point of the argument between him and the believer. The Christian does not have two ultimate authorities for interpreting life and directing his thinking, one that he shares with the unbeliever and one that is unique to his religious stance. "The Christian knows that he would interpret nature wrongly, due to the sin that is within him, unless he be enlightened by Scripture and guided by the Holy Spirit. Strictly speaking, he should therefore not refer to two sources with respect to his general interpretation of life. If he says, 'Scripture and reason convince me that this or that is true,' he should mean by this that his reason, as it looks at everything in the light of Scripture, has convinced him. If, therefore, he appeals to the unbeliever on the ground that nature itself reveals God, he should do this in such a manner as to make it appear in the end that he is interpreting nature in the light of Scripture."[15]

Apologetics involves a conflict over ultimate authorities—that is, a conflict over our presuppositions or final standard. What should be the source of a person's presuppositions? For the unbeliever, it will be some authority for reasoning other than the word of God, while for the believer it is God's revelation. "For science and philosophy, as well as for theology, we frankly take our basic presuppositions from Scripture. . . . There are no central truths on which all [believer and unbeliever] agree.[16] The disagreement is fundamental and goes to the heart of the matter."[17]

---

13. Reason—in the sense of the tool of intellectual analysis (reasoning)—must indeed be used to read, understand, and believe what God's revelation says, and yet the final authority that directs this reasoning process is God's revelation itself; moreover, the tool of reasoning is only intelligible in terms of what God's revelation teaches in the first place.
14. *Introduction to Systematic Theology*, 29, 15.
15. Ibid., 197.
16. Van Til held that even where there was the appearance of agreement on fundamental points in the reasoning, science, or philosophy of believer and unbeliever, there was nonetheless and ultimately a difference between them in both the broader understanding and the more specific application of those points.
17. *Common Grace*, 63.

DIFFERENT FINAL COURTS OF APPEAL [18]

When man fell it was therefore his attempt to do without God in every respect. Man sought his ideals of truth, goodness and beauty somewhere beyond God, either directly within himself or in the universe about him. God had interpreted the universe for him, or we may say man had interpreted the universe under the direction of God, but now he sought to interpret the universe without reference to God; we mean of course without reference to the kind of God defined above. . . .

What then was the result as far as the question of knowledge is concerned on man's rebellion against God? The result was that man tried to interpret everything with which he came into contact without reference to God. The assumption of all his future interpretation was the self-sufficiency of intra-cosmical relationships.[19] . . .

We have felt ourselves compelled to take our notions with respect to the nature of reality from the Bible. It will readily be conceded that such a notion of reality as we have presented could be received upon authority only. Such a notion of being as we have presented is to be found nowhere except in the Bible. The Bible is taken so seriously that we have not even left any area of known reality by which the revelation that comes to us in the Bible may be compared, or to which it may be referred as to a standard. We have taken the final standard of truth to be the Bible itself.

It is needless to say that this procedure will appear suicidal to most men who study philosophy. Is it not by the help of man's own reason that we are to think out the nature of reality and knowledge? To accept an interpretation of life upon authority is permissible only if we have looked into the foundations of the authority we accept. But if we must determine the foundations of the authority, we no longer accept authority on authority.[20] Authority could be authority to us only if we already knew that it had the right to claim authority. Such could be the case only if we knew in advance the nature of that authority. Thus we would have a theory of being already taken for

---

18. Excerpts from *Defense of the Faith*, 31, 64, 49–52, 309, 158–59, 162–63, 165, 306.
19. Man, in rebellion against God, takes the world and the relationships therein (between things or events) to be quite intelligible without making reference to anything that transcends the world or human experience.
20. In the nature of the case, God is the final authority. But if God's authority must be authorized or validated by the authority of human reasoning and assessment, then human thinking is more authoritative than God Himself—in which case God would not have final authority, and indeed would no longer be God. The autonomous man who insists that God can only be accepted if His word first gains the approval or agreement of man has determined in advance that God will never be acknowledged as God (the final authority).

granted at the outset of our investigation. In this manner we could not give a fair hearing to opposing views.

A modern way of stating this objection to our position is found in the words of Dr. Edgar A. Singer's *Notes on Experience and Reflection*.[21] Dr. Singer tells us it is the business of philosophy to ask, *How do we know?* In other words, according to Singer the epistemological question can and must be asked without saying anything with respect to the ontological question.

Is this position of Dr. Singer tenable? Suppose it is true, for argument's sake, that such a being as we have described God to be, does actually exist. Would not such a God have the right to speak to us with authority? Are we not, by saying that the question of knowledge is independent of the question of being, excluding one possible answer to the question of knowledge itself? If the Being of God is what, on the basis of Scripture testimony we have found it to be, it follows that our knowledge will be true knowledge only to the extent that it corresponds to his knowledge. To say that we do not need to ask about the nature of reality when we ask about the nature of knowledge is not to be neutral but is in effect to exclude the Christian answer to the question of knowledge.

That Singer has in effect excluded from the outset the Christian answer to the question of knowledge appears from the fact that in his search for an answer to this question he affirms that we must go to *as many as possible* of those reputed to *have* knowledge (p. 5). The notion of going to One whose opinion may be more valuable than the opinion of others even to the extent of being authoritative over the opinion of others is not even considered. In paradise, Eve went to *as many as possible* of those who were reputed to have knowledge. God and Satan both had a reputation for knowledge. Apparently God did not think well of Satan's knowledge, and Satan did not think well of God's knowledge—but each thought well of his own knowledge. So Eve had to weigh these reputations. It was for her a question as to, How do we know?

The problem that Eve faced was a difficult one. God told her that she would surely die if she ate of the forbidden tree. Numerically there was only one in favor of one and only one in favor of the opposite point of view. Thus she could not settle the matter of reputation by numbers. She herself had to decide this matter of reputation by a motion and a vote. God claimed that he was the Creator. He claimed that his being was ultimate while Satan's being was created and therefore dependent upon God's being. Satan said in effect that she should pay no attention to this problem of being. He told her she should decide the question, *How do we know?* without asking the question,

21. CVT: An unpublished class syllabus.

What do we know? He said she should be neutral with respect to his inter-pretation and God's interpretation of what would take place if she ate of the forbidden tree. Eve did ignore the question of being in answering the ques-tion of knowledge. She said she would gather the opinions of as many as she could find with a reputation for having knowledge and then give the various views presented a fair hearing.[22]

We should observe particularly that in doing what she did Eve did not re-ally avoid the question of *What do we know?* She gave by implication a very definite answer to that question. She made a negation with respect to God's Being. She denied God's Being as ultimate being. She affirmed therewith in effect that all being is essentially on one level.

At the same time she also gave a definite answer to the question *How do we know?* She said we know independently of God. She said that God's au-thority was to be tested by herself. Thus she came to take the place of ulti-mate authority. She was no doubt going to test God's authority by *experi-ence* and *reflection* upon experience. Yet it would be *she* herself, who should be the final authority.

It would appear then that the theory of being that we have presented fits in with the notion of the Bible as an authoritative revelation of God. Such a being as the Bible speaks of could not speak otherwise than with absolute authority.[23] *In the last analysis we shall have to choose between two theo-ries of knowledge. According to one theory God is the final court of appeal; according to the other theory man is the final court of appeal.*[24] . . .

Sin will reveal itself in the field of knowledge in the fact that man makes himself the ultimate court of appeal in the matter of all interpretation. He will refuse to recognize God's authority. We have already illustrated the sinful per-son's attitude by the narrative of Adam and Eve. Man has declared his au-tonomy as over against God.

---

22. CVT: Van Halsema's charge that for me "the metaphysical situation is of only secondary sig-nificance" *(Calvin Forum*, Dec. 1953, p. 85) is here, as throughout my writings, shown to be contrary to fact.

23. Thus, the very thing that most unbelievers demand—a neutral and autonomous investigation of the facts to see whether God's word can be recognized as true and authoritative—already precludes the kind of God of which the Scripture speaks. Apologists need to come to grips with this, lest their method of defend-ing the faith betray the object of their faith.

24. Emphasis added. Apologetical argument is directed by one's more general the-ory of knowing (one's epistemology). Because the believer and the unbeliever have different ultimate authorities, they of necessity have ultimately different the-ories of knowledge. It is shameful for apologists to pretend otherwise, hoping that unbelievers will not be conscious of (or come to realize) the conflict in episte-mology that separates them in principle from believers.

This means that in the total picture that man must seek for himself, he must go to Scripture as the final court of appeal. He learns from nature still, but what nature teaches him must be brought into relationship with what the Scriptures teach in order that it may be properly understood. . . .

In other words, on Montague's scheme[25] of things the mind of man must, for all practical purposes, take the place of God in the Christian scheme of things. To talk about what can or cannot exist according to logic is but to swing a sword in the sky unless it is first determined at what point logic meets reality.[26] According to the Christian story, logic and reality meet first of all in the mind and being of God. God's being is exhaustively rational. Then God creates and rules the universe according to his plan. Even the evil of this world happens according to this plan. The only substitute for this Christian scheme of things is to assert or assume that logic and reality meet originally in the mind of man. The final point of reference in all predication must ultimately rest in some mind, divine or human. It is either the self-contained God of Christianity or the would-be autonomous man that must be and is presupposed as the final reference point in every sentence that any man utters. . . .

The entire idea of inscripturated supernatural revelation is not merely foreign to but would be destructive of the idea of autonomy on which the modern man builds his thought. If modern man is right in his assumption with respect to his own autonomy then he cannot even for a moment logically consider evidence for the fact of the supernatural in any form as appearing to man. The very idea of God as self-contained[27] is meaningless on his principles. The idea of such a God, says the modern follower of Kant, is fine as a limiting notion.[28] Taken as a limiting notion it is quite innocent and even use-

25. Van Til is here drawing from "Does the Universe Have a Mind?" *His* 8, no. 4 (April 1948): 28–30, in which he answers an article of the same title by William Pepperell Montague in the *Saturday Review of Literature* for September 6, 1947.
26. This refers to one of the perennial problems in philosophy, which is expressed in various ways. The subject of knowledge—the knower—thinks in a particular way; the way in which he thinks, even if it is a matter of logically organizing his beliefs, is internal to his mind. However, the object of knowledge—what he is thinking about—is (usually) the world outside his mind. What warrant is there for assuming that the subject and the object in this knowledge transaction correspond to each other? In terms of Van Til's question, why should unchanging concepts or laws of logic be thought appropriate for understanding the constantly changing world outside the mind?
27. The self-sufficiency or independence of God refers to the fact that He needs nothing outside of Himself and is not subject to or determined by anything outside of Himself; that is, God is "self-contained." As such, He is the Creator of all things and the determiner of all events; everything depends upon Him. "In Him we live and move and have our existence" (Acts 17:28).
28. In Kant's philosophy, certain ideas—the ideas of reason—are not in themselves

ful. For then it stands merely for the ideal of exhaustive rationality. And science requires such an ideal. But the idea of such a God as taken by orthodox Christians, that is as a constitutive rather than as a limiting concept, is meaningless; it would kill the idea of pure facts as the correlative to pure rationality. And the idea of pure fact as a limiting concept is as necessary to modern science as is the idea of pure rationality.[29]

It is therefore logically quite impossible for the natural man, holding as he does to the idea of autonomy, even to consider the "evidence" for the Scripture as the final and absolutely authoritative revelation of the God of Christianity. . . .

Their position allows for sacred books and even for a superior book. But the one thing it does not allow for is an absolutely authoritative book.[30] Such a book presupposes the existence and knowability of the self-contained God of Christianity. But such a God, and the revelation of such a God in the universe and to man, are notions that, as has already been observed, the natural man must reject. So he will naturally also reject that which is simply the logical implicate of the idea of such a God and of such a revelation. . . .

Hence the idea of human autonomy can find no place in the truly Christian system any more than can the idea of chance. The human being is analogical rather than original in all the aspects of its activity. And as such its activity is truly significant. . . .

When we deal with the non-regenerate consciousness, we must think of it as it is according to its adopted monistic assumption.[31] Hence we cannot

---

false, but can be used in an erroneous fashion. If they are used as though they denoted something that is metaphysical and yet known by the immanent categories of human reasoning (that is, used "constitutively"), they lead to illusions. However, if such ideas are used in a regulative fashion—as "limiting notions"— they set ideal conditions and curb the extreme application of universal principles, thereby helping to bring coherence and unity to human experience. Limiting notions give guidance to human thinking and knowing; man is to proceed as if there were objects denoted by them. Such ideas can regulate our thinking, whether or not they correspond to any transcendent objects.

29. A "pure" fact is a raw and uninterpreted experience (or, alternatively, the object that is experienced). "Pure" rationality refers to the categories and unifying principles utilized by the mind in interpreting experience. In Kant's philosophy, the mind of man is active in constituting its objects, not simply a passive receiver of sense data. So the mind's pure rationality is "imposed" upon the pure facts.

30. Remember here that Van Til speaks of an "absolutely" authoritative book—one whose authority is beyond challenge and has no qualifications or limits. Unbelievers may see the Bible as enshrining the advanced wisdom of many good men over the ages, and in that sense may see it as bearing some authority, but never an authority that in itself establishes what is true and right, no matter what.

31. "Monistic" refers to the fact that the unregenerate man will not take account of

grant that it has *any right to judge* in matters of theology, or, for that matter, in anything else. The Scriptures nowhere appeal to the unregenerated reason as to a qualified judge. When Scripture says: "Come, let us reason together," it often speaks to the people of God, and, if it does speak to others, it never regards them as equal with God or as really competent to judge. The unregenerate man has knowledge of God, that is of the revelation of God within him, the sense of deity which he seeks to suppress. Scripture does appeal to this sense of deity in man, but it does so and can do so only by denying that man, when acting on his adopted monistic assumption, has any ability or right to judge of what is true or false, right or wrong.

MAN NOT AN AUTONOMOUS AUTHORITY[32]

The second attribute of Scripture the Reformers spoke of is that of *authority*. This authority is involved in the idea of necessity. Scripture is necessary because an authoritative revelation is necessary. We have seen that the sinner will not of himself recognize that he is abnormal in his interpretation of life. Hence he also refuses to recognize that God is the ultimate while he himself should be nothing but the immediate starting point in the knowledge situation.[33] The sinner seeks to be *autonomous*. He will, therefore, seek to set himself up as a judge over that which presents itself to him as revelation. Now if the revelation of God came to men in such a way as to recognize the sinner as autonomous and able to judge about the truth of revelation of himself, it is certain that the sinner would never escape his position of autonomy. There would then be no one to challenge it. God himself would be strengthening man in his self-conceit. Accordingly we find that revelation comes to the sinner with a claim of absolute authority over man. It asks man to submit his thought captive to it in obedience. Thus the concepts of necessity and authority are involved in one another. There would be no necessity for anything but for an authoritative revelation while, on the other hand, there was an absolute necessity for an authoritative revelation.

---

the Creator-creature distinction when it comes to thinking and reasoning. The conditions of knowing are singular, he insists, applying equally to God and man. For Van Til, however, man's thinking must follow after or replicate God's thinking on the level of a creature, thus being "analogical" and recognizing two levels of knowing (original and derivative, absolute and subordinate).

32. An excerpt from *Introduction to Systematic Theology*, 134–35.
33. In the process of knowing anything, man begins with his own experience and questions—the "immediate" starting point. However, that which man knows metaphysically begins with God (who preinterprets, creates, and governs everything man could know), and God's mind is epistemologically the standard of truth— thus being the "ultimate" starting point.

3.2 An Implicit Clash of Entire Worldviews (Thus Methods Too)

The disagreement between believer and unbeliever extends to the very heart of their differing outlooks on life, which includes their contrary convictions about the nature of reality, and thus involves their fundamental division over the proper method for knowing anything (learning, interpreting, proving, etc.).

Van Til saw that the dispute in apologetics was not simply over isolated religious claims or conclusions, but was in principle a dispute regarding entire worldviews. "It is indeed impossible for any man to make any statement about any fact of experience without doing so in terms of an all-inclusive view of reality. And we can only rejoice if there seems today to be some measure of appreciation of this fact, for to the extent that this is the case we need no longer concern ourselves with the idea of 'neutrality.' And to the extent that such is the case, we may start from the assumption that every bit of scientific search for facts already proceeds upon a basic view with respect to reality. . . . All men presuppose, whatever the name they use for it, a synoptic view of reality as a whole. We continue to call it metaphysics."[34] Alternatively: "For convenience we speak of this total outlook on reality as a world and life view."[35]

"The fight between Christianity and non-Christianity is, in modern times, no piece-meal affair. It is the life and death struggle between two mutually opposed life and world-views."[36] The Christian, perhaps thinking that his argument with the non-Christian is simply over the truth of such external matters as creation (versus evolution), may set out to prove from science that the alternative is simply implausible, but he soon realizes (if he is at all thoughtful) that the two of them also disagree over the genuine character of science and scientific theorizing. The Christian, perhaps thinking that his argument with the non-Christian is simply over a fact such as Christ's resurrection from the dead, may set out to prove from history that this event occurred, but he soon realizes (if he is at all thoughtful) that the two of them also disagree over the proper character of historical research, reasoning, and evaluation. The Christian, perhaps thinking that his argument with the non-Christian is simply over the philosophical coherence and practicality of the biblical perspective, may set out to defend it or offer reasons in support of it, but he soon realizes (if he is at all thoughtful) that

---

34. *Case for Calvinism*, 115.
35. *Protestant Doctrine of Scripture*, 103.
36. *Introduction to Systematic Theology*, 6.

the two of them also disagree over the nature of meaning, utility, possibility, explanation, etc.

Because they operate out of the context of conflicting worldviews, the believer and the unbeliever will find—if they are consistent and their dialogue pushes into deeper reasons for differing with each other—that their disagreement covers their theory of knowledge (method and criteria of knowing) as well as what they claim to know (or what cannot be known) about God, the world, man, life, conduct, or values. Thus, Van Til taught: "If man does not own the authority of Christ in the field of science, he assumes his own ultimate authority as back of his effort. The argument between the covenant-keeper and the covenant-breaker is never exclusively about any particular fact or about any number of facts. It is always, at the same time, about the nature of facts. And back of the argument about the nature of facts, there is the argument about the nature of man. However restricted the debate between the believer and the non-believer may be at any one time, there are always two world views ultimately at odds with one another."[37]

This explains why the apologist must not see his dispute with the unbeliever as a matter of *faith* (the Christian perspective) versus *reason* (the non-Christian perspective). It is rather one worldview (a faith that controls reasoning) versus another worldview (a different faith that controls reasoning). The worldviews may not be explicitly explained or acknowledged in the dispute, but they determine the course of the argument. "All men do their thinking on the basis of a position accepted by faith. If your faith is not one which has God in Christ speaking infallibly in Scripture for its object, then your faith is in man as autonomous. All of one's reasoning is controlled by either of these presuppositions."[38] In apologetics we must become accustomed to thinking in terms of "package deals." The unbeliever has a certain view of reality, man, etc., and his theory of knowledge and method of reasoning not only are used to support that particular view, but also are determined by it; it is a package deal. Likewise, the believer has a certain view of reality, as well as a theory of knowledge that supports, and is determined by, that view of reality; it too is a package deal.

The believer's "package" should not be reduced to some isolated or abstract elements of it, as though what we defend is "theism in general" rather than the specific character of the full Christian concep-

37. *Protestant Doctrine of Scripture*, 5.
38. *Case for Calvinism*, 128–29.

tion of God.[39] "From the point of view of the sinner, theism is as objectionable as is Christianity. Theism that is worthy of the name is Christian theism. Christ said that no man can come to the Father but by him. No one can become a theist unless he becomes a Christian. Any God that is not the Father of our Lord Jesus Christ is not God but an idol."[40] Nor does the believer's "package" (worldview) allow for an isolation or abstraction of its epistemology and metaphysic. Van Til denounced an apologetical strategy that says, "First the inspired Bible and secondly the divine Christ," because you cannot intelligibly have one without the other. "We must rather take the Bible simultaneously with Christ and with God as its author."[41] As we say, it is a package deal.

Accordingly, in apologetics the believer's package deal (worldview) stands over against and challenges the unbeliever's package deal (worldview). In principle, if the advocates of the two differing positions were cognizant of their unspoken assumptions about reality and knowledge, and if they were completely consistent with their presuppositions, they would disagree on everything with each other. "Insofar as men are aware of their most basic alliances, they are wholly for or wholly against God at every point of interest to man."[42] Van Til explained: "It is the idea of the interrelatedness of every aspect of the revelation of God [in nature and in word] to man that is all important. It is only when this interrelatedness is stressed that, as Christians, we can effectively challenge the wisdom of the world and show that it has been made foolish by God. Only thus can the *total* interpretation of life and the world, as given by Christ in Scripture, be that on which alone every aspect of human experience must be based in order to have significance. . . . If then the Christian is to fulfill his calling he must set the Christian approach to men and things over against that

39. This does not mean that we can say everything about God simultaneously with everything else that can be said about God. Obviously, we can only talk about "one thing at a time." Nevertheless, when we talk about the existence or intelligence or power (etc.) of God, the object of our discussion is specifically or concretely that Being for whom there is a full Christian conception (in accordance with His self-revelation in Scripture). There is, for instance, no abstract divine sovereignty that is not the sovereignty of the covenant-keeping God of Scripture—any more than there is any divine covenant that is not enacted by the sovereign God of Scripture. Whenever the Christian talks about the aspect of covenant or about the aspect of sovereignty, he always keeps in mind the fuller *and implicitly definitional* context of what he is narrowly discussing. The only omniscient God whom the Christian defends is the one who is simultaneously omnipotent, omnipresent, etc.
40. "Nature and Scripture," in *The Infallible Word*, ed. N. B. Stonehouse and Paul Woolley (Philadelphia: Presbyterian and Reformed, 1946), 280.
41. *Protestant Doctrine of Scripture*, 61.
42. *Introduction to Systematic Theology*, 29.

of modern science, philosophy, and theology. If he does not do so in *all* three fields he cannot effectively do so in *any* one of these fields."[43] The Christian apologist must become "epistemologically self-conscious" about the broader philosophical implications and influences on his method of reasoning, and he must—in pursuit of the very task of apologetics—seek to draw out into the open the details of the worldview that comes to expression in the non-Christian's method of reasoning, making the unbeliever epistemologically self-conscious as well.

TOTAL PICTURES OF LIFE, REALITY, AND METHOD[44]

Our view of reality or being involves a view of knowledge and of ethics even as our view of knowledge and ethics involves and is based on our view of being.[45] . . .

The philosophers have sought for a unified outlook on human experience. Philosophers have sought for as comprehensive a picture of the nature of reality as a whole as man is able to attain. But the universe is composed of many things. Man's problem is to find unity in the midst of the plurality of things. . . .

When seeking to persuade men to accept the truth of the system of doctrine revealed in Scripture, we speak of our Christian view of life. And we subdivide this Christian view of life into three main sections, the Christian theory of being, the Christian theory of knowledge and the Christian theory of ethics or behavior. We must set off the Christian view of life sharply from the non-Christian view of life.[46] Basic to all the differences between the Christian and the non-Christian views of life is the fact that Christians worship and serve the Creator, while non-Christians worship and serve the creature.[47] Through the fall of mankind in Adam, the first man, the representative of all men, all became creature-worshippers. But through the redemption wrought by Christ and applied to his people by the Holy Spirit, the chosen ones have learned,

---

43. *Protestant Doctrine of Scripture,* 12, 57.
44. *Defense of the Faith,* 41, 48–49, 113, 115–16.
45. "Theory of being" is another way of designating one's theory of reality (what kinds of things exist, their origin, relationships, etc.), called "metaphysics." One's "theory of knowledge" is his "epistemology," involving the nature, limits, methods, and standards of knowing. For Van Til, one's epistemology and one's metaphysics mutually influence and are adjusted to each other, thus forming a "network" of presuppositions.
46. That is, the Christian worldview or "system" must be set in contrast to the non-Christian's worldview or "system."
47. The Christian and non-Christian worldviews are divided because they involve different religions—different ultimate commitments in life, with different points of reference.

be it only in principle, to worship and serve the Creator more than the creature. They now believe the theory of reality offered in Scripture. They now
believe in God as self-sufficient, in the creation of all things in this universe
by God, in the fall of man at the beginning of history and in the "regeneration of all things" through Christ.

But it is just as important to have a Christian theory of knowledge as it is
to have a Christian theory of being. One cannot well have the one without
at the same time also having the other. Modern thought is largely preoccu-
pied with the theory of knowledge. As Christians we shall therefore find it
necessary to set the Christian theory of knowledge over against the modern
form of the non-Christian theory of knowledge. Even so we shall have to make
it plain that our theory of knowledge is what it is because our theory of being
is what it is. As Christians we cannot begin speculating about knowledge by
itself. We cannot ask *how* we know without at the same time asking *what*
we know. . . .

The Christian view of man and the Christian view of method are alike
aspects of the Christian position as a whole. So also the non-Christian view
of man and the non-Christian view of method are alike aspects of the non-
Christian position as a whole. That such is indeed the case will appear as we
proceed. . . .

The Reformed apologist cannot agree at all with the methodology of the
natural man.[48] Disagreeing with the natural man's interpretation of himself
as the ultimate reference-point, the Reformed apologist must seek his point
of contact[49] with the natural man in that which is beneath the threshold of

48. Van Til is here speaking of the unbeliever's methodology—his understanding or
view of the method to use in knowing, interpreting, or proving things. He has a
different theory of method than the believer. Nevertheless, in actual practice the
two of them follow a procedure or method that will be very similar (e.g., they open
their eyes and look, compare conflicting accounts for inconsistencies, etc.). Van
Til often said that regeneration does not give men different noses, but it surely
changes their understanding and use of their noses! (Substitute for "noses" the
words "brains," "logic," etc., to get the crucial point.)
49. The "point of contact" is something that two opponents have in common and
which, as such, is a point that one person can use to make contact with the other
person and build toward greater agreement in outlook. If two former basketball
players who have now become businessmen have a dispute over a business
arrangement, one of them might seek to resolve their dispute by first finding a
point of contact in their common, previous experiences as basketball players.
("Remember how you had to learn to work together on the court with that team-
mate you did not personally like, all for the greater good of putting together a
winning season? Well, that is kind of what we are going to have to do if this snag
in our contract is going to get cleared up.") What Van Til wanted us to see, however, is that the believer's point of contact with the unbeliever—what they have
in common as rational creatures of God who know their Creator—is something

his working consciousness, in the sense of deity which he seeks to suppress. And to do this the Reformed apologist must also seek a point of contact with the systems constructed by the natural man. But this point of contact must be in the nature of a head-on collision. *If there is no head-on collision with the systems of the natural man there will be no point of contact with the sense of deity in the natural man.*[50] So also, disagreeing with the natural man on the nature of the object of knowledge, the Reformed apologist must disagree with him on the method to be employed in acquiring knowledge. According to the doctrine of the Reformed faith all the facts of nature and of history are what they are, do what they do and undergo what they undergo, in accord with the one comprehensive counsel of God. All that may be known by man is already known by God. And it is already known by God because it is controlled by God.

The significance of this for the question of method will be pointed out soon. For the moment this simple fact must be signalized as the reason which precludes the possibility of agreement on methodology between the Reformed theologian and the non-Christian philosopher or scientist.

CONFLICTING THEORIES OF REASON AND EVIDENCE[51]

The third and final legitimate use of reason, according to Hodge, is that it must judge of the evidences of any revelation that comes to it. Faith, he argues, is "an intelligent reception of the truth on adequate grounds" ([*Systematic Theology*] Vol. I, p. 53), and Scripture never demands faith "except on the ground of adequate evidence" (*ibid.*).

On the surface at least this manner of statement again seems to assume that all men, regenerate and non-regenerate, agree on the nature of reason and evidence. But this is contrary to fact. The average philosopher and scientist today holds to a non-theistic conception of reason and therefore also to a non-theist conception of evidence. Assuming the ultimacy of the human

---

that the unbeliever wants to suppress and deny. ("What do you mean? I never played basketball"—even though you have his records, press releases, and on-court pictures in your briefcase.) Stubbornness in maintaining a dispute sometimes means that the point of contact becomes a point of confrontation.

50. The "systems" of the natural man represent the philosophies or worldviews that the unbeliever will openly espouse and attempt to defend—in contrast to the "sense of deity," which the unbeliever attempts to suppress. What Van Til means here is that what the believer and the unbeliever genuinely have in common— their true point of contact (the sense of deity)—brings about a confrontation between their espoused "systems."

51. Excerpts from *Introduction to Systematic Theology*, 41, 42.

mind and of impersonal laws of logic he must and does reject that which is, objectively, the best of evidence for what revelation teaches, for example with respect to the existence of the transcendent God and his creation of the universe. Following Kant he simply asserts that evidence, to be intelligible, must not go beyond experience, and that to assert that a God exists who is not subject to the categories of space and time, is to assert that which is without meaning. If therefore we say to him that Revelation does not expect him to accept anything that is not credible according to his rules of evidence, this is, in effect, to ask him to reject the gospel.

It is accordingly necessary in our day, if we wish to bring out the truth for which Hodge is contending, to argue that only in theism can we find a true theory of reason and of evidence, and therefore true harmony between reason and revelation. To this must then be added that deep down in his heart even the natural man knows that theism is true and that he has concocted a false theory of reason and of evidence which he should reject.[52] . . .

But on the monistic assumption of the non-Christian it would be contradictory to believe in the resurrection of Jesus as the Son of God. The whole idea of God as transcendent is contradictory of the monism that underlies the unbeliever's views. Hence also he can allow no evidence to be genuine that pretends to prove the activity of the transcendent God of Christianity in human history.[53]

3.3 The Refutation of the Unbeliever's Presuppositions

A popular evangelical apologist once told me that he appreciated the way in which presuppositional apologetics diligently exposes the unspoken assumptions of the unbeliever, as well as its reminder to us all that defending the faith is ultimately a matter of entire worldviews encountering one another.[54] The problem, he said, is that we are then

---

52. This short paragraph contains two essential components of Van Til's presuppositional apologetic: (1) Only the Christian worldview can provide an intelligible theory of evidence and produce reasoning on the basis of it. (2) This worldview is known, but suppressed, by the unbeliever, who attempts (unsuccessfully) to formulate an alternative worldview to account for reasoning and evidence.
53. The unbeliever insists that God must be subject to the same conditions as man; so he is "monistic," rejecting any true transcendence for God. Thus, if a corpse is resuscitated, it could not be due to the transcendent action of God, but must simply be an unusual biological event awaiting explanation. *In advance* the unbeliever rules out transcendent explanations, for he is a naturalist in his espoused presuppositions.
54. Van Til observes: "Every non-Christian has an a priori. And the a priori of every non-Christian is different, radically different, from that of the Christian" (*Introduction to Sys-*

left in something of a "presuppositional standoff." Neither worldview (with its final standards) can disprove the other worldview (with its final standards). With that he also indicated how little perceptive reading he had done in Van Til's works.

Van Til's point is not simply that everybody has assumptions. There is little specific help for a successful program of apologetics in that observation (which nearly anybody can make). Indeed, left there, the insight might woefully suggest that nature and history could be just as well interpreted on a non-Christian basis as on a Christian one—a thought that was abhorrent to Van Til. Having referred to the blindness of the natural man, he wrote: "We dare not say that nature and history lend themselves quite as well to the non-Christian as to the Christian interpretation. . . . All looks yellow to the jaundiced eye. But for all this we would still maintain . . . that he who reads nature aright reads it as the Christian reads it." And then Van Til immediately added that the apologist must "press the objective validity of the Christian claim at every point."[55] The job of apologetics is to move beyond the recognition of the presuppositional nature of the disagreement between the believer and the unbeliever and show whose presuppositions are correct. Thus Van Til wrote: "We ought to find small comfort in the idea that others too, for example, non-Christian scientists, have to make assumptions. . . . We all make assumptions, but we alone do not make false assumptions. The fact that all make assumptions is in itself a mere psychological and formal matter. The question is as to who makes the right assumptions or presuppositions."[56]

In Van Til's outlook, it is not sufficient for the apologist merely to combat the claims that Christianity is not reasonable, merely to neutralize the criticisms that arise from science and history, and merely to exhibit and vindicate the Christian's ultimate assumptions. The best defense of the faith would require taking the offensive. Thus, the apologist "may be quite proficient in warding off the attack as far as details are concerned, but he will forever have to be afraid of new attacks as long as he has never removed the foundation from the enemy's position."[57] Apologetics requires us to *remove the foundation* of the unbeliever's argument. When the non-Christian criticizes the Christian worldview, the de-

---

tematic Theology, 115). An "a priori" is something that someone claims can be known as true (or false) "prior to"—or apart from, or without reference to—observation or experience.

55. *Common Grace*, 94–95.
56. Ibid., 50.
57. *Introduction to Systematic Theology*, 7.

fender of the faith should "ask his critics to show him the epistemological foundation on which they stand when they raise their objection. Can they, on their foundation, even have any such thing as an intelligible philosophy of fact?"[58] When the two presupposed worldviews are explicated and set over against each other, Van Til contended, "We as Christians alone have a position that is philosophically defensible."[59]

We can rehearse briefly why this is the case. The thing that is most characteristic of the philosophy of the unbeliever is its presumption of moral and intellectual autonomy from God. The non-Christian is not philosophically self-sufficient and cannot make sense out of experience apart from God, but he still desires (and claims) to be independent of his Creator. Van Til pointed out: "Man has declared his independence from God. We may therefore call him the *would-be autonomous man*. This *would-be* autonomous man assumes that he is ultimate and properly the final reference point in predication, i.e., reality must be interpreted by man in terms of man."[60] Van Til said of the natural man, who is dead in trespasses and sin, that he "wants to be something that he cannot be. He wants to be 'as God,' himself the judge of good and evil, himself the standard of truth. . . . The non-regenerate man takes for granted that the meaning of the space-time world is immanent[61] in itself, and that man is the ultimate interpreter of this world"[62]—instead of receiving God's revelation as the ultimate point of reference for his thinking, reasoning, and interpretation of the world or experience. While perhaps not explicitly declaring it to be so, the would-be autonomous man conducts his reasoning and living as though he were not a creature of God and under obligation to the word of His Creator. Van Til said: "I have frequently explained that by the term 'autonomous man' I mean the idea of a man who *virtually* denies his createdness. . . . With the entrance of sin man was no longer willing to obey the law of his maker. He became a covenant breaker. He sought to be a law unto himself, that is, he sought to be autonomous. . . . Men *virtually* assume or presuppose that they are non-created. . . . Is this too broad and sweeping a statement to make about all sinners? The daily newspaper is unintelligible on any other basis. There are

---

58. *Protestant Doctrine of Scripture*, 62.
59. *Common Grace*, 8.
60. *Protestant Doctrine of Scripture*, 125. Cf. the position espoused by the ancient Sophists that "man is the measure of all things."
61. Something is "immanent" if it is near at hand or inherent in human experience (as opposed to being "transcendent"—originating beyond or exceeding human experience).
62. *Introduction to Systematic Theology*, 26.

those who worship and serve the creature and there are those who worship and serve the Creator. This is the simple differentiation with which I am concerned. I try to call men back to the recognition of the fact that they are creatures of God by challenging their false assumption of their non-createdness, their autonomy or ultimacy."[63]

The Christian worldview maintains the indelibly revelational character of every fact of the created universe and the all-controlling providence of God in governing every event of history. The non-Christian's autonomous philosophy is not "neutral" on such crucial points, but obviously works on assumptions that are quite contrary to them. "Why live in a dream world, deceiving ourselves and making false pretense before the world? The non-Christian view of science: (a) presupposes the autonomy of man; (b) presupposes the non-created character, i.e., the chance-controlled character, of facts;[64] and (c) presupposes that laws rest not in God[65] but somewhere in the universe."[66] In defending the faith, the Christian cannot allow the suitability or legitimacy of using such autonomous presuppositions with respect to any aspect of knowledge, as though they can make sense of the natural world but must then be set aside when one thinks about the supernatural aspects of God's revelation in Scripture. As Van Til noted, "If we claim that we are independent in our knowledge, and think we can do without God at any point, we may as well assert that we are ready to do without him at every point."[67]

How can the apologist refute the presuppositions of autonomous reasoning? Van Til taught that it could certainly not be by adopting

63. *Defense of the Faith*, 247–48.
64. If the mind of God does not sovereignly determine the relationship of every event to every other event according to His wise plan, then the way things are in the world and what happens there are random and indeterminate. In that case, there is no intelligible basis for holding that any experience is like any other experience, there is nothing objectively common to the two of them, and there is no causal connection between any two events—and thus they are meaningless and indescribable.
65. If the laws of science, the laws of logic, and the laws of morality are not seen as expressions of the unchanging mind of God, then the notion of universal and absolute "laws" or the concept of order in the contingent, changing world of matter makes no sense whatsoever. In what way could anything truly be universal and law-abiding when every event is isolated and random? If universality is supposed to be objective, then there is no justification for holding to it on the basis of man's limited experience, whereas if universality is subjective (internal to man's thinking), then it is arbitrarily imposed by man's mind on his experience without warrant.
66. *Common Grace and the Gospel* (Philadelphia: Presbyterian and Reformed, 1972), 195.
67. *Introduction to Systematic Theology*, 199.

them as our own! "How can we call unbelieving man to repentance by belief in what Jesus Christ the Son of God and Son of man suffered on the cross of Calvary and through his resurrection from the dead, if we ourselves have first so largely emasculated our thinking by adopting the very humanism[68] from which we are seeking to save them?"[69] Van Til cautioned that the defender of the faith "all too frequently employs uncritically the conceptions of 'reason' and 'fact' as these are understood by those who make no profession of Christianity. The result is that there is no teaching of Christianity as a challenge to unbelief."[70]

Rather than accepting the deceptive invitation of the unbeliever to approach the apologetical dialogue in a neutral fashion—which in fact is to approach it in an autonomous fashion—the Christian must argue that the unbeliever's outlook renders such philosophically crucial and critical notions as fact, reason, experience, science, necessity, meaning, and morality unintelligible, due to the incoherence of the unbeliever's professed worldview. "If then a non-Christian should urge our pastor to take off his 'rose-colored glasses' and look at the cosmos 'with the naked eye of reason,' or should appeal to conscience to refute the interpretation of human experience as given in Scripture, our pastor knows that to do so would be to take the ground from under his own feet. Reason would then be truly 'naked' or formal; its assertions would be as meaningless as the gyrations of a propeller of an airplane engine without the airplane. If the facts could be said to exist at all, they would be utterly interchangeable with one another. . . . It is only in Reformed theology that we have a method of apologetics that meets the requirements of the hour. It alone challenges the natural man in the very citadel of his being. It alone is able to show how he who will not accept God's interpretation of life has no coherence in his experience."[71]

So in presuppositional apologetics we seek to "remove the enemy's foundation" by reducing his worldview to absurdity, thereby rendering the claims that constitute his case against the gospel unintelligible and demonstrating the necessity of the Christian worldview if we are to make sense of argumentation about, reasoning about, and interpretation of, any element of human experience. Without the as-

---

68. "Humanism" is a term susceptible to a variety of definitions. Van Til uses it to refer to the view that man is the highest value and authority in ethics and knowledge, which makes it functionally equivalent to "autonomy."
69. *Reformed Pastor and Modern Thought*, 222.
70. *Introduction to Systematic Theology*, 7.
71. *Reformed Pastor and Modern Thought*, 30–31.

sumption of Christian theism, there would be no basis for believing that there is order, connection, predictability, or necessity anywhere in human experience. Van Til put it this way: "The scientist who is a Christian therefore has the task of pointing out to his friend and colleague, who is not a Christian, that unless he is willing to stand upon the Christian story with respect to the world which has been redeemed through Christ, there is nothing but failure for him. Scientific effort is utterly unintelligible unless it is frankly based upon the order placed in the universe of created facts by Christ the Redeemer. . . . To those who are committed to the position which interprets man in terms of a supposedly intelligent procedure not based on biblical principles . . . the answer to this must be that the procedure of science and the procedure of philosophy cannot be shown to be intelligible unless they are carried on on the presupposition of the God who speaks to man in Scripture."[72]

Given the presuppositions of autonomous reasoning, it is not hard to see why this is the case. In the first place, the "knower" is no different than anything else in his environment; he is not distinguished by a "mind" that has the self-consciousness and freedom to search for the truth, evaluate options, and make intellectual commitments, for man has nothing more than a physical brain, which—like every other natural object—is determined by chemistry, biology, and physics. The "thinking" of this product of chance cannot warrant the notion of universals, necessity, causal connections, or moral prescriptions. In the second place, the "facts" that man encounters are likewise random and unconnected in any way that would justify categorization, laws, or predictability. The "standards" of logic or reasoning cannot be taken as objective or justified as to their universality—or even applicability to the world of contingent material facts, which is so different from them in character. The apologist must be honest in pointing out how philosophically pathetic this "total picture" really is, rather than flattering it by adopting such assumptions as a springboard for proving the completely *contrary* viewpoint of Christianity. Van Til delighted in describing the absurdity of what autonomous philosophy ends up with; for instance: "If you have a bottomless sea of Chance, and if you, as an individual, are but a bit of chance, by chance distinguished from other bits of chance, and if the law of contradiction has by chance grown within you, the imposition of this law on your environment is, granted it could take place, a perfectly futile activity."[73]

72. *Protestant Doctrine of Scripture*, 6, 39.
73. *Case for Calvinism*, 141–42.

The would-be autonomous man begins by taking for granted that he and God would have to be on a par when it comes to interpreting the world, knowing anything, or making moral judgments, but this "monistic assumption" (which denies the significance of the Creator/creature distinction for epistemology and ethics) results in the destruction of the intelligibility of reasoning, science, and ethics. Therefore, as Van Til maintained, Scripture does not grant that the unregenerate man has any right to judge anything whatsoever, consistently *"denying that man, when acting on his adopted monistic assumption, has any ability or right to judge of what is true or false, right or wrong."*[74]

How can any sense, then, be made of the claims and argumentation to which the unbeliever has appealed in his case against God or the gospel? His reasoning against Christianity could only be intelligible if what he were trying to disprove were instead true. This is the strongest form of argument in favor of the Christian worldview: it must be secretly presupposed even in the attempt to argue against it. The most compact and dramatic way of summarizing Van Til's apologetic that I have seen (or can imagine) is simply these three words: "Antitheism presupposes theism."[75] Van Til immediately explained: "One must stand upon the solid ground of theism to be an effective antitheist." This demonstrates the Christian worldview to be true from the impossibility of the contrary. Or, as Van Til succinctly expressed it elsewhere: "The only 'proof' of the Christian position is that unless its truth is presupposed there is no possibility of 'proving' anything at all."[76]

Does this mean that for Van Til unbelievers know nothing whatsoever and cannot make any useful contribution to culture? Not at all. It means that the would-be autonomous man can never give an intelligible, coherent, or meaningful *account* of how he is able to know anything or accomplish anything culturally. The unbeliever's failure is a rational or philosophical failure to make sense out of knowledge, morality, beauty, etc. But because the unbeliever is not actually what he thinks he is—and the world is not what he takes it to be—he can within God's world, as a creature made in God's image, make intellectual and cultural progress. Van Til held that "as for the cultural products of those who are not Christians, we would follow Calvin

---

74. *Introduction to Systematic Theology*, 29.
75. *A Survey of Christian Epistemology*, In Defense of the Faith, vol. 2 (Philadelphia: Presbyterian and Reformed, 1969), xii.
76. "My Credo," in *Jerusalem and Athens*, ed. E. R. Geehan (Philadelphia: Presbyterian and Reformed, 1971), 21.

in ascribing this to the common grace of God that works in them. True, the natural man is not blind in every sense. True, he is not as bad as he could be and as he will one day be. Modern science, so far as it has been carried on by those who are not Christians, has made marvelous discoveries of the true state of affairs in the phenomenal world. But the whole point . . . is that unless it were for the common grace of God there would be no discovery of any truth and no practice of any goodness among those who are not born again."[77] Even the achievements of the non-Christian contribute to the Christian's apologetic, therefore, since such things would be unintelligible apart from the explanation of them which the Christian worldview can offer.

This indicates that the unbeliever has actually been working and thinking in terms of two conflicting worldviews—one which he openly professes and which is autonomous in character, and another which he does not wish to acknowledge, but which makes it possible to make sense out of language, math, science, history, logic, ethics, and everything else in his experience and reasoning. Accordingly, Van Til taught that when we defend the faith, our appeal is made to the unbeliever's suppressed knowledge of God, not to the professed presupposition or point of reference that the unbeliever advocates. The apologist must recognize, as Scripture teaches, that the natural man sins "against his better knowledge." In his heart of hearts, he is aware that what the Christian proclaims and defends is the truth of God. Why is it that we as believers acknowledge this truth and submit to the authority of the Savior, while others resist admitting the truth and giving their lives over to Him? It cannot be because we are better or wiser than others, according to Van Til; rather, "we shall, of course, remember that all that we have received has been by grace . . . , [in which case we] ought to be the humblest of all men."[78] Van Til's approach to defending the faith was, therefore, an intriguing combination of the strongest and most aggressive attack upon the intellectual foundations of the unbeliever's reasoning and at the same time an exhibition and gracious acknowledgment of the believer's own grateful dependence upon God for everything he enjoys—from the hope of eternal life to the philosophical ability to make sense out of human experience. *"Christians can bear witness of this God only if they humbly but boldly make the claim that only on the*

77. *Protestant Doctrine of Scripture,* 43.
78. *Common Grace and the Gospel,* 129.

presupposition of the existence of this God and of the universe in all its aspects as the revelation of this God is there any footing and verge for the interpretive efforts of man."[79]

THE ONLY RATIONAL FAITH[80]

In all this we have already been dealing with philosophy as well as with science. No one can be a scientist in any intelligible way without at the same time having a philosophy of reality as a whole.[81] Christian apologists often speak of scientism as being objectionable but of science as being innocent with respect to the claims of Christianity. But surely this cannot be the case. Anyone who has a philosophy of nature that is not based upon the presupposition of what the Bible says about nature at the same time has a view of God that is hostile to that which Christianity proclaims.

Frequently Christian apologists plead with the scientists for a hearing by saying that they are merely offering something *additional* to what the scientist himself offers. Science, say these apologetes, gives us truth *as far as it goes,* but it does not include the spiritual *aspect* of reality in its vision.[82] So Christianity merely asks men to see that they must *add* the person-to-person or spiritual dimension to that of the impersonal and mechanical. After all, these apologetes say, science deals and can deal only with the quantitative aspects of reality. It is faith and faith only that has a vision for spiritual things.

And then it is added that science, too, needs to build itself on faith.[83] Did not Aristotle show how all first principles are adopted by faith? The fact that logic applies to reality is something that all men must *believe,* is it not? So then Christians are only doing what non-Christians do. Both put faith in something.

---

79. *Defense of the Faith,* 198. (A "verge" is a threshold, border, or outer boundary.)
80. An excerpt from *Protestant Doctrine of Scripture,* 51–52.
81. Van Til insisted that science does not operate apart from philosophical presuppositions. This is one of the reasons why it is naive for apologists to attempt to argue with unbelievers "simply on scientific grounds."
82. This outlook fails to challenge the intelligibility of science even when it is dealing with mundane (nonreligious) topics of interest and, therefore, grants the autonomy of the unregenerate man. If man is allowed to be an intellectual law unto himself, he can (with good reason) simply dismiss the "spiritual dimension" as unnecessary (or uninteresting) to him. Christian conversion is not simply adding something new to one's life; it is the complete reversal of one's life, indeed, the gracious reception of a new life from God. And reasoning is part of life.
83. Notice here how all claims about "faith" are taken as referring to the same kind of thing, namely, adopting an outlook that is mysterious, unreasoned, or unprovable. Different people do not necessarily mean the same thing by "faith" any more than they do by "love."

In this whole approach it is forgotten that the question is not one of having or not having faith but of having the *proper* faith. Of course all men start from faith. But the point is that the non-Christian starts from faith in man as not a creature of God and as not a sinner before God, while the Christian starts with his faith in Christ. It is the *object* of faith that gives meaning to the faith one professes. There are only two alternatives. The object of the non-Christian's faith is man as autonomous, while the object of the Christian's faith is God as revealed in Christ and in Christ as revealed in Scripture. "There is no person on earth," says Wolthuis, "who lives without faith of some sort" *(Op. cit.,* p. 48).[84] This is true, but it is not true that therefore the Christian's faith stands on a par with the non-Christian's faith as far as validity is concerned. It is the Christian's faith in God as revealed in Christ that is *true* faith. It *alone* gives an intelligible foundation to scientific procedure. The Christian and the non-Christian position are never to be thought of as intellectually on a par with one another. The Christian's faith is not a blind faith, as is the faith of the non-Christian. The non-Christian scientist may and does believe in the presence of order, but he has no warrant for doing so.[85] His assumed philosophy of chance points to the opposite. The Christian's position is not merely just as good as the non-Christian's position. Christianity is the *only* position that does not *per se* take away the very foundation for intelligible scientific and philosophical procedure. Christianity is the only rational faith!

CHANCE CANNOT PROVIDE A CRITERION[86]

How could unbelievers, unbelievers just because they have already rejected God's revelation in the universe about them and within them by a philoso-

84. Van Til's reference is to Enno Wolthuis, *Science, God and You* (Grand Rapids: Baker, 1965).
85. This is a key thrust in Van Til's challenge to unbelievers (as will be illustrated below in his "Why I Believe in God"). Various types of claims made by the unbeliever assume "order" in human experience (logical, causal, moral, etc.), but the unbeliever cannot warrant any claims about reality as a whole—or even about the whole of what is possible for human experience. Thus, whether such order exists (or is properly characterized in human thinking) is a question that exceeds the unbeliever's ability to answer with rational warrant. Van Til goes on to say that belief in order is not only unsupported by the unbeliever, but also contradicted by the assumption that there is nothing "behind" the events of history or "behind" the thinking of men that could provide such order; thus, everything is random ("chance").
86. An excerpt from *Protestant Doctrine of Scripture,* 61–62.

phy of chance and of human autonomy, ever concede that the claims of the New Testament writers with respect to their inspiration by God are true? The criterion they employ will compel them to deny it.[87] It is their criterion that must be shown to involve a metaphysics of chance. Then, if the Spirit opens their eyes, they will see the truth.

To be sure, if Warfield's appeal to the natural man were of an *ad hominem nature*, then it would be well.[88] Christ does ask the natural man to judge with respect to the truth of his claims. But then he asks them to admit that their own wisdom has been made foolishness with God. Only the Christian theory of knowledge, based as it is upon the absolute authority of the Word of God speaking in Scripture, makes communication of any sort possible anywhere between men. Without this presupposition men would have no integrated selves and the world would be a vacuum.[89] Without this presupposition of the Christian theory of being there would be no defensible position with respect to the relation of men and things. Neither men nor things would have discernible identity. There would be no science and no philosophy or theology, for there would be no order. History would be utterly unintelligible. Finally, without the presupposition of the Christian theory of morality there would be no intelligible view of the difference between good and evil. Why should any action be thought to be better than any other except on the supposition that it is or is not what God approves or disapproves? Except on the Christian basis there is no intelligible distinction between good and evil.

87. The standard or "criterion" that the unbeliever uses to judge what is true or not is a presupposition that rules out in advance the biblical claim to inspiration. Accordingly, the apologist must attack that presupposed criterion. He does so by examining the view of reality (the metaphysical assumptions) that is supposed to provide the context for this criterion's use (this epistemological commitment and practice).

88. In the context, Van Til has been criticizing Warfield's notion that the Christian faith does not rest upon the foundation of the doctrine of biblical inspiration. Rather, said Warfield, as apologists we simply appeal to the books of the Bible as historical records—and then challenge the natural man to explain the claim to inspiration within these records written by sober men. Evidentialist critics of Van Til often overlook the fact that Van Til sees some use in that kind of challenge. However, it is *ad hominem* (exposing the man's inconsistency of character or practice), rather than an independent proof of what is claimed.

89. Remember what was said above about principles of "order." Van Til perceived that the unbeliever's random (chance) view of the world, history, and man would make it unintelligible or unwarranted to use communication (ordered semantics and syntactics), to assume continuing personal identity and harmony between the various aspects of man's personality, or to think of the world as a "cosmos" (ordered things and events).

PRECLUDING CHRISTIANITY IS TO PRECLUDE JUSTIFIABLE ORDER[90]

Man was told, in effect [when God gave the cultural mandate to Adam], to be *religiously* engaged when he was making his experimentation in the laboratory as well as when he is singing psalms in the church on Sunday. If then science deals with the laws of nature it *does* give an interpretation of the facts. If the scientist does not see the laws of nature as manifesting the Creator redeemer, he is guilty before God.

As a sinner man seeks to suppress the revelation of God that speaks to him through the created world. He holds under the truth in unrighteousness. And when modern science is trying to understand nature without placing it, from the outset, in relation to its creator and redeemer, it is engaged in the sinful enterprise of repression. . . .

Modern science as a whole assumes that what Christianity teaches with respect to nature *cannot* be true. Experimentation, we are told, needs or presupposes the idea of an open universe.[91] Immanuel Kant's position with respect to the idea of pure contingency underlies the method of the average non-Christian scientist today. The ideas of creation and of providence as controlling all that comes to pass are therefore *assumed* to be intolerable. The idea of experiment, we are told, assumes that at the beginning of one's research one hypothesis is as good as another. If the Christian therefore wants to get a hearing for his ideas of creation and providence he must present them as one hypothesis among many.[92] But how can the Christian do this without betraying his own most basic conviction? His own conviction is to the effect that the possibility of successful scientific procedure *depends* upon the idea that God through Christ controls whatsoever comes to pass. Nature is orderly because it is the order of God[93] that appears in it. He who does not hold this to be true has not seen nature for what it is. "Nature" apart from God is, for the Christian, a meaningless term.[94] The non-Christian must tell us how he will make it meaningful apart from God in Christ.

90. An excerpt from *Protestant Doctrine of Scripture*, 48–49.
91. That is, the universe must be looked upon in such a way as not to preclude any event or hypothesis as an explanation of events. No restrictions are imposed in advance.
92. That is, the unbeliever insists in advance that such beliefs may not be warranted by divine authority, but must be placed on the same level—and treated in the same way—as any other hypothesis that autonomous man might test for acceptability or truth.
93. The "order of God," as opposed to some imaginary order inherent in the world itself, or in the properties of matter, or in the principles of "nature," etc.
94. The very idea that the spatio-temporal realm or the realm of man's temporal ex-

Again, modern science holds not only to the idea of pure contingency or indeterminacy, but also to that of pure determinism.[95] Modern science insists that the order which it discovers cannot be that of a God who wills it to be a certain way. The order of nature, we are told, is what it is because of an impersonal unchangeable regularity (Cf. Morris Cohen, *Reason and Nature*).

APPEALING TO THE UNBELIEVER'S BETTER KNOWLEDGE[96]

The reason why these differences [between the believer and the unbeliever with respect to the foundation and application of the concepts of fact, logic, possibility, etc.] do not appear on the surface is that, as a matter of fact, all men are human beings who were created in the image of God. Even the non-regenerate therefore have in their sense of deity, though repressed by them, some remnant of the knowledge of God and consequently of the true source and meaning of possibility and probability. It is to this remnant of a truly theistic interpretation of experience that Hodge[97] really appeals when he speaks of the laws of belief that God has implanted in human nature. It is, of course, not only quite legitimate, but absolutely imperative to appeal to the "common consciousness" of men in this sense. But in order really to appeal to this "common consciousness" that is repressed by the sinner we must refuse to speak of a "common consciousness" that is not suppressed by the sinner.[98]

---

perience constitutes a "nature" assumes that it can be described and accounted for according to some unifying principles. The order that is found in the physical world may be attributed to the particles of which it consists (atomism), or laws governing events (Stoicism), or an internal dialectic (Hegel), or whatever. But all such theories of "nature" assume something—a universal order of some kind—that cannot be justified by the worldviews in which they appear. Thus, when unbelievers speak of "nature," they are either personifying disconnected events or, given their own presuppositions, speaking nonsense (using assumptions without referent or justification).

95. Van Til found in non-Christian attempts to formulate a worldview a contradictory commitment to the view that "anything can happen" (the open universe of indeterminism) right alongside the view that everything happens according to the strict laws of scientific explanation (the natural world of determinism, to which even man's psyche and behavior must be subject). This kind of "dialectical" tension renders the unbeliever's worldview incoherent. Cf. Van Til's discussion elsewhere of a rational-irrational dialectic in unbelieving worldviews.

96. An excerpt from *Introduction to Systematic Theology*, 38.

97. In the context, Van Til has been discussing the claim of Charles Hodge (in his *Systematic Theology* [New York: Charles Scribner's Sons, 1872], 1:51ff.) that for Christians "reason" has the prerogative of determining whether a thing is possible or not (the *"judicium contradictionis"*).

98. To put it another way, the only proper appeal to what the believer and the unbeliever hold in common regarding reasoning is one which realizes that the un-

The non-regenerate man seeks by all means to "keep under" this remnant of a true theistic interpretation that lingers in his mind. His real interpretative principle, now that he is a covenant-breaker, is that of himself as ultimate and of impersonal laws as ultimate. It is he himself as ultimate, by means of laws of logic that operate independently of God, who determines what is possible and probable. To the extent, then, that he proceeds self-consciously from his own principle of interpretation, he holds the very existence of God, and of the creation of the universe, to be not merely improbable, but impossible.[99] In doing so he sins, to be sure, against his better knowledge. He sins against that which is hidden deep down in his own consciousness. And it is well that we should appeal to this fact. But in order to appeal to this fact we must use all caution not to obscure this fact. And obscure it we do if we speak of the "common consciousness" of man without distinguishing clearly between what is hidden deep down in the mind of natural man as the revelation and knowledge of God within him and what, in rejecting God, he has virtually adopted as being his final interpretative principle.

3.4 An Example of Presuppositional Proof of Christianity

The presuppositional approach to defending the faith which is summarized above was once illustrated by Van Til in a short pamphlet aimed at a popular audience and entitled *Why I Believe in God*.[100] It was not intended to be philosophically complex in content or overly scholarly in its style. It is conversational and easy to follow—and devastating in its power (once one understands the nature of the presuppositional defense pursued there). It offers a profound and readable illustration of the "transcendental" argument for the truth of the Christian worldview, but without resorting to calling it that or using other philosophical parlance.

Later in his life, Van Til wrote a booklet that indicates the chief purpose for which he had written the various books, syllabi, and pamphlets that were published during his long career. In it, the very

---

believer is suppressing it in unrighteousness, rather than openly and correctly incorporating it in his espoused philosophy.

99. CVT: See e.g., E. Frank, *Philosophical Understanding and Religious Knowledge*.

100. It was originally published by the Orthodox Presbyterian Church's Committee on Christian Education (Tracts for Today, no. 9) in 1948. Subsequently it was reprinted as a promotional brochure by Westminster Theological Seminary (and is presently distributed by P&R Publishing). Although no indication is made of the fact, there are enough stylistic alterations or deletions in Westminster's publication of the pamphlet to qualify as a revised edition.

first one of his publications that he chose to annotate was *Why I Believe in God*. About it he said: "I was brought up on the Bible as the Word of God. Can I, now that I have been to school, still believe in the God of the Bible? Well, can I still believe in the sun that shone on me when I walked as a boy in wooden shoes in Groningen? I could believe in nothing else if I did not, as back of everything, believe in *this* God. Can I see the beams underneath the floor on which I walk? I must assume or presuppose that the beams are underneath. Unless the beams were underneath, I could not walk on the floor."[101] This was Van Til's homey way of expressing the penetrating truth declared by the psalmist David: "In thy light shall we see light" (Ps. 36:9). Unbelievers cannot bring together both order (unity) and change (diversity) in their reasoning or in their view of reality. They thereby make nonsense of both, and all arguments against God are intellectually self-defeating. If you cannot believe in God, then you cannot logically believe in anything else. This is the subtle message that he drove home in this imaginary dialogue with an unbeliever.

WHY I BELIEVE IN GOD[102]

You have noticed, haven't you, that in recent times certain scientists like Dr. James Jeans and Sir Arthur Eddington, as well as some outstanding philosophers like Dr. C. E. M. Joad, have had a good deal to say about religion and God? Scientists Jeans and Eddington are ready to admit that there may be something to the claims of men who say they have had an experience of God, while Philosopher Joad says that the "obtrusiveness of evil" has virtually compelled him to look into the argument for God's existence afresh. Much like modernist theologian Dr. Reinhold Niebuhr who talks about original sin, Philosopher Joad speaks about evil as being ineradicable from the human mind.

Then, too, you have on occasion asked yourself whether death ends all. You have recalled, perhaps, how Socrates the great Greek philosopher, struggled with that problem the day before he drank the hemlock cup. Is there anything at all, you ask yourself, to the idea of a judgment after death? Am I quite sure, you say, that there is not? How do I know that there is no God?

In short, as a person of intelligence, having a sense of responsibility, you have from time to time asked yourself some questions about the foundation

---

101. *Toward a Reformed Apologetics* (Philadelphia: privately printed, 1972), 1–2.
102. What follows is the entire content of the pamphlet by the same name, following the text of the original publication.

of your thought and action.[103] You have looked into, or at least been concerned about, what the philosophers call your theory of reality. So when I suggest that you spend a Sunday afternoon with me discussing my reasons for believing in God, I have the feeling that you are basically interested in what I am proposing for discussion.

To make our conversation more interesting, let's start by comparing notes on our past. That will fit in well with our plan, for the debate concerning heredity and environment is prominent in our day. Perhaps you think that the only real reason I have for believing in God is the fact that I was taught to do so in my early days. Of course I don't think that is really so. I don't deny that I was taught to believe in God when I was a child, but I do affirm that since I have grown up I have heard a pretty full statement of the argument against belief in God. And it is after having heard that argument that I am more than ever ready to believe in God. Now, in fact, I feel that the whole of history and civilization would be unintelligible to me if it were not for my belief in God. So true is this, that I propose to argue that unless God is back of everything, you cannot find meaning in anything.[104] I cannot even argue for belief in Him, without already having taken Him for granted. And similarly I contend that you cannot argue against belief in Him unless you also first take Him for granted.[105] Arguing about God's existence, I hold, is like arguing about air. You may affirm that air exists, and I that it does not. But as we debate the point, we are both breathing air all the time. Or to use another illustration, God is like the emplacement on which must stand the very guns that are supposed to shoot Him out of existence. However if, after hearing my story briefly, you still think it is all a matter of heredity and environment, I shall not disagree too violently. My whole point will be that there is perfect harmony between my belief as a child and my belief as a man, simply because God is Himself the environment by which my early life was directed and my later life made intelligible to myself.[106]

103. As the name would indicate, "presuppositional" apologetics directs the dialogue with the unbeliever into a consideration of the issue of foundational principles in thinking and behavior.
104. Already, at this early stage, Van Til indicates to his hypothetical and unbelieving opponent just what his overall argument will be: human experience of anything whatsoever (in this case, of history and civilization) would be unintelligible or meaningless apart from a foundational belief in the Christian God.
105. The "transcendental" necessity of belief in God is indicated in the claim that even arguments against Him already presuppose Him for the intelligibility of argumentation itself.
106. Here Van Til held that the charge of "environmental" influences on the early childhood faith of a Christian is—within the Christian worldview—not a terribly damaging thing, even if true, because God's all-controlling sovereignty is the

THE "ACCIDENT OF BIRTH"

We are frequently told that much in our life depends on "the accident of birth." In ancient time some men were said to spring full-grown from the foreheads of the gods. That, at any rate, is not true today. Yet I understand the next best thing happened to you. You were born, I am told, in Washington, D. C., under the shadow of the White House. Well, I was born in a little thatched roof house with a cow barn attached, in Holland. You wore "silver slippers" and I wore wooden shoes.

Is this really important for our purpose? Not particularly, but it is important that neither of us was born in Guadalcanal or Timbuktu. Both of us, I mean, were born in the midst and under the influence of "Christian civilization." We shall limit our discussion, then, to the "God of Christianity." I believe, while you do not believe or are not sure that you do believe, in this particular kind of God. That will give point to our discussion. For surely there is no sense in talking about the existence of God, without knowing what kind of God it is who may or may not exist.

So much then we have gained. We at least know in general what sort of God we are going to make the subject for our conversation.[107] If now we can come to a similar preliminary agreement as to the standard or test by which to prove or disprove God's existence, we can proceed. You, of course, do not expect me to bring God into the room here so that you may see Him. If I were able to do that, He would not be the God of Christianity. All that you expect me to do is to make it reasonable for you to believe in God. And I should like to respond quickly by saying that that is just what I am trying to do. But a moment's thought makes me hesitate. If you really do not believe in God, then you naturally do not believe that you are his creature. I, on the other hand, who do believe in God also believe, naturally, that whatever you yourself may think, you really are his creature. And surely it is reasonable for God's creature to believe in God. So I can only undertake to show that, even if it does not appear reasonable *to* you, it is reasonable *for* you, to believe in God.[108]

---

broader context of such influences. Upon later reflection, the young believer will realize that God's all-controlling sovereignty is likewise the necessary context for the intelligibility of anything he thinks about.

107. The apologetical debate must focus on the concrete nature of God as revealed in the Scriptures, rather than trying to do justice to some vague and generalized concept of a deity that fits into a wide range of religions. There is, in fact, no such concept that is universally adequate or acceptable, and, therefore, the pretense that the apologist intends to defend such a notion is simply hidden prejudice and arbitrariness.

108. Presuppositionalism recognizes that the atheist (and the agnostic) have one conception of what amounts to a "reasonable" belief, while the Christian theist has

I see you are getting excited. You feel a little like a man who is about to undergo a major operation. You realize that if you are to change your belief about God, you will also have to change your belief about yourself.[109] And you are not quite ready for that. Well, you may leave if you desire. I certainly do not wish to be impolite. I only thought that as an intelligent person you would be willing to hear the "other side" of the question. And after all I am not asking you to agree with what I say. We have not really agreed on what we mean by God more than in a general and formal way. So also we need not at this point agree on the standard or test in more than a general or formal way. You might follow my argument, just for argument's sake.[110]

CHILDHOOD

To go on, then, I can recall playing as a child in a sandbox built into a corner of the hay-barn. From the hay-barn I would go through the cow-barn to the house. Built into the hay-barn too, but with doors opening into the cow-barn, was a bed for the working-man. How badly I wanted permission to sleep in that bed for a night! Permission was finally given. Freud was still utterly unknown to me, but I had heard about ghosts and "forerunners of death." That night I heard the cows jingle their chains. I knew there were cows and that they did a lot of jingling with their chains, but after a while I was not quite

---

another conception of reasonableness. Yet it should be clear even to the atheist that if the Christian God exists, it is "reasonable" to believe in Him. Thus, Van Til wrote that it may not appear reasonable to the unbeliever to believe in God, even though (given the Christian worldview) it would still be reasonable for the unbeliever to believe. The debate ultimately involves the proper standard of reasonableness.

109. This point is crucial. When a presupposition as significant as one's belief about God changes, there will of necessity be monumental changes throughout the belief structure of an individual. Given intellectual laziness and personal prejudices, the unbeliever will resist altering his professed belief about God. The presuppositional apologist will want to keep the unbeliever apprised of this natural inclination against changing his mind, especially since such a change of belief will extensively affect his own self-conception. In this kind of situation, where personal matters are at stake, it is entirely unrealistic for the unbeliever to pretend to be psychologically neutral or indifferent to the outcome of the dialogue.

110. Because the unbeliever is made in God's image and has a knowledge of God suppressed deep within himself (although admitting none of this, of course), he can "follow the argument" that the Christian presents to him. However, if the unbeliever fully and consistently reasoned in terms of his espoused presuppositions, he could not understand the Christian's claims and arguments—indeed, he could not understand anything at all. In order to display this truth to the unbeliever, the presuppositionalist is willing to "think things through" in terms of what the unbeliever claims are his basic assumptions, and then, for the sake of comparison, he invites the unbeliever to "think things through" in terms of the Christian's basic assumptions.

certain that it was only the cows that made all the noises I heard. Wasn't there someone walking down the aisle back of the cows, and wasn't he approaching my bed? Already I had been taught to say my evening prayers. Some of the words of that prayer were to this effect: "Lord, convert me, that I may be converted." Unmindful of the paradox, I prayed that prayer that night as I had never prayed before.

I do not recall speaking either to my father or mother about my distress. They would have been unable to provide the modern remedy. *Psychology* did not come to their library table—not even *The Ladies Home Journal!* Yet I know what they would have said. Of course there were no ghosts, and certainly I should not be afraid anyway, since with body and soul I belonged to my Saviour who died for me on the Cross and rose again that His people might be saved from hell and go to heaven! I should pray earnestly and often that the Holy Spirit might give me a new heart so that I might truly love God instead of sin and myself.

How do I know that this is the sort of thing they would have told me? Well, that was the sort of thing they spoke about from time to time. Or rather, that was the sort of thing that constituted the atmosphere of our daily life. Ours was not in any sense a pietistic family. There were not any great emotional outbursts on any occasion that I recall. There was much ado about making hay in the summer and about caring for the cows and sheep in the winter, but round about it all there was a deep conditioning atmosphere. Though there were no tropical showers of revivals, the relative humidity was always very high. At every meal the whole family was present. There was a closing as well as an opening prayer, and a chapter of the Bible was read each time. The Bible was read through from Genesis to Revelation. At breakfast or at dinner, as the case might be, we would hear of the New Testament, or of "the children of Gad after their families, of Zephon and Haggi and Shuni and Ozni, of Eri and Areli." I do not claim that I always fully understood the meaning of it all. Yet of the total effect there can be no doubt. The Bible became for me, in all its parts, in every syllable, the very Word of God. I learned that I must believe the Scripture story, and that "faith" was a gift of God. What had happened in the past, and particularly what had happened in the past in Palestine, was of the greatest moment to me. In short, I was brought up in what Dr. Joad would call "topographical and temporal parochialism." I was "conditioned" in the most thorough fashion. I could not *help believing* in God—in the God of Christianity—in the God of the whole Bible![111]

111. The reader can observe here how presuppositional apologetics will attempt (and not be shy) to place the argument about God and the Bible into a larger and personal context. Matters of testimony cannot take the place of reasoning

Living next to the Library of Congress, you were not so restricted. Your parents were very much enlightened in their religious views. They read to you from some *Bible of the World* instead of from the Bible of Palestine. No, indeed, you correct me, they did no such thing. They did not want to trouble you about religious matters in your early days. They sought to cultivate the "open mind" in their children.

Shall we say then that in my early life I was conditioned to believe in God, while you were left free to develop your own judgment as you pleased? But that will hardly do. You know as well as I that every child is conditioned by its environment. You were as thoroughly conditioned *not* to believe in God as I was to believe in God.[112] So let us not call each other names. If you want to say that belief was poured down *my* throat, I shall retort by saying that unbelief was poured down *your* throat. That will get us set for our argument.

EARLY SCHOOLING

To the argument we must now shortly come. Just another word, however, about my schooling. That will bring all the factors into the picture.

I was not quite five when somebody—fortunately I cannot recall who—took me to school. On the first day I was vaccinated and it hurt. I can still feel it. I had already been to church. I recall that definitely because I would sometimes wear my nicely polished leather shoes. A formula was read over me at my baptism which solemnly asserted that I had been conceived and born in sin, the idea being that my parents, like all men, had inherited sin from Adam, the first man and the representative of the human race. The formula further asserted that though thus conditioned by inescapable sin I was, as a child of the covenant, redeemed in Christ. And at the ceremony my parents solemnly promised that as soon as I should be able to understand they would instruct me in all these matters by all the means at their disposal.

It was in pursuance of this vow that they sent me to a Christian grade school. In it I learned that my being saved from sin and my belonging to God

---

and argument, but they do strengthen the persuasive effect of the argument—especially if that argument aims to present God as the conditioning context for the intelligibility of everything in life and experience.

112. This is a distinctive of Van Til's presuppositional apologetic approach. The unbeliever is not allowed to proceed on the false (and vain) assumption of his intellectual neutrality, which, if true, would (he thinks) put him in a superior position to judge the rationality of faith. The unbeliever will not be "set for our argument," as Van Til goes on to say, until he realizes that the apologetical conflict is between two "prejudiced" parties (i.e., parties with their personal background and influences, but especially with their respective philosophical commitments).

made a difference for all that I knew or did. I saw the power of God in nature and His providence in the course of history. That gave the proper setting for my salvation, which I had in Christ. In short, the whole wide world that gradually opened up for me through my schooling was regarded as operating in its every aspect under the direction of the all-powerful and all-wise God whose child I was through Christ. I was to learn to think God's thoughts after him in every field of endeavour.[113]

Naturally there were fights on the "campus" of the school and I was engaged in some—though not in all—of them. Wooden shoes were wonderful weapons of war. Yet we were strictly forbidden to use them, even for defensive purposes. There were always lectures both by teachers and by parents on sin and evil in connection with our martial exploits. This was especially the case when a regiment of us went out to do battle with the pupils of the public school. The children of the public school did not like us. They had an extensive vocabulary of vituperation. Who did we think we were anyway? We were goody goodies—too good to go to the public school! "There! Take that and like it!" We replied in kind. Meanwhile our sense of distinction grew by leaps and bounds. We were told in the evening that we must learn to bear with patience the ridicule of the "world." Had not the world hated the church, since Cain's time?

How different your early schooling was! You went to a "neutral" school. As your parents had done at home, so your teachers now did at school. They taught you to be "open-minded." God was not brought into connection with your study of nature or of history. You were trained without bias all along the line.

Of course, you know better now. You realize that all that was purely imaginary. To be "without bias" is only to have a particular *kind* of bias. The idea of "neutrality" is simply a colorless suit that covers a negative attitude toward God. At least it ought to be plain that he who is not *for* the God of Christianity is *against* Him. You see, the God of Christianity makes such prodigious claims. He says the whole world belongs to Him, and that you are His creature, and as such are to own up to that fact by honoring Him whether you eat or drink or do anything else. God says that you live, as it were, on His estate. And His estate has large ownership signs placed everywhere, so that he who goes by even at seventy miles an hour cannot but read them. Every fact

113. Given the teaching of the Bible about God, man, and salvation, the believer is expected to use God's revelation as his basic standard and guide for interpreting every aspect of human experience. Christianity is not "added on" to his independent study of human life or the world, but is rather the "reference point" for understanding anything about human life or the world.

in this world, the God of the Bible claims, has His stamp indelibly engraved upon it. How then could you be neutral with respect to such a God?[114]

Do you walk about leisurely on a Fourth of July in Washington wondering whether the Lincoln Memorial belongs to anyone? Do you look at "Old Glory" waving from a high flagpole and wonder whether she stands for anything? Does she require anything of you, born an American citizen as you are? You would deserve to suffer the fate of the "man without a country" if as an American you were neutral to America. Well, in a much deeper sense you deserve to live forever without God if you do not own and glorify Him as your Creator. You dare not manipulate God's world and least of all yourself as His image-bearer, for your own final purposes. When Eve became neutral as between God and the Devil, weighing the contentions of each as though they were inherently on the face of them of equal value, she was in reality already on the side of the Devil!

There you go again getting excited once more. Sit down and calm yourself. You are open-minded and neutral, are you not? And you have learned to think that any hypothesis has, as a theory of life, an equal right to be heard with any other, have you not? After all I am only asking you to see what is involved in the Christian conception of God. If the God of Christianity exists, the evidence for His existence is abundant and plain so that it is *both* unscientific and sinful not to believe in Him.[115]

When Dr. Joad, for example, says: "The evidence for God is far from plain," on the ground that if it were plain everybody would believe in Him, he is begging the question. If the God of Christianity does exist, the evidence for Him *must* be plain. And the reason, therefore, why "everybody" does not believe in Him must be that "everybody" is blinded by sin.[116] Everybody wears

114. What need to be underlined here are the "prodigious claims" made by the particular kind of God who is revealed in nature and Scripture. Not every conception of God advanced by men in religious debates would exclude the possibility of neutrality, but the kind of God who created and controls all things with the effect of making Himself inescapably known to man as a rational creature either is or is not just that clearly revealed in all things. To say that He is not (in which case a neutral mind-set is appropriate in seeking evidence for or against God) is already to maintain that this Christian conception of God as found in the Bible is false.

115. Presuppositional apologetics maintains that the unbeliever's outlook is not simply immoral (being unfaithful to, and rebellious against, God), but also intellectually indefensible (unscientific or irrational). Sometimes those who have little familiarity with this approach to defending the faith mistakenly reduce the presuppositional challenge to the first kind of remark.

116. Here is a good example of the determinative influence of one's presuppositions on the inferences that one will draw. Both the believer and the unbeliever recognize that not all men claim to believe in the Christian God. From this fact,

colored glasses. You have heard the story of the valley of the blind. A young man who was out hunting fell over a precipice into the valley of the blind. There was no escape. The blind men did not understand him when he spoke of seeing the sun and the colors of the rainbow, but a fine young lady did understand him when he spoke the language of love. The father of the girl would not consent to the marriage of his daughter to a lunatic who spoke so often of things that did not exist. But the great psychologists of the blind men's university offered to cure him of his lunacy by sewing up his eyelids. Then, they assured him, he would be normal like "everybody" else.[117] But the simple seer went on protesting that he did see the sun.

So, as we have our tea, I propose not only to operate on your heart so as to change your will, but also on your eyes so as to change your outlook. But wait a minute. No, I do not propose to operate at all. I myself cannot do anything of the sort. I am just mildly suggesting that you are perhaps dead, and perhaps blind, leaving you to think the matter over for yourself. If an operation is to be performed it must be performed by God Himself.

LATER SCHOOLING

Meanwhile let us finish our story. At ten I came to this country and after some years decided to study for the ministry. This involved preliminary training at a Christian preparatory school and college. All my teachers were pledged to teach their subjects from the Christian point of view. Imagine teaching not only religion but algebra from the Christian point of view! But it was done. We were told that all facts in all their relations, numerical as well as others, are what they are because of God's all comprehensive plan with respect to them.[118] Thus the very definitions of things would not merely be incomplete

---

the non-Christian infers that not all men believe, while from the same fact the Christian infers that this belief is being suppressed and rationalized away by those who profess atheism. It all depends upon the worldview in terms of which the facts are recognized and interpreted. I once taught a seminar on a well-known philosophical polemic against the existence of God: Michael Martin's *Atheism: A Philosophical Justification* (Philadelphia: Temple University Press, 1990). The very first sentence of the book (in the introduction) states: "Nonbelief in the existence of God is a worldwide phenomenon." To the surprise of the students, I stopped to observe that with this declaration the author had already begged the crucial question—in his very first utterance on the subject. Given the Christian conception of God, there are no genuine atheists.

117. Because of their conflicting fundamental presuppositions, the believer and the unbeliever do not in principle even agree on what is "normal" in human reasoning and experience.

118. Subtly tucked away in this apparently autobiographical account is the major philosophical point that Van Til will later exploit: when education and reason-

but basically wrong if God were left out of the picture. Were we not informed about the views of others? Did we not hear about evolution and about Immanuel Kant, the great modern philosopher who had conclusively shown that all the arguments for the existence of God were invalid? Oh, yes, we heard about all these things, but there were refutations given and these refutations seemed adequate to meet the case.[119]

In the seminaries I attended, namely Calvin, and Princeton before its reorganization along semi-modernist lines in 1929, the situation was much the same. So for instance Dr. Robert Dick Wilson used to tell us, and, as far as we could understand the languages, show us from the documents, that the "higher critics" had done nothing that should rightfully damage our child-like faith in the Old Testament as the Word of God. Similarly Dr. J. Gresham Machen and others made good their claim that New Testament Christianity is intellectually defensible and that the Bible is right in its claims. You may judge of their arguments by reading them for yourself. In short, I heard the story of historic Christianity and the doctrine of God on which it is built over and over from every angle by those who believed it and were best able to interpret its meaning.

The telling of this story has helped, I trust, to make the basic question simple and plain. You know pretty clearly now what sort of God it is of which I am speaking to you.[120] If my God exists it was He who was back of my parents and teachers. It was He who conditioned all that conditioned me in my early life. But then it was He also who conditioned everything that conditioned you in your early life. God, the God of Christianity, is the *All-Conditioner!*

---

ing take place within the context of the Christian worldview, there is no problem explaining the universality and necessity of the laws of mathematics, etc.

119. The Christian apologist is not to be an obscurantist who does not listen to the objections and arguments of those who oppose Christianity, dismissing them with a cavalier claim that unbelievers have their own presuppositions and can therefore be ignored. Critics of presuppositionalism who have suggested that it adopts such an attitude could not be further from the truth. Unbelievers who portray Christians as "only knowing one side of the story" are likewise mistaken in their generalizations. The opposite is for the most part usually the case. Unbelievers who study in unbelieving institutions hardly ever give serious attention to (or are tested on) the arguments of Christian scholars. Whose education and research is then lopsided?

120. In comparing the worldviews of the Christian and the non-Christian, the apologist must make "the basic question" very clear: what is the nature of the God whose existence and revelation the Christian defends? This kind of God is the necessary precondition for the meaningfulness of believing anything whatsoever—for believing that He exists, as well as for believing that He does not! Belief is meaningless without God as your presupposition. This is the argument to which Van Til will eventually return.

As the All-Conditioner, God is the *All-Conscious* One. A God who is to control all things must control them "by the counsel of His will." If He did not do this, He would Himself be conditioned. So then I hold that my belief in Him and your disbelief in Him are alike meaningless except for Him.

OBJECTIONS RAISED

By this time you are probably wondering whether I have really ever heard the objections which are raised against belief in such a God. Well, I think I have. I heard them from my teachers who sought to answer them. I also heard them from teachers who believed they could not be answered. While a student at Princeton Seminary I attended summer courses in the Chicago Divinity School. Naturally I heard the modern or liberal view of Scripture set forth fully there. And after graduation from the seminary I spent two years at Princeton University for graduate work in philosophy. There the theories of modern philosophy were both expounded and defended by very able men. In short I was presented with as full a statement of the reasons for disbelief as I had been with the reasons for belief. I heard both sides fully from those who believed what they taught. You have compelled me to say this by the look on your face. Your very gestures suggest that you cannot understand how any one acquainted with the facts and arguments presented by modern science and philosophy can believe in a God who really created the world, who really directs all things in the world by a plan to the ends He has in view for them. Well, I am only one of many who hold to the old faith in full view of what is said by modern science, modern philosophy, and modern Biblical criticism.

Obviously I cannot enter into a discussion of all the facts and all the reasons urged against belief in God. There are those who have made the Old Testament, as there are those who have made the New Testament, their life-long study. It is their works you must read for a detailed refutation of points of Biblical criticism. Others have specialized in physics and biology. To them I must refer you for a discussion of the many points connected with such matters as evolution.[121] But there is something that underlies all these discussions. And it is with that something that I now wish to deal.

You may think I have exposed myself terribly. Instead of talking about God as something vague and indefinite, after the fashion of the modernist, the

---

121. Van Til explicitly endorses detailed work in "evidences" here, favorably pointing out to the unbeliever that Christians who have done advanced historical and scientific research can adequately deal with the "factual" criticisms brought against Christianity. Nevertheless, as he goes on to say, the "underlying" issue that controls debates over factual matters cannot be ignored by the apologist. The deeper question has to do with one's presuppositions or worldview.

Barthians, and the mystic, a god so empty of content and remote from experience as to make no demands upon men, I have loaded down the idea of God with "antiquated" science and "contradictory" logic. It seems as though I have heaped insult upon injury by presenting the most objectionable sort of God I could find. It ought to be very easy for you to prick my bubble. I see you are ready to read over my head bushels of facts taken from the standard college texts on physics, biology, anthropology, and psychology, or to crush me with your sixty-ton tanks taken from Kant's famous book, *The Critique of Pure Reason*. But I have been under these hot showers now a good many times. Before you take the trouble to open the faucet again there is a preliminary point I want to bring up. I have already referred to it when we were discussing the matter of test or standard.

The point is this. Not believing in God, we have seen, you do not think yourself to be God's creature. And not believing in God you do not think the universe has been created by God. That is to say, you think of yourself and the world as just being there. Now if you actually are God's creature, then your present attitude is very unfair to Him. In that case it is even an insult to Him. And having insulted God, His displeasure rests upon you. God and you are not on "speaking terms." And you have very good reasons for trying to prove that He does not exist. If He does exist, He will punish you for your disregard of Him. You are therefore wearing colored glasses. And this determines everything you say about the facts and reasons for not believing in Him. You have as it were entered upon God's estate and have had your picnics and hunting parties there without asking His permission. You have taken the grapes of God's vineyard without paying Him any rent and you have insulted His representatives who asked you for it.[122]

I must make an apology to you at this point. We who believe in God have not always made this position plain. Often enough we have talked with you about facts and sound reasons as though we agreed with you on what these really are. In our arguments for the existence of God we have frequently assumed that you and we together have an area of knowledge on which we agree. But we really do not grant that you see any fact in any dimension of life truly. We really think you have colored glasses on your nose when you talk about chickens and cows, as well as when you talk about the life here-

122. Once again Van Til explains why the unbeliever cannot credibly claim to be intellectually and psychologically neutral in his opinions and in his reasoning about God. Even the unbeliever should be able to follow this "for argument's sake." Requisite self-examination would lead the unbeliever to question his own reliability and "objectivity" when it comes to reasoning about a God with whom, if He exists, the unbeliever is not at all "on speaking terms."

after. We should have told you this more plainly than we did. But we were really a little ashamed of what would appear to you as a very odd or extreme position. We were so anxious not to offend you that we offended our own God.[123] But we dare no longer present our God to you as smaller or less exacting than He really is. He wants to be presented as the All-Conditioner, as the emplacement on which even those who deny Him must stand.[124]

Now in presenting all your facts and reasons to me, you have assumed that such a God does not exist. You have taken for granted that you need no emplacement of any sort outside of yourself. You have assumed the autonomy of your own experience. Consequently you are unable—that is, unwilling—to accept as a fact any fact that would challenge your self-sufficiency. And you are bound to call that contradictory which does not fit into the reach of your intellectual powers. You remember what old Procrustus did. If his visitors were too long, he cut off a few slices at each end; if they were too short, he used the curtain stretcher on them. It is that sort of thing I feel that you have done with every fact of human experience. And I am asking you to be critical of this your own most basic assumption.[125] Will you not go into the basement of your own experience to see what has been gathering there while you were busy here and there with the surface inspection of life? You may be greatly surprised at what you find there.

To make my meaning clearer, I shall illustrate what I have said by pointing out how modern philosophers and scientists handle the facts and doctrines of Christianity.

Basic to all the facts and doctrines of Christianity and therefore involved in

123. Van Til is here alluding to the traditional apologetical efforts of natural theology and evidential apologetics, both of which have failed to issue a transcendental challenge to the very intelligibility of the unbeliever's attempt to use science, logic, morality, etc., against the faith. Such a challenge, it has been thought, makes "too big" a claim and insults the unbeliever's intellect. But Van Til observes that the failure to make this honest claim actually diminishes the believer's conception of God and is offensive to Him.
124. Recall here Van Til's words: "Antitheism presupposes theism."
125. The presuppositionalist wants the unbeliever to realize that he has not been nearly critical enough in his mind-set and approach. He has never honestly examined the philosophical sufficiency of his pretended autonomy. Because so many other "scholars" around him take their autonomy for granted with unthinking gullibility, and because it is the "respectable" thing to do in secular institutions and media, the unbeliever will comfort himself that "everybody is doing it"—in which case the question of man's intellectual adequacy in interpreting the world on his own hardly needs to be asked. In any other setting, the educated unbeliever would recognize this line of thinking as fallacious, prejudicial, and even dangerously arrogant. But here he permits himself to indulge in the very thing he elsewhere would condemn.

the belief in God, is the creation doctrine. Now modern philosophers and scientists as a whole claim that to hold such a doctrine or to believe in such a fact is to deny our own experience. They mean this not merely in the sense that no one was there to see it done, but in the more basic sense that it is logically impossible. They assert that it would break the fundamental laws of logic.

The current argument against the creation doctrine derives from Kant. It may fitly be expressed in the words of a more recent philosopher, James Ward: "If we attempt to conceive of God apart from the world, there is nothing to lead us on to creation" *(Realm of Ends,* p. 397). That is to say, if God is to be connected to the universe at all, he must be subject to its conditions. Here is the old creation doctrine. It says that God has caused the world to come into existence. But what do we mean by the word *cause?* In our experience it is that which is logically correlative to the word *effect*. If you have an effect you must have a cause, and if you have a cause you must have an effect. If God caused the world, it must therefore have been because God couldn't help producing an effect. And so the effect may really be said to be the cause of the cause. Our experience can therefore allow for no God other than one that is dependent upon the world as much as the world is dependent upon Him.

The God of Christianity cannot meet these requirements of the autonomous man. He claims to be all-sufficient. He claims to have created the world, not from necessity but from His free will. He claims not to have changed in Himself when He created the world. His existence must therefore be said to be impossible, and the creation doctrine must be said to be an absurdity.

The doctrine of providence is also said to be at variance with experience. This is but natural. One who rejects creation must logically also reject providence. If all things are controlled by God's providence, we are told, there can be nothing new and history is but a puppet dance.

You see then that I might present to you great numbers of facts to prove the existence of God. I might say that every effect needs a cause. I might point to the wonderful structure of the eye as evidence of God's purpose in nature. I might call in the story of mankind through the past to show that it has been directed and controlled by God. All these evidences would leave you unaffected. You would simply say that however else we may explain reality, we cannot bring in God. *Cause* and *purpose*, you keep repeating, are words that we human beings use with respect to things around us because they seem to act as we ourselves act, but that is as far as we can go.[126]

126. In terms of his own way of thinking, the unbelieving philosopher justly points out that, if the premises of a theistic proof refer to the realm of natural experience, it would be unwarranted and fallacious to draw conclusions about an altogether different realm that goes beyond natural experience (the supernatural).

And when the evidence for Christianity proper is presented to you the procedure is the same. If I point out to you that the prophecies of Scripture have been fulfilled, you will simply reply that it quite naturally appears that way to me and to others, but that in reality it is not possible for any mind to predict the future from the past. If it were, all would again be fixed and history would be without newness and freedom.

Then if I point to the many miracles, the story is once more the same. To illustrate this point I quote from the late Dr. William Adams Brown, an outstanding modernist theologian. "Take any of the miracles of the past," says Brown, "the virgin birth, the raising of Lazarus, the resurrection of Jesus Christ. Suppose that you can prove that these events happened just as they are claimed to have happened. What have you accomplished? You have shown that our previous view of the limits of the possible needs to be enlarged; that our former generalizations were too narrow and need revision; that problems cluster about the origin of life and its renewal of which we had hitherto been unaware. But the one thing which you have not shown, which indeed you cannot show, is that a miracle has happened; for that is to confess that these problems are inherently insoluble, which cannot be determined until all possible tests have been made" (*God at Work,* New York, 1933, p. 169). You see with what confidence Brown uses this weapon of logical impossibility against the idea of miracle. Many of the older critics of Scripture challenged the evidence for miracle at this point or at that. They made as it were a slow, piece-meal land invasion of the island of Christianity. Brown, on the other hand, settles the matter at once by a host of Stukas from the sky. Any pillboxes that he cannot destroy immediately, he will mop up later. He wants to get rapid control of the whole field first. And this he does by directly applying the law of non-contradiction. Only that is possible, says Brown, in effect, which I can show to be logically related according to my laws of logic. So then if miracles want to have scientific standing, that is, be recognized as genuine facts, they must sue for admittance at the port of entry to the mainland of scientific endeavour. And admission will be given as soon as they submit to the little process of generalization which deprives them of their uniqueness. Miracles must take out naturalization papers if they wish to vote in the republic of science and have any influence there.

Take now the four points I have mentioned—creation, providence, prophecy and miracle. Together they represent the whole of Christian theism. Together they include what is involved in the idea of God and what He has done round about and for us. Many times over and in many ways the evidence for all these has been presented. But you have an always available and effective answer at hand.[127] It is impossible! It is impossible! You act like a postmaster who has received a great many letters addressed in foreign languages. He says he will deliver them as soon as they are addressed in the King's English by the people who sent them. Till then they must wait in the dead letter department. Basic to all the objections the average philosopher and scientist raises against the evidence for the existence of God is the assertion or the assumption that to accept such evidence would be to break the rules of logic.

I see you are yawning. Let us stop to eat supper now. For there is one more point in this connection that I must make. You have no doubt at some time in your life been to a dentist. A dentist drills a little deeper and then a little deeper and at last comes to the nerve of the matter.

Now before I drill into the nerve of the matter, I must again make apologies. The fact that so many people are placed before a full exposition of the evidence for God's existence and yet do not believe in Him has greatly discouraged us. We have therefore adopted measures of despair. Anxious to win your good will, we have again compromised our God. Noting the fact that men do not see, we have conceded that what they ought to see is hard to see. In our great concern to win men we have allowed that the evidence for God's existence is only *probably* compelling. And from that fatal confession we have gone one step further down to the point where we have admitted or virtually admitted that it is not really compelling at all.[128]

And so we fall back upon testimony instead of argument. After all, we say, God is not found at the end of an argument; He is found in our hearts. So we simply testify to men that once we were dead, and now we are alive, that once we were blind and that now we see, and give up all intellectual argument.

Do you suppose that our God approves of this attitude of His followers? I do not think so. The God who claims to have made all facts and to have placed His stamp upon them will not grant that there is really some excuse

127. Proofs of God and evidences for Christianity can always be countered by the unbeliever's controlling presuppositions or worldview. That is why the presuppositional approach to apologetics teaches us to be prepared to argue with and refute the underlying philosophy that the unbeliever uses to evade the force of the evidences and proofs.

128. This is the sad end product of weak forms of apologetical argument that share an autonomous outlook with the unbeliever in an effort to win him over to Christ. Since the presuppositions connected with man's autonomy are diametrically opposed to the Christian message, it is only to be expected that apologetical arguments patterned after them will fail to prove Christianity. Rather than abandoning the fatal presuppositions, however, many apologists simply lower their claims about what such arguments can prove. Van Til saw in this despairing attempt to win the approval of autonomous thinkers a compromise with the Christian's religious commitment.

for those who refuse to see. Besides, such a procedure is self-defeating. If someone in your hometown of Washington denied that there were any such thing as a United States Government would you take him some distance down the Potomac and testify to him that there is? So your experience and testimony of regeneration would be meaningless except for the objective truth of the objective facts that are presupposed by it. A testimony that is not an argument is not a testimony either, just as an argument that is not a testimony is not even an argument.

Waiving all this for the moment, let us see what the modern psychologist of religion, who stands on the same foundation with the philosopher, will do to our testimony. He makes a distinction between the *raw datum* and its cause, giving me the raw datum and keeping for himself the explanation of the cause. Professor James H. Leuba, a great psychologist of Bryn Mawr, has a procedure that is typical. He says, "The reality of any given datum—of an *immediate* experience in the sense in which the term is used here—may not be impugned: When I feel cold or warm, sad or gay, discouraged or confident, I *am* cold, sad, discouraged, etc., and every argument which might be advanced to prove to me that I am not cold is, in the nature of the case, preposterous; an immediate experience may not be controverted; it cannot be wrong." All this seems on the surface to be very encouraging. The immigrant is hopeful of a ready and speedy admittance. However, Ellis Island must still be passed. "But if the raw data of experience are not subject to criticism, the causes ascribed to them are. If I say that my feeling of cold is due to an open window, or my state of exultation to a drug, or my renewed courage to God, my affirmation goes beyond my immediate experience; I have ascribed a cause to it, and that cause may be the right or the wrong one" (*God or Man,* New York, 1933, p. 243). And thus the immigrant must wait at Ellis Island a million years.

That is to say, I as a believer in God through Christ, assert that I am born again through the Holy Spirit. The psychologist says that is a raw datum of experience and as such incontrovertible. We do not, he says, deny it. But it means nothing to us. If you want it to mean something to us you must ascribe a cause to your experience. We shall then examine the cause. Was your experience caused by opium or God? You say by God. Well, that is impossible since as philosophers we have shown that it is logically contradictory to believe in God. You may come back at any time when you have changed your mind about the cause of your regeneration. We shall be glad to have you and welcome you as a citizen of our realm, if only you take out your naturalization papers!

We seem now to have come to a pretty pass. We agreed at the outset to tell each other the whole truth. If I have offended you it has been because I dare not, even in the interest of winning you, offend my God. And if I have not offended you I have not spoken of my God.[129] For what you have really done in your handling of the evidence for belief in God, is to set yourself up as God. You have made the reach of your intellect, the standard of what is possible or not possible. You have thereby virtually determined that you intend never to meet a fact that points to God. Facts, to be facts at all—facts, that is, with decent scientific and philosophic standing—must have your stamp instead of that of God upon them as their virtual creator.

Of course I realize full well that you do not pretend to create redwood trees and elephants. But you do virtually assert that redwood trees and elephants cannot be created by God. You have heard of the man who never wanted to see or be a purple cow. Well, you have virtually determined that you never will see or be a created fact. With Sir Arthur Eddington you say as it were, "What my net can't catch isn't fish."

Nor do I pretend, of course, that once you have been brought face to face with this condition, you can change your attitude. No more than the Ethiopian can change his skin or the leopard his spots can you change your attitude. You have cemented your colored glasses to your face so firmly that you cannot even take them off when you sleep.[130] Freud has not even had a glimpse of the sinfulness of sin as it controls the human heart. Only the great Physician through His blood atonement on the Cross and by the gift of His Spirit can take those colored glasses off and make you see facts as they are, facts as evidence, as inherently compelling evidence, for the existence of God.[131]

129. Many apologetical strategies fostered today make it a point to tone down the demands of the gospel and avoid the rough edges of true theology. The Christian message is made more and more like the natural thinking of men so that natural men will not resist it so much. Van Til taught, rather, that the Christian worldview must be seen and presented as the antithesis of the unbeliever's thinking and living. That means that the apologist should expect his position to seem outlandish, demanding, and unreasonable to the unregenerate; the message, if faithfully portrayed, cannot help but "offend" the sinner's pride and self-sufficiency. (This does not mean, of course, that the demeanor or manner of the apologist is permitted to be offensive on a personal level.)

130. Van Til constantly reminded unbelievers that they were not at all religiously neutral, as they may have thought of themselves. However, the "prejudice" that the unbeliever brings to all experience is so pervasive that he never sees anything differently enough to recognize that he is actually prejudging everything about the facts and reasoning.

131. The worldview that the Christian sets before the unbeliever cannot be reduced (in something like a deistic manner) to those aspects which make an understanding of natural experience possible. Because of man's sin and suppression of God's revelation (which is necessary to making experience intelligible), there must be within an adequate worldview some provision for his salvation from guilt

It ought to be pretty plain now what sort of God I believe in.[132] It is God, the All-Conditioner. It is the God who created all things, who by His providence conditioned my youth, making me believe in Him, and who in my later life by His grace still makes me want to believe in Him. It is the God who also controlled your youth and so far has apparently not given you His grace that you might believe in Him.

You may reply to this: "Then what's the use of arguing and reasoning with me?" Well, there is a great deal of use in it. You see, if you are really a creature of God, you are always accessible to Him. When Lazarus was in the tomb he was still accessible to Christ who called him back to life. It is this on which true preachers depend. The prodigal thought he had clean escaped from the father's influence. In reality the father controlled the "far country" to which the prodigal had gone. So it is in reasoning.

True reasoning about God is such as stands upon God as upon the emplacement that alone gives meaning to any sort of human argument.[133] And such reasoning, we have a right to expect, will be used of God to break down the one-horse chaise of human autonomy.

But now I see you want to go home. And I do not blame you; the last bus leaves at twelve. I should like to talk again another time. I invite you to come to dinner next Sunday. But I have pricked your bubble, so perhaps you will not come back. And yet perhaps you will. That depends upon the Father's pleasure.

Deep down in your heart you know very well that what I have said about you is true.[134] You know there is no unity in your life. You want no God who

---

and pollution. The redemptive features of the Christian worldview are thus—in man's current fallen situation—not simply an appendix to the rational, scientific, and moral necessity of the Christian's outlook, but at its very heart. Man needs to be "saved," according to Van Til, to make an intelligible use of reason.

132. It is vital to presuppositional apologetics to keep pointing out the larger picture in terms of which the Christian challenge is advanced. It is not simply an abstract "god," devoid of content, with which the unbeliever must contend. Given the kind of God for whom the Christian contends, it is perfectly reasonable that He speaks with ultimate and unchallengeable authority, that He sovereignly controls all things (including responses to His revelation), and that the unbeliever cannot rationally escape Him.

133. This is the heart of Van Til's transcendental argument for God's existence. All argumentation involves presuppositions, but only the presupposition of the Christian God renders any kind of argument meaningful. In that case, the unbeliever's "argument" against God or the gospel, if it can make any sense whatsoever, already "stands upon the emplacement" of belief in God's existence. Rational argumentation already assumes the Christian position to be true, even when unbelievers argue against that truth.

134. Presuppositional apologetics does not hesitate to point to the unbeliever's inward recognition of the truth of the Christian claims, even though the unbe-

by His counsel provides for the unity you need. Such a God, you say, would allow for nothing new. So you provide your own unity. But this unity must, by your own definition, not kill that which is wholly new. Therefore it must stand over against the wholly new and never touch it at all. Thus by your logic you talk about possibles and impossibles, but all this talk is in the air. By your own standards it can never have anything to do with reality. Your logic claims to deal with eternal and changeless matters; and your facts are wholly changing things; and "never the twain shall meet." So you have made nonsense of your own experience.[135] With the prodigal you are at the swine trough, but it may be that, unlike the prodigal, you will refuse to return to the father's house.

On the other hand, by my belief in God I do have unity in my experience. Not of course the sort of unity that you want.[136] Not a unity that is the result of my own autonomous determination of what is possible. But a unity that is higher than mine and prior to mine. On the basis of God's counsel I can look for facts and find them without destroying them in advance. On the basis of God's counsel I can be a good physicist, a good biologist, a good psychologist, or a good philosopher. In all these fields I use my powers of logi-

---

liever may not be willing to admit to that conviction. He does, after all, suppress the truth in unrighteousness. In particular at this point, Van Til presses upon the unbeliever that he is quite cognizant that his professed presuppositions do not provide an intelligible basis for unity in his experience (causal connections between events, conceptual continuity, logical necessity, moral absolutes, etc.). On the other hand, the unbeliever knows that his rejection of the Christian outlook is a matter of personal choice and desire (he does not "want" the God who can provide the order he needs), not intellectual necessity. The apologist should continue to appeal to the unbeliever's inward awareness of such truths (as well as showing that his reasoning and behavior betray this awareness).

135. It should be noticed that this is an internal critique of the unbeliever's worldview, one made from within the context of his assumptions and aims—rather than an external criticism of the unbeliever's position simply for disagreeing with the Christian position. Van Til points out that the unbeliever has, in terms of his own presuppositions, "made nonsense" of his experience. By refusing to think in terms of the truth revealed by God, he undermines his own rational efforts. He is refuted from within his own philosophy of life.

136. The believer's attempt to organize and interpret his experience is successful when it reflects the original order of God's mind, by which all things are defined and all events work together; he seeks to "think God's thoughts after Him." The unbeliever, by contrast, either imposes the unifying ideas of his own mind on an external reality not controlled by his mind (subjectivism) or respects the particularity and novelty of every fact in the world, in which case nothing can be said about it using unifying concepts or uniform principles (irrationality). Imposing a "system" in advance discards the need for scientific research; respecting the individuality and novelty of experience destroys the intelligibility of facts in advance.

cal arrangement in order to see as much order in God's universe as it may be given a creature to see. The unities, or systems that I make are true because genuine pointers toward the basic or original unity that is found in the counsel of God.

Looking about me I see both order and disorder in every dimension of life.[137] But I look at both of them in the light of the Great Orderer who is back of them.[138] I need not deny either of them in the interest of optimism or in the interest of pessimism. I see the strong men of biology searching diligently through hill and dale to prove that the creation doctrine is not true with respect to the human body, only to return and admit that the missing link is missing still. I see the strong men of psychology search deep and far into the sub-consciousness, child and animal consciousness, in order to prove that the creation and providence doctrines are not true with respect to the human soul, only to return and admit that the gulf between human and animal intelligence is as great as ever. I see the strong men of logic and scientific methodology search deep into the transcendental for a validity that will not be swept away by the ever-changing tide of the wholly new, only to return and say that they can find no bridge from logic to reality, or from reality to logic. And yet I find all these, though standing on their heads, reporting much that is true.[139] I need only to turn their reports right side up, making God instead of man the center of it all, and I have a marvellous display of the facts as God has intended me to see them.

137. Those aspects of experience which afford "order" are those characterized by unity, connections, sameness, generalization, universality, lack of change, or continuity. Those aspects of experience which display "disorder" are those that have diversity, particularity, individuality, novelty, uniqueness, change, or discontinuity.

138. By contrast, all unbelieving worldviews look at unity and diversity in terms of a fundamental "disorder" behind everything: there is no plan, purpose, or sovereign control that orders events, provides universality for laws, or coordinates mind (logic) and its objects (reality).

139. Van Til consistently held that unbelievers are not mindless, ignorant, and useless in understanding the world that God has made. However, their professed "point of reference" (their presuppositions or perspective) is skewed. They need to be "turned around" (converted).

140. By "my unity" Van Til meant his Christian conception of what gives unity to life and reasoning. It is important to see that the Christian worldview does not simply claim to explain its own perspective (seeing things in a Christian way), but also accounts for the non-Christian's perspective (why he sees things the way he claims to see them). We do not end up with a plurality of "unities" (worldviews that unify experience) competing with each other, as though there were a number of equally self-satisfactory presuppositions. There is one worldview that truly provides unity (and includes an explanation of the competing claims of unbelievers) and a variety of professed worldviews that reduce to disunity (disorder, chance, chaos, etc.).

And if my unity[140] is comprehensive enough to include the efforts of those who reject it, it is large enough even to include that which those who have been set upright by regeneration cannot see. My unity is that of a child who walks with its father through the woods. The child is not afraid because its father knows it all and is capable of handling every situation. So I readily grant that there are some "difficulties" with respect to belief in God and His revelation in nature and Scripture that I cannot solve. In fact there is mystery in every relationship with respect to every fact that faces me, for the reason that all facts have their final explanation in God, whose thoughts are higher than my thoughts, and whose ways are higher than my ways. And it is exactly that sort of God that I need. Without such a God, without the God of the Bible, the God of authority, the God who is self-contained and therefore incomprehensible to men, there would be no reason in anything.[141] No human being can explain in the sense of seeing through all things, but only he who believes in God has the right to hold that there is an explanation at all.[142]

So you see when I was young I was conditioned on every side; I could not help believing in God. Now that I am older I still cannot help believing in God. I believe in God now because unless I have Him as the All-Conditioner, life is chaos.[143]

141. Thus, everyone must choose between two kinds of mystery at the center of their reasoning endeavors. The Christian accepts what is mysterious to him as a man, a revelation that transcends his reasoning, but knows that it is not mysterious to his Creator, whereas the non-Christian accepts an ultimate mystery that is devoid of explanation or meaning.

142. As the apologetical argument begins, it might appear that the question has to do with which "side" can offer a better explanation of the way things are. In reality, said Van Til, it comes down to whether unbelieving worldviews can, in terms of what they maintain, offer any genuine explanation at all. Using logic and inductive reasoning in order to explain things is futile if there is no explanation for the uniformity of nature (induction) or universal validity of reasoning (logic) themselves.

143. Van Til has turned the unbeliever's criticism (namely, that Christians simply cannot help believing) into a commendation of the Christian worldview. Of course, the reason we "cannot help" believing is no longer, if it ever was, due (as the unbeliever thought) to psychological and social conditions, but due to the sovereignty of God, who "gives order" to everything by His controlling plan and purpose. This too might seem to be a basis for objection from the unbeliever (confusing it with fatalism and the denial of human responsibility). Instead, Van Til shows that this worldview alone—where God conditions all things—rescues life and reasoning from chaos (meaninglessness). Because God orders every detail of life and history, there is an objective basis for people to reason about causes, logical necessity, moral absolutes, etc. As a child, perhaps, the believer like Van Til could not help believing, but now, as a grown-up, and from the standpoint of what is necessary to reason about anything, the believer still "cannot help" believing.

I shall not convert you at the end of my argument. I think the argument is sound. I hold that belief in God is not merely as reasonable as other belief, or even a little or infinitely more probably true than other belief; I hold rather that unless you believe in God you can logically believe in nothing else. But since I believe in such a God, a God who has conditioned you as well as me, I know that you can to your own satisfaction, by the help of the biologists, the psychologists, the logicians, and the Bible critics reduce everything I have said this afternoon and evening to the circular meanderings of a hopeless authoritarian. Well, my meanderings have, to be sure, been circular; they have made everything turn on God. So now I shall leave you with Him, and with His mercy.[144]

144. This excellent closing paragraph sets forth salient points in Van Til's presuppositional apologetic. (1) The Christian worldview is not presented simply as a viewpoint that explains the facts somewhat better than others; rather, it is—objectively speaking—the only perspective that makes reasonable sense of believing or judging anything. (2) Nevertheless, the unbeliever will follow any number of lines of thought in order to rationalize—to his own subjective satisfaction—his refusal to submit to the Christian God. (3) In the end, everyone must choose an ultimate authority and then regiment his reasoning in terms of it ("circularly"): the Christian looks to God to make sense of things (cf. #1), while the non-Christian looks to himself (cf. #2). (4) Apologists must recognize that the subjective change of the unbeliever, his conversion, cannot be achieved by the power of our argument alone, but depends on the sovereign mercy of God. (5) At the end of our discussions with them, unbelievers should be left with a clear picture of the true nature of the disagreement and with a sense that they must deal with God over it, not merely with their human opponent. This is objectively true, whether they wish subjectively to acknowledge it or not. If God is merciful, they will be saved not only for eternal life, but also in their reasoning.

Chapter 4

The Epistemological Side of Apologetics

4.1 Apologetics as Epistemological Disagreement

In the nature of the case, an apologetical discussion is not merely an exchange of personal opinions. It eventually focuses on questions like "How do you *know* this to be true?" or "How can that belief be justified?" That is, apologetics entails the application (even if the unwitting application) of one's basic theory of knowledge—one's *epistemology*. Because epistemology is at the heart of apologetics, and because there continue to be significant disagreements between men over epistemological questions, the apologist must begin with a clear and firm understanding of his own position as a Christian—in particular, his distinctive Christian convictions touching matters of epistemological importance. If he is muddled or mistaken about these basic issues pertaining to the Christian faith, he can hardly raise a clear and effective defense of that very faith. He is more likely to resort to argumentative tactics that do not epistemologically comport with the system of truth he seeks to vindicate.

Both the unbeliever and the believer operate with epistemological convictions about the nature of truth, belief, meaning, knowledge, evidence, proof, etc. The unbeliever will say that he does not "believe" that the claims of Christianity are "true," that there is no "proof" of miracles, that he "knows" Jesus was merely a man, or other such things. Likewise, believers who defend the faith make use of epistemological notions, saying that we "believe that God raised Jesus from the dead" (Rom. 10:9), that "I know my Redeemer lives" (Job 19:25), that God "has furnished proof" that Jesus will judge the world (Acts 17:31), that God's "word is truth" (John 17:17), etc.

It should be clear, moreover, that we find not only enduring, unresolved disagreements about epistemology between schools of thought and between individuals throughout the history of philosophy (including our own day), but also—more fundamentally and relevantly—significant conflicts between the Christian and the non-Christian over crucial epistemological matters. In light of biblical teaching about the intellectual renewal of the believer (Rom. 12:2; Eph. 4:23–24) and the all-pervasive depravity of the unbeliever (Rom. 8:7; Eph. 4:17–19), this philosophical discord should not surprise us. The apologist must not naively take for granted that everyone shares a common view of knowledge, truth, language, logic, evidence, etc. If they did, basic philosophical or religious disputes could be more readily settled, simply by making sure that everyone has the same information or raw data available. But such disputes persist, since men disagree over more fundamental epistemological issues—indeed, even over whether there is "raw data" or not. As the Christian knows from reading his Bible, men are divided by epistemological conflicts concerning such matters as the nature of "truth" (John 18:38), what is "believable" (Acts 26:8), the reliability of our senses (Matt. 28:17; Luke 24:16; John 21:4, 12), the difference between knowledge and "pseudoknowledge" (1 Tim. 6:20) or between wisdom and folly (1 Cor. 1:18–29), and the evidential value and power of miracles (Luke 16:31; Matt. 28:11–15).

Van Til realized that the epistemological disagreements between believers and unbelievers could not be resolved in a neutral fashion, as though the issue of God's existence and character (and man's relationship to Him) could be treated as secondary—and thus temporarily set aside without any commitment one way or another—while abstract philosophical issues were debated and settled. It is often, but vainly, imagined that once we come to agreement on our epistemology, we can apply those epistemological standards to the questions of whether God exists, whether miracles occur, whether the Bible is true, etc. By contrast, Van Til taught that abstract epistemological neutrality is an illusion and that, given the kind of God revealed in the Bible, imagined neutrality is actually prejudicial against God. If God exists and is as the Christian worldview claims, then His existence has an undeniable bearing on how we understand the process of knowing, the standards of truth and evidence, ultimate authority, and other crucial matters in epistemology.

Moreover, if the Christian outlook is correct, then the spiritual condition of man himself affects the manner in which he reasons and the ideals or standards of knowledge to which he tries to conform. "By the sinner's epistemological reaction," wrote Van Til, "I mean his reaction as an ethically responsible creature of God."[1] There is no pristine, religiously neutral, abstract "reason" to which all men first swear their allegiance, only then to turn to such secondary matters as man's nature, moral character, relation to God, destiny, etc. The kind of man who is doing the reasoning already determines something about the way in which he thinks about reason and engages in reasoning. Thus Van Til stated, "It is impossible to speak of the intellect per se, without taking into consideration whether it is the intellect of a regenerate person or of a non-regenerate person."[2]

Van Til simply called for honesty and realism here. The metaphysical situation and object of knowledge (e.g., God's existence, the relation of created things to Him), as well as the psychological/moral situation and the subject of knowledge (i.e., man as a knower, someone using reasoning ability), cannot be ignored as we develop our views of knowing. "Reason" is simply an intellectual tool, rather than an ultimate standard of knowledge (more authoritative even than God), and as such will be affected by the regenerate or unregenerate condition of the man using it. A person's epistemological behavior and commitments are ethical in character. According to Van Til, one's theory of knowledge is not neutral, but subject to moral assessment in terms of the ultimate authority to which one submits and which one attempts to honor.

For reasons such as these, it is simply naive to run to the philosophers as the first step toward resolving the disagreement between the believer and the unbeliever, thinking that they can referee the conflict and provide an agreed-upon and neutral approach to epistemology. This is evident from the history of philosophy, even in matters that are not explicitly religious. Philosophers have conspicuously

1. *The Defense of the Faith* (Philadelphia: Presbyterian and Reformed, 1955), 259.
2. *A Survey of Christian Epistemology*, In Defense of the Faith, vol. 2 (Philadelphia: Presbyterian and Reformed, 1969), 187.

differed with one another over such basic issues as the nature of mind, of logic, and of truth. Those who have emphasized that the world is comprised of separate and discontinuous things (sharply different in kind and number) have conceptualized thinking as an activity that occurs *in* the mind, with the basic problem being how to get independent minds into "correspondence" with independently existing objects outside the mind. By contrast, philosophers who have emphasized the similarities, unities, and continuities in the world—in which case different things blend together in the process of history and are basically different in degree—have conceptualized thinking as itself *being* the mind, whose reasoning develops and unfolds in continuity with all of man's faculties (e.g., perception, volition, imagination) and in connection with the object of knowledge itself. Accordingly, for this second group of philosophers, the problem is not to explain how minds and objects correspond (for they are already inherently related, the differences between them being only of degree), but to explain how a finite mind can have a wide enough (inclusive enough) system to know any particular or limited truth. These two different approaches to philosophy even see logic differently from each other. For the first, every statement must be neatly classified into one of two quite distinct categories, the consistent or the contradictory. For the second, such categories are merely tentative and provisional, standing in dynamic tension (because of our limited conceptualizations) while we await progress toward more adequate integration of the various aspects of what we know.

Now then, can advocates of these two conflicting approaches to philosophy—with their disagreements even over mind, truth, and logic— arrive at an agreed-upon theory of knowledge at the outset of dialogue, so that their disagreements about the nature of reality can later be addressed and resolved? Not at all. Arguments between these schools of thought have always been unrewarding just because their epistemological differences are a reflection of, and are coordinated with, their differences over the nature of reality. The first school (which emphasizes sharp differences and discontinuities) accuses the second school (which emphasizes differences of degree and continuities) of being muddled in their thinking and failing to draw clear contrasts, while the second school accuses the first of falsifying the whole truth by reductionism and oversimplification. Arguments between conflicting schools of philosophy, to put it simply, tend already to incorporate epistemological arguments concerning method, the proper kind of analysis, the nature of truth, the use of logic, etc.[3] Philosophers do not reach a consensus in epistemology, and their arguments with each other continue to be inconclusive, as Van Til perceptively taught, because their differences are ultimately and profoundly differences in their presuppositions—their network of ultimate assumptions about reality, knowledge, and ethics. This network cannot be readily separated into component parts (such as epistemology) that can be discussed in neutral isolation.

This should be all the more obvious when the disagreement with which we begin is openly religious in character, as it is when the believer and the unbeliever get into an apologetical argument. The apologetical disagreement is itself a reflection of an implicit disagreement in respective theories of knowledge. Accordingly, the early Greek philosophers, as Van Til noted, were not wide-eyed innocents who approached the questions of knowledge and reality with presuppositionless detachment. Nor are their modern disciples and counterparts. Regardless of their educational level or sophistication, unbelievers who challenge the truth of Christianity today do not employ a neutral epistemology developed in isolation from metaphysical and ethical considerations. Their understanding and use of "reason" discloses something of their vision of reality and the values by which they have chosen to live.

NEUTRALITY AS ANTITHEISTIC [4]

No fact in the world can be interpreted truly except it be seen as created by God. The Greeks were among those of whom Paul speaks when he says that they hinder or repress the truth in unrighteousness. The significance of the fact that Greek speculation began with a definitely antitheistic bias cannot be stressed too much because of the common misunderstanding on this score. The usual presentation is that the Greeks naturally began to look around them at the physical universe and to ask questions about it as a child asks questions about any strange or new thing that it sees. Hence, it is argued that no more than you would accuse a child of starting with an antitheistic bias should you accuse the Greeks of beginning with anything but an open mind. Naturally they would begin with the things that were nearest to them, and only

---

3. For more extensive discussion and illustration, see W. T. Jones, "Philosophical Disagreements and World Views," *Proceedings and Addresses of the American Philosophical Association* 43 (1969–70): 24–42.

4. An excerpt from *Survey of Christian Epistemology*, 18–22.

afterward could they pass on to the more remote questions of metaphysics. They began with physics and thereupon turned to *metaphysics*.

These objections, however, are themselves based upon the self-same antitheistic bias noted above. In these objections it is taken for granted that the Greeks may fairly be compared to children who begin to wonder about things around them. But this comparison would be fair only if antitheism were true. The comparison presupposes that the human race was for the first time emerging into self-consciousness in the persons of the Greeks. The comparison takes for granted that the human race had never been in close contact with a God who was nearer to them than the universe. In other words, the comparison takes for granted that the physical facts would naturally be knowable first, and that if God is to be known he must be known later.

But this is exactly the point in dispute. If the theistic view is true, then man was originally as close to God as he was to any physical fact. If theism is true, man once realized the fact that the animals and the trees were known to him *because* God was known to him. If theism is true, the revelation of the absolute God was everywhere found in the created universe, so that no matter where man would turn, to himself or to nature about him, he would meet God. This is implied in the idea of creation. The idea of creation carries with it a definite view of being and of becoming, the two main questions of Greek philosophy. The idea of creation makes a distinction of being between God and man. Anyone holding to the idea of creation (we speak of temporal and not of logical creation) must also hold to the idea of a God who existed apart from the world and had meaning for himself apart from the world. And this point goes counter to the first assumption of Greek speculation spoken of, that all things are at bottom one. If theism is right, all things are at bottom two, and not one. In the second place, anyone holding to the idea of creation must also hold that the world of becoming cannot be taken for granted as an ultimate with which as a given the human mind must begin its speculation. Being is before becoming and independent of becoming.[5] Thus the creation idea also runs counter to the second and third assumptions of Greek philosophy, that the fact of change should be taken for granted, and that the manifold generated from the one is all the while identical with the one.[6]

We should add that according to Scripture, God spoke to man at the outset of history. In addition to revealing himself in the facts of the created universe, God revealed himself in Words, telling man about what he should do

---

5. That is, the unchanging Creator, who exists of Himself ("being"), preceded the separate realm of changing and contingent things ("becoming"), which He created.
6. The "manifold" is the universe of many, varied things. The "one" is the singular, unique, and distinct Creator.

with the facts of the universe. Since the fall, all men, as fallen in Adam (Rom. 5:12), continue to be responsible for this twofold revelation of God given to man at the beginning of history.

From these considerations it follows that if theism is true the Greeks are not a race of innocent children just beginning to look around in the world. If theism is true, there has been an original monotheism or, as we may now say, an original theism from which the race has fallen away. This truth is usually given no more serious thought than one of the myths of the Greeks. In fact it is usually regarded as being nothing but a myth to which none but the hopeless traditionalists will pay any attention. Even Christians themselves often feel as though this creation story is something they must carry along in order to have the other advantages of theism, but something which in itself is of no importance. For this reason we have sought to point out that the creation idea is an integral part of the Christian theistic system of thought. We accept it because it is in the Bible and *we believe that which is in the Bible to be the only defensible philosophical position*.[7] Our opponents have no right to reject the creation story unless they can prove that it is not essential to Christianity or that Christianity is not the only position that makes human predication intelligible. Yet the ordinary textbook on philosophy presents the beginning of Greek speculation as something entirely neutral. But to try to be neutral is to speak against God and his Christ.

If the theistic position be defensible *it is an impossibility for any human being to be neutral*. This is quite readily admitted when a centrally religious question is discussed. We need only recall the words of Jesus, "He that is not against me is for me," to remind ourselves of this fact. When two nations are at war no citizens of either of these two nations can be neutral. It may be reasonable for citizens of a third nation to be neutral, but this cannot be the case for citizens of countries actually at war. We may apply this analogy to the relation between theism and antitheism. Of course the applicability of such an analogy will at once be denied by every red-blooded antitheist. But this very fact shows that it is a point in dispute between the two systems of thought, for it is equally true that every red-blooded theist will affirm that

---

7. Emphasis added. This represents the essential "defense of the faith" for presuppositional apologetics, namely, that only Christianity has a defensible philosophical position that can give an intelligible account of the ability to speak meaningfully, to "predicate" (as Van Til goes on to say here), to be rational, to know anything, etc. Christianity is not one of many internally reasonable worldviews from which men may choose, but the only candidate if one is committed to rationality (a defensible philosophy of life and epistemology). This fact helps to explain why modern non-Christian scholarship and culture show a predilection for irrationality, meaninglessness, and subjectivism.

there is a definite warfare between the two. True, the antitheist may speak of a war and of a clash of opinions, but what he means by war is not to be identified with the theist's conception of war. The antitheist cannot, because of the very doctrines that he holds, consider it a matter of the greatest importance which system of thought one feels inclined to embrace. Certainly for him there are no eternal destinies of men involved. For a Christian theist the entire outlook is different. For him it is as important that men should be theists as that they should be Christians, for the obvious reason that for him a true theism and a true Christianity are identical. Hence a true theist is always a missionary, even when engaged in the most "abstruse" speculations about eternal things. A Christian will engage in no speculation.[8] He has no "metaphysics" as metaphysics is usually understood. He does not even start his thinking with God as his master concept in order to deduce his "system" of truth from this master concept. His thinking is always and only an attempt to integrate the various aspects of biblical teaching. In doing so he is deeply conscious of the fact that every "concept" he employs must be limited by every other "concept" he employs, and that therefore his "system" is an effort to restate in his confession the truth as it is in Jesus.[9]

From these considerations it ought to be evident that one cannot take the possibility of neutrality for granted. To be philosophically fair, the antitheist is bound first of all to establish this possibility critically before he proceeds to build upon it.[10] If there is an absolute God, neutrality is out of the question, because in that case every creature is derived from God and is therefore directly responsible to him. And such a God would not feel very kindly disposed to those who ignore him. Even in human relationships it is true that to be ignored is a deeper source of grief to him who is ignored than to be opposed. It follows then that the attempt to be neutral is part of the attempt to be antitheistic. For this reason we have constantly used the term antitheistic instead of *non*theistic. To be nontheistic is to be antitheistic.

---

8. Van Til means here that the Christian worldview (and its interrelated aspects of metaphysics, epistemology, and ethics) is not developed by standing outside a commitment to God's revelation and attempting by neutral reasoning to arrive at a satisfactory conception of knowledge, reality, and moral behavior abstracted (mentally separated) from each other. The believer does not "speculate" in general—but submits to the concrete and detailed information revealed by God—about reality, knowledge, and ethics.

9. It is worth noting that Van Til's allusion here is to Eph. 4:21 (the context of which should be consulted and reflected upon as well). His conception of what it is to develop a philosophical "system" is derided by critics for being "biblicistic."

10. If the atheist, for instance, has not first critically defeated the alternative outlook (the Christian position), his intellectual method proceeds with an unsupported prejudgment (a prejudice against Christianity)—and thus he is not "neutral" at all.

The narrative of the fall of man may illustrate this point. Adam and Eve were true theists at the first. They took God's interpretation of themselves and of the animals for granted as the true interpretation. Then came the tempter. He presented to Eve another, that is, an antitheistic theory of reality, and asked her to be the judge as to which was the more reasonable for her to accept. And *the acceptance of this position of judge constituted the fall of man.*[11] That acceptance put the mind of man on an equality with the mind of God. That acceptance also put the mind of the devil on an equality with God. Before Eve could listen to the tempter she had to take for granted that the devil was perhaps[12] a person who knew as much about reality as God knew about it. Before Eve could listen to the tempter, she had to take it for granted that she herself might be such an one as to make it reasonable for her to make a final decision between claims and counter-claims that involved the entire future of her existence. That is, Eve was obliged to postulate an ultimate epistemological pluralism and contingency before she could even proceed to consider the proposition made to her by the devil. Or, otherwise expressed, Eve was compelled to assume the equal ultimacy of the minds of God, of the devil, and of herself. And this surely excluded the exclusive ultimacy of God. This therefore was a denial of God's absoluteness epistemologically. *Thus neutrality was based upon negation. Neutrality is negation.*

This negation was bound to issue in a new affirmation of the supremacy of the human mind over the divine mind. Eve did not ask God, let alone her husband, to decide the issue placed before her. When there are claims and counter-claims someone must assume the role of absolute ultimacy. Eve was definitely placed before an "either or" alternative. Of course she would have denied this if you had told her so at the time. She would have resented being placed before any such alternative. She naturally thought that the issue was not irrevocable, but that she could experiment with the Satanic attitude for a while, and if it did not seem to work she could turn back to her old position of theism again. She thought that evil or sin was at the worst a stepping-stone to higher things, and that she could do all the stepping herself. In all this she was quite wrong. Whether she liked it or not she was, as a matter of fact, standing before an exclusive alternative.[13] Only an action proceeding

11. Emphasis added. Cf. Edward J. Young, *Genesis 3* (London: Banner of Truth Trust, 1966), 25–45.
12. "Perhaps" is a quite significant word here. In behaving as she did, Eve's view of what was "possible" was not in accord with God's viewpoint, position, and authority. Her view of possibility was not innocent. According to it, God could no longer be taken to have absolute authority or "exclusive ultimacy" in the realm of knowing (as Van Til goes on to say).
13. The point is that Eve's rebellious choice was not one that could be reversed by

from the bosom of the eternal could place her on the right track again. It was God who had to reinterpret her deed and place it in its true setting in the universe. And this reinterpretation by God was a reversal of the interpretation given by man. Man had to be brought back to God. This in itself is proof sufficient that the decision on the part of man was *anti*theistic and not merely *non*theistic.

The devil insinuated the idea that an intelligent and decisive interpretation can be made only if reality is purely contingent. God cannot exist and be your creator, for if he did, your choices would be those of a puppet. Don't let the abstract or formal idea of an all-controlling providence of God control your thought. Stand up for your rights as a *free* person. This was, in effect, Satan's argument.

When Eve listened to the tempter, she therefore not only had to posit an original *epistemological pluralism*, but also an *original metaphysical pluralism*. She had to take for granted that as a time created being she could reasonably consider herself to be sufficiently ultimate in her being, so as to warrant an action that was contrary to the will of an eternal being. That is, she not only had to equalize time and eternity, but she had to put time above eternity. It was in time that Satan told her the issue was to be settled. He said that it still remained to be seen *whether* God's threats would come true. The experimental method was to be employed. Only time could tell. This attitude implied that God was no more than a finite God. If he were thought of as an absolute, it would be worse than folly for a creature of time to try out the interpretation of God in the test tube of time. If he were thought of as eternal, such an undertaking was doomed to failure, because in that case history could be nothing but the expression of God's will. And in that case man's humanity would be destroyed.

It is true that this story of man's fall is cast away as a relic of a mythological age by the average student of philosophy. But surely this is unjust. The question is not merely one of the historicity of the book of Genesis. It is that, but it is also more than that. The whole philosophy of theism is involved in it. Anyone rejecting the Genesis narrative must also be prepared to reject the idea of an absolute God. The history includes the philosophy, and the philosophy includes the history. Or we may say that those who reject the Genesis narrative begin their investigation of Greek philosophy with a definite antitheistic bias. It is only because they are themselves not neutral, that they

---

her own wisdom and strength, because the choice deprived her of wisdom and strength. Only the power of God's grace can restore the heart and mind of men so that they see things correctly again.

claim the Greeks to have been neutral. It is an example of identification of neutrality with a fundamental antitheistic bias. And as Christian theists we do not at all wonder at this. It is just what we would expect. *The fact that present-day antitheistic philosophers seem to be totally unaware of their bias, and constantly insist that their starting point is that of neutrality, is itself the best possible proof of the complete control the bias has of them.*[14] In other words, the amazement with which the average student of philosophy or science looks at you if you dare to tell him that, according to your conviction, neutrality is not only undesirable but impossible, is sufficient proof that he has never questioned the reasonableness or the possibility of neutrality. Then the more necessary it is that we challenge this colossal assumption at the outset when it is applied to the study of the Greeks.

REASON AS A TOOL, NOT AN ABSTRACT JUDGE[15]

Accordingly every one of fallen man's functions operates wrongly.[16] The set of the whole human personality has changed. The intellect of fallen man may, as such, be keen enough. It can therefore formally understand the Christian position. It may be compared to a buzz-saw that is sharp and shining, ready to cut the boards that come to it. Let us say that a carpenter wishes to cut fifty boards for the purpose of laying the floor of a house. He has marked his boards. He has set his saw. He begins at one end of the mark on the board. But he does not know that his seven-year-old son has tampered with the saw and changed its set. The result is that every board he saws is cut slantwise and thus unusable because too short except at the point where the saw first made its contact with the wood. As long as the set of the saw is not changed the result will always be the same. So also whenever the teachings of Christianity are presented to the natural man they will be cut according to the set of sinful human personality. The keener the intellect the more consistently will the truths of Christianity be cut according to an exclusively immanentistic pattern.[17] The result is that however much they may formally understand the

---

14. Emphasis added. This is a crucial insight to which students of philosophy should cling as they pursue their studies with instructors who "appear perfectly reasonable" and seem to manifest (or claim) religious indifference in their work.
15. Excerpts from *Defense of the Faith*, 91, 98–101.
16. This is what Reformed theology means by "total" depravity.
17. The noetic effect of sin (the depravity of man's intellect) does not imply, for Van Til, that the unbeliever cannot have a keen intellect. He may be very smart indeed, and thus all the more dangerous to himself and others. Depravity gives a distorted and destructive *orientation* to the sinner's mental functions.

truth of Christianity, men still worship "the dream and figment of their own heart."[18] . . .

It is not our purpose here to deal fully with the question of reason and revelation. Suffice it to note the ambiguity that underlies this approach to the question of the point of contact. When Hodge speaks of *reason* he means "those laws of belief which God has implanted in our nature."[19] Now it is true, of course, that God has planted such laws of belief into our very being. It is this point on which Calvin lays such great stress when he says that all men have a sense of deity. But the unbeliever does not accept the doctrine of his creation in the image of God. It is therefore impossible to appeal to the intellectual and moral nature of men, as *men themselves interpret this nature*, and say that it must judge of the credibility and evidence of revelation. For if this is done, we are virtually telling the natural man to accept just so much and no more of Christianity as, with his perverted concept of human nature, he cares to accept.[20]

To use once again the illustration of the saw: the saw is in itself but a tool. Whether it will move at all and whether it will cut in the right direction depend upon the man operating it. So also reason, or intellect, is always the instrument of a person. And the person employing it is always either a believer or an unbeliever. If he is a believer, his reason has already been changed in its set, as Hodge has told us, by regeneration. It cannot then be the judge; it is now a part of the regenerated person, gladly subject to the authority of God. It has by God's grace permitted itself to be interpreted by God's revelation. If, on the other hand, the person using his reason is an unbeliever, then this person, using his reason, will certainly assume the position of judge with respect to the credibility and evidence of revelation, but he will also certainly find the Christian religion incredible because it is impossible and the evidence for it is always inadequate. Hodge's own teaching on the blindness and hardness of the natural man corroborates this fact.[21]

---

18. Van Til here footnotes Calvin's *Institutes*, 1.4.1.
19. Van Til is here discussing Charles Hodge's view that reason must judge the credibility of a revelation, as expressed in his *Systematic Theology* (New York: Charles Scribner's Sons, 1872), 1:50–53.
20. It is hard to overstate the apologetical importance of this insight. If rebellious, autonomous men have the epistemological right to judge the truth and believability of God's words, they have the right to accept only as much of Scripture as matches their preconceived opinions. This is exactly what we see unbelievers doing all the time.
21. It is good to remember here that there exists no such thing as "reason" in itself, abstracted from and common to both believing and unbelieving ways of thinking. Van Til poses a telling alternative, which reveals that reason cannot simultaneously be subordinate to God and stand in judgment over God. As Van Til goes

Accordingly he also speaks about "reason" as something that seems to operate rightly wherever it is found. But the "reason" of sinful men will invariably act wrongly. Particularly is this true when they are confronted with the specific contents of Scripture. The natural man will invariably employ the tool of his reason to reduce these contents to a naturalistic level. He must do so even in the interest of the principle of contradiction. For his own ultimacy is the most basic presupposition of his entire philosophy. It is upon this presupposition as its fulcrum that he uses the law of contradiction. If he is asked to use his reason as the judge of the credibility of the Christian revelation without at the same time being asked to renounce his view of himself as ultimate, then he is virtually asked to believe and to disbelieve in his own ultimacy at the same time and in the same sense. Moreover this same man, in addition to rejecting Christianity in the name of the law of contradiction, will also reject it in the name of what he calls his intuition of freedom.

It is only to follow out the lead which Hodge in his theology, following Calvin, has given, if we seek our point of contact not in any abstraction whatsoever, whether it be reason or intuition. No such abstraction exists in the universe of men. We always deal with concrete individual men. These men are sinners. *They have "an axe to grind." They want to suppress the truth in unrighteousness. They will employ their reason for that purpose.*[22] And they are not formally illogical if, granted the assumption of man's ultimacy, they reject the teachings of Christianity. On the contrary, to be logically consistent[23] they are bound to do so.

THE INTELLECTUAL IS ITSELF ETHICAL [24]

Christ came to restore us to true knowledge, righteousness and holiness (Col. 3:10; Eph. 4:24). We call this the image of God in the narrower sense. These two [senses of the image of God, wider and narrower] cannot be completely separated from one another. It would really be impossible to think of man having been created only with the image of God in the wider sense;[25] every

---

on to say here, the unbeliever cannot both believe and disbelieve at the same time that his reasoning has ultimacy.

22. Emphasis added. As the subsequent reading selection teaches, reasoning is part of man's behavior and, as such, is subject to the same considerations of motive and purpose as the rest of his behavior.

23. To act as though man's reasoning is the ultimate authority and yet believe by such reasoning that it is not the ultimate authority would be logically inconsistent.

24. Excerpts from *Defense of the Faith*, 29, 63, 52, 189–90, 33–34.

25. While we can distinguish the image of God in the wider sense (namely, the rational and moral character of man, which sets him apart from the lower creation)

act of man would from the very first have to be a moral act, an act of choice for or against God. Hence man would even in every act of knowledge manifest true righteousness and true holiness. . . .

When we say that sin is ethical we do not mean, however, that sin involved only the will of man and not also his intellect. Sin involved every aspect of man's personality. All of man's reactions in every relation in which God had set him were ethical and not merely intellectual; the intellectual itself is ethical. . . .

Sin will reveal itself in the field of knowledge in the fact that man makes himself the ultimate court of appeal in the matter of all interpretation. He will refuse to recognize God's authority. We have already illustrated the sinful person's attitude by the narrative of Adam and Eve. Man has declared his autonomy as over against God. . . .

So far then as men self-consciously work from this principle they have no notion in common with the believer.[26] Their epistemology is informed by their ethical hostility to God. . . .

Christ's work as priest cannot be separated from his work as prophet. Christ could not give us true knowledge of God and of the universe unless he died for us as priest. The question of knowledge is an ethical question at the root. It is indeed possible to have theoretically correct knowledge about God without loving God. The devil illustrates this point. Yet what is meant by knowing God in Scripture is *knowing and loving* God: this is *true* knowledge of God: the other is *false*.[27]

In the third place the catechism asks: "How does Christ execute the office of a King?" The answer is: Christ executeth the office of a King, in subduing us to himself, in ruling and defending us, and in restraining and conquering all of his and our enemies." Again we observe that this work of Christ as king must be brought into organic connection with his work as prophet and priest. To give us true wisdom or knowledge Christ must *subdue* us. He died for us to subdue us and thus gave us wisdom. It is only by emphasizing this organic connection of the aspects of the work of Christ that we can avoid all me-

---

from the image in the narrower sense (namely, man's proper use of that capability, seen in righteousness and fellowship with God), Van Til correctly notes that we cannot separate the two. Man's moral and rational abilities are always being used either to imitate God's thinking and character or not to imitate them.

26. Van Til allows that sinners do not always act in character, deliberately and consistently thinking in accordance with their principles of autonomy. But according to those principles, they do not have the same standards and conceptions as the believer.

27. In a variety of ways, Van Til contrasts the believer's knowledge of God and the unbeliever's knowledge of God (e.g., knowing "deep down," partially "self-conscious" knowing). The expression used here—"false knowledge"—is not the most helpful or clear way to express it.

chanical separation of the intellectual and the moral aspects of the question of knowledge.

4.2 Knowing as Having Belief, Truth, and Evidence

Apologetics involves epistemological disagreement. The believer claims to "know" that God exists and that the gospel is "true," while the unbeliever claims that the Bible is "false," or that the existence of God is "unknowable." The apologetical arena is not the place for arbitrary opinions and purely subjective, unsupported claims back and forth between the believer and the unbeliever. Van Til was resolute in teaching that philosophical opinions that stand opposed to each other "ought to be refuted by a reasoned argument, instead of by ridicule and assumption."[28] Accordingly, the conflicting claims about what is known or not known with respect to Christianity call for analysis and cogent reasoning. In seeking an appropriate approach to apologetics, then, it would serve us well to analyze just what we mean when we speak of "knowing" something.

Knowing. The word "epistemology," which derives from the Greek words *episteme* and *logos*, means "a discourse on (or study of) knowledge." So let us begin by reflecting a bit on the nature of knowledge. What do people ordinarily mean when they say that they "know" something? There is no single, simple answer to that question because the verb "to know" is used in such a wide variety of ways. This is obvious enough in twentieth-century English parlance, but it is also true of the biblical use of the term. The richness of usage is due to the different kinds of objects that are said to be "known." We speak of knowing truths (facts, claims, propositions), as in "He knows *that* the car needs repair"; the Bible also uses the word in this fashion (e.g., Matt. 24:32). We also speak of knowing in the sense of having an ability, as in "He knows *how* to fix the carburetor"; the Bible speaks this way, too (e.g., Luke 11:13). Finally, we speak of knowing persons in the sense of acquaintance or intimacy, as in "I have known *him* for many years"; this usage is common in the Bible (e.g., Gen. 4:1; Matt. 7:23).

The last two senses of "knowing" (as ability and as interpersonal relationship) cannot be reduced merely to the first sense (as intellectual comprehension). However, sometimes when the common locu-

28. *Survey of Christian Epistemology*, 23.

tion for knowing truth ("know that . . .") is utilized, the intended sense is not limited to a barely intellectual or theoretical one. The statement "Be still and know that I am God" (Ps. 46:10) goes beyond an intellectual apprehension and entails both a personal relationship of trust (cf. the context) and the ethical ability to obey the Lord (cf. Jer. 22:16). The last two senses can never be completely divorced from the first sense, either, as though they were independently intelligible. Knowing *how* to fix the carburetor involves knowing *that* it mixes fuel and air, what its parts are, etc.; similarly, knowing *how* to please God involves knowing *that* His precepts require certain things (cf. Rom. 7:7; 8:4–9). Knowing someone *personally*, even in the sexual sense, minimally entails knowing some *facts about* that person; similarly, those who personally "know God" must believe certain propositions about Him (e.g., Heb. 11:6). We should notice that the reverse is not necessarily the case: knowing all the facts in a carburetor manual does not automatically confer ability to fix one, and knowing many personal facts about a famous celebrity does not involve knowing him personally. Likewise, knowing certain facts about God or His law does not automatically give one the ability (know-how) to please Him (e.g., Hos. 2:13; Rom. 2:13) or a personal, saving knowledge of Him (e.g., Hos. 4:6; Gal. 3:24; 4:5, 8). Accordingly, for simplicity and clarity, our discussion of knowledge will focus on the intellectual sense of "knowing" since it is at least part of (although not everything important about) all instances of knowledge.

Knowing in the intellectual sense involves "knowing propositions." The word "proposition" is used here in its strict sense as *that which is expressed* by an indicative sentence in a natural language. This means that two different sentences in the same language (e.g., "He stopped the car" and "The car was stopped by him") and a sentence in a different language (e.g., *"Er hielt das Auto an"*) may express the same proposition. Thus, if we say that all (verbally competent) people have a knowledge of God, this does not mean that they all believe certain sentences in a certain language. Rather, it means that they all believe certain claims that are expressed in various ways in various languages.

Belief. What then is knowledge (in the intellectual sense)? In the first place, knowledge is a subcategory of belief: to know something is, at least, to believe it. We do have to allow for idiomatic expressions that gain their punch by departing from ordinary usage, as in expressing shock: "I know we won the lottery, but I still can't believe it!" But even here the statement would not be intelligible—or convey its sense of amazement—if the word "know" did not entail believing, in which case the statement implies: "I believe it, but still find it unbelievable." In ordinary discourse, it makes no sense to say literally that you know a proposition to be true, but do not believe it to be true. Knowledge involves belief. Of course, there are many kinds of belief of which people are capable and many interesting aspects of belief.

Sometimes we speak of a mental event as a belief, while at other times we think of belief as a disposition to act in certain ways. Beliefs are held with differing degrees of confidence (cf. suspicions, opinions, convictions). Some beliefs are spontaneous, but others are derived by mental investigation and inference. Some beliefs are subject to voluntary control, while not all seem to be so. Some beliefs are given personal avowal; some are held without much reflection at all. Some beliefs have numerous or important consequences, whereas others are relatively insignificant. Some beliefs are normative for us, some are even incorrigible, but some are maintained only by concentrated effort. Some beliefs are irrational or held inconsistently. In all these cases, however, we are still dealing with what is legitimately called "belief."

Attempting to take this diversity into account, we might characterize belief as a positive cognitive attitude toward a proposition, an action-guiding mental state on which a person relies (whether intermittently or continuously) in his theoretical inferences or practical actions and plans.

The different aspects of this characterization can be briefly explained. The mental states or cognitive attitudes that we call a person's "beliefs" are distinguished from each other by the propositions that are their intended objects. Belief is not merely the entertaining of a thought or hypothesis, but a positive attitude toward a proposition, meaning that one relies upon it—whether self-consciously (as in assent) or not—in guiding one's actions. Those actions can be mental (e.g., drawing an inference from certain propositions), verbal (e.g., asserting something to be the case), or physical (e.g., purchasing the item you believe to be the best buy). Actions that are consequent upon a belief are not always of all three kinds, though; people have been known to behave outwardly in terms of a belief that is too painful to assert verbally. Also, verbal assertions of one's beliefs may involve deception and error (e.g., your friends may recognize, in light of your social behavior, the hollowness of your avowal of racial equality, even when you do not suspect yourself of insincerity). It should be further noted that a belief need not always be manifesting itself: the mental state can often be quiescent, and even its active mode may be merely periodic (depending upon the person's changing circumstances and other attitudes or desires). However, the capacity of the mental state to cause mental, verbal, and physical activity is not dependent upon some outside stimulus (as a behaviorist might suggest), but can be exercised at will by the person who believes the proposition in question.

The various aspects of this conception of belief are reflected in Scripture. Knowledge is not separated from belief (cf. the interchangeability of terms in Titus 1:1; 1 John 4:16; 5:5, 20), and belief is a positive attitude ("assurance . . . conviction" in Heb. 11:1; cf. James 1:6) toward propositions that have been heard or read (Rom. 10:14; cf. John 5:24; Acts 24:14; 1 Cor. 1:21; 1 Thess. 2:13; 2 Thess. 2:13). Belief is treated as a dateable event (e.g., Rom. 13:11; 1 Thess. 2:13) as well as a state of mind (e.g., Rom. 15:13; Col. 1:23; 1 Tim. 1:5, 13). That state of mind may be temporary (Luke 8:13; Heb. 10:35, 38–39) or enduring. This depends upon whether the faith comes from God and is grounded in Him (e.g., Eph. 2:8–9; 1 Cor. 2:5; 1 Thess. 2:13; 2 Thess. 2:13; 2 Tim. 1:12; 1 Peter 1:4–5, 9) or not. When men live in faith, their belief comes to expression whenever an occasion requires it (e.g., Abraham and Moses in Heb. 11:8–9, 17, 23–28; cf. James 1:2–3); however, in another sense their faith is continuously operative in life (e.g., 1 Tim. 6:12; 2 Tim. 4:7; Heb. 4:1–11; 10:38–39). Belief carries different degrees of confidence (e.g., Mark 9:24; Luke 17:5; Rom. 4:19–21). It expresses itself in one's mental inferences (e.g., Heb. 11:3; Rom. 4:20–21), in one's verbal remarks (e.g., Rom. 10:9–10; 2 Cor. 4:13), and in one's actions (e.g., James 2:14–20; Heb. 11:4ff.; cf. Luke 8:15; 1 Thess. 2:3; 1 Tim. 4:10). Finally, there is a sense in which belief is not simply a passive response to external stimuli, but an active expression of one's will—since it is morally enjoined upon men, both at its inception (e.g., Mark 1:15; John 20:27; Acts 16:31) and in its continuing operation (e.g., 1 John 3:23; Eph. 6:16; Col. 1:23; 2:7; cf. 2 Tim. 3:14).

Truth. At any rate, knowing something is a case of believing it. Yet knowledge is clearly more than a mere belief. It often happens that two people believe propositions that contradict each other; one asserts a claim (e.g., Winston Churchill was elected to Parliament in 1900), while the other denies it. In such a case, both people cannot "know" what they have asserted (thus, it either is the case that Churchill was elected in 1900, or it is not); at least one of them is mistaken. As experience shows only too often, not everything that people believe proves to be true. And whenever a proposition or claim turns out to be false, nobody can be said to have "known" that proposition—even though someone sincerely believed that it was true. A man may honestly "believe" that Mount Rushmore is located in California, but he cannot really "know" it, for the simple reason that the claim is not accurate. So then, instances of knowing are instances of believing, but one can know a proposition only if it is true. Most everybody has an intuitive understanding of what it means for a proposition to be "true." In commonsense or ordinary usage, we say that a proposition is true if it states "what is the case," conforms to "the facts" (or to reality), accords with "the actual state of affairs," or is "correct."

It is one thing to offer an adequate synonym for "true," but quite another to set forth a theory of truth—something that philosophers have struggled to do. It should be noted, though, that different philosophical theories of truth are not necessarily in conflict with each other, since they may address different aspects of the matter. For example, the correspondence theory attempts to explain the nature of the property called "truth." The coherence or pragmatic theories attempt to explain the evidence for the presence of that property. And the semantic and performative theories attempt to explain the logical structure or function of sentences using the term.

Each of these theories has its own drawbacks. For instance, the correspondence theory (that true sentences parallel or picture extramental reality) either rests upon a crude and unworkable metaphor or speaks of correspondence with abstract entities (e.g., states of affairs, "facts") that cannot be explained and individuated apart from reference to true propositions—which the theory was supposed to explain in the first place. Similarly, the coherence theory relies on the premise that two inconsistent propositions cannot both be true, thus unwittingly invoking the very thing (truth) that the theory was to explain.

The pragmatic theory (that true sentences are corroborated by their practical results) presupposes that we know in advance what results should truly be expected from any sentence—or (worse) allows that any sentence is true just as long as somebody believes that the satisfying conditions for its practical effect(s) have been fulfilled.

The semantic theory basically lays down a condition of material adequacy for any interpretation in a language, namely, that the proposition named *p* is true if and only if *p*. That is, the value "true" should be assigned to all and only those sentences that are regarded as true—regardless of how one determines that! A definition of truth in English would then call for assigning names to all objects, giving satisfaction conditions for every predicate, and then recursively determining the values of every possible English sentence. The semantic theory requires recourse to a formal language (so as to distinguish between an object language and a metalanguage), so it is unworkable (inapplicable) in natural languages like English, where truth-claims are normally debated.

According to the performative theory, to assert that a sentence is true is not to ascribe any property to it, but rather to perform the action of offering personal reassurance or confirmation with regard to it. But this notion is unhelpful, for a sentence obviously offers reassurance of its own truth. It is also linguistically inaccurate. For example, the sentence "Every statement made by Napoleon was true" does indeed ascribe a property to Napoleon's statements, but it does not convey the same message as "I confirm every statement made by Napoleon."[29]

The Christian's approach to the notion of truth is both more basic than those usually considered and also less formal (more substantial, more personal). The believer understands that truth fundamentally is whatever conforms to the mind of God (cf. Ps. 111:7–8; John 14:6; 16:13). Thus, the Bible applies the term not only to the facts (e.g., Deut. 17:4; Eph. 4:25)—since they are all predetermined by the mind of God (Eph. 1:11; Isa. 46:9–11; Matt. 10:29–30)—but also to what is eternal and absolute (e.g., John 6:32, 35; 15:1; Heb. 8:2), as well as to what is ethically right (e.g., Ps. 26:3; John 3:21; 2 John 4). Because God is faithful, His word (reflecting His mind) is not contradictory (2 Cor. 1:18), and He Himself never contradicts it (Heb. 6:18). Propositions that correspond to God's mind will therefore be coherent with each other. Moreover, as the book of Proverbs drives home over and over

29. For a more extensive critique of the pragmatic and performative theories, see Greg L. Bahnsen, "Pragmatism, Prejudice, and Presuppositionalism," in *Foundations of Christian Scholarship: Essays in the Van Til Perspective*, ed. Gary North (Vallecito, Calif.: Ross House Books, 1976), 243–58, 271–84.

again in numerous ways, the most "pragmatic" way to live in God's world—the most efficient and successful strategy for living—is to submit to the guidance of God's wisdom.

Van Til's presuppositional approach to apologetics has often been misconstrued as endorsing one of the theories of truth that have been advanced by different schools of philosophy, when in fact Van Til condemned (and endorsed) them all in terms of the broader worldview that gives them their particular character. Van Til did not endorse one or the other, but was content to incorporate them all within a broader *revelational epistemology*. Even more fundamentally, Van Til realized that the revelational (or Christian) approach to the theory of knowledge and the nonrevelational (non-Christian) approach do not see the problems of epistemology in the same light. They differ over what are the most basic issues, the relevant problems to be solved, and the way in which they understand successful methods of knowing.

Christian philosophy is a way of restating what God has authoritatively revealed about Himself, the world, man, etc.—the Christian worldview—and thus the way in which we know anything at all is first and foremost a matter of revelation. Once this revelational context is understood, the Christian philosopher does not advocate (in the secular sense) a coherence theory of truth over a correspondence theory, or vice versa. Indeed, the Christian understands the most important kind of "correspondence" and the most important kind of "coherence" in ways that are quite different from—and objectionable to—unbelieving philosophers. Furthermore, the Christian does not choose "deductive" reasoning over "inductive" reasoning,[30] nor inductive over deductive.[31] This is a false dilemma from Van Til's perspective. As understood and used by men who presuppose their autonomy from God, both kinds of reasoning are hostile to Christianity. Understood within the Christian framework, both kinds of reasoning are equally acceptable and necessary for the believer.

---

30. Clark Pinnock seriously misrepresents Van Til when he says that Van Til is opposed to empirical investigation and gives a veto to any inductive approach to knowing ("The Philosophy of Christian Evidences," in *Jerusalem and Athens*, ed. E. R. Geehan [Philadelphia: Presbyterian and Reformed, 1946], 421–22; *Biblical Revelation: The Foundation of Christian Theology* [Chicago: Moody Press, 1971], 38; cf. Daniel Fuller and Clark Pinnock, "On Revelation and Biblical Authority," *Christian Scholars Review* 2 [1973]: 331–33).

31. Deductive reasoning begins with general principles or truths and assimilates particular observations or instances to them; the conclusions of deductive arguments simply display what was already implicit in their premises. It is generally

REVELATIONAL EPISTEMOLOGY[32]

The subject of a Christian View of Life must be studied historically and sys-tematically in order to understand it comprehensively. If we study it thus we find that we face an ultimate choice between Christian and non-Christian epis-temology. Especially because of the modern emphasis on the immanence of God, it is necessary to become clearly aware of the deep antithesis between the two main types of epistemology. . . .

The question we must ask constantly is how anyone has conceived of the relation of the human mind to the divine mind. It is on this point that the great-est difference obtains between the theistic and the non-theistic position. The former cannot think of the human mind as functional at all except when it is in contact with God; the latter presupposes it to be possible that the human mind functions normally whether or not God exists. . . .

We must seek to bring the theistic and the non-theistic positions face to face with one another on the central issue of the relation of the finite con-sciousness to God. We may begin the argument by discussing what is involved in the ordinary knowledge transaction of man. Christian theism claims that finite consciousness can know nothing about anything except upon the pre-supposition of the absolute self-consciousness of God.[33] The non-theistic po-sition holds to the opposite of this. . . .

The main question in dispute between Christians and their opponents comes out most clearly when the subject of knowledge is discussed. It is then that we must give an answer to the question whether the human mind is able in itself to interpret reality.[34] On this important point we note that the oppo-nents of Christian theism have taken for granted that which they ought to

---

held, then, that the acquiring of new knowledge relies on inductive reasoning, which generalizes or projects conclusions on the basis of particular observations or cases. The conclusions reached by inductive arguments are less than conclu-sive because new (or newly discovered) data could affect their strength.

32. Excerpts from *Survey of Christian Epistemology*, v, viii, ix, xiii–xiv, 1–3, 4–10.

33. In God's thinking, there are no facts that are newly discovered or contingent (or, as Van Til sometimes put it earlier in his career, God's knowledge is exclusively analytical, not synthetical). This is because God is the Creator of all facts, and the facts are what they are in terms of God's sovereign plan; thus, to know anything "outside" Himself, God need only "analyze" or consult His own mind. His knowl-edge is universal, unalterable, and self-sufficient. These are the sort of truths that Van Til summarized in his expression "the absolute self-consciousness of God."

34. Cf. *Survey of Christian Epistemology*, 210: "Naturally, the main point in dispute is whether our opponents can get along without God. All of our opponents have said *in effect* that human categories [of thought] are ultimate. With respect to all of them we would then ask what happens if they seek to face the more ultimate questions of philosophy on this basis" (emphasis added).

have proved, namely, the independence and therefore the ultimacy of the human mind.[35] . . .

Every system of philosophy must tell us whether it thinks true knowledge to be possible.[36] Or if a system of philosophy thinks it impossible for man to have a true knowledge of the whole of reality or even of a part of reality, it must give good reasons for thinking so.[37] From these considerations, it follows that if we develop our reasons for believing that a true knowledge of God and, therefore, also of the world, is possible because actually given in Christ, we have in fact given what goes in philosophy under the name of epistemology. It will then be possible to compare the Christian epistemology with

35. With this piercing observation, Van Til indicates that non-Christian philosophy, by its very choice (or exclusion) of which questions need to be answered, is not at all ideologically neutral, but is at the outset already prejudiced in favor of an autonomous theory of knowledge—despite a lack of evidence for it and a lack of answers to obvious challenges (arising from man's finitude, questions of objectivity in a subject-object relationship like knowing, recognized distorting and relativizing influences, etc.). Van Til wrote that "there is a bias involved in the question of epistemology even at the very starting point" (ibid., 116).

36. This takes us to the heart of presuppositional apologetics. In the conflict between "systems of philosophy" (worldviews), Van Til urged defenders of the faith to challenge the non-Christian epistemologically—not simply about knowing (or not knowing) God, but about the possibility of knowing anything whatsoever. "The struggle between Christian theism and its opponents covers the whole field of knowledge. It is not as though we are at the outset dealing with the question of the knowledge of the world about us and that the only point in dispute is whether or not God can be and need be known. We may indeed make the question whether God need be and can be known so inclusive that it coincides with the question whether anything can be known. *Christian theism's fundamental contention is just this, that nothing whatsoever can be known unless God can be and is known.* . . . The important thing to note is this fundamental difference between theism and antitheism on the question of epistemology. There is not a spot in heaven or on earth about which there is no dispute between the two opposing parties" (p. 116, emphasis added). Non-Christian worldviews cannot give a cogent account of the possibility of rational justification for any belief—that is, cannot make sense out of objective, self-consistent, evidence-warranted "knowledge."

37. When it comes to scholarship and attempting to be rational in one's convictions, arbitrariness is a cardinal sin. Thus, in the apologetical dispute between believer and unbeliever, neither side should be allowed to get by with asserting things for which no reasons are offered (or could be offered). Presuppositional apologetics does not (contrary to misrepresentations) endorse taking a philosophical position at will, then "protecting" it by claiming its presuppositional status, and refusing to argue (give reasons) for it. Quite the contrary. Van Til taught us that unbelievers repeatedly take the most controversial or question-begging stances simply for granted, and that this should be exposed as unreasoning prejudice. At this point in the reading selection, he teaches that both those who claim that genuine knowledge is possible and those who are skeptical about it must be pressed for their reasons. Likewise, Christians must "develop our reasons" for the answer we give to this basic question.

any and with all others. And being thus enabled to compare them all, we are in a position and placed before the responsibility of choosing between them. And this choosing can then, in the nature of the case, no longer be a matter of artistic preference. *We cannot choose epistemologies as we choose hats.*[38] Such would be the case if it had been once for all established that the whole thing is but a matter of taste. But that is exactly what has not been established. That is exactly the point in dispute. . . .

REVELATION

According to Scripture, God has created the "universe." God has created time and space. God has created all the "facts" of science. God has created the human mind. In this human mind God has laid the laws of thought according to which it is to operate. In the facts of science God has laid the laws of being according to which they function. In other words, the impress of God's plan is upon his whole creation.

We may characterize this whole situation by saying that the creation of God is a revelation of God. God revealed himself in nature and God also revealed himself in the mind of man. Thus it is impossible for the mind of man to function except in an atmosphere of revelation. And every thought of man when it functioned normally in this atmosphere of revelation would express the truth as laid in the creation by God. We may therefore call a Christian epistemology a revelational epistemology. . . .

We must now seek to define this revelational epistemology more closely by relating it still more definitely to the conception of him who gives the revelation. *The* all-important question is what kind of a God reveals himself. Pantheistic thinkers also speak of God revealing himself, and might therefore also speak of a revelational epistemology if they desired. But for the sake of clearness, the term revelation should really be reserved for biblical thought. According to this view God has been, and is, eternally self-conscious. There is no fringe of ignorance or darkness in him.

CORRESPONDENCE

It is this concept of a completely self-conscious God that is all-important in epistemology. This appears at once from the implications of such a concept for the fact of human knowledge.

True human knowledge corresponds to the knowledge which God has of

---

38. Emphasis added. Van Til did not hold that people arbitrarily choose their presuppositions, rendering the conflict between worldviews an irresolvable matter rooted in personal preferences. A rational vindication is required of one's epistemology—and thus of one's conception of rationality itself.

himself and his world. Suppose that I am a scientist investigating the life and ways of a cow. What is this cow? I say it is an animal. But that only pushes the question back. What is an animal? To answer that question I must know what life is. But again, to know what life is I must know how it is related to the inorganic world. And so I may and must continue till I reach the borders of the universe. And even when I have reached the borders of the universe, I do not yet know what the cow is. Complete knowledge of what a cow is can be had only by an absolute intelligence, i.e., by one who has, so to speak, the blueprint of the whole universe. But it does not follow from this that the knowledge of the cow that I have is not true as far as it goes. It is true if it corresponds to the knowledge that God has of the cow.

From this presentation of the matter, it is clear that what we mean by correspondence is not what is often meant by it in epistemological literature. In the literature on the subject, correspondence usually means a correspondence between the idea I have in my mind and the "object out there." In the struggle between the "realists" and the "subjective idealists" this was the only question in dispute. They were not concerned about the question uppermost in our minds, i.e., whether or not God has to be taken into the correspondence. We may call our position in epistemology a *Correspondence Theory of Truth,* if only we keep in mind that it is opposed to what has historically been known under that name.

COHERENCE

In opposition to the historical correspondence theory of truth there arose in the Kant-Hegel tradition the so-called Coherence Theory of Truth. The Idealists argued in the way that we have argued above about the cow. They said that true knowledge cannot be obtained by a mere correspondence of an idea of the mind to an object existing apart from the mind. The mind and the object of which it seeks knowledge are parts of one great system of reality and one must have knowledge of the whole of this reality before one has knowledge of any of its parts. Accordingly, the Idealists said that the thing that really counted in knowledge was the coherence of any fact with all other facts. To know the place of a fact in the universe as a whole is to have true knowledge. This position, as we shall see more fully later, approaches, in form, what we are after in our position. Yet it is *only in form* that it approaches our position. That this is true can be seen from the determining fact that the Absolute to which the Idealist seeks to relate all knowledge is not the completely self-conscious God of Christianity. We cannot prove this point here. We only state it as our conviction here in order to clear the ground. The Absolute of Idealism, we believe, is not really an absolute because he exists as merely correlative to the space-time world. Accordingly there are new facts arising for him as well as for us. God becomes a *primus inter pares,* a One among others. He can no longer be the standard of human knowledge.

It is our contention that only the Christian can obtain real coherence in his thinking.[39] If all of our thoughts about the facts of the universe are in correspondence with God's ideas of these facts, there will naturally be coherence in our thinking because there is a complete coherence in God's thinking. On the other hand we hold that the Idealistic coherence theory of truth cannot lead to coherence because it omits the source of all coherence, namely, God.

In a way it might be well for us to call our position the *Coherence Theory of Truth* because we claim to have true coherence. Whether we call our position a correspondence theory or whether we call it a coherence theory, we have in each case to distinguish it sharply from the theories that have historically gone by these names. Accordingly, the determining factor must be a consideration of that which is most fundamental in our theory of correspondence or of coherence. Now this depends upon the question whether we have God's knowledge in mind first of all, or whether we begin with human knowledge. For God, coherence is the term that comes first. There was coherence in God's plan before there was any space-time fact to which his knowledge might correspond, or which might correspond to his knowledge. On the other hand, when we think of human knowledge, correspondence is of primary importance. If there is to be true coherence in our knowledge there must be correspondence between our ideas of facts and God's ideas of these facts. Or rather we should say that our ideas must correspond to God's ideas.[40] Now since we are dealing with opponents who speak of human knowledge almost exclusively, we can perhaps best bring out the distinctiveness of our position by calling it the *Correspondence Theory of Truth.* An additional reason for this choice is that at the present time the old correspondence theory has pretty well died down, leaving the coherence theory in control of the field. Hence

39. Notice here that attaining logical consistency is important in Van Til's approach to epistemology. Indeed, presuppositional apologetics challenges unbelieving schools of philosophy with the claim that only Christianity exhibits logical consistency.

40. This is an important sentence to keep in mind when one interprets (or criticizes) Van Til's doctrine of "analogy"—that man knows anything he knows (whether the world or God Himself) by thinking "analogously" to God's thinking. God and man know the same objects or truths, according to Van Til, and the standard of truth for both God and man is the same, namely, God's thoughts about whatever we know. This is far from being an avenue to theological skepticism or irrationality, as unsympathetic critics insist. Rather, Van Til said quite categorically that "our ideas must correspond to God's ideas"—even though, metaphysically speaking, man's mind (and ideas) are not the same as God's mind (and ideas).

we have the advantage of a different name from the current name, since we are interested in making it clear that we really have a different theory from the current theory. . . .

METHOD

Finally we must discuss the question of method. At this stage we are interested only in seeing what sort of method of investigation is involved in Christianity. *At the outset it ought to be clearly observed that every system of thought necessarily has a certain method of its own. Usually this fact is overlooked. It is taken for granted that everybody begins in the same way with an examination of the facts, and that the differences between systems come only as a result of such investigations. Yet this is not actually the case.*[41] It *could not* actually be the case. In the first place, this could not be the case with a Christian. His fundamental and determining fact is the fact of God's existence. That is his final conclusion. But that must also be his starting point.[42] If the Christian is right in his final conclusion about God, then he would not even get into touch with any fact unless it were through the medium of God.

And since man has, through the fall in Adam, become a sinner, man cannot know and therefore love God except through Christ the Mediator. And it is in Scripture alone that he learns about this Mediator. Scripture is the Word of Christ, the Son of God and Son of man. No sinner knows anything truly except he knows Christ, and no one knows Christ truly unless the Holy Ghost, the Spirit sent by the Father and the Son, regenerates him.[43]

If all things must be seen "in God" to be seen truly, one could look ever so long elsewhere without ever seeing a fact as it really is. If I must look through a telescope to see a distant star, I cannot first look at the star to see whether there is a telescope through which alone I could see it. If I must look through a microscope to see a germ, I cannot first look at the germ with the naked eye to see if there is a microscope through which alone I can see it. If it were a question of seeing something with the naked eye and seeing the same object more clearly through a telescope or a microscope, the matter

41. Emphasis added.
42. "Circularity" in one's philosophical system is just another name for "consistency" in outlook throughout one's system. That is, one's starting point and final conclusion cohere with each other.
43. Van Til clearly identified the redemptive character of the presuppositional worldview that the Christian defends. Christians do not defend a bare worldview that supports the intelligibility of logic, science, etc., and leaves the work of Christ out of the picture; for Van Til, that redemptive work is crucial to fallen man finding intelligibility in anything he does or thinks.

would be different. We may see a landscape dimly with the naked eye and then turn to look at it through a telescope and see it more clearly. But such is not the case with the Christian position. According to it, nothing at all can be known truly of any fact unless it be known through and by way of man's knowledge of God.

But if it be readily granted that a Christian begins with a bias, it will not so readily be granted that his opponents also begin with a bias. Yet this is no less the case. And the reason for this is really the same as that given above in the case of the Christian. We may again illustrate with our telescope analogy. The antitheist is one who has made up his mind in advance that he will never look through a telescope. He remains steadfast in his conviction that there are *some* facts that can be known truly without looking through a telescope. This much is implied in the very idea of starting to see *whether* there is a God. It will be observed that *even to say that there are some facts that can be known without reference to God, is already the very opposite of the Christian position.*[44]

It is not necessary to say that all facts can be known without reference to God in order to have a flat denial of the Christian position. The contention of Christianity is exactly that there is not one fact that can be known without God. Hence if anyone avers that there is even *one* fact that can be known without God, he reasons like a non-Christian. It follows then that such a person in effect rejects the whole of the Christian position, the final conclusions as well as the starting point. And that means that such a person has at the outset taken for granted that there is no God in whom alone "facts" can be known.[45] In other words, such a person has taken for granted that God is at least not such a "fact" that he is related to every other "fact" so that no other fact can be understood without reference to the "fact" of God.

It was needful to make this point that every human being must necessarily begin with a "bias" clear, at this stage, because it is often assumed that the real difference between the traditionally Christian position and the ordinary philosophical and scientific methods exists in the fact that the traditional position alone is prejudiced, while all others are open-minded. It was necessary, too, to emphasize the universality of "prejudice" at this point because it will thus become clear that when the Christian and his opponent use the same terminology they do not mean the same things. Both speak of inductive, deductive and transcendental methods, but each of them presupposes his own starting point when he uses these terms, and that fact gives these

---

44. Emphasis added. "Without reference to God" means not appealing or alluding to God within the chain of reasoning by which we explain or justify what is known.
45. The emphasis in this claim is on the particular *kind* of God proclaimed and intellectually defended by the Christian.

terms a different meaning in each case. It follows from this too that what the Christian is opposing is not these methods, as such, but the anti-Christian pre-suppositions at the base of them.[46]

KNOWLEDGE

Which method fits with a certain system of thought depends upon the idea of knowledge a system has. For the Christian system, knowledge consists in understanding the relation of any fact to God as revealed in Scripture. I know a fact truly to the extent that I understand the exact relation such a fact sustains to the plan of God. It is the plan of God that gives any fact meaning in terms of the plan of God. The whole meaning of any fact is exhausted by its position in and relation to the plan of God.[47] This implies that every fact is related to every other fact. God's plan is a unit. And it is this unity of the plan of God, founded as it is in the very being of God, that gives the unity that we look for between all the finite facts. If one should maintain that one fact can be fully understood without reference to all other facts, he is as much antitheistic as when he should maintain that one fact can be understood without reference to God.

IMPLICATION

From this conception of knowledge it will appear which method a Christian would naturally be bound to use. That method we may perhaps best designate as the *method of implication*.[48] What we seek to do in our search for

46. These presuppositions determine not only the particular and precise meaning, but also the meaningfulness, of such terms (and the methods they name).
47. In unbelieving philosophical circles, a dispute continues to rage over the proper nature of "explanation." Some philosophers argue that all explanation follows the pattern of natural science (with reference to initializing conditions and covering laws), while others maintain that especially in history explanation must incorporate reference to intentions or purpose (thus accounting for what is unique about human behavior). The one side "explains" in terms of past conditions and relations, while the other "explains" in terms of future aims. Whatever kind of explanation one pursues, however, Van Til says that the "fact" is explained by its place in God's plan—since God's plan is philosophically necessary to make sense out of both "causation" (natural explanation) and "purpose" (teleological explanation).
48. The word "implication" has been used in a wider variety of ways than many students of philosophy today are aware, and thus Van Til's vocabulary will seem strange here. Philosophers have given different accounts, for instance, of the relationship between the notion of implication and the notion of entailment (as also conditional statement, deduction, inference, etc.). Philosophers have spoken of "strict implication" (C. I. Lewis), "formal implication" (Bertrand Russell), "material implication" (texts in first-order predicate logic), etc. We can speak of logical implication, definitional implication, conceptual implication (and pre-

understanding the universe is to work ourselves ever more deeply into the relations that the facts of the universe sustain to God. That is, we seek to *implicate* ourselves more deeply into a comprehension of God's plan in and with every fact that we investigate. Suppose that I am a biologist, studying the color of certain frogs. In order to do so, I must seek to know all about frogs in general. I must have some conception about the species as a whole, before I can intelligently study the individual. Or if I am studying some animal about which no information is available from the records of science, it is still necessary that I have a theory about animal life in general, in order to engage in fruitful research. Thus in starting any investigation the *general precedes the particular.* No one without any general notion about animal life would ever think of investigating a point of detail. Then when I continue my investigation, I must seek to relate this particular frog to other frogs, then the frogs to other animal life, and then animal life as such to human life, and human life to the conception of God that I have.

Now this approach from the bottom to the top, from the particular to the general is the *inductive aspect* of the method of implication. *The greater the amount of detailed study and the more carefully such study is undertaken, the more truly Christian will the method be.*[49] It is important to bring out this point in order to help remove the common misunderstanding that Christianity is opposed to factual investigation. That the opponents of Christianity are still seeking to spread this misunderstanding may be seen, for instance, from such a book as that of Stewart G. Cole, *The History of Fundamentalism.* Throughout the book it is stated time and again that the believers in the

---

supposition), causal implication, volitional implication, contextual implication, etc. For some absolute idealist philosophers, "implication" is a way of speaking of any knowledge-gaining activity or method. This way of speaking is natural in light of the title of the two-volume work by Bernard Bosanquet, *Logic or the Morphology of Knowledge* (1888), and his earlier essay, "Logic as the Science of Knowledge" (1883). Bosanquet sought to diminish the differences between judgments and inferences, as also between induction and deduction. When we gain knowledge we go beyond isolated perceptions or individual qualities in things, gaining "depth and complexity of insight into a sub-system of the world."

49. Once again we must note here how far afield some of Van Til's critics have strayed in understanding him. Presuppositionalism is not simply interested in philosophical or abstract principles, but in empirical detail and research as well. For example, John W. Montgomery claims that Van Til offers the unbeliever "an a priori dogmatic" demand, in contrast to "the factually compelling evidence for the Christian truth-claim" ("Once upon an A Priori," in *Jerusalem and Athens*, ed. Geehan, 392). And according to Clark Pinnock, Van Til "refuses to have anything to do with . . . empirical demonstrations," and indeed "recoils from" detailed evidence that can verify the faith ("The Philosophy of Christian Evidences," in *Jerusalem and Athens*, ed. Geehan, 421, 424–25).

traditionally Christian position are opposed to the spread of the knowledge of all the facts discovered by chance. Now it were a great deal better for Liberalism itself if it were willing to fight openly and *admit that the whole fight is one about two mutually opposite philosophies of life*,[50] instead of about the hiding or non-hiding of certain facts.

DEDUCTION AND INDUCTION

Then, corresponding to the inductive aspect of the method of implication is the *deductive aspect.* We may define this as the control of the general over the particular. Our conception of God controls the investigation of every fact. We are certain, as certain as our conviction of the truth of the entire Christian position, that certain "facts" will never be discovered. One of these, for example, is "the missing link." The term "missing link" we take in its current meaning of a gradual transition from the non-rational to the rational. As such, it is an anti-Christian conception, inasmuch as it implies that the non-rational is more ultimate than the rational. At least the anti-Christian wants to leave the question of the relative ultimacy of the rational to the non-rational an open question, while the Christian can never afford to do this. For the Christian, it is a settled and not an open question.

And this difference between the Christian and his opponents comes to the fore in the method of investigation of facts. The anti-Christian holds that any sort of fact may appear. He thinks this to be one of the most important requirements of a truly scientific attitude. On the other hand, the Christian holds that no fact will appear that could disprove the ultimacy of the fact of God, and therefore of what he has revealed of himself and his plan for the world through Christ in the Scriptures. We may illustrate this point by the example of a mathematician who finds that three points are related to one another by the arc of a circle. Then when he proceeds to draw the circle he follows a definitely "prescribed" course, even if he has made no mark on his paper yet. If it is the circle that relates the points, and if the circle exhausts the relation of the points, the mathematician cannot reasonably expect to find other points on a tangent to the circle that are nevertheless related to the points of the circle. Now we may compare the circle of the mathematician to the Christian concept of God. We hold that the meaning of any one finite fact is exhausted by its relation to the plan of God.[51] Hence this same thing will hold for any two or three facts. And it follows that no other facts can stand in any possi-

50. Emphasis added.
51. That is: although the Christian does not know all the facts (as the mathematician does not have all the points), he does know the pattern (as the mathematician has the arc) in which alone they make sense (are connected).

ble relation to these facts unless they too are related to this one comprehensible plan of God. In other words, only Christian facts are possible. For any fact to be a fact at all, it must be what Christ in Scripture says it is.

This is the main point in dispute between Christians and non-Christians. The difference between the two does not only appear in the interpretation of facts after they have been found, but even in the question what facts one may *expect* to find. And it does not go without saying, as is all too often assumed, that the non-Christian is right in looking for any kind of fact. If the Christian position should prove to be right *in the end,* then the anti-Christian position was wrong, not only at the end, but already at the beginning.

From the description given of the deductive and the inductive aspects of the method of implication, it will now appear that *what has historically been known by the deductive and inductive methods are both equally opposed to the Christian method.*[52] By the deductive method as exercised, e.g., by the Greeks, was meant that one begins his investigations with the assumption of the truth and ultimacy of certain axioms, such as, for example, that of causal relation. The question whether these axioms rest in God or in the universe was in that case not considered to be of great importance. Not as though the question was not raised. Plato did consider the question whether God was back of the ideas or whether the ideas were back of God. Yet this question was not given the importance that we give to it. We must put the point more strongly. The question was, in effect, given the wrong answer. It was assumed that the true, the beautiful and the good rest in themselves, and that God is subordinate to them. For us the question is all-important. If the axioms on which science depends are thought of as resting in the universe, the opposite of the Christian position is in effect maintained. The only rationality they know of in the universe is then the mind of man.[53] Hence the alternative may be stated by saying that according to the Christian position, the basis of human investigation is in God, while for the antitheistic position the basis of human investigation is in man.

Similarly with the more modern method of induction. What is meant by induction as a method of science is the gathering of facts without reference to any axioms, in order to find to what these facts may lead us. Many scientists claim this method to be *the* method of science. But we have already seen that the usual assumption underlying this method is the antitheistic one, that

52. Emphasis added.
53. This is the critical epistemological question in our apologetical challenge to unbelief. Is rationality (science, logic, intention, etc.) to be accounted for in terms of the mind of man or the mind of God? Compare the last sentence in the next paragraph by Van Til.

there may be any kind of fact. Hence *the difference between the prevalent method of science and the method of Christianity is not that the former is interested in finding the facts and is ready to follow the facts wherever they may lead, while the latter is not ready to follow the facts.*[54] The difference is rather that the former wants to study the facts *without God,* while the latter wants to study the facts in the light of the revelation God gives of himself in Christ. Thus the antithesis is once more that between those for whom the final center of reference in knowledge lies in man, and those for whom the final center of reference for knowledge lies in God, as this God speaks in Scripture.

Accordingly, we pay scant attention to the historic quarrel between the apostles of deduction and the apostles of induction. Our quarrel is not with either of them in particular but with both of them in general. To us the only thing of great significance in this connection is that it is often found to be more difficult to distinguish our method from the deductive method than from the inductive method. But the favorite charge against us is that we are still bound to the past and are therefore employing the deductive method.[55] Our opponents are thoughtlessly identifying our method with the Greek method of deduction. For this reason it is necessary for us to make the difference between these two methods as clear as we can.

From our discussion it will also appear that even the method of implication, as employed by Idealistic philosophy, is quite the opposite of ours.[56] Here especially it is of paramount importance to distinguish clearly. We have purposely chosen the name implication for our method because we believe that it really fits in with the Christian scheme, while it fits in with no other scheme. Hence we must take particular pains to note that the method of implication as advocated especially by B. Bosanquet and other Idealists, is really as fundamentally opposed to our method as is the method of ancient deductivism and of modern inductivism. The difference is once more that we believe the Idealists to have left God out of consideration.

54. Emphasis added.
55. Years ago Van Til realized that opponents of presuppositionalism tend to think that there are only two kinds of reasoning: inductive and deductive. Deductive reasoning stands opposed to inductive. However, there is also transcendental reasoning, in which the preconditions for the intelligibility of what is experienced, asserted, or argued are posed or sought. It, too, stands opposed to a purely inductive approach to knowledge. Critics seem to think that, since presuppositionalism does not endorse pure inductivism, it must favor deductivism instead. This logical fallacy is known as false antithesis.
56. Note this well. Far from following idealism, Van Til maintained that it did not have a worldview in which its endorsement of "implication" could be made intelligible.

A PRIORI AND A POSTERIORI

Closely related to the terms inductive and deductive are the terms *a posteriori* and *a priori*. The literal meaning of these terms is "from that which follows or is subsequent," and "from that which is before" respectively. An a posteriori method is one that is practically identical with the empirical or inductive method. The a priori method is usually identified with the deductive method. We need only observe that a priori reasoning, and a posteriori reasoning, are equally anti-Christian, if these terms are understood in their historical sense. As such they contemplate man's activity in the universe but do not figure with the significance of God above the universe.

4.3 The Inescapable Knowledge of God in Nature

Let us recap where we have been. Apologetics is necessarily epistemological in its concerns. There can be no religious neutrality when it comes to the position one takes in epistemology, and the Christian worldview has a unique approach to the problems and standards of epistemology. With this in mind, we continue our analysis of "knowing" (in the intellectual sense).

We have already noted above that for someone to know a proposition, at least two conditions must be met: the person must believe the proposition in question, and the proposition must be true. However, even this is an inadequate analysis of knowledge. At first sight, it might seem that if we believe what is in fact true, then we have knowledge; but on further reflection, to define knowledge as true belief proves to be too broad.

Having Evidence. The reason for this is that true beliefs can sometimes be arrived at by invalid means, or from false premises, or without requisite regard for evidence at all. Consider some examples. Suppose that Sam believes that "In 1985 the initials of the president of the United States were R. R.," but he believes it because he believes that Roy Rogers was president in 1985. The specimen sentence is indeed true (since Ronald Reagan was president), but no one would credit Sam with "knowing" it to be true. Similarly, if Sam looks at a clock that is not running, but at the very moment when the hands are pointing to the correct time, Sam does not in such a circumstance gain "knowledge" of what time it is. If Sam mistakenly remembers the testimony of a liar, he may accidentally turn out to believe what happens to be true, but he is not properly said to "know" it. In cases like these, Sam's beliefs are based on false reasons. Other people believe some things that turn out to be true, but for no apparent reason at all; they follow some alternative at a venture, without a rational means of deciding to do so (e.g., the person who is "just sure" he is going to win the lottery, and does). Beliefs that are arbitrarily adopted or based upon faulty grounds, even when they turn out to be true, do not qualify as instances of "knowledge."

What is the additional ingredient, besides being correct, that a belief must have in order to count as knowledge? It must be substantiated, supported, or justified by evidence. Knowledge is true belief held on adequate grounds, rather than held fallaciously or haphazardly. To put it traditionally, knowledge is justified, true belief.

It should be noted here that by "justified" we mean that the person actually has sound reasons (good evidence), not simply that he thinks his evidence is good or sufficient in light of the pool of information available to him. Socially speaking, we might deem a medical doctor "justified," by what he learned in medical school or read in reputable journals, in believing that a particular therapy, surgical procedure, or prescribed medicine will benefit his patient; epistemologically speaking, though, if advances in research correct certain ideas taught in medical school (or if the journal articles prove to be based on fraudulent research reports), we would say that the doctor's belief was not, after all, "justified"—i.e., not based on good evidence.

The human enterprise that we honor with the name of "knowledge" (or "science" in the broadest sense) pursues the goal of eliminating personal prejudice, unreasoning conjecture, and distorting bias in our beliefs. Accordingly, having a warrant for one's belief(s) is essential to knowledge. This explains why the issue of justification has always been a critical one throughout the history of epistemology. E.g., when and how are claims that we make well founded? Or, how do we acquire, or what is the source of, reliable beliefs? On what basis is intellectual authority conferred upon our ideas? By what standard are our judgments to be evaluated? How do we know what we know? Philosophers have found it difficult to agree on a general description of what should count as good, adequate, or justifying evidence for beliefs (cf. rationalism, empiricism, pragmatism, positivism, common sense). But regardless of how such disputes are resolved, knowledge should be taken to be true belief for which one has good evidence.

Of course, it is one thing to "have" (be in possession of) good evidence for a belief and another thing to "realize" (acknowledge to one-self) or be able to "give" that evidence to others. It is simplistic to take it as a universal truth that a person does not have something unless he realizes it (e.g., money, cancer) or unless he can give it to others (e.g., insecurity, incentive, reputation). Obviously we "have" direct experiences (e.g., of the snows of Kilimanjaro) that we cannot "give" to others, and even some beliefs that we may not be able to give to others (e.g., that the Republican candidate is the best man for the office).

People often know more than they are able to say. Sometimes this is because a person who is unquestionably in a position to know (e.g., an experienced medical doctor, or a woman with repeatedly confirmed intuitions about human character) may be unable to formulate for himself or others the precise evidence or reason(s) for believing something—yet the judgment has arisen from his perception of relevant factors. Then again, "having evidence" for a proposition is a matter of having a belief that, among other things, functions for the person to support a further belief. Yet not all of a person's beliefs are acknowledged to himself (i.e., given conscious, inward assent)—because no one can mentally entertain all of his beliefs simultaneously, because some are too painful to face, because some are too trivial or too commonly assumed to focus upon, etc. To maintain that introspection invariably accompanies every "belief," or that self-awareness is essential to "believing" a proposition, or that conscious assent necessarily accompanies "belief" is to erect artificial terminological rules that only serve to screen off from ourselves the complexity of human nature and behavior. Thus, we may sometimes have evidence (beliefs supporting beliefs) that we do not realize or are not able to give to others. To put it another way, we may sometimes "know" something without "knowing that we know" it. Naturally, in such cases a person will not assert, assent to, or openly confess what he knows.

The Unbeliever Knows God Without Confessing It. Perhaps the foundational epistemological insight that is most significant for the practice of Christian apologetics, yet is most often ignored, is that all men *already know* God—long before the apologist engages them in conversation—and cannot avoid having such knowledge. Applying our initial observations above, this "personal knowledge" of God, which every human being has, can be minimally analyzed or rationally reconstructed. We include the need for "rational reconstruction" of the experience of personally knowing God, in order to account for the fact that some individuals who have not learned a natural language (e.g., very young children) still have this experience or relationship to the Lord. Apologetics does not deal directly with such cases because these individuals do not openly challenge the faith. Yet it is important to remind (and comfort) ourselves that they, like all men, in some sense know their Creator—even if it is difficult for us to talk about their experience except by way of analogy to adult knowledge (with its verbal orientation and competence).

Based on our previous observations about knowledge, we would analyze the concept of intellectually knowing God as *believing* certain propositions concerning God that are *true* and for which one has *good evidence*. Scripture teaches that nobody is ignorant of the living and true God. People lack neither information nor evidence. Everybody believes important things about God that are true and well supported. Thus, all men *know* that God exists, that He is almighty and all-knowing, that His holy character forbids theft and murder, that we will all be judged by Him, etc. Accordingly, the apologist embarks on the wrong road altogether if he thinks his task requires, for instance, providing data and proofs about God to someone who does not possess such things and simply needs them cogently brought to his attention in order to become a believer. In a crucial sense, all men already are "believers"—even "unbelievers" who will not respond properly by openly professing and living obediently in accordance with the knowledge they have of God. In the end, the work of the apologist is not simply an intellectual mission (akin to a scientist trying to convince colleagues about his new research conclusions), but embodies as well the work of *morally convicting* the non-Christian for not owning up to the truth that he already knows and cannot escape. The apologist is not simply challenging the unbeliever's reasoning, but in the process also (inherently) challenging the unbeliever's controlling personal attitudes, intellectual behavior, and lifestyle.

Romans 1 speaks definitively on this subject. The apostle Paul there describes the natural man as *gnontes ton theon* (v. 21)—"knowing the God." The verb indicates an intellectual awareness and understanding. The definite article ("the") indicates that this is not a vague awareness of "some kind of supernatural power or person somewhere out there," but rather a distinct awareness of a familiar or well-defined object of knowledge, namely, the living and true, one and only God. It is "because" (*dioti* at the beginning of v. 21) men have this knowledge of the true God that they are *anapologetous* (v. 20)—"without an excuse" (literally, "without an apologetic") for their unrighteous, idol-atrous, and reprobate living (vv. 18, 23–31), for their thanklessness (v. 21), and for their foolish thinking (vv. 21–22). God's wrath justly rests upon such men, taught Paul, because He has "manifested" Him-self to them in such a way that they themselves show "that which is known about God" (v. 19). They "clearly see and understand" God's divine attributes (v. 20) and are in possession of "the truth of God" (v. 25), but they did not deem it worthwhile to "retain God in their knowledge" (v. 28), choosing rather to "suppress the truth" by means of their unrighteousness (v. 18). The non-Christian has definite be-liefs about God that are true, and he possesses full and overwhelm-ing warrant for those beliefs.

The knowledge (justified, true belief) that all men have of their Creator has a very special feature and importance that do not attach to other, commonplace cases of knowing. Scripture indicates that to know that God exists is, from an epistemological standpoint (not sim-ply from a spiritual, ethical, or eschatological perspective), far more significant than knowing that my shirts are in the closet, that Harry Truman won reelection in 1948, that caffeine is addictive, that the sun rises in the east, etc. Our knowledge of God is not just like the rest of our knowledge. The psalmist wrote, "In Thy light we see light" (Ps. 36:9). The knowledge that all men have of God because of natural revelation provides the framework or foundation for any other knowl-edge they are able to attain. The knowledge of God is the necessary context for learning anything else. One can gain enlightenment ("see light") about the world or oneself only in terms of the more funda-mental revelation of God about Himself ("in Thy light"). Even pagan philosophers cannot miss the fact that it is in Him that we live and move and have our existence (Acts 17:28). Apart from Him, there is only ignorance (vv. 23, 30).

In Romans, Paul summarizes the sinful rebellion of the unbeliever with the words, "There is no fear of God before their eyes" (3:18), al-luding to the psalm we have just noted (Ps. 36:1). Paul was well aware of the theology and wisdom of the Old Testament, how it drove home the theme that "The fear of Jehovah is the beginning of knowledge, but fools despise wisdom and instruction" (Prov. 1:7). Although all men clearly know God, having no excuse for confusion (Pss. 19:1; 97:6–9), they all go astray by refusing to reverence and obey Him (Pss. 14:2–3; 55:19). By saying in their heart that there is no God, they have become fools (Pss. 14:1; 53:1). Their lips cannot disperse knowledge

(Prov. 15:7). Paul applied this insight when he taught in Romans 1 that all men have clear and persuasive evidence before them and within them that God exists. The rebel denies the obvious. The non-Christian refuses to profess his knowledge of God or behave consistently and appropriately in terms of it. This effort to evade God cannot be successful intellectually, and this is where the apologist gains direction for his argument with unbelievers. Seeking to suppress his knowledge of the truth about God, the unbeliever's professed wisdom is reduced to vain reasoning and foolishness (vv. 21–22). When men deny having this knowledge, their thinking and attempts to gain knowledge can be reduced to absurdity. This biblical insight is at the heart of Van Til's presuppositional defense of the faith.

The Character of the Unavoidable Evidence for God. When we say that men "know" that the living and true God exists, we are (in part) asserting that they "have evidence" that justifies the belief that He exists. A word should be added here about the general nature of the warrant for believing, to which we implicitly allude in claiming that all men know God.

We do so because of a common but simplistic (and thus misleading) tendency to make inferential or discursive knowledge the model for all cases of knowing. If Sam knows that milk gives him indigestion, he came to this conclusion through certain "steps of reasoning." He recalled a number of past experiences in which indigestion followed his drinking of milk, but could not remember any cases of indigestion where milk had not been in his diet, so he made a general association and interpreted it in a causal fashion, etc. Sam did not simply look at milk and immediately apprehend its indigestion-producing quality (although some children claim to have this kind of intuitive ability when they encounter new vegetables); rather, he inferred the truth from his experience. Likewise, if Sam knows that 487 multiplied by 139 equals 67,693, it would be highly unusual if he did not gain this knowledge by making a mathematical computation. In a large number of cases, our knowledge of a proposition is warranted by a discursive process of inference. For example, all of the union truckers are on strike; Sam is a union trucker; therefore, Sam must be on strike. Such inferential or discursive knowledge is common, but that does not mean that knowledge arises only from such reasoning. There are obvious cases of noninferential knowledge; it is implausible and artificial to insist that they must somehow be the product of an "unconscious" inference.

Surely there are times when one believes certain propositions with good reason, without inferring them from other propositions—as when one believes that one is typing with both hands, or believes that the music is painfully loud, or believes that one is not the same person as one's neighbor, or believes the times tables in math. When Sam knows that a black cat is in his path, he does not infer it from propositions about his sensations, about forms of appearance, about animal categories, etc. His knowledge is not discursive, following certain steps of reasoning to a likely conclusion; he *immediately* (without mediating lines of inference) apprehends the truth that a black cat is in his path. (We need not concern ourselves here with debates over how to account for such noninferential cognition, whether by linguistic conventionalism, behaviorism, an intuitive faculty, etc.) Such a non-propositional experience (an acquaintance with an object) is not something mystical and ineffable; rather, people have the ability to express and define the experience propositionally (thus describing it and relating it to other beliefs so that it is available for reference, memory, assertion, inference, application, etc.). The "immediate" apprehension may very well be caused ("mediated") by natural factors, but the recognition takes place in the absence of discursive inference (drawing a conclusion through the mediation of reasoning from premises).

When we encounter a person at the store and "know" that he is our friend Sam, our belief can indeed be warranted without being derived or reached by a series of mental arguments, computations, or inferences. The same is true when we directly identify his signature on a letter. There is evidence that justifies what we believe, but it is noninferential and direct. This claim should not be too controversial, but it does require some attenuation. In those cases where "knowing" is immediate or noninferential, we are speaking of the evidence as it is apprehended by a particular individual at the initial time of assenting to the proposition warranted by it. No doubt somebody else who is unfamiliar with Sam might not immediately apprehend that this letter is from Sam. And if someone should raise some doubt whether the letter is, after all, from Sam, the kind of "evidence" that would be brought forth to defend or vindicate the challenged belief would be the discursive or inferential kind, rather than the initial evidence of direct apprehension.

Philosophers have argued for years over what kinds of things (or truths about what kinds of things) can be "known" or justified by direct apprehension, rather than by the self-conscious process of demonstrations and inferences. Candidates have ranged from sensations and perceptions to universals, clear concepts, self-evident truths, and obligations. Van Til maintained, following the teaching of Paul in Romans 1–2, that all men have a knowledge of God that is justified by direct apprehension of His handiwork in the world and within themselves. Even without a discursive argument or a chain of inferences from elementary observations about experience, all men see and recognize the signature of their Creator in the world that He created and controls, as well as in themselves as His created image. Van Til wrote, "Man is internally certain of God's existence only because his sense of deity is correlative to the revelation of God about him. And all the revelation of God is clear."[57] This knowledge of God is mediated in the sense of being caused by the stimulus of the external world and man's internal constitution, but it is apprehended immediately without argumentation, computation, or self-conscious reasoning.

The philosophically sophisticated chains of inference or argument (the "theistic proofs") that have been advanced by scholars to justify belief in God cannot by any stretch of the imagination be what the apostle Paul is referring to in Romans 1, because he says that all men have this knowledge, and yet not all men have the training or intellect to engage in philosophical argumentation. Thus, Van Til insisted on distinguishing between "natural revelation" and "natural theology." God has revealed Himself to all men, providing evidence that justifies belief in His existence and character; this revelation is "mediated" through the evidence of the created order and man's personality. However, this evidence or justification for belief is not inferential or discursive. Rather, the evidence for God is immediately perceived—indeed, it is inescapable and undeniable (even though men in their perversity attempt to deny it). This conception of natural revelation should not be confused with natural theology, which consists of discursive arguments that begin with observations about the *natural* world (e.g., that there is motion, or that there is order in nature) and then draw inferences about the *supernatural* existence or character of God.[58] Van Til explained:

---

57. *Defense of the Faith*, 196.
58. For example, Thomas Aquinas maintained that there are some truths about God "which the natural reason is . . . able to reach. . . . In fact, such truths about God

It is of basic importance that what has just been said about God's revelation in the world of nature and of man be not confused with what is called natural theology. Natural theology is the result of the interpretive reaction that sinful man has given to the revelation of God to him in the created world. When we speak of revelation in nature we speak of an act of God directed manward. When we speak of natural theology we speak of a reaction on the part of man directed Godward. This distinction is all important for a proper exegesis of Romans one.[59]

Careful reading shows that Romans 1–2 does not teach that men can develop a "natural theology" from the uninterpreted raw data of the natural realm, if they will rationally reflect upon it and formulate appropriate chains of argument, leading to the conclusion that God very probably exists. Rather, Van Til maintained that Romans 1 teaches a "natural revelation" whereby the created order is a medium of constant, inescapable, clear, preinterpreted information about God, with the effect that all men, at the outset of their reasoning, possess an actual knowledge of God and his character.

I have *never* denied that there is a common ground of *knowledge* between the believer and the unbeliever.[60] I have *always* affirmed the kind of common ground that is spoken of in Scripture, notably in Romans 1 and 2, and in Calvin's *Institutes*. As creatures made in God's image man cannot help but know God. It is this revelation *to* man through "nature" and through his own constitution that Paul speaks of in Romans.

But as I have always *affirmed* the fact that all men, even the most wicked of men, have this *knowledge* so I have always *denied* that fallen man's *interpretation of this revelation* of God to him is *identical* with the revelation itself. *Natural revelation must not be identified with natural theology.*[61]

---

have been proved demonstrably by the philosophers, guided by the light of the natural reason" (*Summa Contra Gentiles*, 1.3.2).

59. *The Protestant Doctrine of Scripture,* In Defense of the Faith, vol. 1 (Philadelphia: Presbyterian and Reformed, 1967), 56.

60. Van Til was here strongly objecting to a misrepresentation of his viewpoint by J. Oliver Buswell, Jr., in "The Fountainhead of Presuppositionalism," *Bible Today* 42 (November 1948): 41–64.

61. *A Christian Theory of Knowledge* (Philadelphia: Presbyterian and Reformed, 1969), 301 (emphasis original).

The failure to draw this distinction between natural revelation and natural theology has led many apologists astray, and the failure to note the importance of this distinction in Van Til's approach to apologetics has led many of his critics into misconceptions of presuppositionalism.

Van Til simply insisted that:

> As Christian theists, we could certainly never allow that the universe was originally known to man before God was known to man. The *cosmos-consciousness*, the *self-consciousness*, and the *God-consciousness would naturally be simultaneous*. . . . Man would at once with the first beginning of his mental activity see the true state of affairs as to the relation of God to the universe as something that was known to him. . . . *He would know that God is the Creator of the universe as soon as he knew anything about the universe itself.*[62]

Van Til correctly distinguished between God's *revelation* and man's *reaction to revelation*. Attempts at "natural theology" fall into the latter category. For the unregenerate man, Van Til noted, attempts at natural theology ironically amount to a kind of "natural atheology"— which should be an eye-opening contrast to be noticed and appreciated in the well-intended efforts of apologists to devise theistic proofs in the traditional style of natural theology. But apart from the favorable or unfavorable, cogent or fallacious "reactions" of men to it, Van Til insisted that there is the directly apprehended revelation of God. "In the *sensus deitatis*, then, we find a welling up within the consciousness of man an *immediate awareness* of the fact that God is the creator and sustainer of this world."[63]

EVEN PROFESSING ATHEISTS CLEARLY KNOW THAT GOD EXISTS[64]

(A) We shall not attempt to give an exegesis of this most difficult passage [Romans 1:18–21]. It may suffice to call attention to the following matters.

---

62. *An Introduction to Systematic Theology*, In Defense of the Faith, vol. 5 (Philadelphia: Presbyterian and Reformed, 1974), 72–73 (emphasis original).
63. Ibid., 90 (emphasis added).
64. The following excerpts are taken from:

    (A) *Introduction to Systematic Theology*, 93–95;
    (B) *Defense of the Faith*, 114–15, 154, 172, 254–55, 285;

In the first place we observe that Paul says that men do actually in some sense see the truth. We do not do justice to this passage by merely saying that all men or most men believe in *a* god or believe that God probably exists. Paul says that the revelation of the only existing God is so clearly imprinted upon man himself and upon his environment that no matter how hard he tries he cannot suppress this fact. As psychologically active self-conscious creatures they must see something of the truth. They hold down the truth, to be sure, but it is the truth that they hold down. Nor is it that this truth is objectively placed before them only in nature and in the make-up of man. It is, to be sure, on this that Paul does lay the emphasis. But knowledge is also *in man* in the sense that his subjective reaction to that which he sees shows some acquaintance with the truth. The invisible things of God *are perceived* (*kathoratai*). Knowing God (*gnontes ton theon*), they have not glorified God.

In the second place, it is primarily in this fact that men know and do not live up to what they know that Paul sees the greatest folly. Though they knew God, yet they glorified him not. They hold down *the truth* that is in them as well as round about them. It is in this immediate connection that Paul speaks of the revelation of God's wrath. He says that God's wrath is displayed on men just because they hold down the truth in unrighteousness. It is true that God's wrath is displayed on whatever form unrighteousness may take, but it is specifically mentioned here that God displays his wrath because men hold down the truth. . . .

As far as the intellectual aspect of the matter is concerned, we have now the following factors: In the first place, the body of man is, since the entrance of sin, in a weakened condition. In the second place, the functions of the soul are weakened. In the third place, and in spite of this, the invisible things of God, that is the nature of God, his power and divinity, are still displayed in man as well as round about him, in the fact of the self-conscious activity of his person, in his own negative moral reaction to the revelation about and within him, in his sense of dissatisfaction with all non-theistic interpretations,[65] and in a measure of involuntary recognition of the truth of the theistic interpretation as the true interpretation of the origin of the world. In spite of all this, man has not accepted for himself what he himself must admit to be the true interpretation of the origin of the world.

(C) *Common Grace* (Philadelphia: Presbyterian and Reformed, 1947), 53–55, 88–89.

65. The epistemological issue that the Christian apologist makes explicit is that the unbelieving worldviews are not satisfactory from an intellectual standpoint, primarily because they cannot make knowing intelligible in terms of the very worldviews which are posed.

In this respect man's knowledge is characterized by the same folly that marks Satan's knowledge of God. The first act of man's antitheistic interpretation consisted in the attempt on his part to be something that he knew he could not be. It is this folly that man has carried on through the ages, and it is this that still makes sin so foolish. And it is upon this foolishness that Paul says that the wrath of God is revealed.

This revelation is (a) partly objective to man in the narrow sense of being outside his person, as is the case with revelation in nature, (b) partly subjective to man in the narrow sense of consisting of his psychological constitution, and (c) partly subjective in the sense of consisting of his own involuntary ethical approval or disapproval (conscience). Over against that which is thus objective (1. outside man, 2. within man psychologically, 3. within man as involuntary ethical relation) we call that "subjective" which gives expression self-consciously, even if not with full consistency, to what that sinner as sinner does with that which comes to him objectively. As sinner, he seeks to suppress the objective revelation of God within him. . . .

We can readily see that all these matters, taken together, produce a very complex situation. There are three main things to be taken into consideration. In the first place, we must think of what was the original situation in paradise and what remained of this after the fall of man. In the second place, we must think of the wrath of God and the great complexity that this introduced into the situation. In the third place we must think of non-saving grace and, especially, of the great civilization that has flourished by it as a means.

Under the first head, we have the fact that man's rationality is, as a matter of fact, a creation of God. When man tries to make of himself an ultimate instead of a proximate starting point in knowledge, he somehow feels that he is doing something that he cannot do and that he ought not to try to do. Under the second head, we have the fact that man's mind is, as a matter of fact, now that sin has entered into it, abnormal. When man acts as though his mind were normal, he frustrates himself, and he senses something of this self-frustration. He somehow feels that his ideal of absolute comprehension in knowledge is a false ideal. Under the third head, we have the fact that, in spite of the fact that man has tried to set himself up as a metaphysically ultimate starting point, and in spite of the fact that he considers his mind to be normal, he has been able to do as much as he has. He ought to recognize the fact, says Calvin, that he lives by grace.[66]

The highest point of revelation outside of Scripture as it is found after the

---

66. It is worth noting again that presuppositionalism stresses the moral, personal, and redemptive character of the worldview that makes reasoning intelligible. That is the context of the argument carried out with the unbeliever in defense of the faith.

entrance of sin is just this point, that, together with the objective clarity of all these matters comes the fact that men, in some sense, at bottom recognize them to be true. The truth, as it were, penetrates into men's minds against their will and in spite of themselves.

(B) The Reformed apologist, on the other hand, would compromise what he holds to be of the essence of Christianity if he agreed with Taylor.[67] For him the whole of created reality, including therefore the fields of research with which the various sciences deal, reveals the same God of which Scripture speaks. The very essence of created reality is its revelational character. Scientists deal with that which has the imprint of God's face upon it. . . .

To change the figure, compare the facts of nature and history, the facts with which the sciences are concerned, to a linoleum that has its figure indelibly imprinted in it. The pattern of such a linoleum cannot be effaced till the linoleum itself is worn away. Thus inescapably does the scientist meet the pattern of Christian theism in each fact with which he deals. The apostle Paul lays great stress upon the fact that man is without excuse if he does not discover God in nature. Following Paul's example Calvin argues that men ought to see God, not a god, not some supernatural power, but the only God, in nature. They have not done justice by the facts they see displayed before and within them if they say that a god exists or that God probably exists. The Calvinist holds to the essential perspicuity of natural as well as Biblical revelation. . . .

Disagreeing with the natural man's interpretation of himself as the ultimate reference-point, the Reformed apologist must seek his point of contact with the natural man in that which is beneath the threshold of his working consciousness, in the sense of deity which he seeks to suppress. . . .

Now it is this fact that Rome is always and everywhere committed to the idea of brute fact as such, to eventuation apart from the counsel of God, that is all-determinative on the question of its conception of the relation of reason to authority. Rome simply has not the materials with which to build a really Christian concept of authority. A truly Christian concept of authority presupposes that in all he does man is face to face with the requirement of God. But how could man be face to face with the requirement of God if God does not control all things? How could God face man with his requirements there where he has no power to rule? It is only on the idea of the com-

---

67. Van Til is referring to A. E. Taylor's book, *Does God Exist?* (London: Macmillan, 1947), and particularly the claim that natural science is limited to discovering uniformities in the course of events and thus "can throw no light on the question . . . whether God exists."

prehensiveness of the plan of God that a true concept of authority can be based. And this is to say, in effect, that only on the idea of the covenant as all-comprehensive with respect to every phase of human life can the idea of authority find a footing. . . .

Secondly, man has round about him the clearest possible evidence of the power and divinity of God.

> In attestation of his wondrous wisdom both the heavens and the earth present us with innumerable proofs, not only of those more recondite proofs which astronomy, medicine, and all the natural sciences, are designed to illustrate, but proofs which force themselves on the notice of the most illiterate peasant, who cannot open his eyes without beholding them.[68]

Thus the knowledge of God is inherent in man. It is there by virtue of his creation in the image of God. This may be called innate knowledge. But as such it must be distinguished from the innate ideas of idealist philosophy. For the innate knowledge as Calvin thinks of it is based upon the idea of man's creation in the image of God. And as such it is correlative to the idea of revelation to man mediated through the facts of his environment which are also created by God. In contrast with this the innate knowledge of Descartes and idealist philosophy is based on the idea of the autonomy of man.

Following Calvin, then, Kuyper did not tone down the clarity of the revelation of God to man. In this respect he is in agreement with Warfield. Both men are equally anxious to follow Calvin as Calvin simply followed St. Paul in the idea that God has never left himself without a witness to men. He witnessed to them through every fact of the universe from the beginning of time. No rational creature can escape this witness. It is the witness of the triune God whose face is before men everywhere and all the time. Even the lost in the hereafter cannot escape the revelation of God. God made man a rational-moral creature. He will always be that. As such he is confronted with God. He is addressed by God. He exists in the relationship of covenant interaction. He is a covenant being. To not know God man would have to destroy himself. . . .

Everything in the created universe therefore displays the fact that it is controlled by God, that it is what it is by virtue of the place that it occupies in the plan of God. The objective evidence for the existence of God and of the comprehensive governance of the world by God is therefore so plain that he who runs may read. Men cannot get away from this evidence. They see it round

68. Van Til cites Calvin's *Institutes*, 1.5.2.

about them. They see it within them. Their own constitution so clearly evinces the facts of God's creation of them and control over them that there is no man who can possibly escape observing it. If he is self-conscious at all he is also God-conscious. No matter how men may try they cannot hide from themselves the fact of their own createdness. Whether men engage in inductive study with respect to the facts of nature about them or engage in analysis of their own self-consciousness they are always face to face with God their maker.

Having taken these two, revelation in the created universe, both within and about man, and revelation by way of supernatural positive communication as aspects of revelation as originally given to man, we can see that natural revelation is even after the fall perspicuous in character. "The perspicuity of God's revelation in nature depends for its very meaning upon the fact that it is an aspect of the total and totally voluntary revelation of a God who is self-contained" (*Idem*, p. 269).[69] . . .

Calvin argues that as created in God's image every man, of necessity, has a knowledge of God. This "innate knowledge" is correlative to God's revelation in man's environment. And try as he may the sinner cannot efface this knowledge. He can only seek to suppress it. Without first knowing God he could not seek to deny it. He must be originally in contact with the truth in order to love and propagate the lie.

(C) As made in the image of God no man can escape becoming the interpretative medium of God's general revelation both in his intellectual (Romans 1:20) and in his moral consciousness (Romans 2:14, 15). No matter which button of the radio he presses, he always hears the voice of God.[70] Even when he presses the button of his own psychological self-conscious activity, through which as a last resort the sinner might hope to hear another voice, he still hears the voice of God. "If I make my bed in hell, behold, Thou are there." It is in this sense that we must, at least to begin with, understand the matter when we are told that there are no atheistic peoples and no atheistic men. Psychologically there are no atheistic men; epistemologically every sinner is atheistic.[71] . . .

Then, too, Paul tells us, in effect, that the voice of the *true* God, the only

---

69. Van Til here quotes his article "Nature and Scripture," in *The Infallible Word*, ed. N. B. Stonehouse and Paul Woolley (Philadelphia: Presbyterian and Reformed, 1946).

70. In his intellectual endeavors, there is no subject (or "radio station") that a man can choose to consider ("button he presses") which does not bring him to the revelation of God. He cannot escape being confronted by God if he is self-conscious at all.

71. Van Til distinguishes here between the way men actually think ("psychologically") and their proposed pictures of themselves as thinkers ("epistemologically"). No

existent God, is everywhere present. He does not, to be sure, say that this God is present in the fulness of His revelation. Yet it is the true God, *the* God, not *a* God, that is everywhere to be heard, whatever button we may press. It is the *what*, not merely the *that*, of God's existence that the heathen find impressed upon them.[72] To this *what* they, willingly or not, give interpretative expression, thereby increasing the pressure of God's requirements upon their ethical powers of reaction. . . .

Sin has not been able to efface all this requisitional material from the consciousness of man. The very activity of his consciousness is a daily reminder to him of the will of God. Though he has tried over and over again to choke the voice of God he has not been able to do so. His evil nature would fain subdue the voice of the creation in nature, but it cannot wholly do so. Involuntarily men think back, with the prodigal, to the father's home.

NATURAL REVELATION DISTINGUISHED FROM NATURAL THEOLOGY[73]

In the first place there is a basic difference concerning the nature of revelation. For Calvin, revelation is always and everywhere clear. The facts of natural revelation, both within and about man, are so clearly revelatory of God that he who runs may read. The *indicia divinitatis* (marks of divinity) of Scripture are equally clear. In fact, the revelation of God to man is so clear that no man can help but know God. Thus man is *from the beginning* in contact with the truth. Moreover, he cannot separate the *existence* of God from the *character* of God. *The intelligibility of anything, for man, presupposes the existence of God*—the God whose nature and character are delineated in God's revelation, found both in nature and in Scripture.[74] It is this God— the only God—whom all men, of necessity, "know." . . .

According to Aquinas[75] the revelation of God to man is not inherently clear.

---

man actually thinks rationally without God, but in terms of their systems of philosophy they try to account for thinking without making reference to God.

72. The "that" refers to the *existence* of God, while the "what" refers to the *nature* or *character* of the God who is said to exist. According to Van Til, one cannot consider or argue about the former without some conception of the latter.

73. Excerpts from *The Reformed Pastor and Modern Thought* (Philadelphia: Presbyterian and Reformed, 1971), 12–13, 24.

74. Emphasis added. This sentence serves as a compact summary of the presuppositional challenge in apologetics. Men necessarily know God (His existence and nature), whether from nature or Scripture or both, and if He is not presupposed in their thinking, nothing they think about can be made intelligible.

75. The medieval philosopher and Benedictine monk Thomas Aquinas is a prime example of someone proposing to reach a "natural" knowledge of God by means of

As finite, man lives on the verge of non-being;[76] and as such a mixture, man's knowledge is derived from the senses. Man is also, therefore, enmeshed in an environment which is not *exclusively* determined by the plan of God, but rather a combination of the forces of God and of chaos.[77] Accordingly, Aquinas thinks that man can intelligently discuss the question of the existence of God without at the same time presupposing the nature of God as revealed in Scripture. Thus the attitude of doubt with respect to the existence of God is assumed to be legitimate. Ignorance is not basically culpable.

Involved in this original separation of the existence and the nature of God is the idea that, for man, the nature of God is not exclusively determined by the revelation of God. The nature of God is, in part, determined by man himself.

It is thus that the scholastic notion of natural theology is born. If man, without special revelation, partly determines the nature of God, then this nature of God is, to an extent, defined by the supposed demands of logic and fact, *as man knows these independently of the revelation of God*.[78] Thus the distinction between the revelation of God *to* man and the interpretation of this

---

theistic proofs ("the five ways," as he called them). By importing Aristotelian presuppositions into his apologetic and theology, as Van Til goes on to observe (see his footnotes), Aquinas allowed that "nature" does not clearly and inescapably reveal God, for the natural man's questions and arguments about God's existence are intelligible apart from assuming God. Moreover, "nature" cannot be clear in itself about God because it is not completely determined by God in an Aristotelian outlook; it participates in nonbeing or chaos (matter). The tradition of natural theology and even the philosophy of Aquinas (following Aristotle) are inappropriate for an evangelical or Reformed approach to theology, according to Van Til, but some evangelicals are willing to embrace both (e.g., Norman Geisler, *Thomas Aquinas: An Evangelical Appraisal* [Grand Rapids: Baker, 1991]).

76. CVT: Man is a mixture of form (Being) and matter (non-Being). Except for his participation in God (Being), a participation which God himself sustains, man would be wholly absorbed into matter or pure Chaos (non-Being), which is the polar opposite of God and therefore evil. It is, however, equally ultimate with God. (By "equally ultimate" we mean that neither in any way is dependent on the other for existence.)

77. CVT: Since both man and nature are in some *combinations* of the finite (Chaos) and infinite (Rationality), the witness of both man and nature is *unclear*. Therefore the existence of God, for Aquinas, is a matter of *question* and can be answered only in terms of rational and empirical argumentation. Of course, Aquinas thought that his arguments for the existence of God were completely valid. Many modern orthodox apologists, however, recognizing the inadequacies of the "theistic proofs," generally maintain that, when all the arguments are taken together, God's existence is seen to be highly probable. However, they still hold to Aquinas' belief in (1) the lack of clarity in God's revelation; and (2) the ability of man's intellect to reason about God correctly prior to, and independently of, the revelation of God.

78. Note well that Van Til does not set aside considerations of fact and logic, but considers illegitimate the "demands" of fact and logic as they are conceived autonomously.

revelation *by* man is obscured. *Natural revelation* then tends to be identified with *natural theology*. This idea of natural theology assumes that without Scripture and the testimony of the Spirit men generally can have a measure of morally and spiritually acceptable knowledge of God. It assumes that there can be an interpretation[79] of the natural revelation of God with which both believers and unbelievers are in basic agreement.

The difference between the knowledge of the Christian and the knowledge of the non-Christian [would] consist, then, primarily [of] the former being more comprehensive than the latter. The Christian *adds* to his knowledge of facts obtained by his own empirical research without reference to Scripture, the information about these facts that he gets from supernatural revelation. On the Thomistic basis the difference between the knowledge of the Christian and the knowledge of the non-Christian is primarily quantitative. To be sure, according to Thomas, sin has *wounded* the natural capacities of man. Accordingly the supernatural must, to some extent, be *remedial* as well as supplementative. This fact, however, does not change the fact that for Thomas supernatural revelation is *primarily* supplementative. . . .

Calvin makes a sharp distinction between the revelation of God to man and man's response to that revelation. This implies the rejection of a natural theology such as Aquinas taught.[80]

4.4 The Redemptive Self-Attesting Revelation of God in Scripture

Van Til, following the guidance of Scripture, taught that all men directly apprehend more than sufficient evidence in nature and in man's rational-moral personality for the existence and character of

---

79. The "interpretation" of God's natural revelation by man refers to a self-conscious development of a system of thought or philosophy.

80. The natural man's "response" to God's revelation is not to develop a natural theology, but to develop a natural atheology. "There is none who seeks after God" (Rom. 3:11; cf. Pss. 14:2–3; 53:2–3). Calvin wrote: "As experience shows, God has sown a seed of religion in all men. But scarcely one man in a hundred is met with who fosters it, once received, in his heart, and none in whom it ripens—much less shows fruit in season. . . . All degenerate from the true knowledge of him. . . . I do not mean by this that their ingenuousness should free them from blame. For the blindness under which they labor is almost always mixed with proud vanity and obstinacy. Indeed, vanity joined with pride can be detected in the fact that, in seeking God, miserable men do not rise above themselves as they should, but measure him by the yardstick of their own carnal stupidity, and neglect sound investigation; thus out of curiosity they fly off into empty speculations. They do not therefore apprehend God as he offers himself, but imagine him as they have fashioned him in their own presumption" (*Institutes of the Christian Religion*, ed. John T. McNeill, trans. Ford Lewis Battles [Philadelphia: Westminster, 1960], 1.4.1, p. 1:47).

God, thus giving them the fundamental knowledge they need in order to gain further knowledge about the world in which they live. However, Van Til also had a unique appreciation for the fact that, from the very beginning of man's experience in the world, this unspoken and immediate evidence was accompanied by authoritative and interpretative verbal revelation from God to man.[81] In the Garden of Eden, God spoke with man right after his creation, explaining who he was, what his environment was, and how he should use his mind and conduct his life in that environment to glorify God and enjoy Him. Natural revelation was never intended to operate on its own without God's verbal communication as a supplemental and necessary context for understanding. "God's revelation in nature, together with God's revelation in Scripture, form God's one grand scheme of covenant revelation of himself to man. The two forms of revelation must therefore be seen as presupposing and supplementing one another. . . . Revelation in nature and revelation in Scripture are mutually meaningless without one another and mutually fruitful when taken together."[82]

Van Til made this point repeatedly and drew out its great apologetical significance—that the epistemological defense of natural revelation and the epistemological defense of special revelation must even now continue to be integrated and work together, rather than treated as separate religious claims that are intelligible and justifiable apart from each other. Supernatural verbal revelation is, according to Van Til, inherent in the human situation and the intended concomitant to supernatural revelation in nature and in man's inner constitution. In that case, man was never—and is not now—expected simply to observe the natural world or consider his own rational, moral personality and figure out for himself how they are to be interpreted and how their truths are to be verbally expressed. Man's Creator has provided the linguistic framework for "exegeting" the truth of God in natural revelation and in man himself.

Now that sin has entered the picture, however, the evidence for God that men encounter in the natural order and in human personality is universally distorted and suppressed "by means of unrighteousness," and this introduces a moral and soteriological dimension into the treatment

81. See especially his crucial article, "Nature and Scripture." In the first half of this discussion, Van Til draws a brilliant parallel between the attributes of Scripture—necessity, authority, sufficiency, perspicuity—and the corresponding attributes of natural revelation.
82. Ibid., 267, 269.

of man's epistemological pursuits. This means that the linguistic revelation of God, which was always prerequisite for man's intellectual interpretation of God's natural revelation (and knowing anything), must now become redemptive in character. Being lost in sin and thus mentally turning away from God, man has lost his bearings with respect to knowing anything; he cannot really justify the things he claims to know, even though in some sense he clearly does continue to know things about himself and the world. His ability to warrant his beliefs has, at the most basic level, become confused and corrigible; he no longer has a sure sense of the reason (purpose) for things, of their cause, or of appropriate norms or standards. He pretends that he is intellectually authoritative in a world where, nevertheless, his lack of epistemic self-sufficiency and normative authority is conspicuous. He now walks about with a "vain mind," "darkened understanding," and "ignorance" (Eph. 4:17–18); he lives with the empty words of mental darkness, self-congratulatory foolishness, empty and pointless philosophy—and prefers it (Eph. 5:6–8; 1 Cor. 1:18–25; Col. 2:8; John 3:19). Any satisfactory theory of knowledge must offer an account of why men are so capable of error, why they disagree with each other even over fundamental issues of method and interpretation, why they deny the obvious (such as the evidence for God, or whatever else is thought to be the precondition for the possibility and procedures of learning anything), why they sometimes prefer irrationality, why interpretive mistakes are so pervasively made, etc. The Christian view is that this is a personal matter of insubordination against God and His authority. Sinful men thus act like "fools" in trying to evade God, with the result that their mental lives are afflicted with logical inconsistency, incorrectly interpreted perceptions, misleading conceptualizations, fallacies in reasoning, mistakes in computation, personal bias and error, inappropriately chosen standards, inability to resolve disputes, purposeful lies and deception—and, above all, an inability to make sense of their methods of knowing. Since man has suppressed the light and chosen to proceed in darkness, he now needs to be saved epistemologically (as well as spiritually). His reasoning is as lost in sin as any other part of his personality.

Accordingly, if God is to be properly known and the intellectual effects of man's fallen condition are to be corrected, a deistic or redemptionless worldview is inadequate.[83] It is not enough for man to

83. Sometimes students begin to grasp the presuppositional approach to defending the faith by appreciating its successful challenge to unbelieving philosophies on such issues as the foundations of scientific inference, the laws of logic, and the

think that he can take as the context and foundation of his episte-mological efforts God as Creator and final Judge. He also needs a Re-deemer who can deal with his guilt and pollution, especially as they bear upon his intellectual life. As the Westminster Confession of Faith puts it, Christ's work as the mediator of the covenant of grace en-compasses His saving ministry, not only as priest and king, but also as our prophet. Man will not return to thinking aright without this di-vine provision. The necessity of noetic salvation is integral to the Christian worldview and has an enormous bearing upon the defense of the faith. Men cannot get their "rational lives" in order without get-ting right with God spiritually, and they cannot get back to the nec-essary and fundamental knowledge of their Creator (in terms of which any other knowing can make sense) without being graciously restored to Him by the work of the Redeemer. Therefore, Paul did not set forth the "treasures of wisdom and knowledge" as "deposited" in God sim-ply conceived of as the Creator; it is rather and more particularly that they are deposited in the "Messiah" (Christ: Col. 2:3). Any philoso-phy that takes its presuppositions ("rudimentary principles") from the world instead of from the Messiah will be deprived of such treasures (v. 8). The possibility of saving man's intellectual endeavors from ar-bitrariness and absurdity has been graciously provided by Christ com-ing into the world to save sinners who have rebelled against the knowl-edge of God in nature. They have turned from the Light in which anyone can see light (cf. Ps. 36:9) and sunk into darkness, but, ac-cording to God's gracious promise, His creative "Word" (cf. Prov. 8:22–31) has arrived as "the true light which enlightens every man coming into the world" (John 1:9). Through His saving work, men can now be "renewed unto knowledge after the image of the Creator" (Col. 3:10) and can repent "unto the knowledge of the truth" (2 Tim.

---

absolutes of morality. They prematurely think that this is the whole story, and that a worldview would be philosophically adequate as long as it simply made sense of science, logic, and morality—but thereby overlooking the need for a world-view to have a credible and integrated view of *man himself*, the knower, with re-gard to his personal failings and character (particularly his perversity in behav-ior and reasoning), as well as providing a solution that rescues him from them. A merely "natural religion," without supernatural interference in this world (that is, without miracles, special revelation, or atonement), as promoted by the sev-enteenth- and eighteenth-century deists, is philosophically inadequate because man now corrupts and mishandles natural revelation and does not have the means in himself to rescue himself from this plight. God's grace is required— and thus the historical provisions for a Savior and His redemptive work cannot be left out of the Christian worldview.

2:25). Christ as the way back to the Father is simultaneously man's way
back to knowledge of the Father's world.

God's saving work in history was once known by men in terms of
redemptive *events* (from Old Testament miracles and anticipations of
the incarnation, life, death, and resurrection of the promised Messiah, together with the spiritual inception of the church) as well as in
terms of the contemporaneous, inspired proclamation or teaching by
His chosen servants (by prophets, apostles, and, above all, His own
Son speaking on earth). These are all past, of course. Later generations have learned of these redemptive events and the saving proclamation of God's grace in the inspired message that is recorded in the
Scriptures. Naturally enough, then, the teaching of the Bible continually becomes the focal point of apologetical dispute between believers and unbelievers. To recapitulate, the Christian maintains that
all men have been given, as the necessary context for knowing anything whatsoever, clear and direct evidence of God in nature and in
man's personality, but by turning away from this evidence and attempting to suppress it, sinners have come to need the saving work
of the Messiah, which is necessary even for saving their ability to justify knowing things. This salvation is revealed to us in the pages of
Scripture. How do we "know" that God's verbal revelation found there
is true? For us who did not see the miracles or speak to the Savior,
what is the evidence that warrants believing the claims made by the
Bible about that Savior? Van Til's apologetic insists that Christian
faith is not "blind faith." It is fully warranted—and not simply in the
subjective sense that the inward testimony of the Holy Spirit per-
suades the believer.[84] The justifying evidence, taught Van Til, is public, objective, and perfectly adequate to establish the truth of the
claims made by Scripture. Where, however, is this evidence found?

Van Til realized that there are "confirmatory" but inconclusive in-

---

84. Far too often those who are only slightly familiar with Reformed theology and
   presuppositional apologetics mistakenly collapse the concept of the Holy Spirit's
   internal testimony into the concept of Scripture's self-attestation. The two are
   clearly distinguished by Van Til. One is the objective and self-evidencing testimony
   of the Bible itself as a written message, regardless of the subjective response given
   to that testimony by men. The other is the work of the Third Person of the Trinity and determines the subjective personal response given by men to the Bible's
   own testimony. When critics interpret Van Til's references to Scripture being self-
   attesting as references to some kind of mystical experience or inward satisfaction,
   they are confusing the self-attestation of Scripture with the internal testimony of
   the Holy Spirit.

dications that the Bible is the word of God. These evidences can, when viewed in the alien context of unbelieving presuppositions, be reinterpreted and pushed aside by those who are attempting to escape facing God. As the Westminster Confession of Faith puts it, such things as the testimony of the church to the Bible, the consent of its parts, and indeed its entire perfection would be things that "abundantly evidence" the Bible to be "the word of God." As indirect testimonies (involving disputable steps of reasoning and human assessments), they do not carry the force of direct divine encounter. The unbeliever may respond with alternative lines of reasoning (rationalizing) and refuse to be persuaded (1.5).[85] This evidence, like "sideline endorsements," is valuable, but it is not the most basic and inescapably authoritative evidence.

For that, Van Til directs us back to the previous section in the Confession of Faith (1.4), which is the essential context for the "abundant evidences" mentioned next (1.5). Who is in a position to tell us what the proper indications of divinity would be when it comes to a purported revelation from God? If an opinion poll discloses that sixty-three percent of Americans believe the Bible to be God's word in some special sense, does that count as relevant evidence for the conclusion that it is God's word? Should the percentage rather be at least eighty-five? Should those surveyed rather be Asians or Europeans? One person opines that the Bible's "beautiful and comforting words" indicate that it came from God, while another takes such features as a kind of contrived and self-serving artificiality that lacks the rough realism or (alternatively) the ecstatic frenzy that one would "expect" of inspiration. Who is in an authoritative position to say? The answer is that only God could tell us reliably and authoritatively what qualities mark out His word as really His. But where would God say this? If some document purported to be God's word answering this crucial question, what adequate evidence could man have that this second message is a divine message to us? At some point, the message claiming to be from God would have to be its own authority, and there is no reason, then, why that should not be at the first point. Thus, *only God is adequate to bear witness to Himself or to authorize His own words.* As Heb. 6:13 teaches, God can swear by nothing greater than Himself, in which case His word can be truly authorized only by His own word. God's word

85. Note that presuppositional apologetics "cuts off" the very availability of alternative reasoning; that is, it undermines the intelligibility of reasoning that does not submit to the divine authority of Scripture.

is the ultimate authority, and as such it can be authorized only by itself. Thus the Confession rightly says: "The authority of the holy Scripture, for which it ought to be believed, and obeyed, dependeth . . . *wholly* upon God (who is truth itself) the author thereof: and therefore it is to be received, because it is the word of God" (1.4). The fundamental evidence that Scripture is the word of God is its own testimony to that effect. Thus Van Til taught that the Bible is *self-attesting.*[86]

Whenever God reveals Himself, He does so with persuasive evidence and authority, as we have already seen to be the case with natural revelation according to Romans 1. But the psalmist readily speaks of God's revelatory work through both nature ("the heavens") and Scripture ("the law"). It is the same God who discloses Himself in both cases, through His works as well as His word. And God does not mumble. Men have been made to recognize His voice. Experience can "condition" us to identify a signature on a letter as the signature of a good friend. Similarly, God has so created men that, as it were, they are "conditioned" to see and understand His signature throughout the created world. The evidence is directly apprehended, and it is persuasive—leaving men without any excuse. What we have said here about God's revelation in the natural order is just as true of God's revelation in Scripture. Men are so constituted as to recognize these words as the authoritative voice of their Maker speaking to them.

86. Ronald Nash argues against Van Til's claim that Scripture carries self-attesting authority: "As I see it, a self-attesting truth is one that cannot be questioned. A good example . . . would be an analytic statement like 'All bachelors are unmarried men' " ("Attack on Human Autonomy" [a review of Van Til's *A Christian Theory of Knowledge*], *Christianity Today* 14 [Jan. 16, 1970]: 349). But Nash needs to rethink, for this is *not* a defining mark of a self-authenticating truth, as Nash's own example shows. Individuals can (and have) questioned the truth or certainty of "All bachelors are unmarried men." Nash would respond that the only ones who question it are poorly trained students, muddled thinkers, or those not yet adept at the English language. Perhaps so, but the claim is "questioned" nonetheless. Nash more likely meant that his example of an analytic truth cannot "rationally" be questioned—that is, cannot properly be questioned *within the context* of certain fundamental convictions or linguistic stipulations (certain presuppositions!). But the fact remains that a self-evident truth does not gain its self-evidency from the impossibility of questioning it or the impossibility of being confused over its meaning. The fact that non-Christians ("irrationally") question biblical authority, and the fact that Christians sometimes misinterpret the Bible's meaning, take nothing away from the Scripture's own possession of self-attesting authority (authority for which there is none higher). (In passing, the notion that only "analytic" truths enjoy unquestionable status is examined in my essay "Revisionary Immunity," in which I discuss the apologetical implications of the defeat of any autonomous attempt to draw the analytic-synthetic distinction.)

Scripture's divine quality is perceived directly, just as the sweetness of candy or the wetness of water is immediately experienced without discursive argumentation.

God's testimony is greater than that of any man—just because it is God's own testimony (1 John 5:9). Anyone who believes in the Son of God, according to Scripture, has this self-attesting testimony of God in his heart (v. 10). When all is said and done, he has come to believe God's word on God's own say-so. That word is "more sure" and more persuasive than even miracles (e.g., Luke 16:31; 2 Peter 1:19; John 20:29, 31). Christ's works bore testimony to Him, to be sure, but even apart from them the Father has also borne a plain and simple testimony that is even more authoritative (John 5:36–37). The word of Christ carried such evidential warranting power within itself that He could say that whoever rejected His word would be judged on the final day by that very word itself (John 12:48). The astonishing thing was that Christ taught as someone who possessed authority in Himself, not needing (as was customary) to rest on the authority of others (Matt. 7:29). When Christ speaks, the very words themselves carry the justifying evidence that they are God's, which is obvious to men and is acknowledged by God's people. "They know his voice" (John 10:4, 27), and men show it by following Him (unless they are personally set against Him). The gospel as God's own effective disclosure presents clear and convincing evidence in itself that it is the word of God.

It should be plain to see that when God reveals Himself—whether in nature, Scripture, or His very Son—the identification of His word (or Word) must be authoritative, not resting on relativistic human opinion or unreliable endorsement. Why should anyone believe that Jesus was in fact "very God of very God"? Could any mere man's evaluation establish such a claim? Even the estimation of a large percentage of people would be insufficient to establish that Jesus was more than a man. Even his miracles and resurrection do not in themselves imply deity (think of the other miracle workers in Scripture); they constitute evidence of divine status only because He authoritatively interprets them as such. So the only authority by which the identification of Jesus as God could be warranted would have to be the authority of Jesus Himself, taken as the one whom He claims to be. Such self-identification or self-authorization is, in the very nature of the case, "circular." And this is true of the divine information conveyed in other forms of revelation as well. In them God "testifies to

Himself" because there is nothing more epistemologically authoritative or morally ultimate that could authorize what He discloses.

Van Til taught that the self-attesting authority of God's revelation in Scripture pertained to the entire Bible, Old and New Testaments alike; the word of Christ is heard in them both as one message. Moreover, the testimony of Scripture to itself is not simply an isolated, narrow, and formal claim that it comes with divine authority; it is the entire testimony that it offers to the character, plan, and works of God—the details of the whole gospel story. The substantial message of the Bible taken as a whole as God's word (its content)—not simply the claim that it is God's word—is referred to when "the testimony" is said to be authorized by the divine testimony itself.[87] The biblical testimony, furthermore, is relevant to more than matters of eschatological and eternal salvation. As we have already said, supernatural verbal revelation is the interpretative context for God's revelation of Himself in nature and events. Accordingly, the self-attesting word of Christ in Scripture is crucial for properly submitting to, interpreting, and applying the divine disclosure in the external world. In this way, presuppositional apologetics maintains that every fact of the universe needs to be understood in the light of Christ.

Nevertheless, just as we saw above with respect to God's revelation in nature, when unbelievers encounter the clear, direct, and obvious evidence that it is God speaking with self-authorizing authority in the Scriptures (the gospel message), they will again seek to evade or sup-

---

87. The most serious misinterpretation of Van Til's presuppositionalism in John W. Montgomery's article "Once upon an A Priori" (in *Jerusalem and Athens*, ed. Geehan, 380–92) is that the challenge of the presuppositional apologist is reduced to a narrow, formal, and contentless demand to submit to abstract authority because it is authoritatively demanded. Naturally, when such a hollow "presupposition" is compared to any formally similar, hollow "presupposition" of authority, there is no intellectual basis for a choice between them. However, what Van Til taught was miles apart from such nonsense. According to him, the content of the Christian worldview, with all its claims about God, man, the universe, history, redemption, ethics, etc.—as well as its claims about the source and authority of these claims—must be defended over against the full-fledged and presupposed worldview of the unbeliever. For Van Til, "the heavenly content" of God's word is just as much part of its self-attesting truth as its being pronounced "from above." That is why apologists should, as much as possible, make sure that those to whom they defend the faith have first read the Bible. This may seem extremely elementary, but its importance is obvious when (as often) the requirement is overlooked. Without an awareness of the Bible's rich texture and weighty message, the unbeliever naturally tends to get mired in argumentation over *a priori* and abstract authority for an apparently arbitrarily chosen book.

press it. Doing so, however, only produces for them intellectual folly (as well as spiritual damnation). *There are epistemological consequences to rejecting the good news about Christ.* Those who refuse to base their thinking and living on the words of Christ are styled "fools" who build instead on ruinous sand (Matt. 7:24–27). In the same vein, when Paul speaks of unbelievers who encounter the gospel—"the word of the cross"—and despise it as foolishness (1 Cor. 1:18, 23), even though it comes "by powerful demonstration of the Spirit" (2:4–5, 13), he again asserts (just as he did in Romans 1) that "God has made foolish the wisdom of this world" (1 Cor. 1:20). Because "the foolishness of God is wiser than men" (1:25), the believer can "put to shame" the unregenerate people who profess to be wise (1:27), since we speak "not in words which man's wisdom teaches" (2:13).

So then, God's revelation of Himself, whether in nature (showing His holy character and wrath) or in the gospel (showing His redemptive love), comes with such clear evidence and persuasive power that those who repudiate what He has revealed have their professed "wisdom" reduced to sheer folly and irrationality. They can only maneuver mentally to avoid—that is, work at hindering—(without hope of success) their inescapable knowledge of God. This truth is indispensable and basic to Van Til's presuppositional method of apologetics.

VERBAL REVELATION NATURALLY UNITED WITH NATURAL[88]

To what has been said one further point needs to be added. It has been stressed that the Reformed concept of Scripture and the Reformed view of history imply one another. It has been stressed that the inscripturation of the Word of God is necessary because of the sin of man. Thus we have the idea of an authoritative revelation of God as self-attesting in a world of sin. But the world was not always a world of sin. Before the fall of Adam, man walked and talked with God in intimate fellowship. Then no Bible was required. Man was not alienated from God. No Christ was needed for man's redemption. But shall we add that therefore no supernatural authoritative revelation was necessary for him? Shall we say that man could originally identify himself and the facts of the universe without supernatural thought communication on the part of his Creator? The answer must be in the negative.

The necessity of an authoritative self-revelation of God in supernatural fashion is inherent in the human situation. It is "natural" that there should

88. An excerpt from *Christian Theory of Knowledge*, 29–30.

be supernatural revelation. Apart from and prior to the entrance of sin, God actually spoke to man. God *identifies* one tree among many in order to indicate to man his task on earth.[89] Man's task is to cultivate the earth and subdue it. He can do so only if he thinks and acts in obedience to his Maker. So his obedience must be tested. He must become even more self-consciously desirous of keeping the covenant with his God than he was. Hence supernatural thought communication is from the outset of history added to revelation through the facts of the universe in order thus to intimate to man his cultural task. Self-conscious covenantal reaction on the part of man presupposes identification of the facts of history and nature as clearly and directly carrying the will of God.

Man was to deal covenantally with every fact of history. He must therefore have available to him in history the direct confrontation of God and his requirements. Man must be able to identify all facts about him as the bearers of God's requirements; hence he needs a special supernatural test at the outset. He needs to learn by way of one example what he is to do with all the facts of history.

Thus the idea of supernatural thought communication on the part of God to man is inherent in the human situation. It is important to emphasize this point. Without clearly seeing that such is the case, there is no good argument for the necessity of Scripture. The idea of the Bible as the infallible Word requires, as has been noted, the idea of God's complete control over history. In similar fashion the idea of the Bible as supernatural revelation and as self-attesting, presupposes the idea that God's supernatural identification of his will in history took place before the fall of man. *It was against such a specific self-identification that man sinned*. The idea of sin is precisely that of the wilful setting aside of that which has been clearly identified to him as the will of God by God himself. So *pre-redemptive* supernatural revelation is the presupposition of *redemptive* supernatural revelation.

THE MIND, NOT NOW NORMAL, NEEDS REGENERATION[90]

It is at this irreducible epistemological level that we must face the question of error as a whole. We have already spoken of it by implication in our discus-

89. In the history of philosophy, there has been considerable attention given to the notion that knowing something is knowing "what it is for"—that is, knowing its aim or purpose (e.g., Aristotle, Leibniz, Kant, pragmatism, modern philosophy of science). For Van Til, if God had not revealed to man his task on earth (his purpose)—and thus his relation to the things in his environment—he would never have "known" or understood the world.
90. Excerpts from *Survey of Christian Epistemology*, 22–23, 28, 32, 184–86.

sion of the impossibility of neutrality. But the antitheist will continue to urge that it was natural for the Greeks that they should make mistakes in their investigation, and that we should not expect them to appear at once with a full-fledged theism. Even if they were to come to the theistic position at the end, they had to find their way and therefore had to be given time.

The assumption at the basis of this objection is that the Greek mind was the normal human mind. Yet this is not the case if the Christian theistic interpretation as a whole is tenable. In that case the Greek mind was a manifestation of the human mind as it has become abnormal through sin. Antitheistic thought identifies sin [with] finite limitation. It takes for granted that because man is a limited being he could not at once have a satisfactory knowledge of God. Consequently the many mistakes man made in his search for God are not regarded as sinful but as entirely normal. The analogy of the child that is beginning to learn is once more employed. But according to theism there can be no such identification of the finite and the sinful or evil. According to theism original man, though finite, was not sinful. Consequently he had at the outset a true and adequate knowledge of God.[91] His finite limitations in no way prevented him from having such adequate knowledge. . . .

And this lack of any notion of reconciliation that at all approaches the Christian idea on that subject corroborates what was said above about the assumption on the part of the Greeks, that the mind of man is naturally sound. It is assumed that there is no reconciliation to be made between God and man. And if there is any reconciliation to be made at all, it is the mind of man that is to do the reconciling. Thus the mind of man does not need any reconciliation to God by God, but it can itself reconcile the physical universe to God. Instead of needing a Mediator, the mind of man sets itself up as a mediator[92] if there is to be any mediator at all. . . .

Paul says that the world by its wisdom—that is, by the effort of its own unaided intellect—had not found God. To the Greek mind the gospel was foolishness because it implied that the mind of the "natural man" is radically corrupt. Paul presented the gospel, not as a source of wisdom in coordination with other sources, but as something before which men were to bow as before an absolute authority. The Christ Paul preached was an absolute Christ, and hence the gospel of Christ was an absolute gospel. If the Greek was to

91. CVT: By "adequate" we do not mean *comprehensive*. We mean "sufficient for his needs as a creature."

92. In Plato's philosophy, man's mind (acquainted with and recollecting the eternal forms or ideas) becomes "incarnate"—that is, is united with a material body. Thus, the reconciliation of spirit and matter (achieved by making the transcendent immanent) takes place in man's thinking, not in God's work.

accept this gospel of Christ he had to admit that his own wisdom was fool-ishness. And to do that would imply an entire reversal of his previous mode of thought. Naturally such a reversal of thought could not be effected unless it was effected by God, that is by the Holy Spirit. But the existence of such a Holy Spirit the Greek would have to deny if true to his own viewpoint. For him the spirit of generic man is holy. . . .

In the first place, Christian theism maintains that the subject of knowledge [i.e., man as the knower] owes its existence to God. Accordingly, all its inter-pretative powers are from God and must therefore be reinterpretative pow-ers. In the second place, when the subject of knowledge is to come into con-tact with the object of knowledge, the connection is possible only because God has laid it there. In other words, the subject-object relation has its va-lidity via God. Theologically expressed, we say that the validity of human knowledge in general rests upon the *testimonium Spiritus Sancti*.[93] In addi-tion to this, Christian theism maintains that since sin has come into the world, no subject of knowledge can really come into contact with any object of knowledge, in the sense of interpreting it properly, unless the Scripture give the required light and unless the regeneration by the Spirit give a new power of sight.

In opposition to this, the antitheist holds it to be self-evident that the sub-ject of knowledge exists in its own right and can interpret truly without any reference to God. The "natural man" claims to be able to interpret nature and history properly without the need of any reference to God, to Scripture, or to regeneration.

It follows from this clear-cut difference, a difference that goes to the bot-tom so that not a single "fact" or "law" is left for neutral territory, that the one group must naturally regard the other as being blind. Accordingly, it is when the question of the subject-subject relation[94] comes up, that this prob-lem as to what one group thinks of the other group, becomes acute. The rea-son why Christians have not always been alive to this difficulty is that they have not always been consistent in drawing the distinction between the Christian theistic and the antitheistic system of epistemology clearly and fully. All too often they have allowed a hazy fringe to remain when it came to the question of whether unbelievers really know material facts aright. Christian-ity has all too often been interpreted in a narrowly soteriological fashion.[95]

93. That is, the "testimony of the Holy Spirit."
94. That is, the relation of one knower to another knower.
95. Again, the mistake is in thinking that unbelieving philosophy can know, explain, and interpret the "natural" world and needs only to *supplement* that knowledge with the claims of Christianity.

Accordingly, the territory of nature and of history was left vacant for any first comer to occupy. If, however, we take Christianity seriously with its philosophy of nature and of history, it becomes at once apparent that a life and death struggle is set in motion.

It follows then that the question of the subject-subject relation cannot be discussed in peace. There is, of course, a sense in which this can be done. In the first place, when the question of the subject-subject relation is limited to that of one regenerated subject to another regenerated subject the answer is not difficult. In that case, the communication between one subject and another subject is possible through God once more. Taken in the soteriological sense, we say that it is the Holy Spirit who is the agent of communication, and that communication is effected as communion of the saints through the mystic union with Christ. Taken in a more comprehensive and cosmic sense, this communion does not stop till it has enveloped heaven and earth. There is then a Christian consciousness which is aware of the fact that it alone has the true interpretation of nature and of history. All too often it happens that scientists who are Christians are not aware of this Christian consciousness and, therefore, do not place their labors at the foot of the cross. On the other hand, all too often theologians have been to blame for this neglect on the part of scientists because they have spoken as though Christianity has no direct bearing upon science.[96] . . .

What we must deal with then is the clash between the two great opposing systems of epistemology. We now ask not *how* the two should reason together, but *whether* they should seek to reason together.

For the antitheist, this question is not difficult. For him the only cause of our blindness[97] is that we have been brought up in unfortunate circumstances. It may take quite some time and may often require measures of force as well as of ridicule to force upon us the light that they claim to have. But there is for them no inherent difficulty such as we have with respect to them. With respect to them, we have the conviction that they will not see our point of view till the Holy Spirit pleases to regenerate them. So the question narrows itself down to this, whether we shall, in view of our convictions with respect to the necessity of regeneration, nevertheless continue to reason with unbelievers.[98]

---

96. The aim of the presuppositionalist apologist is not simply to get Christianity added to the results of autonomous scientific investigation, but to challenge unbelievers to justify or account for science without a Christian worldview.

97. That is, man's epistemological foibles and failures in theory and/or in practice.

98. This question was addressed above in chap. 2.1 and will appear again in chap. 6.

REDEMPTIVE REVELATION NEEDED
TO READ NATURE RIGHTLY[99]

The necessity of special revelation appears not only with respect to man's failure to know and react to *spiritual* things aright, but also with respect to his inability to interpret "natural" things aright. Calvin brings out this point fully when, after laboring to show that God is marvelously revealed in his creation, he inserts a chapter on "The Need of Scripture, as a Guide and Teacher, in Coming to God as a Creator." He begins this chapter (I, 6) by saying:

> Therefore, though the effulgence which is presented to every eye, both in the heavens and on the earth, leaves the ingratitude of man without excuse, since God, in order to bring the whole human race under the same condemnation, holds forth to all, without exception, a mirror of his Deity in his works, another and better help must be given to guide us properly to God as a Creator.

No one, on the basis of present general revelation alone, actually knows God aright as the Creator. It is not as though man by himself and on the basis of natural revelation alone can truly know God as the creator, but that he cannot truly know God as Savior. Man *ought*, to be sure, from nature to know God as creator, seeing that nature clearly displays the creator. But since man has become a sinner, he has become a willing slave of sin (*ethelodoulos*). (Calvin's *Institutes*, II, 2.) He therefore never reads the "book of nature" aright even with respect to "natural" things. He may, to be sure, by virtue of the sense of deity within him, give involuntary, adventitious interpretations of natural revelation that are, so far forth, correct. In this sense every man knows God and knows himself to be a creature of God (Rom. 1:19). But to the extent that he interprets nature according to his own adopted principles, he does not speak the truth on any subject.[100] . . .

Yet the willing disobedience on the part of man is itself the greatest dam-

---

99. An excerpt from *Introduction to Systematic Theology*, 112–13.
100. It is important to understand that, according to Van Til, the unbeliever has two things going on inside him as he attempts to understand the world. Because he already knows God, he can gain further knowledge of the world; but as he attempts to use his "adopted" principles (where God is suppressed), he would be unable to understand anything correctly. What the unbeliever successfully accomplishes, he credits to his adopted principles. This is precisely what the presuppositional apologist wishes to challenge (that those adopted principles could make sense out of knowing anything about the world), arguing instead that the unbeliever's understanding must be credited to his unacknowledged knowledge of God.

age done to God's creation; it is this that must be repaired. This cannot be done unless creation is really seen as God's creation and man is really seen as the creature of God. It is only if man is the creature of God that he can be saved by God. Salvation means that man, the sinner, must be brought back to the knowledge of himself as the creature of God and therefore, to the knowledge of God as the Creator. Being a sinner, man will not read nature aright unless he does it in the light of Scripture. "If true religion is to beam upon us, our principle must be, that it is necessary to begin with heavenly teaching, and that it is impossible for any man to obtain even the minutest portion of right and sound doctrine without being a disciple of Scripture" (*Institutes*, I, 6:2).

We should accordingly avoid the error of separating too sharply between science and religion as is often done. The world of natural and historical fact with which science deals cannot be truly interpreted by anyone who is not a Christian, any more than can the world of spiritual things. Every statement about the physical universe implies, in the last analysis, some view about the "spiritual" realm. Scientists frequently say that in their statements they will limit themselves to the phenomenal world. But every assertion they make about the "phenomenal" world involves an attitude toward the "noumenal" world.[101] Even the mere assumption that anything can intelligently be asserted about the phenomenal world by itself presupposes its independence of God, and as such is in effect a denial of him.

SCRIPTURE CARRIES ITS OWN EVIDENCE IN ITSELF[102]

Thus the Bible, as the infallibly inspired revelation of God to sinful man, stands before us as that light in terms of which all the facts of the created universe must be interpreted. All of finite existence, natural and redemptive, functions in relation to one all-inclusive plan that is in the mind of God. Whatever insight man is to have into this pattern of the activity of God he must attain by looking at all his objects of research in the light of Scripture. "If true religion is to beam upon us, our principle must be, that it is necessary to begin with heavenly teaching, and that it is impossible for any man to obtain even the minutest portion of right and sound doctrine without being a disciple of Scripture."[103] . . .

---

101. These labels come from the philosophy of Kant and were used by him to differentiate between the realm of things as they appear in man's immediate experience (phenomenal) and the realm of things as they really are in themselves (noumenal). The latter is a transcendent or metaphysical realm.
102. Excerpts from *Defense of the Faith*, 124–26, 254–56.
103. Van Til cites Calvin's *Institutes*, 1.6.2.

In the first place it must be affirmed that a Protestant accepts Scripture to be that which Scripture itself says it is on its own authority. Scripture presents itself as being the only light in terms of which the truth about facts and their relations can be discovered. Perhaps the relationship of the sun to our earth and the objects that constitute it, may make this clear. We do not use candles or electric lights in order to discover whether the light and the energy of the sun exist. The reverse is the case. We have light in candles and electric light bulbs because of the light and energy of the sun. So we cannot subject the authoritative pronouncements of Scripture about reality to the scrutiny of reason because it is reason itself that learns of its proper function from Scripture. . . .

All the objections that are brought against such a position spring, in the last analysis, from the assumption that the human person is ultimate and as such should properly act as judge of all claims to authority that are made by any one. But if man is not autonomous, if he is rather what Scripture says he is, namely, a creature of God and a sinner before his face, then man should subordinate his reason to the Scriptures and seek in the light of it to interpret his experience.[104]

The proper attitude of reason to the authority of Scripture, then, is but typical of the proper attitude of reason to the whole of the revelation of God. The objects man must seek to know are always of such a nature as God asserts they are. God's revelation is always authoritarian. This is true of his revelation in nature no less than of his revelation in Scripture. The truly scientific method, the method which alone can expect to make true progress in learning, is therefore such a method as seeks simply to think God's thoughts after him.[105]

When these matters are kept in mind, it will be seen clearly that the true method for any Protestant with respect to the Scripture (Christianity) and with respect to the existence of God (theism) must be *the indirect method of reasoning by presupposition. In fact it then appears that the argument for the Scripture as the infallible revelation of God is, to all intents and purposes, the same as the argument for the existence of God.*[106] Protestants are required

---

104. Refusing to subordinate one's reasoning to the claims of Scripture is already to deny the fallen character and the dependent (creaturely) character of one's reasoning—and thus to reject the biblical message in advance. It is true that God calls sinful men to consider the truth about Him and the evidence supporting His word, but God does not bid sinners to evaluate His word and evidence *as His epistemological equal.*

105. Cf. sec. 4.5 below.

106. Emphasis added. We have noted above that Paul's challenge is the same with regard to both natural revelation (4.3) and Scripture (4.4): by rejecting them, the unbeliever is reduced to foolish and futile reasoning. The Christian worldview

by the most basic principles of their system to vindicate the existence of no other God than the one who has spoken in Scripture. But this God cannot be proved to exist by any other method than the indirect one of presupposition. No proof for this God and for the truth of his revelation in Scripture can be offered by an appeal to anything in human experience that has not itself received its light from the God whose existence and whose revelation it is supposed to prove.[107] One cannot prove the usefulness of the light of the sun for the purposes of seeing by turning to the darkness of a cave. The darkness of the cave must itself be lit up by the shining of the sun. When the cave is thus lit up each of the objects that are in it "proves" the existence and character of the sun by receiving their light and intelligibility from it. . . .

To begin with then I take what the Bible says about God and his relation to the universe as unquestionably true on its own authority. . . .

Having taken these two, revelation in the created universe, both within and about man, and revelation by way of supernatural positive communication as aspects of revelation as originally given to man, we can see that natural revelation is even after the fall perspicuous in character. "The perspicuity of God's revelation in nature depends for its very meaning upon the fact that it is an aspect of the total and totally voluntary revelation of a God who is self-contained" (*The Infallible Word*, p. 269). . . .

At this point we may add the fact of Scriptural revelation. God has condescended to reveal himself and his plan in it to sinners. It is the same God who speaks in Scripture and in nature. But in Scripture he speaks of his grace to such as have broken his covenant, to such as have set aside his original revelation to them. And as the original revelation of God to man was clear so is the revelation of grace in Scripture. "The Scriptures as the finished product of God's supernatural and saving revelation to man have their own evidence in themselves" (*Idem*, p. 271).

In all of this there is one thing that stands out. It is that man has no excuse whatsoever for not accepting the revelation of God whether in nature, including man and his surroundings, or in Scripture. God's revelation is always clear.[108]

---

is "indirectly" proven by the inability of those who reject Christianity to make reason and ethics intelligible.

107. "In Thy light shall we see light" (Ps. 36:9).

108. Since God's revelation is always and everywhere clearly evident as God's revelation, it never needs support from "outside" considerations in order to bolster its credibility. We might contrast this to corroborating evidence in the case of a crime. Because even eyewitnesses are able to make mistakes in identifying, interpreting, or remembering their experience, the testimony that is brought against the accused needs to be corroborated by an independent line of evidence

The first and most basic point on which my approach differs from the traditional one is therefore that . . . I start more frankly from the Bible as the source from which as an absolutely authoritative revelation[109] I take my whole interpretation of life.[110]

NATURAL AND SUPERNATURAL
REVELATION SELF-ATTESTING[111]

The first point about a truly Protestant or Reformed doctrine of Scripture is that it must be taken exclusively from Scripture. It is, says Bavinck, exclusively from the Scriptures that we learn about Christ and his work of redemption for man. From the Scriptures alone do we learn about God's work of redemption for man. On its authority as the Word of God do we know the whole "system" of Christian truth. Therefore also, on its authority alone do we believe what the Scripture says about itself.[112] The Scripture testifies to itself because in it Christ testifies of himself. "Now, in order that true religion may shine upon us, we ought to hold that it must take its beginning from heavenly doctrine and that no one can get even the slightest taste of right and sound doctrine unless he be a pupil of Scripture. Hence, there also emerges the beginning of true understanding when we reverently embrace what it pleases God there to witness of himself."[113]

Reformed theologians have pointed out that the idea of Scripture as self-

---

against him (e.g., another eyewitness or fingerprints). But the evidence that God presents of Himself in His revelation leaves man without any excuse whatsoever. The sinner cannot legitimately claim that God's revelation requires external corroboration.

109. Because the authority of revelation is "absolute," it is not qualified by, or contingent upon, authorization or independent support outside of itself. The highest or ultimate (and thus absolute) authority must necessarily authorize itself. This is true for all systems of philosophy and all interpretations of life.

110. Other approaches start "outside" the Bible and work from that (allegedly) self-sufficient position toward the Bible, seeking to determine intellectually whether the Bible might qualify for inclusion in one's interpretation of life.

111. Excerpts from *Christian Theory of Knowledge*, 25–27, 28, 30–34, 39–40.

112. The alternative to this is theologically and epistemologically unacceptable. The teaching of Scripture about itself is the source and authority for our doctrine of Scripture, just as much as it is for any other doctrine. Anybody who advocates the inerrancy of Scripture must recognize this, since nobody can corroborate each and every claim made in the Bible. If Scripture is not presented as self-attesting in some apologetical methods, then the unbeliever has every right to hold that the other doctrines of Christianity need not be accepted on Scripture's say-so.

113. CVT: Calvin: *Institutes of the Christian Religion*, ed. by John T. McNeill, tr. by Ford Lewis Battles ("The Library of Christian Classics," Vol. XX, XXI, ed. by J. Baillie, J. T. McNeill and H. P. Van Dusen; Philadelphia: Westminster Press), I:6.2.

attesting is involved in the fact that in it we have the message of redemption for man. This message of redemption is not a piecemeal affair. It centers around the person and work of Jesus Christ. His incarnation, his death and resurrection, Bavinck points out, cannot be repeated. They are historically unique.[114] The Son of God became like unto men in all things, sin excepted. So the question of identification becomes at once important. Who is the Christ? Is it this man Jesus of Nazareth? But he does not seem to differ greatly from other men. How can he be identified as being the Son of God as well as the son of Mary?

Can there be identification unless there be complete or exhaustive description? How is he, if he is wholly unique, to be indicated for what he is to those who are wholly different from him? Or, if he is not wholly different, if he is like them and yet also unlike them, where is the boundary line between likeness and difference? When we can only recognize him at the point where he is like us or identical in nature with us, we cannot recognize him where he is different from us.

The upshot of such considerations is that the identification of Jesus Christ must be by his own authority. Without authoritative identification, the Christ is lost in the ocean of relativity.

A distinction must be made at this point. Authority is needed for purposes of identification in history. But the authority of Scripture, as has already been mentioned, has to do with the question of redemption through Jesus Christ as the Son of God. Christ came to redeem sinners. Sinners are covenant-breakers. They are descendants of Adam in whom, as their representative, they turned against God. The natural man, the sinner, the covenant-breaker in Adam, is spiritually blind. He is wilfully blind. He cannot see the truth because he will not see it. He seeks to suppress the truth in unrighteousness (Rom. 1:18). *Sinners hate the idea of a clearly identifiable authority over them.*[115] They do not want to meet God. They would gladly make themselves believe that there is no clearly discernible, identifiable revelation of their Creator and Judge anywhere to be found in the universe. God's work of redemption through Christ, therefore, comes into enemy territory. It comes to save from themselves those who do not want to be saved, because they think that they do not need to be saved.

It is this situation, as has been indicated by Reformed theologians, that ac-

---

114. Van Til cites Herman Bavinck, *Gereformeerde Dogmatiek*, vol. 1 (Kampen: J. H. Kok, 1928), 399.

115. Emphasis added. As long as it were vague, uncertain, or only a hypothesis in need of confirmation, "revelation" would not threaten man's autonomy by asserting prior authority over all his thinking.

counts for the need of inscripturation of the authoritative and redemptive Word of God.

But this view of sin itself comes from Scripture as authoritative. Experience apart from Scripture does not teach such a doctrine. Only he who accepts the Scripture as the authoritative revelation of God and of the self-identifying Son of God, will accept what it says about himself as a sinner. So we are of necessity moving about in circles.[116] Those who accept the fully biblical conception of sin will accept the Bible as authoritative. And those who accept the fully biblical view of sin do so because they accept the Bible as the authoritative Word of God. . . .

It thus appears afresh that a specifically biblical or Reformed philosophy of history both presupposes and is presupposed by the idea of the Bible as testifying to itself as being the source of its own identification. . . .

A further point remains to be made. It has been pointed out that the Bible tells the story of God's redemptive work for man. This work is accomplished through Christ, the Son of God, who is also completely human. The Word tells us of the person and work of Christ. But Christ himself tells about the Word as being authoritative because it is the Word of God. Christ testified to the Old Testament as being the Word of God that cannot be broken. He performed his work on earth in accordance with the program outlined for him in the Word. Thus the Christ as testifying to the Word and the Word as testifying to the Christ are involved in one another.[117]

But the work of Christ was not finished while he was on earth. He accomplished much of his work through his apostles after him. So he promised them his Spirit that they might write the New Testament as a supplement to the Old Testament. But who should identify the New Testament as being the Word of God after it was written? Should the church do this? Protestant theologians have replied that the church cannot and did not authenticate the New Testament Scriptures as being the Word of God. The New Testament as well as the Old is self-attesting. The church merely recognized the Word in its self-attestation. It is Christ whose voice the church hears in Scripture.[118]

---

116. Critics who have faulted Van Til for committing the fallacy of circular reasoning have failed to understand his position properly. Van Til is simply making the point that the Christian worldview is a *coherent and unique system* in which every part assumes every other part. The doctrine of sin assumes what Scripture says about the Savior, just as the doctrine of the Savior assumes the doctrine of sin.

117. Without the Bible as God's authorized testimony, we would not know of Christ, but without Christ as God authorizing what Scripture says about Him, we would have no authoritative revelation.

118. Van Til is here addressing the issue of biblical canonicity. Cf. Greg Bahnsen, "The Concept and Importance of Canonicity," *Antithesis* 1, no. 5 (September–October 1990): 42–45.

It is only if, in this manner, both the Old and New Testaments are regarded as a unit, and as a self-attesting unit, that justice is done to the idea of the Scriptures as the Word of God.

It is only thus, too, that the unity of the work of Christ can be maintained. The work of Christ is the work of establishing and perfecting the covenant of grace in a world of sin. He came to redeem a people for the Father. That people is a unit by virtue of their common redemption through Christ. But they are taken out of a broader unit, namely the human race. This work has the greatest possible significance for the human race as a whole. Christ's work is of cosmic significance. He came to save the *world*. So there is through him and through his Word an authoritative interpretation given to mankind of the whole of the cosmic scene. Every fact in the universe must be Christologically interpreted.[119] Through Christ the new heavens and the new earth are to come into being, as sprung from the old, through the redemptive power of the risen Christ. In greater or lesser degree, all the facts of the universe are what they are because of the work of Christ. For it is through the work of Christ that God accomplishes his plan for the world.

Accordingly, the Bible must be identified in its entirety in all that it says on any subject as the Word of God. It is, again, only if history is considered to be what it is because of the ultimate controlling plan of God, that such a relationship between God's Word and all the facts of the universe can be obtained.

In several of the preceding sections we have seemingly gone beyond the matter of Scripture's self-attestation. It has been impossible to avoid dealing with the question of what Scripture teaches even in a discussion of where the Scriptures may be found. In other words, the question of the identity of Scripture could not be discussed without asking about the truth of the content of which it speaks. The *that* and the *what* overlap. Unless we conjoin the message of the Scripture and the idea of Scripture, the latter becomes an abstraction.[120]

This is but to be expected. *It is of the utmost apologetical importance. It is precisely because God is the kind of God he is, that his revelation is, in the nature of the case, self-attesting. In particular, it should be noted that*

---

119. In order to be intelligible, any fact that is known presupposes a view of man (the knower), the objects of knowledge, the course of nature and history, etc. Van Til's point is that only the worldview that centers on the person and work of Christ can render facts intelligible to sinful men.

120. Van Til repeats here that Scripture's claim to authority is not an empty, abstract claim, but rather the claim (or authoritative proclamation) of the whole worldview that is revealed in Scripture.

such a God as the Scripture speaks of is everywhere self-attesting.[121] To see the import of this doctrine it must be noted that man cannot look anywhere but that he confronts God, and God as self-attesting. Natural or general revelation speaks with as much authority and as directly as does the Bible, albeit in a different manner and not on redemption.

It is this complementary and supplementary character of supernatural and natural revelation that must be borne in mind when approach is made to the question of the indications of the divinity of Scripture. The Westminster Confession of Faith speaks eloquently of the heavenly character, the consent of all the parts, etc., of Scripture.

Says Calvin on this subject: "What wonderful confirmation ensues when, with keener study, we ponder the economy of the divine wisdom, so well ordered and disposed; the completely heavenly character of its doctrine, savoring of nothing earthly; the beautiful agreement of all the parts with one another—as well as such other qualities as can gain majesty for the writings."[122]

Then after considerable discussion on the various matters he adds: "There are other reasons, neither few nor weak, for which the dignity and majesty of Scripture are not only affirmed in godly hearts, but brilliantly vindicated against the wiles of its disparagers; yet of themselves these are not strong enough to provide a firm faith, until our Heavenly Father, revealing his majesty there, lifts reverence for Scripture beyond the realm of controversy. Therefore Scripture will suffice for a saving knowledge of God only when its certainty is founded upon the inward persuasion of the Holy Spirit."[123]

In this passage Calvin brings into contact the fact that objectively the Scriptures have on their face the appearance of divinity while yet none will accept its self-attestation unless the Holy Spirit, himself divine, witnesses to the Word which he has inspired the prophets and apostles to write.

First then, argues Calvin, we are not to separate the fact of Scripture from the nature of Scripture. The identification of the fact of Scripture is an identification accomplished by the setting before us of the content of Scripture, the system of truth centering in the ideas of God as self-contained and of his plan for the universe which controls whatsoever comes to pass. The identity is not that of an unknown quantity. Faith is not blind faith. "The nature of

---

121. Emphasis added. Other approaches to apologetics may seem appropriate only because the kind of God who is presented and defended in them is not an ultimate authority necessary for knowing anything whatsoever. But if God *is* that kind of God, only His own authority could authorize His revelation, not the secondary, limited, and dependent "authority" of human reasoning.

122. CVT: *Institutes*, I:8.1.

123. CVT: *Ibid.*, I:8.13.

faith is acceptance on the basis of testimony, and the ground of faith is therefore testimony or evidence. In this matter it is the evidence God has provided, and God provides the evidence in his Word, the witness the Bible itself bears to the fact that it is God's Word, and our faith that it is infallible must rest upon no other basis than the witness the Bible bears to this fact. If the Bible does not witness to its own infallibility, then we have no right to believe that it is infallible. If it does bear witness to its infallibility then our faith in it must rest upon that witness, however much difficulty may be entertained with belief. If this position with respect to the ground of faith in Scripture is abandoned, then appeal to the Bible for the ground of faith in any other doctrine must also be abandoned."[124]

It is this interdependence of the idea of *the fact* and *the content* of Scripture that is all important. The *that* and the *what* are correlative or supplementative the one to the other. It is this interdependence that enables Calvin to exult in the absolute assurance that he has before him in the Bible, not the word of man, not the word of man as it speaks in a church that claims to authenticate the Word, but the very Word of God himself. "As to their question—How can we be assured that this has sprung from God unless we have recourse to the decree of the church?—it is as if someone asked: Whence will we learn to distinguish light from darkness, white from black, sweet from bitter? Indeed, Scripture exhibits fully as clear evidence of its own truth as white and black things do of their color, or sweet and bitter things do of their taste."[125]

It is through the heavenly content of the Word that God speaks of himself. Faith is not blind faith; it is faith in the truth, the system of truth displayed in the Scriptures.

At the same time the interdependence of the *that* and the *what* of Scripture fits in with the idea of the witness of the Holy Spirit to the divinity of Scripture as alone able to convince men of its divinity.

It is this whole system of truth that is set forth in the Bible. The writers of Scripture were inspired by the Holy Spirit to set forth this system of truth. *Thus the system is self-attesting.*[126] The testimony or influence of the Spirit in the heart of man cannot be in the nature of new information. The whole

---

124. CVT: John Murray, "The Attestation of Scripture," *The Infallible Word*, a symposium by the members of the Faculty of Westminster Theological Seminary, ed. by N. B. Stonehouse and Paul Woolley (Philadelphia: The Presbyterian Guardian, 1946), pp. 7–8. Revised, Presbyterian and Reformed Publishing Co., 1968.
125. CVT: Calvin, *Institutes*, I:7.2.
126. Emphasis added. Van Til does not say that the individual doctrines taken in isolation are self-attesting, but that the system as a whole is self-attesting.

system of truth is already contained in Scripture and is being identified as such. It would not be identified by the Spirit as such if the Spirit gave other additional revelation. The Scripture would no longer be self-attesting if the Spirit gave additional information.[127] On the other hand it is by the sovereign act of the Holy Spirit that the Scripture can be seen to be the self-attesting Word of God. For sin is that by which men seek to interpret facts apart from the revelation of God. The sinner seeks a criterion of truth and knowledge independent of the revelation of God. The sinner wants to test that which presents itself as the revelation of God by a standard not itself taken from this revelation. He complains of the circular reasoning that would be involved in accepting the word of Scripture about the nature of Scripture.[128] So then, to overcome this hostile attitude of the sinner it is necessary that the Holy Spirit convict him of his sin in not accepting the Bible as the Word of God. The miracles, the prophecies fulfilled, the symmetry of its parts, etc., will all be misinterpreted because interpreted by the wrong standard, unless the Spirit convicts and convinces the sinner that he is dealing with the Word of God.[129]

"For as God alone is a fit witness of himself in his Word, so also the Word will not find acceptance in men's hearts before it is sealed by the inward testimony of the Spirit. The same Spirit, therefore, who has spoken through the mouths of the prophets must penetrate into our hearts to persuade us that they faithfully proclaimed what had been divinely commanded."[130]

It should be noted that this view of Scripture thinks of God as here and now speaking to men through his Word. "Scripture is not a dry tale or an old chronicle, but it is the ever living, ever youthful Word which God at the present time and always sends out to his people. It is the ever continuing speech of God to us."[131] . . .

In conclusion it should be pointed out that the doctrine of Scripture set forth above sets before men the fact of God. God requires of men that they love

---

127. That is, the Holy Spirit does not add to the evidence already available in the word itself—not even the assertion of the Bible's truth. Rather, the Spirit changes the resistant and doubting heart, granting the gift of faith in what the Bible says about itself (and especially about the Savior).

128. Likewise, some apologists complain about this kind of "circularity," as though each doctrine sues for acceptance on its own, and as though the ultimate authority of the collected system could rest somewhere outside the system itself.

129. The evidences that we usually think of presenting to the unbeliever are not truly evidential of scriptural veracity unless they are interpreted by proper presuppositions. Without those presuppositions, these things are not intelligible as evidences of anything.

130. CVT: *Ibid.* [Calvin, *Institutes*], I:7.4.

131. CVT: Bavinck, *op. cit.* [*Gereformeerde Dogmatiek*], p. 405.

and obey him. He made them perfect in his image. They rebelled against him. Now he is, in grace, calling them to repentance through his Son. He tells them about this call to repentance through his Son. He tells them about this call to repentance and love in the Bible. So Christ, the Redeemer, the Son of God, speaks directly to us in the words of Scripture.

It follows that those who take the Bible to be what it says it is, must present this Bible as conveying a challenge of Christ to men. They must use it always as a means with which to send forth a clarion call of surrender to those who are rebels against God. To be sure, it is the grace of God that is offered to men. Just as Jesus wept over Jerusalem and her children, desiring that they might repent, so those who are believers must be filled with deep concern and love for the lost. But in their love for the lost they must, none the less, not lower the claims of God revealed in Christ who calls upon "all men everywhere" to repent (Acts 17:30). This call to repentance has application for the whole of human life and for all the activities of men.[132]

"The authority of Scripture extends itself over the whole man and over the whole of humanity. It stands above mind and will, above heart and conscience; it cannot be compared to any other authority."[133]

Men must therefore be asked to repent for the way they have carried on their scientific enterprises, no less than for the way they have worshiped idols. Scripture is the Word, the living Word of God who is the Creator and Redeemer of men and of mankind. It presupposes that he to whom it comes is ". . . corrupted in his religious attitude and therefore in need of redemption. It would therefore be to deny itself if it recognized the natural man as its competent judge. If Christianity is in the full sense of the term a religion of redemption and therefore wants to redeem man from the error of his intellect as well as from the impurity of his heart, if it wants to save man from the death of his soul as well as from that of his body, then it can in the nature of the case not subject itself to the criticism of man, but must subject man to the criticism of itself."[134] "The revelation of God in Christ does not seek support or justification from men. It posits and maintains itself in high majesty. Its authority is not only normative but also causative. It fights for its own triumph. It conquers for itself the hearts of men. It makes itself irresistible."[135]

---

132. God demands total surrender and admission of guilt at the very outset of one's thinking—even the guilt of previous intellectual rebellion and deceit.
133. CVT: *Ibid.* [Bavinck, *Gereformeerde Dogmatiek*, vol. 1], p. 492.
134. CVT: *Ibid.*, p. 533.
135. CVT: *Ibid.*

4.5 Thinking God's Thoughts After Him

In the previous two sections, we spoke of men "knowing" God—having justified, true beliefs about His existence and character that are gained through natural revelation (for all men) and special verbal revelation (for those who have encountered Scripture or its proclamation). The evidence in nature and Scripture that justifies our beliefs about God is ultimately noninferential. It is not derived by a psychological and discursive process of drawing inferences from other propositions, but rather is immediately apprehended. God is disclosed and recognized simultaneously with any consciousness of the natural order. The truth that God is speaking in Scripture is self-attesting. We have likened these direct apprehensions of the "marks of deity" to directly identifying a friend's "signature" or discerning his "voice." Once you are familiar with somebody well enough, you just "know" him when you see him or hear from him, although such knowledge is not reached by inference. When men see the world around them or hear the message of Scripture, they realize that they are dealing with their God as the Creator or author of what they are encountering. They immediately apprehend His "signature" or "voice."[136]

If the analogy used here is to be appropriate, however, we must assume that men are already familiar with God when they encounter the world or His word. They come to their experiences prepared to recognize the indications in nature and Scripture as indications of God. Such preconditioning is necessary in all cases of direct, noninferential knowing. Whenever we gain knowledge in the form of immediate awareness, there has been prior training or preparation (linguistic, conceptual, behavioral, etc.). So by holding that there are some cases of noninferential knowing, Van Til was not at all endorsing a naive empiricist theory of concept formation or an artificial verificationist criterion of meaningfulness. To put it simply, the mind is not a *tabula rasa*, and there are no "pure" observations. There is no such thing as the passive, neutral reception of stimuli that somehow bear meaning all by themselves. Observation always involves interpretation and is bound to theory. Broadly speaking, we bring a "cognitive background" to our experiences, so that we identify objects,

---

136. Remember, immediate apprehension is the (initial) warrant or justification for some (but not all) of our beliefs. But to repeat what was said above, even in those cases, where there is doubt about or argument over the belief in question, the "evidence" now used to justify (i.e., defend) the belief is not that of immediate apprehension. Arguments (even within ourselves) involve lines of reasoning or inference.

events, and relations in terms of a theoretical perspective, cluster of beliefs, or state of mind.[137] This cognitive background is partly a matter of intellectual/linguistic ability (a potentiality not always or fully developed), but also partly a matter of propositional truths capable of expression (in degrees of precision, accuracy, and scope), which mature along with the development of intellectual/linguistic ability.

> The mind of man as created by God cannot be a *tabula rasa*. . . . Accordingly we cannot say that the innate knowledge of God in man is the merely formal ability, the capacity or potentiality, in view of man's creation as an intellectual being, to recognize revelation if and when it comes. There can be no finite human consciousness that is not stirred to its depths by the revelational content within itself as well as about itself. Thus the innate knowledge deals with a thought-content, and not with a mere formality. The finite human consciousness is itself revelational of God. . . . This thought-content is, at bottom, involuntary. It springs up within man in spite of himself. It is for this reason that it appears most clearly at the intuitional or non-ratiocinative level of man's consciousness. . . . We should therefore rather speak of the innate knowledge of God in man as the revelational thought-content that arises with his self-consciousness, inasmuch as his own constitution is revelational of God.[138]

As we see in this quotation, Van Til was cautiously willing to speak of an "innate knowledge" of God: "Thus the knowledge of God is inherent in man. It is there by virtue of his creation in the image of God. This may be called innate knowledge. But as such it must be distinguished from the innate ideas of idealist philosophy. . . . In contrast with this the innate knowledge of Descartes and idealist philosophy is based on the idea of the autonomy of man."[139] In scriptural terms, human beings come into this

137. It is not our interest or purpose to delve into discussions of the development of adolescent cognition. Suffice it to say that, regardless of the explanatory theory that should be adopted, we are not here claiming that developing children self-consciously or linguistically identify the "beliefs" in terms of which they gradually interpret their experiences. But with the development of linguistic ability comes the developing ability to express the propositions that describe the content of that "cognitive background" with which they have interpreted themselves and the world. Their sinful nature, however, distorts, obscures, and rebels against the truths that have become expressible—thus suppressing and/or perverting their expression of them.
138. *Introduction to Systematic Theology*, 195–96.
139. *Defense of the Faith*, 172. "Descartes followed the idealist line of thought in maintaining

world as "the image of God." They are already conditioned to recognize their Maker as He is revealed in the world around them and in their intellectual and moral constitution. As Van Til indicated, this involves not only intellectual *capacity* (a formal ability), but also definite thought *content.*[140]

Calvin taught at the very beginning of the *Institutes*—something to which Van Til repeatedly alluded—that our knowledge of God and our knowledge of ourselves are "mutually connected" (1.1.1–3). Without the one there could not be the other. This is a fundamental principle in Van Til's approach to knowledge: "For man self-consciousness presupposes God-consciousness. Calvin speaks of this as man's inescapable sense of deity. For Adam in paradise God-consciousness could not come in at the end of a syllogistic process of reasoning. God-consciousness was for him the presupposition of the significance of his reasoning on anything. . . . Even when he closed his eyes upon the external world his internal sense would manifest God to him in his own constitution."[141] Accordingly, Van Til held that in order for us even to exist as self-conscious beings, "we *must* have true knowledge of Him [God]. . . . All this we express theologically when we say that man is created in God's image. This makes man like God and *assures* true knowledge of God."[142]

Throughout the history of philosophy, the typical questions and critical issues in epistemology have revolved around how we are to "picture" ourselves as knowers. For example, what is mind and its relation to body? What is man's place in the cosmos? How do we relate to objects of knowledge? How does one mind relate to another? What are bearers of meaning? What is appropriate and reliable intellectual procedure? Plato's picture of knowing (recollection) was opposed by Aristotle's picture of knowing (abstraction); similarly, Locke's picture of knowing (cf. *tabula rasa*) was opposed by Kant's picture of knowing (active mental formation). How should we look upon ourselves as knowers in order to give an account of the possibility and

that man has knowledge within himself. His position is contrary to the Christian position in that it does not recognize that all knowledge of man presupposes revelation. With Plato, Descartes assumes that man can, to a large extent, obtain knowledge by simply eliciting what is in himself, apart from God, . . . [and that] the natural man's principles of interpretation . . . rest in themselves instead of in God" (*Introduction to Systematic Theology*, 195–96).

140. "Scripture clearly teaches that it [the innate knowledge of God] is not a mere matter of form, but very definitely a matter of content. The heathen, according to Paul, deal with a certain thought-content that comes up in them" (*Introduction to Systematic Theology*, 196).
141. *Defense of the Faith*, 107–8.
142. Ibid., 57 (emphasis added).

process of knowing? According to Van Til, we need to picture our-selves, having been made in the image of God, as "thinking God's thoughts after Him." Because we are created as the image (reflection) of God, we not only come into this world cognitively "conditioned" or prepared to recognize the indications of our Creator in nature and Scripture, but *all* of our knowing, whether about God, ourselves, or the world, is a matter of "imaging" (reflecting) God's thinking about the same things. "True human knowledge corresponds to the knowledge which God has of himself and his world. . . . We should say that our ideas must correspond to God's ideas."[143]

God knows Himself, of course, perfectly and comprehensively. He knows His holy character. He knows all propositional truths and possibilities, as well as their conceptual or logical relations. He knows His plan for every detail of creation and history, as well as the relations between all events and objects. His understanding is infinite and without flaw. Moreover, it is in terms of His creative and providential activity that all things and events are what they are. God's thinking is what gives unity, meaning, coherence, and intel-ligibility to nature, history, reasoning, and morality. In terms of this picture of the knowing process, man can search for causal re-lationships and laws (thinking God's thoughts after Him about His providential plan). He can think in terms of shared properties, similarities, or classes (thinking God's thoughts after Him about the patterns, classifications, or kinds of things He creates and provi-dentially controls). He can draw logical inferences (thinking God's thoughts after Him about conceptual and truth-functional rela-tions). He can make meaningful normative judgments (thinking God's thoughts after Him about the demands of His righteous-ness). He can account for man's mind knowing extramental objects (thinking God's thoughts after Him about created man's control over the created environment in which God placed him). He can account for the public or objective character of the truth available to many finite minds (thinking God's thoughts after Him about the community of minds created and providentially planned to reflect His thinking), etc.

How does man think God's thoughts after Him? First, by receiving the information that God discloses in His self-revelation through na-ture and Scripture. Within that context, man then seeks to know "the

---

143. *Survey of Christian Epistemology*, 1, 3.

mind of God" further by using the rational and empirical abilities with which God has equipped him as His own image. Because God placed man in the world with the calling to understand and control it, we have a God-given ability to observe (with our senses), check, generalize, and apply truths about the cosmos. Because God's plan and purpose (and not our imaginations) determine whatever comes to pass, we need to explore, research, and gather details about nature and history to "know God's mind" regarding them. Because God's thinking is faithful and coherent, we must seek to be conceptually clear and logically consistent in our reasoning, so that we might "think as God thinks" about truths and their relationships. So when we learn things through empirical research and logical reasoning—and not simply when we receive preinterpreted information through divine revelation—we are coming to think thoughts on the creaturely level which God originally thought (or thinks) as Creator and providential Governor of the world, and to reach such truths by means of the intellectual tools He has granted us as His image bearers. "Man was to gather up in his consciousness all the meaning that God had deposited in the universe and be the reflector of it all. The revelation of God was deposited in the whole creation, but it was in the mind of man alone that this revelation was to come to self-conscious re-interpretation. Man was to be God's re-interpreter, that is, God's prophet on earth."[144]

Unbelieving philosophy disdains such a view, of course, and insists on approaching the knowing process in a way (whether through randomness, materialism, egocentrism, relativism, etc.) that ends up destroying unity, universality, causality, community, and moral absolutism—in short, resulting in skepticism. Against all unbelieving worldviews and their conceptions of knowing, Van Til presented the epistemological alternative of picturing man as thinking God's thoughts after Him: "It is this fact of the priority of the positive relation of God to the world in the way of creation and providence, in the way of man's creation in the image of God, that saves from scepticism. The Christian idea of human knowledge as analogical of God's knowledge is therefore the only position in which man, who cannot control or know anything in the ultimate comprehensive sense of the term, can nevertheless be assured that his knowledge is true."[145]

Notice in the above quotation that Van Til speaks of human knowl-

144. *Introduction to Systematic Theology,* 69.
145. Ibid., 185.

edge as being "analogical" of God's knowledge.[146] This may not be a familiar way of speaking,[147] but by it Van Til stressed the "agreement, correspondence, resemblance, or similarity" (the analogous relation) between God's knowledge and man's knowledge, while recognizing at the same time the elements of discontinuity or difference between God's knowing and man's knowing. The fact that God is the transcendent Creator and sovereign controller of all things, and the fact that He (and thus his knowledge) is incomprehensible to man, must not lead anyone to think that He cannot be known or apprehended by man. Much less should these facts suggest theological (and thus philosophical) skepticism, according to Van Til. Just the opposite is the case when we think analogously to God's thinking. "When on the created level of existence man thinks God's thoughts after him, that is, when man thinks in self-conscious submission to the voluntary revelation of the self-sufficient God, he has therewith the only possible *ground of certainty* for his knowledge."[148] Van Til called the relationship between God's knowledge and man's knowledge "analogical" in order to express and guard the truthfulness and reliability of what man knows. "Since the human mind is created by God and is therefore in itself naturally revelational of God,

---

146. The two relevant expressions here were used interchangeably by Van Til. For instance: "We must think His thoughts after Him. We must think analogically, rather than univocally" (*Common Grace*, 28).

147. From a pedagogical perspective, I would not have preferred to use this kind of summary tag-word for what Van Til was trying to teach. Although it is certainly possible to understand what he meant by the expression, this way of speaking probably occasioned more avoidable misunderstanding and misrepresentation from a small circle of critics than anything else he wrote. The historical context was a controversy over the incomprehensibility of God that took place in the Orthodox Presbyterian Church during the 1940s, with Gordon H. Clark and Van Til being the primary spokesmen for the two antagonistic parties. Personalities and politics added fuel to the antagonism, which only tended to muddy the theological debate that was already muddled by unclear polemics on both sides. After an extended analysis of the issues and verbal disputes involved in that unhappy debate (one which I highly recommend to readers interested in the matter), John Frame writes: "The 'Clark Case' is a classic example of the hurt that can be done when people dogmatize over difficult theological issues without taking the trouble first to understand one another, to analyze ambiguities in their formulations, and to recognize more than one kind of theological danger to be avoided" (*The Doctrine of the Knowledge of God* [Phillipsburg, N.J.: Presbyterian and Reformed, 1987], 40). Van Til's own assessment of the theological and philosophical issues that were traversed can be found in chap. 13 of *An Introduction to Systematic Theology*, although he refers to and discusses "analogical knowledge" and the "incomprehensibility of God" in a number of his other publications as well.

148. "Nature and Scripture," 278.

the mind may be sure that its system is true and corresponds on a finite scale to the system of God. That is what we mean by saying that it is analogical to God's system."[149]

In knowing anything, according to Van Til, man thinks what God Himself thinks: there is continuity between God's knowledge and man's knowledge,[150] and thus a theoretical basis for the certainty of human knowledge. At the same time, of course, when man knows something, it is man doing the thinking and not God—which introduces a discontinuity between the two *acts* of knowing, a discontinuity that is greater and more profound than the discontinuity between one person's act of knowing something and another person's act of knowing it. "For as the heavens are higher than the earth, so are . . . my thoughts higher than your thoughts" (Isa. 55:9). Not only is there "a difference between God's *manner* of knowing and man's manner of knowing," but God's knowledge and man's knowledge "coincide at no point *in the sense that* in his awareness of [the] meaning of anything, in his mental grasp or understanding of anything, man is at each point dependent upon a *prior act* of unchangeable understanding and revelation on the part of God."[151] The dis-

---

149. *Introduction to Systematic Theology*, 181.
150. Difficulty arises when we fail to be requisitely analytical and overlook the different senses in which the English word "knowledge" can be used. It can be used for *what* is known (to share knowledge is to know the same object—say, the rose in the garden or the laws of physics). The word "knowledge" can mean the *methods or criteria* of knowing; to say of two persons that "their knowledge is the same" can indicate that they go about gaining knowledge in the same way. The word can also signify the actual *act* of knowing as a personal event; in this sense my knowledge (act of knowing) is not identical with your knowledge (act of knowing), just as my driving a car cannot be identical with your driving a car (since we are different "actors"). Other distinctions could be discussed. However, the reason for this reminder about the multiple uses of the word "knowledge" is that some critics of Van Til, even those who are philosophically trained, create problems by falling into careless equivocation. For example, Ronald Nash writes: "I once asked Van Til if, when some human being knows that 1+1=2, that human being's *knowledge* is *identical* with God's knowledge. The question, I thought, was innocent enough. Van Til's only answer was to smile, shrug his shoulders, and declare that the question was improper in the sense that it had no answer" (*The Word of God and the Mind of Man* [Grand Rapids: Zondervan, 1982], 100 [emphasis added]). I can understand Van Til's perceptive smile. Nobody should let himself be beguiled by an equivocal question (which is indeed improper and misleading), for which there can be no answer. My best guess is that Nash wanted to know if *what* God and man know is "identical"—to which the answer is (too) obviously yes.
151. *Introduction to Systematic Theology*, 172, 165 (emphasis added). Given the tremendous philosophical and linguistic confusion (on all sides) that has swirled around this debate, it is important to notice that Van Til speaks of "no coincidence" in the "act"

continuity between God's knowing and man's knowing is obvious as a metaphysical truth: "Man could not have the same thought content[152] in his mind that God has in his mind unless he were himself divine. *Man can never experience the experience of God. . . .* It is only on the assumption that the human mind is not the mind of a creature but is itself the mind of the Creator

---

of understanding or knowing—not in the meaning, referent, or truth of any proposition known to both God and man. To say that the Creator's act of knowing does not coincide with the creature's act of knowing should be noncontroversial.

152. The vague expression "thought content" has played havoc in many a theological and philosophical dispute, and its ability to generate confusion was conspicuous in the Clark–Van Til controversy as well. I believe that by "thought content" Van Til meant the *thinking activity* in which the mind of God engages, which mental "experience" (notice the very next sentence in Van Til's text) is metaphysically different from the operations of man's mind.

To understand Van Til, the reader must remember his resistance to the notion of "abstract knowledge" or "abstract truth"—the notion that there are ideas that exist in themselves, apart from God's mind or man's mind, and to which both minds must look (or conform) in order to possess the truth (knowledge). This is not really idiosyncratic. The problems of "knowledge" are construed in the idealist tradition (within which Van Til matured philosophically) with a concern for relating the subject of knowing to that which is known; discussions of "the nature of thought" take a special place, all of them focusing on knowledge as an act of mind. Knowing is an activity relating a mind to the truths known by it. Anyway, in Van Til's perspective, all cases of knowledge are concrete acts of knowing, either by God or by man. For man to know the proposition that "2 is the square root of 4" or that "Mecca fell to the forces of Mohammed in 630" is to know something of God's thinking. If they are called "ideas," they are ideas "in God's mind" (about things that are, nonetheless, not identical with God). God's "thought content" actively makes these things so (i.e., actively makes the truth), while man's "thought content" does not (being passive with regard to the truth).

Gordon Clark unnecessarily cast Van Til's terminology in a highly negative light. Likewise, Ronald Nash deems "the most serious objection" to Van Til's position to be Clark's criticism, namely: "According to Van Til, God's knowledge and man's knowledge do not (and cannot) coincide at a single point, from which it follows that no proposition can mean the same thing to God and man" ("Attack on Human Autonomy," 349). Similarly, after expressing extensive appreciation for the apologetical work of Van Til, Robert L. Reymond says that, nevertheless, his major concern is with Van Til's doctrine of "analogical" knowledge because by it God's knowledge and man's knowledge do not "coincide" at a single point "as to content" (*The Justification of Knowledge* [Nutley, N.J.: Presbyterian and Reformed, 1976], 98–105). But Reymond has not taken the reference to "content" in the way Van Til intended (namely, referring to the active experience of the mind's knowing something). This misreading is evident when Reymond, indicating how he had interpreted Van Til, writes: "The solution to all of Van Til's difficulties is to affirm, as Scripture teaches, that both God and man share the same concept of truth and the same theory of language" (p. 105). But it is clear from Van Til's own words that "no coincidence" in "content" never meant a difference in the knowledge, truth, theory of truth, meaning, or theory of meaning regarding that which God and man both know.

that one can talk consistently of identity of content between the mind of man and the mind of God."[153]

Man cannot do what God does, except by way of finite imitation or reflection. This applies to the act of knowing things. Because the word "analogy" refers to (and indeed stresses)[154] the element of agreement or identity between two things that are different, it seemed an appropriate word to describe the relationship between God's knowing and man's knowing. Man knows what God knows, even though the two are metaphysically much different. The relationship of a "microcosm" to a "macrocosm" might be helpful as a teaching device here.[155] Van Til once put it this way: "God's knowledge is archetypal and ours ectypal. . . . God is the original and man is the derivative."[156] God "must be taken as the prerequisite of the possibility and actuality of relationship between man's various concepts and propositions of knowledge. Man's system of knowledge must therefore be an analogical replica of the system of knowledge which belongs to God."[157] Van Til spoke of man's gaining knowledge as "using the gift of logical manipulation given . . . for the purpose of thinking God's thoughts after him *on a created scale . . .* that in some measure reflects the plan of God."[158]

God and man are metaphysically different, which is evidenced in their differing acts of knowing, but man is to think the same things that God does. What man knows is literally the truth (not an analogy of truth)[159]—the *same truth* known by God, accepted or verified by the

153. *Introduction to Systematic Theology*, 184, 165 (emphasis added).
154. "To draw an analogy between two or more entities is to indicate one or more respects in which they are similar" (Irving M. Copi and Carl Cohen, *Introduction to Logic*, 8th ed. [New York: Macmillan, 1990], 359).
155. Van Til's classroom students will remember the larger circle above the smaller circle. These were different circles, but the points in one figure were nevertheless related to each other within that figure in the same way that the points in the other figure were related to each other within that other figure. That is, they are both circular, but at different magnitudes, proportions, or levels.
156. *Introduction to Systematic Theology*, 203.
157. *Defense of the Faith*, 138.
158. *Reformed Pastor and Modern Thought*, 79. In context, Van Til points out that the unbeliever takes the "created scale" version of knowledge and "absolutizes" it. He treats it as his own original thinking through, or organizing of, the truth; he demands—as a principle of continuity—that reality must match his creative, constructive way of thinking. As Van Til observes, the unbeliever tries, epistemologically speaking, to "take to himself the place ascribed to God in a true Christian theology."
159. In the 1940s dispute, the Clarkian opponents of Van Til seriously misconstrued what he taught. The "Answer" to the "Complaint" (against Clark's views and ordination) charged the Van Tillians with holding that "man can grasp only an

same standard or "point of reference" for both man and God (namely, God's own mind). Yet there is, to use Van Til's way of putting it, an important "qualitative difference" between God's knowing and man's knowing. God's incomprehensibility is not simply a quantitative matter of His knowing more truths than man or coming to know them faster (intuitively) than man. Van Til wanted to guard the Creator-creature relationship even in the realm of knowing,[160] and thus spoke in terms of "analogical" knowing. "All his [man's] knowledge is analogical of God. God is the original knower and man is the derivative re-knower. Man knows in subordination to God; he knows as the covenant-keeper."[161] In rebellion against "analogical" thinking, unbelievers insist that their knowing anything is "univocal" (disregarding the Creator-creature distinction): "We do not think God's thoughts after Him, but together with God we think out thoughts that have never been thought either by God or by man."[162] In contrast to the Christian doctrine of God's incomprehensibility, said Van Til, "the non-Christian view is monistic."[163]

God and man are not on a par in seeking to attain knowledge of

---

analogy of the truth itself." Van Til did not teach that what we know is only an analogy of God (or truth about Him), much less that univocal predication regarding God must be rejected, but rather that we know God (as well as His creation) *analogously* to His knowing Himself (and His creation). A few years following the dispute, Gordon Clark again portrayed Van Til as holding that propositions have a different meaning (equivocation) for God and man, and that man is ignorant of the truth that is in God's mind, possessing only an analogy of the truth rather than the truth itself. Thus he charged Van Til with unrelieved skepticism and neoorthodox existentialism ("The Bible as Truth," *Bibliotheca Sacra* 114 [April–June 1957]: 157–70; see also Ronald H. Nash, "Gordon Clark's Theory of Knowledge," in *The Philosophy of Gordon H. Clark*, ed. Ronald H. Nash [Philadelphia: Presbyterian and Reformed, 1968], 162). Clark acknowledged that his negative characterizations of Van Til's position were contrary to what Van Til himself said, but he reasoned that the way Van Til expressed certain things implied those characterizations—in which case Van Til must have been "retracting" his affirmations of man's knowledge of the very truth in God's mind. In other words, Clark thought that Van Til was confused. A handful of contemporary disciples of Clark have perpetuated this dubious line of argument. For example, John W. Robbins has declared that Van Til was an irrationalist who asserted "that we do not know the same truth as God knows, but only an analogy of the truth" (letter to the editor, *Journey Magazine* 3, no. 3 [May-June 1988]: 15).

160. "But [by] asserting a qualitative difference between the knowledge of God and the knowledge of man the *Complaint* [against Gordon Clark's view of God's incomprehensibility] was merely asserting the Creator-creature relationship and the idea of the basic significance of revelation for all predication" (*Introduction to Systematic Theology*, 171).

161. *Introduction to Systematic Theology*, 167.

162. *Defense of the Faith*, 65.

163. *Introduction to Systematic Theology*, 174.

the world (or of God Himself). As Van Til put it: "Christians believe in two levels of existence, the level of God's existence as self-contained and the level of man's existence as derived from the level of God's existence. For this reason, Christians must also believe in two levels of knowledge, the level of God's knowledge which is absolutely comprehensive and self-contained, and the level of man's knowledge which is not comprehensive but is derivative and re-interpretive."[164] What we must take account of is the fact that God does not discover truths about Himself or about the world and history. Nor does He observe data (receive sensations, etc.) that He organizes into an interpretation.[165] Rather, God is the "original knower" in that He has comprehensively known Himself from all eternity and has created the world, as well as planning every detail of history, according to His own "pre-interpretation." He is and He makes the truth that man comes to know. He did not simply find out the truth earlier, more intuitively, or in greater scope than man. He is the Creator, and man is the receiver. Thus, God's interpretation of the world and history is constructive of that world and history, whereas when man properly interprets (or knows) the world and history, he is "reconstructive" of God's original interpretation or thinking about them. The same holds for truths about God or man: man's self-knowledge and theological knowledge are gained by "receptive reconstruction" of what God originally knows.

Accordingly, man can never think of his mind as ultimate, but must recognize its dependency. All of man's thinking must take place in humble subordination to thoughts which God has first and originally thought. For that reason, man could never be in an epistemological position to question or challenge anything that God has verbally interpreted and revealed to him (even when that revelation is admittedly anthropomorphic in character). God's word must be, in the nature of the case, the ultimate standard for judging claims to truth, and God's word must be the preconditioning context in which man goes out to discover more truth about himself and his world. Furthermore,

164. Ibid., 12.
165. "God is completely self-comprehensive. God is absolute rationality. He was and is the only self-contained whole, the system of absolute truth. God's knowledge is, therefore, exclusively analytic, that is, self-dependent. There never were any facts existing independent of God which he had to investigate. . . . In him . . . fact and interpretation of fact are coterminous. . . . Either one thinks of God as the wholly self-conscious being for whom there are no brute facts, or one makes God dependent upon brute facts. It is on the basis of his own decree with respect to the world that God has full knowledge of the world" (*Introduction to Systematic Theology*, 10, 236; cf. p. 235).

even when God and man know the same truth, God's knowledge retains a quality of wonder or awe about it that is not attributable to man's knowledge. Perhaps this will illustrate the point. When a student begins his course of education, he may deeply respect his professor's expertise and scope of knowledge; there is a "sense of distance" between him and the teacher. As the student learns more and more of what the professor knows—and even becomes an expert in the same field—he may still respect his professor, but the original sense of intellectual distance has diminished.[166] Just the opposite holds, however, for man coming to know more and more of what God knows. As man's knowledge of God's increases, his sense of distance does not diminish, but actually increases. He stands in even greater awe and wonder at God's mind. He is humbled even more than when he began to learn of Him.

God's knowledge is thus original, creative and constructive, all-determinative, normative, beyond challenge, and productive of ever deepening awe and wonder.[167] These are profound qualities that pertain uniquely to God's "thought content"; they stress how His thinking is transcendent in character and incomprehensible to man's thinking.[168] God's knowledge is different from man's with respect to

---

166. Van Til observed that "there is only a gradational difference between" a teacher and a pupil; they "both are operating under the same conditions and limitations." Moreover, the teacher does not control everything, much less the pupil's mind; "so there is mystery for him in the same way that there is mystery for the pupil" (*Introduction to Systematic Theology*, 183).

167. In light of such qualities as these, one can understand why Van Til held that "the fact that man is given more and ever more revelation of God does not tend to reduce the incomprehensibility of God." Dr. Clark had said, by contrast, that God is incomprehensible *except* when He reveals Himself (*Introduction to Systematic Theology*, 165, 169).

168. During the Clark–Van Til debate, the concern of those opposing Clark was that his description and explanation of God's incomprehensibility minimized the difference between God's thinking and man's, not taking sufficient account of His status as Creator or its implications in the realm of knowing. Whether they effectively articulated their misgivings about Clark's teaching at that time or not, it seems to me that Clark subsequently confirmed the validity of such misgivings when he proposed the linguistically dubious, theologically reductionistic translation of John 1:1, "In the beginning was Logic . . . and Logic was God" (*Philosophy of Gordon H. Clark*, ed. Nash, 67). While differing with Aristotle's theology and epistemology, Clark nevertheless found his phrase "thought thinking thought" to be a "helpful" description of God. However, it is one thing to hold that logic is a reflection of God's thinking, but a debasement of His person to assert an identity, as Clark does: "God and logic are one and the same first principle" (p. 68). Likewise, in the dispute of the 1940s, Clark underplayed the "qualitative" transcendence of God's thoughts. (To put Clark's treatment of

the subject (the knower) and the act of knowing. Nevertheless, God's knowledge and man's knowledge are identical with respect to both the objects (or truths) that are known and the standard by which claims to knowledge are judged.

In this sense, then, Van Til held that for man to know anything is to "think God's thoughts after Him"—to think "analogously" to God's mind. This is not a thesis about theological language, as if the sentences by which God has expressed His thoughts to man (say, in Scripture) were merely literary analogies.[169] The meaning of those sentences, with respect to their sense (intention) and referent is the same for God and man; God uses the precisely appropriate expressions in human language that will communicate the truth for human thinking. While the meaning (i.e., the idea or propositional import and the specific designation) is the same for God and man, however, in certain respects the meaning may be greater or deeper for God than it is for man. God may have intended functions or expected effects ("meanings") for an expression that individual men in particular situations do not fully grasp. The connotational feelings, emotions, commitments, and attitudes associated with a sentence for God may certainly exceed those experienced by individual men. God surely knows more of the implications (logical, causal, and volitional) of a sentence than does any man, in which case its meaning is much broader and richer for Him. God better understands the explanatory and operational

---

John 1:1 in the best possible light, the reader should consult his later study, *The Johannine Logos* [Philadelphia: Presbyterian and Reformed, 1972], where he concedes that "Logic" is relatively accurate, but that "it would make a somewhat inadequate translation" [p. 16]. Clark does a valuable job of placing the Greek term *logos* in its historical context of Greek philosophy and the Septuagint, suggesting that John was warning his gentile readers "against false forms of the Logos doctrine" [p. 18].)

169. Although Van Til's doctrine of analogical knowing was not a thesis about religious language, it does have some noteworthy implications about such language. Since all of our knowledge of God must be based on His revelation to us, God must teach men how to speak about Him—and He can speak to them with human words that perfectly communicate how they are to think about Him. The words used by God to teach us about how to think and speak of Him can, therefore, utilize figures of speech without jeopardizing the veracity and adequacy of what we learn and know about God from His revelation. Thus, Van Til could assert: "We are entitled and compelled to use anthropomorphism not apologetically but fearlessly. . . . We hold that we are able to affirm that our words have meaning for no other reason than that we use them analogically" (*Common Grace*, 73). Because we must think God's thoughts after Him (analogously), there can be no objection if "Scripture . . . has no hesitation in speaking anthropomorphically of God" (*Introduction to Systematic Theology*, 212; cf. p. 205).

meanings of sentences than men do: their evidential basis, how they index referents, how they function to accomplish particular purposes, the conditions under which they can do so, etc.[170] Accordingly, it should be uncontroversial, as Van Til maintained, that the human mind cannot know "even one proposition in its minimal significance with the same depth of meaning with which God knows that proposition." And, just as importantly, "man can yet truly know the meaning of a proposition," even though he cannot "state it exhaustively," as can God.[171]

So the meaning of linguistic expressions for God and for man overlap, in some respects being identical for them and in other respects being much greater for God than for man. For Van Til, the same can be said for the concepts with which man and God think. Where men "think God's thoughts after Him"—either by heeding His verbal revelation or responsibly using their logical and empirical abilities to know things—there is conceptual continuity between their thinking and God's. Our concepts are accurate as far as they go and adequate for our needs as creatures made as God's image and living in His world. Yet we would not want to deny that God's thinking is more "conceptually adequate,"[172] since it, unhindered by man's limited focus and mental ability, takes everything into account, making it comprehensive and unlimited. For instance, human concepts of divine foreordination (patterned after the human experience of causing things to happen) and of human freedom make it difficult to understand conceptually how God foreordains the free acts of men—how these two can be conceptually integrated (or tie together). In this and many other cases, human knowledge may have a paradoxical cast to it,

---

170. For explanatory background on "the meaning of meaning," consult the first three tapes in my course entitled "Hermeneutics and Exegesis."
171. *Introduction to Systematic Theology*, 172, 185.
172. A helpful illustration of what we mean by conceptual adequacy or inadequacy is afforded by the offbeat movie *The Gods Must Be Crazy*. Imagine taking a product of Western culture—say, a Coke bottle—and literally dropping it into the midst of an aboriginal culture that has had no experience with soda pop, glass bottles, etc. Will the natives "understand" the Coke bottle from their first encounter with it? Yes and no. Certainly they will understand some things about it, and yet, because they apply a limited range of experience and mental categories to it, their initial conclusions will be "conceptually inadequate" (somewhat humorously, no doubt). This surely does not indicate that the Coke bottle is absurd or irrational, or that any attempt to understand it must be freighted with contradictory sentences. However, until the experiences of the natives and their ways of living and thinking are broadened, they will continue to apply to this unfamiliar object concepts with which they are familiar and whose appropriate range of use is limited.

then; we affirm as truths things that may appear to be contradictory.[173] God's concepts are more insightful and adequate than ours, however, since He made and controls all things; what is mysterious to our limited vision and thinking is perfectly clear and harmonious within His thinking.

What we have rehearsed in the discussion above is Van Til's attempt to take honest account of the transcendent (incomprehensible) character of God's knowledge. God's experience or act of knowing anything is not identical with man's; there are profound qualities about it that cannot be attributed to any man's thinking. God's grasp of the meaning of sentences that express the truth (including those revealed by Him to man) is broader and deeper than man's—even as God's thinking about anything is more conceptually adequate than could be the case for man's limited intellect. In all of this, however, Van Til's point was to maintain that man can think God's thoughts after Him on the level or scale of a creature (made in God's image) and genuinely know the truth that God knows about Himself or the

---

173. Van Til went out of his way to make it clear that he was talking only about the *appearance* of contradiction to man—not that there is actually any logical contradiction. Indeed, "we hold that our position is the only position that saves one from the necessity of ultimately accepting the really contradictory. . . . We shun as poison the idea of the really contradictory" (*Common Grace*, 9). "All the truths of the Christian religion have of necessity the appearance of being contradictory. . . . We do not fear to accept that which has the appearance of being contradictory. We know that what appears to be so *to us* is not really so" (*Defense of the Faith*, 399 [emphasis added]). We cling to God's revelation, "knowing that that which appears contradictory to man because of his finitude, is not really contradictory to God" (ibid., 228).

Although the sentences by which the things we know (particularly based on scriptural revelation) can be shown to be free of verbal contradictions, there can still be a conceptual difficulty for us in understanding how those truths "work together." Believers humbly accept the difficulty (as due to their finitude and/or sin) and see it as divinely mysterious—exalting God's more comprehensive knowledge and greater conceptual adequacy. They realize that it is only "natural that there should be in all that pertains to our relation to God (and what does not?) an element of mystery" (*Common Grace*, 27). "We should have to be God ourselves in order to understand God in the depth of his being. God must always remain mysterious to man. . . . The difference between the Christian and the non-Christian conception of mystery may be expressed in a word by saying that we hold that there is mystery for man but not for God" (*Defense of the Faith*, 30). However, unbelievers arrogantly expect that any conceptual difficulties that they have must be as difficult for God as well (disregarding the Creator-creature distinction), and thus conclude that apparent contradictions must be real contradictions. Of course, the unbeliever must eventually concede that, given his worldview, there is mystery at the base of everything he says or claims to know: "The non-believer admits mystery, too. In fact for him mystery is ultimate, enveloping God as well as man. His position therefore is rationalistic first and irrationalistic last" (*Common Grace*, 28).

world and history—and in some cases know it with certainty. Man can apprehend God truly and can therefore apprehend further truths about "the works of God"—about himself (as man), about the world, and about history. Because man genuinely knows God, through nature and Scripture, there is a theoretical basis as well as a personal responsibility for man to use his God-given gifts of logical and empirical reasoning to extend his knowledge. When he successfully does so, he is—to use the picture of knowing appropriate to the Christian worldview—"thinking God's thoughts after Him" on the creaturely level, that is, reflecting or reconstructing in his own human mind what God the Creator originally thought or foreordained. Man grows in knowledge by coming to think what God thinks (as well as created and providentially ordered) about the natural world, historical events, human personality, social order, art, morality, etc.

Logical and Conceptual Reasoning. Van Til pictured human knowing as "thinking God's thoughts after Him." He also maintained that God's thinking represents perfect coherence. Therefore, in order for men to know things, taught Van Til, they too must think coherently or with logical consistency. *"The law of contradiction, therefore, as we know it, is but the expression on a created level of the internal coherence of God's nature."* So in all of our thinking about Scripture and the world, believers are obligated to think logically, thinking God's thoughts after Him. "Christians should employ the law of contradiction, whether positively or negatively, as a means by which to systematize the facts of revelation, whether these facts are found in the universe at large or in the Scripture." Van Til goes on to indicate that in contrast to unbelieving thought, the Christian views logic as a reflection of God's own thinking, rather than as laws or principles that are "higher" than God or that exist "in independence of God and man."[174] To explain by applica-

---

174. *Introduction to Systematic Theology*, 11 (emphasis original in the first quotation). Van Til's words expose a fundamental misconception of his position by Ronald Nash, who wrote in 1963 that for Van Til the law of contradiction is "an arbitrary human law" (*The New Evangelicalism* [Grand Rapids: Zondervan, 1963], 140–41). Seven years later, in "Attack on Human Autonomy," Nash acknowledged that Van Til recognized the importance of the Christian worldview not falling into logical contradictions. He wrote: "For the life of me, I cannot understand this vacillating use of logic. . . . Van Til introduces logic when it is convenient and ushers it out the back door when it is no longer needed" (p. 350). But it is not really so difficult to understand. One must distinguish between the actual principles or laws of logic (as they really are) and the theories and argu-

tion what this means (in part), Van Til held that God's word must be interpreted logically—that is to say, using God's thoughts (logical ordering) to interpret God's thoughts (in Scripture)—but cannot (and may not) in the nature of the case be subject to criticism or rejection on the basis of some supposedly higher logic.[175] Van Til said that there is "no impersonal law of logic" that dictates to God what He can or cannot say;[176] the logical constraints of God's thinking are the constraints of His own personal nature, which man is to emulate. Man's logical reasoning, then, must always be pursued as a servant, subordinating his thoughts to the thinking of his Lord. Because Van Til declared that believers and unbelievers have different conceptions of logic, some critics have misunderstood him as holding that the laws of logic are different for believers and unbelievers. But that could not have been his position, for he held that there is only one God and that the laws of logic are a reflection of His thinking. Van Til wrote: "I do *not* maintain that Christians operate according to new laws of thought any more than that they have new eyes or noses."[177]

Indeed, according to Van Til, only the Christian worldview can *account for* the objective validity and the demands of logical consistency. "The law of contradiction cannot be thought of as operating anywhere except against the background of the nature of God."[178] One's use of and account of logic is not something religiously neutral, but indicates something about one's fundamental view of reality. "One's conception

---

ments about such things developed by philosophers. Van Til was aware that "logic" can refer to the genuine thing (reflecting God's mind) and can also be debated as a developing theory (reflecting the minds of men). Van Til likewise recognized that an allegedly "autonomous" use of logic destroys its foundations or intelligibility, while the true foundation for the intelligibility of logic (God's mind revealed to men) cannot as such be subordinate to man's use of logic for its own acceptability.

175. One biblical doctrine cannot be denied in favor of another biblical doctrine in the name of the law of contradiction (cf. *Common Grace*, 202, 231).

176. *Defense of the Faith*, 247.

177. Ibid., 296.

178. *Introduction to Systematic Theology*, 11. Cf.: "The law of contradiction, to operate at all, must have its foundation in God" (*Defense of the Faith*, 297). Van Til advised that the apologist "should ask them [unbelievers] to show him the foundation in reality on which their philosophy of logic rests. If they answer that logic is logic and has nothing to do with reality, he can ignore what they say. . . . To talk about the law of contradiction without asking with respect to the metaphysical foundation upon which it rests is to talk in the air [to reduce logic to contentless formalities]" (*Protestant Doctrine of Scripture*, 62). For an illustration of the apologetical application of this insight, see my debate with Gordon Stein at the University of California, Irvine (1985).

of reality is one's conception of the foundation of the laws of logic. If men are 'neutral' in their methodology . . . the law of contradiction does not necessarily have its foundation in God."[179] By suppressing the truth about God, modern thought is committed to the ultimate mysteriousness of the universe, there being no plan or purpose for what exists or transpires, nor any necessary connection between events (causality) or truths (logic). "Modern thought believes in an ultimate irrationalism, while Christianity believes in an ultimate rationality. It is difficult to think of two types of thought that are more radically opposed to one another. It is the most fundamental antithesis conceivable in the field of knowledge. . . . The very foundation of all Christian theology is removed if the concept of the ultimate rationality of God be given up."[180] Even though God's word reveals deep mysteries that leave us with conceptual difficulties—and which *appear* contradictory—because as human beings we cannot fully explain the relation of the infinite to the finite, Van Til firmly and clearly maintained that "faith abhors the really contradictory; to maintain the really contradictory is to deny God. . . . [We have] the right and the courage to say that Christianity does not contradict the laws of logic. . . . [We are certain] that Christianity is objectively valid and that it is the only rational position for man to hold."[181] At another point, Van Til very clearly declared: "The Christian finds, further, that logic agrees with the [biblical] story. Human logic agrees with the story, *because it derives its meaning from the story*."[182]

When we reason logically—organizing and testing truth claims according to certain laws of logic, and attempting to draw inferences without falling into fallacious ways of thinking—we assume the reality or normativity of something that is abstract, universal, and invariant. That is, our reasoning presupposes something that is not concrete—something that transcends individual objects or particulars. The generalizations and laws that logicians refer to are not particular experiences, thoughts, sentences, or objects, but rather are somehow a unity "common to" the plurality of such experiences, thoughts, sentences, and objects. The "laws" of logic are not treated as momentary and particular mental events. This raises a question that has persisted throughout the history of philosophy, which pertains to logic (and mathematics), but is not at all restricted to it.

This question has to do with the reality of abstract entities or no-

179. *Defense of the Faith*, 299.
180. *Introduction to Systematic Theology*, 13.
181. *Common Grace*, 67, 27, 82.
182. *Defense of the Faith*, 308 (emphasis added).

tions. It is raised in a variety of forms, in connection with universals, ideas, general concepts, essences, categories, classes, set definitions, resemblances, predicates, properties, etc.—all of which are said to be applicable to, or inclusive of, many particulars. Although our observational experience is always of concrete, particular things, we often reason and speak in terms of abstract entities or concepts. In the sentence "The tree has green leaves," there is a reference to a particular tree, yet the term "tree" does not itself name that specific object; other objects take the designation as well. Likewise, many things have the term "green" applied to them, not simply the particular leaves on this particular tree. The sentence "Fleas are carriers of bubonic plague" is not about any specific or individual instance of fleas or plague, but rather is a generalization. And the sentence "Categorical syllogisms that use a term equivocally draw unreliable inferences" is not critical of one particular argument that someone formulated, but is supposed to hold for all such arguments in all times and places—to be universally normative. How can such references to (unobserved) generalities, universals, and laws be made intelligible? Van Til noted, "The whole problem of knowledge has constantly been that of bringing the one and the many together."[183] Or again: "The whole problem of philosophy may be summed up in the question of the relation of unity to diversity; the so-called problem of the one and the many receives a definite answer from the doctrine of the simplicity of God."[184] Non-Christians have stumbled badly over this philosophical problem (and have sometimes wished simply to ignore it), and thus a persistent effort has been made throughout the history of philosophy to reduce all such abstract, general, or universal entities (or talk about them) to concrete or particular things (or talk about them).[185] All such attempts have proved to be unpersuasive or lacking in cogency. We regularly think and speak and reason in terms of general concepts.

183. *Introduction to Systematic Theology*, 10.
184. *Defense of the Faith*, 26.
185. The enduring thorn in the side of philosophers who wish to dismiss universals (etc.) is the need to "talk" about them in terms of particulars of some sort, when such talk is comprised of words that are not simply a series of names (for particulars). Eventually the problem of universals resurfaces as a problem about general terms—e.g., how one word "flea" can be applied to different particular pests. The most stringent attempts at a nominalist reduction to particulars still get foiled by the existence of sets, the reality of resemblances, and the inadequacies of a behaviorist analysis of language.

In Van Til's outlook, we engage in conceptual reasoning (utilizing universals and laws) because we have been created in God's image and thus can think His thoughts after Him on the finite, creaturely level.

> If we wish to know the facts of this world, we must relate these facts to laws. That is, in every knowledge transaction, we must bring the particulars of our experience into relation with universals. . . . As Christians, we hold that in this universe we deal with a derivative one and many, which can be brought into fruitful relation with one another because, back of both, we have in God the original One and Many. If we are to have coherence in our experience, there must be a correspondence of our experience to the eternally coherent experience of God. Human knowledge ultimately rests upon the internal coherence within the Godhead; our knowledge rests upon the ontological Trinity as its presupposition. . . .
>
> In paradise Adam had a true conception of the relation of the particulars to the universals of knowledge with respect to the created universe. He named the animals "according to their nature," that is, in accordance with the place God had given them in his universe. Then, too, Adam could converse truly about the meaning of the universe in general and about their own life in particular with Eve. . . . In paradise man's knowledge was self-consciously analogical; man wanted to know the facts of the universe in order to fulfill his task as a covenant-keeper.[186]

For Van Til, the "universals" must not be conceived of as absolutely abstract, existing impersonally in themselves apart from God. "The question is as to what the Greeks meant by universals. They meant self-existing, eternal, impersonal laws . . . [that] did not rest upon the nature of the Creator God. They existed in themselves. Accordingly, no amount of

---

186. *Introduction to Systematic Theology*, 22, 23, 25. In this quotation, Van Til speaks of our knowledge "resting upon" God's internal coherence, but not in the sense that our knowledge of God's internal coherence (or of the Trinity) is a foundational truth or premise upon which is based or inferred further specific knowledge-claims (having a particular content or character). Rather, our knowing in general is made intelligible by—"rests upon" (in order to make sense)—the knowledge we have that particularity and universality (plurality and oneness) are related in an equally ultimate way within God. Likewise, man's knowledge of individual things—say, an individual frog (particularized by being created by God)—is appropriately taken to yield knowledge of general or "universal" categories—in this case, that of "frogness" (reflecting God's preinterpretation of what it is to be a frog).

trimming can bring them into shape for Christian use."[187] To separate the universals in the Godhead from the person of God is, for Van Til, to oppose the doctrine of the simplicity of God (which states that God is not made up of parts), to assume the ultimacy of human thinking, and to "impersonalize the ultimate foundation of predication."[188]

For the Christian, universals exist in a concrete (not an abstract) fashion within the mind of the personal Creator Himself. God "thinks universally" and such thinking is found in man "analogically." The Christian's presuppositions about God provide a rationale or basis for the intelligibility of conceptual reasoning (with generalizations, categories, laws, etc.). In dealing with the problem of knowing universals (the "one") in the experience of particulars (the "many"), Van Til found the key to a proper philosophical orientation in the triunity of God: "So then, though we cannot tell why the Godhead should exist tri-personally, we can understand something of the fact, after we are told that God exists as a triune being, that the unity and the plurality of this world has back of it a God in whom unity and the plurality are equally ultimate."[189] Our interpretation of experience and of the world should proceed in that light.

> The ontological trinity will be our interpretative concept everywhere. God is our concrete universal; . . . in Him the problem of knowledge is solved. If we begin thus with the ontological trinity as our concrete universal, we frankly differ from every school of philosophy . . . not merely in our conclusions, but in our starting-point and in our method as well. For us the facts are what they are, and the universals are what they are, because of their common dependence upon the ontological trinity. Thus, as earlier discussed, the facts are correlative to the universals.[190]

187. Ibid., 46. On the same page, Van Til faults even the "moderate realism" of Herman Bavinck as "not a specifically Christian position based upon the presupposition of the existence of the God of Scripture." Moderate realism (cf. Aristotle) answers the question about universals by saying (like Plato) that they are "real"—i.e., definite elements in particular, sensible substances, distinguishable from matter— but (unlike Plato) that they are not absolutely or independently real; human reason "abstracts" the universal from the individual substance, in which case it exists "conceptually" in the mind.

188. Ibid., 216.

189. Ibid., 230.

190. *Common Grace*, 64. Van Til refers to the "ontological Trinity" (as God exists in reality, from all eternity), where there is equal ultimacy among the three Persons, as distinguished from the "economical Trinity" (as God works in relation to man within history), where there is subordination among the Persons. God's

Because the particulars are correlative ("equally derived and equally dependent upon God"), they are not unrelated and unknowable (*"abstract* particulars"!), and the unity we reach by abstracting or generalizing from them has "not stripped these particulars of their particularity" (which would amount to "an *abstract* universal"). Van Til realized in this matter that all unbelieving philosophy destroys the possibility of knowledge. "As Christians we hold that there is no answer to these problems from a non-Christian point of view. . . . It is only in the Christian doctrine of the triune God, as we are bound to believe, that we really have a *concrete universal* . . . [where] there are no particulars not related to the universal and there is nothing universal that is not fully expressed in the particulars."[191] The Christian worldview, therefore, does not face the problem of irrational particulars (which cannot be interpreted according to unifying categories, generalizations, or laws) standing over against abstract universals (blank formalities, empty of any detailed content regarding the concrete particulars).

Empirical Knowledge. Thus, for Van Til, if we picture man's knowing as a matter of thinking God's thoughts after Him on the creaturely level, we have an intelligible basis for reasoning logically and conceptually. Likewise, if knowing is a matter of thinking God's thoughts after Him, human beings have a rationale and a requirement for seeking to know things by means of observation (i.e., by using their senses). Van Til maintained quite clearly: "We do not go to the Bible itself for the facts with which we deal [in the laboratory or the field]. . . . We do not limit ourselves entirely to the Bible when we study anything."[192]

---

thinking is the thinking of a particular or concrete entity, about particular facts and specific details in nature and history (not simply about abstractions), without compromising the universality of the way He thinks (in terms of essences, categories, laws, etc.)—the "concrete universal." As Van Til once explained, "The very ideal of the *Concrete Universal* . . . boasts of the fact that the individual and the universal, the temporal and the eternal, are always present together in every experience of man" (*Reformed Pastor and Modern Thought*, 133). This is possible, held Van Til, because God foreordains (preinterprets) every experience of man, and man has been created as the image of God to think His thoughts after Him. At this point (and at many others, e.g., *Defense of the Faith*, 241), Van Til distinguishes his use of the term "concrete universal" from its use within Hegelian or idealistic philosophy. Early critics mentioned in *The Defense of the Faith* (e.g., the DeBoers, Van Halsema, Daane) had been too quick to make Van Til out to be an idealist, because of his use of similar terminology.

191. *Defense of the Faith*, 43–44.
192. *Introduction to Systematic Theology*, 15.

God created man with eyes, ears, hands, etc., in order that he might experience His glory, wisdom, and power as it is manifested through the creation (see, e.g., Pss. 8:1; 19:1–6), and also that he might learn about the creation in order to exercise dominion over it in serving God's ends (Gen. 1:26–28; 2:15, 19–20; Ps. 8:6–9). Man's possession of this intellectual power is specifically tied to his being "the image of God." "The hearing ear and the seeing eye, Jehovah has made even both of them" (Prov. 20:12). Scripture always takes for granted that men were given their senses to gain knowledge; notice how readily this function is assumed: "He who formed the eye, shall He not see? . . . He that teaches man knowledge?" (Ps. 94:9–10). Jesus did not hesitate to say that men "know" summer is near from their observation of the leaves budding on a tree (Matt. 24:32; cf. 7:20). Likewise, Scripture acknowledges that people can "know" the events of history (e.g., Acts 2:22; 15:7; 26:26). With their senses, they can know other human beings (e.g., Acts 12:14), and can know what is true about them (e.g., Acts 26:3) and even something of their inward spiritual character (e.g., John 13:35). Accordingly, even though he recognized that sin has weakened man's senses,[193] Van Til asserted that "man's knowledge of nature depends to a large extent upon the keenness of his sensations. . . . [W]e marvel that in his non-saving grace God has left to man such a large measure of ability in this respect." He was never sympathetic to the artificial epistemology of Christian scholars (even some labeled "presuppositionalist") who denied the possibility of empirical knowledge.[194] Rather, he quite openly taught:

193. "It is all too apparent that man is constantly making mistakes in his observations of the universe around him. Man's eye and ear and all his senses have been greatly weakened through the effects of sin. . . . Even the great in this field have great weaknesses too" (*Introduction to Systematic Theology*, 91).

194. Van Til disagreed with Gordon Clark most pointedly on this matter. Clark rejected "inductive logic" (a well-known subject in books on argument and right reasoning—to which 125 pages are given, for instance, in Copi's 8th edition of *Introduction to Logic*), asserting that "all inductive arguments are formal fallacies" (*Three Types of Religious Philosophy* [Nutley, N.J.: Craig Press, 1973], 116). According to Clark, science is "incapable of arriving at any truth whatever" (*Christian View of Men and Things* [Grand Rapids: Eerdmans, 1952], 227; cf. *The Philosophy of Science and Belief in God* [Nutley, N.J.: Craig Press, 1964]). Scripture reveals truth to us, according to Clark, but "there are no other sources of truth" (*Three Types of Religious Philosophy*, 8). Clark argued that "there is no knowledge otherwise obtainable" (*Philosophy of Gordon H. Clark*, ed. Nash, 91), but that reduced him to skepticism because he could not "know" what the truths of Scripture were without using his senses. In defense of his position, Clark argued that we do not learn anything through sensation of the words in Scripture, but are

We then study the hawks and handsaws and all things else by means of our powers of observation, strengthened by various means. We use our God-given power of imagination and of reasoning to devise hypotheses with respect to the behavior of the facts we study. We test these hypotheses again and again. But in it all we presuppose that God, the creator and controller of all things, is the source of possibility.[195]

Because God has already thought out or planned the details of nature and the events of history, there are causal connections, meaning, and purpose to be discovered by man when he uses his powers of observation and applies his intellect to what he finds. Except where God has verbally revealed things about the natural order or the course of history, man cannot determine God's thoughts regarding them and so must "look and see" with his senses. In this, again, he is "thinking God's thoughts after Him," even though the immediate object of his investigation is the world around him or the course of history preceding him. God's thoughts make the world what it is and determine what happens—which is why all facts are revelatory of God, according to Van Til. Given the presuppositions of creation, providence, and revelation, empirical knowledge is both possible and important to man. However, Van Til was just as insistent that because the unbeliever

---

simply "reminded" by them of what "was already in our knowledge . . . which God reveals within the soul" (*Philosophy of Gordon H. Clark*, ed. Nash, 415–16). However, a large portion of the Bible—telling about the grace of God and the history of His redemptive work to save His people—is not the content of general revelation or what men know as the image of God (which pertains, more narrowly, to God's wrath and condemnation: Rom. 1:18–32; 2:14–16; 3:5–6, 9–19). Clark's antiempirical epistemology kept him from "knowing" not only the words of Scripture, but also anything outside of biblical propositions (which he enthusiastically affirmed)—such as that he was a Christian (which can be deduced only from biblical propositions and extrabiblical information). I broached this criticism to him in 1977, and he insisted that in fact nobody can "know" that he is saved—which contradicted both Scripture (e.g., 1 John 5:13) and what Clark himself had written elsewhere (*What Do Presbyterians Believe? The Westminster Confession: Yesterday and Today* [Philadelphia: Presbyterian and Reformed, 1965], 176, 178). Clark's philosophy is self-contradictory, results in skepticism, and/or (most likely) rests on an entirely artificial notion of knowledge.

195. *Defense of the Faith*, 301. So then, hypotheses that deny "the facts and teachings directly revealed in Scripture" are not relevant to the Christian historian or scientist. His empirical methods are a gift from God to "find out God's mind (plan)" with respect to nature and history outside of (but not contrary to) what God has spoken to us. "We therefore devise such hypotheses and only such as are within that which is possible according to the plan of God so far as it is known to us" (pp. 301–2; cf. *Introduction to Systematic Theology*, 15).

pretends to be religiously neutral and has thereby "presupposed chance [as] back of the facts," any secular "form of empiricism . . . is utterly out of accord with Christian theism" and reduces to irrationalism.[196] Empirical methods of knowing can be made intelligible only within the Christian worldview. This is especially obvious when one considers that such methods assume that nature is uniform and that the knower's powers of observation correlate with or adapt to the extramental objects of knowledge. Unbelieving worldviews cannot make sense of the possibility of empirical knowledge.[197]

If we could offer a brief summation of Van Til's religious epistemology, we would begin, as he did, by saying that all men know God. They have true beliefs about God that are justified by the direct apprehension of His revelation of Himself in the world and within themselves, as well as (for some) by the self-attesting revelation of Christ in Scripture. Because he has been created in God's image, man brings with him into the world the intellectual ability and cognitive background to apprehend immediately the indications of God in nature and Scripture. When man knows things revealed in Scripture or in the natural world, he is thinking God's thoughts after Him. God's thoughts are transcendent and incomprehensible, to be sure, yet man can (and has been created to) think God's truths on a creaturely level (analogously to God's act of thinking them). Thinking God's thoughts after Him requires that men think logically and conceptually, as well as learn things through observation (using their senses). The Christian worldview provides a context within which rational and empirical knowing are intelligible.

Because Van Til took this kind of approach to epistemology, he could write very appropriately: "I do not artifically separate induction from deduction, or reasoning about the facts of nature from reasoning in *a priori* analytical fashion about the nature of human-consciousness. I do not artifically abstract or separate them from one another. On the contrary I see induction and analytical reasoning as part of one process of interpreta-

---

196. *Introduction to Systematic Theology*, 115. Cf.: "If the world and its facts are not what they are, ultimately, by the counsel of God . . . then there can be no distinguishing between a hawk and a handsaw. As already discussed, the only alternative to the counsel of God as the ultimate principle of individuation is that of Chance. In Chaos and Old Night all is blank" (*Defense of the Faith*, 300).

197. For presuppositional apologetical use of this in public debate, the reader may consult my debate with Edward Tabash at the University of California, Davis, in 1993.

tion."[198] Although Christian philosophy rules out the rationalism of a Leibniz and the empiricism of a Locke, said Van Til, "the Bible does not rule out every form of empiricism any more than it rules out every form of *a priori* reasoning."[199] What is philosophically crucial is that rational and empirical reasoning take place within the presupposed framework of God's revelation or the Christian worldview. Neither innate knowledge (rational methods of knowing) nor acquired knowledge (empirical methods) is intelligible "by itself." Such was Van Til's persistent witness to philosophers and apologists. As rationalism and empiricism have been understood within autonomous philosophy, the Christian "is equally opposed to both of these systems of philosophy because neither of them has any place for the Christian doctrine of revelation. . . . Only if first we presuppose God and therefore think of all created reality, including the self-consciousness of man, as revelational of God can we think truly of both innate and acquired knowledge. We may then think of them as limiting concepts, the one of the other."[200] Van Til urged us to recognize the distinctiveness of the Christian method—that rational and empirical reasoning mean something very different within the Christian worldview than they do within non-Christian worldviews.

> But what is of the utmost importance to note is that the main criticism of these methods is not on points of detail, but on the fact that they have not been analogical, and more specifically, that they have not been theological. A rationalistic method, that is, a method in which the *a priori* predominates, is itself no worse than an exclusively empirical or *a posteriori* method. Both are equally unacceptable if they do not have the Christian conception of the *a priori* and *a posteriori*. So, also, no combination of rational and empirical aspects will produce a method that is any better than either a rationalistic or an empirical method. If we add ever so many zeros to zero, we have zero still.[201]

---

198. *Defense of the Faith*, 258.
199. *Introduction to Systematic Theology*, 45.
200. Ibid., 195, 197.
201. Ibid., 19–20. Van Til hints at his distinctive apologetical argument—the transcendental method of proof—when he speaks of autonomous rationalism producing a zero (philosophical skepticism) and autonomous empiricism likewise producing a zero; no combination of autonomous notions will ever escape that zero. Rational and empirical reasoning can be saved only by placing them within the presupposed framework of the Christian worldview (God's revelation).

We can turn to some excerpts from Van Til's writings to see his affirmation of rational and empirical methods of knowing[202] in the context of God's incomprehensibility and the need for thinking "analogically"—thinking God's thoughts after Him.

GOD'S MIND IS INCOMPREHENSIBLE[203]

Nothing can exist in man just as it exists in God. Therefore God is incomprehensible in all that he reveals with respect to himself. Everything with respect
to God is on the plane of the absolute, while everything with respect to man
is derivative. On the other hand, we have in man a copy, something of that
which God has revealed with respect to himself. Man's being is analogical of
God's being.[204] . . .

It is this fact of the priority of the positive relation of God to the world in
the way of creation and providence, in the way of man's creation in the image
of God, that saves from scepticism. The Christian idea of human knowledge
as analogical of God's knowledge is therefore the only position in which man,
who cannot control or know anything in the ultimate comprehensive sense
of the term, can nevertheless be assured that his knowledge is true.

To say therefore that the human mind can know even one proposition in
its minimal significance with the same depth of meaning with which God
knows that proposition is an attack on the Creator-creature relationship and
therewith an attack on the heart of Christianity. . . .

In the Christian doctrine of the incomprehensibility of God, the Creator-
creature distinction is made fundamental. In the non-Christian view this is not
the case. The non-Christian view is monistic. . . .

For the [Christian] this distinction implies that the triune God, as he has
from all eternity existed apart from any relationship to the universe of space
and time, is wholly sufficient to himself in his being and knowledge. It implies therefore that God is wholly knowable and wholly known to himself.
God is light and in him is no darkness at all.

---

202. These and other portions of Van Til's writings show that there is a fundamental misunderstanding on the part of Ronald Nash when he asserts that Van Til's
approach to apologetics would require us "to defend the authority of the Scriptures without making any appeal to logic or to 'facts' " ("Attack on Human Autonomy," 349). It should rather be said that Van Til's apologetic argues that,
without the presupposition of the scriptural worldview, appeals to logic and facts
are not epistemologically intelligible (see chap. 5 following).
203. Excerpts from *Introduction to Systematic Theology*, 205, 185, 174–75, 164–65, 171,
172, 173, 181–82, 184.
204. That is, man is created as "the image" of God.

The orthodox idea of the Creator-creature distinction involves further the idea that the world of space and time has been brought into existence by the forthputting of God's power, by creation out of nothing, by the mere exercise of his will, and not as a necessity of his being. Thus there is no power of any sort operative in the course of the history of the world as man knows it, that is not without any qualification under the control and direction of God. . . . For to admit that anything happens outside the will of God is to admit the pagan notion of chance. God by his plan controls *whatsoever* comes to pass. . . .

Without the presupposition of God's revelation to man there could be no predication of God at all. God would be not incomprehensible, but inapprehensible. . . .

If we speak therefore of the incomprehensibility of God, what is meant is that God's revelation to man is never exhaustively understood by man. As by his revelation to man God says something about himself, so that man knows something about everything that exists, so it is equally true that there is nothing that man knows exhaustively. It is as impossible for man to know himself or any of the objects of the universe about him exhaustively as it is impossible for man to know God exhaustively. For man must know himself or anything else in the created universe in relation to the self-contained God. Unless he can know God exhaustively he cannot know anything else exhaustively.

It is only if these two points be taken together, the fact that man knows something about everything, including the very essence of God, and on the other hand that he does not know anything exhaustively, that the doctrine of the incomprehensibility of God can be seen for what it is.

In the first place, it is possible in this way to see that the knowledge of God and the knowledge of man coincide at *every* point in the sense that always and everywhere man confronts that which is already fully known or interpreted by God. *The point of reference cannot but be the same for man as for God.* There is no fact that man meets in any of his investigation where the face of God does not confront him.

On the other hand, in this way it is possible to see that the knowledge of God and the knowledge of man coincide at no point in the sense that in his awareness of meaning of anything, in his mental grasp or understanding of anything, man is at each point dependent upon a prior act of unchangeable understanding and revelation on the part of God. The form of the revelation of God to man must come to man in accordance with his creaturely limitations. . . .

This is true with respect to every bit of revelation that God gives to man.

Accordingly, the fact that man is given more and ever more revelation of God does not tend to reduce the incomprehensibility of God. For man any new revelational proposition will enrich in meaning any previously given revelational proposition. But even this enrichment does not imply that there is any coincidence, that is, identity of content[205] between what God has in his mind and what man has in his mind. If there is no identity of content in the first proposition that God gives to man there can be no identity of content attained by means of any number of additional propositions of revelation that God gives to man.[206] And there could be identity of content on the first proposition only if there were no first proposition. That is to say, if there *could* be an identity of content there *would* be and always has been an identity of content. There could and would be an identity of content only if the mind of man were identical with the mind of God. It is only on the assumption that the human mind is not the mind of a creature but is itself the mind of the Creator that one can talk consistently of identity of content between the mind of man and the mind of God. . . .

The Reformed faith teaches that the reference point for any proposition is the same for God and for man. It holds that this identity of reference point can be maintained only on the presupposition that all human predication is analogical re-interpretation of God's pre-interpretation. Thus the incomprehensibility of God must be taught with respect to *any* revelational proposition. . . . [By] asserting a qualitative difference between the knowledge of God and the knowledge of man the *Complaint* was merely asserting the Creator-creature relationship and the idea of the basic significance of revelation for all predication. . . .

For to "state clearly" can mean nothing but to "explain exhaustively" unless one presupposes the doctrine of revelation. . . . It is [our] contention that without stating clearly, i.e. exhaustively, man can yet truly know the meaning of a proposition. . . .

But if truth is really thought of as dependent upon God then we are back to the Christian method. Then we cannot at the same time maintain the exact identity of content as between the mind of man and the mind of God. For

205. That is, as Van Til explains, God's mind as a mind (or God's act of knowing as an act) always transcends man's creaturely mind (or act of knowing). "Content" is not used here for subject matter or the objects (truths) that are known by God and man; according to Van Til, these are identical, to the limited degree that man knows things at all.

206. This is an awkward and easily misunderstood statement. It could be better expressed like this: If man's mind does not become identical with God's mind (achieving mental "identity of content") with regard to the first proposition revealed by God to man, it will not do so with additional revealed propositions.

the truth then comes to man exclusively by revelation as noted above. It is God, by an eternal intuition knowing himself, who reveals himself. Man has no approach to the knowledge of the nature of God—on which truth is admittedly dependent—except by the self-conscious activity of God as expressed in revelation. And this revelation is a revelation about the manner of God's knowing or it is not a revelation about God at all. God's nature is self-conscious activity. Only on this basis is there an identity of reference point. On this basis man may know the proposition that two times two is four as part of the "system" of knowledge that is God's. Thus only is there identity of reference point between man's knowledge and God's knowledge. Only thus can man know truly without knowing exhaustively. . . .

Therefore when God tells me something that pertains directly to his own being apart from the world, I may repeat on the level of my experience the words that he has spoken. When he, for instance, tells me that he has existed from all eternity before the foundation of the world, I may repeat his words and say 'God is eternal,' but it is evident that God has, and I have not, grasped fully what God means. God knows himself exhaustively, and I know him truly but not exhaustively. Moreover, what holds true of things that God tells me about himself holds true of everything God tells me about myself or the world. Even of the things that I observe with my senses, with respect to the things that you are accustomed to speaking of as belonging to the realm of science or to the realm of the phenomenal world, it remains true on my presuppositions that I do not comprehend them exhaustively. All the facts of the phenomenal world are incomprehensible to me precisely because they are what they are by virtue of the voluntary action of the will of God with respect to them. They are what they are, they occupy a place in the scheme of things spatio-temporal, because God by his plan and by the execution of his plan in the works of creation and providence makes them what they are. They are in the last analysis as incomprehensible to me as is God himself. *My idea of the incomprehensibility of God, therefore, presupposes his true knowability*. And his true knowability is based on the fact that I am his creature and that all things created are made by him. I could therefore not even assert the incomprehensibility of God unless I presupposed the knowability of God. *I cannot assert the knowability of anything in the phenomenal world unless I presuppose the knowability of God.*[207] It is therefore upon the idea that all phenomenal reality, whether within the mind of man or surrounding it, is what it is because of the result of the activity of the will of God as revelational of his character. Upon this I base the doctrine of the incomprehensibility of God. . . .

207. Emphasis added here and in the preceding italicized sentence.

Thus the two positions, the Christian and the non-Christian, stand squarely over against one another. Affirming the primacy of the Creator-creature relationship, the Christian position, consistently expressed in the Reformed faith, maintains that man does not at any point have in his mind exactly the same thought content that God has in his mind. When his God makes a revelational proposition to him such as that he, God, is eternal, man in repeating this proposition says that God is eternal. The reference point is the same but the content is not. Being subject to no conditions, himself the source of all conditions for man, God at once sees the significance of such a proposition in all the depth of its meaning. God knows the meaning of this proposition in all the fulness of its significance because he knows it in relationship to all other propositions that he will make or will not make to man.

If God had made all the revelational propositions that he will ever make to man about himself, even then man could not have the same thought content in his mind that God has in his mind unless he were himself divine. Man can never experience the experience of God. An endless number of added propositions does not change the matter in the least. Added revelation has in the past enriched and no doubt will hereafter enrich the fulness of meaning that man possesses when he responds to this revelation in his confession and adoration, but added revelation cannot wipe out the difference between the experience of the self-contained ontological Trinity and the experience of the created man.

MAN KNOWS ANALOGOUSLY TO GOD'S KNOWING[208]

(A) Why, first of all, is the question of *analogy* so important? What is involved in the question of analogy? It is the question of the relation of God to man. It is the question, more specifically, as to the *priority* of these two. There are those who worship and serve the creature rather than the Creator. There are also those, having been saved by grace, who worship and serve the Creator rather than the creature. . . .

There are only *two* kinds of people in the world, covenant-breakers and covenant-keepers. Covenant-breakers are such in all that they do, and

208. The following excerpts are taken from:

   (A) *Reformed Pastor and Modern Thought*, 78–79;
   (B) *Introduction to Systematic Theology*, 101, 181, 206;
   (C) "Nature and Scripture," 273, 277–78, 280–81;
   (D) *Defense of the Faith*, 55–58, 64–66, 138, 165;
   (E) *Introduction to Systematic Theology*, 167, 69–70, 87–88.

covenant-keepers are such in all that they do.[209] Covenant-breakers make God in man's image, and covenant-keepers make man in God's image. This distinction, thus baldly stated, indicates the antithesis between the believer and the unbeliever *in principle*. Of course, this principle does not come to full expression in this life. . . .

[The unbeliever] will try to make himself believe that he can explain to himself the nature of the world and himself without God. Taking to himself the place ascribed to God in a true Christian theology, he assumes that reality must be of such a nature as he says it is. Using the gift of logical manipulation given to him for the purpose of thinking God's thoughts after him on a created scale (in order thus to form an analogical system that in some measure reflects the plan of God), he absolutizes himself and compels the nature of reality to be equal to the reach of his logical thought.

(B) As indicated at the outset of this work, we speak of all forms of reasoning in which man is assumed to be the final or ultimate reference point of predication as *univocal* reasoning. In contrast to this we speak of the form of reasoning employed by the Christian who recognizes that God is the ultimate reference point of predication as *analogical* reasoning. . . .

If then every fact that confronts me is revelational of the personal and voluntary activity of the self-contained God, it follows that when I try to think God's thoughts after him, that is to say, when by means of the gift of logical manipulation which this Creator has given to me, I try to make a "system" of my own, my system will . . . at every point be analogical[210] of the system of God. . . . On the other hand, since the human mind is created by God and is therefore in itself naturally revelational of God, the mind may be sure that its system is true and corresponds on a finite scale to the system of God. That is what we mean by saying that it is analogical to God's system. It is *dependent* upon God's system, and by being dependent upon God's system it is of necessity a true system. . . .

When we speak of our concept or notion of God, we should be fully aware that by that concept we have an analogical reproduction of the notion that God has of himself. Our notions or concepts are finite replicas of God's notions.

---

209. CVT: I John 2:3, 4, 5; 3:4, 6, 9, 10, 23, 24.
210. In the source for this excerpt, Van Til indicates that an "analogical" system is not simply a "direct replica." Yet, as he goes on to say here, it does "correspond on a finite scale" to God's system—thus amounting to a "finite replica." He seems to be affirming a truly functional equivalence in man's thinking on the creaturely scale ("correspondence"), while denying that this amounts to simply making man's mind a smaller version of the divine mind (a "direct replica").

(C) Man was created as an analogue of God; his thinking, his willing and his doing are therefore properly conceived as at every point analogical to the thinking, willing and doing of God. It is only after refusing to be analogous to God that man can think of setting a contrast between the attitude of reason to one type of revelation and the attitude of faith to another type of revelation. . . .

Created man may see clearly what is revealed clearly even if he cannot see exhaustively. Man does not need to know exhaustively in order to know truly and certainly. When on the created level of existence man thinks God's thoughts after him, that is, when man thinks in self-conscious submission to the voluntary revelation of the self-sufficient God, he has therewith the only possible ground of certainty for his knowledge. When man thinks thus he thinks as a covenant creature should wish to think. That is to say, man normally thinks in analogical fashion. He realizes that God's thoughts are self-contained. He knows that his own interpretation of nature must therefore be a re-interpretation of what is already fully interpreted by God. . . .

When man fell, he denied the naturally revelatory character of every fact including that of his own consciousness. He assumed that he was autonomous; he assumed that his consciousness was not revelational of God but only of himself. He assumed himself to be non-created. He assumed that the work of interpretation, as by the force of his natural powers he was engaged in it, was an original instead of a derivative procedure. He would not think God's thoughts after him; he would instead think only his own original thoughts.

Now if anything is obvious from Scripture it is that man is not regarded as properly a judge of God's revelation to him. Man is said or assumed from the first page to the last to be a creature of God. God's consciousness is therefore taken to be naturally original as man's is naturally derivative. Man's natural attitude in all self-conscious activities was therefore meant to be that of obedience. . . .

(D) All of this may again be expressed from another point of view by saying that human knowledge is analogical of divine knowledge. We cannot avoid coming to a clear-cut decision with respect to the question as to whose knowledge, man's or God's, shall be made the standard of the other. The one must be original and the other analogical of the original. The one must be determinative and the other subordinate. Roman Catholic theology seeks to serve two masters here. It too speaks of created being and human knowledge as being analogical of divine being and divine knowledge but it does not really take this seriously. In its philosophy and apologetics Romanism reasons as though man can, by himself, determine the nature and possibility of knowledge without reference to God. On the other hand it refers to mysteries as being above the understanding of man. But as Protestants we should definitely choose to make God the original in the knowledge situation.

The first thing to note in the question of our knowledge of God is that it must be true or objective. That this is so is once more involved in our God-concept. God knows himself analytically and completely and therefore must know all things beyond him analytically and completely. God certainly must have true knowledge of us and of the universe in general. Our existence and our meaning, our denotation and our connotation are derived from God. We are already fully interpreted before we come into existence. God knows us before and behind; he knows the thoughts of our hearts. We could not have existence and meaning apart from the existence and meaning of God. All this is the road from God to us. But surely we can get back to God by the road that he has used to create us. If I lay a road in order to build a city somewhere the inhabitants of that city can come back to me by the road that I have built. Of course we might say that some one could destroy that road. In this case the city would still exist and yet its inhabitants could not get back to me. But this cannot be applied in the case of our relationship to God. It is not that we are merely brought into existence by God, but our meaning also depends upon God. Our meaning cannot be realized except through the course of history. God created man in order that man should realize a certain end, that is, the glory of God, and thus God should reach his own end. For that reason if we could think of the road between God and man as broken, it would mean also that we should no longer exist and thus the whole question would disappear.

We may safely conclude then that if God is what we say he is, namely a being who exists necessarily as a self-complete system of coherence, and we exist at all as self-conscious beings, we must have true knowledge of him. (We are not now speaking of the question of sin. That is an ethical and not a metaphysical question. Our metaphysical dependence upon God has not been wiped out by sin.) All this we express theologically when we say that man is created in God's image. This makes man like God and assures true knowledge of God. We are known of him and therefore we know him and know that we know him. God is light and therefore we have light.

Important as it is to insist that our knowledge of God must be true, because God is what he is, it is equally important to insist that our knowledge of God is not and cannot be comprehensive. We are God's creatures. We cannot know God comprehensively now nor can we hope to know God comprehensively hereafter. We may know much more in the future than we know now. Especially when we come to heaven will we know more than we know now, but we will not know comprehensively.

We are therefore like God so that our knowledge is true and we are unlike God and therefore our knowledge can never be comprehensive. When we say that God is a mystery for us we do not mean that our knowledge of him is not true as far as it goes. When we say that God is transcendent above us or when we say that God is "the absolutely Other" we do not mean that there is not a rational relation between God and us. As God created us in accordance with his plan, that is, as God created us in accordance with his absolute rationality, so there must be a rational relationship from us to God. Christianity is, in the last analysis, not an absolute irrationalism but an absolute "rationalism." In fact we may contrast every non-Christian epistemology with Christian epistemology by saying that Christian epistemology believes in an ultimate rationalism while all other systems of epistemology believe in an ultimate irrationalism.

When we say that as Christians we believe in an ultimate rationalism we are, naturally, not intending anything like the idea that we as human beings have or may at some time expect to have a comprehensive rational understanding of God. We have just asserted the contrary. Here too every non-Christian epistemology may be distinguished from Christian epistemology in that it is only Christian epistemology that does not set before itself the ideal of comprehensive knowledge for man. The reason for this is that it holds that comprehensive knowledge is found only in God. It is true that there must be comprehensive knowledge somewhere if there is to be any true knowledge anywhere but this comprehensive knowledge need not and cannot be in us; it must be in God. . . .

What then was the result as far as the question of knowledge is concerned of man's rebellion against God? The result was that man tried to interpret everything with which he came into contact without reference to God. The assumption of all his future interpretation was the self-sufficiency of intra-cosmical relationships. This does not signify that man would immediately and openly deny that there is a God. Nor does it mean that man would always and everywhere deny that God is in some sense transcendent. What he would always deny, by implication at least, would be that God is self-sufficient or self-complete. At best he would allow that God is a correlative to man. He might say that we need God to interpret man but he would at the same time say that in the same sense we need man to interpret God. He might say that the temporal cannot be interpreted without reference to the eternal but he would at the same time say that the eternal cannot be interpreted without reference to the temporal. He might say that we need God in order to obtain unity in our experience, but he would at the same time say that God needs the historical many in order to get diversity into his experience. All these forms of correlativity amount in the end to the same thing as saying that the finite categories are self-sufficient. For that reason we can make a very simple and all comprehensive antithesis between the knowledge concept of all non-Christian philosophies and the Christian view. Scripture says that some men worship and serve the Creator; they are the Christians. All other men worship and serve the creature rather than the Creator.

Christian-theism says that there are two levels of thought, the absolute and the derivative. Christian-theism says that there are two levels of interpreters, God who interprets absolutely and man who must be the re-interpreter of God's interpretation. Christian-theism says that human thought is therefore analogical of God's thought. In opposition to all this, non-Christian thought holds in effect that the distinction between absolute and derivative thought must be wiped out. . . .

[In univocal thinking] we do not think God's thoughts after him, but together with God we think out thoughts that have never been thought either by God or by man. Non-Christian philosophies hold that human thought is univocal instead of analogical.

Thus the Christian concept of analogical thought and the non-Christian concept of univocal thought stand over against one another as diametrical opposites.

Non-Christian thought holds to the ultimacy of the created universe. It holds therefore to the ultimacy of the mind of man itself and must in consequence deny the necessity of analogical thought. It holds to the normalcy of the human mind as well as to its ultimacy. It holds to the normalcy of the human mind as it holds to the normalcy of everything else in the world.

Naturally this conception of the normalcy of the human mind does not imply that the human mind never makes mistakes. It only means that mistakes are thought of as natural and to be expected and have nothing to do with sin.

We can readily see from this that the non-theistic mind must set for itself the ideal of absolutely comprehensive knowledge as long as it has not become fully conscious of the implications of its own thought. However, it will maintain that it is unnecessary for man to have any comprehensive universal in order to live. As long as non-theistic thought still thinks it necessary for man to have an absolute universal it naturally has to set for itself the task of finding this universal, inasmuch as God has been put out of the picture. Then when it appears impossible for man ever to find a universal, inasmuch as the particulars of the time are by definition always ahead of any time-generated universal, man says that he does not need any absolute universal anyway except as a limiting concept.

It may be useful in this connection to point out that in the whole situation we have therefore to deal with three types of consciousness.

In the first place there is the Adamic consciousness. When man was first created he was perfect. He recognized the fact that he was a creature; he was actually normal. He wanted to be nothing but a re-interpreter of the inter-pretation of God. He was receptive to God's revelation which appeared within him and round about him; he would reconstruct this revelation. He was re-ceptively reconstructive. For that reason he had real though not comprehen-sive unity in his experience.[211]

In the second place we deal with the fallen or non-regenerate conscious-ness. It builds upon the non-theistic assumption. It in effect denies its crea-turehood. It claims to be normal. It will not be receptive of God's interpreta-tion; it wants to create its own interpretation without reference to God. It will not reconstruct God's interpretation. It will construct only its own interpreta-tion. It seeks to be creatively constructive. It thus tries to do the impossible with the result that self-frustration is written over all its efforts. There is no unity and never will be unity in non-theistic thought; it has cut itself loose from the only existing source of unity. Yet since it could not cut itself loose from God metaphysically and since God, for the purpose of realizing his plan of redemption, *rudera* or *scintillae* of the knowledge of God and of the uni-verse remain in man. Non-Christians know after a fashion, as Paul tells us in Romans. Thus also there is a relative good in those who are ethically totally evil. The unity that they have in experience is a shadow unity, a unity that prevents them from falling into complete disintegration in this world. Here-after complete disintegration will follow, though even hereafter the disinte-gration can only be ethical and not metaphysical; there must be a kingdom or mock-unity even in hell.

In the third place there is the regenerate consciousness. This regenerate consciousness has in principle been restored to the position of the Adamic con-sciousness. It recognizes anew that man is God's creature and that he has fallen into sin. It recognizes the fact that it has been saved by grace. It there-fore wants to be receptively reconstructive once more. It wants to interpret reality in terms of the eternal one and many. It therefore does have unity in its experience, though not comprehensive unity. . . .

If man's necessarily discursive thought is not to fall into the ultimate irra-tionalism and scepticism that is involved in modern methodology we must presuppose the conception of the God that is found in Scripture. Scripture

211. CVT: The reader may observe again how basically important Adam's place in history is said to be. James Daane had criticized Van Til for allegedly reducing the historical particularity of Adam to a generality of mankind (cf. pp. 17–19).

alone presents the sort of God whose intuition of system is not bought at the price of his knowledge of individuality, and whose knowledge of individuality is not bought at the expense of intuitional knowledge of system. But such a God must really be presupposed. He must be taken as the prerequisite of the possibility and actuality of relationship between man's various concepts and propositions of knowledge. Man's system of knowledge must therefore be an analogical replica of the system of knowledge which belongs to God. . . .

Hence the idea of human autonomy can find no place in the truly Christian system any more than can the idea of chance. The human being is analogical rather than original in all the aspects of its activity. And as such its activity is truly significant.

(E) By presupposing the God of eternal self-affirmation man can get on the way to learning because he knows God when he first appears upon the scene. He has knowledge of self for what he really is. He also can add to his knowledge since the new facts that he learns about are already known and not new to God. Therefore they are related to what man already knows in true coherence. In setting out a series of propositions about the revelation of God, as the church has done in its confessions, the Christian may rest assured that he has "the system of truth" while yet he may add to his knowledge of that system. All his knowledge is analogical of God. God is the original knower and man is the derivative re-knower. Man knows in subordination to God; he knows as the covenant-keeper. If he is not a covenant-keeper he will set the false ideal of knowing even as God knows, by complete coincidence with the contents of the mind of God, and end up by knowing that what he calls knowledge is no true knowledge at all. . . .

At this point, it is again necessary that we distinguish most carefully between the Christian theistic position and non-Christian thought. We can do so if we note first of all that the thought activity of man's consciousness as it was originally in paradise was genuinely revelational in the sense that the whole of the created universe of God is revelational of God. We deal here with the subject of human knowledge, that is, with the mind that knows. As we have seen, the relation of the human mind to objects of its knowledge is founded on the Logos of creation. We ought to note in addition to this that man was created the only self-conscious re-interpreter in this universe. Man was to gather up in his consciousness all the meaning that God had deposited in the universe and be the reflector of it all. The revelation of God was deposited in the whole of creation, but it was in the mind of man alone that this revelation was to come to self-conscious re-interpretation. Man was to be God's re-interpreter, that is, God's prophet on earth.

We may perhaps clarify what is meant by the consciousness of man as being originally revelational if we say that man would naturally, by virtue of his thought activity, know and come to know ever more fully the true state of affairs about the universe in general and about himself in particular. He would, in the field of metaphysics, know and recognize the fact that he was a creature. Hence he would know, in the field of knowledge, that, in the nature of the case, he could be no more than a re-interpreter. That is, he would recognize at once that the possibility of predication presupposed the existence of God as absolute.

In paradise, man made his self-consciousness the *immediate but wholly derivative* starting point while he made the self-consciousness of God the *remote* but *wholly ultimate starting point* of all his knowledge. Hence he saw that his knowledge was, though finite, yet true. Hence he did not set before himself the false ideal of absolute comprehension. Hence, too, he did not despair and conclude to irrationalism simply because he himself could not fully comprehend the whole of reality.

In opposition to this, the non-Christian interpretation of the human mind is based upon the presupposition that it is the ultimate and not merely the derivative starting point for man. Hence it has set before itself the ideal of comprehensive knowledge. This was done especially in the earlier stages of human thought. The Greek thinkers were as children who thought they could do everything. Even in modern times we have, in such systems as that of Leibniz, a striking manifestation of the pride, "hubris" of the sinner who wishes to be as God. In more recent times, however, men have become more sophisticated. They have given up the quest for certainty and the quest for comprehension, except as a limiting concept. In modern irrationalism, the prodigal has recognized that he is at the swine trough, but still refuses to return to the father's house. His "hubris" never forsakes him. . . .

The first point of importance to note is that Calvin, in the first chapter of his first book begins the whole discussion of his *Institutes* by bringing forward the conception of the close connection between man's knowledge of himself and of God. We quote the first lines of his book:

> Our wisdom in so far as it ought to be deemed true and solid wisdom, consists almost entirely of two parts: the knowledge of God and of ourselves. But as those are connected together by many ties, it is not easy to determine which of the two precedes, and gives birth to the other. For, in the first place, no man can survey himself without forthwith turning his thoughts toward God in whom he lives and moves; because it is perfectly obvious, that the endowments which

we possess cannot possibly be from ourselves, nay, that our very being is nothing else than subsistence in God alone.

From this quotation, certain things are clear. Calvin never did start a chain of reasoning about man's nature and destiny by taking man by himself. He did not start with man as with an ultimate starting point. Calvin did start with a general a priori position. His position is as radically opposed to that of Descartes as it is to that of Hume. Most apologetic writers who have come after Calvin have allowed themselves to be influenced unduly by Cartesian philosophy on this matter. Calvin recognized fully that if man is to have true knowledge of himself he must regard God as original and himself as derivative. He did not place God and man as correlatives next to one another, but he recognized from the outset two levels of existence and two levels of interpretation, on the one hand the divine and eternal, and on the other hand the human or temporal. To him it is perfectly obvious that the endowments that we possess are not of ourselves, but of God. Hence he says that "not a particle of light, or wisdom, or justice, or power, or rectitude, or genuine truth, will anywhere be found, which does not flow from him: and of which he is not the cause . . ." (I, 2, 2).

It is this thought of Calvin, rooted as it is in the Scriptural doctrines of creation and providence, that we tried to express in the previous chapter by saying that originally man was able to see the true state of affairs with respect to his own thought. He saw himself as a reinterpreter of God's interpretation.

RATIONAL AND EMPIRICAL KNOWLEDGE AFFIRMED[212]

When we study physics, we do not usually think of the fact that we are dealing with revelation. We study the individual objects in the physical universe. We try to see in accordance with what laws they work. We try to bring the particulars and the universals together. We deal, therefore, first of all with the object-object relation. But we also deal with the object-subject or the subject-object relation. It is the human mind or subject that seeks to get information about the objects of knowledge. We hold that God has so created the objects in relationship to one another that they exist not as particulars only, but that they exist as particulars that are related to universals. God has created not only the facts but also the laws of physical existence. And the two are meaningless except as correlatives of one another. Moreover, God has adapted the objects to the subjects of knowledge; that the laws of our minds

212. An excerpt from *Introduction to Systematic Theology*, 65–66.

and the laws of the facts come into fruitful contact with one another is due to God's creative work and to God's providence, by which all things are maintained in their existence and in their operation in relation to one another.

It is of particular significance to see clearly that the laws of mathematics are but modes of the created universe. They are not, as theologians have all too often held, existences that are independent of God. Many theologians have followed Plato in thinking of the laws of mathematics as somehow existing from all eternity alongside of God. And what holds true for the laws of mathematics holds equally true for the conception of time. Time is not a moving image of the abstract notion of eternity. It is God-created as a mode of finite existence.

Now since we think of nothing as having existence and meaning independently of God, it is impossible to think of the object and the subject standing in the fruitful relation to one another that they actually do unless God is back of them both. Hence, the knowledge that we have of the simplest objects of the physical universe is still based upon the revelational activity of God.

It is customary on the part of some orthodox theologians to depreciate the objects of sensation as a source of knowledge. They have become deeply convinced of the scepticism involved in historical empiricism. They would therefore substitute an a priori approach for that of the empiricist, thinking that thus they represent biblical thought.

Two points may be mentioned with respect to this. In the first place, to flee to the arms of an a priorism from those of empiricism is in itself no help at all. It is only if an a priori is self-consciously based upon the conception of the ontological Trinity rather than upon the work of Plato or some other non-Christian philosopher that it can safeguard against scepticism. The a priori of any non-Christian thinker will eventually lead to empiricism. It can keep from doing so only if it keeps within the field of purely formal predication. In the second place, if we do place the ontological Trinity at the foundation of all our predication then there is no need to fear any scepticism through the avenue of sense. Sensation does "deceive us" but so does ratiocination. We have the means for their corruption in both cases. The one without the other is meaningless. Both give us true knowledge on the right presupposition; both lead to scepticism on the wrong presupposition.

Chapter 5

The Apologetical Side of Epistemology

5.1 Epistemological Disagreements Entail Worldview Debate

As explained in the previous chapter, unbelievers have a true knowledge of the existence and character of God, which is justified by the evidence directly apprehended in God's clear and inescapable natural revelation of Himself. This is immediate knowledge, rather than knowledge derived by inferences and discursive arguments. Moreover, whenever the unbeliever encounters the gospel in Scripture, he recognizes the voice of God speaking authoritatively in its words; the divine character, convincing testimony, and self-authorizing quality of its message cannot be evaded. Since any self-revelation by God (whether in nature or in Scripture) would be clear and persuasive, and man was created by God to be His image (and thus was "preconditioned" to identify the characteristics of his Creator), unbelievers immediately discern and understand the evidence about God in their natural experience and recognize the voice of God when they read the Bible. They thus "know" God and within that context can make sense of their rational and empirical reasoning about themselves, their world, history, values, etc. The picture we have of ourselves as knowers is that of thinking God's thoughts after Him on a creaturely level.

However, to belabor the obvious, the unbeliever flatly denies apprehending any direct evidence of God's existence and character in nature or encountering any self-attesting evidence for the gospel in Scripture, and he rejects any overtly religious model of man as a knower. This is where apologetics comes in. The picture of man as one who thinks God's thoughts after Him, and the claim that "God's signature" is found in every fact of the external world and in man's personality, just like the claim that "God's voice" is clearly heard in the message of Scripture, cannot remain mere claims. As we have seen, Van Til taught that reasons must be provided for the statements a person makes when they are subject to dispute. Arbitrariness is philosophically unacceptable, even if it is widespread. People who indulge themselves in unwarranted opinions are, as Van Til once put it, "epistemological loafers." Christians cannot be satisfied with intellectually lazy and ultimately subjective beliefs. They must offer proof for what they assert about God, man, salvation, etc. How can this be done?

According to Van Til, the Christian claim (that non-Christians already know God from natural revelation and also recognize the voice of God in Scripture) is justified because the knowledge of God is *the context and prerequisite for knowing anything else whatsoever*. Without presupposing God, it is impossible to make theoretical sense out of any rational method for "justifying" beliefs of any kind on any subject. As the apostle Paul indicated, by suppressing the truth about God that they clearly and directly know, unbelievers have their reasoning reduced to foolishness (Rom. 1:21–22). If they do not acknowledge knowing God, they cannot make intellectual sense out of God's world or out of themselves as God's image-bearers. Likewise, Paul taught that those who reject the word of the cross (which is needed to repair man's stubborn refusal to submit to the light of God) are reduced to foolishness in their thinking and living (1 Cor. 1:20). Their attempts to warrant what they believe and do—indeed, to know anything—are futile deceptions apart from that philosophy which is "according to Christ," in whom "all the treasure of wisdom and knowledge are deposited" (Col. 2:3, 8). The Christian message, whether it be the truth about the Creator communicated in natural revelation or the saving truth of the gospel declared in Scripture, was defended by Van Til as the necessary precondition for rationally justifying any claim to knowledge about anything else. "In fact it then appears that the argument for the Scriptures as the infallible revelation of

God is, to all intents and purposes, the same as the argument for the existence of God."[1]

But before we can understand this aspect of presuppositional apologetics better, we must first grasp something else about arguments pertaining to epistemology. In our preceding discussions, we found that
a person's theory of knowledge (epistemology) is but part (or an aspect) of a whole network of presuppositions that he maintains, which
includes beliefs about the nature of reality (metaphysics) and his
norms for living (ethics). Consider someone's commitment to a certain method of knowing (learning, reasoning, proving, etc.). That
method will not be set forth by its advocate simply in a *descriptive* fashion, as though we were just observing what happens when people
come to know things. Rather, the method will be treated as *normative*—
as the proper and obligatory way in which to gain or justify knowledge.
It carries prescriptive force, then, and becomes a standard for evaluating or judging claims to knowledge. The choice of such an epistemological norm and the choice to conform in particular cases to it are
part of a person's broader lifestyle, reflecting his ultimate authority for
conduct and attitudes (ethics). Moreover, a commitment to this particular method of knowing already assumes certain beliefs about the
nature of reality (metaphysics). If one is attempting to be philosophically reasonable (rather than arbitrary), one's method of knowing has
presumably been chosen, from among conflicting methods, because
it "works" well in identifying the beliefs that reflect reality (the way
things are) and separating out the beliefs that fail to do so. In that case,
then, our choice of an epistemological method is adjusted to what we
take as paradigm instances of beliefs reflecting the actual metaphysical state of affairs. As Van Til was quoted earlier: "Our theory of knowledge is what it is because our theory of being is what it is. . . . We cannot ask
how we know without at the same time asking *what* we know."[2]

It will not be possible, then, to resolve disputes of a basic epistemological character between individuals without engaging in argumentation at the level of presupposed worldviews as a whole. An ancient idealist like Plato believed that men could know things by

---

1. *The Defense of the Faith* (Philadelphia: Presbyterian and Reformed, 1955), 126. This
argument is the transcendental presuppositional argument that is explained in
chap. 7 below, namely: "No proof for this God and for the truth of his revelation in Scripture can be offered by an appeal to anything in human experience that has not itself received
its light from the God whose existence and whose revelation it is supposed to prove."
2. Ibid., 49.

intuition ("recollection") of the universals ("forms" or ideas) of things that are encountered in this world, while the British empiricist David Hume maintained that no idea was meaningful unless it could be analyzed and its component parts could be traced to sensation. Imagine the two famous philosophers arguing with each other. A debate between Plato and Hume could hardly be restricted to epistemology, since their conflicting theories of knowledge reflect a simultaneous disagreement on the nature of things that exist (metaphysics). For Plato, universals (ideas) were transcendent and real, distinct from the particulars in this world, which were imperfect instances of them. Hume, by contrast, presupposed as a metaphysical dogma that only particulars encountered in man's temporal experience exist. An epistemological dispute between Plato and Hume would be "the other side of the coin" of their metaphysical dispute.[3] They had radically different worldviews. In light of this fact, epistemological disagreements at the most fundamental level must be seen in a broader perspective as a clash of worldviews. As Van Til recognized, arguments about the theory of knowledge should and must incorporate considerations of both metaphysical and ethical matters.

Van Til wrote that "every metaphysics has an implicit, if not an explicit, epistemology," and "every man educated or not educated has an epistemology implied in his practice."[4] Different views of reality, its characteristics and relations, like differing lifestyles and rules of conduct, incorporate similarly different views on how one knows about reality. A "distinctively Christian conception of reality implies a distinctively Christian conception of scientific methodology. . . . One's conception of reality is one's conception of the foundation of the laws of logic."[5] Thus, in a self-conscious and full-ranging argument between a Christian and a non-Christian, they will inevitably debate issues of both metaphysics and epistemology. "It really makes very little difference in this connection whether one begins with metaphysics and ends with epistemology, or whether one begins with epistemology and ends with metaphysics. The important thing to observe is that the one is involved in the other."[6]

3. Similarly, Van Til noted about Aristotle that "his logic was involved in his metaphysics as his metaphysics was involved in his logic" (ibid., 298).
4. *A Survey of Christian Epistemology*, In Defense of the Faith, vol. 2 (Philadelphia: Presbyterian and Reformed, 1969), 15.
5. *Defense of the Faith*, 299. For an illustration of how presuppositional apologetics puts this insight into practice in challenging unbelief, consult my debate with the atheist Gordon Stein at the University of California, Irvine, in 1985.
6. *Survey of Christian Epistemology*, 29.

So then, given its particular view of God and of how man ought to live (its unique metaphysical and ethical commitments), the Christian position should also be expected to have its own understanding of knowledge and reasoning. "The question of starting-point then is largely determined by one's theology . . . the Reformed life and world view."[7] Likewise, Van Til said that the Christian method of reasoning is involved in, and springs from, the Christian message itself.[8] That is, our apologetic approach (with its implicit epistemological method) is governed by the message that we defend, even as the unbeliever's conception of epistemology is impacted by his beliefs in the areas of metaphysics and ethics. In seeking "a method of defense of the Christian philosophy of life," Van Til explained to his students that:

> Every system of philosophy [must have an epistemological position, but] in the second place every system of philosophy has a theory of metaphysics . . . a complete theory of reality. . . . It should be noted further that, as in epistemology so in metaphysics, the matter of choice comes up again. We shall find that the Christian theory of metaphysics is the only one that really takes the matter of metaphysics seriously. For the others it has really become a question of taste. . . . The conviction at the basis of such an attitude must be that it is rationally impossible for man to have any knowledge of ultimate things. It will be necessary for us to insist that our opponents make reasonable to us this claim that man can have no knowledge of ultimate things. Unless they are able to do this they have no right to their attitude of carelessness. So then, we are necessarily led once more into a dialogue.[9]

In his dialogue with unbelievers over epistemological matters, the apologist must look into the metaphysical and ethical context of the unbeliever's epistemological convictions, contrasting them with his own Christian integration of metaphysics, ethics, and epistemology, so as to demonstrate that the dispute is ultimately and implicitly between entire philosophical systems or schools of thought. Each school of thought has its own way of conceptualizing difficulties, choosing

7. *Defense of the Faith*, 96.
8. *The Case for Calvinism* (Philadelphia: Presbyterian and Reformed, 1963), 110, 131.
9. *Survey of Christian Epistemology*, xiv.

which problems are most relevant and important,[10] determining what the accepted way of solving them is, setting standards of accomplishment, etc.[11] Van Til wrote that "the starting point, the method, and the conclusion are always involved in one another"; this integrated philosophical outlook determines the "formulation of problems" and the "relevance of hypotheses."[12] "Even the description of facts in the lowest dimension presupposes a system of metaphysics and epistemology."[13] Accordingly, Van Til held that the difference between the Christian and the non-Christian positions in every area of philosophy and interpretation was systematic:

> It will now be plain that our conception of the nature of reality goes counter to every theory of reality that the history of philosophy affords. . . .
>
> We are at this juncture merely concerned to point out that as a matter of fact we deal here with the most basic contrast conceivable between a Christian and a non-Christian theory of knowledge. Christianity interprets reality in terms of the eternally self-conscious divine personality; non-Christian thought interprets reality in terms of an existence independent of God. . . .
>
> This then is the most basic and fundamental difference between Christian and non-Christian epistemology, as far as it has a direct bearing upon questions of ethics, that in the case of non-Christian thought man's moral activity is thought of as *creatively constructive* while in Christian thought man's moral activity is thought of as being *receptively reconstructive*. According to non-Christian thought, there is no absolute moral personality to whom man is responsible and from whom he has received his conception of the good, while according to Christian thought God is the infinite moral personality who reveals to man the true nature of morality. . . .
>
> The Christian philosophy of nature and the Christian philosophy of history are the diametrical opposites of the non-Christian philosophy of nature and the non-Christian philosophy of history. . . .

10. Notice how one aspect of Van Til's criticism of the apologetic of E. J. Carnell is precisely that "from such men as Kant, Kierkegaard and Niebuhr, Carnell has learned to ask the proper questions" (*Case for Calvinism*, 94).
11. Similar insights about disputes between different schools of science were made a number of years later by Thomas Kuhn, *The Structure of Scientific Revolutions* (Chicago: University of Chicago Press, 1962; 2d ed., 1970).
12. *Defense of the Faith*, 118, 228, 301–2.
13. *Common Grace* (Philadelphia: Presbyterian and Reformed, 1947), 85.

> Either one holds the entire system of orthodox Christianity . . . or one denies the entire system.[14]

To put it very simply, Van Til always described the apologetical dialogue between believer and unbeliever in terms of "the radical difference which exists between the world-views of Christians and non-Christians." The apologist takes Christianity as "a totality view of man and his environment, a view including every fact in the universe, involving them all in one grand drama of redemption or condemnation." In apologetical argument, if such is well thought out, "this totality view stands over against the totality view" that arises from the different unbelieving approaches to and motifs in philosophizing.[15] "It will be our business then to take the totality picture of Christianity, and compare it with the totality picture of non-Christian thought."[16]

Because of the critical importance of worldviews in apologetical/epistemological disputes between believers and unbelievers, Van Til was critical of "atomistic" or "piecemeal" defenses of isolated elements of the complete Christian position. Such a procedure accepts the natural man's desire to assess individual Christian doctrines or claims in the wider and alien philosophical context of his own unbelieving framework. "And herewith they have at the same time lost all power to challenge the non-Christian methodology at the outset of its career."[17] Van Til stressed "the interdependence of the various aspects of" God's supernatural revelation of Himself as crucial to the self-attesting character of Scripture. He wrote:

> As soon as the elements of the special principle, such as the indications of divinity, the testimony of the Spirit, or the words of Christ are set next to one another, as largely independent of one another, the natural man is given an opportunity to do his destructive work. He is then allowed to judge at least with respect to one or more of these elements. And if he is allowed to judge of the legitimacy or meaning of any one of them he may as well be given the right to judge of all of them.[18]

14. *Defense of the Faith*, 47, 55, 70, 37, 218–19.
15. *The Reformed Pastor and Modern Thought* (Philadelphia: Presbyterian and Reformed, 1971), 36, 218.
16. *Defense of the Faith*, 41.
17. Ibid., 139.
18. Ibid., 361.

The Christian faith should not be defended one isolated belief after another isolated belief—as though a "block house" were being built up, one block at a time. Instead, the whole system should be presented and defended as a unit. Its epistemology should be defended in terms of its metaphysics and ethics (including anthropology and soteriology), and its metaphysics and ethics (including anthropology and soteriology) should be defended in terms of its epistemology.

ENTIRE SYSTEMS IN OPPOSITION[19]

Since the natural man assumes the idea of brute fact in metaphysics[20] and the idea of the autonomy of the human mind in epistemology,[21] the Reformed apologist realizes that he should first challenge these notions. He must challenge these notions in everything that he says about anything. It is these notions that determine the construction that the natural man puts upon everything that is presented to him. They are the colored glasses through which he sees all the facts. . . . [The Reformed apologist] will first present the facts for what they really are and then he will challenge the natural man by arguing that unless they are accepted for what they are according to the Christian interpretation of them, no facts mean anything at all.[22]

Here then are the facts, or some of the main facts that the Reformed apologist presents to the natural man. There is first the fact of God's self-contained existence. Second, the fact of creation in general and of man as made in God's image in particular. Third, there is the fact of the comprehensive plan and providence of God with respect to all that takes place in the universe. Then there is the fact of the fall of man and his subsequent sin. It is in relation to these facts and only in relation to these facts that the other facts pertaining to the redemptive work of Christ are what they are. . . . Thus there is one system of reality of which all that exists forms a part. And any individual fact of

19. Excerpts from *Defense of the Faith*, 164, 165, 166–67.
20. This is the view that there is no plan or purpose for events, and that the facts have no necessary relationship to each other and require no interpretive context to be known and understood; everything happens randomly, "by chance."
21. That is, man's mind does not depend upon divine thought and revelation in order to make sense out of things or know anything.
22. This is a synopsis of the "indirect" or two-step apologetical procedure that presuppositional apologetics advocates. The first step is to lay out the Christian worldview, in terms of which human experience is intelligible and the objections of the unbeliever can be contextually defeated. The second step is to show that within the unbeliever's worldview, nothing is intelligible—not even objections to the Christian's viewpoint. (The order in which these two steps in the argument are taken is not important.)

this system is what it is in this system. It is therefore a contradiction in terms to speak of presenting certain facts to men unless one presents them as parts of this system. . . .

It is natural that only the supernatural revelation of God can inform man about such a system as that. For this system is of a nature quite different from the systems of which the natural man speaks. For the latter a system is that which man, assumed to be ultimate, has ordered by his original structural activity. . . .

The idea of supernatural revelation is inherent in the very idea of this system of Christianity which we are seeking to present to the natural man. But if this is so then the idea of a supernatural, infallible inscripturated revelation is also inherent in this system. Man as the creature of God needs supernatural revelation and man, become a sinner, needs supernatural redemptive revelation. . . .

As a rational creature he [the sinner] can understand that one must either accept the whole of a system of truth or reject the whole of it. . . . He knows right well as a rational being that only the Reformed statement of Christianity is consistent with itself and therefore challenges the non-Christian position at every point. He can understand therefore why the Reformed theologian should accept the doctrine of Scripture as the infallible Word of God. He can understand the idea of its necessity, its perspicuity, its sufficiency and its authority as being involved in the Christian position as a whole.

But while understanding them as being involved in the position of Christianity as a whole, it is precisely Christianity as a whole, and therefore each of these doctrines as part of Christianity, that are meaningless to him as long as he is not willing to drop his own assumptions of autonomy and chance.

It follows that on the question of Scripture, as on every other question, the only possible way for the Christian to reason with the non-believer is by way of presupposition.[23]

ATOMISTIC APOLOGETICS A MISTAKE[24]

It has been pointed out that the difference between a Roman Catholic–Arminian and a Reformed type of argument[25] lies in the fact that the former is direct

23. That is, the Christian should compare the fundamental principles or most basic beliefs that determine the antithetical, general character and content of the whole worldviews advocated by the Christian and the non-Christian.
24. Excerpts from *Defense of the Faith*, 122–23, 131–32.
25. Van Til was here pointing to the difference between nonpresuppositional and presuppositional approaches to defending the faith, taking it for granted (in his la-

and the latter is indirect.[26] The former grants the essential truthfulness of the non-Christian theory of man and of method, while the latter challenges both. This difference will appear again and appear in its fundamental importance still more strikingly if the question of the place of Scripture in apologetics is brought up for consideration. A few remarks on this subject must suffice.

For better or for worse the Protestant apologist is committed to the doctrine of Scripture as the infallibly inspired final revelation of God to man. This being the case, he is committed to the defense of Christian theism as a unit. For him theism is not really theism unless it is Christian theism. The Protestant apologist cannot be concerned to prove the existence of any other God than the one who has spoken to man authoritatively and finally through Scripture.

The entire debate about theism will be purely formal unless theism be taken as the foundation of Christianity. But if it is so taken it is no longer theism as such but Christian theism that is in debate. Pantheists, deists and theists (that is bare theists) may formally agree that God exists. Socrates, in arguing about the nature of piety within Euthyphro says that men "join issue about particulars."[27] So if the whole debate in apologetics is to be more than a meaningless discussion about the *that* of God's existence and is to consider *what kind* of God exists, then the question of God's revelation to man must be brought into the picture. . . .

We have also seen that the method of presupposition requires the presentation of Christian theism as a unit. But the theology of Roman Catholics compels them to deal with theism first and with Christianity afterwards. As-

---

beling) that (1) Reformed doctrine represents the most consistent form of Protestant theology, and (2) that a consistent commitment to Reformed theology will lead one to see the need for arguing presuppositionally.

26. Two parties who disagree with each other can take a "direct" approach to "the facts" when they share the same basic assumptions or presuppositional framework for identifying and interpreting them. When they disagree in their presuppositions, however, what they identify as the facts and how they understand them will differ as well, in which case no direct appeal will be decisive. Instead, an "indirect" line of argument must be used, which discredits the opponent's presuppositions, for instance by showing that they are incoherent, entail something false, or have destructive consequences (e.g., the method of "reductio ad absurdum"). In an indirect argument, the two positions are compared with each other, thinking each one through "for argument's sake."

27. Verbal abstractions are conducive to the deceptive appearance of agreement between two conflicting schools of thought; given their generality or vagueness, abstractions can be readily endorsed by people. Who, after all, would want to stand against "love" or "fair play"? Nevertheless, when people who have conflicting philosophies of life say that they are all in favor of, say, "fair play," their agreement does not amount to much. Obviously, the dispute between them is about the particulars—about the specific content or application of "fair play."

signing to reason the task of interpreting nature without dependence upon Scripture, this theology is bound to prove the truth of theism first.[28] The theism that is proved in this way cannot be the only theism that any Christian should want to prove, namely, Christian theism. Yet having proved some sort of theism by reason, the Roman Catholic is bound by virtue of his theology to prove a type of Christianity that will fit on to the deformation of theism it has "established." And what holds true of Roman Catholicism holds true fundamentally also of Arminianism.

It remains now to indicate more fully than has been done that the Roman Catholic and Arminian method of reasoning is bound, not merely to cut the unity of Christian theism in two, but is bound even to prove its theism piece by piece. Romanism and Arminianism lead not merely to dualism but to atomism in methodology.[29]

A truly Protestant method of reasoning involves a stress upon the fact that the meaning of every aspect or part of Christian theism depends upon Christian theism as a unit. When Protestants speak of the resurrection of Christ

---

28. The Roman Catholic apologist (following the tradition of natural theology and theistic proofs) seeks first to prove to the natural man, by means of natural reason, that study of, and reflection upon, the realm of nature should lead him to conclude that there is a supernatural realm as well. That is, he seeks to prove the existence of *some kind of a god*. However, this supernatural force, principle, or person has already been adjusted to the preconceptions of reason and reality utilized by the unbeliever. Then, secondly, when the apologist tries to push further and argue for the adoption of Christianity in particular, the conception of Christianity that is defended must fit in with the theism that was previously established— that is, the distorted and stunted supernaturalism that natural theology laid down.

29. If the natural man, with his presumed autonomy, is granted the right to judge the credibility of any aspect of the Christian outlook—say, whether God exists or is personal and all-powerful—there is no good reason why he cannot demand the right to judge the rationality and acceptability of each and every doctrine that makes up the Christian faith. If it initially seems rational to conclude that Jehovah exists, but there are irrational premises that are essential to describing His character or actions (e.g., unbelievers will often object to the Trinity, predestination, the hypostatic union, and blood atonement), then belief in Jehovah is not rational after all. The whole system needs to be free of intellectually objectionable elements, the natural man can consistently contend, if the system is to be judged unobjectionable. At that point, Christian theology would have to be defended point by point, not as a whole. Nonpresuppositional apologists delude themselves when they think that the unbeliever, having been granted intellectual autonomy at the outset, will willingly abandon that autonomy at some point and bow his heart and mind to anything and everything in the Bible. Presuppositionalists are not willing to grant autonomy in the first place, arguing that biblical religion—the Christian worldview—must be adopted as a whole (even if only in principle and in the personal commitment of the convert, who subsequently needs to grow in detailed understanding of its specific teachings).

they speak of the resurrection of him who is the Son of God, the eternal Word through whom the world was made. The truth of theism is involved in this claim that Christians make with respect to the domain of history. And what is true of the resurrection of Christ is true with respect to all the propositions about historical fact that are made in Scripture. No proposition about historical fact is presented for what it really is till it is presented as a part of the system of Christian theism that is contained in Scripture.[30] To say this is involved in the consideration that all facts of the created universe are what they are by virtue of the plan of God with respect to them. Any fact in any realm confronted by man is what it is as revelational through and through of the God and of the Christ of Christian theism.

But if this is true—and it would seem to be of the very essence of the Biblical point of view to say that it is true—then it follows that *the whole claim of Christian theism is in question in any debate about any fact.*[31] Christian theism must be presented as that light in terms of which any proposition about any fact receives meaning.

5.2 The Antithesis in Attitude and Outlook

Christians and non-Christians, to repeat what has been said earlier, have an epistemological disagreement with each other. Christians claim that all men know God—that is, they believe important truths about the Creator and directly apprehend evidence that justifies those beliefs. Christians claim further that God as the Redeemer has given a saving and self-attesting revelation of Himself in the Scriptures, which is necessary to restore fallen man's rebellious mind and wayward reasoning. *Faith is thus prerequisite for a genuinely rational understanding of anything.* This is the evidence for the previous claims that men directly grasp the God-given evidence in nature for the Creator, and in Scripture for the Redeemer.

30. Van Til was concerned that evidentialist approaches to apologetics constantly overlook this salient fact. To demonstrate the historical likelihood that a particular human corpse was once resuscitated would not establish the biblical doctrine of Christ's resurrection—not simply because it does not say enough, but because the bare claims that are being expressed are not conceptualized in a Christian fashion. Without the broader framework of Christian theology, all that would be demonstrated would be a freak event in a world of chance.
31. Emphasis added. The apologetical argument pertains to the intelligibility of any facts, not simply the truth or significance of certain "special" facts. Van Til insisted that the unbeliever does not simply miss the factuality and import of, say, miraculous events; given his presuppositions, he misses the possibility of the meaningfulness of each and every fact of experience (including miracles in history).

But non-Christians reject these claims, asserting instead that Christians do not know these things to be true (that is, are not justified in what they allege)—and/or that certain things that men do know disprove the Christian position. So believer and unbeliever disagree with each other epistemologically. Their dispute over epistemological matters, however, must inevitably be carried out in the wider context of the conflicting philosophical systems that coordinate what they maintain about reality, ethics, and epistemology. According to presuppositional apologetics, within the worldview of the unbeliever one cannot devise and sustain an intelligible account of human knowledge or rationality, whereas just such a grounding and rationale for epistemology is provided by the biblical worldview. *Faith is the necessary foundation or framework for rationality and understanding.*

In order to press this epistemologically oriented apologetic argument for the truth of Christianity successfully, the apologist must clearly grasp the principial conflict in philosophical positions, think and reason in terms of it, and constantly lay out for the unbeliever this fundamental clash in perspectives as the *defining and determinative context* for their argument with each other. The Christian should intellectually defend his faith in terms of, and with a clear conceptualization of, the ideological and personal antithesis between believers and unbelievers.

To begin with, we can hardly forget (even if we sometimes overlook) the fact that interpreting the world, reasoning about life, and developing philosophical convictions are things done by persons, not by mechanical devices like computers. Personal qualities and factors (attitudes, desires, aims, prejudices, and defects) will be operative in any expression of opinion, line of reasoning, system of thought, or interpretation. Because there is a fundamental moral and spiritual contrast between believer and unbeliever—one is seeking to glorify God and understand the world in the light of God's word, while the other is self-seeking and in rebellion against God's word—the way in which they reason and argue will manifest an antithesis in attitude. Their subjective difference in attitude will affect everything they touch—everything about which they think and express themselves. "Their epistemology is informed by their ethical hostility to God," as Van Til said.[32]

Thus, Van Til held that there are no main points, systematically basic principles, or central truths in philosophy where the disagree-

---

32. *Defense of the Faith*, 189.

ment between the believer and the unbeliever will not be seen. The conflict between their attitudes always goes hand in hand with an antithesis in their philosophical outlooks. Abraham Kuyper had taught that there is a conflict between "the natural principle" of interpretation and "the supernatural principle" of interpretation, which makes antithesis inevitable, but then he pulled back from applying the antithesis to intellectual reasoning pertaining to "external" or merely "formal" matters, like weighing or counting or logic. Attempting to be more consistent with Kuyper's basic insights and teaching, Van Til disagreed with Kuyper at this point,[33] saying that the antithesis between the thinking of the believer and the thinking of the unbeliever must be systematic and total.

Of course, we must distinguish between the actual operating beliefs of a person and the systems of philosophy or interpretation that he professes and advocates. According to Van Til, the philosophical systems of the believer and the unbeliever are in principle (that is, with regard to their essential character and consistent claims) utterly antithetical to each other. Although men themselves *as men* may not be entirely true to their fundamental presuppositions about reality, knowledge, and ethics, the positions that they espouse as a presuppositional perspective have a distinctive identity *as ideas*. The philosophical conception of life, reality, and knowing that is promoted by the non-Christian stands in irresolvable opposition (as well as personal antagonism) to the philosophical conception of the Christian. The ideal positions of the two opponents are diametrically opposed to each other with regard to their presuppositions or worldviews. As systems of philosophy, they have different starting points, methods, standards, and conclusions. According to what believers and unbelievers say, there is a stark contrast between the ways in which they fundamentally understand man, the world, and knowing—as well as formal logic, counting, etc.

Van Til taught that this antithesis is not perfectly carried out in the practice and thinking of the unbeliever (or the believer, for that matter). Indeed, the antithesis cannot be consistently and self-consciously realized until the consummation of history—the day of final judgment, when believers and unbelievers will be definitively and eternally separated. Until that time, the Spirit of God continues to strive with men, keeping them from working out their intellectual and moral re-

33. See ibid., 288–300.

bellion against God to its bitter end. Because of the common grace (restraint) of God, both the intellectual disagreement (antithesis) and the intellectual agreement (commonality, cooperation) between believers and unbelievers throughout the course of history must be spoken of in a qualified fashion. In practice, there is no unqualified antithesis, or unqualified commonality (that is, no agreement unaffected by differences in contextual understanding, personal attitude, and application).[34] Because of these qualifications in practice, thought Van Til, we can allow for a wider area of cooperation than did Kuyper (going beyond formalities or external matters and pertaining with qualification to all thinking). At the same time, we must insist against Kuyper that the antithesis is more inclusive (it applies in qualified form even to weighing, counting, and logic). In terms of philosophical systems, and as a matter of principle, the antithesis between Christianity and its challengers is unconditional and uncompromising. On peripheral and incidental matters, however, the unbeliever does not "live up to his principles" and ends up agreeing with the believer, especially on mundane matters of everyday life. This incongruity was seen by Van Til as an issue of personal biography or psychology.

Van Til urged Christians to be ever cognizant of the uniqueness of what God has revealed about Himself, developing their theology and apologetics with utter consistency and personal loyalty to His word. Moreover, to prevent any weakening of the intellectual challenge of the gospel, apologists must press their unbelieving opponents likewise to be fully, logically, and unsparingly consistent with their own espoused presuppositions. When this is done, there is no room for dividing the field of knowledge into two compartments, one dealing with nature and secular concerns, and the other touching the personal, sacred, or supernatural dimension of reality. It would be deadly to the aims of apologetics to suggest to the unbeliever that he is basically right about himself (as a knower) and basically right about the world (the objects of knowledge), and simply needs to add the supernatural dimension of grace to his outlook. He will understandably expect that, as he has been intellectually competent to be the judge in secular matters, any hypotheses about sacred issues are subject to

---

34. In this regard, Van Til called for believers to be very careful when talking about generalizations or abstractions (e.g., "mankind," "reason," "existence," "possibility," "justice") that by their very nature tend to gloss over relevant and important philosophical differences in the way that conflicting worldviews understand them.

his autonomous judgment as well—and must be "trimmed" to accommodate his personal expectations. That is why Van Til insisted that the Christian not compromise with the basic principles of non-Christian philosophical conceptions and commitments, not even to make common cause with the "best" or "highest" of unbelieving systems of thought. If we fail to keep the principial conflict always in view when we defend the faith, we grant undeserved intellectual favors to the unbeliever (not squeezing the philosophical problems with his position as tightly as it deserves) and tempt ourselves to adopt with the unbeliever a measure of autonomous intellectual authority (not bringing *every* thought captive to the obedience of Christ).

Presuppositional apologetics calls for believers to be steadfast about the antithesis if they would defend the uniqueness, exclusivity, and indispensability of the Christian faith. This explains why Satan's ploy throughout history has been to get God's people to neglect or minimize the enmity (the antithesis) between themselves and the seed of the serpent. That antagonism is a persistent and profoundly important biblical theme.[35] Its significance for apologetics is illustrated by the way Scripture speaks of non-Christians as "enemies in their minds" (Col. 1:21). Elsewhere, Paul wrote that "the mind of the flesh is enmity against God; for it is not subject to the law of God, neither indeed can it be" (Rom. 8:7). The Christian apologist must take realistic appraisal of the intellectual antagonism and contrast between the believer and the unbeliever. "The implication of all this for Christian apologetics is plain. There can be no appeasement between those who presuppose in all their thought the sovereign God and those who presuppose in all their thought the would-be sovereign man."[36]

Van Til's proposal, therefore, for a consistent method in defending the faith was that "we no longer make an appeal to 'common notions' which Christian and non-Christian agree on, but to the 'common ground' which they actually have because man and his world are what Scripture says they are." And then, he proposed that we "set the non-Christian principle of the rational autonomy of man against the Christian principle of the dependence of man's knowledge on God's knowledge as revealed in the person and by the Spirit of Christ."[37] As Van Til was previously quoted to

35. Cf. Greg L. Bahnsen, "At War with the Word: the Necessity of Biblical Antithesis," *Antithesis* 1 (January–February 1990): 6–11, 48–54.
36. *The Intellectual Challenge of the Gospel* (London: Tyndale Press, 1950; reprint, Phillipsburg, N.J.: Lewis J. Grotenhuis, 1953), 40.
37. "My Credo," in *Jerusalem and Athens*, ed. E. R. Geehan (Philadelphia: Presbyterian and Reformed, 1971), 21.

say: "It is necessary to become aware of the deep antithesis between the two main types of epistemology. . . . [T]he whole fight is one about two mutually opposite philosophies of life."[38]

In Van Til's perspective (as in Scripture as well), there are only two fundamental outlooks: the Christian and the non-Christian. "*Every method, the supposedly neutral one no less than any other, presupposes either the truth or the falsity of Christian theism.*"[39] One either has "the mind of Christ" (1 Cor. 2:16) or is an "enemy in your mind" (Col. 1:21). If you are not taught the truth in Jesus and "renewed in the spirit of your mind," then you necessarily "walk in the vanity of [your] mind" (Eph. 4:17–24; on intellectual "vanity," cf. Rom. 1:21; Col. 2:8). One either begins his thinking with the triune God who has clearly revealed Himself as the one who created and providentially controls all things, and who graciously saves His people by the redemptive work of the incarnate Son applied by the Holy Spirit—or one does not begin one's thinking with this presupposition. Middle ground is excluded. At base, there are only two options. Of course, there are numerous variations and "family squabbles" within the two fundamental positions. Those whose starting point is the Christian worldview do not all see eye to eye on every subordinate doctrinal point within the biblical system of truth (e.g., on infant baptism or eschatology).[40] Those whose

38. *Survey of Christian Epistemology*, v, 7.
39. *Defense of the Faith*, 117. It is absolutely crucial that transcendental argumentation begin by positing that Christian theism is either true or false (see chap. 7 below). Van Til's defense of the faith does not require the apologist to be aware of and refute every single variation of unbelieving philosophy, but only the presupposition common to them all (namely, the rejection of Christian theism). Many apologists mistakenly imagine that there are really three options available: one may accept Christianity, reject it, or be "undecided." But, as Van Til recognized, to be undecided about the claim that Christian theism is the presupposition necessary to make sense out of any reasoning whatsoever, is to begin one's reasoning on the operational assumption that this claim is false (and can be laid aside as one proceeds to research and develop one's views). Since there are only two options at the most fundamental level—the truth or falsity of Christian theism as a presupposition—the refutation of the unbelieving one (in whatever illustrative variation it appears) is an indirect proof of the other.
40. However, they do maintain that there is objective truth regarding these matters, and that truth is part and parcel of the overall Christian worldview. Should the Bible be mistaken in what it teaches about such an issue (regardless of what that teaching turns out to be), the Christian worldview as a system of truth resting upon the authority of divine revelation would be refuted. "The Scripture cannot be broken," as Jesus declared (John 10:35). Every truth revealed in Scripture is part and parcel of the Christian worldview that we defend as a whole; every one is "necessary" to the position we defend, in the sense that if it should fail to be true, the system itself (which claims that truth as an integral part) would not be infallible. This does not

starting point is not the Christian worldview revealed in Scripture, while sharing this attitude with each other, differ from one another on other points—for instance, whether reality is basically changing or unchanging (Heraclitus versus Parmenides), whether knowledge is conceptual or empirical (Descartes versus Locke), whether reasoning gives insight into reality or distorts it (Hegel versus Schopenhauer), etc. The various non-Christian schools of philosophy display interesting and relevant disagreements, but their fundamental agreement in repudiating the Christian starting point is what is of utmost significance for apologetics.[41] Unbelieving positions are simply a series of illustrations of the same underlying position that rejects Christianity as its presupposition. This may not be how things are pictured in most histories of philosophy (since most of them were not written from a distinctively Christian perspective), but it is the conceptual scheme of the wisest man who ever lived: "He who is not with me is against me" (Matt. 12:30).

What, then, are some of the crucial philosophical differences between the Christian and the non-Christian that have a bearing upon epistemology and display the stark antithesis in outlook between them? Van Til would have us begin by noting the personalism of Christian theism as a philosophical perspective grounded in revelation, over against the impersonalism of non-Christian philosophical speculation. The Christian thinks about himself and about everything in the world as being intimately related to God—created, controlled, and preinterpreted by Him. Our aim is to know Him better, to see His glory and wisdom worked out in the world, to respond in obedience and praise, etc. This is not at all the primary perspective of the unbeliever. He holds that we must begin with the "hard, cold, dry, lifeless" facts that are found in an impersonal environment of randomness; any "personal" considerations (self-consciousness, man as a free personality, creativity, dignity, purpose, moral standards, etc.) must be

mean that every biblical doctrine will be as directly relevant as any other in dealing with specific philosophical issues; the apologist obviously refers more often to the sovereign providence of God than to infant baptism when confronting the philosophical problem of inductive reasoning. But that sovereign providence is, nevertheless, the sovereign providence of the covenant-keeping God who calls for the children of believers to be baptized. The overall system conditions how we understand each of its parts.

41. Van Til would find an example of this disagreement-within-agreement in the fact that the Jews and the Romans—who despised each other in certain respects— were at one with each other and cooperated in the broader context of rejecting and crucifying the Lord of glory (cf. Acts 4:27).

secondary qualities or realities that somehow evolved by chance from the more fundamental building blocks of matter or energy. As Christians, everything we do and everything we think about must be understood in the context of God's personal character and activity (creation of all things, providential and sovereign government in history, clear revelation of Himself, etc.): "In Him we live and move and have our existence" (Acts 17:28). For non-Christians, none of that is relevant—certainly not from the outset of philosophical reasoning or interpretation. Speculation takes impersonal matter, particles, motion, physical events, natural laws (or whatever) as the ultimate elements of reality, in terms of which we are to explain everything and guide our thinking and living. The universe is basically impersonal, and thus all questions that occupy our thinking are viewed in an impersonal framework or context.

For the Christian, all the facts are part of God's personal plan and serve His personal purpose; all of the laws by which we relate the facts (whether conceptually, logically, or causally) are a reflection of God's personal mind and His ordering of reality. Man's mind was created to imitate God's thinking with respect to these personally qualified facts and personally qualified laws. God's personal influence over all the objects of knowledge as well as the mind of man, and His purpose to have man understand and control the facts of his environment, provide for the possibility of the mind accurately apprehending the extramental world. Every thing and every event must be ultimately related to God (who controls the relations between things and between events) in order to be part of a coherent and intelligible system. But for the non-Christian, the impersonal, spatio-temporal universe either exists by itself or is intelligible in itself, without reference to God. Things and events are simply what they are, with no need for (or possibility of) more basic explanation. The facts are "brute"—that is, particulars unrelated to any plan or interpretation. The universe consists of purely random matter, moving completely according to chance. The connecting links between brute facts—whether concepts or laws—exist apart from God as abstract, impersonal, and apparently self-existent universals. Facts and events cannot be known, much less interpreted, in advance, thus making any hypothesis as credible as any other hypothesis prior to investigation and/or prior to historical eventuation. "On a non-Christian basis facts are 'rationalized' for the first time when interpreted by man. But for one who holds that the facts are already part of an ultimately rational system by virtue of the plan of God it is clear that such hypotheses as presuppose the non-existence of such a plan must, even from the outset of his investigation, be considered irrelevant."[42]

The Christian submits to the self-identifying, self-authorizing, final authority of God for all he does or thinks, but the non-Christian takes for granted that this kind of authority belongs to himself. Man presumes to interpret and explain himself by his own internal principles and to give the original interpretation to the brute facts in a random universe. Indeed, every aspect of reality is subject to the reference point, prescriptive values, and autonomy of man's interpretive efforts. The Christian, by contrast, takes God to be the ultimate interpreter and God's mind to be the appropriate reference point for reasoning. The unbeliever seeks abstract and general principles about truth, about reality, and even about whatever gods there may be, while the Christian follows principles that are concrete and personal, revealed by and revelatory of God Himself. The unbeliever assumes that man and the facts of his environment can be understood intelligibly whether or not there is a God who created the universe. Both the facts and the mind of man are assumed to be self-existent and independent of any God. Finally, the unbeliever takes man to be morally innocent, even if as yet ignorant. He is certainly not, as the Christian worldview maintains, willfully blind, morally rebellious, and spiritually lost.

The antithesis (in principle) between the philosophical systems of unbelievers and the philosophical system of believers is so broad and basic that it even affects the way they deal with central philosophical notions like logic, possibility, and objectivity (to mention but a few). This observation should not be misunderstood. The presuppositionalist does not say that Christians and non-Christians inevitably accept and operate with completely different, specific laws of logic in their practical exercises of reasoning. Yet they do clearly disagree with each other concerning the nature, source, and authority of the laws of logic. Both worldviews may endorse and utilize the disjunctive syllogism or De Morgan's theorems, but when we inquire into what they are talking about, the evidence that is appropriate or persuasive for their claims (about syllogisms, theorems, etc.), or the necessity of the truths about logic, we get radically different answers—which almost always betray differing convictions regarding metaphysics.

---

42. *Defense of the Faith*, 116. Cf. p. 165: "For the [natural man] a system is that which man, assumed to be ultimate, has ordered by his original structural activity. The natural man virtually attributes to himself that which a true Christian theology attributes to the self-contained God."

Similarly, both Christians and non-Christians seem to have similar concepts of "possibility" (or, correspondingly, "impossibility" and the related idea of "necessity"), and yet the differences in their understanding of possibility turn out to be fundamental. Throughout the history of philosophy, the notion of possibility has been handled in various ways. Philosophers have first discussed conceptual possibility, but have disagreed on whether to understand it psychologically (that which is clearly conceivable), logically (that which is describable without contradiction), or linguistically (that which fits conventional usage)—or whether to simply dismiss the notion as muddled and mysterious. Philosophers have also argued over physical (or "nomological") possibility, but have disagreed strongly on how to analyze something like a law of nature. Events (or truths) have also been considered "possible" relative to some set of conditions. Accordingly, "abilities" or "capacities" are considered possibilities for achieving some effect under particular circumstances (described hypothetically or with subjunctive conditionals). Truths or states of affairs have likewise been spoken of as "possible" when the speaker is implicitly referring to our present state of knowledge or the available evidence for such truths or states of affairs—which (ironically) makes possibility contingent, changing, or subject to degrees. The important point is that throughout the history of philosophy, views on possibility have been strongly influenced by metaphysical convictions—for instance, about forms or ideals, essences, potentialities, laws of nature, determinism, the plenitude of Being, God's freedom, the perfection of reality (or the world), striving toward actuality, the uniqueness and discreteness of men's minds, various materialistic dogmas—or by antipathy toward metaphysical discussion.

Van Til did not address specific disputes between philosophers or contemporary debates regarding possibility, but he realized that Christians are committed to hold certain beliefs about possibility that unbelievers will reject. "It is today more evident than ever before that it is exactly on those most fundamental matters, such as possibility and probability, that there is the greatest difference of opinion between theists and antitheists."[43] To put it simply and memorably: "Non-believers have false assumptions about their *musts*."[44] Van Til was particularly keen to observe

---

43. *An Introduction to Systematic Theology*, In Defense of the Faith, vol. 5 (Philadelphia: Presbyterian and Reformed, 1974), 36.
44. *Defense of the Faith*, 264. That is, they utilize a false philosophical outlook regarding "necessity," "possibility," etc.

that "abstract possibility" must not be "placed higher than God"[45]—a metaphor for asserting that God is not enveloped (and does not have His source) in a broader kind of "possibility"; rather, there are no "possibilities" that are independent of Him, His knowledge, or His plan.[46] "The meaning of the word *possibility* is first determined by the God who has spoken to sinners through *the* book [the Bible]. That, and only that, is possible which the God of the Bible determines."[47] So the antithesis with unbelieving thought is felt at this most basic philosophical level. "For the Christian, God legislates as to what is possible and what is impossible for man. For the non-Christian, man determines this for himself. Either positively or negatively the non-Christian will determine the field of possibility and therewith the stream of history by means of the law of contradiction. This means that for the non-Christian the concepts that he employs while using the law of contradiction are taken to be exhaustive of the 'essence of the thing' they seek to express."[48] Van Til detected subtle intellectual arrogance even in the way unbelievers treat possibility. "The law of non-contradiction employed positively or negatively by man assuming his own ultimacy, is made the standard of what is possible or impossible, both for men and for whatever 'gods' may be. But on this basis the Bible cannot speak to man or any God whose revelation and whose very nature is not essentially penetrable to the natural intellect of man."[49] Neither man's mind nor "reason" has the prerogative of deciding whether a thing is possible or impossible.[50] According to the Christian perspective, "the God of Christianity is the God whose counsel or plan is the source of possibility. The word 'possibility' has no possible meaning except upon the presupposition of the existence of the self-contained ontological Trinity as the source of it."[51] So one takes possibility to be determined either by God's plan or by "chance" (variously called

45. Ibid., 274.
46. See *Introduction to Systematic Theology*, 37, 38, 235; *Defense of the Faith*, 297, 417.
47. *Intellectual Challenge of the Gospel*, 20.
48. "A Reply to Criticism," in *Common Grace and the Gospel* (Philadelphia: Presbyterian and Reformed, 1972), 200–201.
49. *Reformed Pastor and Modern Thought*, 33. An obvious example would be when men say that God cannot foreordain the freely chosen actions of men—that it is not possible because they do not understand how He could do so. (Notice here that even the alleged contradiction involved—that a man "could," yet "could not" do other than he actually does—rests upon words pertaining to some doctrine of metaphysical possibilities.)
50. *Defense of the Faith*, 298. Even when the Christian rules out something as a logical contradiction, he finds the normativity and authority of the standards of logic in the character of God—in which case "it is logically impossible" is shorthand for "God's thinking and standards for our reasoning in subservience to Him render it impossible."
51. *Introduction to Systematic Theology*, 114–15.

"experience" or "logic"), said Van Til,[52] but the latter is ruled out because the existence of God must be presupposed as the basis for the *intelligibility* of any possibility or probability.[53] Accordingly, "the true God is not surrounded by, but is the source of, possibility. *He could not possibly not exist*. We cannot intelligently think away God's existence."[54] "From the Christian point of view, it is impossible to think of the non-existence of God."[55] "He himself exists as a necessary being."[56] None of this will be acceptable to the thinking of the unbelieving philosopher (to understate the obvious), which only underscores the point we are making in this section—namely, that there is an utter antithesis in outlook between the worldview of the Christian and that of the non-Christian.

This can again be seen in the case of "objectivity." Philosophers have typically sought to defend propositions that are true in a public sense, regardless of any particular person's feelings or attitudes or beliefs. To collapse truth into personal belief (subjectivism), with the corollary adoption of relativism, has spelled death for the respectability and authority of philosophical reasoning; the critical examination of ourselves and of what we believe is hardly relevant or important unless objective truth and objective values are attainable. But since the person who believes whatever propositions we wish to consider has prejudices, feelings, aims, blind spots, a personal perspective, etc., the influence of subjectivity poses difficulties for the very possibility of objectivity. Both believer and unbeliever—to the degree they take apologetical dispute seriously—want to maintain that their positions are objectively true (or at least closer to the objective ideal of truth than the other's). However, as Van Til realized, this should not lure us into thinking naively that the conflicting worldviews will understand the concept of objectivity (or how to achieve it) in the same way. A difference is to be expected because objectivity is a fundamental value, and is therefore defined by the presuppositions of the worldview itself.

For Plato, objectivity exists independently of the will or expression of God (the gods), as well as independently of the world and man's

---

52. "Particularism and Common Grace," in *Common Grace and the Gospel*, 102–3.
53. *Reformed Pastor and Modern Thought*, 98.
54. "Common Grace and Witness-Bearing," in *Common Grace and the Gospel*, 131 (emphasis added).
55. *Introduction to Systematic Theology*, 9–10.
56. Ibid., 235. Advanced students may want to reflect on the implications of Van Til's remarks here for a revised, presuppositional version of an "ontological argument."

experience of it—in a realm above both man and God.[57] Man's mind participates in this transcendent ideal realm (recollecting the forms), according to Plato, and thus objectivity (unchanging and universal truth) depends upon man's reasoning, not upon divine revelation.[58] In the history of philosophy, empiricists have disagreed with Plato's metaphysics, his epistemology, and (not surprisingly) his view of objectivity. For them, objectivity is still centered in the mind of man, but now as it passively receives sensations and observes the facts (as a *tabula rasa*, as John Locke put it); "the objectivity of knowledge is thus guaranteed, because the mind receives the facts *just as they are.*"[59] But Kant knew better than this. The reasoning mind is not in fact passive, but plays an active role in forming its ideas, imposing conditions and concepts upon the external stimuli. For Kant, objects are partly a product of the mind's own activity, and thus he found the objectivity of phenomenal truth "in the organizing activity of the mind," which stands over against (and never knows in itself) the realm of space-time factuality.[60] The irony here is that Kant "saved science" (and the objective, universal validity of causation, for instance) by psychologizing it—by making it the result of what the mind imposes upon raw experience. Things have become so philosophically perverse that objectivity is saved by subjectivity!

Van Til wanted apologists who aimed to be thoroughly self-conscious in their philosophical reasoning and faithful to their Christian worldview to realize that different schools of thought maintain different conceptions of objectivity (in accordance with their underlying metaphysical, epistemological, and ethical commitments). Christians reject any idea that truth is subjective. Indeed, it would be selling out the Christian faith to defend it as only subjectively true (or to suggest that religious truth is a matter of one's subjective choices or feelings). Nevertheless, if we hold consistently to our Christian commitments, we find ultimate objectivity in God's point of view—in divine revelation, not in human reason. The non-Christian will not accept God's revelation as the ultimate standard of truth, and he will therefore accuse the believer of "subjective prejudice" for evaluating all things according to that presupposition. Inevitably, arguments over objectivity become "circular," for the way in which one views it

57. *Case for Calvinism*, 118–20.
58. *Reformed Pastor and Modern Thought*, 81.
59. Ibid., 108.
60. Ibid., 114.

stems from one's controlling presuppositions. There are really no two ways about it, nor is there any middle ground. The two worldviews operate with different notions of objectivity.

Apologists are led into errant and compromising methodologies, taught Van Til, when they fail to recognize this and therefore adopt non-Christian conceptions of objectivity (along with related elements of the non-Christian worldview). For instance:

> For Beegle, objectivity is found in the facts as they exist, whether or not God controls them. After all, says Beegle, the human mind does not create the evidence. All that "human reason can do is to function properly with the data that are furnished it" (*Ibid.*, p. 64).[61] But then for Beegle the same thing is true for God, who has created the facts of the world. According to Beegle man must not identify objectivity with anything that God says in the Bible. . . . But whatever Beegle may mean when he says that the statements of Scripture with respect to inspiration are *primary* data, this much is clear: in merely regarding these statements as *data* which must be correlated with other data, man, to all intents and purposes, becomes the arbiter of truth and error. In spite of what Beegle says about man finding objectivity rather than making it, his view makes man the final arbiter of truth. . . .
>
> On such a view as Beegle offers nobody knows objectivity, nobody knows truth [in advance]. Beegle starts with the idea of abstract truth in order to escape circular reasoning. The only way to escape the process of circular reasoning with respect to the authority of Jesus and the Scriptures, argues Beegle, "is to employ our reason objectively with respect to all the evidence, Biblical or otherwise" (*Ibid.*, p. 63). Of course, says Beegle, even when we employ reason objectively with respect to all the evidence we cannot attain "perfect objectivity." For "in spite of our sincere efforts we bring to the task of interpretation certain unconscious presuppositions that have become a part of us during our formative years" (*Ibid.*, p. 63). . . .
>
> Having made his concession with respect to the restricting influence of unconscious presuppositions on the interpretive activity of the human mind, Beegle goes on to say that "we are nonetheless

---

61. Van Til is here analyzing Dewey M. Beegle's book, *The Inspiration of Scripture* (Philadelphia: Westminster, [1963]). Beegle endorsed an inductive method of testing or evaluating the truth-claims of the Bible.

dependent on reason; for we must use it to help isolate and set aside, as far as possible, even our restricting assumptions" (*Idem*).[62]

We note now that all of this sorting activity of reason is supposed to pertain to an activity of reason which, as noted, has no effect on the question of objectivity at all, for as noted, "the factor of truth and error is settled before human reason comes on the scene" (*Ibid*., p. 64). And yet reason must sift and sort *in order to find objectivity*.[63]

By working with the notion that objectivity is the presuppositionless (neutral) activity of reason as it sorts "the facts" that are outside the mind and isolates "our restricting assumptions" that are within the mind, Beegle had to admit that reason is not really objective (neutral), but influenced by unconscious assumptions. To save his concept of objectivity, then, Beegle assigned to reason the task of isolating and setting aside our assumptions. Somehow reason, which is not objective in itself, is supposed to regain objectivity for itself! And under this artificial and incoherent conception of objectivity, Beegle subjects God's word to an assessment of its objectivity by man's reason as it explores the facts (a process that is admittedly nonobjective, but feigns self-objectification). For Van Til, objectivity in the Christian worldview is not a matter of having *no* presuppositions (and letting a pretended neutral reason find the pretended external truth, which is actually organized by the subjective mind of man), but a matter of having the *right* presuppositions—that is, having the divine point of view gained through revelation.

So then, if we may summarize, the worldview of the Christian and the worldview of the non-Christian—the context within which their epistemological disagreements will be debated—subtly, yet profoundly disagree with each other. There is an antithesis in philosophical outlook that touches on the personal or impersonal nature of both reality and reasoning, the random or divinely preinterpreted (preplanned) character of events, final authority and value, the self-sufficiency of man's mind as an interpreter, man's nature and envi-

---

62. The careful reader should not overlook in this remark by Beegle the equivocating shift from using reason as a tool of the intellect (reasoning) to using reason as the judge (say, of the objectivity) of whatever the intellect reasons about. We reason about our assumptions, to be sure, but that does not make reason somehow the value or authority by which we assess our assumptions (as to their objectivity or anything else).

63. *The Protestant Doctrine of Scripture*, In Defense of the Faith, vol. 1 (Philadelphia: Presbyterian and Reformed, 1967), 80–81.

ronment, facts, abstract concepts or principles, universals, logic, possibility, objectivity, etc. The following selections from Van Til throw light on the antithesis between the believer and the unbeliever in both their different religious attitudes and their different philosophical perspectives.

CHRISTIANITY IN CONFLICT[64]

And Christ can only be seen for what he is and for what he has done through the Scriptures as his Word.

Of course there has been a struggle about this Word as the Word of Christ. Satan is today doing his best to have men believe that no such thing as a transition from wrath to grace *can* take place in the person and work of Christ. As an aspect of this effort, he is also doing his best to have men believe that even if such a transition had taken place in history we could not learn of it in Scripture, for Scripture is itself a product of human experience.[65]

There is then not a square inch of space where, nor a minute of time when, the believer in Christ can withdraw from the responsibility of being a soldier of the cross. He must put on the whole armor of Christ for defensive warfare, to be sure, but ultimately for offensive warfare. Satan must be driven from the field and Christ must rule. . . .

The whole of the story of Christianity in conflict must start from this self-identification of Jesus.

In saying this, we are already in the midst of conflict. In fact, in saying this we are at the center of the conflict as it has always been carried on and as it is being carried on today. Current, *i.e.* post-Kantian, philosophy of history insists that, to be truly scientific, we must say that we *can* have no knowledge of either man or God and of a personal relation between them. And the rea-

---

64. Excerpts from *Christianity in Conflict* (Philadelphia: Westminster Theological Seminary, 1962–64), vol. 1, pt. 1, pp. ii, 1–3, 5, 17, 18, 27, 33, 43. The syllabus at this point discusses the earliest days of apologetic endeavor in the history of the church. The interested reader is strongly encouraged to obtain this massive work.

65. The reason for this is that no merely human authority is sufficient to speak universally, absolutely, and with divine prerogative about man, his place and purpose, and his guilt, much less about his redemption and destiny. Thus, Satan's strategy is to reduce any putative revelation to human experience that must be identified and verified by human experience and reasoning. Over against this, the Christian receives revelation as God's word (in human words), which is identified as such and verified by God's own selfsame word (in human words). Accordingly, as Van Til goes on to say, apologetics is at base the conflict between self-identifying and self-attesting interpreters: the sinner on the one hand and the Creator-Redeemer on the other.

son why we *can* have no knowledge of God is, on Kant's basis, in the last analysis, based on the assumption that man must first identify himself in terms of himself before he can say anything about God. In other words, in Kant's philosophy it is man who takes the place of God. In Christianity, God is the original self-affirming one; in Kant's philosophy it is man who is the original self-affirming one. In Christianity, it is God who in Christ calls men away from the folly of his would-be ultimate self-assertion. He tells men that no one knows the Father but the Son and no one knows the Son or can come to the Son except the Father draw him. It is with this background of utter self-affirmation that Christ says, "Come unto me, all ye that labour and are heavy laden, and I will give you rest." . . .

Only Christ himself can tell us this news. He testifies to himself in the Bible as a whole and in the New Testament in particular. Therefore as the acts or works of redemption performed for us by Christ in history were finished once for all, so his testimony to these acts was finished once for all. Herein lies the reason, says Herman Ridderbos, that it is impossible to be confronted with the acts of God elsewhere than through the witness of Christ to himself in the New Testament.[66] . . .

Shall we first interpret ourselves, our finitude, our sin, our evil plight in terms of criteria taken from ourselves or from the world and then turn to Jesus Christ for help in time of need?

We can well understand and must deeply sympathize with those who have attempted to follow either of these ways. The question of the "human factor" in Scripture allows of no easy solution. There are detailed questions of text and there is the general question of the nature and extent of the canon. But back of all these questions lies the much deeper, the ultimate question, with respect to the nature of Christ. We appear to have no way of knowing who and what he is unless he tells us about himself. And if he tells us that he was from all eternity "in the form of God," that he was "with God" and that for our sins and our salvation he "was made in the likeness of men, and being found in fashion as a man, he humbled himself, and became obedient unto death, even the death of the cross" then we dare not say that such a Christ *cannot* exist.

On the other hand we dare not assert that because as the eternal Son of God, equal in power and glory with the Father and the Holy Spirit, he is not fully comprehensible to us that therefore he cannot clearly reveal himself to us. In short, we dare not think that we already largely know who and what we are, and what the environment we live in consists of, how fact is related

66. CVT: *Heilsgeschiedenis en Heilige Schrift*, Chapter 11.

to logic or logic to fact, and then turn to Christ for further light or further help.[67] It is that point of view precisely from which we have been saved by the grace of God in Christ.

Right gladly do we then, by the help of his Spirit, submit our thoughts, our interpretation of the whole of human life and cosmic history, to the obedience of Christ. . . .

The Christ who tells us what he is and what we are, what he has done and what we have done and must do, the Christ whose face as Creator and Redeemer we cannot but see in the words of Scripture, this Christ we would teach all men to proclaim, to witness to, and to explain in secondary and subservient fashion. Heralds, witness-bearers, truth-proclaimers they must be.

The whole world lieth in darkness. All men keep down the truth confronting them, even the truth of Christ, the Son of God through whom the world is made, in unrighteousness.[68] Hence the wrath of God abides upon them. To teach men everywhere to flee from the wrath to come, to be saved for this life and for the life to come, and all to the praise of his grace, that is what the followers of Christ must learn to do. It is easy for any of us to think that we have good reasons, reasons of fact, reasons of logic, reasons derived from our moral consciousness and our sense of freedom, to depart from this historic position with respect to the Person of Christ. But if we thus depart, then we must also assume the responsibility for supplying a positive foundation from which life and history may be seen to have meaning without this Christ.[69] . . .

But if men insist that the Christ of the Scriptures cannot be accepted because of the facts of history, because of the demands of logic, and, basic to all, because of the rightful requirements of human personality, then we beg of them, in Christ's name, lest facts, logic and human personality all be lost, to permit themselves and the whole world to be interpreted by Christ as he continues to confront them in the words of Scripture. The Christ that has determinate character as *vere deus, vere homo*, the Son of God incarnate, the

---

67. If the word of Christ is merely supplemental to, and depends for its acceptability on, man's self-sufficient understanding of himself, his world, facts, logic, etc., then man is not in need of salvation in the first place (and so can dispense with the supplement).

68. As this sentence indicates, Van Til believed that the sinful dynamic of "suppressing the truth in unrighteousness" applies not only to the truths of natural revelation (to which Paul applies this expression in Rom. 1:18), but also to the truths of special revelation (e.g., Christology).

69. The presuppositional challenge is propounded here in a nutshell: either accept the word of Christ as your philosophical foundation, or otherwise leave logic, fact, reason, personality, etc., without any intelligible interpretation or intellectual basis in your philosophy.

crucified Saviour, the risen Lord, the ascended Christ, the judge of all men to come, the Christ before all history, come into history, and Lord of history, the Christ with saving relevance to all the problems of modern man in history, we cannot know him and confront him unless we confront him in the Scriptures. . . .

The main outlook of recent philosophy of history is that of a general process-philosophy. And this fact itself shows clearly that the conflict between those who believe in historic Christianity and those who do not cannot be carried by a discussion of "facts" without at the same time discussing the philosophy of fact.

When Rudolf Bultmann[70] discusses the "facts" of the New Testament he presupposes a philosophy of fact similar to that which is held by such as Heidegger and Collingwood.[71] [Likewise] the Roman Catholic and the traditional Protestant position in Apologetics as set forth by Bishop Butler and his followers tends to betray the Christ of Scripture because it does not start with the self-asserting Christ in order to show that any philosophy of history that does not do this makes human predication meaningless. . . .

As through his servants among men Satan sought to destroy the Christ and his work while he was on earth, so he continued to do so after he returned to heaven. In particular did Satan seek to destroy the church founded by Christ on the basis of his finished work on earth.

There was first the effort to destroy the church by means of physical persecution. This physical persecution was, to begin with, leveled at the apostles and later at those who through the message of the apostles carried on the message of Christ. In the early church there were many martyrs. These men paid the supreme penalty for their faith in Christ. They proved to the world that Christ was all in all to them. Their testimony could not fail and did

70. Rudolf Bultmann (1884–1976) was a German existentialist theologian who taught New Testament at the University of Marburg, promoted the interpretive technique of "form criticism," and made famous the alleged necessity to "demythologize" the New Testament and make it "speak to" the modern mentality (with its concerns over angst, authenticity, and freedom).

71. Martin Heidegger (1889–1976) was a German existentialist philosopher who sought a phenomenological analysis of human existence and uniqueness (as a "being-unto-death," living in anxiety, needing authenticity, etc.). In a mystical fashion, "Being" can be discerned in man's use of words. R. G. Collingwood (1889–1943) was an English philosopher and historian who stressed the need to find the presuppositions of human thought peculiar to one period of history in contrast to another; the statement of any scholarly viewpoint was for him always to be interpreted in the context of the particular interests, conceptions, and values that controlled the culture in which it arose—thus tending toward historical relativism in philosophy.

not fail to have, in the last analysis, the reverse effect of that which was intended by Satan.

Martyrdom was not the final nor the most effective weapon of the devil. He must prove to men that those who gave their lives for their Saviour were following a delusion. He must prove that it is contrary to reason and the facts to hold to the self-attesting Christ for which believers are giving their lives. It must be shown that Jesus Christ did not come in the flesh because if he were truly and unchangeably God he could not deny himself and become one with changing man. Above all, it must be shown that it is an insult to man's self-conscious personality to accept such teaching as would reduce him to a puppet in the hand of God.

Still further, if the policy of showing men that the very idea of God becoming man is logically impossible, contrary to fact, and insulting to man's self-respect does not work, then a concession must be made.[72] The concession to be made is that Christianity is to be given equal status with other religions. Or if believers get too strong at any sector of the front, they may even be told that Christianity is the best or the highest of all religions. It also does better justice to the idea that, in striving for the realization of this highest Christ-ideal in themselves, men are on the way to the highest that is possible for any man. And if the so-called Christian Church can itself be made to believe this illusion of Satan, then the entire self-testimony of Christ to man will be absorbed in the self-testimony of man to himself. . . .

Throughout the history of the Christian church one of the greatest dangers, if not the greatest danger, threatening it has been the idea that there are high and noble forms of non-Christian thought that stand ready to join a common expedition against secularism and materialism. This is especially true now that Kant's idea of the primacy of the practical over the theoretical reason has invaded and permeated the Protestant church. The common slogan is that all religious people, all that are interested in spiritual values, all that believe in some God or in some Christ should join hands in a joint effort to save the human race from falling back into servitude to lower ideals. . . .

Justin[73] was also quite mistaken when he assumed that Trypho was really a Jew in the true sense of the term. Paul has told us plainly that only he is a

---

72. The "concession" represents an attempt to weaken or break down the antithesis between Christianity and other outlooks.

73. Justin Martyr (c. 105–65) was a Neoplatonist who converted to Christianity and attempted to show educated pagans that Christ is the aim of true philosophy. He argued that Greek philosophy was illumined by the divine Logos and served as a preparation for the truth that was fulfilled in Christianity. One of his key writings was entitled *Dialogue with Trypho*.

true Jew who is one inwardly. Those who have circumcision of the flesh but not of the heart must be challenged in their basic assumption. If they are not challenged in their basic assumption, then the evidence is not presented for what it really is. The Old Testament really points to Christ as all the facts of the universe really reveal God. But since this is true, then Christians dare not present the evidence for the claim of Christ as the Son of God as though this evidence may possibly be accounted for even if Jesus were not the Christ.

It may be objected that Jesus himself pointed to his works as evidence for the truth of his claim to Messiahship. This is true, but it does not prove that Jesus pointed to his works as possibly intelligible on some other presuppositions than that of his Messiahship.[74] . . .

From the battles of the [early church] Apologists with Greek theism it became clear that the way to victory lies not through compromise. The Greek *paideia*[75] typifies the non-Christian *paideia* as a whole. The idea of human autonomy is therefore its basic assumption. But this principle of autonomy is never satisfied unless all reality, both God and man, are made subject to its laws. The Apologists did not realize this fact, and so they tried to strike a bargain. They attempted to build theism with the Greeks in order to lead them on to Christianity from that common point. The Apologists did not clearly challenge the Greeks to forsake their total *paideia* and to accept in its place the Christian *paideia*.

NO COMMONALITY WITHOUT QUALIFICATION[76]

Man by his sinful nature hates the revelation of God. Therefore every concrete expression that any sinner makes about God will have in it the poisoning effect of this hatred of God. His epistemological reaction will invariably be negative, and negative along the whole line of his interpretative endeavor. There are no general principles or truths about the true God—and that is the only God with whom any man actually deals—which he does not falsify. The very idea of the existence of abstract truths is a falsification of the knowledge of the true God that every sinner involuntarily finds within himself. . . .

There are no *capita communissima*, on which believers and non-believers

---

74. This is a very important point, which nonpresuppositional approaches to apologetics tend to overlook. According to Van Til, there is abundant evidence for the truth of the gospel. However, all evidence has a philosophical framework or network of presuppositions by which it is seen as evidence and interpreted.

75. *Paideia* is a Greek term that refers to the discipline or training of a child (a *paidion*)—and, by extension, to a *conception of education* (or learning, instruction).

76. Excerpts from *Common Grace*, 57, 63, 42–44, 84–87.

can agree without a difference. There are no central truths on which all agree. The disagreement is fundamental and goes to the heart of the matter. . . .

Kuyper argues for the commonness of the territories on the ground of their interpretative insignificance. It is because of the *externality* of weighing and measuring, and it is because of the *formality* of logic, that the three territories are said to be common to believer and non-believer. We are to hold, according to Kuyper's argument, that where sin has not changed the metaphysical situation, the difference between believer and unbeliever need not be brought to the fore. This is, in effect, to say that to the extent that the objective situation has not changed, the subjective change need not be taken into account. To point out the ambiguity in the argument is, therefore, at the same time to point out its invalidity.

What do we mean when we say that the metaphysical situation has changed because of sin? What do we mean when we say that even after the Fall man is a rational and moral creature still? We surely do not mean to deny total depravity. Accordingly there is no sinner who, unless regenerated, does not actually seek to interpret himself and the universe without God. The natural man uses his logical powers to describe the facts of creation as though these facts existed apart from God. He has rejected the common mandate. It is therefore in conjunction with the sinner's subjective alienation from God, as a limiting concept merely, that we can speak of anything as not having been destroyed by sin. In the interpretative endeavor the "objective situation" can never be abstracted from the "subjective situation." If we do abstract it, we fall back on the Scholastic position.[77] . . .

No valid answer can be given the Scholastics by the device of reducing the area of commonness to ever smaller proportions. Any area of commonness, that is, any area of commonness without qualification however small, is a justification for larger areas of commonness, till at last there is but one common area. The only valid answer to the Roman Catholic is to say that in the whole of the area of interpretative endeavor the subjective difference makes its influence felt. Weighing and measuring and formal reasoning are but aspects of one unified act of interpretation. It is either the would-be autonomous man who weighs and measures what he thinks of as brute or bare facts by the help of what he thinks of as abstract impersonal principles, or it is the believer, knowing himself to be a creature of God, who weighs and measures what he thinks of as God-created facts by what he thinks of as God-created laws. Looking at the matter thus allows for legitimate cooperation. Looking at the

---

77. The Scholastic position was that "nature" and man's "natural understanding" of it have not been affected by supernatural matters (such as sin).

matter thus allows for a larger "common" territory than Kuyper allows for, but this larger territory is common with a qualification. Looking at the matter thus allows us to do full justice to "antithesis," which Kuyper has taught us to stress. . . .

What has been said may also help us to some extent in an intelligent discussion of the attitude of believers toward unbelievers. That attitude should, if our general approach be at all correct, be a conditional "as if" attitude. The attitude of Christ's followers is, as Christ has told us, to be in positive imitation of God's attitude. Hence we are to make practical use of the concept of "mankind in general." We are to use this notion as a limiting concept. We are not to forget for a moment that no such thing exists in any pure state. We are therefore to witness to men that in themselves they are enemies of God. We are to witness to them that this enmity appears even in such dimensions as that of counting and weighing. This is done if, among other things, we build separate Christian day schools. And we are to oppose men more definitely to the extent that they become epistemologically more self-conscious. To say to the antichrist that God loves sinners, and therefore may love him, is to cast pearls before swine. For all that, we still need the concept of "mankind in general." We are to think of non-believers as members of the mass of humankind in which the process of differentiation has not yet been completed. It is not to the righteous and to the unrighteous as fully differentiated that God gives His rain and sunshine.[78] It is not to unbelievers as those that have with full self-consciousness expressed their unbelief that we are to give our gifts. We are to give our "rain and sunshine" as God gives them, on the basis of the limiting concept, to the as-yet-undifferentiated (or at least not fully differentiated) mass of mankind.

By thus substituting the ideas of earlier and later for lower and higher[79]

78. Men will not be fully differentiated until the Day of Judgment, when God will separate the sheep from the goats. At that time, each man's character will be fully revealed. Prior to that, men will continue to show an inconsistent mixture of good and bad traits (true and false ideas), and it is to the mass of undifferentiated men in this preconsummation state that God grants His undeserved and nonsaving favors—His "common grace."

79. The issue of common grace, and thus (in some sense) of the commonality between covenant keepers and covenant breakers, has usually led theologians to draw a distinction of some sort. Van Til was dissatisfied with the misleading distinction between "lower" and "higher" realms—between nature (where men know and enjoy things in common) and grace (where they differ). He declared that the commonality among men is accounted for by their "earlier" union (in Adam, for all), which goes back to the Creation and the Fall, and that their differentiation has to do with their "later" union (in Christ, for some), to be fully revealed at the Day of Judgment.

we may get something approaching a solution to the question of territories. There is no single territory or dimension in which believers and non-believers have all things wholly in common. As noted above, even the description of facts in the lower dimension presupposes a system of metaphysics and epistemology. So there can be no neutral territory of cooperation. Yet unbelievers are more self-conscious epistemologically in the dimension of religion than in the dimension of mathematics. The process of differentiation has not proceeded as far in the lower as it has in the higher dimensions. Does not this fact explain to some extent our attitude in practice? We seek, on the one hand, to make men epistemologically self-conscious all along the line. As Reformed Christians we do all we can, by building our own educational institutions and otherwise, to make men see that so-called neutral weighing and measuring is a terrible sin in the sight of God.[80] To ignore God anywhere is to insult the God who has told us that, whether we eat or drink or do anything else, we are to do all to His glory. But when all the reprobate are epistemologically self-conscious, the crack of doom has come.[81] . . .

It is thus that we finally come to some fruitful insight into the problem of civil righteousness or the works of non-regenerate men. It is not that in some lower dimension no differentiation, epistemological or psychological, needs to be made by believers. It is not that there is even a square foot of neutral territory. It is not that in the field of civics or justice, any more than in any other particular dimension, men, to the extent that they are epistemologically self-conscious, show any righteousness. The problem, as already suggested, faces us in every dimension.

RELIGIOUS ANTITHESIS EVEN AFFECTS THE STUDY OF NATURE[82]

The entrance of sin involved a false interpretation of reality. Man thought that he, though a creature, could actually become as God the creator. This was a serious miscalculation. It was but to be expected that when man once fell into sin his power of true interpretation would, from an absolute point of view, disappear altogether. No *sinner* can interpret reality aright. This is the first

---

80. The apologist aims to make the unbeliever more clearly aware of the character and implications of his theory of knowledge—to promote his "epistemological self-consciousness"—in which case the unbeliever must be shown that neutrality is not simply intellectually impossible, but even more is a form of rebellion against God in the use of one's mind (i.e., a "terrible *sin*").

81. Full awareness and acknowledgment of the implications of one's epistemology will come at the end of history, at the Day of Judgment (i.e., "the crack of doom").

82. Excerpts from *Introduction to Systematic Theology*, 92, 81, 82, 83–84, 85, 113, 98–99.

point to keep in mind in this connection. It will not do to separate the logical powers of man from his moral powers and say that though man is morally unwilling to serve God, he can intellectually know God aright. . . .

With the entrance of sin, however, man cut his study of himself loose from God, and therewith also cut his study of nature loose from himself. For this reason all the study of nature that man has made since the fall of man has been, in a basic sense, absolutely false. As far as an ultimate point of view is concerned, the sinner has been mistaken in his interpretation of the physical universe no less than in his interpretation of God. The physical world cannot be truly known when it is cut loose from God. We may say that the phenomena cannot be truly known without the noumena. It is not enough to say that the [understanding of the] phenomenal world can be wholly true if the phenomenal world be not set in relation to God. . . .

Men can read nature aright only when it is studied as the home of man who is made in the image of God.

Note: This point that the knowledge of "phenomena" is as basically mistaken from an *ultimate* point of view as the knowledge of God, if the phenomena are not brought into relation to God, has been greatly obscured in the history of Christian thought by a common distinction made between knowledge of natural things and knowledge of heavenly things. It is often presented as though Christians and non-Christians would then be different only in that the former, in addition to knowing earthly things also know heavenly things, while the latter know earthly things only. . . .

[T]hough all of the natural man's interpretations are from an ultimate point of view equally unsatisfactory, there is a sense in which he knows something about everything, about God as well as about the world, and that in this sense he knows more about the world than about God. This distinction is not only true, but important to make. Many non-Christians have been great scientists. Often non-Christians have a better knowledge of the things of this world than Christians have.

It is important to keep these things in mind, in view of the all too common practice on the part of Christian apologists to make a hard and fast distinction between the field of religion and the field of science. The assumption of this division is that as Christians we need only to claim that we know about heavenly things, and that scientists, whether Christians or non-Christians, know about earthly things. In this way, apologists hope to gain a free territory for religion. It is obvious, however, that such an attempt is foredoomed to failure.

Non-Christian scientists cannot study the phenomenal world without some reference to the noumenal. And this is true when ministers secretly, if not openly, conceding their ability to speak on ultimate matters, ask them whether science has discovered God. Nothing is so evident from the writings of scientists today as the fact that they are constantly making statements about and drawing conclusions about the noumenal world on the ground of their studies of the phenomenal world which they are first supposed to have undertaken without reference to the noumenal world. They are constantly speaking about the nature of Reality as a whole. On the other hand it is equally true that our religion is not confined to information about the noumenal world without reference to the phenomenal world. Christianity says something very definite about the phenomenal world, both as to its origin and as to its destiny. The only distinction that will really help us is the one that Calvin developed, namely, that from an ultimate point of view the natural man knows nothing truly, but that from a relative point of view he knows something about all things. He knows all things *after a fashion*, and his fashion is best when he deals with earthly things such as electricity, etc.

Paul assures us in Romans that all men know God. Calvin calls this knowledge the sense of deity. All men at bottom know that theism is the only true interpretation of life. But it is precisely this knowledge which they do their best to repress in the actual self-conscious efforts that they make at interpreting human experience. And it is of these systems of their own interpretation that we speak when we say that men are as wrong in their interpretation of trees as in their interpretation of God. . . .

If even in paradise man was meant to interpret nature in terms of self, and both in the light of the supernatural communication of God's thoughts with respect to the course of history as a whole, how much the more should man as sinner seek to understand nature in relation to self and to this self as interpreted in Scripture.

The idea of theologico-physics is naturally the object of great ridicule on the part of non-Christian scientists. To them the idea that one must interpret nature in terms of and in subordination to scriptural revelation is to give up scientific or rational inquiry altogether. Non-Christian investigators of nature are as successful as they are because they work with stolen capital.[83]

Roman Catholicism has been unwilling to submit the study of nature to the light of Scripture in any consistently Christian way. The result has been either that there has been no harmony between Roman Catholic science and Roman Catholic theology or that the harmony has been accomplished at

---

83. That is, the non-Christian makes use of "intellectual capital," which is "stolen" from the Christian worldview. That is, the unbeliever secretly rests his case upon Christian presuppositions, even while outwardly denying that he holds to them (and sometimes even putting up a show of opposition to them).

the price of the reduction of its theology to suit the naturalistic pattern of its science.

It is highly unfortunate that the Reformation principle has not been carried through with any great consistency in many Protestant circles. The scientific study of nature has all too frequently been carried on, even by avowedly Protestant scholars, as though they could stand on neutral ground with non-believers and simply study the facts of nature. It is then forgotten that in the study of nature the basic question is as to what the facts of nature are, or, to put it otherwise, what the facts are about the "facts." Every student of nature approaches the task of a description of nature and its facts in terms of the presuppositions of a philosophy of fact. The Christian can obtain his philosophy of fact from no other source than Scripture. . . .

Failure to see this fact involves a compromise with the naturalistic principle. No Christian can escape facing the fact that many non-Christian scientists have discovered much truth about nature. If he does not explain this fact with Calvin by virtually saying that this is true *in spite of* their immanentistic view of life and *because of* the fact that they cannot help but work with the "borrowed" capital of Christianity, then he must grant that the naturalist is *partially* right. Speaking of the Christian, [Bernard] Ramm says, "He does not deny the naturalistic explanation completely" (p. 67), and that in spite of the fact that naturalism is said to explain nature without God. There is no escape from such compromise unless one makes the claim that only in terms of the God of the Scripture can science do its work. . . .

Yet the willing disobedience on the part of man is itself the greatest damage done to God's creation; it is this that must be repaired. This cannot be done unless creation is really seen as God's creation and man is really seen as the creature of God. It is only if man is the creature of God that he can be saved by God. Salvation means that man, the sinner, must be brought back to the knowledge of himself as the creature of God and therefore, to the knowledge of God as the Creator. Being a sinner, man will not read nature aright unless he does it in the light of Scripture. "If true religion is to beam upon us, our principle must be, that it is necessary to begin with heavenly teaching, and that it is impossible for any man to obtain even the minutest portion of right and sound doctrine without being a disciple of Scripture" (*Institutes*, I, 6:2).

Note: We should accordingly avoid the error of separating too sharply between science and religion as is often done. The world of natural and historical fact with which science deals cannot be truly interpreted by anyone who is not a Christian, any more than can the world of spiritual things. Every statement about the physical universe implies, in the last analysis, some view about the "spiritual" realm. Scientists frequently say that in their statements they will limit themselves to the phenomenal world. But every assertion they make about the "phenomenal" world involves an attitude toward the "noumenal" world. Even the mere assumption that anything can intelligently be asserted about the phenomenal world by itself presupposes its independence of God, and as such is in effect a denial of him. . . .

That even Reformed philosophers and theologians do not always make full use of the riches found in Calvin's *Institutes* may be briefly pointed out by a reference to the work of Gordon H. Clark, *A Christian Philosophy of Education*. He says that the position of the atheist and pantheist in actually or virtually denying that there is a creator is untenable. If a discoverer of an uninhabited island were to search its confines for a particular form of animal life he might fail to find it. "He could not be sure, however, that the particular animal had never lived on the island, because, even though the search had been diligent, still tomorrow the remains might be discovered. Similarly, it is clear that no finite amount of searching could rationally lead one to deny the existence of God. During the time of the atheist's investigation of this earth, it just might be that God was hiding on the other side of the moon, and if some rocket should take the atheist to the moon, there is no reason to hold that God might not go over to Jupiter—for the express purpose of inconveniencing the atheist" (p. 44). But a God who can thus escape to the moon or to Jupiter is not inconveniencing the atheist at all. On the contrary, he shows himself to be so finite, so insignificant, that the atheist can cover the whole earth without being confronted by him. This is the exact reverse of the teaching of Calvin, based on Paul, that God is divinity and power, being always and everywhere so obviously present that he who says there is no God is a fool. The foolishness of the denial of the creator lies precisely in the fact that this creator confronts man in *every* fact so that no fact has any meaning for man except it be seen as God's creation.

In his book *Notes on the Doctrine of God*, Carl F. H. Henry follows an approach similar to that of Clark. Though admitting in a note (p. 72) that from a biblical point of view the "fool" is entitled to no comfort, he starts out his first chapter under the heading, "Giving the Fool Some Comfort," with the following words: "The case for the existence of God is not so obvious that it cannot be doubted. . . " (p. 23). In the note referred to this is said to be a "temporary acceptance of his approach" presumably for pedagogical purposes. In the text this "temporary acceptance" turns out to be a permanent acceptance of the validity of the non-believer's immanentistic method at least in the "phenomenal" realm of experience. Henry is careful not to introduce his God so as to inconvenience the scientist even at the outset of his career.

The scientist is not to be molested though he works with an exclusively immanentistic method.

THE DISAGREEMENT IN "SYSTEMS" IS IN PRINCIPLE AND ALL-INCLUSIVE[84]

Disagreeing with the natural man's interpretation of himself as the ultimate reference point, the Reformed apologist must seek his point of contact with the natural man in that which is beneath the threshold of his working consciousness, in the sense of deity which he seeks to suppress. And to do this the Reformed apologist must also seek a point of contact with the systems constructed by the natural man. But this point of contact must be in the nature of a head-on collision. *If there is no head-on collision with the systems of the natural man there will be no point of contact with the sense of deity in the natural man. . . .*

To the theism set forth above,[85] Christianity must now be added. Due to the sin of man the curse of God rests upon the whole creation. Man has joined Satan in his opposition to God. At the same time God has inserted a remedial influence against sin into the world. This remedial work centers in the Christ.[86]

He came forth "to destroy the works of the evil one." He came to bring peace, to be sure, but the peace that he came to bring must be built upon the complete destruction of the power of darkness. "I came not to bring peace upon the earth but the sword." Such was the message of the Prince of Peace. To herald this message, he sent prophets before him and apostles after him. When most enveloped in this message, when most enthusiastic about this peace, the psalmist cries out: "Shall I not hate those that hate thee? I hate them with a perfect hatred." When he was on earth Christ entered the arena with Satan single-handed and triumphed. He is seen by John the Apostle, riding upon his white horse, conquering and to conquer. When he sees his armies languish, weary of the fight, his clarion voice bids them put on the whole armour of God. They may not waver, it is the church militant, this people of God. Only those who fight to the end receive the crown. And then there

84. Excerpts from *Defense of the Faith*, 115–16, 45–46, 189–92, 295, 306, 318.
85. This refers to the theistic metaphysical outlook that has not as yet taken into consideration the implications of sin and its curse.
86. In this paragraph and the one that follows, we find a good illustration of how, for Van Til, biblical teaching (theology) and philosophical perspective were readily interwoven. He takes what Scripture teaches and "translates" it into recognition of the systematic antithesis that exists between the scholarship of believers and that of unbelievers.

is peace indeed. In the "regeneration of all things" he that sits upon the throne is surrounded by the twenty-four elders and the four living creatures. The whole creation is there; the whole creation is redeemed. No discordant voice is heard. All sing the great song of the redeemed creation. Through redemption creation's purpose was accomplished. Where are the enemies? They are sealed in a soundproof exclusion chamber. . . .

For it is not till after the consummation of history that men are left wholly to themselves. Till then the Spirit of God continues to strive with men that they might forsake their evil ways. Till then God in his common grace, in his long-suffering forbearance, gives men rain and sunshine and all the good things of life that they might repent. The primary attitude of God to men as men is that of goodness. It is against this goodness expressing itself in the abundance of good gifts that man sins. And even then God prevents the principle of sin from coming to full fruition. He restrains the wrath of man. He enables him by this restraint to cooperate with the redeemed of God in the development of the work he gave man to do.

But all this does not in the least reduce the fact that as far as the principle of the natural man is concerned, it is absolutely or utterly, not partly, opposed to God. That principle is Satanic. It is exclusively hostile to God. If it could it would destroy the work and plan of God. So far then as men self-consciously work from this principle they have no notion in common with the believer. Their epistemology is informed by their ethical hostility to God. . . .

Moreover, only if both parties, the unbeliever and the believer, have equal natural ability to use the gifts of God can there be an all-inclusive antithesis between them. The argument between Christians and non-Christians involves every fact in the universe. If it does not involve every fact it does not involve any fact. If one fact can be interpreted correctly on the assumption of human autonomy then all facts can. If the Christian is to be able to show the non-Christian objectively that Christianity is true and that those who reject it do so because they hold to that which is false, this must be done everywhere or else it is not really done anywhere. . . .

Thus there is *nowhere* an area where the second factor, that of man's ethical hostility to God, does not also come into the picture. This factor is not so clearly in evidence when men deal with external things; it is more clearly in evidence when they deal with the directly religious question of the truth of Christianity. But it is none the less present everywhere. . . .

Thus the idea of the antithesis involves nothing extreme or absurd. It simply asserts that Christianity saves the whole man, it saves him with his culture. It saves even the culture of unbelievers. It provides for its absorption into the Christian view of things without resulting in the destruction of the essence of Christianity itself. It makes Kuyper's slogan of *Pro Rege* apply to the whole of life, not merely to worship. It provides for the intelligent relationship of common grace to special grace in Christ.

None of these things can be accomplished if we cling to classic realism, scholasticism, modern dimensionalism, natural theology and a common grace concept built on natural theology. In all these cases we have assumed that the Christian principle and the non-Christian principle can in some areas be combined.[87] At least we have ignored the fact that they can nowhere be combined. . . .

In so far as men are aware of their most basic alliances, they are wholly for or wholly against God at every point of interest to man. . . .

His [the Reformed apologist's] argument is that unless this [Creator/creature] distinction is made basic to all that man says about anything, then whatever man says is fundamentally untrue. The natural man, who assumes that he himself and the facts about him are not created, therefore assumes what is basically false. Everything he says about himself and the universe will be colored by this assumption. It is therefore impossible to grant that he is right, basically right, in what he says about any fact. If he says what is right in detail about any fact, this is *in spite of, not because of* his basically false assumption.

TWO MUTUALLY EXCLUSIVE PRINCIPLES OF INTERPRETATION[88]

In view of the facts mentioned above we shall have to concern ourselves first and primarily with the two opposing *principles* of interpretation. The Christian principle of interpretation is based upon the assumption of God as the final and self-contained reference point. The non-Christian principle of interpretation is that man as self-contained is the final and self-contained reference point. It is this basic difference that has to be kept in mind all the time. It will be difficult at times to see that such is actually the case. The very fact that by God's common grace fallen man is "not as bad as he could be" and is able to do that which is "morally good" will make the distinction between two mutually exclusive principles seem an extreme oversimplification to many.

87. Van Til's concern here is that Christian scholars often misapply the biblical doctrine of "common grace" in order to establish a neutral area of "nature" that can be commonly and correctly interpreted by both believers and unbelievers—that is, a kind of "common ground" that need not take into account religious differences.
88. An excerpt from *A Christian Theory of Knowledge* (Philadelphia: Presbyterian and Reformed, 1969), 44–45.

In fact, it is *in spite of appearances* that the distinction between the two principles must be maintained. The point is that the "facts of experience" must actually be interpreted in terms of Scripture if they are to be intelligible at all. In the last analysis the "facts of experience" must be interpreted either in terms of man taken as autonomous, or they must be interpreted in terms of God. There is no third "possibility." The interpretation which takes the autonomous man as self-interpretive is an "impossible possibility." . . .

It is our task now to indicate how fallen man, the man who *in principle* assumes himself to be a law unto himself, will estimate the idea of Scripture as outlined in the preceding chapter. The Scriptures speak of the self-identifying Christ as the self-identifying God and therefore of his self-attesting revelation to man. Scripture requires that man renounce himself as autonomous and submit himself to the will of God as expressed in Christ. The Scripture requires repentance. It says to the natural man that he is blinded in mind and rebellious in heart. It tells him that he cannot of himself see the truth which he yet ought to see, and that he cannot do that which he yet ought to do.

AGREEMENTS ARE POSSIBLE, BUT ARE INCIDENTAL AND PERIPHERAL[89]

The reason why these differences do not appear on the surface is that, as a matter of fact, all men are human beings who are created in the image of God. Even the non-regenerate have by virtue of common grace some remnant of what *should be, though it is not*, the general consciousness of mankind. Accordingly, it happens that there is *incidental agreement* on many matters of the moral life. It is in a general sense true that everyone holds murder to be wrong. But the agreement is no more than incidental. A theist holds murder to be wrong because it violates the justice of God. A non-Christian holds murder to be wrong because it is not in the best interest of the human race. According to theism, the idea of justice has its foundation in the nature of God. According to Pragmatism, the idea of justice is a historical development in the consciousness of the race. Accordingly, there is nothing that the two conceptions of justice have in common except the name. "What is morally wrong" is therefore not a phrase into which everybody spontaneously pours the same thought content. The agreement on this matter then between theists and antitheists, in addition to being merely incidental, is also merely formal and abstract. This formal and abstract agreement we expect because man, by virtue of his creation in God's image, cannot be metaphysically alienated from God, however much he may be ethically alienated.

89. An excerpt from *Survey of Christian Epistemology*, 190.

In the second place, we may mention as a reason why these fundamental differences are not easily observed, the fact that the incidental and abstract agreement between theists and antitheists on moral and intellectual matters usually deals with things that are proximate rather than with things that are ultimate.[90]

DIFFERING VERSIONS OF OBJECTIVITY[91]

(A) Another term that needs description before we can proceed with our historical survey is that of "objectivity." In ordinary speech we understand by an "object" anything that exists "out there," that is, independently of the human mind. We then claim to have objective knowledge of something if the idea that we have in our minds of that thing corresponds to the thing as it exists independently of the mind. We may have false ideas about a thing. In that case we say that it is only subjective and does not correspond to reality. The controversy between Berkeley and his opponents hinged on the point whether or not there are objects "out there" to which our knowledge corresponds. Berkeley said that to be is to be perceived. He said, therefore, that all knowledge is subjective only. His opponents maintained the contrary. Johnson is said to have tried to refute Berkeley by kicking against a stone.

The coherence theory of truth implied a new conception of objectivity. For it, objectivity no longer was the correspondence of an idea to a certain object supposed to exist in total independence of the mind. For it, objectivity meant a significant reference to the whole system of truth. One would have a true idea of a cow not by having a replica of the cow in one's mind, but by understanding the place of the cow in the universe.

Now it will be readily understood that as far as the form of the matter is concerned the Christian conception of objectivity stands closer to the latter than to the former position. For us, too, the primary question is not that of the out-thereness of the cow. What we are chiefly concerned about is that our idea of the cow shall correspond to God's idea of the cow. If it does not, our knowledge is false and may be called subjective. But the exact difference between the idealistic conception of objectivity and ours should be noted. The

90. That is, the agreement has to do not with "ultimate" principles of thinking or living—the presuppositions pertaining to reality, knowing, and conduct—but rather with matters that are closer at hand ("proximate") and have less significance or impact throughout one's system of beliefs.
91. The following excerpts are taken from:

(A) *Survey of Christian Epistemology*, 3–4;
(B) *Defense of the Faith*, 60, 297, 386, 76–77.

difference lies just here, that for the Idealist, the system of reference is found in the Universe inclusive of God and man, while for us, the point of reference is found in God alone.

When therefore we examine the various epistemological views with regard to their "objectivity," we are interested most of all in knowing whether or not these views have sought the knowledge of an object by placing it into its right relation with the self-conscious God. The other questions are interesting enough in themselves but are comparatively speaking not of great importance. Even if one were not anxious about the truth of the matter, it ought still to be plain to him that there can be no more fundamental question in epistemology than the question whether or not facts can be known without reference to God. Suppose for argument's sake that there is such a God. And surely the possibility of it anybody ought to be willing to grant unless he has proved the impossibility of God's existence. Suppose then the existence of God. Then it would be a fact that every fact would be known truly only with reference to him. If then one did not place a fact into relation with God, he would be in error about the fact under investigation. Or suppose that one would just begin his investigations as a scientist, without even asking whether or not it is necessary to make reference to such a God in his investigations; such a one would be in constant and in fundamental ignorance all the while. And this ignorance would be culpable ignorance, since it is God who gives him life and all good things. It ought to be obvious then that one should settle for himself this most fundamental of all epistemological questions, whether or not God exists. Christ says that as the Son of God, he will come to judge and condemn all those who have not come to the Father by him.

(B) Our argument for the objectivity of knowledge with respect to the universe can never be complete and satisfactory unless we bring in the relation of both the object and the subject of knowledge to God. We may debate endlessly about psychological problems without fruitage if we refuse to bring in the metaphysical question of the nature of reality.[92] If the Christian position with respect to creation, that is, with respect to the idea of the origin of both the subject and the object of human knowledge is true, there is and must be objective knowledge. In that case the world of objects was made in order that the subject of knowledge, namely man, should interpret it under God. Without the interpretation of the universe by man to the glory of God the whole world would be meaningless. The subject and the object are therefore adapted

92. CVT: Note the basic importance assigned to the doctrine of creation and therewith to a basically Christian, in distinction from an idealist, metaphysic.

to one another. On the other hand if the Christian theory of creation by God is not true then we hold that there cannot be objective knowledge of anything. In that case all things in this universe are unrelated and cannot be in fruitful contact with one another. This we believe to be the simple alternative on the question of the objectivity of knowledge as far as the things of this universe are concerned. . . .

If God has an absolutely self-determinate character, then the universe also has an "objectivity" to which the mind of man must submit itself. Then man cannot by the power of his logic determine the nature of God. And that is what he, as a sinner, wants to do.

To seek to control reality, to be the source of "objectivity," is not the ideal of the modern idealists only; it was the ideal of classic realism just as well. It is the ideal of all non-Christian thought. . . .

[Kuyper] says that faith is formal only in the field of the exact or external sciences. In what he calls the spiritual sciences he asserts that the fact of sin makes its presence felt. . . .

But how are we to draw the line between physical or objective and spiritual sciences? In both cases the human subject is involved. There is no "unifying power of the object" that can do away with this fact. Kuyper himself has insisted that even in observation of facts the subjective element enters into the picture. There is not the least harm in this. It is a purely metaphysical and psychological fact. It is not the fact that a subject is involved in the knowledge situation that makes for skepticism. It is only when this subject does not want itself interpreted in terms of God that skepticism comes about. . . .

[C. S.] Lewis seeks for objective standards in ethics, in literature, and in life everywhere. But he holds that objectivity may be found in many places. He speaks of a general objectivity that is common between Christians and non-Christians and argues as though it is mostly or almost exclusively in modern times that men have forsaken it. Speaking of this general objectivity he says: "This conception in all its forms, Platonic, Aristotelian, Stoic, Christian, and Oriental alike, I shall henceforth refer to for brevity simply as 'the *Tao*.' Some of the accounts of it which I have quoted will seem, perhaps, to many of you merely quaint or even magical. But what is common to them all is something we cannot neglect. It is the doctrine of objective value, the belief that certain attitudes are really true, and others really false, to the kind of thing the universe is and the kind of things we are."[93] But surely this general objectivity is common to Christians and non-Christians in a formal sense only. To say that

93. CVT: *The Abolition of Man*, London, 1947, p. 17.

there is or must be an objective standard is not the same as to say what that standard is. And it is the *what* that is all important. Granted that non-Christians who hold to some sort of something somewhere above men are better than non-Christians who hold to nothing whatsoever above man, it remains true that in the main issue the non-Christian *objectivists* are no less subjective than are the non-Christian *subjectivists*. There is but one alternative that is ulti-mate; it is that between those who obey God and those who please them-selves. Only those who believe in God through Christ seek to obey God; only they have the true principle in ethics.[94]

SOME SYSTEMATICALLY BASIC POINTS OF DISAGREEMENT[95]

In the preceding chapters in which we have dealt with the starting point of knowledge, there is one thought that has occurred constantly, namely, that antitheistic and anti-Christian writers have at the outset of their argument taken their position for granted. Now if this is true, the question that comes up at once is whether it is then of any use to argue about the Christian the-istic position at all with those who are of contrary convictions.

It is this problem that must be discussed under the heading of the subject-subject relation. Before doing so, let us bring afresh to our minds what we have found so far in the matter of the starting point of knowledge. We must do this inasmuch as we come now to the climax of the whole question, and we must have all the factors clearly in mind.

We have so far discussed the question of the object of knowledge. Under that heading we saw that we may speak of the object of knowledge as such and that we must also consider the relation of one object to other objects. And if we consider the relation of one object to another object as they exist simultaneously, we have the question of *space*. On the other hand, when we consider the object of knowledge in its relation to other objects of knowledge that have existed at an earlier time or will exist at a later time, the whole ques-tion of *time* is up for consideration. The final question, then, when consider-ing the object of knowledge, is whether the spatial-temporal universe exists by itself or whether we must presuppose the existence of God in order to think intelligently of the spatial-temporal world. We found that, according to Chris-tian theism, every individual object of knowledge to be known at all must be known in its relation to God. Then if one spatial object is to be known in its relation to another spatial object, the connection must be thought of as made

---

94. And only they have the true principle in epistemology or any other field of in-quiry, as Van Til would say.
95. An excerpt from *Survey of Christian Epistemology*, 183–84.

by God. In other words, the universals of knowledge have their source in God. Similarly, if one object of knowledge is to be known in its relation to other objects of knowledge that have existed or will exist at another period of time, we must think of the connection as being made by the plan of God.

On all these points the antitheist not only took the opposite position, but he took the opposite position for granted as being so obviously the true position that he did not at all need to discuss it.[96] The antitheist took for granted the self-existence of the objects of knowledge to begin with. He speaks of them as the "facts" from which it is obviously necessary that we should begin as from something ultimate, for it is they that need [no] explanation.[97]

In the second place, it was taken for granted that if one object of knowledge was to be known in its relation to other objects of knowledge, it is entirely unnecessary to resort to God to furnish the connecting links. These connecting links either exist between the objects themselves so that they are given with the facts, or the human mind furnishes them. In other words, the universals are as ultimate as the facts. They think nobody would dream of the law of self-contradiction as having anything to do with God. They hold this to be so patently absurd as to require no more than ridicule for disproof.

Similarly, if one object of knowledge is to be known in its relation to other objects of knowledge that have occurred or will occur at another time, it is taken for granted that the connection is somehow found between the facts themselves without the necessity of reference to any mind, or if reference to mind is considered necessary, it is at least taken for granted that the human mind can furnish the universal in this case also.

From these assumptions of antitheistic thought it follows that if God is to have any significance for the objects of knowledge at all he must be reduced to one individual object of knowledge among many others.[98] Christian theism

96. Van Til advised defenders of the faith to confront the prejudice and question begging that is found at the outset of the unbeliever's approach to reasoning, research, scholarship, argumentation, etc. The unregenerate man displays his opposition to God not simply at the end of his lines of thinking, but already at the beginning.

97. As explained in the preface, I have occasionally taken the editorial liberty to "smooth out" some elements in the reading selections from Van Til. However, adding a negation to a sentence (as here) should be flagged as going much further than making a reading more readable! However, the author clearly intended the negation.

98. This observation is of great importance. The would-be autonomous man (and, sadly, some schools of apologetics) requires that God be treated as any other object of belief (or any other proposition that is subject to inspection and verification before being affirmed), thereby denying in advance the Christian's fundamental claim that God has a special status as the Creator, Controller, Redeemer,

on the contrary says that God is the one supreme object of knowledge. He is the most ultimate fact and the most ultimate universal. It is from him that all facts and all universals that we ordinarily deal with derive their meaning.

LOGICALLY INCOMPATIBLE ASSUMPTIONS[99]

It is only when this interrelatedness [between all aspects of God's revelation to man, in facts and in words] is stressed that, as Christians, we can effectively challenge the wisdom of the world and show that it has been made foolish by God. Only thus can the *total* interpretation of life and the world, as given by Christ in Scripture, be that on which alone every aspect of human experience must be based in order to have significance. . . .

According to Christ speaking in the Scripture, man has sinned against him by declaring his independence. When man listened to the temptation of Satan it was, in effect, to deny his own creaturehood. Adam was no longer willing to love his Creator and to show this love by obedience to his voice. He wanted to make himself the center of his own interpretative effort.

Involved in this was the idea that man rejected God's prediction with respect to what we now, after Kant, call the phenomenal realm. He said in his heart that God did not know that death would be the consequence of eating the forbidden fruit. Why did Adam think that God did not know? There were no records of what had happened to people who had eaten this fruit in the past. Could not Satan's hypothesis be as good as God's? Does not the scientific method require that, at the outset of any investigation of the facts of the physical universe, any hypothesis be placed on a par with any other hypothesis? Surely any hypothesis that anyone makes with respect to the future configuration of facts must be tested by those future facts themselves. And these future facts must not be interpreted in advance.

---

and Judge of mankind—the truths about whom constitute the "transcendentals" that make thinking and reasoning about all other matters intelligible. It should be apparent, however, that the metaphysical character of any object has a bearing upon the way in which it is known, discovered, proven, interpreted, etc. Different kinds of things are known (reasoned about) in different ways. The way in which we find out if there are crackers in the pantry is decidedly different from the way in which we determine the reality of, and rationally interpret, political obligations, quasars, memories, numbers, elasticity, names, love, etc. There are crucial differences in the argumentation and types of evidence used by biologists, grammarians, physicists, lawyers, mathematicians, mechanics, merchants, artists, etc. When the unbeliever refuses to grant that there is a special way in which we would know and interpret any truth about God—a unique Being who has a unique metaphysical status and character—he shows from the outset that he has determined not to allow God to be God.

99. An excerpt from *Protestant Doctrine of Scripture*, 12–14.

Here then are the marks of the natural man in his attitude toward the interpretation of the facts (events) of the world:

(1) He thinks of himself as the ultimate judge of what can or cannot be. He will not allow any authority to stand above him revealing to him what may or may not have happened in the past or what may or may not happen in the future.

(2) This assertion or assumption of autonomy on the part of man makes a covert, if not an overt, assertion about the nature of God. God (it is assumed if not asserted) *cannot* be of such a nature as to control any and all phenomena.

(3) These two assertions or assumptions imply a third: that man's thought is, in the final analysis, absolutely original. Whatever his ultimate environment may be, the area of interpretation that man makes for himself will be true for him because his thought is in effect legislative with respect to that environment.

(4) The facts of man's environment are not created or controlled by the providence of God. They are *brute* facts, uninterpreted and ultimately irrational. The universe is a *Chance* controlled universe. It is a wholly open universe. Yet, at the same time, it is a closed universe.[100] It is so in this sense: it cannot be what Christ says it is, namely, created, governed, and redeemed by him. In this one respect the cosmos is closed—there can be no such God as the Bible reveals. This is the universal negative of the open-minded men of philosophy and science.

Herbert Feigl[101] seems to see this great gulf fixed between the men of science and philosophy and the people of God when he says: "If by religion one refers to an explanation of the universe and a derivation of moral norms from theological premises, then indeed there is logical incompatibility with the results, methods, and general outlook of science" (H. Feigl, "The Scientific Outlook: Naturalism and Humanism," *Readings in Philosophy of Science*, ed. Brodbeck and Feigl, New York, 1953, p. 16).

The basically important point about all this is that the scientist as well as the philosopher and the theologian, unless he be converted to Christ by his Spirit, follows the method that was introduced into the world by Adam when he listened to Satan. The essence of this method is that man starts and finishes his interpretation about any and every aspect of life with the assump-

---

100. This is an example of the rational-irrational dialectic that Van Til sought to expose in all unbelieving thought.

101. Herbert Feigl (1902–88) was an Austrian and American philosopher, steeped in physicalism and behaviorism, and famous for being one of the original members of the "Vienna Circle" that promoted logical positivism.

tion of his own autonomy, with the assumption of the brute factuality of the material with which he deals, and with the assumption of abstract formality of the logic which he uses to relate the brute facts to one another.

The Christian, on the other hand, has been saved by the blood and tears of Christ from this God-insulting and self-destroying methodology.

5.3 The Epistemological Failure of Unbelief

Apologetical disputes between believers and unbelievers depend upon, include by reference, and arise out of conflicting epistemologies. Conflicts over the theory of knowledge in turn incorporate, function within, and must address differing world-and-life views (with divergent concepts of man as a knower), if they would be resolved. The bold defense of the faith offered by Van Til's presuppositionalism is that the unbeliever's worldview fails to provide an adequate or workable theory of knowledge in terms of which the non-Christian can intellectually challenge the truth of Christianity. His presuppositions preclude the unbeliever from making claims to know anything intelligible or meaningful.

The Christian worldview begins with the personal, self-sufficient, sovereign, and triune God, who created all things from nothing and made man to be His image. God knows all things and directs all events by His wise, providential plan. Thus, all objects, properties, minds, events, general laws, and moral prescriptions are determined, controlled, and related to each other by the mind of the Lord. Whatever the Lord says is utterly truthful and unfailing in its purposes, and that includes every passage of the Old and New Testaments. Human behavior and reasoning have become immoral and futile, due to self-centered rebellion against God. Man is biased against and hostile to the Lord and His revelation, wishing to be his own ultimate authority (autonomous). He needs the redemptive work of God's incarnate Son (as a prophet, priest, and king) and the regenerating work of God's Holy Spirit to be saved from intellectual foolishness, moral guilt, and eternal damnation. Given this overall "picture" of God, the world, man, value, history, and salvation—the basic biblical world-and-life view—the Christian can give an account of the objectivity of truth; the mind's correspondence to objects and other minds; the possibility of knowledge; the rational and empirical procedures by which we learn, test, and justify propositions; the possibility of our finite minds knowing universal, absolute, and prescriptive concepts and laws; the human tendency toward disagreement, prejudice, and irrationality, etc.

There is *at base* only one non-Christian worldview; logically speaking, it is the negation of the overall picture described above—the denial of some or all of the propositions used to summarize biblically-based Christianity (e.g., the Trinity, creation, providence, sin, incarnation, redemption, regeneration). Most pointedly, every non-Christian philosophical position takes for granted that man, not God, must function with ultimate intellectual authority, being the measure or "reference point" for all that he believes to be true. As Van Til observed:

> There are many schools of philosophy with which the college student has to make his acquaintance. The textbooks speak of some of them as objective and of others as subjective. Some are spoken of as monistic and others as pluralistic. Some are said to be pantheistic and others deistic, some rationalist and others irrationalist. Recently we have existential, analytical and positivist systems of philosophy. But all these schools must be seen in the light of the analysis made of them in Scripture. The main question that can be asked about any system of thought is whether it is man-centered or God-centered. Does it make the Creator-Redeemer or the creature the final reference point in prediction? If an answer to this question is found, then the problematics presented by the various schools of philosophy become [intelligible] to us.[102]

The unbeliever, whoever he may be at whatever time or place, utilizes and develops a theory of knowledge that is controlled by his hostility to God. He takes his own mind as the autonomous, self-attesting authority for knowledge; his mind (or to some degree that of his fellow men) is the reference point and basic interpretive guide to anything that may be known. The unbeliever assumes his own freedom and personality, while admitting that the environment in which he lives is not personal. He presumes that man is innocent and unbiased in this thinking (not seeking to avoid the light out of shame and fear). He does not believe that he needs at the outset of his reasoning to take account of the existence of the triune God, of the creation of all things, of God's providential control of every

102. *Christian Theory of Knowledge,* 49.

event, or of himself as created in God's image and answerable to God in all that he does. (These things may perhaps, upon examination, be added to his worldview at a later point, he might say, but they cannot be necessary from the start.) In the non-Christian outlook, the space-time universe exists and is intelligible apart from God; whatever happens is random, and facts are not preinterpreted, related, or controlled by a personal mind. Values stem from man himself or are somehow inherent in nature. The individual's own mind thus provides the connections between himself, objects, events, or other minds—as well as contributing the (purely formal) principles or laws by which he thinks and evaluates and by which he orders and interprets his experience. If there is any divine revelation, his mind must first be satisfied as to its identity, credibility, and subsequent authority over him.[103]

This generic non-Christian worldview is not, of course, propounded by unbelievers in such a bare-bones fashion. There are a plethora of ways in which unregenerate minds have expressed these underlying assumptions. At the more detailed or enriched level of presentation, which is the usual mode of its communication, the unbelieving worldview appears in a vast array of variations on the themes mentioned here. The Platonic version of the unbelieving worldview differs from the Aristotelian version, as the Hegelian version of the unbelieving worldview stands out from the Kierkegaardian version of it, etc. There is good reason to study and compare the many philosophical viewpoints, even while we recognize that the different schools are giving their own peculiar spin to the underlying non-Christian worldview. The specific weaknesses of one type of unbelieving philosophy are (usually) distinct in a number of ways from the particular weaknesses of other types. Nevertheless, as Van Til taught, at the most basic level there are only two philosophical viewpoints: "In trying to teach men Christian apologetics, and in that process briefly surveying the history of philosophy, a basic issue must be made between those who by grace believe and those who do not believe the story of the Bible."[104] Regardless of the variations, the generic worldview with which

103. In neither the simple description of the Christian worldview nor the basic non-Christian worldview has an attempt been made to be systematic or thorough in detailing what each holds as its presuppositions. But enough has been given to see their fundamental difference.
104. *Defense of the Faith*, 239.

each unbeliever begins is fatally flawed when it comes to offering an account of the possibility or intelligibility of what we take as "knowing" anything.

The various schools of philosophy set forth by unbelievers cannot explain man's personal and intellectual freedom in a mechanical world. They cannot provide for a reliable connection between the mind and its objects—or the mind and other minds. They cannot escape the egocentric predicament, subjectivism, and relativism.[105] They would require the individual mind to know everything to be certain of anything, and then simultaneously plead the limitations, inescapable biases, and fallibility of the human mind. Van Til explained:

> In all non-Christian forms of epistemology there is first the idea that to be understood a fact must be understood exhaustively. It must be reducible to a part of a system of timeless logic. But man himself and the facts of his experience are subject to change. How is he ever to find within himself an a priori resting point? He himself is on the move. The futile effort of Descartes stands out from the efforts of other non-Christian thinkers not because it is essentially different but only because it is more consistent. Every effort of man to find one spot that he can exhaustively understand either in the world of fact about him or in the world of experience within, is doomed to failure. If we do not with Calvin presuppose the self-contained God back of the self-conscious act of the knowing mind of man, we are doomed to be lost in an endless and bottomless flux.

105. Just think of the Continental rationalists (Descartes, Spinoza, Leibniz), who began with supposedly clear and distinct, "self-evident" ideas (notice their internal, subjective character), and yet derived from them radically and embarrassingly divergent conclusions about reality (dualism, monism, pluralism). Then consider the British empiricists (Locke, Berkeley, Hume), who traced the mind's ideas back to individual sensations (notice again the internal, subjective locus), only to render a "substance" that unites properties inexplicable (Locke), to dispense with material substance (Berkeley), and then to lose altogether any mental substance or "self" that unites perceptions (Hume). As Kant concluded, to the degree the mind knows its own inner contents (constituted by its own activity in forming the input of the senses), it still has no knowledge of things-in-themselves outside the mind. The predicament is that man as a knower can never "get outside" the ideas formed within himself. When the unbeliever begins his philosophizing with himself at the center, he ends up unable to escape himself (subjectivism); and since every unbeliever faces the same dilemma, nobody can speak with authority about objective reality for anybody else (relativism).

> But granted that man could get started on the way to learning by experience on a non-Christian basis, he could add nothing new to what he already knows. There would be nothing new. If it was known it would be no longer new. As long as it was new it would be unknown. Thus the old dilemma that either man must know everything and he need ask no questions, or he knows nothing and therefore cannot ask questions, remains unsolved except on the basis of the Reformed Faith.[106]

Non-Christians cannot give a philosophically adequate account of the universality and invariance of the laws of logic or the laws of morality—much less how the unchanging abstract laws or concepts could accurately reflect the completely different realm of constantly changing, brute, physical facts outside the mind. They fail to provide a justification for the scientific or inductive reasoning that is utilized in virtually everything we know and can communicate. The meaningfulness, communicability, and creativity of language are mutually inexplicable. Unbelievers cannot determine whether diversity and particulars in motion are to be emphasized or rather similarities and continuity found in unchanging principles. They cannot escape arbitrariness and inconsistency, cannot establish legitimate intellectual authority for what they say or believe, and cannot counter the skeptic effectively. In short, the unbelieving worldview renders personality, self-consciousness, mind, logic, science, and morality unintelligible. When unbelievers criticize the Christian faith, they have in themselves no cogent theory of knowledge in terms of which to formulate or advance their criticisms.

Throughout his writings at various points, Van Til would pick out one or another illustration of the underlying non-Christian worldview to make his point that unbelief represents an epistemological failure. He was bold to declare: "We believe that which is in the Bible to be the only defensible philosophical position . . . the only position that makes human predication intelligible." And the history of autonomous thought bears this out: "We shall have to approach the matter of a Christian world-and-life view from an historical point of view. . . . [W]e are naturally persuaded that in history lies the best proof of our philosophy of human life."[107] As the history of philosophy illustrates repeatedly, given his worldview, the

106. *Introduction to Systematic Theology*, 167.
107. *Survey of Christianity Epistemology*, 19, xiii.

unbeliever cannot explain the possibility or account for the actuality of man's knowing anything at all.[108] In the reading selections below, we will sample some of Van Til's discussions of this epistemological failure throughout the history of autonomous philosophy. These are valuable for their variation and details. Following them, we will consider a few of the more general lines of criticism that Van Til would address in a blanket fashion to any and all unbelieving worldviews and their theories of knowledge: the problem of brute (random) facts without meaning, the problem of continuity and contingency (a closed, yet open universe), the problem of relating logic to facts, the problem of phenomenalism (the mind knowing only itself, not the external world), and then—the critique for which Van Til is best remembered by his students—the "rational-irrational tension" that afflicts all unbelieving thought.[109]

Every school of epistemology stumbles over how to relate formal or logical principles (continuity) to chance particulars or facts (contingency). Likewise, every variation of unregenerate philosophy evidences the tendencies of both rationalism and irrationalism in one form or another, taking the autonomous mind of man as the ultimate standard or authority regarding truth and knowledge, and yet admitting its unsuitability or inability to function as the final judge. Non-Christian philosophies always turn out to be an unstable mixture of arrogance and humility. The autonomous man is arrogant regarding the authority and competence of his rational ability to figure

108. In his writings and classroom lectures, Van Til, especially earlier in his teaching career, took for granted (perhaps mistakenly) that his students were familiar with the key issues and philosophical positions in the history of philosophy. His habit was thus to lump together the various problems in secular epistemology under a convenient or paradigmatic label—e.g., the problem of relating "facts and laws," or the problem of "predication," or the "one and many" problem (unity and diversity).

109. The terms "rational" and "irrational" are given a wide variety of definitions in philosophical (and quasi-philosophical) literature and teaching. For instance, "rational" can describe what pertains to man's intellect, or to the attitude of autonomy from God, or to a specific school of epistemology that affirms the possibility of knowledge independent of observation, etc. As Van Til uses this pair of terms to describe the dialectical tension in autonomous theorizing, the "rational" tendency is to view man's mind as competent to describe reality accurately and serve as the final authority for all claims to knowledge; the "irrational" tendency in any philosophy is its admission of intellectual unreliability and limitations, its inability to comprehend everything (or even to anticipate what factors it may be unaware of), and its lack of certainty in the face of skepticism and mystery.

out what is real, how we should conduct ourselves, and what can be known; by his rational standards, he dismisses the truthfulness of Christianity (in one way or another). On the other hand, the autonomous man, living in a random universe that no mind can comprehend or fathom, must confess in all humility that intellectual certainty is not available to anybody.

> The modern man is in the first place a rationalist. All non-Christians are rationalists. As descendants of Adam, their covenant-breaking representative (Rom. 5:12), every man refuses to submit his mind in the way of obedience to the mind of God. He undertakes to interpret the nature of reality in terms of himself as the final reference point. But to be a rationalist man must also be an irrationalist. Man obviously cannot legislate by logic for reality. Unwilling to admit that God has determined the laws of reality, man, by implication, attributes all power to chance. As a rationalist he says that only that is possible which he can logically grasp in exhaustive fashion. As an irrationalist he says that since he cannot logically grasp the whole of reality, and really cannot legislate for existence by logic at all, it is chance that rules supreme. It is to this rationalist-irrationalist man that the gospel comes with its doctrine of creation and revelation, its doctrine of redemption through grace in Christ. It is quite impossible to challenge the modern man with the gospel of Christ unless this gospel of Christ be set in its widest possible setting. It is that which the Reformed faith tries to do.[110]

On the one hand, the unbeliever will be a rationalist who is committed to the competence of the human mind, while on the other hand he will resort to an irrationalist mind-set that cannot find a secure starting point in a changing universe or escape the deadly challenge of skepticism. This tension or incoherence in the unbeliever's approach to knowledge manifests itself not simply as a philosophical quandary for the unbeliever, but also expresses itself in his intellectual attempts to repudiate the Christian faith. In this memorable summary of the would-be autonomous man's declaration to the Christian, Van Til highlights the conflicting rational and irrational themes of unbelief: "Nobody knows anything for sure, but we know that you are wrong"!

---

110. *Introduction to Systematic Theology*, 174.

ANCIENT IDEALISM: PLATO [111]

(A) In his doctrine of reminiscence as well as in his doctrine of ideal identification of man with God[112] through intuition, Plato laid great emphasis upon the principle of *changeless unity*. Man had himself to be participant in this principle in order to have unity in his experience. Accordingly, he tended to deny either the existence, or at least the real significance, of change. The world

111. The following excerpts are taken from:
  (A) *Reformed Pastor and Modern Thought*, 81;
  (B) "Nature and Scripture," in *The Infallible Word*, ed. N. B. Stonehouse and Paul Woolley (Philadelphia: Presbyterian and Reformed, 1946), 284–85;
  (C) *Survey of Christian Epistemology*, 25–43.

    The importance of Plato (c. 428–c. 348 B.C.) for the history of philosophy (and for the theory of knowledge in particular) is evident; as A. N. Whitehead once put it, the history of Western philosophy is a series of footnotes to Plato. As a graduate student, Van Til read Plato's writings in the original Greek. As brilliant a thinker as Plato was, according to Van Til, if this would-be autonomous man could not develop a cogent and coherent theory of knowledge, there would be few (if any) who could improve on his effort.
    For Plato, to understand anything (from justice to cows) is to relate it to its class concept—to be able rationally to define the general nature of that which manifests itself in all the individual acts (of justice) or objects (particular cows). Mere opinion (derived from perception and imagination) is characterized by experience of a plurality of particulars or things that are only partly real because they are constantly changing and imperfect; our beliefs here are always subject to qualification or refutation. "Knowledge," on the other hand, pertains to what unifies the many particulars of experience (the Idea of duck, rather than the plurality of ducks on the pond), what is ideal (perfect and unchanging), and what is fully real and (thus) can be stated without qualification. The definable objects of knowledge (Ideas) must be essential or universal (e.g., triangularity as opposed to the many drawings of triangles in this world) and stable; thus, their existence is distinguishable from the perceptible or sensed world of time and space, which is always diverse (characterized by multiplicity), changing, and imperfect. A person cannot learn the unchanging and perfect conceptual essence of any thing (its Idea, ideal, or form) through sense experience of the changing particulars in this world; such knowledge is innate within him or "recollected" (intuited) from his soul's preexistent life (prior to becoming "entombed or imprisoned" in the physical body) in the realm of changeless, universal, and abstract Ideas. The particulars "participate" in the Idea of which they are instances or imperfect approximations (as different actors "participate" in the role of the scripted character in a play). The world of our experience is a cross between the unchanging realm of being and the changing realm of nonbeing. That is, the chaotic and irrational realm of matter was "in-formed" (formed into particular, temporal, and imperfect instances of the eternal prototypes or Ideas of things) by the divine activity of a "demiurge"—an explanation which Plato fully admitted to be mythical (and philosophically desperate).
112. In describing Plato's view, Van Til does not use the terms "God" and "the divine" in a personalistic and Christian fashion, nor does he use the terms that Plato

of "becoming" had only a quasi-existence and knowledge of it was only a quasi-knowledge. In man, however, there was a rational soul which was not part of this quasi-existent world of chance, but was participant in the divine.

Plato spoke much of the reality of that which is above man in the way of eternal truth. In order for man to exist and to know at all, he had to be essentially divine; that is, in his intellectual soul man had to be participant in the very being of the ideal world. The world of temporal reality was not, for Plato, the revelation of the self-contained God. If, therefore, he could prove that his worldview could make intelligible the nature of reality, thereby making the world understandable without reference to the Creator-Redeemer, he would have justified to himself and to his followers his covenant-breaking attitude.

(B) As for Plato this [monistic assumption] may be observed first from the hard and fast distinction that he makes between the world of being that is wholly known and the world of non-being that is wholly unknown. For Plato any being that is really to exist must be eternal and changeless. Similarly any knowledge that really can be called knowledge must be changeless, comprehensive knowledge. It is in terms of these principles that Plato would explain the world of phenomena. This world is intermediate between the world of pure being that is wholly known and the world of pure non-being that is wholly unknown. The being that we see constitutes a sort of tension between pure being and pure non-being.[113] So also the learning process constitutes a sort of tension between pure omniscience and pure ignorance.

Plato's view of the relation of sensation and conceptual thought corresponds to this basic division between the worlds of pure being and pure non-being. The senses are said to deceive us. It is only by means of the intellect as inherently divine that man can know true being. The real philosopher bewails his contact with the world of non-being. He knows he has fallen from his heavenly home. He knows that he is real only to the extent that he is divine. He seeks to draw away from all contact with non-being. He seeks for identifica-

---

himself would have chosen. They refer to what is transcendent, unchanging, and eternal. Only God (as Christians would say) could know such things, but Plato presents man as knowing them (by intuition and preexistence), and thus being identified with or participating in the prerogatives or abilities of God. Reality is intelligible to man, according to Plato, because he is "essentially divine" (being preexistent and comprehending eternal truths).

113. Pure being is represented by the Ideas or forms (particularly the unifying Idea of the Good), and pure nonbeing is represented by the realm of matter (which is evil). Things in the "phenomenal" world of experience are a cross between unintelligible matter (nonbeing) and intellectually comprehensible Ideas or forms (being).

tion with the "wholly Other," which, for the moment, he can speak of only in negative terms. When Socrates speaks of the Good he can only say what it is not. The Ideal table is never seen on land or sea. Piety must be defined as beyond anything that gods or men may say about it. True definition needs for its criterion an all-inclusive, supra-divine as well as supra-human, principle of continuity. Ultimate rationality is as much above God as above man.[114]

The result is that for Plato, too, nature is revelational. But it is revelational as much of man as of God.[115] To the extent that either of them is real, and known as real, he is wholly identical with the rational principle that is above both. On the other hand, as real and known in the rational principle, both are face to face with the world of non-being. And this world of non-being is as ultimate as the world of pure being. So God and man are wholly unknown to themselves. Thus both God and man are both wholly known and wholly unknown to themselves. Reality as known to man is a cross between abstract timeless formal logic and equally abstract chance. Yet in it all the ideal pure rationality as pure being dominates the scene.

(C) We have thus far been speaking of the beginnings of Greek philosophy. Under that general heading it was necessary also to look at the questions of neutrality and evil. It remains now to look at the highest development of Greek thought as far as it has bearing upon our subject.

In order to reach our goal, it will not be essential that we review every one of the Greek philosophers in order to see what they have to say on the subject of epistemology. We are not interested in the historical development of Greek epistemology except insofar as it throws light on the highest spot reached by Plato and Aristotle. And of these two philosophers we shall consider Plato rather than, or at least more than, Aristotle. The reason for this is that we are chiefly interested in knowing what the Greek genius has to say on the place of the human mind in the universe, and this may be more easily ascertained from a study of Plato than from a study of Aristotle. And even

114. Ideas exist in themselves and are definitive for the thinking of whatever gods there may be, according to Platonism. If a god declares something to be good or pious, it is only because he has "looked up" to the definitional Idea or standard of goodness or piety, which is above himself and men alike.
115. If the natural world is intelligible, it is only because the realm of matter has been "in-formed." The forms or Ideas that organize the unintelligible realm of matter are "divine" in Van Til's sense that they are self-existent, transcendent, unchanging, and eternal. Thus, the mind of man (with its innate awareness of Ideas) is completely knowable, while the material realm in itself (non-being) is completely unknowable (beyond rational understanding, not being form or Idea).

if we are mistaken on this point, it is of no great moment. No one will gainsay that a study of Plato gives a fair crosscut of Greek thought. . . . We hold that both Plato and Aristotle stood diametrically opposed to Christianity, and that it is out of the question to speak of Christianity as having developed out of either of their philosophies. This does not deny the fact that Greek thought in general and the philosophy of Plato and Aristotle in particular has been of great *formal* value to Christianity. Nor do we mean to intimate that Christianity has, in many of its exponents, not actually been influenced by the pagan motif. But the genius of Christianity is a reversal of the genius of the Greeks.

It is to Plato's doctrine of the soul that we must turn to find what may be called the high-water mark of Greek epistemological speculation. In it we have before us the ripest fruits of Greek speculation on the place of man's mind in the universe. . . .

Greek philosophy as a whole tends to depersonalization and abstraction. . . . It was characteristic of the genius of the Greek mind to run into abstractions. It is inherent in all apostate thought to think abstractly.

A third general remark to be made is that Greek thought in general was intellectualistic. The emotional and volitional aspects of man are given scant attention. The essence of the soul is found in the contemplation of the "Ideas." Plato was firmly convinced that the world of sense is not the most real world. It has its reality, to be sure. But its reality was adequately known through the senses. The more real world was the world of Ideas, and that could not be known through the senses; it had to be known through contemplation by the mind.

It will be found upon careful scrutiny that all three of these characteristics just enumerated, (a) a tendency to identification of the human mind with the laws of the universe as a whole, (b) a tendency toward depersonalization and abstraction, and (c) a tendency toward intellectualism, will be found to be characteristic of all non- or anti-theistic thought. . . .

The form of the presentation here [in the *Symposium*] is metaphorical, but we can already see the direction in which Plato's thought is moving. The true nature of man is his soul, and not his body. A dualism is developing. Moreover, the true nature of man is the intellect and not the senses. Only through the intellect can man come into contact with the universals, and these universal Ideas have more reality than the particulars of sense experience. Another dualism is developing. The true function of man's soul is contemplation of the Ideas, and its highest destiny is separation from the world of sense in order to be wholly absorbed in the contemplation of Ideas. . . .

In the *Phaedo* this line of argument is pursued in still more detail. True knowledge is of universals only, and it is the soul in its intellectual capacity that is fitted to come into contact with this world.

Still we must not draw this argument too sharply. Even in the *Protagoras*, an early dialogue, Plato has made Socrates admit that if virtue is teachable, there must be a stage of learning. And this could not be the case if there is too sharp a separation between the world of sense and the world of Ideas. In that case one either knows or does not know; one is either in contact with the Ideal world and therefore in possession of it as knowledge, or one is a poor earthworm and knows nothing at all. Some reality must be given to the world of sense inasmuch as learning seems to be possible. Perhaps the in-dwelling of the soul in the body is not altogether in vain. . . .

The nasty problem why there should be an incarnation of the Ideas at all is not here discussed.[116] . . . Even in Plato's maturest thought as expressed in the *Timaeus*, there is only a faintest suggestion of the idea that it is perhaps the soul's function to bring together two opposing forces in the universe, namely, spirit and matter. And this lack of any notion of reconciliation that at all approaches the Christian idea of the subject corroborates what was said above about the assumption on the part of the Greeks, that the mind of man is naturally sound. It is assumed that there is no reconciliation to be made be-tween God and man. And if there is any reconciliation to be made at all, it is the mind of man that is to do the reconciling. . . . Instead of needing a Me-diator, the mind of man sets itself up as mediator if there is to be any medi-ator at all.[117] . . .

For all practical purposes [Plato's] conception of time as "the moving image of eternity" amounts to saying that the eternal and the temporal are equally ultimate aspects of one general Reality. . . . [A]ccording to Plato, time and eternity are equally underived.[118] . . .

116. That is, even if one granted Plato's point that the Ideas (forms) would have needed to organize or form the material realm in order to make the world of sense knowable, and then granted that it is knowable to human souls which, in-nately aware of the forms, are imprisoned in bodies, he has still given no ratio-nale or explanation for why the Ideas (forms) or human souls ever became "in-carnated" in the lower realm of time and space at all. Thus, Plato's epistemology is ultimately arbitrary and rests on unwarranted assumption.

117. That is, Plato grants to the mind of man the function of the divine Messiah, in being a mediator between the transcendent (heavenly, eternal) and immanent (earthly, temporal) realms; every man is a little "incarnation" of the divine (the forms innate in the soul) within a fleshly body. Were it not for this divine soul in him, man could never know anything in his present temporal-spatial experi-ence. The "reconciliation" between "heaven" and "earth" (forms and matter), however, is not for Plato a soteriological matter dealing with redemption from sin and guilt.

118. The criticism here is that, even on Plato's own terms, what is unintelligible

Plato was still willing to attribute some possible meaning to the myths of which the forefathers spoke. . . . Plato, of course, as a philosopher begins by assuming that the human mind is capable of meeting the riddles of the universe, but that when man sees more deeply into the limitations of human thought he is willing to listen with some respect to those who claim to have had revelations from the gods. . . . There might possibly be something to these myths after all. . . .

So Plato's chief argument is here that the soul partakes of the Idea of life and therefore is immortal. Soul is in intimate relation with Ideas but is not itself an Idea.[119] . . . Here we strike the heart of the matter. The Idea of life partakes of the general characteristics of all Ideas, namely, that it is eternal and self-existent. Now of this Idea of life the soul is a concrete manifestation or particularization. The soul "participates" in the Idea of life and is therefore underived . . . [in which case] the notion *of change is taken right into the realm of Ideas.*[120] . . .

In Plato's thought man as such is, as it were, substituted for the second person in the Trinity. Man as ultimate is as God; only it is he that appears in the temporal sphere and seems to be no different from God. What the Chalcedon Creed confesses about the Theanthropos[121] identified with the person of Christ, Plato confesses about the Theanthropos identified with generic man.[122] For orthodox Christianity it is *Christ* who "somehow" combines the eternal and the temporal into a close union *without intermixture.*[123] In the

---

(change, chaos, time) is as basic as what is intelligible (stability, unity, eternity). Thus, there could never be epistemological certainty. Rationalism would be canceled by irrationalism.

119. If soul were an Idea, it would not be active and part of the changing world (imprisoned in the body)—which is the linchpin of Plato's epistemology. By its very nature ("life"), the soul must be subject to movement or activity. But if the soul is not an Idea, it must be unintelligible (being singular in nature, neither abstract nor universal). In that case, Plato's view of the intelligibility of the world to man hangs on something which is itself unintelligible.

120. The objects of knowledge must exist in an unchanging realm, as Plato insisted. But by introducing the active soul of man into that realm, Plato rendered it changing and—on his own presuppositions—unknowable.

121. That is, the "God-man."

122. There is a crucial insight here which bears on apologetics. In the nature of the case, philosophical speculation seeks general principles or universal truths, and thus whatever "way of salvation" it would devise must focus on "generic man" or truths that any man could work out on his own for all other men. The particularity and exclusivity of the Christian gospel, centered on one historical individual, is offensive to Greek speculation and all unbelieving philosophy.

123. Van Til is reflecting here an aspect of the mystery of the hypostatic union (between the divine and human natures in one person) as declared and defined by the Chalcedonian formula—"without confusion, division, mixture, or separation."

case of Plato's thought it is *man* who "somehow" combines the eternal and the temporal *by way of an admixture.* . . .

Platonism *does* and Christianity *does not* admit a final mystery in its system. . . . Platonism on the other hand must maintain that the divine mind as well as the human mind is surrounded with a universe which neither of the two minds has penetrated or can penetrate. Hence mystery exists equally for God and man.[124] . . .

But now we are to observe carefully that, according to Plato, altogether different laws obtain in the eternal world of Ideas than in the temporal world of sense. In the sense world there is nothing upon which one can depend. There is no telling but that things may turn into their very opposites. There is no underlying unity that controls and gives meaning to the diversity of the sense world.[125] There is here an ultimate plurality without an equally ultimate unity. It was for this reason that there was no guarantee to be found in empirical reasoning for the immortality of the soul. But in the world of Ideas everything is different. There nothing changes. There we seem to meet with an ultimate unity without an equally ultimate diversity. The soul which partakes of the nature of the Idea of life also partakes of the nature of the unchangeability which is characteristic of the Idea of life, as well as of all other Ideas. Hence things can never change into their opposites. More than that, things can never change at all. In the world of Ideas qualities are absolute.

To which of these two worlds, then, does the soul really belong? Surely it cannot belong to both, if the qualities of the Ideal world are summed up in complete unchangeability and the qualities of the sense world are summed up in complete changeability.[126] On the other hand it is equally certain that the soul must belong to both worlds or there would be no unity in its thought.

Plato cannot escape this difficulty and he does not wish to do so. Hence he admits in the end that it might not be so foolish after all to listen to the ancients who claimed to have a revelation of the gods on the subject. . . .

Plato would at one time conceive of the Ideas as immovable, so that in-

---

124. Plato could not give a "rational" account of how the Ideas come to organize the chaotic realm of matter, nor could he give a "rational" account of how man's mind comes to occupy a physical body. In the end, Plato resorted to admitted myths to save his "rationality." There is no reason for the way things are or how things happen; thus, mystery surrounds the thinking of man as well as the gods.

125. In popular parlance, everything is random and unconnected—a matter of "chance."

126. If man is simply matter in motion, then his thinking apparatus (the brain) must be characterized by what is true of matter and motion. If his brain is finite, particular, and changing, its operations or results will not manifest the opposite characteristics (pertaining to truth, laws, principles, etc.) of universality and immutability.

carnation[127] would be impossible. Then again, seeing that incarnation was a fact notwithstanding its theoretical impossibility, he would hold that the eternal had entered into the temporal, so that there was no longer an essential difference between time and eternity. . . .

In the second place, Plato tried to find knowledge by seeking it in the Ideal world alone. But this attempt, too, he recognized to be a failure. There was, to begin with, trouble in the heavenly realm itself. There seemed to be a fundamental and an underlying unity there in the Idea of the Good.[128] That Idea seemed to rule as king over all the other Ideas. But the question was, by what right did the Idea of Good rule over all the others? Was it because the Idea of the Good was more ultimate? That was out of the question. The other Ideas were just as ultimate and not at all derived from the Idea of the Good. That this is so can be noted from the fact that there were Ideas of mud and hair and filth; that is, there were Ideas of evil things as well as of good things.[129] But since it was of the very nature of all Ideas to be unchangeable and to oppose their opposites, it would certainly be intolerable to contemplate the Idea of the Good as bringing forth the Idea of the Bad. This proves conclusively that there was for Plato a fundamental diversity as well as a fundamental unity in the world of Ideas. And this would offhand seem to be all to the good, inasmuch as that is just what we are looking for in a true theory of knowledge. But the point is that this very fact that there was a fundamental evil as well as a fundamental good proves that there was *really no underlying and controlling unity in the world of Ideas after all*.[130] . . .

On the other hand, one could never seek to account for the reality of the world of senses (sensuous world), if one would limit his knowledge to the standard of the Ideal world only. These could not be kept separate. And what was most important, Plato had the true insight that unless one could relate the two worlds in one comprehensive scheme of knowledge, one could not ex-

---

127. Van Til is referring here to the "incarnation" of the individual's soul in a body.
128. Attempting to follow his assumptions consistently, Plato realized that if plurality were ultimate in the realm of Ideas (forms), then this realm would be unknowable, not being related or reducible to a general unity. Thus, he proposed (in a sense that is unclear) that all the Ideas are really "united" in, and expressible as instances of, the Idea of "the Good."
129. This is embarrassing for Plato because he conceived of the realm of Ideas (the Ideal realm) as that which is good or of positive value. For evil things to be intelligible, there must be an Idea for them, but that awkwardly suggests that such Ideas are in their nature both evil (as to substance) and good (as to form) simultaneously.
130. Emphasis added. This is a very good illustration of what Van Til takes to be an "internal critique" of the unbeliever's worldview and theory of knowledge—showing that it is a failure even on its own terms.

pect to know anything about either of the two worlds.[131] He felt that in the human soul the two worlds were somehow united, and one would have to understand this union to understand either the soul itself or anything else. . . .

Plato assumed that it was possible for man to reason with the categories of eternity. This is in the nature of the case impossible for a time-conditioned creature such as man finds himself to be.[132] . . . Hence if he cannot reason with any but temporal categories, his knowledge is useless. The only way then for man to have any knowledge of either temporal or eternal things is for a God to think for us in eternal categories and reveal to us the Measure of truth we can fathom. Thus we hold that Christian theism is the only alternative to skepticism. . . .

In other words, the doctrine of Ideas left the problem of the one and the many, and therefore that of creation, unsolved. If the Ideal world was itself an ultimate plurality, it could be of no service in an attempt to explain the plurality of the world we live in.

Still further, if the Ideas were to be divided there would be no end to this process. An Idea would be required for every participation of an Idea in a sensuous object. And this process would have to go on indefinitely. Thus knowledge would be face to face with an infinite regression.[133]

131. If there is an ultimate and irresolvable plurality (dichotomy, duality) of explanatory principles in one's philosophy, then it is impossible to be certain of the relationship between the principles and the appropriate application of them, leaving (at best) an irrationally divided "field of knowledge" or (at worst) ultimate skepticism. Plato realized this, thus attempting to devise an epistemology in which unity is recognized as necessary and final. But the unremitting dualism of time and eternity destroyed his "comprehensive scheme" (to use Van Til's words). For the Christian, the ultimate unifying principle is the self-sufficient, eternal, sovereign, personal, and triune Creator of heaven and earth. And within this Creator there is an equal ultimacy of unity and plurality (three persons in one essence). The impersonal, particular, and causal features of the physical universe are subordinate to this God—see the doctrines of creation and providence—in the Christian's "comprehensive scheme of knowledge." This is not so for Plato, who could not make the realms of Idea and matter mutually intelligible.

132. This problem reappears over and over again down through the history of epistemological theorizing. Men will take, for instance, the "laws of logic" to be necessary to rational thinking, characterizing them as universal and absolute. However, the brain of man who uses these laws, given its limitations and foibles, is neither universal in the scope of its experience nor absolute in its accuracy. So how does the eternal and unchanging (laws, concepts, ideas) ever comport with the finite and changing (individual man)?

133. If relationships are intelligible on Plato's terms, they must be an instance of a general Idea. The relationship between particular things and their Idea is that of "participation," said Plato. Similarly, each participation must itself participate in an Idea of participation, and that participation must in turn participate in its

In desperation, Plato asks himself whether we may then think that the Ideas are no more than our thoughts, that is, only subjective. But he finds that this offers no escape. If in such a case the Ideas were to remain in contact with the world of sense and have meaning for it, we would have to conclude . . . that all our thought about reality is merely subjective, that is, that there is nothing more to reality than our subjective thought. Thus knowledge would be reduced to an illusion.

On the other hand, if Ideas are no more than thoughts, we might think of them as not having penetrated [or covered] the whole of reality, in order thus to save ourselves from subjectivism. But in that case there would be an area of reality totally unknown to anyone. And yet this area might have some influence upon the reality that we seem to have knowledge of. Hence we would not even have knowledge of that of which we thought we had knowledge. We would once more be face to face with an infinite regress. . . .

The final conclusion drawn from this renewed investigation of the theory of Ideas is that the fact of knowledge cannot be explained with it. And the reason for this was that the logic employed throughout was too abstract and exclusive. It was impossible to get a set of immovable qualities to explain anything in an inherently moving body such as the temporal universe was. . . .

In our criticism of this Platonic logic it is not imperative that we discuss the question to what extent Plato thought this attempt at a solution of the problem of knowledge successful. We may say that Plato felt the problem of knowledge to be unsolved even after this modification of the doctrine of Ideas. He practically says that much when he makes the statement that not all forms will intermingle with all forms.[134] If all forms intermingled with all forms, there would once more be a completely colorless mass. In that case it would be as difficult to make any statement about reality as it would be if all things were immovable as the world of Ideas was formerly thought of as immovable. In either case we would be at the place where the Megarians were, who said that all things were One, and concluded that predication was consequently impossible. And then we would be face to face with the question whether this One were to be thought of as temporal or as eternal. If as eternal, then the whole of temporal reality remained unaccounted for. If as tem-

---

own Idea of participation, and so on *ad infinitum.* Thus, as Van Til indicates, on Plato's own terms a man cannot know any one particular thing without having infinite knowledge. This is a *reductio ad absurdum* that confronts the variations of idealistic epistemology that appear throughout the history of philosophy.

134. If all the forms (Ideas) "intermingle," then they are not truly distinct from one another or ultimately diverse at all. They are not a plurality, but just one confused Idea (an ultimate, but irrational unity)!

poral, we could not help but think of an ultimate plurality. Thus an ultimate
plurality would mean the same thing as an ultimate unity. And this amounts
to saying once more that our predication as a whole is without meaning.[135] . . .

Plato insisted that the Idea of evil was as original as the Idea of the Good.
He also insisted that the Idea of plurality was as original as the Idea of unity.
And more than that, he insisted that the Idea of time was as fundamental as
the Idea of eternity. This amounted to saying that the Idea of time is as *eternal* as the Idea of eternity itself. Or it amounts to saying that the Idea of eternity is as temporal as the Idea of temporality. All of which comes to a complete confusion and stultification of thought. Plato cannot escape the criticism
of the *third man*.[136] If there must be an Idea of man to explain the Socrates
who walked in Athens, there must be once more an Idea of the participation
of Socrates in the Idea of Socrates, and so on ad infinitum. Plato himself clearly
saw this difficulty when he criticized his first and second positions. He has in
no way escaped these difficulties in his third position.[137] The Neoplatonists
demonstrated this fact when they tried to work out this platonic principle with
respect to the Mediator. When they tried to find a Mediator that was to be
an intermixture between the unapproachable Eternal and the Temporal they
had to continue making more Mediators all the time.[138]

135. If everything is timelessly the same (forming an ultimate oneness), it would be
    unintelligible to predicate greenness of the grass ("The grass is green"), because
    grass and greenness could not be differentiated. On the other hand, if every-
    thing is constantly different (an ultimate plurality), it would still be unintelli-
    gible to predicate greenness of the grass, because the single term "grass" (as
    also the single term "green") could not be used for a multiplicity of things or
    experiences; each separate experience (or event) would call for its own dif-
    ferent term.
136. Van Til refers here to the most famous criticism of the doctrine of Ideas, which
    was raised by Plato himself in the dialogue named *Parmenides*. Any plurality of
    things designated by a single term (e.g., "man") has a corresponding Idea (of
    man), in terms of which each particular deserves to be designated. But the orig-
    inal class of men plus the Idea of man—all of which are designated "man"—
    forms an expanded class or greater plurality, which calls for a further Idea ("the
    third man") to unify the new class, and so on *ad infinitum*. Thus, in order to know
    any one thing, given Plato's analysis, one must have infinite knowledge. This is
    one of the many ways in which it can be shown that Plato's distinguishable realm
    of Ideas—separate from the world of time and space, as well as from the indi-
    vidual's soul—cannot account for the individual's ability to know anything.
137. Van Til, like most interpreters of Plato, divides up the career of the philosopher
    into different (usually three) phases. Van Til taught that Plato tried a first posi-
    tion, found it epistemologically inadequate and modified it—only to apply fur-
    ther criticism to his second position as well. The final position adopted by Plato,
    according to Van Til's assessment, did not escape the difficulties of the first two.
138. If two original "terms" in a polar duality (A–B) require a connecting interme-
    diary (A–C–B), then the duality between the first term and the intermediary

All antitheistic thought has to face the third man argument because all antitheistic thought . . . [is] based upon abstract reasoning.

ANCIENT EMPIRICISM: ARISTOTLE[139]

(A) In a non-Christian scheme of thought abstract universals and particulars stand over against one another in an unreconcilable fashion. Such was the case in Plato's philosophy. Aristotle sought to remedy the situation by teaching that the universals are present in the particulars. But he failed to get genuine contact between them, inasmuch as for him the lowest universal (*infima species*), was, after all, a supposed abstraction from particulars. Hence the particulars that were presupposed were bare particulars, having no manner of contact with universality. And if they should, *per impossible*, have contact with universality, they would lose their individuality.[140] . . .

(A–C), as well as the duality between the intermediary and the second term (C–B), will themselves require further intermediaries (A–D–C–E–B), and so on *ad infinitum*.

139. The following excerpts are taken from:

(A) *Common Grace*, 81;
(B) "Nature and Scripture," 285–86;
(C) *Reformed Pastor and Modern Thought*, 82–83, 85–86, 88–90.

    Aristotle (384–322 B.C.) was the most famous student in Plato's Academy and was an instructor there until Plato's death; after tutoring young Alexander the Great, he returned to Athens and founded his own school, the Lyceum. His collected works cover nearly all the "sciences" of that era and are characterized by a breadth of empirical data. While appropriately calling his viewpoint "empiricism," we should nevertheless distinguish it from the more stringently observational epistemology of (say) Epicurus; Aristotle still retained the Platonic presupposition that reality resides in Idea (or form). But Aristotle was critical of Plato's theory of a mysterious, transcendent realm of Ideas, finding such Ideas useless as an explanatory instrument—especially for explaining the most common feature of natural experience, change or motion. For Aristotle, individual, sensible things are the "primary substances" which alone have separate existence; the species (concepts, forms) of such things, which make them intelligible, are embodied in the particulars themselves. Every natural object is a compound of intelligible form and individuating matter. An object is known through sensation (acting on the "passive intellect"), followed by the "active intellect" drawing out of it the object's intelligible form or Idea—a process of mental abstraction. There are two kinds of being for Aristotle, then: actuality (found in the definable, universal form or Idea) and passive potentiality (found in the particularizing or individuating principle of matter). Change in a sensible particular (say, an acorn) is a process by which a dynamic potentiality in it (say, an oak tree) becomes actualized ("realized").

140. Is the individual substance or particular dog, Fido, knowable or intelligible in his individuality? For Aristotle, what is "knowable" is the definable concept that

(B) As over against Plato, Aristotle contends that we must not look for rationality as a principle wholly beyond the things we see. Universals are to be found within particulars. All our troubles come from looking for the one apart from the other. We must, to be sure, think of pure form at the one end and of pure matter at the other end of our experience. But whatever we actually know consists of pure form and pure matter in correlativity with one another. Whenever we would speak of Socrates, we must not look for some exhaustive description of him by means of reference to an Idea that is "wholly beyond." Socrates is numerically distinct from Callias because of pure potentiality or matter.[141] Rational explanation must be satisfied with classification. The definition of Socrates is fully expressed in terms of the lowest species. Socrates as a numerical individual is but an instance of a class. Socrates may weigh two hundred pounds and Callias may weigh one hundred pounds. When I meet Socrates downtown he may knock me down; when I meet Callias there I may knock him down. But all this is "accidental."[142] None of the perceptual characteristics of Socrates, not even his snub-nosedness, belong to the Socrates that I define.[143] By means of the primacy of my intellect I know Socrates as he is, forever the same, no matter what may "accidentally" happen to him. And what is true of Socrates is true of all other things.

Aristotle's philosophy, then, as over against that of Plato, stresses the correlativity of abstract rationality and pure Chance. Aristotle takes Plato's worlds of pure being and pure non-being and insists that they shall recognize a need of one another. Neither Plato nor Aristotle speaks of limiting concepts in the sense that modern philosophers use this term. Yet both Plato and Aristotle in effect use such limiting concepts, and Aristotle more so than Plato.

---

is common to the many particulars (e.g., the many "dogs"). Thus, even the most specific thing that you could say in order to differentiate Fido from the genus (the lowest species) would still be an abstraction. If Fido stands in his bare particularity, he cannot be known. To the degree that Fido is known, he loses his individuality.

141. Socrates and Callias are both instances of the "form" (universal) of humanity, but they are different from each other because they have different material bodies.

142. In philosophical terminology, "accidental" qualities or properties are those that are not "essential" to what a thing is. For example, a fish tail is essential to a mermaid, but the color of her hair is an accidental or incidental quality; if her hair color were different, she would still be a mermaid.

143. If one devised a "complex" universal (e.g., the form or Idea of man weighing two hundred pounds, having a snub nose, etc.) for every particular met in one's experience, there would be as many universals as particulars and no point to distinguishing between universals and particulars. Moreover, the problem would then arise of how the universal of snub-nosedness relates to the complex universal of Socratesness (and to every other universal that incorporates snub-nosedness).

(C) Thus, in contradistinction from Parmenides, Aristotle holds that being is not all of one kind; it is inherently various and hierarchical. At the bottom of the ladder is pure matter or potentiality. At the top of the ladder is pure form. But we never meet with either pure form or pure matter in actual experience. *Reality as we see it is always composite.* The matter in it contributes the individuating, and the form in it, the universalizing, element. Thus Aristotle thinks that he can do justice to individuality and universality alike.

The relation of Aristotle to his predecessors is therefore very similar to that of Kant to the empiricist, Hume, and the rationalist, Leibniz. Aristotle's position may, we think, not unfairly be said to be a sort of pre-phenomenalist phenomenalism.[144] Of course Aristotle's position is not modern; it is realistic, not critical. Our contention is that he takes the first important step in the direction of modern phenomenalism, and that there was nowhere else that anyone, who wanted to maintain the non-Christian concept of the autonomy of man, could go.[145] The autonomous man must on the one hand seek to explain reality exhaustively; he must hold that unless he does so, he has not explained it at all.[146] By definition, he has no Creator-Redeemer Mind back of his own mind. On the other hand, the autonomous man must hold that any diversity that exists is independent of God.[147] . . .

It should be noted that Aristotle himself never separated sharply between the passive and active intellect in man. He was indeed anxious to develop realism, the reality of facts and their true existence apart from the activity of the human mind with respect to them. . . . In Aristotelianism *God is pure ac-*

---

144. CVT: Phenomenalism: "The theory that all we know is a phenomenon, that is, reality present to consciousness, either directly or reflectively; and that phenomena are all that there are to know, there being no thing-in-itself or object out of relation to consciousness" (*Dictionary of Philosophy and Psychology*, ed. James Baldwin, Gloucester: 1960).

145. That is, autonomous realism degenerates into its opposite, namely, phenomenalism. For a philosopher like Aristotle who is attempting to defend the knowledge of "real" objects that are public or external to the mind, this is a devastating critique by Van Til. On Aristotle's own assumptions, what an individual man knows (i.e., the abstraction, the intelligible species) is the result of the internal activity of his own mind and thus private to himself.

146. If there is a segment of reality that he is not aware of and cannot account for or understand (and who could know how extensive it is?), then he cannot be sure that there are not factors that are relevant to, or would interfere with, the adequacy of the explanations he has offered for what he experiences. If his explanatory principles cannot be thought of as universal, but are subject to possible qualification, he cannot say in any particular case that it is appropriate to use those principles or that he is not being arbitrary or shortsighted.

147. The particularity of objects and events is simply random and unintelligible—a matter of chance, rather than produced by the creative and providential work of God.

tive intellect. He is pure act. Man's mentality *shares* in the nature of the divine activity. It is only on the basis of this *sharing in the divine activity* that abstraction from the sensible world, or the making of generalizations, so essential to the Aristotelian scheme, can be effected. The intellect of man abstracts the intelligible species that are said to be found in the facts that surround him. All *certain* knowledge is exclusively of universals. The intellect cannot deal with sensible facts otherwise than in terms of *concepts*. But facts *are* not concepts; they are *individuations of concepts*. Matter as such, pure matter as opposed to pure ACT, is non-rational and cannot be the object of intellectual knowledge.[148] It is the *species* that exist in the facts of sense that are said to be discovered by the intellect, and this discovery is not merely a passive something. . . . [N]o non-Christian can finally escape the virtual identification of the human mind with the divine mind. So Aristotle, in thinking of the human mind as discovering the intelligible species in the things, is virtually attributing the same powers to the human mind that he attributes to the divine mind. The active mind of man is ideally identical with the active mind which is God. . . .

What this position[149] really amounts to is that man can by these self-evident principles interpret reality correctly without taking God into consideration from the outset.

This position is, to be sure, not the same as that of Parmenides, or even of Plato. For convenience we may say that whereas Parmenides wanted to use the law of contradiction positively, Aristotle wanted to use it more in the way modern philosophy uses it—negatively. We do not say that he was doing what Kant did when he formalized and subjectivized universality entirely. Aristotle was still a realist and not critical in the modern Kantian sense of the term. But he was working in the direction of Criticism.[150] He was frankly allowing that there was a reality beyond that which can be conceptualized by man.[151] But

148. Accordingly, Aristotle's version of empirical epistemology renders the particularity of facts (or individual objects) nonrational or unintelligible—another disastrous internal failure.

149. In context, Van Til has just mentioned the view that the first principles of reasoning are self-evident, but that the existence of God is not—a view advanced by Thomas Aquinas, following Aristotle.

150. Immanuel Kant's scrupulous attempt to investigate the nature and limits of human understanding is often called "Criticism"—following the titles of his important treatises: *The Critique of Pure Reason*, *The Critique of Practical Reason*, and *The Critique of Judgment*.

151. In Aristotle's approach, what can be conceptualized are the formal or universal aspects of an object. Beyond what is rationally known, however, there is also the "material"—the irrationally individuating—principle, which accounts for what the particular sensible substance is. As with Kant, there is a mysterious realm be-

he was also saying that for any such reality to be known by man, it had to lose its uniqueness and be subjected to the classification of formal logic.

The essential point, then, about the human mind as active, in the way Aristotle conceived of it, is that it is virtually *taken out of its temporal conditions*. The intellect of man is absolutized. Its ultimately legislative character is taken for granted. When it is compelled to admit that there is anything in reality that is beyond its control, it assumes that this something can have no determinative significance for the knowledge that man has. . . .

The Thomistic notion of the mind of man as potentially participating in the mind of God,[152] leads to an impersonal principle that is purely formal, and as such is correlative to brute factual material of a non-rational sort. It follows that it is only by abstraction from individuality that the facts can be *known*. The whole scheme of the philosophy of nature is made into a "Chain of Being"[153] idea, fitted into a pattern of ever-increasing universality. Inasmuch as anything is higher in the scale of being than something else, it is to that extent less individual. All knowledge is of universals. And, as already observed, it is the mind conceived of as ultimate and as correlative to these facts that has to abstract from particularity in order to know them.

The point we are now most concerned to make here is that the position of Aristotle and Thomas is essentially no more realistic than is any form of modern idealism.[154] The pure intelligible essences of Thomistic philosophy are virtually intellectual constructs. If they did exist, they would be eternal and unchangeable and as such destructive of the Christian teaching about history.[155]

---

yond appearances that is not accessible to rationality, which might popularly be called the realm of "chance."

152. In the gradation of being from "pure actuality" at the top—as Aristotle would put it, God as "thought thinking thought"—and "pure potentiality" or matter at the bottom, there are different levels or degrees of reality and intelligibility. Man is a mixture of form, matter, and soul (*psyche*), which is active and intellectual—like God in this respect. Man's "active intellect" discovers what is knowable or intelligible about the world that we sense.

153. CVT: Cf. A. O. Lovejoy's *The Great Chain of Being* (Cambridge, 1942).

154. CVT: J. Maritain, a Roman Catholic philosopher, has attempted in his *Degrees of Knowledge* (London, 1959), to establish, unsuccessfully from our point of view, this more "realistic" nature of Thomas' thought.

155. Since eternal and unchangeable things are entirely unlike—indeed, contrary to the character of—brute and contingent facts, they would be destructive of the non-Christian's conception of history as well. This is the dialectical tension inherent in Aristotle's version of empirical knowledge. If the historical facts are knowable, they are eternal and unchangeable—and thus not historical at all. But if the facts are brute, contingent, and always changing, they are "historical" (in the sense given to that term in unbelieving worldviews), but unknowable.

MODERN RATIONALISM AND EMPIRICISM[156]

(A) If the "facts" of scientific knowledge had, each and all of them, charac-teristics of their own prior to their being known by man, they would, argues Kant, be forever unknowable.

The rationalists before Kant attempted to know such facts, but in the process of knowing them, reduced their individuality or uniqueness to blank identity. For Spinoza the "facts" simply *had* to be what the intellect of man, using the laws of logic, and especially the law of contradiction, said they must be. Accordingly for Spinoza, the order and connection of things is said to be identical with the order and connection of thought. Similarly Leibniz aimed at finding the individuality of facts by means of complete description.[157]

---

156. The following excerpts are taken from:

    (A) *Reformed Pastor and Modern Thought*, 107–9;
    (B) "Nature and Scripture," 293–94.

      The Continental rationalists were René Descartes (1596–1650), Baruch Spin-oza (1632–77), and Gottfried Leibniz (1646–1716). They maintained that there are self-evident truths from which we can deduce with certainty (taking mathe-matics as their model for method) substantive conclusions about reality. Spin-oza came to the conclusion that the laws of physics are implicative relations (under the attribute of spatial extension), reflecting the rational deductions of our minds, which are only in confused ways (at the level of sense perception) personally unique; at the level of pure thought, all minds are but one. Leibniz sought to protect the reality of individuals, arguing that what physics studies is actually a continuum of infinitely small units or centers of psychic activity ("mon-ads"), which differ from each other not physically, but in terms of different lev-els of thought (a unity of inner consciousness and awareness), but which all mir-ror the whole universe of monads. The "dream-philosophy" speculations of the rationalists were intellectually abhorrent to the British empiricists: John Locke (1632–1704), George Berkeley (1685–1753), and David Hume (1711–76). Ac-cording to them, there are no innate ideas; the mind starts out as a "blank tablet," which passively receives sense impressions. Only concrete particulars exist— which can be known (with probability) by means of observation. Given this em-pirical approach, Locke argued that ultimate realities (the individuals that com-bine various properties) or "substances" could not be known, even though they exist. Berkeley argued against material substance (as an abstract idea that is un-perceived), and Hume eventually argued against even mental substance (argu-ing that the mind is but a "bundle of perceptions"). Neither school of thought could make rationality and individual identity mutually intelligible, nor could either escape sliding into skepticism.

157. Leibniz held that every substance has its "complete concept," consisting of all the true propositions that apply to it. Every predicate that can be truly attributed to any subject is contained in the concept of that subject (thus making all true pred-icates essential, not accidental). Because a genuinely "complete" concept would provide adequate grounds to identify and distinguish one substance from an-other, a complete concept can only have one instance. The reason that one thing

According to these rationalists, therefore, there was not and there could not be anything new in science.[158]

Yet the very idea of science presupposes that genuinely new facts are discovered and that in being discovered they are not lost in a net of abstract logical relations but really add to a fund of existing knowledge. If the rationalists were right, logic itself would be reduced to an eternal changeless principle of identity. All facts would be wholly known by abstract thought thinking itself. Thus not only would there be no facts not wholly known but the idea of the "wholly known" would become an abstract contentless principle. Logic itself would become meaningless. There would be no longer any process of reasoning; such a process would be absorbed in identity.

The empiricist also believed in facts that had characteristics in themselves, prior to their being known in terms of relations between them and in terms of their relation to the one who knows them. Moreover, the empiricists saw what happened to these facts in the hands of angry rationalists. To keep the facts and their individuality from being swallowed up by logic, the empiricist proposed to bring the facts into relation with one another by means of *induction* rather than by *deduction*. To make sure that logic would do no damage to the individuality of space-time facts, John Locke, the father of empiricism, insisted that the mind is a *tabula rasa*. The mind simply *receives* and therefore does not destroy the uniqueness of the facts as it brings them together. The objectivity of knowledge is thus guaranteed, because the mind receives the facts *just as they are*.

However, the troubles of empiricism appeared clearly when its most brilliant exponent, David Hume, insisted that in receiving facts the mind is so passive, that its "concepts" are but faint replicas of its "percepts." This was evidence for Hume of the fact that the mind has no organizing power at all. Even if all the facts were brought into the mind in the forms of concepts they would still be utterly unrelated. It would be as though the human mind, like a modern Noah's ark, had gathered together all facts which the womb of chance has produced in the past and would produce in the future, only to realize that the concept of the ark is itself nothing but the faint replica of a percept. Thus all the facts would still be not partially but *wholly* hidden.

One step more needs to be taken in our analysis of rationalism and empiricism. If the rationalists were not to defeat their own purposes by being

---

differs from another is that their rational descriptions are not exactly alike. (Contrast this with Aristotle, for whom matter is the principle of individuation.)

158. For Spinoza, the results of science are rationally deducible and thus in principle knowable apart from observation. For Leibniz, from knowledge of any true property of a substance one can infer all its other properties.

wholly successful, i.e., in attaining the realization of their ideal of exhaustive reduction of all space-time factuality to a Parmenidean notion of abstract identity, then they would have to fall back on the idea of an unknown and unknowable realm of facts, in which each fact differs from all other facts by characteristics *wholly* unknowable. This would apply both to the supposed objects and to the supposed subjects of knowledge. If each of the objects of knowledge were to retain its identity, it would have to be impervious to other objects and to the mind of any knower. Similarly if the mind of the individual knower were not to be absorbed in advance by the Universal Mind, it would have to be *wholly* unaffectable by other, equally impervious, individual minds, and wholly inexplicable by any supposed universal mind.

The empiricists must fall back on the notion of the facts as being *wholly* and exhaustively known and reduced to one block of identity. Otherwise they would defeat themselves by being too successful in their attempt to attain absolute objectivity. The mind of the knower, the subject of knowledge, is said to be purely passive instead of creative, and the objects of knowledge are said to exist independently of the subject of knowledge. Without this rationalist notion of a logic that swallows up all facts, the empiricists could not explain how they could identify one fact in distinction from any other fact. The post-Kantian idealist critics of empiricism have pressed this point by saying that there is no possibility of counting without the presupposition of an absolute system of truth.[159]

(B) The rationalistic view, exhibited at its highest and best by Leibniz, represents the idea of univocal reasoning in its first modern garb. By means of refined mathematical technique, Leibniz hopes to reach that for which the ancients strove in vain, namely, individuation by complete description. God stands for the idea of pure mathematics by means of which all reality may be described as seen at a glance. All historical facts are essentially reducible to the timeless equations of mathematical formulae. Such is the nature and consequence of his ontological proof for the existence of God. There could be no revelation of God to man on such a basis. How could God tell man anything that he was not able eventually to discover by means of the differential calculus? God becomes wholly revealed to man, but with the result that he is no longer God.[160]

In opposition to the position of Leibniz, the rationalist, stands that of

159. Without the conceptual context of a "sequence" (or system that orders the particulars), there could be no intelligibility to "counting" something as a particular.
160. Recall that for Leibniz each individual substance (including God) is individuated by its "complete concept" (or description). From the knowledge of any true

Hume, the skeptic. Concepts, he argued, are but faint replicas of sensations, and the laws of association by which we relate these concepts are psychological rather than logical in character.[161] As Leibniz sought to be wholly univocal, so Hume sought to be wholly equivocal in his reasoning. As in the philosophy of Leibniz God lost his individuality in order to become wholly known, so in the philosophy of Hume God maintained his individuality but remained wholly unknown.

To be sure, neither Leibniz nor Hume was able to carry his position to its logical conclusion. Leibniz paid tribute to brute fact as Hume paid tribute to abstract logic. Leibniz maintained the necessity of finite facts and therefore of evil, lest his universal should be reduced to the blank identity of Parmenides, lest he should have all knowledge of a being that is interchangeable with non-being. Hume, on his part, virtually makes universal negative propositions covering all objective possibility. To make sure that no God such as is found in the [Westminster] Confession, a God who controls all things by the counsel of his will, would speak to him, Hume had virtually to assert that such a God cannot possibly exist and that there cannot at any point in the past or future be any evidence of such a God. So Leibniz, the rationalist, was an irrationalist and Hume, the irrationalist, was a rationalist. It is impossible to be the one without also being the other.

RESULTANT SKEPTICISM: HUME[162]

Basic to all of Hume's opposition to Christianity and to theism is his conception of knowledge as derived from the senses. His objections to miracles as

---

property of an individual, we can infer all of its properties. If God is known at all, then, He must in theory be known completely.

161. For Hume, there is no empirical (and thus no rational) basis for attributing necessity to the regular sequences of events we have experienced. We expect a heavy object to drop to the ground when we let go of it, not because of sound scientific reasoning, but simply because of the psychological habit of associating one event with another. We have become accustomed to things happening in that way, even though there is no intellectual basis for predicting that they will do so in the (unperceived) future.

162. Excerpts from *Christian-Theistic Evidences*, In Defense of Biblical Christianity, vol. 6 (Phillipsburg, N.J.: Presbyterian and Reformed, 1978), 17–22, 25.

The Scottish philosopher David Hume hated the "abstruse speculations" of philosophers, and said that the way to be liberated from them was seriously to analyze the nature of human understanding. Hume had the intellectual honesty to reach the conclusions to which a consistently empirical epistemology leads, namely, skepticism as to science (causality as a necessary relation is not perceived), as to selfhood (a personal unity of experience is not perceived), as to ethics (obligations are not perceived), and of course as to religion. Hume set

well as his objections to natural religion are based upon his theory of knowledge. He marched right up to the very citadel of his opponents in order to attack them there.

> All the perceptions of the human mind resolve themselves into two distinct kinds, which I shall call *impressions* and *ideas*. The difference betwixt these consists in the degrees of force and liveliness, with which they strike upon the mind, and make their way into our thought or consciousness. Those perceptions, which enter with most force and violence, we may name *impressions:* and under this name I comprehend all our sensations, passions and emotions, as they make their first appearance in the soul. By *ideas* I mean the faint images of these in thinking and reasoning; such, as, for instance, are all the perceptions excited by the present discourse, excepting the immediate pleasure or uneasiness it may occasion. (*A Treatise of Human Nature*, being an attempt to introduce the experimental method of reasoning into moral subjects, and *Dialogues Concerning Natural Religion*, by David Hume, edited by T. H. Green and T. H. Grose, London, 1874, Vol. I, p. 311).

In this opening sentence of the *Treatise* we have the gist of the matter. All knowledge comes from sensation; that is basic to Hume's theory of knowledge. We have no ideas which are not faint copies of previous impressions. Ideas, as copies of sensations, Hume argues, are discrete. He is in entire agreement with Berkeley that "all general ideas are nothing but particular ones, annexed to a certain term."[163] He holds that Berkeley's "discovery"[164]

---

forth his philosophical approach in *An Enquiry Concerning the Human Understanding* (1748), a revised version of his earlier *Treatise of Human Nature* (which, he said, "fell dead-born from the press"). It was a watershed in the history of autonomous philosophy. Immanuel Kant would later confess that Hume's strikingly bold concession to skepticism "awakened me from my dogmatic slumbers."

163. Disagreeing with Locke's view of abstraction, Berkeley held that it is not possible to have general ideas—for instance, the idea of an apple in general—which would have to be the idea of an object with color, weight, etc., but no particular color, weight, etc., so that all possible apples would be covered by the general idea. Instead, said Berkeley, we have a group of ideas about particular apples, which are associated in our mind (by their resemblance or similarity) and given a name.

164. Van Til places the word in quotation marks to alert the reader to the absurdity of an empiricist claiming that someone "discovered" (by sense impressions) the truth of a non-sensed abstract principle (namely, that "all" general ideas resolve into particular ones)!

of this point is "one of the most valuable discoveries that has been made of late years in the republic of letters" (*op. cit.*, p. 325).

The far-reaching significance of Hume's point of view appears at a glance. Since all knowledge is of sensation there is no *a priori* reasoning. To be sure, in the field of algebra, when we are merely concerned with the manipulation of figures, we may speak of *a priori* knowledge, but when we pretend to deal with factual knowledge, *a priori* reasoning is taboo.[165]

But what of the *a posteriori* reasoning such as Butler has employed in his *Analogy*?[166] Granted we are willing to forego the certainty and universality that *a priori* reasoning was supposed to bring, can we not at least depend upon probability? May we not reasonably expect that the "constitution and course of nature" will continue in the future as it has in the past? Such questions, though not asked by Hume with direct reference to Butler, are yet asked by him with respect to the type of argument used by Butler.

The answer to such questions, says Hume, depends upon the nature of the connection between our various ideas. One particular idea simply recalls another particular idea. It is thus that we obtain our general ideas. There is no necessary connection between our various particular ideas. There is no systematic relation between them. There is no systematic relation between them because there is no systematic relation between our sensations.

It will be observed that in this way there is no basis for the notion of cause and effect. There is no "impression, which produces an idea of such prodigious consequence" (377). Yet all ideas must come from impressions. My impressions are simply of contiguity and succession. Hence my ideas too are merely of contiguity and succession.

> Tho' the mind in its reasonings from causes or effects carries its view
> beyond those objects, which it sees or remembers, it must never lose

---

165. Hume maintained that the demonstrable knowledge that we have in mathematics or geometry could not arise from sensible images in our minds since there is no necessary connection between such images. Mathematical knowledge is demonstrative because it involves only an analysis of how we use our terms. Distinguishing between analytic and synthetic truths, Hume held that any truth that is "instructive" (a matter of fact) could not be certain, and any truth that is certain could not be instructive (but merely semantic).

166. Bishop Joseph Butler (1692–1752) wrote *The Analogy of Religion, Natural and Revealed, to the Constitution and Course of Nature* in 1736. In it, he argued that observations of the natural world confirm the revealed doctrines of Christianity. Butler touched on the subject of probability in the introduction to his treatise, saying that it (unlike demonstration) admits of degrees and (against the rationalists) must be for us "the very guide of life."

sight of them entirely, nor reason merely upon its own ideas, without some mixture of impressions, or at least of ideas of the memory, which are equivalent to impressions. When we infer effects from causes, we must establish the existence of these causes; which we have only two ways of doing, either by an immediate perception of our memory or sense, or by an inference from other causes; which causes again we must ascertain in the same manner, either by a present impression, or by an inference *from their causes*, and so on, till we arrive at some object, which we see or remember. 'Tis impossible for us to carry on our inferences *in infinitum;* and the only thing that can stop them is an impression of the memory or senses, beyond which there is no room for doubt or enquiry (p. 384).

Absolutely all our reasoning about cause and effect goes back to sensation, and sensations are discrete. To this basic point Hume returns again and again.

'Tis therefore by EXPERIENCE only, that we can infer the existence of one object from that of another. The nature of experience is this. We remember to have had frequent instances of the existence of one species of objects; and also remember, that the individuals of another species of contiguity and succession with regard to them. Thus we remember, to have seen that species of object we call *flame*, and to have felt that species of sensation we call *heat*. We likewise call to mind their constant conjunction in all past instances. Without any farther ceremony, we call the one *cause* and the other *effect*, and infer the existence of the one from that of the other (p. 388). From the mere repetition of any past impression, even to infinity, there never will arise any new original idea, such as that of a necessary connexion; and the number of impressions has in this case no more effect than if we confin'd ourselves to one only (p. 389).

It is easy to sense the implication of all this for the argument of Butler. Butler holds that we may reasonably expect the course and constitution of nature to remain the same in the future as it has been in the past. Hume says that if we expect this it is because of custom only. *There is simply no logical relation between the past and the future*.

To see this point clearly we may follow Hume still further when he enters upon a discussion of probability. Continuing from the passage we have just quoted, Hume says:

. . . If reason determin'd us, it would proceed upon that principle, *that instances, of which we have had no experience, must resemble those, of which we have had experience, and that the course of nature continues always uniformly the same.* In order therefore to clear up this matter, let us consider all the arguments, upon which such a proposition may be supposed to be founded; and as these must be deriv'd either from *knowledge* or *probability*, let us cast our eye on each of these degrees of evidence, and see whether they afford any just conclusion of this nature.

Our foregoing method of reasoning will easily convince us, that there can be no *demonstrative* arguments to prove, *that those instances, of which we have had no experience, resemble those, of which we have had experience.* We can at least conceive a change in the course of nature; which sufficiently proves, that such a change is not absolutely impossible. To form a clear idea of anything, is an undeniable argument for its possibility, and is alone a refutation of any pretended demonstration against it.

Probability, as it discovers not the relations of ideas, consider'd as such, but only those of objects, must in some respects be founded on the impressions of our memory and sense, and in some respects on our ideas. Were there no mixture of ideas the action of the mind, in observing the relation, wou'd, properly speaking, be sensation, not reasoning. 'Tis therefore necessary that in all probable reasonings there be something present to the mind, either seen or remember'd, and that from this we infer something connected with it, which is not seen nor remember'd.

The only connexion or relation of objects, which can lead us beyond the immediate impressions of our memory and senses, is that of cause and effect; and that because 'tis the only one, on which we can found a just inference from one object to another. The idea of cause and effect is deriv'd from *experience*, which informs us, that particular objects, in all past instances, have been constantly conjoin'd with each other. And as an object similar to one of these is suppos'd to be immediately present in its impression, we thence presume on the existence of one similar to its usual attendant. According to this account of things, which is, I think, in every point unquestionable, probability is founded on the presumption of a resemblance betwixt those objects, of which we have had experience, and those, of which we have had none; and therefore 'tis impossible this presumption can arise from probability.[167] The same principle cannot be both the cause and effect of another; and this is, perhaps, the only proposition concerning that relation, which is either intuitively or demonstratively certain (pp. 389, 391). . . .

This passage deals with the central concept of Butler's *Analogy*, namely, that of the presumption that the constitution and course of nature will be the same in the future as we have seen it to be in the past. Hume finds no justification for this presumption except in custom. It is important to note that his argument here is, if sound, as destructive of Butler's reasoning as it is of *a priori* reasoning. To be sure, his argument appears to be primarily against the idea of a necessary connection of an *a priori* sort. Yet his argument is (p. 21) equally opposed to the idea of a presumptive rational connection of a probable sort. The whole point of Hume's argument is that there is no rational presumption of any sort about future events happening in one way rather than in another. We may expect that they will, but if we do, we do so on non-rational grounds. Our reasoning is based upon past experience. Past experience is nothing but an accumulation of brute facts which have been observed as happening in a certain order. Why should not the events of the future be entirely different in nature from the events of the past? . . .

Hume's empiricism was far more critical and consistent than that of Butler. We proceed to see what happens to the conception of probability on the basis of Hume's empiricism. If all knowledge is based upon experience, and experience is interpreted without the presupposition of the "Author of nature" as Hume claims it is, we cannot expect that one thing rather than another will happen in the future. From the point of view of logic, one thing as well as another might take place in the future. But why is it then that we expect the course and constitution of nature to remain the same? *"Wherein consists the difference betwixt incredulity and belief?"* asks Hume (395). The answer is once more that it is in nothing but custom and feeling.

Now as we call every thing CUSTOM, which proceeds from a past repetition, without any new reasoning or conclusion, we may es-

---

167. To put it simply, the notion of probability presupposes the uniformity of nature (i.e., the resemblance between events that we have experienced and events that we have not experienced), in which case probability cannot be the foundation for a belief in the uniformity of nature. This insight of Hume's has major importance. When an apologist points out to an unbeliever that his naively empirical approach to knowledge renders scientific reasoning (relying as it does on causal or inductive principles—"the uniformity of nature") unfounded, he will often thoughtlessly retort that, while we cannot be certain of uniformity, it is probable based on past experience. But, as Hume noted, probability itself assumes uniformity, and thus probability cannot justify belief in uniformity.

tablish it is a certain truth, that all the belief, which follows upon any present impression, is deriv'd solely from that origin (p. 403).

Custom gives vividness to an idea, and the vividness of the idea is the source of our belief in the existence of the object of the idea. "Thus all probable reasoning is nothing but a species of sensation. 'Tis not solely in poetry and music, we must follow our taste and sentiment, but likewise in philosophy" (p. 403). . . .

Grant an infinite number of possibilities, to begin with, as an absolutely pure empiricism must presuppose, then there is an infinite number of improbabilities to cancel every infinite number of probabilities. That is, there is no probability at all. Such is Hume's argument. Hume is right when he says again and again that "an entire indifference is essential to chance." The idea of a law of chances is, strictly speaking, a contradiction in terms. *It is to this position of total indifference with respect to the future that anyone embracing a pure empiricism is driven.*[168] By Hume's argument Butler would be driven to accept a pure empiricism with the consequences now before us, or to accept the "Author of nature" as a real and effective principle of interpretation.[169]

CRITICAL PHILOSOPHY: KANT[170]

(A) Kant himself says that on the basis of empiricism we can have only brute facts and more brute facts but no systematic relation between them. He adds that on the basis of rationalism we would have only order, but it would be

168. The devastating conclusion to which Hume's consistent empiricism drove him was that we can have no rational basis for scientific knowledge, and therefore (given Hume's chosen prejudice for such knowledge) all philosophy reduces to personal preferences (as in poetry and music). With this admission, unbelieving epistemology became a complete intellectual failure.
169. The latter alternative would be unacceptable to any evidentialist apologetics that claims to be presuppositionally neutral; it refuses to presuppose God as its principle of interpretation. It tries to follow a purely empirical approach to knowledge, and thus, with Hume, should be driven to utter skepticism and arbitrariness: "An entire indifference is essential to chance."
170. The following excerpts are taken from:

   (A) *Protestant Doctrine of Scripture*, 53–54;
   (B) *Case for Calvinism*, 112–14;
   (C) "Nature and Scripture," 296–99;
   (D) *Reformed Pastor and Modern Thought*, 113, 114, 116, 128–30;
   (E) *Christian-Theistic Evidences*, 35–39 [with a mistyped sentence on p. 37 reconstructed from p. 40 of the 1961 edition], 68–69, 79–80, 94–95, 134.

   Immanuel Kant (1724–1804) never left the town of Königsberg, Prussia, where he was born and later served as a university professor, but his thought revolutionized philosophy. Kant considered it a "Copernican revolution" to intro-

merely the idea of order without any ordering of facts. Kant sought to remedy the situation by means of his Copernican revolution. No one had ever conceived the idea that the mind itself was doing the ordering even as it was doing the observing. Facts cannot be observed, argues Kant, except they are observed as being incorporated into systematic arrangement. So it is the mind itself that imposes its categories of substance and causality upon nature even as it observes nature. Nature means causally related facts. And causally related facts are brute facts observed and arranged by the mind of man.

Thus the whole knowledge transaction with respect to nature is complete without any reference to God. More than that, God must not interfere with this knowledge process. If he does interfere, there is no more knowledge, properly speaking.

Yes, indeed, Kant thinks that he has made room for faith even as he has limited science. For by thinking of man as the source of the ordering process of nature, man's knowledge is limited to what he does thus order. Through the intuition of time and space man gets the stuff of his experience. By the imposition of his categories man supplies the order in this stuff. Therefore the knowledge that results as the product of this activity of the mind upon the raw stuff of experience *by definition* excludes knowledge of God and of anything that God might do directly in relation to nature. A God who has cre-

---

duce the notion that the mind is not passive in knowing, but is active in forming or constituting its objects. Kant felt that his "critical" philosophy (also known as "transcendental idealism") could "save science" (by synthesizing elements of rationalism and empiricism) and "make room for faith" (by taking account of human freedom and ethics). With the empiricists, Kant agreed that nothing can be known apart from the input of sense experience (there are no innate ideas), but with the rationalists Kant agreed that the mind is not a *tabula rasa*, but rather imposes on the sensations the perceptible forms of time and space and the conceptual forms of quantity, quality, relation (including causation), and modality. "Concepts without percepts are empty," he said, and "percepts without concepts are blind." These mental impositions are "transcendentally" necessary—that is, they are presupposed for the intelligibility of any experience. Thus, "the understanding is itself the lawgiver of nature"; man's active mind provides the order and regularity necessary for rational and scientific knowledge. Of course, such rational and scientific knowledge is only of things as they *appear* to us (phenomena), rather than of reality as it is "in itself" (noumena). In the very manner that Kant "saved science" (rendering all rational knowledge phenomenal only), he left plenty of room for a realm that transcends the mind's activity, namely, the noncognitive and nonrational experience of human freedom and moral obligation. Kant is said to have "salvaged" personality (freedom) and science (determinism) simultaneously by decreeing an irresolvable dichotomy between them. But since they contradict each other—one cannot be interpreted in light of the principles of the other—the price of Kant's solution was an incoherent worldview and the failure of epistemology (making it the mere psychologizing of "science").

ated and who by his providence controls nature, and a Christ who as the Son of God redeems nature, may be believed in if people wish. But they must not say that they *know* or *can* know any such thing. For knowledge is, by definition, limited to the field of science, to the field of phenomena. The world of religion is the world of the wholly other, of the wholly unknown and unknowable.

To be sure, Kant does speak of having a *practical* knowledge of God. But this practical knowledge is a faith-construct. It is a limiting notion. As men we have no theoretical, that is, real conceptual knowledge of God. Such real knowledge is, argues Kant, limited to the space-time world. For that very reason everybody is free to believe what he wishes about that other world. Nobody can interfere with him in that field. All religious statements are *in principle* non-cognitive statements.

(B) Kant's idea of man is best expressed in his own notion of autonomy. And the first thing to note about this idea of autonomy is that it cannot be stated without involving a construction of reality as a whole in terms of this autonomy. Of course Kant says that he starts merely from *facts* of experience. He wants no metaphysics. He starts from the *fact* of science. He starts from the *fact* of the moral experience. But he finds these facts because he has from the outset placed them where they are in terms of his own autonomy. If man is autonomous, then he acts as autonomous when he is engaged in intellectual interpretation. That is to say, in assuming man's autonomy Kant virtually takes for granted the essentially legislative character of human thought. . . . On Kant's view man's autonomous intellectual activity can tell us what ultimate reality *cannot* be. And to say what ultimate reality *cannot* be is, in effect, the same as to say what it *can* and *must* be. Kant's rejection of metaphysics simply leads him to the adoption of a new metaphysics.[171] . . .

Kant keeps God out of the world of the phenomenal by establishing the validity of science in terms of the ultimate organizing activity of the autonomous man. In other words, the man of Kant takes over, in effect, the functions of God as these are set forth in Scripture. On Kant's view, man's organizing activity, as this is expressed through the logical function of man, is assumed to be the final source of order in the facts of nature and history. . . .

Kant also makes man the ultimate source in the realm of the noumenal. . . . The whole message of Christianity, the story of the transition from

171. This kind of internal critique of unbelieving philosophy is possible for any viewpoint that declares that metaphysical knowledge is impossible. Van Til taught that it is not a question of whether men will adopt a metaphysical position, but only a question of which metaphysic they will adopt. Kant was no exception.

wrath to grace in history, must therefore be symbolical of transactions that take place within the moral self as wholly self-dependent.[172]

(C) Kant's great contribution to philosophy consisted in stressing the activity of the experiencing subject. It is this point to which the idea of a Copernican revolution is usually applied. Kant argued that since it is the thinking subject that itself contributes the categories of universality and necessity, we must not think of these as covering any reality that exists or may exist wholly independent of the human mind. By using the law of non-contradiction we may and must indeed determine what is possible, but the possibility that we thus determine is subjective rather than objective. It is a possibility *for us*. To save rationality, Kant argues, we must shorten the battle-line and reduce its claims even in its own domain. Hereafter reason must claim to legislate only in that area that can always be checked by experience, and even in this area it must ever be ready to receive the wholly new. The validity of universals is to be taken as frankly due to a motion and a vote; it is conventional and nothing more. Thus the univocation of Leibniz is to be saved by casting it into the sea of equivocation stirred up by Hume.

Again stressing the original activity of the thinking subject, Kant argued that it is impossible ever to find the entirely single thing of Hume. Like a sausage-grinder, the mind of man forms things into molds as it receives them. We never see either pork or beef; we see only sausages that, according to the butcher's word, contain both. Thus we always make facts as much as we find them. The only facts we know are instances of laws.

Kant's argument against the rationalists was like the argument of Aristotle against the "definition mongers" who wanted to know all things. His argument against Hume was like Aristotle's arguments against Protagoras,[173] the skeptic, who went on speaking even when his principle allowed him to say nothing determinate. Science, Kant argued, does not need and could not

172. That is, the gospel story cannot be true with respect to the world that we know by rational and scientific means; miracles are clearly contrary to causal necessity. So the gospel is not true of the world of experience (the phenomenal world), but applies only to the "inner" experience of freedom and morality, which is noncognitive. The "outer story" of the gospel is thus "symbolical" of an inner religious experience.

173. Protagoras (ca. 490–410 B.C.) was a famous Sophist who claimed the ability to refute any proposition since there was no absolute truth. His most famous aphorism was "Man is the measure of all things," the premise of epistemological subjectivism and ethical relativism. Van Til points to the internal inconsistency in his philosophy: he went on asserting things to be true, even though his philosophical principle was that there is no absolute truth. All skeptics likewise refute themselves.

exist with such objective universality as Leibniz desired, but it does need and actually has the subjective validity that the autonomous man supplies in the very act of interpretation. Kant argues, as it were, that Aristotle was right in seeking for universals in the particulars rather than above them, but that he did not have the courage of his convictions and did not go far enough. Science requires us to have done once and for all with all antecedent being, with all metaphysics except that which is immanentistic. Hereafter the notions of being, cause and purpose must stand for orderings we ourselves have made; they must never stand for anything that exists beyond the reach of our experience. Any God who wants to make himself known, it is now more clear than ever before, will have to do so by identifying himself exhaustively with his revelation. And any God who is so revealed, it is now more clear than ever before, will then have to be wholly hidden in pure possibility. Neither Plato nor Aristotle were entitled, by the methods of reasoning they employed, to reach the Unconditioned. The Unconditioned cannot be rationally related to man.

There is no doubt but that Kant was right in this claim. Plato and Aristotle no less than Kant assumed the autonomy of man. On such a basis man may reason univocally and reach a God who is virtually an extension of himself or he may reason equivocally and reach a God who has no contact with him at all. Nor will adding two zeros produce more than zero. The addition of pure pantheism to pure deism will not bring forth theism. It was Kant's great service to the Christian church to teach us this. No theistic proof, either of the *a priori* or of the *a posteriori* sort, based on Platonic Aristotelian assumptions could do anything but disprove the God of the [Westminster] Confession.

But if Kant has done so great a service, his service has of course been wholly negative. Orthodox apologists have all too often overlooked this fact. Did not Kant make room for faith? Did he not challenge the pride of the rationalist in its denial of a God whose thoughts are higher than man's thoughts? Is not the scientist who today works on the basis of his principles a very humble sort of person, satisfied with the single dimension of the phenomenal, leaving the whole realm of the noumenal to the ministers of religion? And does not Scripture itself ascribe to reason the power and right to interpret at least an area of reality, restricted though it be, in its own right? Surely the God of Scripture does not mean to dictate to the man who merely describes the facts as he sees them in the laboratory.

In all this there is profound confusion. Nor is this to be blamed primarily on Kant. Kant knew well enough what sort of Christianity is involved in the natural theology of his *Critique of Pure Reason*. His own statement of it is unmistakable and frank. To him the only Christianity that accords with the principles of his thought is a Christianity that is reduced from its historic uniqueness to a universal religion of reason. And modernist theologians working with his principles today make similar reductions of historic Christianity. We can but admire their consistency. The very idea of Kant's Copernican revolution was that the autonomous mind itself must assume the responsibility for making all factual differentiation and logical validation. To such a mind the God of Christianity cannot speak. Such a mind will hear no voice but its own. It is itself the light that lighteth every man that comes into the world. It is itself the sun; how can it receive light from without? If Plato and Aristotle virtually identified the mind of man with that of God, Kant virtually identified the mind of God with that of man. Such a mind describes all facts as it sees them, invariably through colored lenses. The miracles of Scripture are always reduced to instances of laws, and laws themselves are reduced to conventional and purely contingent regularities. Prophetic prediction that has come true is always reduced to pure coincidence in a world of chance. Conventional law and brute fact are the stock in trade of the Kantian philosopher and scientist. His phenomenal world is built up of these.

(D) Struggling with this situation [how synthetic *a priori* judgments are possible],[174] Kant's eyes were finally opened to the astounding insight that the reason for the failure of every dogmatic approach, whether rationalist or empiricist, lay in the fact that the empiricists were not empirical enough and the rationalists were not rationalist enough.

The empiricist's "stuff," or material of knowledge, had too much form in it. The "facts," even though still utterly unknown by the mind of man, were already structured to some extent. This already structured nature of facts acted like an immovable roadblock to the beginning, the progress, and the completion of man's knowledge of these facts. To know is to conceptualize. But the facts of empiricism were unconceptualizable. *To be conceptualizable the facts must be pliable, so pliable as to admit of complete formalization.*

In insisting on this point Kant merely expressed the demands of the Parmenidean position in relation to space-time factuality. How could the facts of the space-time world be *completely* conceptualized unless they had, previous to being known, no individual distinctiveness whatsoever?

Moreover, if the legitimate claim of the empiricist is to be met, then his "facts" must not only be without character before meeting the mind that

174. That is, how can judgments that are informative (giving substantial information about the way things are) be known apart from experience or observation of the world? This is the central concern of Kant's masterpiece, *The Critique of Pure Reason* (1781).

knows them, but this mind itself must then not be thought of as passive. The only movement possible must spring from the subject of knowledge. The movement of things is movement of things because it is, first of all, a movement of mind.

The movement of cause and of purpose within and between things is what it is, because it is, first of all, a movement within the mind. If the empiricists wish to preserve and protect the objectivity of the knowledge of the acts of the space-time world in relation to one another, they had better give up looking for the holy grail of "facts in themselves" and find their objectivity within the organizing activity of the mind.

But while Kant, as it were, thus lectures the empiricists, he has also a criticism of the rationalists. The mind is inherently active. Would that the rationalists had understood this fact. Then they would have realized that objectivity of knowledge is inherently a matter of growth. If the rationalists wish to preserve and protect the objectivity of the knowledge of the facts of space and time in relation to one another, then they too must find this objectivity in the organizing activity of the mind. Only by looking for objectivity in the organizing activity of the mind will they see that their notion of knowledge, as a universal changeless system, will forever stand dualistically over against a world of unrelated space-time factuality. They must think of their system as a growing and developing system. . . .

To save science and make room for religion means then that we must think of science as the field where our categories of thought create order in an utterly non-interpreted realm of pure contingency. Man's categorical thinking is absolutely legislative in the sense that it, and it alone, furnishes the forming element of experience.

Suppose you take the tray out of your refrigerator and fill it with water. Then you place a divider in the tray of water and return it to the refrigerator. When, after a while, you take the tray out of the refrigerator and the divider out of the tray, you have ice cubes. Are you surprised because all the ice cubes are of the same size? Not at all. Your divider has seen to that. *Similarly* in the world of science, the unbeliever will *always* see "raw stuff" ordered and arranged by himself by means of his logical activity. He will never find any providentially controlled facts such as the Reformers saw everywhere about them. He will never hear about such miracles as the virgin birth of Christ or his resurrection from the dead. There *could* be no such things as the regeneration of men's hearts by the recreating work of the Holy Spirit, or even providence.

This does not mean that you cannot be religious as well as scientific at the same time. On the contrary, science is saved by limiting it to the realm in which man's conceptual organizing activity rules, i.e., the realm of the *phenomenal*. But beyond the realm of the phenomenal is the realm of the *noumenal*. And, as before noted, in this realm of the noumenal man is negatively free from all conceptualizing control, and man is positively free to determine what is good and what is evil. In this realm of the noumenal man is free to determine the nature of the true, the good, and the beautiful in the way that Socrates insisted on doing it. . . .

From the foregoing we note first that Kant has developed the principle of apostate thinking till it has attained a large measure of internal consistency. As noted before, Socrates expressed this principle well when he said he must know the nature of the holy regardless of what the gods say about it. Even so, when he sought to answer the scepticism of the Sophists, Socrates appealed to a self-existing realm of truth in which the knowing subject of man participated. Socrates did not yet dare to identify the knowing subject as *itself* the source, the goal, and the standard of knowledge. Nor did Descartes dare to go this far. He let the world of fact and the world of law stand dualistically over against the knowing subject. As for the rationalists and empiricists, though they, as followers of Descartes, were more subjective than the Greeks, yet they did not have the courage of their convictions. Their "science-ideal," as Dooyeweerd calls it, tended to swallow up the individual knowing subject. The activity, and with it the individuality, of the knowing subject was lost as soon as it was "successful" in reaching its object.[175] It is not till the generating activity of the knowing self is thought of as the ultimate source of meaning that the spirit of apostasy reaches its climax.[176]

All "objective" existence must be thought of as the projection of the self-sufficient self. Accordingly, even the "objective" existence of the self as phenomenal must be a projection of the noumenal self.[177] All the "laws" of the

---

175. Given the ideal of science, the object of knowledge must be known by means of the principle of causal determinism (every event is theoretically predictable and thus an instance of the operation of some law or laws). But if this could be successfully attained, the presupposed causal determinism would preclude the notion of a free, inquiring person who pursues the ideal of science; his apparent individuality would be dissolved into lawlike generalities.

176. To Van Til's way of thinking, Kant had the unflattering honor of developing more consistently than previous philosophers what is inherent in the spirit of autonomy. If philosophy begins with man and his own authority, then the conclusion of philosophy cannot transcend this source—all of man's thinking reflects his own subjective ordering and interpretation, but nothing of the objective world of reality. If you start with man's thoughts as your point of reference, you cannot escape phenomenalism and thus skepticism—the egocentric predicament.

177. The "phenomenal" self is the self as it must appear in our experience of it. But

space-time world, relating the "objects" of the space-time world to one another, must be projections of the noumenal self. As such these laws are *purely* formal. They are in consequence *purely* correlative to *purely* contingent stuff.

Only thus can Kant "save" science and make room for religion. As for Kant, both science and a truly moral religion would be destroyed if man had to think of a God such as historic Protestantism has. If the laws of science and of religion are to be valid for man, they must ultimately be projections of himself. The universals and the particulars of science cannot be thought of as deriving their differentiation from one another in the noumenal self. So too, the laws of God for morality and religion cannot be thought of as properly related to the particulars of man's space-time experience, unless they be thought of as deriving their differentiation from one another in the noumenal self. If science is to be taken for what it is, a growing system of knowledge, and if religion is to be moral, then they both must have their common source in the self-sufficient noumenal self. The noumenal self is the ultimate self-sufficient point of departure, the standard and the goal for anything that may or must be said by man about anything.

Kant is so basically hostile to historic Protestantism that his description of it is, as seen earlier, largely a caricature. Nowhere does he present its teachings for what they claim to be. Its view of science and religion are portrayed as both contradictory and immoral.

But on what does Kant himself stand when he swings the logician's postulate and declares that historic Protestantism is contradictory? He stands on the noumenal self, and the noumenal self itself asserts that it stands on nothing.[178]

Nothing less than this will do if Kant is to "save science and make room for religion." Kant needs the idea of pure contingency if he is to escape ra-

---

this apparent self is the projection of the organizing activity of the mind—that is, the product of a "noumenal" self which is "in itself" free and undetermined. In the nature of the case, this noumenal self could not be rationally understood or interpreted (by the categories of understanding imposed by the active mind). It is a "transcendental unity of apperception," a mere place-marker for one's mental activity. In the "transcendental dialectic," Kant discussed the "psychological paralogism" (or fallacy) that there is a substantial self, with continuing personal identity, that does the thinking.

178. To put it simply, in order to refute the Christian's claim to knowledge about God (man, redemption, etc.), Kant had to develop a philosophical perspective that destroys the intelligibility of any objective knowledge at all. This reflects the desperation of those who intellectually oppose the faith. They would rather be reduced to subjectivism (e.g., the projections of an unknowable "noumenal" self) than to acknowledge their responsibility before God, whom they very well know and cannot escape.

tionalism and empiricism—and especially if he is to escape the everywhere-present claims of the God and the Christ of Christianity.

The idea of the noumenal self as the source of the idea of a genuine scientific development is admittedly utterly mysterious. This noumenal self, springing moment by moment from the womb of pure contingency, must therefore, on the one hand, know God, the world, and itself exhaustively, and, on the other hand, know nothing about God or the world or itself at all. All reality must be thought of as both wholly revealed and as wholly hidden to man.

Here we have the modern equivalent of the idea of Parmenides to the effect that *being is one* and static. Here we have also the modern equivalent to the idea of Heraclitus that opposites turn into one another. Here, in short, the Greek notion finds its modern expression: All Being is One: change is ultimate, and therefore all things emanate from this One, and finally, all things that have emanated from the One return to the One.

Modern man, following Kant, now feels sure that the God and the Christ of the Reformers does not exist because he *cannot* exist. It is now *absolutely certain* that this God and this Christ *cannot* exist. All the assertions of Scripture to the effect that sinful man will come into judgment for his rejection of God as his creator and of Christ his redeemer may now be safely set aside. We may now smile with condescension at the *naivete* of early man who still fears a coming judgment in the way he fears spooks.

E) There are first, those who have sought help from Kant by dividing, as he did, the field between science and religion. Kant claims to have made room for faith by giving to it the whole of the noumenal realm, reserving for science only the phenomenal realm. It appears, however, that such a division is based upon the idea of an appeal to brute fact. We are free in the noumenal realm, though determined in the phenomenal realm. . . .

Kant's phenomenalism is the typically modern expression of the philosophy of the would-be autonomous man. This man virtually makes the man the measure of reality. He boldly claims that only that is significantly real which he can categorize. . . .

Kant's phenomenalism is but the natural out-growth of ancient philosophy. Once man assumes the virtual identity of his intellect with that of God he is driven to maintain with even greater clarity that all rationality is purely formal and that, correspondingly, all differentiation is purely non-rational. Aristotle virtually maintained this, and Thomas Aquinas followed him. It remained for Kant and his followers to assert the exhaustive correlativity of pure logic and pure fact, thus banishing the God of Christianity from any intellectually ascertainable contact with the universe. . . .

The . . . question we must ask, however, is whether the particular schematism of Kant itself avoided landing us once more into the realm of chance or brute fact. And here, too, we are happy to be in agreement with Orr[179] when he seeks to go beyond Kant. It is apparent that the whole realm of the noumenal as Kant conceives it is a realm of brute facts. And since that noumenal realm surrounds the phenomenal realm and has a possible influence on it, the result is that the phenomenal realm is really also a realm of chance and brute fact. Kant's phenomenal realm is but an island, and that a floating island on a bottomless and shoreless sea. After all, the human mind can furnish at most a finite schematism or *a priori*. We do not admit that the human mind can furnish any *a priori* at all unless it is related to God. But suppose for a moment that it could, such a schematism could never be comprehensive. Even Kant himself, besides setting his noumenal realm over against the phenomenal, admits that those facts for which the human mind furnishes the *a priori* are at the outset brute facts. Without the percepts the concepts of the mind are blind, says Kant. This, he should have argued, points to the need of God in whom there is no correlative relation between percepts and concepts, because his concept includes all possible percepts of his creatures.[180] . . .

We may agree at the outset that idealism is right as over against empiricism in claiming that bare facts are in themselves unintelligible. We may also rejoice in the fact that Hegelian idealism has outgrown the eighteenth century rationalism in that it has recognized the fact that an *a priori* that stands in no relation to the facts is unintelligible. All this Kant taught idealism. He sought "die Bedingungen die die Erfahrung möglich machen," i.e., "the presuppositions that make learning by experience possible" (see *Experience and Reflection*, by Edgar A. Singer, Chapter II, p. 15, mimeographed). He held that we could not recognize or individuate objects without an *a priori* equipment furnished by the mind. That was the death blow to empiricism. On the other hand, he recognized as over against Leibniz that individuation is not by minute description, but by space-time coordinates. On this point Kant agreed with Hume. *Brute facts occupy as fundamental a place in the philosophy of Kant as in that of Hume. And Kant's philosophy is, in consequence, fully as sceptical as that of Hume.*[181] Retaining the idea of brute fact, or pure chance

179. Van Til is referring here to the Scottish theologian James Orr (1844–1913) and two of his books: *David Hume and His Influence on Philosophy and Theology* (1903) and *The Christian View of God and the World* (1893).

180. Van Til makes the point that in nothing that God knows is He utterly passive and receptive; He has no "percepts" from which He constructs His knowledge. Rather, by His own original and constructive (creative) concepts, God determines the nature of reality and all the facts of history.

181. Emphasis added.

differentiation, he was driven to reduce the idea of absolute rationality to that of a merely contingent rationality *for us.* He "saved" universality by subjectivising it. He "saved" causality within the world by denying God as the creator of the world. That is to say, from the Christian point of view he destroyed rather than saved universality.

We must go on briefly to note the nature of the idealistic development that went beyond Kant. Hegelian idealism is usually called objective idealism inasmuch as it is by *inclusion* rather than by *exclusion* of the "facts" that it seeks to interpret experience. It looks for a "concrete" rather than an "abstract" universal. It wishes to bring the phenomenal and the noumenal world of Kant into one world explained by one principle of interpretation. That is the principle of dialecticism.

Kant's view, valuable as it was, would, if tested by its own standard, defeat itself. We quote the admirable statement of Singer on this point:

> But no sense of the cogency of the reasons driving Kant to the doctrine of *a priori* science should blind one to the difficulties facing this philosophy. . . . The following objections are as obvious as they are serious: The sciences to which *a priori* knowledge is confined are (1) such science as enables us to order our experience in space-time coordinates—the science of geometry, and (2) such as furnish us with the concepts by means of which we recognize an object as an object—the science of logic. Since we bring these abilities to experience, we must in some sense bring to experience the sciences, not to possess which is to lack such abilities. But we all know—and Kant was willing to concede, even to insist on the point—that these sciences are the possession of none but the mature, which is to say, the highly experienced mind. We might even go farther and maintain that no human mind has yet won a complete insight into the ways of either geometry or logic. The technical journals are filled with patient efforts to put science in more masterful possession of these disciplines: one would not be risking much in predicting that if this cooling planet ever comes to its last day, and if in that day there still appear technical journals, their tables of contents will continue to include such titles as 'On the axioms of Geometry,' 'On the Postulates of Logic.' How then and in what sense can that science which is beyond the grasp of a Euclid or of an Aristotle be the possession of a newborn babe? Or to render the matter still more preposterous, does it not seem that a Euclid or an Aristotle must have spent his life in a none too successful struggle to possess himself of

a science the possession of which was the condition of his beginning the struggle? (Chap. IV, p. 5).

The point of difficulty to which Singer calls attention is our old friend *hard*
or *brute fact*. Kant was not willing to go with the rationalists in identifying the
particular facts with the *infima species,* i.e., in individuating by minute description. His principle of individuation was non-rational. The space-time coordinates by which facts are brought into contact with the rational principles
of the mind are themselves non-rational; they are intuitions.[182] Thus, the rational principle of the mind, i.e., the *a priori*, is still set abstractly over against
the non-rational facts. The result is that the hard facts are still with us. The
Ding an sich selbst[183] escapes us. Hume has not really been answered. . . .

We must go on to a consideration of post-Kantian science. In what does
it differ from pre-Kantian science? There is no basic difference. Post-Kantian
science has shown an even greater respect for brute fact than pre-Kantian
science did. This appears primarily in the fact that the scientific ideal was reduced by Kant from an absolute ideal to that of a limiting concept. For Kant
the space-time coordinates formed the principle of individuation. In this he
opposed Leibnizian rationalism. Leibniz thought of complete description as
the principle of individuation. Every individual could be set into its logical
niche. For Kant logic had no such comprehensive sweep. It was balked by a
buzzing-blooming confusion of temporal facts. This factual realm could never
be wholly reduced to logical relations. The categories of the understanding
can, according to Kant, at most show us aspects of truth. What a fact in itself
is we can never fully know. We can do no more than make approximations
to the knowledge of facts.

The far-reaching significance of this position of Kant requires careful attention. It still means that facts are not created but are just there somehow.
The mind of man can never by its utmost efforts get back of this just-thereness of facts. If the mind of man attempts to get back of the brute facts, argues Kant, it winds itself into a knot of hopeless antinomies.[184] Here we hit
upon the source of Kant's criticism of the "theistic proofs." Kant's criticism of
these proofs cannot be met unless we lay bare the spectre of brute fact. *This*

---

182. By "intuition" Kant meant an immediate awareness of a sensible object.
183. That is, the "thing-in-itself."
184. According to Kant, when we attempt to extend our ideas beyond the realm of
    experience, we are led into hopeless contradictions, called the "antinomies of
    reason" (e.g., not everything in the world takes place according to natural laws),
    where the mind takes a particular position but is then forced by countervailing
    reasons to take up the opposite position instead—only to be forced back again
    to the original position.

spectre can be banished only if we take the Christian conception of God as the Creator of the space-time world as the presupposition of all knowledge. A true science will have to build itself upon this Christian foundation. Unless one builds upon this foundation, complete scepticism stares us in the face.[185]

Post-Kantian science has not faced this fact. It has simply reduced the ideal of complete comprehension for human knowledge from an absolute to a limiting concept. It has taken for granted with Kant that it is up to the human mind as such, itself a brute fact, to arrange these brute facts into universals or laws as best it can. It has taken for granted that in this procedure it is on the way to truth, forgetting that the whole structure of "truth" is then built upon brute facts. Thus modern science has virtually assumed that the addition of zeros will produce something more than zero. . . .

It is a well-known fact that Kant had essentially the same type of criticism to make on all three of the theistic proofs. In fact he led them all back to the ontological proof. His criticism was that the "proofs" imply an illegitimate jump from man's knowledge of the phenomenal world to reality beyond possible experience. Thought as such is an abstraction, says Kant. It is only in connection with the intuitions of sense-experience that it has meaning. Therefore it is impossible to extend thought to a realm beyond experience.

Applying this criticism to the concept of causality Kant finds that it is a category that is immanent in experience. The concept of causation is subordinate to that of explanation and explanation must be immanent within the universe. Explanation must be something that is within reach of the human mind.

Kant holds that if we seek to conclude from a series of causes that we observe in the phenomenal world to a cause of the world itself we contradict our own principle of explanation. It would mean that there is a God who is not penetrable to the human mind. He would be beyond our possible experience. In this manner we should involve ourselves in contradiction. We should then have a God who was supposed to have caused or determined all things. That would destroy our freedom. That would destroy the contingency of temporal events. We would then be back to a position similar to that of Leibniz. We would also be doing violence to brute fact.

Just now we said that Kant thinks of the creation idea as bringing us back to a position similar to that of Leibniz. In reality Leibniz and Kant agree in holding to an exclusively immanentistic principle of interpretation. Both would sub-

---

185. Emphasis added. Here is a brief summary of Van Til's challenge to unbelieving philosophy. Either one presupposes God, or one must deal with random and meaningless factuality—in which case the unbeliever is reduced to skepticism.

stitute *reason for causation* when the universe as a whole is up for discussion. Both would follow a principle of continuity that avoids any real transcendence. But Kant does not think reason can envelop the whole area of brute fact. More than that, he does not think reason can comprehensively interpret even one brute fact. Reason deals with universals. It must deal with universals. It seeks to bring individual brute facts into relation with one another. To do this it must subtract from the uniqueness of individuals. When an individual is treated as a member of a class and we make general statements about the class we have subtracted from the uniqueness of that individual. I may put an individual into ever so many classes. Then I may add what I have said about each one of those classes. Still I will not have begun to exhaust the meaning of the individual.

Accordingly I must give up the notion of absolute truth. With all my categories I can but express aspects of the truth. Brute fact will never allow itself to be completely caught in the net of my categories. There will always be more of brute fact for me to catch. When I apply the category of causality to the brute facts that meet me I do throw light on an aspect of the behavior of brute fact. But I can never apply the category of causality to the existence of brute fact itself. That would mean that I had explained the whole of brute fact. But when I claim to have explained the whole of brute fact I involve myself in contradiction and thus deny my own principle of explanation. If I am to continue to claim that I can explain anything at all I shall have to give up claiming to be able to explain everything, and give up the idea that everything is essentially explicable by the human mind.

Thus modern thought, as it is based upon Kant, is in no sense a return to Christian theism. It is rather a desperate effort to save the principle of exclusively immanentistic interpretation from bankruptcy. In the hands of the rationalists the principle had involved itself in complete self-contradiction. To avoid this contradiction and yet save the immanentistic character of interpretation, Kant emphasized more than ever the bruteness of brute facts. . . .

It will now be apparent that modern thought and Christianity stand squarely opposed to one another on the creation concept. If anywhere, the contrast ought to be clear at this point. Brute fact is the issue. Modern thought assumes it. Assuming brute fact, it thereby reduces God to the level of man. He is at most a co-interpreter, with man, of brute fact. His thought is therefore not on a higher level than the thought of man. Man does not need to await the interpretation of fact by God before he gives his own final interpretation.

Over against this, Christianity holds that God is the creator of every fact. There are no brute facts. Thus God's thought is placed back of every fact. . . .

It follows from this that there is purpose *within* the universe because the triune God has a purpose *for* the universe. Every purpose within the universe must, in the last analysis, be referred to God. Without this reference to God, no purpose within the universe has meaning. . . . Mechanical laws are, from the ultimate point of view, completely teleological. . . .

In complete contrast with this Christian view of teleology is the non-Christian view. The non-Christian view denies the doctrines of creation and providence. It denies any reference to a transcendent, self-sufficient God. It is based upon a philosophy of chance. Bare possibility is taken as the most basic metaphysical category. Frequently all teleology is denied.[186] But even if some sort of teleology is affirmed it is a teleology that is a chance collocation of brute facts. It is always an exclusively immanentistic teleology.

The modern form of this non-Christian immanentistic teleology is strikingly expressed by Kant. As noted above, he virtually reduced all the theistic proofs to the ontological one. According to Kant, speculative theology made an un-justifiable leap beyond the realm of possible experience. He said it took abstract thought and concluded to a Being that is beyond experimental proof. As against this he held to what he called the transcendental nature of thought. Thought, says Kant, is an abstraction, unless brought into connection with space time facts. Accordingly the categories of thought can never go beyond the phenomenal world. So then the category of purpose, like the categories of substance and causality, apply within our experience of the phenomenal world. Purpose cannot be spoken of in connection with the universe as a whole.[187] . . .

Kant has enabled us to see that by the idea of true inwardness of the human self we may overcome the hopeless reduction of fact to logic or of the hopeless reduction of logic to fact. We now see that the notions of pure contingency and of pure system are correlative and therefore necessary to one another. In the on-going process of human experience man needs both, the ideal of absolute openness of the universe and the ideal of the absolute comprehension of experience. But he cannot have both unless he takes them as correlative to one another.[188]

186. To hold that reality (or man) is teleological in nature is to say that its events or objects (or man's behavior) serve an "end," aim, or purpose.
187. The significance of this commentary is that on Kant's own terms, there can be no knowledge of objective purpose (beyond what is subjectively imposed by the mind of man) in the events of history or the facts of the world. This renders the external world "in itself" completely random and incoherent. On the one hand, we have "pure contingency" (the noumenal realm), and on the other hand, "pure system" (the phenomenal realm actively but "inwardly" constructed by the mind).
188. Kant had set out to "save" the rationality of science and the free personality of man from the skepticism of Hume, but his effort failed. Science was subjec-

RECENT IDEALISM[189]

(A) In many quarters the idea seems to prevail that Idealism and Christianity have found an alliance against all forms of Pragmatism. Both Idealism and Christianity, it is claimed, stand for the maintenance of absolute truth and value while Pragmatism has frankly embraced the relativity of truth and value. Is this presentation correct? I think it is not. Idealism as well as Pragmatism, it seems to me, has embraced the relativity of truth and value. Idealism as

---

tivized, and personality (teleology) could at best be noncognitive and lost in utter contingency. The Christian apologist should be interested to find out from the intellectual despisers of Christian faith who it is, then, that has provided the rational rebuttal to the skepticism of Hume. Perhaps to his surprise he will find that most contemporary philosophers—having little taste for idealism (with its speculative complexities and flights from common sense)—acquiesce to Hume (and thus to skepticism), either by trivializing the problems he raised ("Nobody can answer them, so they are not important") or by giving up on epistemological certainty in favor of "pragmatic" approaches to knowledge or science. The supremely pragmatic spirit was found in Friedrich Nietzsche (1844–1900), who had an instrumentalist theory of knowledge (and a "perspectivist" theory that all truth is interpretation), which led him to assert that "the falsity of a judgment is no objection to it"! What is important is not whether a proposition is true, but whether it is useful and life-affirming, and serves man's "will to power."

189. The following excerpts are taken from:

(A) *Christianity and Idealism* (Philadelphia: Presbyterian and Reformed, 1955), 7, 34;
(B) *Reformed Pastor and Modern Thought*, 133;
(C) *Christianity and Idealism*, 22, 29–30, 14, 32, 26, 16, 21, 24, 26–27, 17.

Post-Kantian idealism (particularly neo-Hegelian idealism) was the dominant school of thought in Anglo-American philosophy at the beginning of the twentieth century, but it is now virtually abandoned. Although the idealists differed from each other in interesting ways, their basic outlook can be reasonably summarized. In contrast to subjective and phenomenalistic idealism (e.g., Berkeley and Kant, respectively), "absolute" or "objective" idealism held that everything that exists (all plurality) is a form of one mind (thus transcending the individual minds of particular, and thus limited, individual persons) coming by degrees to perfect self-consciousness. The universe is not fragmented and atomistic (except in appearance), but unified and one according to the whole and completely adequate concept or idea of it. The universe (or reality) is rational; however, since every particular assertion is at best a conditioned and partial truth (exhibiting a limited perspective), we never grasp the world as a whole, and contradictions are generated in our thinking. The absolute and single truth (or idea) embraces the integrated whole of reality, expressed now as simultaneously concrete (completely detailed and empirical) and universal (rational and perfectly unified); in it all contradictions are rationally resolved, and there is no longer a dichotomy between thought and reality. Reality is not only rational, but identical with reason itself. F. H. Bradley (1846–1924) conceded that the Absolute is ultimately unknowable; a finite in-well as Pragmatism is a foe of Biblical Theism. Together they form a secret alliance against Theism. Such will be the contention of this paper. . . .

It would seem that the forgoing discussion has explained why it is that so often Theism and Idealism are considered to be close allies while in reality they are enemies. Idealism has constantly avowed its friendship towards Theism. Idealism has maintained the necessity of presupposing (a) a unity basic to diversity, (b) a timeless unity basic to diversity, and (c) one ultimate subject of interpretation. On these points Idealism only *seems* to stand with Theism for Idealism has *also* maintained we must have (a) a plurality as basic to unity, (b) a temporal plurality as basic to unity, and (c) a plurality of interpreters of Reality. These two conflicting tendencies cannot but seek to destroy one another. Logic demands that Idealism choose between the theistic and pragmatic motifs. Logic also demands that if the pragmatic motif is entertained seriously at all, it will win out altogether in time. History has amply justified the demands of logic. The Absolute of Idealism is today no more than a logical principle and that a changing one. The "obsolescence of the eternal" has taken place. Idealism as well as Pragmatism is a foe of Theism; the "Absolute" is not God.[190]

---

dividual could never fully realize the existence of the Absolute without ceasing to be an individual. Any effort to gain systematic knowledge is doomed in advance, said Bradley, and all attempts to avoid this conclusion must prove "illusory." Other idealists to whom Van Til alludes in these reading selections are Georg W. F. Hegel (1770–1831), Johann G. Fichte (1762–1814), Friedrich W. J. Schelling (1775–1854), Bernard Bosanquet (1848–1923), Josiah Royce (1855–1916), J. E. McTaggart (1866–1925), and Andrew Seth Pringle-Pattison (1856–1931).

The writings of the idealists (as well as those of their critics, like Van Til) can be very abstruse and difficult to follow. Van Til urged various objections against idealism. He faulted idealism for denying true transcendence and setting forth simply another immanent perspective of autonomous thinking. For that reason, it cannot avoid an ultimate plurality (or gain rational unity and coherence), reduces to metaphysical relativism (like pragmatism, its supposed foe), fails as a transcendental program, and ultimately becomes a kind of pantheism (where God's thoughts are not distinguished in kind from man's thoughts, and God is identified with the "developing whole").

190. Van Til first published these words in 1930, in "God and the Absolute," *Evangelical Quarterly* 2 (October 1930): 358–88. His first footnote explained: "We use the term Theism to signify biblical Theism, of which we take the notion of an absolute, self-sufficient, personal God to be the central metaphysical concept" (p. 358). His last words were that the "Absolute" of idealistic philosophy is not God. Various critics through the years (from Cecil DeBoer to Clark Pinnock) have tried to dismiss Van Til as a redressed idealist; such criticism betrays serious misunderstanding (probably of both the idealists and Van Til himself). Van Til addressed the charge that he promotes "the God of idealism" in *Defense of the Faith*, 228–32.

(B) We cannot give a survey here of the development of the post-Kantian idealism in such men as Fichte, Schelling, and Hegel.[191] One remark may be made in passing. When Hegel says that the real is the rational and the rational is the real, he is not reverting to pre-Kantian rationalism. Hegel despises the *alte Metaphysik*. His is a post-Kantian "rationalism." It is "rationalism" that has built the Kantian notion of contingency into its "system."

The very ideal of the *Concrete Universal* which constitutes the central notion of the idealism of such men as F. H. Bradley, Bernard Bosanquet, and Josiah Royce, presupposes that the irrational has been given its rightful place. Modern idealism, therefore, boasts of the fact that the individual and the universal, the temporal and the eternal, are always present together in every experience of man.

(C) Theism may also say that diversity is basic to unity. Theism may contend that the Trinity is not a burdensome encumbrance to a theology already heavily loaded with irrationalities but the very foundation of rational thought. Formally the Theist and Bosanquet agree, but materially they differ. Bosanquet seeks for his diversity not within Absolute Number One, but within Absolute Number Two, the Universe.[192] . . .

With this attempt Bosanquet tried to do the impossible. His was a search for a self-generating *a priori;* the search seems as hopeful as that for the Holy Grail. We may dislike "either-or" alternatives, but here we must face one: your *a priori* is either in the timeless self-conscious God with the result that history realizes the purpose of God, or your *a priori* is to develop in a Universe inclusive of God, with the result that history is self-dependent.

We shall soon see this aspect of Idealism run into an open avowal of Pluralism in the case of McTaggart and Pringle-Pattison. Suffice it here to have pointed out that a metaphysical Pluralism is embedded in the heart of Bosanquet's logic.[193] . . .

---

191. CVT: Cf. the writer's *Christianity and Idealism* (Philadelphia: Presbyterian and Reformed Publishing Co., 1955).
192. Earlier in the article, where he identified two concepts that were used ambiguously by F. H. Bradley and the idealists, Van Til distinguished "Absolute Number One," which is called the "Beyond" or "God," from "Absolute Number Two," which turns out to be "the Universe or the Whole" (p. 17). Van Til's criticism here is that Bosanquet does not have diversity (as well as unity) in a transcendent absolute (the "Beyond"), but only in an immanent absolute (the "Whole" or the Universe, inclusive of God and man).
193. This is a deadly internal critique of the logic utilized in idealism. According to it, the intelligibility of any plurality depends upon an absolute unity within which the diversity or plurality exists. However, if that absolute unity is not found in the transcendent, personal God (as it is in Christianity), then idealism must

A frank acceptance of temporalism in metaphysics, [J.] Watson tells us, is not only the logical outcome of idealistic logic, but it is also the only safeguard against agnosticism. Hegel and some of his followers still asked the question why the Absolute should reveal himself, assuming that he was beyond. Watson, on the other hand, tells us that: "If it is asked *why* the Absolute reveals itself gradually in the finite, I should answer that the question is absurd: we cannot go beyond reality in order to explain why it is what it is; we can only state what its nature, as known to us, involves."[194] What the Theist asserts of God, that is, that it cannot be asked who made him, Watson asserts of temporal reality. In other words, the space-time continuum is frankly accepted as the matrix of God. Metaphysically we are coming very close to the position maintained by S. Alexander in *Space, Time and Deity*.[195] All reality "implies succession, and hence we must say that there is no conceivable reality which does not present the aspect of succession or process."[196] . . .

It is this emphasis on time and succession as an inseparable aspect of the whole of reality that leads Idealism far away from Theism and very close to Pragmatism. . . .

The Idealist has not presupposed his Absolute[197] and therefore his Absolute is or tends to become the God of the Pragmatist. Such is our main contention. The Idealist has recognized the necessity of presupposing the Absolute but has not been able to do so because of the neutrality involved in his logic. As in the case of the Pragmatist "neutrality" leads the Idealist to, and is itself an evidence of, his metaphysical relativism. . . .

In the philosophy of C. C. J. Webb we have a case in point. In his work, "Problems in the Relation of God and Man," Webb clearly pronounces his

---

look to this "absolute" unity to evolve or develop immanently within the contingencies of history—in which case it never escapes plurality and diversity.

194. CVT: *Phil. Rev.*, v. 4, 1895, p. 367.
195. The embarrassing thing about this observation is that Samuel Alexander (1859–1938) was an emergent evolutionist, who took the origin of all existing things to be the space-time matrix. For Alexander, truth is not absolute, but relative—and may even turn into its opposite (falsehood). Reality is moving and changing, with every next stage or higher level representing transcendent "deity" to the earlier stage. Given such affirmation of materialism, change, and relativism, Alexander's philosophy was hardly congenial to that of the absolute idealists. However, according to Van Til, the idealists end up very close to Alexander anyway.
196. CVT: *Phil. Rev.*, v. 4, 1895, p. 497.
197. What Van Til means here is that idealism is at odds within itself—it wants to presuppose an Absolute, yet one that will allow it to be neutral. Idealism thus maintains a metaphysical relativism, being open-minded about the definite character of ultimate reality, as well as epistemologically "neutral."

general agreement with the idealist theory of logic. The usual idealistic argument for the necessity of a system is advanced fully. Still he thinks it quite possible to study the phenomena of the religious consciousness without any metaphysical presuppositions. Webb wants to have an Absolute and still be "neutral." He tries like Bosanquet to serve two masters. He wishes to assume no metaphysics at the beginning of his investigation, which means that he has assumed the metaphysics of relativity. Webb has as a matter of fact assumed that religion must be worship of the whole.

Surely on this issue Idealism ought to choose which master it will serve. If its demand for a presupposed Absolute be taken seriously then its "neutral" method in the philosophy of religion stands condemned. On the other hand if Idealism wishes to be "scientific" or "neutral" in its investigations of the religious and moral consciousness it must say farewell to the Absolute. The solution is sought by gradually immersing the Absolute. The idealistic philosophy of religion is built upon a metaphysical relativism throughout.

Thus we see that the view of the moral consciousness as determinative of the Absolute is the natural result of the Kantian creative theory of thought[198] which is inherent in idealistic as well as Pragmatic logic. . . .

Bosanquet represents the high-water mark of recent idealistic thought. He has worked out the implications of idealistic logic more fully than anyone else. In his Logic he has clearly shown that the unrelated pluralistic universe of Pragmatism as it corresponds to and is the necessary correlative of the so-called "scientific," "open-minded," "neutral" method of research is destructive of knowledge itself. God is a fact that must be presupposed or he cannot be harmonized with other facts. Accordingly neutrality is impossible. But if "neutrality" be still adhered to, God is denied and with him the rationality which we need as much as breath. "Neutrality" we saw to be inherent in the heart of Bosanquet's essential creativity theory of thought by virtue of which he constantly speaks of laws that hold for "all possible experience." The result has been that Bosanquet has forsaken the transcendental method, returned to the false *a priorism* imbedded in every "scientific method," when it determines what is possible and impossible. What was actually proved impossible on this assumption of the essential unity of human and divine thought is the presupposition of God.[199] . . .

198. Recall that Kant maintained that the chaotic input of the senses is actively formed into concepts by the human mind. The mind thus constitutes its own objects in the midst of a chance world which is "in itself" beyond cognition and rational order. It is the "lawgiver" which determines the conditions for all intelligible experience.

199. This is a crucial observation. According to Van Til, although idealism sets out on a transcendental project (to find the preconditions of intelligible experi-

The burden of his argument is that our knowledge or experience in general needs to presuppose system and this can be presupposed in the Absolute only. Now we found that the Absolute of Bosanquet is not absolute but is after all an aspect of a self-developing whole. . . .

Bradley speaks of comprehensibility *per se* while Theism distinguishes between comprehensibility for God and comprehensibility for man. Bradley has assumed that all thought must be measured by one standard, that all thought, human and divine, is of one type. . . .

From the Theistic standpoint this assumption of the unity of type of all thought is the cancer working its deadly work in the Idealistic organism. . . . From the idealistic assumption that all thought is of one type it follows that the Universe is a wider concept than "God." It is the Universe in the case of Bradley as in the case of other Idealists, that is really the Absolute. "God" and man operate within this Universe. They are aspects of this Universe, correlatives one of the other. They are really *equally ultimate* aspects, or they could not be aspects of one Reality at all. . . .

[A]ll thought was assumed to be of one type. Similarly with Bosanquet. The acosmic tendency in his thinking which demands that human beings be considered "connections of content" or "foci" of the Absolute is pantheistic, not theistic. And more important still the reason for Bosanquet's acosmism is the assumption of the identity of the nature of human and divine thought. The Absolute cannot think in terms of purpose since purpose is a temporally conditioned category. This sounds theistic. But when it is added that our thought, to be genuine, must be like God's thought, beyond time, the Pantheism is apparent. It seems as though we are exalting "God" very highly when we say that his thoughts are not temporally conditioned, but when we add that our thoughts also are not temporally conditioned the exaltation of "God" is neutralized. . . .

"God" must be the self-developing Whole. Only it may well be questioned whether "God" can be a self-developing Whole. Does not this controvert the basic demand of Idealism that the actual precede the potential? Bosanquet's great desire for inclusiveness has led him to compromise his principle. One cannot have his cake and eat it. The unity for which he seeks, which he says we must even presuppose, turns out to be merely a member of the plurality, or an abstract principle within it, or thirdly the Whole plurality itself and all these in flux. . . .

Our conclusion is that Bosanquet has tried to serve two masters. As a great

---

ence), it cannot successfully or consistently pursue that project because it does not take God as its presupposition. Idealism represents a false or failed transcendentalism.

logician he saw that a temporal plurality, or the open universe, cannot account for our knowledge; the "neutrality" that is the invariable concomitant of metaphysical relativism is but an apotheosis of negation operating in a vacuum. But when he assumed without question the identity of the nature of "all possible experience," when he made synthesis as fundamental as analysis, and the possible as fundamental as the actual, he took the "ultimacy," the underived character of time for granted and with it the Universe as a wider concept than God. He tried to be "neutral," after all. Reality is that which thought (that is, our thought operating on experience) finds it to be. After this assumption of the Universe as the subject of all predication *God could not be presupposed.* Bosanquet desperately seeks for a God within the Universe and therefore could not presuppose him beyond the Universe. . . .

In our criticism of Bosanquet we saw that as the result of his view of the inherent creativity of thought the Absolute which he feels he needs will have to respect (*a*) an ultimate plurality, (*b*) a plurality in flux, that is, self-developing Universe, and therefore (*c*) the final interpretation of experience by man. Has subsequent history justified our criticism?

In seeking to answer this question we limit ourselves to a discussion of a few representative Idealists. Our contention is that recent exponents of Idealism have themselves felt the ambiguity in Bosanquet's position. They are frankly denying transcendence and embracing immanence.

We may begin with the philosophy of McTaggart. McTaggart has keenly felt that Idealism must do either of two things: it must admit a temporalism in metaphysics or it must deny the reality of time. For, and this is highly significant, McTaggart simply assumes that the Absolute of Idealism is Absolute Number Two, that is, the Universe inclusive of God and Man.

The demand of Bosanquet's logic that the Universe is the subject of all predication is rigidly carried through by McTaggart. Hence he no longer seeks for a timeless basis of the universe. That would involve the application of two contradictory predicates to the same subject. For him the Universe is either wholly temporal or wholly non-temporal.

The Universe is non-temporal. Time is an illusion. Such is McTaggart's position.[200] Only a timeless reality is complete and therefore furnishes the system necessary to thought. We might develop a criticism here that to prove the unreality of time, be it objective, subjective or merely as an illusion, is highly artificial. We might add that McTaggart has not proved the unreality of time and is therefore seeking to interpret one ultimate in terms of another

---

200. CVT: McTaggart, J. E., *Mind*, N.S. 524, p. 326, in articles on "Time and the Hegelian Dialectic."

ultimate. We pass these criticisms by to observe that granted McTaggart has proved his case even so the Absolute is in no sense Beyond. . . .

Add to this the observation that the idealistic assumption in epistemology that man's thought is on the par with God's is the "neutrality" of Pragmatism since it seeks to make the interpretation of reality a co-operative enterprise between God and man which implies that man ultimately interprets reality for himself,[201] and we already see "neutrality" chasing "relativity" as a dog chases its tail.

Bradley seems to have felt something of the difficulties involved in his position. He ends up one argument after another with an appeal to mystery. "Somehow" Reality will absorb all the difficulties of Appearance. His Reality becomes much of a Moloch, requiring the sacrifices of the Appearance. There is in Bradley an acosmic strain. But the Theist fears this acosmic strain; to him it is an evidence of a false *a priorism* that says man cannot be man unless he is God. A Moloch demanding human sacrifice is an idol; by that token can one know it. Moreover Idealism has no right to appeal to mystery. One who assumes that the Real is the Rational and at the same time makes man a charter member with "God" in the Universe cannot, without destroying his basic principle, appeal to mystery.[202] There may be, on an idealistic basis, a sphere of the unknown to man, but never one of the unknowable. By this token too is Idealism distinguished from Theism. Theism says there is nothing unknown or unknowable for God, but there is for man one territory unknown but knowable and another unknown and also unknowable. If it were not so man would be one with God. Thus if Theism appeals to mystery it appeals to the ultimate rationality as it is in God. Theism does not, as does Idealism, by its appeal to mystery neutralize its basic demand that there must be an ultimate rationality back of our experience.

RECENT EMPIRICISM: LOGICAL POSITIVISM[203]

For a brief description of *Logical Positivism* as it originated in the so-called *Vienna Circle*, we listen to A. J. Ayer.

201. CVT: *Vide* discussion in previous pages on the differences between Pragmatism and Theism.
202. This is another biting internal critique. The very principle of idealism (i.e., the real is the rational) precludes the appeal to mystery (the nonrational) that Bradley and other idealists must make in order to account for the intellectual difficulties with the developing and contingent realm of historical plurality— the realm of "appearance" that is not yet the fully developed reality (or idea).
203. An excerpt from *Christian-Theistic Evidences*, 139–46 (an appendix added to the 1975 and subsequent editions, based on a 1968 lecture at Calvin College).
    In 1895 a chair in the philosophy of the inductive sciences was established at the University of Vienna in the name of Ernst Mach (1836–1916), whose philo-

It is remarkable, says Ayer, in speaking of the *Vienna Circle,* "how many of their most radical doctrines are already to be found in Hume" (*ibid.,* p. 73).[204] "The positivist flavour of their thought," Ayer continues, "comes out most strongly in their hostility to metaphysics" (*ibid.,* p. 74). Any attempt to describe Reality as a whole, or to find the purpose of the Universe, or to reach beyond the everyday world to some supra-sensible spiritual order was thought of as metaphysics (*ibid.,* p. 74). They condemned metaphysics "not as being unduly speculative, or even as being false, but as being literally nonsensical. They reached this conclusion by the application of a criterion of meaning which is known as the verification principle" (*ibid.,* p. 74). Roughly stated, says Ayer, this principle "lays it down that the meaning of a statement is de-

---

sophical aim was to eliminate all unobserved entities and unify the "sciences" in their commitment to the study of sensations. In the first two decades of the twentieth century, a group of scholars dedicated to the same perspective developed in Vienna, including Otto Neurath (1882–1945) and Rudolf Carnap (1891–1970), who together advanced the thesis of physicalism (that all assertions of fact can be formulated as statements about publicly observable objects and events). In 1922 Moritz Schlick (1882–1936) was named to the Mach chair, and he gave leadership to the group through Thursday meetings of philosophers and scientists. In the 1920s, the group became enamored of the *Tractatus Logico-Philosophicus,* by Ludwig Wittgenstein (1889–1951), due to its insistence that the world is made up of elementary facts (the objects of empirical study), that the job of language is to state (indeed, to picture) those facts or tautologies, and that every other type of proposition (e.g., ethical and metaphysical ones) is, strictly speaking, "nonsense"—an assessment that Wittgenstein had the honesty to pin on the *Tractatus* itself. The group published a position paper entitled "Scientific Worldview" and identified itself as "The Vienna Circle" in 1929, and in 1939 it started the *Journal of Unified Science.* The outlook of the Vienna Circle is known as "logical positivism," and it was most enthusiastically propounded by the Oxford philosopher Alfred J. Ayer (1910–89), particularly in his popular work *Language, Truth, and Logic* (1936, rev. 1946). In it, Ayer maintained that any genuinely meaningful and factual statement must pass the "verifiability criterion" (which he could never successfully formulate)—to the effect that any meaningful statement is in theory verifiable by observation, either directly or indirectly (by observation of what can be deduced from it along with other "legitimate" statements). The philosopher does not have available to him any truths that are not accessible by the other sciences, and so the job of philosophy becomes that of clarifying the language of science, developing logical sophistication, and purifying the field of the nonsense of metaphysics and ethics. Although the radical empiricism and antireligious character of logical positivism gave intellectual respectability to the popular prejudices of many unbelievers, the Christian apologist can be glad for its explicit advocacy. This has made possible the very public and painful discrediting of that viewpoint (even at the hands of other unbelieving philosophers) as self-refuting, prejudicial, and a veiled faith-commitment to its own particular kind of metaphysics.

204. Van Til quotes from *The Revolution in Philosophy,* ed. Gilbert Ryle (New York: Macmillan, 1960).

termined by the way in which it can be verified, where its being verified consists in its being tested by empirical observation" (*ibid.*, p. 74). Judged by the verification principle, statements of metaphysics as above described "are ruled out as factually meaningless. Statements of metaphysics, that is, are not capable of stating facts. Wittgenstein expressed this contention succinctly in the last sentence of his *Tractatus* by saying: "Of that of which we cannot speak we should be silent" (*ibid.*, p. 75). Neurath, one of the members of the circle, wants to go further than this. He wants to make sure not only that we cannot *speak* of metaphysical entities, but that there *are* no such entities. "When it comes to metaphysics," said Neurath, "one must indeed be silent, but not *about* anything." Or as the Cambridge philosopher, F. P. Ramsey, an enthusiastic but critical follower of Wittgenstein, puts it: "What we can't say we can't say, and we can't whistle it either." Ayer himself adds: "A great deal of bad philosophy comes from people thinking that they can somehow whistle what they cannot say" (*ibid.*, 75).[205]

On what, someone may ask, does the verification principle itself rest? Could one verify the verification principle? Of course not, says Ayer. "It was put forward as a definition, not as an empirical statement of fact.[206] But it is not an arbitrary definition. It purports to lay down the conditions which actually govern our acceptance, or indeed our understanding, of common sense

---

205. That is, thinking that there is some other kind of communication or connection with real states of affairs that is not verbalizable and rational in the preferred scientific sense.

206. This would be, of course, a tremendous embarrassment to logical positivism on its own terms, because definitions are mere tautologies (with the help of semantic facts) and thus entirely trivial or noninformative. Thus, Ayer must immediately add that the verification principle is not an "arbitrary" definition, but stipulates the conditions that govern the practice of scientific discussion. Does he mean that it is prescriptive, then? If so, it again suffers the disdain of logical positivism, which, according to its own strictures, deems ethical statements (of obligation) emotive or factually meaningless. Does Ayer then mean that the verification principle simply "defines" (describes) the actual past practice of scientists? If so, so what? One could as readily and as arbitrarily define the verifying procedures of religious mystics (although Ayer seems to think, rather naively, that metaphysicians recognize no procedures or tests for what they will allow as believable). Resorting to a pragmatic defense at this point, Ayer might contend that the verification principle "defines" the past practice of the naturalistic scientists because that practice has proven so successful in achieving their aims. This would be a philosophical *faux pas*, however, because then Ayer would have to defend a value judgment (namely, that the aims of the naturalistic scientists are the right aims to choose) and make metaphysical judgments (namely, that science has been more successful than other procedures in the past, and that the future will resemble the past). But value judgments and metaphysical judgments are the very things that logical positivism seeks to banish from meaningful discourse.

and scientific statements, the statements which we take as describing the world 'in which we live and move and have our being' " (*ibid.*, p. 75).

If a metaphysician replies that there "may be other worlds besides the world of science and common sense, and that he makes it his business to explore them," then we reply that "the onus is on him to show by what criterion his statements are to be tested; until he does this we do not know how to take them" (*ibid.*, pp. 75, 76).

What we insist on, argues Ayer, is that the statements made by the metaphysician must not be entered as scientific hypotheses. If they enter their statements as something other than scientific hypotheses, "then we want some information about the conditions under which this different race is run" (*ibid.*, p. 76).

We have done with metaphysics. Now to the task of interpreting science and daily life by observation of facts and by testing any statement of observation by the verification principle.

It is obvious that in scientific interpretation of facts we must connect our individual observations by means of logic and mathematics. Now if logic and mathematics are themselves empirical generalizations, as was held, e.g., by John Stuart Mill, then how do we account for their necessity? Without necessity we have no firm ground under our own position. How then shall we deny metaphysics?

Well, the Vienna Circle allowed that logic and mathematics are necessary "but only because they were true by definition. They were said to be tautologies, in Wittgenstein's somewhat special use of this term" (*ibid.*, p. 76). "Logic and mathematics have, on this theory, the important function of making it clear to what our use of symbols commits us. . . . [A] priori statements are not themselves descriptive of anything, but their use enables us to pass securely from one descriptive statement to another. Wittgenstein, like Eddington, applies to our conceptual system the simile of a fisherman's net. Logic and mathematics are concerned only with the structure of the net, and, therefore, only with the form of the fish. Their truths are certain because we do not admit the possibility of their being falsified" (*ibid.*, p. 77).

The Vienna Circle has now accomplished the exclusion of all metaphysics and has shown us the foundation on which it stands when it accomplishes this exclusion. If the theologian wants to continue to make statements about a world beyond the world of science, he may be permitted to do so on condition that he regards his statements as emotive rather than informational. As for the philosopher, since he too must cease to be metaphysical, we assign to him the task of "a sort of intellectual policeman, seeing that nobody trespasses into metaphysics" (*ibid.*, p. 79). "It is science that gives us our knowledge of the world; there is not, there cannot be, a philosophical brand of knowledge which would compete with science in this field" (*ibid.*, p. 78). This was, says Ayer, essentially Wittgenstein's view in the *Tractatus*.

The Vienna Circle wanted to give the philosopher a second, a positive form of employment. The task of the philosopher would be to refine scientific statements by analysis (*ibid.*, p. 79). The result of philosophizing is not to establish a set of philosophical propositions but to "make other propositions clear" (*ibid.*).

At this point Ayer asserts that the Vienna Circle had not solved the basic epistemological problem. What is really meant when we say that a statement is verifiable? Does it mean merely that statements about facts are internally coherent with one another? Does it not also mean that statements must be verifiable in relation to facts? Then, if I make statements about my experience of facts, how can I convey the meaning of my experience to you? For my experience is private to me, and your experience is private to you; how then, if we each have to interpret every statement of fact as referring to our own experience, do we ever succeed in communicating with each other?[207]

Morris Schlick's solution of this difficulty was to say that while the content of our experiences is indeed incommunicable, their structure is not. What I call "red" may look quite different to me from the way what you call "red" looks to you; we can never tell. It is doubtful even if the question whether they are or are not the same has any meaning. But we can at least discover that we apply the word on the same occasions; so that whatever may be the difference in the content of our private worlds, their structure is the same (*ibid.*, p. 81). This answer of Schlick's, says Ayer, does not withstand analysis. Here are a number of people "immured within the several fortresses of their own experience . . . considering what they can convey to one another." It is obvious that if they are so immured as Schlick says they are, "there would be nothing they could convey, not even structure" (*ibid.*).

In connection with this problem a difference of opinion developed within the members of the Vienna Circle. They disputed between themselves about what they called "protocol statements." Protocol statements are "the basic reports of direct observations, by reference to which the truth of all other empirical statements is to be tested" (*ibid.*). But must not these protocol statements themselves "be inter-subjectively verifiable?" (*ibid.*, p. 82). And to be inter-subjectively verifiable "was taken to imply that they must refer to physical events; for it was assumed without argument that physical events were

207. This is one illustration or application of the old problem of phenomenalism and the egocentric predicament. The public or objective nature of truth is subject to question in empirically anchored epistemologies.

accessible to all alike" (*ibid.*, p. 82). The language of physics, Neurath argued, "is a universal language; universal in the sense that every empirical statement can be expressed in it" (*ibid.*). This, says Ayer, "is the old doctrine of materialism, in a modern guise" (*ibid.*). It may also be called physicalism.

In opposition to Neurath, others of the Circle thought protocol statements need not be inter-subjectively verifiable. "They alone were verified directly; all other empirical statements were verified indirectly through them" (*ibid.*, p. 82).

The physicalists "took away from protocol statements their special character as records of experience; and they then went on to deny their function. It makes no sense, they said, to speak of comparing statements with facts.[208] Statements can be compared only with one another. Accordingly, they were led to adopt a coherence theory of truth; they maintained that the criterion by which it is to be decided whether a statement is true is not its correspondence with fact but its consistency with other statements" (*ibid.*, p. 83).

Then, if someone objected by saying that "many incompatible systems of statements may each be internally consistent; and since they are mutually incompatible, they cannot all be true," then Carnap is ready with his reply. "Carnap's answer to this was that we were to regard as true that system which was accepted by the scientists of our culture" (*ibid.*, p. 83). Finally, if each of several competing systems claimed that it alone is accepted by the scientists of our culture, then Carnap is ready again with his reply. "What Carnap meant was that the true system was that which they *in fact* accepted" (*ibid.*). Ayer's comment on this final answer of Carnap's is: "But if a reference to fact is to be allowed in this case, why not in others also? Experience might even show that contemporary scientists sometimes make mistakes" (*ibid.*).

"On any view of philosophy," says Ayer near the end of his discussion of the Vienna Circle, "this inner-outer problem is extremely difficult, and I shall not attempt to give a solution here" (*ibid.*, p. 84). . . .

Ayer can point to plenty of evidence to prove that the problem of inner-outer has proved not only difficult but impossible of solution by referring to such efforts as we have discussed.

Bacon[209] and his followers wanted to study the facts of nature "as they are"

---

208. This is the crucial point. If "facts" are the actual states of affairs as they are directly experienced (say, the sensation of redness and roundness at this place and at this time), but "statements" are verbal utterances (consisting of written or voiced words like "red" or "round"), in what sense can we "compare" facts and statements? They are completely different kinds of things. (For instance, the word "round" does not look—is not physically sensed as—round.)

209. Francis Bacon (1561–1626) was an early English advocate of the empirical and inductive method in science; see his *The New Organon* (1620), obviously intended to replace the old *Organon* (tool of learning) written by Aristotle on logic.

without any preinterpretation. Their exclusion of the creative-redemptive activity of the Triune God of Scripture in the world was, in principle, as absolute as any member of the Vienna Circle might wish. But in excluding the self-identifying Christ of Scripture from their enterprise they encumbered themselves with a problematics that is inherently artificial and insoluble. Separating man from God they also separated man from man and man from "nature." They made for themselves a false ideal of knowledge. Man must know all reality exhaustively or he knows nothing at all. Then if man would know everything, he would know everything about nothing. All diversity would be reduced to blank identity.

Modern scientists inherited this false ideal of knowledge from the Greeks. Parmenides saw the vision of reality as one, to which nothing had ever been or could ever be added. Kant followed his modern predecessors; the idealists followed Kant; the "logical atomists"[210] and the "logical positivists" in turn follow the idealists. The "revolution in philosophy" which we have traced so far is a revolution within the Kantian revolution, within the Renaissance revolution, within the Greek revolution, within the revolution of Adam.

To escape the nemesis of success by showing that nature must be what mathematics based on the notion of human autonomy says it must be, modern scientists and philosophers, like Heraclitus before them, must assume that all reality is flux. The idea that *all* reality is flux is as necessary to modern science and philosophy as is the idea that all reality is changeless. These two ideas, that all reality is changeless and that all reality is flux, underlie the various schools of modern science and philosophy[211] as well as the various schools of ancient philosophy.

There is, therefore, one false problematics that underlies all these schools, as there is one basic ethical hostility that comes to expression in them. Men are victimized intellectually by their ethical opposition to the self-identifying Christ of Scripture.

If Christian believers would evaluate various schools of modern science or

210. Logical atomism was an early thesis of Bertrand Russell (1872–1970), who held that the world consists of simple or "atomic" facts, which can be expressed by elementary propositions that combine first-level predicates and a proper name (standing for a sense datum). This "picture theory" of language (where every word in a sentence mirrors an element of an experienced fact) was intended as a reform program whereby ordinary language could be "purified"; all complex sentences, if legitimate, could be broken down into simple or atomic statements.
211. For an example of this, taken from John Dewey's pragmatism, see Greg L. Bahnsen, "Pragmatism, Prejudice, and Presuppositionalism," in *The Foundations of Christian Scholarship: Essays in the Van Til Perspective*, ed. Gary North (Vallecito, Calif.: Ross House Books, 1976), 241ff.

philosophy, they would be well advised if they took note of this basic similarity between them. Taking note of this similarity may keep them from thinking that one school of man-centered science or philosophy is less sympathetic to Christianity than another.

It is often thought that because of its anti-metaphysical bias, modern positivism is more hostile to Christianity than were the idealist, the spiritualist and the theist philosophies of the modern and the ancient past. To think so is to deceive oneself. Modern anti-metaphysical speculation is simply more openly and perhaps more honestly, more outspokenly "immanentistic" in its view. The great service that such movements as logical atomism and logical positivism may render is to show that the more consistently the principle of human autonomy works itself out, the more clearly it appears that once man leaves the father's home, he cannot stop till he is at the swine trough. The verification principle of modern positivism can verify nothing. It has separated absolutely between a formal rationality that is like a turnpike in the sky and a bottomless swamp of factual ooze on which the turnpike must somehow rest. . . .

The "Vienna Circle," says Ayer, "did not accomplish all that they once hoped to accomplish. Many of the problems which they tried to settle still remain unsolved" (*ibid.*, p. 86). We may add that they will always remain unsolved so long as men seek to solve them in terms of (a) human autonomy, of (b) brute factual reality, and of (c) self-subsistent and self-sufficient logic. There will, on this basis, always be an absolute dichotomy between contingent factuality and purely formal logic.

Yet it is upon the basis of an interpretation of the world of everyday experience in terms of these principles that many recent scientists and philosophers boldly assert that "metaphysics" is a meaningless phrase.[212] We readily grant the truth of this point if by "metaphysics" is meant the speculations of Greek and of modern philosophy from Descartes to Dewey. But the reason why the metaphysics of these men is meaningless is because it is built upon the same anti-Christian assumptions as those on which recent "anti-metaphysical" speculation is built. Recent anti-metaphysical schools of philosophy and science are just as metaphysical as was what is actually called metaphysics of the past. And, more importantly, the various forms of anti-metaphysical positivism constitute, in effect, a type of metaphysics that *excludes* Christianity. It not merely *ignores* the God and Christ of Scripture but, in effect, *denies* him. It is as though men picked the fruits and vegetables of a garden, ignoring the signs of the owner that are obvious everywhere.[213]

---

212. Or better: the work of metaphysics produces meaningless phrases.
213. Logical positivists carry out their discussions and advance their viewpoints in a way that is intelligible only because they live in God's world and know their

Recent positivisms still deal, in effect, with "the ponderous enigmas of metaphysicians." There is the same sort of "system construction" which leads to purely *a priori* logic which, by definition, says nothing and, by definition, never will be able to say anything about facts. There is the same sort of fact which forever recedes as one seeks to say something about it.

In terms of recent scientific and philosophic theory no fact can ever be identified in its uniqueness. As soon as it is identified it is no longer unique. Again in terms of recent scientific and philosophic theory, no fact can be intelligently related to any other fact. There is no intelligible principle of verification by which scientific hypotheses may be tested in terms of experience.

When Ayer, as a young man, wrote his book, *Language, Truth and Logic*, he was quite certain that he had discovered a principle of verification by which a solid body of scientific knowledge could be built up. A number of years later he was less sure of himself. He no longer claims that a proposition can be "conclusively established in experience." He now says that a proposition is said to be verifiable "in a weak sense, if it is possible for experience to render it probable" (Alfred Jules Ayer, *Language, Truth and Logic*, Dover Publ., p. 10). He now knows that the truth of a scientific proposition can never be established. It "never could be; for however strong the evidence is in its favor, there never would be a point at which it was impossible for further experience to go against it" (*ibid.*, p. 11). How else can science discover what is new unless the universe be completely open at every point? Ayer had, apparently, in his zeal to exclude all metaphysics, for a moment forgotten this. But Ayer hastens on to tell us that the universe is not so open, but that there are some "basic propositions" which can be verified conclusively. These basic propositions can be "verified conclusively" because "they refer solely to the content of a single experience" (*ibid.*). Such basic propositions may therefore be said to be "incorrigible." It is impossible to be mistaken about them "except in a verbal sense" (*ibid.*). In short, it is a case of "nothing ventured, nothing lost." Ayer adds: "It is, however, equally a case of 'nothing ventured, nothing won,' since the mere recording of one's present experience does not serve to convey any information either to any other person or, indeed, to oneself; for in knowing a basic proposition to be true one obtains no further knowledge than what is already afforded by the occurrence of the relevant experience" (*ibid.*).

Obviously Ayer is in great straits. He is frank and honest enough to say so. He needs an absolutely open universe in which the future might prove every-

---

Maker, and yet their discussions aim to show that it does not make sense to speak of this God. They farm the garden and ignore the signs of ownership.

thing that has been said in the past to be wrong, except for the fact that there are "basic propositions" which could never be shown to be wrong. That is, they could never be shown to be wrong because they could never be shown to have any communicable meaning to anyone. Of course a "dictionary" might be written by means of which statements can be shown to be verifiable. But then "the statements which constitute the dictionary" must be regarded as "analytic"[214] (*ibid.*, p. 13). By means of this dictionary we could keep the metaphysicians from invading the realm of science (*ibid.*, p. 14). But then the dictionary itself can, on Ayer's view, at best be composed of an infinite number of descriptions of "basic propositions" which, as Ayer insists, not even he who makes them knows what they mean.

Thus Ayer's dictionary records the usage of words conventionally agreed upon by a group of scientists and philosophers, even though none of these scientists or philosophers has been able to give himself or others an intelligible account as to the reason for his usage of words. There is a common assumption on the part of the contributors to this dictionary that though the "basic propositions" on which every possible use of the dictionary depends are utterly meaningless to those who make them, yet, together, they prove that the presence of the activity of God and of Christ in their own consciousness and in the facts must be denied as meaningless.

To Ayer's imaginary dictionary we may write an imaginary "Introduction" to the effect:

(a) None of the contributors knows what the basic propositions they report mean to themselves. They have no intelligible notion of themselves; when they seek to identify themselves to themselves, they must do so by concepts which generalize and therewith destroy their uniqueness. What all of the contributors do know is that every man is in the same position of not being able to identify himself and of communicating with himself or with others.

(b) It follows that the historic Protestant claim with respect to Jesus Christ as the self-identifying one, who has from all eternity been in full self-conscious communication with the Father and the Son and who offers himself as the Savior of all those who have entangled themselves in mental and spiritual confusion, *cannot* be true. If it were true, then man would not be the one who makes "basic propositions" and he would not hide himself in a position where he could say "nothing ventured, nothing lost" or "nothing ventured, noth-

214. An analytic statement, according to a reigning dogma of empiricism, is one that is true by virtue of semantic facts (meanings) and the laws of logic. For example, "All bachelors are unmarried males" is an analytic truth. It gives no new or significant factual information about the world beyond what we know from the definitions of "bachelor," "unmarried," and "male."

ing won," for in that case his very attempt to make "basic statements" constitutes an insult to the self-identifying Christ. No one can steal tomatoes in God's garden while in his deepest heart knowing that it is God's garden (*gnontes ton Theon*) and expect to escape the wrath of God by claiming that he does not know what he is doing.

The name of the self-identifying Christ must therefore be pressed anew upon the men of science and of philosophy in our day in order that they might be saved. If Roman Catholic and Arminian thinkers fail to do this, they therewith do not press the breadth and depth of the liberating power of the gospel upon men. Christ came to save the whole man. Christ came to save science and philosophy. Kant was not able to save it by his Copernican revolution; the recent scientists have not been able to save it by their revolution. Each new scientific-philosophic revolution, short of the revolution that springs from the work of Christ and his Spirit, leads the non-Christian scientist and philosopher more deeply into his hopeless program of interpreting reality in terms of a self which can never identify itself.

There is evidence to show that at least some modern scientists and philosophers realize that they have not come in sight of solving their problems. In concluding his survey of the Vienna Circle, Ayer says, "It will be seen that the Vienna Circle did not accomplish all that they had once hoped. Many of the philosophical problems which they tried to settle still remain unsolved" ("The Vienna Circle" in *The Revolution in Philosophy*, p. 86). Ayer might better have said that they have solved *no* problem. No problem *can* be solved if the problem of the relation between concept and fact is not solved. So long as an infinite number of wholly independent "things" must be related to one another by an infinite number of wholly independent "minds" by their being reduced to a oneness that absorbs all things and all minds, so long there is no solution for any problem.

BRUTE FACTS ARE MUTE FACTS[215]

To begin with Conklin[216] tells us that no one knows. Secondly, in effect, he tells us as Christians, "But you are wrong." Thirdly he adds, in effect, "I as an evolutionist and believer in chance am right." No one knows, but you are wrong and I am right; this is typical of the current scientific method.[217]

---

215. Excerpts from *Christian-Theistic Evidences*, 64–65, 78, 80–81, 88.
216. Van Til is referring to Edwin G. Conklin, "A Biologist's Religion," in *Has Science Discovered God?* ed. Edward H. Cotton (New York: Thomas Y. Crowell, 1931), 75–89.
217. Modern thought is aware of its inability to respond to the challenge of skepti-

We do not wish to suggest that there is intentional fraud in this matter. It only points to the actual exigency of scientific methodology. It cannot proceed differently. Nor does our criticism imply that we are not very appreciative of the great accomplishments of scientists who are not Christians. We readily allow that non-Christian science has done a great work and brought to light much truth. But this truth which science has discovered is in spite of and not because of its fundamental assumption of a chance universe. Non-Christian science has worked with the borrowed capital of Christian theism, and for that reason alone has been able to bring to light much truth. . . .

Something similar to this [Solomon using the Phoenicians as his servants, not his architects, in building the temple] should be our attitude to science. We gladly recognize the detail work of many scientists as being highly valuable. We gladly recognize the fact that "science" has brought to light many details. But we cannot use modern scientists and their method as the architects of our structure of Christian interpretation. We deny the legitimacy of the ideal of science;[218] we deny its principle with respect to the relevancy of hypothesis; and we deny the legitimacy of its appeal to brute facts. We challenge its whole procedure. Instead we offer the God and the Christ of the Bible as the concrete universal in relation to which all facts have meaning. We maintain that there can be no facts but Christian-theistic facts. We then go to the "facts," the phenomena of experience, and find again and again that if we seek to interpret any "fact" on a non-Christian hypothesis it turns out to be a brute fact, and brute facts are unintelligible. . . .

But we have seen that the scientific method is based upon the philosophy of chance. This philosophy of chance, or of brute fact, destroys human predication. Upon its basis there is no connection between one fact and another fact.[219] We shall have to bring the matter back to this fundamental point again and again. Christian theism alone can vanquish the spectre of brute fact. . . .

---

cism with a cogent and systematic theory of knowledge. It thus denies that intellectual certainty is available to anyone (and, today, usually adds that such certainty is actually unimportant). However, modern thought is—by contrast—also quite dogmatic about the certainty of evolution, the impossibility of miracles, etc. It thus condemns Christianity, "knowing" that it must be mistaken. This epistemological inconsistency (and hypocrisy) is "typical," according to Van Til.

218. Remember that Van Til is here referring to the aims and procedures of science as it is conceived of in an autonomous fashion that will not presuppose God.

219. If the "facts" (external events or states of affairs) are completely a matter of "chance"—random and unconnected, having no rationale, no preestablished order, no intended pattern or preceding interpretation, no necessity—then they are indeed "brute" or untamed, not subject to reason. In that case, speaking of something (e.g., "the horse") as an instance of a class wherein members are connected or part of a definable order, and speaking of its relations or prop-

It will now be apparent that modern thought and Christianity stand squarely opposed to one another on the creation concept. If anywhere, the contrast ought to be clear at this point. Brute fact is the issue. Modern thought assumes it. Assuming brute fact, it thereby reduces God to the level of man. He is at most a co-interpreter, with man, of brute fact. His thought is therefore not on a higher level than the thought of man. Man does not need to await the interpretation of fact by God before he gives his own final interpretation. Over against this, Christianity holds that God is the creator of every fact. *There are no brute facts. Thus God's thought is placed back of every fact. Thereby man's thought is made subject to God's thought in the interpretation of every fact.*[220] There is not a single fact that man can interpret rightly without reference to God as the creator of that fact. Man cannot truly apply the category of causality to facts without the presupposition of God. It is God who has "caused" all facts to stand in a certain relation to one another. Man must seek to discover that relation as far as he can.

As Christians we join the battle with modern thought at this point in a life and death struggle. We maintain that unless God has created the existence of the universe, there would be no possibility of scientific thought. Facts would then be utterly unrelated. No two of them could be brought into any sort of relation with one another. We could not even think of the categories of human thought as revealing aspects of reality without the presupposition of God.

This implies that God must really be taken as the presupposition of the possibility of human interpretation. If with [Bishop Joseph] Butler we first allow the non-theistic principle of exclusively immanentistic interpretation for an area of human life, we have no further argument against modern thought. For us to allow that we can interpret any one fact without God is to maintain the bruteness of that fact. It is also to reduce God's thought to the level of man's thought. It is to make of God a finite God.[221] We can then at best prove the

---

erties ("is a gray mare") in general terms that are applicable to other particular things, would be contrary to the isolated and brute character of chance facts. Brute facts would have to be mute—that is, not subject to predication or communication.

220. Emphasis added. Because facts are preinterpreted by God's plan and purpose, they are connected, ordered, classifiable, and related in conceptual and causal ways; they reflect God's thought "back of" them (preceding and controlling them). Thus, they cannot be mute, but communicate the mind of God. To be knowable at all, they must be knowable in reference to God as the Creator and governor of all things.

221. Since God would not be in control of all facts, and since He would need to search out and interpret the raw data in the way man must do, He would not be self-sufficient, sovereign, or infinite in knowledge and power—in which case He could not be the Creator, or indeed "God" at all.

existence of a finite God. We can in that case never prove the existence of the Creator of heaven and of earth. He has been excluded from the outset.[222] . . .

We have already quoted from [James H.] Jeans' book *The Mysterious Universe* [London, 1930] to show that for Jeans there is nothing but chance back of the universe. It does not help us then if modern scientists do hold to "creation" if they think of this creation as springing into being by chance out of the void.

The total picture we obtain from both modern science and modern philosophy is a complete rejection of the biblical notion of creation. It matters not whether this rejection comes in the form of an outright negation, in the form of agnosticism, or in the form of substituting another meaning for the word "creation." As orthodox Christians we have to face the fact that we are at this point, as along the whole line of thought, out of accord with modern thought. And it is at this point that the weakness of the method of defense of Christianity as advocated by Butler appears most clearly. It was based upon the assumption of brute facts and man's ability, apart from God, to explain at least some of them. If one grants this much one cannot present any argument against modern science on the question of creation. The assumption of brute fact is itself the most basic denial of the creation doctrine. And the assumption that man can himself interpret brute facts is itself the denial of God as creator. We need therefore to challenge the very idea of brute fact. We need to challenge man's ability to interpret any fact unless that fact be created by God and unless man himself is created by God.

THE OPEN-CLOSED UNIVERSE[223]

Everything that man does with respect to nature, he does either as *keeping* or as *breaking* the covenant of grace that God has made with man. Thus the scientist in the laboratory and the philosopher in his study are both dealing with their materials either as a covenant-keeper or as a covenant-breaker. All of man's acts, all of man's questionings, all of man's affirmations, indeed all of his denials in any dimension of his interests, are covenantally conditioned. . . .

Naturally, if all of man's acts with respect to nature, as well as with respect

---

222. The unbeliever presupposes "from the outset" that a personal God who is self-sufficient, sovereign, and infinite in knowledge and power—and thus necessary and authoritative for anything that would be intelligible in man's experience—cannot exist. This would be inconsistent with his presumed autonomy to think freely for himself about the brute (as yet uninterpreted) facts, whatever they may be.

223. Excerpts from *Protestant Doctrine of Scripture*, 4–5, 16–17.

to Scripture, are covenantally conditioned, this is because everywhere Christ speaks to him, and speaks always with absolute authority. The scientist may or may not recognize this fact. If he is not a Christian, he will argue that any such thing as Christ having authority—an absolute authority—with respect to his scientific procedure, is utterly destructive of the very idea of science. The idea of science, he will argue, presupposes freedom on the part of the scientist to make any hypothesis that he thinks may fit the facts. Any such absolute authority also excludes, he will continue, the idea that the words of Christ may and must be tested by facts and the order of facts, i.e., by natural laws already known to man from his earlier experience and experimentation. Suppose, he may say, that I had to work under the absolute restriction of the idea of an all-controlling redemptive providence of God such as the Bible teaches. That would be against the idea of an absolutely open universe. My hypothesis would then have to be of such a nature as to be in accordance with, and even subordinate to, the idea of this all-controlling Providence. This would exclude all newness in science. All would be already fixed.

On the other hand, the idea of an all over-arching and redemptive providence would require me to allow that God could arbitrarily come into the "unity" of nature which science has discovered through many toiling efforts, and destroy this "unity" with miraculous insertions. We would then have to allow for the arbitrary createdness of every fact with which we deal. We would have to interpret the idea of scientific "law" as being subservient to that of the biblical account of sin and of redemption controlled by the fiat of the sovereign God. This cannot be, and we will not have it!

Put in other words, the methodology of science which is not definitely based upon the redemptive story of the Bible is based upon the assumption that on the one hand the universe must be wholly open and on the other hand that it must be wholly closed.[224] . . .

If man does not own the authority of Christ in the field of science, he assumes his own ultimate authority as back of his effort. The argument between the covenant-keeper and the covenant-breaker is never exclusively about any particular fact or about any number of facts. It is always, at the same time, about the nature of facts. And back of the argument about the nature of facts,

224. The autonomous concept of freedom requires an "open" universe, where things are not determined in advance or subject to absolute, rational prediction or control (as they would be, assuming God's sovereign foreordination of whatsoever comes to pass). The autonomous concept of scientific rationality requires a "closed" universe, where everything is determined in advance and is (theoretically) subject to absolute, rational prediction and control (so that miraculous intrusions by God can be ruled out in advance).

there is the argument about the nature of man. However restricted the debate between the believer and the non-believer may be at any one time, there are always two world views ultimately at odds with one another.[225] . . .

Paul teaches that every man is created in the image of God. Being thus created, in the image of God, man cannot help but know God as his Creator. But having become a sinner, he does not want to own God as his Creator. He therefore makes his interpretations of life in terms of a principle of abstract rational continuity, i.e., of abstract logic, which is above both God and man ("being in general"). Parmenides[226] says that reality must be that which rational thought, that is divine-human thought, can without contradiction say that it must be. Applying this principle to the facts of the world, he says that there can be no reality to what appear to us as changing facts of experience. Yet on the basis of fallen man, the idea of absolute *change* has as good a right to be thought of as ultimate as has the idea of the *changeless*. Heraclitus[227] had as good a right to say that all things change as Parmenides had to say that nothing changes. When others at later times said that all things are both wholly changeless and wholly changing, they had as much right to do so as did either Parmenides or Heraclitus to say what they said. Those who hold that everything changes can be refuted negatively up to a point by those who hold that nothing changes. It is obvious that if everything changes, predication ceases. Again, those who hold that nothing changes can be refuted negatively up to a point by those who say that all things change. It is obvious that if nothing changes, predication again ceases. Moreover, it is obvious that any *modus vivendi* between the two extreme views has as much right as any other *modus vivendi* or as either the idea of pure staticism or the idea of pure flux.

225. Notice again that there are basically only two worldviews—Christian and non-Christian—in Van Til's perspective. This follows from the opening of this reading selection as well. In all of man's activity (including reasoning and scientific endeavor), he acts either as a covenant-keeper (submitting to and loving God with all his mind) or a covenant-breaker (loving and respecting his own authority instead).

226. Parmenides (c. 515–c. 450 B.C.) from Elea was an early philosophical defender of motionless monism. For him, it would be irrational to hold that "nothingness" exists, for "nothing" could not even be thought (given that all thought has an existing referent). If there is not a "nothing" for the universe to come from or go to, it must be an uncreated, indestructible, and unchangeable substance. Reality was for him, then, singular and unmoving: all is one.

227. Heraclitus (c. 540–475 B.C.) from Ephesus maintained that everything is in flux (constantly changing), so that it would be impossible to step into the "same" river twice. Where there is a coordinated orderliness to the way in which different things change, we have the appearance of permanence—a cosmic process he likened to eternal fire and called "logos" (from which the Stoics developed the nonmoral concept of "natural law" or reason controlling the natural process).

All non-Christian positions have equal rights with respect to one another just because none of them have any right to their views.[228] If any of them are going to say anything definite about any fact in this world in relation to any other fact in this world, they must flatly contradict themselves in every sentence which they utter. They must use a static principle of continuity and a purely contingent principle of discontinuity in everything that they say about anything. If they say anything about any fact in the space-time world, they must say how the one fact differs from the other fact in terms of the space-time relations that both occupy. But to say how one fact differs from another fact in terms of the space-time continuum requires one to have some intelligible conception of this space-time continuum as a whole. Immanuel Kant was quite right in demanding this. But Kant himself was unable to say anything intelligible about the space-time continuum as a whole. The reason for this inability lay in the fact that he sought to do so in terms of man as the final reference point in predication. For all the advances that he may be said to have made upon Descartes in certain respects, Kant's view of man, as well as that of Descartes', is that of autonomy. It is this idea of autonomy that brings internal discord into the very nature of man. On the one hand he must, on this view, interpret himself in terms of a system of changeless laws, and therefore must know himself exhaustively. On the other hand he must regard himself as wholly free from the laws he has himself imposed upon the field of knowledge, and therefore must be unable to know himself at all. According to Kant, therefore, man must be at the same time both wholly known and wholly unknown to himself.

If then, on Kant's basis, science is to be saved from having to do with, on the one hand, an infinite number of unrelated particulars—like beads that have no holes in them—and, on the other hand, having to do with pure abstract logic—like an infinitely long string which has no ends and certainly no end that can be found by man—then science must be saved by this very same man who does not understand himself and who never will understand himself.

TENSION BETWEEN INTERNAL RATIONALITY AND EXTERNAL FACTS[229]

(A) [Samuel Alexander, Henri Bergson, Martin Heidegger, Nicholas Berdyaev, and John Dewey] all express the recent spirit of opposition to modern ideal-

---

228. Emphasis added. In one way or another, all non-Christian positions are intellectually arbitrary and/or inconsistent. They tend to cancel each other out, all of them together lacking rational warrant for their presuppositions.
229. The following excerpts are taken from:

   (A) *Christian-Theistic Evidences*, 237;
   (B) *Defense of the Faith*, 142, 144, 157–58, 193.

ist absolutism, and back of that to Greek absolutism, and back of that to the only absolute who is not a virtual projection of self-sufficient man, namely, the God of historic Christianity. When these various writers are out, as Kant was, to *save science*, they are seeking to save it from the destructive principles of historic Protestant thought from which their predecessors had not been altogether able to liberate themselves. It is this God and only this God who controls in advance all that the space-time continuum produces and thus at one stroke kills the very idea of open factuality[230] which the scientist needs as bread and butter. It is this God and only this God who insists that man's principle of coherence as it rests on the activity of the mind of man rests, back of this, upon the activity of the mind of God.

The modern scientist and philosopher have no other tools with which to save science than that of human autonomy, of pure contingent factuality, and of abstract self-existent rationality. The Greeks operated with these principles, Renaissance man operated with these principles, Kant and [F. H.] Bradley operated with these principles. In each case science was not saved and the Christian religion was arbitrarily excluded as not even possibly needed by science and philosophy—in fact as destructive of science. In each case the problematics was how to get a network of purely conceptual and absolutely comprehensive relations into significant contact with an endless number of unrelated facts.

(B) Given the non-Christian assumption with respect to man's autonomy the idea of chance has equal rights with the idea of logic.[231] . . .

It is by means of universal timeless principles of logic that the natural man must, on his assumptions, seek to make intelligible assertions about the world of reality or chance. But this cannot be done without falling into self-contradiction. About chance no manner of assertion can be made. In its very idea it is the irrational. And how are rational assertions to be made about the irrational? If they are to be made, then it must be because the irrational is itself wholly reduced to the rational. That is to say if the natural man is to make any intelligible assertions about the world of "reality" or "fact" which, according to him is what it is for no rational reason at all, then he must make the virtual claim of rationalizing the irrational. To be able to distinguish one fact from another fact he must reduce all temporal existence (all factuality)

---

230. "Open factuality" is another way of speaking of what was called in the previous reading selection "the open universe"—one where anything at all can happen by chance.

231. To put it another way, the denial of any necessity (chance) is on a par with the affirmation of necessity (logic).

to immovable timeless being. But when he has done so he has killed all individuality and factuality as conceived of on his basis. *Thus the natural man must
on the one hand assert that all reality is non-structural in nature and on the
other hand that all reality is structural in nature.*[232] He must even assert on
the one hand that all reality is non-structurable in nature and on the other
hand that he himself has [in his own mind] virtually structured all of it. Thus
all his predication is in the nature of the case self-contradictory. . . .

Thus we are back at that arch foe of Christianity, namely, the idea of
human ultimacy or autonomy. This idea of autonomy expresses itself in modern times by holding that in all that comes to man he gives as well as takes.
Modern philosophy has, particularly since the day of Kant, boldly asserted that
only that is real for man which he has, in part at least, [mentally] constructed
for himself.[233]

Nor is this modern form or manifestation of the would-be autonomous
man illogical. In every non-Christian concept of reality brute facts or chance
plays a basic role. This is so because any one who does not hold to God's counsel as being man's ultimate environment has no alternative but to assume or
assert that chance is ultimate. Chance is simply the metaphysical correlative
of the idea of the autonomous man. The autonomous man will not allow that
reality is already structural in nature by virtue of the structural activity of God's
eternal plan. But if reality is non-structural in nature then man is the one who
for the first time, and therefore in an absolutely original fashion, is supposed
to bring structure into reality. But such a structure can be only "for him."[234] . . .

It is merely the non-rational that is given to him; he himself rationalizes it
for the first time. And so that which appears to him as rationally related reality is so related primarily because he himself has rationalized it.

The modern form of autonomy expresses itself then both in a negative and
in a positive fashion. Negatively it assumes or asserts that that which is "out
there," that is, that which has not yet come into contact with the human mind,

232. Emphasis added. For the would-be autonomous man, there are no necessary
     causal or rational connections between things or between truths (i.e., everything
     is contingent, a matter of chance)—and thus reality is nonstructured. Yet he
     wishes to engage in logical reasoning and scientific inference, so he insists that
     there are conceptual and causal connections—that reality is indeed structured.
     These two autonomous perspectives contradict and destroy the intelligibility of
     each other.
233. Kant contended that the mind of man is active in constituting the objects that
     it rationally knows; the mind "gives" the "order" to the disorder and chaotic sen-
     sations that it "receives."
234. And, accordingly, phenomenalism, subjectivism, and relativism are inherent to
     autonomous (chance-affirming) worldviews.

is wholly non-structural or non-rational in character. We are not now concerned so much to point out that this assumption is itself not very reasonable to make for one who claims to limit his assertions to what human experience can control.[235] . . .

It is this irrationalist-rationalist idea of fact that appears, with variations, in the writers on the philosophy of science. Generally speaking they follow the lead of Kant's philosophy of fact and of logic. There is for them first the abstract possibility of any sort of fact existing. Facts in this sense have no determinable nature. They belong in Kant's noumenal realm. They are unknown and unknowable.[236] This idea is directly and completely destructive of the doctrines of creation and providence. Secondly the facts that are known, that is those that somehow come into contact with the human mind, are known by virtue of the original ordering effect of the human mind upon the raw stuff of experience. These are the facts of science. They are *taken* as much as given. What they are depends not upon the ultimate determinative character of God but upon the ultimate determinative character of man, who virtually takes the place of God. Every fact then that has scientific standing is such only if it does not reveal God, but does reveal man as ultimate. No other facts are allowed as being facts unless they are as raw material generalized into a system that keeps out God. They are "statistically standardized correlations of existential changes." Existential changes as such are irrational. But they are standardized by the original, not derivative, organizing action of man as autonomous. Only then are they facts with scientific standing. It is thus that in the very act of the observation of facts the non-Christian does, so far as he works according to his principle, do what Kuyper says the natural man always does, namely, suppress the truth of God into naturalistic categories.

DEGENERATION INTO PHENOMENALISM AND THE IMPOSSIBILITY OF A RATIONAL SYSTEM[237]

Even the mere counting of particular things presupposes a system of truth of which these particulars form a part. Without such a system of truth there would be no distinguishable difference between one particular and another. . . .

---

235. This is yet another devastating internal contradiction in the thinking of unbelievers. They limit themselves to what can be experienced by finite minds (or brains), and then make universal statements—especially, about what finite minds can discover.
236. That is, they are unknowable as things-in-themselves, rather than as things as they are internally experienced (things as they appear).
237. An excerpt from *Defense of the Faith*, 133–38.

It may be objected that one fact differs from other facts precisely because none of them are rationally controlled. . . . Has not Kant taught us that, if we are to have logical concatenation between the individual facts of our experience at all, we can have it just to the extent that we give up the impossible ideal of knowing individual things *in themselves*?[238] . . .

The historical forms of rationalism have done either of two things. If they were reasonably consistent then they were ready to deny the existence and meaning of individuality in history altogether. . . . Parmenides was therefore ready to assert the non-existence and meaninglessness of individual historical factuality. On the other hand, if rationalists were [less] consistent they held to the same ideal of individuation by means of complete logical description on the part of man, but they realized that such a description cannot be accomplished. Leibniz was not less a rationalist in his hopes and ambitions than was Parmenides. . . . Yet Leibniz questioned whether man could ever attain to the perfect analysis. . . . Thus, in spite of himself, Leibniz has to allow for the actual existence of individual, ultimately changing things. But then to do so he has to sacrifice his system of logic. He recognizes temporal individuality but can do so only at the expense of logical system. *Thus the rationalist agrees with the irrationalist that individuality in fact can exist only at the expense of logical system.*[239] And the idealist logicians, such as F. H. Bradley and Bernard Bosanquet, are no exceptions to this rule.

But in contradistinction from the rationalist and the irrationalist, and in contradistinction from the forms of thought that seek some sort of combination between these two, the Reformed apologist must hold both to the idea of absolute system and to that of genuine historic fact and individuality. He does not hold to "truths of fact" at the expense of "truths of reason." . . .

Over against this Christian theistic position, any non-Christian philosophy virtually denies the unity of truth. It may speak much of it and even seem to contend for it, as idealistic philosophers do, but in the last analysis non-Christian philosophy is atomistic. This follows from the absolute separation between truth and reality that was introduced when Adam and Eve fell away from God. . . . Reality, Satan practically urged upon man, was to be conceived of as something that is not under rational control [by God]. Every non-Christian philosophy makes the assumption made by Adam and Eve and is therefore irrationalistic. This irrationalism comes to most consistent expres-

---

238. Emphasis added. The point is that individual things are not known for what they are in and of themselves, but only as they are rationalized or ordered by the human mind. Thus, they are known as they appear, not as they "really" are.
239. Emphasis added.

sion in various forms of empiricism and pragmatism. In them predication is frankly conceived of in atomistic fashion.

On the other hand when Satan tempted Eve he virtually asked her to become a rationalist. He asked her to take the position that she needed not to obtain any information about the course of factual eventuation from any source but her own mind. Prior to any tendency that had developed in the course of historical events she, following Satan's advice, made what was tantamount to a universal negative judgment about temporal reality. She took for granted that punishment could not come as a consequence of her eating of the forbidden fruit. This rationalism appears most consistently in such men as Parmenides. But even the inconsistent rationalists are really *a priorists*; they make concessions only because they cannot realize their ideal.

In modern times Kant has combined the principles of rationalism and empiricism. "He described the contribution of reason to knowledge as exactly so and so and the contribution of sense as exactly such and such."[240] This position of Kant is the dominating position that confronts us today. It is usually spoken of as phenomenalistic. It is characterized by an attempt to bridge the gulf between fact and mind (that was brought into the world as the consequence of the sin of Adam). But it cannot be a remedy for this dualism. Phenomenalism is still basically atomistic inasmuch as it still maintains that factuality in itself is non-rational in character. At the same time phenomenalism is still rationalistic in that whatever of unity it thinks it finds in this atomistically conceived reality virtually proceeds from the human mind. At least this rationality is not taken as proceeding from the mind of God. The rationalizing effort that is inherent in phenomenalism would, if successful, destroy all individuality. Its rationalizing effort is admittedly a step-by-step affair. *That this is so is evident from the fact that its rationalizations are rationalizations of admittedly non-rational material. . . .*

The dilemma that confronts the non-Christian methodology in general, and that of modern phenomenalism in particular, is therefore that one must either know everything or one cannot know anything. . . . "A completed rational system having nothing outside of it nor any possible alternative to it, is both presupposed and beyond the actual attainment of any one moment."[241]

The point we are now concerned to stress is the atomistic character of the non-Christian methodology. The idea of system is for it merely a limiting notion. It is merely an ideal. What is more, it must forever remain but an ideal. To become a reality this ideal would have to destroy science itself. It would

240. CVT: Gordon H. Clark in *Christian Opinion*, January, 1945.
241. CVT: Cohen, *Reason and Nature*, New York, 1931, p. 158.

have to demolish the individuality of each fact as it became known.[242] Thus there would no longer be knowledge of a fact that is different from any other fact. The method of non-Christian science then requires that to be known facts must be known-as-part-of-a-system. And since the Christian idea of system as due to the counsel of God is by definition excluded, it is man himself that must know this system. But to know the system he must know it intuitively. He cannot know it discursively because discursive thought, if it is to be in contact with reality at all, must partake of the piecemeal character of non-rational being. Each individual concept that pretends to be a concept with respect to things that have their existence in the world of time must partake of the *de facto* character of these facts themselves.[243] In consequence each judgment or each proposition that is made by discursive thought about temporal existence is also characterized by the *de facto* character of temporal existence itself. Each proposition then, as far as all practical purposes are concerned, would have to be thought of as standing essentially by itself and as intelligible by itself.[244] There could be no

242. Emphasis added.
243. That is, the facts are simply and arbitrarily what they are, without any necessary, planned, or preestablished connection between them. There could be no objective basis for predictability or for giving any causal explanation for each new fact, nor could there be any objective basis for seeing any given fact as an instance of a "kind" of thing (and thus categorizable as a "barn," as something "red," etc.).
244. Without any other beliefs whatsoever, could you consider the proposition "The monkey ate the banana" and, standing all by itself, find it intelligible? Of course not. (Indeed, even to understand any assertion requires certain beliefs about words, syntax, etc.) For something to be designated a "monkey" (rather than a dog, a mountain, a disease, a postal regulation, an Olympic event, etc.), it has to have certain features or properties that make it like some things but unlike others; so you would need to have beliefs about some things and other things. The same could be said regarding the noun "banana" and the verb "ate"; they too have defining and differentiating features or properties. Events in the world (and experiences of them) must be connected in various nonrandom ways to have (or to be thought of and characterized as having) the features or properties of eating, monkeys, and bananas. But in a disconnected or chance world, where every event is individual, detached, and thus new, every fact would stand on its own and be intelligible only in itself—which, as we have just noted, is not rationally possible. What Van Til here notes is that in a chance universe, the piecemeal character of both extramental facts and mental thoughts about them—where there is no contextual system of knowledge—would preclude any organization of a system of truths about monkeys, eating, and bananas such that the particular proposition about a specific event, "The monkey ate the banana," could be intelligible.
   But, on the other hand, if, on an autonomous human basis, the full system is available in advance of experience or observation of what actually happens (thus making individual propositions intelligible), there would then (absurdly) no longer be any need for scientific study of, or inquiry into, particular mon-

logically necessary connection between the various judgments of discursive thought; there could only be an intuition that, as F. H. Bradley puts it, *somehow* Reality contains the harmony that is not found in appearance. . . .

It is not difficult to see that the Christian position requires the apologist to challenge this whole approach in the interest of the knowledge of the truth. If man's necessarily discursive thought is not to fall into the ultimate irrationalism and scepticism that is involved in modern methodology we must presuppose the conception of the God that is found in Scripture. Scripture alone presents the sort of God whose intuition of system is not bought at the price of his knowledge of individuality, and whose knowledge of individuality is not bought at the expense of intuitional knowledge of system.

AUTONOMY'S RATIONAL-IRRATIONAL TREATY, REGARDLESS OF ITS MUTUALLY DESTRUCTIVE INTERNAL TENSION[245]

(A) Strange as it may seem at first sight, the irrationalism of the idea of pure contingency requires for its correlative the rationalism of the most absolute

---

keys, particular meals thereof, or particular bananas. The system could not simply be a knowledge of generalities, with the individual chance facts not being included and thus absorbed into the generalities of the system. In order to grasp this, consider a question that (on an autonomous basis) seems unanswerable in advance of the details of what actually happens in this random universe. Imagine we have a specific situation where a particular monkey refuses to eat a banana and, instead, declares in a humanlike voice, "I eat only spinach soufflé." Different systems of belief (about monkeys, eating, bananas, and many other things) would analyze this particular event differently. Given one system of beliefs, we would say that this is clearly not a monkey after all. Another system of beliefs would indicate that this illustrates for us a new and unusual breed of monkeys. Yet another system of beliefs would not even countenance such a preposterous and bizarre example. Now then, if one could determine (in a rational, nonarbitrary fashion) in advance of actual, particular events which of the three systems should be adopted, then it would certainly seem to follow that scientific research or study of the individual monkeys and their behavior would be irrelevant.

Given the non-Christian's presuppositions about man, reason, the world, history, etc., a knowledge of particulars (science) and a system of knowledge are in irreconcilable tension with each other, dissolving into skepticism. Without knowing everything, the unbeliever cannot be certain that he knows any one thing, but he would need to come to know each thing one by one before he could cumulatively know everything.

245. The following excerpts are taken from:

(A) *Intellectual Challenge of the Gospel*, 16-19;
(B) *Defense of the Faith*, 142–43, 237, 271–72, 274, 297–98, 310–11;
(C) *Introduction to Systematic Theology*, 114–15;
(D) *Christian Theory of Knowledge*, 47–49, 56–58, 65, 68–70.

determinism. The idea of pure contingency requires the rejection of the Christian doctrine of creation and providence as logically impossible. Thus the statement that *anything* may happen must be qualified by adding[246] that anything but Christianity is possible. Theoretically speaking, any hypothesis is relevant, but practically speaking, the Christian "hypothesis" is excluded at the outset of any investigation. Men will follow the facts wherever they may lead so long as they do not lead to the truth of Christianity.

There is nothing surprising in the fact that modern man is utterly irrationalist and utterly rationalist at the same time. He has to be both in order to be either. And he has to be both in order to defend his basic assumption of his own freedom or ultimacy. About the idea of freedom or contingency pure and simple, nothing can be said. It is the idea of pure, bare, brute, or mute factuality. It is the idea of existence without essence;[247] the idea of being without meaning. Yet modern man must say something about his freedom. Above all he must be defended against those who attack it. And who are they that attack it? Are they the determinists and the rationalists? Not at all. The determinists and rationalists are what they are in the interest of defending the same autonomy or freedom of man that the indeterminists and irrationalists are defending. The determinist or rationalist differs from the indeterminist or irrationalist merely *in the way that he defends* the ultimacy or autonomy of man. They therefore have their internal family quarrels. These quarrels center on the one question of how best to fend off the common enemy, which is Christianity.

But how then, it will be asked, does the determinist seek to defend the idea of man's ultimacy or freedom and therewith the idea of contingency? He does this by seeking to show that Reality *cannot* allow for the Creator-creature distinction. Creation out of nothing is said to be *impossible*. It is said to be impossible because it is *contradictory*. It would require us to hold that God changed from the status of not being a Creator to the status of being the Creator of the universe and that without any change in His being. Reality must therefore be of one nature. And if man is contingent, as is assumed, then God must also be contingent. If God is ultimate, man is also ultimate. If God is free, man is free with the same freedom with which God is free. It is thus that

246. That is, irrationalism (anything is possible; there is pure contingency) is now "qualified" by adding rationalism to it (certain things are impossible).
247. For example, the modern apostle of freedom, Jean-Paul Sartre, stated the first premise of existentialism as, "Existence precedes essence." Man first exists, and only thereafter can any defining limits (any essence) be placed upon him by his own free choice of what he will be (and thus how he will conduct himself).

the irrationalist may employ the rationalist or determinist to do battle for him in a field where he says he does not feel at home.[248]

In fact the "free man" of modern non-Christian thought is Janus-faced.[249] He turns one way and would seem to be nothing but an irrationalist. He talks about the "fact" of freedom. He even makes a pretense of being hotly opposed to the rationalist. With Kierkegaard[250] he will boldly assert that what cannot happen according to logic has happened in fact. Then he turns the other way and would seem to be nothing but a rationalist. Surely, he says, the "rational man" will accept nothing but what has intelligible meaning for him in accord with the law of contradiction. There must be coherence in experience. It is meaningless to talk about the "entirely single thing."[251]

But both in his irrationalist and in his rationalist features, the would-be autonomous man is seeking to defend his ultimacy against the claims of the Christian religion. If he is right as an irrationalist then he is not a creature of God. If he were a creature of God, he would be subject to the law of God. He would thus be "rationally related" to God. He would know that he was a creature of God and that he should obey the law of God. If he is right as a rationalist, then too he is not a creature of God. The law that he then thinks of as above him, he also thinks of as above God; God and he are, for him, subject to a common law. If he were a creature of God, he would grant that what God has determined, and only that, is possible. He would then subject his logical manipulation of "reality" to the revelation of God.

It is this Janus-faced covenant-breaker, then, who must be won for the gospel. It is he who walks the streets of New York and London. And no one but he does. All men are sinners; all are interested in suppressing the fact of their creaturehood. The irrationalist and rationalist have become friends in the face of their common foe. And this common foe is historic Christianity.

---

248. What Van Til is describing here is the selective way in which the indeterminist (holding that there are no necessities) is willing to utilize the reasoning of the determinist (holding that man necessarily exists under the same conditions as any alleged god) to defend the ultimacy (and thus the "freedom") of autonomous man.

249. Janus was the Roman god of beginnings. He was portrayed with a head having two faces, facing different directions from each other.

250. Søren Kierkegaard (1813–55) was a Danish existentialist who, like Sartre (despite preceding him by half a century and being of a religious temperament), stressed the authenticity and freedom of the "existing individual" as an individual—in protest against the universalizing concepts (essences) and irresistible logic of Hegelian rationalism.

251. That is, something that is completely individual or particularized (unique in and to itself).

(B) In the second place modern irrationalism has not in the least encroached upon the domain of the intellect as the natural man thinks of it. Irrationalism has merely taken possession of that which the intellect, by its own admission, cannot in any case control. Irrationalism has a secret treaty with rationalism by which the former cedes to the latter so much of its territory as the latter can at any given time find the forces to control. Kant's realm of the noumenal has, as it were, agreed to yield so much of its area to the phenomenal, as the intellect by its newest weapons can manage to keep in control. Moreover, by the same treaty irrationalism has promised to keep out of its own territory any form of authority that might be objectionable to the autonomous intellect.[252] The very idea of pure factuality or chance is the best guarantee that no true authority, such as that of God as the Creator and Judge of men, will ever confront man. . . .

It is not merely that the Greeks had not yet heard of such a God. It is rather that in Adam, they had heard this God speak to them and in Adam they had virtually denied his existence. They had with all men in Adam, their representative, denied that space-time reality is dependent upon God, created and controlled by him. They had with all men in Adam assumed that possibility is not subject to God but that God is subject to abstract possibility. When Adam, for all men, refused to take God's prediction of punishment for disobedience seriously, he virtually said that the facts and laws of the universe are not under God's control but operate by virtue of Chance. This is ultimate and utter irrationalism. At the same time, in the same act of disobedience Adam virtually assumed that what God threatened would come to pass could not come to pass. Assuming that he did not want to die, we must think of him as rejecting the idea that physical and spiritual death could come as the result of eating the forbidden fruit. This was ultimate and utter rationalism.

Now all men, since Adam, have been both utterly irrationalistic and utterly rationalistic. I hold this to be the direct implication of the idea that Adam's fall involved all men.[253] . . .

---

252. Kant claimed to "save science and leave room for faith." However, the "science" that he saved was limited to the realm of the mind's own active construction from sensation (its imposing of a rational, but subjective order). And the "faith" for which he left room was beyond rationality or cognitive meaningfulness—beyond the rationalizing and constructive activity of man's mind. Thus, man was declared to be the authority for "rationality," and God was not allowed to speak to man with rational authority.

253. Emphasis added. Van Til conceived of the Fall, in which all of Adam's posterity participated by their representative, as a rejection of the sovereign, personal authority of the self-sufficient Creator. All men thus reject the counsel of God as foreordaining whatsoever comes to pass; they are irrationalists who say every-

To be sure, if you ask him about his method he will insist that he is open-minded, that he will follow the facts wherever they may lead him, even if they should lead him to the position of the Christian. But to begin with, he must be allowed to make any hypothesis he pleases. And this assumption of the theoretical relevancy of any hypothesis already excludes the Christian position. The Christian believes on the authority of Scripture that "there is no contingency for God" because he controls all things. The relevancy of scientific hypotheses for man therefore falls within the idea of God's providence.

But Cohen, quite consistently from his point of view, finds that the idea of providence must be ruled out if science is to be free in the making of hypotheses. He posits a metaphysics of chance as the foundation of the scientific method.

Contrary to the usual views of it, the principle of sufficient reason as actually relied on in scientific procedure is not only compatible with a domain of chance, contingency or indetermination, but positively demands it as the correlative of the universality of law.[254]

Now in a universe of chance it might seem that anything might happen. Might then the Christian position be true, by chance? Cohen replies that though in scientific procedure we need the idea of chance or indeterminism we also need, as its correlative, the idea of determinism. Otherwise we could not exclude the absurd. . . .

> Thus ruling out ghostly, magical, and other supernatural influences, it would seem that scientific method impoverishes our view of the world. It is well, however, to remember that a world where no possibility is excluded is a world of chaos, about which no definite assertion can be made. Any world containing some order necessarily involves the elimination of certain abstract or ungrounded possibilities such as fill the minds of the insane.[255]

Now all this is, to be sure, not metaphysics in the pre-Kantian sense of the term. Cohen, like many other modern thinkers, disavows man's ability to know ultimate reality. In this they follow Kant in limiting human knowledge to the

---

thing is contingent, unplanned, and a matter of chance. At the same time, all men are rationalists who reject the authority of God expressed in His verbal revelation (e.g., of what will happen if they rebel against Him), arguing that such claims could not be true or authoritative for them. Because of the nature of sin, then, all men are rationalistic-irrationalistic in perspective.

254. Van Til cites Morris R. Cohen, *Reason and Nature* (Glencoe, Ill: Free Press, 1931), 151.

255. CVT: *Idem*, p. 159.

realm of the phenomenal. But for all its disavowal of having anything to do with the *alte Metaphysik*[256] this modern phenomenalism does rest upon an assumed metaphysics. It could not well be otherwise. Cohen's exposition is itself a clear indication that phenomenalism requires the exclusion of the idea of the supernatural and even of providence. Cohen seeks to make sure that his island of reality is safe from any possible attack by the supernatural, in short by God as Christianity thinks of him. Involved in his phenomenalism is a universal negative judgment to the effect that the God of Christianity cannot exist. . . .

Sir James Jeans tell us that some millions of years ago certain stars wandered blindly through space. "In course of time, we know not how, when, or why, one of these cooling fragments gave birth to life." Thus in the same breath we have an assertion of agnosticism, a denial of Christianity, and the assurance that Chance rules the world.[257] . . .

When therefore the non-Christian employs the law of contradiction upon the facts of Christianity these facts are "naturalized." Quite likely the admission will first be made that Christianity may possibly be true. Anything can happen. The existentialist philosopher, Kierkegaard, tells us that this is precisely the meaning of existence: its absolute freedom to be or not to be . . . ; all of which is to say that Reality (inclusive of God and the world) is contingent, ruled by Chance.

Then secondly, this irrationalism and indeterminism will be supplemented by rationalistic determinism. The sinner, assuming himself by its means to be the determiner of the nature of reality, will assert that orthodox Christianity cannot be true. To be true it would have to become part of this indeterminist-determinist system which, according to the would-be autonomous man, can alone exist.

Now some such thing is bound to happen when the natural man is allowed to stand as judge above the revelation of God. . . .

Knowing [that as a finite being he cannot by means of logic legislate what reality should be] the non-Christian none the less constantly attempts the impossible:

1. Negatively he says in effect that reality is not rationally constituted at all and that the Christian story therefore cannot be true. This is in-

---

256. That is, "the old metaphysic" found in philosophers prior to Kant's criticism.
257. CVT: James Jeans, *The Mysterious Universe* (N. Y., 1931), p. 3. This is a brief but blistering example of Van Til's internal critique of an unbeliever's rationalism (a scientific explanation of the origin of life . . .) allied with irrationalism (agnosticism: we know not how . . .) for the purpose of precluding Christianity (this much is clear about any possible explanation: it was not religious).

volved in his idea of "facts" as springing from "Chaos and Old Night."[258]

2. Positively he assumes that reality is after all rationally constituted and answers exhaustively to his logical manipulations. This is involved in his idea that any "cosmic mind" or God that is to be tolerated must be manipulable by categories devised by man without reference to "him" or "it." . . .

The non-Christian also interprets the facts in terms of his presuppositions. One of these presuppositions is that of ultimate non-rationality. On such a basis any fact would have a nature that is different in all respects from all other facts. Here is "Chaos and Old Night" with a vengeance. The second of these presuppositions is the rationality of all reality in terms of the reach of logic as manipulated by man. On such a basis the nature of any fact would be identical with the nature of every other fact. In practice the procedure of the non-Christian is that of keeping in careful balance the utter equivocism involved in his first and the utter univocism involved in his second presupposition.[259] In any case the non-Christian can never so much as discover any fact. On his principles he knows nothing of its nature. But when he has discovered what he cannot discover he can tell us everything about it. On his principles he knows everything if he knows anything.

(C) Even the curse of God that fell upon the created universe did not basically change this radically revelatory character of the universe. Man *ought* always to regard the universe as revelatory of God; there is no excuse whatsoever for his not doing so.

Now it is this basically and exclusively revelatory character of all the facts of the universe that is either openly or covertly denied by both rationalist and irrationalist forms of heresy. Both hold to a non-Christian view of *possibility*. Both hold that it is at least *possible* that the facts of the universe can be something other than revelatory of God. And this is, in effect to posit *chance* as equally ultimate with God. And positing chance as equally ultimate with God is virtually the same as denying the existence of God. To say that the evidence, when fully and fairly considered, merely shows that God *probably* exists, is

258. In ancient Greek cosmological speculation, for instance as found in the poetry of Hesiod, Chaos is the eternal, dark, and windy chasm that did not become manifest until the separating of heaven and earth. It is the mysterious and unintelligible background state which conditioned and preceded the emergence of natural order (the "cosmos").

259. The presupposition of "equivocism" is that everything is utterly different from everything else, completely individualized, a matter of chance—and thus cannot be clearly conceptualized or spoken of. The presupposition of "univocism" is that everything is completely conceptualized and subject to the rational unifying or universalizing principles imposed by man's mind.

tantamount to saying that he does not at all exist. The God of Christianity is the God whose counsel or plan is the source of possibility. The word possibility has no possible meaning except upon the presupposition of the existence of the self-contained ontological Trinity as the source of it.

It should be noted, too, that in presupposing chance, rationalism is as irrationalistic as is irrationalism. Rationalism is secretly while irrationalism is frankly and openly addicted to a philosophy of chance. Both rationalism and irrationalism are therefore committed to a form of empiricism that is utterly out of accord with Christian theism. Though both are committed to a supposedly neutral attitude, an attitude that is willing to find in the facts whatsoever there is to be found. It is a foregone conclusion that they will never find Christian theism there. Having presupposed chance back of the facts it is chance and nothing but chance that they can find in the facts.

And this leads to the obvious observation that irrationalists no less than rationalists are rationalistic; both have adopted their ultimate positions not after but before they have investigated the facts.[260] No human being can escape making an assumption about the nature of possibility at the outset of his investigation.

(D) Now since it was in Adam as their representative that men have sinned, it is well that the implications of this fall for the Christian theory of knowledge be ascertained as far as possible.[261]

The story of Adam in paradise is familiar. It is part of the orthodox view of things to regard this story as historical. It is so presented in Scripture, and it is in accord with the idea of Scripture as identifying to man in this story a clear-cut expression of the will of God. Those who would make a myth or a *saga* out of this narrative do so in the interest of a philosophy that holds that no clear and direct revelation of God to man can be given in and through the facts of history.[262]

260. "Rationalism" is characterized as the view that at least some things can be known apart from observation or experience—that is, *a priori* (prior to), rather than *a posteriori* (after) what we observe. Even "irrationalists" (like empiricists who hold that only particulars exist) hold *a priori* beliefs and thus are "rationalistic."

261. This is something that nearly all philosophers, and even most Christian philosophers, overlook or disregard at the very outset of their philosophical theorizing. The normalcy and competence of human reasoning, as well as the honorific "rationality" of man (or at least one's own personal "rationality"), are taken for granted. Van Til urged apologists to give serious consideration to the noetic effects of the Fall.

262. CVT: Neo-orthodox theologians do not take the Genesis creation and fall accounts seriously as historical narratives in the common sense notion of "historical" (events in the phe-

The tree of the knowledge of good and evil was indicated [pointed out] to Adam as a test by which God would bring man to a fully self-conscious reaction to his will. Man was created good. He was not created with a will that could as well turn in the direction of evil as in the direction of the good;[263] even so God would have man become fully and wholly spontaneous and self-conscious in every sense of the word in his attitude toward God. God wanted man to accept God's judgment or criterion as that to which man would gladly and lovingly submit.

At the instigation of Satan man decided to set himself up as the ultimate standard of right and wrong, of the true and false. He made himself, instead of God, the final reference point in predication.[264]

For the question of knowledge this implied the rejection of God as able to identify himself in terms of himself to man and with it the rejection of God as the source of truth for man. Instead of seeking an analogical system of knowledge, man after this sought an original system of knowledge.[265] This means that God was reduced with him to the necessity of seeking truth in an ultimately mysterious environment. In other words, it implied that in setting up himself as independent, man was declaring that there was no one above him on whom he was dependent. But man even then knew that he was not ultimate. He knew that he had no control of reality and its possibilities. So what his declaration of independence amounted to was an attempt to bring God down with himself into an ocean of pure contingency or abstract possibility.

Moreover, pure contingency in metaphysics and pure irrationalism in epistemology go hand in hand. Abstract possibility in metaphysics and ultimate mystery in epistemology are involved in one another. To this must be added that in ethics this involved the denial of God's right to issue any commandment for man. For the natural man reality, truth and goodness must be what he thinks they must be. They cannot be what Christ says they are.

At the fall then, man virtually told God that he did not and could not know what would happen if he (man) should eat of the "forbidden tree." Why was

---

nomenal world). In recent years some Reformed theologians under the influence of neo-orthodoxy are trying to make adjustments on this point.
263. The Reformed view regarding man's original condition is that man was created with positive righteousness, whereas the Arminian view is that man was created merely innocent, with a free will that could as readily have chosen good as evil.
264. That is, man looked to himself for the fundamental orientation and authority ("reference point") in making judgments about what is true ("predicating" one thing of another).
265. For an explanation of "analogical" thinking (versus "original" thinking) and of the view that God does not "seek" (or discover) truth along with man, see chap. 4.5 above.

this called a "forbidden" tree? Was it not perhaps because God arbitrarily called it thus? God was first upon the scene of history. No one had as yet had any experience with eating of this tree; there were no inductively gathered records to indicate even as much as a tendency to evil being involved in the use of the fruit of this tree. It was the "inductive method" with its assumption of ultimate mystery involved in pure possibility that Adam introduced. This was utter irrationalism. It was therefore by implication a flat denial of God's being able to identify himself. It was in effect a claim that no one, neither God nor man, can really know what he is or who he is. How could there be any ultimate or final distinction or preference made in an ocean of Chance? Anyhow why should one "rational being" who had become rational by Chance, seek to lord it over another "rational being" who also had become rational by Chance? In a world of Chance there can be no manner of self-identification. There can be no system of truth and therefore no intelligible use of the "law of contradiction." There can therefore certainly be no authoritative identification of truth and law by one "rational being" for another "rational being." There can be no such thing as authority in the biblical sense of the term.

But there is another side to the story of the fall of man. How could man be sure that he could safely ignore the command of God? How did he presume to know that God did not know what would come to pass should he eat of the forbidden tree? If there was to be any seeming sense to such an action, it would have to be on the assumption that man himself knew that the evil threatened would not take place. Satan told man that the issue would be quite otherwise than God said it would be. He said that God knew that it would be otherwise. Satan suggested that God too knew that man would be as God, knowing good and evil, if man should eat of the tree. Reality, said Satan in effect, is wholly lit up, lit up for the "creature" as well for the "Creator." Man therefore does not need to live by the authoritative assertions of the Creator. He can discover by his own independent inspection, by *Wesensschau*, what will take place in the course of time. Man as well as God can ascertain the laws of being by means of the laws of rationality in his mind. Is not the law of rationality in the minds of men and of gods ultimately one with the law of being in reality as a whole? Surely reality cannot be "deeper than logic."

It was thus that man, in rejecting the covenantal requirement of God, became at one and the same time both irrationalist and rationalist. These two are not, except formally, contradictory of one another. They rather imply one another. Man had to be both to be either.[266] To be able to identify himself apart from God, man had to distinguish himself as an individual from all the

---

266. Emphasis added.

relationships of the system of which he actually is a part. If he were not part of the God-ordained system of relationships, he would be an entity in a vacuum; he would not be distinguishable to himself from any one or anything else. In fact he would not be self-conscious at all. He or it would be part of "the great buzzing blooming confusion" that would constitute Chaos. On the other hand, being part of a system of relations "created" by himself man would have to know this system exhaustively in order to know it at all. Reality then must be "wholly lit up" to himself without any appeal to authority. Only then can he rightly say that he does not need to be identified and set in a system of relationships by God his Creator. . . .

It has been intimated that fallen man is both irrationalist and rationalist, and at the same time. His irrationalism rests upon his metaphysical assumption that reality is controlled by or is an expression of pure Chance. His rationalism is based upon the assumption that reality is wholly determined by laws with which his thought is ultimately identical. It is to be expected that on such assumptions fallen man cannot allow for biblical authority. For this idea, as noted above, rests upon the idea of the self-contained God. This involves the idea that God himself is wholly known to himself and that the created universe is also wholly known to him because wholly controlled by him. This is the Christian principle of continuity. The natural man would call this rationalism and determinism. He would say that the idea of freedom and significance for human knowledge has, on this view, disappeared. At the same time the Christian idea of authority maintains that God's thoughts are not open to the inspection of man. God must reveal himself. This is the Christian principle of discontinuity. The natural man would call this irrationalism and indeterminism. He would say that it cuts off all reasonable continuity between God and man. It requires man to be subject to the purely arbitrary pronouncements that God may make upon him.

Thus it is that a combination of the non-Christian principle of continuity correlative to the non-Christian principle of discontinuity stands over against the Christian principle of continuity correlative to the Christian principle of discontinuity.[267] . . .

267. Van Til observed that both the unbeliever and the believer maintain correlative views of continuity (rationalism) and discontinuity (irrationalism), and that these two sets of correlative views stand in contradiction to each other. The previous paragraph has defined these contradictory sets of correlative views. The Christian holds that God knows and controls all things (resulting in rationality and continuity), which contradicts the non-Christian's view that reality is an expression of pure chance (resulting in irrationality and discontinuity). The Christian holds that God must reveal Himself and does so with authority over man's reasoning (stressing discontinuity and "irrationality" or man's rational inade-

In the beginning of the modern era he [apostate man] seemed to have won for himself absolute freedom. At the same time he was using modern mathematics in order by means of it to control the whole of reality, including man himself. The ideal of his science was to know and control all things, including the internal movements of the human mind. But if this ideal should succeed, man would have lost his freedom which he wishes to maintain at all costs. So in the philosophy of Kant there is a sort of compromise between the ideal of science and the ideal of free personality. To the former is assigned the realm of the *phenomena*, to the latter is reserved the realm of the *noumena*. But this is merely a *modus vivendi;* it is no solution to the problem. No solution is possible on a non-Christian foundation.

From the non-Christian point of view then, the idea of biblical authority is impossible. This idea is impossible if human experience is to be interpreted by the adopted principle of apostate man. On the basis of apostasy it is impossible that there should be the sort of God who speaks with authority. Kant made room for "faith" but not for biblical faith. To be sure, the non-Christian principle of discontinuity demands that one hold to abstract possibility. "Anything" is possible on this principle. Thus it would seem that the existence of such a God as the Bible speaks of may also be possible. But when the natural man says that for him anything is possible and that therefore he has an open mind for the evidence of anything that may be presented to him, this assertion has a basic limitation. When he says that anything is possible, this is for him an abstraction or a limiting concept. He knows that cows cannot jump over the moon except in fairy tales. So the idea of a God whose experience is not subject to the same conditions as those that control man is not *practically* possible. Such an idea, he says, is meaningless. It is without intelligible content. It is the mere assertion of a *that* without an intelligible *what*. It is therefore pure irrationalism to say that such a God exists.

On the other hand, the Christian notion of biblical authority is said to be

---

quacy), which contradicts the non-Christian's view that reality is controlled and (in principle) completely knowable by the laws of his own mind (stressing rationality and continuity).

John Frame has often capitalized on this significant insight by Van Til. He elaborates on it in fruitful ways as the dialectic of irrationalism-rationalism (or mystery-rationalism or transcendence-immanence) in his "Lecture Outline" for the course "Doctrine of the Knowledge of God" (pp. 3, 6–7, 9, 15–16) and his "Lecture Outline" for "Christianity and the Great Debates" (pp. 1–3). It is found in "the square of religious opposition" in his *The Doctrine of the Knowledge of God* (Phillipsburg, N.J.: Presbyterian and Reformed, 1987), 14–15, and is reflected in the section on "The Unbeliever's Twin Strategies" (of atheism and idolatry) in *Apologetics to the Glory of God* (Phillipsburg, N.J.: Presbyterian and Reformed, 1994), 193–201.

pure rationalism. It would require a view of rationality as controlling what-soever comes to pass. It would give man no measure of independence, his own reason would be of a piece with that which is predetermined from all eternity by God. Thus there would be no authority at all because authority implies the freedom of one person over against another.

The non-Christian is quite consistent with his own principles when he thus rejects the Christian claim to authority as well as the Christian claim to the necessity of Scripture. How could there be any necessity for that which is in-herently meaningless and outside the realm of practical possibility? How can we say that man has sinned against a God who exists in isolation from man and yet places irrational demands upon him, out of accord with the nature of human personality? . . .

Thus the idea of the sufficiency of Scripture as well as that of its neces-sity is charged [by modern man] with being both irrationalistic and ratio-nalistic. This charge is based upon the assumption of the ultimacy of man. Thus man's ultimate irrationalism requires that he charge the Christian po-sition with rationalism because it holds to a God who controls all things. Thus man's ultimate rationalism requires that he charge the Christian position with irrationalism because it holds that God controls all things by his counsel that is itself above and prior to and therefore not involved in the "relativity" of history. . . .

In terms of this rationalism he must therefore deny that any system can be called perspicuous or clear that is not open to complete inspection by man. . . .

On the other hand the natural man, as indicated repeatedly, insists that reality is ultimately "open." It constantly produces the wholly new. It cannot then be controlled by a plan of a God who exists apart from the world. God himself must, together with the world and as an aspect of the world, be in-volved in a process or he cannot be honored as God. Thus the idea of a sys-tem of truth, such as orthodox Christianity pretends to have, which clearly, in readily identifiable and in directly available fashion, tells man what is true and what he ought to do, cannot exist. We must think of mystery as some-thing ultimate, as something that envelops God as well as man. This idea of mystery as inclusive of God as well as man is taken as correlative to the no-tion that all reality, again inclusive of both God and man, is exhaustively lit up and wholly penetrable to man. The two notions must be taken as sup-plementative of one another. . . .

Summing up now what has been said on the attitude of "modern man" to the Scripture, we have the following:

(a) Basic to all the various views present is the common assumption of man as autonomous.

(b) This basic assumption is *in principle* the exact opposite of the view that the Bible, God's Word, is autonomous.

(c) By and large, modern man therefore cannot allow for: 1. The idea of a Bible that testifies to itself by identifying itself as alone the Word of God. 2. The idea that there is in this Bible a system of truth that requires men to interpret the world and themselves in terms of it.

(d) The ideas of the Bible as identifying itself and of containing the divine system of truth are correlative to one another. They are together involved in the idea of God as self-contained.

(e) These ideas will therefore be charged with being both irrationalistic and rationalistic by those who make man the final reference point in predication.

1. They will be said to be irrationalistic in terms of what is actually the rationalistic notion of fallen man. Fallen man putting himself virtually in the place of God also virtually demands essential continuity between himself and God. He speaks of thought in general and of the laws of being in general. He therewith subjects the thought and being of God to the same limitations to which man is subject. In consequence the Christian's view of Scripture appears to break the continuity between God and man, as being irrationalistic.

2. On the other hand, the biblical idea of self-identification as containing the ultimate system of truth will be charged with being rationalistic by the natural man. This is the case because such an idea of Scripture involves the notion that God knows all things because he controls all things. Thus, it is argued, the sacredness of human personality and human freedom would be violated. In the name of the idea of science, the ideal of complete comprehension and continuity, the idea of Scripture is said to be irrationalistic. In the name of the idea of personality—the idea of freedom—the idea of Scripture is said to be rationalistic.

(f) Modern science, modern philosophy and modern theology are, broadly speaking, in agreement with one another in their assumption of the autonomy of man.

THE CONDEMNING TESTIMONY
OF THE HISTORY OF PHILOSOPHY[268]

(A) Can they not observe the fact that the wisdom of this world is but foolishness in the sight of God? Has not the whole of the history of human phi-

---

268. The following excerpts are taken from:

  (A) *Protestant Doctrine of Scripture,* 2;
  (B) *Introduction to Systematic Theology,* 75–76, 94.

losophy shown that if the "facts" of the world were not created and controlled by the redemptive providence of God, they would be utterly discrete and therefore undiscoverable? Has not the whole history of philosophy also shown that when man regards his logical powers as positively legislative for reality, he winds himself into a knot of contradictions? Has not the history of thought displayed the fact that if man takes the laws of logic as negatively legislative with respect to the facts with which they deal, then his logic and his reality stand over against one another in an absolute contrast, or else, when they do come into contact, they immediately destroy one another?

In other words, it is the Christian's task to point out to the scientist that science needs to stand on Christ and his redeeming work if it is not to fall to pieces. Without Christ he has no foundation on which to stand while he makes his contradictions. A scientific method not based on the presupposition of the truth of the Christian story is like an effort to string an infinite number of beads, no two of which have holes in them, by means of a string of infinite length, neither end of which can be found.

(B) It is difficult to know just what Paul means [in Romans 1:18ff.] by this revelation of God's wrath on the folly of man. We may sense something of his meaning, it would seem, if we think again of a man far removed in time from Adam. He would have before him the endless repetition of the folly of man's interpretations. He would have before him those things of which Calvin speaks when he says that the Epicureans concluded from the diversity of interpretations given by philosophers that no interpretation could be true. The folly of man has devised all manner of seemingly plausible interpretations. This fact itself would complicate matters for anyone who came long after Adam. And this would constitute a manifestation of God's wrath.[269] . . .

It should be remembered that the universe has actually been created by God and is actually sustained by his providence. This precludes the possibility of any non-Christian philosopher, however profound, offering a system of interpretation of the universe that would seem satisfactory even to himself.[270] Naturally the sinner will try his best to find an exclusively immanen-

269. The apostle Paul wrote in Romans 1 that, because men refused to have God in their knowledge and suppressed the truth regarding Him (vv. 18, 28), they became fools who are futile in their reasoning (vv. 21–22). Van Til identifies the intellectual failures throughout the history of philosophy as illustrations of God's wrath upon the rebellious and arrogant mind of the sinner.

270. This is an important theme in Van Til's presuppositional criticism of any purported foundation on which the unbeliever might stand to launch his objections to the truth of Christianity. Not only will that purported foundation be intellectually unacceptable to the believer, but even the non-Christian philosopher

tistic principle of interpretation.[271] Yet he can never succeed in finding one that will do his work. It is as Job said: "But where shall wisdom be found? And where is the place of understanding? Man knoweth not the price thereof; neither is it found in the land of the living. The deep saith, It is not in me; and the sea saith, It is not with me" (Job 28:12–14). Or, again: "Whence cometh wisdom? And where is the place of understanding? Seeing it is hid from all living, and kept from the fowls of the air? Destruction and death say, We have heard a rumor thereof with our ears" (Job 28:20–22).

The history of philosophy abundantly testifies to the fact that men have tried to interpret the universe immanentistically. At the same time, history testifies with equal clarity that no system of philosophy has ever been able to make its composer feel that he had reached a satisfactory solution of the problems of life. Modern pessimism and agnosticism are but the climax of the long-felt dissatisfaction in the ranks of the foremost thinkers of the world.

---

must (if open and honest) admit the defects and inadequacy of it. The unbeliever can be shown to be wrong even on his own terms. That is, the would-be autonomous thinker can be shown that his would-be autonomous reasoning is unintelligible in itself (and thus that his ability to come to this correct realization shows that he has not been consistently thinking in an autonomous fashion after all, but resting on the very revelation of God that his autonomy resists).

271. An "immanentistic" principle is one found within man's experience and reasoning, as opposed to a principle that is revealed authoritatively from a "transcendent" God (beyond human experience or reasoning).

Chapter 6

The Psychological Complexities of Unbelief

6.1 Speaking Epistemologically, Speaking Psychologically

The apologist must understand his opponent, especially what he actually knows and what claims to knowledge he can philosophically justify. Unbelievers challenge the truth of the Christian faith, objecting to its credibility and reasoning critically about it (at different levels of sophistication). The Christian who responds in defense of the faith is much more likely to do so faithfully and effectively if he has a realistic appraisal of the person with whom he is arguing. Accordingly, in chapter 4 we discussed what unbelievers actually do know (the "psychological" perspective), while in chapter 5 we discussed whether the unbeliever's knowledge is intelligible, given his philosophical theories (the "epistemological" perspective). Together, these two chapters conveyed three important points that Van Til's presuppositional apologetics maintains about the thinking and reasoning of the unbeliever. (The first two points come from chapter 4; the third comes from chapter 5.)

First, all men know God, regardless of what they may say about this. Even unbelievers have direct and compelling evidence that warrants their (unacknowledged) belief not only that God exists, but also that He is all-powerful, holy, the Creator and sovereign determiner of all events, etc. This evidence is supplied to all men by the clear revelation of God in nature and to many men by the self-attesting revelation of God in Scripture.

Second, because all men know God from His works of creation and providence, even those who will not profess and glorify Him are able, and actually do, gain considerable knowledge about themselves and about the world. Their knowledge of God justifies their logical and empirical reasoning. It provides the needed philosophical context and the personal operational basis for their coming to know anything else. Thus, unbelievers actually possess a knowledge of God (His sovereign power, holy character, etc.) and extensive knowledge of the world (history, science, art, etc.).

Third, because unbelievers personally deny knowing God (that is, they repudiate the first point above), they are unable to give an epistemological or philosophical account of their knowledge of the world and of themselves that is intelligible. The knowledge of God is necessary in order to justify any knowledge of the world. The unbelieving philosophical assumptions and systems of thought that non-Christians profess to follow render their reasoning and interpretations unintelligible (lacking meaning, coherence, etc.). Unbelievers have no cogent explanation for their ability to know the things they actually know.

When Van Til discussed matters pertaining to the third point, he said he was speaking about the unbeliever "epistemologically." Epistemology is the theory of knowledge. In terms of their professed theories, unbelievers cannot provide a cogent justification of the truths that they believe. Of course, the inadequacies of the unbeliever's reflective theories about himself as a knower or about knowing itself do not cancel, deny, or preclude the actual knowledge that he happens to possess. A ten-year-old child may very well be able to swim the length of the pool—and actually do it over and over again—without being able to offer an adequate scientific account of how this is possible (with respect to body densities, buoyancy, friction, displacement, propulsion in a medium, coordination of limbs, etc.). Van Til was quite clear about this:

> The point I am interested in is to show that all the knowledge non-Christians have, whether as simple folk by common sense, or as scientists exploring the hidden depths of the created universe—they have because Christianity is true. It is because the world *is not* what non-Christians assume that it is, a world of Chance, and *is* what the

Christian says that it is, a world run by the counsel of God, that even non-Christians have knowledge. . . .

Now the question is not whether the non-Christian can weigh, measure, or do a thousand other things. No one denies that he can. But the question is whether *on his principle* the non-Christian can account for his own or any knowledge.[1]

As Van Til liked to quip: unbelievers can very well count, but they cannot "account for counting." When it comes to knowing things, then, the unbeliever is an "epistemological" failure; he has no adequate theory, or philosophy, or worldview that makes his knowing intelligible.

On the other hand, turning from philosophical theory to actual personal behavior and accomplishments, the unbeliever is not always a failure at all. He may very well know a great deal about history, science, art, etc. When Van Til discussed the things that are covered in the first and second points above (positive knowledge of God and of His world), he would say that he was speaking about the unbeliever "psychologically"—with respect to what actually goes on within him.[2] To do so is to speak of the real internal thoughts and reasoning of the unbeliever, as opposed to the imagined theories that he externally professes and in terms of which he attempts to regiment his thinking and arguments.[3] Van Til relied heavily upon the distinction between "speaking epistemologically" and "speaking psychologically (metaphysically)," particularly when he handled the difficult issue, which every apologist must face, of the common ground and common notions of the believer and the unbeliever. The terminology used to ex-

---

1. *The Defense of the Faith* (Philadelphia: Presbyterian and Reformed, 1955), 286, 288.
2. Van Til also spoke "metaphysically" about the actual psychological processes of thinking and reasoning within the unbeliever (what is *really* happening), as opposed to speaking of him "epistemologically"—referring to the unbeliever's own theories (about knowing, about himself as a knower, etc.).
3. The unbeliever also speaks silently to himself about these thoughts and theories, of course. Thus, it is not entirely correct to contrast the unbeliever's "internal" thoughts from his "external" thoughts. However, it does help students begin to draw the distinction between epistemological and psychological analyses. To be more precise, though, we need to distinguish between thoughts that are self-reflective and those that are not. There are many times when I am, operationally speaking, thinking about English semantics and syntax (in order to use them in communication), but not reflecting in the forefront of my attention upon my thinking about the English language; at other times (as when writing this particular sentence), I am self-consciously thinking about the fact that I am thinking about the English language.

press this problem varies, but it boils down to a question of whether, and to what extent, the believer and the unbeliever share a common knowledge or interpretation of the world, their experience, or God.

> What has been said up to this point may seem to be discouraging in the extreme. It would seem that the argument up to this point has driven us to a denial of *any* point of contact whatsoever with the unbeliever. . . .
>
> If a man is wholly ignorant of the truth he cannot be interested in the truth. On the other hand if he is really interested in the truth it must be that he already possesses the main elements of the truth. It is in the interest of escaping the horns of this dilemma that Rome and evangelical Protestantism seek a point of contact in some area of "common knowledge" between believers and unbelievers. Their argument is that in teaching the total depravity of man in the way he does the Calvinist is in the unfortunate position of having to speak to deaf men when he preaches the gospel.[4]

The issue of "common ground" or "point of contact" is a troubled one because a number of significant theological doctrines bear upon it, but in ways that create tension or seem to lead to opposite conclusions. All men are made in the image of God, but all men are fallen and totally depraved (even in their reasoning). No man can escape the clear revelation of His Maker through the natural order and inward conscience, but there is no man who does not suppress and distort that revelation as well. All men rebel against God and seek to flee from the light of His revelation, suppressing the truth in unrighteousness, and yet the common, restraining grace of the Holy Spirit keeps men from consistently and successfully working out to the end their resistance to God's revelation.

So do believers who submit to God's word have "common ground" with unbelievers who ignore or despise that word? Do Christians and non-Christians share "common notions" (the very same principles, ideas, truths, propositions, etc.) in their beliefs and reasoning? To answer such questions, said Van Til,

> we do well to take careful note of a distinction . . . between the psychological and the epistemological. If there be such things as "com-

---

4. *Defense of the Faith*, 103.

mon notions," psychologically speaking, it does not follow that there are such things as "common notions," epistemologically speaking. . . .

After the fall this revelational interpretation was invariably accompanied by an attitude of hostility [man's ethical *reaction*]. Paul tells us that knowing God, having engaged in interpretative activity, psychologically speaking, the heathen yet glorified Him not as God. . . .

We shall need to make a sharp distinction between that which is merely psychological, and that which is epistemological in man's interpretative activity. . . . "Common notions" may be thought of as nothing more than revelation that comes to man through man. As an ethical subject man, after the fall, acts negatively with respect to this revelation. As made in the image of God no man can escape becoming the interpretative medium of God's general revelation both in his intellectual (Romans 1:20) and in his moral consciousness (Romans 2:14, 15). No matter which button of the radio he presses, he always hears the voice of God. Even when he presses the button of his own psychological self-conscious activity, through which as a last resort the sinner might hope to hear another voice, he still hears the voice of God. "If I make my bed in hell, behold, thou art there."

It is in this sense that we must, at least to begin with, understand the matter when we are told that there are no atheistic peoples and no atheistic men. Psychologically there are no atheistic men; epistemologically every sinner is atheistic.[5]

Sinners cannot avoid believing in God and actually using revealed notions in their reasoning and beliefs about the world, with the result that Christians and non-Christians "psychologically" share some common knowledge. Nevertheless, sinners suppress the truth about God and therefore "epistemologically" offer a distorted theoretical interpretation of these things, which invariably conflicts with the Christian's interpretation.

It is this fact, that the natural man, using his principles and working on his assumptions, must be hostile in principle at every point to the Christian philosophy of life, that was stressed in the writer's little book, *Common Grace*. That all men have all things in common metaphysically and psychologically, was definitely asserted, and further, that the natural man has epistemologically nothing in common with

5. *Common Grace* (Philadelphia: Presbyterian and Reformed, 1947), 52, 53–54.

the Christian. And this latter assertion was qualified by saying that this is so only *in principle*. . . . As far as the principle of the natural man is concerned, it is *absolutely* or utterly, not partly, opposed to God. . . . So far then as men self-consciously work from this principle they have no notion in common with the believer. Their epistemology is informed by their ethical hostility to God.[6]

6.2 The Unbeliever's Mixed Status (Which Is Awkward to Articulate)

Water is water. That should be obvious enough. So we would think that talking intelligently about water or using the word "water" unequivocally would not be complicated or confusing. So it might seem. But our communications employing the word "water" are not ordinarily problematic only because certain unspoken qualifications and distinctions are taken for granted (in most cases). A science teacher may say to his class, "Water freezes at thirty-two degrees Fahrenheit," but the truth of his assertion depends upon the way in which he is using this (supposedly unproblematic) word "water." As an empirical generalization, the sentence is in fact quite false. In most cases on earth, what we call "water" does not freeze at precisely thirty-two degrees Fahrenheit. Most of what we call "water" includes a variety of minerals (if not also traces of other chemicals), and is not located where the atmospheric pressure is exactly the same as it is at sea level. Yet we do not fire the science teacher for his inaccuracy or empirical error. When he states the freezing point of water, he is referring to pure, distilled water. When we talk about a particular case of water ("actual water" in ordinary experience, with its impurities), the discussion gets more complicated and generalizations call for a range of qualifications. (If we traced the linguistic habits of our science teacher, we would undoubtedly find that he uses the simple word "water" in both ways, sometimes for distilled water and sometimes for unpurified water, relying upon the context to indicate for his hearers the way in which he is speaking.)

All of us, including Van Til, are in similar straits when it comes to speaking about the "unbeliever" (or "natural man," "unregenerate man," "fallen man," "autonomous man," "apostate," "sinner," "non-Christian," etc.). It might be thought that we could use such a designation easily, with unequivocal and clear meaning. However, there is

6. *Defense of the Faith*, 189–90.

more to particular unbelievers whom we meet in actual experience than "chemically distilled," pure unbelief. From the standpoint of religious epistemology, the unbeliever represents something of a mixture, according to Van Til:

> To the extent that he works according to this monistic assumption he misinterprets all things, flowers no less than God. Fortunately the natural man is never fully consistent while in this life. . . . The natural man "sins against" his own essentially Satanic principle. . . . The actual situation is therefore always a mixture of truth with error. Being "without God in the world" the natural man yet knows God, and, in spite of himself, to some extent recognizes God. By virtue of their creation in God's image, by virtue of the ineradicable sense of deity within them and by virtue of God's restraining general grace, those who hate God, yet in a restricted sense know God, and do good.[7]

Your pagan next-door neighbor, Mr. Smith, is not only a rebel against God, but also a creature of God, made as His image, inescapably in possession of a knowledge of Him, and restrained in his rebellion by the common grace of the Holy Spirit. So you find in him intellectual traits and personal conduct that are not altogether consistent with unbelief or unregeneracy; a full psychological profile of him would be an impure and sometimes baffling mixture. This makes for complications (or possible misunderstandings) when we speak of an individual unbeliever (or generalize about unbelievers) as though he exhibited merely the traits of unbelief. Nevertheless, we need to understand the characteristics of unbelief, know what makes it what it is, know what it is capable of, and know how it may be expected to behave (or respond to our witness), etc.—and be careful to distinguish from these traits the characteristics that result from being made as God's image, being restrained by common grace, etc. Since the unbeliever has "two principles working inside him," it would be a serious error to assume that the effects of common grace (for instance) are characteristics of unregeneracy in itself.

Keenly aware of the significance of the antithesis between belief and unbelief, Van Til felt it was crucial to warn his students and readers about the characteristics—both ethical and (by extension) epis-

---

7. *An Introduction to Systematic Theology*, In Defense of the Faith, vol. 5 (Philadelphia: Presbyterian and Reformed, 1947), 27.

temological—of unbelief or unregeneracy. In order to do this, he generalized, as any instructor would, about the ethical and epistemological nature of unbelief or unregeneracy. He could thus say: "On account of the fact of sin man is blind with respect to the truth wherever the truth appears."[8] Or: "No sinner can interpret reality aright."[9] Or: "It is therefore impossible to grant that he [the natural man] is right, basically right, in what he says about any fact."[10] Likewise, in consideration of the inherent nature of sinful rebellion, he could say that the sinner's "epistemological reaction will invariably be negative, and negative along the whole line of his interpretative endeavor."[11] When Van Til said things of this nature, he did not for a moment lose sight of the fact that, in the case of the particular unbelievers we encounter in experience (like Mr. Smith), there is more to them than the rebellious, blind, epistemologically destructive, and spiritually dead condition that is characterized by such statements. It would be unfair, then, to dismiss those statements as "simplistic"[12] and "extreme" antithetical formulations[13]—just as it would be unfair to criticize a science teacher for telling his class that water freezes at thirty-two degrees Fahrenheit.

---

8. *Defense of the Faith*, 90.

9. *Introduction to Systematic Theology*, 92.

10. *Defense of the Faith*, 318. On the same page, he likewise says: "Whatever man says is fundamentally untrue," if he does not take into account the Creator-creature distinction. Also compare Van Til's comments that "basically proper" (p. 100) and "essentially correct" (p. 110) interpretations are beyond the unbeliever. As I understand him, such expressions were used to denote the fact that the *fundamental* or *central* beliefs held by the non-Christian—that is, his presuppositions—keep him from a proper understanding of whatever he is talking about. According to Van Til, the unbeliever often gets many proximate details correct, but never arrives at a satisfactory overall interpretation (incorporating those details) because he does not have the "basic" ("essential") beliefs that can make those details coherent, intelligible, or meaningful.

11. *Common Grace*, 57.

12. Van Til himself anticipated this criticism. The fact that God's common grace keeps fallen man from being as bad as he could be, said Van Til, "will make the distinction between two mutually exclusive principles seem an extreme oversimplification to many" (*A Christian Theory of Knowledge* [Philadelphia: Presbyterian and Reformed, 1969], 44). While the principles are in themselves mutually exclusive, the psychological fact is (strange though it may be) that spiritual confusion makes people attempt to work from both principles.

13. This is, oddly enough, charged against Van Til by John M. Frame, "Van Til on Antithesis," *Westminster Theological Journal* 57 (1995): 81–102. The article expands upon criticism issued by Frame in his essay "Cornelius Van Til," contributed to the *Handbook of Evangelical Theologians*, ed. Walter A. Elwell (Grand Rapids: Baker, 1993), where he alleges that Van Til "goes on to characterize unbelievers in various ways which are neither adequate to the biblical data nor consistent with one

Van Til openly pointed out that, because of the psychological and spiritual complexity of the unbeliever's personal condition, we "must allow for the value of the knowledge of non-Christians. This has always been a difficult point. . . . All that we can do with this question . . . is to hem it in in order to keep out errors."[14] Accordingly, when Van Til reflected on the ethical and epistemological defects of the unbeliever, he repeatedly specified and qualified the sense in which his words applied.

---

another" (p. 164). After examining various explanations by Van Til of the unbeliever's paradoxical status (of knowing God, yet not knowing Him), Frame says: "It is difficult to make sense out of all this. Clearly we need to go back to the drawing board" (p. 165).

    According to Frame's article "Van Til on Antithesis," Van Til was "fond" of his "extreme" formulations of the antithesis between the believer and the unbeliever (p. 100) and "often" spoke "in ways that suggest the unbeliever knows no truth at all and therefore has literally no area of agreement with the believer" (p. 87); these extreme formulations were "simplistic" (suggesting that every utterance of the unbeliever is false), were not "careful," and indeed were not very "defensible scripturally" (p. 102). Frame even charges that they are "inconsistent with" or "contradict" (pp. 86, 94, 98) what Van Til says elsewhere about the "complexity" of the unbeliever's situation: e.g., unbelievers have a revealed knowledge of God, are unable to suppress it completely, recognize Him against their wills, presuppose Him even while denying it, and recognize the unsatisfactory character of their philosophical systems! This is an odd criticism. It would seem far more reasonable and fair to conclude that these latter statements by Van Til demonstrate rather convincingly that the previous statements were not properly interpreted as "extreme" in the first place. After all, Frame himself must acknowledge that, taken literally and out of context, those statements do not represent the "complexity," "flexibility," "subtlety," and "richness" of Van Til's views (pp. 99, 100, 101, 102). No contradiction has been demonstrated to exist between Van Til's various explanations (or "strategies for reconciling antithesis with common grace") when they are interpreted in the light of each other. Since Frame characteristically takes just such a charitable approach in his analysis of other authors, it is hard to understand why he fails to do so here. In describing Van Til's "extreme" formulations of antithesis, Frame attributes to him—without any specific textual substantiation (but resting instead on what "seems" to be an implication of what Van Til actually wrote, or on what Van Til "suggests")—the views that the unbeliever's "conclusions" are always false, that he never utters a true sentence "except" formally, and that believers and unbelievers are speaking "different languages" (cf. p. 91).

14. *Introduction to Systematic Theology*, 26. Since this statement is also quoted by Frame in "Van Til and Antithesis" (p. 86), it is even more odd that he would fault Van Til for allegedly making some (very few, actually) "extreme" and unqualified statements of the antithesis. Van Til tipped off his readers that his statements about the unbeliever's personal condition (as it relates to ethics and epistemology) were generalizations which, for the sake of accuracy, are "hemmed in" by other descriptions; these other descriptions, then, were intended to qualify his preceding generalizations. But even if he had not said as much, any author deserves to be interpreted in the fuller context of his words. Nevertheless, even after extensively

Here are some conspicuous examples: "Insofar as men are aware of their most basic alliances, they are wholly for or wholly against God at every point of interest to man." "To the extent that [the sinner] interprets nature according to his own adopted principles, he does not speak the truth on any subject."[15] He could write that "all the study of nature that man has made since the fall of man has been, in a basic sense, absolutely false," but then in the next sentence add the qualification, "as far as an ultimate point of view is concerned."[16] When he stated that unbelievers (as such) would mistakenly interpret nature as well as God, Van Til specified the scope of his remark: "It is *of these systems* of their own interpretation that we speak when we say that men are as wrong in their interpretation of trees as in their interpretation of God."[17] The qualified and focused way in which Van Til thought of the antithesis between the believer's reasoning and the unbeliever's reasoning was repeatedly made plain: "The absolute contrast between the Christian and the non-Christian in the field of knowledge is said to be that of principle." Accordingly, he clearly drew "the distinction . . . between the regenerated consciousness which by its *principle* sees the truth and the unregenerate consciousness which by its *principle* cannot see the truth."[18]

Van Til stressed the absolute personal hostility and philosophical opposition between the essential nature of unbelief (resistance to God) and that of belief (submission to God's word and authority). In distilled form, we have death set over against life, or utter ignorance versus genuine knowledge. This kind of antithetical teaching left Van Til vulnerable to misinterpretation and criticism. Critics could easily construct a straw man out of his hard-hitting words, and then knock

---

noting the ways in which Van Til himself qualifies his general statements about the unbeliever's inability to interpret reality correctly (etc.), Frame charges that "Van Til sometimes forgot that his doctrine of antithesis was a doctrine about the human heart. He sometimes thought that he could identify it exhaustively with various conceptual oppositions. In this belief he was wrong" (p. 102). It appears, rather, that Frame is wrong. Surely one could not reasonably expect every "hemming in" qualification to appear in each and every sentence Van Til wrote on the subject.

15. *Introduction to Systematic Theology*, 29, 113. Notice especially "insofar as" and "to the extent that," which are explicit expressions of qualification and delimitation. Van Til was neither simplistic nor forgetful of the complexity of the unbeliever's internal character and thinking.

16. Ibid., 81.

17. Ibid., 84 (emphasis added). By "system" Van Til designates the philosophical or theoretical outlook of the unbeliever, taken in its ideal and consistent expression or outworking.

18. *Defense of the Faith*, 67, 290.

it down. For example, William Masselink claimed that Van Til's position "results in an *absolute antithesis*." "For the natural man," he alleged, "the fact that $2 \times 2 = 4$ is just as certain as it is for the Christian. The Reconstructionists[19] however assert that also this is annihilated by sin."[20] But Van Til never taught that the natural man is so consistent and successful in his rebellion against God that he actually reaches the stage of knowing nothing whatsoever, becomes a blithering idiot, and never reaches true conclusions (or believes true propositions) in any sense on any subject at all. Asked whether he means to assert that unbelievers do not actually discover any truth by the methods they employ, Van Til replied firmly and categorically: "We mean nothing so absurd as that."[21] Indeed, if the unbeliever were to be utterly ignorant on everything, he would no longer be responsible before God for his sin and rebellion. Because he is made as God's image, confronted with God's inescapable revelation, and restrained by the common grace of the Holy Spirit, the unbeliever cannot fail to know God and, by extension, to understand something of himself and God's world. Van Til thus taught: "There is a sense in which he knows something about everything, about God as well as about the world. . . . Many non-Christians have been great scientists. Often non-Christians have a better knowledge of the things of this world than Christians have. . . . From a relative point of view he knows something about all things."[22]

From Van Til's viewpoint, then, the unbeliever exists in a state of conflict with respect to knowing, and that mixed condition is awkward to articulate. Simple designations and generalizations, while facilitating communication, tend to tone down the real complexity of what we are talking about. At least three things need to be kept in mind, according to Van Til, if we are to understand the unbeliever for apologetical purposes: (1) all men inescapably know God (cf. chapter 4.3–4 above); (2) because of this, men can gain rational and empirical knowledge (cf. chapter 4.5); (3) and yet by their opposition to the Christian faith, un-

---

19. Although I rather like this term, it was not used here in the sense that is current in American Reformed circles today. Masselink distinguished the views of the "Reconstructionists" Van Til, Schilder, Vollenhoven, and Dooyeweerd (as he amalgamated them) from what he called "the Historic Reformed view" of men like Kuyper, Warfield, Bavinck, Hodge, Machen, Hepp, and Berkhof.
20. *General Revelation and Common Grace* (Grand Rapids: Eerdmans, 1953), 161. Claims such as this are found throughout the book. In his copy of Masselink's book, Van Til at various places scrawled comments like "Outrageous!" and "I do not."
21. *Defense of the Faith*, 120.
22. *Introduction to Systematic Theology*, 83.

believers cannot offer an adequate epistemological theory to account for what they know (cf. chapter 5). Moreover, the resulting antithesis that exists between believers and unbelievers with respect to their fundamental personal attitudes and philosophical outlook is also a complicated matter, calling for explanation and qualification (cf. chapter 5.2). For instance, although there can be no appeasement of unbelief at the presuppositional or worldview level, the antithesis is not as immediately obvious in external or peripheral matters. Likewise, it is evident from the way they speak and live that believers and unbelievers utilize and affirm some common concepts, and yet these prove upon analysis to be somewhat abstract or formal in nature, given the very different assumptions, context, and concrete applications that they make of them. On the one hand, the ethical hostility of non-Christians always adversely affects their epistemology and interpretations of experience, the world, and God; the poisoning effect of sin is involved in everything they think and say. On the other hand, specific unbelievers in real life often speak, believe, and behave in ways with which Christians agree. But this should not confuse or mislead us, Van Til would say. As far as they are self-conscious unbelievers, they have no notions in common with believers; theoretically or epistemologically speaking, there are no neutral "common notions" to which both the believer and the unbeliever can unequivocally appeal.

For the sake of our own faithfulness to God, and for the sake of pressing home the apologetical challenge upon the unbeliever, Van Til always urged apologists to seek to make men ever more epistemologically self-conscious and thereby exhibit with increased clarity the antithesis between believers and unbelievers with respect to their basic character and espoused systems of thought. But he did not forget or disregard the unbeliever's mixed status in this life—and thus understood both the epistemological antithesis and the common knowledge between believers and unbelievers in a qualified way.

THE ANTITHESIS CANNOT BE UNQUALIFIED[23]

All men, even after the fall, know, deep down in their hearts, that they are creatures of God; that they should therefore obey, but that they have actually broken, the law of God.

---

23. An excerpt from "A Reply to Criticism" in *Common Grace and the Gospel* (Philadelphia: Presbyterian and Reformed, 1972), 196–97.

After the fall, therefore, all men seek to suppress this truth, fixed in their being, about themselves. They are opposed to God. This is the biblical teaching on human depravity. If we are to present the truth of the Christian religion to men we must take them where they are. They are: (a) creatures made in God's image, surrounded by a world that reveals in its every fact God's power and divinity. Their antithesis to God can never be metaphysical. They can never be anything but image bearers of God. They can never escape facing God in the universe about them and in their own constitution. Their antithesis to God is therefore an *ethical* one. (b) Because of God's common grace, this ethical antithesis to God on the part of the sinner is *restrained*, and thereby the creative forces of man receive the opportunity of constructive effort. In this world the sinner does many "good" things. He is honest. He helps to alleviate the sufferings of his fellow men. He "keeps" the moral law. Therefore the "antithesis," besides being ethical rather than metaphysical, is limited in a second way. It is one of *principle*, not one of full expression. If the natural man fully expressed himself as he is in terms of the principle of ethical hostility to God that dwells within his soul, he would then be a veritable devil. Obviously he is often nothing of the sort. He is not at all as "bad as he may be."

THE ANTITHESIS IS "IN PRINCIPLE"[24]

Just now we spoke of "elements of truth" that may be found in the non-Christian diagnosis of sin and evil. This points to the necessity of qualifying the analysis of fallen man given above. What we have said of him is true only *in principle*. Fallen man does *in principle* seek to be a law unto himself. But he cannot carry out his own principle to its full degree. He is restrained from doing so. God himself restrains him; God is long-suffering toward him. He calls man to repentance. He keeps fallen man from working out the full consequence of his sin. Reformed theologians speak of this restraint of God upon mankind in general as due to *common grace*.

The restraint of God upon fallen mankind enables it to help build the culture of the race. At the beginning of history man was given the task of subduing the earth. He was to subdue it "under God" and thus to the glory of God. But as a sinner man seeks to make himself instead of God, the ultimate aim as well as the ultimate standard in life. Yet he cannot ultimately change the practical situation. He is still a creature. The universe is still what God has made it to be, and it will be what God intends it to be. So fallen man cannot

24. An excerpt from *Christian Theory of Knowledge*, 43–44.

destroy the program of God. He cannot even destroy himself as inherently a builder of culture for God. In spite of what he does against God, he yet can and *must* work for God; thus he is able to make a "positive contribution" to human culture.

Thus it comes to pass that they of whom Scripture says that their minds are darkened can yet discover much truth. But this discovery of truth on their part is effected *in spite* of the fact that *in principle* they are wholly evil. Their discovery of truth is adventitious so far as their own principle is concerned. They are not *partly* evil, they are not just sick; they are *wholly* evil, they are spiritually *dead*. But in spite of being dead in sins, they can, because of God's common grace, discover truth. The universe is what the Scripture says it is, and man is what the Scripture says he is. On both of these points it says the opposite of what fallen man says. Fallen man knows truth and does "morally good" things in spite of the fact that *in principle* he is set against God.

METAPHYSICAL COMMON GROUND AND PSYCHOLOGICALLY COMMON KNOWLEDGE[25]

Whatever may happen, whatever sin may bring about, whatever havoc it may occasion, it cannot destroy man's knowledge of God and his sense of responsibility to God. Sin would not be sin except for this ineradicable knowledge of God.[26] Even sin as a process of ever-increasing alienation from God presupposes for its background this knowledge of God.

This knowledge is that which all men have in common. For the race of men is made of one blood. It stood as a unity before God in Adam. This confrontation of all men with God in Adam by supernatural revelation presupposes and is correlative to the confrontation of mankind with God by virtue of creation. If then the believer presents to the unbeliever the Bible and its system of truth as God speaking to men, he may rest assured that there is a response in the heart of every man to whom he thus speaks. This response may be, and often is, unfavorable. Men will reject the claims of God but, none the less, they will own them as legitimate. That is, they will in their hearts, when they cannot suppress them, own these claims. There are no atheists, least of all in the hereafter. *Metaphysically speaking then, both parties, be-*

---

25. Excerpts from *Defense of the Faith*, 173, 174, 179, 191, 192, 286, 292.
26. This sentence establishes how crucial it is to presuppositional apologetics to maintain that unbelievers genuinely possess some knowledge. If they absolutely knew nothing at all, then they would not be responsible for their sinful behavior—and thus would not be in need of any evangelistic witness or apologetical defense of the truth of the gospel.

*lievers and unbelievers, have all things in common; they have God in com-
mon, they have every fact in the universe in common. And they know they
have them in common.*[27] All men know God, the true God, the only God.
They have not merely a capacity for knowing him but actually do know him.

Thus there is not and can never be an absolute separation between God
and man. Man is always accessible to God. There can be no *absolute* antithesis
in this sense of the term. . . .

And where there is no true basis for a common knowledge there is no true
basis for the unity of science. Only in Protestant thought, and more particularly in Reformed thought, with its insistence that God controls whatsoever
comes to pass, and with its insistence that every man as man is an addressee
of God, is there unity of science. On this basis only the unity of science is guaranteed. Every man can contribute to the progress of science. Every man must
contribute to it. It is his task to do so. And he cannot help but fulfill his task
even if it be against his will. . . .

In particular sin did not destroy any of the powers that God gave man at
the beginning when he endowed him with his image. To be sure, here too
there have been weakening results. But man still has eyes with which to observe and logical ability with which to order and arrange the things that he
observes. . . .

If sin is seen to be ethical alienation only, and salvation as ethical restora-
tion only, then the question of weighing and measuring or that of logical reasoning is, of course, equal on both sides. All men, whatever their ethical relation to God, can equally use the natural gifts of God. How could men abuse
the gift of God if they could not even use it? And what an easy way of escape
for sinners it would be if the result of their folly was nothing more serious than
the loss of their natural powers, and with it the loss of responsibility. . . . As
far as natural ability is concerned the lost can and do know the truth and could
contribute to the structure of science. . . .

Men on both sides can, by virtue of the gifts of God that they enjoy, contribute to science. The question of ethical hostility does not enter in at this
point. Not merely weighing and measuring, but the argument for the existence of God and for the truth of Christianity, can as readily be observed to
be true by non-Christians as by Christians. . . .

---

27. Emphasis added. Van Til always held that there is abundant common ground between the believer and the unbeliever—namely, all of reality, both the Creator
and His entire creation. This is metaphysical common ground, but Van Til also
asserted that the believer and the unbeliever, as creatures made in the image of
God, can have in common a knowledge (psychologically speaking) of the metaphysical situation, to whatever degree they know God or His world.

God calls men to conversion. His natural gifts to them are calculated to make them return to God.[28] And even as they continue to operate in opposition to God, they are restrained from working out to the fullest extent the principle of wickedness within them. And as they are thus restrained by God's Spirit striving with them, their natural powers are, so to speak, set at liberty for constructive work. . . .

Often non-Christians have a better knowledge of the things of this world than Christians have. . . .

Why waste words on the idea that non-Christians do not have good powers of perception, good powers of reasoning, etc. Non-Christians have all these. If that were the issue, then the contention should be made that non-Christians are blind, deaf, and have no powers of logical reasoning at all; in fact, they should be non-existent.

YET NO EPISTEMOLOGICALLY SELF-CONSCIOUS COMMON NOTIONS[29]

(A) The "presuppositionalist" does not, as Hamilton[30] thinks he does, deny that there is common ground between the believer and the unbeliever. Neither party denies the fact of the existence of common ground. The question pertains to the *nature* of the common ground. The present writer has repeatedly asserted that metaphysically believers and unbeliever have *all reality in common*. The unbeliever and believer are, alike, image-bearers of God. Together they operate in the God-created and Christ-redeemed world. . . .

It is, therefore, because all men are image-bearers of God and because the "facts" and "laws" of the world are what they are, as revelatory of God's acts of revelation in and through them, that the natural man remains accessible to God. No man can escape the call of God which confronts him in his own constitution as well as in every fact of the world that surrounds him.

On the other hand, the unbeliever does *not* believe that he is a creature of God and that he is spiritually blind because of his fall in and with Adam. The unbeliever *assumes* his non-createdness, his autonomy. He *assumes* the non-createdness, the just-thereness, of the facts of the universe. He *assumes*

---

28. CVT: Romans, chapter 2.
29. The following excerpts are taken from:

   (A) *Christian Theory of Knowledge*, 258–59;
   (B) *Defense of the Faith*, 84–86, 90, 102, 183, 188, 288, 304, 353.

30. Van Til here responds to criticism found in Floyd E. Hamilton, *The Basis of Christian Faith*, 4th ed. (New York: Harper, 1964). He had earlier replied to Hamilton in *Defense of the Faith*, chap. 13, sec. 3.

the existence of the laws of "causality" and of "logic" as having no reference to the Creator-redeemer God of Scripture.

Such being the case, the "presuppositionalist" refuses to speak of a common ground between believers and unbelievers, in which this all-determinative difference between them is ignored. When the believer *interprets* the world he interprets it in terms of the biblical teaching with respect to God and his relation to man and his world, and therefore every word he speaks when ultimately considered is colored by this fact. When the unbeliever *interprets* the world, he interprets it in terms of his assumption of human autonomy, and with it a non-created or purely contingent factual space-time cosmos and of a non-created, timeless, abstract principle of logic. In consequence every word he utters, when it is completely "talked out,"[31] is seen to receive its definition from this underlying structure.

The unbeliever is the man with yellow glasses on his face. He sees himself and his world through these glasses. He cannot remove them. His *interpretation* of himself and of every fact in the universe relating to himself is, unavoidably, a *false* interpretation. . . .

It is therefore the idea of a common ground of *interpretation* that the "presuppositionalist" rejects. Such common ground would be a meaningless monstrosity. Can any one intelligently assume that he is both a creature and not a creature, a sinner and not a sinner? Can any one intelligently assume with Hamilton, the Reformed theologian, that God is the source of possibility and with Hamilton, the apologist, that possibility is the source of God?

(B) Is there an area known by both from which, as a starting point, we may go on to that which is known to believers but unknown to unbelievers? And is there a common method of knowing this "known area" which need only to be applied to that which the unbeliever does not know in order to convince him of its existence and its truth? It will not do to assume at the outset that these questions must be answered in the affirmative. For the knower himself needs interpretation as well as the things he knows. The human mind as the knowing subject, makes its contribution to the knowledge it obtains. It will be quite impossible then to find a common area of knowledge between believers and unbelievers unless there is agreement between them as to the nature of man himself. But there is no such agreement. . . .

---

31. This is an important qualifier. Van Til asserts that the interpretations of reality that are propounded by the believer and the unbeliever, if completely talked out or reasoned through to their consistent conclusions, would not be common at all—and that the unbeliever's interpretation would render itself unintelligible (thus "unavoidably false").

The conception of man as entertained by modern thought in general cannot be assumed to be the same as that set forth in Scripture. It is therefore imperative that the Christian apologist be alert to the fact that the average person to whom he must present the Christian religion for acceptance is a quite different sort of being than he himself thinks he is. A good doctor will not prescribe medicines according to the diagnosis that his patient has made of himself. The patient may think that he needs nothing more than a bottle of medicine while the doctor knows that an immediate operation is required.

Christianity then must present itself as the light that makes the facts of human experience, and above all the nature of man himself, to appear for what they really are. Christianity is the source from which both life and light derive for men. . . .

But without the light of Christianity it is as little possible for man to have the correct view about himself and the world as it is to have the true view about God. On account of the fact of sin man is blind with respect to the truth wherever the truth appears. And truth is one. Man cannot truly know himself unless he truly knows God. . . .

There seems to be for Hepp, as for Hodge, something in the way of a common sense philosophy which the natural man has and which, because intuitive or spontaneous, is, so far forth, not tainted by sin. It appears, however, even from the brief quotation given, that the "common notions" of men are sinful notions. For man to reflect on his own awareness of meaning and then merely to say that a higher power, "a god," exists, is in effect to say that God does not exist. It is as though a child, reflecting upon his home environment would conclude that *a* father or *a* mother exists. And to "recognize the reality of the world and of man" is in itself not even to recognize the elemental truths of creation and providence. It is not enough to appeal from the more highly articulated systems of non-Christian thinkers to the philosophy of the common consciousness, of common sense, of intuition, that is to something that is more immediately related to the revelational pressure that rests upon men. Both Hepp and Hodge seem to be desirous of doing no more than Calvin does when he appeals to the sense of deity present in all men. But this notion, seeking to set forth as it does the teaching of Paul, that God's revelation is present to every man, must be carefully distinguished from the *reaction* that sinful men make to this revelation. . . .

When they do this they seek for *common notions* between believers and unbelievers that are not exclusively based upon the idea of the *sensus deitatis*. They then ignore the difference between the idea of fact and logic as it springs from the position that is based upon the notion of the autonomous man, and the idea of fact and logic which springs from the position that is based upon the notion of the ontological trinity.

Yet the idea of fact as it is based upon the notion of the autonomous man is that of utterly irrational differentiation. And the notion of logic as it is based upon the idea of man as autonomous is that of system that is above and inclusive of the distinction between God and man. . . .

It is this actual possession of the knowledge of God that is the indispensable presupposition of man's ethical opposition to God. There could be no *absolute ethical antithesis* to God on the part of Satan and fallen man unless they are self-consciously setting their own common notions, derived from the folly of sin, against the common notions that are concreated with them. Paul speaks of sinful man as suppressing within him the knowledge of God that he has. How does he do this? He does this by assuming his own ultimacy. . . . It is these notions of human autonomy, of irrational discontinuity and of rationalistic continuity that are the *common notions* of sinful or apostate mankind. . . .

Now the question is not whether the non-Christian can weigh, measure, or do a thousand other things. No one denies that he can. But the question is whether on *his* principle the non-Christian can account for his own or any knowledge. I argued that when two people, the one a Christian and the other not a Christian, *talk things out* with one another, they will appear to differ at every point.

In the interpretative endeavor the "objective situation" can never be abstracted from the "subjective situation."[32] . . .

The Reformed apologetic, therefore, does not take for granted, as does the Humanist and the Evangelical, that because men have "common notions" about God by virtue of their creation in God's image, that sinners and saints also have common notions when they are epistemologically self-conscious. . . .

All their [Van Til's critics'] detailed criticisms are based on the assumption that apologetics requires an area of interpretation which the unbeliever and the believer have in common. When I point out that this view leads inevitably to a compromise of the Reformed Faith, they take no notice of it. If the natural man can correctly interpret the realm of the phenomenal on the assumption of man's autonomy, the non-createdness of facts, and the idea of a system of logic that envelops God as well as man, it is too late to ask him to accept Christianity.

When I point out that in terms of "common notions" which ignore the difference between the Christian and the non-Christian principle of interpre-

---

32. CVT: *Common Grace*, p. 43.

tation, it is impossible to show the non-Christian why he should become a Christian, my critics again take no notice.[33]

6.3 Common Grace Does Not Dilute the Apologetical Challenge

As Van Til stated, apologists must be aware that Christians and non-Christians would have no common notions (or self-conscious interpretations) if unbelievers were completely consistent in their unbelief—that is, apologists must understand the fundamental opposition between Christian and non-Christian ultimate principles—so that they can effectively drive home the epistemological challenge to unbelievers that their autonomous systems of thought render it impossible to know anything at all. Given the antithesis between faith and unbelief, there is no truth that is religiously neutral, or of which believers and unbelievers could have a common theoretical knowledge or interpretation. And yet unbelievers do actually (psychologically) know much about many things, a fact for which they have no intelligible explanation. Thus, the apologist, based upon an intelligent dialogue with the non-Christian and a patient analysis of this situation, can call on the unbeliever to strip off his intellectual mask of pretended autonomy. He can demonstrate that it is both personally immoral and philosophically unreasonable for the unbeliever to resist professing the truth of Scripture and embracing the Christian faith.

On the other hand, Van Til taught that if believers and unbelievers share common notions, epistemologically speaking, and do so regardless of the presuppositional antithesis between them, it will be impossible to show the non-Christian, from the standpoint of intellectual argument, why he needs to become a Christian. (He may wish to sup-

---

33. The reason why apologists must be aware that there would be no common notions between Christians and non-Christians if the latter lived consistently with their ("distilled") character as unbelievers—that is, why apologists must understand the antithesis in terms of ultimate principles—is that they can thereby drive home the epistemological challenge to unbelievers that their autonomous systems of thought render it impossible to know anything at all. Theoretically, the believer and the unbeliever could have no common knowledge. Therefore, since such unbelievers do actually know (psychologically) much about many things, the apologist can call on the unbeliever to strip off his intellectual mask of pretended autonomy and can tell him that it is both unreasonable and immoral for him to resist the Christian faith. But, Van Til taught, if believers and unbelievers share common epistemological notions, despite their presuppositional antithesis, it is impossible to show the non-Christian through intellectual argument why he needs to become a Christian.

plement his system of thought with some new beliefs, but he will regard his system as perfectly all right as far as it goes.) This is precisely
what has (unintentionally) resulted in many Christian circles, thought
Van Til, because of distorted and defective views of common grace.[34]

Theologians commonly misunderstand common grace as something positive or constructive, rather than as God's restraining influence on the sinner's rebellion. Because common grace is common,
the interpretation of it as the empowering of the unregenerate man
to come to true conclusions suggests that these truths are universally
understood, and that all men are intellectually entitled to them, regardless of any underlying differences in their ethical condition or
philosophical outlook. Being "neutral" truths, they supposedly provide a common platform for daily work or apologetical dialogue with
the unbeliever. This is, of course, the perspective of natural theology.
It is imagined that the autonomous man can, by means of some ability granted by common grace, examine the natural world and, in full
agreement with the regenerate as far as these matters are concerned,
develop a correct interpretation of this world—which can then be
used as a stepping stone to demonstrate truths about the supernat-

---

34. It is important to take note of the fact that in Van Til's outlook, common grace
is not the only factor that contributes to the "common knowledge" (psychologically speaking) that is shared by believers and unbelievers. Other factors include
man being made in the image of God and God's compelling and clear revelation
of Himself in nature and Scripture. However, in Van Til's lifetime it was especially
through the door of misconceived ideas about common grace that so many Christians were bringing in flawed views of apologetics. In "Van Til on Antithesis," John
Frame lumps together under the rubric of "common grace" all the formulations
or distinctions by which Van Til mitigated the effects of "the antithesis." (E.g.,
"We may call these formulations 'strategies for reconciling antithesis with common grace' " [p. 87].) When he then considers Van Til's teaching about inescapable revelation (p. 87) and man's created natural abilities (p. 88), his faulty
categorization leads him astray, so that he mistakenly criticizes Van Til for suggesting that "common grace" is God's revelation itself and that "common grace"
preserves the metaphysical situation. Van Til did not combine these different factors. As he is quoted above: "By virtue of their creation in God's image, by virtue of the
ineradicable sense of deity within them and by virtue of God's restraining general grace, those
who hate God, yet in a restricted sense know God, and do good" (*Introduction to Systematic Theology*, 27). Again, in explaining how unbelievers can contribute to discovering truth in science and thus cooperate with believers, Van Til separates these
factors: "They can contribute by virtue of their metaphysical constitution; they can cooperate by virtue of the ethical restraint of common grace" (*Defense of the Faith*, 194). Likewise: "To be sure I do deny that this natural knowledge of God and of morality is the result
of common grace. I think it is the *presupposition* of common grace. . . . So too, if we take
common grace to be that which has to do with the restraint of sin, then it is an *ethical* not
a *metaphysical function* that it performs" (*Common Grace*, 159, 174).

ural world. In this view, then, the common notions shared by believers and unbelievers do not themselves challenge the unbeliever. That is, they do not rationally require a supernatural context or Christian presuppositions in order to be intelligible.

By contrast, Van Til held that man is naturally (i.e., as created) in possession of rational and moral abilities, but that, because of the Fall, these abilities are used by sinful men in a way that is always categorically hostile to serving and glorifying God (cf. the doctrine of "total" depravity). The unregenerate man has nothing in himself to keep this hostility from becoming consistent and full blown—in which case he would never do anything remotely moral and would never be able to rationally justify any claim to knowledge. Common grace does not enable him to justify his truth-claims, nor does it establish religiously neutral truths that are intelligible regardless of one's attitude toward and beliefs about God. Rather, for Van Til, "common grace is the means by which God keeps man from expressing the *principle* of hostility to its full extent."[35]

If common grace is understood as divine power that restrains the hostility and rebellion of unregenerate men, it accounts for their not becoming as intellectually destructive as they could be, rather than attributing to them any sin-neutralized proficiency in producing constructive accomplishments. The very real accomplishments of unbelievers are not their own and cannot be accounted for apart from the grace of God. But there is no "neutral" common ground, equally explainable or accessible on unbelieving and believing terms. According to Van Til, the doctrine of common grace ought not to be formulated or interpreted in such a way that the unbeliever's development of science or culture is thought to be "all right as far as it goes," or that the intellectual challenge of the gospel becomes irrelevant in the science lab or any other human endeavor.

COMMON FAVOR AND SINCERE INVITATION[36]

It is only if we think concretely of God that we can also think concretely of the things of the created world. And therefore we can think scripturally about the much-disputed doctrine of "common grace." If we think concretely of the question, we see at once that the term "common" is really applicable only

---

35. *Common Grace*, 174.
36. Excerpts from *Introduction to Systematic Theology*, 240, 241, 243–44.

in a very loose sense to the idea of grace. God's attitude toward the saved and the unsaved can at no point be strictly common. It is well that we begin at this point. God always regards the reprobate as reprobate. When, therefore, he gives to the reprobate certain gifts in this life, of which they are undeserving, and these same gifts (as, for instance, rain and sunshine) also come to the saved, we cannot conclude that, with respect to rain and sunshine, God has the same attitude toward the believer and the unbeliever. When we speak of the attitude of God toward unbelievers we must take into consideration the total picture of the unbeliever's relationship to God. Thus the gifts of rain and sunshine to the believer are the gifts of a covenant God who has forgiven the sins of his people, and who knows that his people need these gifts. In a similar way, the gifts of rain and sunshine to unbelievers are gifts to those whom God hates, and are given because they too have need of those things to fulfill the purpose that God has with them. God gave Pharaoh life and ability to rule, that he might be able to do that for which God had raised him up.

Both the wheat and the tares receive rain and sunshine so that both may reach the day of judgment for the revelation of the glory of God. In all this, God gave a witness to his presence (Acts 14:16). Men are through this witness without excuse. Thus God gave men and nations everywhere what they needed for a natural life and civilization, that they might accomplish the purposes of God. He restrained them in their natural tendency to do only evil continually, so that they, in spite of their own inherent evil nature, do that which externally resembles the requirements of the law of God (Rom. 2:14, 15). It was thus by the gifts of God to sinners that the full demoniacal character of sin appeared and shall appear. When the world by its wisdom shows itself to be ignorant of God, God by his grace saves sinners unto himself. When the righteousness of men is shown to be but as filthy rags, God reveals his righteousness from heaven among men.

We conclude then, that "common grace" is not strictly *common*. The "common" grace that comes to believers comes in conjunction with their forgiven status before God; the "common" grace that comes to unbelievers comes in conjunction with their unforgiven status. Externally considered, the facts may be the same, but the framework in the two cases is radically different. . . .

We say that this is one factor of the whole situation. We do not say that it is the only factor. God loves the works of his hands, and the progress that they make to their final fulfillment. So we may and should rejoice with God in the unfolding of the history of the race, even in the unfolding of the wickedness of man in order that the righteousness of God may be most fully displayed. But if God tells us that, in spite of the wickedness of men, and in spite of the fact that they misuse his gifts for their own greater condemnation, he is longsuffering with them, we need not conclude that there is no sense in which God has a favor to the unbeliever. There is a sense in which God has a disfavor to the believer because, in spite of the new life in him, he sins in the sight of God. So God may have favor to the unbeliever because of the "relative good" that God himself gives him in spite of the principle of sin within him. If we were to think of God and of his relation to the world in a univocal or abstract fashion, we might agree with those who maintain that there is no qualitative difference between the favor of God toward the saved and toward the unsaved. Arminians and Barthians virtually do this. Or, we might agree with those who maintain that there is no sense in which God can show a favor to the reprobate. On the other hand, if we reason concretely about God and his relation to the world, we simply listen to what God has told us in his Word on the matter. It may even then be exceedingly difficult to construct a theory of "common grace" which will do justice to what Scripture says. We make Scripture the standard of our thinking, and not our thinking the standard of Scripture. All of man's activity, whether intellectual or moral, is analogical; and for this reason it is quite possible for the unsaved sinner to do that which is "good" in a sense and for the believer to do what is "evil" in a sense.[37]

With respect to the question, then, as to whether Scripture actually teaches an attitude of favor, up to a point, on the part of God toward the non-believer, we can only intimate that we believe it does. Even when we take full cognizance of the fact that the unbeliever abuses every gift of God and uses it for the greater manifestation of his wickedness, there seems to be evidence in Scripture that God, for this life, has a certain attitude of favor to unbelievers. . . .

So also ought we to think of what is often called the universal well-meant offer of salvation. We know that there are those whom God, in his secret counsel does not intend to save. Of those round about us, we do not always know who are saved and who are not. In a sense, therefore, our ignorance accounts for the necessity of using a general formula in preaching the gospel. Yet this is not the only reason why Christ wept over Jerusalem, over a Jerusalem which he knew would, for the most part, reject him. So God calls those whom he knows will harden their hearts. He labored with Pharaoh to let his people go before the final time of destruction should come. Yet he had raised up Pharaoh for that final destruction. It is the duty of men to repent, as it was originally their duty not to sin. It is always the duty of man to obey the voice of God.

---

37. CVT: Cf. the writer's booklet, *Common Grace*.

The call to repentance that unbelievers receive will add to their judgment be-cause they do not heed it. But to be able to add to their judgment, it must have had a real meaning in their case. To say this is not to fall into individual-istic Arminianism. Those who have not heard the call of redemption will be judged because they are sinners in Adam and with Adam. Yet those who have heard the call and have not accepted it will receive the greater damnation. Thus, there must be a genuine meaning in the call that comes to them. It is only if we really think analogically or concretely of the attributes of God that we can thus do justice to all the aspects of Scripture truth. . . .

All in all the idea of *commonness*, whether applied to grace or to the gospel call, should be closely connected with the idea of earlier and later. Com-monness is always commonness up to a point and with a difference. But com-monness is more common earlier than later. Men in general, believers and un-believers, are regarded and treated similarly according as the process of differentiation between them has not come to development. There is a com-mon wrath upon elect and non-elect to the extent that the difference between the elect and the non-elect has not yet come to expression. So also with com-mon grace and the common gospel call. It is to men regarded in their more or less undifferentiated state that the term commonness is applicable. History has genuine meaning; the doctrine of election may not be interpreted so as to destroy its meaning, but rather so as to be the foundation of it.

AVOIDING OPPOSITE EXTREMES REGARDING COMMON GRACE [38]

For Hoeksema[39] all grace is grace to the elect. For the Arminians all grace is grace to men as men, to men as creatures of God. For Hoeksema all grace is special grace; for the Arminians all grace is common grace.

Both Hoeksema and the Arminian allow abstract logic to rule over Scrip-ture to a point. Both charge us with being self-contradictory because we hold to both election and common grace. There is no contradiction between them.

---

38. Excerpts from *Defense of the Faith*, 400–401, 169–70, 189, 191–92, 194–95.
39. In a number of books, pamphlets, and magazine articles, Herman Hoeksema vig-orously opposed the doctrine of common grace as taught by Abraham Kuyper. To Hoeksema it was inconceivable that God would in any sense show favor to the nonelect; the gifts He gives to them are not evidences of favor, but ordained means toward final condemnation. Moreover, held Hoeksema, if we said that men were enabled by common grace to do any good, we would be forced to deny total de-pravity. In 1924 the Synod of the Christian Reformed Church issued a three-point pronouncement on common grace which, in effect, condemned the views advo-cated by Hoeksema.

We do not hold to the "common grace" of the Arminian. To do so would be *ipso facto* to deny election. But we do hold to the idea that God has an attitude of favor to men as men, whether they be elect or reprobate. . . .

Now the question is whether we are to have a theory of common grace that will fit in with a scholastic type of natural theology and with a type of apologetics pursued by old Princeton or whether we shall have a theory of common grace that fits naturally into the system of truth called the Reformed Faith.

We have on the one side those who deny common grace. They employ, to some extent, a non-Christian principle of interpretation in doing so. We have on the other side those who affirm a scholastic theory of common grace. Our hope would seem to lie in following neither the one nor the other. . . .

The present advocates of this semi-scholastic theory of common grace are seeking to suggest that their view is "the traditional view" and therefore also that of the "three points" of 1924. But this remains to be proved. It cannot be proved. To say that God has a favorable attitude to all men, including the reprobate, already calls attention to the fact that there is no sameness without qualification. To say that God restrains the sin of men presupposes the idea of total depravity and excludes the notion of a neutral territory of interpretation. To say that the unregenerate do civic righteousness is again to reject the idea that the works of the regenerate and the non-regenerate proceed at any point from the same principle. . . .

For it is not till after the consummation of history that men are left wholly to themselves. Till then the Spirit of God continues to strive with men that they might forsake their evil ways. Till then God in his common grace, in his long-suffering forbearance, gives men rain and sunshine and all the good things of life that they might repent. The primary attitude of God to men as men is that of goodness. It is against this goodness expressing itself in the abundance of good gifts that man sins. And even then God prevents the principle of sin from coming to full fruition. He restrains the wrath of man. He enables him by this restraint to cooperate with the redeemed of God in the development of the work he gave man to do. . . .

Not that they were, while building, wholly self-conscious of their own ethical hostility. They were restrained from being fully self-conscious by common grace. They were restrained by common grace, employing the pressure of God's presence in his revelation to men upon them. . . .

And by the striving of the Spirit men cannot be wholly insensitive to this goodness of God. Their hostility is curbed in some measure. They cannot but love that which is honest and noble and true. They have many virtues that often make them better neighbors than Christians themselves are. And as such they can *cooperate* with believers in seeking the truth in science. They can contribute by virtue of their metaphysical constitution; they can cooperate by virtue of the ethical restraint of common grace.

Thus it is that the idea of the unity of science is conceived of along Christological lines. For common grace is then itself conceived of along Christological lines. All men have not only the ability to know but actually know the truth. This is so even in the case of those who do not know all the truth that they would need to know in order to be saved. All men know that God exists and is their judge. Secondly, all men have become sinners through Adam's fall. All men therefore suppress the truth that they know. This suppression is perfect in principle. It is due to hatred of God; it is due to deadness in sin. Sinners use the principle of Chance back of all things and the idea of exhaustive rationalization as the legitimate aim of science. If the universe were actually what these men assume it to be according to their principle, there would be no science. Science is possible and actual only because the non-believer's principle is not true and the believer's principle is true. Only because God has created the universe and does control it by his providence, is there such a thing as science at all. Thus the unity of science cannot be built on "common notions" that are common between believers and non-believers because their difference in principle has not been taken into consideration. Common grace is not a gift of God whereby his own challenge to repentance unto men who have sinned against him is temporarily being blurred.

Common grace must rather serve the challenge of God to men to repentance. It must be a tool by means of which the believer as the servant of Christ can challenge the unbeliever to repentance. Believers can objectively show to unbelievers that unity of science can be attained only on the Christian theistic basis. It is the idea of God's controlling whatsoever comes to pass that forms the foundation of science. And no one can or does believe that idea unless by the sovereign grace of God through Christ he has repented from his sin. Thus it is Christianity that furnishes the basis of the structure of science.

MASSELINK'S TWILIGHT ZONE [40]

In his book *General Revelation and Common Grace*,[41] Dr. William Masselink, formerly of the Reformed Bible Institute at Grand Rapids, Michigan, takes exception to the position of the present writer. . . . The question hinges largely

40. An excerpt from *Christian Theory of Knowledge*, 21–22.
41. William Masselink, *General Revelation and Common Grace* (Grand Rapids: Eerdmans, 1953).

on the problem of the value of the knowledge of the non-Christian. Masselink's contention is that, on the basis of the position taken by this writer, no value can be assigned to the knowledge of the unbeliever at all. This, he argues, is against the Reformed confessions. For these confessions speak of the natural light of reason by which men, though they are sinners against God, yet have natural knowledge of God and morality. In particular, God has, by his "common grace," not only restrained the sin of man but maintained the image of God in him. He thus enables him to make contributions to science and to practice "moral virtue."

In dealing with this contention an attempt will be made to show that the doctrine of general revelation and of common grace must not be taken as justifying a neutral area between the non-Christian and the Christian. There is no escape from taking it as such unless, with Calvin, appeal is made to the knowledge of God which the natural man inescapably has (Rom. 1:19, 1:20, and 2:14), but which he seeks to, but cannot wholly, suppress (Rom. 1:18).

As far as the principle of interpretation is concerned, the natural man makes himself the final point of reference. So far, then, as he carries through his principle, he interprets all things without God. In *principle* he is hostile to God. But he cannot carry through his principle completely. He is restrained by God from doing so. Being restrained by God from doing so, he is enabled to make contributions to the edifice of human knowledge. The forces of creative power implanted in him are to some extent released by God's common grace. *He therefore makes positive contributions to science in spite of his principles and because both he and the universe are the exact opposite of what he, by his principles, thinks they are.*

As against this method of approaching the question of the knowledge of the non-Christian, Masselink argues, with the late Dr. Valentine Hepp of Amsterdam, that there are *central* truths about God, man, and the world on which Christians and non-Christians do not greatly differ. That is to say, Masselink, following Hepp, does not signalize, first, the difference between the two principles of interpretation, the one based on the assumption that man is the creature of God. Common grace, is, in effect, used to blur the differences between these two mutually exclusive principles. There is supposed, then, to be some area where the difference between these two mutually exclusive principles does not very greatly count. There is a "twilight zone" where those who are enemies fraternize and build together on the common enterprise of science; there is an area of commonness without difference, or at least without basic difference. It is the contention of this writer that in this manner the doctrine of common grace becomes a means by which a specifically Reformed conception of apologetics, and therefore a consistently Christian method of apologetics, is suppressed.

COOPERATION BETWEEN ADVOCATES OF CONFLICTING WORLDVIEWS [42]

It should be remembered in this connection that when we say that all nontheistic thought ends in Babylonian confusion, this conclusion is not contradicted by the obvious fact that there are sciences, and that there is philosophy in history, and that there is communication of thought on all these subjects. We grant that all these things are there *after a fashion*. We maintain, however, and this is in entire harmony with the whole theistic position, that all these things as they are and as far as they are what they ought to be, exist by the common grace of God which has not allowed matters to work themselves out to their logical conclusion on this earth. For this reason, it is entirely consistent for a Christian to take the position that we have taken with respect to the more fundamental question of the relation of the two mutually exclusive life and world views, and at the same time be interested in and cooperate with scientists and historians who are opposed to the theistic system by virtue of their presuppositions.

The biblical analogy that serves our purpose here is that of Solomon hiring foreign help for the building of the temple. In the case of the Samaritans who wished to help the Jews rebuild the temple, it was the business of the true Jew to reject the offer. In the case of the Phoenicians, it was the privilege and the duty of the true Jew to accept the service. The difference is simply that in the case of the Samaritans there was an effort to have a voice in the interpretation of the plans of God for his temple. On the other hand, in the case of the Phoenicians there was no such attempt. There it was no more than a case of skilled workmanship. And skilled workmanship is often, by God's common grace, found more abundantly in the camp of the antitheists than in the camp of the theists.

COMMON GRACE LEADS NOT TO NATURAL THEOLOGY BUT TO A CALL FOR REPENTANCE [43]

But there is another side to the story. If we are to witness to the God of Scripture we cannot afford to deny common grace. For, as noted, common grace

42. An excerpt from *A Survey of Christian Epistemology*, In Defense of the Faith, vol. 2 (Philadelphia: Presbyterian and Reformed, 1969), 217–18.
43. An excerpt from *Common Grace*, 142–45.

is an element of the general responsibility of man, a part of the picture in which God, the God of unmerited favor, meets man everywhere. But neither can we afford to construct a theory in which it is implicitly allowed that the natural man, in terms of his adopted principles, can truly interpret any aspect of history. For the natural man seeks to interpret all the facts of this world immanentistically. He seeks for meaning in the facts of this world without regarding these facts as carrying in them the revelation and therewith the claims of God. He seeks to determine what can and cannot be, what is or is not possible, by the reach of human logic resting on man himself as its foundation.

Now surely, you say, no Reformed person would have any commerce with any such view as that. Well, I do not think that any Reformed person purposely adopts such a view. But we know how the Roman Catholic conception of natural theology did creep into the thinking of Reformed theologians in the past. And the essence of this natural theology is that it attributes to the natural man the power of interpreting some aspect of the world without basic error. Even though men do not recognize God as the Creator and controller of the facts of this world, they are assumed to be able to give as true an interpretation of the laws of nature as it is possible for finite man to give. It is admitted that man as a religious being needs additional information besides what he learns by means of his own research. But this fact itself indicates that on this basis the knowledge of God about salvation has no bearing upon the realm of nature. The realm of nature is said to be correctly interpreted by the natural man.

On this basis it is quite possible for Christians to join with non-Christians in the scientific enterprise without witnessing to them of God. The Christians and non-Christians have, on this basis, a certain area of interpretation in common. They have *common ideas* in the sense that they agree on certain meanings without any difference. It is not merely that they are together confronted with the natural revelation of God. It is not merely that men are, all of them together, made in the image of God. It is not merely that they have in them the ineradicable sense of deity so that God speaks to them by means of their own constitution. It is not merely that, as Kuyper stressed, all men have to think according to the rules of logic according to which alone the human mind can function. It is not merely that all men can weigh and make many scientific discoveries.

All these things are true and important to maintain. But it is when in addition to these it is said that there are *common notions*, common *reactions*, about God and man and the world to all this speech of God, on which there is no basic difference between Christians and non-Christians, that natural theology is confused with natural revelation. And it is allowed that those who assume that the facts of this world are come from chance and those who presuppose that the facts of this world are created and controlled by God, have essentially the same interpretation of these facts. Thus the Christian and the non-Christian scientist could work together in the laboratory for days, for weeks and years and the Christian would have no other witness to give to his friend than to invite him to the prayer meeting or the Sunday service. . . .

Thus the Christian working in the laboratory is confronted with the necessity of leaving the laboratory, giving it over entirely to the unbeliever or witnessing to the fact that only if Christianity is true is science possible and meaningful.

Are we then to fail to witness for our God in the field of science? Is it only because the unbeliever has never been confronted with the full implication of Christianity for the field of science that he tolerates us in his presence still? And are we to have a theory of common grace that prohibits us from setting forth the witness of God before all men everywhere? Is not the Christ to be set forth in His cosmic significance by us after all? Is it not true that there could be no science if the world and all that is therein is controlled by chance? Is it not true that the non-Christian does his work by the common grace of God? A theory of common grace based on a natural theology is destructive of all grace, common or special.

Surely the witness to the God of the Scriptures must be presented everywhere. It must be, to be sure, presented with wisdom and with tact. But it must be presented. It is not presented, however, if we grant that God the Holy Spirit in a general testimony to all men approves of interpretations of this world or of aspects of this world which ignore Him and set Him at naught.

The non-Christian scientist must be told that he is dealing with facts that belong to God. He must be told this, not merely in the interest of religion in the narrower sense of the term. He must be told this in the interest of science too, and of culture in general. He must be told that there would be no facts distinguishable from one another unless God had made them and made them thus. He must be told that no hypothesis would have any relevance or bearing on these same facts, except for the providence of God. He must be told that his own mind, with its principles of order, depends upon his being made in the image of God. And then he must be told that if it were not for God's common grace he would go the full length of the principle of evil within him. He would finish iniquity and produce only war. His very acts of courtesy and kindness, his deeds of generosity, all his moral good is not to be explained, therefore, in terms of himself and the goodness of his nature but from God's enabling him to do these things in spite of his sinful nature. "Will you not then repent in order to serve and worship the Creator more than the creature?"

6.4 Intellectual Affinity and Rapport

We have just taken note of the fact that the common (restraining) grace of God keeps unbelievers from pursuing as radically as they might like their moral rebellion and intellectual opposition to God and His revelation. We can add to this salient truth another apologetically significant observation about the unbeliever. The unbeliever remains a person created in the image of God, even while he is doing everything he can, ethically and intellectually, to destroy that image or escape from it. The unbeliever is not what he pretends to be (uncreated, autonomous, etc.). Because Van Til drew the distinction between understanding the unbeliever *epistemologically* (according to his professed theories) and understanding him *psychologically* (according to what really goes on within him), he had a ready explanation for why the antithesis between the worldview of the non-Christian and the worldview of the Christian does not—indeed, could not—destroy the possibility of the two understanding each other in an argument.

If pressed to utter consistency, the unbeliever's theories of reality, knowledge, and ethics would render meaning, logic, science, absolutes, and personality incoherent and unintelligible. In that case, *in principle* the unbeliever could not think rationally or speak cogently about anything, much less about such ultimate issues as God, man's place in the cosmos, and how we should live. Moreover, if the unbeliever were to carry out to the extreme his professed metaphysical, epistemological, and ethical convictions, the antithesis between him and the believer would keep the two from communicating with each other since their fundamental perspectives would be completely different; the one's orientation would always be disoriented to the other. But the unbeliever does not actually live and reason entirely consistently with his professed theories. He thinks (psychologically) in a particular way that does not comport (epistemologically) with his argumentation.[44]

44. It is likewise true that believers do not in actual practice live and reason in perfect harmony or consistency with their professed theology (or, even more, the full truth of God's revealed word). Accordingly (but sadly), because we lack full sanctification, all believers will at times go along with behavior and opinions of the unbeliever that we should self-consciously resist.

The rationale for this distinction and observation should be obvious. A person's theories and beliefs are about the state of affairs (reality), but they do not control or determine the nature of reality. A man may have a very sophisticated argument (in theory) that air does not exist, but he still (in reality) breathes air while he is arguing. Another man may refuse to believe that he has cancer, but the actual disease can still destroy his body. Likewise, the unbeliever may argue at length that God does not exist and that man is not a creature responsible to his Maker, but none of that argumentation and mental gymnastics does anything to determine (or change) the actual state of affairs. He remains the image of God, being both able and responsible to think God's thoughts after Him. Whenever he discovers, reflects upon, or communicates the truth, he is in fact thinking God's thoughts as God's created image.

Because men are always—*qua* men—the image of God, and because they psychologically think and reason in terms of that image (with concomitant natural abilities), even when their epistemological arguments repudiate those realities, the unbeliever can still understand and communicate with believers who affirm them. There is always an intellectual affinity between believers and unbelievers just because they are both made in God's image. Unbelievers are guilty of making errors in their philosophical systems, even as they are guilty of outright rebellion against God in their moral conduct. Thus, we might expect their philosophical antagonism to raise an insurmountable obstacle to finding any kind of rapport with our reasoning as believers. However, unbelievers never escape knowing the God whom they deny or ignore—indeed, they know God to some extent just in knowing themselves. And they never escape reasoning in terms of this awareness of God, to the degree that they reason at all.

The unbeliever to whom you are defending the faith may never *outwardly* express a philosophical sympathy for what you are saying or arguing (although occasionally one does), since his theories do not permit such sympathy, and yet *inwardly* ("psychologically") he can understand what you are saying and in his "heart of hearts" he involuntarily concurs with it. The believer and the unbeliever are not on different intellectual wavelengths; rather, the unbeliever wants to garble and block the "wavelength" that brings home to his conscience the truth of God's word. But he was made by God precisely to receive and acknowledge that cognitive signal, whether it comes to him directly through divine revelation in nature or Scripture, or indirectly through the testimony and argument of the Christian. The message cannot fail to get through, even when the unbeliever speaks to himself or others about it. God has created him to be His own rational and moral image, and He maintains or preserves the unbeliever's status as such. The unbeliever cannot change who he actually is, certainly not by verbalizing theories contrary to it.

AN EVER PRESENT POINT OF CONTACT [45]

What point of contact is there in the mind and heart of the unbeliever to which the believer may appeal when he presents to him the Christian view of life? . . .

It is to this sense of deity, even this knowledge of God, which, Paul tells us (Romans 1:19–20) every man has, but which, as Paul also tells us, every sinner seeks to suppress, that the Christian apologetic must appeal. . . .

The apostle Paul speaks of the natural man as actually possessing the knowledge of God (Rom. 1:19–21). The greatness of his sin lies precisely in the fact that "when they knew God, they glorified him not as God." No man can escape knowing God. It is indelibly involved in his awareness of anything whatsoever. Man *ought*, therefore, as Calvin puts it, to recognize God. There is no excuse for him if he does not. The reason for his failure to recognize God lies exclusively in him. It is due to his willful transgression of the very law of his being. . . .

Of course, when we thus stress Paul's teaching that all men do not have a mere capacity for but are in actual possession of the knowledge of God, we have at once to add Paul's further instruction to the effect that all men, due to the sin within them, always and in all relationships seek to "suppress" this knowledge of God (Rom. 1:18, *American Standard Version*). The natural man is such a one as constantly throws water on a fire he cannot quench. He has yielded to the temptation of Satan, and has become his bondservant. When Satan tempted Adam and Eve in paradise he sought to make them believe that man's self-consciousness was ultimate rather than derivative and God-dependent. He argued, as it were, that it was of the nature of self-consciousness to make itself the final reference point of all predication. [46] . . .

It is not to be wondered at that neither Romanism nor Evangelicalism has

---

45. Excerpts from *Defense of the Faith*, 84, 102, 109, 110–12, 257, 266.
46. That is, the unbeliever reasons that in the very nature of his self-consciousness as a rational agent he must be intellectually self-sufficient and the one who determines what he will believe. In both his inner reasoning and his outward communication (in all predication), he must presuppose his own autonomy (making himself the final reference point).

much interest in challenging the "philosophers" when these, as Calvin says, interpret man's consciousness without being aware of the tremendous difference in man's attitude toward the truth before and after the fall. *Accordingly they do not distinguish carefully between the natural man's own conception of himself and the Biblical conception of him.*[47] Yet for the question of the point of contact this is all-important. If we make our appeal to the natural man without being aware of this distinction we virtually admit that the natural man's estimate of himself is correct. We may, to be sure, even then, maintain that he is in need of information. We may even admit that he is morally corrupt. But the one thing which, on this basis, we cannot admit, is that his claim to be able to interpret at least some area of experience in a way that is essentially correct, is mistaken. We cannot then challenge his most basic epistemological assumption to the effect that his self-consciousness and time-consciousness are self-explanatory. We cannot challenge his right to interpret all his experience in exclusively immanentistic categories. And on this everything hinges. For if we first allow the legitimacy of the natural man's assumption of himself as the ultimate reference point in interpretation in any dimension we cannot deny his right to interpret Christianity itself in naturalistic terms.

The point of contact for the gospel, then, must be sought within the natural man. Deep down in his mind every man knows that he is the creature of God and responsible to God. Every man, at bottom, knows that he is a covenant-breaker. But every man acts and talks as though this were not so. It is the one point that cannot bear mentioning in his presence. A man may have internal cancer. Yet it may be the one point he will not have one speak of in his presence. He will grant that he is not feeling well. He will accept any sort of medication so long as it does not pretend to be given in answer to a cancer diagnosis. Will a good doctor cater to him on this matter? Certainly not. He will tell his patient that he has promise of life, but promise of life on one condition, that is, of an immediate internal operation. So it is with the sinner. He is alive but alive as a covenant-breaker. But his own interpretative activity with respect to all things proceeds on the assumption that such is not the case. Romanism and Evangelicalism, by failing to appeal exclusively to that

---

47. Emphasis added. This observation is important, especially if we would resolve the paradox that those who do not believe in God are actually believers in Him nonetheless. The unbeliever's *self-conception* is that of an unbeliever, and so he acts in ways that evidence unbelief, and we talk about him as an unbeliever. But in fact—according to the *biblical* conception of him—he really does psychologically believe in God; there is evidence of this in his actions as well. The psychological situation of the unbeliever is extremely complex (and in tension).

which is within man but is also suppressed by every man, virtually allow the legitimacy of the natural man's view of himself.[48] They do not seek to explode the last stronghold to which the natural man always flees and where he always makes his final stand. They cut off the weeds at the surface but do not dig up the roots[49] of these weeds, for fear that crops will not grow.

The truly Biblical view, on the other hand, applies atomic power and flame-throwers to the very presupposition of the natural man's ideas with respect to himself. It does not fear to lose a point of contact by uprooting the weeds rather than by cutting them off at the very surface. It is assured of a point of contact in the fact that every man is made in the image of God and has impressed upon him the law of God. In that fact alone he may rest secure with respect to the point of contact problem.[50] For that fact makes men always accessible to God. That fact assures us that every man, to be a man at all, must already be in contact with the truth. He is so much in contact with the truth that much of his energy is spent in the vain effort to hide this fact from himself.[51] His efforts to hide this fact from himself are bound to be self-frustrative.[52]

Only by thus finding the point of contact in man's sense of deity that lies

48. Van Til criticized the traditional method of doing apologetics as it is found in Roman Catholic and Arminian circles. For them, an epistemological "point of contact" can be found with the unbeliever—that is, found in some element of the worldview or philosophical theory espoused by the unbeliever. To allow for this, Romanists and Arminians must accept that the unbeliever's self-conception is not basically wrong, and that he can autonomously interpret some areas of human experience in a way that is essentially correct. But then, as Van Til noted, the apologist can no longer challenge the rationality of interpreting reality in exclusively immanentistic categories. By allowing for epistemological common ground, Romanist and Arminian apologetics concede the legitimacy of the natural man's view of himself. Refusing to do that, the presuppositionalist appeals, instead, "exclusively to that which is within man but is also suppressed"—that is, only to what is psychologically and actually the case about the unbeliever: his being made in the image of God and in possession of a knowledge of God.

49. Not to "dig up the roots" is not to challenge the presuppositions of the unbeliever's thinking and reasoning about anything whatsoever (and not just about religion or God).

50. CVT: Here, as throughout this chapter, it appears that I do not start my analysis of the knowledge of the natural man from the "absolute ethical antithesis" as Masselink contends, but from the sense of deity in the way Calvin does.

51. Cf. "The lady doth protest too much, methinks" (Shakespeare, *Hamlet*, act 3, sc. 2, line 242).

52. One must understand this observation if one is to understand Van Til's presuppositional apologetic. Men work hard to hide from themselves the fact that they are the creatures of God, responsible to think His thoughts after Him; instead, they pretend to be autonomous. However, presuppositionalism does not allow that men are successful in their intellectual rebellion against God. Their efforts must in the nature of the case "frustrate themselves." The very ability to reason cogently or meaningfully requires that God exist and man be made as His image,

underneath his own conception of self-consciousness as ultimate can we be both true to Scripture and effective in reasoning with the natural man. . . .

With Calvin I find the point of contact for the presentation of the gospel to non-Christians in the fact that they are made in the image of God and as such have the ineradicable sense of deity within them. Their own consciousness is inherently and exclusively revelational of God to themselves. No man can help knowing God for in knowing himself he knows God. His self-consciousness is totally devoid of content unless, as Calvin puts it at the beginning of his *Institutes*, man knows himself as a creature before God. There are "no atheistic men because no man can deny the revelational activity of the true God within him" (*Common Grace*, p. 55). Man's own interpretative activity, whether of the more or less extended type, whether in ratiocination or intuition, is no doubt the most penetrating means by which the Holy Spirit presses the claims of God upon man" (*Idem*, p. 62).[53] Even man's negative ethical reaction to God's revelation within his own psychological confusion is revelational of God. His conscience troubles him when he disobeys; he knows deep down in his heart that he is disobeying his Creator. There is no escape from God for any human being. Every human being is by virtue of his being made in the image of God accessible to God. And as such he is accessible to one [the apologist] who without compromise presses upon him the claims of God. . . .

One then makes the claims of God upon men without apologies though always *suaviter in modo*. One knows that there is hidden underneath the surface display of every man a sense of deity. One therefore gives that sense of deity an opportunity to rise in rebellion against the oppression under which it suffers by the new man of the covenant breaker.[54] One makes no deal with this new man. One shows that on his assumptions all things are meaningless.

---

and therefore all meaningful or cogent argumentation against these truths can only defeat itself. The pretended autonomous man strives to be what he can never be. This is precisely the point at which the apologist directs the thrust of his argument. It is every person's vulnerable spot, intellectually speaking.

53. It was Van Til's contention that the transcendental challenge to the cogency or intelligibility of autonomous reasoning (interpretation, predication, communication, etc.) was the most philosophically devastating and biblically warranted argument that the apologist could use in answering unbelief. If this form of argument is most faithful to the Christian faith, both rationally and revelationally, then the apologetical analysis of man's interpretative activity (asking about its necessary presuppositions) would be "no doubt the most penetrating means by which the Holy Spirit presses the claims of God upon man"—for the Spirit works through the word, not through the independent "wisdom of men" (cf. 1 Cor. 2:4–5).

54. Van Til here uses, ironically, the figure of the "new man" for the unbeliever. The unbeliever's "old man" was man as God created him, a covenant-keeping man

6.5 Unbelievers Suppress the Truth, and Thus Work with Two Mind-Sets

As we have seen in this chapter, when Van Til spoke of the antithesis between the thinking of the believer and the thinking of the unbeliever, and when he spoke of the inability of the unbeliever to know anything in terms of his espoused presuppositions, he was speaking of the unbeliever *epistemologically*—that is, speaking in principle, about systems of thought and their self-conscious implications. When Van Til spoke of the unbeliever inescapably knowing God and knowing things about His world, when he spoke of common grace making co-operation possible between the believer and the unbeliever, and when he spoke of common ground between the two or of the point of contact that the believer always has with the unbeliever, he was speaking of the unbeliever *psychologically*—that is, speaking about the actual (though unadmitted) inner thoughts and practices of the person who wants to (but cannot) escape from his awareness of God and the authority of God over him. It is necessary to draw this distinction between speaking of the unbeliever's knowledge and reasoning psychologically and speaking of it epistemologically because, according to the diagnosis of God's unfailing word, the natural man "suppresses the truth by means of unrighteousness" (Rom. 1:18).

To say that the unbeliever suppresses the truth is to say both that he possesses it and that he suppresses it. On the one hand, the unbeliever has a measure of truth about God (His nature and character, His moral demands, etc.), understands this truth, and believes it. He cannot change the fact that he is the image of God, nor can he block out the revelation of God (with its clarity and compelling power). And because of the common restraint of the Spirit, he cannot successfully work out his pretended autonomy from God. He is a possessor of the truth and psychologically knows God. On the other hand, the unbeliever wants to be his own authority, hates and fears God, carries a grudge against his Maker, and thus approaches everything in his experience and in his reasoning "with an ax to grind" against God. Therefore, he now becomes a suppressor of the truth,

---

who would submit his thoughts and actions to the authority of God's word and seek to glorify His Creator. This is now suppressed by the sinful, fallen nature, which has become his "new man." Van Til urged apologists to reason with the "old man" who psychologically knows God, but never to make any intellectual deals with the epistemological reasoning and claims of the covenant-breaking "new man."

epistemologically developing and intellectually professing[55] systems of philosophy or interpretations of the world and of life that will facilitate and exhibit his resistance to what he knows about God. The unregenerate man suppresses the truth of God's revelation, not only as it comes to him through the natural order, but also as it comes to him through the gospel. According to Van Til, Scripture carries self-attesting authority and power (proof within itself), but the unbeliever does not wish to deal with the God who is revealed in it. Accordingly, he suppresses the message of Scripture, just as he suppresses the message of nature and conscience.

The two points that are implicit in the fact that non-Christians suppress the truth from and about God reinforce what we have seen above, namely, that the unbeliever is a very complicated, complex, and confusing person from a religious perspective.[56] He both possesses and suppresses the truth about God. Does the unbeliever then "know God"? Seeking to follow Scripture faithfully (cf. Rom. 1:21 with v. 28, or Ps. 19:2 and Acts 17:27–28 with 2 Thess. 1:8), Van Til realized that the answer to this question is both yes and no. "Deep down in his mind every man knows that he is the creature of God and responsible to God. . . . But every man acts and talks as though this were not so."[57] Van Til could say that the unbeliever "sins against better knowledge,"[58] and that man knows God in an "original sense," even though he is spiritually blind. "He will not see things as he, in another sense, knows that they are."[59] As

55. We do not lose sight of the fact that unbelievers exhibit widely varying degrees of philosophical sophistication. Some systems of non-Christian thinking are much more well thought out, self-conscious, and sophisticated. Some non-Christians make little effort to reflect on their convictions, think through their beliefs consistently, or seek a warrant for them. Some people would be surprised to be told that they have a philosophy of life at all. Nevertheless, even if it is only implicit in their comments and actions, all unbelievers have beliefs about the nature of reality, how we know what we know, and how we ought to behave. It will often be the task of the apologist to help an unbeliever become more self-conscious about his convictions—and the kind of system of thought they (ideally) represent.

56. Compare here the apparently purposeful ambiguity in Paul's word to the Areopagus council, describing the men of Athens as being in all things *deisidaimon-esterous:* both (positively speaking) "religious" and (negatively speaking) "excessively superstitious" (Acts 17:22). Their "piety" was at the same time an exhibition of "ignorance" (v. 23). Cf. Greg L. Bahnsen, "The Encounter of Jerusalem with Athens," *Ashland Theological Bulletin* 13 (Spring 1980): 4–40.

57. *Defense of the Faith,* 111.

58. Ibid., 100.

59. *Christian Theory of Knowledge,* 46. It is important to notice the willfulness of the unbeliever in not seeing things as he (actually) sees them—the purposeful

we explained above (in chapter 4.2), to know something is (among other things) to believe it, and consequently the paradox that the non-Christian both knows and yet does not know God can also be stated in terms of faith or belief. To put it bluntly, unbelievers are in some sense believers! Van Til wrote:

> To be sure, all men have faith. Unbelievers have faith as well as believers. But that is due to the fact that they too are creatures of God. Faith therefore always has content. It is against the content of faith as belief in God that man has become an unbeliever. As such he tries to suppress the content of his original faith. . . . [W]hen this faith turns into unbelief this unbelief cannot succeed in suppressing fully the original faith in God. Man as man is inherently and inescapably a believer in God. Thus he can contribute to true knowledge in the universe.[60]

There is no question that Scripture teaches this complex view of the unbeliever. He does not know God, being an unbeliever who repudiates the truth of God's revelation; nevertheless, he does in fact know God very well—well enough to be responsible for his rebellion and under God's condemnation. He believes the truth revealed by God, and yet he is an unbeliever. How can these scriptural truths, appropriated by Van Til's presuppositional apologetic, be reconciled? They appear to be contradictory.

Because both sides of this complex situation are biblically based, Van Til is to be commended for incorporating them into the heart of his apologetic. He recognized that the non-Christian *does not* believe or know God and needs a clear testimony to the gospel and a rigorous defense of the faith; at the same time, he realized that the non-Christian *does* clearly believe and know God, which alone can intelli-

---

skewing or distorting of the way he looks at things. His epistemology is controlled by his sinful reaction against God and God's revelation.

60. *Defense of the Faith*, 385, 386. The "faith" that all men have in common pertains to the content of natural revelation; the unbeliever is thus said to "believe" that God exists as Creator and providential controller of all things, that He has a particular nature (all-powerful, all-knowing, etc.), and that His holy character requires righteousness of men. Van Til did not mean that unbelievers are underneath it all really believers in the gospel, trusting Jesus Christ as their Savior. Even when unbelievers are aware that the gospel is true, they are not, in Van Til's outlook, secretly saved (without their being aware of it). Quite the contrary. They are more fully subject to the wrath of God (for not acknowledging the gospel as true).

gibly account for his knowing anything else. Nevertheless, Van Til admitted that the paradoxical character of the unbeliever's knowledge and belief was difficult to understand. He once called Romans 1:18–21 "this most difficult passage."[61] And when declaring that sin affects man's intellectual reasoning, and yet that unbelievers are able to know many things, Van Til observed:

> We need to recognize this complexity, and to see the problem it involves. . . . [T]here is a sense in which we can and must allow for the value of the knowledge of non-Christians. *This has always been a difficult point.* It is often the one great source of confusion on the question of faith in its relation to reason. We should admit that we cannot give any wholly satisfactory account of the situation as it actually obtains.[62]

Those who are antagonistic to presuppositional apologetics would readily criticize this fundamental point, realized Van Til:

> It is ambiguous or meaningless, says the Arminian, to talk about the natural man as knowing God and yet not truly knowing God. Knowing is knowing. A man either knows or he does not know. He may know less or more, but if he does not "truly" know, he knows not at all.[63]

Van Til did not for a moment consider this to be a genuine contradiction, and thus he did what he could to draw some kind of distinction that would adequately explicate the difference between the two different senses of "knowing."

Van Til indicated that some kind of distinction was called for when he spoke of the unbeliever knowing God: "Non-Christians know *after a*

---

61. Ibid., 93.
62. *Introduction to Systematic Theology*, 25, 26 (emphasis added). Because people often think that autonomous reason is able to make things intelligible, they wrestle with how to relate, incorporate, or integrate with reason the truths that are believed by faith. In terms of presuppositional apologetics, however, all men have faith in God (with respect to the truths of natural revelation), and only in terms of that can man's reasoning be intelligible. Thus, faith is not added to the foundation of reason; rather, reason operates upon and requires the foundation of faith. The unbeliever is able to gain knowledge because, in an important sense, he is yet a believer. Cf. Greg L. Bahnsen, "The Problem of Faith," *Biblical Worldview* 8, no. 5 (May 1992): 10–12; no. 6 (June 1992): 9–12, and my taped radio dialogue with George H. Smith, author of *Atheism: The Case Against God* (Buffalo: Prometheus, 1979).
63. *Defense of the Faith*, 363–64.

fashion, as Paul tells us in Romans," and "there is *a sense in which* all men have faith and all men know God. All contribute to science."[64] Van Til recognized that the knowledge of God needed to be understood in two related but distinct ways, as he explained in this passage:

> True, as noted above, Paul says that man knows God and that he recognizes, in a sense, the difference between right and wrong. But when Paul speaks of the natural or fallen man as knowing God and as knowing and even in a sense doing good, he is not speaking of that knowledge which is according to truth, that knowledge which man needs in order to be what God at the first made him to be. *There are two senses to the word "knowledge" used in Scripture.* There is the sense in which Paul uses it when he says that men by virtue of their creation by God in his image have knowledge of God. They cannot at any point of their interest succeed in escaping from the face of God. Their sin is always sin against better knowledge.
>
> This point is of the utmost importance for Christian apologetics. It alone offers a point of contact with the mind and heart of natural man. For the moment it may suffice to stress the fact that the Bible itself would come to man in a vacuum and its whole claim would be without meaning except for the assumption that all the facts of the universe, including man himself, are revelational of God. The revelation of grace comes to those who have sinned against the revelation that came to man previous to his need for grace. Men could not have sinned in a vacuum. The very idea of sin is sin against the revelation of God.
>
> Though it is of the greatest possible importance to keep in mind that man knows God in this original sense, it is of equally great importance to remember that he is now, since the fall, a sinner without *true* knowledge of God. He is spiritually blind. He will not see things as he, in another sense, knows that they are. He hates to see them that way because if he admits that they are what they really are, then he therewith condemns himself as a covenant-breaker. He therefore cannot see the truth till he at the same time repents.[65]

"True" or genuine knowledge of God is that knowledge which accompanies repentance and which is necessary for a man to become

64. Ibid., 66, 388 (emphasis added).
65. *Christian Theory of Knowledge*, 45–46 (emphasis added).

what God originally made men to be; it loves and submits to the truth, openly professes it, and seeks to live consistently with it, thus bringing God's blessing. The other kind of knowledge is an awful awareness of the truth about God that no man can successfully escape; it hates this truth and willfully chooses not to see things in terms of it, will not profess it, and refuses to live consistently with it, thereby calling for divine condemnation.

Thinking in these terms, Van Til was able to assert simultaneously that unbelievers "know" God (hatefully, in condemnation), and yet do "not know" Him (lovingly, in blessing); that is, there is damning faith, as well as saving faith. Van Til drew the same distinction with respect to how men know God when he wrote, "The natural man does not know God. But to be thus without knowledge, without living, loving, true knowledge of God, he must be one who knows God in the sense of having the sense of deity (Romans 1)."[66] Likewise: "The gospel of God's grace to sinners comes to creatures who know God but who have rebelled against God and therefore *do not know God lovingly.*"[67] The sinner has a sense of deity that condemns him, but he does not have the "living, loving, true knowledge of God" that brings salvation. This explanation is insightful and helpful to a point, even though it does not resolve all the problems.[68]

At some points Van Til explained the conundrum of the unbeliever knowing and yet not knowing God in terms of a popular psychological model of "subconscious" motives or drives.[69] He spoke of the nat-

---

66. *Defense of the Faith*, 364.
67. *Christian Theory of Knowledge*, 227 (emphasis added).
68. It does not explicate the knowledge of God that believers and unbelievers have in common, but provides insight into the different ways in which believers and unbelievers *respond to* that common knowledge. (It is beneficial to look upon knowing God in a covenantal fashion, namely, as something which, though called the same thing, brings either blessing or curse.) Believers and unbelievers do not share the knowledge of God in condemnation, for believers are not condemned. Nor do they share the knowledge of God in salvation, for unbelievers are not saved. To some extent, the unregenerate man has the same knowledge as the regenerate man, but he suppresses it. That is, he reacts to it much differently than the believer. Scripture does not seem to treat the suppression of the truth *as* knowing God, but rather treats it as something done *to* that knowledge.
69. We do not speak of "subconscious awareness" of the truth, for that would be nonsensical—amounting to "subconscious consciousness." However, if subconscious drives are not a matter of some intellectual awareness or "way of seeing" things, how could they personally motivate or activate behavior? We seem to be left with impersonal biological or physical forces that propel or constrain involuntary action (like breathing or heart beating). And yet that conception would be contrary to the theoretical framework within which "subconscious" forces are hypothe-

ural man's knowledge of God as being "beneath the threshold of his working consciousness"—that is, "deep down in" his mind or heart, where he borrows Christian ideas "without recognizing it."[70] But this explanation is not altogether satisfactory, either. In the first place, Van Til himself was wary of the distinction it employs: "We should, however, be on our guard not to make too much of the distinction between unconscious (or preconscious) and self-conscious action."[71] Moreover, this kind of explanation seems to imply that the unbeliever is not conscious of his suppressing of God's revelation, and thus not morally responsible for doing it. Sinners are somehow conscious of the character of their rebellion. "What needs to be done then in presenting the Scriptures to the natural man is to appeal to his 'sense of deity,' to the fact that *in the very pentralia of his consciousness* he does always confront the same God who now asks him to yield obedience to Him."[72] Denying the truth of God and suppressing it unrighteously is something of a self-conscious act, according to Van Til, even if the lost are not in this life "*wholly* self-conscious of their own ethical hostility."[73] Another time Van Til put it this way:

> Again it must be borne in mind that when we say that fallen man knows God and suppresses that knowledge so that he, as it were, sins self-consciously, this too needs qualification. Taken as a generality and in view of the fact that all men were represented in Adam at the beginning of history, we must say that men sin against better knowledge and also self-consciously. But this is not to deny that when men are said to be without God in the world they are ignorant. . . . There is therefore a *gradation* between those who sin more and those who sin less self-consciously.[74]

sized, and it would place the action in question outside of personal responsibility, control, and moral assessment. The whole notion of the subconscious has come into disrepute in the philosophical analysis of psychology.

70. *Defense of the Faith*, 115, 111, 257, 325, 355.

71. *Introduction to Systematic Theology*, 90.

72. *Christian Theory of Knowledge*, 227 (emphasis added).

73. *Defense of the Faith*, 191 (emphasis added).

74. *Christian Theory of Knowledge*, 46 (emphasis added). In their moral and intellectual rebellion against the revealed truth of God, unbelievers differ from each other in the degree of self-conscious opposition. For Van Til, the factors that explain the variations would include their place within the unfolding of history (there being greater cognizance of, and greater willingness openly to pursue, the wickedness of sin as time goes on) and the extent of their education, especially in philosophical awareness or refinement (cf. *Defense of the Faith*, 99, where Van Til contrasts "the sophistications of the philosophers" to "the common sense of . . . the masses of men").

So we see, once again, how awkward it is to articulate the unbeliever's status, character, or mental conduct. But however we describe the situation, Van Til insisted that when the sinner reacts epistemologically improperly to the revelation of God, he does so "as an ethically responsible creature of God." He emphasized that "the Scriptures continue to hold man responsible for his blindness"—that "the reason for his failure to recognize God lies exclusively in him. It is due to his willful transgression."[75] The sinner's suppression of the truth about God is not an involuntary act of blinding oneself; rather, it is a matter of "culpable ignorance."[76]

Regardless of the difficulty that Van Til felt in conceptualizing the situation, the bits and pieces necessary for an adequate analysis of the unbeliever's suppression of the truth—knowing while not knowing God—can be found in Van Til's writings. For instance, he was quite right to describe unbelievers in this fashion: "Every man, at bottom, knows that he is a covenant-breaker. But every man *acts and talks as though* this were not so. . . . His conscience troubles him when he disobeys; he knows deep down in his heart that he is disobeying his Creator. . . . [Sinners] do not want to keep God in remembrance. They keep under the knowledge of God that is within them. That is they try as best they can to keep under this knowledge *for fear* they should look into the face of their judge."[77] That is, the unbeliever's response to God's revelation is a deliberately self-serving or self-protecting effort to act out being what he desperately wants to be, an unbeliever. But he cannot admit to himself that he is purposely making such an effort. "He is so much in contact with the truth that much of his energy is spent in the vain effort to hide this fact from himself"—like a cancer patient who refuses to admit that he has it.[78] The unbeliever's desire and policy is to hide the dreaded truth from himself by rationalizing the evidence—as well as rationalizing his motivation for rationalizing the evidence—and thereby to convince himself that he does not believe what he believes. To put it simply, he deceives himself.[79] This is deception of the self, by the self, and for the sake of preserving one's self-conception. Recall this profound insight by Van Til that was noted earlier, namely, that we must "distin-

---

75. *Defense of the Faith*, 259, 306, 109.
76. *Survey of Christian Epistemology*, 4.
77. *Defense of the Faith*, 111, 257, 259 (emphasis added).
78. Ibid., 111–12.
79. Cf. *Defense of the Faith*, 324 (emphasis added): "He lives in a stupor (Romans 11:8). To him the wisdom of God is foolishness. The truth about God, and about himself in relation to God, is obnoxious to him. He does not want to hear of it. He seeks to close eyes and ears to those who give witness of the truth. *He is, in short, utterly self-deceived.*"

guish carefully between the natural man's own conception of himself and the Biblical conception of him."[80]

With these elements of the complex situation at hand, we can adequately resolve the paradox of saying that the unbeliever believes or (by extension) that the man who does not know God knows God. We will take Sam as our hypothetical unbeliever. When we say that Sam does not believe in (or know) God, we are describing him according to certain features of his behavior and thinking: for example, his immoral conduct and attitudes, his refusal to glorify God, and especially his profession not to believe in God. After all, Sam acts and talks like a person who sincerely disbelieves; indeed, he argues vehemently against believing in God's existence. However, the fact of the matter is that Sam actually does believe in God. When we say that he believes in God, we are (in accordance with the diagnosis of God's word) describing him according to certain features of his behavior and thinking that manifest belief: for example, his living in terms of some kind of moral standards, his acceptance of the need for logical consistency, his expectation of uniformity in nature, his fear of death, and his assuming of freedom of thought.[81] As in the case of believers, we say that Sam knows God in the sense that he has justified, true beliefs about Him. So then, it turns out that Sam's belief in his own unbelief is mistaken. He rationalizes the evidence, motivated by his desire to avoid facing up to God, whose condemnation he fears and whose authority over him he resents. Nevertheless, he sincerely and constantly pursues unbelief as his self-deluded life's project.[82]

It thus appears that the unbeliever works with two different sets of fundamental beliefs or presuppositions, one acknowledged and one unacknowledged (or denied)—one which he makes his regulating ideal, and the other which makes it possible for him to know anything. He inescapably knows the truth (one set of beliefs) and yet suppresses it (endorsing a second set of beliefs). When the apologist speaks of the unbeliever's "presuppositions," then, he must keep in mind the difference between the presuppositions that the non-Christian es-

---

80. Ibid., 110.
81. In ascribing beliefs to a person, we often act on the reasonable policy that "actions speak louder than words." Sometimes a person's public behavior indicates beliefs that belie his quite sincere utterances to the contrary.
82. For further details and an explanation of this analysis of the unbeliever's suppression of the truth, see Greg L. Bahnsen, "The Crucial Concept of Self-Deception in Presuppositional Apologetics," *Westminster Theological Journal* 57 (1995): 1–31.

pouses epistemologically (those propounded in his argumentation against the faith) and the presuppositions that he employs psychologically in order to be intelligible (which are contrary to what he propounds). According to Van Til's analysis, the unbeliever operates with two conflicting mind-sets. As created by God in His image and confronting His inescapable revelation, the unbeliever sees the world in a particular way that enables him to gain knowledge and live a somewhat successful life; however, as a rebel against God who pretends to be autonomous, the unbeliever "puts on colored glasses" and sees the world in a different way, which, though popularly espoused, cannot consistently make sense of knowledge or make successful living possible. To change the metaphor, the unbeliever has intellectually "cooked the books." He operates in terms of presuppositions that accord with God's revelation, but in his philosophical accounts he represents himself as reasoning in terms of presuppositions that do not comport with the others. But in this case it is not the "cooked books" that are consistent and balanced, offering a true and reasonable account of his (intellectual) affairs, but rather the hidden ones (his suppressed presuppositions).

Van Til emphasized that unbelievers work from two sets of presuppositions (or two systems of thought). As he was quoted above, Van Til taught that the natural man is never fully consistent in this life.[83] The non-Christian will argue against the Christian faith, resting upon and propounding some kind of autonomous theory of knowledge and interpretation of experience, utilizing presuppositions that are antithetical to the Christian faith. And yet, said Van Til, "non-Christians are never able and therefore never do employ their own methods consistently. . . . The natural man does not thus self-consciously work from his principles."[84] Unbelievers talk in terms of one kind of philosophical system or set of presuppositions (and try to work within them), but "no man is actually fully consistent in working according to these assumptions."[85] If he were, he would destroy all meaning, logic, science, human personality, and morality. Still, the non-Christian "makes positive contributions to science in spite of his principles."[86] This is because he reasons and behaves in terms of a different kind of philosophical system or set of presuppositions, which expresses the truth about God (etc.), and he

---

83. *Introduction to Systematic Theology*, 27.
84. *Defense of the Faith*, 120, 193.
85. Ibid., 260.
86. *Christian Theory of Knowledge*, 22.

does so without acknowledging the fact or giving thanks to God for what the knowledge of Him makes possible. Non-Christians argue against the very Christian presuppositions that they utilize.

Van Til maintained that self-consciousness on the part of any man presupposes God-consciousness,[87] so that "even in his [the non-Christian's] virtual negation of God, he is still really presupposing God."[88] This is a startling realization, and one that is momentous for apologetics. The unbeliever is presupposing the revealed truth of God even when he is attempting to work out and apply contrary presuppositions in order to argue against God's truth. Van Til's pungent insight was precisely: "Antitheism presupposes theism."[89] In order to argue or reason at all, in order to have any intellectual achievements whatsoever, the unbeliever is unknowingly relying upon Christian presuppositions. As Van Til said, he is "borrowing, without recognizing it, the Christian ideas of creation and providence."[90] The upshot of this with regard to the natural man is that "there is a conflict of notions within him. But he himself is not fully and self-consciously aware of this conflict within him. . . . Thus the ideas with which he daily works do not proceed consistently either from the one principle [the knowledge of God] or from the other [human autonomy, which suppresses the knowledge of God]."[91]

It now appears that the complexity and confusion that characterize the unbeliever's knowledge of God are the result of an internal contradiction or tension in the unbeliever himself—one which he is unwilling to recognize or confess, lest his guilt before God become evident. He lives out of two conflicting frameworks of thought or two mind-sets. He works with two antagonistic sets of presuppositions, and that leaves him in a terrible personal and intellectual state of conflict. One set of presuppositions makes his reasoning, convictions, and commitments possible and intelligible; however, his reasoning, convictions, and commitments constitute a conflicting system of thought and presuppositions which would, if followed out consistently, destroy the intelligibility of his thinking and experience. The unbeliever is a living contradiction. "But herein exactly lies the contradiction of Satan's personality that though he knows God he yet does not really know God. His very intellect is constantly devising schemes by which he thinks he may over-

87. *Defense of the Faith*, 107, 257.
88. *Christian Theory of Knowledge*, 13.
89. *Survey of Christian Epistemology*, xii.
90. *Defense of the Faith*, 355.
91. Ibid., 190 (emphasis added).

throw God, while he knows all too well that God cannot be overthrown. . . . In like manner, too, man's thought since the entrance of sin has been characterized by self-frustration."[92]

Thus, in defending the faith to any particular unbeliever, the Christian must be aware that his opponent already believes in God, and indeed is borrowing the Christian's own beliefs in order to make sense of experience or to reason and argue at all. Nevertheless, this unbeliever will set forth conflicting beliefs and rest upon conflicting presuppositions in his argument with you as a believer, even though he continually exhibits a failure to be fully and epistemologically self-conscious of what he says and assumes. Non-Christians simply cannot employ their methods consistently—a fact that makes the presuppositional apologetical challenge decisive, clear-cut, and overpowering. Unbelievers cannot make sense of reasoning, meaning, science, ethical absolutes, self-consciousness, or mental freedom without resting upon the presuppositions of the Christian worldview. "Thus there is absolutely certain proof for the existence of God and the truth of Christian theism. Even non-Christians presuppose its truth while they verbally reject it. They need to presuppose the truth of Christian theism in order to account for their own accomplishments."[93]

POSSESSING YET SUPPRESSING THE TRUTH[94]

Accordingly Calvin argues that though mankind generally does not have the knowledge that comes from being "taught of God," men do have a knowledge that is created within them and inherited from Adam. It is the knowledge which they have as image bearers of God. Men generally seek to suppress this knowledge of God. They would gladly live where the searchlight of God's revelation does not constantly expose them to themselves. But there is no such place. This searchlight never ceases to shine. It shines particularly *within them*. There is no hiding from it. The knowledge of God is infixed in their being. . . .

Men in general are, therefore, truth *suppressors*. They are not those who are first of all *without* knowledge of the truth. They are indeed such, if one thinks of the knowledge that must come from Scripture. But they are first of all truth *possessors*, or truth-knowers, who have, by sinning, become truth

92. *Introduction to Systematic Theology*, 92.
93. *Defense of the Faith*, 120.
94. Excerpts from *The Reformed Pastor and Modern Thought* (Philadelphia: Presbyterian and Reformed, 1971), 16, 17, 32.

suppressors. Having taken to themselves the right to define the nature of God and of themselves, they have mingled the idea of their new god with that of the God they know by virtue of their creation. In their natural theology, that is, in what, as sinful men, they set forth as their view about God, they never state the truth without adulteration. They do not completely succeed in suppressing the truth, but they never assert the truth without an overwhelming admixture of error. The god of the philosophers is *never* their Creator and the Creator of the universe. He is always of necessity bound up with his creation. Hence sinful unregenerate men never worship the true God as they ought. In practice they do not know him because when they think of him they, of necessity, think falsely of him; they always degrade him to the level of the creature. . . .

To be sure, there is a sense in which it must be said that all men have all facts "in common." Saint and sinner alike are face to face with God and the universe of God. But the sinner is like the man with colored glasses on his nose. The Scriptures tell us that the facts speak plainly of God (Rom. 1:20; 2:14, 15). But all is yellow to the jaundiced eye. As the sinner speaks of the facts, he reports them to himself and others as "yellow." There are no exceptions to this. It is the facts as reported to himself by himself, as distorted by his own subjective condition, which he assumes to be *the facts as they really are.*

SUPPRESSION BY CHOICE, BUT UNSUCCESSFUL[95]

As I have followed Calvin closely in stressing the fact that men *ought* to believe in God inasmuch as the evidence for his existence is abundantly plain, so I have also closely followed Calvin in saying that no sinner reacts properly to God's revelation. Is this too sweeping a statement? It is simply the doctrine of total depravity. All sinners are covenant breakers. They have an axe to grind. They do not want to keep God in remembrance. They keep under the knowledge of God that is within them. That is they try as best they can to keep under this knowledge for fear they should look into the face of their judge. And since God's face appears in every fact of the universe they oppose God's revelation everywhere. They do not want to see the facts of nature for what they are; they do not want to see themselves for what they are. Therefore they assume the non-createdness of themselves and of the facts and the laws of nature round about them. Even though they make great protestations of serving God they yet serve and worship the creature more

95. Excerpts from *Defense of the Faith*, 259, 260, 308.

than the Creator. They try to make themselves believe that God and man are aspects of one universe. They interpret all things immanentistically. . . .

What then more particularly do I mean by saying that epistemologically the believer and the non-believer have nothing in common? I mean that every sinner looks through colored glasses. And these colored glasses are cemented to his face. He assumes that self-consciousness is intelligible without God-consciousness. He assumes that consciousness of facts is intelligible without consciousness of God. He assumes that consciousness of laws is intelligible without God. And he interprets all the facts and all the laws that are presented to him in terms of these assumptions. . . . I am now speaking of him as the covenant breaker. Neither do I forget that no man is actually fully consistent in working according to these assumptions. . . .

The Christian finds that his conscience agrees to the truth of the story. He holds that those who deny the truth of the story have an axe to grind. They do not want the story to be true; they do not want the facts to be what the story says they are. They "protest too much." And by protesting too much they testify, in spite of themselves, that their conscience does not tell them that the story is untrue. Their conscience tells them the reverse of what they say it does.

GOD'S REVELATION OF GRACE LIKEWISE SUPPRESSED [96]

The worst of men, says Calvin, cannot wholly efface from their memory the fact that from the beginning of history man has walked in the light of the revelation of God. Throughout history, since the fall of all men in Adam, men have tried to suppress and push aside the truth in unrighteousness. They have blinded their eyes and then complained that God has created them in darkness. They search with great diligence for the existence of a God, while they are walking every minute in the light of his presence. The natural theologian is like a child who daily and constantly sees his father in the father's home and yet who takes a lantern in order to search for him.

To be sure, the sinner needs new light as well as a new power of sight. He needs the light of the grace of God in Christ. If the water supply of a city is sufficient for the ordinary needs of its citizens, it none-the-less takes the fire hose to put out a conflagration started by mischievous hands. So the light of the grace of God in Christ as redemptive is given to those who have wilfully taken out their own eyes and are trying to blame their darkness on the God

---

96. An excerpt from *The Case for Calvinism* (Philadelphia: Presbyterian and Reformed, 1963), 108.

who had created them in a relation of light and love to himself. But when the natural man is confronted with this new, yet more brilliant light of the grace of God he quickly seeks to put out this light too.

UNBELIEVERS KNOW AND YET DO NOT KNOW[97]

(A) Men must be told that the revelation of God round about them and the revelation of God within their own constitution is clear and plain, rendering them without excuse. "For the invisible things of him from the creation of the world are clearly seen, being understood by the things that are made, even his eternal power and Godhead; so that they are without excuse, because that, when they knew God, they glorified him not as God, neither were thankful; but became vain in their imaginations, and their foolish heart was darkened" (Rom. 1:20, 21).

All men know God. Every fact of the universe has God's stamp of ownership indelibly and with large letters engraved upon it.

All men know not merely that a God exists, but they know that God, the *true* God, the *only* God, exists. They cannot be conscious of themselves, says Calvin, except they be at the same time conscious of God as their creator. This general revelation of God stays with man whatever his attitude toward God may be. When he sins against God, he must sin against this God whom he knows. Otherwise sin would be sin in a vacuum. Even in the hereafter, the lost and the evil angels still know God.

Yet these same men to whom we must testify that they know God, must also be told that they *do not* know God. They walk in the midst of this world which is an exhibition house of the glories and splendors of God, full as it is of the works of his hands, and they ask, mind you, *whether* God exists. They profess to be open-minded on the question. They say that they will follow the facts wherever these may lead them. But invariably they refuse to follow these facts. They constantly conclude that God does not exist. Even when they conclude that a god exists and that with great probability, they are virtually saying that God does not exist. For the true God is not surrounded by, but is the source of, possibility. He could not possibly not exist. We cannot intelligently think away God's existence.

When working in the laboratory as scientists, men act as though they are not dealing with materials that belong to God. They are like a thief who, en-

---

97. The following excerpts are taken from:

    (A) *Common Grace*, 130, 131;
    (B) *Introduction to Systematic Theology*, 26, 27.

tering into your home and exploring all kinds of things within it, claims that the question of the ownership of the house is of no concern to him. They are like those who go hunting in a woods clearly marked "No Gunning," without a permit from the owner.

How absurd, says the objector. Do you mean to say that men really know that they are creatures of God, and that there is punishment awaiting them if they are not thankful and obedient to Him and yet pretend to be looking for Him if haply they may find Him? Do they know God and yet not know Him? How contradictory, how utterly absurd is this religion which you are asking me to believe.

(B) We are well aware of the fact that non-Christians have a great deal of knowledge about this world which is true as far as it goes. That is, there is a sense in which we can and must allow for the value of knowledge of non-Christians. This has always been a difficult point. It is often the one great source of confusion on the question of faith in its relation to reason. We should admit that we cannot give any wholly satisfactory account of the situation as it actually obtains. We cannot do that with respect to this question any more than we can with respect to the question of how it is possible that God can give to those who are children of his wrath such natural blessings as rain and sunshine, or physical prosperity in general. All that we can do with this question as with many other questions in theology, is to hem it in in order to keep out errors, and to say that truth lies within a certain territory.

In order to hem in our question we are persuaded that we must begin by emphasizing the *absolute ethical antithesis* in which the "natural man" stands to God. This implies that he knows nothing truly as he ought to know it. It means, therefore, that the "natural man" is not only basically mistaken in his notions about religion and God, but is as basically mistaken in his notions about the atoms and the laws of gravitation. From this ultimate point of view the "natural man" knows nothing truly. He has chains about his neck and sees shadows only.

It is this point on which many theologians are vague. They maintain, to be sure, that the natural man cannot truly know God, but they will not maintain that the natural man cannot truly know the flowers of the field. Now it may seem as though it is straining at a gnat to insist on the point that the natural man does not even know the flowers truly, as long as it is maintained that he does not know God truly. The point is, however, that unless we maintain that the natural man does not know the flowers truly, we cannot logically maintain that he does not know God truly. . . .

The difficulty with respect to the natural man's knowledge of God may be somewhat alleviated if we remember that there are two senses in which we may speak of his having knowledge. The natural man has knowledge, true knowledge of God, in the sense that God through nature and man's own consciousness impresses his presence on man's attention. So definitely and inescapably has he done this that, try as he may, man cannot escape knowing God. It is this point that Paul stresses in the first two chapters of Romans. Man has the sense of deity indelibly engraved upon him. He knows God and he knows himself and the world as God's creation. This is objective revelation to him. Even to the extent that this revelation is in man, in his own constitution, and as such may be called "subjective," it is none the less objective to him as an ethically responsible creature, and he is bound to react as an ethical person to this objective revelation.

But it is this objective revelation both about and within him that the natural man seeks to suppress. Having made alliance with Satan, man makes a grand monistic assumption. Not merely in his conclusion but as well in his method and starting point he takes for granted his own ultimacy. To the extent that he works according to this monistic assumption he misinterprets all things, flowers no less than God. Fortunately the natural man is never fully consistent while in this life. As the Christian sins against his will, so the natural man "sins against" his own essentially Satanic principle. As the Christian has the incubus of his "old man" weighing him down and therefore keeping him from realizing the "life of Christ" within him, so the natural man has the incubus of the sense of deity weighing him down and keeping him from realizing the life of Satan within him.

The actual situation is therefore always a mixture of truth with error. Being "without God in the world" the natural man yet knows God, and, in spite of himself, to some extent recognizes God. By virtue of their creation in God's image, by virtue of the ineradicable sense of deity within them and by virtue of God's restraining general grace, those who hate God, yet in a restricted sense know God, and do good.

UNBELIEVERS INCONSISTENTLY RELY UPON BELIEVING PRESUPPOSITIONS[98]

To be sure, the Christian view of life is true and all other views are false; that is to say, the Bible presents a view of God, of man and of Christ which is exclusive of all other views. The natural man serves and worships the creature

---

98. Excerpts from *Defense of the Faith*, 20, 120, 259, 260, 190, 409, 66, 385, 386, 355, 67.

more than the Creator. The Christian has by the grace of God learned to serve the Creator more than the creature. And this fact expresses itself in whatever he does. But even those who worship and serve the creature more than the Creator are not "finished products" in this world. They can and therefore do make their positive contribution to the realization of the cultural mandate given to Adam, the first man of history, the representative of all succeeding generations. . . .

The first objection that suggests itself may be expressed in the rhetorical question "Do you mean to assert that non-Christians do not discover truth by the methods they employ?" The reply is that we mean nothing so absurd as that. The implication of the method here advocated is simply that non-Christians are never able and therefore never do employ their own methods consistently. . . .

You ask what person is consistent with his own principles. Well I have consistently argued that no one is and that least of all the non-Christian is. I have even argued in the very booklet that you review that if men were consistent they would be end products and that then there would be no more reasoning with them. However since sinners are not consistent, and have what is from their point of view an old man within them, they can engage in science and in the general interpretation of the created universe and bring to light much truth. It is because the prodigal is not yet at the swine trough and therefore still has of the substance of the Father in his pockets that he can do that and discover that, which for the matter of it, is true and usable for the Christian. . . .

This is not to forget that he also, according to the old man within him, knows that God exists. But as a covenant breaker he seeks to suppress this. And I am now speaking of him as the covenant breaker. Neither do I forget that no man is actually fully consistent in working according to these assumptions. The non-believer does not fully live up to the new man within him which in his case is the man who worships the creature above all else. . . .

But in the course of history the natural man is not fully self-conscious of his own position. The prodigal cannot altogether stifle his father's voice. There is a conflict of notions within him. But he himself is not fully and self-consciously aware of this conflict within him. He has within him the knowledge of God by virtue of his creation in the image of God. But this idea of God is suppressed by his false principle, the principle of autonomy. This principle of autonomy is, in turn, suppressed by the restraining power of God's common grace. Thus the ideas with which he daily works do not proceed consistently either from the one principle or from the other. . . .

[S]o the natural man has the incubus of the sense of deity weighing him down and keeping him from realizing the life of Satan within him.

The actual situation is therefore always a mixture of truth with error. Being "without God in the world," the natural man yet knows God, and, in spite of himself, to some extent recognizes God. By virtue of their creation in God's image, by virtue of the ineradicable sense of deity within them and by virtue of God's restraining general grace, those who hate God, yet in a restricted sense know God, and do good. . . .

Non-Christians know after a fashion, as Paul tells us in Romans. Thus also there is a relative good in those who are ethically totally evil. The unity that they have in experience is a shadow unity, a unity that prevents them from falling into complete disintegration in this world. Hereafter complete disintegration will follow, though even hereafter the disintegration can only be ethical and not metaphysical; there must be a kingdom or mock-unity even in hell. . . .

To be sure, all men have faith. Unbelievers have faith as well as believers. But that is due to the fact that they too are creatures of God. Faith therefore always has content. It is against the content of faith as belief in God that man has become an unbeliever. As such he tries to suppress the content of his original faith. . . .

Then when this faith turns into unbelief this unbelief cannot succeed in suppressing fully the original faith in God. Man as man is inherently and inescapably a believer in God. Thus he can contribute to true knowledge of the universe. Add to this the fact of common grace and he can in a measure cooperate with the believer in building the edifice of science. . . .

I account for the non-Christian's scientific accomplishments by virtue of the fact that in spite of his principle of Chance, he is borrowing, without recognizing it, the Christian ideas of creation and providence. . . .

All this makes the matter of apologetical argument very complicated. Only a clear recognition of the three types of consciousness, of the total inability of the non-regenerate consciousness of itself to accept the truth of Christianity, of the necessity of a consistent presentation of the Christian position together with firm reliance on the grace of God, can help us to reason fruitfully with men.[99]

99. CVT: The absolute contrast between the Christian and the non-Christian in the field of knowledge is said to be that of principle. Full recognition is made of the fact that in spite of this absolute contrast of principle, there is relative good in those who are evil in principle and relative evil in those who are good in principle. Is it possible to set forth the fully Biblical or Reformed position without maintaining both of these points? Some of my critics deny the necessity of maintaining both points at all times. In this, I feel, they depart from generic Calvinism.

Chapter 7

The Presuppositional Apologetical Argument

7.1 Presuppositions Are the Crux

Van Til's approach to apologetics is popularly known as "presuppositionalism." Van Til realized that when the believer encounters intellectual objections or challenges to his Christian faith from unbelievers, the dispute between them is almost always generated by, and will be controlled by, their different fundamental assumptions—their presuppositions.[1] The basic convictions that people hold determine how they will live and how they will use their minds.

Presuppositions have an impact on the thinking of believers and unbelievers alike, often in ways that are relevant and crucial for apologet-

---

1. Presuppositional differences are not mentioned in every apologetical discussion. The conversation may not get that far (e.g., the coffee break is over, or the conversation has only begun to clarify and examine differences of opinion), or other questions may require attention (e.g., what is meant by a miracle, which Bible version does the believer use, or why are there different denominations?). If pursued with clarity of analysis, even these conversations will end up addressing the difference in ultimate standards of interpretation and justification for beliefs—that is, differences in presuppositions. Moreover, in rare cases the "intellectual difficulty" that has been keeping an unbeliever from confessing what the Bible declares about Christ is a rather peripheral matter of fact (e.g., how the resurrection accounts in the Gospels fit together) or of personal misunderstanding (e.g., whether Christian have to believe that holy water can effect exorcisms).

ics. Consider the subject of evolution. There is no lack of teachers and books today that will tell us that scientific research strongly suggests that the human species descended from related life forms by mutation and adaptation to the environment. Such an idea poses difficulties for believers and unbelievers alike, and the way they handle those difficulties is an indicator of their different presuppositions. Some believers take the pronouncements of science as a reason to modify their commitment to the inerrancy or inspiration of the Bible, others change their hermeneutics so as to allow for an evolutionary interpretation of the book of Genesis, and yet others challenge the research and reasoning that lead to evolutionary conclusions. Which is the proper response? That depends on your presuppositions. Evolution poses difficulties for the world of unbelieving scholarship, too. Presumably, if you adopt the evolutionary outlook, you should seek an evolutionary account of man's behavior and social relations—the notion of "sociobiology." However, nearly all sociobiological research and reflection has interpreted man (like any other animal) as being selfish, violent, and antiegalitarian in order to perpetuate his species or his own offspring. Such a view is embarrassing to liberal scholarship, especially its traditional views on human nature and sociopolitical programs. Some thus denounce sociobiology ("mere pseudoscience!"), others reject evolution as contrary to proper political ideals, and yet others conclude that liberalism must be set aside as contrary to nature (to "reality"). Which is the right response for an unbeliever? It all depends upon his presuppositions.

An apologist must not ignore the fact that believers and unbelievers work (outwardly anyway) with espoused sets of presuppositions that are contrary to each other. The notion that their argument with each other could be pursued in a "neutral" fashion is naive and thoroughly misleading. The Christian's commitment to Christ as his Lord leads him to see everything in the light of who Christ is and what Christ has revealed in His word; his reasoning and evaluations are subject to the authority of God, speaking infallibly in the Scriptures. The non-Christian's commitment to himself as his own autonomous authority leads him, by contrast, to spurn the light of Christ and see everything according to his own patterns of interpretation, observation, reflection, or experience; his reasoning and evaluations are subject to his own intellectual authority.[2] Accordingly, believers and un-

2. This can be quite an act, and it usually means blindly following college professors or other "experts" who say what he would like to hear. The apologist needs to keep

believers do not always agree about what the "facts" are—whether historical or current. And even when they do agree, their respective assessments of the meaning or interpretation of those facts are at odds with each other.

The Christian reads in God's word, and thus believes, that Jesus Christ ascended into heaven; the non-Christian says that this claim in a merely human book is unbelievable precisely because such things do not—or cannot—take place. It should be obvious that they are working with different assumptions—about the nature of the Bible, about the nature and workings of the external world, etc. The Christian prays to God and his friend is "miraculously" healed of cancer, but the unbeliever may scoff and say, rather, that there is no God with whom to speak and that, given more information, doctors could explain how the cancer suddenly disappeared. Why do they disagree? Clearly, they are living by different guidelines and thinking in terms of different underlying beliefs—about the existence of God, about how things must take place in the natural world, etc. Because of their different assumptions, even the "facts" that believers and unbelievers agree upon (in a vague or formal way) will be interpreted in vastly different ways. They may agree on the fact that the unbeliever feels a sense of exhilarating freedom in his atheism, but the believer interprets that as what we would expect of a man who wants to rationalize his licentious lifestyle and elude fear of judgment. They may agree on the fact that the believer feels an important psychological need for comfort and care that is satisfied by his belief in God; the unbeliever interprets that as emotional weakness, while the believer says that Scripture teaches that God made us to feel this need for Him. What about something that seems less subjective, like historical facts—such as biblical passages that accurately describe historical events in advance? The believer sees this as evidence of predictive prophecy, but the unbeliever is sure that the "prophecy" must have been written after the fact.

It is not hard to understand, then, that the assumptions that each

---

challenging the would-be autonomous man to think for himself! If he will not, he should certainly not get away with portraying the religious debate as a conflict between those who live by faith and those who are guided by reason; it is rather a matter of the unbeliever's chosen trust in his experts, over against the believer's trust in Christ and His word. Even then, the apologist should not leave matters in a subjective standoff. As Christians, we claim that our faith is rational and objective, not simply preferential and subjective (as is claimed by the non-Christian).

party brings to a religious (or any fundamental) disagreement will both define their difference of opinion and determine how each one responds to the arguments of the other. An intelligent approach to apologetics cannot miss this feature of the debate between Christians and non-Christians. We should also recognize that there are different levels of assumptions within each person's conceptual outlook. When Sam looks at the clock and then hurries to fill the freezer tray with water so that there will be ice cubes for the party tonight, he assumes a large number of things: that the freezer is working, that ice cubes are made from water, etc. But there are other assumptions more basic than these. For instance, he assumes that the world exhibits regularity and predictability, and that causation will remain as it has been in the past (water in an ice cube tray, when placed in the freezer, will turn into ice cubes). But we can press further and find even deeper assumptions than these in Sam's outlook. For instance, the longer he waits, the less time he has to let the water freeze; that is, he does not believe that the time or opportunity for freezing the water increases if he refrains from acting (that is, time does not "move backward"). For that matter, Sam assumes that there is a difference between himself (and his thoughts about the need for ice cubes) and the ice cubes themselves.[3] Now this illustration allows us to see very clearly that certain assumptions are held more tenaciously than others by Sam. When he goes to the freezer tonight and finds no ice cubes, his most likely reaction is to question whether the freezer was really working after all. He is far less likely to repudiate his belief that regularity characterizes this area of his experience ("evidently, the realm of ice cubes is just a great mystery that nobody can explain or predict"). Sam is even less likely to blame the absence of ice cubes on himself, either for hurrying to put the trays in the freezer ("if I had only waited longer, the water would have had more time to freeze"), or for not thinking correctly ("my thoughts are ice cubes, so my mind is at fault for the fact that we cannot have cold drinks").

So all assumptions can affect a person's reasoning and conclusions, but all assumptions do not have the same strength or influence. They

3. The last couple of illustrations may strike more "practically minded" people as the abstract and ridiculous reflections that only philosophers worry about. This is because in our day-to-day affairs, such fundamental assumptions are not ordinarily questioned, and (from one perspective) need not be. But these beliefs are genuinely assumed, and they illustrate the difference between levels of assumption or the different degrees of authority that different beliefs are afforded by us.

are held with varying levels of tenacity; they occupy different places within a person's conceptual scheme (more or less central, more or less peripheral); they control other beliefs to different extents. Presuppositional apologetics pays attention, not simply to the influence of just any assumptions on a person's thinking, but more especially to his most fundamental or basic philosophical assumptions. These deeper beliefs control how a person reasons and how he interprets and evaluates experiences and evidence. These deeper beliefs or assumptions are what Van Til usually called "presuppositions." They determine how a person sees his experience (as colored glasses affect our vision). They provide a general orientation and are taken as a reliable guide for a person's reasoning—a "point of reference." Everything is organized and interrelated in one's system of thought by one's presuppositions. They exercise pervasive and systematic control over one's interpretation of experience, and they govern how one lives one's life.

It is because of a person's particular presuppositions (even when he does not self-consciously identify them) that he has the kind of worldview he does, in terms of which he understands everything from his momentary experiences to the overall meaning of life. These presuppositions, just like any other beliefs, are not isolated, freestanding convictions that are unconnected with other presuppositions. We do not come to them one by one or understand them apart from the way they integrate with other fundamental beliefs. They are coordinated with each other so as to be coherent with, and mutually supportive of, each other. That is why a worldview is thought of as a network of presuppositions—fundamental and systematically influential beliefs about metaphysics, epistemology, and ethics. Because a person's presuppositions determine his conception of science, rationality, evidence, etc., one does not ordinarily appeal to scientific procedures, abstract reasoning, or experiential verification in order to "prove" one's presuppositions; the notion of proof itself takes its meaning from those presuppositions. Van Til noted:

> The Reformed method of apologetics . . . would "presuppose" God. . . . Before seeking to prove that Christianity is in accord with reason and in accord with fact, it would ask what is meant by "reason" and what is meant by "fact." It would argue that unless reason and fact are themselves interpreted in terms of God they are unintelligible. . . . Reason and fact cannot be brought into fruitful union

with one another except upon the presupposition of the existence of God and his control over the universe.[4]

Now, not all apologists use the word "presupposition" in the same way that Van Til did.[5] Carnell and Schaeffer spoke of the Christian "presupposition" as though it were a hypothesis subject to verification by independent considerations and reasons (logic, historical evidence, personal satisfaction, etc.)—thus obviously not the most basic epistemological, metaphysical, or ethical assumptions to which a person is committed. Gordon Clark, on the other hand, used the word to designate the "axioms" of a person's system of thought, which are unprovable because they are dogmatically posited as a first principle for which there is nothing more basic by which to demonstrate it. Naturally, that conception led Clark to a fideistic stance that precludes the apologist from offering the unbeliever rational grounds for believing the Christian's presupposition.[6] Van Til differed with both Carnell and Clark in the use of the word "presupposition." In his view, a presupposition is more basic than a hypothesis, and yet the network of presuppositions that form a person's worldview is not beyond rational proof. Because presuppositions are the most fundamental and coordinated convictions that a person has regarding reality, knowing, and conduct, they are the transcendentals by which (it is hoped) a person's experience can be made coherent, meaningful, and intelligible. Accordingly, Van Til could write: "A truly *transcendental* argument takes any fact of experience which it wishes to investigate, and tries to determine what the *presuppositions* of such a fact must be, in order to make it what it is."[7] The presuppositions espoused or utilized by the believer (on the one hand) and the unbeliever (on the other hand) were con-

---

4. *A Christian Theory of Knowledge* (Philadelphia: Presbyterian and Reformed, 1969), 18.
5. There is nothing amiss about that fact; Van Til had no copyright to the word or authority to stipulate how it must be used. The word "presupposition" is used in a variety of ways in contemporary English, and not even Van Til always used it in the particular way being discussed here. Nevertheless, if we do not distinguish between the various uses of the word by different apologists, we will only be confused when they use it.
6. Clark did endorse rational discussion with the unbeliever and criticism of the unbeliever's theory of knowledge, ethical stand, etc. But the only "reason" (cause) for an unbeliever choosing the Bible over the Koran is the regenerating work of the Holy Spirit (*Three Types of Religious Philosophy* [Nutley, N.J.: Craig Press, 1973], 121–23).
7. *A Survey of Christian Epistemology*, In Defense of the Faith, vol. 2 (Philadelphia: Presbyterian and Reformed, 1969), 10 (emphasis added); cf. p. 201.

sidered by Van Til to be their "reference point" for interpreting any experience and guiding all reasoning. They are intended to be preconditions for making sense out of any thinking or experience. As Van Til wrote, they should be understood as "the conditions which make experience intelligible."[8]

PRESUPPOSITIONS AS ONE'S BASIC GUIDING POINT OF REFERENCE[9]

Roman Catholic theology agrees with the essential contention of those it seeks to win to the Christian faith that man's consciousness of himself and of the objects of the world is *intelligible without reference to* God.

But herein precisely lies *the fundamental point of difference* between Romanism and Protestantism. According to the principle of Protestantism, man's consciousness of self and of objects *presuppose for their intelligibility* the self-consciousness of God. In asserting this we are not thinking of psychological and temporal priority. *We are thinking only of the question as to what is the final reference point in interpretation*. The Protestant principle finds this in the self-contained ontological trinity. By his counsel the triune God controls whatsoever comes to pass. If then the human consciousness must, in the nature of the case, always be the proximate starting-point, it remains true that God is always *the most basic and therefore the ultimate or final reference point in human interpretation*.

This is, in the last analysis, the question as to what are one's ultimate presuppositions. When man became a sinner he made of himself instead of God the *ultimate or final reference point*. And it is precisely *this presupposition*, as it *controls* without exception all forms of non-Christian philosophy, that must be brought into question. If this presupposition is left unquestioned in any field all the facts and arguments presented to the unbeliever will be *made over by him according to his pattern*. The sinner has cemented colored glasses[10] to his eyes which he cannot remove. And all is yellow to the jaun-

---

8. *Christian Theory of Knowledge*, 286.
9. An excerpt from *The Defense of the Faith* (Philadelphia: Presbyterian and Reformed, 1955), 94–95, taken from the syllabus *Apologetics* (reprint, Nutley, N.J.: Presbyterian and Reformed, 1976), 45. Emphasis is added to highlight what Van Til usually meant by someone's "presuppositions."
10. It should be noted that when Van Til used the metaphor of "colored glasses" for the unbeliever's presuppositions, he emphasized that these are willfully adopted by the sinner so that he can see the world differently, as he wishes to do. But Van Til did not teach that all presuppositions are a matter of voluntary choice, or that any set of glasses (presuppositions) distorts reality. He maintained that all men

diced eye. There can be no intelligible reasoning unless those who reason to-gether understand what they mean by their words.

In not challenging *this basic presupposition with respect to himself as the final reference point* in predication the natural man may accept the "theistic proofs" as fully valid. He may construct such proofs. He has constructed such proofs. But the god whose existence he proves to himself in this way is al-ways a god who is something other than the self-contained ontological trin-ity of Scripture. The Roman Catholic apologete does not want to prove the existence of this sort of God. He wants to prove the existence of such a God as will leave intact the autonomy of man to at least some extent.

CHRISTIANITY NOT ONE HYPOTHESIS AMONG MANY[11]

[T]he statement [is] often made that we must present Christianity as an hy-pothesis which men are to try in the interpretation of the facts of experience. One form of this contention appears when preachers appeal to men to take Christ because he will satisfy them best. Now it goes without saying that a drunkard cannot be tempted into accepting Christ in this way if it be under-stood as meaning nothing more than that the drunkard is himself, as he is, to be the judge of what really satisfies him. But it is exactly this that the preacher does not want. He wants the drunkard to allow Jesus to tell him what satisfies him, and if he does, then Jesus will satisfy him.

Similarly we may certainly present Christianity as an hypothesis *if we do it while reasoning with our opponents in an* ad hominem *fashion*, i.e., if we allow him to try what he can make of Christianity as an hypothesis among many by the process of univocal reasoning.[12] He will then soon find that if he is going to accept Christianity he must *give up the idea of treating it as an hypothesis and ask forgiveness for having done so*.

On the other hand, if he continues to regard Christianity as one hypoth-esis among many, it is a foregone conclusion that he will not accept this hy-pothesis rather than another. And if he did accept Christianity as the most likely hypothesis, he would not be accepting Christianity, but a substitute for it. To reason about anything as an hypothesis for the explanation of any fact

---

know God by His unavoidable and clear revelation, and that this knowledge gives them the presuppositions by which to see God's world correctly. They have, nev-ertheless, put on colored glasses instead.

11. An excerpt from *Survey of Christian Epistemology*, 208–9.
12. "Univocal" reasoning does not honor the Creator-creature distinction, but as-sumes that God and man approach knowing in the same way and under essen-tially the same conditions. It refuses to "think God's thoughts after Him" (cf. chap. 4.5 above) and asserts its intellectual autonomy.

or facts means that there may be other hypotheses that should eventually prove to be true. And if it is conceivable that an interpretation other than God should finally be given for the facts of the universe, then it is also true that these facts are now considered as being apart from God. So then our conclusion must be that if we present Christian theism as an hypothesis, it *must always be done by us as a part of our analogical reasoning process*, even if it be at that point where we are reasoning for argument's sake.[13]

7.2 The Need to Argue over Contrary Epistemologies

If the thinking and reasoning of the Christian and the non-Christian are guided by contrary presuppositions, and if those presuppositions determine each one's conception of knowledge, rationality, and proof, then it might appear that reasoning with unbelievers is a useless enterprise. A number of Van Til's critics have mistakenly tried to draw that inference for his system of apologetics.[14] But he never looked at defending the faith that way at all. We are not left in some irresolvable presuppositional standoff. As Van Til put it: "To all this we must humbly but confidently reply by saying that we have the best of philosophical justification for our position. It is not as though we are in a bad way and that we must seek for some comfort from others who are also in a bad way."[15] Some men rebel against God and pursue that rebellion in their intellectual activities, while other men submit to God's revelation and bow to its authority in their intellectual activities, but Van Til also insisted that it is objectively true that God is one, that His image (in which all men are created) is one, and that the truth is one. Auton-

---

13. The significance of this last sentence will become apparent when we shortly take up the matter of Van Til's "indirect" method of proving the faith by analyzing the internal consistency of the believer's and unbeliever's worldviews and comparing their ability to make sense of the world. This will involve thinking through the implications of the unbeliever's outlook "for argument's sake." But even when we are arguing "within" the unbeliever's espoused worldview, we will still "think God's thoughts after Him" (using "analogical" reasoning). That is, we will follow Christian presuppositions while investigating the nature of the unbeliever's system of thought.

14. Sometimes this has arisen from limited exposure to Van Til's full viewpoint (unwittingly taking certain tenets out of context). Sometimes people have failed to comprehend or reflect upon broader philosophical and theological issues, and thus have drawn unwarranted conclusions. And, sadly, sometimes straw men have been set up for easy (but irrelevant) refutation. Whatever the explanation, there is no justification for such misrepresentations.

15. *Common Grace* (Philadelphia: Presbyterian and Reformed, 1947), 8.

omy is a futile pretense, is wishful thinking, and is practiced only outwardly "as a show" in the professed systems that unbelievers develop. They nevertheless know God and inwardly interpret their experience and engage their reasoning on the basis of that knowledge.

Therefore, acknowledging the espousal and use of contrary presuppositions in the public dispute between believers and unbelievers does not lead to the conclusion that there are different kinds of argument or rationality, one for the believer and a contrary one for the unbeliever—and "ne'er the twain shall meet." Van Til taught that there is only one genuine type of argument for all men, despite their espousal of conflicting presuppositions. Having been made by God and being controlled by His sovereign providence, the natural man has the formal or intellectual ability to receive and understand the testimony and argument of the Christian. And by the gracious power of the Holy Spirit, who can regenerate and enlighten, he can be granted the substantial or spiritual ability to adopt, profess, and obey the truth of that testimony and argument.

We must argue, then, with people who espouse conflicting presuppositions in their outward reasoning and attempts to develop a system of thought. And in particular we must press men to address the epistemological issues that separate the believer from the unbeliever in their reasoning and conclusions. Given their respective worldviews, how can either perspective make sense out of man's ability to know things? How are the criteria and methods of knowing successful and intelligible? Van Til taught that the apologist must avidly pursue the question "How do you know?" with men who oppose the truth claims of the Christian faith.

Not all unbelievers openly reveal or explicitly lay out a theory of knowledge "up front" in their disputes with believers, however. Indeed, the larger share of non-Christians whom the apologist encounters either do not care about (what we call) "epistemological" matters or have never been forced to grapple with them and make self-conscious choices regarding them. Thus, much of the work done by a presuppositional apologist, especially in the early phases of dialogue with a critic of Christianity, must involve questioning, analysis, and cross-examination, in order to make manifest the unbeliever's implicit assumptions about knowledge and reasoning. Much of our apologetical task consists of making men face up to the critical issues pertaining to their theories of knowledge. As Van Til said, there are too many "epistemological loafers," and it is the job of those who defend the faith to prod and challenge them, rather than letting them continue to take crucial issues for granted or consenting to their intellectual arbitrariness. The apologist who is willing to satisfy the unbeliever's unexamined prejudices about science, logic, rationality, factuality, proof, etc., is—to his detriment and without realizing it—submitting to the unspoken network of other philosophical convictions that form the interpretive context for those epistemological prejudices. Unbelievers who oppose the truth of the Christian message, regardless of their level of philosophical sophistication or intellectual training, must be challenged to open up and critically evaluate their presuppositions about the process, standards, and possibility of knowing anything.

Unbelievers cannot be content to proceed as "agnostics." For all of its outward display of intellectual humility, the agnostic position carries its own epistemological prejudices. It is, as Van Til indicated, actually a very closed-minded or proud attitude. Even more, maintaining an agnostic stance entangles the unbeliever in self-contradiction, which the apologist should bring out into the open. Moreover, unbelievers cannot be content simply to adopt whatever epistemological perspective they wish, thinking that "if the presuppositions in all worldviews are ultimately defended in a circular fashion (a matter of coherence in outlook), then we may choose according to our desires." Presuppositional apologetics is utterly opposed to voluntarism.[16] Van Til frowned upon the fact that in modern times matters of epistemology (and metaphysics) have "really become a question of taste." They need, rather, to be matters of philosophical criticism and rational proof, so that when men self-consciously choose their theory of knowledge, "this choosing can then, in the nature of the case, no longer be

---

16. A more inappropriate and misleading label for Van Til's presuppositionalism could hardly be imagined than Stuart Hackett's "voluntaristic rationalism" (*The Resurrection of Theism* [Chicago: Moody Press, 1957], 154, cf. p. 158). Hackett calls it "*voluntaristic*, because the acceptance of the basic postulate is a volitional or willful act for which, in the final analysis, no rational evidence can be given" (p. 155). Equally bad is Clark Pinnock's designation, "metaphysical voluntarism" ("The Philosophy of Christian Evidences," in *Jerusalem and Athens*, ed. E. R. Geehan [Philadelphia: Presbyterian and Reformed, 1971], 422). Pinnock writes that Van Til "demands the non-Christian make a total and *ungrounded* commitment to the absolute God of Scripture. . . . Men must *decide* to become Christians and not think about it first. . . . Thus the decision is voluntaristic, an existential leap of faith" (p. 423, emphasis partly added). Hackett and Pinnock are woefully misinformed, for Van Til wrote, e.g., "Thus there is absolutely certain proof for the existence of God and the truth of Christian theism" (*Defense of the Faith*, 120).

a matter of artistic preference. *We cannot choose epistemologies as we choose hats."*[17]

To sum up, Van Til's apologetic maintains that, although presuppositions are the crux of the dispute between believers and unbelievers, it is necessary and appropriate to reason with unbelievers. In particular, they must be pressed to consider their assumptions regarding epistemology (perhaps unspoken and unanalyzed) and to face the challenge of justifying them with good reasons.

THE NECESSITY OF REASONING, DESPITE CONTRARY PRESUPPOSITIONS[18]

If it is true that the difference between Christian and antitheistic epistemology is as fundamental as we have contended that it is, and if it is true that the antitheist takes his position for granted at the outset of his investigations, and if it is true that the Christian expects his opponent to do nothing else inasmuch as according to Scripture the "natural man" cannot discern the things of the Spirit, we must ask *whether* it is then of any use for the Christian to reason with his opponent.

The answer to this question must not be sought by toning down the dilemma as is easily and often done by the assumption that epistemological terminology means the same thing for theists and non-theists alike.[19] The answer must rather be sought in the basic concept of Christian theism, namely, that God is absolute. If God is absolute man must always remain accessible to him. Man's ethical alienation plays upon the background of his metaphysical dependence. God may therefore use our reasoning or our preaching as a way by which he presents himself to those who have assumed his nonexistence. . . .

In the first place, our discussion has brought out that we must clearly recognize the fact of the fundamental difference between the two types of consciousness. If we do not do this we argue in the blue. It does us no good to talk about reason in the abstract. Such a thing does not exist.

Yet we must recognize the truth contained in the contention that there is

---

17. *Survey of Christian Epistemology,* xiv (emphasis added). Cf. p. xiii: "Every system of philosophy must tell us whether it thinks true knowledge to be possible. Or if a system of philosophy thinks it impossible for man to have a true knowledge of the whole of reality or even of a part of reality, *it must give good reasons for thinking so"* (emphasis added).

18. Excerpts from *Survey of Christian Epistemology,* x–xi, 195–98.

19. Van Til is here indicating that the philosophical conceptions of the things designated with common epistemological terminology (e.g., "induction," "logic," "proof,' "objectivity") differ between the Christian and the non-Christian worldviews.

a general consciousness of man. We can do this first of all by recognizing that *there once was* such a consciousness. We must go back to the Adamic consciousness as being the fundamentally human consciousness. We speak now of the Adamic consciousness previous to the entrance of sin in the world. As such it was entirely able to judge, for the good reason that it was not ethically alienated from God. Not as though man's original ethical consciousness was able, by and of itself, to judge between right and wrong. Even before the fall man's ethical consciousness needed the instruction directly given it by God's speaking with man. But because of its inherently right attitude toward God and his revelation, man's moral consciousness could judge between right and wrong. The fact that man was a temporal creature did not hinder him from seeing the truth about the relation of God to the universe. It is true that the *range* of his knowledge never could be as comprehensive as the range of the knowledge of God. But this was not necessary. Validity did not depend upon range. We cannot say then that because man was a finite creature, he could not relate man properly to the existence of God but had to live by revelation from the outset. There is no such contrast between revelation and reasoning in the case of Adam. He could reason soundly just because he reasoned in an atmosphere of revelation. His very mind with its laws was a revelation of God. Accordingly, he would reason analogically and univocally. He would always be presupposing God in his every intellectual operation. He did not reason from nature or from himself as existing independently, to God as the "first cause." He reasoned as one seeing all things from the beginning for what they are, i.e., dependent upon God.

As entirely dependent upon God metaphysically and as perfect ethically, man, at the beginning of history, recognized that all about him and within him was revelational of God. Moreover, from the beginning God spoke with man about his handling of the facts of his space-time environment. Accordingly, Adam reasoned within an environment which was exhaustively revelational, and in obedience to a supernatural word revelation that was supplemental to his created environment. At the beginning, therefore, Adam could not start from the facts of the space-time world and ask himself whether or not they were related to God. A child in a home does not ask *whether* he has a father.

It follows then that because we hold that there once was no ethical alienation between God and the consciousness of man, but perfect harmony, we can now say that *the consciousness of man should be perfect too*. In other words, we hold that the Christian theistic system is as a matter of fact *the truth*. Accordingly, to be truly human one must recognize this truth. Just as God continues in the Scriptures to hold before the sinners' eyes the duty of being perfect though man in himself can never be perfect, so it follows that it is the task of the Christian apologist to hold before man the truth, and God's requirement that men should accept the truth, even though he knows that it requires the grace of God for man to see it. There is in this matter nothing else to consider but the command of God.

Since it is upon God's command that the work must be undertaken, it is God's command that gives one the assurance that *the work will accomplish its purpose*. Looking at matters by themselves, it would be worse than useless to undertake reasoning with unbelievers. But it is the deep conviction of the total depravity of man that makes one throw his whole reliance upon God in all respects, and not the least in this question of reasoning with unbelievers. It is only he who deeply believes in the total depravity of man that can really preach with conviction that his work will not be in vain. Since he is convinced that the ethical alienation has been against God and against nothing else, he also knows that God is able to remove the ethical alienation. He, therefore, trusts that the Holy Spirit to whom, in the economy of redemption, the task has been assigned of convicting the world of judgment, will use the means of rational argumentation to accomplish his task. This hope is not inconsistent with the conception of the immediacy of the work of the Holy Spirit. That immediacy is complete. Our arguments taken by themselves effect nothing, while the Holy Spirit may very well convict without the use of our argument as he may convict without the use of our preaching. *Yet because God is himself a completely rational God and has created us in his image, there is every reason to believe that he will make argumentation effective.*[20]

Then further it should be remembered in this connection that because man is a creature of God, it is impossible that he should ever be alienated from God metaphysically. He can never actually become the independent being that he thinks he is. Even the king's heart is in the hand of God as the watercourses. We have seen above that it was exactly because of this fact that man is, as a matter of fact, utterly dependent upon God, that a complete ethical alienation could take place. And it is for the same reason that the ethical alienation can be removed. It is this that had entered so deeply into Augustine's soul when he told God to command him anything whatsoever, because it was God who first had to give what he commanded. And God can give

---

20. Emphasis added. Man can be expected to argue in a rational fashion—and be effectively convinced by rational argumentation—because he is created as the image of God, who is Himself completely rational. But in order to pursue autonomy and suppress the knowledge of God, men inevitably distort true rationality and replace it with somewhat irrational imitations.

what he commands because man has always remained his creature. There is then even in the consciousness of the non-regenerate a *formal power of receptivity*. It is this that enables him to consider the Christian theistic position and see that it stands squarely over against his own, and demands of him the surrender of his own position.

Still further we should recall that the ethical alienation, though complete and exclusive in principle, is not yet complete in degree. It is this conception of the relatively good in the absolutely evil that underlies the contention of Hodge that there is a general moral consciousness of man that may be trusted in moral matters to some extent. Everybody admits that murder is wrong. Even the non-regenerate admit that. And though this fact must ever be taken in connection with the fundamental difference between the two types of consciousness, it is, taken together with the metaphysical considerations of the preceding paragraph, once more a *formal power of receptivity* on the part of the non-regenerate by virtue of which he can consider Christianity as a challenge to himself.

If we thought of the non-regenerate consciousness what it thinks of itself, we should not attempt to reason with it. By that we mean that the non-regenerate consciousness thinks itself to be independent of God metaphysically and ethically. If we thought there was any truth in this we could not argue with it, because with a being metaphysically independent, it would not be possible to come into any intellectual or moral contact at all. We hold, then, that though the ethical miracle of regeneration must occur before argumentation can be really effectual, such an ethical miracle will certainly occur. Not as though we know this with respect to every individual with whom we reason. To hold that would be to deny the free grace of God in connection with the miracle of regeneration. But we do know that it is true, in a general sense, that God will bring sinners to repentance, since the whole work of redemption would fail if he did not. It is thus in *this higher unity of the comprehensive plan and purpose of God* which rests upon his being, that we must seek the solution of the difficulty encountered when we think of the complete ethical alienation of man from God, and the efforts of the redeemed to reason with those who are not redeemed. The problem is, after all, logically beset with no greater difficulties than is the whole problem of the relation of the absolute consciousness of God to the finite consciousness of man. It is but a subdivision of this more general problem. The completeness of the ethical alienation of man does not make it any more difficult than before for God to come into moral contact with man. If then we only consider our argumentation as an instrument of the Holy Spirit, we may partake of the assurance that God's power is in our work. On the other hand, the moment we begin to think of our work as something that is independent of the Spirit, we have no more right to expect anything from it.

It is not, then, as though the clear recognition of the fundamental ethical difference between the regenerate and the non-regenerate consciousness implies that there is a two-fold truth, or that we must use one type of argument for one type of consciousness and another type of argument for the other type of consciousness. It is exactly the deep conviction that there is metaphysically only one type of consciousness, and that the non-regenerate and the regenerate consciousness are but ethical modifications of this one fundamental metaphysical consciousness, that leads us to reason with unbelievers. And it is exactly because of our deep conviction that God is one and truth is therefore one, that we hold that *there is only one type of argument for all men*. All that the recognition of the deep ethical difference does is to call attention to this very fact that it is *God who must make this one truth effective* in the hearts of men.[21]

PRODDING THE "EPISTEMOLOGICAL LOAFERS"[22]

We must therefore briefly seek to understand what the consequences are if one takes this [non-Christian] position to the bitter end. First we should notice, however, that there are all too many who are not willing to accept responsibility for their epistemological attitude. There are perhaps more epistemological loafers than any other kind.

We see them in those who say we cannot be sure about this question of whether the Bible is a revelation of God. We see them in the ordinary medical man who says that he does not wish to be dogmatic, because nobody knows. In Scripture this attitude is exemplified in Ahab's time when men were taught that Baal and Jehovah were equally valuable. So today many parents are willing to have their children attend Sunday school because they ought to learn something about religion. The religious tolerance that we find Modernism advocating today is based upon this epistemological indifference and ignorance, rather than upon any broadmindedness.

Indifferentists of this sort are hard to deal with. To some extent, it is a matter of temperament. Yet where it is based upon temperament we should attempt to have them see that they may not indulge in any sort of temperament they please. They are rational beings, and should ask themselves questions about the rationale of their temperaments. In such extreme cases the only

21. Emphasis added in this paragraph.
22. An excerpt from *Survey of Christian Epistemology*, 211–12.

method that may approach their thought at all is a vigorous testimony to one's own convictions about the truth of Christianity, and specifically its implications with respect to the judgment day. If they are too intellectually lethargic to do any thinking on their own account, if they have so far succeeded in drowning the voice of humanity within them, there seems to be nothing left to do but to testify. In a sense, of course, the whole presentation of the Christian theistic system to those who believe it not is a matter of testimony. But we mean here testimony that is no more than a vigorous statement of one's belief of the truth without expediting any immediate intellectual response. Testimony *to* such and prayer *about* such is about all that we can do. It may be that our testimony and our prayer will *lead them to begin some intellectual operation of some sort, so that we may begin to reason with them.*[23]

In the second place we should notice that there are thousands who do not engage in intellectual consideration of the truth to any great extent, not so much because they are necessarily indifferent to such things by nature as because they are unsuited to it. With respect to these, it is obvious that it would be useless to present the intellectual argument for Christian theism in any subtle and detailed form. Nor is this necessary. A simple presentation of the truth in positive form, and once more largely by way of testimony, may be all that is required. *Christianity is not for a few elite intellectuals. Its message is to the simple and to the learned. The argument must therefore be adapted to each one's mental capacity.*[24] And it should not be forgotten that the difference between the learned and the unlearned is, after all, very small when it comes to a consideration of ultimate questions. The learned may have many more facts at his disposal and be more skilled in the use of the syllo-

---

23. Emphasis added. As rational creatures of God, unbelievers must be encouraged and led—by vigorous testimony (to them) and prayer (to God)—to engage their intellectual abilities and to "begin to reason" about matters pertaining to God and their destiny.

24. Emphasis added. This wise and probing observation cannot be stressed enough. Unfortunately, in books like Van Til's (or this one), where somewhat advanced and sophisticated philosophical issues must be addressed to explain apologetics as a self-conscious science to an educated audience, the impression can easily be left that the practice of defending the faith is only for intellectuals or philosophers. This impression is wrong, and Van Til wanted that to be understood clearly. (Van Til's students will remember with warmth how he would in classroom lectures "speak to the giraffes" [eating the lofty foliage] as well as "to the bunny rabbits" [nibbling on the lower grass].) The academic argument for the truth of Christianity can and must be "adapted to each one's mental capacity." One of the features that was compelling about presuppositionalism for me was precisely its adaptability to every kind of audience and every kind of person, regardless of intelligence or education. It can be taught to children (without fancy labels) and used for debating worldly intellectuals (with philosophical acumen).

gism, but when it comes to a consideration of the meaning of any one fact or of all facts put together, all this refinement does not bring him very far. *Many a man of ordinary intelligence can reason with himself about the reasonableness of thinking of the existence of the facts apart from God,*[25] as well as the most learned scholar. To say this is not to disparage scholarship. Scholarship is necessary in its place, but it is not necessary for every man.

THE CLOSED-MINDEDNESS OF AGNOSTICISM[26]

In the third place, there are many who are avowed agnostics. These are not intellectually indifferent or unable. On the contrary, they are often very sophisticated. They are the men with a little learning, which is a dangerous thing. They may be experts in the field of medicine and daubers in the field of epistemology. They will tell you that it is patent that nobody knows anything about the origin of matter and of life, and that it is therefore a conceit to say that he does. They therefore think it to be truly humble to say that they do not know. It is this attitude that underlies much of present-day scientific method which wants to limit its investigations to the facts and draw no great conclusions from them about ultimate matters.

This attitude is usually coupled with the felt or stated assurance that, after all, man has no metaphysical need. All that man needs is to get along for his three score years and ten in the environment in which he finds himself. He may wonder what is going to happen after this life, but he surely need not worry about it because it is certain that he can do nothing about it.

With such as these it would seem that the point we should be most anxious to drive home is that in trying to be agnostic, and in trying to say that they have no need of metaphysics, *they have already given one of the two possible answers to every question of epistemology that may be asked.*[27]

---

25. Emphasis added. People who lack philosophical training or experience in abstract reasoning can, nevertheless, reason about things. Elitist prejudices aside, ordinary men are just as much "philosophers" and intellectually equipped as those with formal training or degrees. Van Til was confident that the man in the street could be brought to use his intellectual endowments to see how "unreasonable" it would be to think he could know anything or make sense of it apart from the God who is revealed in the Bible.

26. An excerpt from *Survey of Christian Epistemology*, 212–15.

27. Over and over again Van Til observed that those who imagine themselves to be neutral have not set the major questions aside or refused to take sides regarding them. The apologist must not, therefore, be deceived by the outward appearance and profession of agnosticism by unbelievers. They have indeed answered crucial questions and chosen between options, without wanting to draw attention to the fact (either to themselves or to others).

They have, as a matter of fact, said that all the facts—or, in epistemological language, they have said that the object and the subject of knowledge—
exist apart from God and are able to get along without God. They think they
have said nothing at all about ultimate matters, while as a matter of fact they
have in effect said everything that could be said about them, and, we believe,
more beside. They have tried to be so modest that they did not dare to make
a positive statement about anything ultimate, while they have made a universal negative statement about the most ultimate consideration that faces
the mind of man. That this charge is fair is apparent from the consideration
of the opposite. Suppose that the object and the subject of knowledge *do
not* exist apart from God. Suppose, in other words, that the Christian theistic conception of philosophy is true. In that case, it is not only possible to know
something about ultimate things, but in that case the knowledge of proximate things depends upon the knowledge of ultimate things. In that case,
not a single fact can be known unless God is known.

*What the present-day agnostic should do then is to make his position rea-
sonable by showing that God does not exist. The burden of the proof is upon
him. He claims, of course, that the burden of the proof is upon us when we
hold that God exists. Yet this is clearly not the case, since his own position,
to be reasonable, must presuppose the non-existence of God. If God does
exist, man can know him, for the simple reason that in that case all knowledge depends upon him. Hence an agnostic position must first prove that
God does not exist.*[28]

From these considerations it follows that agnosticism is completely
self-contradictory. And it is self-contradictory not only upon the assumption of the truth of theism, but it is self-contradictory upon its own
assumptions. Agnosticism wants to hold that it is reasonable to refrain
from thorough epistemological speculations because they cannot lead to
anything. But in order to assume this attitude, agnosticism has itself make

---

28. Emphasis added. The issue of the burden of proof is often misconstrued. If we
   are arguing over something whose existence or nonexistence has no bearing on
   the intelligibility of our experience and reasoning (say, unicorns), then understandably the burden of proof rests on those who affirm its existence; without evidence, such things should be dismissed as figments of their imagination. But the
   existence of God is not on this order. God's existence would have tremendous
   bearing on the possibility of man knowing anything at all, having self-conscious
   intelligence, properly interpreting his experiences, or making his reasoning intelligible—even making sense out of what we call "imagination." In this special
   case, the burden of proof in the argument between a theist and an antitheist
   would shift to the person denying God's existence, since the possibility and intelligibility of that very debate is directly affected by the position taken.

the most tremendous intellectual assertion that could be made about ultimate things. In the second place, agnosticism is epistemologically self-contradictory on its own assumptions because its claim to make no assertion about ultimate reality rests upon a most comprehensive assertion about ultimate reality. This is, of course, the point of pivotal importance. It is hard to make men see that they have, as a matter of fact, in effect made a universal statement about the whole of reality when they think that they have limited their statements to only a few facts in their immediate vicinity. We should attempt to make plain that the alternative is not between saying something about ultimate reality or not saying anything about it, but that the alternative is rather between saying one thing about it or another. Every human being, as a matter of fact, says something about ultimate reality.

It should be noted that those who claim to say nothing about ultimate reality not only do say something about it just as well as everybody else, but they have assumed for themselves the responsibility of saying *one definite thing* about ultimate reality. They have assumed the responsibility of excluding God. We have seen again that a God who is to come in afterward is no God at all. Agnosticism cannot say that it is open-minded on the question of the nature of ultimate reality. It is absolutely closed-minded on the subject. It has one view that it cannot, unless its own assumption be denied, exchange for another. It has started with the assumption of the non-existence of God and must end with it. Its so-called open-minded attitude is therefore a closed-minded attitude. *The agnostic must be open-minded and closed-minded at the same time. And this is not only a psychological self-contradiction, but an epistemological self-contradiction.*[29] It amounts to affirmation and denial at the same time.

Accordingly, they cancel out one another, if there is cancellation power in them. But the predication of agnosticism cannot be said to have cancellation power unless the whole antitheistic system be first proved true. And the whole position could never be proved true because every fact would have to be in before the agnostic should be willing to make any statement about any other fact, since one fact may influence other facts. Now since clearly no individual agnostic can hope to live till all the facts are in, every individual agnostic must die with an "open" mind and at the same time with a closed mind on the subject of God's existence. On his death bed he must make not one, but two pronouncements. He cannot say science has no pronouncements to make and let it go at that. He must

29. Emphasis added.

make first a universal negative statement which, we have seen, is involved in his agnostic position. Then he must at the same time be completely open-minded on the question of God's existence. He must say that there cannot be a judgment, and at the same time he must look around the corner for it as the next fact that *might*, for all his own position allows him to hold, appear.

The only way, then, that the agnostic can seek to harmonize his mutually exclusive statements that he finds himself constantly making about ultimate reality is to hold that none of them mean anything because all of them operate in a void. And he could not say anything about the void unless there were something beyond the void. In other words, *he cannot argue for the truth of the agnostic or the generally non-theistic position except upon the assumption of the truth of the Christian theistic system.*[30]

It is on this wise, then, that we shall have to deal with agnosticism. We can first show that it is self-contradictory since Christian theism is true. Then we must show that it is self-contradictory if antitheism were true. And finally we must show that it would not even have power to show itself self-contradictory upon its own assumption unless theism is true. The anti-theistic conception of the self-contradictory presupposes the theistic conception of the self-contradictory for its operation.[31]

Incidentally, we may point out that, in addition to being psychologically and epistemologically self-contradictory, the agnostic is morally self-contradictory. His contention was that he is very humble, and for that reason unwilling to pretend to know anything about ultimate matters. Yet he has by implication made a *universal* statement about reality. He therefore not only claims to know as much as the theist knows, but he claims to know much more. More than that, he not only claims to know much more than the theist, but he claims to know more than the theist's God. He has boldly set bare possibility above the theist's God and is quite willing to test the consequences of his action. It is thus that the *hubris* of which the Greeks spoke so much, and upon which they invoked the wrath of the gods, appears in new and seeming innocent garb.

---

30. Emphasis added.
31. It is extremely important to notice and reflect upon the point being made by Van Til at this juncture. As we shall see shortly, a "transcendental" argument has this special "logical feature" about it, that it can draw its conclusion from the affirmation of some position (or premise) as well as from the denial of that position (or premise). This exhibits the "necessity" of what the transcendental argument proves. This is not, then, the same as deductive necessity, since the denial of a crucial premise in a deductive argument would render the argument invalid.

7.3 How to Prove One's Presuppositions: Indirectly

We saw in chapter 4.1 above that apologetical dialogue between the believer and the unbeliever draws them both into epistemological reflection and disagreement. For example, one says that he "knows" that God exists and has revealed Himself in the Bible, but the other says that he "knows"[32] that the Bible is in error because it reports miraculous events that could not have happened, since God does not exist. Both the believer and the unbeliever, in contradiction to each other, claim to hold true beliefs, for which they have justification or good evidence (cf. chap. 4.2). As we have just seen (chap. 7.1), it is their opposing presuppositions—their contradictory points of reference and final authorities (cf. chap. 3.1)—which make the critical difference in what each opponent will accept as justified or intellectually warranted. Such a religious dispute is by its very nature a dispute between different final courts of appeal. The resolution of disputes in apologetics, therefore, turns on whether the believer or the unbeliever can rationally justify his ultimate standards (or methods) of justification, which amounts to exhibiting the "rationality of one's conception of rationality." How could that possibly be done? (There is no shortage of religious and irreligious philosophers who would maintain that it cannot be done.) How can the Christian prove his presuppositions and disprove the espoused presuppositions of the non-Christian?

In chapter 5.1 (cf. chap. 3.2) we ascertained that disagreements over theories of knowledge necessarily take place in the wider context of debate over contrary worldviews—contrary networks of presuppositions pertaining to the nature of reality, ethical standards, and how we know what we know. Christianity and its rival philosophies of life represent mutually exclusive principles of interpretation, criteria of truth, conceptions of objectivity, values and ideals, etc. Ultimately, then, the details of one's theory of knowledge are "justified" in terms of their coherence within the distinctive and broad theory

---

32. If the believer and the unbeliever do not claim to have knowledge, but are content simply to exchange personal opinions ("I believe the Bible about Christ's virgin birth"; "I do not believe it is possible for a virgin to give birth"), they are not rationally addressing religious issues or engaging in apologetics. They are simply sharing autobiographical details that can be ignored. The issue is whether either side's personal beliefs are known to be true or not. To argue about knowledge is to argue about the objective state of affairs, not simply about subjective commitments or feelings.

of which they are a part;[33] they will be warranted in light of the fundamental metaphysical and ethical assumptions that are themselves warranted by those same epistemological assumptions. The arguments on both sides are "circular" in the sense that each worldview attempts to regiment its presuppositions as a consistent and coordinated perspective on experience. Hypothetically, if both were consistent with their fundamental assumptions, the believer and the unbeliever would end up with an all-inclusive antithesis in their personal attitude and conceptual systems or outlooks (chap. 5.2), in which case they could not effectively exhibit to each other the rationality, coherence, or justification of their conceptions of rationality, coherence, or justification.[34]

However, the unbeliever is not (and cannot be) consistent with his espoused presuppositions. He argues one thing outwardly in terms of his epistemological or philosophical system, but inwardly or psychologically he reasons in terms of contrary presuppositions (cf. chap. 6.1, 2, 5). Despite his intellectual opposition to the Christian faith, he

---

33. It should be noted that a worldview is indeed a very broad theory, ultimately made up of all the beliefs held by a person, not simply the most basic or central convictions (presuppositions). There is a misconception abroad (e.g., John W. Montgomery, "Once upon an A Priori . . .," and Clark Pinnock, "The Philosophy of Christian Evidences," in *Jerusalem and Athens*, ed. Geehan, 382–83, 387, 421, 425) that recognizing coherence as the mark or condition of a true theory means that the requirement of correspondence between any proposed theory and experience (observation of the "facts") has been discarded, in which case any number of arbitrary, conflicting, but internally consistent theories would qualify as true— "which is absurd!" (ah, but only absurd if the truth must be coherent!). But this is not at all the case. Among one's beliefs will be found one's observations of the world of experience (the "facts"), and therefore to say that one's theory does not correspond to the facts of experience is simply to say that one part of the theory is not coherent with another part of it—so that it is (after all) untrue. The criticism that a coherence criterion allows any consistent crackpot theory to be deemed true, even though it is "unconnected to reality," is simply not true. To judge a theory by coherence is not to allow that beliefs (about entities, events, etc.) may be generated arbitrarily, nor is it to maintain that the truth is constituted by the coherence of beliefs (rather than marked by it).

34. The problem for the unbeliever is that he keeps committing himself to some (quite proper and unavoidable) requirement of "rationality" and insisting upon it being honored, only to find upon analysis that only the Christian worldview coheres with it (makes it intelligible). The unbeliever has been borrowing essentially Christian ideas in epistemology, without giving God the glory and thanks. After all, given the unbeliever's worldview, why should reasons be required for what we believe? Why should logical consistency be demanded? Why should arbitrariness be disreputable? There is no reason for the normativity of rationality (however it is conceptualized).

cannot escape knowing God through nature (cf. chap. 4.3) and recognizing the voice of His Maker when he encounters the message of Scripture (cf. chap. 4.4). In terms of his knowledge of God, the unbeliever has an affinity for the Christian's position and can both understand and appreciate his apologetical argumentation (cf. chap. 6.4). But he suppresses the truth in unrighteousness, offering any number of arguments and objections to the Christian worldview in order to rationalize his rebellion. He has become a man who lives with two mind-sets (cf. chap. 6.5), uncomfortable with the one and intellectually frustrated by the other. The worldviews of unbelievers have always proven to be epistemological failures (cf. chap. 5.3). Nevertheless, the thinking of the unbeliever with whom the apologist deals has not become as futile as it could be if it were entirely consistent. God's common grace restrains the immorality and irrationality of the unbeliever, providing a context for a forceful apologetical challenge from the believer (cf. chap. 6.3). Non-Christians commonly uphold fruitful and appropriate standards of conduct and knowing[35]. This provides a "*pou sto*"[36] for refuting their system of thought. If we analyze and compare the competing worldviews, we find that the outlook of the would-be autonomous man makes facts, logic, objectivity, experience, etc., unintelligible (cf. chap. 5.3). Only the Christian apologist has a philosophical system within which the standards or beliefs to which the unbeliever assents in common with the believer (e.g., logic, induction, self-consciousness, mental freedom, conceptual reasoning, moral absolutes, human dignity) are intelligible (cf. chap. 4.5). And this is the source of the essential apologetical argument by which the unbeliever's ultimate presuppositions and worldview are refuted (cf. chap. 3.3).

To put it in compressed form, apologetical disputes hinge on the conflicting presuppositions (worldview) of the believer and the unbeliever, but the believer can argue for the rationality of his presup-

---

35. Unbelievers who have for the most part abandoned rationality (not desiring to make sense or think clearly) or have become indifferent to "giving reasons" for what they believe, have thereby stepped outside of the circle of apologetical concern. Apologetics arises because of the unbeliever's attack upon or questioning of the reasonableness of faith. When people care little for reasonableness, they care little about what apologetics is all about. They still need to be evangelized, of course, but the evangelizing of them at this point has little or nothing to do with intellectually defending Christianity as rational.

36. Speaking of the lever, Archimedes (d. 212 B.C.) said: "Give me a place to stand [Greek, *pou sto*], and I will move the earth."

positions (and demonstrate the irrationality of the opposing outlook) by means of an "internal comparison and critique" of the two contrary sets of presuppositions. This is what is known as an *indirect argument*— an argument "from the impossibility of the contrary." We can clarify this by considering what a direct argument is like. A direct argument is possible between two people who share relevant assumptions. Within the context of that interpretive agreement, they can directly appeal to observed facts, personal values and standards, or lines of reasoning that should "carry weight" with the other person; no entrenched "interpretive" disagreement would be expected. (Think of two friends going to a mutually accepted textbook in botany to settle their disagreement over the kind of flower growing in a garden.) However, when the argument involves disagreement over one's ultimate assumptions (e.g., the existence of God, man's nature and place in the cosmos, or the standards of right and wrong), there is nothing to which direct appeal can be made which is not itself weighed or interpreted in terms of the very standards or values that are being debated.

Therefore, we are left with indirect proof or refutation. The two fundamental theories or worldviews must be compared, being analyzed "from within" themselves, with a view to reducing to absurdity the position that opposes your own. The autonomous position of the unbeliever must be shown to be intellectually untenable on its own grounds. Here is how Van Til described his apologetical procedure:

> Since on the Reformed basis there is no area of neutrality between the believer and the unbeliever, the argument between them must be *indirect*. Christians cannot allow the legitimacy of the assumptions that underlie the non-Christian *methodology*. But they can place themselves upon the position of those whom they are seeking to win to a belief in Christianity for the sake of the argument. And the non-Christian, though not granting the presuppositions from which the Christian works, can nevertheless place himself upon the position of the Christian for the sake of the argument.[37]

37. *Christian Theory of Knowledge*, 18. David P. Hoover criticizes this element of Van Til's apologetical strategy since it falls short of demonstrating the absolute (unqualified) necessity that Christianity is true (thus placing Van Til in no better position than the traditionalists in apologetics). But to consider a viewpoint "for argument's sake" is not to grant that the viewpoint is in fact true ("stating a reality," in Hoover's words), but only to treat it as though it were true in order to see the

> [T]he method of reasoning employed must be consistent with and flow out of the position defended. . . . If this fundamental canon of Christian reasoning be always kept in mind, we can begin reasoning with our opponents at any point in heaven or earth and may *for argument's sake* present Christian theism as one hypothesis among many,[38] and may for argument's sake place ourselves upon the ground of our opponent in order to see what will happen. In all this it will remain our purpose to seek to reduce the non-theistic position, in whatever form it appears, to an absurdity. In our preaching we say that those who do not accept Christ are lost. Our reasoning can do nothing less.[39]

The "reason for the hope" that is within us (cf. 1 Peter 3:15) is that without the lordship of Christ, there could be no intelligible reason given by the unbeliever for anything at all. God has made foolish the wisdom of this world (cf. 1 Cor. 1:20). The Bible, stating the *reductio ad absurdum* advocated by Van Til, says very pointedly and powerfully, "Professing themselves to be wise, they become fools" (Rom. 1:22).

---

consequences of doing so. So Hoover writes: "The Christian necessarily both starts and finishes his argument at the level of hypothesis" ("For the Sake of Argument" [Hatfield, Pa.: Interdisciplinary Biblical Research Institute, n.d.], 7). This observation is quite unobjectionable, except that Hoover deems it a criticism of Van Til. Since Van Til concludes that Christianity is actually (and not simply hypothetically) true, Hoover thinks that he must have "shifted the logical ground" by taking Christianity as asserting what is really the case, not simply as true for argument's sake (p. 8). However, Hoover has missed two important aspects of Van Til's apologetical approach. First, although Hoover alludes to its intended transcendental character, he has not taken its significance into account (proving, if successful, the impossibility of the contrary). Second, to express it differently, because this is an apologetical dialogue (giving reasons, expecting argument, etc.), both parties have assumed that the true viewpoint must affirm rationality. Van Til argues that if the unbeliever's worldview were true, rationality would be repudiated, whereas if Christianity were true, rationality would be affirmed and required. So while the whole argument may be stated in hypothetical terms, the conclusion is actually established as true, since the hypothetical condition was granted from the outset by both parties. (If the unbeliever realizes this and now refuses to grant the legitimacy, demand, or necessity of rationality, he has stepped outside the boundaries of apologetics. Furthermore, he forfeits the right to assert or believe that he has repudiated rationality, since without rationality assertion and belief are unintelligible.)

38. As indicated earlier, even when the apologist, for the sake of protocol and polite discussion with the unbeliever, goes through the motions of treating Christianity as a hypothesis to be considered, he is not actually taking it as such. He intellectually rests upon Christian presuppositions even when reviewing, analyzing, and assessing those presuppositions with the unbeliever.

39. *Survey of Christian Epistemology*, xi.

The indirect apologetical argument is evident on previous pages of this book. As has already been indicated in previous analyses and discussions, the believer's worldview can be internally compared with the unbeliever's worldview to see if either one has a cogent theory of knowledge. When we do this, the results are of great apologetical significance (since believers and unbelievers are arguing over what they do and do not "know"). Within the Christian worldview, knowledge (along with rational and empirical methods) can be affirmed and made intelligible (cf. chap. 4.5). But when we "for argument's sake" look into the character and consequences of non-Christian philosophies, we encounter the repeated epistemological failure of unbelief (cf. chap. 5.3). Christianity is therefore epistemologically necessary; that is, it must be true because of the impossibility of the contrary.

In the argument between Christian faith and unbelief, it is important to remember that the two positions are mutually exclusive: one submits to the authority of God's revelation; the other asserts human autonomy. Despite the variety of unbelieving philosophical positions, there are fundamentally only two options (cf. chap. 5.2). As Christ asserted: "He who is not with Me is against Me" (Matt. 12:30). At root, one either has the mind of the "old man" who walks in ignorance and futility, or one has the mind of the "new man" renewed by Christ (Eph. 4:17–24). Van Til noted, "We have constantly sought to bring out that all forms of antitheistic thinking can be reduced to one."[40] It would be incorrect, then, to conceive of Van Til's presuppositional apologetic as an inductive project to find and then refute every "imaginable" alternative to Christianity—every single variation, past or future, on the worldview of autonomous reasoning.[41] A wise and inspired man who

---

40. Ibid.
41. John W. Montgomery trips himself up with this misconception of presuppositional apologetics when he writes: "And even if it were possible in some fashion to destroy all existent alternative world-views but that of orthodox Christianity, the end result would still not be the necessary truth of Christianity; for in a contingent universe, there are an *infinite* number of possible philosophical positions, and even the fallaciousness of infinity-minus-one positions would not establish the validity of the one that remained (unless we were to introduce the gratuitous assumption that at least one *had* to be right!)" ("Once upon an A Priori . . .," 387–88).
  But if that "gratuitous assumption" were not made, then the entire argument between the believer and the unbeliever would make no sense. Both parties assume that some philosophical perspective renders reasoning intelligible and possible, or else there would be no point to communicating and arguing with each other. Now then, since the dialogue between the believer and the unbeliever assumes the meaningfulness of their words and the intelligibility of their reason-

surveyed the field concluded, "There is no new thing under the sun" (Eccl. 1:9–10; cf. 12:12). Logically and theologically, at the most basic presuppositional level there is only one option outside of Christian commitment, and that is rejection of (or failure to make) such a commitment. Either the living and true God (concretely characterized by His self-revelation)[42] is a person's philosophical point of reference

---

ing, the unbeliever either (1) implicitly assumes the Christian's presuppositions, (2) considers it a mystery that not everything is mysterious or nonsensical, or (3) offers a worldview in which his words and reasoning are meaningful. If he admits to (1) or (2), he has conceded defeat in his attempt to prove Christianity wrong. If he attempts (3), the apologist proceeds to reduce his autonomous outlook to absurdity. If the unbeliever realizes this absurdity, he may try and try again, but in each case the apologist redoubles his effort and again reduces autonomy to absurdity. Eventually the unbeliever should get the point and recognize that his efforts always fail because they presuppose human autonomy.

Alternatively, he may make an admittedly "blind leap of faith" and hold out the hope that someday, somewhere, someone will furnish an adequate autonomous worldview to protect unbelievers against the compelling rationality of Christianity—in which case he has reverted to position (2) and loses anyway. The kind of necessity for which presuppositional apologetics argues is transcendental or inherent in the arguing itself (showing that the precondition of intelligibility makes any unbelieving argument impossible), not a matter of exhaustively eliminating unbelieving worldviews (all of which share the critical point of presumed autonomy).

Think once again of the battered and often refuted opponent of the Christian worldview. Montgomery imagines that this opponent could now argue that "this is a contingent universe, so the philosophical options are infinite." But in a completely contingent universe, in which there would be no logic, causality, or morality, this very declaration would not be intelligible. The finite and fallible unbeliever has no intellectual authority to make declarations about a range of possibility (much less about what is "infinite"!). He cannot continue to argue against Christianity in any meaningful way (even by placing his trust in hypothetical possibilities) without assuming the Christian worldview.

Similar replies would be appropriate, *mutatis mutandis*, for David Hoover ("For the Sake of Argument," 4, 8–9), who thinks that "discursive finitude" (lack of omniscience) would preclude "a finite human intellect" from "achiev[ing] the perspective necessary to run an argument of such great consequence." That is, presuppositional argumentation might show that Christianity is a sufficient condition for rationality, uniformity, etc., but it cannot show Christianity to be a necessary condition. However, it has never been held (from Kant onward) that a transcendental argument establishes necessity only by the exhaustive elimination of all real and imaginary *ways of expressing* the alternative (of which there is logically only one: the conclusion's negation).

42. Recall Van Til's opposition to "abstract" reasoning in apologetics. The word "God" is not to be treated as a merely formal expression or an empty placeholder in our thinking, with the question of God's specific character being a distinct matter—as though the abstraction can be "colored in" at some other time. We always argue for, and in terms of, a definite concept of God (based on Scripture) and not merely a generic deity (whatever he, she, or it may be).

and final authority, or in some fashion man (individually or collectively, atheistically or by conjuring up idolatrous substitutes) takes over that position and function. Despite "family squabbles" and secondary deviations among unregenerate men in their thinking, they are united at the basic level in setting aside the Christian conception of God. The indirect manner of proving the Christian position is thus to exhibit the intelligibility of reasoning, science, morality, etc., within the context of biblical presuppositions (as well as showing how unbelievers' objections are resolvable, given that context of thought[43]), and then to make an internal criticism of the presuppositions of autonomous thought (in whatever form it is presently being discussed) in order to show that it destroys the possibility of proving, understanding, or communicating anything.

REDUCING THE NON-CHRISTIAN'S PRESUPPOSITIONS TO ABSURDITY[44]

Since antitheistic thinking takes this univocal method of reasoning to be so evidently the only possible method of reasoning, since univocal reasoning is the reasoning of "the natural man," which he will not and cannot forsake till he is no longer a "natural man" but a regenerated man, the one thing of im-

---

43. For example, non-Christians might fault the Christian worldview for teaching such nonsense as that an ax head can float or a storm can be stilled upon command. The apologist needs to point out that this is not a problem *within* the biblical worldview, in which a personal, omniscient, and almighty Creator exercises sovereign control over the natural environment and providentially directs events within it.

   Alternatively, the unbeliever might argue that there is a problem with the Bible's teaching about God, for it would be "fundamentally unfair" for Him to show love and compassion to one ethnic group (e.g., the Old Testament Jews) while overlooking other groups and consigning them to perdition. Again, the apologist should reply that this is not a problem *within* the biblical worldview, where the controlling premises are that all men are guilty before God and deserve His wrath, and that a gracious God by the very nature of grace may show mercy on whom He will.

   It is not uncommon for an unbeliever to offer objections to the faith that carry weight only within his own worldview—thus *begging the question*. For example, I once debated a well-educated lawyer on the existence of God, and he asked me how I could possibly believe in the inerrancy of the ancient books of the Bible, when the people who wrote and transcribed them did not have modern computers and copiers. I replied that within the Christian worldview, this presents no problem at all, since God controls all events and outcomes (even those that come about by human choice and activity) and is far more capable and powerful than modern machines.

44. An excerpt from *Survey of Christian Epistemology*, 203–8.

portance to remember is that we must set over against this natural man not something that is a little modification of that which he already holds. We must hold before him the necessity of a total reversal of his attitude of mind.

It is this that Paul did when he preached the gospel to the wise men of Athens, steeped as they were in Plato and Aristotle. The Christian epistemologists have been all too remiss in fearing to follow Paul's example boldly.[45] They have feared that they would have no results if they were thus fearless in their approach. Yet if anything would seem to follow from the Christian position as a whole, it is that we could expect no results at all unless bold measures be taken. If the whole head is sick and the whole heart faint, it is not a snuffbox that is needed, but a lively stimulant. If men are dead in their sins and trespasses they are dead epistemologically too, and no demonstration of health will do any good, but only the gift of new life. Accordingly, we must reason in such a way that the Holy Spirit can give life through our reasoning as an avenue.

Our reasoning then *must always and everywhere be truly analogical.*[46] It matters not whether we are reasoning inductively or deductively, whether we analyze or synthesize, whether we reason in a priori or a posteriori fashion, if we only reason analogically we are true to our principle and may expect results, and if we do not reason analogically we are not true to our principle and may not expect any results.

The necessity of reasoning analogically is always implied in the theistic conception of God. If God is to be thought of at all as necessary for man's interpretation of the facts or objects of knowledge, he must be thought of as being determinative of the objects of knowledge. In other words, he must then be thought of as the only ultimate interpreter, and man must be thought of as a finite reinterpreter. Since, then, the absolute self-consciousness of God is the final interpreter of all facts, man's knowledge is analogical of God's knowledge. Since all the finite facts exist by virtue of the interpretation of God, man's interpretation of the finite facts is ultimately dependent upon God's interpretation of the facts. Man cannot, except to his own hurt, look at the facts without looking at God's interpretation of the facts. Man's knowledge of the facts is then a reinterpretation of God's interpretation. It is this that is meant by saying that man's knowledge is analogical of God's knowledge.

We must now consider more fully the question how one who has thus become convinced that analogical reasoning is the only type of reasoning that

45. Cf. Greg L. Bahnsen, "Socrates or Christ: The Reformation of Christian Apologetics," in *Foundations of Christian Scholarship: Essays in the Van Til Perspective*, ed. Gary North (Vallecito, Calif.: Ross House Books, 1976), 191–239.
46. Cf. chap. 4.5 above.

gives us truth at all, must face one who is convinced that univocal reasoning is the only type of reasoning that can possibly bring one into contact with truth.

In the preceding chapter we have seen that the point of contact that we may presuppose is that man, as a matter of fact, never exists in such independence as he thinks he does. *He remains accessible to God always.* It is this that gives us courage to proceed. And with this conviction we proceed with assurance of success. It is this that gives us courage not to condescend to any form of univocal reasoning.

When we approach the question in this way we should be willing to start anywhere and with any fact that any person we meet is interested in. The very conviction that there is not a single fact that can really be known unless it is interpreted theistically gives us this liberty to start anywhere, as far as a proximate starting point is concerned. If we thought that the fact of God's existence had no significance for physics, we would have to seek to bring our opponents at once into contact with the more specifically religious problem. But that is exactly what we need not do.

We can start with any fact at all and challenge "our friends the enemy," to give us an intelligible interpretation of it. Since the non-theist is so heartily convinced that univocal reasoning is the only possible kind of reasoning, we must ask him to reason univocally for us in order that we may see the consequences.[47]

In other words, we believe it to be in harmony with and a part of the process of reasoning analogically with a non-theist that we ask him to show us first what he can do. We may, to be sure, offer to him at once a positive statement of our position. But this he will at once reject as quite out of the question. So we may ask him to give us something better. The reason he gives for rejecting our position is, in the last analysis, that it involves self-contradiction. We see again as an illustration of this charge the rejection of the theistic conception that God is absolute and that he has nevertheless created this world for his glory. This, the non-theist says, is self-contradictory. And it no doubt is, from a non-theistic point of view.

But the final question is not whether a statement appears to be contradictory. *The final question is in which framework or on which view of reality—the Christian or the non-Christian—the law of contradiction can have application to any fact.*[48] The non-Christian rejects the Christian view out of hand as being contradictory. Then when he is asked to furnish a foundation for the law of contradiction, he can offer nothing but the idea of contingency.

47. Emphasis added.
48. Emphasis added.

What we shall have to do then is to try to reduce our opponent's position to an absurdity. Nothing less will do. Without God, man is completely lost in every respect, epistemologically as well as morally and religiously.[49] But exactly what do we mean by reducing our opponent's position to an absurdity? He thinks he has already reduced our position to an absurdity by the simple expedient just spoken of. But we must point out to him that upon a theistic basis our position is not reduced to an absurdity by indicating the "logical difficulties" involved in the conception of creation. Upon the theistic basis it must be contended that the human categories are but analogical of God's categories, so that it is to be expected that human thought will not be able to comprehend how God shall be absolute and at the same time create the universe for his glory. If taken on the same level of existence, it is no doubt a self-contradiction to say that a thing is full and at the same time is being filled. But it is exactly this point that is in question—whether God is to be thought of as on the same level with man. What the antitheist should have done is to show that even upon a theistic basis our conception of creation involves self-contradiction.

We must therefore give our opponents better treatment than they give us. We must point out to them that univocal reasoning itself leads to self-contradiction, not only from a theistic point of view, but from a non-theistic point of view as well. It is this that we ought to mean when we say that *we must meet our enemy on their own ground.* It is this that we ought to mean when we say that we reason *from the impossibility of the contrary.* The contrary is impossible only if it is self-contradictory when operating on the basis of its own assumptions. It is this too that we should mean when we say that we are arguing *ad hominem.* We do not really argue *ad hominem* unless we show that someone's position involves self-contradiction, and there is no self-contradiction unless one's reasoning is shown to be directly contradictory of or to lead to conclusions which are contradictory of one's own assumptions.

It will be seen that when we reason *ad hominem* or when we say that we place ourselves upon our opponent's position *we are still reasoning analogically.* We would not be reasoning analogically if we really placed ourselves upon our opponent's position. Then we would, with him, have to reason univocally, and we would drown with him.[50] We use the figure of drowning in

49. Emphasis added.
50. If an apologist truly adopted and thought in terms of the unbeliever's presuppositions, his thinking would become as meaningless and senseless as the unbeliever's system of thought. If it were possible to show the internal flaws of the non-Christian's position while truly abandoning all believing presuppositions (the knowledge of God), then the non-Christian position would not be essentially

order to suggest what it is that we really do when we say that we are placing ourselves upon someone else's position. We may then compare ourselves to a lifesaver who goes out to save someone from drowning. Such a lifesaver must be bound to the shore to which he wants to rescue the other party. He may depend upon his power to swim, but this very power to swim is an invisible cord that connects him to the shore. Similarly, if we reason when we place ourselves upon our opponents' position, we cannot for a moment do more than argue thus for "argument's sake."

When we reason thus we are not reasoning on the basis of some abstract law of self-contradiction. We have seen that the very question between theists and antitheists is as to the foundation of the law of contradiction.[51] When they criticize our position and think they have reduced it to the place where it falls under the law of self-contradiction, we do not give in to defeat or appeal to irrationality in the name of faith, but we challenge their interpretation of the law of contradiction. We hold that they have falsely assumed that the self-contradictory is to be identified with that which is beyond the comprehension of man. But this takes for granted that human categories are ultimate categories—which is just the thing in question. We must maintain that we have the true conception of the law of contradiction. According to that conception, only that is self-contradictory which is contradictory to the conception of the absolute self-consciousness of God. If there were in the Trinity such a self-contradiction, there would also be in the matter of God's relation to the world. But, since the Trinity is the conception by which ultimate unity and diversity is brought into equal ultimacy, it is this conception of the Trinity which makes *self-contradiction impossible for God and therefore also impossible for man.* Complete self-contradiction is possible only in hell, and hell is itself a self-contradiction because it feeds eternally on the negation of an absolute affirmation. Accordingly, we must hold that the position of our opponent has in reality been reduced to self-contradiction when it is shown to be hopelessly opposed to the Christian theistic concept of God.

Yet in order to bring this argument as closely to the non-regenerate consciousness as we may, we must seek to show that the non-theist is self-contradictory upon his own assumptions, as well as upon the assumption of the truth of theism, and that he cannot even be self-contradictory upon a non-theistic basis, since if he saw himself to be self-contradictory he would be self-contradictory no longer.

---

flawed after all—and the Christian position would not be psychologically or epistemologically necessary (cf. chaps. 5.2–3; 6.1–2, 5 above).

51. Emphasis added. Compare the taped Bahnsen-Stein debate (held at the University of California at Irvine), "Does God Exist?"

Now when this method of reasoning from the impossibility of the contrary is carried out, there is really nothing more to do.[52] We realize this if we call to mind again that if once it is seen that the conception of God is necessary for the intelligible interpretation of any fact, it will be seen that this is necessary for all facts and for all laws of thought. If one really saw that it is necessary to have God in order to understand the grass that grows outside his window, he would certainly come to a saving knowledge of Christ, and to the knowledge of the absolute authority of the Bible. It is true, we grant that it is not usually in this way that men become true Christian theists, but we put it in this way in order to bring out clearly that the investigation of any fact whatsoever will involve a discussion of the meaning of Christianity as well as of theism, and a sound position taken on the one involves a sound position on the other. It is well to emphasize this fact because there are Fundamentalists who tend to throw overboard all epistemological and metaphysical investigation and say that they will limit their activities to preaching Christ. But we see that they are not really preaching Christ unless they are preaching him for what he wants to be, namely, the Christ of cosmic significance. Nor can they even long retain the soteriological significance of Christ if they forsake his cosmological significance. If one allows that certain facts may be truly known apart from God in Christ, there is no telling where the limit will be. It soon appears that the elephant wants to warm more than his nose. He will soon claim that the truths of the religious consciousness may also be known apart from Christ, and may therefore become the standard of what is to be accepted of the Bible.

In this connection we must also say a word about the contention often made by Christians that we must be positive rather than negative in our presentation of the truth to those who have not yet accepted it. We have no fault to find with this statement if it be correctly understood. We must certainly present the truth of the Christian theistic system constantly, at every point of the argument. But it is clear that if you offer a new wife to one who is perfectly satisfied with the one he has now, you are not likely to be relieved of your burden.

In other words, it is the self-sufficiency of the "natural man" that must first be brought under some pressure, before there is any likelihood of his even considering the truth in any serious fashion at all. The parable of the prodigal helps us here. As long as the son was at home there was nothing but a positive argument that was held before him. But he wanted to go out of the father's house in order to indulge in "riotous living." Not till he was at the

52. Emphasis added.

swine trough, not till he saw that he had made a hog of himself and that he could not be a hog because he was a man, did he at all begin to consider the servants of his father who had plenty of bread. The kingdom of God must be built upon the destruction of the enemy. God increases his plagues upon those that "dwell upon the earth" in order to make them think analogically. And though they cry for the mountains and the hills to fall upon them rather than turn to him that chastises them, yet God continues to increase the weight of his plagues. Now this is more than an analogy. Univocal reasoning is itself a part of the manifestation of sin. Hence it too must be destroyed. And if it is destroyed the natural result is analogical reasoning. And it matters not how far may seem the way, once one reasons analogically one will arrive at the father's house at last. The *far* country into which the prodigal had gone and where he thought he was beyond the father's control was nevertheless the father's country, and the father was "pulling the strings" there.

It is this, it will be noticed, that leads us to victory. If it were not true that it is the father who "pulls the strings," we would reason in vain. For we need not flatter ourselves that even if the non-theist be shown that his position is self-contradictory in the sense that it contradicts his own assumptions and breaks to pieces his own law of contradiction, he will turn from his ways of himself. Instead, he will conclude that man must remain in such complete ir-rationality, rather than turn to analogical reasoning. *The miracle of regeneration has to occur somewhere, and all that we are arguing for is that we must ask where it is that the Holy Spirit will most likely perform this miracle. And then there can be no doubt but that the likelihood is in favor of that place where the non-theist has to some extent seen the emptiness and vanity of his own position.*[53]

THE TWO-STEP PROCEDURE IN APOLOGETICS[54]

We are told over and over again [by unbelieving critics] that we must make no metaphysical assumptions when we study the phenomena of the religions. We are told that the traditional position constantly makes such assumptions. It has, we are told, a whole scheme of metaphysics in light of which it interprets the religious experience. In contrast to this we are to go to the facts and study them with unbiased mind. In the first place we must go to history to find out about the origin of religion. We find that man gradually evolved from the beast. Religion and morality somehow sprung from the non-moral and

53. Emphasis added.
54. An excerpt from *Christian Theistic Evidences*, In Defense of Biblical Christianity, vol. 6 (Phillipsburg, N.J.: Presbyterian and Reformed, 1978), 127–28.

the non-religious. Men evolved the religious attitude in response to their physical needs. . . .

We need not enlarge upon this matter. It is too well known to need further elucidation. What does not need elucidation is the fact that men can seriously offer such a presentation and still think they are not taking for granted a complete scheme of metaphysics and epistemology. . . .

To say that we can find the origin of religion by simply historical study is to assume the non-Christian position. It takes for granted that history is self-explanatory. It therefore at the outset excludes God as the creator of history. . . . We cannot [hereby] reach to the high position of the Biblical account. That account speaks of an originally perfect man. Where is the factual historical evidence that such a man ever existed?

We cannot [in apologetical response] resort to possibilities and probabilities. The Bible requires absolute faith in its truthfulness. We cannot resort to a dualism between our faith and our rational interpretation of life. The Bible says that we are created as unified personalities. The only method of dealing with this whole problem is that spoken of repeatedly. We should allow men to work out a complete interpretation of life upon the basis of the principles they have assumed. They will then run into a blind alley. So in the present instance. Starting with self-sufficiency it cannot find in history any criterion with which to judge between better or worse. Starting with the normalcy of the mind of sinful man, the abnormal is made an aspect of the normal. Truth cannot be distinguished from error. Light cannot be distinguished from darkness.

When the bankruptcy of the non-Christian interpretation of the origin of religion thus appears we point out that the "facts" are in accord with the Christian position. We presuppose God. That gives meaning to history as a whole. God is the maker of all things. He created man in his own image. Man's consciousness could therefore function fruitfully when it sought to interpret life in accordance with God's interpretation of it.

7.4 The Transcendental Nature of Presuppositional Argument

To understand the character of Van Til's presuppositional apologetical argument for the truth of Christianity, it will be instructive to review a short segment of the history of philosophy: the beginning of the "modern period" (the seventeenth and eighteenth centuries) in Europe and England. Along with other influences, Descartes had situated epistemology at the center of philosophical speculation. For example, what can we know for certain (beyond doubt)? How do we psychologically come to know what we do? How do we justify (prove) our claims to knowledge? Prior to the arrival of Kant's critical approach to such questions (especially, how are synthetic *a priori* judgments possible?), two major schools of epistemological thought competed with each other. There was the "rationalist" approach to learning, knowing, and proof, advocated by the "Continental rationalists" René Descartes, Baruch Spinoza, and Gottfried Leibniz. The competing school of thought took an "empiricist" approach to epistemology and was represented by John Locke, George Berkeley, and David Hume. Both rationalism and empiricism adopted the autonomous point of reference that was assumed by Descartes' attempt to escape skepticism or doubt, namely, man's intellectual self-sufficiency as his own starting point for philosophical reasoning. (According to Descartes, the first clear and indisputable truth is that the individual man who is thinking or doubting must exist in order to think or doubt.)

How do we know what we know, and how can we prove our beliefs to be true? The autonomous rationalists maintained that there are self-evident truths from which we can deduce substantial conclusions about the nature of reality. The wildly different conclusions about reality at which they arrived made it rather incredible that their premises were genuinely self-evident and that their deductions were genuinely necessary. The autonomous empiricists rejected all innate ideas, maintained that only particulars exist, and said that we know and prove things by common sense and observation of the world. This too led to philosophical embarrassment, in that the empirical demand for verification (or the tracing of our particular ideas back to their origin) was not itself a truth that could be empirically verified, and the nature of the particulars that were acknowledged to exist was hotly disputed. Was there a particular substance underlying the particular attributes of things (Locke), or did material substance exist only as a mental idea or internal experience (Berkeley), or—empirically speaking—must we not also reject the existence of a mental substance (the mind being only a bundle of perceptions), as well as enduring extramental objects (made up of isolated, experienced traits) and any causal relation between them (Hume)? Enlightenment epistemology was a shambles in both Europe (the rationalists) and Great Britain (the empiricists). Hume could comment: "If reasoning be considered in an abstract view, it furnishes invincible arguments against itself"! The vaunted "Age of Reason" had collapsed into subjectivism and skepticism, failing to find a reliable method of knowing—and even disagreeing sharply over the nature of "reasoning" itself. There would seem to be no intellectual basis for confidence in man's ability to gain objective knowledge of the real and orderly world outside (or inside) the mind.

Thus, as the story runs, Immanuel Kant was "awakened from dogmatic slumbers" by the shocking skepticism to which Hume was driven, and he pursued a "Copernican Revolution" in the way we should view the mind and its reasoning. The memorable opening line of the preface to the first edition of the *Critique of Pure Reason* stated: "Human reason has this peculiar fate that in one species of its knowledge it is burdened by questions which, as prescribed by the very nature of reason itself, it is not able to ignore, but which, as transcending all its powers, it is also not able to answer."[55] It was scandalous, said Kant, to philosophy and human reason that "if anyone thinks good to doubt" the existence and nature of things outside us, "we are unable to counter his doubts by any satisfactory proof" and must accept those things "merely on faith."[56] The rationalist and empiricist conceptions and methods of "proof" were obviously inadequate to counter the skeptic, but Kant felt that a different program of philosophical analysis could very well "save science" (as well as leave room for mystical and moralistic religious faith). Kant's *particular* recommendation for doing this was philosophically (and religiously) abhorrent to Van Til (cf. chap. 5 above),[57] but the *general kind of program* (or approach to the proof of fundamental beliefs) that Kant recom-

---

55. Immanuel Kant, *Critique of Pure Reason,* trans. Norman Kemp Smith (German original, 1781; English translation, 1929; reprint, New York: St. Martin's Press, 1965), A vii.

56. Ibid., B xl.

57. Kant did not depart from the man-centered and autonomous standpoint of Descartes, but actually intensified its inwardness, making the mind of man the source of order or law in the world of experience. The mind, previously viewed as passive in the knowing process, is actually active in the acquisition of knowledge, held Kant; it imposes order (that is, the forms of time and space, and categories such as substance and causality) on the chaotic raw data of sensations. Against the rationalists, Kant taught that nothing could be known apart from experience or observation; against the empiricists, he held that the mind is not a blank tablet, but constructive of its objects of knowledge. Kant's scheme was arbitrary, offering no proof that the structure of the mind is universally the same or that our physical cognitive faculties do not change from time to time in a contingent world. It also capitulated to subjectivism and skepticism, since the mind "knows" objects only as they appear in experience, not as they are in themselves. Kant's metaphysical agnosticism with respect to extramental things of "this world" (the noumenal realm) and things "beyond this world" (nonempirical ideas such as God) renders his autonomous philosophy thoroughly unacceptable, both philosophically and religiously.

mended to improve upon rationalism and empiricism was convincing and effective, according to Van Til. Kant proposed to engage in "transcendental" analysis, which asks what the preconditions are for the intelligibility of human experience. Under what conditions is it possible, or what would also need to be true in order for it to be possible, to make sense of one's experience of the world? To seek the transcendental conditions for knowing is to ask what is presupposed by any intelligible experience whatsoever. This kind of analysis takes us beyond the methods of rationalism and empiricism to see what is presupposed by them both. Kant wrote, "I entitle *transcendental* all knowledge which is occupied . . . with the mode of our knowledge of objects in so far as this mode of knowledge is to be possible *a priori*."[58] Beliefs that are genuinely transcendental, then, cannot be false, and their certainty is ascertainable apart from specific empirical experiences that suggest or confirm them. Kant explained that the conclusion of a transcendental argument (or an analysis of some item of experience) "has the peculiar character that it makes possible the very experience which is its own ground of proof, and that in this experience it must always itself be presupposed."[59]

The transcendental method of knowing one's fundamental beliefs or proving one's presuppositions, in which Van Til took a keen interest and advocated for apologetics in the late 1920s (when there was, as yet, a background of continuing appreciation for idealism in philosophical circles), has again come somewhat into vogue as a matter of some fascination (both negative and positive) among philosophers.[60]

58. *Critique of Pure Reason*, A 12.
59. Ibid., B 765. Note well that not all claims that a belief or idea is transcendental are in fact true. Saying so does not make it so. For instance, a dedicated opponent of the Christian faith might allege that his empiricism is a "transcendental" truth. But the principle "All knowledge is based on observational experience" is hardly one that could not possibly be false. Furthermore, it does not make possible its own ground of proof! Far from being self-authorizing or self-attesting, the empirical principle actually testifies against itself and betrays its own lack of authority. That is, we do not empirically know that all knowledge is based on observational experience.
60. The contemporary catalyst has been the analysis offered by P. F. Strawson in books such as *Individuals* (London: Methuen, 1959) and *The Bounds of Sense* (London: Methuen, 1965), but one could also consider Ludwig Wittgenstein's argument against the impossibility of a private language (*Philosophical Investigations*) and his argument for the possibility of knowledge (*On Certainty;* cf. Greg L. Bahnsen, "Pragmatism, Prejudice, and Presuppositionalism," in *Foundations of Christian Scholarship*, ed. North, 258–71). Other important contributions to the discussion of transcendental arguments are A. C. Grayling, *The Refutation of Scep-*

They disagree over the proper scope of transcendental arguments (how broad or ambitious should be their aim?) and the metaphysical character of what they prove (does it exist objectively or is it simply necessary to our conceptual scheme?). But others have been critical of the very notion of a transcendental kind of analysis or argument that is distinct from the methods of rationalism or empiricism (or their more refined modern counterparts). Similarly, John Frame has taken a critical position regarding this type of argument, holding that "there is probably not a distinctively 'transcendental argument' which rules out all other kinds of arguments." He questions whether they are "really distinct from direct arguments," and suggests that only rhetorical form or phrasing (the order in which things are mentioned) makes them different from deductive or inductive arguments that move "directly" from some observation or principle to what can be inferred from it.[61] In my judgment, however, Frame is mistaken about this.

The difference between the kind of philosophical analysis and argument that was engaged in and advanced by Kant and the kind of analysis or argument set forth by Descartes or Locke cannot credibly be reduced to a matter of rhetorical phrasing. The same holds for the difference between the kind of apologetical argumentation offered by Van Til and that which has been proposed by rationalistic and evidentialist apologists. The rationalist and empiricist philosophers se-

---

ticism (London: Duckworth, 1985) and R. Harrison, *On What There Must Be* (Oxford: Clarendon Press, 1974). There have been numerous relevant articles in the journals, some supportive and some critical of the notion of transcendental proof. They include Barry Stroud, "Transcendental Arguments," *Journal of Philosophy* 65 (1968): 241–56; John Kekes, "Transcendental Arguments and the Sceptical Challenge," *Philosophical Forum* 4 (1973–74): 422–31; A. Phillips Griffiths and J. J. MacIntosh, "Transcendental Arguments," *Proceedings of the Aristotelian Society*, supp. vol. 43 (1969): 165–93; T. E. Wilkerson, "Transcendental Arguments," *Philosophical Quarterly* 20 (1970): 200–212; Stephen W. Arndt, "Transcendental Method and Transcendental Arguments," *International Philosophical Quarterly* 27 (1987): 43–58; Charles Crittenden, "Transcendental Arguments Revived," *Philosophical Investigations* 8 (1985): 229–51; Moltke S. Gram, "Transcendental Arguments," *Nous* 5 (1971): 15–26; Jaakko Hintikka, "Transcendental Arguments: Genuine and Spurious," *Nous* 6 (1972): 274–80; Charles Taylor, "The Validity of Transcendental Arguments," *Proceedings of the Aristotelian Society*, n.s. 79 (1978–79): 151–65. A convenient and competent overview of the contemporary discussion can be found in *A Companion to Epistemology*, edited by Jonathan Dancy and Ernst Sosa (Oxford: Basil Blackwell, 1992).

61. *Apologetics to the Glory of God* (Phillipsburg, N.J.: Presbyterian and Reformed, 1994), 73, 76.

lected a starting point (for Descartes, self-evident or clear ideas; for Locke, simple ideas caused by sensation),[62] whereas Kant's analysis encourages one to start with any idea or fact whatsoever. The earlier philosophers also employed methods of reasoning different from Kant's: Descartes connected and unpacked concepts, and Locke connected ideas by inductive generalization and analyzed complex ideas into their simple components. Kant, however, did not take items of phenomenal experience (whether conceptual or perceptual) themselves and connect them to others or break them down (unpack them); rather, he asked about something distinct from them, namely, the conditions (additional beliefs) that are necessary for them to be intelligible. Kant's argument about the "necessity" of a causal understanding of our experience is not at all a rhetorical variation on the kind of analysis and argumentation we find in the work of Descartes or Locke (or especially Hume); they are concerned with different types of issues and appeal to different kinds of support for the positions they take on those issues.

But we realize even more clearly and definitively the distinctiveness of transcendental arguments when we contrast their logical character (that is, the truth-functional relation of their conclusions to their premises) with that of rational and empirical arguments. A deductive demonstration takes particular premises and draws a necessary conclusion from them; but if, in this rational argument, one of the relevant premises were to be negated, the conclusion would no longer follow or be established. Likewise, in an inductive or empirical argument, the premises include particular claims (or instances) of a definite sort; from them the conclusion draws a generalization with probability. However, if a component or relevant premise (or sets of instances) were to be negated, the general conclusion would no longer be the same as before (or would no longer be drawn with the same degree of probability). To put it simply, in the case of "direct" arguments (whether rational or empirical), the negation of one of their premises changes the truth or reliability of their conclusion. But this is not true of transcendental arguments, and that sets them off from the other kinds of proof or analysis. A transcendental argument

62. Likewise, rational proofs for God's existence do not start with just any truth, principle, or concept at all, but with an especially important one—like cause or purpose or perfection. Evidential proofs do not start with just any fact whatsoever, but with an especially important one—like Christ's resurrection or fulfilled prophecy.

begins with *any* item of experience or belief whatsoever and proceeds, by critical analysis, to ask what conditions (or what other beliefs) would need to be true in order for that original experience or
belief to make sense, be meaningful, or be intelligible to us. Now then,
if we should go back and negate the statement of that original belief
(or consider a contrary experience), the transcendental analysis (if
originally cogent or sound) would nevertheless reach the very same
conclusion.[63] Clearly then, transcendental demonstration has a very
distinct kind of argument over against rational and empirical proofs.[64]

A number of the features of transcendental argumentation commended themselves to Van Til as an apologist. In the first place, it is
a forceful, all-or-nothing intellectual challenge to unbelief in all of its

63. Van Til's stunning application of this feature of transcendental argumentation
    to apologetics is that the truth of the Christian worldview is established not only
    by theistic premises and opinions, but also by antitheistic beliefs and opinions.
    As Van Til said, "Antitheism presupposes theism" (*Survey of Christian Epistemology*,
    xii). Even if the unbeliever wants to start with the assertion that "God does not
    exist," a transcendental analysis of it would show that the possibility of its coher-
    ence or meaningfulness assumes the existence of the very God that it denies.
64. In passing, it should be noted that there is no transcendental argument that "rules
    out all other kinds of arguments," as Frame puts it (*Apologetics to the Glory of God*,
    73)—either in general philosophy and scholarship or particularly in apologetics
    (cf. chap. 8.3, 4 below).
       However, when Frame says that transcendental arguments "require supple-
    mentation"—the help of other, "subsidiary" arguments—because he does "not
    think that the whole of Christian theism can be established by a single argument"
    (pp. 71, 72, 73), he fails to grasp that at stake in the transcendental argument is
    nothing less than the *whole* of the Christian worldview as revealed in Scripture.
    Frame criticizes Van Til by saying, "We must prove more than that God is the au-
    thor of meaning and rationality," and then says, "Besides proving that God is the
    author of meaning, we must . . . prove that God is personal, sovereign, . . . just,
    loving, omnipotent, omnipresent, etc." (p. 73). Or again: "There is no single ar-
    gument that will prove the entire biblical doctrine of God" (p. 73). Remarks like
    these misconstrue the transcendental argument, as if it were one part of an atom-
    istic or "blockhouse" apologetic, in which the defender of the faith proves the
    various features of the Christian worldview one by one. Rather, Van Til taught that
    when we engage in the internal critique of worldviews (the indirect argument with
    the unbeliever), we set forth for comparison the entire biblical worldview with
    all its features and details. In the dialogue with the unbeliever, we cannot speak
    of everything simultaneously (and it is convenient and polemically effective to
    get into the issues of meaning and rationality from the start), but the position for
    which we are arguing is nothing less than all of Christianity. The Christian apol-
    ogist may choose to focus on meaningfulness with one opponent, but turn to con-
    siderations of justice or love with a different opponent. These are simply "illus-
    trations" of the broader project laid out by the transcendental approach. The
    illustration that is used in a particular circumstance is "person variable" (cf.
    Frame, p. 72).

manifestations. Our method of apologetics should not be concessive or compromising. As Van Til put it:

> The natural man must be blasted out of his hideouts, his caves, his last lurking places. . . .
>
> Calvinism makes no compromise with the natural man either on his views of the autonomy of the human mind or on his views of the nature of existence as not controlled by the plan of God. Therefore Calvinism cannot find a direct point of contact in any of the accepted concepts of the natural man. . . . He disagrees with the basic immanentistic assumption of the natural man. For it is this basic assumption that colors all his statements about individual teachings. It is therefore this basic assumption of the natural man that meets its first major challenge when it is confronted by the statement of full-fledged Christianity.
>
> The Reformed apologist throws down the gauntlet and challenges his opponent to a duel of life and death from the start.[65]

Secondly, this form of argumentation covers the entire field. The transcendental, presuppositional argument does not allow that the unbeliever "can interpret *any aspect* of experience in terms of his principles without destroying the very idea of intelligibility." To put it another way, Van Til maintained "that the philosophy of the non-Christian cannot account for the intelligibility of human experience *in any sense.*"[66]

And thus, thirdly, the transcendental argument upholds the exclusivity or singularity of Christianity as the answer to man's woes:

> Thus the Christian-theistic position must be shown to be not *as defensible as* some other position; it must rather be shown to be *the position which alone does not annihilate intelligent human experience.* . . . He must therefore present the facts . . . as proving Christian theism because they are intelligible as facts in terms of it and in terms of it alone.[67]

Transcendental apologetics need not yield to the competing virtues of other worldviews: "We as Christians alone have a position that is philo-

---

65. *Defense of the Faith,* 122, 129–30.
66. Ibid., 198, 354 (emphasis added).
67. Ibid., 197, 264 (emphasis original).

sophically defensible. . . . We are [certain] that Christianity is objectively valid and that it is the only rational position for man to hold."[68]

In that case, fourthly, the transcendental form of defending the faith can deal with anything that the unbeliever brings up as an objection or challenge.

> One shows that on his [the unbeliever's] assumptions all things are meaningless. Science would be impossible; knowledge of anything in any field would be impossible. No fact could be distinguished from any other fact. No law could be said to be law with respect to facts. . . . Thus every fact—not *some* facts—every fact *clearly* and not probably proves the truth of Christian theism. If Christian theism is not true then nothing is true.[69]

Indeed, given the force of the transcendental argument, the apologist is justified in rejecting in advance any hypothesis whose assumptions contradict the Christian outlook.[70]

A fifth virtue that commends transcendental apologetics is, accordingly, that it is not forced to agree to anything in the unbeliever's position or argument—as though future research might affect its validity,[71] or as though Christianity is merely more probably correct than its competition. The argument for it is "objectively valid," regardless of the attitude of the person to whom it comes. "Christianity is the only reasonable position to hold. It is not merely as reasonable as other positions, or a bit more reasonable as other positions; it alone is the natural and reasonable position for man to take."[72] If the transcendental project is properly pursued, the position of those who do not believe in the self-authenticating Christ "is reducible to absurdity."[73] "Our argument, then, is that those who . . . stop short of maintaining the fundamental conceptions of an absolute Christ, an absolute Scripture, and regeneration, reduce experience to an absurdity."[74]

Finally, then, in light of the foregoing features that make tran-

68. *Common Grace,* 8, 82.
69. *Defense of the Faith,* 266–67. The last sentence is elliptical; to put it more precisely, substitute "nothing is known to be true" for "nothing is true."
70. Ibid., 116.
71. *Common Grace,* 50.
72. *Defense of the Faith,* 256; cf. *The Reformed Pastor and Modern Thought* (Philadelphia: Presbyterian and Reformed, 1971), 98.
73. *The Case for Calvinism* (Philadelphia: Presbyterian and Reformed, 1963), 144.
74. *Survey of Christian Epistemology,* 221.

scendental reasoning so attractive to a Christian apologist, Van Til considered it to have great personal and spiritual strength. "By stating the argument as clearly as we can, we may be the agents of the Holy Spirit in pressing the claims of God upon men," for a transcendental analysis of man's interpretive activity "is no doubt the most penetrating means by which the Holy Spirit presses the claims of God upon men." Indeed, although it may be couched in academic terms and be part of an intellectual dialogue, the transcendental argument for the truth of Christianity is an avenue by which "God calls men to conversion."[75]

It is easy to understand why Van Til and others have found the transcendental approach to defending the faith compelling and attractive. To understand how Van Til utilized it, however, it is important to see that his version of transcendental argumentation was unique. Van Til pointed out that he was applying the method of Kant or of the logic of idealism, but in a way which they could not.[76] In investigating the preconditions for the intelligibility of man's experience, Van Til introduced significant changes in the method employed by unbelieving philosophers when pursuing a similar aim:

> Again, we may speak of our method as being transcendental, but if we do, we should once more observe that our meaning of that word is different from the Kantian, or modern, meaning. Kantian thought does not really find its final reference point in God. Modern thought in general does not really interpret reality in eternal categories. It seeks to interpret reality by a combination of eternal and temporal categories. . . . It is only the Christian who really interprets reality in exclusively eternal categories because only he believes in God as self-sufficient and not dependent upon temporal reality.[77]

Van Til held that Valentine Hepp was wrong to say "that Kant sought the solution of the question of certainty *in the same direction* in which a Christian should seek it." And the reason why Van Til made a point of insisting on this and distinguishing transcendental apologetics from

---

75. *Defense of the Faith*, 256, 257, 285 (in the first two citations, Van Til was quoting from *Common Grace*, 62).

76. *An Introduction to Systematic Theology*, In Defense of the Faith, vol. 5 (Philadelphia: Presbyterian and Reformed, 1974), 9.

77. Ibid., 14. The significance of the remarks about introducing temporal categories into one's point of reference is that they are, as such, contingent and subject to change, thereby excluding their conceptual necessity.

Kant was that "Kant's foundation of reasoning is wrong inasmuch as it is based upon the assumption of the ultimacy of the human mind, and inasmuch as it has assumed the existence of brute fact."[78]

Van Til's *kind* of transcendental critique was not a philosophically neutral or autonomous, abstract intellectual analysis, in which any unbeliever could participate without objection. It was not a project that started with no definite assumptions and reflected on immanent factors to discover the general foundations of thought in a way that any philosophers might do in formal cooperation with each other. "We do not first set out without God to find our highest philosophical concept in terms of which we think we can interpret reality and then call this highest concept divine."[79] God does not come in at the end of the process, having earned the intellectual right to a place in our thinking. The very process of transcendental thinking or analysis must itself begin with belief in the living and true God. Advocates of autonomous transcendental critique consider transcendental apologetics distasteful, because Van Til's transcendental reasoning has a transcendent and concrete starting point in the presupposition of the truth of Scripture. "It is not enough for a Christian to point to the mere fact of the necessity of an *a priori* element in science. He must also show that unless that *a priori* be given the Christian-theistic basis, it is no true *a priori*."[80] This is considerably too religious, too personal, and too specific for autonomous philosophers and thinkers—as Van Til knew very well. He stated:

> We accept this God upon Scriptural authority. In the Bible alone do we hear of such a God. Such a God, to be known at all, cannot be known otherwise than by virtue of His own voluntary revelation. . . .
>
> The frank acceptance of our position on authority, which at first blush, because of our inveterate tendency to think along non-Christian lines, seems to involve the immediate and total rejection of all philosophy—this frank acceptance of authority is, philosophically, our very salvation.[81]

The would-be autonomous man openly disdains bringing the Scriptures into a philosophical dialogue. He likewise derides any effort to give serious consideration to a complex, general worldview, insisting

78. Ibid., 55.
79. *Common Grace,* 8.
80. *Introduction to Systematic Theology,* 45.
81. *Common Grace,* 8.

that limited analytical details are the only proper subject for philosophical discussion. The kind of transcendental comparison or indirect argument that is encouraged by the Christian apologist is odious to him. He may ridicule it, but by the demands of philosophy itself, he cannot ignore it.

So, as we see, in Van Til's conception and use of transcendental argumentation, his own position rests upon authority (not upon autonomous analysis, starting from scratch). Further, the reasoning is concrete, rather than formal or abstract. That is why Van Til was critical of Kuyper for attempting to counter skepticism with the notion of mere "formal faith." Kuyper had argued that "general faith"—firm conviction "previous to investigation" or "prior to all proof"—was inherent in a human being and necessary to maintain one's own existence, the reliability of observation by our senses (as a bridge from the phenomenal to the noumenal), the truth of the laws of logic, the uniformity of nature, and the unity of all truth. Without this faith, a person would land in subjectivism and be overwhelmed by skepticism.[82] Van Til's trenchant critique was right on target:

> Kuyper insists that the concept of faith that he here speaks of is without content. It is inherent in the subject, therefore, not because the subject is *unavoidably confronted with God*, but simply *as such*. By means of this purely formal faith the human subject is first to become conscious of its own existence. Then by means of this formal faith a bridge is to be laid to the external world. The laws of thought by which the environment of man is to be manipulated also rest on this formal faith. . . .
>
> To be sure, all men have faith. Unbelievers have faith as well as believers. But that is due to the fact that they too are creatures of God. *Faith therefore always has content.* It is against the *concept of faith as belief in God* that man has become an unbeliever. As such he tries to *suppress the content* of his original faith. *He tries to reduce it to something formal.*[83] Then its content can take any form

82. *Defense of the Faith*, 384.
83. For instance, instead of saying "Jehovah is the Creator and controller of the world, of me as His image and responsible servant, and of my cognitive faculties so that I can reliably know His world and serve Him there," the unbeliever wants to reduce this to something less definite and theological—to the more "formal" belief that "there must be a 'me' who exists, with reliable cognitive faculties to know some kind of external world." The latter belief does not entail responsibility to acknowledge, thank, and glorify God for one's existence and abilities or to think of oneself as God's responsible servant.

he wants it to have. Then its content is actually indeterminate. And thus there is [to be philosophically honest] no foundation for man's knowledge of himself or of the world at all. . . .

Kuyper speaks as though the merely formal idea of faith is a dam against skepticism. . . . But how can this be? For this very formal idea of faith says nothing about the content or *object of faith*. Or rather, by its formality [an "unsaturated" function without defining value or subject] it allows for and even demands the correlative notion of pure non-rational factuality and of logic as an abstract system that includes both God and man. *Thus the formal idea of faith is the very source of skepticism itself.*[84]

The apologist commends to the unbeliever a very specific philosophical outlook or theory, with definite content—not simply abstract and formal ideas—for internal analysis and contrast to the concrete position of the unbeliever.

Hence, Van Til wrote that "the process of transcendental reasoning as employed by Christian theism is of necessity and inherently concrete."[85] Thus, the argument is that "the intelligibility of anything, for man, presupposes the existence of God—the God whose nature and character are delineated in God's revelation"[86]—not simply *a god* of some indeterminate character who (or which) might be transcendentally necessary. To simply posit a god about whom (or which) theoretical reason says nothing more (as with Kant) leaves the mind of man free to exercise its presumed autonomy by filling in the details.[87] The whole issue in apologetics is over *the specific kind* of God we are seeking to prove. "We must first ask what kind of a God Christianity believes in before we can really ask with intelligence whether such a God exists. The *what* precedes the *that*."[88] Likewise, the presuppositional argument does not first debate the formal possibility of a book from God, but rather begins the argument from the outset with the actuality of the Bible—whose worldview is offered for internal comparison with any other contrary viewpoint:

84. *Defense of the Faith*, 384–85 (emphasis added).
85. *Survey of Christian Epistemology*, 33.
86. *Reformed Pastor and Modern Thought*, 12.
87. "Particularism and Common Grace," in *Common Grace and the Gospel* (Philadelphia: Presbyterian and Reformed, 1972), 104.
88. *Defense of the Faith*, 25; cf. pp. 25–29.

We must begin with the actuality of the book. We must not pretend that we have established the possibility of the book and the necessity of it in terms of a philosophy that we did not get from the book. We have as Christians indeed learned with Calvin to interpret ourselves in terms of the book, and that on the authority of the book, and then we have looked to the book for the interpretation of the meaning of the facts. . . . We know nothing but such facts as are what the book, the authoritative revelation of God, says they are. And we *challenge unbelievers by saying that unless the facts are what the Bible says they are, they have no meaning at all.*[89]

So then, the extraordinary use of the transcendental project in Van Til's presuppositional apologetic includes beginning with a position that is based on transcendent authority (and is presented as such) and which is concrete in content (and not merely formal or abstract).

A further unique feature of Van Til's version of transcendental argumentation is that it is much broader in scope than what most philosophers today want to discuss. Van Til was not simply analyzing and arguing about the contours, formal features, or isolated and broad kinds of beliefs that are necessary as the precondition for intelligible experience and reasoning—that is, not simply narrow issues or aspects of one's conceptual scheme or detached prerequisite assumptions. For him, a truly transcendental argument must be about an extensive network of concrete and systematic beliefs. To put it simply, *the argument is over entire worldviews.* Accordingly, the "cogito" argument of Descartes ("I think, therefore I am"—because I cannot argue to the contrary without existing to think) is too limited and not adequate as a truly transcendental justification:

89. *Introduction to Systematic Theology*, 190–91 (emphasis added). Note well that the transcendental challenge begins with the Bible as a written, complete expression of a philosophical point of view—and then calls for any other philosophical outlook to be set next to it for comparison, so that it will be evident that *without that finished product with which we began*, the facts could have no meaning at all. The apologist does not start his reasoning outside the context of the Scriptures in order to somehow prove, first, that it is possible that there might be a book revealed by God, for the only "place to stand" where facts could be meaningful in proving that possibility is within the position revealed by the Bible. (Those who are without the written oracles of God still know God by natural revelation, which is the cognitive context in which they receive and are convinced that God also speaks to them in Scripture.)

[Those who seek to flee the voice of God] start with the "cogito" as though it were a rock in a bottomless ocean. They cannot individuate. They cannot show how one fact, if it could be found, can be related to another fact. They cannot account for the uniformity of nature. They cannot use the law of contradiction except they abuse it, making it destroy individuality as it succeeds in its reduction to abstract unity. They cannot find intelligible meaning in the words *"cause,"* *"substance,"* or *"purpose"*; there is no coherence in all their thought.[90]

Thus, because of its limited range, Descartes' transcendental proof does not show his existence to be intelligible after all. Isolated from a broader theory, his conclusion is useless and meaningless.[91] By contrast, Van Til challenged the unbelieving world with the broad and detailed theory or system of thought revealed by the Christian Scriptures as that which is transcendentally necessary for a cogent epistemology. He said that it should not be atomistically divided into component parts for separate argumentation and then reassembled.

90. *Defense of the Faith*, 393. Descartes' argument, "I think; therefore I am," only proves that thinking is occurring. It does not prove the existence of separate substances or the existence of personal substances, much less the existence of Descartes himself as a personal substance. It does not prove (but simply assumes), or demonstrate the proper use of, the law of contradiction; thus, it would be equally valid to assert that thinking is not occurring, even though it is. The argument does not establish the uniformity of nature, and so the connection between thinking and a personal thinking substance may be broken tomorrow. Descartes' seemingly solid conclusion, then, is still unintelligible. It is, as Van Til expressed it, "a rock in a bottomless ocean."

91. This observation is relevant to answering the question of those who, having read or heard a particular illustration of the transcendental project of showing Christianity to be the precondition for intelligibility (say, an argument or debate centering on logic, inductive reasoning, or moral absolutes), wonder why such a presuppositional apologetic does not simply prove that the unbeliever must incorporate (as isolated items) logic, induction, or absolutes into his thinking and not necessarily concern himself with the entire Christian worldview. While a specific transcendental argument cannot say everything at once or deal with every detail of Christian theology simultaneously, it is intelligible only within the *entire* Christian system, which it seeks to prove by indirectly comparing whole worldviews. If the unbeliever wants to accept the point of the specific illustration (say, logic), but not place it within the wider theory, it will be meaningless and useless as a philosophical outlook. (For example, "All I believe in is logic" already says much more than something about logic!). Presuppositional apologetics does not gradually build up the Christian worldview one step at a time, because if that worldview alone provides the context for intelligible reasoning, there cannot be another worldview that provides a context for intelligibly reasoning one's way to the exclusive Christian position!

Presuppositional apologetics orients the transcendental argument to *entire worldviews* that are in conflict with each other. This explains why it is, then, that "the argument for the Scripture as the infallible revelation of God is, to all intents and purposes, the same as the argument for the existence of God."[92] Transcendental presuppositionalism does not attempt to prove that some kind of god exists, apart from proving that it is the God who has revealed Himself in Scripture; nor does it try to prove that Scripture is a revelation from God, apart from proving that the God revealed in Scripture exists. It is a package deal (cf. chap. 3.2 above), and Christianity must be defended as a unit (cf. chap. 2.1 above):

> As a rational creature he [the unbeliever] can understand that one must either accept *the whole of a system* of truth or reject the whole of it. . . . He can understand the idea of [Scripture's] necessity, its perspicuity, its sufficiency and its authority as being involved in *the Christian position as a whole*.
>
> But while understanding them as being involved in the position of *Christianity as a whole*, it is precisely Christianity as a whole, and therefore each of these doctrines as part of Christianity, that are meaningless to him as long as he is not willing to drop his own assumptions of autonomy and chance. . . .
>
> [T]he only possible way for the Christian to reason with the nonbeliever is by way of presupposition. He must say to the unbeliever that unless he will accept the presuppositions and with them the interpretations of Christianity there is no coherence in human experience. . . . [I]t will be impossible to find meaning in anything.[93]

Van Til's "holistic" approach to apologetical argument distinguishes his transcendental method from what his idealist counterparts would have done or approved:

> The whole claim of Christian theism is in question in any debate about any fact. Christian theism must be presented as that light in terms of which any proposition about any fact receives meaning. Without the presupposition of the truth of Christian theism no fact can be distinguished from any other fact. To say this is but *to apply the method*

---

92. *Defense of the Faith*, 126.
93. Ibid., 166–67 (emphasis added).

of idealist logicians in a way that these idealist logicians, because of their own anti-Christian theistic assumptions, cannot apply it.[94]

Because of the nature and content of the Christian's own fundamental presuppositions—involving the authority of God and His revelation—even his conception and method of transcendental argumentation will be a transformed interpretation or understanding which distinguishes his outlook from that of the would-be autonomous man.

Here then is how the presuppositional (transcendental) method of defending the faith would proceed, once the preliminary discussions and clarifications have taken place with the unbeliever—and the two outlooks now come head-to-head.[95] The unbeliever says that he knows that miracles are impossible, that a personal, almighty God does not exist, that ethical principles are not normative across cultural boundaries, etc. Or the unbeliever says that the believer cannot know that the Bible is God's word, or that Jehovah exists, or that Christ was His Son, etc. The Christian apologist must seek to uncover what this unbeliever's personal convictions are regarding relevant metaphysical and epistemological matters: e.g., what is the nature of things that are real, how does the world operate, where did it come from, what is man's place in the world, what is man's nature, are there moral or epistemological norms that are not chosen by the individual, what are the criteria of truth, what are the proper methods of knowing, is certainty possible, etc.? Once the believer has a fairly good grasp of the general kind of worldview assumed (or explicitly advocated) by the unbeliever, it should be compared to the worldview of the Christian. The Christian can show that the particular objections raised by the unbeliever would, *within the Christian outlook*, not prove to be legitimate objections or intellectual problems at all. Thus, who really "knows" what he is talking about, the Christian or the non-Christian? The cogency of each side's theory and practice of knowing must be tested within the broader worldviews of which

94. Ibid., 132–33 (emphasis added).
95. It should be clear that what follows is a highly compressed and artificially programmatic summary of what the procedure aims to be. In actual conversations, the order in which things are discussed, the relevant illustrations, the irrelevant sidebars, personal quirks, and unpredictable mental associations will all contribute to a specific dialogue that will likely differ from other ones and wander in many different directions.

they are a part. The apologist explains how rationality, communication, meaning, science, morality, and man's redemption and renewal are quite understandable, meaningful, coherent, or intelligible within the biblical worldview—within the framework of thinking God's thoughts after Him. The apologist then subjects the unbeliever's worldview to an internal critique to show that it is (1) arbitrary, and/or (2) inconsistent with itself, and/or (3) lacking the preconditions for the intelligibility of knowledge (language, logic, science, morality, redemption, etc.). Since that is the case, the unbeliever cannot "know" the things that he urges against Christianity—indeed, he could not know anything at all and loses all claim to rationality. Thus, the Christian has proved the rationality and necessity of His scripturally based worldview.

The specific questions or philosophical issues with which an apologist chooses to press the unbeliever, and the particular aspects of experience that he selects for application of these issues, are wide, varied, and not prescribed in advance by the transcendental program of proving Christianity and disproving any version of autonomous unbelief. Take anything about which the unbeliever is committed or concerned—anything that seems uncontroversial and agreed upon by the unbeliever and the believer alike—and from that point show that it would be unintelligible, meaningless, or incoherent if the unbeliever's worldview, instead of the believer's, were true. The illustrations are as wide as human experience—from the curing of polio, to the composing of an opera, to the condemnation of police brutality, to the balancing of your checkbook. The philosophical issues about which Van Til wrote were extensive and varied, and we should make use of his arguments to prove the believer's epistemology and discredit the unbeliever's. For example, we read about the problem of making sense of (or the possibility of) predication,[96] reason,[97] explanation,[98] interpretation,[99] learning,[100]

96. *Introduction to Systematic Theology,* 229; *Common Grace,* 49; *The Protestant Doctrine of Scripture,* In Defense of the Faith, vol. 1 (Philadelphia: Presbyterian and Reformed, 1967), ii.
97. "Nature and Scripture," in *The Infallible Word,* ed. N. B. Stonehouse and Paul Woolley (Philadelphia: Presbyterian and Reformed, 1946), 301; *Common Grace,* 9–10; *Introduction to Systematic Theology,* 163; *Case for Calvinism,* 142; *Reformed Pastor and Modern Thought,* 30, 97.
98. *Defense of the Faith,* 259.
99. *Protestant Doctrine of Scripture,* ii.
100. *Case for Calvinism,* 132, 141, 148–49.

certainty,[101] universals,[102] possibility,[103] cause, substance, being, and purpose,[104] counting,[105] coherence, unity, and system in experience or in a conception of a universe,[106] logic,[107] individuating of facts,[108] unchanging natures or laws in a chance universe,[109] uniformity,[110] science,[111] connecting logic and facts or predication to reality,[112] avoiding contradictions,[113] avoiding the irrationalism or skepticism that arises from the tension between knowing discursively and knowing systematically,[114] etc.

In short, the transcendental critique of unbelieving worldviews aims to show that, given their presuppositions, there could be no knowledge in any field whatsoever[115]—that it would be impossible to find meaning or intelligibility in anything at all.[116] As an example of this kind of criticism directed at worldly systems of philosophy or autonomous thinking (at its best), the reader can review chapter 5.3.

Once again it is important to recall that Van Til's presuppositional apologetic does not argue that unbelievers in fact do not count, reason, learn, communicate, engage in science, explain, seek purpose and order, etc. Because they psychologically know God, they are both concerned about the issues listed above and are to some extent successful in negotiating or applying them to understand the world and their personal experiences. The issue is not what unbelievers can do intellectually, but *whether they can give an account of it* (epistemologically) within their worldview. Their autonomous worldview takes man's interpretation of the world to be "original"—to provide the primary ordering of particulars or the "rationalizing" of (that is, making systematic sense of) brute facts. But when the would-be autonomous

101. *Common Grace,* 50; *Introduction to Systematic Theology,* 46.
102. *Common Grace,* 5–6; *Introduction to Systematic Theology,* 46.
103. *Introduction to Systematic Theology,* 114–15.
104. *Common Grace,* 49; *Defense of the Faith,* 393.
105. *Defense of the Faith,* 294, 354.
106. Ibid., 66, 167, 258, 354, 393; *Survey of Christian Epistemology,* 218.
107. *Common Grace,* 28; *Defense of the Faith,* 311, 393; *Introduction to Systematic Theology,* 11; *Case for Calvinism,* 129; *Protestant Doctrine of Scripture,* 62.
108. *Defense of the Faith,* 267, 300, 393.
109. *Introduction to Systematic Theology,* 40.
110. *Defense of the Faith,* 120, 393; *Reformed Pastor and Modern Thought,* 31.
111. *Common Grace,* 50; *Defense of the Faith,* 194, 195, 266, 268, 283–84, 285, 354.
112. *Defense of the Faith,* 131, 164–65; *Introduction to Systematic Theology,* 39, 60.
113. *Common Grace,* 9.
114. *Defense of the Faith,* 137–38.
115. Ibid., 266.
116. *Survey of Christian Epistemology,* 18; *Defense of the Faith,* 164, 167, 264.

man is put at the center of the knowing process, and his presuppositions are consistently driven to their logical outcome, he ultimately slips into subjectivism and skepticism. The only alternative—the Christian worldview—places the creative and providential activity of the triune God "in back of" all of man's experiences and intellectual efforts, and that solves the fundamental problems of epistemology that leave the unbelieving critic nowhere to stand.[117] Only Christianity can account for or make sense of the intellectual accomplishments of the unbeliever. The critic of Christianity has been secretly or unknowingly presupposing the truth of the faith even as he argues against it; his own arguments would be, upon analysis, meaningless unless they were wrong and Christian theism were true.

Van Til memorably encapsulated the essence of the transcendental argument in apologetics in the "Credo" which he wrote for his *Festschrift*. In his proposal for a "consistently Christian methodology of apologetics," Van Til's suggestion was that "we claim . . . that Christianity alone is reasonable for men to hold. It is wholly irrational to hold any other position than that of Christianity. Christianity alone does not slay reason on the altar of 'chance.' " Accordingly, said Van Til, we must reason by presupposition. And the powerful essence of that presuppositional argument is just this: "The only 'proof' of the Christian position is that unless its truth is presupposed there is no possibility of 'proving' anything at all."[118] What the Christian sets forth as the Bible's worldview—as authoritatively revealed by God—is the indispensable foundation for proof itself—for the intelligibility of reason and experience, for the ability to make sense of knowing anything. At this point, the unbeliever's choices are either to acknowledge the truth revealed by God's word (and repent of his sins, including intellectual autonomy) or to reject rationality itself. He had demanded that the Christian "give a reason" for his firm conviction ("hope") about Christ and His word (cf. 1 Peter 3:15), and he must now either accept the Christian's reasoning or retreat from the task and normativity of "giving reasons" (for rationality, intelligibility, meaning, logic, science, morality, etc.). In either case, the apologetical encounter has been successful for, and has ended in favor of, the Christian position.

---

117. *Defense of the Faith*, 116, 165; *Reformed Pastor and Modern Thought*, 89; *Common Grace*, 64.
118. "My Credo," in *Jerusalem and Athens*, ed. Geehan, 21.

THE MEANING OF "TRANSCENDENTAL" METHOD[119]

One more point should be noted on the question of method, namely, that from a certain point of view, the method of implication may also be called a *transcendental method.* We have already indicated that the Christian method uses neither the inductive nor the deductive method as understood by the opponents of Christianity, but that it has elements of both induction and deduction in it, if these terms are understood in a Christian sense. Now when these two elements are combined, we have what is meant by a truly transcendental argument. *A truly transcendental argument takes any fact of experience which it wishes to investigate, and tries to determine what the presuppositions of such a fact must be, in order to make it what it is.* An exclusively deductive argument would take an axiom such as that every cause must have an effect, and reason in a straight line from such an axiom, drawing all manner of conclusions about God and man. A purely inductive argument would begin with any fact and seek in a straight line for a cause of such an effect, and thus perhaps conclude that this universe must have had a cause. Both of these methods have been used, as we shall see, for the defense of Christianity. Yet neither of them could be thoroughly Christian unless they *already presupposed God.* Any method, as was pointed out above, that does not maintain that not a single fact can be known unless it be that God gives that fact meaning, is an anti-Christian method. On the other hand, if God is recognized as the only and the final explanation of any and every fact, neither the inductive nor the deductive method can any longer be used to the exclusion of the other.

That this is the case can best be realized if we keep in mind that the God we contemplate is an absolute God. Now *the only argument for an absolute God that holds water is a transcendental argument.* A deductive argument as such leads only from one spot in the universe to another spot in the universe. So also an inductive argument as such can never lead beyond the universe. In either case there is no more than an infinite regression. In both cases it is possible for the smart little girl to ask, "If God made the universe, who made God?" and no answer is forthcoming. This answer is, for instance, a favorite reply of the atheist debater, Clarence Darrow. But if it be said to such opponents of Christianity that, unless there were an absolute God their own questions and doubts would have no meaning at all, there is no argument in return. There lies the issue. It is the firm conviction of every *epistemologically*

---

119. Excerpts from *Survey of Christian Epistemology*, 10–12, 201–2 (emphasis partly added). This passage that defines Van Til's message comes from his earliest syllabus; it was not a later development of his thought.

self-conscious Christian that *no human being can utter a single syllable, whether in negation or in affirmation, unless it were for God's existence.*[120] Thus the transcendental argument seeks to discover what sort of foundations the house of human knowledge must have, in order to be what it is. It does not seek to find *whether* the house has a foundation, but it presupposes that it has one. . . .

It should be particularly noted, therefore, that only a system of philosophy that takes the concept of an absolute God seriously can really be said to be employing a transcendental method. *A truly transcendent God and a transcendental method go hand in hand.* It follows then that if we have been correct in our contention that Hegelian Idealism does not believe in a transcendent God, it has not really used the transcendental method as it claims that it has.

Now at this juncture it may be well to insert a brief discussion of the place of Scripture in all this. The opponent of Christianity will long ago have noticed that we are frankly prejudiced, and that the whole position is "biblicistic." On the other hand, some fundamentalists may have feared that we have been trying to build up a sort of Christian philosophy without the Bible. Now we may say that if such be the case, the opponent of Christianity has sensed the matter correctly. *The position we have briefly sought to outline is frankly taken from the Bible.* And this applies especially to the central concept of the whole position, viz., the concept of an absolute God. Nowhere else in human literature, we believe, is the concept of an absolute God presented. And this fact is once more intimately related to the fact that nowhere else is there a conception of sin, such as that presented in the Bible. According to the Bible, sin has set man at enmity against God. Consequently it has been man's endeavor to get away from the idea of God, that is, a truly absolute God. And the best way to do this was to substitute the idea of a finite God. And the best way to accomplish this subordinate purpose was to do it by making it appear as though an absolute God were retained. Hence the great insistence on the part of those who are really anti-Christian, that they are Christian.

It thus appears that we must take the Bible, its conception of sin, its conception of Christ, and its conception of God and all that is involved in these concepts together, or take none of them. *So also it makes very little difference whether we begin with the notion of an absolute God or with the no-*

---

120. Van Til is not making the metaphysical point here (true though it may be) that if God did not really exist, then human beings would not actually have linguistic abilities. His point is an epistemological one: God must be believed (presupposed, made part of one's conceptual scheme) in order to make intelligible the possibility and the actuality of human communication.

*tion of an absolute Bible. The one is derived from the other. They are to-
gether involved in the Christian view of life.* Hence we defend all or we defend none. Only one absolute is possible, and only one absolute can speak
to us. Hence it must always be the same voice of the same absolute, even
though he seems to speak to us at different places. The Bible must be true
because it alone speaks of an absolute God. And equally true is it that we believe in an absolute God because the Bible tells us of one.[121]

And this brings up the point of circular reasoning. The charge is constantly
made that if matters stand thus with Christianity, it has written its own death
warrant as far as intelligent men are concerned. Who wishes to make such a
simple blunder in elementary logic, as to say that we believe something to be
true because it is in the Bible? Our answer to this is briefly that we prefer to
reason in a circle to not reasoning at all. We hold it to be true that circular
reasoning is the only reasoning that is possible to finite man. The method of
implication as outlined above is circular reasoning. *Or we may call it spiral
reasoning.* We must go round and round a thing to see more of its dimensions and to know more about it, in general, unless we are larger than that
which we are investigating. Unless we are larger than God we cannot reason
about him any other way, than by a transcendental or circular argument. The
refusal to admit the necessity of circular reasoning is itself an evident token
of opposition to Christianity. *Reasoning in a vicious circle is the only alternative to reasoning in a circle as discussed above.*[122] . . .

In this respect the process of knowledge is a growth into the truth. For this
reason we have spoken of the Christian theistic method as the method of *implication* into the truth of God. *It is reasoning in a spiral fashion rather than
in a linear fashion.* Accordingly, we have said that we can use the old terms
deduction and induction if only we remember that they must be thought of

---

121. CVT: In some of his recent publications—particularly in his work *De Heilige Schrift*,
1966–1967—Dr. G. C. Berkouwer warns orthodox Christians against having a formal view
of Scripture. He stresses the fact that the content of biblical teaching and the idea of the
Bible are involved in one another. It is this point that the syllabus made in 1939.

122. The "circularity" of a transcendental argument is not at all the same as the fallacious "circularity" of an argument in which the conclusion is a restatement (in
one form or another) of one of its premises. Rather, it is the circularity involved
in a coherent theory (where all the parts are consistent with or assume each
other) and which is required when one reasons about a precondition for reasoning. Because autonomous philosophy does not provide the preconditions for
rationality or reasoning, its "circles" are destructive of human thought—i.e., "vicious" and futile endeavors. (Because there is more than one kind of "circularity," Van Til sometimes repudiated and sometimes tolerated the notion that his
apologetics was circular—which has undoubtedly been confusing to his readers
and students.)

as elements in this one process of implication into the truth of God. If we begin the course of spiral reasoning at any point in the finite universe, as we must because that is the proximate starting point of all reasoning, we can call the method of implication into the truth of God a *transcendental method.* That is, *we must seek to determine what presuppositions are necessary to any object of knowledge in order that it may be intelligible to us.* It is not as though we already know some facts and laws to begin with, irrespective of the existence of God, in order then to reason from such a beginning to further conclusions. It is certainly true that if God has any significance for any object of knowledge at all, the relation of God to that object of knowledge must be taken into consideration from the outset. It is this fact that the transcendental method seeks to recognize.

The charges made against this type of reasoning we must turn upon those who made them. It will be said of this type of reasoning that it introduces the subjective element of belief in God, which all men do not share. Of this we can only say that all men should share that belief, and before the fall of man into sin man did have that belief. Belief in God is the most human attitude conceivable. It is abnormal not to believe in God. We must therefore hold that *only the Christian theist has real objectivity, while the others are introducing false prejudices, or subjectivity.*

The charge is made that we engage in circular reasoning. Now if it be called circular reasoning when we hold it necessary to presuppose the existence of God, we are not ashamed of it because we are firmly convinced that all forms of reasoning that leave God out of account will end in ruin. Yet *we hold that our reasoning cannot fairly be called circular reasoning, because we are not reasoning about and seeking to explain facts by assuming the existence and meaning of certain other facts on the same level of being with the facts we are investigating, and then explaining these facts in turn by the facts with which we began.* We are presupposing *God,* not merely another fact of the universe. . . .

Even in paradise it was God's verbal self-disclosure, and the disclosure of his will for man's activity in relation to the created cosmos, that was indispensable for man's ability to identify any fact and to relate any fact properly to any other fact. Applying this to the Scripture, it is but natural that we should accept the Scripture testimony about itself. If we did anything else we would not be accepting Scripture as absolute. The only alternative then to bringing in a God who testifies of himself and upon whose testimony we are wholly dependent, is not to bring in God at all. And not to bring in God at all spells nothing but utter ruin for knowledge. In that case knowledge may be said to be reduced to the pass of drawing circles in a void. *Hence we must return the charge of circular reasoning to those who made it.* On the other hand, we are happy to accept the charge of circular reasoning. Our reasoning frankly depends upon the revelation of God, whose "reasoning" is within the internal-eternal circularity of the three persons of the Trinity. *It is only if we frankly depend for the validity of our reasoning upon this internal circular reasoning in the triune God that we can escape trying in vain to reason in circles in a vacuum of pure contingency.*

The charge has been made that it is an *a priori* procedure to bring in God at the beginning of the process of knowledge. This too is a charge that acts as a boomerang. A priori reasoning is reasoning that does not start with the facts. *Now antitheism has arbitrarily taken for granted that God is not a fact, and that if he is a fact that fact does not have any bearing upon the other facts.* This we must hold to be an a priori procedure. We hold that the so-called "facts" are wholly unintelligible unless the supreme fact of God be brought into relation with them. We are willing to start with any fact as a proximate starting point, but refuse to admit before the investigation has begun that there can be no such fact as God.

Summing up, we may observe that all the various methods of investigation that have been advanced may be used theistically or they may be used antitheistically, according as God is taken into or is left out of consideration at the outset. . . . [A]ntitheistic thinking was constantly taking for granted that its position was correct. It did this by taking for granted that the object and the subject of knowledge exist apart from God and can come into fruitful relation with one another without any reference to God. Therewith antitheistic thinking reduced God, *if he was later to be taken into consideration at all, to a quantitative addition to man.*

A SAMPLE[123]

The argument must be the same in principle with all the various forms of antitheistic speculation. . . .

Naturally, *the main point in dispute is whether our opponents can get along without God.* All of our opponents have said in effect that human categories are ultimate. With respect to all of them we would then ask what happens if they seek to face the more ultimate questions of philosophy on this basis. . . .

All of these and many other nuances of modern thought and scientific method have this in common—that *they naively take for granted that the*

123. Excerpts from "A Sample of Christian Theistic Argument," chap. 16 in *Survey of Christian Epistemology*, 210, 211, 215, 216–17, 218 (emphasis partly added).

"facts" are there as ultimates from which we must begin our research. The object and the subject of knowledge are taken for granted without the question of reference to God. It is *assumed, therefore, that human categories are in themselves quite able to interpret reality.* . . .

We must therefore briefly seek to understand what the consequences are if one takes this position to the bitter end. First we should notice, however, that there are all too many who are not willing to accept the responsibility for their epistemological attitude.[124] . . .

Agnosticism of the type criticized is characteristic of all the movements in physics, biology, psychology, and philosophy spoken of above. Not all of them are usually spoken of as agnostics, because many of them claim to know about finite things even if they disclaim knowledge of ultimate things. But it is itself a sign of agnosticism not to classify as agnostics not only all who disclaim knowledge about ultimate reality, but also all those who claim to have knowledge about finite matters without having knowledge about God. *The assumption of those who say they are not agnostic about finite things, but only about God, is that finite things can be known apart from God.* From the Christian theistic point of view, such as claim knowledge of finite things and disclaim knowledge of God are as much agnostics as those who disclaim knowledge of both. This is involved in our argument which showed that to attempt to know a finite object apart from God involves one in self-contradiction upon one's own assumptions. . . .

[We] begin our argument against all of them on essentially the same point, that is, that they have taken for granted that the object and the subject of knowledge exist and can come into relation with one another without taking God into consideration. We cannot agree with the attitude taken by Charles Harris that, since there has been a reaction against some of the more extreme forms of materialism, etc., there is now no serious opponent to Christianity in the field of philosophy today. He holds that because the *contingency of the universe* has become "an accepted philosophical doctrine" there is not much else to fear (cf. his *Pro Fide*, p. xviii). We hold that if it is true that the contingency of the universe is an established philosophic doctrine, then philosophy is as much opposed to Christianity as ever Materialism was, since it then leaves God's plan out of consideration.

If God is left out of the picture it is up to the human mind to furnish the unity that must bind together the diversity of factual existence. It will not do to think of laws existing somehow apart from the mind. And even if this were possible it would not help matters any, because even these laws would

---

124. See the readings above on epistemological loafers and agnosticism.

be thought of as independent of God and as just there somehow. In other words, the only alternative to thinking of God as the ultimate source of the unity of human experience as it is furnished by laws or universals is to think that the unity rests in a void. Every object of knowledge must, therefore, be thought of as being surrounded by ultimate irrationality. It is this that is involved in the position A. E. Taylor represents when he constantly avers that there is a surd in everything historical or temporal, that is, in all factual existence. On the other hand, if the more subjective position be taken, it is the human mind that furnishes the universal element of experience, and the human mind must itself be thought of as swimming in a void.

In the second place, it should be noticed that if the object and the subject must both be thought of as somehow being in the void, it is inconceivable that there should be any relation of any sort between them. Aristotle admitted to being baffled at the question of the *infima species*, i.e., the relation of the individual to the lowest universal. There he found ultimate mystery. On the one hand you cannot say that the individual is subsumed under the species entirely, lest there be nothing but species, and the whole individual disappear. On the other hand, you cannot have complete individuality without bringing the individual into relation with others. Aristotle therefore admitted that, as far as he could see, the relation of the individual and species, or the relation of the fact to law, remained a mystery. And since the day of Aristotle there has not been any advance made on this score, because modern philosophy has continued to build upon the same assumption that Greek philosophy built upon, namely, that all things are at bottom one and return unto one. If there is to be any relation between the one and the many, it must be, according to all non-theistic thought, a relation of identity, and if identity is seen to lead to the destruction of knowledge, *the diversity that is introduced is thought of as being ultimate*. In other words, according to all non-theistic thinking, the facts and the laws that are supposed to bind the facts together into unity are first thought of as existing independently of one another and are afterward patched together. It is taken for granted that the temporal is the ultimate source of diversity. Accordingly, Reality is said to be essentially synthetic. The real starting point is then an ultimate plurality. And *an ultimate plurality without an equally ultimate unity will forever remain a plurality*.

It is this that is especially apparent in all forms of pragmatic thought. There the necessity of having any such ultimate unity is openly denied. And the only way we can meet that contention is to show that by denying ultimate unity they have also denied to themselves the possibility of having a proximate unity. There is no guarantee that the human mind can in any sense know reality that is near unless it knows reality that is far away. For all I know, the next fact that I must adjust to a previous fact is a fatal automobile accident. How then do I know that it is not the most pragmatically valuable thing for me to know whether the fact of death does not immediately connect me with another fact, namely, the judgment?

It is clear that upon pragmatic basis, and for that matter *upon antitheistic basis in general, there can be no object-object relation, i.e., there can be no philosophy of nature, so that the sciences become impossible, and no philosophy of history, so that the past cannot be brought into relation with the present nor the future with the present.* Then there can be no subject-object relation, so that even if it were conceivable that there were such a thing as nature and history, *I would be doomed to ignorance of it.* In the third place, there can be no subject-subject relation, so that even if there were such a thing as nature and history, and even if I knew about it, *I could never speak to anyone else about it.* There would be Babylonian confusion. . . .

Our conclusion then must be that the various devotees of the open universe, who take for granted that the human mind can furnish all the universals that the facts require, must be regarded as having reduced human experience to an absurdity.

REASONING BY PRESUPPOSITION [125]

These things being as they are it will be our first task in this chapter to show that a consistently Christian method of apologetic argument, in agreement with its own basic conception of the starting point, must be by presupposition. To argue by presupposition is to indicate what are the epistemological and metaphysical principles that underlie and control one's method. The Reformed apologist will frankly admit that his own methodology presupposes the truth of Christian theism. Basic to all the doctrines of Christian theism is that of the self-contained God, or, if we wish, that of the ontological trinity. It is this notion of the ontological trinity that ultimately controls a truly Christian methodology. Based upon this notion of the ontological trinity and consistent with it, is the concept of the counsel of God according to which all things in the created world are regulated.[126]

125. *Defense of the Faith*, 116–20, 134–35. The reading selection, bearing the same title as used here, first appeared in Van Til's early and main syllabus, *Apologetics* (pp. 61ff.), from which it was reproduced in the chapter on "The Problem of Method" in what has become his best-known publication, *The Defense of the Faith*. It may deservedly be looked upon as the essence of his instruction on how to defend the truth-claims of Christianity.

126. It is imperative to bear in mind that Van Til described the presuppositional method as working from the outset with the distinctive doctrines of Christian

Christian methodology is therefore based upon presuppositions that are quite the opposite of those of the non-Christian. It is claimed to be of the very essence of any non-Christian form of methodology that it cannot be determined in advance to what conclusions it must lead. To assert, as the Chris-

---

theism (e.g., the Trinity, divine providence). Earlier in this chapter, it was pointed out that Van Til's transcendental method is concrete, not abstract or formal. He never offered to discuss with the unbeliever merely the worldview of a god of some undetermined nature and character; rather, he always put forward the specific and full worldview of biblical Christianity. That is why the syllabus *Apologetics* and the book *The Defense of the Faith* both begin with detailed statements of Christian theology. These statements were not intended simply as a review, warming up to apologetics; they were for Van Til a defining part of the apologetical task. Accordingly, his presuppositional method could not be used in defense of "any other religion," as many critics have mistakenly suggested.

In dealing with the advocates of other religions, the Christian apologist should use the presuppositional method in the same way that he would use it with atheists and materialists. That is, he makes an internal examination of the worldview that is offered by whatever religious devotee he is having the dialogue with. The fact that the opposing religionist speaks formally of "God" (or "gods") is not a difficulty here, for he must define his specific concept of deity. His deity is not the Christian God, for Scripture says, "Their rock is not as our Rock" (Deut. 32:31). Recall the devastating prophetic critique of the heathen's lifeless idols, which are (contradictorily) under the control of those who bow down to them. The use of religious vocabulary does not change the applicability of the indirect method of disproving non-Christian presuppositions.

Most of the unstudied and superficial comments by people about comparative religion—for instance, that "all religions are alike" or "you can have your pick of sacred books"—can be easily contradicted by the apologist. Indeed, if anybody is tempted to be the spokesman and defender of "just any" non-Christian religion (so as to silence the Christian apologetic), it should be politely observed that the vast majority of world religions cannot even offer epistemological competition to the Christian worldview. There are indeed other sacred books, but they are not at all like the Bible. An internal analysis of the metaphysical and epistemological presuppositions of non-Christian religions shows that they teach, metaphysically, that there is no god, or no personal god, or no god who is omniscient, sovereign, etc. Accordingly, from an epistemological perspective, these sacred books are not and cannot be anything like what the Bible claims for itself, namely, to be the personal communication and infallible verbal revelation from the only living, completely sovereign, and all-knowing Creator. The other religious books, *on their own presuppositions*, give no reason to accept them as true or normative. And as for their own worldviews, these books as pieces of literature can have no epistemological or ethical authority. What they offer (when you can make sense of it at all) is simply one opinion against another.

The remaining world religions or cults that might seem at first to offer something in competition with Christianity (namely, a personal deity and a verbal revelation) are usually poor imitations of Christianity (using "borrowed capital") or Christian heresies (departing from biblical teaching in a crucial way). Ordinarily, the best tactic is to reason with the advocates of these groups from Scripture, refuting their errors from the Scripture itself. This amounts to an internal

tian apologist is bound to do if he is not to deny the very thing he is seeking to establish, that the conclusion of a true method is the truth of Christian theism is, from the point of view of the non-Christian, the clearest evidence of authoritarianism. In spite of this claim to neutrality on the part of the non-Christian the Reformed apologist must point out that every method, the supposedly neutral one no less than any other, presupposes either the truth or the falsity of Christian theism.

The method of reasoning by presupposition may be said to be indirect rather than direct. The issue between believers and non-believers in Christian theism cannot be settled by a direct appeal to "facts" or "laws" whose nature and significance is already agreed upon by both parties to the debate. The question is rather as to what is the final reference-point required to make the "facts" and "laws" intelligible.[127] The question is as to what the "facts"

---

critique of the opposing worldview. For example, Sun Myung Moon tries to authorize certain of his teachings by simply appealing to the Bible, but he has no justification for doing so, since he rejects other teachings of the Bible and refuses to grant its claim to plenary authority. Unless he accepts the Bible's plenary authority, no simple appeal to what it says (that is, without outside warrant) can authorize the point he is attempting to make. There must be some outside warrant for it, and so the apologist will then want to examine the credentials of this extrabiblical authority.

In some people's minds, the Muslim faith presents the greatest challenge to presuppositional apologetics because, it is imagined, Islam can counter each move in the Christian's argument. But this is a mistaken notion. The worldviews of Christianity and Islam are dissimilar in pivotal ways. For example, Islam teaches unitarianism and fatalism, has different moral concepts, and lacks redemption. It can be critiqued internally on its own presuppositions. Take an obvious example. The Koran acknowledges the words of Moses, David, and Jesus to be the words of prophets sent by Allah; therefore, the Koran, on its own terms, is refuted because of its contradictions with earlier revelation (cf. Deut. 13:1–5). Sophisticated theologies offered by Muslim scholars interpret the Koran (cf. 42:11) as teaching the transcendence (*tanzih*) of unchanging Allah in such an extreme fashion that no human language (derived from changing experience) can positively and appropriately describe Allah—in which case the Koran rules out what it claims to be. The Islamic worldview teaches that God is holy and just with respect to sin, but that (unlike the Bible—see the words of Moses, David, and Jesus) there can indeed be "salvation" where guilt remains unremitted by the shedding of the blood of a substitute for the sinner. The legalism of Islam (i.e., good works are weighed against bad) does not address this problem because bad works remain on one's record in the very sight of Allah (who supposedly cannot tolerate sin, but must punish it). Compare my lectures on Islam and the debate (at Orange Coast College) with a leading Muslim scholar in America, entitled "Sister Faiths?"

127. Van Til's apologetic is often set forth and illustrated in terms of epistemological and metaphysical issues, but a very simple and understandable example of it can be given in the area of ethics. In my experience, the most popular argu-

and "laws" really are. Are they what the non-Christian methodology assumes that they are? Are they what the Christian theistic methodology presupposes they are?

The answer to this question cannot be finally settled by any direct discussion of "facts." It must, in the last analysis, be settled indirectly. The Christian apologist must place himself upon the position of his opponent, assuming the correctness of his method merely for argument's sake, in order to show him that on such a position the "facts" are not facts and the "laws" are not laws. He must also ask the non-Christian to place himself upon the Christian position for argument's sake in order that he may be shown that only upon such a basis do "facts" and "laws" appear intelligible.

To admit one's own presuppositions and to point out the presuppositions of others is therefore to maintain that all reasoning is, in the nature of the case, *circular reasoning*. The starting-point, the method, and the conclusion are always involved in one another.

Let us say that the Christian apologist has placed the position of Christian theism before his opponent. Let us say further that he has pointed out that his own method of investigation of reality presupposes the truth of his position. This will appear to his friend whom he is seeking to win to an acceptance of the Christian position as highly authoritarian and out of accord with the proper use of human reason. What will the apologist do next? If he is a Roman Catholic or an Arminian he will tone down the nature of Christianity

---

ment urged against Christianity is "the problem of evil." Unbelievers declare that the Christian worldview is logically inconsistent since it holds that God is powerful enough to prevent evil, that God is good enough not to want evil, and yet that evil exists. Suppose one asks, "How can you believe in a God who permits child molestation to take place?" The believer and the unbeliever apparently agree that molesting innocent children is morally outrageous and objectively wrong. But Van Til would ask what "reference point" (final standard, authority) is necessary to make this moral judgment "intelligible." Surely no autonomous or unbelieving presupposition or fundamental outlook will suffice, since each one, upon analysis, reduces to subjectivism in ethics, in which case child molestation could not be condemned as absolutely or objectively immoral, but simply taken as generally not preferred. Notice also that the usual presentations of the apparent contradiction within the Christian premises about God omit the equally important premise that God always has a morally sufficient reason for the suffering and evil that He foreordains. With the addition of that biblical premise, there is no *logical* problem of evil left. Everyone struggles *psychologically* to take God on His word here, to be sure, but that is different from there being an intellectual incongruity within the Christian faith. Unbelievers will not give up their psychological resistance to that premise until God offers His rationale for evil to them for inspection and approval—which is subtle but incontestable evidence that they beg the question, holding that God cannot be proven to be the final authority until *they* are first acknowledged as the final authority.

to some extent in order to make it appear that the consistent application of his friend's neutral method will lead to an acceptance of Christian theism after all. But if he is a Calvinist this way is not open to him. He will point out that the more consistently his friend applies his supposedly neutral method the more certainly he will come to the conclusion that Christian theism is not true. Roman Catholics and Arminians, appealing to the "reason" of the natural man as the natural man himself interprets his reason, namely as autonomous, are bound to use the direct method of approach to the natural man, the method that assumes the essential correctness of a non-Christian and non-theistic conception of reality.

The Reformed apologist, on the other hand, appealing to that knowledge of the true God in the natural man which the natural man suppresses by means of his assumption of ultimacy, will also appeal to the knowledge of the true method which the natural man knows but suppresses. The natural man at bottom knows that he is the creature of God. He knows also that he is responsible to God. He knows that he should live to the glory of God. He knows that in all that he does he should stress that the field of reality which he investigates has the stamp of God's ownership upon it. But he suppresses his knowledge of himself as he truly is. He is the man with the iron mask. A true method of apologetics must seek to tear off that iron mask.

The Roman Catholic and the Arminian make no attempt to do so. They even flatter its wearer about his fine appearance. In the introductions of their books on apologetics Arminian as well as Roman Catholic apologists frequently seek to set their "opponents" at ease by assuring them that their method, in its field, is all that any Christian could desire. In contradistinction from this, the Reformed apologist will point out again and again that the only method that will lead to the truth in any field is that method which recognizes the fact that man is a creature of God, that he must therefore seek to think God's thoughts after him.

It is not as though the Reformed apologist should not interest himself in the nature of the non-Christian's method. On the contrary he should make a critical analysis of it. He should, as it were, join his "friend" in the use of it. But he should do so self-consciously with the purpose of showing that *its most consistent application not merely leads away from Christian theism but in leading away from Christian theism leads to destruction of reason and science as well.*[128]

An illustration may indicate more clearly what is meant. Suppose we think of a man made of water in an infinitely extended and bottomless ocean of

128. Emphasis added.

water. Desiring to get out of water, he makes a ladder of water. He sets this ladder upon the water and against the water and then attempts to climb out of the water. So hopeless and senseless a picture must be drawn of the natural man's methodology based as it is upon the assumption that time or chance is ultimate. On his assumption his own rationality is a product of chance. On his assumption even the laws of logic which he employs are products of chance. The rationality and purpose that he may be searching for are still bound to be products of chance. So then the Christian apologist, whose position requires him to hold that Christian theism is really true and as such must be taken as the presupposition which alone makes the acquisition of knowledge in any field intelligible, must join his "friend" in his hopeless gyrations so as to point out to him that his efforts are always in vain.

It will then appear that Christian theism, which was first rejected because of its supposed authoritarian character, is the only position which gives human reason a field for successful operation and a method of true progress in knowledge.

Two remarks may here be made by way of meeting the most obvious objections that will be raised to this method of the Reformed apologist. The first objection that suggests itself may be expressed in the rhetorical question "Do you mean to assert that non-Christians do not discover truth by the methods they employ?" The reply is that we mean nothing so absurd as that. The implication of the method here advocated is simply that non-Christians are never able and therefore never do employ their own methods consistently.

Says A. E. Taylor in discussing the question of the uniformity of nature, "The fundamental thought of modern science, at any rate until yesterday, was that there is a universal reign of law throughout nature. Nature is rational in the sense that it has everywhere a coherent pattern which we can progressively detect by the steady application of our own intelligence to the scrutiny of natural processes. Science has been built up all along on the basis of this principle of the uniformity of nature, and the principle is one which science itself has no means of demonstrating. No one could possibly prove its truth to an opponent who seriously disputed it. For all attempts to produce 'evidence' for the 'uniformity of nature' themselves presuppose the very principle they are intended to prove."[129] Our argument as over against this would be that the existence of the God of Christian theism and the conception of his counsel as controlling all things in the universe *is the only presupposition which can account for the uniformity of nature which the scientist needs*.

But the best and only possible proof for the existence of such a God is that

---

129. CVT: *Idem* [*Does God Exist?* (London: Macmillan, 1947)], p. 2.

his existence is required for the uniformity of nature and for the coherence of all things in the world. We cannot *prove* the existence of beams underneath a floor if by proof we mean that they must be ascertainable in the way that we can see the chairs and tables of the room. But the very idea of a floor as the support of tables and chairs requires the idea of beams that are underneath. But there would be no floor if no beams were underneath.[130]

Thus there is absolutely certain proof for the existence of God and the truth of Christian theism. *Even non-Christians presuppose its truth while they verbally reject it. They need to presuppose the truth of Christian theism in order to account for their own accomplishments.*[131] . . .

The true Christian apologist has his principle of discontinuity; it is expressed in his appeal to the mind of God as all-comprehensive in knowledge because all-controlling in power. He holds his principle of discontinuity then, not at the expense of all logical relationship between facts, but because of the recognition of his creaturehood. His principle of discontinuity is therefore the opposite of that of irrationalism without being that of rationalism. The Christian also has his principle of continuity. It is that of the self-contained God and his plan for history. His principle of continuity is therefore the opposite of that of rationalism without being that of irrationalism.

Conjoining the Christian principle of continuity and the Christian principle of discontinuity we obtain the Christian principle of reasoning by presupposition. It is the actual existence of the God of Christian theism and the infallible authority of the Scripture which speaks to sinners of this God that must be taken as the presupposition of the intelligibility of any fact in the world.

This does not imply that it will be possible to bring the whole debate about Christian theism to full expression in every discussion of individual historical fact. Nor does it imply that the debate about historical detail is unimportant. It means that no Christian apologist can afford to forget the claim of his system with respect to any particular fact. He must always maintain that the "fact" under discussion with his opponent must be what Scripture says it is, if it is to be intelligible as a fact at all. . . . It is only as manifestations of that system that they are what they are. If the apologist does not present them as such he does not present them for what they are.

---

130. In using this particular illustration, Van Til was envisioning home construction as it was familiar to folks living on the East Coast. There are also houses built without elevated foundations or basements. The analogy is thus limited, but it still makes the point if the assumption about houses is granted for the sake of getting the point. This kind of house requires beams under the floor, and we readily accept that they exist, even though we do not observe them in the way that we observe that there are tables and chairs in the room.
131. Emphasis added.

Chapter 8

Comparisons and Criticisms of Apologetical Methods

8.1 Departure from the "Traditional" Method

There are precedents in the history of Christian apologetics for the kind of presuppositional defense of the faith that Van Til advocated, especially in the antithetical boldness of Tertullian in the ancient church, the mature and challenging theological epistemology advanced by Augustine and Calvin, and the counterbalancing insights about the relationship between Christianity and genuine science in Kuyper and Warfield. Nevertheless, if we look at the general trend in apologetics over the years—what we can broadly call "the traditional method"—we are bound to recognize the distinctiveness and re-forming nature of Van Til's presuppositional approach.[1]

Traditionally, apologists have encouraged all parties to lay aside their religious assumptions; neither the believer nor the unbeliever should take for granted what they aim to prove about religion, but argue in a religiously neutral fashion, starting with criteria and facts that are commonly accepted by "reasonable" men. The different as-

---

1. Cf. Greg L. Bahnsen, "Socrates or Christ: The Reformation of Christian Apologetics," in *Foundations of Christian Scholarship: Essays in the Van Til Perspective*, ed. Gary North (Vallecito, Calif.: Ross House Books, 1976), 191–239. This article surveys in condensed form the history of Christian apologetics.

pects of the Christian position—what we believe "on faith," listening to God's revelation—are separated into isolated truth-claims (from general to specific) and defended one by one, from bottom to top. Assuming that man's reasoning is epistemologically intelligible in itself, and seeing no need to consider the possibility of its abnormality, the traditional method of apologetics seeks then to interpret the natural world (or man's experience) apart from any need for the light of scriptural revelation. The argument usually proceeds in two major steps. (1) Autonomous, self-sufficient, unaided reason (it is imagined) can establish from nature that there is most probably a supernatural realm as well—and, with further refinements, that a God of some sort exists. Theistic proofs are then followed by (2) appeals to natural and historical evidences (empirical facts) which inductively support the likelihood that the Bible is historically accurate, especially about Jesus, including His miracles and resurrection—and, therefore, is right about whatever else it says (because He believed that it was). This traditional method of defending the faith, thought Van Til, was lacking in both philosophical cogency and good theological foundations.

Van Til taught that the Christian faith is best defended by that method of argumentation which is based upon, and directed by, the theological character of the faith we defend. Moreover, for him, the fullest and most accurate expression of biblical Christianity is to be found in Reformed theology. Thus: "If there is not a distinctively Reformed method for the defense of every article of the Christian faith, then there is no way of clearly telling an unbeliever just how Christianity differs from his own position and why he should accept the Lord Jesus Christ as his personal Savior."[2] The traditional way of defending the Christian faith reflects either a non-Reformed version of the faith or (if the apologist is Reformed) an isolation of apologetical method from theology.

Since apologetics is a defense of the truths presented in Christian theology, and since the method used for defending any system of thought grows out of the nature of that system, it is only natural that defective theology will beget a defective apologetical strategy. As Van Til taught, "One's theology and one's apologetics go together."[3] Van Til's studied and humble judgment was that non-Reformed theologies—that

---

2. *The Defense of the Faith* (Philadelphia: Presbyterian and Reformed, 1955), 335.
3. *The Reformed Pastor and Modern Thought* (Philadelphia: Presbyterian and Reformed, 1971), 31.

is, Roman Catholic, Lutheran, and Arminian theologies—incorporate a number of "foreign elements" into their systems of thought, which cause them to depart (in greater and lesser ways) from the authoritative and unfailing truth of Scripture, whose authority and message the apologist is called upon to defend. These elements, being foreign to the Christian method and message (i.e., to revelational authority and to the revealed truth about God, the world, man, etc.), are unwittingly elements of the sinner's self-serving and autonomous method and message (i.e., the natural man's authority and his views of God, the world, man, etc.).

For instance, non-Reformed theologies compromise the distinction between the Creator and the creature (having inadequate views of God's aseity, His incomprehensibility, and His sovereignty), do not see every event of history (including man's choices) and every aspect of reality as foreordained by God, and misconstrue man's original condition (either the image of God or man's original righteousness). They likewise have inadequate views of the fall of man and the noetic effects of sin. In various ways the necessity, the clarity, the sufficiency, and thus the authority of Scripture are diminished in non-Reformed theologies. These significant flaws in the non-Reformed Christian's views of reality, knowledge, and ethics weaken his apologetic, for his apologetic reflects his metaphysical, epistemological, and moral presuppositions. Moreover, it is not irrelevant that Roman Catholic and Arminian approaches to defending the faith proceed on false theological assumptions about God, man, knowledge, sin, etc., for Scripture teaches that the Holy Spirit bears witness to the truth (cf. John 15:26; 16:8–15) in our testimony, not to false or flattering notions.

Roman Catholic and Arminian theologies lead to ways of reasoning with unbelievers that make concessions to the pretended autonomy of the unbeliever, thereby obscuring the clear difference between the Christian and the non-Christian worldviews. As Van Til put it:

> Thus we have something of both the irrationalism and the rationalism of the Romanist position carried over into the theology of Protestantism.[4] And it is these foreign elements both of irrationalism and of rationalism that keep the adherents of Arminian theol-

4. As "rationalists," the Romanist and the Arminian determine that it is impossible that God should control and predetermine the genuinely free actions of men; the doctrine of election is said to be contrary to the demands of logic. But as "irrationalists," the Romanist and the Arminian hold to the contingent character of re-

ogy from making every thought subject to the obedience of the revelation of God.

Naturally it is also these legacies of foreign or non-Christian thought that make it impossible for the Arminian to challenge the wisdom of this world effectively. For the thought of modern man begins with the assumption of his own ultimacy. That for him is the fact of all facts. It is his *basic* fact. It follows that for him "God" cannot be ultimate. . . .

[B]oth Romanism and Arminian Protestantism leave the root assumption of the modern man untouched. And they leave this root assumption unchallenged because the root assumption of their own theology partakes in a measure of the root assumption of the foes of the Christian religion.[5]

Non-Reformed theologies blur the difference between the Christian and the world. For instance, by compromising the doctrine of God's providential control of every detail of nature and history (including the choices of men), non-Reformed theologies conceive of possibility apart from (and even as more basic than) God and to some extent incorporate chance into their view of reality—which makes facts and logic meaningless, even as they are within non-Christian systems of thought. Non-Reformed theologies seek (in vain) to be neutral in their approach to truth and knowledge, to judge the various claims of Christianity in isolation from one another (as though individual facts can be assessed apart from the system that gives them their meaning or interpretation), and to prove them by a direct appeal to the facts of experience and logical inferences—as though such reasoning and interpretation may be properly, and can be intelligibly, employed apart from the light of the Bible. Non-Reformed theologies do not recognize the depth and extent of man's spiritual problem, and thus they assume that his thinking is unobjectionable as far as it goes (not suppressing the truth unrighteously) and simply needs to be supplemented with further information (and then persuasion) about the gospel. Non-Reformed thought resists requiring the unsympathetic rebel against God to recognize a self-attesting ("circular"

---

ality; facts are not predetermined or preinterpreted, and thus anything can happen (except, of course, God controlling the free actions of men).

5. *The Intellectual Challenge of the Gospel* (London: Tyndale Press, 1950; reprint, Phillipsburg, N.J.: Lewis J. Grotenhuis, 1953), 16, 19.

and transcendent) source of information that is not itself subject to the authorization of man's own (immanent) experience and reasoning. Non-Reformed thought does not demand unconditional, rational, and moral surrender from the unbeliever and would even leave the astute unbeliever with the realization that in basic principles his way of thinking is not that much different from the Christian's way of thinking.

Such features in an apologetic method are not out of character for the theological system that non-Reformed believers sincerely defend. But they simply will not comport with the nature, content, and implications of Reformed theology, according to Van Til. He grieved to see men who advocated Reformed doctrine employ the traditional method of apologetics, since it stood in tension with their theological outlook. He confronted them with a heartfelt call to greater personal consistency, but it was not always appreciated.[6]

For Van Til, theology must guide apologetics. Because (in Reformed theology) God has ultimate authority over everything, including man's reasoning, it follows that religious neutrality in philosophy and argumentation—even with regard to the realm of nature—is neither permissible nor possible. Indeed, man's sinfulness is epitomized by his supposed autonomy, which despises or ignores the revelation of God, especially its inherently self-attesting authority. A self-consciously biblical theory of knowledge is needed, therefore, in order to challenge head-on the foolish foundations of the natural man's reasoning and his rebellious attempts to gain knowledge or make sense of experience apart from God. The apologist must understand that his non-Christian critic, despite his protestations to the contrary, already knows the revealed truth about God and is now desperately attempting to suppress it by his arguments against the faith. Thus, the presuppositional method sets out the contrasting worldviews of Christianity and its opponents, insists that one's professed worldview have a cogent epistemology, and uses a transcendental

---

6. Many of Van Til's critics professed to be Reformed in their theological outlook. But for them theology was one thing and apologetics was another. Apologetics was pretheological, even as it was preevangelistic. Naturally, then, apologetics was considered to be neutral with respect to one's theological presuppositions and heart commitments. Granted this neutrality, the only intellectual and moral authority by which an unbeliever could decide for or against the faith would have to be autonomous—even though Reformed theology consistently and steadfastly opposes the autonomy of man, especially sinful man.

method rationally to prove the truth and certainty of Christianity. The apologist pits the Christian doctrines of creation and providence against the pagan doctrine of chance (to which all unbelieving philosophies, in one form or another, are presuppositionally committed). He shows that the unbeliever's position reduces to absurdity, being unable to make experience or knowledge of it intelligible. To argue against the Christian worldview at all, then, the unbeliever must already presuppose it.

The traditional approach to apologetics does not work in terms of the commitments and insights laid out above. Roman Catholics, Lutherans, and Arminians obviously disagree with them outright. But sometimes even Reformed apologists do not take them into account or work according to them when arguing with unbelief. Nevertheless, there is a stark contrast (in principle) between traditional apologetics and presuppositionalism precisely because of the distinctive Reformed doctrines. This is not to say, of course, that there is no value in the scholarship and research of nonpresuppositionalists, but only that their underlying method needs correction. Van Til put it this way:

> Our aim is not to depreciate the work that has been done by believing scholars in the Arminian camp. Our aim is rather to make better use of their materials than they have done by placing underneath it an epistemology and metaphysic which make these materials truly fruitful in discussion with non-believers. . . .
>
> As for the results of evangelical scholarship, the Reformed apologist should gratefully employ all that is true and good in it.[7] . . . But when it comes to the master plan of procedure, the Reformed apologist must go his own way; and it is only of the master plan that we speak when we deal with the question of apologetics in general. . . .
>
> The basic difference between the two types of apologetics is to be found, we believe, in the primary assumption that each party makes. The Romanist-evangelical type of apologetics assumes that man can first know much about himself and the universe and *afterward* ask whether God exists and Christianity is true. The Reformed

7. Given a statement such as this, Frame's assertion that we "must reject the claim [by Van Til?] that his suggested method must replace everything that was done by the more traditional apologists" is at best misleading ("Cornelius Van Til," *Handbook of Evangelical Theologians*, ed. Walter A. Elwell [Grand Rapids: Baker, 1993], 166). After all, Frame himself cites Van Til's own contrary view, which we have just quoted.

apologist assumes that nothing can be known by man about himself
or the universe unless God exists and Christianity is true.[8]

The traditional method does not challenge the presumed autonomy
of the unbeliever's thinking and assumes that he has made his experience intelligible, as far as it goes. "He only needs to accept something
additional to what he has always believed." The presuppositionalist
replies that it is then "too late to ask him to accept Christianity,"[9] for if
the legitimacy and epistemological cogency of his autonomy have
been granted, then God's revelation and grace are not fundamentally
necessary. The absolute demand of the gospel is lost, since all the treasures of wisdom and knowledge are not, after all, deposited in Christ
(cf. Col. 2:3), who "has made foolish the wisdom of this world" (1 Cor.
1:20). The lost condition of the unbeliever is not fully recognized,
since he is not seen to be one whose mind is vain and darkened with
ignorance (cf. Eph. 4:17–18), who is unable to know the things of the
Spirit (cf. 1 Cor. 2:14), and whose reasoning has been rendered futile (cf. Rom. 1:21–22). With heartache Van Til therefore observed:
"So the traditional method of Apologetics compromises Christianity in order
to win men to an acceptance of it."[10]

Sometimes efforts born of goodwill and commendable ecumenical spirit are made to minimize the differences between the traditional
and the presuppositional methods of apologetics. Everyone whose
heart graciously belongs to our common Lord should be easy to en-
treat and should recognize legitimate unity.[11] We do not wish to ex-

8. *Defense of the Faith*, 163, 317.
9. Ibid., 323, 353 (emphasis added).
10. Ibid., 351.
11. Cf. John M. Frame, *Apologetics to the Glory of God* (Phillipsburg, N.J.: Presbyterian
and Reformed, 1994). Frame is mistaken to suggest that "there is less distance
between Van Til's apologetics and the traditional apologetics than most partisans
on either side (including Van Til himself) have been willing to grant" (p. 85)—
as my analysis will attempt to illustrate.
    Frame does concede that all the differences are not removed between the two
approaches, particularly the "high barrier" of the issue of neutrality (p. 86). For
him, this particular point is an "issue of piety," revealing that "perhaps presuppositionalism is more of an attitude of heart" (p. 87). He believes that Van Til
was confused, however, and mistakenly treated the difference between presuppositionalism and the traditional approach as a difference not only of heart, but
also of method. And Frame conceives of this difference in method simply as a
matter of the "order" in which things are mentioned: "What comes first in my
[apologetical] argument?" (Compare how Frame likewise downplays the objection of presuppositionalism to the traditional approach as merely aiming to "pre-

aggerate our differences. Nonetheless, it is equally true that we cannot ignore certain profound and irresolvable points of disagreement between the two distinct approaches to defending the faith. In the context of such issues as these, Van Til said, "But witnessing is a matter of the head as well as of the heart,"[12] and, accordingly, the way in which the apologist uses his head—his method of reasoning and arguing—must be assessed for its cogency and its fidelity to God's word.

The following points set forth the basic disagreement between the traditional and the presuppositional approaches to defending the faith. Each point is anything but trivial or of minimal philosophical significance. Each point is illustrated by quotations from apologists. And in order to demonstrate the distinctiveness of Van Til's position, most of these quotations are taken from the writings of Edward J. Carnell or Francis Schaeffer.[13]

1. *The traditional method assumes that sinners can be—and ought to be—intellectually autonomous and religiously "neutral" in approaching, examining, and reasoning about the truth-claims of Christianity.*

> There are moments when man is free to evaluate one ultimate over against another with a genuine (though never absolute) freedom from prejudice.[14]

---

vent the apologist from discussing 'cause' *before* discussing God" in "Cornelius Van Til," 166 [emphasis added].) As the list of points offered below will indicate, there was a profound epistemological difference between Van Til and the traditional apologists—one which went beyond heart attitudes and rhetorical order in our apologetical method.

Particular objection must be made to Frame's assertion that Van Til, in criticizing other apologetical methods, was confused and "in effect imput[ing] evil motives" to their adherents (*Apologetics to the Glory of God*, 87). Van Til himself was forthright and transparent about his own personal attitude: "We are not judging men's hearts. . . . The point is that we are now speaking of theological systems. . . . We are happy and thankful, of course, for the work of witnessing done by Evangelicals . . . [because] in presenting the Christian testimony, something, often much, of the truth of the gospel shines through unto men, and they are saved" (*Defense of the Faith*, 316, 335).

12. *Defense of the Faith*, 335.
13. Carnell and Schaeffer both identified themselves as Reformed in theology, and both were at one time students under Van Til. Since many people have called Carnell and Schaeffer "presuppositionalists," these two apologists might be thought of as close to Van Til, even though they departed from his distinctive method. The illustrative quotations taken from such writers, then, can hardly be looked upon as artificial or extreme, as though the traditional method were here being unnecessarily portrayed at its worst (that is, at its furthest distance from Van Til).
14. E. J. Carnell, *A Philosophy of the Christian Religion* (Grand Rapids: Eerdmans, 1952), 24.

A normal person does not submit his life to any authority until, guided by reason, he is fully assured in his mind that the authority in question is trustworthy.[15]

But thinking individuals will not outrage their dignity by defying the verdict of a critically disciplined understanding. Whatever else faith may be, it is at least a "resting of the mind in the sufficiency of evidences." The extent of this sufficiency is measured by a cool and dispassionate use of reason.[16]

Bring on your revelations! Let them make peace with the law of contradiction and the facts of history, and they will deserve a rational man's assent.[17]

2. *The traditional method assumes that presuppositions are merely hypotheses to be tested by factual observation or logic, rather than a person's most fundamental assumptions—functioning as preconditions of intelligibility—in terms of which hypotheses are tested.*

If one will proceed to reality with a humble attitude, he will discover that the presuppositions of Christianity are friendly to the highest tests of reason.[18]

[The Christian] believes the postulate of a rational God to be a workable hypothesis in the light of the evidence.[19]

What I urge people to do is to consider the two great presuppositions—the uniformity of natural causes in a closed system and the uniformity of natural causes in an open system . . . and to consider which of these fits the facts of what is. . . . But as I have said, it is a question of which of these two sets of presuppositions really and empirically meets the facts as we look about us in the world.[20]

15. E. J. Carnell, *An Introduction to Christian Apologetics* (Grand Rapids: Eerdmans, 1948), 73.
16. E. J. Carnell, *Christian Commitment: An Apologetic* (New York: Macmillan, 1957), 76.
17. Carnell, *Introduction to Christian Apologetics*, 178.
18. Carnell, *Christian Commitment: An Apologetic*, 197.
19. Carnell, *Introduction to Christian Apologetics*, 164.
20. Francis Schaeffer, *He Is There and He Is Not Silent* (Wheaton, Ill.: Tyndale House, 1972), 65, 66.

Accordingly, with the traditional method, Christianity has no special epistemic status, but is tested like everything else.

> Why should faith be exempted from the general rule that all belief is subjected to the law of contradiction in the light of the facts of history? What higher floor in the building of knowledge is there than coherence?[21]

> If this credible individual be oneself, the man across the street, or God, one should follow exactly the same rule.[22]

3. *The traditional method assumes that there are brute, observable, common facts (outside of any interpretive theory) by which hypotheses can be tested.*

> Facts just *are*. . . . A fact is any unit of being which is capable of bearing meaning. . . . Each of these fact-situations must be explained. . . . Meaning is what the mind entertains when it passes judgment upon the facts.[23]

Apparently, then, for the traditional method scientific observations are not affected by ultimate presuppositions or commitments.

> Science seeks for the natural meaning of a thing. . . . [S]cientific conclusions as such do not depend for their meaning upon one's logical starting point. . . . As long as the scientist confines his judgments to an impersonal description of what objectively exists in the world of flux, the problem of common ground has no relevance.[24]

The traditional method sees facts as more ultimate than worldviews, in which case they can be used to test worldviews.

> One must move to the fitting of the facts as the ultimate test of a world view.[25]

21. Carnell, *Introduction to Christian Apologetics*, 119.
22. Carnell, *Philosophy of the Christian Religion*, 30.
23. Carnell, *Introduction to Christian Apologetics*, 92, 213.
24. Ibid., 214.
25. John Warwick Montgomery, "Survey of Evangelical Apologetes," *Christianity Today* 21 (April 1, 1977): 771.

In that case, the traditional method teaches that human experience of the facts can be used to verify the Christian hypothesis.

> The mark of an acceptable hypothesis is its ability to explain the facts as we experience them. . . . [Is] it not good science to postulate the existence of God to account for the known data in human experience?[26]

> [The question is:] does the Christian answer conform to and explain what we observe concerning man as he is (including my knowledge of myself as man)?[27]

> We are not asked to believe until we have faced the question as to whether this is true on the basis of space-time evidence.[28]

4. The traditional method proceeds as though the unbeliever, in terms of his own professed philosophical perspective, has intelligible concepts or standards by which he may judge, test, or verify the Christian hypothesis.

> We must strain through the grid of reason everything that comes into our mind.[29]

> There must be a pre-evangelism before evangelism is meaningful to twentieth century people. . . . This pre-consideration falls into two areas: the first is in the area of epistemology.[30]

> Before a man is ready to become a Christian, he must have a proper understanding of truth.[31]

> The Bible as a system must stand openly and by itself in the arena, in the forum, of the thought of men. Never, never, never will I say "You must believe it because the Bible teaches it." . . . We cannot expect twentieth century men to take the

26. Carnell, *Philosophy of the Christian Religion*, 270–71.
27. Francis Schaeffer, *The God Who Is There* (Chicago: Inter-Varsity Press, 1968), 109.
28. Ibid., 141.
29. Francis Schaeffer, *The Church at the End of the 20th Century* (Downers Grove, Ill.: Inter-Varsity Press, 1970), 104.
30. Francis Schaeffer, "Historic Christianity and Twentieth Century Man" (unpub. manuscript, 1965), 1.
31. Schaeffer, *The God Who Is There*, 143.

authority of the Scripture as a reason for believing the Christian system.[32]

The truth that we let in first is not a dogmatic statement of the truth of the Scriptures but the truth of the external world and the truth of what man himself is. . . . This, I am convinced, is the true order for our apologetics in the second half of the twentieth century.[33]

All pretenses to revelation must be put through a scrutinizing test. . . . [T]he Bible should be tested in the light of relevant criteria.[34]

Like any hypothesis, it [special revelation] is verified when it results in an implicative system which is horizontally self-consistent and which vertically fits the facts.[35]

The only proof [anyone] can offer, both for his system of philosophy and for the actions which flow from it, is *systematic coherence* [according to the law of contradiction and the concrete facts of history]. . . . It is in this framework that the Christian offers proof for his system. . . . Faith must be founded in objectively verifiable metaphysical theories.[36]

If the meaning of God's character cannot be anticipated by information drawn from our own conception of decency, what significance is conveyed by the term "God"?[37]

The reason why we are able to trust Christ is that he spoke and lived in a way which is congenial with our axiological expectations. . . . Jesus Christ is worthy of our faith . . . because both his person and his doctrine are rationally continuous with the values which we have already accepted in ordinary experience.[38]

---

32. Schaeffer, "Historic Christianity and Twentieth Century Man," 10.
33. Schaeffer, *The God Who Is There*, 129.
34. Carnell, *Philosophy of the Christian Religion*, 31, 41.
35. Carnell, *Introduction to Christian Apologetics*, 174–75.
36. Ibid., 107, 117.
37. Carnell, *Christian Commitment: An Apologetic*, 138.
38. Carnell, *Philosophy of the Christian Religion*, 474, 495.

5. The traditional method appeals to concepts or standards that are assumed to be intelligible on the unbeliever's presuppositions—and presumed to be commonly understood or interpreted, and thus uncontroversial as yet—as a basis for a line of argument that leads the unbeliever, if he would simply reason cogently, out of his unbelieving perspective into the antithetical conclusions of Christianity.

> Christian apologetics do not start somewhere beyond the stars. They begin with man and what he knows about himself. . . . He knows something of the external world, and he knows something of himself.[39]

We thus notice the traditional method's sympathy for Thomistic scholasticism: reason operating in the realm of nature serves as the vestibule to faith.

> Surely he [the unbeliever] must first have Scriptures authenticated to him as such, before he can take his standpoint in them. . . . [Faith has its] grounds in right reason.[40]

> First we know [rationally] in order that we might believe; then we believe in order that we might know [experientially].[41]

> Knowledge precedes faith. . . . Only the faith which believes God on the basis of knowledge is true faith.[42]

According to the traditional method, the unbeliever's perspective is all right as far as it goes, but simply needs to be taken further.

> Like a ship which has ten good days at sea but sinks on the eleventh, so paganism develops profound truths in various spheres, only to fail in answering how a man may be just with God. . . . If Christianity cannot complete what is valid in the wisdom of the ages, then the unbeliever will be offended, not

39. Schaeffer, *The God Who Is There*, 123.
40. B. B. Warfield, "Introduction to Francis R. Beattie's *Apologetics*," in *Selected Shorter Writings of Benjamin B. Warfield*, vol. 2, ed. John E. Meeter (Nutley, N.J.: Presbyterian and Reformed, 1973), 98.
41. Carnell, *Philosophy of the Christian Religion*, 515.
42. Schaeffer, *The God Who Is There*, 142.

challenged, by the gospel. He will spew out any system that negates elements which, by nature and common sense, are foundations of the true, the good and the beautiful.[43]

Some apologists try to safeguard the finality of Christianity by repudiating the possibility of truth outside of Christianity. But their effort, as one might suspect, is a failure. Christ himself defended degrees of truth in the natural man. . . . Non-Christians can develop relative truths about nature and life, but they cannot answer the profound question "How can a sinner be just before God?"[44]

While rejecting the humanistic ideal as incomplete, therefore, [Christ] nevertheless *built* upon its insights rather than derogating it as untruth.[45]

For the traditional method, then, there is wisdom, intelligence, science, etc., that is common to both the believer and the unbeliever.

General wisdom is not a threat to the gospel. . . . Aristotle said many wise things about logic, Confucius many wise things about morals. When a Christian attacks general wisdom in the name of the gospel, the natural man will attack the gospel in the name of general wisdom.[46]

The traditional method maintains that the Bible is verified by the common concepts and standards used in our thinking or reasoning elsewhere.

Truth is systematically construed meaning, and if the Bible fulfills this standard, it is just as true as Lambert's law of transmission.[47]

---

43. Edward John Carnell, "Perfect Assurance," *The Christian Century* 73 (Jan. 4, 1956), 15. Carnell was here reviewing Van Til's *The Defense of the Faith.* He later repeated these arguments in *Christian Commitment: An Apologetic.*
44. Carnell, *Christian Commitment: An Apologetic,* viii.
45. Carnell, *Philosophy of the Christian Religion,* 276.
46. E. J. Carnell, *The Case for Orthodox Theology* (Philadelphia: Westminster, 1959), 128.
47. Carnell, *Introduction to Christian Apologetics,* 175.

545 COMPARISONS AND CRITICISMS OF APOLOGETICAL METHODS

Scientific proof, philosophical proof and religious proof follow the same rules. . . . The theory must be non-contradictory and must give an answer to the phenomena in question. We must be able to live consistently with our theory. . . . [T]he answer must conform to what we observe.[48]

[What demonstrates the truth of historic Christianity?] Christianity . . . constitutes a non-self-contradictory answer that does explain the phenomena and which can be lived with, both in life and scholarly pursuits.[49]

6. The traditional method portrays and defends aspects (parts) of the Christian worldview (message) in a way that is not distinctively Christian in conception—as though they were truths that may be properly understood in isolation from the overall Christian worldview (message) and thus as theoretically compatible with other, presumably similar, worldviews.

In accordance with this, the traditional method thinks that Christianity can be appropriately defended piece by piece: from broad theism to historic Christianity. First we argue for theism in general, then unitarianism, then trinitarianism. Then we argue for God's personality, and then His intelligence, and then His love, and then His causal interaction with the world, and then His performing of miracles. We move on to argue that man is a physical being, then that he has a spiritual nature, then that he is free, and then that he is a creature possessing dignity. We turn to arguing for Christ as a good man, then as a miracle worker, then as one who was raised from the dead, and then as the very God-man.

Firstly, he needs to bow in the realm of Being (metaphysically). . . . Secondly, he needs to bow in the realm of morals. . . . Now he is faced with God's propositional promise, "Believe on the Lord Jesus, and thou shalt be saved."[50]

For the traditional method, one can rationally work up from lower religious values to Christianity.

48. Schaeffer, *The God Who Is There*, 109.
49. Ibid., 111.
50. Ibid., 134.

> A consistent venture in the religious life must lead a person
> step by step from lower to higher commitments. . . . [R]eli-
> gion reaches its perfection with faith in the person of Jesus
> Christ. . . . Reasons will be suggested in each case why one *must*
> move on from the lower to the higher on the one hand, and
> from the higher to faith in the person of Christ on the other.[51]

In terms of the traditional method, the unbeliever's problem is that
his knowledge is incomplete. For example, Schaeffer portrays materialistic science as being fine as far as it goes:

> Finally the Christian turns to the materialist and says, "Well,
> this is a tremendous work. You really told me a great deal
> about my universe that I wouldn't have known. However,
> my friend, this is all very fine, but it's drastically incom-
> plete." . . . "It's as if you had taken an orange, sliced it in
> half, and only concerned yourself with one of the halves.
> To really understand reality in our universe, you have to
> consider both halves—both the seen and the unseen. . . .
> You are completely unbalanced. You only know half of your
> own universe."[52]

*7. The traditional method proposes to show only that the truth of Christianity
is "highly probable," rather than infallible and certain.*
   Accordingly, in terms of the traditional method, Christianity is
comparatively better than other options, but not absolutely necessary
or the *only intelligible option.*

> The task of any philosophy of life is to construct an adequate
> explanation for the whole course of reality. . . . The aim of this
> volume is to discharge the obligation which this verse [1 Peter
> 3:15] lays upon us by showing how Christianity is able to an-
> swer the fundamental questions of life as adequately as, if not
> more adequately than, any other world-view.[53]

51. Carnell, *Philosophy of the Christian Religion*, pref.
52. Francis Schaeffer, *Death in the City* (Chicago: Inter-Varsity Press, 1969), 128–31.
53. Carnell, *Introduction to Christian Apologetics*, 10.

> The Christian finds his system of philosophy in the Bible . . .
> [and he accepts this] because, when tested, it makes *better*
> sense out of life *than other systems* of philosophy make.[54]

> Proof for the Christian faith, as proof for any world-view that is
> worth talking about, cannot rise above rational probability. . . .
> If the scientist cannot rise above rational probability in his em-
> pirical investigation, why should the Christian claim more?[55]

The ultimate philosophical fallback position for those adhering to the
traditional method is to say that, after all, nobody can really know anything for sure.

> This admission . . . is not a form of weakness. . . . The system
> of Christianity can be refuted only by probability. Perhaps our
> loss is our gain?[56]

As we can see from the above points, the presuppositional defense
of the faith, in contrast to the traditional defense of it, amounts to an
all-out *methodological* (epistemological) as well as *moral* challenge to the
unbeliever's presumed neutrality and autonomy (his rational self-
sufficiency). Because that kind of challenge is missing in the traditional approach, the difference between it and presuppositionalism
cannot rightly be minimized. It is not simply a crack in the sidewalk
which separates the two methods in apologetics, but rather a discrepancy (in principle) as wide as the Grand Canyon. They are at their
root as disparate in apologetics as are Reformed and non-Reformed
conceptions in theology.

In view of this "great divide" in apologetical outlook and strategy,
Van Til grieved when he saw men who advocated Reformed theology
standing on the other side of the canyon in their apologetic method.
He wanted very much to win them back to greater consistency in their
reasoning and scholarship. He wished they would realize that, given
the traditional approach to defending the faith, the unbeliever has
all the philosophical tools and ploys available to him—and actually
endorsed by the apologist—by which he can readily and legitimately

54. Ibid., 10 (emphasis added).
55. Ibid., 113–14.
56. Ibid., 115n.

defeat any intellectual challenge of the gospel.[57] A good example is found in the career of Edward John Carnell. Although influenced in certain ways for a time by the teaching of Van Til, Carnell moved away from that perspective,[58] eventually writing five books and numerous articles that set forth a defense of Christianity which was in the vein of the traditional method[59] and which was widely popular for more

57. This is not to say that the unbeliever will in fact always utilize his own pagan philosophical presuppositions or consistently follow his pretended autonomous method when interacting with the Christian apologist. The traditional approach to apologetics may very well, therefore, "win some arguments" or be used by God as the occasion of a person turning to faith. If we would have intellectual integrity and be open before the Lord, however, this should hardly comfort or encourage us in continuing to use the traditional approach. Apologetics cannot be satisfied with taking advantage of an unbeliever's philosophical naivete or personal inconsistencies ("catching him off guard") in reasoning and debate; apologists cannot be content to rely on the Holy Spirit to make weak arguments seem strong to the unwary.

In this connection, I believe that John Frame ("Van Til on Antithesis," *Westminster Theological Journal* 55 [1995]: 85, 92, 98–99) misinterprets Van Til's statement that "the natural man will *invariably* employ the tool of his reason to reduce these contents [of Scripture] to a naturalistic level" (*Defense of the Faith*, 100 [emphasis added]). Frame takes this to mean that, according to Van Til, we can *always* predict the unbeliever's response to an apologetic, and that he will *necessarily* reject evidences for the resurrection of Christ and twist them into a naturalistic scheme of thinking (cf. *Defense of the Faith*, 24; cf. pp. 331–34). However, Van Til never actually said that we can always predict the unbeliever's response, and he never drew that conclusion from the sentence Frame quotes. What Van Til meant is that the natural man as such "invariably" naturalizes the evidence in order to avoid facing God; it is his character to do so. But, as we saw in chap. 6, Van Til understood quite well that the unbeliever does not always act in character, but is inconsistent with his espoused presuppositions. In terms of the contrast between the traditional and the presuppositional methods of apologetics, however, Van Til's point would be that, as long as we utilize the traditional approach, *the unbeliever always has every right to turn our presuppositions against our arguments*, if he should choose to do so. It is obviously counterproductive and spiritually scandalous for a defender of the faith to make such an argument or put himself in such a position in his debate with unbelief.

58. It is clear, especially in *An Introduction to Christian Apologetics*, that Carnell picked up certain themes and pointers from Van Til—for instance, a focus on the problem of the one and the many. However, there is no evidence that he ever grasped the transcendental character of Van Til's presuppositional apologetic. If he did, we find no expression of it or explanation of why he considered it philosophically or exegetically objectionable. The same failure to understand clearly and interact meaningfully with Van Til's transcendental presuppositionalism is found in proponents of Carnell's work, such as Gordon Lewis and Ronald Nash.

59. These are mentioned above in the footnotes to the list of seven features of the traditional method of apologetics, but to them could be added Carnell's *The Kingdom of Love and the Pride of Life* (Grand Rapids: Eerdmans, 1960).

than two decades in the evangelical world. Van Til wrote at a number of places in criticism of Carnell's apologetic, perceiving it as "a typical sample of [the] procedure generally followed in conservative or evangelical circles today."[60]

Carnell attempted to improve upon the traditional method, only to slip back into it (as illustrated by the quotations of him above) and become subject to the very philosophical futility that an apologetic should expose in unbelieving thought. Van Til explained:

> That this traditionalist type of apologetics is particularly impotent in our day I have shown in my review of . . . Dr. Carnell's book on Apologetics. . . . Dr. Carnell is an orthodox believer. To an extent he has even tried to escape from the weaknesses of the traditional method of apologetic argument. But he merely rejects its inductivist form. By and large he falls back into traditional methodology. . . . To the extent that he admits the type of coherence [founded upon autonomous human experience] he has no argument against [autonomous modernist thought]. To the extent that he admits [this] type of coherence . . . to be valid, he has to give up the uniqueness of the events of Christianity as he himself holds them. On the other hand, to the extent that he holds to the uniqueness of events the way [an autonomous modernist] holds to them, to that extent he has to give up the coherence to which he himself as an orthodox Christian should hold.[61]

In Van Til's estimation, Carnell misused the doctrines of common grace and of man being created in God's image in order to justify having his apologetic method cater to sinful man's presumed intellectual

---

60. *Defense of the Faith*, 321. The critique of Carnell in this text is reproduced below; it takes the form of a mock dialogue. Van Til reviewed Carnell's *An Introduction to Christian Apologetics* in the *Westminster Theological Journal* 11 (1948): 45–53, and the review was reprinted in a collection of Van Til's reviews entitled *Christianity in Modern Theology* (Phillipsburg, N.J.: Lewis J. Grotenhuis, 1955). Van Til analyzed Carnell (along with Billy Graham, Bernard Ramm, and Carl Henry) in *The New Evangelicalism* (Philadelphia: Westminster Theological Seminary, 1960). Carnell's *The Case for Orthodox Theology* was one of three key books that were criticized by Van Til in *The Case for Calvinism* (Philadelphia: Presbyterian and Reformed, 1963), esp. chap. 3. Van Til also addressed the differences between himself and Carnell in his response to Gordon R. Lewis in *Jerusalem and Athens*, ed. E. R. Geehan (Philadelphia: Presbyterian and Reformed, 1971), chap. 19—which is reproduced below.
61. *A Christian Theory of Knowledge* (Philadelphia: Presbyterian and Reformed, 1969), 299.

authority, as though his reasoning could be intelligible apart from submission to the revelation of God:

> His method pulls him down into compromise. His method is to start with man as autonomous. Starting from man as autonomous, Carnell worked up a modern form of natural theology under the guise of common grace. Starting from man as autonomous and therefore inherently good . . . Carnell again caters to the idea that God is identical with the projected ideals of the "good man."[62]

Here is the heart of the matter.[63] Carnell erroneously imagined that a person's most fundamental convictions regarding epistemology (e.g., one's criterion of truth and one's method of knowing) could be isolated from the various metaphysical options and used as an independent test for choosing between them.[64] The traditional approach to apologetics wants to begin with elements of a theory of

---

62. *Case for Calvinism*, 95.
63. In *The New Evangelicalism* (Grand Rapids: Zondervan, 1963), Ronald Nash expounded what was essentially Carnell's approach to apologetics. According to it, the method of rationally investigating and verifying basic assumptions, to see which ones are "more probably true," is similar to the method used by scientists in "testing an hypothesis." Epistemology is independent of, and more basic than, metaphysics. "The problem is to discover criteria of truth by which we may test world views or metaphysical systems" (pp. 117–18). Likewise, Millard Erickson wrote that "Carnell particularly has stressed the rational demonstration of the truth of the Christian world-view. He has appealed to a method which verified the Christian system like a broad hypothesis, much as does the scientific method" (*The New Evangelical Theology* [Westwood, N.J.: Revell, 1968], 226). Erickson acknowledged that this leads scholars coming from different angles, like Van Til and William Hordern, to see Carnell as a conservative utilizing the methodology of theological liberalism—and thus attempting to combine two fundamentally opposed methodologies (with two final authorities: reason and the Bible).
64. In Carnell's confusing terminology, the "synoptic starting point" (i.e., the *epistemological* criterion of systematic consistency for testing truth-claims) is utilized to "prove" or "test the credentials" of the "logical starting point" (i.e., the ultimate *metaphysical* belief defining and unifying one's worldview, which in the case of the Christian is the triune God of the Bible). According to Gordon Lewis, Van Til "falsely charges Carnell with starting with autonomous man" because he failed "to give due importance to Carnell's distinction between the logical starting point and the synoptic starting point" ("Van Til and Carnell—Part I," in *Jerusalem and Athens*, ed. Geehan, 351, 359). On the contrary, it is just because of that distinction that Van Til charged Carnell with catering to autonomy. The Christian worldview, as Van Til never tired of emphasizing, must be defended as a unit (comprising metaphysics, epistemology, and ethics in an unbreakable system) over against the sinful worldviews of the natural man.

knowledge that all men can agree upon—common ground, the interpretation of which does not depend on whether God exists or not—in order to prove whether or not God exists. In a word, man is presumed to be epistemologically and morally autonomous, and both competent and authorized to judge God by man's own ideals. And since these criteria must be religiously neutral (common to believers and unbelievers alike), the traditional apologist is reduced to the same hopeless plight of the natural man in attempting to combine abstract rationality (coherence) with brute factuality (uniqueness) to know anything at all. For Van Til, it is by means of exhibiting the intellectual hopelessness of this plight that the apologist "makes evident" the impossibility of autonomy to the would-be autonomous man.[65] But for Carnell, Christianity is not the transcendental necessity that makes tests or methods of proof intelligible, but is merely one hypothesis among others to be tested by man's autonomous standards. The profound difference between Carnell's traditional method and Van Til's presuppositional method cannot be glossed over.

In one of Van Til's best remembered passages, he offers an extended dialogue between a Reformed believer ("Mr. White"), an intelligent and self-conscious unbeliever ("Mr. Black"), and a believer who wants to defend the faith using traditional apologetical arguments ("Mr. Grey"). The illustration demonstrates the differences between a Reformed approach to apologetics and a non-Reformed approach, and shows how easy it is for the would-be autonomous

65. Some critics of Van Til (such as James Daane, cited by Gordon Lewis, "Van Til and Carnell," 356) claim that if Van Til in any way appealed to the unbeliever in an attempt to make the truth of Christianity appear "evident," he himself thereby condoned and even reintroduced the autonomous man as a judge over God's revelation. However, the central thrust of Van Til's apologetical argument to make Christianity's truth evident was to demolish the pretense of any intellectual autonomy from God! An appeal to the unbeliever need not be an appeal to autonomous reasoning on its own terms; it can just as easily be, as it was for Van Til, a rational refutation of autonomous reasoning. Thus, John Gerstner, R. C. Sproul, and Arthur Lindsley are quite mistaken to allege "that Van Til has an 'autonomy' of his own" since he "argues" for the need to presuppose God. They miss the crucial distinction between arguments that assume and reinforce the rational autonomy of man and arguments that refute or disprove the rational autonomy of man. It is preposterous to declare that Van Til has "become a traditionalist" in apologetics simply because he is found to "give a reason for believing" the Bible! They have no reason to conclude, then, "that there is no real difference on the matter of autonomy" after all (*Classical Apologetics: A Rational Defense of the Christian Faith and a Critique of Presuppositional Apologetics* [Grand Rapids: Zondervan, 1984], 233, 238, 239).

man ("Mr. Black") to deflect and destroy the arguments of the traditional apologist (whether he be Arminian or Reformed). This dialogue is easy to read and forceful; it appears at the end of the following set of reading selections.

KEY POINT: METHOD MUST MATCH CONTENT [66]

The emphasis, therefore, on human autonomy in non-Reformed evangelical theology not only plays havoc with the scriptural message of salvation by grace alone, but distorts the doctrine of Scripture itself by finding the ultimate exegetical tool in the subjective experience of human freedom and by denying to Scripture and the Holy Spirit the power, authority, and necessity of invading the souls of men. . . .

From these examples of Roman Catholic, Arminian-Wesleyan-Lutheran, and finally modern theology, it is clear (1) that the idea of Scripture can never be separated from the message of Scripture, and (2) that none of these non-Reformed evangelical and modern theologies have a view of Scripture such that the Lord Christ speaks to man with an absolute authority. The self-attesting Christ of Scripture is not absolutely central to these theologies. Just so, he will not be central in any apologetic form to defend them.

TOWARD A CHRIST-CENTERED APOLOGETIC

Deciding, therefore, to follow the Reformers in theology, it was natural that I attempt also to do so in apologetics. I turned to such Reformed apologists as Warfield, Greene, and others. What did I find? I found the theologians of the "self-attesting Christ," defending their faith with a method which denied precisely that point! That this was the case may be shown by a brief survey of what I call the "traditional" method of Christian apologetics.

The traditional method, offered first in detail by Thomas Aquinas in its Catholic form and by Joseph Butler in its Protestant form (but being in principle that offered by the very earliest of apologists), is based upon the assumption that man has some measure of autonomy, that the space-time world is in some measure "contingent" and that man must create for himself his own epistemology in an ultimate sense.

The traditional method was concessive on these basic points on which it should have demanded surrender! As such, it was always self-frustrating. The traditional method had explicitly built into it the right and ability of the natural man, apart from the work of the Spirit of God, to be the judge of the

66. Excerpts from "My Credo" in *Jerusalem and Athens*, ed. Geehan, 9, 10–11, 14, 15.

claim of the authoritative Word of God. It is man who, by means of his self-established intellectual tools, puts his "stamp of approval" on the Word of God and then, only after that grand act, does he listen to it. God's Word must first pass man's tests of good and evil, truth and falsity. But once you tell a non-Christian this, why should he be worried by anything else that you say? You have already told him he is quite all right just the way he is! Then the Scripture is not correct when it talks of "darkened minds," "wilful igno-rance," "dead men," and "blind people"! With this method the correctness of the natural man's problematics is endorsed. That is all he needs to reject the Christian faith. . . .

For Calvin speculation about God, independently of Scripture, is excluded. Natural theology, therefore, is also excluded. Natural theology starts with man as autonomous and with the world as "given." Natural theologians assume that "reason" and "logic" and "fact" are "religiously neutral." They are but "tools" by which man may and must determine what is and what is not possible. . . .

Calvin explicated the person of Christ solely in scriptural terms, i.e., his method is exegetical rather than speculative. As such his method is simple: who Christ is depends on Christ's self-identification. If Christ is who he says he is, then all speculation is excluded, for God can swear only by himself. To find out what man is and who God is, one can only go to Scripture. Faith in the self-attesting Christ of the Scriptures is the beginning, not the conclusion, of wisdom! It was, therefore, not until the fully developed trinitarian theol-ogy of Calvin, which says that Christ is authoritative because [*autotheos*], that there was therewith developed a truly Christian *methodology* of theology and of apologetics, the method by which a Christian develops the content. Calvin, seeing this, denied all speculation and natural theology as "avenues" to faith. Rather, faith and understanding are pure gifts of free grace.

A DISTINCTIVELY REFORMED METHOD [67]

All Protestants will agree with one another that the doctrines of Protestantism must be defended as over against Romanism. But not all agree that there is a distinctly Protestant method of defending Christianity as a whole. Some hold that Protestants should first join the Romanists in order with them to defend the doctrines that they have in common. All Christians, we are told, believe in God. All believe that God has created the world. All Christians hold that God controls the world by his providence. All believe in the deity of Christ. These and other doctrines may therefore be defended in the same way by all

67. Excerpts from *Christian Theory of Knowledge*, 11–14, 17–18.

Christians. There is no specifically Protestant way of defending the Christian doctrine of God. How could there be since this is the common property of all Christians?

Other Protestants contend that there must be a specifically Protestant defense of all Christian doctrines. Their argument is that all Christian doctrines are interdependent. Each major doctrine implies all of the others and colors all of the others. A Protestant's doctrine of the atonement will, to some extent, color his doctrine of God and vice versa. In fact, the difference with respect to all other doctrines rests ultimately on a difference with respect to the notion one has of God.

But what, it will then be asked, is the difference between a Protestant and a Romanist doctrine of God? The answer given is that the Protestant doctrine of God stresses his self-sufficiency and therefore his ultimate control over all that comes to pass in the course of the history of the world. The Romanist doctrine of God, while also speaking of God's self-sufficiency, none-the-less compromises it to some extent. It does this by virtually ascribing to man a measure of self-sufficiency. And by ascribing a measure of self-sufficiency or ultimacy to man, God is in a measure made dependent upon man.

It is natural, then, to ask how this difference between the Romanist and the Protestant concept of God should necessitate a specifically Protestant defense of Christianity as a whole. . . .

The Romanist method of defending God . . . does not, to be sure, agree with the non-Christian position in assuming that *man* must deliberately be made the final reference point of human predication. On the other hand, it does not clearly insist that *God* be made the final reference point. In other words, the Romanist position is a compromise between the Christian and the non-Christian view on the matter of the final reference point of human experience. Hence it cannot distinguish clearly between the two positions. On the one hand, it cannot consistently show that the non-Christian view is ruinous to man. On the other hand, it cannot consistently show that the Christian position means salvation for human experience.

Up to this point in our discussion it has been assumed that all Protestants agree in thinking of God as all-sufficient and as self-explanatory. This assumption must now be examined. Why does one group advocate the idea that there is a distinctly Protestant method of defending Christianity in all of its doctrines? Why does the other group maintain that Protestants should first join Roman Catholics in defending doctrines they have in common with them in order then to go on to the defense of the specific Protestant teachings? The only reason that can be found is that the second group is basically sympathetic to the Romanist view of man as being, in part, autonomous.

We refer now to those Protestants who are usually spoken of as *evangelicals* as distinct from those who embrace the Reformed Faith. Under the term *evangelicals* we include all those who hold to the Remonstrant or Arminian view of man in his relation to God. We include also the Lutherans. To be sure, Lutherans are not by any means to be identified as Arminian in every respect. But on the point at issue their view is basically the same as that of the Arminians. The point is that both Arminians and Lutherans maintain that man has a measure of ultimacy or autonomy. In this respect they resemble the Roman Catholics. The measure of autonomy ascribed to man is much smaller in the case of many Arminians and Lutherans than it is in the case of the Roman Catholics. Even so, *any* measure of autonomy ascribed to man implies a detraction from the self-sufficiency of God. It implies that God can no longer be taken as the final reference point in human predication.

It is expected, then, that evangelicals, holding as they do in their theology to the idea of man as having some measure of ultimacy, will also maintain that Protestants may and even must join with Roman Catholics in defending certain doctrines that they have in common. They will hold that only after certain doctrines that Roman Catholics and Protestants hold in common have been defended against the non-Christian by both groups standing side by side, will there be occasion for Protestants to go on to the defense of their own teachings. Then this defense of their own teachings will have to be against Roman Catholics as well as against unbelievers.

Over against these convictions of the evangelicals with respect to the method of defense of the Christian Faith stands the position of Reformed theology. Reformed theology holds to the self-sufficiency of God without compromise. It therefore rejects every form of human autonomy. *Only on the assumptions of divine self-sufficiency and man's complete dependence upon God can the difference between the Christian and the non-Christian points of view be clearly made out.*[68] Only thus can the issue be clearly drawn. . . .

The difference between a Christian system that seeks to be consistently analogical and one, like that of Romanism and evangelicalism, that does not, is that only in the former is the *false ideal of knowledge* of the unbeliever rejected. *If one does not make human knowledge wholly dependent upon the original self-knowledge and consequent revelation of God to man, then man will have to seek knowledge within himself as the final reference point.* Then he will have to seek an exhaustive understanding of reality. Then he will have to hold that if he cannot attain to such an exhaustive understanding of reality, he has no *true* knowledge of anything at all. Either man must then know

68. Emphasis added here. Elsewhere in this reading, the emphasis is original.

everything or he knows nothing. This is the dilemma that confronts every form of non-Christian epistemology. The Romanist or evangelical type of argument for Christianity is not able to indicate this fact with clarity. The only way by which this dilemma can be indicated clearly is by making plain that the final reference point in predication is God as the self-sufficient One.

So far in this chapter the general difference between a consistently Protestant or Reformed and a more generally evangelical method of reasoning has been pointed out. The Romanist-evangelical method would start reasoning with the non-Christian on a neutral basis. It would not challenge the presuppositions of the non-Christian at the outset of the argument. The reason for this is obvious. The Romanist and the evangelical are in some measure in agreement with the non-Christian on his presuppositions. They, too, attribute a measure of autonomy to man. They therefore hold that the non-Christian quite legitimately demands that Christianity shall be shown to meet the demands of the autonomous man.

These demands are, first of all, that Christianity shall be shown to be in "accord with reason." By "reason" is meant the reason of man as the determiner of the possible and the impossible by means of "logic." Only that is said to be possible which is in accord with, or at least is not against, the law of contradiction. Secondly, Christianity must be shown to be "in accord with the facts." These facts are the facts as reason, the determiner of the possible and impossible, has "discovered" or observed them.

The Romanist-evangelical method of defending Christianity therefore has to compromise Christianity while defending it. If the demands of "reason" as the non-Christian thinks of it are assumed to be legitimate, then Christianity will be able to prove itself true only by destroying itself. As it cannot clearly show the difference between the Christian and the non-Christian view of things, so it cannot present any clear-cut reason why the non-Christian should forsake his position.

DEFECTIVE THEOLOGY BEGETS WEAK APOLOGETICS[69]

They [Roman Catholics] divide the field of factual research between autonomous Reason and Faith. "The natural" is said to be the territory of Reason and "the supernatural" is said to be the territory of Faith. In the territory of Reason believers and non-believers are said to have no difference. The question whether the mind of man is created or is not created, we are told in effect, need not be raised in this area. Rome is willing, in what it calls the field

---

69. An excerpt from *Common Grace* (Philadelphia: Presbyterian and Reformed, 1947), 6–7.

of Reason, to employ the ideas of brute fact, of abstract impersonal law and autonomous man, not merely for argument's sake, but without qualification.

Arminians have, by and large, adopted a similar position. It is but natural that they should. Their theology allows for autonomy in man at the point of salvation. Their philosophy, running in the same channel, ascribes autonomy to man in other fields.

It is therefore in Reformed thinking alone that we may expect to find anything like a consistently Christian philosophy of history. Romanism and Arminianism have virtually allowed that God's counsel need not always and everywhere be taken as our principle of individuation. This is to give license to would-be autonomous man, permitting him to interpret reality apart from God. Reformed thinking, in contrast with this, has taken the doctrine of total depravity seriously. It knows that he who is dead in trespasses and sins lives in the valley of the blind, while yet he insists that he alone dwells in the light. It knows that the natural man receives not the things of God, whether in the field of science or in the field of religion. The Reformed believer knows that he himself has been taken out of a world of misinterpretation and placed in the world of truth by the initiative of God. He has had his own interpretation challenged at every point and is ready now, in obedience to God, to challenge the thinking and acting of sinful man at every place. He marvels that God has borne with him in his God-ignoring and therefore God-insulting endeavors in the field of philosophy and science as well as in the field of religion. He therefore feels compelled to challenge the interpretation the non-Christian gives, not merely of religion but of all other things as well.

WEAKENED BY "FOREIGN ELEMENTS" [70]

Why not have the Romanist help us build the first story of the house of Christian theism? After they have helped us build the first story of our house, we can dismiss them with thanks for their services and proceed to build the second story, the story of Protestantism, ourselves.

The answer to this is that if Romanists have helped us in building the first story of our house, then the whole house will tumble into ruins. It has already been noted that when they build the first story of their house the Romanists mix a great deal of the clay of paganism with the iron of Christianity. . . . Warfield's point is that Evangelicalism is inconsistent Protestantism. It has car-

---

70. Excerpts from *Defense of the Faith*, 315–16, 318–19, 304, 256–58, 261–62, 264–66, 351–53, 355–56. The section from pp. 351–53 also appears in *Reformed Pastor and Modern Thought*, 69–70.

ried into its system certain foreign elements—elements ultimately derived by way of Romanism from paganism.

"But," someone will exclaim, "look where you have brought us! To what extremes you have gone! Not to speak of Romanists, are we not even to co-operate with Evangelicals? I know many Evangelicals who are much better Christians than are many Calvinists." But this is not the issue. The question is not as to who are Christians and who are going to heaven. We are not judging men's hearts. Many Evangelicals are no doubt better Calvinists in practice than other men who are officially known as Calvinists. . . .

Thomas Aquinas, the Roman Catholic, and Bishop Butler, the Arminian, both talk a great deal about the nature of man and of reality as a whole before they approach the question of the existence of God or of the truth of Christianity. At least, they assume much about the nature of man and of reality as a whole while they are speaking about the possibility of the existence of God or of the truth of Christianity. . . .

Since the Romanist-evangelical apologist *does not* make the Creator-creature distinction basic to the very first thing that he says about man or the universe, he is willing to join hands with the natural man, and together with him "discover" many "truths" about man and the universe. He will make common ground with the unbeliever as in science or in philosophy they investigate together the nature of Reality as a whole. He will agree with the natural man as he speaks about "being in general," and only afterward argue against the unbeliever for the necessity of introducing the Creator-creature distinction. . . .

Of course, the reason why the one type of apologetics *does* and the other *does not* wish to make the Creator-creature distinction basic at the outset of all predication is to be found in the differing conceptions of sin. The natural man does not want to make the Creator-creature distinction basic in his thought. The sinner does not want to recognize the fact that he is a creature of God, and as such responsible to God, and because of his sin under the judgment of God. This is to be expected. But why should Christians who have confessed their sins to God, who have therefore recognized him as Creator and Lord, and especially why should evangelicals who confess that they hold to the Bible as their only infallible rule of authority, not wish to bring their every thought captive to the obedience of Christ? In other words, how do you account for the fact that evangelicals carry into their theology and into their apologetics so much foreign material? It is, of course, because of their defective view of sin. . . .

Christians must present the truth in terms of God the Creator, of man his creature and also of this man's rebellion against God. Romanism and Evangelicalism do not want to think of the fall of man as having immediate significance for an argument between a Christian and a non-Christian. The Reformed view of theology alone takes the Bible story of Adam's representation seriously. Hence the Reformed view alone appreciates fully the significance of the fall of man for Apologetics. . . .

The first and most basic point on which my approach differs from the traditional one is therefore that: (a) I start more frankly from the Bible as the source from which as an absolutely authoritative revelation I take my whole interpretation of life. Roman Catholicism also appeals to Scripture but in practice makes its authority void. Its final appeal is to the church and that is, in effect, to human experience. Even Arminianism rejects certain Scripture doctrines (e.g., election) because it cannot logically harmonize them with the general offer of salvation. (b) I stress the objective clarity of God's revelation of himself wherever it appears. Both Thomas Aquinas and Butler contend that men have done justice by the evidence if they conclude that God probably exists. . . . (c) With Calvin I find the point of contact for the presentation of the gospel to non-Christians in the fact that they are made in the image of God and as such have the ineradicable sense of deity within them. . . . But I could not thus speak with assurance that the natural man could have any such apprehension of the truth of the gospel if I held with the traditional view of Apologetics that man's self-consciousness is something that is intelligible without reference to God-consciousness. If man's self-consciousness did not actually depend upon his God-consciousness there would be no meaning to Romans 1:20. . . .

Yet it is the very essence of the positions of Aquinas and Butler that human self-consciousness is intelligible without God-consciousness. Both make it their point of departure in reasoning with the non-believers that we must, at least in the area of things natural, stand on the ground of neutrality with them. And it is of the essence of all non-believing philosophy that self-consciousness is taken as intelligible by itself without reference to God. . . .

For them the human self therefore is supposed to be able to think of itself as intelligible and of the facts and laws of the world as manipulable and therefore intelligible apart from their relationship to God. I have already pointed out that for this reason the traditional view of apologetics has no universe and has no real point of contact in the unbeliever. If either Romanism or Arminianism were right in their view of the self-consciousness of man there could be no apologetics for Christianity at all. There would be no all-comprehensive plan of God. This much being clear it can be seen that the Romanist and the Arminian will, in consistency with their own theology, not be able to challenge the natural man's false assumptions. The traditional apologist must somehow seek for a point of contact within the thinking of the natural man as this thinking has been carried on upon false assumptions. He cannot seek to stir up the old man in opposition against the new man in the non-Christian. He makes no use of such a distinction. He will allow for gradational differences within the natural man. He will even make a great deal of these. To him therefore the passages of Paul to the effect that every man knows God and that man is made in the image of God are interpreted so as to do injustice to other equally important teaching of Scripture to the effect that the natural man knoweth not God. All this is compromising theology. It is no wonder that the Romanist and the Arminian will also follow a compromising apologetics.

The basic falseness of this apologetics appears in the virtual if not actual denial of the fact that the natural man makes false assumptions. Aquinas and Butler hold that the natural man, whom the Calvinist knows to be a covenant breaker and as such one who interprets God himself in terms of the universe, has some correct notions about God. I mean correct notions as to content, not merely as to form. . . .

But when he thus talks about what *must* exist and when he refuses even to admit that non-believers have false assumptions about their *musts*, let alone being willing to challenge them on the subject, he has in reality granted that the non-believer's conception about the relation of human logic to facts is correct. It does not occur to him that on any but the Christian theistic basis there is no possible connection of logic with facts at all. When the non-Christian, not working on the foundation of creation and providence, talks about *musts* in relation to *facts* he is beating the air. His logic is merely the exercise of a revolving door in a void, moving nothing from nowhere into the void. But instead of pointing out this fact to the unbeliever the traditional apologist appeals to this non-believer as though by his immanentistic method he could very well interpret many things correctly. . . .

[T]his traditionalist type of apologetics is particularly impotent in our day. . . .

The general conclusion then is that on the traditional method it is impossible to set one position clearly over against the other so that the two may be compared for what they are. Certainly there can be no confrontation of two opposing positions if it cannot be pointed out on what they oppose each other. On the traditional basis of reasoning the unbeliever is not so much as given an opportunity of seeing with any adequacy how the position he is asked to accept differs from his own. . . .

The traditional method was constructed by Roman Catholics and Arminians. It was, so to speak, made to fit Romanist or Evangelical theology. And since Roman Catholic and Evangelical theology compromises the Protestant doctrines of Scripture, of God, of man, of sin and of redemption, so the traditional method of Apologetics compromises Christianity in order to win men to an acceptance of it.

The traditional method compromises the Biblical doctrine of God in not clearly distinguishing his self-existence from his relation to the world. The traditional method compromises the Biblical doctrine of God and his relation to his revelation to man by not clearly insisting that man must not seek to determine the nature of God, otherwise than from his revelation.

The traditional method compromises the Biblical doctrine of the counsel of God by not taking it as the only all-inclusive ultimate cause of whatsoever comes to pass.

The traditional method therefore compromises the *clarity* of God's revelation to man, whether this revelation comes through general or through special revelation. Created facts are not taken to be clearly revelational of God; all the facts of nature and of man are said to indicate no more than that *a god probably* exists.

The traditional method compromises the *necessity* of supernatural revelation in relation to natural revelation. It does so in failing to do justice to the fact that even in paradise man had to interpret natural revelation in the light of the covenantal obligations placed upon him by God through supernatural communication. In consequence the traditional method fails to recognize the necessity of redemptive supernatural revelation as concomitant to natural revelation after the fall of man.

The traditional method compromises the *sufficiency* of redemptive supernatural revelation in Scripture inasmuch as it allows for wholly new facts to appear in Reality, new for God as well as for man.

The traditional method compromises the *authority* of Scripture by not taking it as self-attesting in the full sense of the term.

The traditional method compromises the Biblical doctrine of man's creation in the image of God by thinking of him as being "free" or ultimate rather than as analogical.

The traditional method compromises the Biblical doctrine of the covenant by not making Adam's representative action determinative for the future.

The traditional method compromises the Biblical doctrine of sin, in not thinking of it as an ethical break with God which is complete in principle even though not in practice.

In spite of these things, this traditional method has been employed by Reformed theologians. This fact has stood in the way of the development of a distinctly Reformed apologetic. . . .

The Holy Spirit surely testifies only to the truth. It testifies to the revelation of God in all the facts of the created universe. I take it that Christians must give their testimony to the world of unbelievers in subservience to this general testimony of the Spirit. Christians must therefore be servants of the Spirit in seeking to convict the world of sin, of righteousness and of judgment. They can do so only if they point out to men that it is sin to serve and worship the creature more than the Creator. And do not scientists and philosophers worship the creature when they interpret reality in terms of man as the ultimate point of reference?

How can you, on your basis, prevent the Holy Spirit from wiping out the difference between truth and falsehood? If you defend the traditional method of apologetics you are committed to an area of common or neutral interpretation, and thus you would destroy the testimony of the Holy Spirit to the truth.

CONCESSIONS TO AUTONOMY IN APOLOGETICAL METHOD[71]

But if this be true, it becomes quite impossible for the apologist to do what Roman Catholics and Arminians must do on the basis of their view of Christianity, namely, agree with the non-Christian in his principles of methodology to see whether or not Christian theism be true. From the Roman Catholic and the Arminian point of view the question of methodology, like that of starting-point, is a neutral matter. According to these positions the Christian apologist can legitimately join the non-Christian scientist or philosopher as he, by his recognized methods, investigates certain dimensions of reality. . . .

What will the apologist do? If he is a Roman Catholic or Arminian he will tone down the nature of Christianity to some extent in order to make it appear that the consistent application of his friend's neutral method will lead to an acceptance of Christian theism after all. But if he is a Calvinist this way is not open to him. He will point out that the more consistently his friend applies his supposedly neutral method the more certainly he will come to the conclusion that Christian theism is not true. Roman Catholics and Arminians, appealing to the "reason" of the natural man as the natural man himself interprets his reason, namely as autonomous, are bound to use the direct method of approach to the natural man, the method that assumes the essential correctness of a non-Christian and non-theistic conception of reality. . . .

Now the Roman Catholic is not committed to any such doctrine of Scripture as has been expressed above. He can therefore build up his apologetics by the direct method. He can, as has already been shown, to a large extent

71. Excerpts from *Defense of the Faith*, 113–14, 118, 126–29, 131, 138–39.

agree with the natural man in his conception of both the starting point and the method of human knowledge. He can therefore join the non-Christian in his search for the existence or non-existence of God by the use of reason without any reference to Scripture. That is, he and the natural man can seek to build up theism quite independently of Christianity. Then when the Romanist has, together with his friend the natural man, built the first story of the house to the satisfaction of both, he will ask his friend to help in building the second story, the story of Christianity. He will assure his friend that he will use the same principles of construction for the second story that they have together employed in their common construction of the first story. The second story is, according to Rome, to be sure, the realm of faith and of authority. But then this authority is but that of the expert. Rome knows of no absolute authority such as Protestantism has in its doctrine of Scripture. Rome's authority is the authority of those who are experts in what they say are reported to be the oracles of God. These oracles receive their authoritative illumination from the expert interpreters of them, from the Pope first of all. But such a concept of authority resembles that which Socrates referred to in *The Symposium* when he spoke of Diotima the inspired. When the effort at rational interpretation failed him, Socrates took refuge in mythology as a second best. The "hunch" of the wise is the best that is available to man with respect to that which he cannot reach by the methods of autonomous reason. No "wise man" ought to object to such a conception of the "supernatural." It merely involves the recognition that he has not yet discovered the truth about all of reality by means of reason. So then the natural man need not really object, even from his own point of view, to the presentation of supernatural revelation as it is offered to him by the Roman Catholic apologist.

If the Roman Catholic method of apologetic for Christianity is followed then Christianity itself must be so reduced as to make it acceptable to the natural man. Since Rome is more than willing to grant the essential correctness of the starting point and method of the natural man in the "realm of nature" he cannot logically object to the conclusion of the natural man with respect to supernatural reality. The natural man need only to reason consistently along the lines of his starting point and method in order to reduce each of the Christian doctrines that are presented to him to naturalistic proportions.

As for the Arminian way of reasoning, it is, as already noted, essentially the same as that of Rome. The method followed by Bishop Butler follows closely that of Thomas Aquinas. According to Butler some of those who have no belief in or knowledge of Christianity at all have, none the less, quite rightly interpreted the "course and constitution of nature." The cave has already been lit up by means of light that was not derived from the sun. By the use of the empirical method those who make no pretense of listening to Scripture are said or assumed to have interpreted nature for what it really is. It is no wonder then that the contents of Scripture too must be adjusted to the likes of the natural man. He will not accept them otherwise. And Butler is anxious to win him. So he says to him: "Reason can, and it ought to judge, not only of the meaning, but also of the morality and the evidence, of revelation. First, it is the province of reason to judge of the morality of Scripture; i.e., not whether it contains things different from what we should have expected from a wise, just, and good Being; for objections from hence have now been obviated; but whether it contains things plainly contradictory to wisdom, justice, or goodness—to what the light of nature teaches us of God."[72] Since even in the interpretation of "nature" the natural man must and does himself admit that he cannot know everything, he can certainly, without compromising himself in the least, allow that what Scripture claims about "supernatural" things may *probably* be true. Already accustomed to allowing for a measure of discontinuity even in his interpretation of the "course and constitution of nature" why should he not allow for a little more of this same sort of discontinuity in realms about which he admits that he still may learn? Such a concession will not break the principle of continuity that he has employed in all his interpretations of things that he knows; his principle of continuity needs merely to be stretched. The natural man does not object to stretching his principle of continuity if he is compelled to do so by virtue of the irrationality of reality; the only thing to which he strenuously objects is the submission of his own principles of continuity and of discontinuity to the counsel of God.

It appears then that as Arminianism together with Roman Catholicism is willing to join the natural man in his supposedly neutral starting point and method, so also Arminianism is forced to pay for these concessions by having the natural man to some extent dictate to him what sort of Christianity he may or may not believe. If the natural man is given permission to draw the floor-plan for a house and is allowed to build the first story of the house in accordance with his own blueprint, the Christian cannot escape being controlled in a large measure by the same blueprint when he wants to take over the building of the second story of the house. Arminianism begins by offering to the natural man a Christian theology that has foreign elements in it. As over against the Reformed faith the Arminian has fought for the idea of man's ultimate ability to accept or reject salvation. His argument on this score amounts to saying that God's presentation of his claims upon mankind can-

72. CVT: *The Works of Bishop Butler*, edited by W. E. Gladstone, New York, 1896, Vol. 1, p. 238.

not reach down to the individual man; it can only reach to the *infima species*. God has to await the election returns to see whether he is chosen as God or is set aside. God's knowledge therefore stands over against and depends to some extent upon a temporal reality which he does not wholly control. When the Arminian has thus, as he thinks, established and defended human responsibility against the Calvinist he turns about to defend the Christian position against the natural man. But then he soon finds himself at the mercy of the natural man. The natural man is mercilessly consistent. He simply tells the Arminian that a little autonomy involves absolute autonomy, and a little reality set free from the plan of God involves all reality set free from the plan of God. After that the reduction process is simply a matter of time. Each time the Arminian presents to the natural man one of the doctrines of Christianity, the natural man gladly accepts it and then "naturalizes" it. . . .

Thus in the whole business he has dishonored his God (a) by practically admitting that his revelation is not plain and (b) by himself running away from God in his interpretation of natural revelation and in his subjection of supernatural revelation to the illegitimate requirements of the natural man. Meanwhile he has failed in his purpose of persuading the natural man to go in the right direction. The Roman Catholic and Arminian views of theology are compromising; in consequence the Roman Catholic and the Arminian method of apologetics is both compromising and self-frustrative. . . .

We need not now pursue this matter further. It must rather be pointed out in this connection that since Roman Catholicism and Arminianism are committed to a neutral starting point and methodology they are bound also to fall into the atomism of non-Christian thought. Since they will not look at all the facts as facts of the Christian theistic system, and flatly refuse to maintain that anything but a Christian theistic fact can exist at all, and with this claim challenge the non-Christian methodology from the outset of the argument, they are bound to be carried away to a non-Christian conclusion. It is of the essence of both the Romanist and the Arminian method of argumentation to agree with the non-Christian that individual propositions about many dimensions of reality are true whether Christianity is true or not. Neither Roman Catholics nor Arminian apologists are in a position to challenge the natural man's atomistic procedure. Their own theologies are atomistic. They are not built along consistently Christian lines. Their individual doctrines are therefore not presented as being what they are exclusively by virtue of their relation to the main principles of the Christian position. Their contention that the Reformed faith is wrong in thinking of all things in the world as being what they are ultimately in virtue of God's plan with respect to them compels the Roman Catholic and the Arminian apologist to admit the essential correctness of non-Christian atomism. And herewith they have at the same time lost all power to challenge the non-Christian methodology at the outset of its career. Instead they themselves become the victims of this method. Since the principles of their theology will not permit them to argue by way of presupposition, their own piece-meal presentation of Christian theism constantly comes to a sorry end. It is as though an army were sending out a few individual soldiers in order to wrest some atoll from a powerful concentration of an enemy's forces. There can be no joining of issues at the central point of difference, the interpretation by exclusively immanentistic categories or the interpretation in terms of the self-sufficient God, unless it be done by way of presupposition. And the Reformed apologist has a theology that both permits and requires him to do this.

THE DISCREPANCY IN METHODS: CARNELL AND VAN TIL[73]

Dear Dr. Lewis:

Your carefully articulated essay on the differences between the apologetic methodology of the late Edward J. Carnell and that which I have advocated deserves a full answer. I shall do my best to clarify the situation to some extent in my limited space.

You assert: "If my analysis has any truth at all, Van Til seriously misinterprets his former student." In view of your serious analysis it is proper that I ask myself whether I have done Dr. Carnell such grievous injustice as you suggest. The issue certainly is not merely academic.

May I tell you that Carnell was a student of mine for four years and that he was a friend as well? His Master's examination was a brilliant one and there was in it every indication that we were in agreement regarding apologetic methodology.

When I picked up my copy of his prize book, *An Introduction to Apologetics*, I read in it: "The Word of God is self-authenticating. It bears its own

73. This excerpt is Van Til's response to the essay "Van Til and Carnell—Part I," by Gordon R. Lewis, in *Jerusalem and Athens*, ed. Geehan, 361–68. Lewis claimed that Van Til, having misunderstood Carnell and having "conveniently ignore[d]" the points where their positions agree or are identical, falsely charged Carnell with making man autonomous. Lewis rhetorically asks, "How can Van Til find such a *similar method* so 'destructive of Christianity'?" (p. 360 [emphasis added]). But then he insists upon their *dissimilarity* after all—and concludes about Van Til that "in the name of defending the faith he left the faith defenseless" (p. 361)! For Lewis's own critique of Van Til's apologetic method as "biblical authoritarianism," see his book *Testing Christianity's Truth Claims: Approaches to Christian Apologetics* (Chicago: Moody Press, 1976), chap. 5.

testimony to truth; it seals its own validity. If the Word required something more certain than itself to give it validity, it would no longer be God's Word. If God, by definition, is that than which no greater may be conceived, then his Word is that than which no truer may be conceived."[74]

Well, why then do men not believe on the self-authenticating Word of God? Surely all "men have the *rationes* by which they know that God exists. But, being in defection by their sins, what they see is vitiated. Thus, they are not able to see and appreciate that one of the peculiar characteristics of this God is that he is the Creator of the world and the Saviour of men. God, therefore, gives men up, for they 'exchanged the truth about God for a lie and served the creature rather than the Creator, who is blessed forever! Amen' (Rom. 1:25)." Here Carnell adds the word of Calvin, to the effect that, "notwithstanding the clear representations by God in the mirror of his works, both of himself and of his everlasting dominion, such is our stupidity, that, always inattentive to these obvious testimonies, we derive no advantage from them."[75]

In line with this general notion of the Scriptures as the self-authenticating Word of God and of the clarity of God's revelation in his works, Carnell has this to say of those who do not accept it as such: "Observe, that a fundamental presupposition of the higher critic is that the Bible is just another piece of human writing, a book to which the scientific method may safely be applied, not realizing that the Bible's message stands pitted in judgment against that very method itself. It does not occur to the higher critic that he has started off with his philosophy of life in a way that makes the consistency of redemptively conceived Christianity impossible."[76]

Then he goes on to show that the non-Christian, because be does not begin with the self-attesting Christ, has no intelligible foundation for human predication: "Technically speaking, whenever a man talks and expects something to be meant by it, he is resorting to a prerogative which belongs to a Christian alone."[77]

Carnell quotes from Colossians: "In Christ all things hold together." Christ is the *I am*. Possession of the knowledge of Christ, thus, is possession of the highest form of reality. For this reason, the Christian admonishes men that there is a difference in value between the two levels of being. Being contingent upon God's will, it is this will, and not an antecedent system of logic,

74. CVT: Edward John Carnell, *An Introduction to Apologetics* (Grand Rapids: Eerdmans, 1st ed., 1948), p. 66.
75. CVT: *Ibid.*, p. 72.
76. CVT: *Ibid.*, p. 194.
77. CVT: *Ibid.*, p. 212.

which gives meaning to the movement of the space-time world. The many are theologically related to each other according as God has decreed the end (*telos*) of things."[78]

Thus it appears that according to Carnell, it is the theology of the self-authenticating God of Scripture that alone enables man to put logic and fact together in a proper relationship to one another. Here, then, was my young, formerly confused, fundamentalist student broadening out so as to see that only in terms of the fully biblical Reformed philosophy of history is there a metaphysics, an epistemology, and an ethics that is intelligible.

In my little book, *The Case for Calvinism,* I therefore thought it was sufficient to make one general statement on Carnell's faithfulness to the historic Christian faith: "When he says that the 'Word of God is self-authenticating' he does not refer with the New Reformation theology to some word hidden behind the words of Scripture. Carnell believes in the direct revelation of God in history and in the Bible as the direct revelation of God. No further evidence need be given of this fact. [Carl F. H.] Henry is also right when he says that Carnell seeks to tell the Christian story as that which alone gives meaning to life."[79]

Again, "Of course Carnell believes in total depravity. He believes in the whole story of Christianity as told in Scripture. For him there is a genuine transition from wrath to grace in history."[80] And, "Carnell is no Arminian."[81] I am at one with Dr. Carnell when he says, "When God says something, it is true, for God cannot lie; and when man reposes in God's Word, he has faith. If he fails to rest in it as truth, we call him an infidel, i.e., he is not one of the faithful. The power by which the heart is enabled to see that the Word of God is true is the Holy Spirit. The Word of God is thus self-authenticating."[82]

THE RATIONAL MAN

My disappointment with Carnell's book on apologetics sprang from his presenting the idea of the God of the Bible—the God who controls all things, who cannot lie and who, therefore, appeals to nothing beyond himself in order to establish the truth of what he says—as *a hypothesis which may or may not be true.*

Carnell presents to us two mutually exclusive views of God. First, there is the biblical God who is the source of all space-time possibility and actuality,

78. CVT: *Ibid.*, p. 40.
79. CVT: C. Van Til, *CFC [The Case for Calvinism]*, p. 65.
80. CVT: *Ibid.*, p. 91.
81. CVT: *Ibid.*, p. 111.
82. CVT: Carnell, *op. cit.*, p. 66.

the God whom Carnell, as a simple believing Christian, worshiped and served to the day of his death. Second, is the god of apostate man, produced by his sinful imagination, a god surrounded by abstract possibility. The first God is, as Carnell said, standing shoulder to shoulder with Calvin and Paul, the God whose face is inescapably present to every living man. As image bearers of God, all men know God (Rom. 1:19). No matter how desperately apostate man seeks to escape from the face of God, he cannot do so. Every fact in the universe, whether within man's own intellectual and moral constitution, or around him on every hand, has, as it were, God's signature on it in plain view. The world is God's estate. This Carnell believed, professed, and gloried in.

No doubt, from his deep desire to win over the cultured despisers of this truth, he tried to do so by starting with them in their interpretation of the universe. Can they not be really open-minded and consider this Christian—this conservative—point of view as a hypothesis that may possibly do better justice to the universally agreed upon requirements of logic and factuality?

As I read certain sections of his *Apologetics* I can hear Carnell saying to E. Brightman, his professor at Boston, "Look here, I as a conservative ardently defend *a* system of authority, but I agree with you that it is up to us as free human personalities to choose between authorities by means of a criterion that, in the nature of the case, must be within ourselves. Plato was surely right when he said that the only place to begin any investigation of our experience is our own drifting raft of experience itself. Descartes and Kant stood firmly on Plato's shoulders and now you have worked out their implied notion of personality in detail. You have spoken of a formal and a material aspect of it, attempting to avoid the 'definition-mongers' such as Spinoza on the one hand and the modern 'flux' theologians on the other. You have, therefore, a 'rational basis' for science and also adequate room for personal faith. There is a primacy of the spiritual over the material. With Buber you speak of the I-thou dimension as taking precedence over the I-it dimension.

"But now look, I think my conservative position does *even better justice* to both logic and fact than does yours. 'The Christian believes that a judgment is true when it corresponds to the mind of God, since God is the author of all facts and their meaning.' You might think that when I say this I am, like a fundamentalist, swinging my Bible over my head saying, 'The Bible says so and therefore it is true.' Certainly not! 'The test to which he [the Christian] proposes to subject his propositions, to know when he does correspond to God's mind, is, as Professor Brightman phrases it, "systematic consistency."' [83] 'Truth, therefore, is correspondence with the mind of God. The test for truth is sys-

83. CVT: *Ibid.*, p. 56.

tematic consistency, for God is consistent and the world that he teleologically orders gives system to this consistency. As we unite validity with experience, we have a perfect test for truth.'[84] 'The Christian, by systematic consistency, will be privileged to speak not only of the other side of the moon and of an absolute good, but also of creation, the flood, angels, heaven and hell.' "[85]

As a *conservative* Carnell is now willing, despite all he has said indicating the contrary, to submit the absolute authority of the living Redeemer-God of the Bible to an examination administered by Mr. Natural Man, who no longer thinks of himself as a creature of God, who has never sinned against the grace and love of God, and who is now, supposedly, a fairly innocent seeker for truth in a universe so "open" "that there may be many other gods who have as much right to be candidates for the throne of the universe as does the God of the Bible."[86] What sort of "system of authority" is this where the Creator must pass a test set by his creature who has worked out a system of logic by which he, all on his own, decides what can and what cannot exist, who assumes that any and all facts are thoroughly explicable whether or not God exists, for the existence of God is irrelevant to our understanding of any fact? Carnell seems to answer in this fashion: "Without reason to canvass the evidence of a given authority, how can one segregate the right authority from the wrong one? Shall we count the number of words used, to distinguish between the worth of the Vedas, the Shastras, the writings of Confucius, the Koran, the Book of Mormon, the works of Mary Baker Eddy, the Scriptures, and the *ex cathedra* pronouncements of the popes?"[87] "Any theology which rejects Aristotle's fourth book of the *Metaphysics* is big with the elements of its own destruction."[88] "If Paul were teaching that the crucified Christ were objectively foolish, in the sense that he cannot be rationally categorized, then he would have pointed to the insane and the demented as incarnations of truth."[89] Clearly Carnell believed in a system of authority which was stamped with "Man's Seal of Approval"! For Carnell, as for St. Thomas of the past, faith must have a rational foundation. Both men find a common aid, although in different ways, in Aristotle.

Dr. Lewis, it should be clear by now that my criticism of Dr. Carnell was but an extension and "updating" of my continual criticism of the Aquinas-Butler form of Christian apologetics which I began in the late 1920's. The fatal

84. CVT: *Ibid.*, p. 63.
85. CVT: *Ibid.*, p. 64.
86. CVT: *Ibid.*, p. 71.
87. CVT: *Ibid.*, p. 72.
88. CVT: *Ibid.*, p. 78.
89. CVT: *Ibid.*, p. 85.

mistake of this methodology has always been that it expresses, at the very beginning, *areas of ultimate agreement* with the systems of unbelievers. Butler told the deists that he was in accord with them on the interpretation of the "course and constitution of nature." He only wanted them to go on with their method and *add* belief in God the Son to their belief in God the Father.

Now Carnell attempted to say the same thing to the personalists. They must simply see that the *conservative* notion of personalism is even better than theirs. Carnell knew well enough that the starting-point of the self-attesting Christ in Scripture brings with it the prerequisite of regeneration, the effort of basic exegesis, and a theology closely akin to that of the Reformers. He also knew that the starting-point of personalism transforms the kingdom of Christ into the kingdom of man, and conceives of Christ as the inherent, universal salvation of mankind. Carnell could only establish a common ground with personalism by ignoring the falseness of the Christ of personalism.

Although I have, in my response to Dr. Pinnock,[90] attempted to clarify my criticism of the Butler-Aquinas method, I would like to make a couple of additional observations on this method of a more theological nature.

Any form of a Butler method is both unbiblical and futile.

It is unbiblical because it denies the clarity of God's revelation in man and in his surroundings. The evidence for God's existence is crystal clear, but because of his sinful blindness man does not see it. To ask *whether* God exists and *whether* God realizes his plan for the world through his works of creation and providence, is, in effect, to deny the perspicuity of revelation.

Basic to this approach is the conviction that man is intelligible to himself and can intelligibly ask questions about himself and his world even though God does not exist. But if this were so, wherein would the need of God or of revelation and salvation consist? To tell man that his *mind* does not need to be saved, is to tell him that he does not need to be saved at all.

The Christian should, rather, show that *unless* what God through Christ in Scripture says is true, man's whole effort at asking and answering questions ceases to have significance, and, worse than that, he himself remains under the wrath of the Lamb. Human predication is reduced to prattle unless it is based upon the truth of what God says in his Word. Idealism, as I have observed in the past, correctly maintained that bare facts are in themselves unintelligible.[91] But "bare facts" are the only facts which the natural man, including the Idealists themselves, have. Only Christianity brings fact and reason into meaningful relation, not through some kind of pan-logism of Parmenides,

90. Van Til refers here to the response he made to Clark Pinnock's contribution to *Jerusalem and Athens;* this response is reproduced below.
91. CVT: Cf. C. Van Til, *CI [Christianity and Idealism].*

but in the organic plan of God. Reason is not the autonomous arbiter of truth, but the servant of the heart, believing or not. Despite what may be appearances to the contrary, as I have said before, "No Christian apologetic can be based on the destruction of rationality itself."[92] The Bible shows us the proper place of reasoning, whether philosophical or theological. "Out of the heart are the issues of life!" Reasoning is an activity of a religiously oriented heart, whether undertaken as a covenant-keeper or as a covenant-breaker.

The gospel of the self-authenticating God speaking through Christ in Scripture offers man salvation, not only for his life, but for his science and philosophy and theology as well. The would-be self-authenticating man must be challenged to repent and return to God. The natural man whose wisdom has, in the course of history, shown itself to be foolishness, must be taken out of his hall of mirrors, out of Topsy-Turvy Land into the open sunlight. He will then see for the first time that it is not Chance but God's providence that constitutes man's principle of individuation and that it is not some abstract principle of rationality or logic but God's plan which constitutes his proper principle or unity.

We therefore must follow the example of Paul, who lays down the gauntlet with, "Where is the wise man, where is the scribe? Where is the debater of this age? Has not God made foolish the wisdom of the world? For since in the wisdom of God, the world through its wisdom did not come to know God, God was well pleased through the foolishness of the message preached to save those who believe" (I Cor. 1:20, 21, NASB). As made in the image of God, and therefore "knowing God" (Rom. 1:19), men can intellectually understand the contrast between a view of human predication based on man having sprung from Chance and one based on man as God's image. They can intellectually understand the difference between the God of Scripture who is the source of all possibility and who controls whatsoever comes to pass in history and a god who is catapulted out of the void by the logic of man who has himself come from the void. Preaching to men who are, according to Scripture, spiritually dead, is not in vain. God can and does give men light and life and a new heart in the presence of his Word. The same is true of reasoning with them, when that reasoning receives its primary orientation from the Word of God.

Dr. Lewis, you have said: "Van Til's criticism of testing revelation-claims by systematic consistency assumes that the Bible is self-authenticating, a claim which begs the apologetics question. That question asks which among the contradictory alleged revelations, if any, is God's Word." Perhaps you will now

---

92. CVT: C. Van Til, *CTEv [Christian-Theistic Evidences]*, 1961 ed., p. 50.

see that to face such a problem, in a manner such as you suggest, would be, already, to give the wrong answer. Such a question, as well as any man-made method devised to answer it, would be blasphemous. I remind you of Carnell's own words which I quoted earlier, "If the Word required something more certain than itself to give it validity, it would no longer be *God's* Word."[93]

I wish Carnell had held on to this position, but his book on apologetics exhibits this inconsistency throughout. The fact that all other religions fail Carnell's test (at least he hoped they did) and that Christianity passed it *magna cum laude* is not to the point. The point is that the man who is a creature of God and who has sinned against God is accorded the prerogative of setting the examination which the Creator and Redeemer must pass before he may become what he is.

I hope I have made somewhat more clear to you, Dr. Lewis, why I think I have not seriously misinterpreted my brother in Christ. I have said again, as I have tried to say before, that Dr. Carnell believed in the gospel in the way I believe in it. Secondly, I have said more plainly than before, I hope, that he and I were in basic disagreement on the question of methodology in apologetics. He was sure, as he told me during a whole day we spent together discussing these matters, that since I did not do justice to Aristotle's fourth book of the *Metaphysics,* my faith must be a blind faith. He was sure I could make no intelligible contact with the unbeliever. Everything he wrote in his first book on apologetics, and in all those to follow, he wrote with full consciousness of the differences which arose between us during his days at Boston.

I must leave this discussion now. I hope, above all things, that you now see that the differences between me and the late Dr. Carnell were not imaginary or even semantic, but differences which we *both* saw.

THE TRADITIONAL METHOD'S COMPROMISES AND DEFEAT ILLUSTRATED: THE DIALOGUE OF MR. WHITE, MR. BLACK, AND MR. GREY [94]

THE BELIEVER MEETS THE UNBELIEVER

To see clearly what is meant, think of a dentist. You go to him with a "bad tooth." Does he take care of your tooth in two operations? To be sure, you may have to come back to have him finish the job. But it is one job he is doing. He takes all the decayed matter out before he fills the cavity. Well, Mr. Black

---

93. CVT: Carnell, *op. cit.*, p. 66.
94. Excerpts from *Defense of the Faith*, 319–27, 331–51. This discussion originally appeared as a series of articles on "Reformed Apologetics" in *Torch and Trumpet*, vols.

is the man with the toothache, and you, as a Reformed Christian, are the dentist. Would you first convert him to Evangelicalism and then to the Reformed Faith? Then you would be like a dentist who would today take half the decayed matter out and fill the cavity, and tomorrow or next week take out the rest of the decayed matter and fill the cavity again. Or, rather, you would be like the dentist who takes part of the decayed matter out, fills the cavity, and then lets the patient go until a long time later he returns complaining again of a toothache.

Indeed, it is no fun to have the dentist drill deep into your tooth. And it is the last and deepest drilling that hurts most. So Mr. Black is likely to feel more at home in the office of the "evangelical" dentist than in the office of the "Reformed" dentist. Will the latter have any customers? He is likely to fear that he will not. He is ever tempted, therefore, to advertise that he is cooperating with all good "conservatives" in all good dentistry, but that he has a specialty which it would be very nice for people to see him about.

Let us now ask by what means we may diagnose Mr. Black. For that purpose we use the X-ray machine. Whence do you know your misery? Out of the law, the revealed will of God, answers the Reformed Christian. Let us call him Mr. White. It is by means of the Bible, not by personal experience, that he turns the light on himself, as well as on Mr. Black. He does not appeal to "experience" or to "reason" or to "history" or to anything else as his source of information in the way that he appeals to the Bible. He may appeal to experience, but his appeal will be to experience as seen in the light of the Bible. So he may appeal to reason or to history, but, again, only as they are to be seen in the light of the Bible. He does not even look for *corroboration* for the teachings of Scripture from experience, reason or history except insofar as these are themselves first seen in the light of the Bible. For him the Bible, and therefore the God of the Bible, is like the sun from which the light that is given by oil lamps, gas lamps and electric lights is derived.

Quite different is the attitude of the "evangelical" or "conservative." Let us call him Mr. Grey. Mr. Grey uses the Bible, experience, reason or logic as equally independent sources of information about his own and therefore about Mr. Black's predicament. I did not say that for Mr. Grey the Bible, ex-

1–2 (1951–53). It reappeared with a new introduction in *Reformed Pastor and Modern Thought*, 36–69. There Van Til appropriately explained: "On the other hand we have a representative of those who have, by the grace of God, become worshipers of the Creator-Redeemer, called Mr. White. Mr. White is far from what, judging him by his name, we should expect him to be. But he is washed in the blood of the Lamb. *In Christ* he is whiter than snow. Mr. White is the Reformed Christian. . . . [T]here is a third party, an Arminian, called Mr. Grey. Of course, *in Christ*, Mr. Grey is as white as is Mr. White" (p. 36).

perience and reason are *equally* important. Indeed they are not. He knows that the Bible is by far the most important. But he none the less constantly appeals to "the facts of experience" and to "logic" without first dealing with the very idea of fact and with the idea of logic in terms of the Scripture.

The difference is basic. When Mr. White diagnoses Mr. Black's case he takes as his X-ray machine the Bible only. When Mr. Grey diagnoses Mr. Black's case he first takes the X-ray machine of experience, then the X-ray machine of logic, and finally his biggest X-ray machine, the Bible. In fact, he may take these in any order. Each of them is an independent source of information.

Let us first look briefly at a typical sample of procedure generally followed in conservative or evangelical circles today. Let us, in other words, note how Mr. Grey proceeds with an analysis of Mr. Black. And let us at the same time see how Mr. Grey would win Mr. Black to an acceptance of Christianity. We take for this purpose a series of articles which appeared in the January, February and March, 1950, issues of *Moody Monthly*, published by the Moody Bible Institute in Chicago. Edward John Carnell, Ph.D., author of *An Introduction to Christian Apologetics* and the Professor of Apologetics at Fuller Theological Seminary, Pasadena, California, wrote this series. Carnell's writings are among the best that appear in evangelical circles. In fact, in his book Carnell frequently argues as we would expect a Reformed apologist to argue. By and large, however, he represents the evangelical rather than the Reformed method in Apologetics.

When Mr. Carnell instructs his readers "How Every Christian Can Defend His Faith," he first appeals to facts and to logic as independent sources of information about the truth of Christianity. Of course, he must bring in the Bible even at this point. But the Bible is brought in only as a book of information about the fact of what has historically been called Christianity. It is not from the beginning brought in as God's Word. It must be shown to Mr. Black to be the Word of God by means of "facts" reasoning in a circle. He does not want Mr. Black to point the finger at him and say: "You prove that the Bible is true by an appeal to the Bible itself. That is circular reasoning. How can any person with any respect for logic accept such a method of proof?"

Carnell would escape such a charge by showing that the facts of experience, such as all men recognize, and logic, such as all men must use, point to the truth of Scripture. This is what he says: "If you are of a philosophic turn, you can point to the remarkable way in which Christianity fits in with the moral sense inherent in every human being, or the influence of Christ on our ethics, customs, literature, art and music. Finally, you can draw upon your own experience in speaking of the reality of answered prayer and the witness of the Spirit in your own heart. . . . If the person is impressed with this evidence, turn at once to the gospel. Read crucial passages and permit the Spirit to work on the inner recesses of his heart. Remember that apologetics is merely a preparation. After the ground has been broken, proceed immediately with sowing and watering."[95]

It is assumed in this argument that Mr. Black agrees with the "evangelical," Mr. Grey, on the character of the "moral sense" of man. This may be true, but then it is true because Mr. Grey has himself not taken his information about the moral sense of man exclusively from Scripture. If with Mr. White he had taken his conception of the moral nature of man from the Bible, then he would hold that Mr. Black, as totally depraved will, of course, misinterpret his own moral nature. True, Christianity is in accord with the moral nature of man. But this is so only because the moral nature of man is first in accord with what the Bible says it is, that is, originally created perfect, but now wholly corrupted in its desires through the fall of man.

If you are reasoning with a naturalist, Carnell advises his readers, ask him why when a child throws a rock through his window, he chases the child and not the rock. Presumably even a naturalist knows that the child, not the rock, is free and therefore responsible. "A bottle of water cannot ought; it must. When once the free spirit of man is proved, the moral argument—the existence of a God who imposes moral obligations—can form the bridge from man to God."[96]

Here the fundamental difference between Mr. Grey's and Mr. White's approach to Mr. Black appears. The difference lies in the different notions of the free will of man. Or, it may be said, the difference is with respect to the nature of man as such. Mr. White would define man, and therefore his freedom, in terms of Scripture alone. He would therefore begin with the fact that man is the creature of God. And this implies that man's freedom is a derivative freedom. It is a freedom that is not and cannot be wholly ultimate, that is, self-dependent. Mr. White knows that Mr. Black would not agree with him in this analysis of man and of his freedom. He knows that Mr. Black would not agree with him on this any more than he would agree on the Biblical idea of total depravity.

Mr. Grey, on the other hand, must at all costs have "a point of contact" in the system of thought of Mr. Black, who is typical of the natural man; just as Mr. Grey is afraid of being charged with circular reasoning, so he is also afraid of being charged with talking about something that is "outside of experience." And so he is driven to talk in general about the "free spirit of man."

95. CVT: *Moody Monthly*, January 1950, p. 313.
96. CVT: *Idem,* p. 343.

Of course, Mr. Black need have no objections from his point of view in allowing for the "free spirit of man." That is at bottom what he holds even when he is a naturalist. His whole position is based upon the idea of man as a free spirit, that is, a spirit that is not subject to the law of his Creator God. And Carnell does not distinguish between the Biblical doctrine of freedom, as based upon and involved in the fact of man's creation, and the doctrine of freedom, in the sense of autonomy, which makes man a law unto himself.

Of course, Mr. Black will be greatly impressed with such an argument as Mr. Grey has presented to him for the truth of Christianity. In fact, if Christianity is thus shown to be in accord with the moral nature of man, as Mr. Black himself sees that moral nature, then Mr. Black does not need to be converted at all to accept Christianity. He only needs to accept something additional to what he has always believed. He has been shown how nice it would be to have a second story built on top of the house which he has already built according to his own plans.

To be sure, the Evangelical intends no such thing. Least of all does Carnell intend such a thing. But why then does not the "Evangelical" see that by presenting the non-Christian with Evangelicalism rather than with the Reformed Faith he must compromise the Christian religion? And why does he not also see that in doing what he does the non-Christian is not really challenged either by fact or by logic? For facts and logic which are not themselves first seen in the light of Christianity have, in the nature of the case, no power in them to challenge the unbeliever to change his position. Facts and logic, not based upon the creation doctrine and not placed in the context of the doctrine of God's all-embracing Providence, are without relation to one another and therefore wholly meaningless.

It is this fact which must be shown to Mr. Black. The folly of holding to any view of life except that which is frankly based upon the Bible as the absolute authority for man must be pointed out to him. Only then are we doing what Paul did when he said: "Where is the wise? where is the scribe? where is the disputer of this world? hath not God made foolish the wisdom of the world?" (I Corinthians 1:20.)

As a Reformed Christian Mr. White therefore cannot cooperate with Mr. Grey in his analysis of Mr. Black. This fact may appear more clearly if we turn to see how Mr. Black appears when he is analyzed by Mr. White in terms of the Bible alone.

Now, according to Mr. White's analysis, Mr. Black is not a murderer. He is not necessarily a drunkard or a dope addict. He lives in one of the suburbs. He is every whit a gentleman. He gives to the Red Cross and to the Red Feather campaigns. He was a boy scout; he is a member of a lodge; he is very much civic minded; now and then his name is mentioned in the papers as an asset to the community. But we know that he is spiritually dead. He is filled with the spirit of error. Perhaps he is a member of a "fine church" in the community, but nevertheless he is one of a "people that do err in their heart" (Psalm 95:10). He lives in a stupor (Romans 11:8). To him the wisdom of God is foolishness. The truth about God, and about himself in relation to God, is obnoxious to him. He does not want to hear of it. He seeks to close eyes and ears to those who give witness of the truth. He is, in short, utterly self-deceived.

Actually, Mr. Black is certain that he looks at life in the only proper way. Even if he has doubts as to the truth of what he believes, he does not see how any sensible or rational man could believe or do otherwise. If he has doubts it is because no one can be fully sure of himself. If he has fears it is because fear is to be expected in the hazardous situation in which modern man lives. If he sees men's minds break down he thinks this is to be expected under current conditions of stress and strain. If he sees grown men act like children he says that they were once beasts. Everything, including the "abnormal," is to him "normal."

In all this Mr. Black has obviously taken for granted that what the Bible says about the world and himself is not true. He has *taken this for granted*. He may never have argued the point. He has cemented yellow spectacles to his own eyes. He cannot remove them because he will not remove them. He is blind and loves to be blind.

Do not think that Mr. Black has an easy time of it. He is the man who always "kicks against the pricks." His conscience troubles him all the time. Deep down in his heart he knows that what the Bible says about him and about the world is true. Even if he has never heard of the Bible he knows that he is a creature of God and that he has broken the law of God (Romans 1:19, 20; 2:14, 15). When the prodigal son left his father's house he could not immediately efface from his memory the look and the voice of his father. How that look and that voice came back to him when he was at the swine trough! How hard he had tried to live as though the money with which he so freely entertained his "friends" had not come from his father! When asked where he came from he would answer that he came "from the other side." He did not want to be reminded of his past. Yet he could not forget it. It required a constant act of suppression to forget the past. But that very act of suppression itself keeps alive the memory of the past.

So also with Mr. Black. He daily changes the truth of God into a lie. He daily worships and serves the creature more than the Creator. He daily holds the truth in unrighteousness (Romans 1:18). But what a time he has with himself! He may try to sear his conscience as with a hot iron. He may seek to escape the influence of all those who witness to the truth. But he can never escape himself as witness bearer to the truth.

His conscience keeps telling him: "Mr. Black, you are a fugitive from justice. You have run away from home, from your father's bountiful love. You are an ingrate, a sneak, a rascal! You shall not escape meeting justice at last. The father still feeds you. Yet you despise the riches of his goodness and forbearance and longsuffering; not recognizing that the goodness of God is calculated to lead you to repentance (Romans 2:4). Why do you kick against the pricks? Why do you stifle the voice of your conscience? Why do you use the wonderful intellect that God has given you as a tool for the suppression of the voice of God which speaks to you through yourself and through your environment? Why do you build your house on sand instead of on rock? Can you be sure that no storm is ever coming? Are you omniscient? Are you omnipotent? You say that nobody knows whether God exists or whether Christianity is true. You say that nobody knows this because man is finite. Yet you assume that God cannot exist and that Christianity cannot be true. You assume that no judgment will ever come. You must be omniscient to know that. And yet you have just said that all man declares about "the beyond" must be based upon his brief span of existence in this world of time and chance. How, then, if you have taken for granted that chance is one of the basic ingredients of all human experience, can you at the same time say what *can* or *cannot* be in all time to come? You certainly have made a fool of yourself, Mr. Black," says Mr. Black to himself. "You reject the claims of truth which you know to be the truth, and you do that in terms of the lie which really you know to be the lie."

It is not always that Mr. Black is thus aware of the fact that he lives like the prodigal who would eat of the things the swine did eat, but who knows he cannot because he is a human being. He is not always thus aware of his folly—in part at least, because of the failure of evangelicals, and particularly because of the failure of Reformed Christians to stir him up to a realization of his folly. The Evangelical does not want to stir him up thus. It is in the nature of his own theology not to stir him up to a realization of this basic depth of folly. But the Reformed Christian should, on his basis, want to stir up Mr. Black to an appreciation of the folly of his ways.

However, when the Reformed Christian, Mr. White, is to any extent aware of the richness of his own position and actually has the courage to challenge Mr. Black by presenting to him the picture of himself as taken through the X-ray machine called the Bible, he faces the charge of "circular reasoning" and of finding no "point of contact" with experience. And he will also be subject to the criticism of the Evangelical for speaking as if Christianity were irrational and for failing to reach the man in the street.

Thus we seem to be in a bad predicament. There is a basic difference of policy between Mr. White and Mr. Grey as to how to deal with Mr. Black. Mr. Grey thinks that Mr. Black is not really such a bad fellow. It is possible, he thinks, to live with Mr. Black in the same world. And he is pretty strong. So it is best to make a compromise peace with him. That seems to be the way of the wise and practical politician. On the other hand, Mr. White thinks that it is impossible permanently to live in the same world with Mr. Black. Mr. Black, he says, must therefore be placed before the requirement of absolute and unconditional surrender. And surely it would be out of the question for Mr. White first to make a compromise peace with Mr. Black and then, after all, to require unconditional surrender! But what then about this charge of circular reasoning and about this charge of having no point of contact with the unbeliever? . . .

A CONSISTENT WITNESS

It must always be remembered that the first requirement for effective witnessing is that the position to which witness is given be intelligible. Evangelicalism, when consistently carried out, destroys this intelligibility.

The second requirement for effective witnessing is that he to whom the witness is given must be shown why he should forsake his own position and accept that which is offered him. Evangelicalism, when consistently carried out, also destroys the reason why the unbeliever should accept the gospel. Why should the unbeliever change his position if he is not shown that it is wrong? And, in particular, why should he change if the one who asks him to change is actually encouraging him in thinking that he is right? The Calvinist will need to have a better method of defending the doctrine of the atonement, for example, than that of the Evangelical.

We have dealt with the doctrine of the atonement. That led us into the involved question whether God is the source of possibility, or whether possibility is the source of God. It has been shown that the "evangelical" or Arminian fundamentalist holds to a position which requires him to make both of these contradictory assertions at once. But how about the realm of fact? Do you also hold, I am asked, that we need to seek for a specifically Reformed method of defending the facts of Christianity? Take the resurrection of Christ as an example—why can there be no common witness on the part of the Evangelical and the Calvinist to such a fact as that?

Once more Mr. Grey, the Evangelical, punches the doorbell at Mr. Black's home. Mr. Black answers to admit him.

"I am here again, Mr. Black," begins Grey, "because I am still anxious to have you accept Christ as your personal Savior. When I spoke to you the other time about the atonement you got me into deep water. We got all tangled up on the question of 'possibility.'

"But now I have something far simpler. I want to deal with simple facts. I want to show you that the resurrection of Jesus from the dead is as truly a fact as any that you can mention. To use the words of Wilbur Smith, himself a Calvinist but opposed to the idea of a distinctively Reformed method for the defense of the faith: 'The *meaning* of the resurrection is a theological matter, but the fact of the resurrection is a historical matter; the nature of the resurrection body of Jesus may be a mystery, but the fact that the body disappeared from the tomb is a matter to be decided upon by historical evidence.'[97] And the historical evidence for the resurrection is the kind of evidence that you as a scientist would desire.

"Smith writes in the same book: 'About a year ago, after studying over a long period of time this entire problem of our Lord's resurrection, and having written some hundreds of pages upon it at different times, I was suddenly arrested by the thought that the very kind of evidence which modern science, and even psychologists, are so insistent upon for determining the reality of any object under consideration is the kind of evidence that we have presented to us in the gospels regarding the resurrection of the Lord Jesus, namely, the things that are seen with the human eye, touched with the human hand, and heard by the human ear. This is what we call empirical evidence. It would almost seem as if parts of the gospel records of the resurrection were actually written for such a day as ours when empiricism so dominates our thinking.'[98]

"Now I think that Smith is quite right in thus distinguishing sharply between the *fact* and the *meaning* of the resurrection. And I am now only asking you to accept the fact of the resurrection. There is the clearest possible empirical evidence for this fact. The living Jesus was touched with human hands and seen with human eyes of sensible men after he had been crucified and put into the tomb. Surely you ought to believe in the resurrection of Christ as a historical fact. And to believe in the resurrected Christ is to be saved."

"But hold on a second," says Mr. Black. "Your friend the Calvinist, Mr. White, has been ahead of you again. He was here last night and spoke of the same thing. However, he did not thus distinguish between the fact and the meaning of the resurrection. At least, he did not for a moment want to separate the fact of the resurrection from the system of Christianity in terms of which

97. CVT: *Therefore Stand*, Boston, 1945, p. 386.
98. CVT: *Idem*, pp. 389, 390.

it gets its meaning. He spoke of Jesus Christ, the Son of God, as rising from the dead. He spoke of the Son of God through whom the world was made and through whom the world is sustained, as having risen from the dead. And when I asked him how this God could die and rise from the dead, he said that God did not die and rise from the dead but that the second person of the Trinity had taken to himself a human nature, and that it was in this human nature that he died and rose again. In short, in accepting the fact of the resurrection he wanted me also to take all this abracadabra into the bargain. And I have a suspicion that you are secretly trying to have me do something similar."

"No, no," replies Mr. Grey. "I am in complete agreement with you over against the Calvinist. I have a common witness with you against him. I, too, would separate fact and system. Did I not agree with you against the Calvinist, in holding that possibility is independent of God? Well then, by the same token I hold that all kinds of facts happen apart from the plan of God. So we Evangelicals are in a position, as the Calvinists are not, of speaking with you on neutral ground. With you, we would simply talk about the facts of Christianity without bringing into the picture anything about the meaning or the significance of those facts.

"It makes me smile," continues Mr. Grey, "when I think of Mr. White coming over here trying to convert you. That poor fellow is always reasoning in circles. I suppose that such reasoning in circles goes with his determinism. He is always talking about his self-contained God. He says that all facts are what they are because of the plan of this God. Then each fact would of necessity, to be a fact at all, prove the truth of the Christian system of things and, in turn, would be proved as existing by virtue of this self-same Christian system of things. I realize full well that you, as a modern scientist and philosopher, can have no truck with such horrible, circular reasoning as that.

"It is for this reason that, as Evangelicals, we have now separated sharply between the resurrection as a historical fact and the meaning of the resurrection. I'm merely asking you to accept the fact of the resurrection. I am not asking you to do anything that you cannot do in full consistency with your freedom and with the 'scientific method.' "

"Well, that is delightful," replies Mr. Black. "I always felt that the Calvinists were our real foes. But I read something in the paper the other day to the effect that some Calvinist churches or individuals were proposing to make a common witness with Evangelicals for the gospel. Now I was under the impression that the gospel had something to do with being saved from hell and going to heaven. I knew that the modernists and the 'new modernists,' like Barth, do not believe in tying up the facts of history with such wild speculations. It was my opinion that 'fundamentalists' did tie up belief in historical facts, such as the death and the resurrection of Jesus, with going to heaven or to hell. So I am delighted that you, though a fundamentalist, are willing to join with the modernist and the neo-modernist in separating historical facts from such a rationalistic system as I knew Christianity was.

"Now as for accepting the resurrection of Jesus," continued Mr. Black, "as thus properly separated from the traditional systems of theology, I do not in the least mind doing that. To tell you the truth, I have accepted the resurrection as a fact now for some time. The evidence for it is overwhelming. This is a strange universe. All kinds of 'miracles' happen in it. The universe is open. So why should there not be some resurrections here and there? The resurrection of Jesus would be a fine item for Ripley's *Believe It or Not*. Why not send it in?"

Mr. Gray wanted to continue at this point. He wanted to speak of the common witness that he had, after all, with the Calvinist for the gospel. But it was too late. He had no "common" witness left of any sort. He had again tried to gallop off in opposite directions at the same time. He had again taken away all intelligibility from the witness that he meant to bring. He had again established Mr. Black in thinking that his own unbelieving reason was right. For it was as clear as crystal to Mr. Black, as it should have been to Mr. Grey, that belief in the fact of the resurrection, apart from the system of Christianity, amounts to belief that the Christian system is not true, is belief in the universe as run by Chance, is belief that it was not Jesus Christ, the Son of God, who rose from the dead.

To be sure, in practice the "evangelical" is much better in his witness for the resurrection of Christ than he has been presented here. But that is because every Evangelical, as a sincere Christian is at heart a Calvinist. But witnessing is a matter of the head as well as of the heart. If the world is to hear a consistent testimony for the Christian faith, it is the Calvinist who must give it. If there is not a distinctively Reformed method for the defense of every article of the Christian faith, then there is no way of clearly telling an unbeliever just how Christianity differs from his own position and why he should accept the Lord Jesus Christ as his personal Savior. We are happy and thankful, of course, for the work of witnessing done by Evangelicals. We are happy because of the fact that, in spite of their inconsistency in presenting the Christian testimony, something, often much, of the truth of the gospel shines through unto men, and they are saved.

THE AUTHORITY OF SCRIPTURE

"But how can anyone know anything about the 'Beyond'?" asks Mr. Black.

"Well, of course," replies Mr. Grey, "if you want absolute certainty such as one gets in geometry, Christianity does not offer it. We offer you only 'rational probability.' 'Christianity,' as I said in effect a moment ago when I spoke of the death of Christ, 'is founded on historical facts, which, by their very nature, cannot be demonstrated with geometric certainty. All judgments of historical particulars are at the mercy of the complexity of the time-space universe. . . . If the scientist cannot rise above rational probability in his empirical investigation, why should the Christian claim more?' And what is true of the death of Christ," adds Mr. Grey, "is, of course, also true of his resurrection. But this only shows that 'the Christian is in possession of a world-view which is making a sincere effort to come to grips with actual history.' "[99]

By speaking thus, Mr. Grey seeks for a point of contact with Mr. Black. For Mr. Black, history is something that floats on an infinitely extended and bottomless ocean of Chance. Therefore he can say that *anything* may happen. Who knows but the death and resurrection of Jesus as the Son of God might issue from this womb of Chance? Such events would have an equal chance of happening with "snarks, boojums, splinth, and gobble-de-gook." God himself may live in this realm of Chance. He is then "wholly other" than ourselves. And his revelation in history would then be wholly unique.

Now the Evangelical does not challenge this underlying philosophy of Chance as it controls the unbeliever's conception of history. He is so anxious to have the unbeliever accept the possibility of God's existence and the fact of the resurrection of Christ that, if necessary, he will exchange his own philosophy of fact for that of the unbeliever. Anxious to be genuinely "empirical" like the unbeliever, he will throw all the facts of Christianity into the bottomless pit of Chance. Or, rather, he will throw all these facts at the unbeliever, and the unbeliever throws them over his back into the bottomless pit of Chance.

Of course, this is the last thing that such men as Wilbur Smith, Edward J. Carnell, and J. Oliver Buswell, Jr., want to do. But in failing to challenge the philosophy of Chance that underlies the unbeliever's notion of "fact," they are in effect accepting it.

This approach of Mr. Grey is unavoidable if one holds to an Arminian theology. The Arminian view of man's free will implies that "possibility" is above God. But a "possibility" that is above God is the same thing as Chance. A God surrounded by Chance cannot speak with authority. He would be speaking into a vacuum. His voice could not be heard. And if God were surrounded by Chance, then human beings would be too. They would live in a vacuum, unable to hear either their own voices or those of others. Thus the whole of history, including all of its facts, would be without meaning.

99. CVT: E. J. Carnell: *An Introduction to Christian Apologetics*, p. 113.

It is this that the Reformed Christian, Mr. White, would tell Mr. Black. In the very act of presenting the resurrection of Christ or in the very act of presenting any other fact of historic Christianity, Mr. White would be presenting it as authoritatively interpreted in the Bible. He would argue that unless Mr. Black is willing to set the facts of history in the framework of the meaning authoritatively ascribed to them in the Bible, he will make gobble-de-gook of history.

If history were what Mr. Black assumes that it is, then *anything* might happen and then *nobody* would know what may happen. No one thing would then be more likely to happen than any other thing. David Hume, the great skeptic, has effectively argued that if you allow any room for Chance in your thought, then you no longer have the right to speak of probabilities. Whirl would be king. No one hypothesis would have any more relevance to facts than any other hypothesis. Did God raise Christ from the dead? Perchance he did. Did Jupiter do it? Perchance he did. What is Truth? Nobody knows. Such would be the picture of the universe if Mr. Black were right.

No comfort can be taken from the assurance of the Conservative that, since Christianity makes no higher claim than that of rational probability, "the system of Christianity can be refuted only by probability. Perhaps our loss is gain." How could one ever argue that there is a greater probability for the truth of Christianity than for the truth of its opposite if the very meaning of the word probability rests upon the idea of Chance? On this basis nature and history would be no more than a series of pointer readings pointing into the blank.

In assuming his philosophy of Chance and thus virtually saying that *nobody knows* what is back of the common objects of daily observation, Mr. Black also virtually says that the Christian view of things is wrong.

If I assert that there is a black cat in the closet, and you assert that nobody knows what is in the closet, you have virtually told me that I am wrong in my hypothesis. So when I tell Mr. Black that God exists, and he responds very graciously by saying that perhaps I am right since nobody knows what is in the "Beyond," he is virtually saying that I am wrong in my hypothesis. He is obviously thinking of such a God as could comfortably live in the realm of Chance. But the God of Scripture cannot live in the realm of Chance.

Mr. Black's response when confronted with the claims of God and his Christ, is essentially this: Nobody knows, but nevertheless your hypothesis is certainly wrong and mine is certainly right. Nobody knows whether God exists, but God certainly does not exist and Chance certainly does exist.

When Mr. Black thus virtually makes his universal negative assertion, saying in effect that God *cannot* possibly exist and that Christianity *cannot* possibly be true, he must surely be standing on something very solid. Is it on solid rock that he stands? No, he stands on water! He stands on his own "experience." But this experience, by his own assumption, rests again on Chance. Thus standing on Chance, he swings the "logician's postulate" and modestly asserts what cannot be in the "Beyond," of which he said before that nothing can be said.

Of course, what Mr. Black is doing appears very reasonable to himself. "Surely," he says, if questioned at all on the subject, "a rational man must have systematic coherence in his experience. Therefore he cannot accept as true anything that is not in accord with the law of noncontradiction. So long as you leave your God in the realm of the 'Beyond,' in the realm of the indeterminate, you may worship him by yourself alone. But as soon as you claim that your God has revealed himself in creation, in providence, or in your Scripture, so soon I shall put that revelation to a test by the principle of rational coherence.

"And by that test none of your doctrines are acceptable. All of them are contradictory. No rational man can accept any of them. If your God is eternal, then he falls outside of my experience and lives in the realm of the 'Beyond,' of the unknowable. But if he is to have anything to do with the world, then he must himself be wholly within the world. I must understand your God throughout if I am to speak intelligently of any relationship that he sustains to my world and to myself. Your idea that God is both eternal and unchangeable and yet sustains such relationships to the world as are involved in your doctrine of creation and providence, is flatly contradictory.

"For me to accept your God," continues Mr. Black, "you must do to him what Karl Barth has done to him, namely, strip him of all the attributes that orthodox theology has assigned to him, and thus enable him to turn into the opposite of himself. With that sort of God I have a principle of unity that brings all my experience into harmony. And that God is wholly within the universe. If you offer me such a God and offer him as the simplest hypothesis with which I may, as a goal, seek to order my experience as it comes to me from the womb of Chance, then the law of noncontradiction will be satisfied. As a rational man I can settle for nothing less."

All this amounts to saying that Mr. Black, the lover of a Chance philosophy, the indeterminist, is at the same time an out-and-out determinist or fatalist. It is to say that Mr. Black, the irrationalist, who said that nobody knows what is in the "Beyond," is at the same time a flaming rationalist. For him only that can be which—so he thinks—he can exhaustively determine by logic must be. He may at first grant that anything may exist, but when he says this he at the same time says in effect that nothing can exist and have meaning for man but that which man himself can exhaustively know. Therefore, for

Mr. Black, the God of Christianity cannot exist. For him the doctrine of creation cannot be true. There could be no revelation of God to man through nature and history. There can be no such thing as the resurrection of Christ.

Strangely enough, when Mr. Black thus says that God cannot exist and that the resurrection of Christ cannot be a fact, and when he also says that God may very well exist and that the resurrection of Christ may very well be a fact, he is not inconsistent with himself. For he must, to be true to his method, contradict himself in every statement that he makes about any fact whatsoever. If he does not, then he would deny either his philosophy of Chance or his philosophy of Fate. According to him, every fact that he meets has in it the two ingredients: that of Chance and that of Fate, that of the wholly unknown and that of the wholly known. Thus man makes the tools of thought, which the Creator has given him in order therewith to think God's thoughts after him on a created level, into the means by which he makes sure that God cannot exist, and therefore certainly cannot reveal himself.

When Mr. White meets Mr. Black he will make this issue plain. He will tell Mr. Black that his methodology cannot make any fact or any group of facts intelligible to himself. Hear him as he speaks to the unbeliever:

"On your basis, Mr. Black, no fact can be identified by distinguishing it from any other fact. For all facts would be changing into their opposites all the time. All would be gobble-de-gook. At the same time, nothing could change at all; all would be one block of ice. Hath not God made foolish the wisdom of this world? He clearly has. I know you cannot see this even though it is perfectly clear. I know you have taken out your own eyes. Hence your inability to see is at the same time unwillingness to see. Pray God for forgiveness and repent."

But what will be the approach of the Conservative, Mr. Grey, on this question of logic? He will do the same sort of thing that we saw him do with respect to the question of facts. Mr. Grey will again try to please Mr. Black by saying that, of course, he will justify his appeal to the authority of the Bible by showing that the very idea of such an appeal, as well as the content of the Bible, are fully in accord with the demands of logic.

"You are quite right in holding that nothing meaningful can be said without presupposing the validity of the law of noncontradiction," says Mr. Grey.[100] " 'The conservative ardently defends a system of authority.'[101] But 'without reason to canvass the evidence of a given authority, how can one segregate a right authority from a wrong one? . . . Without systematic consistency to aid us, it appears that all we can do is to draw straws, count noses,

---

100. CVT: *Idem*, p. 114.
101. CVT: Cf. Carnell, *op. cit.*, p. 57.

flip coins to choose an authority. Once we *do* apply the law of contradiction, we are no longer appealing to *ipse dixit* authority, but to coherent truth.'[102] 'The Scriptures tell us to test the spirits (I John 4:1). This can be done only by applying the canons of truth. God cannot lie. His authority, therefore, and coherent truth are coincident at every point. Truth, not blind authority, saves us from being blind followers of the blind.'[103]

" 'Bring on your revelations!' " continues Mr. Grey. " 'Let them make peace with the law of contradiction and the facts of history, and they will deserve a rational man's assent.'[104] 'Any theology which rejects Aristotle's fourth book of the *Metaphysics* is big with the elements of its own destruction.'[105] 'If Paul were teaching that the crucified Christ were objectively foolish, in the sense that he cannot be rationally categorized, then he would have pointed to the insane and the demented as incarnations of truth.' "[106]

"Well," says Mr. Black, "this is great news indeed. I knew that the modernists were willing with us to start from human experience as the final reference point in all research. I knew that they were willing with us to start from Chance as the source of facts, in order then to manufacture such facts of nature and of history as the law of noncontradiction, based on Chance, will allow. I also knew that the new modernist, Karl Barth, is willing to make over his God so that he can change into the opposite of himself, in order that thus he may satisfy both our irrationalist philosophy of Chance and our rationalist philosophy of logic. But I did not know that there were any orthodox people who were willing to do such a thing. But you have surprised me before. You were willing to throw your resurrection into the realm of Chance in order to have me accept it. So I really should have expected that you would also be willing to make the law of noncontradiction rest upon man himself instead of upon God.

"And I am extremely happy that not only the Arminian Fundamentalists but also you less extreme or moderate Calvinists, like Buswell and Carnell, are now willing to test your own revelation by a principle that is wholly independent of that revelation. It is now only a matter of time until you will see that you have to come over on our side altogether.

"I do not like the regular Calvinists. But they are certainly quite right from their own point of view. Mr. White claims that I am a creature of God. He says that all facts are made by God and controlled by the providence of God.

---

102. CVT: *Idem*, p. 71.
103. CVT: *Idem*, p. 72.
104. CVT: *Idem*, p. 73.
105. CVT: *Idem*, p. 178.
106. CVT: *Idem*, pp. 77, 78.

He says that all men have sinned against God in Adam their representative. He adds that therefore I am spiritually blind and morally perverse. He says all this and more on the basis of the absolute authority of Scripture. He would interpret me, my facts, and my logic in terms of the authority of that Scripture. He says I need this authority. He says I need nothing but this authority. His Scripture, he claims, is sufficient and final. And the whole thing, he claims, is clear.

"Now all this looks like plain historic Protestantism to me. I can intellectually understand the Calvinist on this matter of authority. I cannot understand you. You seem to me to want to have your cake and eat it. If you believe in Scriptural authority, then why not explain all things, man, fact, and logic in terms of it? If you want with us to live by your own authority, by the experience of the human race, then why not have done with the Bible as absolute authority? It then, at best, gives you the authority of the expert.

"In your idea of the rational man who tests all things by the facts of history and by the law of non-contradiction, you have certainly made a point of contact with us. If you carry this through, you will indeed succeed in achieving complete coincidence between your ideas and ours. And, with us, you will have achieved complete coincidence between the ideas of man and the ideas of God. But the reason for this coincidence of your ideas with ours, and for the coincidence of man's ideas with God's, is that you then have a God and a Christ who are identical with man.

"Do you not think, Mr. Grey, that this is too great a price for you to pay? I am sure that you do not thus mean to drag down your God into the Universe. I am sure that you do not thus mean to crucify your Christ afresh. But why then halt between two opinions? I do not believe Christianity, but, if I did, I think I would stand with Mr. White."

PROOFS FOR THE EXISTENCE OF GOD

When Mr. Black objects against Mr. White that unconditional surrender to the authority of Scripture is irrational, then Mr. Grey nods approval and says that, of course, the "rational man" has a perfect right to test the credibility of Scripture by logic. When the Bible speaks of God's sovereign election of some men to salvation this must mean something that fits in with his "rational nature." When Mr. Black objects to Mr. White that unconditional surrender to Scripture is rationalistic, then Mr. Grey again nods approval and says that, of course, genuine human personality has a perfect right to test the content of Scripture by experience. When the Bible speaks of God by his counsel controlling whatsoever comes to pass, this must mean something that fits in with man's freedom. God created man and gave man a share in his own freedom; men therefore participate in his being.

But what of natural or general revelation? Here surely there can be no difference, you say, between the requirements of Mr. White and Mr. Grey. Here there is no law and no promise; here there is only fact. How then can you speak of requirement at all? Here surely Mr. White can forget his "five points of Calvinism" and join Mr. Grey in taking Mr. Black through the picture gallery of this world, pointing out its beauties to him so that with them he will spontaneously exclaim, "The whole chorus of nature raises one hymn to the praises of its Creator."

Let us think of Mr. White as trying hard to forget his "five points." "Surely," he says to himself, "there can be nothing wrong with joining Mr. Grey in showing Mr. Black the wonders of God's creation. We believe in the same God, do we not? Both of us want to show Mr. Black the facts of creation so that he will believe in God. When Mr. Black says: 'I catch no meaning from all I have seen, and I pass on, quite as I came, confused and dismayed' Mr. Grey and I can together take him by plane to the Mt. Wilson observatory so he may see the starry heavens above. Surely the source of knowledge for the natural sciences is the Book of Nature, which is given to everyone. Do not the Scriptures themselves teach that there is a light in nature, per se, which cannot be, and is not, transmitted through the spectacles of the Word? If this were not so, how could the Scriptures say of those who have only the light of nature that they are without excuse?"

So the three men, Mr. White, Mr. Grey, and Mr. Black, go here and there and everywhere. Mr. White and Mr. Grey agree to share the expense. Mr. Black is their guest.

They go first to the Mt. Wilson observatory to see the starry skies above. "How wonderful, how grand!" exclaims Mr. Grey. To the marvels of the telescope they add those of the microscope. They circle the globe to see "the wonders of the world." There is no end to the "exhibits" and Mr. Black shows signs of weariness. So they sit down on the beach. Will not Mr. Black now sign on the dotted line?

As they wait for the answer, Mr. Grey spies a watch someone has lost. Holding it in his hand he says to Mr. Black: "Look round the world: contemplate the whole and every part of it: you will find it to be nothing but one great machine, subdivided into an infinite number of lesser machines, which again admit of subdivisions, to a degree beyond that which human senses and faculties can trace and explain. All these various machines, and even their minute parts, are adjusted to each other with an accuracy which ravishes into admiration all men who have ever contemplated them. The curious adapting of means to ends, throughout all nature, resembles exactly, though it much exceeds, the productions of human contrivance; of human designs, thought, wisdom and intelligence. Since, therefore, the effects resemble each other, we are led to infer, by all the rules of analogy, that the causes also resemble one another; and that the Author of Nature is somewhat similar to the mind of man; though possessed of much larger faculties, proportioned to the grandeur of the work, which he has executed.

"Now, Mr. Black, I don't want to put undue pressure on you. You know your own needs in your own business. But I think that as a rational being, you owe it to yourself to join the theistic party. Isn't it highly probable that there is a God?

"I'm not now asking you to become a Christian. We take things one step at a time. I'm only speaking of the Book of Nature. Of course, if there is a God and if this God should have a Son and if this Son should also reveal himself, it is not likely to be more difficult for you to believe in him than it is now to believe in the Father. But just now I am only asking you to admit that there is a great accumulation of evidence of the sort that any scientist or philosopher must admit to be valid for the existence of a God back of and above this world. You see this watch. Isn't it highly probable that a power higher than itself has made it? You know the purpose of a watch. Isn't it highly probable that the wonderful contrivances of nature serve the purpose of a God? Looking back we are naturally led to a God who is the cause of this world; looking forward we think of a God who has a purpose with this world. So far as we can observe the course and constitution of the universe there is, I think, no difficulty on your own adopted principles, against belief in a God. Why not become a theist? You do want to be on the winning side, don't you? Well, the Gallup poll of the universe indicates a tendency toward the final victory of theism."

When Mr. Grey had finished his obviously serious and eloquent plea, Mr. Black looked very thoughtful. He was clearly a gentleman. He disliked disappointing his two friends after all the generosity they had shown him. But he could not honestly see any basic difference between his own position and theirs. So he declined politely but resolutely to sign on the dotted line. He refused to be "converted" to theism. In substance he spoke as follows: "You speak of evidence of rationality and purpose in the universe. You would trace this rationality or purpose back to a rational being back of the universe who, you think, is likely to have a purpose with the universe. But who is back of your God to explain him in turn? By your own definition your God is not absolute or self-sufficient. You say that he probably exists; which means that you admit that probably he does not exist. But probability rests upon possibility. Now I think that any scientific person should come with an open mind to the observation of the facts of the universe. He ought to begin by assuming that any sort of fact may exist. And I was glad to observe that on this all important point you agree with me. Hence the only kind of God that either of us can believe in is one who may not exist. In other words, neither of us do or can believe in a God who cannot *not* exist. And it was just this sort of God, a God who is self-sufficient, and as such necessarily existent, that I thought you Christian theists believed in."

By this time Mr. White was beginning to squirm. He was beginning to realize that he had sold out the God of his theology, the sovereign God of Scripture by his silent consent to the argument of Mr. Grey. Mr. Black was right, he felt at once. Either one presupposes God back of the ideas of possibility or one presupposes that the idea of possibility is back of God. Either one says with historic Reformed theology on the basis of Scripture that what God determines and only what God determines is possible, or one says with all non-Christian forms of thought that possibility surrounds God. But for the moment Mr. White was stupefied. He could say nothing. So Mr. Black simply drew the conclusion from what he had said in the following words:

"Since you in your effort to please me have accepted my basic assumption with respect to possibility and probability it follows that your God, granted he exists, is of no use whatsoever in explaining the universe. He himself needs in turn to be explained. Let us remember the story of the Indian philosopher and his elephant. It was never more applicable than to the present subject. If the material world rests upon a similar ideal world, this ideal world must rest upon some other; and so on, without end. It were better, therefore, never to look beyond the present material world. In short, gentlemen, much as I dislike not to please you, what you offer is nothing better than what I already possess. Your God is himself surrounded by pure possibility or Chance; in what way can he help me? And how could I be responsible to him? For you, as for me, all things ultimately end in the irrational."

At this point Mr. Grey grew pale. In desperation he searched his arsenal for another argument that might convince Mr. Black. There was one that he had not used for some time. The arguments for God that he had so far used, he labeled *a posteriori* arguments. They ought, he had thought, to appeal to the "empirical" temper of the times. They started from human experience with causation and purpose and by analogy argued to the idea of a cause of and a purpose with the world as a whole. But Mr. Black had pointed out that if you start with the ideas of cause and purpose as intelligible to man without God when these concepts apply to relations within the universe, then you cannot consistently say that you need God for the idea of cause or purpose when these concepts apply to the universe as a whole. So now Mr. Grey drew out the drawer marked *a priori* argument. In public he called this the argument from finite to absolute being. "As finite creatures," he said to Mr. Black, "we have the idea of absolute being. The idea of a finite being involves of necessity the idea of an absolute being. We have the notion of an absolute being; surely there must be a reality corresponding to our idea of such a being; if not, all our ideas may be false. Surely we must hold that reality is ultimately rational and coherent and that our ideas participate in this rationality. If not how would science be possible?"

When Mr. Grey had thus delivered himself of this appeal to logic rather than to fact, then Mr. White for a moment seemed to take courage. Was not this at least to get away from the idea of a God who probably exists? Surely the "incommunicable attributes of God," of which he had been taught in his catechism classes, were all based upon and expressive of the idea of God as necessarily existing. But Mr. Black soon disillusioned him for the second time. Said he in answer to the argument from Mr. Grey, "Again I cannot see any basic difference between your position and mine. Of course we must believe that reality is ultimately rational. And of course, we must hold that our minds participate in this rationality. But when you thus speak you thereby virtually assert that we must not believe in a God whose existence is independent of our human existence. A God whom we are to know must with us be a part of a rational system that is mutually accessible to and expressive of both. If God is necessary to you then you are also necessary to God. That is the only sort of God that is involved in your argument."

"But Mr. Black, this is terrible, this is unbearable! We do want you to believe in God. I bear witness to his existence. I will give you a Bible. Please read it! It tells you of Jesus Christ and how you may be saved by his blood. I am born again and you can be born again too if you will only believe. Please do believe in God and be saved."

Meanwhile Mr. White took new courage. He realized that he had so far made a great mistake in keeping silent during the time that Mr. Grey had presented his arguments. The arguments for the existence of God taken from the ideas of cause and purpose as set forth by Mr. Grey had led to pure irrationalism and Chance. The argument about an absolute being as set forth by Mr. Grey had led to pure rationalism and determinism. In both cases, Mr. Black had been quite right in saying that a God whose existence is problematic or a God who exists by the same necessity as does the universe is still an aspect of or simply the whole of the universe. But now he felt that perhaps Mr. Grey was right in simply witnessing to the existence of God. He thought that if the arguments used are not logically coercive they may at least be used as a means with which to witness to unbelievers. And surely witnessing to God's existence was always in order. But poor Mr. White was to be disillusioned again. For the witness bearing done by Mr. Grey was based on the assumption that the belief in God is a purely non-rational or even irrational matter.

Mr. Black's reply to the words of Mr. Grey indicated this fact all too clearly. Said Mr. Black to Mr. Grey: "I greatly appreciate your evident concern for my eternal welfare. But there are two or three questions that I would like to have you answer. In the first place I would ask whether in thus witnessing to me you thereby admit that the arguments for the existence of God have no validity? Or rather do you not thereby admit that these arguments, if they prove anything, prove that God is finite and correlative to man and therefore that your position is not basically different from mine?"

Mr. Grey did not answer because he could not answer this question otherwise than by agreeing with Mr. Black.

"In the second place," said Mr. Black, "you are now witnessing to Christ as well as to God, to Christianity as well as to theism. I suppose your argument for Christianity would be similar in nature to your argument for theism, would it not? You would argue that the Jesus of the New Testament is probably the Son of God and that he quite probably died for the sins of men. But now you witness to me about your Christ. And by witnessing instead of reasoning you seem to admit that there is no objective claim for the truth of what you hold with respect to Christ. Am I right in all this?" Again Mr. Grey made no answer. The only answer he could consistently have given would be to agree with Mr. Black.

"In the third place," said Mr. Black, "you are now witnessing not only to God the Father, to Jesus Christ the Son, but also to the Holy Spirit. You say you are born again, that you know you are saved and that at present I am lost. Now if you have had an experience of some sort it would be unscientific for me to deny it. But if you want to witness to me about your experience you must make plain to me the nature of that experience. And to do that you must do so in terms of principles that I understand. Such principles must need be accessible to all. Now if you make plain your experience to me in terms of principles that are plain to me as unregenerate, then wherein is your regeneration unique? On the other hand, if you still maintain that your experience of regeneration is unique, then can you say anything about it to me so that I may understand? And does not then your witness bearing appear to be wholly unintelligible and devoid of meaning? Thus again you cannot make any claim to the objective truth of your position.

"Summing up the whole matter, I would say in the first place, that your arguments for the existence of God have rightfully established me in my unbelief. They have shown that nothing can be said for the existence of a God who is actually the Creator and controller of the world. I would say in the second place that using such arguments as you have used for the existence of God commits you to using similar arguments for the truth of Christianity with similar fatal results for your position. In both cases you first use intellectual argument upon principles that presuppose the justice of my unbelieving position. Then when it is pointed out to you that such is the case you turn to witnessing. But then your witnessing is in the nature of the case an activity that you yourself have virtually admitted to be wholly irrational and unintelligible."

When Mr. Black had finished, Mr. White was in a great distress. But it was through this very distress that at last he saw the richness of his own faith. He made no pretense to having greater intellectual power than Mr. Grey. He greatly admired the real faith and courage of Mr. Grey. But he dared keep silence no longer. His silence had been sin, he knew. Mr. Black had completely discomfited Mr. Grey so that he had not another word to say. Mr. Black was about to leave them established rather than challenged in his unbelief. And all of that in spite of the best intentions and efforts of Mr. Grey, speaking for both of them. A sense of urgent responsibility to make known the claims of the sovereign God pressed upon him. He now saw clearly first that the arguments for the existence of God as conducted by Mr. Grey, are based on the assumption that the unbeliever is right with respect to the principles in terms of which he explains all things. These principles are: (a) that man is not a creature of God but rather is ultimate and as such must properly consider himself instead of God the final reference point in explaining all things; (b) that all other things beside himself are non-created but controlled by Chance; and (c) that the power of logic that he possesses is the means by which he must determine what is possible or impossible in the universe of Chance.

At last it dawned upon Mr. White that first to admit that the principles of Mr. Black, the unbeliever, are right and then to seek to win him to the acceptance of the existence of God the Creator and judge of all men is like first admitting that the United States had historically been a province of the Soviet Union but ought at the same time to be recognized as an independent and all-controlling political power.

In the second place, Mr. White now saw clearly that a false type of reasoning for the truth of God's existence and for the truth of Christianity involves a false kind of witnessing for the existence of God and for the truth of Christianity. If one reasons for the existence of God and for the truth of Christianity on the assumption that Mr. Black's principles of explanation are valid, then one must witness on the same assumption. One must then make plain to Mr. Black, in terms of principles which Mr. Black accepts, what it means to be born again. Mr. Black will then apply the principles of modern psychology of religion to Mr. Grey's "testimony" with respect to his regeneration and show that it is something that naturally comes in the period of adolescence.

In the third place Mr. White now saw clearly that it was quite "proper" for Mr. Grey to use a method of reasoning and a method of witness-bearing that is based upon the truth of anti-Christian and anti-theistic assumptions. Mr. Grey's theology is Arminian or Lutheran. It is therefore based upon the idea that God is not wholly sovereign over man. It assumes that man's responsibility implies a measure of autonomy of the sort that is the essence and foundation of the whole of Mr. Black's thinking. It is therefore to be expected that Mr. Grey will assume that Mr. Black needs not to be challenged on his basic assumption with respect to his own assumed ultimacy or autonomy. From now on Mr. White decided that, much as he enjoyed the company of Mr. Grey and much as he trusted his evident sincerity and basic devotion to the truth of God, yet he must go his own way in apologetics as he had, since the Reformation, gone his own way in theology. He made an appointment with Mr. Black to see him soon. He expressed to Mr. Grey his great love for him as a fellow believer, his great admiration for his fearless and persistent efforts to win men to an acceptance of truth as it is in Jesus. Then he confessed to Mr. Grey that his conscience had troubled him during the entire time of their travels with Mr. Black. He had started in good faith, thinking that Mr. Grey's efforts at argument and witnessing might win Mr. Black. He had therefore been quite willing, especially since Mr. Grey was through his constant efforts much more conversant with such things than he was, to be represented by Mr. Grey. But now he had at last come to realize that not only had the effort been utterly fruitless and self-frustrating but more than that it had been terribly dishonoring to God. How could the eternal I AM be pleased with being presented as being a god and as probably existing, as necessary for the explanation of some things but not of all things, as one who will be glad to recognize the ultimacy of his own creatures? Would the God who had in paradise required of men implicit obedience now be satisfied with a claims and counter-claims arrangement with his creatures?

From the quotations given above the reader can for himself discern why I have advocated what seems to me to be a Reformed as over against the traditional method of Apologetics. The traditional method was constructed by Roman Catholics and Arminians. It was, so to speak, made to fit Romanist or Evangelical theology. And since Roman Catholic and Evangelical theology compromises the Protestant doctrines of Scripture, of God, of man, of sin and of redemption so the traditional method of Apologetics compromises Christianity in order to win men to an acceptance of it.

8.2 Agreeing and Disagreeing with Warfield and Kuyper

In Van Til's judgment, the ineffectiveness and flaws of the traditional method of defending the faith are tied to an underlying theological outlook that is biblically deficient, such as Roman Catholicism or Arminianism. Reformed theology, which is more scripturally sound, would lead, if one were faithful to its tenets, to a presuppositional conception and practice of apologetics. Now, in the early decades of the twentieth century, the Reformed world had two exceptional elder statesmen. During this era when Van Til was gaining his education and developing his outlook, perhaps the two most influential and famous, if not the greatest, Reformed scholars and theological stalwarts were Abraham Kuyper (1837–1920) of the Free University of Amsterdam and Benjamin B. Warfield (1851–1921) of Princeton Theological Seminary.

Both Kuyper and Warfield exercised a formative influence on the thinking of Van Til as he sought a rigorously consistent, Reformed understanding of apologetics. But they did not see eye to eye on every point, and on the subject of apologetics their disagreement was readily apparent. Warfield gave expression to this disagreement particularly in the introduction that he penned for Francis R. Beattie's *Apologetics*.[107] The two leaders in Reformed scholarship had different conceptions of the nature of science and different convictions about the relationship of Christianity to the work of science.

There are two good reasons for examining Van Til's own analysis of, and response to, the conflict between Warfield and Kuyper regarding apologetics. The first reason is that it is so widely misunderstood and mistakenly portrayed. This is surprising, since Van Til wrote specifically and substantially on the subject, addressing "Warfield and Kuyper" in *The Defense of the Faith* (pp. 358–64) and "Kuyper and Warfield on Apologetics" in *A Christian Theory of Knowledge* (pp. 229–54). He compared his view of apologetical methodology with theirs in this way: "To the extent that these [Reformed theologians] differ

107. Warfield's introductory note to Beattie's *Apologetics; or, The Rational Vindication of Christianity*, vol. 1: *Fundamental Apologetics* (Richmond: Presbyterian Committee of Publication, 1903), 19–32, is reprinted in *Selected Shorter Writings of Benjamin B. Warfield*, vol. 2, ed. Meeter, 93–105. Warfield's personal respect and appreciation for Kuyper's work can be seen in his introductory note to Kuyper's *Encyclopedia of Sacred Theology*, trans. J. Hendrik de Vries (New York: Charles Scribner's Sons, 1898), xi–xix. This work was reprinted as *Principles of Sacred Theology* (Grand Rapids: Eerdmans, 1954), and Warfield's note was again reprinted in *Selected Shorter Writings of Benjamin B. Warfield*, vol. 1, ed. John E. Meeter (Nutley, N.J.: Presbyterian and Reformed, 1970), 447–54.

among one another I have been compelled to choose between them. Even so these differences have not been of such a basic nature that I could not appeal to a common view held by both parties. I have tried to use elements *both* of Kuyper's and of Warfield's thinking."[108] It is sometimes said that Van Til sided completely with Kuyper against Warfield, yet that view is simplistic and misinformed.

The second reason for examining Van Til's evaluation of the strengths *and* weaknesses in *both* Kuyper's viewpoint and Warfield's viewpoint is that we thereby gain a beneficial insight into the unique character and genius of Van Til's own conception of apologetics. He combined the strongest features of both the Amsterdam and the Princeton schools of thought and left aside features of both systems that did not comport with the best Reformed principles. A person who can explain the ways in which Van Til agreed and disagreed with both Warfield and Kuyper, is a person who understands presuppositional apologetics.

According to Van Til, we find these three things in both Warfield and Kuyper: (1) a brilliant conviction of central importance which is relevant to our theory of knowledge and apologetics, (2) another notion, which is inconsistent with the first conviction, and then (3) a view of apologetics that is mistakenly inferred from that first conviction.

(W1) Warfield's prominent and irreproachable principle of apologetics was his stress on the objective, intelligible, and clear revelation of God to all men in nature and history. God's revelation to men is so objectively clear that it is not "rational" (or scientific) for men to reject the Christian faith. This is true for all men, no matter who they are or with what prejudices they begin. The case for Christianity is objectively compelling if one is genuinely scientific. *Ideally* speaking, then, there is but "one science." Therefore, Christianity is the only intelligible system of truth.

(W2) Warfield's grand principle was compromised, however, when he maintained that the evidence for Christianity warrants only the *probability* of its truth. If it is not really rational to reject Christianity, and if the revelation of God is objectively and fully clear, then one would think that the Christian faith attains the level of epistemic certainty. Moreover, while there is only one science, ideally and objectively speaking, the practical and personal fact is that those engaging in scientific work are subjectively and spiritually at war in their prin-

---

108. *Defense of the Faith*, 20 (emphasis added).

ciples and goals. If unbelievers contribute to a great singular edifice of truth, it is because they depart from their principles or presuppositions. The "advantage of regeneration," which Warfield taught us to press in our conflict with unbelief, does more than give the believer "stronger and purer" thinking than the unbeliever. On the natural man's principles, there would be no intelligible thinking (no rationality) at all.

(W3) The inference that Warfield incorrectly drew from his outstanding first principle is that the natural man is able to give a correct interpretation of God's natural revelation. That is, anybody using "right reason" could properly develop a natural theology from his experience of the world. Indeed, we must do this first—assuring ourselves that there is a knowledge of God in the world—before we take our standpoint in the Scriptures and develop our theology. By thus giving apologetics epistemic primacy over personal faith and over the veracity of theology, Warfield erred. First, he confused the objectivity and inescapability of natural revelation with the autonomous and discursive results of "natural theology." Second, there is no "right reason" available to the natural man in his total depravity, and for that reason he is unable to find elementary religious truth that might lead him to accept the Scriptures as the crowning point of his reflections. Sinners must receive the Scriptures as God's word, correcting their distorted perception of nature and history.

(K1) Kuyper's distinctive and masterful insight into apologetics was that the two conflicting principles that are at work in the believer and the unbeliever—submission to God versus autonomy—produce two opposing theories of knowledge (two "sciences"). He recognized the significance of the alienation of the natural man from God, in contrast to the regenerating and enlightening work of the Holy Spirit in the believer. Kuyper maintained that there is an antithesis between belief and unbelief, exhibited in their different orientations of heart and different lifestyles. The regenerate and unregenerate minds have different conceptions of "science"; they are committed to two different types of knowing. Those who have been graciously regenerated by God regard the way they see things as normal and correct; they enjoy true knowledge or science. The unregenerated man's mind is darkened and he refuses the light of revelation, yet nevertheless he considers his viewpoint to be natural, normal, and true. These two "sciences" operate on conflicting principles and cannot even grant the honorable name of "science" to the way in which the other is thinking.

(K2) Kuyper's profound insight into the antithesis between the regenerated and the unregenerated minds was somewhat undercut, however, by two other ideas. First, he believed that some of man's abilities to deal with external matters (e.g., weighing, measuring, and using logic) are not affected by his depravity. Second, he interpreted common grace in such a way that there is a limited area of neutral common ground where the regenerate and the unregenerate meet on equal terms and arrive at common interpretations of the facts. But since human depravity is comprehensive ("total"), and the antithesis between depravity and regeneration is radical (going to the root of life and death), it is hard to see how Kuyper could allow for such exceptions.

(K3) The mistaken inference that Kuyper drew from his correct principle (K1) was that, given the antithesis between belief and unbelief and the resulting two sciences, apologetics aimed at the unbeliever is virtually useless and deserves only a narrow place in the theological curriculum. There is little use or justification for reasoning with an unbeliever, since he has a depraved understanding of reasoning itself; meaningful communication between belief and unbelief is not naturally going to occur. But here Kuyper stumbled, thought Van Til. First, God has clearly revealed Himself in nature and history, and so men have not done justice to the objective facts when they do not submit to Him in praise. Second, unbelievers never cease being the image of God, and only by acting as such—thinking God's thoughts after Him—can they find an intelligible foundation for their knowledge and experience. The unbeliever needs to be challenged to see that by suppressing the truth of God, his pursuit of science is futile, being an epistemological failure at the presuppositional level.

Kuyper's insight that believing science is in principle antithetical to unbelieving science (K1) contradicted Warfield's inference that the natural man can use "right reason" to interpret nature and history correctly (W3). Likewise, Warfield's insistence upon the objective rationality of Christianity (W1) contradicted Kuyper's inference that apologetics aimed at the unregenerate is virtually useless (K3). By endorsing the fundamental points of Warfield and Kuyper (W1, K1), as well as repudiating the false inferences drawn from them (W3, K3), Van Til engineered a system of apologetics that has tremendous intellectual strength and is free from the inconsistencies of Warfield and Kuyper (W2, K2). According to Van Til's presuppositional apologetic, there are indeed two conflicting worldviews and conceptions of science

(K1), but the objective rationality of the Christian worldview is provable (W1) by the transcendental argument that non-Christian presuppositions render reasoning unintelligible. That is, apologetics is indeed powerful and useful (cf. K3) because it can demonstrate that the unbeliever cannot exercise "right reason" (cf. W3). By the very nature of presuppositional apologetics, there cannot, in consistent philosophical principle, be any neutral interpretations or common ground between the two antithetical sets of professed presuppositions (cf. K2). And by pressing the unbelieving worldview to its consistent conclusions, we come to see the transcendental necessity (and thus the epistemic certainty, not merely the probability) of the Christian worldview (cf. W2).

Van Til sought to develop an approach to apologetics that was consistently based upon the principles of Reformed theology. He would concede nothing to autonomous, non-Reformed thought. He therefore turned away from the traditional method. He drew the best insights from Kuyper and Warfield, and molded them into a transcendental, presuppositional apologetic that presents a crushing philosophical challenge to all those who would argue against the biblical worldview.

KUYPER'S STRENGTH AND WEAKNESS[109]

The broader question involved in both natural theology and common grace is that of the knowledge of the non-believer. Must he be thought of as rightfully judging in terms of his own autonomous principle whether the Bible is the Word of God? Must Christians approach the non-believer on a neutral basis, thereby admitting that the epistemological principles of the natural man are essentially right at least for the interpretation of general revelation?

In old Princeton apologetics the answer given to these questions was in the affirmative; in the view of Abraham Kuyper and his followers the answer given to these same questions was in the negative. . . .

When Kuyper gave this unequivocal negative answer, however, he did not thereby intend to deny that the unbeliever has any true knowledge in any sense of the term. Disclaiming originality Kuyper closely follows Calvin in insisting that every man knows God.

Something more must now be said on this subject, in particular as it pertains to the relation of "Amsterdam" and "old Princeton." . . .

109. Excerpts from *Defense of the Faith*, 171, 357, 358–64, 382–83, 387; then *Christian Theory of Knowledge*, 234–35.

The difference between Warfield and Kuyper appears sharply in their different evaluation of natural theology.

What evaluation is to be placed upon the interpretation of natural revelation, internal and external, that the natural man, who operates with the principle of autonomy, has given? Can the difference between the principle of autonomy and that of Christian theism be ignored so that men can together seek to interpret natural revelation in terms of one procedure?[110]

Kuyper answers in the negative. The idea of two ultimate principles is, he insists, a contradiction in terms.

Either allow that the natural principle has within itself the legitimate powers of self-interpretation and then expect the special principle to be destroyed by it, or else maintain that the natural principle is in any case finite and more particularly sinful and then present the special principle to it with the demand of submission. . . .

The result is, says Kuyper, even worse than that. For the action of sinful human thought is not merely fruitless; it is destructive of the truth. Sinful man is out to destroy the special principle when it comes to him with its challenge. The natural principle takes an antithetical position over against the special principle and seeks to destroy it by means of logical manipulation.[111] The natural principle lives from *apistia;* its faith is fixed upon the creature instead of upon the Creator.[112] . . .

With the light of Scripture it is possible for man to read nature aright. Without that light we cannot, even on the Areopagus, reach further than the unknown God.[113]

It is thus that the enlightened consciousness of the people of God stands over against the natural consciousness of the world. For the believers, Scripture is the principle of theology. As such it cannot be the conclusion of other premises, but it is *the* premise from which all other conclusions are drawn.[114]

From what has been said it is not to be concluded that Kuyper has no great appreciation of the knowledge of God that may be obtained from nature. The contrary is true. He lays the greatest possible stress upon the idea that the Bible is not a book that has fallen from heaven. There is a natural foundation for it. This natural foundation is found in the fact that the natural is itself the

---

110. CVT: *A Christian Theory of Knowledge*, p. 156. [Here and throughout this reading selection, Van Til's references are to the early syllabus by this name, which was later revised and published as a book with the same title.]
111. CVT: *Idem*, p. 242.
112. CVT: *Idem*, p. 254.
113. CVT: *Idem*, p. 332.
114. CVT: *Idem*, p. 517.

602 COMPARISONS AND CRITICISMS OF APOLOGETICAL METHODS

creation of the same God who in the special principle comes to man for his redemption. . . .

It is difficult to see how else the Scriptures can be presented as self-attesting. As soon as the elements of the special principle, such as the indications of divinity, the testimony of the Spirit, or the words of Christ are set next to one another, as largely independent of one another, the natural man is given an opportunity to do his destructive work. He is then allowed to judge at least with respect to one or more of these elements. And if he is allowed to judge of the legitimacy or meaning of any one of them he may as well be given the right to judge of all of them. If the natural man is allowed the right to take the documents of the gospels as merely historically trustworthy witnesses to the Christ and his work, he will claim and can consistently claim also to be the judge of the Christ himself. For it is only if the Christ be taken as the Son of God that he can be said legitimately to identify himself. If he is not presupposed as such then his words too have no power. Then they too are absorbed in what is a hopeless relativity of history.[115] . . .

This head-on collision between the principle of the natural man and the principle of the regenerate man, can it do anything but destroy science? Warfield thought it would. He therefore reduced Kuyper's distinction between two kinds of science to one of degree. Otherwise "there would be no science attainable at all."[116]

Warfield accordingly attributes to "right reason" the ability to interpret natural revelation with essential correctness. This "right reason" is not the reason of the Christian. It is the reason that is confronted with Christianity and possesses some criterion apart from Christianity with which to judge of the truth of Christianity.[117]

Appealing to "right reason" in the sense defined, Warfield asks it to judge in its own terms that Christianity is true. . . .

The result of this method of appealing to "right reason" is that theism and Christianity are shown to be only *probably* true.[118]

It is not, of course, that Warfield himself entertains any doubts about the plenary inspiration of Scripture. He was one of its greatest advocates. Nor is it that he disagrees with Calvin in maintaining the clarity of natural revelation or in holding that all men have the sense of deity. It is only that in Apologetics, Warfield wanted to operate in neutral territory with the non-believer. He

---

115. CVT: *A Christian Theory of Knowledge*, pp. 156–58 [book edition: p. 234].
116. CVT: Cf. Warfield's "Introduction" to Beattie's *Apologetics*, 1903.
117. CVT: Cf. his article on "Apologetics" in the *New Schaff Herzog Encyclopedia of Religious Knowledge*, New York, 1932.
118. CVT: *Idem*, p. 218.

thought that this was the only way to show to the unbeliever that theism and Christianity are objectively true. He sought for an objectivity that bridged the gulf between Kuyper's "natural" and special principles. . . .

It is impossible to hold with Kuyper that the Christian and the non-Christian principles are destructive of one another and to hold with Warfield that they differ only in degree. . . .

For myself I have chosen the position of Kuyper.[119] But I am unable to follow him when from the fact of the mutually destructive character of the two principles he concludes to the uselessness of reasoning with the natural man. . . .

So then[120] after we have identified ourselves, then built a bridge of cause, order, purpose and morality to God, we approach the Biblical writings as we do any other book. The foundation fact to which they testify is the resurrection of Christ. Thus we have reached the risen Christ by neutral approach. *After that* we stand on his authority. He witnessed to the Old Testament as the Word of God. He promised the Spirit to his apostles so they might write the New Testament as the completion of the Word of God.

After that we bow before the Word of the sovereign God and require men to subject their reason to its verdict.

It was the *after that* that Kuyper so vigorously opposed in the sort of apologetics we have before us. If reason is not challenged at the outset it cannot fairly be challenged at all. Why should not "reason" be as anxious to suppress the evidence for the *fact* that the Bible is God's Word as to deny the system of truth of that Word? No one can recognize the fact of Christ's resurrection and the fact of the divinity of Scripture except in terms of the *meaning* of the resurrection and the *content* of the system Scripture presents. In all the stress on the fact that true faith is not blind but is faith in response to the presentation of evidence, this indissoluble unity of the *that* and the *what* of Christianity is overlooked. . . .

To have a balanced view of the relation of the "old Princeton" and the "Amsterdam" apologetics, it is imperative that we turn to the question of "inconsistency" in the views of Kuyper and Bavinck. We have stressed the fact that in his main contention Kuyper strongly opposed the idea of a neutral area of interpretation between believers and unbelievers. And we have shown that

---

119. In context, Van Til was here expressing agreement with Kuyper over Warfield, not on apologetical issues in general, but on the particular question whether Christian and non-Christian principles destroy one another or simply differ in degree.

120. On the pages prior to this, Van Til was analyzing the apologetical method found in Floyd E. Hamilton's *The Basis of the Christian Faith* (New York: George H. Doran, 1927), taking it as representative of the "old Princeton" apologetic advocated by B. B. Warfield.

Warfield was strongly insistent on the necessity of proceeding with unbelievers on a neutral basis with respect to the problem of theism and even with respect to the claims of Scripture to be the Word of God. But we have also indicated that Kuyper too sometimes reasons as though he were on neutral grounds with unbelievers. Even in his *Encyclopedia*, in which he so valiantly defends the idea of a twofold science, even in this work which Warfield so vigorously criticized, Kuyper sometimes does the same thing that Warfield does. Indeed Warfield has pointed out this very inconsistency in Kuyper. . . .

Therefore no corroboration is to be sought for the truth of the idea of Scripture, or for the truth of the system of doctrine it contains, by an appeal to the natural man as he interprets life in terms of his own principles. In fact it cannot be allowed that the natural man can in terms of his principles interpret any aspect of experience correctly. He does, to be sure, contribute to the edifice of true interpretation, but he does this because his principle is false and the Christian principle is true. . . .

The result is that Kuyper cannot carry through the idea that the believer must challenge the unbeliever in his interpretation of the universe at every point. He is vague in his discussion of the natural sciences. His main principle requires him to say that every science is possible only on the presupposition of the truth of Christianity. His main principle therefore requires him to insist that the principle of Scripture be self-attesting. And this involves that man's self-identification and the uniformity of nature be based upon this identification of God's identification of himself to man. If Kuyper is to have an internally consistent picture of the Christian view of things that he has so valiantly set forth, he must dispose of the idea of faith as purely formal. Wherever he maintains this formal idea of faith, he virtually grants that the man who works on the assumption of human autonomy has the right principle with which to interpret not only the external phenomena but even the causes of things (cf. [*Encyclopedia*, vol. 2], p. 95). . . .

There is one main conclusion that Kuyper has drawn from this, his general position, and that is that because of it there is virtually no use in Christian apologetics. Not that Kuyper has himself always been true to his virtual rejection of apologetics. But he frequently argues that since the natural man is not to be regarded as the proper judge of the special principle and since this is true because his understanding is darkened, there is no use and no justification for reasoning with the natural man at all. The question is whether this conclusion can be harmonized with the fact that Christianity is the true religion and has the criterion of truth within itself. In his *Institutes* Calvin greatly stresses that men *ought* to see God's presence as Creator, Provider, Benefactor, and Judge in nature and its history because this presence is clearly there.

Men have not done justice by the facts, by the evidence of God's presence before their eyes, unless they burst out into praise of him who has made all things. Christ himself says that men should believe him as being in and with the Father because of his words, but if not for his words then for his works' sake. Does not the doctrine of Scripture itself maintain that this book has in it the marks of divinity so that it is clearly distinguishable from all other books as being the very Word of God? And does not the Holy Spirit testify to the Word with definite content as being the Word of God?

Shall we then simply say that since the natural man is blind there is no purpose in displaying before him the rich color scheme of the revelation of God's grace? Shall we say that we must witness to men only and not reason with them at all? How would witnessing to them be of any more use to them than would reasoning? If men cannot in the least understand what he who witnesses is speaking of, will the witnessing be any challenge to him at all?

To find an answer to such questions as these it is well that we turn to the objection that Warfield raised against the position of Kuyper.

WARFIELD'S STRENGTH AND WEAKNESS[121]

Apologetics comes for Kuyper at the end of the process whereby Christianity has been set forth thetically. [Warfield replies:] "Meanwhile, as for Christianity itself, it has remained up to this point—let us say frankly—the great Assumption. The work of the exegete, the historian, the systematist, has all hung, so to speak, in the air; not until all their labor is accomplished do they pause to wipe their streaming brows and ask whether they have been dealing with realities, or perchance with fancies only."[122]

Has not Kuyper himself engaged in apologetics of a much more basic sort than he speaks of when he calls it a defense against false philosophy? Has he not defended the idea of the sense of deity independently of Scripture? . . .

Then after noting this "inconsistency" in Kuyper he [Warfield] offers his basic criticism. Kuyper shows how the various disciplines of theology are to be organized, ending with practical theology. Its system of truth may be drawn from Scripture. Warfield says:

> But certainly before we draw it from the Scriptures, we must assure ourselves that there is a knowledge of God in the Scriptures. And,

---

121. Excerpts from *Christian Theory of Knowledge*, 236–44; then *Defense of the Faith*, 364; then *Christian Theory of Knowledge*, 244, 251–53.
122. CVT: *Ibid.* [quoting Warfield's introductory note to Beattie's *Apologetics*], p. 22.

before we do that, we must assure ourselves that there is a knowledge of God in the world. . . . Thus, we inevitably work back to first principles. And, in working back to first principles, we exhibit the indispensability of an "apologetical theology," which of necessity holds the place of the first among the five theological disciplines.

It is easy, of course, to say that a Christian man must take his standpoint not *above* the Scriptures, but *in* the Scriptures. He very certainly must. But surely he must first *have* Scriptures, authenticated to him as such, before he can take his standpoint in them. It is equally easy to say that Christianity is attained, not by demonstrations, but by a new birth. Nothing could be more true. But neither could anything be more unjustified than the inferences that are drawn from this truth for the discrediting of apologetics. It certainly is not in the power of all the demonstrations in the world to make a Christian. Paul may plant and Apollos water; it is God alone who gives the increase. But it does not seem to follow that Paul would as well, therefore, not plant, and Apollos as well not water. Faith is the gift of God; but it does not in the least follow that the faith that God gives is an irrational faith, that is, a faith without grounds in right reason. It is beyond all question only the prepared heart that can fitly respond to the "reasons"; but how can even a prepared heart respond, when there are no reasons to draw out its action? . . .

But we are arguing that faith is, in all its exercises alike, a form of conviction, and is, therefore, necessarily grounded in evidence. And we are arguing that evidence accordingly has its part to play in the conversion of the soul; and that the systematically organized evidence which we call apologetics similarly has its part to play in the Christianizing of the world. And we are arguing that this part is not a small part; nor is it a merely subsidiary part; nor yet a merely defensive part—as if the one end of apologetics were to protect an isolated body of Christians from annoyance from the surrounding world, or to aid the distracted Christian to bring his head into harmony with his heart. The part that apologetics has to play in the Christianizing of the world is rather a primary part, and it is a conquering part. It is the distinction of Christianity that it has come into the world clothed with the mission to *reason* its way to its dominion. Other religions may appeal to the sword, or seek some other way to propagate themselves. Christianity makes its appeal to right reason, and stands out among all religions, therefore, as distinctively "the apologetic religion." It is solely by reasoning that it has come thus far on its way to its kingship. . . .

Nevertheless, there is question here of perfection of performance, rather than of kind. It is "science" that is produced by the subject held under sin, even though imperfect science—falling away from the ideal here, there and elsewhere, on account of all sorts of deflecting influences entering in at all points of the process. The science of sinful man is thus a substantive part of the abstract science produced by the ideal subject, the general human consciousness, though a less valuable part than it would be without sin.[123]

In this passage Warfield rejects the idea of a twofold science so fully developed in Kuyper's work. . . . Warfield argues that the difference between the scientific effort of the regenerated and the non-regenerated consciousness is, though a great difference, yet after all no more than a gradational difference. Otherwise "there would be no 'science' attainable at all." . . .

From this quotation it seems as though Warfield is altogether ignoring the fact that there is a difference of principle between those who work from the basis of regeneration and those who do not. He seems to regard the fact that there cannot in history be any actually complete manifestation of the victory of one principle over the other as sufficient warrant for ignoring Kuyper's contention that the two types of people spoken of see themselves and all things else differently from one another. Yet Warfield realizes full well that there is a conflict of principle going on in the world. What he is deeply concerned to avoid is the separation of the Christian from the non-Christian in the field of knowledge, for then the conflict of principles would be stifled. . . .

Apologetics therefore has great value [for Warfield]. "Though faith is the gift of God, it does not in the least follow that the faith which God gives is an irrational faith, that is, a faith without cognizable ground in right reason. We believe in Christ because it is rational to believe in him. . . ."[124]

From what has been quoted of Warfield's position the following points of importance emerge: . . .

Warfield stresses the objective rationality of the Christian religion. This is not to suggest that Kuyper does not also believe in such an objective ratio-

123. CVT: *Ibid.*, pp. 24–26, 26–27. (In the original publication, this long section from Warfield is not set off as a block quotation.)
124. Van Til here quotes from Warfield, "Apologetics," in the *New Schaff-Herzog Encyclopedia of Religious Knowledge*, ed. Samuel Macauley Jackson (New York: Funk and Wagnalls, 1932), 1:236–37; reprint, Warfield, *Studies in Theology* (New York: Oxford University Press, 1932), 15.

nality. But by pointing out again and again that the Christian faith is belief on evidence not blind belief, Warfield makes plain that Christianity is "rationally defensible." This has direct significance for apologetics. . . . To the extent that Warfield differs on this point with Kuyper and has called us back to Calvin, he has done great service for Christian apologetics. . . .

It is therefore of the utmost importance to stress what Warfield stressed, when he said that we believe Christianity because it is "rational." When the Scriptures are presented to the natural man and with it the system of truth that it contains, he knows at once that he ought to accept it. He knows that if he rejects it he does so in spite of the fact that he knows its claim is true and just. Scripture speaks in the name of God to the sinner asking that he repent from his sin. The natural man, having usurped authority to himself is asked to recognize his legitimate sovereign. . . .

Hence Warfield was quite right in maintaining that Christianity is objectively defensible. And the natural man has the ability to understand intellectually, though not spiritually, the challenge presented to him. And no challenge is presented to him unless it is shown him that on his *principle* he would destroy all truth and meaning. Then, if the Holy Spirit enlightens him spiritually, he will be born again "unto knowledge" and adopt with love the principle he was previously anxious to destroy. . . .

Having stressed the objective rationality of Christianity, Warfield does not adequately stress the difference between the principle of the natural man and the principles of the Christian.

This appears primarily in the fact that he attributes to "right reason" the ability to interpret natural revelation with essential correctness. It is not easy to discover just what Warfield means by "right reason." But clearly it is not the regenerated reason. It is not the reason that has already accepted Christianity. It is the reason that is confronted with Christianity and has some criterion apart from Christianity with which to judge the truth of Christianity. . . .

Unfortunately Warfield recognizes the legitimacy of the idea of abstract possibility in his apologetic methodology. His whole procedure as outlined above is based upon the idea that in studying the facts, either of natural or of special revelation, men have every right to start from the idea that God can possibly not exist and that the Bible at least can possibly be the word of men rather than the word of God. He insists that men have a right and a duty to be open-minded with respect to the claims of God for himself, and the Christian must not claim more than probable certainty for his position.

In thus allowing for the idea of abstract possibility Warfield cannot do justice to the claims of God's revelation either in nature or in history or in Scripture. He cannot do justice to the fact that the God of his own theology is the source of necessity and "possibility" and therefore of necessity self-attesting. He cannot do justice to the evidence of God's existence in nature and history. He cannot say with Calvin that men ought to see God, the true God, in nature and history since this true God and he alone is clearly revealed there. No other God could possibly be revealed there. A theism that is merely said to be more probably true than its rivals is not the theism of the Bible. It is the God who cannot but exist that is the one who is clearly and unavoidably present to every man created by this God. Man's sense of deity speaks of this God, not of a god who *probably* exists and probably does not exist.

Again, in allowing for the idea of abstract possibility, Warfield cannot do justice to his own principle of the trustworthy character of the apostolic witnesses to Christ and his work. It is utterly impossible that there should be trustworthy witnesses to the incarnate Word unless these trustworthy witnesses are trustworthy because they are servants of the self-attesting God, speaking through the Son of God. This is only to say that any identification of any fact can take place in terms of the truth of the Christian religion alone. It is but to say that Christianity *alone* is rational. It is but to say that if one leaves the foundation of the presupposition of the truth of the Christian religion one falls into the quagmire of the utterly irrational. No intelligent predication is possible except on the basis of the truth, that is the *absolute* truth of Christianity. . . .

Finally, how could those who are asked to study the evidence for the divinity of Scripture for themselves, with a method that is not itself clearly based upon the presupposition of this divinity itself, be given an opportunity to identify the Scriptures for what they are at all? The only way by which the Scriptures can be placed before men so that they can even intellectually recognize it as being the Word of God is by placing the sharpest possible contrast before men between the principles involved in the idea of divine ultimacy and human ultimacy. The natural man must be shown that, on his principle, no intelligible identification of any fact in human history is possible. He must not be encouraged to think that he can make such an identification in terms of his principle. If it be allowed that he can make any such identification, he is, by implication, also given the right to identify both the incarnate and the written Word. The result will be that in identifying them he will destroy them by his principles of univocism and equivocism.[125]

---

125. That is, he will destroy them by his principles of abstract logic (pure unity) and brute factuality (pure diversity).

COMBINED STRENGTHS YIELD
THE PRESUPPOSITIONAL CHALLENGE[126]

(A) It is therefore upon this common basis, held by old Princeton and Amsterdam alike, that we build when we contend:

> a. That in apologetics we must use the same principle that we use in theology, namely the principle of the self-attesting Scripture and of the analogical system of truth which it contains.

> b. That therefore we must not make our appeal to the "common notions" of unbelievers and believers but to the "common notions" that, by virtue of creation in God's image, men as men all have in common.

> c. That when appeal is thus to be made to man as man, this can be done only as we set the principle of Christianity squarely in opposition to the principle of the unbeliever. Only when the principle of autonomy, with its irrationalist-rationalist principles of identity and contradiction, is rejected in the name of the principle of analogy, is appeal really made to those common notions which men have as men.

> d. That therefore the claims must be made that Christianity alone is reasonable for men to hold. And it is utterly reasonable. It is wholly irrational to hold to any other position than that of Christianity. Christianity alone does not crucify reason itself. Without it reason would operate in a total vacuum.

> e. That the argument for Christianity must therefore be that of presupposition. With Augustine it must be maintained that God's revelation is the sun from which all other light derives. The best, the only, the absolutely certain proof of the truth of Christianity is that unless its truth be presupposed there is no proof of anything. Christianity is proved as being the very foundation of the idea of proof itself.

> f. That acceptance of the Christian position on the part of sinners who are *in principle* alienated from God, who seek to flee his face, comes when, challenged by the inescapably clear evidence, the Holy Spirit opens their eyes so that they truly see things for what they are. In-

126. The following excerpts are taken from:

(A) *Defense of the Faith*, 396–97;
(B) *Christian Theory of Knowledge*, 253–54.

tellectually sinners can readily follow the presentation of the evidence that is placed before them. If the difference between the Christian and the non-Christian position is only made plain to them, as alone it can be on a Reformed basis, the natural man can, for argument's sake, place himself upon the position of the Christian. But though in this sense he then knows God more clearly than otherwise, though he already knew him by virtue of his sense of deity, yet it is only when by the grace of God the Holy Spirit removes the scales from men's eyes that they know the truth existentially. Then they know him, whom to know is life eternal.

g. That therefore the remnants of the traditional method of apologetics that have been taken over from Romanism and Evangelicalism, in greater measure by old Princeton, in lesser measure by Amsterdam, must no longer be retained.

Standing on the shoulders of Warfield and Kuyper we honor them best if we build on the main thrust of their thought rather than if we insist an carrying on what is inconsistent with their basic position. Then are we most faithful to Calvin and to St. Paul.

(B) It has not been possible to avoid a discussion of the difference between these two great modern Reformed theologians, Kuyper and Warfield. The difference between Kuyper and Warfield on the matter of apologetics is there and it is important. It is impossible to ignore it and to speak as though there were only minor differences of emphasis between them. It is impossible to follow both Kuyper and Warfield, however much lovers of the Reformed Faith may revere them both. On the other hand the difference between them should not be over-stressed.

It was only an inconsistency on Warfield's part to advocate a method of apologetics that is out of accord with the foundation concepts of his own Reformed theology. Kuyper too was inconsistent when, after rejecting such a method of apologetics, he yet sometimes employed it. There is no need here, nor space, to give the evidence for this contention.

Both men have also been most fortunately inconsistent in another direction. Warfield again and again in his writings shows how the principles of those who work with the idea of autonomy lead to the destruction of human experience. When he does this he does basically what Kuyper does, i.e., appeals to the sense of deity in men, rather than to the principles that follow from the idea of autonomy. In other words Warfield then rejects the idea of autonomy. He seems to hold that because of the sense of deity within men they really in practice do not proceed from the idea of autonomy, and that they are therefore in a position to be to some extent ready to recognize the special principle for what it is. And it is this that is also true of Kuyper. He does set forth the idea of autonomy and of its opposition to any manifestation of the truth of God. But he too stresses again and again the fact that no man is a finished product. Man has the sense of deity within him, and in particular he is the recipient of the common grace of God. In practice he is therefore more ready to give consideration of the presentation of the special principle than one would expect him to be.

With grateful acknowledgment of indebtedness to both Kuyper and Warfield, to Herman Bavinck and other associates and followers of Kuyper, to the various associates and followers of Warfield, to J. Gresham Machen in particular, we would take their common basic contribution to the idea of the full Christian faith and the self-attesting Scripture and build as best as we can upon it. The great contribution of Kuyper discussed in this chapter is that of his analysis of the idea of autonomy. Never again can we forget that the natural man, working from his adopted principle, will seek to weave the special principle into the natural principle, and that he will seek to do this in philosophy and science no less than in theology. The great contribution of Warfield discussed in this chapter is his insistence that Christian theism is the only internally intelligible system of truth.

Combining these two great principles, held by both men, but not equally emphasized by both, we shall claim that the Christian system is undoubtedly true, that it is distinguishable intellectually by men because it has been distinguished for them by God through his Word, and that unless one therefore presupposes its truth there is no theology, no philosophy, and no science that can find intelligible meaning in human experience.

8.3 Theistic Proofs: Traditional or Presuppositional?

Van Til turned aside from the traditional method of defending the faith and sought to develop an apologetical strategy that would be rigorously consistent with Reformed theology, namely, the presuppositional method. As we saw in chapter 7, he developed a "transcendental" form of proving the rational necessity of the Christian worldview as based on God's infallible and redemptive revelation (the Bible). The traditional method that we sketched at the beginning of this chapter, when put into actual practice, normally has two steps. These are not, however, the "indirect" two steps of Van Til's presuppositional challenge (comparing worldviews in light of the preconditions of intelligibility). Rather, the traditional apologetic makes two "direct" appeals to the unbeliever, seeking to establish first that God exists, and second that the Bible is reliable (especially about Jesus and His resurrection).

Since presuppositional apologetics opposes the traditional method, does it repudiate theistic proofs and appeal to empirical evidence? An affirmative answer is often given by the opponents of presuppositionalism, yet that is a serious misrepresentation. Would it not be extremely odd for a defender of the faith to be antagonistic to proof and evidence? One should suppose from the outset that an apologist's misgivings would not be about proofs or evidence *per se*, but rather about the *kind* of proof and evidence employed and the *manner* in which it is used. Nonetheless, Clark Pinnock wrote this in opposition to Van Til's presuppositional apologetics: "A philosophy of Christian evidences which employs *theistic argument* and *historical evidence* is needed, lest the gospel be discredited as a grand and unwarranted assumption."[127]

But Van Til himself said this: "I do not reject 'the theistic proofs' but merely insist on formulating them in such a way as not to compromise the doctrines of Scripture. 'That is to say, if the theistic proof is constructed as it ought to be constructed, it is objectively valid, whatever the attitude of those to whom it comes may be.'"[128] Or listen to him again: "There is a natural theology that is legitimate. It is such a theology as, standing upon the basis of faith and enlightened by Scripture, finds God in nature. But Rome's natural theology . . . is illegitimate. Its natural theology is attained by the natural reason without reference to Scripture."[129] Presuppositionalism does not for a moment discourage theistic proof. It recognizes, however,

127. "The Philosophy of Christian Evidences," in *Jerusalem and Athens*, ed. Geehan, 425 (emphasis added)—notice the two phases of the traditional apologetical argument. Pinnock wrongly asserted that Van Til's work as a defender of the Christian faith employs "a curious epistemology," which "requires decision before reflection," thus amounting to "irrational fideism." Pinnock similarly depicted Van Til in a published exchange of letters with Daniel Fuller in the *Christian Scholars Review* 2 (1979): 330–35; cf. Greg L. Bahnsen, "Inductivism, Inerrancy, and Presuppositionalism," *Journal of the Evangelical Theological Society* 20 (1977): 289–305, reprinted in *Evangelicals and Inerrancy*, ed. Ronald Youngblood (Nashville: Thomas Nelson, 1984), 199–216.

128. *Defense of the Faith*, 256. Van Til here quotes his *Common Grace*, 49.

129. *Common Grace*, 44. Van Til's manner of expression could be a little confusing here since he usually uses the term "natural theology" to describe autonomous attempts to reason about nature and reach conclusions about God—without enlightenment from Scripture. In that sense, "natural theology" is distinguished from "natural revelation." Here, however, Van Til uses the term "natural theology" also to refer to learning about God from nature under the self-conscious

that the traditional formulation and understanding of such "proofs" is not the same as a presuppositional formulation or understanding of them. "The proofs may be formulated either on a Christian or on a non-Christian basis."[130] What is at stake here is the way in which the facts and the criteria that are utilized in the arguments are philosophically formulated, whether autonomously or in submission to God's revelation. Unbelievers who pretend to be autonomous have no reason to be threatened by a proof for God's existence that does not disturb their pretense. Van Til wisely observed: "In not challenging this basic presupposition with respect to himself as the final reference point in predication the natural man may accept the 'theistic proofs' as fully valid. . . . But the god whose existence he proves to himself in this way is always a god who is something other than the self-contained ontological trinity of Scripture . . . a God as will leave intact the autonomy of man to at least some extent."[131]

As Van Til labored to teach throughout his career (and as we have said many times in this book), *there simply is no presupposition-free and neutral way to approach reasoning*, especially reasoning about the fundamental and philosophically momentous issues of God's existence and revelation. To formulate proofs for God that assume otherwise is not only foolish and futile, from a philosophical perspective, but also unfaithful to the Lord. Reasoning is a God-given gift to man, but it does not grant to him any independent authority. The Christian concept of God takes Him to be the highest and absolute authority, even over man's reasoning; such a God *could not* be proved to exist by some other standard as the highest authority in one's reasoning. That would be to assume the contrary of what you are seeking to prove. That is why Van Til so clearly announced: "The most absolute God of the [Westminster] Confession can only be presupposed. He cannot be proved to exist *in the way* that the idea of proof is taken by the Romanist-Arminian apologetics."[132] The traditional method of theistic proof endeavors to ig-

---

guidance of "natural revelation," not through autonomous reason. It would appear in context that Van Til uses the expression "natural theology" in this way at this point because he is summarizing and alluding to what Herman Bavinck said (in *Gereformeerde Dogmatiek*).
130. *Defense of the Faith*, 196.
131. Ibid., 94–95.
132. *An Introduction to Systematic Theology*, In Defense of the Faith, vol. 5 (Philadelphia: Presbyterian and Reformed, 1974), 163 (emphasis added). Cf.: "For Adam in paradise God-consciousness could not come in *at the end* of a syllogistic process of reasoning. God-consciousness was for him *the presupposition* [and thus at the beginning] of the significance of his reasoning on anything" (*Defense of the Faith*, 107 [emphasis added]).

nore the presuppositional issue and assumes that neutrality is possible.[133] The presuppositional method, by contrast, focuses precisely upon the issue of presuppositions, showing that neutrality would destroy the possibility or intelligibility of any reasoning whatsoever.

Van Til thus said: "They [the proofs] are formulated on a Christian basis if, with Calvin, they rest clearly upon the ideas of creation and providence. . . . When the proofs are thus formulated they have absolute probative force."[134] Readers and critics who take this kind of comment out of context, and who are ignorant of Van Til's transcendental approach to proving God, are bound to misunderstand (as they often have) what this means—as though Van Til proposed to prove the conclusion "God exists" from a premise which assumes it already ("God created and providentially controls the world"). Van Til in this very place explicitly indicated that he was using an "analogical," rather than "deductive," concept of demonstration. To put it another way, the transcendental (analogical) method of argument, as opposed to the traditional (deductive) method, calls for comparing the two opposing *worldviews* of belief and unbelief. Right in the immediate context of the previous quote, Van Til explains that within the Christian worldview, God is taken as "that One who cannot but exist. And when he is seen to be such, the world is, in the same act, seen of necessity to be existing as the creation of God." The unbeliever may accept that outlook (with its own internal character, logic, and demands) or not. But if the opponent of Christianity dismisses this worldview, and thus refuses to reason analogically (thinking God's thoughts after Him, presupposing

133. Also see the discussion of "natural theology" versus "natural revelation" in chap. 4.3 above. Traditional attempts to prove God's existence are designed to extend the natural man's knowledge from what is evident about nature to what he should infer about supernature, but their formulations and strategies do not take into account that all men already inescapably know God—in which case the work of the apologist should be to expose, rather than extend. Traditional attempts to develop an autonomous natural theology rest on a number of other assumptions as well, which are also theologically and philosophically unacceptable. To wit: some matters are more epistemically certain than God's existence; man's experience and reasoning are intelligible apart from God's existence; the available evidence for God's existence is ambiguous; the god whose existence is proven may or may not be the Christian God; the unbeliever to whom the proofs are directed can be open-minded and fair in assessing them. Cf. Greg L. Bahnsen, "Machen, Van Til, and the Apologetical Tradition of the OPC," *Pressing Toward the Mark*, ed. Charles G. Dennison and Richard C. Gamble (Philadelphia: Committee for the Historian of the Orthodox Presbyterian Church, 1986), 268–69.

134. *Defense of the Faith*, 196.

the truth of biblical revelation), the apologist then shows him that his reasoning cannot make rational sense of itself or anything else. "Thus the Christian-theistic position must be shown to be not *as defensible as* some other position; it must rather be shown to *be the position which alone does not annihilate intelligent human experience.*"[135]

It is in this way that Van Til endorsed theistic proof, and indeed maintained that it is objectively and absolutely sound, and yet did not formulate it in the traditional fashion.

> If the Christian forms the proofs theistically correctly, they are, to be sure, a weapon in his hand with which he may confirm himself and ward off the attack of the enemy. But then this defense and confirmation is on the ground that he has the truth and that his opponents trust in a lie. It cannot be said that at least the enemy has no better weapons; it must then be said that the enemy has wooden guns, while the believer has true guns. If theistically stated, the arguments do nothing but give the content of the revelation of God to man, and argue that it is the only reasonable thing to do for a human being to accept this revelation.[136]

The way he put it elsewhere was to stress "the basic difference between a theistic proof that presupposes God and one that presupposes man as ultimate."[137] Presuppositional theistic proofs openly challenge the autonomy of man, rather than catering to and reinforcing the unbeliever's assumption of autonomy. The challenge to autonomy rests upon a conviction that no man can escape the natural revelation of God (can escape *already* knowing God, although suppressing this knowledge in unrighteousness). Van Til saw this as foundational to the intellectual cogency of the proofs. "God's revelation is everywhere, and everywhere perspicuous. *Hence* the theistic proofs are absolutely valid. They are but the restatement of the revelation of God."[138] Because the transcendental challenge amounts to "restating" God's revelation— the revelation that man is completely dependent upon his Maker for all things, including intelligibility and meaning in experience or thinking—"we should not tone down the validity of this argument to the

135. Ibid., 196–97 (emphasis original).
136. *Introduction to Systematic Theology*, 199.
137. "A Letter on Common Grace," in *Common Grace and the Gospel* (Philadelphia: Presbyterian and Reformed, 1972), 193.
138. Ibid., 181.

probability level.[139] . . . Christianity is the only reasonable position to hold."[140] This is a distinctive feature of transcendental argumentation; where legitimate, it shows the rational necessity of its conclusion. Van Til could put it very powerfully and succinctly: "The only 'proof' of the Christian position is that unless its truth is presupposed there is no possibility of 'proving' anything at all."[141]

Consider, for example, the difference between a traditional conception of the "cosmological" argument and a presuppositional conception of it.[142] The cosmological argument purports to prove the existence of God from a consideration of causation. The traditional approach does not challenge the autonomy of the natural man's thinking, but naively assumes that his experience and understanding of causal relations is intelligible. If everything has a cause, it is argued, then he should admit that this world also has a cause—which can only be God. This argument is credible to Christians, who see the world as the creation of God, but it is not traditionally presented as the internal logic of the Christian worldview. Rather, the traditional argument assumes that the world and causation can be understood outside the context of the theistic worldview (with its own internal logic). By the "common" (external, inherently intelligible) canons of logic used by men, the causal principle is applied to the world in order to prove that God is the creator. Yet in that context the argument is not convincing. Traditional formulations of the cosmological proof for God's existence have always been, as autonomously conceived and interpreted, philosophically embarrassing.

How should we understand the fundamental premise in the cosmological argument, "Everything has a cause" (or "Every object has an origin," or, better, "Every event has a cause")? If this is taken as a

---

139. Cf.: "Following Paul's example Calvin argues that men *ought* to see God, not *a* god, not some supernatural power, but the only God, in nature. They have not done justice by the facts they see displayed before and within them if they say that *a* god exists or that God *probably* exists. . . . I stress the *objective clarity* of God's revelation of himself wherever it appears. Both Thomas Aquinas and Butler contend that men have done justice by the evidence if they conclude that God *probably* exists. . . . I consider this a compromise of simple and fundamental Biblical truth. It is an insult to the living God to say that his revelation of himself so lacks in clarity that man, [who is] himself through and through revelation of God, does justice by it when he says that God *probably* exists" (*Defense of the Faith*, 115, 256).

140. *Common Grace*, 62.

141. "My Credo," in *Jerusalem and Athens*, ed. Geehan, 21.

142. Cf. Greg L. Bahnsen, taped lecture at Virginia Tech (1991), "Proof of God's Existence."

universal metaphysical principle (or even a category of understanding imposed by the mind on anything that would be "rational"), then the embarrassing conclusion reached by the apologist would be that *God too* has a cause or origin. If the premise that "Everything has a cause" is interpreted in a more familiar way, as having an empirical impetus based on observation, then it refers to our ordinary and natural experiences. In that case, the cosmological argument proceeds upon an insecure foundation, for nobody knows from empirical experience that every single object and event in this world has a cause; nobody has observed everything. Moreover, if the causal principle is empirically interpreted, then "everything" means more precisely "each and every particular thing within the universe of experience," and "has a cause" means more specifically "has a natural cause." But the conclusion of the cosmological argument, if we are analytically clear, refers to the universe as a whole (everything together, as a collected set of particular members) and refers to a single cause that is supernatural, beyond the universe. Consequently, when the meaning of its terms is fully disclosed, the cosmological argument amounts to saying: "*Each of the many parts* within experience has a *natural* cause; therefore, *the whole* set of things has a *single* and *supernatural* cause." Thus analyzed, we readily see that the cosmological argument fallaciously moves from the characteristics of the parts to the characteristics of the whole. It fallaciously moves from a multitude of causes to a single cause. And, most damaging of all, it fallaciously moves from a premise about natural causes to a conclusion about a supernatural cause—completely exceeding the scope of the premise.

A presuppositional version of the cosmological argument amounts to the general presuppositional argument (i.e., the transcendental argument that God is the precondition of rational intelligibility), applied to the particular notion of causation. As Christians, we maintain that we can rationally prove God's existence from causation. We can show the unbeliever that causal reasoning or the "inductive principle" (compare the belief in the uniformity of nature) is not only taken for granted by all men, but is rationally necessary for our scientific inferences, our use of language, and our practical experience. However, when the worldview of the Bible is set next to the worldview of unbelief (in whatever form it takes) for mutual analysis, the causal principle is seen to be intelligible only within the Christian framework of thought. Unbelievers who have been both brilliant and honest about this matter[143] have openly conceded that they have no rational basis for believing that the future will resemble the past. We may have observed that event B followed event A many times in the past, but to know that B *necessarily* follows A (i.e., that the relation is causal), calls for reference to a metaphysical principle (namely, the future will be like the past) for which the unbeliever has no warrant or right. As Bertrand Russell was driven to conclude: "The general principles of science, such as the belief in the reign of law, and the belief that every event must have a cause, are as completely dependent upon the inductive principle as are the beliefs of daily life. All such general principles are believed because mankind have found innumerable instances of their truth and no instances of their falsehood. But this affords no evidence for their truth in the future, unless the inductive principle *is assumed*." Assumed? But that is what was supposed to be proved! Russell was aware of his defeat: "Hence we can never use experience to prove the inductive principle without begging the question. Thus we must . . . forgo all justification of our expectations about the future."[144] But the Christian worldview does not have this intellectual dilemma of justifying the causal principle (inductive or scientific reasoning). It is transcendentally justified by the inner coherence of our presupposed worldview, or within its wider context, being entailed by both the nature and promises of God (cf. chap. 4.5 above). The unbeliever may be unwilling to resort to a "theological rationale" to justify the foundational belief (the causal principle) that is necessary to the rationality of science, but it is the only rational alternative to "forgo[ing] all justification of our expectations about the future." The presuppositional cosmological argument points out that unbelief must destroy rationality in order to save it. The unbelieving worldview cannot provide a cogent reason for what we necessarily assume in all of our reasoning. Thus, it is entirely unreasonable not to believe in God.

---

143. The foremost example of this, of course, is David Hume's devastating critique of causal reasoning in *An Inquiry Concerning Human Understanding* (1748). Cf. the segment on Hume's skepticism in chap. 5.3 above.

144. Bertrand Russell, "On Induction," in *The Problems of Philosophy* (1912; reprint, London: Oxford University Press, 1959), 69, 68. (In the omitted part of the quotation, Russell repeats what he has just concluded and offers it as an alternative, saying that we must forgo all justification for our expectations about the future, and thus all scientific knowledge, or be content to accept the inductive principle on the ground of "its intrinsic evidence"—that is, surrender to "begging the question.")

Similarly, transcendental versions of the teleological argument (proving God's existence from a consideration of order) and the ontological argument (proving God's existence as a necessary being) are insinuated or generally developed in Van Til's writings. The transcendental project is applied to the notion of order in his pamphlet *Why I Believe in God:*

> You know pretty clearly now what sort of God it is of which I am speaking to you. . . . [T]he God of Christianity is the *All-Conditioner.* . . .
>
> Deep down in your heart you know . . . there is no unity in your life. You want no God who by His counsel provides for the unity you need. . . . So you have made nonsense of your own experience. . . .
>
> Looking about me I see both order and disorder [novelty] in every dimension of life. But I look at both of them in the light of the Great Orderer Who is back of them. . . .
>
> No human being can explain in the sense of seeing through all things, but only he who believes in God has the right to hold that there is an explanation at all. . . .
>
> I believe in God now because unless I have Him as the All-Conditioner, life is Chaos. . . .
>
> I hold rather that unless you believe in God you can logically believe in nothing else.[145]

The ontological argument begins by asking us to consider the very nature or definition of God, from which it is evident that God necessarily exists. This certainly embodies the presuppositional commitments and internal logic of the Christian worldview. According to Van Til, if the theistic proofs bear witness to the true God, they must bear witness to Him as being what He actually is. "And he is that One who cannot but exist."[146] If God did not exist, the intelligibility of human experience, reasoning, and communication would be lost; indeed, God must exist in order for someone meaningfully to deny His existence. "From the Christian point of view, it is impossible to think of the non-existence of God."[147] When the non-Christian claims that it is possible for him to think of God's non-existence, the Christian apologist ap-

---

145. Pp. 10, 18–20. The entire pamphlet is reprinted above in chap. 3.4.
146. *Defense of the Faith*, 197. Cf. the discussion of "possibility" in chap. 5.2 above.
147. *Introduction to Systematic Theology*, 9–10. Cf.: "He himself exists as a necessary being" (p. 235).

plies the transcendental critique to the non-Christian's worldview in order to reveal that in all of his thinking processes, if they are meaningful or intelligible, he has (without being willing to recognize it) been assuming the existence of God. "Antitheism presupposes theism."[148] Accordingly, Van Til asserted that "we cannot intelligently think away God's existence."[149] God is proved to exist, according to the presuppositional version of the ontological argument, by the impossibility of the contrary.[150]

So, then, we find that Van Til's presuppositional defense of the faith does not repudiate theistic proofs, but simply insists on formulating them in a way that is faithful to Christian presuppositions. His complaint against the traditional versions of the cosmological, teleological, and ontological proofs of God's existence was that they were formulated to accommodate the autonomous reasoning of man, rather than to attack it head-on. This head-on collision is found in the transcendental formulation of the proofs, illustratively applying the challenge, that Christianity is the rational precondition of intelligibility, to the notions of causation, order, and necessary being. To put it in Van Til's own words, "The true theistic proofs undertake to show that the idea of existence (ontological proof), of cause (cosmological proof), and purpose (teleological proof) are meaningless unless they presuppose the existence of God."[151] When properly formulated and used, such theistic proofs have a common thrust or aim, and the various illustrations tend to blend into each other:

> That is to say, if the theistic proof is constructed as it ought to be constructed, it is objectively valid, whatever the attitude of those to whom it comes may be. To be constructed rightly, theistic proof ought to presuppose the ontological trinity[152] and contend that, unless we may make this presupposition, all human predication is meaningless. The words "cause," "purpose," and "being," used as universals in the phenomenal world, could not be so used with meaning unless we may

---

148. *A Survey of Christian Epistemology*, In Defense of the Faith, vol. 2 (Philadelphia: Presbyterian and Reformed, 1969), xii.
149. "Common Grace and Witness-Bearing," in *Common Grace and the Gospel*, 131.
150. *Survey of Christian Epistemology*, 205.
151. "A Letter on Common Grace," in *Common Grace and the Gospel*, 190.
152. Before a hasty critic jumps in, aghast and shocked, claiming that Van Til says we should deductively infer from the premise, "The God who is ontologically triune exists," the conclusion that "God exists" (which is simply begging the question!), read on to the end of the sentence.

presuppose the self-contained God. If the matter is put this way one argument is as sound as the other. In fact, then, each argument involves the others. Nor is any one of the arguments then at any point vulnerable. And future research cannot change their validity.[153]

From what we have seen, then, and contrary to critics who have not thoroughly read or properly understood his presuppositional apologetic, Van Til did not sweepingly and indiscriminately discard theistic proofs. He affirmed quite boldly that the argument for the existence of God, when properly construed, is indeed objectively valid—so that Christianity is the only reasonable position for men to hold.

REASONING FROM NATURE TO NATURE'S GOD[154]

God continued to reveal himself in nature as the self-sufficient and self-subsistent rational God even after man became a sinner. If therefore men would only reason analogically they should be able to reason from nature to nature's God. But sinners until saved by grace do not reason analogically. They reason univocally.[155] And because they reason univocally about nature they conclude that no god exists or that a god exists but never that the true God exists. . . . By univocal reasoning, one can, in the nature of the case, find an immanent God only. . . .

It would at first glance seem as though Scripture itself begins by reasoning from the created universe as something existing independently of God, to the existence and character of God. When Scripture asks whether it be reasonable to think that he that hath planted the ear should not hear, it might seem as though it is starting from the creature as an independent something in order to reason from it to the creator. But this is not the case. The absurdity of thinking of God as not hearing lies in the very fact that God *has planted* the ear of man, that is, that he is the original and that man is the derivative. The argument is, therefore, that it is unreasonable not to *presuppose* in God the originals of those things that we see in us. Thus, when we reason from nature to nature's God, by way of eminence, we must take this eminence seriously. We must take it so seriously that we take it absolutely. That means

---

153. *Common Grace*, 49–50. (The last observation establishes that the formulation of the proofs that he had in mind was not inductive in character.)
154. An excerpt from *Introduction to Systematic Theology*, 101–7.
155. CVT: As indicated at the outset of this work, we speak of all forms of reasoning in which man is assumed to be the final or ultimate reference point of predication as *univocal* reasoning. In contrast to this we speak of the form of reasoning employed by the Christian who recognizes that God is the ultimate reference point of predication as *analogical* reasoning.

that God was self-sufficient before he created the world, and that he is self-sufficient still. Accordingly, we must think of ourselves as proximate, as well as of God as ultimate. We must negate ourselves as ultimates or as correlatives and think of ourselves as derivatives. We must not argue as though we can already know a great deal about nature by itself but that, inasmuch as we cannot know all that ought to be known about it, there must be one who knows infinitely more than we do. We must rather reason that unless God exists as ultimate, as self-subsistent, we could not even know anything, we could not even reason that God must exist, nor could we even ask a question about God.

In order to do this, in order to negate himself as ultimate and as correlative, *the natural man must first negate himself as normal*. This he will not and cannot do. Paul speaks of this inability when he says: "Because the mind of the flesh is enmity against God; for it is not subject to the law of God, neither indeed can be" (Rom. 8:7). But the fact that man cannot do what he ought to do does not make the "ought" any less important, and it is with this "ought" that we now deal.

God has continued to reveal himself in nature even after the entrance of sin. Men ought, therefore, to know him. Men ought to reason analogically from nature to nature's God. Men ought, therefore, to use the cosmological argument analogically in order thus to conclude that God is the creator of this universe. Men ought to realize that nature could not exist as something independent. They ought to sense that if anything intelligible is to be said about nature, it must be in relation to the absolute system of truth, which is God. Hence, they ought at once to see nature as the creation of God. Men ought also to use the ontological argument analogically. Men ought to realize that the word *"being"* cannot be intelligently applied to anything unless it be applied to God without limitation. They ought not, as is usually done in the case of the ontological argument, first assume that the word "being" can be intelligibly applied to this universe in order then and thereafter to conclude that it must also be applied in an unlimited way to a still higher being than ourselves or this world. The better theologians of the church have constantly sensed the fact that the theistic argument must not be used univocally. They have sensed something of the fact that all the theistic arguments should really be taken together and reduced to the one argument of the possibility of human predication. Intelligent predication about anything with respect to nature or with respect to man were impossible unless God existed as the ultimate reference point of it all. God, as self-sufficient, as the One in whom the One and the Many are equally ultimate, is the One in whom the persons of the Trinity are interchangeably exhaustive, is the presupposition for the intelligent use of words with respect to anything in this universe, whether it be the trees of the garden or the angels in heaven.

Accordingly, men ought to reason that the order of nature is due to the providence of God. This providence is actually displayed there. Men ought to reason that natural laws cannot exist in themselves. They ought to reason that the conception of law could never have been applied by the mind of man to the phenomena of nature unless there were a God who is in himself absolute order or absolute system, and who has therefore implanted order upon his creation.

Still further, men ought to reason that the disorder that is found in nature is unnatural. The disorder of nature cannot be part of the originally constituted state of affairs with respect to nature. The God of order would create an orderly universe, if he created one at all. To create a disorderly universe would be to deny himself as a God of order. The disorder of the universe must, therefore, have come into nature by the wilful disobedience of man. Nature itself, not being moral, could not sin. Hence, nature must have been cursed because of the sin of man. Nature must be suffering under the wrath of God, and therefore it must be true that God is a righteous God who executeth judgment upon unrighteousness. Moreover, seeing that it is an absolute God, a sovereign God alone who actually reveals himself, this God may possibly defer the punishment of the iniquity of men. Men ought to conclude from the "unevenness" of the ways of God, not that he actually is "uneven," unstable, or arbitrary, but that he will "even out" things *hereafter*.

Again, because men ought to conclude that the sin of man is the source of the curse of God upon nature, they ought also to conclude that it is by the grace of God that they live at all, and that nature is not fallen into complete disorder. That winter and summer follow one another is actually a matter of God's grace to man, as the covenant with Noah shows. This, men ought to see. The facts are there before them, and they ought to see the facts. Hence they ought to glorify the creator.

As a matter of fact, men have not reasoned and interpreted as they ought to have reasoned and interpreted. They have reasoned univocally instead of analogically. They have used an immanentistic principle of interpretation for the universe as a whole. They have not been willing to admit that it is by the human mind that disorder and misinterpretation have come into the world. They have not negated themselves as normal. Hence, they have also not negated themselves as ultimate. Yet they have sensed through it all that they have, with their exclusively immanentistic principle, not been able to interpret reality satisfactorily. They have shown, therefore, a *desire* for something different. They have recognized that if no interpretation on the part of a self-sufficient God is given them, there is no rest for the mind of man. On the other hand, in the interpretations that they have actually given, they have shown great similarity of form to the truth. In the idealistic tradition philosophy has verbally recognized the need of a timeless absolute. In the higher religions of the world, outside Christianity, men have also glimpsed something of the fact that it is in something above this world that the soul of man must find its peace. So modernism is today constantly seeking that which is above the mechanical and the material. And though this is in itself misinterpretation, it nevertheless shows that men are constantly seeking something or someone beyond the universe. It is remarkable how many scientists have said that they have discovered God in nature. It is, to be sure, not the true God that they discover, because they, generally speaking, use the univocal method of reasoning; but the fact remains that men seek a God. All of this is eloquent testimony that God is, as a matter of fact, revealed in nature and in the mind of man, and that, therefore, men ought to know him. . . .

Moreover, all men everywhere, deep down in their hearts know that the world is created by God. At bottom they know that by all their attempts at explanation of nature they are suppressing within themselves the testimony of the real creator of the universe. The more self-conscious men become with respect to the real meaning of their own position the more clearly do they realize that their systems are escape-mechanisms by which sinners seek to hide the truth from themselves. . . .

At this point, then, we may say that men ought to reason analogically about themselves. They ought to reason analogically about their being (ontological argument), about the cause of their being (cosmological arguments), and about the purpose of their being (teleological argument). Men ought to see themselves concretely for what they are. They cannot in any true sense define or describe themselves except in terms of their derivation from and responsibility to God. They ought to see that the words *being, cause* and *purpose* have no possible meaning when applied to themselves, except in relation to God as their creator and judge.

Accordingly they ought also to attribute disorder to man, not to God. If error were as fundamental as the truth, if negation were as fundamental as affirmation, it would mean that there would be no truth at all. The least bit of rationality anywhere presupposes absolute rationality in God. To this we may add also that the least bit of irrationality anywhere presupposes absolute rationality in God. No irrationality could have meaning except in contrast to rationality. Yet if irrationality were contrasted merely to finite rationality, it would not be really contrasted to rationality at all. Finite irrationality as well as finite rationality needs absolute rationality as its presupposition.

Thus we see that the very least bit of rational interpretation, as well as the possibility of error, presupposes God. This applies both to the intellectual and to the moral realm. That man can to any extent interpret the universe aright, and that he does by nature the "things of the law" are equally significant as evidences of the existence of God. . . .

Order, when viewed from the point of view of the passage of time, is purpose. Men should therefore also have used the teleological argument analogically. It is in connection with the rational and moral activity of the mind of man that the concept of purpose comes out most strikingly. So then man should see that all things in this universe, and, in particular, all things in the mind and moral activity of man, would be at loose ends if it were not for God and his purpose with respect to them. Here we may note again the difference between a univocal and an analogical argument. Suppose we begin with man as a moral being, taking for granted that we know to a large extent, if not fully, what purpose means in his case, in order then to conclude that there must be a God to conserve the purposes or values of man. That would be univocal instead of analogical reason. It would be to make God the derivative of man instead of man the derivative of God. We would be thinking of a god who is but an extension of man, with the result that all things would still be at loose ends. Thus we would defeat the very purpose we had in mind, that is, of showing the necessity of thinking of God when we think of human purpose. It is true, of course, that there is a sense in which we know what purpose means in the case of man, when we do not so plainly know it in the case of God. When we purpose to go to a certain city, we mean that we intend to exert ourselves physically in order to get there. But this only indicates that in this sense we are more immediate to ourselves than to God. Yet, from an ultimate point of view, God is nearer than breathing, and nearer than hands and feet. . . .

[W]e may say that there must be a comprehensive purpose with history if there is purpose anywhere in history. Without a *comprehensive purpose*, every act of purpose on the part of man would be set in a void. And if there must be absolute purpose, it goes without saying that all the evil must one day be abolished. All unrighteousness will one day have to be punished. God will accomplish his purpose with the universe, or he would not be God. Even the devil must be subordinate to the purpose of God. . . . Thus men are a law unto themselves. They condemn themselves, and, to an extent, they excuse themselves. God has shown the wisdom of man to be foolishness and will finally condemn all purposive thought and action not centered on him at the time of the judgment day.

Thus we see that, both with respect to nature and with respect to man himself, men should have known God as Creator, as Preserver, and as Judge. They should have known his divinity. They should have known him as the Absolute One. They should have known him as the one through whom alone all human predication, applied either to nature or to man, has meaning. They should have known him as the presupposition of the intelligibility of the universe. They should have known him as such in his self-testimony, the self-testimony of the Spirit with respect to nature and man.

Instead of knowing him as such, men sought to interpret the universe by an exclusively immanentistic principle. Paul says: "For that they exchanged the truth of God for a lie, and worshiped and served the creature rather than the creator, who is blessed forever. Amen" (Rom. 1:25). Both deistic and pantheistic types of philosophy are immanentistic. Both try to worship the creature rather than the creator. Yet, as we have seen before, men have recognized something of the insufficiency of the immanentistic principle. They have demanded a *Beyond*. The nations have been incorrigibly religious. The *sensus deitatis* has been deeply ingrained in men, says Calvin, and the seed of religion has been so fixed in their being that they have tried in vain to remove the knowledge of God from their hearts.

On the other hand, the nature of the God whom they have formed for themselves, though often brought down to the level of four-footed beasts and creeping things, has, in the higher instances, been similar in form to the conception of the true God. Plato does, to be sure, "lose himself in his globe" so that his idea of God is, from the Christian point of view utterly false, yet, on the other hand, it is most remarkable that his God is as noble as he is. Both the basic differences and the formal similarities between the gods of the nations and the God of truth are evidence of the truth that God revealed himself to men. Both are given that men might be without excuse.

PROBLEMS WITH THE TRADITIONAL PROOFS[156]

(A) A word may first be said about the proof Thomas gives for the existence of God from the fact of *motion* in the universe. The significant point here is that he "proves" the existence of God from motion as something that is neither created, nor an aspect of created reality. In other words, Thomas says

---

156. The following excerpts are taken from:

    (A) *Reformed Pastor and Modern Thought*, 94–98 (emphasis original);
    (B) *Introduction to Systematic Theology*, 27, 100, 56–57, 161, 196, 206, 198 (emphasis partly added).

    For further discussion of attempts to use the theistic proofs, consult Van Til's analysis and critique of J. Oliver Buswell in *Christian Theory of Knowledge*, 276–309.

that creation cannot be proved by reason; it is an article of faith. The import of this point cannot well be overrated. On his assumptions he was right. The probative force of his argument for a first mover depends entirely upon the assumption that the human mind is at least potentially divine, that is, upon an *a priori* which is found in a universal that comes to expression with equal directness, if not with equal intensity, both in the human and in the divine mind.

This *a priori* is an impersonal abstract principle that, in the nature of the case, has no productive power. It is misleading to speak of it as the first mover. It does not move itself or anything else at all. It does not really even stand as an ideal, except as one uses metaphors and similes.

It follows that according to Thomas, motion must be considered as ultimate in order that God's existence may be proved.

The prime mover as the first cause is for Aquinas, following Aristotle, merely one among other ultimate causes of explanation. And this means in effect that the idea of cause is virtually identical with the idea of a principle of explanation. Besides having the non-rational principle of prime matter, one also needs the idea of a *universal form* in relation to which the individuality that springs from matter receives its unification. Individuation by a non-rational principle would lead to pure indetermination—to an infinite regress. If one had billions of beads without any string, how would one ever have a string of beads? On the other hand, it is equally true that if you had nothing but the string, you still would have no string of beads.

The other argument for God's existence from cause and effect, from gradation, from necessity, and from purpose which Thomas propounds are the same in character as the one which he apparently himself considered the most important of them all.

The probative force of these arguments depends upon the measure of their Parmenidean character. That is true of the probative force of any argument on a non-Christian foundation. Spinoza best expressed this fact when he quite fearlessly asserted that the order and connection of ideas is the same as the order and connection of things, and when, in addition, he said that the human mind is of a piece with the divine. On any non-Christian methodology a thing can be known to exist only if it is categorized in a system of timeless logic. When it is so systematized, it has lost all its temporal character and all its individuality. Thus the argument for a first mover in the Thomistic form is to the effect that God's existence as the first mover is proved only if there be no motion, no time, no history at all.

This pure univocism and fatalism is not immediately seen to be the result of his argument because Thomas, following Aristotle, has inserted the fact of prime matter as the actual principle of individuation. The last thing Aristotle and Thomas want is to arrive at a stark identity philosophy. Yet on their principles the only way to escape this is to assume an ultimate non-rational principle of individuation. Thomas is quite willing to sacrifice something for this purpose. He is quite willing to say that man cannot by reason prove the *nature* of God; he can only prove his *existence*. But of course he cannot make this distinction absolute. It would make no sense to prove the existence of something about the nature of which you could have no information at all. Yet the nature of his argument really required him to say that he knew all about the nature of God. On his argument he could not at all prove the *existence* of God unless he fully knew the *nature* of God. . . .

Everybody calls the first cause of reality God. If we have proved the necessity for the idea of a first cause, therefore, we have proved the existence of God. But who, we ask, is "everybody"? It is the whole *massa periditionis*, the millions of covenant-breakers who have suppressed the knowledge of the Creator within themselves. It is they who are subtly making themselves believe that they are doing justice by the revelation of God when talking about a "first cause." They want to be theists if only they do not need to face the Creator and Judge.

We must therefore hold Thomas to his point. He is logically bound to tell us all about the nature of God if we are to accept his proof for the existence of God as valid.

This leads us on to a further consideration. Thomas thought that he could hold onto the creation out of nothing idea as taught to him by faith, at the same time that he could hold onto the probative force of the argument for a first mover. In this he was mistaken. He was not mistaken in holding that one can believe in the sort of God that Thomas himself believed in by faith, while holding to his rational argument for God's existence. But then this only shows that the synthesis he was making was a false synthesis.

We have seen that one of the ingredients in the argument of Thomas is the non-rational principle of individuation. It is by means of it and by it alone that Thomas must seek to escape the nemesis of pure identity. Well then, it is this pure non-rationality that must serve as the sole object of faith, for if reason must reduce everything to blank identity, faith must have the realm of the utterly irrational. If Thomas, the theologian, hears by revelation that God has created the universe out of nothing and he tells this to Thomas, the philosopher, the latter will answer that he cannot know such to be the case, indeed, that he *will never be able* to know such a thing to be so. He must add that the nature of reality *does not allow* for any such thing to be so. For surely faith will never teach anything that is out of accord with right reason, and has not God given reason to man? Thomas maintains that faith takes over where reason cannot go. But what will he do when both "reason" and "faith" make contradictory statements about the nature of reality? In other words, the argument with respect to the first mover is an argument about the nature of the whole of reality that is utterly out of accord with the nature of this reality as it is said to be in the Christian religion. . . .

The grace-nature scheme of Thomas fits in well with the form-matter scheme of Aristotle. The two are equally destructive of faith and of reason. The face of the covenant God cannot shine through this scheme, or it must shine through *in spite of it*, as it no doubt does to some extent.

However, the face of the covenant God does shine in *Calvin's* doctrine of the *sensus deitatis*. It is based on the idea of man's immediate self-awareness, or awareness of meaning as involving or presupposing the awareness of God as Creator and Judge. But this is as much as to say that we cannot (1) accept the mind of man as furnishing in any way the *ultimate* reference point for predication; (2) that we cannot take the *principles of identity* and of non-contradiction as a self-evident principle by which the nature of being is to be determined in any ultimate way; (3) that on the other hand we cannot take the idea of an *ultimate irrational principle* of individuation as contributing to the nature of reality, and that therefore (4) we cannot take the meaning of the word "God," as this is held by mankind generally, as a substitute for that knowledge of the nature of God revealed in Scripture in anything that we seek to prove.

Valid rational activity cannot be carried on by the mind of man with respect to anything in the universe except upon the basis of, and in conjunction with, the supernatural revelation (by means of positive thought communication) of the nature and purpose of God. Even in paradise man could not, by reason, without word-revelation, know his place and task as a covenant creature. The things with which he dealt were what they were precisely because of this ultimate plan of God. Thomas' teaching about the *donum superadditum* in the case of Adam was not wrong insofar as it brought in the supernatural *at the outset* of the human race; it was wrong insofar as it did not think of this supernatural aid as positive word communication from God. The same thought carried through concerning man *after the fall* implies that *no valid interpretation of any fact can be carried on except upon the basis of the authoritative thought communication to man of God's final purposes in Scripture, as this Scripture sets forth in final form the redemptive work of Christ. Every fact must be interpreted Christologically*.

It is the mistaken notion of much Protestant apologetics that a reason which does not from the outset subject itself to the Scriptures may be expected, nonetheless, to be open and ready to receive its revelation at a later date. It is not true that faith can carry us "the rest of the way." It is not true that the theistic proofs establish the *probable* existence of God and that faith must bring us certainty. The existence of God must be *presupposed* as the *basis* of all possibility and probability instead of the reverse. It is not true that these proofs may well establish the believer in his faith and be merely witness to unbelievers. What is objectively valid ought to be proof and witness for both unbeliever and believer, and what is not objectively valid ought to be neither for either.

(B) It will not do to say that the natural man knows nothing of God, though he knows many other things well. Nor is it even sufficient to say that the natural man does know of the *existence* of God but does not know anything about the *character* of God. The existence of God is the existence of the character. Hence Paul says that the heathen see "God's everlasting power and divinity." They see something of the character of God. . . .

This means that *God*, not some sort of God or some higher principle, but *God*, the *true God*, is displayed before men.[157] This is the fact of the matter, whether men recognize it or not. . . . God is simple. God cannot be cut up into several attributes that are kept distinct from one another. . . .

157. Van Til's point is that theistic proofs must be concrete in their conception of the God proved, rather than abstract or merely formal (e.g., "a god of some undefined nature"). "We must first ask what kind of a God Christianity believes in before we can really ask with intelligence whether such a God exists. The *what* precedes the *that*. . . . At least the latter cannot be discussed intelligently without at once considering the former. . . . The attributes of God are not to be thought of otherwise than as aspects of the one simple original being; the whole is identical with the parts. . . . The transcendence we believe in is not the transcendence of deism and the immanence we believe in is not the immanence of pantheism. . . . The Christian doctrine of God implies a definite conception of the relation of God to the created universe. . . . What we have discussed under the attributes of God may also be summed up by saying that God is *absolute personality*. The attributes themselves speak of self-conscious and moral activity on the part of God. . . . There were no principles of truth, goodness, and beauty that were next to or above God according to which he patterned the world. . . . Christianity offers the triune God, the absolute personality, containing all the attributes enumerated, as the God in whom we believe. . . . Accordingly we are not interested to have any one prove to us the existence of any other sort of God but this God. Any other sort of God is no God at all, and to prove that some other sort of God exists is, in effect, to prove that no God exists. . . . Anyone who says 'I believe in God,' is formally correct in his statement, but the question is what does he mean by the word *God?* The traditional view assumes that the natural man has a certain measure of correct thought content when he uses the word God. In reality the natural man's 'God' is always a finite God. . . . The natural man's god is *always* enveloped within a Reality that is greater than his god and himself. . . . [H]e still has a monistic assumption. . . . [On the traditional approach] the Spirit must testify to the contentless *form* of God; it must testify to the fact *that* God exists without any indication as to *what* is the nature of that God" (*Defense of the Faith*, 25–29, 262, 356).

It is necessary to keep this point in mind clearly, inasmuch as all too much has been made of the difference between the mere existence of God and the nature of God. . . .

As the proofs were often stated at the time of Kant, they were not only useless, but worse than useless. Whatever psychological value they may have had, if followed out logically, they would have to lead to the notion of a finite God. Nothing else could be obtained from them for the reason that they were usually built upon the presupposition of the ultimacy of the human mind and the ultimacy of the facts which the mind meets in the world. A god whose existence could be proved by the method in vogue at the time of Kant would be one who would always be face to face with independent human beings and with utterly uninterpreted facts. . . .

Without in the least indicating a difference between a Christian and a non-Christian formulation of the theistic proofs, Hepp[158] says of them that they press upon our consciousness powerfully. All that is lacking in them is that they cannot afford us absolute certainty. . . .

According to Hepp, then, the theistic proofs as historically developed have nothing inherently wrong in them. All they need is supplementation. . . .

There is in all this a very definite proof that Hepp himself has not avoided the mistake of reasoning as those reason who would build a natural theology. The historically formulated arguments would, we believe, prove, if they could prove anything, the existence of a finite God.[159] . . .

Working with this Aristotelian idea of knowledge [i.e., that it is restricted to

---

158. Van Til refers to Valentine Hepp and his work *Het Testimonium Spiritus Sancti;* this was Hepp's doctoral dissertation for promoter Herman Bavinck. Hepp went on to become a professor of theology at the Free University of Amsterdam. He was well known to Van Til, having delivered the Stone Lectures for 1930 at Princeton Theological Seminary.

159. Cf.: "We cannot say [with Bavinck] that the Christian may use these arguments as witnesses, though not as proofs. If they are constructed as all too often they have been constructed, they are neither proofs nor witnesses. Nor can we seek to defend our position with an argument which we really admit to be of doubtful validity. . . .

"As long as he is unwilling to argue along exclusively Christian lines, Hepp is unable to escape making concessions to a Roman type of natural theology. . . . When Hepp deals with the 'theistic proofs' he, like Bavinck, attributes a certain value to them even when they are constructed along non-Christian lines. . . . Hepp says that they cry day and night that God exists. To this we reply that they cry day and night that God does not exist. For, as they have been constructed, they cry that a finite God exists. . . . They take for granted that we already know from our study of the phenomenal world the meaning of such words as "cause" and "being" and "purpose," whether or not we have referred this phenomenal world to God. . . . We cannot say that the heavens *probably* declare the glory of God. We cannot allow that if rational argument is carried forth on true premises, it should come to any other conclusion than that the true God exists" (*Common Grace,* 50, 60–62).

species] Aquinas asserts that man cannot know what God is, but only what he is not. As far as knowledge of God is concerned the primary relation according to Thomas is that of negation. When he says that reason (by an Aristotelian method) can prove that God exists, this is pointless inasmuch as he adds that it cannot say what God is. And if he tones this contrast down sometimes by saying that man by reason can know something of the general characteristics of God, this is merely inconsistency. . . . Aristotle himself was not illogical when he concluded that such a god as he could allow for in his system was one who had not created the world and knew nothing of the world.[160] His conception of cause was basically as immanentistic as is that of Kant. And it is therefore logically as little possible to reach the transcendent God of Christianity by means of the logic of Aristotle as it is to reach this God by the logic of Kant. . . .

It is only if we have a correct view of the innate knowledge of God that we can also have a proper view of the value of *the ontological argument* for the existence of God. We then substitute the idea that the God of Scripture is the presupposition of all true interpretation for the Cartesian idea that man can begin from himself as an ultimate starting point.[161] . . .

160. Cf.: "To the extent that [Aristotle's god] knows intuitively he knows nothing of individual existence. He knows himself and men only to the extent that they are exhaustively classified and when they are so classified and he therefore knows them, he does not know *them*. And Aristotle's man knows nothing of Aristotle's God as Aristotle's God knows nothing of Aristotle's man. . . .

"The God of Aristotle, for instance, is at best an abstract, impersonal, non-creative principle of specific unity. It is quite impossible to identify this principle of cosmic or acosmic unity with the idea that the God of Scripture is One. . . . The one God of Aristotle retains its oneness only if kept in abstraction from the world. Its correlative plurality is the universe of pure non-being or chance" (*Defense of the Faith*, 138, 238).

It might be helpful here to rehearse a bit of the relevant portions of Aristotle's "On the Heavens." The "god" or "unmoved mover" which is "proved" by Aristotle's version of the cosmological argument is an impersonal, abstract principle of rationality ("thought thinking itself"). It is not the "efficient cause" of the world (as the wind is the efficient cause of the windmill turning); rather, it is the "final cause" of the world, the absolute perfection after which the outer ring of heavens strives (loving and thus emulating its perfection). Thus, Aristotle's god "causes" the heavenly (and eventually earthly) motion without itself moving. This motion must be eternal, according to Aristotle, and thus the universe was never created, but always existed—completely beyond the knowledge or concern of "thought thinking thought."

161. Recall that Descartes took as his firm starting point, "I doubt; therefore, I am." From the indubitable point that he himself exists, Descartes went on to reason that God must exist. We have an idea of God as absolute perfection. The self exists as a doubter, however, and is thus limited and imperfect; so it cannot be the cause of the idea of God. Since there is at least as much reality in the cause as in what it effects, nothing less than God could be adequate as the cause of our idea of God as absolute perfection.

[W]e should be careful when we say that God is the being than whom none higher can be thought.[162] If we take the highest being of which we can think, in the sense of *have a concept of*, and attribute to it actual existence, we do not have the biblical notion of God. God is not the reality that corresponds to the highest concept that man, considered as an independent being, can think. Man cannot think an absolute self-contained being; that is, he cannot have a concept of it in the ordinary sense of the term. God is infinitely higher than the highest being of which he can form a concept. . . . When we speak of our concept or notion of God, we should be fully aware that by that concept we have an analogical reproduction of the notion that God has of himself.[163] . . .

So, with respect to the *teleological proof*, Bavinck says that it would have some value even if it should leave unsettled the question of the unity or the plurality of the Godhead. He says that in any case it would have proved the necessity of the idea of intelligence for an interpretation of the world. With this we cannot agree. We hold this to be out of accord with Bavinck's own theology. If the question of the unity or plurality is not settled, the question of intelligibility in and beyond the universe is not settled. Or, rather, it is then settled unfavorably for Christianity. A plurality of gods is, for all practical purposes, equal to no god. He who is a polytheist is an irrationalist; he has no right to claim the rationality of one absolute God as the principle of his interpretation of life. And a similar line of argument holds for the other so-called theistic proofs. They must either be stated in a truly Christian-theistic fashion, or they involve the doctrine of a finite god; and a finite god is no God.

Accordingly, we would not say that these arguments, as they have been historically formulated even by non-Christians, are valid to a point. We do not hesitate to affirm that they are invalid.

8.4 Evidences: Traditional or Presuppositional?

Van Til's view regarding theistic proofs—namely, that he did not reject them, but found fault with the traditional formulation of them—can now be applied to the use of empirical evidences from nature and history in support of biblical claims. History is vitally important for

---

162. Van Til here alludes to the famous definition of "God" with which Anselm began his ontological argument for God's existence.
163. That is, God has revealed to us what we are to think about Him, and thus our thoughts about God can (when faithful to His revelation) be true. However, God has also revealed that He is much greater than anything that we can finitely imagine. His thoughts are higher than our thoughts (without our thoughts being false or misleading).

presuppositional apologetics; a book dropped from heaven, even if it were filled with metaphysical and moral truths that are "transcendental" necessities for our reasoning and living, would not be adequate for our salvation. Van Til wrote:

> The special revelation of God to man came not only by way of intellectual information. It came both as word and as deed. In theophany and in miracle, we have facts of revelation rather than words. *But these facts needed to be explained by God himself.* Sinful man cannot and will not explain them truly. . . . On the other hand word revelation without fact revelation would hover in the air and not reach reality. Special revelation needed actually to dip into this sinful world with redemptive power. Hence special revelation could not come to man in the form of a book dropped from heaven. Revelation had to be historically *mediated.*[164]

Presuppositional apologetics certainly does not imply that historical debates are unimportant; indeed, Van Til was a leading and effective critic of the Barthian or neoorthodox view of "super-history," since it had the effect of "evaporating" ordinary history. For Van Til, history was not to be reduced by the apologist to something meaningless. We are to argue that only the Christian can intelligibly provide an all-embracing pattern in and underneath the changing facts of history.[165]

And yet, despite all that, there have been those who have claimed that presuppositional apologetics is inherently antagonistic or indifferent to the use of evidences.[166] But why, then, would Van Til have declared, "I see induction and analytical reasoning as part of one process of interpretation. I would therefore engage in historical apologetics"?[167] He said

---

164. *Introduction to Systematic Theology*, 133 (emphasis original). On the point that redemptive facts need to be explained by God himself, cf.: "If an authoritative interpretation were not given to the redemptive facts, if the interpretation were left to men, it is certain that the redemptive revelation of God would not be able to reach the ends of the earth and maintain itself to the end of time" (p. 134).

165. *Defense of the Faith*, 135, 418–19; *Reformed Pastor and Modern Thought*, 217; *Common Grace and the Gospel*, 2, 142.

166. This notion is plainly contradicted by what Van Til actually said about the value of historical evidences. Also, it is significant that J. Gresham Machen (the master of the historical defense of Christianity) and Van Til (the presuppositional philosopher of apologetics) gave support to one another. There was no antagonism to facts in Van Til's defense of the faith. Cf. Greg L. Bahnsen, "Machen, Van Til, and the Apologetical Tradition of the OPC."

167. *Defense of the Faith*, 258. This is repeated in *Christian Theory of Knowledge*, 293. For

this not only in his key apologetics textbook in 1955, but published it again (verbatim) in 1969 in another text; he certainly was not shy about endorsing historical study in defense of the truth of Christianity. But if that is so, somebody might wonder, why do we not find extensive historical argumentation in his publications? Van Til's answer was: "I do not personally do a great deal of this because my colleagues in the other departments of the Seminary in which I teach are doing it better than I could do it." When you are working shoulder to shoulder with scholars like Machen, or Ned Stonehouse, or Edward J. Young, it makes sense to recognize a division of God-given gifts. Hence, Van Til focused on philosophical examination and let his colleagues develop the historical details, all as part of a common task of defending the faith.[168] Van Til declared that the evidential work of such colleagues was imperative: "Historical apologetics is absolutely necessary and indispensable to point out that Christ rose from the grave, etc."[169]

Therefore, John W. Montgomery had no reason to chide Van Til by saying, "The non-Christian must not be presented with an a priori dogmatic; he must be offered the factually compelling evidence for the Christian truth-claim."[170] If one reads Van Til carefully, one will find anything but dogmatism, obscurantism, or an aversion to empirical facts in his outlook:

> The point is, we are told, that in an infallible Bible there should not be any discrepancies. There should be no statement of historical fact in Scripture that is contradictory to a statement of historical fact given elsewhere. Yet higher criticism has in modern times found what it thinks are facts that cannot possibly be harmonized with the idea of an infallible Bible. What shall be the attitude of the orthodox believer with respect to this? Shall he be an obscurantist and hold to the doctrine of the authority of the Scripture though he knows that it can empirically be shown to be contrary to the facts of Scripture themselves? *It goes without saying that such should not be his attitude.*[171]

---

an explanation of how Van Til's theory of knowledge calls for an integration of both analysis and induction, see chap. 4.2, 5 above.

168. See chaps. 2.1 and 3.1 above for Van Til's view that apologetics coordinates all the efforts to defend the truth of Scripture, making "apologetics" and "evidences" part of a common undertaking.
169. *Introduction to Systematic Theology*, 146.
170. "Once upon an A Priori . . .," in *Jerusalem and Athens*, ed. Geehan, 392.
171. *Christian Theory of Knowledge*, 35 (emphasis added).

One has to wonder at the way evidentialists like Montgomery and Clark Pinnock misrepresent Van Til's position. According to Pinnock, Van Til would "refuse empirical investigation of the data in question [about God's work in history]," making "the objective data of divine revelation *inaccessible* to the non-Christian." He continued: "For Van Til, it seems, presuppositions are real, and *facts are not.*" Van Til was imagined to "recoil" from the natural man's request for evidence; he would "dismiss his questions without a hearing."[172] But Van Til's published views were quite different:

> Depreciation of [the] sense world inevitably leads to a depreciation of many of the important facts of historic Christianity which took place in the sense world. The Bible does not rule out every form of empiricism any more than it rules out every form of *a priori* reasoning.[173]

> It is quite commonly held that we cannot accept anything that is not the result of a sound scientific methodology. With this we can as Christians heartily agree. . . . The Christian position is certainly not opposed to experimentation and observation.[174]

> The greater the amount of detailed study and the more carefully such study is undertaken, the more truly Christian will the method be. It is important to bring out this point in order to help remove the common misunderstanding that Christianity is opposed to factual investigation. . . . The difference between the prevalent method of science and the method of Christianity is not that the former is interested in finding the facts and is ready to follow the facts wherever they may lead, while the latter is not ready to follow the facts.[175]

The false view that Van Til was opposed to the use of evidences has traveled far and wide. The unstudied belief of many young students of apologetics is that presuppositionalism is opposed to empirical evidences and resorts to mere authoritarian question-begging. Often their teachers are to blame.

172. "The Philosophy of Christian Evidences," in *Jerusalem and Athens*, ed. Geehan, 422, 424, 425 (emphasis partly added).
173. *Introduction to Systematic Theology*, 45.
174. *Christian-Theistic Evidences*, In Defense of Biblical Christianity, vol. 6 (Phillipsburg, N.J.: Presbyterian and Reformed, 1978), ii, 62.
175. *Survey of Christian Epistemology*, 7, 9.

For instance, by presenting "three fables" in his essay "Once upon an A Priori," Montgomery attempted to depict Van Til's apologetic as giving "the impression that our gospel is as aprioristically, fideistically irrational as the presuppositional claims of its competitors"—which we can see if we "consider a reversal of Van Til's approach," since it renders all worldviews "interchangeable."[176] Montgomery's stories pictured presuppositionalism as merely propounding abstract and empty claims and defending them by circular authorizations of themselves. In this situation, believer and unbeliever cannot meaningfully argue, but can only exchange presuppositional claims, with no prospect of rationally resolving their disagreement. Stories can be an effective teaching device, but also very misleading. Montgomery's fables are fables indeed, bearing no relation to Van Til's real position. Van Til taught that the subject of our apologetical efforts—the "presupposition" we defend—is the full, detailed content of biblical revelation, not just the formal claim that a certain book has authority to which we must mindlessly submit. Likewise, he taught that the dispute over conflicting presuppositions or worldviews (with their respective concrete contents) is to be rationally resolved by means of the transcendental argument—which Montgomery does not mention, even though it is the very heart of Van Til's apologetic![177] Consider just these quotations from Van Til, which we have already presented: "We must first ask what kind of a God Christianity believes in before we can really ask with intelligence whether such a God exists. The *what* precedes the *that*."[178] "It is clear that the idea of Scripture can never be separated from the message of Scripture."[179] "The true method for any Protestant with respect to the Scripture (Christianity) and with respect to the existence of God (theism) must be *the indirect method of reasoning by presupposition*"[180]—that is, "what we will have to do then is to try to reduce our opponent's position to absurdity. Nothing less will do."[181] Van Til believed in arguing

176. "Once upon an A Priori . . .," *Jerusalem and Athens*, 391, 381, 383.
177. Montgomery tells us that if everyone sees things through colored glasses (in terms of a worldview), as Van Til maintains, then "no one can criticize another person's spectacles" (ibid., 382–83). But the whole point of Van Til's apologetic has been to teach us how to do this very thing! Van Til's "indirect" approach to proof, where we compare the contrasting worldviews to see if they sustain or destroy the intelligibility of experience and reasoning, is precisely the means by which to criticize the unbeliever's spectacles.
178. *Defense of the Faith*, 25 (emphasis original).
179. "My Credo," 10.
180. *Defense of the Faith*, 125–26 (emphasis added).
181. *Survey of Christian Epistemology*, 204.

for and against presuppositions; he did not regard them merely as hollow claims to authority.

Pushing aside the straw man erected by Montgomery, Pinnock, and others, the truth is that Van Til had great confidence in the evidence:

> Every bit of historical investigation, whether it be in the directly biblical field, archaeology, or in general history is bound to confirm the truth of the claims of the Christian position. . . . A really fruitful historical apologetic argues that every fact *is* and *must be* such as proves the truth of the Christian theistic position.[182]

Van Til did not maintain that we should never look beyond our Bibles for information. He did not deprecate or discourage serious examination of the empirical facts of the world. He declared:

> It is true that in the study of matters of the laboratories and the field, the Bible is only indirectly concerned. We do not go to the Bible itself for the facts with which we deal. . . . We do not limit ourselves entirely to the Bible when we study anything else.[183]

> It is *when* as a physicist I investigate what is proper to my field that I attend to the creatureliness of things. This is not to engage in worship while handling my laboratory equipment. . . .
>
> Naturally the human mind must concentrate on one aspect of reality; when he studies nature, a man must not read his Bible. . . .
>
> Again the claim is not that the believer by being a believer is transformed "into an expert botanist or physicist." To become an expert botanist or physicist one must study botany or physics.[184]

As a competent epistemologist and theologian, however, Van Til simply recognized that all empirical examination has its unavoidable presuppositions and cannot be done in a neutral fashion. Thus, at the end of this last quotation he added: "But to be an intelligent botanist or physicist there should be an *intelligible science* of botany or physics. And no

---

182. *Defense of the Faith*, 258; repeated in *Christian Theory of Knowledge*, 293.
183. *Introduction to Systematic Theology*, 15.
184. *Defense of the Faith*, 279, 284. Van Til was here responding in part to a misrepresentation made of his views by Cecil DeBoer in the *Calvin College Forum* (September 1953), 5.

such intelligible science exists except on a Christian basis."[185] Van Til said explicitly that he did not "disparage the usefulness of arguments for the corroboration of the Scripture" that come from empirical research like archaeology, but he did wish to insist as a philosopher "that such corroboration is not *of independent power.*"[186]

As with the theistic proofs, so also with empirical evidences, Van Til wholeheartedly supported the endeavors, but could not endorse the traditional way in which believers attempted to defend the faith from "the facts." He candidly indicated: "Our aim is rather to make better use of their materials than they have done by placing underneath it an epistemology and metaphysic which make these materials truly fruitful in discussion with non-believers."[187] The traditional method of arguing from evidence does not take into account the presuppositional issues in epistemology and interpretation. "Another form of the weakening of the Christian testimony spoken of is found when men virtually concede that an argument about facts of history, such as archaeology or miracles, between Christians and non-believers can be satisfactorily brought to a conclusion without bringing in the basic presuppositions of the Christian religion."[188]

Traditional evidentialism falsely assumes the intellectual possibility and moral acceptability of neutrality, as well as the intelligibility of autonomous reasoning making examination of "brute (i.e., as yet uninterpreted) facts"; it simply overlooks the crucial significance of the antithesis between believing and unbelieving thought. Van Til was quite aware of the damage that can, on these terms, be easily done to any case made by the apologist. His aim was then to salvage the great apologetical power of the empirical evidences by placing them in a more presuppositionally self-conscious and philosophically adequate context. He said that "when it comes to the master plan of procedure," the presuppositional apologist goes a different way than that of traditional apologetics. "He should present his philosophy of fact with his facts. *He does not need to handle less facts in doing so.* He will handle *the same facts* but he will handle them as they ought to be handled."[189]

Traditional evidentialism does not handle the evidence as it should. It pretends that there are neutral facts or neutral methods

---

185. *Defense of the Faith,* 284 (emphasis added).
186. Introduction to *The Inspiration and Authority of the Bible,* by B. B. Warfield (Philadelphia: Presbyterian and Reformed, 1948), 37 (emphasis added).
187. *Defense of the Faith,* 163.
188. *Introduction to Systematic Theology,* 16.
189. *Defense of the Faith,* 317, 264 (emphasis added).

for examining the facts. Van Til knew that this was naive and mis-leading. "To be 'neutral' is, therefore, to try to be something no human being can be. . . . 'Neutrality' must beg the question."[190] With regard to the traditional method, he noted that "its appeal to 'neutral' reason in apologetics is unintelligible." The "facts" and the "laws" to which men appeal in their argumentation would not be intelligible apart from underlying philosophical presuppositions, and therefore "*every* method, the supposedly neutral one no less than any other, presupposes ei-ther the truth or the falsity of Christian theism."[191] The error of the evi-dentialist can be put another way. He mistakenly believes that there can be an intellectual consideration of the "factuality" of some ob-ject or event apart from the context of the interpretive "system" in which the fact is asserted or denied. Van Til saw the crucial need to repair this far-reaching epistemological error. "No Christian apologist can afford to forget the claim of his system with respect to any particular fact. He must always maintain that the 'fact' under discussion with his op-ponent must be what Scripture says it is, if it is to be intelligible as a fact at all."[192] In short, in every presentation of a factual argument for Chris-tianity, the defender of the faith is implicitly—if not explicitly—challenging the unbeliever with the *entire system* or Christian world-view of which that fact is a part. "Facts" do not stand outside of systems of thought, as though they could help us to choose among them. In any factual argument, whether attention is drawn to it or not, two worldviews are set next to each other for comparison.

An evidentialist apologetic like that of Montgomery's ignores these determinative factors in the debate between believer and unbeliever. He naively refers to "the facts" as brute, uninterpreted, common points of observation, with which worldviews must make their peace. He teaches that "the facts" are powerful enough to stop myth mak-ing, are the "final test of truth," constitute "neutral evidence," and per-mit "objective and factual verification to serve as a court of appeal"; he imagines that "one's view can be judged by the (neutral) facts of 'universal reality' in the public marketplace of ideas." "When world views collide, an appeal to common facts is the only preservative against philosophical solipsism and religious anarchy." He declares that "we must employ inductive procedures to distinguish fact from fiction . . . [and] determine on the basis of the facts themselves which

190. *Christianity and Idealism*, 12.
191. *Defense of the Faith*, 289, 117.
192. Ibid., 135.

interpretation best fits reality." To do this, "the starting-point has to be the common rationality (the inductive and deductive procedures) which all men share."[193]

The inductive, empirical approach to knowing is not philosophically neutral or unproblematic. It does not comport with all views of metaphysics or epistemology. Someone with an uncritical mind-set might confuse the popularity of empirical induction with an absence of distinctive presuppositions, but that notion is (and has been often) discredited by philosophical analysis.[194] All empirical observation and description is unavoidably laden with theory. Van Til put it this way: "Modern scientific description is not the innocent thing that we as Christians all too easily think it is. . . . Description itself is explanation. . . . [E]ven the description of facts in the lowest dimension presupposes a system of metaphysics and epistemology."[195] How is the cognizance of external objects and events to be understood and described? And just how do we metaphysically categorize such objects and events (e.g., as properties, substances, sense data, things in themselves, raw particulars, lowest rational species, etc.)? How are the procedures, norms, and merits of an inductive study of those objects and events of which we have that cognizance to be understood and described? What rational basis is

193. "Once upon an A Priori . . .," 382–91. At one point Montgomery writes: "Our apologetic should be modeled on the Christ who offered objective evidence of his power to forgive sins by healing the paralytic and who convinced unbelieving Thomas that he was God and Lord by the undeniable presence of his resurrected body" (p. 390). But when we are today defending the faith, are we, like Christ, supposed to prove the claims we make by healing people and presenting a resurrected body? Montgomery's incautious statement betrays an underappreciation of the fact that Christian apologists are not in the same position as Christ or the apostles with respect to presenting empirical evidence. Their hearers were presented with miracles, while our hearers are presented with reports of miracles. This important difference has tremendous epistemological implications for the way in which a person defends, or even can defend, the person and claims of Christ. (Montgomery is also wrong to assert that, at least at the time of direct eyewitness encounter with a miracle like Christ's resurrection, the presence of Christ was "undeniable." Montgomery has apparently not given sufficient epistemological consideration to the implications of Matthew 28:17— "but some doubted.")

194. For a list of indications that inductive reasoning does not proceed in a presuppositionless or philosophically neutral fashion, see the discussion of "Unargued Philosophical Baggage" in Bahnsen, "Inductivism, Inerrancy and Presuppositionalism," 296–300. For another summary of the epistemological flaws in the traditional inductivist apologetic, with support from Scripture, see Bahnsen, "Machen, Van Til, and the Apologetical Tradition of the OPC," 272–74.

195. *Common Grace*, 3, 85.

there for the assumption of natural uniformity, which is taken for granted in all inductive reasoning? Regardless of what specific answers are offered in response, they are certainly not based on empirical observation and inductive generalizations! Such answers are philosophical in nature. The same must be said for other controversial presuppositions of an inductive, empirical method of knowing—such as, that the realm of what exists stretches beyond perceivable individuals to include the repetition of kinds of events, unperceived universals such as logical laws and inference, and normative concepts like "normal observer." Evidentialists should not think that philosophically neutral thinking controls their inductive, empirical procedures from beginning to end. Any number of debatable metaphysical assumptions color their methods and criteria, even though they imagine them to be transparent and unbiased. But the make-believe reaches painful proportions when allegedly neutral inductivism is applied to historical study. There are simply no "pure" observational statements (as the critical debunkings of logical positivism have shown). Statements of observation derive their meaning as well as their credibility within a framework or network of background assumptions. These truths have even more critical significance for someone who does not observe events themselves, but reconstructs past events. Historians are not passive observers, but apply particular criteria of credibility, relevance, importance, coherence, and responsibility in examining sources and integrating their results.

Montgomery's supposedly detached, impartial, and philosophically unbiased method of examining "the facts" in order to see which of the conflicting worldviews "fit" is an exercise in wishful thinking, not serious epistemology. By failing to understand what is at stake, he and other evidentialists lose all opportunity to press their apologetical advantage when unbelievers challenge biblical claims on the basis of empirical evidence and inductive reasoning. The apologist should at that point engage the unbeliever in a serious analysis of the presuppositional issues that must be faced by anyone using an empirical, inductive approach to knowing. Van Til wisely observed: "I would not talk endlessly about facts and more facts without ever challenging the nonbeliever's philosophy of fact."[196] At just this juncture in the dialogue, the Christian apologist can use the transcendental argument to demonstrate that the unbeliever's commitment to "the scientific method" is

---

196. *Defense of the Faith,* 258; repeated in *Christian Theory of Knowledge,* 293.

philosophically unintelligible apart from the worldview revealed in Scripture. But Montgomery cannot so argue, since his "neutral" evidentialism is in the same philosophical quandary as the unbeliever's method of reasoning. Not surprisingly, then, he does not want to claim anything more for his arguments than that they show Christianity to be "probably" true.[197]

Van Til said that when unbelievers resist the factual arguments that apologists can and should readily set before them to confirm or defend the Christian position, we must understand that "the battle is not one primarily of this fact or of that fact. The battle is basically with respect to a philosophy of facts. . . . No one can be a scientist in any intelligible way without at the same time having a philosophy of reality as a whole."[198] Evidences are used in transcendental apologetics with the recognition that the intellectual conflict between believers and unbelievers is ultimately a matter of antithetical worldviews. We must show that the unbeliever's worldview, within which he opposes the claims of the faith, precludes not only the facts of Scripture, but also the very intelligibility of any facts about any subject whatsoever. For that reason, Van Til was adamant that the apologist not make the mistake of pretending to be neutral or autonomous in reasoning, but present his factual defense in the right way and in the right light to the unbeliever. "Christianity does not thus need to take shelter under the roof of a scientific method independent of itself. It rather offers itself as a roof to methods that would be scientific."[199] If the inductive, empirical reasoning used by the unbeliever to oppose the faith is to be intelligible in any philosophical sense, he will have to affirm the Christian faith

---

197. Van Til was critical of this move. "If we drop to the level of the merely probable truthfulness of Christian theism, we, to that extent, lower the claims of God upon men" (*Common Grace*, 62; repeated in *Defense of the Faith*, 256). Also: "But even if it be said that Christianity is more probably true than is the non-Christian position this is still to allow that objectively something can be said for the truth of the non-Christian position" (*Defense*, 197). This kind of criticism is often answered by saying that historical facts (especially miraculous ones), just because they are such, cannot be known with any more than a high degree of probability. Such an opinion is contrary to God's inspired word, however. Peter proclaimed this historical event (and miracle): "Let all the house of Israel therefore *know with certainty* that God has made him Lord" by raising Jesus from the dead (Acts 2:24, 36). He did not say that it was highly probable that Christ rose from the dead, but rather that it was "not possible" that death could hold Him (v. 24).

198. *The Protestant Doctrine of Scripture*, In Defense of the Faith, vol. 1 (Philadelphia: Presbyterian and Reformed, 1967), 51.

199. *Christian-Theistic Evidences*, 56.

as his presupposition or worldview! The efforts of unbelievers should be turned against their own unbelief. That is simply the presuppositional way of defending the faith and pressing evidential arguments. Is the evidential power of (say) Christ's resurrection lost when the evidential argument for it is presented to the unbeliever within the context of biblical presuppositions? Not at all. The internal logic of the biblical worldview, in which the resurrection of Christ is an important part, may be pressed upon the non-Christian: given what the Bible teaches, it makes no sense to think that men radically changed their minds (e.g., Paul) or were willing to become martyrs unless Christ rose from the dead (cf. 1 Cor. 15:14, 17); they would not follow cunningly devised fables (2 Peter 1:16), and did not need to do so since the miraculous event they proclaimed "was not done in a corner" (Acts 26:26). Presuppositional apologetics calls for the Christian and the non-Christian to set their worldviews side by side and examine their internal consistency and strength. In such a comparison, the evidential power of Christ's resurrection is easily set forth.[200] Christians should readily say to unbelievers, "Within our worldview, *the evidence shows* that God raised Christ from the dead (and even more amazingly, He did it out of love for sinners like us), but your worldview only makes nonsense out of history and science and reasoning." The choice should be obvious—and it would be, except for the blinding effect of sin.

The monumental mistake of traditional evidentialists is to think that they can grant neutrality and autonomy to the unbeliever, present the resurrection as a brute fact outside the context of biblical presuppositions, and still demonstrate to the non-Christian that the event took place in history. In fact, they have given the unbeliever everything he needs to resist drawing that conclusion. When a supermarket tabloid claims that some weird or miraculous event took place, the unbeliever does not find the publication believable just for that reason—even if its text is well preserved and beyond question. Likewise, the resurrection claims in the Bible—even if the biblical text is early

200. Somebody might wonder, "But if the presuppositions already require that the Bible be true and thus that Christ rose from the dead, how could the evidence be impressive?" Well, after the game-winning shot at the buzzer has become a matter of history, and even though we know the outcome of the game, we are still astounded by that shot and can watch it in awe when we observe the videotape replay of the game. The shot is still impressive, even when we know the context and outcome. And the resurrection of our Lord is far more impressive, even when we approach it within the context of the Bible's presupposed truth.

and reliable—are precisely why the unbeliever finds the book fanciful and unscientific. Why shouldn't he doubt its historical reliability? The traditional apologist appeals to "probability," yet from his own experience the unbeliever knows how extremely improbable a resurrection is. Since the Bible reports such obviously absurd things, it cannot be trusted by a critically minded man. Indeed, how could he accept these documents (however early their date) as reliable reports even of what Jesus said about himself, since we have a mere man claiming divine prerogatives and allegedly predicting his own resurrection? It is just common sense to the autonomous man to believe that the apostles—like so many students are prone to do—did not hear accurately, or misinterpreted what their master had said, or later exaggerated it out of veneration for him. Advocates of the traditional use of evidences have an answer for this: that Christ promised the gift of the Holy Spirit to His followers so that they would recall correctly what He said and meant—an answer that takes for granted that Jesus was God, although this is the very thing the resurrection argument was supposed to prove (circular reasoning!).

Even if the apologist, using autonomous values and patterns of reasoning, does show that the body of Jesus was probably resuscitated, the naturalistic unbeliever need not conclude that Christianity is true, that Jesus is God, or even that God exists—since he need not interpret the event as a miracle at all. The naturalist may, with his presuppositions undisturbed, accept that the body of Jesus came back to life, reasoning that if we had more information, we would be able to understand the "natural factors" that were no doubt involved, however infrequently they occur. At most, we would simply need to broaden our scientific generalities about what takes place in nature. Van Til thus notes: "If we adopt the 'scientific method' [as autonomously interpreted] we must allow that it is quite possible that at some future date all the miracles recorded in the Bible, not excluding the resurrection of Christ, may be explained by natural laws."[201]

The evidentialist might complain, however, that the unbeliever must appreciate how unusual and unique an event like a resurrection must be! To this the unbeliever could simply point out some other statistically infrequent events (e.g., winning the lottery, getting a rare disease) and maintain that Christ's resurrection is not more "miraculous" than these very natural events. The Christian is simply

201. *Christian-Theistic Evidences*, 60 (p. 65 in the syllabus of 1961).

jumping to conclusions from a lack of scientific knowledge of how the resurrection happened—like ancient pagans assumed that the gods were angry when there was thunder. Or, given his open-ended outlook, the would-be autonomous man could respond to the "uniqueness" of Jesus' body resuscitating—as Van Til indicated—by throwing this and other facts "over his back into the bottomless pit of Chance." What would the event tell us? Nothing. "On this basis nature and history would be no more than a series of pointer readings pointing into the blank." In a chance universe where anything can happen, the resurrection is little more than a fine item for Ripley's *Believe It or Not!*[202] The inference, "if Jesus rose from the dead, then he must be God," is quite arbitrary in the eyes of the "neutral" unbeliever; after all, Lazarus is said to have risen from the dead, and Christians do not bow down to him as a god. (And remember, the argument that Jesus predicted his own resurrection begs the question of whether he was God—the very question the resurrection argument was supposed to answer in neutral fashion.) The further inference drawn by the evidentialist apologist—"if Jesus was God, then He always knew and spoke the truth"—is equally prejudicial, for clearly not all of the available conceptions of "God" or the "gods" include the feature of unfailing truth-telling.

We see, now, why Van Til taught so emphatically that evidential arguments could not be presented effectively in the traditional manner, as though the unbeliever could be neutral and had every right to be autonomous in his reasoning. Evidences play an important role in apologetics, but they must be argued in a presuppositional fashion. As Van Til said:

> It is impossible and useless to seek to defend Christianity as an historical religion by a discussion of facts only. We say that Christ rose from the grave. We say further that this resurrection proves his divinity. This is the nerve of the historical argument for Christianity. Yet a pragmatist philosopher . . . will say that this proves nothing more than that something very unusual took place. . . . It is apparent from this that if we would really defend Christianity as an historical religion we must at the same time defend the theism upon which Christianity is based and this involves us in philosophical discussion.[203]

202. *Defense of the Faith*, 336, 337, 334.
203. *Christian Apologetics* (Philadelphia: Westminster Theological Seminary, 1935, 1939), 2; repeated in *Defense of the Faith*, 23–24.

The factual evidences must be presented within the context of the Christian philosophy of life, the worldview revealed in the Bible; there they are properly and authoritatively interpreted.[204] There they make sense, and every competing claim can be reduced to absurdity by showing it destroys the intelligibility of history, science, and reasoning itself.

BUTLER'S METHOD COMPROMISING AND SELF-FRUSTRATING[205]

To be sure, there is a sense in which it must be said that all men have all facts "in common." Saint and sinner alike are face to face with God and the universe of God. But the sinner is like the man with colored glasses on his nose. The Scriptures tell us that the facts speak plainly of God (Rom. 1:20; 2:14, 15). But all is yellow to the jaundiced eye. As a sinner speaks of the facts, he reports them to himself and others as "yellow." There are no exceptions to this. It is the facts as reported to himself by himself, as distorted by his own subjective condition, which he assumes to be *the facts as they really are.*

Failing to keep these things in mind, Butler appealed to the sinner as though there were in his repertoire of "facts" some that he did not see as "yellow," such as the life, death, and resurrection of Christ, or miracles in general. Butler actually placed himself on a common position with his opponents on certain "questions of Fact," i.e., "Did Christ rise from the dead?"

The compromising character of this position is obvious. It is compromising, in the first place, with respect to the *objective clarity* of the evidence for the truth of Christian theism. The psalmist does not say that the heavens *probably* declare the glory of God; they infallibly and clearly do. Probability is not, or at least should not be, the guide of life. Men ought, says Calvin following Paul, to believe in God, for each one is surrounded with a superabundance of evidence with respect to him. The whole universe is lit up by God. Scripture requires men to accept its interpretation of history as true without doubt. Doubt of this is as unreasonable as doubt with respect to the primacy of the light of the sun in relation to the light bulbs in our homes. It is as unreasonable as a child asking whether he has parents and, after looking at the evidence, concluding that he *probably* has!

204. Cf.: "Miracles of the sort the pragmatist can allow for are merely strange events and have therefore lost all their significance as part of the Christian system of truth. . . . The non-Christian scientist and philosopher can allow for the possibility of such facts, and of such facts only as they are free from all alliance with their Christian connotation" (*Introduction to Systematic Theology*, 188).

205. Excerpts from *Reformed Pastor and Modern Thought*, 32–34, 70–71.

But according to Butler, men have done full justice by the evidence if they conclude that God *probably* exists. Worse than that, according to this position, men are assumed to have done full justice by the evidence if they conclude that *a* God exists. But *a* god is a *finite* god, which is *no* god, but an idol. How can they then identify this *probable* God with the God of the Bible on whom all things depend for their existence?

In presupposing a non-Christian philosophy of fact, the Butler type of argument naturally also presupposes a non-Christian principle of coherence, or rationality. The two go hand in hand. The law of non-contradiction employed positively or negatively by man assuming his own ultimacy,[206] is made the standard of what is possible or impossible, both for men and for whatever "gods" may be. But on this basis the Bible cannot speak to man of any God whose revelation and whose very nature is not essentially penetrable to the natural intellect of man.

In the second place, the Butler type of argument is compromising on the *subjective* side. It allows that the natural man has the plenary ability to interpret certain facts correctly even though he wears the colored spectacles of the covenant-breaker. As though covenant-breakers had no axe to grind! As though they were not anxious to avoid seeing the facts for what they really are!

The traditional argument of Butler is, moreover, not only compromising but also self-destructive. Today, more than ever before, men frankly assert that facts are *taken* as much as *given*. Thus they admit that they wear glasses. But these glasses are said to *help* rather than to hinder vision. Modern man assumes that, seeing facts through the glasses of ultimacy, he can really see these facts for what they are. For him it is the orthodox believer who wears the colored glasses of prejudice. Thus the Christian walks in the valley of those who, more than ever before, identify their false *interpretations* about themselves and about the facts, with the facts themselves.

However, the argument of Butler does not challenge men to repentance for their sin of misrepresentation. It virtually grants that they are right. But then, if men are virtually told that they are right in thus identifying their false interpretations of the facts, with the facts themselves, in certain instances, why should such men accept the *Christian* interpretation of other facts? Are not all facts within one universe? If men are virtually told that they are quite right in interpreting certain facts without God, they have every *logical right* to continue their interpretation of all other facts without God.

From the side of the believer in the infallible Word of God, the claim should

---

206. CVT: To hold to the ultimacy of man means to proceed on the basic fundamental supposition that man is the supreme authority in deciding any question. In other words, man is autonomous, rather than dependent.

be made that there are not, because there cannot be, other facts than God-interpreted facts, i.e., facts which are what they are because of their place in the plan of God. In practice, this means that since sin has come into the world, God's interpretation of the facts must come in finished, written form and be comprehensive in character. God continues to reveal himself in the facts of the created world, but the sinner needs to interpret every one of them in the clearer light of Scripture. Every thought on every subject must become obedient to the requirement of God as he speaks in his Word; every thought must be brought into subjection to Christ. The Butler argument fails to make this requirement and thus fatally compromises the claims of Scripture. . . .

Of course we are speaking primarily of systems rather than men. Many Roman Catholics, and especially many Arminians, are much more biblical than are their systems. Therein must all rejoice. But the Reformed Christian must be true to his Lord. He must love sinners with a deep compassion. But he must not love sinners more than he loves Christ. The more truly he loves sinners the more uncompromisingly will he require of them that they must be saved on God's terms, not their own. It is Christ, through his Word in Scripture, who must diagnose their disease even as it is Christ who heals only those who confess that their disease is what the Great Physician says it is.

HISTORICAL APOLOGETICS AND CIRCULAR REASONING[207]

Before proceeding to the development of the scriptural doctrine of inspiration, it may be well to refer briefly at this point to the charge of circular reasoning implied in such a method. It is said that we cannot fairly go first to Scripture to see what it says about inspiration and then say that the Scripture is true because it is inspired.

In order to avoid this charge of circular reasoning, orthodox theology has often offered the following: In the first place, it is proved by ordinary historical evidence that Christ actually arose from the dead and that he performed miracles. This is said to prove his divinity. Secondly, it is noted that this divine person has testified to the Old Testament as the Word of God and that he himself promised the gift of the Holy Spirit who should lead the apostles into the truth and thus be qualified as authors of the New Testament.

Historical apologetics is absolutely necessary and indispensable to point out that Christ arose from the grave, etc. But as long as historical apologetics works on a supposedly neutral basis it defeats its own purpose. For in that case it virtually grants the validity of the metaphysical assumptions of the un-

207. An excerpt from *Introduction to Systematic Theology*, 146–47.

believer. So in this case, a pragmatist may accept the resurrection of Christ as a fact without accepting the conclusion that Christ is the Son of God. And on his assumptions he is not illogical in doing so. On the contrary, if his basic metaphysical assumption to the effect that all reality is subject to chance is right, he is only consistent if he refuses to conclude from the fact of Christ's resurrection that he is divine in the orthodox sense of the term. Now, though he is wrong in his metaphysical assumption, and though, rightly interpreted, the resurrection of Christ assuredly proves the divinity of Christ, we must attack him in his philosophy of fact, as well as on the question of the actuality of the facts themselves. For on his own metaphysical assumptions the resurrection of Christ would not prove his divinity at all.

In addition to showing that Christ actually arose from the grave and that the facts recorded in the Scripture are as they are recorded as being, insofar as this can be ascertained by historical research, we must show that the philosophy of fact as held to by Christian theism is the only philosophy that can account for the facts. And these two things must be done in conjunction with one another. Historical apologetics becomes genuinely fruitful only if it is conjoined with philosophical apologetics. And the two together will have to begin with Scripture, and argue that unless what Scripture says about itself and all things else of which it speaks is true, nothing is true. Unless God as an absolutely self-conscious person exists, no facts have any meaning. This holds not only for the resurrection of Christ, but for any other fact as well.

If this is done, it will be seen that redemption must have come into the world as soon as sin came into the world, because the world, to exist at all, must exist as a theistic world. This redemptive process could originate with no one but God. Accordingly only God himself can testify to the revelation that he has given of himself. Special revelation must, in the nature of the case, be self-testified. Christ did, to be sure, appeal from himself to the testimony of John the Baptist, etc., but, in the last analysis, this was not an appeal to someone else, because John the Baptist and all other prophets were nothing but the emissaries of Christ. With these things in mind, we need not apologize for going to Scripture in order to see what it says about inspiration, in order then to say that the Scriptures are true because they are inspired. The existence of God is the presupposition of all human predication and the idea of biblical self-testimony is involved in this presupposition.

The only alternative to "circular reasoning" as engaged in by Christians, no matter on what point they speak, is that of reasoning on the basis of isolated facts and isolated minds, with the result that there is no possibility of reasoning at all. Unless as sinners we have an absolutely inspired Bible, we have no absolute God interpreting reality for us, and unless we have an absolute God interpreting reality for us, there is no true interpretation at all.

PROBLEMS WITH THE TRADITIONAL RESURRECTION ARGUMENT [208]

The Arminian will speak to the natural man about the historical *fact* of revelation as recorded in Scripture. He will stress the fact that Christianity is a historical religion. To that he will add that therefore it is simply a matter of evidence whether or not, say, the resurrection of Christ is a fact. On this question, he will insist, anybody who is able to use the canons of historical study is as good a judge as any other. The proof for the resurrection is then said to be just the sort of proof that men demand everywhere in questions of history.

But this argument about the facts of supernatural revelation again forgets that the natural man's entire attitude with respect to the facts that are presented to him will naturally be controlled by his notions of possibility and probability as already discussed. He may therefore grant that a man named Jesus of Nazareth arose from the dead. He need not hesitate, on his principles, to accept the *fact* of the resurrection at all. But for him that fact is a different sort of fact from what it is for the Christian. It is not the same fact at all. It is in vain to speak about the fact without speaking of the meaning of the fact. For the factness of the fact is to any mind that deals with it that which he takes it to mean. It is his meaning that is virtually the fact to him. And it is impossible even to present the fact for what it really is, namely, that which it is according to its interpretation as given in Scripture, to the natural man, if one does not challenge his notions of possibility and probability that underlie his views of the facts of history. To talk about presenting to him the fact of the resurrection without presenting its meaning is to talk about an abstraction. The resurrection either *is* what the Christian says it is, or it is not. If it *is*, then it is as such that it actually appears in history.

Yet the Arminian position is committed to the necessity of presenting the facts of Christianity as being something other than he himself as a Christian knows they are. He knows that it is the Son of God who died in his human nature and rose again from the dead. But the fact of the resurrection about

208. Excerpts from *Defense of the Faith*, 161–62, 262–64.

which he speaks to unbelievers is some nondescript something or other about which believers and non-believers are supposed to be able to agree. . . .

All this is bound to lead to self-frustration on the part of the traditional apologist. Let us watch him for a moment. Think of him first as an inductivist. As such he will engage in "historical apologetics" and in the study of archaeology. In general he will deal with the "facts" of the universe in order to prove the existence of God. He cannot on his position challenge the assumption of the man he is trying to win. That man is ready for him. Think of the traditional apologist as throwing facts to his non-Christian friend as he might throw a ball. His friend receives each fact as he might a ball and throws it behind him in a bottomless pit. The apologist is exceedingly industrious. He shows the unbelieving friend all the evidence for theism. He shows all the evidence for Christianity, for instance, for the virgin birth and the resurrection of Christ. Let us think of his friend as absolutely tireless and increasingly polite. He will then receive all these facts and toss them behind him in the bottomless pit of pure possibility. "Is it not wonderful," he will say, "what strange things do happen in Reality. You seem to be a collector of oddities. As for myself I am more interested in the things that happen regularly. But I shall certainly try hard to explain the facts you mention in accord with the laws that I have found working so far. Perhaps we should say that laws are merely statistical averages and that nothing can therefore be said about any particular event ahead of its appearance. Perhaps there are very unusual things in reality. But what does this prove for the truth of your view?"

You see that the unbeliever who does not work on the presupposition of creation and providence is perfectly consistent with himself when he sees nothing to challenge his unbelief even in the fact of the resurrection of Christ. He may be surprised for a moment as a child that grows up is surprised at the strange things of life but then when he has grown up he realizes that "such is life." Sad to say the traditional Christian apologist has not even asked his unbelieving friend to see the facts for what they really are. He has not presented the facts at all. That is, he has not presented the facts as they are according to the Christian way of looking at them and the Christian way of looking at them is the true way of looking at them. Every fact in the universe is what it is by virtue of the place that it has in the plan of God. Man cannot comprehensively know that plan. But he does know that there is such a plan. He must therefore present the facts of theism and of Christianity, of Christian theism, as proving Christian theism because they are intelligible as facts in terms of it and in terms of it alone.

REPLY TO PINNOCK'S EVIDENTIALIST CRITICISM[209]

Dear Dr. Pinnock:

I greatly appreciate your frankness in expressing your opposition to my views. You are quite right in saying of me, "he believes he can begin with God and Christianity without first consulting objective reality." This is the heart of the matter. If I were to attempt to know what "objective reality" was, apart from the all-embracive message of God as Christ speaking in Scripture, I would deny, it seems to me, all that it means to be a "Christian"! I would not pick up a lantern to help me find the sun, to see whether it exists. The whole notion of "light" is based upon our intimate acquaintance with the sun, day after day. Organically speaking, if the sun did not exist I could not be alive to look for it (given God's world as it is). Just so I use reason (induction, deduction, forms of implication): in full recognition that I discover truth by means of them because each individually, and all collectively, operate in *God's* world and therefore as part of the realization of his plan. To attempt to understand such abilities of man in using reason apart from what God has revealed about his plan would be, for the Christian, "unscientific."

I agree with you that Scripture should speak for itself. In fact, I want it to tell us what God is, what the world is, and what we as men are, not *after* but *before* we start speaking of metaphysics, epistemology, and ethics. To think that I conceive of the "Christian faith" as an "abstract metaphysical system supported by presuppositionalism" is to misunderstand completely the whole thrust of Reformed thinking. I observe, rather, that as Christians we must look at the world as Christ himself looked at it and, in so far as any man does not, he views it falsely. Consequently the attempt to find God in the world without looking through the eyes of Christ is fruitless, not because the world does not reveal God (it continually shouts of the existence of God to men), but because men need new eyes!

When I beseech men to forsake their unbelief and accept the Christ of Scripture as God over all and therefore as their Savior, I ask them to forsake the obviously sinking raft of experience as it is assumed to be by would-be autonomous man. David Hume has shown, I think, that Bishop Butler's argument to the effect that Christianity is more probably true than other views is based on a view of the world in which Chance is ultimate. Clearly any view of probability which is based on the ultimacy of Chance cannot possibly contact reality in any way, for it can say nothing about the probability of any par-

---

209. This excerpt is Van Til's response (on pp. 426–27) to the critical essay "The Philosophy of Christian Evidences," written by Clark Pinnock for *Jerusalem and Athens*, ed. Geehan, 420–25.

ticular event, for all events proceed equally from the belly of Chance. Therefore a "probable" argument for any particular event is of no more value than an improbable one, for both arguments are meaningless in terms of that one "event." A probable argument is not better than an improbable one if the very idea of probability is without meaning.

Only on the biblical basis which says that man is made in the image of God and that the world in all its facts manifests the presence of God are science and philosophy intelligible. You say that "Van Til is right to contend that the world is dependable and intelligible because God is its Creator." I take it you understand me to mean the triune God of the Bible. But then you continue, "His existence is basic to the entire rational structure of reality. However, it is the *fact* of his existence, not the awareness or conscious *recognition* of it by man, that makes this so." *Well and good, but it is this "awareness and conscious recognition" that apologetics is all about!*[210] We as Christians are seeking to have men recognize not only the existence of God but, as you so rightly insist, what he has done and is doing in the world. Those whom you are seeking to win to salvation in Christ have *all the facts in common* with you. It is the same God and the same world created and redeemed by Christ which confronts both you and them. If men do not accept what God says about himself and about the world, they will remain under the wrath of God. In presenting *what* God says to them you are calling them to repentance. This is certainly true, is it not? God in Christ says it is true. Paul said, "Therefore, my beloved brethren, be ye steadfast and unmoveable, always abounding in the work of the Lord, forasmuch as ye know that your labor is not in vain in the Lord." To talk about the existence of God, the *fact* of God's existence, without bringing in the whole of what God in Christ through the Holy Spirit has done and is doing for men, and to claim that this barren *fact* is the common ground between believers and unbelievers, is not only an abstraction, but complete distortion. To tell someone *that* God exists means nothing unless you tell him who God is and what he does.

But I must leave this discussion now, although I have appreciated having the opportunity again of clarifying my opposition to the Butler-Arminian form of apologetics. Your essay, of course, contains many more points I might wish to discuss, but I think many of them have been answered in the essay by Prof. Stoker. In addition, I hope "My Credo" corrected what I believe to be several total misunderstandings on your part of my position.

---

210. Emphasis added. The criticism expressed here by Pinnock is so often voiced, that Van Til's pointed reply deserves to be highlighted. Cf.: "It is the fact of God's existence, not the knowledge of it, which makes rational structure, whether in argument or in reality, possible" (Stuart C. Hackett, *The Resurrection of Theism* [Chicago: Moody Press, 1957], 157).

REPLY TO MONTGOMERY'S INDUCTIVIST CRITICISM[211]

Dear Dr. Montgomery:

You bring some imaginary constructions into your article. This is delightful. These are calculated to make the unwary reader think that there is a great gulf fixed between us. Yet if one of your neo-orthodox Lutheran friends and one of my neo-orthodox Reformed friends should meet they would point out to each other the obvious fact that theologically our differences are not too basic. They would regard your article and my response to it as another bit of in-fighting between hopelessly orthodox Christians. Here is a young man still believing in the God, the Christ, and the Bible of Luther attacking an old man who believes in the God, the Christ, and the Bible of Calvin. But what difference does it make whether one believes in the God of Luther or in the God of Calvin? Surely if Van Til and Montgomery would only read Kant they would realize that, in the nature of the case, no man *can* have any knowledge of a God such as that in which either Luther or Calvin believed. If these men would only read post-Kantian theology, especially that of Karl Barth, they would realize that the story of man's creation, his fall into sin, and his redemption from sin through Christ the Son of God and Son of man, as Luther and Calvin believed it, *cannot* be true!

Kant has shown us the significance of the principle of true *inwardness*. Socrates believed in this principle and therefore told Euthyphro that he, Socrates, for all his ignorance, must know what the essence of holiness is, regardless of what gods or men say about it. Following in the footsteps of Socrates, Kant has shown us that on the principle of free human personality we cannot know anything about an "absolute God" and that therefore such an unknowable God cannot be manifest in nature and in history.

Carrying through the principle of *inwardness* of Socrates and of Kant a man like Robert Collingwood, for instance, has shown that when Jesus of Nazareth says that he is one with the Father and that he has come into the world to save men from their sins in the way that Luther and Calvin believed he did, we cannot take this at face value. If a historian took the statements of Jesus about himself at face value, he would disqualify himself as a historian. A true conception of man's inward self-sufficiency implies an inward teleology of history. Thus for the self-respecting historian "the facts of history are present facts. The historical past is the world of ideas which the present evidence creates in the present. In historical inference we do not move from our present

211. This excerpt consists of selections from Van Til's response (on pp. 392–403) to the critical essay "Once upon an A Priori . . .," written by John W. Montgomery for *Jerusalem and Athens.*, ed. Geehan, 380–92.

world to a past world; the movement in experience is always a movement within a present world of ideas. The paradoxical result is that the historical past is not past at all; it is present. It is not a past surviving into the present; it must *be* the present. But it is not the present as such, the merely contemporary. It is present; because all experience whatever is present; but not merely present."[212]

How wonderfully men like Karl Barth and Rudolph Bultmann have learned and applied this Socratic-Kantian principle of *inwardness* to the biblical story. Thus, for instance, Barth has, he says, *actualized* the incarnation. All the externalism and dualism which such men as Luther and Calvin foisted upon the Christian story has been cut off as so much proud flesh. Moreover, what is true with respect to Christ is also true with respect to the Bible. The theology of Luther and Calvin was hidebound to the old pre-Kantian metaphysics and therefore to the old pre-Kantian epistemology. That makes it unbelievable. . . .

How thrilling, too, is the realization that this modern *Umdeutung* of theology is in accord with the principles of all the major schools of modern philosophy. Where do you find any existing or recent school of philosophy that is not based upon the principle of self-sufficient inwardness of Kant? Do you know any school of modern philosophy that allows for the possibility of the truth of the Christian story as Luther and Calvin believed in it? I know not one.

The moral of what I have said so far, Dr. Montgomery, is that the difference of method of apologetics between you and me will appear to modern theologians like the oppositions between the Lilliputian rope-dancers of Dean Swift. Man-mountain was greatly diverted by these rope-dancers. They "performed upon a slender white thread, extended about two feet, and twelve inches from the ground." "These diversions are often attended with fatal accidents, whereof great numbers are on record."

Of course, I must make a qualification here. In the eyes of modern, post-Kantian theologians and philosophers an argument between us appears to them not merely as being superb folly caused by invincible ignorance but also as stubborn opposition to the advancement in intellectual and moral enlightenment of the human race.

Now both of us believe with Luther and Calvin that there is no other name given under heaven by which men must be saved than the name of Jesus. Both of us believe with Luther and Calvin that all men are creatures made in the image of God, and that because of their sin against the law of love of God they are subject to the wrath of God. Both of us believe, together with Luther and Calvin, that Christ Jesus, the Son of God and Son of man, came

---

212. R. G. Collingwood, *The Idea of History* (New York: Oxford University Press, 1946), 154.

to die on the cross to bear the penalty due to us for our sin. Both of us believe that as we died to sin with Christ in his death so we rose with him from
the tomb for our justification. Both of us believe that though the natural man
receives not the things of God because they are Spirit-discerned, we have the
testimony of the Spirit witnessing to our hearts that we are the children of
God and joint-heirs with Christ of eternal life.

Our common concern is, therefore, to tell this story to men who as creatures made in the image of God thus know God (*gnontes ton theon*) but who,
because of their fall into sin, seek to repress the truth about themselves and
the world. The most effective means ever invented by men to date by which
to make themselves believe that they are not creatures of God and are not
sinners against God is the modern process philosophy and theology of which
I have just spoken. It is therefore our task as Christian apologists to seek to
persuade men that the Christian story as told anew and afresh by Luther and
Calvin in their day is true and must be accepted by men as true today if they
would escape the wrath of God to come.

Neither you nor I have accepted the Christian story as being what Luther
and Calvin believed it to be by starting from the principle of human autonomy, and the idea of pure universal cosmic contingency implied in it, as our
absolute standard of truth. Those who have, as you and I have, accepted the
theology of Luther and Calvin have accepted it because with them we have
learned to regard the self-attesting Christ speaking in Scripture as our absolute
standard of truth. Accepting Christ as the Way, the Truth, and the Life implies swearing off allegiance to ourselves, to man as autonomous and as ethically capable of doing what pleases God. Accepting Christ means accepting
him as the one from whom, through whom, and to whom are all things. Behold all things are become new! . . .

When the Calvinists want, none-the-less [according to Montgomery], to
speak of "objective" truth they have to appeal to "the inward work of the
Holy Spirit." Thus their grandiose, presuppositionalist, seemingly deductive
systems reduce to *Schwärmerei*. "The Spirit serves as a *deus ex machina* to
resist the overwhelming pull toward solipsism. But Scripture cautions us to 'test
the spirits.' How? Not by internal consistency (the devil is an exceedingly coherent logician, as are all great liars), but by an empirical comparison of doctrine with the objective, historically given Scriptures. Thus we are brought back
again to the absolute necessity of an objective historiography, for without it
we can establish no scriptural testing-stone."[213] . . .

213. CVT: *Ibid.*, p. 178. Van Til is citing Montgomery's book, *Where Is History Going?*
(Grand Rapids: Zondervan, 1969).

Allow me now first to take up your analysis of the supposedly speculative, deductive, aprioristic system of Calvinism and then turn to your Luther-Butler-analytic method of apologetic. . . .

If you really believe that Calvinists base their thinking on such a *speculative* principle, then you might well have said what Pieper says. That would have saved you the trouble of setting my supposed Christian apriorism over against some form of non-Christian apriorism, each trying to shout louder than the other that his brand of apriorism is right and the other's brand of apriorism is wrong without ever appealing to facts. There would then be only one, namely a non-Christian apriorism, and its boast about itself would then be a shout by a non-entity in the vacuum of pure contingency.

But, after all, you are not (as I am not!) interested in *a priori* deductive systems. I have argued on a number of occasions against various people to the effect that the biblical "system of truth" is based upon the exegesis of the authoritatively given truth content of Scripture. When exegesis seems to lead into so-called "antinomies" such as the relation of the all-controlling sovereignty of God to the freedom or responsibility of man, I simply admit that I cannot logically penetrate the situation. The Bible teaches God's sovereign electing grace. It also teaches the universal offer of the gospel. I cannot logically comprehend the relation between these two, but this fact does not lead me to a denial of either one of them. The "system" of Scripture which I develop takes both elements as "limiting concepts" of one another. . . .

Extreme Calvinists think they can show that the teachings of the Bible can be related to one another in a logically penetrable system. When they construct their logical system they virtually destroy the significance of historical factuality and with it the significance of the Christian story. Arminians think they can show that the teachings of the Bible can be related to one another in the way inductivist philosophers like John Locke and others relate the facts that spring from the womb of chance to one another. When these men construct their inductive systems, believing that all facts "speak for themselves," they build an island of ice floating on a bottomless, shoreless cauldron of chance.

In order to have their non-Christian friends meet their God and the Christ of the Bible my Arminian friends, following Butler, insist that the meeting take place on this island.[214] Jesus, too, goes afloat on this island. On deck he meets the other tourists of the island, among them one representative of each of the post-Kantian "schools" of science, of philosophy, and of theology. The

---

214. To illustrate the problem with Montgomery's approach to defending the faith, Van Til at this point launches into his own imaginary story, which points out the tension between being an evangelical Lutheran, on the one hand, and an inductivist in apologetical method, on the other.

representative of the analytical school of philosophy always walks arm in arm with the representative of the God-is-dead school of theology.

There is harmony everywhere on this island. Everybody agrees that the everlasting arms of pure contingency are underneath. Everybody is present at the evening service of religion. Says the "Calvinist" song-leader for the evening: "Tonight we praise the God of Anaximander; the name we give him is *Apeiron*.[215] Tomorrow night we worship the God of Socrates; the God of pure *Inwardness* we call him. Next Friday evening we shall worship the God of Jesus, whom we are glad to welcome in our midst. Jesus himself will lead the singing of his favorite hymn: 'O Immanuel, Immanuel, how blest thy Vision Glorious.' Special thanks for arranging our evening services are due to our friends here—I forget their names—great positivist-analyst philosophers. By means of their verification principle they make certain that the gods we worship are indeterminate. How else could we all serve the same God? How else could we all have true *togetherness?* How else could we with Plato say that the *Good* is above all and in us all. How else could we rejoice in the fact that *Good* is inherently diffuse. How else could we apply the maxim of our friend Jesus that the Father's love is *unconditional?*[216] . . .

"Before you say anything, Mr. Marty, let me [Martin Luther] go on: 'From which it follows unalterably, that all things which we do, although they may appear to us to be done mutably and contingently, and even may be done thus contingently by us, are yet, in reality, done necessarily and immutably, with respect to the will of God.'[217] 'This asserted truth, therefore, stands and remains invincible—that all things take place according to the immutable will

---

215. The joke may be a bit too subtle if one is not a student of the history of philosophy. The ancient Milesian philosopher Anaximander reasoned that whatever the underlying stuff is that constitutes and unites all reality, it must be without distinguishing characteristics (*apeiron:* "without a boundary, boundless, indefinite"); otherwise, something else with a definite character would need to be the cause of the opposite characteristic (e.g., water would be expected to account for nonwatery things, as in Thales), which is contrary to reason. Van Til's barb is that the "god" of modern philosophy must be completely indeterminate (formal, contentless), if he (or she or it) is going to be acceptable to all men in their ecumenical worship.

216. At this point Van Til's imaginary story turns to a conversation between two Lutherans (like Montgomery): a modern unorthodox one, Martin Marty, and Martin Luther himself. Luther reminds Marty of what he wrote against Erasmus in *The Bondage of the Will* (trans. H. Cole, corr. H. Atherton [1823; reprint, Grand Rapids: Eerdmans, 1933), 38: "This, therefore, is also essentially necessary and wholesome for Christians to know: that God foreknows nothing by contingency, but that he foresees, purposes, and does all things according to his immutable, eternal, and infallible will."

217. CVT: *Ibid.*, pp. 39–40.

of God! Which they call the necessity of consequence. Nor is there any obscurity or ambiguity. In Isaiah he saith, "My counsel shall stand, and my will shall be done" (Isa. XLVI.10).'[218]

"You see, Mr. Marty, I derived my entire position from Scripture. I told 'Madame Reason,' as I called her, how 'absurdly she tacks her conclusions, based on pure speculation, to the Scriptures.'[219] Scripture 'describes man corrupt and captive.'[220] 'It is, therefore, a settled determination with me, not to argue upon the authority of any teacher whatsoever, but upon that of Scripture alone.'[221] I don't even listen to 'Madame Reason' when she wants to apologize for Scripture teaching. Madame Reason softens the biblical teaching on the electing grace of God. I do no such thing for 'if God be thus robbed of his power and wisdom to elect, what will there be remaining but that idol Fortune, under the name of which all things take place at random! Nay, we shall at length come to this: that men may be saved and damned without God's knowing anything at all about it; as not having determined by certain election who should be saved and who should be damned; but having set before all men in general his hardening goodness and long-suffering, and his mercy showing correction and punishment, and left them to choose for themselves whether they would be saved or damned; while he, in the meantime, should be gone, as Homer says, to an Ethiopian feast!' "[222]

"Well, I see," said Mr. Marty, "you are quite right, Dr. Luther. I am still in name a Lutheran, but my God is not your God, my man is not your man, and my Christ is not your Christ. I can see very well that from your purely *a priori,* deductive, authoritarian, absolutistic, deterministic, and rationalistic point of view, you cannot agree with me on anything. I admit too that I presuppose my view of man as free or autonomous, and I interpret every fact in the universe in terms of a purely contingent principle of individuation as correlative to a purely abstract legislative principle of continuity. You are right in saying that on our view God would know nothing about a process of universal electing grace going on in this world. All of this goes on in terms of the overflowing goodness of the principle of chance. We assume that our island floats on an underlying gulf stream of utter goodness. . . .

"This is, I agree with you, the only alternative to your view of the triune God of Scripture and his creative-redemptive work in the world. But everybody agrees today in saying first that nobody knows what is back of us, un-

218. CVT: *Ibid.,* p. 42.
219. CVT: *Ibid.,* p. 145.
220. CVT: *Ibid.,* p. 147.
221. CVT: *Ibid.,* p. 210.
222. CVT: *Ibid.,* p. 217.

derneath us and before us; second, that your position is wrong and that there-fore ours must be right.

"But tell me, Dr. Luther, now that we are frank with one another, tell me, what do you think of the position of our fellow-Lutheran, Dr. Montgomery? I think he is really on your side. He even holds a view of Scripture that is, it seems to me, virtually identical with yours. Yet he also seems to be on my side. I heard him sing lustily, *Ein' feste Burg ist unser Gott,* yet joins us in a method of inductivism that presupposes a purely contingent universe. What do you think?"

"Well, Mr. Marty, as you say, you and I stand on opposite ground. You con-struct a God out of the only materials you have in order to attack my God. Your God resembles the little girl that must sit on her daddy's lap in order to be able to slap her daddy in the face. Your God presupposes not merely the existence but the all-controlling activity in history of my God in order to act at all.

"Well, then, as to our common friend Montgomery? I not only think, but I am certain he is on my side. I heard him singing *Ein' feste Burg* too. How-ever, he seems to think that he can at the same time also be on your side. He does not seem to realize that his inductive method, as he uses it in common with the non-Christian analytic-positivists, implies, as it is implied by, a meta-physics of pure chance. I hope he won't continue to try straddling the fence. Don't you think I may, as an old man, call upon him to forsake a position in which men may be saved or damned 'without God's knowing anything at all about it'? As it is he looks like one of the Lilliputian rope-dancers, divided into two parts, each part rushing into the other seeking to destroy it."

8.5 Van Til's Critics

Given the length of Van Til's career as a teacher and writer in apolo-getics, one might expect that he would have faced his share of criti-cism from adherents of contrary approaches to defending the faith. And, sure enough, we have seen throughout this book (especially the relevant footnotes) that this was in fact the case. For over a quarter of a century (1928–55), Van Til taught apologetics to his seminary stu-dents and distributed a series of classroom syllabi on the subject, but it was not until 1955 that he finally published a book on the subject: *The Defense of the Faith.*[223] One of the main reasons for the book, it turns

223. This was not Van Til's first published book. He had already published *The New Modernism* (Philadelphia: Presbyterian and Reformed, 1946) and *Common Grace* (1947). The first addressed the theological defections in the "crisis theology" of Barth and Brunner, while the second also dealt with a theological controversy

out, was to answer the criticism that his syllabi and views had generated. Van Til said in his preface:

> The present writer has from time to time prepared syllabi for his classes in Christian Apologetics. A number of "outsiders" have taken an interest in these syllabi. Some have used them for classroom teaching; others have subjected them to critical analysis.
>
> The present volume seeks to be of service to both types of readers. In the first place it seeks to set forth in positive fashion what seems to the writer to be the Biblical method of defending the Christian faith. . . .
>
> In the second place this work deals with contemporary objections which have been made against the writer's views of apologetics.

Van Til indicated that answering critics was not the primary purpose of his book, but we can be happy for the impetus given by these critics, for without them Van Til might not have been motivated to organize his syllabi in book format (at least for some time). We can also be happy for the work of those critics because they forced Van Til to clarify his position and make it more accessible and pertinent to the practical work of pastors in particular.

On the other hand, there is also plenty of reason not to rejoice over the criticisms directed at Van Til (both before and after 1955). In the first place, these criticisms usually contained easily avoided misunderstandings and even manifested ill will (bordering on party spirit). In so many cases, the critics simply did not know what they were talking about, often giving evidence of not having read very far (especially missing the crucial context of Van Til's first syllabus, "The Metaphysics of Apologetics" [1932]),[224] and often having a poor grasp of the history of philosophy and its key issues (particularly the nature and significance of transcendental analysis).[225] In the second place, even

---

in Reformed circles. Both of these books had implications for apologetics (especially *Common Grace*), but the first book to take it up directly was *The Defense of the Faith*.

224. This is now available under the title *A Survey of Christian Epistemology*. Many of the central criticisms and basic misconstructions of Van Til's position that appeared later were anticipated and persuasively dealt with by Van Til in this syllabus written at the outset of his career.

225. When I was a graduate student in philosophy, an accomplished professor (whose heart was committed to the evangelical message) commented to me that the scholarship of evangelicals in the past generation who had written about philosophy was deplorable. Christians have given the world ample opportunity to

when misreadings are set aside, the particular criticisms that have been directed at Van Til's presuppositionalism have not displayed either cogent reasoning or careful use of Scripture—and have ended up in the dismaying position of rationalizing the attempt to be neutral or autonomous when it comes to thinking about God or His word. In the third place, the level of rhetoric and exaggeration exhibited in mutual criticism by the "key players" among Christian apologists has been too high on all sides, especially considering how desperately the world needs the gospel's truth. Being cut off from one another has weakened our witness and wasted our resources.

We do not have enough space to examine in detail all of the critics of presuppositional apologetics, but we will at least offer an overview of the field. Most of what this book has to say in reply to the critics can be found scattered throughout the various chapters (particularly in footnotes).[226] The critics can be divided into four general groups.

1. The first set of critics can be grouped together as early Dutch dissenters, like William Masselink, James Daane, and contributors to the *Calvin College Forum* (the De Boers, Orlebeke, Van Halsema). On the one hand, they hammered Van Til for teaching an "absolute antithesis" between Christian thinking and that of the world; on the other hand, they criticized him for compromising with worldly philosophy by substituting for Christianity the outlooks of Hegelian rationalism, idealism, and (or?) modern existentialism! Van Til could reply with some levity:

> Note how completely opposed to one another these charges appear to be. On the one hand the essential structure of my thought is said to be that of total unbelief. On the other hand I am said to classify Aristotle with the devil. . . . On the one hand, I am said to be more sure of idealist logic than of Christianity, and on the other hand I am said to hold that Christians and non-Christians do not even think according to the same laws of thought![227]

Having taken note that his hostile critics nevertheless make numerous "concessions,"[228] Van Til indicated that in the first part of *The De-*

---

disdain our dabblings; our sad level of misrepresentation even of one another provides further reason to disrespect our scholarship.

226. Check the index for particular names: e.g., Daane, Masselink, Clark, Buswell, Carnell, Dooyeweerd, Montgomery, Pinnock, Lewis, Sproul, Frame.
227. *Defense of the Faith*, 7, 9.
228. Ibid., 10–19.

fense of the Faith "I shall deal with the general structure of my thought. I shall attempt to show that it is the exact opposite of what my critics think it to be." Van Til maintained that his apologetical work was simply the philosophical expression of "generic or historic Calvinism." On the one hand, this meant that he had to boldly propound that "the Christian view of life is true and all other views are false." On the other hand, it meant that he believed that "even those who worship and serve the creature more than the Creator are not 'finished products' in this world. They can and therefore do make their positive contribution to the realization of the cultural mandate given to Adam."[229] In assessing the presuppositions and perspective of his Dutch critics, Van Til offered this final summary of his critique:

> In every instance, though with varying degrees, it is the autonomous man that peeps through these criticisms. Knowingly or unknowingly, these men are unwilling to make their stand on the principle of the self-identification of God in the Scriptures. They seek to satisfy the illegitimate demands of the natural man who sets himself up as his own ultimate interpreter. I do not rejoice in this. I do not report it as a victory; God forbid.[230]

Specific replies and analyses are spread throughout the second part of *The Defense of the Faith*.[231]

2. A second group of Van Til's early critics were philosophical Presbyterians: J. Oliver Buswell, Jr., and Gordon H. Clark. Both of these men had at one time been in the Orthodox Presbyterian Church with Van Til. Both men had taught philosophy (overlapping at Wheaton College from 1936 to 1940) and published in the field. But the differences between Buswell and Clark in the area of epistemology were probably more significant for the present purpose than such outward

---

229. Ibid., 19–20.
230. Ibid., 423.
231. Unfortunately, however, one needs a first edition to examine them adequately. The index should be consulted. James Daane had already published a critique of Van Til's doctrine of common grace ("too static," too deterministic), entitled *A Theology of Grace* (Grand Rapids: Eerdmans, 1954). In addition to Van Til's replies to Daane in *The Defense of the Faith* (especially chaps. 9 and 14 in the first edition), one should consult Van Til's *The Theology of James Daane* (Philadelphia: Presbyterian and Reformed, 1959). For more of Van Til's response to William Masselink beyond *The Defense of the Faith*, see his "Letter on Common Grace" in *Common Grace and the Gospel*, app. 2 in *An Introduction to Systematic Theology* (1966 and subsequent editions), and articles in *The Banner* 95 (Aug. 5, 1960) and 96 (Jan. 13, 1961). Also see chap. 6.2–3 above.

similarities. Buswell endorsed a kind of naive empiricism (and a weakened view of predestination), in terms of which he defended the theistic proofs of Thomas Aquinas (when "more inductively formulated").[232] Clark, on the other hand, promoted in the earlier part of his career a kind of epistemological rationalism (with a rather wooden view of predestination) and sharply reproached the Thomistic proofs for their logical defects. From both standpoints, Van Til's apologetic and theology are quite unacceptable since, as we have seen, his presuppositional approach sides with neither rationalism nor empiricism as schools of thought, while endorsing both rational and empirical means of knowing. Van Til was highly critical of the Thomistic approach to proving God's existence, while still holding that there is an objectively valid proof of it. From Van Til's vantage point, if one does not begin with the transcendental presupposition of the Christian worldview (where God is self-identifying and man must think His thoughts after Him), then the pure contingency of Buswell and the abstract logic of Clark both require each other, while nevertheless canceling each other out.

It is difficult to take Buswell's criticisms seriously, since he simply did not understand Van Til. In a review article entitled "The Fountainhead of Presuppositionalism,"[233] Buswell declared Van Til simultaneously a Platonic realist, an advocate of Hegelian pantheistic idealism, in agreement with Aristotle and Spinoza that history is an illusion, someone who utilizes the pagan idol of "analogy" as taught by Aquinas, and an enthusiast for Barthian paradox in theology! Buswell portrayed Van Til as denying the reality of creation, disbelieving that Adam was a historical individual, denying man's dependence upon God, and making God out to be a voluntarist. Buswell maintained that Van Til rejected the law of contradiction in logic, and charged that Van Til denied any common ground of reasoning or knowledge between the believer and the unbeliever. In a review of *The Defense of the Faith*, Buswell wrote that for Van Til "the unbeliever has no genuine, true and valid knowledge . . . [and is] systematically and totally in error."[234] Anybody who would read Van Til's writings for himself would have no difficulty dismissing such an egregious miscon-

232. Cf. Buswell, *A Christian View of Being and Knowing* (Grand Rapids: Zondervan, 1960), esp. pp. 168–73; *A Systematic Theology of the Christian Religion*, 2 vols. (Grand Rapids: Zondervan, 1962–63).
233. *The Bible Today* 42, no. 2 (November 1948): 41–64.
234. In *Eternity* 9, no. 5 (May 1958): 40.

struing of what Van Til taught, but the problem then (as now) was that so few students would take the time to "go to the sources."[235] In an endeavor to set the record straight, Van Til produced a very readable and persuasive digest of his apologetic for the reading public.[236] As just one indication of the disparity between their approaches, as well as a linguistic key to their miscommunication, consider their different understandings of the word *presupposition*. Buswell once wrote that "we take our presupposition as a conclusion arrived at on the basis of what we consider good and sufficient reasons."[237] Buswell meant that we start out ("pre-") with a supposition (hypothesis) to be tested by independent epistemological criteria ("good and sufficient reasons"). By contrast, Van Til spoke of presuppositions as a person's most basic convictions or beliefs (not simply hypotheses), in terms of which he follows a particular epistemology and on the basis of which he determines what counts as good and sufficient reasons to test other (less basic) beliefs. As he observed, "For Buswell presuppositions are not the conditions which make experience intelligible."[238] From that seminal difference, the viewpoints of Buswell and Van Til in apologetics would naturally and progressively diverge.

The case of Gordon Clark would appear to have offered much greater hope for meaningful dialogue and agreement between his apologetic and that of Van Til. Much of what Clark wrote was at least formally identical to Van Til's distinctives. Consider a few examples:

A philosophy that is based on the existence of God will differ throughout from a philosophy that has no place for God; and

---

235. Two years before Buswell's article, Van Til contributed the essay "Nature and Scripture" to the Westminster faculty's symposium *The Infallible Word.*, ed. N. B. Stonehouse and Paul Woolley (Philadelphia: Presbyterian and Reformed, 1946). This one essay alone offers evidence contrary to Buswell's representations in all but two instances.

236. Van Til replied in *The Bible Today* for April and June–September 1949; his reply is reproduced in *The Defense of the Faith*, chap. 10 (pp. 239–67). Van Til replied further to Buswell in chap. 10 of *A Christian Theory of Knowledge*, pp. 273–309 (the latter portion of which reproduces that part of the reply in the first edition of *The Defense of the Faith* [pp. 253–67] which did not make it into the second and third editions). Van Til indicated that Buswell had attributed to him things he never said and had offered "a basic misunderstanding" (p. 288) of the things he had said. Buswell is also assessed critically in *An Introduction to Systematic Theology*, chap. 14.

237. *Systematic Theology of the Christian Religion*, 1:15.

238. *Christian Theory of Knowledge*, 286.

similarly two systems that do not agree as to what sort of Being God is, will also differ in all their details.[239]

Reformed theology, while denying a common epistemological ground [axioms in common with secular thought], has always asserted a common psychological or ontological ground.[240]

Christianity . . . should develop its epistemology and theory of language from the information contained in the Scriptures.[241]

Now, methodology is never neutral. . . . [T]he use of a method presupposes epistemological and metaphysical positions.[242]

Presuppositionless experience is an impossible philosophy.[243]

Because God is sovereign, God's authority can be taken only on God's authority.[244]

The non-Christian arguments regularly assume the point in dispute before they start. The questions are so framed as to exclude the Christian answer from the beginning.[245]

A rational life is impossible without being based upon a divine revelation.[246]

Clark and Van Til might have found ways to reinforce and strengthen each other's apologetical instruction. Nevertheless, there were significant incongruities between them. Clark could readily

239. *A Christian View of Men and Things* (Grand Rapids: Eerdmans, 1952), 85.
240. *Karl Barth's Theological Method* (Philadelphia: Presbyterian and Reformed, 1963), 100.
241. Ibid., 150.
242. "Reply to Arthur F. Holmes," in *The Philosophy of Gordon H. Clark*, ed. Ronald Nash (Philadelphia: Presbyterian and Reformed, 1968), 434.
243. *Historiography: Secular and Religious* (Nutley, N.J.: Craig Press, 1971), 371.
244. "How May I Know the Bible Is Inspired?" in *Can I Trust My Bible?* (Chicago: Moody Press, 1963), 28.
245. *Religion, Reason, and Revelation* (Nutley, N.J.: Craig Press, 1961), 27.
246. Ibid., 152.

speak of "the test of revelation as a postulate."[247] It is apparent from his writings that the biblical worldview was not the transcendental necessity for rationality or any other "test"; rather, possibility was more ultimate than God, and independently intelligible rationality was the test among the various possibilities:

> Strange accidents do indeed occur, and no proof is forthcoming that the Bible is not such an accident. Unlikely perhaps, but still possible.[248]

> If theism is indeed necessary to the intelligibility of history, possibly Mohammedan theism or some other form would function as well as or even better than Christian theism.[249]

> If the Biblical doctrines are self-consistent, they have met the only legitimate test of reason. But before any type of metaphysics can be accepted, another and far more crucial question must be asked and answered. . . . [E]pistemological theory . . . is where we must begin.[250]

> Metaphysics can be established only on an epistemological basis.[251]

> There is no method of understanding superior to deduction.[252]

> This test of logic is precisely the requirement that a set of propositions be meaningful, whether spoken by God or man.[253]

247. E.g., "Several Implications (Wheaton Lecture III)," in *Philosophy of Gordon H. Clark*, ed. Nash, 94.
248. "How May I Know the Bible Is Inspired?" 24.
249. *Christian View of Men and Things*, 231.
250. "Secular Philosophy (Wheaton Lecture I)," in *Philosophy of Gordon H. Clark*, ed. Nash, 27.
251. "Reply to Arthur F. Holmes," in *Philosophy of Gordon H. Clark*, ed. Nash, 435.
252. "The Axiom of Revelation (Wheaton Lecture)," in *Philosophy of Gordon H. Clark*, ed. Nash, 89.
253. "Special Divine Revelation as Rational," in *Revelation and the Bible*, ed. Carl F. H. Henry (Grand Rapids: Baker, 1959), 37.

> The important question is not whether or not the Bible is true, but whether or not all knowledge is deducible by reason, i.e., by logic alone.[254]

It is by now obvious that Clark was not a transcendental presuppositionalist like Van Til at all. He did not recognize the mutual dependence of epistemology and metaphysics in a worldview, and when all was said and done he used rational coherence as the test of various worldviews as hypotheses, including the worldview of divine revelation. God is still "in the dock" in this approach to apologetics.

Clark was extremely critical of Van Til's theological theory of knowledge and even denounced it as neoorthodox irrationalism which makes it impossible to know anything literally true about God[255] and which can only by contradicting itself hold that unregenerate men are not totally ignorant or can have some knowledge in common with the believer.[256] Van Til taught that the Creator God's act of knowing was qualitatively different from man's act of knowing, even though they know the same truth; not having the comprehensive and creative character of God's knowing, finite man's thinking will find certain combinations of biblical truth to appear paradoxical. So Clarkians accused Van Til of denying a cognitive and nonparadoxical knowledge of God. For Van Til, possibility and logic were both to be construed in a distinctively Christian manner, indeed as unintelligible apart from the Christian worldview based on God's self-attesting revelation. Logic could not be used as a self-sufficient epistemological criterion by which to judge the revelation of God since it was the only intelligible context for man's use of logic as a tool of his intellect. So

---

254. *Religion, Reason, and Revelation*, 53.
255. Cf. Gordon H. Clark, "The Bible as Truth," *Bibliotheca Sacra* 114 (April 1957): 157–70. See chap. 4.5 above for a discussion of knowing God "analogously" and allusions to the Clark–Van Til controversy in the Orthodox Presbyterian Church over the incomprehensibility of God. For a fervent perpetuation of Clark's negative assessment of Van Til, see John W. Robbins, *Cornelius Van Til: The Man and the Myth* (Jefferson, Md.: The Trinity Foundation, 1986).
256. "Apologetics," in *Contemporary Evangelical Thought*, ed. Carl F. H. Henry (New York: Channel Press, 1957; reprint, Grand Rapids: Baker, 1968), 142, 155–56. See the discussion in chap. 6.5 above, regarding Van Til's views on the psychological complexities of unbelief. Note especially the distinction between what believers could know in principle (epistemologically) and what they know as a matter of practical fact (psychologically). In the article cited here, Clark actually draws the same kind of distinction—between a person and his system of thought.

Clarkians accused Van Til of denying logic. But such accusations did not interpret Van Til's comments in their context (where harmony would not have been difficult to find). Previous sections of this book may be consulted for a more sympathetic and accurate presentation of Van Til's views on knowing God and on logic.

Clark's antiempirical attitudes in epistemology and his noncognitivist approach to the work of science[257] also clashed with Van Til's affirmation of the knowledge-gaining character of empirical science. By the end of his career, Clark was arguing that genuine knowledge was available only in the Bible, and he was willing to categorize his apologetical outlook as "fideism" (or "dogmatism"),[258] a term from which Van Til recoiled. Clark eventually held that when a secularist challenges the believer's view that God has revealed Himself in the Bible, "a dogmatist does not try to prove it"! One simply *chooses* one's first principle, which is "indemonstrable" (which, again, Van Til's transcendental presuppositionalism denies). Clark realized that the question would thus become, How does one decide between incompatible first principles? What possibility is left for convincing an opponent of Christianity? Clark's answer must be disheartening to even the most ardent Calvinist, and a terrible *faux pas* in the eyes of those trained in philosophy: "The answer is that faith is the gift of God. . . . The initiation of spiritual life, called regeneration, is the immediate work of the Holy Spirit."[259] Here Clark simply confused the difference between reasons (evidence for believing, which is intellectually assessed) and causes (psychological and external factors producing some personal change in attitude or action). He was certainly correct that God sovereignly causes men to be born again and have faith, but the apologetical question put to Clark was what

257. This is essentially a pragmatic theory of knowledge applied specifically to the work of ordinary science. Clark wrote: "Operationalism asserts philosophically . . . that science provides no knowledge of nature itself. . . . Scientific concepts . . . are plans for action" ("The Nature of the Physical Universe," in *Christian Faith and Modern Theology*, ed. Carl F. H. Henry [New York: Channel Press, 1964; Grand Rapids: Baker, 1971], 142–43). "The most certain truth of physics is that physics is . . . not true as an account of what nature is and how nature works. The concepts of physics are the operations of the physicist" (*The Philosophy of Science and Belief in God* [Nutley, N.J.: Craig Press, 1964], 80). The artificiality of operationalism in the philosophy of science comes out by simply asking why some scientific statements or theories are more operationally effective than others. Evidently they are closer to the *cognitive* truth about the world than their competitors.
258. *Three Types of Religious Philosophy* (Nutley, N.J.: Craig Press, 1973), 7, 104.
259. Ibid., 110, 121, 123.

reason men may have (to which the Spirit surely must testify) to believe that biblical revelation is the truth (rather than, say, the Koran). Clark ultimately left Christianity without a rational defense. In the readings reproduced below, there is a sample of Van Til's critique of Clark.

3. A third group of Van Til's critics consists of those who, not having grasped or appreciated the force of his transcendental argument for the rational necessity of Christianity, have applied the inappropriate epithet of "fideism" to him. These critics exhibit different emphases in their own approaches to apologetics, but they are in general agreement in opposing Van Til. This group includes John Gerstner, R. C. Sproul, and Arthur Lindsley,[260] Norman Geisler,[261] E. J. Carnell and Gordon R. Lewis,[262] and the evidentialists John W. Montgomery and Clark Pinnock.[263] Their criticisms revolve around

260. *Classical Apologetics: A Rational Defense of the Christian Faith and a Critique of Presuppositional Apologetics* (Grand Rapids: Zondervan, 1984). Cf. R. C. Sproul, "You Can't Tell a School by Its Name," *Christianity Today* 22 (November 4, 1977): 220. Sproul's misunderstanding of Van Til's presuppositional argument is evident in a taped lecture entitled "Presuppositionalism and Van Til's Apologetics," where he charges it with reducing one's presupposition to a mere "subjective preference." For rebuttal of Sproul, Gerstner, and Lindsley, beyond what is found in the present book, see Greg L. Bahnsen, "A Critique of 'Classical Apologetics'," *Presbyterian Journal* 44, no. 32 (December 4, 1985): 6–8, 11, with a follow-up letter to the editor in vol. 44, no. 34 (December 18, 1985): 2; cf. "Bahnsen-Sproul Debate" (December 1977). An excellent discussion of *Classical Apologetics* can be found in the review article by John M. Frame, originally published in the *Westminster Theological Journal* 47 (1985): 279–99, and reprinted in his *Apologetics to the Glory of God* (Phillipsburg, N.J.: Presbyterian and Reformed, 1994), 219–43. Frame points out that the authors are so inaccurate in their understanding of Van Til that, at one point, they even quote a critic of Van Til and place his words in Van Til's mouth—on a point of major significance in Van Til's system.
261. *Christian Apologetics* (Grand Rapids: Baker, 1976), 56–58.
262. See citations earlier in this chapter. Although Carnell and Lewis obviously defended and adhered to the "traditional" method in apologetics, and both were quite critical of Van Til's version of presuppositionalism, I am not aware of Carnell or Lewis using the explicit epithet of "fideism." In what amounts to the same thing, however, Lewis (for example) says that "characteristically" (though not consistently) Van Til stressed that Christians "start with [their] presuppositions arbitrarily," denied that men have any ability to check conflicting claims to revelation, and thus (for the most part) was "not doing apologetics but theology" (*Testing Christianity's Truth Claims*, 142, 144). In his contribution to Van Til's *Festschrift, Jerusalem and Athens*, Lewis concluded that Van Til's presuppositional apologetic has actually "left the faith defenseless" (p. 361). For Carnell and Lewis, to object philosophically and theologically to *autonomous* epistemologies is one and the same with rejecting any and all "rational argumentation."
263. See the citations of these men in sec. 4 of this chapter. Cf. Clark Pinnock, *Biblical Revelation—The Foundation of Christian Theology* (Chicago: Moody Press, 1971), 38–42.

(1) a defense of autonomous reasoning and of encouraging the unbeliever to apply it to the faith, (2) the priority of epistemological criteria (or method) over metaphysical convictions, (3) an appeal to "natural theology," which proves God's existence, and/or to the "brute facts" of history and science, which verify (with probability) Christianity's truth—(4) all in an intellectually neutral fashion. We have already shown that Van Til's transcendental presuppositionalism was not fideistic (chap. 2.3), that epistemological "methodism" or choosing criteria apart from metaphysical convictions is impossible (chap. 5.1), that neutrality is antitheistic in character (chap. 4.1), that any autonomous attempt to develop an epistemology is self-destructive (chap. 5.3), and that traditional apologetical proofs and evidences are easily refuted (chap. 8.1, 3, 4). Indeed, this book as a whole constitutes an extensive refutation of the kind of criticism that has been popularized by these men.

4. So far, Van Til's critics have been conveniently classified as the early Dutch dissenters, the philosophical Presbyterians, and the epistemological methodists who mistake presuppositionalism as fideism. The members of all three groups failed to comprehend, or at least take into account, the transcendental character of Van Til's apologetic. But that is not so for the last group we consider. In one way or another, the writers in this group are critical of the transcendental feature of Van Til's defense of the faith. They include Herman Dooyeweerd, John Frame, and Stuart Hackett.

As we saw in chapter 2.2, Dooyeweerd promoted a transcendental critique of theoretical thought, attempting to unmask the pretended autonomy of philosophical systems. However, he was dissatisfied with Van Til's transcendental argumentation, for it was a transcendent transcendentalism—beginning with the self-attesting and dogmatic authority of God's verbal revelation in Scripture.[264] Dooyeweerd insisted that transcendental analysis had to begin immanently, within the structure of theoretical thought itself. But Van Til criticized that as falling back into autonomous thinking.[265] Dooyeweerd insisted that "revelational meaning transcends every human concept since it

---

264. See Herman Dooyeweerd, "Cornelius Van Til and the Transcendental Critique of Theoretical Thought," in *Jerusalem and Athens*, ed. Geehan, 74–89.
265. See Van Til's response to Dooyeweerd in *Jerusalem and Athens*, ed. Geehan, 89–127. Cf. Van Til, *Christianity in Conflict* (Philadelphia: Westminster Theological Seminary, 1962–64), vol. 2, sec. 3; Van Til, *Herman Dooyeweerd and Reformed Apologetics* (Philadelphia: Westminster Theological Seminary, 1974).

is of a supra-rational character," and that Van Til's "rationalistic view of the Word-revelation" led him mistakenly to find philosophical or "conceptual thought-contents"[266] in the Bible. Rather than trying to rebut such a criticism, Van Tillians should wear it as a badge of honor. The leveling of such as a charge against Van Til tells us much more about what is wrong with Dooyeweerd's "philosophy of the cosmonomic idea" than what is wrong with presuppositional apologetics.

John Frame, who studied under Van Til and has written extensively in appreciative application and critical interaction with his thought, takes note of the transcendental character of Van Til's presuppositional apologetic.[267] He appreciates certain features of it, but also has some questions about it. In the end, Frame's critical assessment is that a transcendental argument is not really distinctive, and thus that Van Til's apologetic is not as far from the traditional approach as both sides might think. According to Frame, the transcendental argument cannot stand alone, anyway, but must be supplemented with other kinds of arguments. And given that transcendental argumentation is (for Frame) pretty much like the cosmological argument, Frame not surprisingly concludes that Van Til's apologetic fails to deliver the certainty that he claimed for it—leaving him subject to criticism for being too hard on the probabilism that characterizes the traditional apologetic. Frame believes that Van Til was mistaken to think that one argument could accomplish the complete defense of Christianity, as well as mistaken to think that it must be an "indirect" argument. I must disagree with Frame on these points, and my replies to his various criticisms can be found in earlier discussions in this book, especially in chapter 7 on transcendental presuppositionalism.[268]

---

266. It is worth noting that this tortured and ambiguous expression, "thought content," appears again in criticism of Van Til by Reformed thinkers. Ironically, Clark and his followers faulted Van Til for denying the coincidence of the "thought content" of God and man, whereas Dooyeweerd and his followers criticized him for thinking that man can gain transcendent and divine "thought content" from the Bible!

267. E.g., *Apologetics to the Glory of God* (Phillipsburg, N.J.: Presbyterian and Reformed, 1994), 69ff.

268. What differences I have with Frame are real, but should not detract from my appreciation of his work. If you are going to read only one critic of Van Til, your best choice by far would be to read Frame's books, for he tries to be analytically accurate and his criticism is sympathetic. Also, Frame offers a wealth of solid teaching on defending the faith. As he would say about Van Til, I would say about him: even the good can be better!

In his most recent and thorough treatment of Van Til (*Cornelius Van Til: An*

Finally, then, we come to Stuart Hackett, who was well known as a critic of Van Til.[269] I have placed him in this last group of critics because his "rational empiricism" has clear affinities to Kantian philosophy (surprisingly explicit for an evangelical philosopher),[270] suggesting that he would appreciate the possible formal parallel between Kant's "Copernican revolution" in the history of philosophy and Van Til's presuppositionalism in modern apologetics. Kant's "critical" philosophy, like Van Til's "critical" apologetic, stressed a transcendental analysis of thought and aimed to establish the preconditions for the intelligibility of human experience. Van Til thought that Kant failed to carry out that project (because he attempted to do it autonomously),

---

Analysis of His Thought [Phillipsburg, N.J.: Presbyterian and Reformed, 1995]), Frame concludes (pp. 397–99) with some well-seasoned observations about weaknesses in Van Til's work; I would not disagree with them all. (1) Van Til's teaching (just like that of any of us mortals) should not be treated as a seamless garment, as though it must be wholly accepted or wholly rejected. Van Til himself would have been the first to say that only God's word should be treated as a unit. (2) Frame is also not out of place to question the unclear language used in the Clark controversy, as well as the creative conceptualization of common grace being extended by God "earlier" and to "a generality." (3) More widely, "issues of communication" did sometimes became a problem for Van Til; I would add, however, that this was a problem for most twentieth-century Christian apologists. A healthy dose of analytical reflection would help the cause to which we are all committed. (4) Finally, I too wish that Van Til had given more attention to making practical applications of his presuppositional method—to actually defending the faith against the enemy, rather than debating methodology so much within the family of faith.

269. See *The Resurrection of Theism: Prolegomena to Christian Apology* (Chicago: Moody Press, 1957), pt. 2, chap. 3.

270. "Lest there should be any misapprehension, allow me to say that I accept without reservation Kant's contentions both for a synthetic a priori factor in knowledge, and for the derivation of the categories involved in this factor from the basic types of logical judgment. I further accept Kant's doctrine that the synthetical a priori element in knowledge is strictly categorical and relational: i.e., the categories give us, of themselves, no content of knowledge concerning real existences which are independent of the mind; they are simply forms of thought to which such content must be extraneously furnished. . . . But while Kant's epistemology of rational empiricism is thus generally acceptable, its details require alteration along three lines" (ibid., 46). Hackett would reduce the number of categories, while maintaining (in contradiction to what he has just conceded to Kant) that the categories imposed by the mind are actually forms of the way things really are outside the mind as well (noumena) and thus may be applied beyond sense experience. Hackett's discussions may be compared to those of Kant himself in *The Critique of Pure Reason* to decide who really has the better case. (Hackett saw it as an easy task; he thought that in one short paragraph on page 54 he refuted Kant's restriction of the application of the mental categories to phenomenal experience!)

but that the central concern of a truly biblical apologetical method is similarly to show that without presupposing the Christian worldview, all of man's reasoning, experience, interpretation, etc., is unintelligible. Only the transcendent revelation of God can provide the philosophically necessary preconditions for logic, science, morality, etc., in which case those who oppose the faith are reduced to utter foolishness and intellectually have nowhere to stand in objecting to Christianity's truth-claims.

Hackett, being as close to Kant's own outlook as he was, should have discerned and sympathetically assessed Van Til's use of a transcendental method in his apologetic. Instead, he criticized Van Til's apologetic without recognizing its distinctive nature.[271] Van Til, he declared, was a "metaphysical presuppositionalist" (we have seen the misdirection already; cf. chaps. 3.2 and 5.1 above), holding that one's metaphysical ultimate "does not admit of proof" and is simply a voluntaristic (rather than rational) choice[272]—the very opposite of the position actually taken by Van Til (cf. chaps. 2.3, 7, and 8.3 above)! According to Hackett, Van Til denied that there is any real common ground for argument or discussion between believers and unbelievers,[273] which again misrepresented Van Til (see chap. 6.2 and 6.4 above). Hackett charged Van Til with holding that man's intellect is so distorted by sin that it "cannot distill God from [general] revelation," with the result that only a regenerated person can genuinely know the existence of God.[274] Again Hackett reversed a crucial principle in Van Til's apologetical thought (cf. chaps. 4.3, 6.2, and 6.5 above). He also abhorred the "rigid determinism" of Van Til's Calvinistic theology.[275]

It has not been uncommon for teachers and students of Christian apologetics to dismiss Van Til's position in a rather offhand way, simply alluding to Hackett's critique of presuppositionalism as if it were

271. Part of the difficulty stems from the fact that Hackett did not carefully draw important distinctions, choosing to lump together and define as "presuppositionalism" what he thought was the general position taken by apologists with such divergent viewpoints as Van Til, Carl Henry, Carnell, and Clark (p. 158). One wonders why he attempted to do so, when he himself wrote: "It is difficult to define the common position of the contemporary presuppositionalists, since their own ranks are by no means entirely in agreement on the basic approach to Christian apology." There was not a sufficient common position here to define.
272. Ibid., 154, 155, 158, 166.
273. Ibid., 170.
274. Ibid., 171–72.
275. Ibid., 172–74.

accurate and cogent. Van Til twice replied incisively to Hackett. Indeed, in choosing but one critic to answer in his short "Credo," he selected Hackett as expressing the "stock" objections to his position. In the reading selections below, we will include both the longer and the shorter of Van Til's answers to Hackett.

EVALUATION OF A CALVINIST CRITIC: GORDON H. CLARK[276]

Dr. Gordon H. Clark is a firm believer in and a valiant defender of the theology of the Calvinistic Reformation and, more particularly, of the Westminster Confession and Catechisms. For him truth is true and the good is good because God says that they are.

One would think then that Clark would have an organic view of the Scripture and its inspiration such as Warfield and Bavinck have. But this is not the case. Instead of integrating God's general revelation in the created world with his supernatural revelation given by thought and word communication, Clark sets these over against one another.

That this is the case is apparent from his discussion of the "inadequacy of general revelation." Reformed theologians have, of course, spoken of the inadequacy of general revelation. By this they meant first that it is inadequate for men as *sinners*. Sinners need God's revelation of grace in Christ and only Christ himself reveals his work of grace in Scripture. By this they meant, secondly, that general revelation was inadequate even for men as creatures. God therefore spoke to Adam directly even before the Fall, to instruct him with respect to the use he should make of the facts of the created world. Man never knew anything without the interaction of fact and word revelation upon him. His self-awareness is unintelligible without this interaction. But both of these points with respect to the inadequacy of general revelation do not, for Reformed theologians such as Bavinck and Warfield, indicate any lack of *clarity* in this revelation. Quite the contrary. These theologians follow Calvin as Calvin follows Paul when he asserts that "the invisible things of him since the creation of the world are clearly seen, being perceived through the things that are made, even his everlasting power and divinity" (Romans 1:20).

Reflecting this teaching of the apostle Paul, Calvin says: "His essence, indeed, is incomprehensible, utterly transcending all human thought; but on each of his works his glory is engraven in characters so bright, so distinct, and

---

276. An excerpt from *Protestant Doctrine of Scripture*, 62–72. Van Til also criticized Clark's view of the incomprehensibility of God in *Introduction to Systematic Theology*, chap. 13.

so illustrious, that none, however dull and illiterate, can plead ignorance as their excuse" (*Institutes*, Bk. I, Ch. V.I).

Men *ought* to see that God is the creator of the world. God did not leave himself without a witness in that he gave them "from heaven rain and fruitful seasons" (Acts 14:17).

Men *ought* to see that God displays his character in the created world even in *malum partem*. "For the wrath of God is revealed from heaven against all ungodliness and unrighteousness of men who hold down the truth in unrighteousness" (Romans 1:18). God cursed the ground because of the sin of man. Paul says that the whole creation "groaneth and travaileth in pain together until now." Because of man's sin creation is "under the bondage of corruption" (Romans 8:21, 22). Men *ought* to see this too. It is clearly there to be seen. As time went on, after the fall of Adam, and sinful men became exceeding sinful, God revealed his wrath all the more by giving them up "unto vile passions" (Romans 1:26).

Men *ought* to read God's general revelation in the light of the supernatural revelation originally given to Adam as their representative. General revelation *from the beginning*, says Paul, was meant to be read in the light of God's word-communication to man. The fact that originally general revelation needed supernatural revelation does not mean that it lacked clarity. To do their work effectively your hands and feet need eyes to direct them and these eyes, in turn, need the light of day to do their work. But the need of light does not spell any inherent defect in the eyes as the need of eyes does not spell any inherent defect in hands and feet.

The whole teaching of Paul and of Calvin as well as of later Reformed theologians, following Paul, is to the effect that all men, since the Fall, *ought* to see the world as it really is. The world, and therefore every fact in it, is actually created by God and directed by his redemptive providence. All the world, and therefore every fact in it, is actually under the curse of God because of the sin of man. Man was never expected to read his mandate with respect to his created environment from this environment as such. Man was never alone with natural or general revelation by itself. We cannot see the earth producing its abundance apart from the heat and the light of the sun. But this fact does not detract from the capacity of the earth to show its ability to do this thing. So with respect to God's general revelation. Man *ought* to see that it can and does function both in *bonam* and in *malum partem* because of God's supernatural thought communication to man with respect to it.

Now Clark's position with respect to Scripture and the defense of its teaching is defective because he does not *thus* integrate general revelation with special revelation.

Clark does, indeed, *relate* original pre-redemptive supernatural revelation to general revelation. But he fails to relate them in an organic, supplemental fashion.

"When Adam was created and placed in the Garden of Eden," says Clark, "he did not know what to do. Nor would a study of the Garden have led to any necessary conclusion. His duty was imposed on him by a special divine revelation. Thus moral norms, commands and prohibitions were established by a special and not a general revelation" ("Special Divine Revelation as Rational," in *Revelation and the Bible*, ed. Carl F. H. Henry, p. 29).

It is thus that Clark destroys the organic, supplemental view of the relation of special to general revelation. Here is Adam, as first created. He does not know what to do. He looks about him. Adam does not see nature as God's revelation to him. He looks within. Though he is the image-bearer of God, Adam does not see himself as such. He does not know what to do with respect to himself any more than with respect to the world about him.

This entire approach of Clark's overlooks the fact that *from the beginning* God *spoke* to man. There never was a second of time when Adam did not know what to do. There never was a time when he was confronted with the created universe by itself. It is true that if Adam had, at any time, been left to react to God's revelation in nature and to his own constitution without the benefit of supernatural thought and word communication, he would not have known what to do. But such a condition never did exist. God's revelation through man's own constitution must therefore be said to speak of God's attributes to man, *in conjunction with* supernatural revelation. This was true *from the beginning*.

It is only if we thus maintain the original organic relation of natural to supernatural revelation that we can maintain Paul's teaching with respect to natural revelation after the Fall. Paul says that nature and human nature do manifest the *presence* of God. To be sure, nature and human nature do not manifest the *grace* of God. To be sure, nature and human nature were never meant by themselves to be a sufficient revelation of God to man. For all that, nature and human nature have always been *clearly manifestory* of God's presence. It has been sufficient and clear when seen in relation to supernatural revelation, and it was, from the beginning, meant to be seen in this connection.

It is this view of nature and of human nature that is the necessary presupposition of redemptive-supernatural revelation as given in Scripture. The whole of supernatural redemptive revelation is given in conjunction with the revelation of God in nature and in human nature. Supernatural redemptive revelation is integrated with God's revelation in nature and in human nature.

Supernatural revelation is not seen for what it is unless it is seen as thus integrated with revelation in the created universe.

It is impossible to follow Paul's teaching with respect to the guilt of sinners in respect to the revelation of God in the universe unless one begins his whole approach to the question of revelation by thinking of natural and supernatural revelation as thus organically related. Paul holds the sinner responsible for not seeing the presence of God's attributes in nature and in himself. But Paul does this because he thinks of man as inherently a covenantal being. The sinner is a covenant breaker in and with Adam. Every fact that faces man, through his own constitution as well as through his environment, puts him face to face with God. He is therefore to handle every fact with which he deals to the glory of God. As a scientist he is to use such hypotheses and such only as are based upon the presupposition that every fact is what it is because of the place that it occupies in the plan of God. His scientific method is truly scientific and truly productive of the purpose for which it is to be used only if it is used on the presupposition that man knows nature properly now, and always knew nature properly, only in conjunction with God's speech to him about it. Originally man's very self-awareness required the organically revelational environment that comes from the interaction of word and fact revelation. After the Fall, supernatural redemptive revelation must supply what the original word-revelation supplied to Adam.

Precisely here we discover the difference between the Reformed and the Roman Catholic-Arminian view of revelation in general. On the Reformed view, all created reality is *covenantally revelational*. The facts of man's created environment are what they are as the field of operation for the covenantal reaction of man to God. Man, made in the image of God, is either covenantally obedient or covenantally disobedient in all of his reactions to all of the facts of God's revelational material. The sinner is holding down the truth in unrighteousness when, in his "scientific method," he assumes the pure non-relatedness of the facts with which he deals and when he applies hypotheses that assume that the facts could possibly be anything other than revelational of God.

God's revelation which appears to all men in all the facts which they face is creative-redemptive. It is the triune God, Father, Son, and Holy Spirit who is covenantally operative in all of the facts of the world. If man does not recognize this creative-redemptive character of all the facts of the universe, he resists the truth in unrighteousness. If man does not see that *all* the facts are what they are in relation to one another because of the creative-redemptive program of the triune God through them, he abides under the wrath of God.

The Roman Catholic holds to no such view. Because of its use of Aristotelian or Greek methodology, Roman Catholicism does not think of man's self-awareness as covenantal and of "nature" as, from the beginning, revealing God, in conjunction with God's word-revelation in paradise. The facts of nature are not then seen to be what they are as revelational of God.

It is also of the essence of the modern approach to the field of science that the facts are assumed to be non-revelational of God in the sense discussed. It is therefore the responsibility of Christians who are scientists to call other men who are also scientists, to repentance for their assumption of neutrality with respect to the facts with which they deal in the laboratory. The non-believing scientist is actively engaged in breaking God's covenant requirements when he says that he is simply following the facts wheresoever they may lead him. This is as though someone would dig up a piece of ground on the White House lawn and then not only act greatly surprised when the guard taps him on the shoulder and asks him for his permit to do what he is doing, but insist on his right to do what he is doing without any permit at all. If I find a red heifer with the letters LBJ on it, on the LBJ ranch in Texas, I will grant that I need a permit to move it about. If I enter through the gate of the ranch at all, I already know that every fact I will meet within the confines of the ranch belongs to LBJ.

Now Clark, frankly and outspokenly committed to the Reformed faith though he is, fails to thus challenge the unbeliever to show his permit. He does not tell the unbelieving scientist that nature clearly reveals the ownership of God the creator-redeemer. Clark simply gives up asking the natural man to recognize the revelational character of the field of facts in which he makes his research. Clark says simply that science "must not be regarded as cognitive" (*The Philosophy of Science and Belief in God*, Nutley, 1964, p. 93).

Clark thinks that by thus speaking of science as non-cognitive he at least makes room for the Christian religion. But then he makes room for religion in the way that the White House guard might make room for L. B. J. [President Lyndon Baines Johnson] by asking the intruder mentioned above to restrict his activity to a certain small corner of the rose garden. Graciously accepting this arrangement, the illegitimate ground-digger soon digs tunnels underneath the White House itself, its collapse being the inevitable issue. After all, if the ground-digger claims to have the right to dig at one point on the White House lawn, he will at last claim the right to dig wherever he pleases. He will not only claim the right to dig wherever he pleases, but he will claim that he simply *must* dig up the whole ground to accomplish his purpose. After all, he wants to replace the White House with a building of his own.

Having granted this sort of thing, Clark is driven to the position of having to beg for permission to have a place alongside the ground-digger's present operations for his own religious structure of Calvinism. He thinks he is very bold in claiming the right to build his Calvinistic structure alongside that of the anti-Christian ground-digger. He argues vigorously against those who claim that "all truth is to be obtained by one method, the method of science" (*Op. Cit.*, p. 29).

And this is precisely what the modern neo-Protestant does when, in the name of Kant, he claims room for faith as a necessary supplement to an autonomous science. Clark certainly does not want thus to beg for mercy and for permission to *add* his Calvinism to modern phenomenalist science. Yet he cannot, without retracing his steps, escape falling into the trap of the ethical dualism of modern religious thought.

CAN I TRUST MY BIBLE?

We ask now what implication Clark's view of the non-cognitive character of science has on his way of defending the Bible and what the Bible teaches about the triune God and his relation to the world.

"How May I Know the Bible Is Inspired?" is the title of a chapter Clark contributes to a Symposium under the title, *Can I Trust My Bible?* In line with Warfield's approach, Clark wants first to establish the question of the truth of the Bible before he discusses its inspiration. This in itself commits him, as it did Warfield, to a Roman Catholic-Arminian type of apologetics. It commits him to the idea that the natural man can quite correctly interpret nature and the nature of man up to a certain point in terms of his own principles. It commits him to holding some such position as Butler held when he said that the deists and he had in common their interpretation of the course and constitution of nature. The only difference there is between him and the deists, argues Butler, pertains to that which is *beyond* nature.

Now Clark shares the operational view of nature with the non-Christian scientist. Butler still claimed to be able to prove the possibility and probable truth of the Christian teaching with respect to Christ and his relation to nature. But Clark cannot rightfully claim anything in the way of superiority of the Christian teachings with respect to nature over other views. If science is non-cognitive, that is the end of all argument. For that is to say that nature does not clearly reveal the power and divinity of God.

Yet Clark claims that the truth of Christianity can, at least to some extent, be established by an appeal to the facts of nature. Says Clark: "Some of the evidence that the Bible is true is presented in other chapters of this book. Archaeological and historical research has corroborated Biblical history in numerous instances. This material will here be assumed" (*Can I Trust My Bible?* Chicago, 1963, p. 9).

Clark himself deals with the "logical support" for the claim that the Bible is true (*Ibid.*, p. 10). The "attempt to show the Bible's logical consistency is," says Clark, "I believe, the best method of defending inspiration" (*Ibid.*, p. 23). "Is there then," he adds, "any proposition which the believer and the unbeliever will both accept without proof?" (*Ibid.*, p. 23). "In times past," Clark continues, "there have been areas of agreement. Non-Christians would admit that God exists. During the Reformation the truthfulness of the Scripture was so widely taken for granted that the evidences seemed to furnish conclusive proof to any normal mind. But this situation no longer exists. Not only do most people reject the truthfulness of the Bible, but many reject also the belief in God" (*Ibid.*, pp. 23, 24).

As the situation is now, "the doctrine of inspiration, like every other Christian doctrine, cannot be demonstrated to the satisfaction of a clear thinking unbeliever" (*Ibid.*, p. 24). However, we can, as believers, show that the Bible "is logically consistent." The unbeliever must needs regard this fact to be a "most remarkable accident." "It seems more likely that a single superintending mind could produce this result than that it just happened accidentally. Logical consistency therefore is evidence for inspiration; but it is not demonstration. Strange accidents do indeed occur, and no proof is forthcoming that the Bible is not such an accident, unlikely perhaps, but still possible" (*Ibid.*, p. 24).

The following points must be noted with respect to this argument. We must (a) remember that, according to Clark, the unbeliever does justice to nature if he says that its laws are merely operational and not revelatory of God's attributes at all. This excludes the possibility of making any claim even for the more probable truthfulness for the claim that nature is the work of God's creative-redemptive act than for the view that it has come into existence by chance.

Then (b) Clark asserts that non-believers have sometimes agreed with believers in saying that God exists. But this is only formally true. The content of the word *God*, the meaning of the word *God* always differs radically between the Christian and the non-Christian. The same holds for the idea that unbelievers have sometimes held to the "truthfulness of the Scripture." When Clark agrees with the unbeliever on the merely operational view of nature, he virtually asserts that the unbeliever and the believer may still believe in the same God. But then this time the unbeliever is ahead in the game. He has maneuvered Clark into a virtual admission that the triune God is not clearly operative in the space-time world. How can Clark, in view of all this, consistently assert that the Bible is "logically consistent" in what it teaches? Does the Bible teach what Clark, the Calvinist, believes, namely, that God controls whatsoever comes to pass, and at the same time teach that the Bible, teaching this very fact, might have appeared in the world as an accident?

"To deny that God exists is as much a self-contradiction," says Clark, "as to deny the geometrical theorem" ("Special Divine Revelation as Rational," article in *Revelation and the Bible*, 1958, p. 33). Then with respect to the general content of biblical teaching, Clark adds, "If the Biblical doctrines are self-consistent, they have met the only legitimate test of reason. This test of logic is precisely the requirement that a set of propositions be meaningful, whether spoken by God or man. And if propositions have no meaning, obviously they reveal nothing" (*Ibid.*, p. 37). "Logical consistency" is not an "external test of Scripture." It is, rather, "exemplified in the Scripture; and thus the Scripture can be a meaningful revelation to the rational mind of man" (*Ibid.*, p. 39). So then, it is "the rational mind of man," i.e., the rational mind of the unbeliever who determines what propositions made by God in Christ, have meaning. If God wants to convey meaning to man, he must speak according to the requirements of the law of contradiction as the natural man conceives of this law. And the natural man conceives of this law as operating in a non-created, or chance-controlled universe. The natural man today may follow Aristotle's example and think of logical law as *somehow*, quite incomprehensibly, operative in a universe of chance. The natural man today may follow Kant, and assert that the laws of thought constitute the *a priori* equipment of the mind of man, with which equipment he constructs order in the purely contingent material that surrounds him. In any case it is the natural man who is virtually granted the right to settle what God can or cannot do.

In any case the natural man thinks of the laws of logic as constituting abstract principles which are operative in correlative relation to the pure, brute factual stuff of experience.

As a Christian thinker, Clark holds that the laws of logic are the equipment of man as made in the image of God. If Clark carried out his Christian conviction consistently he would contend that the law of contradiction can operate properly only in a universe that is what it is because of the plan of God with respect to it. In that case he would not say that the Bible and what it teaches could *possibly* have appeared as an accident. In that case he would rather have argued that the law of contradiction cannot function in a universe of chance. Then he would have said that the Bible and what it teaches must be presupposed as being what it claims to be, the inspired Word of God, or else there is no significant predication in science, in philosophy or in theology. Then he would not have said that the planets above and the plants below show some of the wisdom and power of God only "to those who already believe that God has created them" (*Revelation and the Bible*, p. 28). He would then rather have said, with Calvin, following Paul, that *all* men *ought* to see God in nature since he is clearly revealed there, but that only he who is given the regenerated heart actually does see this to be the case.

RESPONSE TO AN ANTI-CALVINIST CRITIC: STUART C. HACKETT [277]

(A) It may prove useful if, at this point, we discuss a further effort on the part of an evangelical Christian to base his faith upon a methodology not involved in or based upon the creative-redemptive work of Christ.

We take for our purpose the book of Dr. Stuart Cornelius Hackett with the title, *The Resurrection of Theism* (Chicago, 1957).

Hackett's problem is virtually the same as that of Beegle. He, like Beegle, wants to make Christianity respectable to its cultured despisers. As Beegle takes his inductive method from modern science so Hackett takes his method of *rational empiricism* from modern philosophy. Beegle might well seek support for his inductivism from Hackett's rational empiricism.

Hackett shares Beegle's intense dislike of Calvinism. In particular Hackett shares Beegle's intense dislike of the present writer's *extreme* Calvinism. Hackett asserts that the sinner is able to "believe the Gospel" without the regenerating grace of the Holy Spirit. Says Hackett: "Thus the presuppositionalist approach lands one ultimately in an extreme Calvinistic atmosphere. If one feels comfortable here let him remain with this God who has created rational men as mere puppets of His sovereignty. But if it seem to be the case that man is under obligation to believe the Gospel and that he must accept Christ as Saviour before the Spirit of God regenerates the heart—if, I say, man is a moral and rational agent confronted with a revelation for the acceptance of which he is morally and rationally responsible—then let the presuppositionalist framework be consigned to the irrationalism that is written so plainly through its structure!" (*Ibid.*, p. 174).

Neither Hackett nor Beegle is directly concerned with an exegetical analysis of the biblical teaching on sin and salvation. Both men simply assume that the idea of man's metaphysical independence of God and of his ethical ability to will the good as over against the evil is at once both biblical and intelligible. Both men are convinced that Calvinism is, on the one hand, *determinist* and is, on the other hand, irrationalist. If then we are to present the gospel

277. The following excerpts are taken from:

    (A) *Protestant Doctrine of Scripture*, 91–103;
    (B) "My Credo," in *Jerusalem and Athens*, ed. Geehan, 15–18.

to non-believers we must, according to both Hackett and Beegle, by all means avoid presenting it in its Calvinist form.

In presenting the gospel to unbelievers, Calvinists have no way of meeting them on common ground. How could they? It is of the essence of Calvinism to insist that Christians and non-Christians begin all their reasonings from "opposing first principles." This precludes all intelligible contact between Christians and non-Christians. Says Hackett: "Denial of common ground and the rejection of rational proof for God. It follows at once that if the Christian and the non-Christian part company with the espousal of opposing first principles, there can be no common ground, at the level of philosophical system, in terms of which the two can meet to accept the same implications of the facts with which they are both confronted: there is no area of agreement, therefore, in terms of which the Christian can prove the truth of the Christian God to an unbeliever" (*Ibid.*, p. 160). And, as if it were not enough to break off in advance all possible contact between the Christian and the non-Christian, Van Til pursues his enemies in their own field. Van Til says that "the natural man cannot reason correctly on any level of thought. Even logic is not the same for Christian and non-Christian, and the syllogistic process must be followed in frank subordination to the notion of a self-sufficient God! The Christian view may thus contain even what, from a human logical point of view, are self-contradictory propositions" (*Ibid.*, p. 163). Hackett grants that it is only Van Til who has shown himself so completely ready "thus to sacrifice reason" (*Ibid.*, p. 163). So, for instance, Dr. Gordon H. Clark and Dr. Edward J. Carnell, though they too are presuppositionalists, build their "whole system" "on the universality of logical laws and the rational categories" (*Idem*).

Whatever then may be the concessions to rationality on the part of some of the presuppositionalists, it remains true that its most consistent expression involves the complete rejection of all intelligible apologetics.

As over against this extreme or consistent determinism and irrationalism, we must, argues Hackett, start with "a common basis of rationality and experience in terms of which the validity of one's metaphysical assertion is to be justified. Men—if Christian theism be correct—come to experience with a rational structure of mind which, when consistently applied to that experience, yields the conclusion that God exists as theism construes that existence. On the Christian view experience would be unintelligible if God did not exist: but it is the fact of God's existence, not the original knowledge of it, which makes the intelligibility of experience possible. Unbelievers, after all, do, like Christians, apprehend their experience as rational: what they fail to do is to carry through this apprehension to its highest explanation in the affirmation of God's reality; or else they volitionally reject the conviction they may thus reach by a logical interpretation of the ultimate possibility of existence" (*Ibid.*, p. 167).

On Van Til's view "argument is impossible. Period!" (*Ibid.*, p. 170). If Christians are to engage in argument with unbelievers there must be a "true common ground." And this means that "presuppositionalism is repudiated" (*Ibid.*, p. 175). "I therefore conclude that since metaphysical presuppositionalism is thus entangled in such a mass of self-contradictions, it forms no valid approach to the knowledge of God. And thus perishes the last principal alternative to rational empiricism as a basis for Christian—or any other—apology. With her opponents thus languishing in defeat, reason pushes on to consider experience itself to determine whether God is real!" (*Ibid.*, p. 175).

1. RATIONAL EMPIRICISM

We turn now to look at the Rational Empiricism in terms of which we, as Christians, may, according to Hackett, escape the "mass of self-contradictions" of the most consistent presuppositionalists and establish a genuine apologetic for Christianity.

Turning our eyes away from the determinist-irrationalism of a man like Calvin we at once seek help from Immanuel Kant. "It was in the year 1781 that Immanuel Kant published the *Critique of Pure Reason*. In that book, Kant became the first systematic champion of rational empiricism" (*Ibid.*, p. 39). With Kant we hold that "knowledge would be impossible on either a purely rational or a purely empirical basis" (*Ibid.*, p. 37). Stating his view positively Hackett says: "Rational Empiricism, as I profess it, is the doctrine that knowledge is possible only because it involves the combination of two elements: a mind that comes to experience with a structure of thought in terms of which it is necessarily disposed to understand that experience—this is the a priori or 'before-experience' element; data upon which this structure of thought terminates to gain specific knowledge of particulars—this is the a posteriori or 'after-experience' element" (*Ibid.*, p. 37).

a. Critical Alteration of Kant's Views

While Kant's epistemology of rational empiricism is thus generally acceptable to Hackett, he proposes some alterations of detail (*Ibid.*, p. 46).

We must first, argues Hackett, maintain against Kant that the categories of human thought need not be limited to sensuous content (*Ibid.*, p. 52). We must maintain against Kant that human knowledge need not be limited to the phenomenal realm. "The categories do give us a knowledge of things-in-themselves" (*Ibid.*, p. 55). We must insist that "even God does not snatch the categories out of the blue." If "the categories are actually preconditions of intelligibility they are just as essential for divine thought as for human" (*Ibid.*, p. 55). Thus over against such a man as Van Til who urges "that in order to interpret reality correctly, man must work within the propositional revelation of Scripture" and who says that " 'for the human mind to know any fact truly, it must presuppose the existence of God' " (*Ibid.*, p. 159), our task is "simply to show that every knowledge experience does presuppose a synthetic a priori factor: that even the opponent of rational empiricism can state his case only on the supposition that it is false" (*Ibid.*, p. 56). "The denial of the synthetic a priori is either self-contradictory or meaningless" (*Idem*).

Here Hackett has reached rock bottom. "Intelligible experience presupposes the synthetic a priori" (*Ibid.*, p. 57). "After all, either thought starts with some general principles with which the mind is initially equipped, or it cannot start at all. Thought consists of ideas and judgments, as we have seen: and the very first act of judging presupposes that the thinker has a structure of thought in terms of which subject and predicate may be united according to certain relations" (*Ibid.*, p. 57).

Hackett sets his view over against the position which holds that "one must start with the assumption that the God who has spoken in Scripture is the true God" (*Ibid.*, p. 158).

b. "Men Do Build Garages, Don't They?"

With Kant, Hackett maintains that if we are to explain the fact of knowledge we must presuppose an "innate equipment" in man, "not as ideas of consciousness, but as forms by which thought operates" (*Ibid.*, p. 58).

Suppose that I want to build a garage. To do so "presupposes a knowledge of my environment and the capacity to make judgments about that environment . . ." (*Idem*).

So we conclude that "ultimately, it is just the faculty of judgment itself that is presupposed prior to experience, even for the simple task of building a garage. And men do build garages, don't they?" (*Ibid.*, pp. 58, 59).

According to Hackett, then, rational empiricism is obviously the only position which can explain any simple empirical fact. He who thinks that he can build a garage on any other principle than that of rational empiricism finds himself in the unhappy position of standing upon the position he is seeking to deny. He looks like the man who is trying to lift the cover off a man-hole while standing on it himself. And if Beegle should attempt to use his inductive method without presupposing the "general principles or categories which are presupposed in every act of thought," he too would be in such a ridiculous position. But we may be sure that Beegle would do no such thing. Beegle has told us that induction is merely the first method to use. His induction is not complete in itself. It needs something in the way of deduction. "Sound results are obtained when induction precedes deduction" (*Op. Cit.*, p. 12). Beegle is now in a position to see clearly that Hackett is his friend. Hackett has shown clearly that some "innate principle" is required in the way of furnishing the relationships between the facts of the inductive method. Hackett has also shown him that it is Kant who has first and best among modern men shown how fact and law, particular and universal, are really brought together. Kant has shown how neither pure rationalism nor pure empiricism can account for the fact that men build garages. Thus Kant has saved science by bringing induction and deduction in proper relation to one another. Kant saved science by restricting knowledge to the phenomenal realm. Science can realize its ideal of universality and therefore of predictability if only it will realize that such universality and predictability are inherent in the equipment with which the faculty of judgment comes to the very first fact of experience. At the same time science can also realize its ambition to add what is genuinely new to what is already known at any given time. Kant has shown how synthetic a priori judgments are possible. Kant has explained the methodology of science. Kant has thus shown how science is possible by his great discovery that it is man himself who is the ultimate and therefore active organizer back of scientific activity.

c. Der Seele Atmet Frei Aus

Up to the time of Kant, man found himself in a sad predicament. He knew that he needed absolute freedom if he was to continue to think of himself as morally responsible. And he knew that he needed absolute determinism if he was to have scientific knowledge. How can one have both?

It was Kant who solved this problem and set man free. After Kant man could explain his scientific methodology and at the same time have his moral freedom. Kant proved that the goal of comprehensive and exhaustive rational understanding is the ideal of science but that it must be maintained only as an on-going goal. The laws of science are absolute but they are absolute as relational to the absolutely raw stuff of experience. The laws of science can therefore never reach out beyond the phenomenal realm. And this means further that knowledge, scientific knowledge, can never be attained about man himself as free. The *old metaphysic* is done with forever. There is no more knowledge of man as free, there is no more knowledge of a God who is not correlative to the world.

Of course man "knows" himself to be free but then this knowing is a wholly other sort of knowing than the knowing of which the scientist speaks.

Once this fact is seen for what it is, it appears that now, for the first time, man is really able, without contradiction, to assert both his absolute freedom or autonomy and yet be absolutely true to the ideal of science as the realm of impersonal relations. Man has at last attained to true *inwardness*. He no longer fears any miraculous intrusions in the realm of science. Is he not the absolute lawgiver there? The only law that manifests itself in the realm of science springs from the innate relationizing equipment found in man. Again man no longer fears any "supernatural" intrusions into his moral consciousness. When he bows in reverence before the moral law and when he worships God as the law-giver, he knows that he is bowing to an image of the ideal self. In particular, he now knows that when he pays homage to the Christ incarnate in history, he is bowing to the ideal of realizing, to some extent in the space-time world, something of the brotherhood of man that he has set before himself as an ideal. So also when he speaks of the Church of this Christ-ideal he thinks of it as a continuation of this ideal incarnation. Kant likes to see an increasing realization of the kingdom of God in which all human beings treat each other as persons. And this would, then, include all higher religions and the cause of ecumenism would be making ever-increasing progress.

All of this appears to be involved in the idea of building garages in terms of Kant's philosophy.

2. I AM THE WAY, THE TRUTH AND THE LIFE

But garages cannot be built in terms of Kant's philosophy. Kant did not save science, and he did not make room for true religion.

In the first place Kant did not save science. His idea of science rests upon the idea of ultimate human autonomy. The a priori equipment which he employs in order to identify factuality would, if allowed to function unrestrained, reduce all factuality to one abstract universality. The only way Kant's innate equipment can be kept from thus destroying newness in science is for pure contingency to act as a counteracting instance. But then to the extent that pure contingency acts as a correlative counteracting instance to pure relational universality, to that extent universality is gone.

Then, too, Kant left no room for true religion. It has often enough been pointed out that on Kant's view the world cannot in any sense manifest the presence and activity of God. This is too obviously true to need further elucidation. The space-time world is for Kant what it is because of the combination of pure contingency and pure rationality, and it is the universal human mind that is presupposed as the source of this interrelation. For Kant the heavens *cannot* declare the glory of God. The divine original of nature appears to be man. Man has taken the place of the God of historic Christianity. Man is the one whose action makes nature into what it is. Yet Hackett speaks of the resurrection of "theism" in terms of Kantian Philosophy.

To be sure Hackett has, as noted, sought to alter Kant's philosophy so as to make room for the knowledge of a God who is beyond the world of nature. But this alteration cannot be adjudged successful. Hackett assures us that his alteration of the Kantian categories does not deny that the "synthetic a priori element in knowledge is strictly categorical and relational" (*Ibid.*, p. 46). But if this is true, Hackett's attempt to make the categories apply beyond the realm of sense must fail. For it is this very relational nature of the categories that makes them interdependent with sensuous experience. It is their relational character that guarantees their purely formal nature. It is this purely formal nature that is required if there is to be the possibility of their applicability to space-time factuality at any point. If, with Spinoza, or with Parmenides, Hackett wants speculative knowledge, he must, with them, lose his identity in a world of determinist, timeless being and thought. We may well urge Hackett, then, to stand fast in the liberty wherewith Kant has set him free.

Hackett argues that to accept the Kantian principle of rational empiricism we need not, with him, limit the categories to the phenomenal world. ". . . the categories are forms of things-in-themselves (noumena) as well as forms of thought, or of things as they appear to us (phenomena)" (*Ibid.*, p. 46).

But, on Kant's view, the idea of things-in-themselves would make the genuinely scientific knowledge of even one fact impossible. For Kant, genuine scientific knowledge means *systematic* knowledge. For any finite human "subject" to know itself at all or for any finite "object" to be known at all, their relationships of interdependence and interaction must be exhaustively displayed or predictable. They must be exhaustively rationalizable. "Things-in-themselves" are anything but that. They are like pockets of independent qualities that will *never* submit to generalization. If, together with such men as Locke and his empiricist descendants, Hackett wants to retain things-in-themselves, he must be ready, with them, to sink back into the pool of ultimate irrationality, or to subside into the dogmatic slumber from which Kant was aroused by Hume.

A more basic issue now faces Hackett. He has failed to see that in his attempt to combine the pre-Kantian *Dogmatism* of the Empiricists and Rationalists and Kantian *Criticism*, he has not attained the freedom and rationality that he seeks. Hackett thinks that he has found a theory of knowledge on the basis of which he can make a genuine choice between mutually exclusive systems of metaphysics. Apparently he does not see that his epistemol-

ogy involves a metaphysics. And the metaphysics involved in his epistemology is such as to reduce man to an abstract focus of interaction between an
abstract eternal form that would set man free from absorption into pure temporal being by absorption into itself and an abyss of ultimate contingency that
would set man free from such an absorption into timeless being by means of
its absorption into a bottomless and shoreless ocean of flux.

It scarcely needs to be indicated that Hackett the evangelical believer has
been tricked by Hackett the philosopher into paying too great a price for his
escape from the determinism and irrationalism of Calvinism which he so
dreads.

Hackett the believing Christian bows before the authority of Christ when
he says that his witness to himself as the Son of God and Son of man must
be accepted at his authority. Christ says that through him all things are made
and that by him all things consist. Christ says that no one *can* come to him
except the Father draw him. Christ says that all men are by virtue of their sin
spiritually dead, and, as such, hostile to God their Creator, and that knowing
God, by virtue of their being created in his image, they hold under the truth
in unrighteousness. Christ said that, sent by the Father, he came to save the
world through his being made a curse, through his being made sin for man.
Christ said that all the facts of the universe, the facts of creation and the facts
of redemption, can be seen for what they are only if they are seen thus in the
light of what he is and what he has done.

As noted earlier, in Jesus' day the Pharisees told Jesus that he blasphemed
when, in saying such things, he made himself one with God. They made their
own sinful moral consciousness the ultimate source and standard by which
they judged Jesus' claims. This is precisely what Kant has done in modern
times. The whole of Kant's epistemology presupposes the absolutely free or
autonomous moral self as the source of law both for the phenomenal and for
the noumenal realm. Kant's own work, *Religion Within the Limits of Pure
Reason*, shows that he will accept the claims of Christ only on condition that
he can reinterpret them, reducing them to nothing more than means by
which self-sufficient moral man may lift himself up by his own bootstraps toward the realization of his own humanized ethical ideal. Why then does
Hackett the philosopher virtually take sides with the Pharisees against the
Christ of the Scriptures, and therefore against Hackett the believer, on this
all-important point?

The Pharisees argued, in effect, that Jesus *could not* be the promised Messiah. Their position was, in effect, that there never could be a discernible appearance of any Absolute in the phenomenal realm. To maintain the honor
of God, they argued, one must honor an absolutely formal unity that is above

space-time being. How then could Jesus, a spatio-temporally conditioned man, claim to be one with the Father? If any finite man claims identity with God, all men are in jeopardy every hour. They must then bow before him as Lord. They must then be *made free* by him. But are not the Jews the sons of Abraham? "We have never been in bondage."

In similar fashion the position of Kant denies both man's creation and his fall into sin. Kant, as well as the Pharisees, refuses to allow that Jesus of Nazareth can possibly have been the Son of God except in the sense that all men are potentially the sons of God or participants in the being of God.

Why then does Hackett the philosopher virtually take sides with Kant in denying the possibility of the knowledge of Christ as the Redeemer-God, and therefore against Hackett the believer?

In the second place, Hackett argues that Calvinists, and in particular such extreme Calvinists as C. Van Til, allow for no common ground for discussion between believer and unbeliever. Hackett the philosopher now provides a common ground by means of the epistemology of Kant. But if such an epistemology provides a common ground it does so by destroying the believer altogether. To be sure, the believer is allowed to retain, not merely some, but all, of the major teachings of Christianity, but then all of these teachings must be reinterpreted as being symbols or pointers (*Hinweise*) toward some far off unknown, unknowable and unrealizable ideal that apostate man sets for himself in order thereby to resist the ever-present pressure of the claims of Christ upon him.

Modern ecumenical theology has fallen for this trap of Satan. In *The Confession of 1967*, the United Presbyterian Church, the historic defender of the unqualified sovereign claims of Christ, has capitulated to the demands of Kant's free man. The composers of this Confession have synthesized all true science, all true philosophy and all true theology by following the Pharisees and Kant—thereby virtually denying the Christ of the Scriptures. Hackett the believer surely does not want to follow this lead. Why then does he allow Hackett the philosopher to make him believe that Kant can set man free?

Finally Hackett says that according to Calvinists, and especially according to that extreme Calvinist, Van Til, "man, while he ought to do so, nevertheless cannot distill God from the general revelation . . ." (*Ibid.*, p. 164). How then, he asks, "is any apologetics possible?"

Hackett disagrees with Van Til who says that "it is only when the Holy Spirit gives man a new heart that he will accept the evidence of Scripture about itself and about nature for what it really is . . ." (*Ibid.*, pp. 163, 164). Kant again appears as savior. And this in spite of the fact that for Kant nature is exclusively revelational of man rather than of God. Or if we accept the alteration of Kant's doctrine of the categories, then we may allow that God and man together may find themselves in the nature they are jointly engaged in confronting and creating.

It is thus that Hackett the philosopher attains to the "resurrection of theism." But the God of this theism cannot be the God and Father of our Lord Jesus Christ. The "theism" thus resurrected is destructive of the possibility of intelligent human predication whether with respect to the "phenomenal" or "noumenal" sphere.

(B) The apologetic method thus far outlined will be made clearer if we consider an objection, indeed the "stock" objection, to such an approach as Calvin's. It comes from Stuart Cornelius Hackett in his *The Resurrection of Theism*. We must, says Hackett, have "a rational justification for the metaphysical ultimate" which we believe in. Calvinism denies this. The Calvinists say that God has "created rational men as mere puppets of his sovereignty. But if it seems to be the case that man is under *obligation* to believe the gospel and that he must accept Christ as Savior *before* the Spirit of God regenerates the heart—if, I say, man is a moral and rational agent confronted with a revelation for the acceptance of which he is morally and rationally responsible— then let the presuppositionalist framework be consigned to the irrationalism that is written so plainly through its structure. . . . With her opponents thus languishing in defeat, reason pushes on to consider experience itself to determine whether God is real."[278]

With these words Hackett sums up the issue between himself as an Arminian and myself as a Calvinist very well. It goes without saying that we two have radically different beliefs as to what the Bible says about man and his sinfulness and about the Holy Spirit and his sovereignty. Indeed, the issues between us are total. There are no "fundamentals" in common between us; we will necessarily understand creation-providence, the fall of man, the atonement of Christ, his sinlessness and his resurrection, his second coming and his ultimate triumph, the doctrine of Scripture, the nature of saving faith—we will necessarily understand, I say, these doctrines in different ways. Hackett's Christian faith and my Christian faith, which we both desire non-Christians to accept, are radically different. They are different not only in their *content* but also in the very *method* of their construction.

I make two broad points in reference to this. First, *any non-Christian epistemology, i.e., any theory of knowledge based upon principles acceptable*

---

278. CVT: Stuart Cornelius Hackett, *The Resurrection of Theism* (Chicago: Moody Press, 1957), pp. 174–75.

per se *to the "mind of the flesh" (and therefore those of Hackett's own method), is doomed to utter failure; not only failure as an avenue to Christian faith, but as an avenue to any form of knowledge whatsoever.*[279] This I think can be, and has been repeatedly, shown by myself and many others. Second, Hackett's basic charge that Calvinism is determinist and irrational is simply not true. First, as to the charge that it is determinist and that men are but "puppets," one need only read Calvin himself to be persuaded that such an understanding of Calvinism is false. The Calvinist notion of divine sovereignty has nothing to do with the philosopher's notion of physical, causal determinism. I have developed at length in other places the covenantal, exhaustively personalist view of providence which is clearly part of Calvin's thought.

As to the charge that the Calvinist position is "irrational," I assume that Hackett cannot mean that it is inconsistent. After all, one of the so-called "sins" of Calvin was that he was too deductive, too logical, in drawing implications from this and that in Scripture, that in "logicizing" theology he destroyed its heart. I assume that what Hackett means is that on the Calvinist position man is called upon to repent of his sins and accept Christ *without having reasons* for doing so. The Calvinist cannot give reasons because he has *no point of contact* with the non-Christian. There are, for the Calvinist, no *reasons* to which he might appeal in an effort to get his friend to accept Christ.

In response to this I observe that this also is not the case. Hackett assumes that unless one finds a point of contact with the natural man by way of agreeing with him on his false views of man and the world then one has no point of contact with him at all. Against this position, I maintain, with Calvin following Paul, that my point of contact lies in the *actual state of affairs between men* as the Bible tells us of it. It is Hackett who has no *real* point of contact, for his lies in what men *imagine* (and, to be sure, "agree") to be the case. The Calvinist's point of contact is rooted in the *actual* state of affairs. All things are what they are because of their relation to the work of the triune God as reported in Scripture. Hackett's "point of contact" as an evangelical Arminian is an essentially Kantian epistemology, an epistemology in terms of which men stand utterly unrelated to one another and are, at the same time, reduced to relations of one another.

To look for a point of contact with the unbeliever in the unbeliever's notions of himself and his world is to encourage him in his wicked rebellion and

---

279. Emphasis added. Van Til offers here an excellent encapsulation of his distinctive approach to apologetics.

to establish him in his self-frustration. We have already seen that the natural man is under the self-imposed delusion that he is "free," i.e., independent of the control and counsel of God, and that the facts about him are also "free" in this way. He may pretend to be "open-minded" and ready to consider *whether* God exists. But in being so "neutral" he commits the same sin as Adam and Eve.

Why seek truth where only a lie is to be found? Can the non-Christian tell *us* and therefore the Christ himself *what* the facts are and how they are related to each other, in what way they cohere, while yet excluding creation and providence? If he can, and if he can tell us truly, then the Christian story simply is not true! Because the natural man cannot do this, because the Christian message is true, I have sought and still seek to reap the benefit of a theology in which the triune God of Scripture has the initiative in salvation.

The Calvinist's idea of an *actual* as opposed to an *imagined* point of contact is not just some useless notion. It is the only intelligible point of contact possible. The non-Christian holds that pure chance and absolute fate are equally ultimate and mutually correlative limiting concepts or heuristic principles which man uses to explain the fact that we have learned much about the world, that there is order in the world, a uniformity, while there is also continual change and development. But the non-Christian's "explanation" is no explanation at all. To say "it just happens" as an explanation of an event is really to say, "There is no explanation that I know of."

The Calvinist, therefore, using his point of contact, observes to the non-Christian that if the world were not what Scripture says it is, if the natural man's knowledge were not actually rooted in the creation and providence of God, then there could be no knowledge whatsoever. The Christian claims that non-Christians have made and now make many discoveries about the true state of affairs of the universe simply because the universe is what Christ says it is. The unbelieving scientist borrows or steals the Christian principles of creation and providence every time he says that an "explanation" is possible, for he knows he cannot account for "explanation" on his own. As the image-bearer of God, operating in a universe controlled by God, the unbeliever contributes indirectly and adventitiously to the development of human knowledge and culture.

When Hackett maintains that the Calvinist position is irrational because it cannot give "reasons" for believing, he must mean that on a position such as mine *the Christian does not accept the non-Christian scheme wherein the non-Christian determines what are "good reasons" and "valid proofs." This is perfectly true, but this is not irrational. Rather the Christian offers the self-attesting Christ to the world as the only foundation upon which a man must stand in order to give any "reasons" for anything at all.*[280] The whole notion of "giving reasons" is completely *destroyed* by any ontology other than the Christian one. The Christian claims that only after accepting the biblical scheme of things will any man be able to understand and account for his own rationality.

---

280. Emphasis added. What count as "good reasons" are determined by one's world-view as a whole, and therefore when the argument is over competing worldviews themselves, Van Til's apologetic defends the faith by showing that offering "reasons" itself would be unintelligible in any other framework of thought.

Chapter 9

Concluding Summary:
How to Defend the Faith

9.1 Recapitulation

Cornelius Van Til was a profound and intelligent philosopher who sought above all to be faithful as a minister of God's authoritative word. His heart was devoted to the self-attesting Savior, whose saving love was presented in that word, and he was dedicated to reaching out to a lost world in the most winsome and effective manner of declaring and defending the gospel he cherished. What he taught us about defending the faith has immense value that should not be missed in our generation or lost to future ones.

Van Til's system of thought is not a simple one. For that reason it has taken some space to explain it and present a healthy dose of Van Til's own words. Van Til wrote a large amount of material; his books, syllabi, mimeos, and pamphlets easily fill more than three feet on a book shelf—thousands of pages. There is much to master, and, because Van Til addressed so many issues (often in a crisscrossing fashion), it is hard for many readers to follow. In this book I have tried to present Van Til's challenging apologetic in a way that will be clear, cogent, systematic, and persuasive. Three feet of material have been reduced to less than three inches. The mass of material has been broken down and reorganized into a progressive presentation of his central ideas, exhibiting the structure and strength of his presuppositional approach to defending the faith. I have added commentary, introductions, annotations, and replies to critics. Obviously much more could have been said and many other readings could have been profitably included. But I hope this text has made Van Til's distinctively Reformed apologetic, with its transcendental method of argument, somewhat more clear and more attractive to fellow believers. I am convinced that it should appeal to those who seriously and self-consciously want to become better prepared to "give an answer to every man who asks a reason for the hope that is in you"—in a way in which Christ is "set apart as Lord in your hearts" (1 Peter 3:15).

For a simple presentation of the basic issues in apologetical strategy as Van Til saw them, and for a popular illustration of how his approach is put into practice, the reader can consult chapter 3 above (cf. chap. 1.1–3). The material in that summary is then retraced, analyzing the presuppositional approach to apologetics in greater detail, philosophical depth, and interaction in chapters 4–8.

Van Til's life reflected his desire as a scholar to surrender totally to Christ and to set Him forth without compromise (chap. 1.4). As a result, he developed a presuppositional conception of apologetics, a brief digest of which can be perused in the "Analysis of Contents" at the beginning of this book. The basic issues of apologetics are raised chapter by chapter: the nature and purpose of the apologetical task (chap. 2), the believer's and the unbeliever's respective theories of knowledge (chaps. 4, 5), an analysis of the person to whom we defend the faith (chap. 6), the basic or underlying argument by which the Christian worldview is defended (chap. 7), and a clarification of the presuppositional method's distinctive character by means of comparison and criticism (chap. 8). A section-by-section reflection on the "Analysis" will disclose what issues Van Til understood to be most pivotal in formulating his strategy for defending the faith, and the headings that are provided for the various readings in each section distill the particular features of Van Til's treatment of those issues.

Unbelievers are committed to a different lifestyle than believers, and they advocate (with varying degrees of self-consciousness and consistency) a different point of view than that of the Christian. When the believer presents the gospel to the unbeliever, many times the response is negative and resistance is offered to the claims of Christ. The resistance may be emotional (ridicule, disdain, apathy) or behavioral (living disobediently, refusing to give thanks or offer worship), but sometimes it is intellectual. The unbeliever in some cases will answer that believers do not really know Christianity to be true—expecting the Christian to prove his beliefs. In other cases the non-Christian will claim to know that the Bible is mistaken or that the Christian outlook is erroneous. Regardless of the specific form that the apologetical dispute takes (demands for proof or objections to claims), it is necessary to answer each challenge (chap. 2.1)—and in a way that is both evangelistic and consistent with our theological convictions (2.2). In giving his answer, the apologist endeavors to present the intellectual challenge of the gospel and demonstrate the objective, certain proof of Christianity's truth (2.3).

Whenever we are drawn into a defense of the faith, Van Til observed, there is a dispute between two different ultimate commitments—a conflict between final authorities for living and reasoning (1.1; 3.1). Neither side is or can be neutral, and the unbeliever's bias will be evident by his opposition to any authority that does not leave him autonomous. This is evident in the fact that the believer and the unbeliever disagree, in principle, over the method and criteria for knowing whatever can be known (4.1, 2; 5.2)—which in turn enmeshes them in an overall debate regarding their antithetical worldviews in general (3.2; 5.1). Van Til taught, therefore, that the Christian apologist must be, and must press the non-Christian to become, epistemologically self-conscious (1.2).

The Christian will claim that because God is inescapably and directly known through natural revelation (4.3) and the special revelation of Scripture (4.4), it is possible to "think God's thoughts after Him" and provide an intelligible context for man's gaining of knowledge and for the processes by which our knowledge is extended (4.5). The non-Christian will repudiate this outlook and suppress the truth of it (5.2; 6.5). Nevertheless, because the unbeliever is made in God's image and is restrained by common grace (6.3, 4), he can understand the believer's claims and arguments. Unbelievers already know God psychologically through nature and Scripture (6.1), and therefore can and do contribute much to our understanding of the world. However, *if they were consistent with their espoused assumptions and declared lifestyle,* they would—in epistemological principle—be unable to justify or make sense of any of their beliefs and would disagree with believers at every point (6.2). How can those who deny the truth yet come to know much that is true? Non-Christians do not acknowledge it, but they think, reason, and live in terms of two different mind-sets (two different sets of presuppositions): their philosophy of would-be autonomy and their suppressed knowledge of God (6.5).

The method by which Van Til defended the faith, therefore, was to unmask the intellectual self-deception of those who contended against it. He would not allow unbelievers to be "epistemological loafers." He pressed them to explain why they believed as they did (or did not) and how they could know anything at all. The failure of all unbelieving philosophies to provide a cogent theory of knowledge (5.3) becomes relevant to (and usually part of) such a discussion. The "indirect" way to prove the truth of Christianity, then, is to take the conflicting worldviews of the Christian and the non-Christian—with their opposing presuppositions and theories of knowledge, in terms of which particular claims are disputed back and forth—and press for a critical internal analysis of each one, looking for philosophical inconsistency and absurdity. This is the way to refute the unbeliever's bedrock presuppositions, showing the intellectual impossibility of any worldview that is contrary to Christianity (1.3; 3.3).

The apologetical program can be pursued with the aid of theistic proofs (8.3) or empirical evidences (8.4), provided such arguments are not offered in such a way as to encourage the unbeliever's autonomous reasoning (8.1). The arguments of the Christian apologist should attack the unbeliever's assumed intellectual independence, presenting a "transcendental" challenge to his would-be autonomy. The apologist argues that unless the unbeliever acknowledges God and brings a belief in Him into his theory of knowledge, it is impossible for him to prove anything at all in any field, including religion. We see two conflicting conceptions of knowledge or "science" as the controlling background in any apologetical encounter. Rather than submitting to the unbeliever's conception and criteria, the apologist must demonstrate that only the Christian conception or presuppositions can ultimately make any sense of "science," logic, experience, reasoning, self-consciousness, morality, etc. (8.2). This is what is meant by the "presuppositional" method of defending the faith. It calls upon the unbeliever to confess his intellectual rebellion and ruin, and then to submit in faith, thanksgiving, and obedience to the claims of the self-attesting Christ.

It would be appropriate to conclude with selections from Van Til in which he distills the presuppositional method of defending the faith. We will do this in three ways. First, we will present what amounts to an abridged reader, tracing the contours of Van Til's apologetic through certain important themes that recur in his writings. Second, we will present passages in which Van Til offered students a specific list of the crucial points in his apologetical method. Finally, we will reproduce a succinct outline that Van Til produced for inclusion in his *Festschrift*. This can be taken as a fitting synopsis of this book of readings and analysis. We will conclude with Van Til's recognition that our reasoning with unbelievers requires the powerful grace of God to be successful, and that as a covenantal endeavor it is always successful in God's plan to bring either blessing or curse upon people.

9.2 A Quick Read of Van Til by Key Themes

THE IMPOSSIBILITY OF NEUTRALITY [1]

This insistence on neutrality is highly significant. Neutrality in method is not a mere matter of course, a hallmark of ordinary intelligence. It is imposed upon the metaphysical relativist. He cannot choose to be prejudiced or biased; he must be neutral. Therefore he too is biased and prejudiced, in favor of neutrality. Neutrality is implied in the supposition of the open universe. If the universe is open, the facts new to God and man constantly issue from the womb of possibility. These new facts will constantly reinterpret the meaning of the old. Our method then must be basically synthetic; God's method is also synthetic. He too must wait to see what the facts may bring. God can do no more than man. He cannot interpret the meaning of reality to man since he has not yet interpreted reality for himself. Therefore man must interpret for himself and must be neutral; his thought is *creatively constructive*.

The Theist, on the other hand, cannot be neutral. His conception of God makes him biased. He holds that for God the facts are in: God knows the end from the beginning. He admits that facts may emerge that are new to man; he knows they are not new to God. History is but the expression of the purpose of God. As far as the space-time universe is concerned the category of interpretation precedes that of existence. Man's interpretation must, therefore, to be correct, correspond to the interpretation of God. Man's synthesis and analysis rest upon God's analysis. Strictly speaking, man's method of investigation is that of analysis of God's analysis. We are to think God's thought after him; our thought is *receptively reconstructive*.

Viewed from the side of epistemology the same difference between Pragmatism and Theism appears.

To be neutral in method implies metaphysical relativism. This is the simple converse of the statement that metaphysical relativity implies neutrality. You cannot be neutral unless the universe is open to God as well as to you. If the facts are all in for God you must accept God's interpretation. To be neutral

---

1. Excerpts from Van Til's first published article, "God and the Absolute," in *Christianity and Idealism* (Philadelphia: Presbyterian and Reformed, 1955), 8–9, 10, 11–12.

implies that system is non-existent. To be neutral implies that synthesis is prior to analysis for God as well as for man. It implies that God is then within the universe. It is determined beforehand that you cannot come to the acceptance of an absolute God; metaphysical relativity is assumed.

The Theist, on the other hand, because of his bias must have an absolute God. If God were not absolute, if for him analysis does not have significance prior to and apart from synthesis, man would have to interpret the facts for himself. Interpretation of reality cannot be a co-operative enterprise between God and man. . . .

We are either metaphysical relativists or metaphysical absolutists. If the former, then we are "neutral," if the latter, then "biased." Choose ye this day whom ye shall serve! . . .

The Theist calls upon men to conform to God's plan. He therefore also calls on the Pragmatist to do so. "I'll wait and see," is the answer of the Pragmatist. "Where do you obtain such knowledge as you say you have? I'll be honestly agnostic, humbly scientific."

Again the Theist urges his case and again the Pragmatist replies: " 'All speculations about an Absolute are but miasmatic exhalations of a false intellectualism which has misconstrued its own nature and powers.'[2] Present axioms once were postulates. All that human thought is for is to find our way efficiently from a known fact to an unknown one. No one knows how many are yet to be discovered. No one can tell us that history will terminate in a judgment day. You, my friend, dare not be openminded."

"Quite true," answers the Theist. "I dare not be openminded because I cannot be. Have you been openminded? You have spoken about what *cannot* be. But to the 'openminded' all things should be possible. 'Openmindedness' requires an 'open' universe; and an 'open' universe requires an 'open' mind; your mind is closed against the Absolute. Or was it inconsistency merely? Do you really wish the open universe? Open for the fact of the judgment, that is, for the Absolute? If so then your universe is really one. To be a genuine relativist you must be a brave absolutist; to be really 'openminded' you must be 'closed' minded. You were after all quite logical in seeking by one a *priori* 'cannot' to strike God out of the universe. It cannot be done any other way. Only you have failed to observe that an 'openminded' man must never use 'cannot' as a weapon. An 'open' mind should be 'unstable in all his ways.'

"Moreover, 'neutrality' seems to be an unreasonable position for a finite, time conditioned man to take. It implies, as we have seen, the open universe, where a new fact may appear at any time. Suppose the 'judgment' should prove to be a fact. Could you meet it 'neutrally'? You could not, since the

2. CVT: Schiller, F. C., "Axioms as Postulates," in *Personal Idealism*, p. 54, edited by Sturt.

judgment implies that facts are now in for God so that you ought to be 'prejudiced.' On the other hand, if it be said that the very meaning of the 'open universe' is that the judgment is not to be a fact, this must be established by *a priori* argument. To be 'neutral' implies the 'open universe'; but no human being can establish the openness of the universe by a neutral method. The assumption of a metaphysical relativism and 'neutrality' would seem to be unreasonable except for one who is absolute, which by admission you are not.

"To be 'neutral' is, therefore, to try to be something no human being can be. I see this most clearly when I notice how readily the advocates of Pragmatism turn from radical empiricism to an extreme form of *a priori* reasoning. They constantly tell me what can and cannot be. They tell me, for example, that the very terms 'relative' and 'absolute' are correlatives so that it is impossible for us to think of God otherwise than as correlative to man. This is but one example of the commonest form in which the assumption that all categories of thinking are the same for God and man is stated. The assumption underlying this is once more that of metaphysical relativism. Only upon the basis of this assumption can you maintain that all categories of thinking are the same for God and man and therefore conclude that the correlativity for us of such terms as 'absolute' and 'relative' necessarily implies the correlativity of these terms for God. Now metaphysical relativity is just the question at issue; least of all then have your friends who boast of 'neutrality' a right to assume it. 'Neutrality' must beg the question.

"These considerations have often made me more 'biased' than ever. I feel that it is better to be 'biased' in favor of the Absolute and admit my bias than to be 'biased' against him and deny my bias. I do not close my eyes to the difficulties as they center about God's relation to his temporally created world, but I have yet to find a solution of these difficulties that does not begin by dissolving one of the terms to be related, that does not begin by assuming metaphysical relativism. Is it hard to believe in God? It is far harder not to believe in him."

UNBELIEVERS ALWAYS AIM TO PRESERVE THEIR AUTONOMY[3]

(A) There are those, of course, who deny that they need any form of authority. They are the popular atheists and agnostics. Such men say that they must be shown by "reason" whatever they are to accept as true. But the great thinkers

3. The following excerpts are taken from:

    (A) *The Defense of the Faith* (Philadelphia: Presbyterian and Reformed, 1955), 140–45;
    (B) *A Christian Theory of Knowledge* (Philadelphia: Presbyterian and Reformed, 1969), 59–60.

among non-Christian men have taken no such position. They know that they cannot cover the whole area of reality with their knowledge. They are therefore willing to admit that there may be others who have information that they themselves do not possess. In everyday life this sort of thing is illustrated in the idea of the expert. A medical doctor knows much about the human body that the rest of us do not know. Then among medical men there are those who, because of natural ability, industry and opportunity, make such discoveries as their fellows do not make. So everywhere and in all respects the lesser minds are bound to submit to the authority of greater minds.

In putting the matter in this way the nature of the authority that can be allowed by the natural man is already indicated. The natural man will gladly allow for the idea of authority if only it be the authority of the expert in the use of reason. Such a conception of authority is quite consistent with the assumption of the sinner's autonomy.

On the other hand the conception of authority as something that stands "above reason" is unacceptable to the natural man. But it is not easy to distinguish in every instance when authority is considered to be "above reason." There are some forms of authority that might seem, at first sight, to be "above reason" while in reality they are not. Some discussion of this matter must therefore precede our analysis of the difference between the Roman Catholic and the Protestant methods of presenting the authority of Christianity to the natural man.

Let us note then some of the forms of authority that are quite acceptable to the natural man because, to his mind, they do not violate the principle of autonomy.

First there is the need for authority that grows out of the existence of the endless multiplicity of factual material. Time rolls its ceaseless course. It pours out upon us an endless stream of facts. And the stream is really endless on the non-Christian basis. For those who do not believe that all that happens in time happens because of the plan of God, the activity of time is like to that, or rather is identical with that, of Chance. Thus the ocean of facts has no bottom and no shore. It is this conception of the ultimacy of time and of pure factuality on which modern philosophy, particularly since the days of Kant, has laid such great stress. And it is because of the general recognition of the ultimacy of chance that rationalism of the sort that Descartes, Spinoza and Leibniz represented, is out of date. It has become customary to speak of post-Kantian philosophy as irrationalistic. It has been said that Kant limited reason so as to make room for faith. Hence there are those who are willing to grant that man's emotions or his will can get in touch with such aspects of reality as are not accessible to the intellect. . . .

There is a second kind of authority that the natural man is quite ready to accept. It does not spring, as did the first, from the fact that the intellect can by definition not control the whole realm of chance. It springs from the fact that even that which the intellect does assert about the objects of knowledge is, of necessity, involved in contradiction. . . .

On the assumptions of the natural man logic is a timeless impersonal principle, and facts are controlled by chance. It is by means of universal timeless principles of logic that the natural man must, on his assumptions, seek to make intelligible assertions about the world of reality or chance. But this cannot be done without falling into self-contradiction. About chance no manner of assertion can be made. In its very idea it is the irrational. And how are rational assertions to be made about the irrational? If they are to be made then it must be because the irrational is itself wholly reduced to the rational. That is to say if the natural man is to make any intelligible assertions about the world of "reality" or "fact" which, according to him is what it is for no rational reason at all, then he must make the virtual claim of rationalizing the irrational. To be able to distinguish one fact from another fact he must reduce all time existence, all factuality to immovable timeless being. But when he has done so he has killed all individuality and factuality as conceived of on his basis. Thus the natural man must on the one hand assert that all reality is non-structural in nature and on the other hand that all reality is structural in nature. He must even assert on the one hand that all reality is non-structurable in nature and on the other hand that he himself has virtually structured all of it. Thus all his predication is in the nature of the case self-contradictory.

Realizing this dilemma, many modern philosophers have argued that any intellectual system of interpretation is therefore no more than a perspective. No system, these men assert, should pretend to be more than a system "for us." We have to deal with reality *as if* it will always behave as we have found it behaving in the past. The world of appearance formed by means of the exercise of the intellect must be taken as "somehow" similar to the world of Reality. And thus we seem to have come again upon the idea of mystery, the world of "faith" and of "authority" where prophets and seers may suggest to us the visions they have seen in the night.

Such then seems to be the present situation. Modern philosophy in practically all of its schools admits that all its speculations end in mystery. Speaking generally, modern philosophy (and science) is phenomenalistic. It admits that ultimate reality is unknowable to man. All systems of interpretation are said to be necessarily relative to the mind of man. And so it seems at first sight that modern philosophy ought, on its own principles, to admit that there is a dimension of reality that is beyond its reach and about which it ought therefore to be ready to listen by the avenue of authority. Modern philosophy would seem to be ready therefore to listen to the voice of "religion." So for instance Dorothy Emmet views the matter. . . . On such a view it might seem that one should be able to accept the authority of Jesus. . . . But it is still no more than the authority of the expert. For those who think as she does, Jesus is nothing more than the kind of person they would like to be and could be if only they lived up to their own ideals.

The natural man then assumes that he has the final criterion of truth within himself. Every form of authority that comes to him must justify itself by standards inherent in man and operative apart from the authority that speaks.

(B) A brief indication may be given of the kind of authority that man who does not begin with Scripture will accept. The kind of authority that he will accept must, in short, be consonant with his own ultimacy and with his own right to be the final arbiter of his fate. In other words the kind of authority he will allow for is such as is consistent with his principle of his ultimate self-reference.

1. Man will allow that the matter of finding the meaning of his experience is a joint enterprise. No one man can know all things. Thus there are authorities in this field and in that field. The doctor is expert in the field of medicine. The physicist is expert in his own field, and so on. Such expert authority men will of course readily own. It is quite consistent with their principle to admit that they are finite.

2. When it comes to religion men will agree that there are those who are experts in this field. So the Jews seem to have been a preeminently religious people, and among them Jesus of Nazareth was perhaps the greatest religious expert that the race has seen. He is the kind of man that we should like to be. So we may take him as our guide or authority. He seems to have had a sort of intuition of the nature of God or ultimate reality. Since it is in any case impossible to find exhaustive knowledge because man cannot by the laws of his thought reach further than the world of experience, it is well to appeal to one who has a feeling for the numinous. Perhaps there is more to life than appears to the eye. Perhaps reality is deeper than logic. Perhaps the great mystics were not altogether wrong. No one knows. Perhaps some have valid hunches.

In such views of authority, it is clear, the final point of reference is still the would-be autonomous man. The experts may differ; it is up to every man finally to decide for himself. This is proper; the sanctity of the human person must not be violated. Ask any man to accept anything on pure authority, the sort of authority that the Bible claims for itself, and you are virtually asking him to deny his manhood. You are then asking him to be irrational and therewith to deny him the use of the powers that constitute his personality. With Plato I may look for some great expert, and listen to mythology as a second best, but rational inquiry, for better or for worse, must be my final guide. For better or for worse I must hold that I have the final criterion of truth or falsehood within myself.

A BLOCKHOUSE METHOD OF DEFENSE INEFFECTIVE[4]

It has been pointed out that the difference between a Roman Catholic–Arminian and a Reformed type of argument lies in the fact that the former is direct and the latter is indirect. The former grants the essential truthfulness of the non-Christian theory of man and of method, while the latter challenges both. This difference will appear again and appear in its fundamental importance still more strikingly if the question of the place of Scripture in apologetics is brought up for consideration. A few remarks on this subject must suffice.

For better or for worse the Protestant apologist is committed to the doctrine of Scripture as the infallibly inspired final revelation of God to man. This being the case, he is committed to the defense of Christian theism as a unit. For him theism is not really theism unless it is Christian theism. The Protestant apologist cannot be concerned to prove the existence of any other God than the one who has spoken to man authoritatively and finally through Scripture.

The entire debate about theism will be purely formal unless theism be taken as the foundation of Christianity. But if it is so taken it is no longer theism as such but Christian theism that is in debate. Pantheists, deists and theists, that is bare theists, may formally agree that God exists. Socrates, in arguing about the nature of piety within Euthyphro says that men "join issue about particulars." So if the whole debate in apologetics is to be more than a meaningless discussion about the *that* of God's existence and is to consider *what kind* of God exists, then the question of God's revelation to man must be brought into the picture. . . .

We have also seen that the method of presupposition requires the presentation of Christian theism as a unit. But the theology of Roman Catholics compels them to deal with theism first and with Christianity afterwards. Assigning to reason the task of interpreting nature without dependence upon Scripture, this theology is bound to prove the truth of theism first. The theism that is proved in this way cannot be the only theism that any Christian should want to prove, namely, Christian theism. Yet having proved some sort

4. Excerpts from *Defense of the Faith*, 122–23, 131–32.

of theism by reason, the Roman Catholic is bound by virtue of his theology to prove a type of Christianity that will fit on to the deformation of theism it has "established." And what holds true of Roman Catholicism holds true fundamentally also of Arminianism.

It remains now to indicate more fully than has been done that the Roman Catholic and Arminian method of reasoning is bound, not merely to cut the unity of Christian theism in two, but is bound even to prove its theism piece by piece. Romanism and Arminianism lead not merely to dualism but to atomism in methodology.

A truly Protestant method of reasoning involves a stress upon the fact that the meaning of every aspect or part of Christian theism depends upon Christian theism as a unit. When Protestants speak of the resurrection of Christ they speak of the resurrection of him who is the Son of God, the eternal Word through whom the world was made. The truth of theism is involved in this claim that Christians make with respect to the domain of history. And what is true of the resurrection of Christ is true with respect to all the propositions about historical fact that are made in Scripture. No proposition about historical fact is presented for what it really is till it is presented as a part of the system of Christian theism that is contained in Scripture. To say this is involved in the consideration that all facts of the created universe are what they are by virtue of the plan of God with respect to them. Any fact in any realm confronted by man is what it is as revelational through and through of the God and of the Christ of Christian theism.

But if this is true—and it would seem to be of the very essence of the Biblical point of view to say that it is true—then it follows that the whole claim of Christian theism is in question in any debate about any fact. Christian theism must be presented as that light in terms of which any proposition about any fact receives meaning.

TWO MUTUALLY EXCLUSIVE POSITIONS, ONLY ONE HOPE FOR MEANING AND RATIONALITY[5]

Christianity is the only hope of the world, and therefore the only hope for modern man. However, this cannot be shown to be true unless it be made evident that Christianity not only has its own methodology but also that only its methodology gives meaning to life. . . .

The natural man must not be encouraged to think that he can, in terms of

5. Excerpts from *The Case for Calvinism* (Philadelphia: Presbyterian and Reformed, 1963), 106–7, 116, 134–37, 147–48.

his own adopted principles, find truth in any field. He must rather be told that, when he finds truth, even in the realm of the "phenomenal," he finds it in terms of principles that he has "borrowed," wittingly or unwittingly, from Christianity. The fact of science and its progress is inexplicable except upon the presupposition that the world is made and controlled by God through Christ and that man is made and renewed in the image of God through Christ. . . .

But if Scripture is thus self-authenticating, it is because Christ speaks to us through it. The Bible is, as it were, a letter from Christ to his people, to his Church. But Christ is God. He speaks to his Church so that his Church might speak to mankind. All men are men as standing in covenant relation to the triune God. It is Christ who says "I am the way, the truth and the life." He says this as the Son of God. God identifies himself as the "I am." There are no laws of truth, goodness or beauty above him to which he need or even can make reference. All law, in the "phenomenal" and in the "noumenal" realm alike, proceeds from him. Again, there are no facts of the world of space and time that act as an independent and therefore as a possibly or actually refractory power below him. There is no such thing as pure contingency. The very idea of possibility so far as man deals with it, gets its meaning from God as the self-referential, self-contained *I am*, for he speaks in Christ. It is this God of pure inwardness in terms of which the Christian interprets himself and his cosmic environment. . . .

It is this "Christian story" that is "alone able to resolve the dilemmas of the modern mood." The dilemmas of the modern mood are the false dilemmas of all non-Christian thought. And all these dilemmas reduce to one. They are all based on the assumption that man is the ultimate reference point in all his interpretation. It is the would-be self-sufficient, this would-be autonomous man that sets himself up as judge above the claims of the self-authenticating Christ. The one issue that lies back of all other issues is that between the self-authenticating man and the self-authenticating Christ.

The self-authenticating man has various disguises. He will appear as the "rational man" and demand that the Christian story must make peace with *the laws* of logic, as these are based on his vision of *Truth* above God and man. He will appear as the "moral man" and demand that the Christian story make peace with *the laws* of morality, as these are based on his vision of *Goodness* above God and man. He will appear as the "scientific man" and demand that the Christian story must make peace with the facts of science. For these facts *must* be what the vision of the self-authenticating man says they *can* be. But in whatever guise he may appear, the self-authenticating man assumes that he is to be the judge. The vision originates with him. In his eyes he is the judge of the supreme court. All questions of law and of fact must be settled by him. He alone knows what they can or cannot be. According to his vision, the Christian story cannot be true. And his judgment is final. There is no repeal from his decision. How could there be? The self-authenticating man virtually takes the place that Christ has in the Christian religion. But where is the constitution by which even the chief judge of the supreme court must judge? The answer is that this constitution has been written by the chief judge himself. . . .

[T]he self-authenticating man cannot be modest. His vision is always the same. In this vision, he sees himself as God. He sees himself as alone able to determine what can be and what cannot be. He is, according to his vision, the source of all possibility. Even when, speaking through Kant, he limits reason to make room for faith, he first makes sure that the object of this faith *cannot* be the Christian story. . . .

Thus, the "reason" of the self-authenticating man is the willing servant of the faith of the self-authenticating man. So far as he sincerely thinks that he is open-minded and therefore ready to follow the facts wheresoever they may lead him, he is self-deceived. . . . The self-authenticating man assumes that only in terms of his totality-vision can law and fact come into fruitful union with one another.

It appears then that if there is to be any intelligible encounter between the Christian and the non-Christian, it must be in terms of the two mutually exclusive visions that each entertains. To appeal to the *law of contradiction* and/or to *facts* or to a combination of these apart from the relation that these sustain to the totality-vision of either, the believer or the unbeliever, is to beat the air. It is well to say that he who would reason must pre-suppose the validity of the laws of logic. But if we say nothing more basic than this, then we are still beating the air. The ultimate question deals with the foundation of the validity of the laws of logic. We have not reached bottom until we have seen that every logical activity in which any man engages is in the service of his totality-vision.

It is also well to say that we must follow the facts wheresoever they may lead us. But again we should note that all research into the realm of fact, on the part of any man, is in the service of his totality-vision. The self-authenticating man assumes that if the Christian story were true, then the scientific enterprise would be meaningless. Free scientific inquiry, he assumes, requires that there be no pre-interpretation of facts in terms of the Christian story. On the other hand, the Christian holds that the idea of free scientific inquiry is unintelligible except upon the presupposition of the truth of the Christian story. . . .

By forsaking him who is the way, the truth, and the life, the "world" strangles itself. Its method is fatal to the entire enterprise of human interpretation.

How then may the "world" be saved? Only by adopting the method that is involved in the Christian story. It is this that Christians must tell the world. They must offer Christ as *the* way, the *only* way by which men may be saved. To offer Christ as *the* way is to call men to repentance. It is sin to seek for truth anywhere without seeking it through Christ as the *only* way. The wrath of God rests upon us if, in seeking truth, we ignore and reject him who alone is truth. The search for truth is an existential matter. One's attitude toward Christ is always involved. Our every thought in science, in philosophy, and in theology must be made captive to the obedience of Christ.

The ultimate source of truth in any field rests in him. The world may discover much truth without owning Christ as Truth. Christ upholds even those who ignore, deny, and oppose him. A little child may slap his father in the face, but it can do so only because the father holds it on his knee. So modern science, modern philosophy, and modern theology may discover much truth. Nevertheless, if the universe were not created and redeemed by Christ no man could give himself an intelligible account of anything. It follows that in order to perform their task aright the scientist and the philosopher as well as the theologian need Christ.

It is man with all his cultural interests and tasks who needs the Christ. But Christ, the Saviour of the world, wants to be accepted as the Lord of men. Men do not accept him at all for what he is unless they accept him as such. For men cannot accept him as Lord except by grace they receive the desire to do so. No one comes to the Father except through the Son and no one can come to the Son except the Father draw him.

So long as we do not dare to tell the "natural man" this fact we have not really brought the Christ to him. Unless we do this we have not really offered the world what it most desperately needs. The world by its wisdom knows not God and not knowing God it knows not the world. If then Christians are to be of help to the world even in the field of science, of philosophy as well as in the field of theology, they must confront men with Christ.

MAN ALWAYS IN NEED OF GOD'S SPECIAL REVELATION[6]

True Protestantism will make the Creator-creature distinction fundamental to its thought. This involves the idea of supernatural, positive thought-communication on the part of God to man from the outset of human experience. God spoke to Adam even in paradise. Man was never left to the study

---

6. An excerpt from *The Intellectual Challenge of the Gospel* (London: Tyndale Press, 1950; reprint, Phillipsburg, N.J.: Lewis J. Grotenhuis, 1953), 20–21.

of natural revelation alone. Natural revelation was from the outset of history accompanied and supplemented by supernatural revelation. The two were involved in one another; they were supplemental to one another. They are unintelligible the one without the other. There has been no time in the history of the human race when man was expected to look at nature alone and ask whether God exists. Man was from the beginning confronted with the fact of God's clear-cut communication of Himself to man. Man was to see the place and function of nature in relation to the purpose it was to serve in human life. And the purpose of human life was set forth to man by direct supernatural communication.

The bearing of this on the doctrine of Scripture is clear. Even before man sinned he walked in the light of the supernatural thought-communication given him by God. Supernatural thought-communication is inherent in the human situation. It is involved in the Creator-creature relationship. Without such communication life would be meaningless for man. It is impossible intelligently to think of man without supernatural thought-communication to him on the part of God. The Bible simply carries on this communication after the fall of man into sin. The Bible is the supernatural thought-communication of God to creatures who have become sinners. Sinners would seek to destroy any form of such communication that might come to them. So God made provision for a form of revelation which sinners, try as they may, cannot destroy. This communication, as deposited in Scripture, is one in terms of which human life is alone intelligible. There is no meaningful predication about anything except in the light of the revelation of *the* God who speaks to sinners in *the* book.

It is therefore mandatory that Reformed theologians urge their fellow Protestants everywhere to call upon modern man to interpret his life in terms of *the book* of God and therefore in terms of *the God* of the book. Only thus can there be a real meeting of minds, a real point of contact with those who must be won for the gospel, and a real challenge of the wisdom of the world in its modern form. If Protestantism first asks for permission to believe in the possibility of the book it will surely be given this permission and be assigned a place as a satellite under the dictatorship of the modern mind.

REGARDLESS OF APPARENT BIBLICAL PROBLEMS[7]

There are two remarks that may be made at this point. The first is with respect to the claim made by those who believe the Bible in the traditional sense.

7. An excerpt from *Intellectual Challenge of the Gospel,* 26–28. A common objection to

They do not claim that the versions or translations have been inspired by God; they claim only that the autographs were thus inspired. They do not hold to any dictation theory of inspiration; they hold that the personality of each writer of Scripture was allowed full play. They claim only that the prophets and apostles of Scripture were guided by the Spirit of God and that what they wrote was therefore infallible. Accordingly, orthodox Christians do not expect that they will be able to solve without residue every problem that may be raised with respect to the phenomena of Scripture. But this fact does not make them doubtful of the truth of their fundamental claim. They are willing to wait till the foundations of the rival position are investigated.

This leads to a second remark. On what positive ground, we ask, do men stand when they, with such confidence and assurance, reject the traditional view of Scripture? The confident rejection of this view is unintelligible unless those who make it have themselves offered something better. More than that, such a rejection is without meaning unless men can show that they them-selves have a final interpretation of the facts of the phenomenal world to offer. How do men know that the doctrine of creation out of nothing is not true unless they themselves can take us back of "history" and tell us what is there? Or unless they can assure us that nothing is there. Karl Barth may assure us that he cannot believe in a speaking serpent any more than can anyone else. How does he know that God has not created the physical and the animal world? How does he know that the phenomenal world works according to impersonal laws and is therefore not accessible to special intervention on the part of God? Again, Barth may assure us that the idea of temporal creation must be rejected because it is not possible to think of it in a logically coher-ent fashion. In doing so he rejects historic Christianity because it does not meet the false test of eighteenth-century rationalism. As for his own system, he would not for all the world have its truth or falsity tried by such a test. But more important than this inconsistency is the point that men who say that creation *cannot* have happened, that Christ *cannot* have passed into the clouds toward heaven, must themselves claim omniscience. They must have such an exhaustive knowledge of the facts of the phenomenal world, and of

---

the presuppositional argument for Christianity and against unbelief is that the apol-ogist cannot effectively defend the biblical worldview as the precondition for the intelligibility of logic, science, experience, etc., if there are difficulties in identify-ing the Bible's teaching—difficulties such as determining its proper text (among conflicting readings in the ancient manuscripts) or determining its proper mean-ing (especially with regard to doctrines that are admittedly mysterious). Van Til contended that such difficulties do not deter us from prosecuting an effective pre-suppositional defense of the faith.

the possibilities behind these facts, as to enable them to understand all their relations to all other facts both past and future. They must be sure of what does happen in "ultimate reality" in order to be able to say that God does not have anything to do with the origin and control of the phenomenal world.

In believing the Bible and its teachings as they do, traditional believers humbly offer their interpretation of life in the name of God, whose mind and thoughts are higher than man's mind and thoughts. They do not claim to understand one fact in the phenomenal world exhaustively. They do not claim to understand the facts of nature exhaustively any more than they claim to understand miracles exhaustively. But they appeal to the Creator and Controller of the world as the One who, because of His creation and control of the world, does understand all things in it exhaustively. They admit the existence of mystery in all things for themselves but they do not admit the existence of mystery in anything for God. Accordingly, they do not pretend that they can reduce the relation of God to the world to a system that they themselves can exhaustively understand. The recognize gladly that *all* things end in mystery for them. But they hold that unless they may believe in the Bible and, therefore, in the God of the Bible, who controls whatsoever comes to pass, all things would end in *ultimate* mystery for them. They would rather admit relative mystery from the start and with respect to everything than claim virtual omniscience at the beginning and end with ultimate mystery at the last. They fear that such will be the case with those who claim to know the laws of the phenomenal world so well as to be able to say that God *cannot* have created it and does not control it.

THE PRESUPPOSITIONAL METHOD OF DEFENDING THE FAITH[8]

The Protestant doctrine of God requires that it be made foundational to everything else as a principle of explanation. If God is self-sufficient, he alone is self-explanatory. And if he alone is self-explanatory, then he must be the final reference point in all human predication. He is then like the sun from which all lights on earth derive their power of illumination. You do not use a candle in order to search for the sun. The idea of a candle is derived from the sun. So the very idea of any fact in the universe is that it is derivative. God has created it. It cannot have come into existence by itself, or by chance. God himself is the source of all possibility, and, therefore, of all space-time factuality.

On the other hand, if God is not self-sufficient and self-explanatory then

---

8. Excerpts from *Christian Theory of Knowledge*, 12–13, 14–16, 18–19 (emphasis original).

he is no longer the final reference point in human predication. Then God and man become partners in an effort to explain a common environment. Facts then are not what they are, in the last analysis, by virtue of the plan of God; they are partly that, but they partly exist in their own power. The human mind, then, need not subject itself to the revelation of God as absolutely authoritative for him. Man may then defer to God as to an expert who has had greater experience than himself, but he need not make all thoughts captive to the obedience of Christ.

The Christian cannot, on this view, indicate to the non-Christian that the non-Christian position is destructive of experience. Nor can he make plain to the non-Christian that Christianity will give him, and will *certainly* give him, what he needs. The essence of the non-Christian position is that man is assumed to be ultimate or autonomous. Man is thought of as the final reference point in predication. The facts of his environment are "just there"; they are assumed to have come into being by chance. Possibility is placed above both God and man alike. The laws of logic are assumed as somehow operative in the universe, or at least as legislative for what man can or cannot accept as possible or probable. If a God exists, he must at least be subject to conditions that are similar to, if not the same as, those to which humanity itself is subject.

How then, we ask, is the Christian to challenge this non-Christian approach to the interpretation of human experience? He can do so only if he shows that man *must* presuppose God as the final reference point in predication. Otherwise, he would destroy experience itself. He can do so only if he shows the non-Christian that even in his virtual negation of God, he is still really presupposing God. He can do so only if he shows the non-Christian that he cannot deny God unless he first affirm him, and that his own approach throughout its history has been shown to be destructive of human experience itself. . . .

The non-Christian assumes that man is ultimate, that is, that he is not created. Christianity assumes that man is created. The non-Christian assumes that the facts of man's environment are not created; the Christian assumes that these facts are created. The Christian has derived his convictions on these matters from Scripture as the infallible Word of God. *As self-explanatory, God naturally speaks with absolute authority. It is Christ as God who speaks in the Bible. Therefore the Bible does not appeal to human reason as ultimate in order to justify what it says. It comes to the human being with absolute authority.* Its claim is that human reason must itself be taken in the sense in which Scripture takes it, namely, as created by God and as therefore properly subject to the authority of God.

It is, therefore, required of man that he regard himself and his world as wholly revelatory of the presence and requirements of God. It is man's task to search out the truths about God, about the world and himself in relation to one another. He must seek a "systematic" arrangement of the facts of the universe. But the "system" that he thus tries to form is not the sort of system that the non-Christian is seeking to make for himself.

The two systems, that of the non-Christian and that of the Christian, differ because of the fact that their basic assumptions or presuppositions differ. On the non-Christian basis man is assumed to be the final reference point in predication. Man will therefore have to seek to make a system for himself that will relate all the facts of his environment to one another in such a way as will enable him to see exhaustively all the relations that obtain between them. In other words, the system that the non-Christian has to seek on his assumption is one in which he himself virtually occupies the place that God occupies in Christian theology. Man must, in short, be virtually omniscient. He must virtually reduce the facts that confront him to logical relations; the "thingness" of each thing must give up its individuality in order that it may be known; to be known, a thing or fact must be *wholly* known by man.

It is true that in modern thought there seems to be no such striving after exhaustive knowledge. But the reason for this seeming "irrationalism" of modern thought lies in the fact that it puts great stress upon another non-Christian assumption: that all reality is temporal throughout. Hence all facts are assumed to be what they are simply as products of chance. This assumption was implied in ancient non-Christian thought as well as in modern non-Christian thought. But it was not until modern times, especially since the time of Kant, that this assumption has come clearly to the foreground. In consequence, modern thought speaks of its systems as being limiting concepts or ideals. The ideal is still that of complete comprehension for man.

The system that Christians seek to obtain may, by contrast, be said to be *analogical. By this is meant that God is the original and that man is the derivative. God has absolute self-contained system within himself.* What comes to pass in history happens in accord with that system or plan by which he orders the universe. . . .

For this reason all of man's interpretations in any field are subject to the Scriptures given him. Scripture itself informs us that, at the beginning of history, before man had sinned, he was subject to the direct revelation of God in all the interpretations that he would make of his environment. . . .

The Reformed method of apologetics . . . begins frankly "from above." It would "presuppose" God. But in presupposing God it cannot place itself at any point on a neutral basis with the non-Christian. Before seeking to prove that Christianity is in accord with reason and in accord with fact, it would ask what is meant by "reason" and what is meant by "fact." It would argue that unless reason and fact are themselves interpreted in terms of God they are unintelligible. If God is not presupposed, reason is a pure abstraction that has no contact with fact, and fact is a pure abstraction that has no contact with reason. Reason and fact cannot be brought into fruitful union with one another except upon the presupposition of the existence of God and his control over the universe.

Since on the Reformed basis there is no area of neutrality between the believer and the unbeliever, the argument between them must be *indirect*. Christians cannot allow the legitimacy of the assumptions that underlie the non-Christian *methodology*. But they can place themselves upon the position of those whom they are seeking to win to a belief in Christianity for the sake of the argument. And the non-Christian, though not granting the presuppositions from which the Christian works, can nevertheless place himself upon the position of the Christian for the sake of the argument.

The Christian knows the truth about the non-Christian. He knows this because he is himself what he is by grace alone. He has been saved from the blindness of mind and the hardness of heart that mark the "natural man." The Christian has the "doctor's book." The Scriptures tell him of the origin and of the nature of sin. Man is dead in trespasses and sins (Eph. 2:1). He hates God. His inability to see the facts as they are and to reason about them as he ought to reason about them is, at bottom, a matter of sin. He has the God-created ability of reasoning within him. He is made in the image of God. God's revelation is before him and within him. He is in his own constitution a manifestation of the revelation and therefore of the requirement of God. God made a covenant with him through Adam (Rom. 5:12). He is therefore now, in Adam, a covenant-breaker. He is also against God and therefore against the revelation of God (Rom. 8:6–8). This revelation of God constantly and inescapably reminds him of his creatural responsibility. As a sinner he has, in Adam, declared himself autonomous.

Thus, intellectual argument will not, as such, convince and convert the non-Christian. It takes the regenerating power of the Holy Spirit to do that. But as in the case of preaching, so in the case of apologetical reasoning, the Holy Spirit may use a *mediate* approach to the minds and hearts of men. The natural man is quite able intellectually to follow the argument that the Christian offers for the truth of his position. He can therefore see that the wisdom of this world has been made foolishness by God. Christianity can be shown to be, not "just as good as" or even "better than" the non-Christian position, but the *only* position that does not make nonsense of human experience.

9.3 Van Til's Guidelines for the Presuppositional Method

FOURTEEN POINTS ON THE INTERPLAY OF NATURAL AND
SPECIAL REVELATION AS THEY BEAR ON THE RELATION
BETWEEN BELIEVER AND UNBELIEVER[9]

Let us now look again at the landscape as a whole. We shall do something in the way of showing the connection between such points as Calvin has stressed.

(1) General and special revelation find their unity in God who is self-sufficient. Dr. Valentine Hepp has stressed the idea that Reformed theology is distinguished from other forms of Christian theology by the great emphasis that it places on the fact of God's self-existence. All other theology, says Hepp, is in some measure a correlation-theology. For in other forms of theology God is made to some extent dependent upon man. Only in Reformed theology is man wholly dependent upon God.

(2) Believers accept this view of God because they accept the Scriptures to be the Word of God. They have not first worked up a philosophy of theism in order to find this theism afterwards corroborated by scriptural teaching. With Calvin they have come to know God as the Creator and controller of the universe because they have regarded the works of God in the light of Scripture. And they have, with Calvin, learned to take the Scriptures as the Word of God because they have received the witness of the Holy Spirit to the divinity of the Scriptures. Involved in this second point is the fact that the Reformed system of doctrine is composed of elements that are exegetically taken from Scripture. The Reformed system is not a deduction from a master concept. Nor is it a mere concatenation of individual items of truth. It is a "system" of truth—an analogical system of truth. And the *idea of analogy* is not formed by an independent study of Being, but by an ordering of the Scripture teaching as a whole. . . .

(3) But to speak thus of the necessity and priority of Scripture is not in the least to deny that there is, in another sense, a priority of the works of God. As Polman indicates, Calvin discusses first the works of God and then the Word of God. But, strictly speaking, it is not possible to speak of a temporal priority of the one over the other. Their relation is rather that of supplementation. Paul tells us that *from the beginning* the works of God challenged men to honor God. And the Genesis narrative, while it relates first the creation of man in the image of God, forthwith proceeds to supplement this narrative by

9. An excerpt from *The Protestant Doctrine of Scripture*, In Defense of the Faith, vol. 1 (Philadelphia: Presbyterian and Reformed, 1967), 122–32.

telling us of supernatural communication in the way of the covenant that God made with and ordained for man. Says the Westminster Confession: "The distance between God and man is so great, that although reasonable creatures do owe obedience unto him as their Creator, yet they could never have any fruition of him, as their blessedness and reward, but by some voluntary condescension on God's part which he hath been pleased to express by way of covenant."

Abraham Kuyper also argues for the supplementative character of the two forms of revelation. He does so by vigorously opposing the idea of their juxtaposition. He points out especially that the idea of natural revelation cannot be considered as something that can stand by itself. "It is, indeed, by means of the *cognitio specialis* that the *cognitio naturalis* becomes useful. Only in the light of Scripture is the sinner enabled to account for the *semen religionis* in his heart and of the glory which is patent in the world: where the light of Scripture is hidden I know no more than 'the unknown God' even on the Areopagus" *(Encyclopaedie der Heilige Godgeleerdheid*, Vol. II, p. 332). Even in paradise, he adds, God did not reveal himself to man through natural revelation independently. Even there God spoke to him. But then, he adds that it is *natural* that such should be the case. Supernatural revelation is not inherently and originally a revelation of grace; it is part and parcel of the normal, and in that sense *natural*, relation between God and man.

(4) God therefore addresses man everywhere and always through the one body of his revelation. Through this one body of revelation God assigns to man, generically speaking, his cultural task. And mankind is still responsible for that task (Romans 5:12). Man as sinner is not merely responsible for the revelation that comes to him through the works of God as they now are. The revelation that now comes to men who have not heard the gospel is but one aspect of the full revelation that came to him originally. The idea that God's revelation to man is clear must primarily be said about revelation as a unit, inclusive of both supernatural pre-redemptive and natural revelation. The revelation of God in nature, as it is now, still clearly manifests God. But it is manifestory as a fragment of a whole. It is clear therefore when general revelation is seen as calling out for and needing its supplement in *original* supernatural revelation. How else could the presence of the curse of God now resting upon nature be seen for what it is?

(5) If present general revelation is but an aspect of a revelation which includes supernatural thought communication, then man the sinner must be said to be a covenant breaker. The whole of revelation was given to mankind as the assignment of a task. Man has refused to undertake this task. He broke the arrangement or covenant that God ordained for him.

Man has declared his independence from God. We may therefore call him the *would-be autonomous man*. This *would-be* autonomous man assumes that he is ultimate and properly the final reference point in predication, i.e., reality must be interpreted by man in terms of man. He wants to avoid the address of God that comes to him from his own constitution as well as from the world about him. But he cannot do so fully. "Nevertheless, life does not remain untouched by the power of God's revelation. We understand the *sensus divinitatus* not as an 'organ' of the knowledge of God which conquered the depravity of human nature but as an *inescapable impression* received by man via this power of God" (Berkouwer, *De Algemeene Openbaring*, p. 125). It was by thus stressing the inescapability of God's revelation as it comes to man especially through his sense of deity and through the sinner's effort at suppressing this revelation that Calvin effected in principle a complete break between the idea of general revelation and natural theology. "It was especially Calvin, who interpreted the thoughts of Scripture clearly at this point, when he *denied* the indissolubleness of general revelation and natural theology in allowing himself to be guided by Romans 1" (*Idem*).

By virtue of his creation in the image of God man therefore knows God. He cannot get away from the revelation of God. He knows he is a creature of God. The revelation about him, conjoined with the revelation through his constitution, cries day and night that God is the Creator and controller and therefore Redeemer of the universe.

But day and night the sinner seeks to hold back this revelation of God. When Paul on the Areopagus uses the words "as certain also of your own poets have said," this cannot be explained otherwise than in terms of the idea of suppression. "Paul's words can be understood only in view of the actual suppression supported by *supplanted* truth. Paul's 'as . . . also' certainly does not mean that their ideas are in agreement with the deepest intent of Paul's gospel. He knows the *background* of their words and does not idealize them. And yet he quotes their words. This is to be explained only in connection with their suppression of the truth of God—apostate religion lives antithetically to and in suppression of God's truth" (*Ibid.*, p. 116).

(6) What has been said just now is true of the sinner, the natural man *in principle* but not in consummation. Every form of non-Christian religion, of non-Christian philosophy and science seeks therefore to envelop God in his creation. *In principle* men turn the true process of knowledge upside down; they think of God as made in man's image instead of thinking of man as made in God's image. They worship and serve the creature more than the Creator.

(7) But God continues, in spite of man's sin, to call men to himself through the works of his hands. He pours out his good gifts upon the race asking them

thereby to be grateful to the giver of these gifts. The goodness of God is given to men that it might lead them to repentance. That is the first God-assigned purpose of them. ". . . or despisest thou the riches of his goodness and forbearance and longsuffering; not knowing that the goodness of God leadeth thee to repentance?" (Romans 2:4). At the same time God threatens to send punishment upon men for breaking his precepts. . . .

(8) . . . God gives his good gifts, says Paul, so that men should repent. But when they fail to repent, their continuance in disobedience adds to their condemnation. God's rain and sunshine come upon men first that they might be "saved." But when men reject this salvation they add condemnation to themselves. . . . Man who receives his life in the first place as a free gift of God now continues to receive it, and the generosity of nature that goes with it, in spite of his breaking of the covenant. He continues to receive it though now he has made himself the enemy of God. This is grace.

(9) The sinner's reaction to this gracious revelation, to this call to repentance, can never be right in principle unless and until he is redeemed in Christ. Short of this his basic reaction continues to be that which Berkouwer speaks of as living by the suppression of that revelation. The sinner may and does turn to God adventitiously but never in principle. He cannot even suppress the truth without giving witness to the truth that he suppresses. This is true even of Satan and the lost. They can only love and practice the lie in opposition to the truth. They know the distinction between good and evil too. Their rational and moral constitution is still maintained by God. This maintenance is the presupposition of the nature and eternal endurance of their punishment.

But until the judgment day the revelation of God to man is a revelation of grace as well as of wrath, of long-suffering endurance as well as of punishment of sinners that they might come to repentance. So, in addition to knowing truth and the difference between good and evil, men respond favorably to it in casual fashion. They have a certain love of the truth, and a certain respect for the good in distinction from evil. They do works which "for the matter of them" are things which God commands and are "in themselves praiseworthy and useful." They do the "civil and moral good." Without these "good works" of unregenerate men civilization could not long endure. Not only that, but through these "good works" unregenerate men contribute to the fulfilling of the original mandate God gave to mankind in spite of themselves so far as their principle is concerned.

But to say this, and to say much more that might be said, is not in the least to tone down the fact that *in principle* sinners live by the suppression of the truth. They live *in principle* by the suppression of truth even as adventitiously they love the truth. They do despite to the Spirit of truth even as, up to a point, they follow him. Even the truth which Satan knows but hates, and the righteousness which Satan knows but despises, come from the Spirit of God as the Spirit of revelation. But Scripture teaches that men in this world are not finished products of wickedness; they are not satanic or diabolic in the sense of being consummately wicked in all that they think or do. Due to the irrepressible character of God's revelation to them as gracious, they give some measure of reluctant recognition to God and his truth in this world.

(10) The believer, however, has been changed *in principle* into a covenant keeper. He now seeks to serve the Creator instead of the creature. He is perfect. He is holy. He is righteous. He loves the truth and only the truth. He hates the lie and only the lie. John says he *cannot* sin.

In practice, however, he daily sins against God. He daily comes short of practicing truth and righteousness. But he now serves sin and the body of death adventitiously, in spite of his true self in Jesus Christ. This is what Luther meant when he said of the Christian that he is *simul iustus et peccator* (at the same time just and sinful).

(11) We may therefore with Kuyper speak of twofold science and yet also speak of the unity of science. When Kuyper speaks of twofold science he contrasts the *principle* of those whose primary aim is to serve and worship the creature, with the *principle* of those whose primary aim is to serve and worship the Creator. He speaks of the *principium naturale* and the *principium speciale*. Creature worshipers seek to live by the *natural* principle alone. Those who have no part in the *principium speciale* do not understand themselves. "You yourself acknowledge from your own point of view that he who stands outside does not and cannot understand the actual focus of his own being and consequently of his reason" (Kuyper, *Encyclopaedie*, II, p. 339). The man of the *natural* principle will require that the special principle subject itself to his criterion of truth. On the other hand the idea of the special principle presupposes that the natural principle has, because of sin, disqualified itself as a judge of the special principle. "When special revelation presupposes that as a consequence of sin the *principium naturale* is distorted, it follows that the *principium naturale* has lost its authority to judge" (*Ibid.*, p. 335). It is the nature of the special principle that it cannot submit its claims to a principle that would require its own abdication. Unity of knowledge, accomplishment of man's cultural task, accordingly, cannot be obtained by a compromise of principle between those whose ultimate point of reference is God and those whose ultimate point of reference is man. It is the nature of a principle, argues Kuyper, to be the presupposition of all interpretation. A principle is totalitarian in nature. Two totalitarian principles stand over against one another; no compromise of any sort is possible between them.

How then can unity of knowledge and of science be accomplished? By the fact that the special principle is bound to be victorious. By being victorious it saves the natural principle as *created* by God. The special principle would not be victorious if it did not save the natural principle. It is victorious precisely in saving the natural principle. The believer, as Calvin stresses, is most anxious to explore the works of God. And the unbeliever, in clinging to his rejection of the special principle, is made tributary to the service of the special principle. By being made tributary to the special principle he indirectly contributes to the true development of the natural principle. Those who refuse to submit the natural principle to the special principle are untrue to the natural principle itself. Their discoveries of truth in the area of the works of God, therefore, rightly belong to those who are covenant-keepers in principle. The unity of science is accomplished in Christ, the Savior of the world.

(12) There is in consequence no neutral territory between covenant-keepers and covenant-breakers. The antitheses of principle is equally real and equally basic at every point of contact between them. How could it be otherwise? The antithesis is not basic at any point unless it is basic at every point. The point of battle between two totalitarian powers may be a spot of desert sand. The battle is not any the less violent for all that. The fate of the empire is always involved. If one fact were intelligible without the presupposition of the truth of the special principle, i.e., of Christ as the Savior of the natural principle, then all facts would be. If the unbeliever could, on his principle, discover any meaning in one fact in relation to any other fact, in terms of *his principle*, then the indispensability of supernatural revelation, and in particular of supernatural revelation in its redemptive garb, would disappear.

(13) But though no compromise can be made between the two principles, this constitutes no bar against cooperation between the adherents of these two principles. In a religious ethical sense, says Kuyper, the unbeliever's opposition to the special principle derives from his enmity of God. But this unbeliever need not on that account, as a man of science, be dishonest (*Ibid.*, p. 339). And he has the ability to discover much truth. He can count and weigh and measure. He can gather facts. His logical powers are often greater than those of believers. Even to oppose the truth he must set it forth. His interpretative endeavor is bound to be revelatory of the truth.

Why should the Christian then not gratefully employ, for purposes of advancing knowledge, the funded results of the investigations of scientists, whether they be Christians or not? He may do so, if only he does not, while doing it, thereby concede the autonomy, the juxtaposition of the natural principle as over against the special principle.

(14) This leads us to our final point. The believing scholar will gladly co-

operate with the unbelieving scholar. But the believing scholar cannot excuse himself from the task of witness-bearing. And this witness-bearing must take place at every point of meeting between believers and unbelievers. The wisdom of this world has been made foolishness with God. If the unbelieving scholar's principle were to be adopted there would be no truth, no science, no knowledge. Basic to the unbelieving scholar's position is the notion of possibility as standing above God. If the unbelieving scholar's assumption were true, all would be Chaos and old Night. No fact could then be found. There would be no distinguishing mark that would differentiate one fact from another fact. Anything might happen, except that nothing intelligible could happen. The human mind would itself be a product of chance. Its laws of logic would have no deeper foundation than a derelict adrift on a shoreless sea. Logic and fact could never come into fruitful union with one another. The very concepts of "probability" and "proof" would be meaningless.

The unbelieving scholar may at first appear to be very open-minded. But he is too open-minded. According to him, God, if he exists, may *possibly* not exist. Christ may, but he also *may not*, be the Savior of men. By this "may-or-may-not" of the unbeliever, the special principle has in effect already been rejected. According to Christianity, especially according to Christianity as expressed in the Reformed confessions, God is the *source of possibility*. The believer cannot allow that justice is done to God and to Christ unless it be maintained that all hypotheses about facts and their possible and probable relations must presuppose God and his Christ as self-existent, self-identifying and therewith as the source of the intelligibility and applicability of the idea of fact or of hypothesis.

The believing scholar, therefore, begs the unbelieving scholar not to forego the fruits of his own labor. The believer pleads with the unbeliever no longer to rebel against the truth, which he must, in spite of himself, constantly presuppose. The revelation of God is clear, it is inescapable. If every fact in the universe, even those facts discovered by the unbeliever, were not themselves by their nature the condemnation of the principle of unbelief, they would not be facts at all. There would be no reality to cite against the unbeliever unless unbelief itself as a parasite must feed upon the truth.

This is not merely to say that if truth should perish it would still be true that it is truth that perishes, and so truth did not perish after all. It is rather to say that the revelation of God in the works of God (as interpreted by the principles of the Word of God, and therefore by the motifs of creation and providence as the carrying out of God's all controlling plan) is clear. By presenting the revelation of God in Christ to men in the laboratory as well as in the arena of philosophical and theological discussion, the believer himself manifests the clarity of the natural revelation of God.

FIVE MOST IMPORTANT MATTERS
ABOUT ARGUMENTATION[10]

So then the whole argument between Christian theistic and antitheistic epistemology stands before us. There is much that might still be discussed. It is possible to enter upon a profitable discussion of many details. However, it was our purpose to speak of only the most important matters. These most important matters were somewhat as follows:

(1) First of all, we note the necessity of seeing clearly that Christianity and theism are intricately interwoven. If one is really a theist he cannot stop short of being a Christian; and Christianity cannot build upon any foundation but that of a sound biblical theism. Accordingly, the argument must constantly be for Christian theism as a whole. We cannot separate, except for the sake of emphasis, between an argument for theism and an argument for Christianity. The absoluteness of God and the inspiration of the Bible are involved in one another and one cannot defend the one without defending the other.

(2) In the second place, this whole Christian theistic position must be presented not as something just a little or as a great deal better than other positions, but must be presented as the only system of thought that does not destroy human experience to a meaningless something. This is in accord with the teaching of the Bible that those who do not accept Christ are lost. Accordingly, if Christian theism is defensible at all it must be defensible in this way. And if it is not defensible in this way it is not defensible in any other way, because any other way of defense reduces the uniqueness of Christianity at once. The question is one of "this or nothing."

(3) The argument in favor of Christian theism must therefore seek to prove that if one is not a Christian theist he knows nothing at all as he ought to know anything. The difference is not that all men alike know certain things about the finite universe and that some claim some *additional* knowledge, while the others do not. On the contrary, the Christian theist must claim that he alone has true knowledge about cows and chickens as well as about God. He does this in no spirit of conceit, because it is a gift of God's grace. Nor does he deny that there is knowledge *after a fashion* that enables the non-theist to get along *after a fashion* in the world. This is the gift of God's common grace, and therefore does not change the absoluteness of the distinction made about the knowledge and the ignorance of the theist and the non-theist respectively.

---

10. An excerpt from the concluding pages of Van Til's first syllabus, later printed as *A Survey of Christian Epistemology* (Philadelphia: Presbyterian and Reformed, 1969), 222–23. (The numbering of points has been added.)

(4) The method of argumentation will accord with the general position taken so far. It will seek to show that antitheistic knowledge is self-contradictory on its own ground, and that *its conception of contradiction even presupposes the truth of Christian theism*. It must be the method of the impossibility of the contrary, or that of the destruction of the enemy. It must show that univocal reasoning is self-destructive.

(5) Meanwhile, Christian theism has the solemn duty to implicate itself ever more deeply into the truth of God as it is revealed in nature and in Scripture till the end of time. It must become ever more explicit in the formulation of what it sees to be the truth in order that it may not lose its identity as time goes on, but the rather gain in its distinctiveness and therefore in its testimony to the world.

9.4 Van Til's Most Succinct Synopsis

THE TOTAL PICTURE[11]

A. My problems with the "traditional method."
  1. This method compromises God himself by maintaining his existence is only "possible" albeit "highly probable," rather than ontologically and "rationally" necessary.
  2. It compromises the counsel of God by not understanding it as the only all-inclusive, ultimate "cause" of whatsoever comes to pass.
  3. It compromises the revelation of God by:
    a. Compromising its *necessity*. It does so by not recognizing that even in Paradise man had to interpret the general (natural) revelation of God in terms of the covenantal obligations placed upon him by God through special revelation. Natural revelation, on the traditional view, can be understood "on its own."

11. This outline is Van Til's briefest and clearest exposition of the nature and distinctiveness of the presuppositional defense of the faith. It has special significance as a crowning statement, appearing at the end of Van Til's "My Credo" in *Jerusalem and Athens*, ed. E. R. Geehan (Philadelphia: Presbyterian and Reformed, 1971), 18–21. An earlier version of part A ("My problems with the 'traditional method' ") can be found in *Defense of the Faith*, 351–53, which was reproduced in *The Reformed Pastor and Modern Thought* (Philadelphia: Presbyterian and Reformed, 1971), 69–70. An earlier version of part B ("My understanding of the relationship between Christian and non-Christian, philosophically speaking") appeared in *Defense of the Faith*, 310–12, which was slightly expanded in *Reformed Pastor and Modern Thought*, 27–30. Part C ("My proposal, therefore, for a consistently Christian methodology of apologetics") appears to be original to "My Credo" and is a gem, communicating the gist of Van Til's apologetical method and argument.

      b. Compromising its *clarity*. Both the general and special revelation of God are said to be unclear to the point that man may say only that God's existence is "probable."

      c. Compromising its *sufficiency*. It does this by allowing for an ultimate realm of "chance" out of which might come "facts" such as are wholly new for God and for man. Such "facts" would be uninterpreted and unexplainable in terms of the general or special revelation of God.

      d. Compromising its *authority*. On the traditional position the Word of God's self-attesting characteristic, and therewith its authority, is secondary to the authority of reason and experience. The Scriptures do not identify themselves; man identifies them and recognizes their "authority" only in terms of his own authority.

4. It compromises man's creation as the image of God by thinking of man's creation and knowledge as independent of the Being and knowledge of God. On the traditional approach man need not "think God's thoughts after him."

5. It compromises man's covenantal relationship with God by not understanding Adam's representative action as absolutely determinative of the future.

6. It compromises the sinfulness of mankind resulting from the sin of Adam by not understanding man's ethical depravity as extending to the whole of his life, even to his thoughts and attitudes.

7. It compromises the grace of God by not understanding it as the necessary prerequisite for "renewal unto knowledge." On the traditional view man can and must renew himself unto knowledge by the "right use of reason."

B. My understanding of the relationship between Christian and non-Christian, philosophically speaking.

1. Both have presuppositions about the nature of reality:

      a. The Christian presupposes the triune God and his redemptive plan for the universe as set forth once for all in Scripture.

      b. The non-Christian presupposes a dialectic between "chance" and "regularity," the former accounting for the origin of matter and life, the latter accounting for the current success of the scientific enterprise.

2. Neither can, as finite beings, by means of *logic* as such, say what reality *must* be or *cannot* be.

      a. The Christian, therefore, attempts to understand his world through the observation and logical ordering of facts in self-conscious sub-jection to the plan of the self-attesting Christ of Scripture.

   b. The non-Christian, while attempting an enterprise similar to the Christian's, attempts nevertheless to use "logic" to destroy the Chris-tian position. On the one hand, appealing to the *non-rationality* of "matter," he says that the chance-character of "facts" is conclusive evidence against the Christian position. Then, on the other hand, he maintains like Parmenides that the Christian story cannot possibly be true. Man must be autonomous, "logic" must be legislative as to the field of "possibility" and possibility must be above God.

3. Both claim that their position is "in accordance with the facts."

   a. The Christian claims this because he interprets the facts and his ex-perience in the light of the revelation of the self-attesting Christ in Scripture. Both the uniformity and the diversity of facts have at their foundation the all-embracing plan of God.

   b. The non-Christian claims this because he interprets the facts and his experience in the light of the autonomy of human personality, the ultimate "givenness" of the world and the amenability of matter to mind. There can be no fact that denies man's autonomy or attests to the world's and man's divine origin.

4. Both claim that their position is "rational."

   a. The Christian does so by claiming not only that his position is self-consistent but that he can explain both the seemingly "inexplicable" amenability of fact to logic and the necessity and usefulness of ra-tionality itself in terms of Scripture.

   b. The non-Christian may or may not make this same claim. If he does, the Christian maintains that he cannot make it good. If the non-Christian attempts to account for the amenability of fact to logic in terms of the ultimate rationality of the cosmos, then he will be crip-pled when it comes to explaining the "evolution" of men and things. If he attempts to do so in terms of pure "chance" and ultimate "ir-rationality" as being the well out of which both rational man and a rationally amenable world sprang, then we shall point out that such an explanation is in fact no explanation at all and that it destroys predication.

C. My proposal, therefore, for a consistently Christian methodology of apolo-getics is this:

1. That we use the same principle in apologetics that we use in theology: the self-attesting, self-explanatory Christ of Scripture.

2. That we no longer make an appeal to "common notions" which Christian and non-Christian agree on, but to the "common ground" which they actually have because man and his world are what Scripture says they are.

3. That we appeal to man as man, God's image. We do so only if we set the non-Christian principle of the rational autonomy of man against the Christian principle of the dependence of man's knowledge on God's knowledge as revealed in the person and by the Spirit of Christ.

4. That we claim, therefore, that Christianity alone is reasonable for men to hold. It is wholly irrational to hold any other position than that of Christianity. Christianity alone does not slay reason on the altar of "chance."

5. That we argue, therefore, by "presupposition." The Christian, as did Tertullian, must contest the very principles of his opponent's position. The only "proof" of the Christian position is that unless its truth is presupposed there is no possibility of "proving" anything at all. The actual state of affairs as preached by Christianity is the necessary foundation of "proof" itself.

6. That we preach with the understanding that the acceptance of the Christ of Scripture by sinners who, being alienated from God, seek to flee his face, comes about when the Holy Spirit, in the presence of inescapably clear evidence, opens their eyes so that they see things as they truly are.

7. That we present the message and evidence for the Christian position as clearly as possible, knowing that because man is what the Christian says he is, the non-Christian will be able to understand in an intellectual sense the issues involved. In so doing, we shall, to a large extent, be telling him what he "already knows" but seeks to suppress. This "reminding" process provides a fertile ground for the Holy Spirit, who in sovereign grace may grant the non-Christian repentance so that he may know him who is life eternal.

9.5 The Issue of Success in Apologetics

HUMBLY, BOLDLY REASONING WITH THE WILLFULLY BLIND[12]

As a hater of God he does not want to hear about God. The natural man seeks to suppress the pressure of God's revelation in nature that is about him. He seeks to suppress the pressure of conscience within him. So he also seeks to suppress the idea of the revelation of grace that speaks in Scripture. In every

12. Excerpts from *Defense of the Faith*, 165–66, 198, 306–7.

case it is God as his Creator and as his judge that asks of him to listen and be obedient. How can the autonomous man be obedient on his own assumptions? He cannot be obedient unless he reverses his entire position, and this he cannot do of himself. It takes the regenerating power of the Spirit to do that.

Having reached this point the Roman Catholic and the Arminian may argue that it was in the interest of avoiding this very impasse that they sought to make their point of contact with the natural man on a neutral basis. The reply of the Reformed apologist is as follows. Good preaching, he will say, will recognize the truth of Scripture that man has been blinded by sin, and that his will is perverted toward seeking self instead of God. But how can deaf ears hear, and blind eyes see? That is to say preaching is confronted with the same dilemma as is apologetical reasoning. In both cases the Roman Catholic and the Arminian tone down the facts of the gospel in order to gain acceptance for them on the part of the natural man. In neither case will the Reformed apologist do so. In both cases he will challenge the natural man at the outset. Both in preaching and in reasoning—and every approach to the natural man should be both—the Reformed theologian will ask the sinner to do what he knows the sinner of himself cannot do. The Reformed Christian is often Reformed in preaching and Arminian in reasoning. But when he is at all self-conscious in his reasoning he will seek to do in apologetics what he does in preaching. He knows that man is responsible not in spite of but just because he is not autonomous but created. He knows that the idea of analogical or covenant personality is that which alone preserves genuine significance for the thoughts and deeds of man. So he also knows that he who is dead in trespasses and sins is none the less responsible for his deadness. He knows also that the sinner in the depth of his heart knows that what is thus held before him is true. He knows he is a creature of God; he has been simply seeking to cover up this fact to himself. He knows that he has broken the law of God; he has again covered up this fact to himself. He knows that he is therefore guilty and is subject to punishment forever; this fact too he will not look in the face.

And it is precisely Reformed preaching and Reformed apologetic that tears the mask off the sinner's face and compels him to look at himself and the world for what they really are. Like a mole the natural man seeks to scurry under ground every time the facts as they really are come to his attention. He loves the darkness rather than the light. The light exposes him to himself. And precisely this neither Roman Catholic nor Arminian preaching or reasoning is able to do.

As to the possibility and likelihood of the sinner's accepting the Christian position, it must be said that this is a matter of the grace of God. . . .

"Ye are my witnesses." That is the word of the covenant God to those he has redeemed. They are such and can be such only if they bear witness to a God who cannot do otherwise than bear witness of himself by means of himself. Christians can bear witness of this God only if they humbly but boldly make the claim that only on the presupposition of the existence of this God and of the universe in all its aspects as the revelation of this God is there any footing and verge for the interpretative efforts of man. . . .

Scripture teaches us to speak and preach to, as well as to r eason with blind men, because God, in whose name we speak and reason, can cause the blind to see. Jesus told Lazarus while dead to arise and come forth from the grave. The prophet preached to the dead bones in the valley till they took on flesh. So our reasoning and our preaching is not in vain inasmuch as God in Christ reasons and preaches through us. Once we were blind; God reasoned with us, perhaps through some human agency, and we saw.[13]

THE COVENANTAL WORK OF APOLOGETICS: BLESSING AND CURSE[14]

How awesome then the responsibility of the Christian. He must proclaim the Christ as the only name given under heaven by which man, the whole man, by which mankind, with its cultural task, must be saved from sin unto God. What a joy to tell the scientist and the philosopher that they may labor for eternity if only they will labor for the Christ. But when the Christian does thus witness to the promise of great joy that is in the Christ who saves the whole man with the whole of his culture, then inevitably what is a "promise" to some becomes a "curse" to others. Paul says:

> "Now thanks be unto God, which always causeth us to triumph in Christ, and maketh manifest the savour of his knowledge by us in every place. For we are unto God a sweet savour of Christ, in them that are saved, and in them that perish: to the one we are the savour of death unto death; and to the other the savour of life unto life" (II Cor. 2:14–16).

Even as some accept, so also others reject the word of God's grace. To them the Word becomes a savour of death. Then they, with their culture, are lost. The work of their hands, their science, their art, their philosophy, their theol-

---

13. CVT: *Introduction to Theology* syllabus, pp. 28–30. (This syllabus was mimeographed by Westminster Theological Seminary in Philadelphia in 1947.)
14. An excerpt from *Protestant Doctrine of Scripture*, 2–3.

ogy, in short their culture, will ultimately profit, not themselves, but those who have *obeyed* the word of grace in Christ.

To be sure none of the cultural efforts of any man will be lost, for all things are Christ's and Christ is God's. But there are men who will lose their cultural efforts. They will lose the fruit of their labors because they have refused to labor unto Christ. They will reap the reward of Balaam who sought to curse Israel and, most of all, Israel's God. They will seek in vain to die the death of the righteous.

Bibliography of
Van Til's Works Cited

"Absolute Idealism." In *The Encyclopedia of Christianity,* edited by Jay Green, 1:33–34. Wilmington, Del.: The National Foundation for Christian Education, 1964.

Apologetics. Philadelphia: Westminster Theological Seminary, 1929, 1947, 1953 (syllabus); Nutley, N.J.: Presbyterian and Reformed, 1976 (syllabus).

"At the Beginning, God: An Interview with Cornelius Van Til." *Christianity Today* 22 (December 30, 1977): 414–18.

"Bavinck the Theologian." *Westminster Theological Journal* 24 (1961): 48–64.

Boston Personalism. Philadelphia: Westminster Theological Seminary, 1956.

"Calvin and Modern Subjectivism." *Torch and Trumpet* 9, no. 4 (September 1959): 14–16.

"Calvin as a Controversialist." *Torch and Trumpet* 9, no. 3 (July–August 1959): 5–9.

"Calvinism and Art: Common Grace Does Not Solve All the Problems." *Presbyterian Guardian* 17 (December 1948): 272–74.

The Case for Calvinism. Philadelphia: Presbyterian and Reformed, 1963.

Christ and the Jews. Philadelphia: Westminster Theological Seminary, 1965 (syllabus); Philadelphia: Presbyterian and Reformed, 1968.

Christian Apologetics. Philadelphia: Westminster Theological Seminary, 1935, 1939 (syllabus).

Christian Theistic Ethics. Philadelphia: Westminster Theological Seminary, 1940, 1947 (syllabus); Phillipsburg, N.J.: Lewis J. Grotenhuis, 1952 (syllabus). In Defense of the Faith, vol. 3. Philadelphia: Presbyterian and Reformed, 1974.

Christian-Theistic Evidences. Philadelphia: Westminster Theological Seminary, 1935, 1947, 1966 (syllabus). In Defense of Biblical Christianity, vol. 6. Phillipsburg, N.J.: Presbyterian and Reformed, 1978.

"A Christian Theistic Theory of Knowledge." *The Banner* 66 (November 6, 1931): 984, 995.

"A Christian Theistic Theory of Reality." *The Banner* 66 (November 20, 1931): 1032.

A Christian Theory of Knowledge. Phillipsburg, N.J.: Lewis J. Grotenhuis, 1954 (syllabus); Philadelphia: Presbyterian and Reformed, 1969.

Christianity and Barthianism. Philadelphia: Presbyterian and Reformed, 1962; 2d ed., 1974.

Christianity and Idealism. Philadelphia: Presbyterian and Reformed, 1955.

Christianity in Conflict. 3 vols. Philadelphia: Westminster Theological Seminary, 1962–64 (syllabus).

Christianity in Modern Theology. Phillipsburg, N.J.: Lewis J. Grotenhuis, 1955.

"Common Grace." *Proceedings of the Calvinistic Philosophy Club* (1941).

"Common Grace." *Westminster Theological Journal* 8 (1945–46): 39–60, 166–200; 9 (1946): 47–84.

Common Grace. Philadelphia: Presbyterian and Reformed, 1947.

Common Grace and the Gospel. Philadelphia: Presbyterian and Reformed, 1972.

"Common Grace and Witness-Bearing." *Torch and Trumpet* 4, no. 5 (December 1954–January 1955): 1–10; reprint, Phillipsburg, N.J.: Lewis J. Grotenhuis, 1956.

The Confession of 1967: Its Theological Background and Ecumenical Significance. Philadelphia: Presbyterian and Reformed, 1967.

The Defense of the Faith. Philadelphia: Presbyterian and Reformed, 1955; 2d ed., 1963; 3d ed., 1967.

"Dr. C. Van Til Replies to Dr. Wm. Masselink." *The Banner* 95, no. 32 (August 5, 1960): 22–23.

"The Education of Man—A Divinely Ordained Need." In *Fundamen-*

tals of Christian Education, edited by Cornelius Jaarsma, 39–59. Grand Rapids: Eerdmans, 1953.

Essays on Christian Education. Philadelphia: Presbyterian and Reformed, 1971.

"From Cornelius Van Til" (a response to "Where Do We Go from Here in Theology?" by Nels F. S. Ferré). *Religion in Life* 25 (1955): 22–28.

"The Full-Orbed Life." In *Fundamentals in Christian Education,* edited by Cornelius Jaarsma, 157–70. Grand Rapids: Eerdmans, 1953.

"God and the Absolute." *Evangelical Quarterly* 2 (1930): 358–88.

The God of Hope. Phillipsburg, N.J.: Presbyterian and Reformed, 1978.

The Great Debate Today. Philadelphia: Presbyterian and Reformed, 1970.

"Has Karl Barth Become Orthodox?" *Westminster Theological Journal* 16 (1954): 135–81.

Herman Dooyeweerd and Reformed Apologetics. Philadelphia: Westminster Theological Seminary, 1974 (syllabus).

The Intellectual Challenge of the Gospel. London: Tyndale Press, 1950; reprint, Phillipsburg, N.J.: Lewis J. Grotenhuis, 1953.

Introduction to *The Inspiration and Authority of the Bible,* by B. B. Warfield. Philadelphia: Presbyterian and Reformed, 1948.

An Introduction to Systematic Theology. Philadelphia: Westminster Theological Seminary, 1949, 1952 (syllabus). In Defense of the Faith, vol. 5. Philadelphia: Presbyterian and Reformed, 1974.

An Introduction to Theology. 2 vols. Philadelphia: Westminster Theological Seminary, 1947 (syllabus).

Is God Dead? Philadelphia: Presbyterian and Reformed, 1966.

Jerusalem and Athens: Critical Discussions on the Theology and Apologetics of Cornelius Van Til. Edited by E. R. Geehan. Philadelphia: Presbyterian and Reformed, 1971.

"My Credo," 1–21.
Response to Herman Dooyeweerd, 89–127.
Response to Robert D. Knudsen, 298–305.
Response to Rousas John Rushdoony, 348.
Response to Gordon R. Lewis, 361–68.
Response to John Warwick Montgomery, 392–403.
Response to Clark H. Pinnock, 426–27.

"John J. de Waard Dies Suddenly." *Presbyterian Guardian* 28 (August 25, 1959): 214–15, 222.

"Kant or Christ?" *Calvin Forum* 7 (1942): 133–35.

"Karl Barth and Historic Christianity." *Presbyterian Guardian* 4 (July 1937): 108–9.

"Karl Barth on Creation." *Presbyterian Guardian* 3 (February 27, 1937): 204–5.

"Karl Barth on Scripture." *Presbyterian Guardian* 3 (January 9, 1937): 137–38.

The Later Heidegger and Theology. Philadelphia: Presbyterian and Reformed, 1964.

Letter on Common Grace. Phillipsburg, N.J.: Lewis J. Grotenhuis, 1953.

The Metaphysics of Apologetics. Philadelphia: Westminster Theological Seminary, 1932 (syllabus). Later published as *A Survey of Christian Epistemology.*

"Nature and Scripture." In *The Infallible Word,* edited by N. B. Stonehouse and Paul Woolley, 263–301. Philadelphia: Presbyterian and Reformed, 1946.

The New Evangelicalism. Philadelphia: Westminster Theological Seminary, 1960 (syllabus).

The New Hermeneutic. Philadelphia: Presbyterian and Reformed, 1974.

The New Modernism: An Appraisal of the Theology of Barth and Brunner. Philadelphia: Presbyterian and Reformed, 1946; 2d ed., 1947; 3d ed., 1972.

The New Synthesis Theology of the Netherlands. Philadelphia: Presbyterian and Reformed, 1975.

Particularism and Common Grace. Phillipsburg, N.J.: Lewis J. Grotenhuis, 1952.

"Pierre Teilhard de Chardin." *Westminster Theological Journal* 28 (1966): 109–44.

"Plato." *Proceedings of the Calvinistic Philosophy Club* (1939), 31–44.

"Presuppositionalism: A Reply." *The Bible Today* 42 (1949): 219–28, 278–90.

"Professor Vollenhoven's Significance for Reformed Apologetics." In *Wetenschappelijke Bijdragen,* edited by S. U. Zuidema, 68–71. Franeker: T. Wever, 1951.

The Protestant Doctrine of Scripture. In Defense of the Faith, vol. 1. Philadelphia: Presbyterian and Reformed, 1967.

"Recent American Philosophy." *Philosophia Reformata* 2 (1937): 1–24.

"Reflections on Dr. A. Kuyper." *The Banner* 72 (December 16, 1937): 1187.

"Reformed Apologetics" (a series of six articles). *Torch and Trumpet* 1, no. 1 (April–May 1951): 16–18; 1, no. 2 (June–July 1951): 17–19;

1, no. 3 (August-September 1951): 16–18, 29; 1, no. 4 (October–November 1951): 16–17, 31–32; 2, no. 2 (June–July 1952): 5–8; 2, no. 5 (December 1952–January 1953): 18–20, 29–30.

The Reformed Pastor and Modern Thought. Philadelphia: Presbyterian and Reformed, 1971.

"Religious Philosophy: A Discussion of Richard Kroner's *Book Culture and Faith.*" *Calvin Forum* 18 (1953): 126–28.

Review of *A New Critique of Theoretical Thought,* vol. 1, by Herman Dooyeweerd. *Westminster Theological Journal* 17 (1955): 180–83.

Review of *A Sacramental Universe,* by Archibald A. Bowman. *Westminster Theological Journal* 2 (1940): 175–84.

Review of *An Introduction to Christian Apologetics,* by Edward John Carnell. *Westminster Theological Journal* 11 (1948): 45–53.

Review of *De Noodzakelijkeheid eener Christelijke Logica,* by D. H. Th. Vollenhoven. *Calvin Forum* 1 (1936): 142–43.

Review of *De Triomf der Genade in de Theologie van Karl Barth,* by G. C. Berkouwer. *Westminster Theological Journal* 18 (1955): 58–59.

Review of *Is God a Person?* by Edgar Sheffield Brightman. *Christianity Today* 3, no. 11 (March 1933): 7.

Review of *Geloof en Rechtvaardiging,* by G. C. Berkouwer. *Westminster Theological Journal* 12 (1949): 74–76.

Review of *Geschiedenis der Wijsbegeerte,* vol. 1, by D. H. Th. Vollenhoven. *Westminster Theological Journal* 14 (1951): 86–87.

Review of *Karl Barth en de Kinderdoop,* by G. C. Berkouwer. *Westminster Theological Journal* 11 (1948): 77–80.

Review of *Paedagogische Beginselen,* by Herman Bavinck, and *De Nieuwe Opvoeding,* by Herman Bavinck. *Princeton Theological Review* 27 (1929): 135–36.

Review of *Personality and Religion,* by Edgar Sheffield Brightman. *Presbyterian Guardian* 2 (June 1, 1936): 100.

Review of *Religion in the Making,* by Alfred North Whitehead. *Princeton Theological Review* 25 (1927): 336–38.

Review of *Studies in the Philosophy of Religion,* by Archibald A. Bowman. *Westminster Theological Journal* 2 (1939): 55–62.

Review of *Systematic Theology,* vol. 2, by Paul Tillich. *Westminster Theological Journal* 20 (1957): 93–99.

Review of *The Doctrine of God,* by Albert C. Knudson. *Christianity Today* 1, no. 8 (December 1930): 10–13.

Review of *The Philosophy of Alfred North Whitehead,* edited by Paul Arthur Schilpp. *Westminster Theological Journal* 4 (1942): 163–71.

Review of *The Philosophy of John Dewey,* edited by Paul Arthur Schilpp. *Westminster Theological Journal* 3 (1940): 62–73.

Review of *The Survival of Western Culture,* by Ralph Tyler Flewelling. *Westminster Theological Journal* 6 (1944): 221–27.

Review of *Twentieth Century Philosophy,* edited by Dagobert Runes. *Westminster Theological Journal* 6 (1943): 72–80.

"The Significance of Dort for Today." In *Crisis in the Reformed Churches,* edited by Peter Y. De Jong, 181–96. Grand Rapids: Reformed Fellowship, 1968.

The Sovereignty of Grace: An Appraisal of G. C. Berkouwer's View of Dordt. Philadelphia: Presbyterian and Reformed, 1969.

A Survey of Christian Epistemology. In Defense of the Faith, vol. 2. Philadelphia: Presbyterian and Reformed, 1969.

The Theology of James Daane. Philadelphia: Presbyterian and Reformed, 1959.

Theology of Crisis. Philadelphia: Westminster Theological Seminary, 1935 (syllabus).

Toward a Reformed Apologetics. Philadelphia: privately printed, 1972.

The Triumph of Grace: The Heidelberg Catechism. Philadelphia: Westminster Theological Seminary, 1958 (syllabus).

"Westminster Professor Replies to Criticism of His Theological Views." *The Banner* 96, no. 2 (January 13, 1961): 18.

"What Shall We Feed Our Children?" *Presbyterian Guardian* 3 (October 24, 1936): 23–24.

Who Do You Say That I Am? Philadelphia: Presbyterian and Reformed, 1975.

Why I Believe in God. Philadelphia: The Committee on Christian Education of the Orthodox Presbyterian Church, 1948.

The Works of Cornelius Van Til, 1895–1987. Edited by Eric Sigward. CD-ROM. New York: Labels Army Co., 1997.

Index of Scripture

Genesis
1:26–28—242
2:15—242
2:19–20—242
4:1—158

Exodus
20:3—54

Deuteronomy
6:16—4
13:1–5—525n.126
17:4—163
32:31—524n.126

Job
19:25—145
28:12–14—404
28:20–22—404
40:1–2—4
40:8—4

Psalms
8:1—242
8:6–9—242
14:1—6, 181
14:2–3—181, 194n.80
19:1—181
19:1–6—242
19:2—443
26:3—163
36:1—181
36:9—121, 181, 197
46:10—158
53:1—181
53:2–3—194n.80
55:19—181
94:9–10—242
95:10—577
97:6–9—181
111:7–8—163
119:24—51
119:66—51
119:98–100—51
119:104–5—51

119:128—51
119:130—51
119:160—51

Proverbs
1:7—3, 6, 43, 48, 181
1:29—6, 48
8:22–31—197
15:7—182
20:12—242
26:5—6

Ecclesiastes
1:9–10—488
12:12—488

Isaiah
46:9–11—163
46:10—661
55:9—226

742

Jeremiah
22:16—159

Hosea
2:13—159
4:6—159

Matthew
4:7—4n.9
6:24—44
7:20—242
7:23—158
7:24–27—5, 203
7:29—201
10:29–30—163
12:30—278, 487
15:14—44
22:37—2, 31, 70, 90
23:15—44
24:32—158, 242
28:11–15—145
28:13–15—27
28:17—145, 642n.193

Mark
1:15—161
9:24—161

Luke
8:13—161
8:15—161
11:13—158
16:31—145, 201
17:5—161
24:11—27
24:16—145

John
1:9—197
3:12—36n.6
3:19—196
3:21—163

5:24—161
5:36–37—201
6:32—163
6:35—163
8:31–32—29
10:4—201
10:27—201
10:35—277n.40
12:48—201
13:35—242
14:6—29, 163
15:1—163
15:26—532
16:8–15—532
16:13—163
17:17—145
18:38—145
20:27—161
20:29—201
20:31—201
21:4—145
21:12—145

Acts
2:13—27
2:22—242
2:36—28, 71
3:19—70
4:20–23—27
4:27—278n.41
6:11–14—27
9:22—28, 71
12:14—242
13:45—27
14:2—27
14:11–13—28
14:16—427
14:17—678
15:1—28
15:5—28
15:7—242
16:16–18—28
16:31—161
17—53
17:2—71
17:6–7—27

17:17—71
17:17–18—28
17:18–20—27
17:22–23—443n.56
17:23—181
17:27–28—443
17:28—98n.27, 181, 279
17:30—181, 219
17:31—85n.117, 145
17:32—27
18:4—71
18:9–10—82n.106
19:8—71
19:9—71
20:28–30—29
24:14—161
26:2—28
26:3—242
26:4–8—53
26:8—27, 145
26:13–16—53
26:18–20—53
26:22—53
26:25–27—53
26:26—242, 645

Romans
1—42, 180–81, 182, 200, 203
1–2—184–85
1:8—289n.68
1:18—213, 432, 438, 442, 577, 678
1:18–21—51, 186, 445
1:18–32—243n.194
1:19—84n.115, 208, 568, 571
1:19–20—432, 577
1:19–21—71, 438
1:20—409, 454, 558, 648, 677
1:20–21—456
1:21—48, 72, 277, 443
1:21–22—5, 262, 536
1:22—486
1:25—566, 627

Index of Names

Alexander, S., 362, 382
Allis, Oswald T., 9, 11
Anaximander, 660
Anselm, 634n.162
Aquinas, Thomas, 47, 49n.31, 80,
184n.58, 192–94, 332n.149, 333,
352, 551, 557–59, 562, 569–70,
617n.139, 627–33, 666
Archimedes, 484n.36
Aristotle, 6n.10, 23, 60, 83, 115,
193n.75, 204n.89, 222, 240n.187,
264n.3, 313, 320–21, 329–33,
346–48, 352, 371n.209, 490, 522,
543, 569, 572, 587, 628–30, 632–33,
666, 684
Armstrong, William Park, 9
Arndt, Stephen W., 500n.60
Augustine, 15, 21n.65, 47, 49n.31, 54,
85n.118, 474, 530, 610
Ayer, A. J., 366–76

Bacon, Francis, 371
Bahnsen, Greg L., 7n.11, 11n.18,
72n.69, 73n.70, 79n.98, 163n.29,
214n.118, 276n.35, 372n.211,
443n.56, 445n.62, 450n.82,
490n.45, 493n.51, 499n.60, 530n.1,
613n.127, 615n.133, 635n.166,
642n.194, 672n.260
Barth, Karl, 12, 13, 581, 585, 587,
656–57, 662n.223, 666, 714
Bavinck, Herman, 8, 10, 14, 24, 25,
55, 64n.57, 212–13, 218n.131,
240n.187, 415n.19, 603, 612,
614n.129, 632nn.158,159, 634, 677
Beattie, Francis R., 596
Beegle, Dewey M., 285–86, 685–86,
688–89
Berdyaev, Nicholas, 382
Bergson, Henri, 382
Berkeley, George, 304, 314n.105,
334n.156, 338, 359n.189, 497
Berkhof, Louis, 8, 415n.19
Berkouwer, G. C., 14, 721
Bosanquet, Bernard, 9n.15, 173n.48,
176, 360n.189, 361, 363–65, 386
Bowman, Archibald Allan, 8
Bradley, F. H., 359n.189, 361, 364,
366, 383, 386, 389

745

Index of Subjects

as mediator in Plato, 322
and objects, 147
miracles, 37, 135, 380, 463, 582,
    642n.193, 646–47, 648n.204
"missing link," 174
moderate realism, 240n.187
modern philosophy, 402, 657–58
modern theology, 13, 402, 551,
    656–62
modernism, 41, 131, 476, 581–82,
    587, 625
motion, 627–28
mystery, 142, 715
    unbeliever's use of, 706
mysticism, 50, 132

naive empiricism, 220, 666
natural law, 21n.65, 37
natural man, 79–80, 105, 205–6, 446,
    489–90, 494, 559, 561–63, 684
    knowledge, 457
    self-conception, 439–40
    self-consciousness, 451–52
    without hope, 709–12
natural religion, 197n.83
natural revelation, 181, 192, 208, 435,
    456, 589–90, 600–602, 700,
    712–13, 720, 727
    Clark on, 677–80
    versus natural theology, 184–86,
        193–94, 598, 615n.133
    perspicuous after the fall, 211
    and special revelation, 195, 203–4
natural theology, 80n.103, 133n.123,
    193–94, 271n.28, 302, 425, 454,
    549, 552, 600–601, 613, 673
    versus common grace, 433–35
    and natural revelation, 184–86,
        193–94, 598, 615n.133
naturalism, 32, 65, 274, 575–76
nature, 83n.109, 118–19, 185, 281,
    563, 681
    and God, 622–27
    uniformity, 342n.167, 380, 528–29
nature and grace, 294n.79, 630
necessity, 281, 346

neo-orthodoxy, 396n.262, 635, 656,
    670
    Van Til charged with, 229n.159
neo-Platonism, 291n.73, 328
neutrality, 10, 101, 110, 111, 124n.109,
    126n.112, 127–28, 145–46,
    640–41, 700, 702–4, 718
    challenged by
        presuppositionalism, 546
    in evidentialism, 644–45
    in idealism, 362–66
    impossibility, 56, 150–54, 534,
        614–15
    in Montgomery, 644
    as negation, 152
    in non-Reformed theology, 533
    Rome on, 555, 561
    and traditional apologetics, 537,
        550
    Warfield on, 603–4
noetic effects of sin, 154n.17,
    396n.261, 532
non-Christian. *See* unbeliever
noninferential knowledge, 182–84,
    220
non-Reformed theology, 531–32
noumenal, 65, 209, 296, 345, 350–54,
    384, 392, 400, 498n.57, 691, 694

object-object relation, 259, 523
object-subject relation, 259
"objective facticity" (Montgomery),
    76n.92
objectivity, 283–86, 304–7, 423
    in interpretation, 293
    non-Christian, 307
objects, of knowledge, 307–8
observation, 241–44
Old Princeton, 47–48, 55, 430,
    600–603, 610–11
one and the many, 59, 61, 238–40,
    316n.108, 326–28, 547n.58
ontological argument, 620–21, 623,
    625, 633–34
openmindedness, 126–28, 703–4. *See
    also* neutrality

unbeliever
    ax to grind, 442, 454–55
    cooperation with believer, 275,
        295, 303–4, 431
    complexity in knowledge of God,
        443–44, 450, 452
    contribution to culture, 113
    "creatively constructive," 266, 702
    denies God, 406
    does not know God, 456–57
    epistemology, 166n.36, 254, 266,
        556, 694–95
    faith of, 460
    inconsistency, 274–75, 436–37,
        451–53, 455, 483–84, 547n.57
    knowledge, 406–7, 415, 419–20,
        600
    knowledge of God, 179–82, 244,
        405–6, 415, 418, 442–47,
        456–57, 460, 514
    lifestyle, 699, 700
    mixture of truth and error,
        458–60
    monism, 99–100, 107, 113
    as "Mr. Black," 572–95
    as "new man," 441–42n.54
    philosophical sophistication,
        443n.55
    presuppositions, 107–15
    psychology, 407, 413, 442
    relative good, 460
    self-consciousness, 416, 438–39,
        448n.74
    self-contradiction, 493–95
    standards, 540–41
    as ultimate judge, 310
    worldview, 29–30, 90, 141n.140,
        166n.36, 311–17
unitarianism, 544
United Presbyterian Church, 693
unity, 139–42, 522, 634
    and diversity, 104, 238, 493
    in idealism, 360
universals, 38, 238–41, 264, 308–9,
    321–22, 329–30, 333, 346–47

universe
    open-closed, 316, 379–80,
        383n.230, 703–4
    random, 279–80
univocal reasoning, 62, 225n.146, 251,
    255, 336, 336–37, 468, 489–95,
    491, 609, 622–25, 626, 628
unregeneracy. *See* unbelief

verbal revelation. *See* special revelation
verification principle, 368, 370, 373,
    374, 497
vicious circle, 518
Vienna Circle, 366–76
voluntarism, 471–72, 676
warrant, 178, 262

Wesleyan theology, 551
Westminster Confession of Faith, 197,
    199–200, 216, 337, 347, 614, 720
Westminster Theological Seminary, 11,
    16, 18–20, 73n.70, 120n.100, 636
Wheaton College, 665
will, 70
"will to power," 359n.188
wisdom, of world, 3, 5, 82–87, 402,
    543
witnessing, 52, 60, 579, 593–94, 732
    and apologetics, 537
    and common grace, 434–36
    See also evangelism
Word of God. *See* Bible; revelation;
    special revelation
world religions, 524n.126
worldviews, 6, 11–12, 20n.65, 40, 57,
    63n.55, 701
    conflict of, 114, 267, 484, 509–11,
        644
    environmental influences on,
        122n.106
    and epistemology, 263
    and facts, 539
    network of, 465–66